Shooter's Bible

113TH EDITION

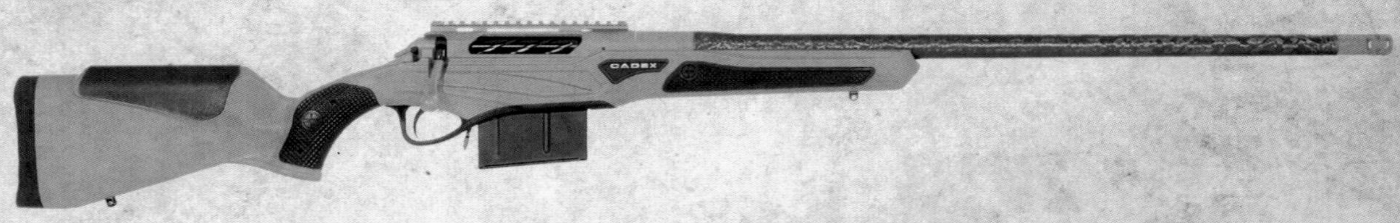

SP
SKYHORSE PUBLISHING

Skyhorse Publishing books may be purchased in bulk at special discounts for sales promotion, corporate gifts, fund-raising, or educational purposes. Special editions can also be created to specifications. For details, contact the Special Sales Department, Skyhorse Publishing, 307 West 36th Street, 11th Floor, New York, NY 10018 or info@skyhorsepublishing.com.

Visit our website at www.skyhorsepublishing.com.

10 9 8 7 6 5 4 3 2 1

Library of Congress Cataloging-in-Publication Data is available on file.

Cover design by Brian Peterson
Cover photos courtesy of Browning, Ruger, and Winchester

Print ISBN: 978-1-5107-6740-9
Ebook ISBN: 978-1-5107-6771-3
ISSN: 0080 9365

Printed in the United States of America

Note: Every effort has been made to record specifications and descriptions of guns, ammunition, and accessories accurately, but the Publisher can take no responsibility for errors or omissions. The prices shown for guns, ammunition, and accessories are manufacturers' suggested retail prices (unless otherwise noted) and are furnished for information only. These were in effect at press time and are subject to change without notice.

CONTENTS

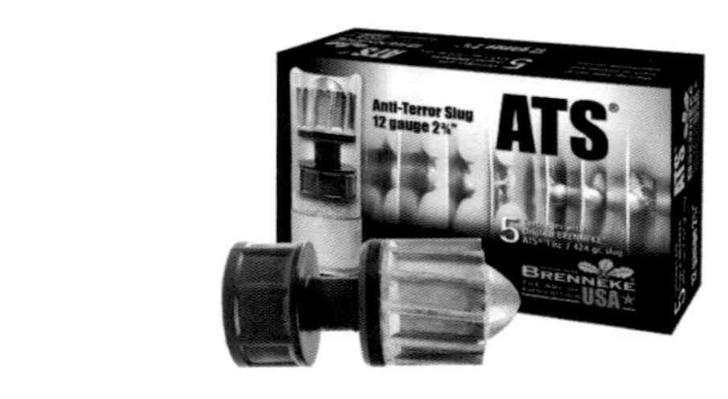

INTRODUCTION

The 113th edition of the *Shooter's Bible* is the most recent version of Skyhorse Publishing's annual, comprehensive firearms reference book. It's the source that millions of people look to when they need information on new firearms, ammunition, optics, and accessories, as well as current prices and specs for thousands of in-production firearms.

As an overview, this past year was an unusual one for the firearms industry. In fact, it was an unusual year for just about every industry in the country, with COVID-19 disrupting everyone's lives. As of this writing, more than 600,000 people have died from the pandemic in the United States alone. The effect on the firearms industry was rampant. The annual SHOT Show was cancelled for the first time in decades. Gun shows across the country were cancelled or postponed. Hunters, unable to fly to remote hunting grounds, mostly stayed close to home. Even local hunting clubs were affected, with members wary about interacting with anyone for fear of contracting the contagious disease.

Some thought that the industry might take a wait and see attitude, holding back new firearms introductions until things returned to some semblance of normalcy. Not so. In fact, firearms and ammo sales were robust across the country, so much so for ammo that some of it became hard to get. Many factors were involved, from the pandemic, protests, looting, and riots, to calls to defund police departments. All contributed to high demand at gun stores across the country. The polarized national elections added to the frenzy. The year 2020 actually ended as a year of record firearm purchases. According to a spokesman for the National Shooting Sports Foundation, "The year 2020 stands apart from all others for the firearm industry because of one number—21 million. That was the total number of background checks related to the sale of a firearm, and it was one for the record books. It was a number hardly anyone in industry would have thought possible at the start of the year. Twenty-one million background checks conducted for the sale of a firearm in 2020 topped 2019's total of 13.2 million by 60 percent. It shattered the previous record from 2016, when 15.7 million background checks were conducted for the sale of firearms.

"The story of firearm sales in 2020 gets even more interesting. NSSF, which is the trade association for the firearm industry, estimates that 8.4 million people bought a firearm for the first time in 2020. That's 40 percent of all purchases. And these new gun owners are increasingly diverse, pushing back against the idea that traditional buyers are the only customers for firearms. Forty percent of 2020's buyers were women. The largest increase of any demographic category was among African Americans, who bought guns at a rate of 58 percent greater than in 2019.

"The record sales year is good news for everyone who enjoys wildlife, wildlands, hunting, and the shooting sports. Excise taxes on the sale of firearms and ammunition have been collected since 1937, and because of the banner sales year in 2020, firearm and ammunition manufacturers paid $792 million to the Wildlife and Sport Fish Restoration program. These funds support wildlife conservation, hunter education, and the building and operation of public shooting ranges—and they're made available to every state.

"Despite production and inventory challenges created by this unprecedented demand for firearms and ammunition, NSSF expects the buying trend to continue into 2021, as more Americans choose to exercise their Second Amendment right to own a firearm for protection, recreational shooting and hunting."

To meet future demand, manufacturers are continuing to come out with a variety of new products, many of which are getting popular acclaim.

Long-range rifles continue to grow in popularity, with new models coming out from a number of firearms makers. Browning now offers a 6.8 Western caliber, chambered in the X-Bolt Western Hunter and X-Bolt Western Long-Range Hunter, while Remington, rebounding from bankruptcy, now offers models chambered for 6.8 Western and 6.5 PCR calibers. Other rifles to pay attention to are also being offered by Savage, J. P. Sauer and Sohn, Franchi, and CZ-USA.

In shotguns, Benelli's new ETHOS Cordoba BE. S. T. shotgun comes at a reasonable price, and is designed

Browning's X-Bolt Western Long-Range Hunter, chambered for 6.8 Western.

for high-volume shooting. Browning has the new Maxus II autoloader, while the Affinity Turkey Elite from Franchi is sure to please gobbler hunters; it's an inertia-driven system, with oversize bolt controls and an enlarged loading port, and is easy to use, even if you're wearing gloves on one of those cold, early season mornings.

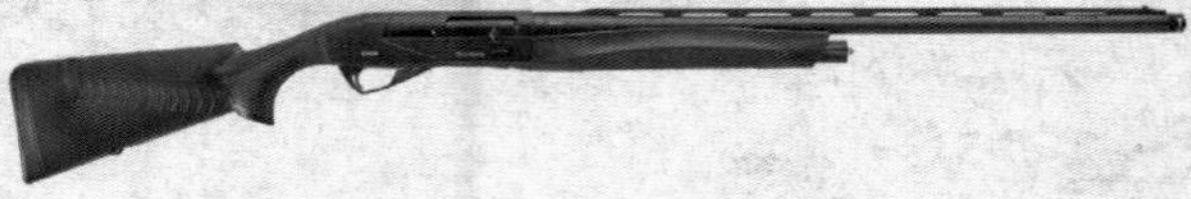

Benelli's ETHOS Cordoba BE. S. T.

A large variety of handguns also entered the market, with models from the likes of FN, CZ-USA, SIG Sauer, and more.

SAR USA SAR9 Optics Ready

Riflescopes are keeping up with the long-range trend, with more magnification power, while Bushnell now has a new RXS-250 red-dot reflex sight designed for pistols, rifles, and shotguns.

As you'll read in Robert A. Sadowski's new product report, "Guns, Optics, and Ammo 2022," beginning on page 6, all of these new introductions and more are examined in detail.

Skyhorse, meanwhile, continues to publish more solid, readable, and useful titles. One book that is going to press as I write this is the *Shooter's Bible Guide to Rifle Ballistics, Second Edition* by Wayne van Zwoll. Completely updated, and with new chapters on .270s, .300s. 6.5s, and 7s, it is the type of book any gun enthusiast will enjoy.

Other books in the works include the *Shooter's Bible Guide to Shotgun Sports for Women* by Laurie Wiles, as well as the *Shooter's Bible Guide to Sporting Shotguns* by Alex Brant. You won't want to miss either one. For a complete lineup of all our firearms books, please refer to www.skyhorsepublishing.com. If you own or are looking to buy currently produced firearms, then you'll want to check out the existing products section in the *Shooter's Bible*, starting on page 113. Here is where you'll find every firearm currently in production, with current prices and specs. If you have a gun that isn't in this section, it is probably out of production, in which case you need to pick up another Skyhorse publication, the *Gun Trader's Guide*. The 423rd edition came off the presses at the same time this edition of the *Shooter's Bible* did.

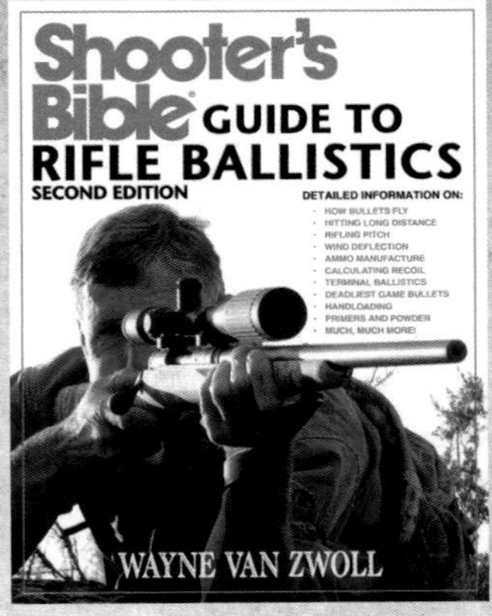

The *Shooter's Bible* has a long, illustrious past. The first numbered edition was published in 1925. It's been published annually, and in some cases biannually, ever since, and continues to be the go-to reference book for millions of people who want information on new guns, ammunition, optics, and accessories.

The Skyhorse staff is proud of this newest edition of the *Shooter's Bible*, a book that has been continually updated and fact checked for the past twelve months. Now that this 113th edition is off the presses, we're already starting to work on the 114th edition. It's an ongoing process, one we have to stay on top of and pay close attention to, given all the changes going on in the world of firearms.

—Jay Cassell
Editorial Director
Shooter's Bible

GUNS, OPTICS, AND AMMO 2022

By Robert A. Sadowski

Bad news is Remington went bankrupt. Good news is all the brands under the Remington umbrella were purchased by other companies and Big Green is back. Rifles are being chambered in 6.8 Western and 6.5 PCR calibers, so long-range hunters and shooters can wring accuracy and power. For shotguns, bronze finishes continue to be popular along with 20- and other sub-gauge models being released. Think less recoil. It's officially a trend with 9mm, a micro-size pistol with a high magazine capacity and red-dot-ready. Ruger and Smith & Wesson just launched their models and follow SIG, Springfield Armory, and FN. Pistol optics and scopes for long distance are hot. Many rifle scopes now feature a higher magnification range power with many new scopes offering 6X and 8X magnification—think long-range shooting. Red-dot optics for pistols are evolving with features that make it easier to use and conserve battery life. Here's what else is new and shiny in the gun world.

Rifles

Browning (browning.com)

A new line of X-Bolt Mountain Pro (MSRP: $2399–$2499) rifles offer features like a carbon fiber stock that is quarter pound lighter than previous versions and the innovative new Browning Recoil Hawg muzzle brake that reduces recoil up to 77 percent. Choose either a Cerakote Burnt Bronze or Tungsten finish. A Picatinny bipod rail on the forend is also included. A new caliber to the X-Bolt series is the 6.8 Western caliber. The 6.8 Western was designed to be the ultimate all-around long-range hunting cartridge and is chambered in the X-Bolt Western Hunter and X-Bolt Western Hunter Long Range. The X-Bolt Western Hunter (MSRP: $1069–$1799) comes equipped with sporter contour barrel, removeable muzzle brake, removeable magazine, top-tang thumb safety, ergonomic bolt handle, composite stock with new adjustable comb system, and A-TACS AU Camo finish. The X-Bolt Western Hunter Long Range features a heavy sporter contour barrel with removeable muzzle brake.

BROWNING X-BOLT MOUNTAIN PRO

CZ-USA (cz-usa.com)

The CZ 557 Eclipse (MSRP: $659) has a push-feed action, cold hammer-forged and lapped 20.5-inch barrel, and it is chambered in 6.5 Creedmoor, .308 Win. and .30-06 Springfield.

Franchi (franchiusa.com)

New to the Momentum Elite series is the Elite Varmint Rifle (MSRP: $999). Chambered in popular varmint calibers like .223 Rem., .22-250 Rem., and .224 Valkyrie, it features an all-new stock designed specifically for varmint hunting and covered in OPTIFADE Subalpine camo. Expect MOA accuracy from the heavy, spiral-fluted barrel.

J. P. Sauer & Sohn (jpsauer-usa.com)

The flagship rifle for this storied German rifle maker is the new S404 Synchro XTC (MSRP: $8199), and it has been updated with a camo-green finish. The stock is hand-laid carbon fiber with a thumbhole grip and adjustable comb. You can get this beauty in nearly any caliber you so desire.

SAVAGE RASCAL MINIMALIST

Savage Arms (savagearms.com)

The introduction of the Impulse rifle is a big deal. Outwardly it looks like a typical bolt action, but the Impulse cycles with a new Hexlock straight-pull action with free-floating interchangeable bolt head. This reduces the time needed for a follow-up shot and makes it easier to work the bolt without removing your cheek from the rifle stock. Three variants are being offered: Impulse Big Game, Impulse Hog Hunter, and Impulse Predator. The Impulse Big Game (MSRP: $1449) is equipped with a fluted, medium-contour barrel and a five-round, flush-fit detachable box magazine. Available in 6.5 Creedmoor, .243 Win., .308 Win., .300 WSM, .30-06 Spfd., and .300 Win. Mag. The Impulse Predator (MSRP: $1379) is available in .22-250 Rem., .243 Win., .308 Win., and 6.5 Creedmoor. It also features an AICS-pattern magazine, matte-finished medium-contour barrel, and the Mossy Oak Terra Gila Camo finish. The pig version, the Impulse Hog Hunter (MSRP: $1379), has a heavy barrel and matte black finish, and is available in 6.5

Creedmoor, .308 Win., .30-06 Spfd.,.300 Win. Mag., and 6.5 Creedmoor. Here piggy, piggy.

The single-shot Rascal Minimalist (MSRP: $289) has a laminate stock in either pink/purple or teal/gray, plus a threaded barrel. Young shooters will think they look super cool. The new .28 Nosler caliber is the most powerful 7mm cartridge commercially available and some new 110 models are making the most of this caliber. The model 110s include the new 110 Timberline (MSRP: $1165) in both left- and right-hand configurations.

Springfield Armory (springfield-armory.com)

The Model 2020 Waypoint (MSRP: $1699–$2399) bolt-action rifle has a tactical heritage and is designed for speed and smoothness. Features include adjustable or non-adjustable AG Composites carbon fiber, hand-painted stocks, adjustable trigger, and either a traditional fluted steel barrel or carbon-wrapped barrel. Yep, you guessed right. Expect sub-MOW accuracy or better. Caliber choices include .308 Win., 6mm Creedmoor, 6.5mm Creedmoor, and 6.5 PRC.

WINCHESTER MODEL 94 DELUXE SPORTING

Winchester Repeating Arms (winchesterguns.com)

The Model 1886 Saddle Ring Carbine (MSRP: $1509) is chambered in .45-90 and .45-70. It features a straight grip Grade I walnut stock with carbine-style forearm, polished blued finish, saddle ring, and a receiver drilled and tapped for Lyman-style rear sight. The Wildcat 22 Combo (MSRP: $309) features include removable lower receiver, ambidextrous magazine release, easy-to-load rotary magazine, integral Picatinny top rail on receiver, and a reflex-style red-dot sight with multiple reticles. The Model 70 Extreme TrueTimber VSX MB (MSRP: $1649) has a receiver and barrel with Tungsten Cerakote finish, a Bell and Carlson synthetic stock with sculpted cheekpiece and TrueTimber VSX finish, jeweled bolt body, knurled bolt handle, and Pachmayr Decelerator recoil pad. XPR Hunter Mossy Oak DNA (MSRP: $629) features Perma-Cote matte finish on the barrel and receiver, composite stock with Mossy Oak DNA camouflage, Inflex Technology recoil pad, MOA trigger system, and a detachable box magazine. The Model 94 Deluxe Sporting (MSRP: $2109) lever-action is a gorgeous rifle with Grade V/VI checkered walnut stock and color case hardened finish.

BENELLI ETHOS CORDOBA BE.S.T.

Shotguns

Benelli (benelliusa.com)

Benelli brings together the best of both style and high performance with the new ETHOS Cordoba BE.S.T. shotgun (MSRP: $2349). Designed for high-volume shooting, the ETHOS Cordoba BE.S.T. has upgraded features along with Benelli's BE.S.T. finish technology for ultimate protection from rust and corrosion.

Browning (browning.com)

The new Maxus II is an autoloader using the tried and true Power Drive Gas System and reliable Maxus action; it features an all-new stock design, enlarged trigger guard that is ramped for fast loading, oversized bolt handle and release that are easier to use, and a traditional threaded magazine cap. Available in a Stalker (MSRP: $1589–$1779, depending on 3- or 3.5-in. chamber) with black synthetic stock; Sporting Carbon Fiber (MSRP: $1859) with Hydrographic dip carbon fiber finish and extended Invector-Plus Midas Grade choke tubes; Wicked Wing with Mossy Oak Shadow Grass Habitat (MSRP: $1939–$2069) with a bronze finish; Mossy Oak Shadow Grass Habitat (MSRP: $1789–$1899) with total camp coverage; and All-Purpose Hunter with Mossy Oak Break-Up Country finish (MSRP: $1979).

FRANCHI AFFINITY 3 TURKEY ELITE

Franchi (franchiusa.com)

Hardcore turkey hunters will appreciate the new 3-inch Affinity 3 Turkey Elite (MSRP: $1249), 20-gauge and 12-gauge shotguns. These turkey killers feature Franchi's inertia-driven system, oversized bolt controls and enlarged loading port for ease-of-use even with gloved hands, 24-inch barrels covered in OPTIFADE Subalpine camo, and pistol grip and forend combined with a Midnight Bronze Cerakote receiver and barrel.

Henry Repeating Arms (henryusa.com)

The Single-Shot Turkey Camo shotgun (MSRP: $687) is a break-action 12-gauge hidden with a Mossy Oak Obsession camo finish. Features include fiber optic sights and extended full-choke tube. Turkeys beware!

Mossberg (mossberg.com)

The new affordable International Gold Reserve series of over/under shotguns are well equipped for upland fields, shooting clays, or 5-stand. Features include shell ejectors, Grade-A black walnut stocks, scroll-engraved receivers, 30-inch blue barrels (26-inch in .410 bore), and a five-piece extended choke tube set. The series includes five models chambered in 12 or 20 gauge or .410 bore. The International Gold Reserve Super Sport (MSRP: $1221) is set up for competitive clay shooting and chambered in 12 gauge with a fully adjustable comb and butt pad. The International Gold Reserve Black Label (MSRP: $983) has a blued receiver with gold inlay. The International Gold Reserve standard model (MSRP: $983) comes equipped with a polished silver receiver. The all new affordable Silver Series of over/unders feature shell extractors, select black walnut (MSRP: $692) or synthetic stock (MSRP: $636), matte blue 26- or 28-inch barrels, and five choke tubes. Model available in in 28, 20, or 12 gauge and .410 bore.

MOSSBERG INTERNATIONAL GOLD RESERVE SUPER SPORT

Pointer by Legacy Sports (legacysports.com)

The new Pointer Acrius series (MSRP: $589) is chambered in 20 or 12 gauge or .410 bore. All feature a Turkish walnut stock, 5 choke tubes, barrel selector, and 28-inch vent rib barrels.

Savage Arms (savagearms.com)

New to the Renegauge line is the Renegauge Competition (MSRP: $1959) 12-gauge autoloader featuring an extended magazine tube for 9+1 capacity, fluted barrel with melonite finish, carbon steel ventilated rib with red Hi-Viz Tri-Comp front sight, competition-ready easy loading magazine port, oversized controls, and more.

Stoeger (stoegerindustries.com)

The semi-auto M3500 Snow Goose (MSRP: $899) was designed for waterfowl hunting and features an 922R-compliant extended 10+1 magazine tube. Made for use in cold weather, this M3500 has an oversized bolt handle and bolt-release button. A specially machined and beveled loading port makes feeding shells into the magazine tube with gloved hands quick and efficient.

STOEGER INDUSTRIES M3500 SNOW GOOSE

Winchester Repeating Arms (winchesterguns.com)

The SX4 autoloader series (MSRP: $1099) is now available in Waterfowl Hunter Woodland finish.

Handguns

Browning (browning.com)

Browning has gone all-in on tricked-out competition-ready .22 LR rimfires. The Buck Mark Plus Vision UFX Black (MSRP: $739) is lightweight with an alloy sleeve around a steel barrel. Sights are a fiber optic front sight and adjustable rear with an integrated optics rail. The Plus Vision UFX Blue (MSRP: $739) features the same sight set-up with a blue finish alloy frame and barrel sleeve with diamond cut outs. The Plus Vision UFX Red (MSRP: $739) is similar to the Black and Blue models but with a red finish and slot cut outs in the barrel sleeve. The Buck Mark Contour Gray URX (MSRP $599) features a 5.5-inch contoured steel barrel with a heft for added stability; it also has a full-length Weaver optics base, so mounting a red dot is an easy option. The adjustable rear sight and partridge-style front sight come standard on the Ultragrip RX (URX) ambidextrous grips, which offer a secure, comfortable hold for most hand sizes.

The .22 LR 1911-22 Compact Gray (MSRP: $639) is built with a lightweight composite frame with alloy subframe. It features an A-TACS AU camo finish, alloy slide with Cerakote Burnt Bronze finish, composite grips, stainless steel barrel block, and steel 3-dot sights. The 1911-22 Speed (MSRP: $639) also features an A-TACS AU camo finish and alloy slide with Cerakote Burnt Bronze finish. It is available in either 3- or 4.25-inch barrel models.

CZ TS2

CZ-USA (cz-usa.com)

CZ knows how to build competition guns. The CZ Tactical Sport has evolved to the TS2 (MSRP: $1699); it has a slide profile as low as possible for better recoil management and a redesigned frame for improved ergonomics for less muzzle flip. Front and rear slide cocking serrations, adjustable rear sight and a fiber optic front post, and a magwell that is easy fast and easy to load are just some of the features. The subcompact P-10 (MSRP: $619) is now available in OD green and FDE finishes and wears tritium night sights.

FN (fnamerica.com)

It's about time FN came out with a 9mm long slide. FN 509 LS Edge (MSRP: $1499) is a long slide striker fire pistol equipped with a 5-inch hammer forged barrel, crisp and flat-faced trigger, flared aluminum magazine well, lightning-cut long slide, low-profile optics-mounting system, and fiber optic sight package. Plus it has the other features from the 509 series, like enhanced texture, two interchangeable backstraps to fit all hand sizes, and a Picatinny accessory rail. The 9mm striker fire FN 509 Compact (MSRP: $679) includes low-profile carry sights and a 12- and 15-round magazine, and it comes in either FDE and matte black finish.

HERITAGE MANUFACTURING BARKEEP WITH WOOD GRIPS

Heritage Manufacturing (heritagemfg.com)

Heritage makes some fun-to-shoot single-action revolvers and the new Barkeep models ($180) offer the same plinking fun. These are equipped with a 2.6-inch barrel and the same full grip as the other Heritage models. One variant comes with a faux case-hardened finish and laser-carved wood grips while the other is blued with imitation pearl grips. These are fun six-shooters for sure.

Kel-Tec (keltecweapons.com)

Do you think a fifty-round magazine is too much? Nope. The new P50 (MSRP: $995) is chambered in the hot and fast 5.7x28mm caliber and was designed around the FN P90 fifty-round, double-stack magazine. The P50 comes with two fifty-round magazines, has an over-all length of 15 inches, and its weight is 3.2 pounds unloaded.

KEL-TEC P50

SAR USA (sarsilmaz.com/en)

The 9mm SAR9 Optics Ready (MSRP: $799) is an optics-ready variant that's equipped with a 4.5-inch hammer-forged barrel with recessed crown, optic-ready mount, and interchangeable backstraps for custom grip fit. The new SAR9 Compact pistol (MSRP: $799) offers a nice balance between a micro and full-size pistol. It's small and light, yet has the capacity of a full-size pistol. Based on the iconic CZ-75 design, the DA/SA Model 2000 (MSRP: $477–$499) has a 4.5-inch hammer-forged barrel, forged stainless-steel frame and slide, ergonomic trigger guard, Picatinny rail for accessories, dovetail rear sight, and changeable front sight. The K12 Sport (MSRP: $799) is also built on the CZ-75 platform and features a 4.7-inch hammer-forged match-grade barrel, oversized and flared magwell, full-length steel dust cover, and a trigger stop.

SAR USA SAR9 OPTICS READY

SIG Sauer (sigsauer.com)

The CustomWorks P320 AXG Scorpion (MARP: $1162) merges the heft and balance of a metal-framed pistol with the performance and reliability of the polymer framed P320 by using the new AXG (Alloy XSeries Grip) metal grip module. It is equipped with Scorpion G10 grips from Hogue, Cerakote Elite coating in FDE finish, skeletonized, flat-bade trigger, and is optic ready.

Stoeger (stoegerindustries.com)

All you need to add is a red dot to the new STR-9 striker-fire 9mm pistol variant. The STR-9S Combat pistol (MSRP: $549) combines high fiber optic suppressor sights, threaded barrel, flared magwell, optics-ready slide, three modular backstraps, and three magazines with a twenty-round capacity.

Taurus (taurususa.com)

I really like the Taurus TX 22 because of the full-size grip and consistent trigger. This year Taurus has kicked it up a notch by adding a red dot. The TX 22 Competition (MSRP: $484) comes out the box optic-ready and has competition features like a 5-inch threaded Bull Barrel, three sixteen-round magazines, adjustable 3-dot iron sights, and two adapter plates to mount a variety of red dot sights. Another new rimfire from Taurus is the Model 942 (MSRP: $369–$384) in .22 WMR and .22 LR. I have been testing a matte stainless steel, 2-inch barrel model and really like this pistol as a kit gun for camping, kayaking, and hiking. You can also get it blued and with a 3-inch barrel. It features an eight-shot cylinder, fixed front sight and drift adjustable rear sight, and comfortable textured rubber grips.

TAURUS MODEL 942

Blackpowder

CVA (cva.com)

The .40 caliber is the new .50 caliber, meaning CVA has a number of models now in .40 caliber that offer longer range and flatter trajectory. The Paramount HTR (MSRP: $1225) is a bolt-action muzzleloader chambered in .40 or .45 caliber with an adjustable cheekpiece designed for long-range hunting. The all new Accura X-Treme LR-X (MSRP: $675) is a break-action muzzleloader chambered in .45 or .50 caliber with a 30-inch barrel. The new Accura X-Treme MR-X (MSRP: $670) is similar except with a 26-inch barrel and adjustable cheek rest.

Taylor's & Company (taylorsfirearms.com)

The new "The ACE" pistol series (MSRP: $358) is a snub-nose version of the .44 caliber 1858 Remington model. The three variants available include a checkered walnut grip, smooth walnut grip, and faux ivory grip. All have a blued finish with a brass trigger guard and short 3-inch barrel.

TAYLOR'S & CO. THE ACE

Traditions Firearms (traditionsfirearms.com)

The next innovation in the affordable Buckstalker line is the Buckstalker XT (MSRP: $219–$403) with a premium-grade chromoly steel 24-inch barrel. The 24-inch barrel provides accuracy further than 200 yards.

Optics

ATN (atncorp.com)

The X-Sight LTV (MSRP: $599–$679) day/night digital rifle scope series come in two models: a 3–9x30mm and a 5–15x50mm. The scopes can record hours of video onto a removable micro SD card, have multiple reticles, and the battery has over a ten-hour life. Uses any 30mm rings.

ATN X-SIGHT LTV 3–9X30

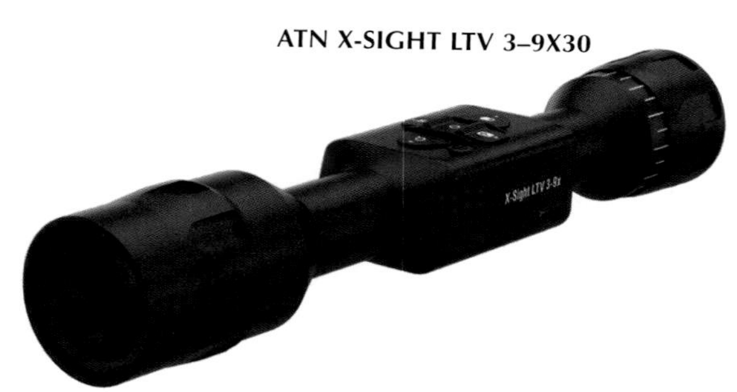

Bushnell (bushnell.com)

The new RXS-250 (MSRP: $249) red-dot reflex sight was designed for pistols, rifles, and shotguns, and it uses a combination of features to extend battery life while offering high brightness settings for day-bright visibility of the 4 MOA dot. The chamfered hood edges help prevent snags on clothing or objects in the environment. Banner 2 riflescopes are designed for hunting and feature improved optical performance with better contrast and clarity along with dusk and dawn low-light performance. Models include a 3–9x40mm (MSRP: $89), 3–9x50mm (MSRP: $99),

4–12x40mm (MSRP: $109), and 6–18x50mm (MSRP: $139). All models are equipped with a DOA Quick Ballistic Reticle that provides five drop points with five mph wind hold lines.

GPO (gpo-usa.com)

The new Spectra 6X riflescope lineup offers six new models that include a 1–6x24i, (MSRP: $799), 1.5–9x32i (MSRP: $899), 1.5–9x44i (MSRP: $899), 2–12x44i (MSRP: $899), 2–12x50i (MSRP: $949), and 3–18x56i (SPR: $1099). All models feature a 30mm main tube, proprietary GPO bright high-transmission lens coating technology, iControl illumination technology, PASSION drop hydrophobic exterior lens coatings and a double HD glass objective lens

Hawke Sport Optics (us.hawkeoptics.com)

The Sidewinder riflescope now has first focal plane (FFP) and second focal plane (SF) models, which feature a 30mm main tube, an ultra-wide 24-degree field of view, and precision locking turrets with 1/10 MRAD clicks that now have a Witness Window that provides instant visual confirmation of your turret position. The SF models (MSRP: $619–$689) include a 4.5–14x44mm, 6.5–20x44mm, 4–16x50mm, 6–24x56mm, and an 8–32x56mm. The two FFP models include a 4–16x50mm (MSRP: $799) and 6–24x56mm (MSRP: $819). SF models are equipped with either an illuminated Half Mil reticle or SR Pro II reticle, and FFP model have Half Mil reticles.

HAWKE SPORT OPTICS SIDEWINDER 30 SF

Holosun (holosun.com)

Varying by model, the new X2 series pistol optics features include lock mode, which prevents unintentional setting changes while the firearm is being carried; Solar Failsafe technology that ensures the optic will operate without battery power; and Shake Awake, which allows an optic to automatically go to sleep when the unit has not detected movement or vibration in a specific amount of time (programmable by the operator). Once the unit senses movement, it will automatically turn itself on and recall the last brightness that was used. All X2 series optics have a side-mounted battery for easy replacement. The HS407C X2 (MSRP: $282) and HE407C-GR X2 (MSRP: $299) feature a 2 MOA red or green dot, respectively. The HS507C X2 (MSRP: $364) and HE507C-GR X2 (MSRP: $399) models feature a multi-reticle system—circle dot, 2 MOA dot, or 32 MOA circle—in red or green, respectively. The HE508T-RD X2 (MSRP: $435) and HE508T-RD X2 (MSRP: $470) models are built with a titanium housing and feature a multi-reticle system—circle dot, 2 MOA dot, or 32 MOA circle—in red or green, respectively. All seven of these models are equipped with Solar Failsafe and Shake Awake technologies. The HS407K X2 (MSRP: $258) features a 6 MOA red dot reticle and Shake Awake technology. The HS507K X2 (MSRP: $341) is equipped with a red multi-reticle system, Shake Awake, and lock mode technologies.

Konus (konuspro.com)

The new second focal plane Glory riflescope series includes a 2–16x50mm and 3–24x56mm configurations (MSRP: $675). Both models provide a versatile 8x zoom system that makes them ideal for shooting at long distance. Reticle options include a German-4 with a dual illuminated center dot, or a fine crosshair reticle with a dual illuminated center dot. Reticles offer dual color illumination in red or blue.

Leica (leica-camera.com)

The Amplus 6 riflescope series features four models 1–6x24mm (MSRP: $1199), 2.5–15x50mm (MSRP: $1399), 2.5–15x56mm (MSRP: $1499), and 3–18x44mm (MSRP: $1399). All feature 6X zoom and reticle illumination in a 30mm tube design. Illuminated reticle options in these SFP scopes include an L-4a, L-4a BDC, and Ballistic BDC.

March Scopes (marchoptics.com)

The new March-F 1–10x24mm Shorty DR model (MSRP: $2650) uses a dual reticle set up, giving it the advantages of both an SFP and FFP reticle. It has the convenience of the FFP reticle scale, which magnifies and reduces according to the magnification, and the usability of the SFP reticle with the constant thickness of the line as the magnification changes. The 4.5–28x52mm (MSRP: $3290–$3590) scopes are FFP with either illuminated or non-illuminated reticles. The illuminated FML-TR1 is a tree-type or grid system reticle, while the FML-3 reticle is a non-tree type. The non-illuminated FML-PDK is also a grid type reticle while the FML-LDK is a simpler non-grid design. These scopes were designed for tactical shooting, such as precision rifle series competitions and can also be used for hunting.

MARCH SCOPES 4.5–28X52MM

NEW PRODUCTS 2021–2022

ACCURACY INTERNATIONAL AT308

ACCURACY INTERNATIONAL AX308

ALLTERRA ARMS ALLTERRA OBSKURA NOX

ALLTERRA ARMS ALLTERRA SAFARI EDITION

ALLTERRA ARMS ARID 1760

ALLTERRA ARMS MOUNTAIN SHADOW 300 SS

ANDERSON MANUFACTURING AM-9

ACCURACY INTERNATIONAL AT308

Action: Bolt
Stock: Synthetic
Barrel: 24 in.
Sights: None
Weight: 12 lb. 13 oz.
Caliber: .308 Win.
Magazine: 10 rounds
Features: "AT" stands for Accuracy Tactical and this short-action .308 features an adjustable cheekpiece; fixed buttplate with spacers; pistol grip; 20 MOA STANAG 4695/Mil Std 1913 rail; double-chamber standard muzzle brake; double-stack magazine; folding stock; barrels finished in choice of Cerakote black, green, or pale brown
MSRP . . . . **$4040.00–$4746.00**

ACCURACY INTERNATIONAL AX308

Action: Bolt
Stock: Synthetic
Barrel: 24 in.
Sights: None
Weight: 13 lb. 11 oz.
Caliber: .308 Win.
Magazine: 10 rounds
Features: A short-action sniper design; two 80mm flush cup accessory rails; 13-in. forend tube and rail; flush cup sling attachment points; adjustable cheekpiece; adjustable buttstock with spacers; right-side folding stock over bolt; double-stack magazine; tactical muzzle brake; High-Performance H series in Cerakote dark earth, green and pale brown options, Elite series in Elite Sand or Elite Midnight
MSRP **$7535.00**

ALLTERRA ARMS ALLTERRA OBSKURA NOX

Action: Bolt
Stock: Synthetic
Barrel: 22 in.
Sights: None
Weight: N/A
Caliber: 6.5 PRC, .28 Nosler, .300 PRC
Magazine: 4 rounds
Features: A very limited edition run of 14 rifles; based off the Mountain Shadow platform; Kryptek Obskura Nox pattern on stock; Leupold VX-6HD 3–18x44mm scope with ½-MOA clicks and illuminated T-MOA reticle; spiral-fluted, match-grade, hand-lapped stainless barrel; metalwork in flat dark earth and black Cerakote; stainless steel directional muzzle brake; two front swivel studs, one rear
MSRP **$7745.00**

ALLTERRA ARMS ALLTERRA SAFARI EDITION

Action: Bolt
Stock: Walnut
Barrel: 22 in.
Sights: Standing, folding rear; barrel band front with hood
Weight: 9 lb. 2 oz.
Caliber: .416 Ruger
Magazine: 3 rounds
Features: TriggerTech Primary trigger; stock of California English walnut by 2 Lazy 2, hand-rubbed with 25 coats of oil and checkered at 24 lpi; AllTerra Arms Convergence Series receiver; Ruger-style quarter-rib; barrel band sling swivel; muzzle brake; scope rings; spiral bolt
MSRP **$12,495.00**

ALLTERRA ARMS ARID 1760

Action: Bolt
Stock: Synthetic
Barrel: 24 in.
Sights: None
Weight: 10 lb. 10 oz.
Caliber: 6.5 SST
Magazine: 4 rounds
Features: A dedicated one-miler; Axial Precision Convergence Series receiver; TriggerTech Diamond trigger; match-grade fluted steel barrel; Race bolt; Heavy Hitter 3-port muzzle brake; adjustable cheekpiece; Manners MCS-EH1A stock in green and tan camo; detachable box magazine; topside and underside Picatinny rails
MSRP **$2495.00**

ALLTERRA ARMS MOUNTAIN SHADOW 300 SS

Action: Bolt
Stock: Synthetic
Barrel: 20 in.
Sights: None
Weight: 6 lb. 6 oz.
Caliber: .300 Sherman Short
Magazine: 4 rounds
Features: You'll need to handload for this one, thanks to the .300 Sherman Short wildcat chambering, but what you get is the power of a long-action cartridge in a short-action receiver; match-grade carbon fiber-wrapped barrel; TriggerTech Primary trigger; Carbon Hunter stock in Everglades camo; metwalwork in graphite Cerakote; Axial Precision Convergence Series receiver; titanium directional muzzle brake; supplied with choice of Talley rings or rail; comes with 40 rounds of ammo to get you started on the reloading
MSRP **$5295.00**

ANDERSON MANUFACTURING AM-9

Action: Semiautomatic
Stock: Synthetic
Barrel: 16 in.
Sights: None
Weight: 7 lb.
Caliber: 9mm
Magazine: 10, 17, 19 rounds
Features: Super fun PCC rifle that takes Glock magazines and features a forged aluminum upper and lower receiver; blowback operating system; M4 contour barrel with a parkerized finish; open trigger guard; six-position buffer tube; six-position carbine stock
MSRP **$793.89**

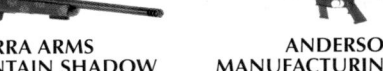

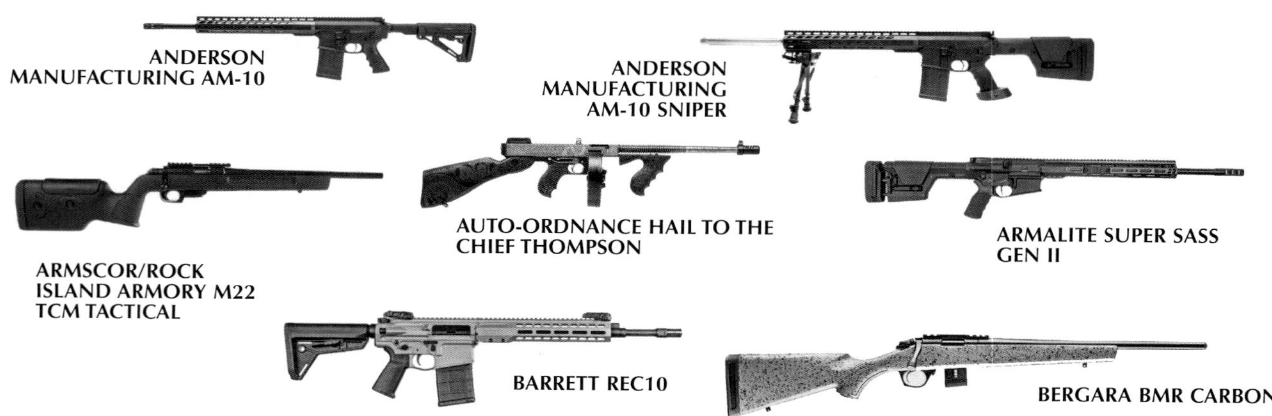

ANDERSON MANUFACTURING AM-10

Action: Semiautomatic
Stock: Synthetic
Barrel: 18 in.
Sights: None
Weight: 10 lb.
Caliber: .308 Win.
Magazine: 10 rounds
Features: Manageable barrel length while still having enough weight to tamp recoil; collapsible stock; M-LOK handguard; muzzle brake; lots of accessory rail
MSRP $1218.29

ANDERSON MANUFACTURING AM-10 SNIPER

Action: Semiautomatic
Stock: Synthetic
Barrel: 24 in.
Sights: None
Weight: 12 lb.
Caliber: .308 Win.
Magazine: 10 rounds
Features: A solid contender for those looking for a long-range gun, one that features acres of rail; adjustable stock; stabilizing pistol grip; M-LOK handguard; bipod
MSRP $2006.59

ARMALITE SUPER SASS GEN II

Action: Semiautomatic
Stock: Synthetic
Barrel: 20 in., 22 in.
Sights: None
Weight: 11 lb. 14 oz.
Caliber: 7.62 NATO, 6.5 Creedmoor
Magazine: 20 rounds
Features: Magpul mag; Armalite-designed upper, lower, 15-in. free-floating Gen II handguard; POF two-stage trigger; Armalite Tac Brake on a stainless steel match grade barrel
MSRP . . . . N/A

ARMSCOR/ROCK ISLAND ARMORY M22 TCM TACTICAL

Action: Bolt
Stock: Synthetic
Barrel: 20 in.
Sights: None
Weight: 7 lb.
Caliber: .22 TCM
Magazine: 5 rounds
Features: Adjustable comb and length of pull; metal top rail; compatible with 17-round magazines from Armscor/RRI's .22 TCM 1911
MSRP $449.00

AUTO-ORDNANCE HAIL TO THE CHIEF THOMPSON

Action: Semiautomatic
Stock: Wood
Barrel: 16.5 in.
Sights: Blade front, notch rear
Weight: N/A
Caliber: .45 ACP
Magazine: 20, 50 rounds
Features: For fans of former President Donald Trump with this heavily embellished Thompson; engravings include the White House, "45th President of the United States," "MAGA" slogan, members of the former first family, presidential seal, American flag, "Keep America Great," and event notations; lavish scrollwork engraving; Cerakote Armor Black with PVC gold highlights
MSRP $12,500.00

BARRETT REC10

Action: Semiautomatic
Stock: Synthetic
Barrel: 16 in.
Sights: Flip-up front and rear
Weight: 8 lb.
Caliber: .308 Win.
Magazine: 20 rounds
Features: This one might find favor with the 3-gun crowd with its direct impingement gas system; anti-tilt bolt carrier; Barrett gas block and barrel; Barrett three-prong flash hider or muzzle brake; Barrett M-LOK rail handguard; ALG QMS trigger; Radian charging handle; Magpul stock, pistol grip, magazine and flip-up sights; available in black, flat dark earth, or tungsten grey
MSRP $2565.00

BERGARA BMR CARBON

Action: Bolt
Stock: Synthetic
Barrel: 18 in., 20 in.
Sights: None
Weight: 5 lb.–5 lb. 7 oz.
Caliber: .22 LR, .22 WMR, .17 HMR
Magazine: 5, 10 rounds
Features: A delightful rimfire, the BMR (Bergara Micro Rimfire) comes with a carbon fiber Bergara barrel in a No. 6 profile; 30 MOA rail; Bergara Performance trigger; synthetic stock in black with gray speckling; steel barrel is optional
MSRP . . . . $565.00–$659.00

BLACKWATER FIREARMS/ IRON HORSE FIREARMS DMR

BROWNING BAR MK III DBM ATACS LE

BROWNING BAR MK III DBM STALKER LEFT-HAND

BROWNING BL-22 GRADE II MAPLE

BROWNING SEMI-AUTO 22 CHALLENGE

BROWNING BLR GOLD MEDALLION

BLACKWATER FIREARMS/ IRON HORSE FIREARMS DMR

Action: Semiautomatic
Stock: Synthetic
Barrel: 18 in.
Sights: None
Weight: 8 lb. 7 oz.
Caliber: .223 Wylde
Magazine: 30 rounds
Features: Designated Marksman Rifle; 4150 steel button-rifled barrel in nitride coating; billet 7075 aluminum upper and lower; rifle-length gas system; A2 buffer, spring, and tube; adjustable length of pull and cheekpiece; ambidextrous charging handle and safety selector; 15.25-in. aluminum handlock with 3, 6, and 9 o'clock M-LOK points; oversized magazine release; supplied with 2 MFT magazines
MSRP $1999.00

BROWNING BAR MK III DBM ATACS LE

Action: Semiautomatic
Stock: Composite
Barrel: 18 in.
Sights: None
Weight: 7 lb. 6 oz.
Caliber: .308 Win.
Magazine: 10 rounds
Features: With a 10-round detachable box magazine (DBM), this rifle has a stock in A-TACS LE camo; matte blue/black metalwork; gas operating system; overmolded grip panels; aluminum alloy receiver; front sling swivel stud; quick-detach swivel cups with swivels; stock is shim adjustable for cast/drop
MSRP $1599.99

BROWNING BAR MK III DBM STALKER LEFT-HAND

Action: Semiautomatic
Stock: Composite
Barrel: 18 in.
Sights: None
Weight: 7 lb. 6 oz.
Caliber: .308 Win.
Magazine: 10 rounds
Features: This a contender for southpaw 3-gun competitors, with a quick-handling design; fluted barrel; detachable box magazine; Inflex recoil pad; bipod stud; recessed quick-detach sling swivel cups; sling swivels; overmolded grip panels; non-reflective matte blue metalwork
MSRP $1539.99

BROWNING BL-22 GRADE II MAPLE

Action: Lever
Stock: Maple
Barrel: 20 in.
Sights: Blade front, leaf rear
Weight: 5 lb.
Caliber: .22 LR, .22 WMR, .17 HMR
Magazine: 15 rounds
Features: Loads of fun and a gun you'll want to pass down to the next generation, with it's blond AAA-grade maple stock; lightly engraved stainless steel receiver in a satin nickel finish; polished blue barrel and magazine tube; plastic butt plate; light sporter barrel contour; not drilled and tapped for scope mount
MSRP $899.99

BROWNING BLR GOLD MEDALLION

Action: Lever
Stock: Walnut
Barrel: 20 in., 22 in.
Sights: Iron sights
Weight: 6 lb. 8 oz.–7 lb. 4 oz.
Caliber: .243 Win., 6.5 Creedmoor, .308 Win., .270 Win., .30-06 Spfd., .300 Win. Mag.
Magazine: 4 rounds
Features: Browning's long-lived lever gun gets the Medallion treatment with Grade III/IV walnut stock in a high-gloss finish; metalwork in high-polish blue; aluminum alloy receiver; four-position folding hammer; Pachmayr Decelerator pad; detachable magazine
MSRP . . . . $1539.99–$1629.99

BROWNING SEMI-AUTO 22 CHALLENGE

Action: Semiautomatic
Stock: Walnut
Barrel: 16.25 in.
Sights: None
Weight: 6 lb. 10 oz.
Caliber: .22 LR
Magazine: 10 rounds
Features: Certainly one for rimfire competition, with metal buttplate; satin-finished Grade 1 walnut stock; fixed bull barrel with threaded-on muzzle brake; matte blued metalwork; topside Picatinny rail
MSRP $939.99

BROWNING SEMI-AUTO 22 MAPLE

BROWNING T-BOLT COMPOSITE SPORTER

BROWNING T-BOLT TARGET WITH MUZZLE BRAKE

BROWNING X-BOLT GOLD MEDALLION

BROWNING X-BOLT HELL'S CANYON LONG RANGE MCMILLAN TUNGSTEN AMBUS

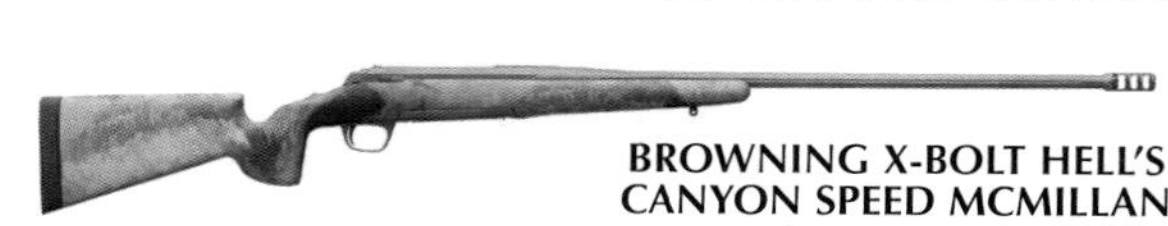

BROWNING X-BOLT HELL'S CANYON SPEED MCMILLAN LEFT-HAND

BROWNING SEMI-AUTO 22 MAPLE

Action: Semiautomatic
Stock: Maple
Barrel: 19.25
Sights: Gold bead front blade, adjustable folding leaf rear
Weight: 5 lb. 3 oz.
Caliber: .22 LR
Magazine: 10 rounds
Features: This special takedown is in a AAA-grade maple stock and has a tubular magazine; steel receiver with a satin nickel finish and engraving; polished blue barrel drilled and tapped for scope mounts
MSRP $939.99

BROWNING T-BOLT COMPOSITE SPORTER

Action: Bolt
Stock: Composite
Barrel: 22 in.
Sights: None
Weight: 4 lb. 9 oz.
Caliber: .17 HMR, .22 LR, .22 WMR
Magazine: 10 rounds
Features: Nimble straight-pull bolt rimfire with a sleek, modern composite stock; medium sporter contour barrel; Double Helix magazine; sling swivel studs; free-floating barrel with a semi-match chamber and recessed crown; spare magazine storage in buttstock
MSRP . . . . $749.99–$779.99

BROWNING T-BOLT TARGET WITH MUZZLE BRAKE

Action: Bolt
Stock: Black walnut
Barrel: 16.5 in.
Sights: None
Weight: 6 lb. 2 oz.
Caliber: .22 LR, .22 WMR, .17 HMR
Magazine: 10 rounds
Features: Handy rimfire for ranch work, casual target practice, or rimfire competition with a Grade 1 black walnut stock in a satin finish; Monte Carlo cheekpiece; free-floating heavy bull target barrel with a semi-match chamber and a threaded-on in-profile muzzle brake; steel receiver; sling swivel studs; straight-pull action; top-tang safety; Double Helix magazine
MSRP . . . . $669.99–$699.99

BROWNING X-BOLT GOLD MEDALLION

Action: Bolt
Stock: Walnut
Barrel: 22 in., 26 in.
Sights: None
Weight: 6 lb. 8 oz.–7 lb.
Caliber: 6.5 Creedmoor, 6.5 PRC, .270 Win., 7mm Rem. Mag., .28 Nosler, .30 Nosler, .300 Win. Mag., .300 RUM, .300 PRC
Magazine: 3, 4 rounds
Features: A more traditional take on the X-Bolt; Grade III/IV black walnut stock in a gloss finish; gloss blue metalwork; rosewood pistol grip cap; sporter contour barrel with threaded-on in-profile muzzle brake; detachable rotary magazine; Feather trigger; X-Lock scope mounts
MSRP . . . . $1339.99–$1379.99

BROWNING X-BOLT HELL'S CANYON LONG RANGE MCMILLAN TUNGSTEN AMBUSH

Action: Bolt
Stock: Composite
Barrel: 26 in.
Sights: None
Weight: 7 lb. 7 oz.–7 lb. 12 oz.
Caliber: 6.5 Creedmoor, 6.5 PRC, 7mm Rem. Mag., .28 Nosler, .300 Win. Mag.
Magazine: 3, 4 rounds
Features: Wears a McMillan Game Scout stock dressed in Urban Carbon Ambush camo; Cerakote tungsten metalwork; threaded in-profile muzzle brake; heavy sporter contour barrel; textured grip panels; 20 MOA topside rail with bubble level; detachable magazine; bipod/accessory rail under forend
MSRP . . . . $2499.99–$2559.99

BROWNING X-BOLT HELL'S CANYON SPEED MCMILLAN LEFT-HAND

Action: Bolt
Stock: Composite
Barrel: 22 in., 24 in., 26 in.
Sights: None
Weight: 6 lb. 9 oz.–7 lb. 1 oz.
Caliber: 6.5 Creedmoor, 6.5 PRC, 6.8 Western, .308 Win., .270 Win., .30-06 Spfd., 7mm Rem. Mag., .30 Nosler, .300 Win. Mag., .300 PRC
Magazine: 3, 4 rounds
Features: A nice choice of long-range and everyday calibers in a left-hand rifle featuring a McMillan Game Scout stock dressed in A-TACS ACU camo; metalwork in burnt bronze Cerakote; fluted sporter barrel with a threaded on Recoil Hawg muzzle brake
MSRP . . . . $2269.99–$2339.99

BROWNING X-BOLT MAX FLAT DARK EARTH LONG RANGE

BROWNING X-BOLT MOUNTAIN PRO LONG RANGE BURNT BRONZE, MOUNTAIN PRO LONG-RANGE TUNGSTEN

BROWNING X-BOLT MEDALLION CARBON FIBER

BROWNING X-BOLT PREDATOR HUNTER

BROWNING X-BOLT MOUNTAIN PRO BURNT BRONZE, MOUNTAIN PRO TUNGSTEN

BROWNING X-BOLT PRO LONG RANGE

BROWNING X-BOLT MAX FLAT DARK EARTH LONG RANGE

Action: Bolt
Stock: Composite
Barrel: 26 in.
Sights: None
Weight: 8 lb. 3 oz.–8 lb. 7 oz.
Caliber: 6.5 Creedmoor, 6.5 PRC, 6.8 Western, .280 Ackley Improved, .300 Win. Mag., .300 PRC
Magazine: 3, 4 rounds
Features: Long-range target option with an adjustable cheekpiece and length of pull stock spacers; fluted heavy sporter barrel with threaded on Recoil Hawg muzzle brake; extended bolt handle with a 60-degree lift; detachable rotary magazine; X-Lock scope mounts; bolt unlock button; Feather trigger
MSRP . . . . $1199.99–$1239.99

BROWNING X-BOLT MEDALLION CARBON FIBER

Action: Bolt
Stock: Carbon fiber
Barrel: 22 in.
Sights: None
Weight: 6 lb. 1 oz.
Caliber: 6.5 Creedmoor
Magazine: 4 rounds
Features: A lightweight Medallion model with a second-generation carbon fiber stock in a gloss finish; gloss blue metalwork; Inflex recoil pad; Feather trigger; X-Lock scope mounts; detachable rotary magazine
MSRP $2069.99

BROWNING X-BOLT MOUNTAIN PRO BURNT BRONZE, MOUNTAIN PRO TUNGSTEN

Action: Bolt
Stock: Carbon fiber
Barrel: 22 in., 23 in., 24 in., 26 in.
Sights: None
Weight: 5 lb. 14 oz.–6 lb. 6 oz.
Caliber: 6.5 Creedmoor, 6.5 PRC, 6.8 Western, .300 WSM, .30-06 Spfd., 7mm Rem. Mag., .28 Nosler, .300 Win. Mag., .30 Nosler, .300 PRC, .300 RUM
Magazine: 3, 4 rounds
Features: Browning says that this is a limited production gun and one that gives the company entry into the semi-custom production category, with features like a carbon fiber stock; Cerakote burnt bronze finish on metalwork; spiral-fluted, lapped sporter contour barrel; removable Picatinny rail; Feather trigger; X-Lock scope mounts; bolt unlock button; detachable rotary magazine
MSRP . . . . $2399.99–$2459.99

BROWNING X-BOLT MOUNTAIN PRO LONG RANGE BURNT BRONZE, MOUNTAIN PRO LONG-RANGE TUNGSTEN

Action: Bolt
Stock: Carbon fiber
Barrel: 26 in.
Sights: None
Weight: 6 lb. 12 oz.–7 lb. 1 oz.
Caliber: 6.5 Creedmoor, 6.5 PRC, 6.8 Western, .300 WSM, .30-06 Spfd., 7mm Rem. Mag., .28 Nosler, .300 Win. Mag., .30 Nosler, .300 PRC, .300 RUM
Magazine: 3, 4 rounds
Features: Similar to the Mountain Pro, but with the barrel standardized at 26 inches across all calibers; fast-twist rifling in some calibers
MSRP . . . . $2439.99–$2499.99

BROWNING X-BOLT PREDATOR HUNTER

Action: Bolt
Stock: Composite
Barrel: 22 in.
Sights: None
Weight: 6 lb. 11 oz.
Caliber: .204 Ruger, .223 Rem., .22-250 Rem., 6.5 Creedmoor
Magazine: 4, 5 rounds
Features: A coyote, prairie dog, and other varmint-getter that won't break the bank; barrel and stock clad in A-TACS AU camo; receiver, bolt, and trigger guard in Elite Sand Cerakote; heavy sporter barrel with threaded-on in-line profile muzzle brake; textured grip panels; Feather trigger; X-Lock scope mounts; extended bolt handle
MSRP $1099.99

BROWNING X-BOLT PRO LONG RANGE

Action: Bolt
Stock: Composite
Barrel: 26 in.
Sights: None
Weight: 6 lb. 12 oz.–7 lb. 1 oz.
Caliber: 6.5 Creedmoor, 6.5 PRC, 6.8 Western, .280 Ackley Improved, 7mm Rem. Mag., .28 Nosler, .300 Win. Mag., .300 PRC, .300 RUM
Magazine: 4, 5 rounds
Features: With a standardized 26-inch barrel across the caliber choices, this rifle features a skip-fluted heavy sporter contour barrel threaded and equipped with the Recoil Hawg muzzle brake; removable Picatinny rail on forend underside; spiral-fluted bolt; natural finish on stock; Carbon Gray Elite Cerakote on metalwork; gun is quarter-pound lighter than previous iterations
MSRP . . . . $2179.99–$2299.99

BROWNING X-BOLT PRO MCMILLAN

BROWNING X-BOLT WESTERN HUNTER

BROWNING X-BOLT PRO MCMILLAN LONG RANGE

BROWNING X-BOLT WESTERN HUNTER LONG RANGE

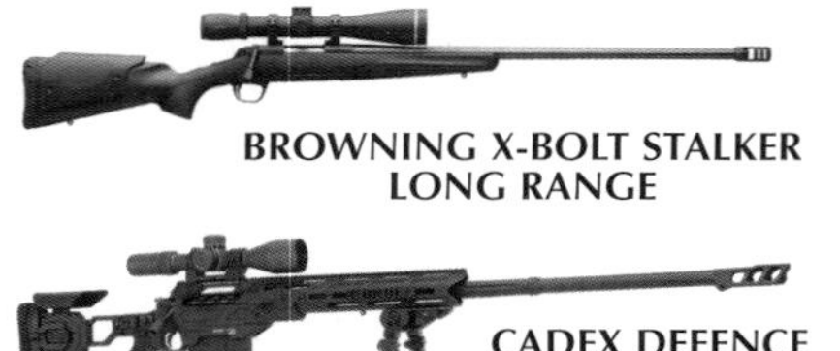
BROWNING X-BOLT STALKER LONG RANGE

CADEX DEFENCE CDX-40 SHADOW

BROWNING X-BOLT PRO MCMILLAN

Action: Bolt
Stock: Carbon fiber
Barrel: 22 in., 23 in., 24 in., 26 in.
Sights: None
Weight: 6 lb. 5 oz.–6 lb. 12 oz.
Caliber: 6.5 Creedmoor, 6.5 PRC, 6.8 Western, .280 Ackley Improved, .300 WSM, .30-06 Spfd., 7mm Rem. Mag., .28 Nosler, .300 Win. Mag., .300 PRC, .300 RUM
Magazine: 3, 4 rounds
Features: This X-bolt wears a McMillan Game Scout stock in Sonoran Carbon Ambush finish; metalwork in Cerakote carbon gray; a skip-fluted sporter contour barrel wearing a threaded-on Recoil Hawg muzzle brake; spiral fluted bolt and fluted bolt knob; 20 MOA Picatinny rail topside plus more under the forend; quick-detach sling attachments
MSRP . . . . $2599.99–$2699.99

BROWNING X-BOLT PRO MCMILLAN LONG RANGE

Action: Bolt
Stock: Carbon fiber
Barrel: 26 in.
Sights: None
Weight: 7 lb.–7 lb. 7 oz.
Caliber: 6.5 Creedmoor, 6.5 PRC, 6.8 Western, .280 Ackley Improved, 7mm Rem. Mag., .28 Nosler, .300 Win. Mag., .300 PRC, .300 RUM
Magazine: 3, 4 rounds
Features: Similar to the X-Bolt Pro McMillan, but with the barrel standardized to 26 inches across all available calibers
MSRP . . . . $2629.99–$2699.99

BROWNING X-BOLT STALKER LONG RANGE

Action: Bolt
Stock: Composite
Barrel: 26 in.
Sights: None
Weight: 7 lb. 7 oz.–7 lb. 12 oz.
Caliber: 6.5 Creedmoor, 6.5 PRC, .270 Win., 7mm Rem. Mag., .28 Nosler, .30 Nosler, .300 Win. Mag., .300 RUM, .300 PRC
Magazine: 3, 4 rounds
Features: Composite stock in A-TACS AU camo; adjustable comb; heavy sporter contour barrel with threaded-on muzzle break consistent with barrel profile; two swivel studs; metalwork in matte blue finish; extended ergonomic bolt handle; new three-lever Feather trigger; free floating action bedded at front and rear; X-Lock scope mounts have four screws per mount; 60-degree bolt lift and bolt unlock button; detachable rotary magazine
MSRP . . . . $1099.99–$1179.99

BROWNING X-BOLT WESTERN HUNTER

Action: Bolt
Stock: Synthetic
Barrel: 22 in., 24 in., 26 in.
Sights: None
Weight: 6 lb. 5 oz.–7 lb. 7 oz.
Caliber: 6.5 Creedmoor, 6.5 PRC, 6.8 Western, .308 Win., .280 Ackley Improved, 7mm Rem. Mag., .28 Nosler, .300 Win. Mag., .300 PRC
Magazine: 3, 4 rounds
Features: Composite stock in A-TACS AU camo has adjustable comb; threaded sporter contour barrel with included thread protector; two swivel studs; metalwork in Cerakote burnt bronze finish; new three-lever Feather trigger; free floating action bedded at front and rear; X-Lock scope mounts have four screws per mount; 60-degree bolt lift and bolt unlock button; detachable rotary magazine
MSRP . . . . $1069.99–$1179.99

BROWNING X-BOLT WESTERN HUNTER LONG RANGE

Action: Bolt
Stock: Synthetic
Barrel: 26 in.
Sights: None
Weight: 7 lb. 8 oz.–7 lb. 13 oz.
Caliber: 6.5 Creedmoor, 6.5 PRC, .270 Win., 7mm Rem. Mag., .28 Nosler, .30 Nosler, .300 Win. Mag., .300 RUM, .300 PRC
Magazine: 3, 4 rounds
Features: A no-frills rifle for those getting started in the long-range game; heavy sporter barrel with a threaded on Recoil Hawg muzzle brake; adjustable comb; matte blued metal on a matte blue composite stock; extended bolt handle; Feather trigger; X-Lock scope mounts; also available in flat dark earth
MSRP . . . . $999.99–$1029.99

CADEX DEFENCE CDX-40 SHADOW

Action: Bolt
Stock: Synthetic
Barrel: 29 in., 32 in.
Sights: None
Weight: 18 lb. 8 oz.
Caliber: .375 CT, .375 EnABLER, .408 CT
Magazine: 5 rounds
Features: Designed for anti-materiel shooting and other targets out to 4,000 yards; tool-less adjustable at cheek, length of pull, and buttplate; V-shaped bedding system that eliminates action movement in the chassis; mirage control tube; three-lug bolt with 60-degree throw; DX2 Evo single-/double-stage selectable trigger; Bartlein heavy straight-taper fluted barrel with a threaded muzzle, and 5R mil-spec match-grade single-point cut rifling; Ergo rubberized finger-groove grip; reverse folding stock; oversized trigger guard; detachable base for easy trigger care; full-length dual top rail in 20, 40, or 60 MOA
MSRP . . . . $7359.95–$7369.95

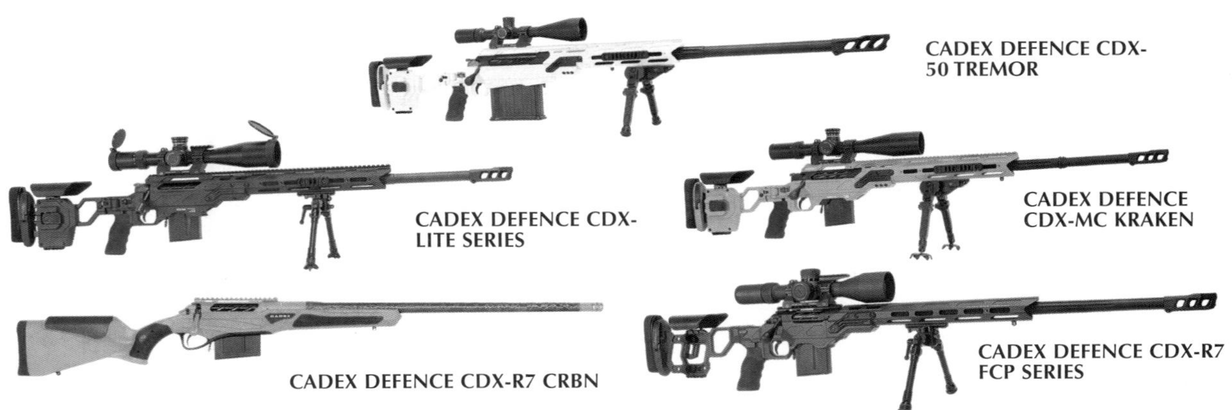

CADEX DEFENCE CDX-50 TREMOR

CADEX DEFENCE CDX-LITE SERIES

CADEX DEFENCE CDX-MC KRAKEN

CADEX DEFENCE CDX-R7 CRBN

CADEX DEFENCE CDX-R7 FCP SERIES

CADEX DEFENCE CDX-50 TREMOR

Action: Bolt
Stock: Synthetic
Barrel: 29 in.
Sights: None
Weight: 22 lb. 7 oz.
Caliber: .50 BMG
Magazine: 5 rounds
Features: Tool-less adjustable cheek, length of pull, and buttplate; V-shaped bedding system that eliminates action movement in the chassis; mirage control tube; four-lug bolt with 50-degree throw; DX2 Evo single-/double-stage selectable trigger; Bartlein straight-taper fluted barrel with a threaded muzzle, and 5R mil-spec match-grade single-point cut rifling; Ergo rubberized finger-groove grip; full-length dual top rail in 20 or 40 MOA
MSRP . . . . $8069.95–$8109.95

CADEX DEFENCE CDX-LITE SERIES

Action: Bolt
Stock: Synthetic
Barrel: 24 in., 26 in., 27 in.
Sights: None
Weight: 13 lb. 7 oz.–14 lb. 8 oz.
Caliber: 6mm Creedmoor, .260 Rem., 6.5 Creedmoor, 6.5x47 Lapua, 6.5 PRC, .308 Win., .300 Win. Mag., .300 PRC, .300 Norma Mag., .338 Lapua Mag., .338 Norma Mag.
Magazine: 10 rounds
Features: Designed for long-range sniper work; V-shaped bedding eliminates action movement in the chassis; mirage-control tube; Bartlein straight-taper fluted barrel with threaded muzzle, 5R mil-spec match-grade single-point cut rifling; built-in recoil lug; DX2 Evo single-/double-stage selectable trigger; Ergo rubberized finger-grooved grip; full-length lite top rail; Cerakote finishing
MSRP . . . . $5599.95–$5719.95

CADEX DEFENCE CDX-MC KRAKEN

Action: Bolt
Stock: Synthetic
Barrel: 24 in., 26 in., 27 in.
Sights: None
Weight: 15 lb. 3 oz.
Caliber: 6mm Creedmoor, .260 Rem., 6.5 Creedmoor, 6.5x47 Lapua, .308 Win., .300 Win. Mag., .300 PRC, .300 Norma Mag., .338 Lapua Mag., .338 Norma Mag.
Magazine: 10 rounds
Features: V-shaped bedding that eliminates action movement in the chassis; mirage-control tube; three-lug bolt with 50-degree throw and choice of round bulb or cross-hatched pattern knob; Bartlein straight-taper heavy barrel with barrel band, threaded muzzle, 5R mil-spec single-point cut rifling; built-in recoil lug; DX2 Evo single-/double-stage selectable trigger; Ergo rubberized finger-grooved grip; full-length top rail; Cerakote finishing
MSRP . . . . $7174.95–$7195.95

CADEX DEFENCE CDX-R7 CRBN

Action: Bolt
Stock: Synthetic
Barrel: 24 in., 26 in.
Sights: None
Weight: 8 lb. 3 oz.–8 lb. 4 oz.
Caliber: 6.5 Creedmoor, 6.5 PRC, .308 Win., .300 WSM, 7mm Rem. Mag., .28 Nosler, .300 Win. Mag., .300 PRC, .338 Lapua Mag.
Magazine: 3, 4 rounds
Features: Hunting-style in-profile muzzle brake; aluminum bedding blocks; choice of 20 or 30 MOA top action rails; four-lug spiral-fluted bolt with 50-degree throw and slim round knob; Proof Research carbon fiber match-grade barrel with a stainless core; CX2 Evo single-/two-stage selectable trigger; neoprene cheekpiece; rubberized grip insert; oversized trigger guard; numerous stock colors
MSRP . . . . $3359.95–$4169.95

CADEX DEFENCE CDX-R7 FCP SERIES

Action: Bolt
Stock: Synthetic
Barrel: 24 in., 26 in., 27 in.
Sights: None
Weight: 12 lb. 15 oz.–13 lb. 2 oz.
Caliber: 6mm Creedmoor, .260 Rem., 6.5 Creedmoor, 6.5x47 Lapua, 6.5 PRC, .308 Win., .300 Win. Mag., .300 PRC, .300 Norma Mag., .338 Lapua Mag., .338 Norma Mag.
Magazine: 10 rounds
Features: Fixed skeleton stock; tool-less adjustable at cheek, length of pull, and buttplate; DX2 Evo single-/double-stage selectable trigger; Bartlein heavy straight-taper barrel with barrel band, threaded muzzle and 5R mil-spec single-point cut rifling; Ergo rubberized finger-groove grip; oversized trigger guard; detachable base for easy trigger care; multiple stock color options
MSRP . . . . $4459.95–$4649.95

CADEX DEFENCE CDX-R7 LCP SERIES

CADEX DEFENCE CDX-R7 SHP SERIES

CADEX DEFENCE CDX-R7 SPTR

CADEX DEFENCE CDX-TAC SERIES

CHIAPPA FIREARMS 1892 WILDLANDS MH, WILDLANDS MH TAKEDOWN

CADEX DEFENCE CDX-R7 LCP SERIES

Action: Bolt
Stock: Synthetic
Barrel: 24 in., 26 in., 27 in.
Sights: None
Weight: 12 lb. 15 oz.–13 lb. 2 oz.
Caliber: 6mm Creedmoor, .260 Rem., 6.5 Creedmoor, 6.5x47 Lapua, 6.5 PRC, .308 Win., .300 Win. Mag., .300 PRC, .300 Norma Mag., .338 Lapua Mag., .338 Norma Mag.
Magazine: 10 rounds
Features: Designed for Precision Rifle Series competition; four-lug bolt with a 50-degree throw and oversized knob in choice of round bulb or crosshatch design; Cerakote finish; Bartlein straight-taper heavy barrel with a barrel band, threaded muzzle, and 5R mil-spec single point cut rifling; Ergo finger-grooved and rubberized pistol grip; reverse folding buttstock; DX2 Evo single-/double-stage selectable trigger; choice of 0, 20, or 30 MOA rail; numerous stock colors
MSRP . . . . $4899.95–$5069.95

CADEX DEFENCE CDX-R7 SHP SERIES

Action: Bolt
Stock: Synthetic
Barrel: 20 in., 24 in., 26 in., 27 in.
Sights: None
Weight: 13 lb.–13 lb. 8 oz.
Caliber: 6mm Creedmoor, .260 Rem., 6.5 Creedmoor, 6.5x47 Lapua, 6.5 PRC, .308 Win., .300 Win. Mag., .300 PRC, .300 Norma Mag., .338 Lapua Mag., .338 Norma Mag.
Magazine: 10 rounds
Features: Cerakoting; MX2 Tactical muzzle brake; aluminum micro-chassis; choice of 0, 20, or 30 MOA action rails; spiral-fluted bolt with a 50-degree throw; oversized bolt knob in choice of round bulb or cross-hatch body; straight taper fluted match-grade barrel; DX2 Evo single-/two-stage selectable trigger; tool-less adjustable spring-loaded cheekpiece; dual-sided built-in quick-detach sling attachment flush cups; ambidextrous palm swell grip; oversized trigger guard; numerous stock colors available
MSRP . . . . $3269.95–$3369.95

CADEX DEFENCE CDX-R7 SPTR

Action: Bolt
Stock: Synthetic
Barrel: 24 in., 26 in.
Sights: None
Weight: 8 lb. 8 oz.
Caliber: 6.5 Creedmoor, 6.5 PRC, .308 Win., .300 WSM, 7mm Rem. Mag., .28 Nosler, .300 Win. Mag., .300 PRC, .338 Lapua Mag.
Magazine: 3, 4 rounds
Features: Hunting-style in-profile muzzle brake; aluminum bedding blocks; choice of 20 or 30 MOA top action rails; four-lug spiral-fluted bolt with 50-degree throw and slim round knob; Cadex sporter-profile stainless steel barrel; CX2 Evo single-/two-stage selectable trigger; neoprene cheekpiece; rubberized grip insert; oversized trigger guard; numerous stock colors
MSRP . . . . $2769.95–$3079.95

CADEX DEFENCE CDX-TAC SERIES

Action: Bolt
Stock: Synthetic
Barrel: 24 in., 26 in., 27 in.
Sights: None
Weight: 12 lb. 3 oz.–13 lb. 5 oz.
Caliber: 6.5 Creedmoor, 6.5 PRC, .300 Win., .300 WSM, .28 Nosler, .300 Win. Mag., .300 PRC, .300 Lapua Mag.
Magazine: 10 rounds
Features: Fixed skeleton stock; tool-less adjustable at cheek, length of pull, and buttplate; V-shaped bedding system that eliminates action movement in the chassis; mirage control tube to reduce visual mirage from barrel heat; DX2 Evo single-/double-stage selectable trigger; Bartlein heavy straight-taper barrel with barrel band, threaded muzzle, and 5R mil-spec single-point cut rifling; Ergo rubberized finger-groove grip; oversized trigger guard; detachable base; full-length lite top rail in 20, 30, or 40 MOA; multiple stock colors
MSRP . . . . $4989.95–$5139.95

CHIAPPA FIREARMS 1892 WILDLANDS MH, WILDLANDS MH TAKEDOWN

Action: Lever
Stock: Synthetic
Barrel: 16.5 in.
Sights: Fiber optic front, leaf rear
Weight: 6 lb. 13 oz.
Caliber: .44 Mag.
Magazine: 5 rounds
Features: Handy, short-barreled rifle with a black synthetic stock and black embossed-finish metalwork; half-cock capability; topside Picatinny rail; wide loop lever with paracord wrap; paracord sling
Standard: $1579.00
Takedown: $2069.00

CHRISTENSEN ARMS CA5FIVE6

CHRISTENSEN ARMS MESA LONG RANGE

CHRISTENSEN ARMS TFM

CIMARRON FIREARMS COMPANY 1859 SHARPS MCNELLY

CIMARRON FIREARMS COMPANY 1873 TRAPPER

CIMARRON FIREARMS COMPANY 1876 CENTENNIAL TOM HORN

CHRISTENSEN ARMS CA5FIVE6

Action: Semiautomatic
Stock: Synthetic
Barrel: 16 in.
Sights: None
Weight: 6 lb. 5 oz.
Caliber: .223 Wylde
Magazine: 10 rounds
Features: Maneuverable carbine; Trigger Tech single-stage trigger; match chamber; ½X28 threaded muzzle with a stainless 3-prong flash hider; carbon fiber-wrapped stainless barrel; forged aluminum upper and lower; 15-in. aluminum hybrid carbon fiber M-LOK handguard; direct impingement system; adjustable MFT minimalist buttstock
MSRP $1495.00

CHRISTENSEN ARMS MESA LONG RANGE

Action: Bolt
Stock: Carbon fiber
Barrel: 24 in., 26 in., 27 in.
Sights: None
Weight: 8 lb. 14 oz.
Caliber: 6.5 Creedmoor, 6.5 PRC, .308 Win., .28 Nosler, 7mm Rem. Mag., .300 Win. Mag., .300 PRC, .338 Lapua Mag.
Magazine: 3, 4 rounds
Features: Stainless steel, medium Palma contour barrel that's hand lapped and button rifled; threaded-on seamless side-baffle brake in stainless steel; CA's own carbon-fiber composite long-range stock with spacer-adjustable comb; match chamber; spot bedding and Invar pillars; internal magazine with hinged floorplate; Trigger Tech trigger; twin-lug spiral fluted bolt and fluted bolt knob; dual ejectors in magnum calibers; M16-style extractor
MSRP $1595.00

CHRISTENSEN ARMS TFM

Action: Bolt
Stock: Carbon fiber
Barrel: 16 in., 24 in., 26 in., 27 in.
Sights: None
Weight: 7 lb. 4 oz.
Caliber: 6mm Creedmoor, 6.5 Creedmoor, 6.5 PRC, .300 Win. Mag., .338 Lapua Mag., .300 PRC
Magazine: 3, 4 rounds
Features: Carbon fiber-wrapped barrel in a target profile; removable and adjustable titanium side-baffle brake; integrated 20 MOA Picatinny rail; fully adjustable match trigger; oversized and fluted bolt knob; tactical mag release; AICS-compatible magazines; CA's carbon fiber long-range tactical stock with thumb-wheel adjustable comb and length of pull; modified beavertail forend, tactical grip with palm swell and thumb shelf; tactical hook; full-length bedding with carbon fiber pillars; nitride-treated, twin-lug, spiral-fluted bolt; dual ejector in magnum calibers; M16-style extractor; barrel is hand lapped, button rifled, free-floating, has a match chamber and a 5/8x24 threaded muzzle
MSRP $4895.00

CIMARRON FIREARMS COMPANY 1859 SHARPS MCNELLY

Action: Lever single-shot
Stock: American black walnut
Barrel: 26 in.
Sights: Blade front, ladder rear
Weight: 10 lb. 14 oz.
Caliber: .45-70 Gov't.
Magazine: 1 round
Features: A centerfire conversion based on the 1859 Sharps Military Carbine; round barrel in a polished blue finish; case-colored receiver
MSRP $1387.10

CIMARRON FIREARMS COMPANY 1873 TRAPPER

Action: Lever
Stock: Walnut
Barrel: 16 in.
Sights: Blade front, leaf rear
Weight: 7 lb. 2 oz.
Caliber: .44-40 (.44 WCF), .32-20 (.32 WCF), .45 LC
Magazine: 9 rounds
Features: Handy short-barreled lever with a straight stock in a polished finish; blued round barrel and magazine; case-colored receiver and action
MSRP $1392.77

CIMARRON FIREARMS COMPANY 1876 CENTENNIAL TOM HORN

Action: Lever single-shot
Stock: Walnut
Barrel: 28 in.
Sights: Blade front, aperture rear
Weight: 10 lb.
Caliber: .45-60
Magazine: 1 round
Features: Inspired by the movie Tom Horn starring Steve McQueen, this single-shot wears a polished blue finish; Tom Horn "signature" engraved on the receiver sideplate; storage in the stock accessed through the crescent buttplate; folding leaf rear for use when the user does not wish to employ the wrist-mounted aperture rear
MSRP $1846.25

CMMG BANSHEE 100 MK4

CMMG BANSHEE 200 MK4

CMMG BANSHEE 300 MK4

CZ-USA CZ 557 ECLIPSE

DANIEL DEFENSE DD5 V4 HUNTER

DANIEL DEFENSE DD5 V5 HUNTER

DANIEL DEFENSE DDM4 HUNTER

CMMG BANSHEE 100 MK4

Action: Semiautomatic
Stock: Synthetic
Barrel: 9 in.
Sights: None
Weight: 4 lb. 15 oz.
Caliber: .22 LR
Magazine: 25 rounds
Features: An SBR (NFA rules apply) in .22 LR; forged M4-type upper with an AR-15-type lower; CMMG RML7 M-LOK handguard; CMMG anti-jam charging handle; Magpul MOE pistol grip and trigger guard; six-position CMMG M4 buttstock with six-position receiver extension; medium taper barrel with an A2 comp threaded ½X28; hard-coat anodized receiver in black with Cerakote upgrade available in numerous colors
MSRP $899.95

CMMG BANSHEE 200 MK4

Action: Semiautomatic
Stock: Synthetic
Barrel: 9 in.
Sights: None
Weight: 5 lb. 1 oz.
Caliber: .22 LR
Magazine: 25 rounds
Features: An SBR (NFA rules apply) in .22 LR; forged M4-type upper with an AR-15-type lower; CMMG RML7 M-LOK handguard; CMMG anti-jam charging handle; Magpul MOE pistol grip and trigger guard; six-position CMMG RipStock with enhance receiver extension and ambidextrous sling plate; medium taper barrel with A2 comp threaded ½X28; hard-coat anodized receiver in black with Cerakote upgrade available in numerous colors
MSRP $1049.95

CMMG BANSHEE 300 MK4

Action: Semiautomatic
Stock: Synthetic
Barrel: 4.5 in.
Sights: None
Weight: 4 lb. 7 oz.
Caliber: .22 LR
Magazine: 25 rounds
Features: An SBR (NFA rules apply) in .22 LR; forged M4-type upper with AR-15-type lower; CMMG RML4 M-LOK handguard with Magpul MVG; oversized ambidextrous charging handle; Magpul MOE pistol grip and trigger guard; collapsible stock; KAK Slim Flash Can threaded ½x28; single-stage mil-spec trigger; Cerakote finish in numerous color options
MSRP $1199.95

CZ-USA CZ 557 ECLIPSE

Action: Bolt
Stock: Synthetic
Barrel: 20.5 in.
Sights: None
Weight: 6 lb. 13 oz.
Caliber: 6.5 Creedmoor, .308 Win., .30-06 Spfd.
Magazine: 5 rounds
Features: Push-fed action; cold hammer-forged and lapped barrel wearing 5/8x24 threads; fixed magazine with hinged floorplate; integrated 19mm dovetail optic mounting grooves; fully adjustable trigger
MSRP $659.00

DANIEL DEFENSE DD5 V4 HUNTER

Action: Semiautomatic
Stock: Glass-filled polymer
Barrel: 18 in.
Sights: None
Weight: 8 lb. 10 oz.
Caliber: 6.5 Creedmoor, .260 Rem., .308 Win.
Magazine: 10 rounds
Features: Buffered bolt carrier; cold hammer-forged, steel chrome-lined barrel in a 2SW—strength-to-weight—profile; direct impingement gas system with a pinned user adjustable gas block; two-stage trigger, 15-in. DD5 rail with M-LOK attachment; soft-touch overmolding on stock and pistol grip; takes all SR-25 magazines
MSRP $2933.00

DANIEL DEFENSE DD5 V5 HUNTER

Action: Semiautomatic
Stock: Glass-filled polymer
Barrel: 20 in.
Sights: None
Weight: 8 lb. 15 oz.
Caliber: 6.5 Creedmoor, .260 Rem.
Magazine: 10 rounds
Features: This camo-clad rifle gets a CNC machined 7075-T6 aluminum upper and lower; two-stage Geissele Super Semiautomatic trigger; direct impingement gas system with heavy phosphate coating; flared magazine well; four-bolt connection system for improved accuracy; Grip-N-Rip ambidextrous charging handle with anti-gas feature; DD's Superior Suppression Device; 15-in. DD5 rail; soft-touch overmolding on stock and pistol grip; takes all SR-25 magazines
MSRP $2933.00

DANIEL DEFENSE DDM4 HUNTER

Action: Semiautomatic
Stock: Glass-filled polymer
Barrel: 16 in.
Sights: None
Weight: 6 lb. 8 oz.
Caliber: .300 BLK, 6.8 SPC
Magazine: 5 rounds
Features: Lightweight and nimble, this rifle clad in Kryptek Highlander camo gets a mil-spec upper and lower; flared magwell; mid-length direct impingement gas system; pinned low-profile gas block; M16 profile gas block; H buffer; staked gas key; Grip-N-Rip charging handle; soft-touch overmolding on stock and pistol grip; DD MFR 15-in rail with M-LOK points; takes PRI magazines
MSRP $1946.00

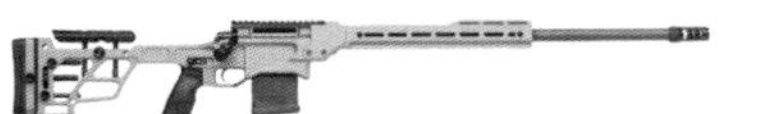
DANIEL DEFENSE DELTA 5 6.5 CREEDMOOR PROOF/DANIEL DEFENSE TORNADO

DANIEL DEFENSE DELTA 5 PRO HPALMA

DANIEL DEFENSE DELTA 5 PRO VARMINT

DEL-TON DT SCOUT

DEL-TON DTI SXT

DEL-TON SIERRA 316L

DANIEL DEFENSE DELTA 5 6.5 CREEDMOOR PROOF/ DANIEL DEFENSE TORNADO

Action: Bolt
Stock: Carbon fiber–reinforced polymer
Barrel: 24 in.
Sights: None
Weight: 9 lb.
Caliber: 6.5 Creedmoor
Magazine: 10 rounds
Features: DD paired with Proof to provide a long-range rifle with both a carbon fiber-reinforced stock and a carbon fiber barrel in an H-Palma profile; barrel is threaded 5/8X24; takes Magpul PMag magazines; stock finished in DD Tornado Cerakote; removable bolt knob; 20 MOA of Picatinny rail; 14 M-LOK attachment points; three M-LOK quick-detach sling points; mechanically bedded stainless steel action with integral recoil lug; Timney Elite Hunter adjustable single-stage trigger
MSRP $2566.00

DANIEL DEFENSE DELTA 5 PRO HPALMA

Action: Bolt
Stock: Chassis
Barrel: 24 in.
Sights: None
Weight: 11 lb. 6 oz.
Caliber: 6.5 Creedmoor
Magazine: 10 rounds
Features: Interchangeable barrel in a heavy Palma profile and with a Cerakote finish; Area 419 Hellfire muzzle brake; Timney Elite Hunter adjustable single-stage trigger; chassis base; interchangeable AR-15 grip attachment; adjustable left/right thumb rest; three-lug bolt with removable bolt knob; 10 quick-detach sling points; six M-LOK attachment points on forend, one on buttstock bottom; adjustable buttstock and cheekpiece; 20 MOA Picatinny rail
Black: $2499.00
Cerakote color: $2673.00

DANIEL DEFENSE DELTA 5 PRO VARMINT

Action: Bolt
Stock: Chassis
Barrel: 26 in.
Sights: None
Weight: 13.3 lb.
Caliber: 6.5 Creedmoor, 6mm Creedmoor
Magazine: 10 rounds
Features: A varmint gun with a chassis foundation; interchangeable barrels; Area 419 Hellfire muzzle brake; three-lug bolt with removable bolt knob; 20 MOA Picatinny scope base; 10 M-LOK quick-detach sling points; integral ARCA lock along entire lower rail; interchangeable AR-15 grip attachment; left/right adjustable thumb rest; tool-less adjustable cheekpiece ad buttstock; single-stage adjustable Timney Elite Hunter trigger; in black or Cerakote olive drab or coyote tan
Black: $2499.00
Cerakote color: $2673.00

DEL-TON DT SCOUT

Action: Semiautomatic
Stock: Synthetic
Barrel: 16 in.
Sights: A2 front sight, flip-up rear
Weight: 5 lb. 14 oz.
Caliber: 5.56 NATO
Magazine: 30 rounds
Features: Lightweight MSR in A3 flattop configuration; forged aluminum upper and lower; chrome-lined carrier and carrier key; lightweight barrel profile with a threaded-on A2 flash hider; mid-length gas system with staked and sealed gas key; mid-length aluminum Delta Ring handguard with heat shield; ejection port cover; round forward assist; A2 grip; carbine buffer
MSRP $680.00

DEL-TON DTI SXT

Action: Semiautomatic
Stock: Synthetic
Barrel: 16 in.
Sights: None
Weight: 6 lb. 3 oz.
Caliber: 5.56 NATO
Magazine: 30 rounds
Features: Forged aluminum upper and lower in Cerakote flat dark earth; 15-in Samson free-floating handguard with M-LOK attachment points; lightweight profile barrel of chrome moly vanadium; M4 feed ramp; DTI low-profile gas block; M4 five-position buttstock with a mil-spec buffer tube; round forward assist; ejection port cover
MSRP $750.00

DEL-TON SIERRA 316L

Action: Semiautomatic
Stock: Synthetic
Barrel: 16 in.
Sights: None
Weight: 6 lb. 3 oz.
Caliber: 5.56 NATO
Magazine: 30 rounds
Features: Optics-ready MSR with a mid-length lightweight barrel; A2 flash hider; DTI low-profile gas block; threaded muzzle; M4 feed ramp; forged aluminum upper and lower receiver hard anodized and mil-spec; M4 five-position buttstock with mil-spec buffer tube; 15-in M-LOK free-floating handguard
MSRP $675.00

DESERT TECH MDRX

DESERT TECH SRS A2 COVERT

DESERT TECH SRS A2 STANDARD

DESERT TECH SRS A2 ULTRA-LIGHT

EUROPEAN AMERICAN ARMORY TANGFOLIO APPEAL

FRANCHI MOMENTUM ELITE VARMINT

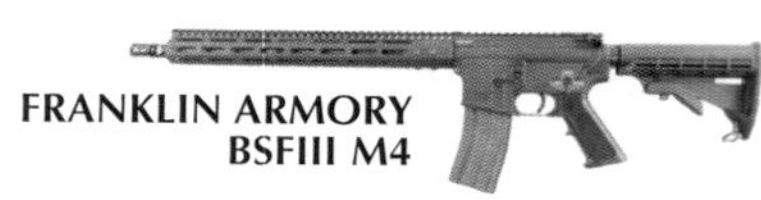
FRANKLIN ARMORY BSFIII M4

DESERT TECH MDRX

Action: Semiautomatic
Stock: Synthetic
Barrel: 16 in., 20 in.
Sights: None
Weight: 8 lb. 8 oz.–8 lb. 14 oz.
Caliber: .223 Wylde, 6.5 Creedmoor, .300 BLK, .308 Win.
Magazine: 10, 20, 30 rounds
Features: This is a convertible bullpup available in either forward-eject or side-eject configurations, both options in state-compliant models as well; trigger pull weight set at 4.7 lb.; ambidextrous controls; barrel threaded ½X28 or 5/8x28 depending on caliber
MSRP . . . . $1889.98–$2199.99

DESERT TECH SRS A2 COVERT

Action: Bolt
Stock: Synthetic
Barrel: 16 in., 18 in.
Sights: None
Weight: 8 lb.–8 lb. 4 oz.
Caliber: .308 Win., 6.5 Creedmoor, .300 Win.
Magazine: 5, 6, 8, 10 rounds
Features: Buffered bolt carrier; cold hammer-forged, steel chrome-lined barrel in a 2SW (strength-to-weight) profile; direct impingement gas system with a pinned user adjustable gas block; Daniel Defense Superior Suppression Device; two-stage Geissele Super Semiautomatic trigger; 15-in. DD5 rail with M-LOK attachment; soft-touch overmolding on stock and pistol grip; takes all SR-25 magazines
MSRP . . . . $4295.00–$4495.00

DESERT TECH SRS A2 STANDARD

Action: Bolt
Stock: Synthetic
Barrel: 22 in., 26 in.
Sights: None
Weight: 8 lb. 15 oz.–9 lb. 8 oz.
Caliber: .308 Win., 6.5 Creedmoor, .300 Win. Mag., .300 Norma Mag., .338 Lapua Mag., .338 Norma Mag.
Magazine: 5, 6, 8, 10 rounds
Features: Similar to the Covert model, but with more caliber choices, including several in the very long-range game; 6-second reload time; adjustable trigger; monopod-ready stock; integral tripod mount; barrel threaded 5/8x24; handguard with M-LOK attachment points; integral Picatinny rails top and bottom
MSRP . . . . $4295.00–$4645.00

DESERT TECH SRS A2 ULTRA-LIGHT

Action: Bolt
Stock: Synthetic
Barrel: 24 in., 26 in.
Sights: None
Weight: 8 lb. 4 oz.–9 lb.
Caliber: 6.5 Creedmoor, .300 Win. Mag. .300 RUM, 7mm Rem. Mag.
Magazine: 5, 6, 8, 10 rounds
Features: Rifle weight is marginally less than the standard; 6-second reload time; adjustable trigger; monopod-ready stock; integral tripod mount; barrel threaded 5/8x24; handguard with M-LOK attachment points; integral Picatinny rails top and bottom
MSRP . . . . $4295.00–$4495.00

EUROPEAN AMERICAN ARMORY TANGFOLIO APPEAL

Action: Semiautomatic
Stock: Synthetic
Barrel: 18 in.
Sights: None
Weight: 4 lb. 14 oz.
Caliber: .22 LR, .22 WMR
Magazine: 10 rounds
Features: Tangfolio's first long-gun, a rimfire in a bullpup configuration; carry handle with topside Picatinny rail; muzzle brake; underside accessory rail; detachable integral sling swivels
MSRP $462.00

FRANCHI MOMENTUM ELITE VARMINT

Action: Bolt
Stock: Synthetic
Barrel: 24 in.
Sights: None
Weight: 9 lb.–9 lb. 7 oz.
Caliber: .223 Rem., .22-250 Rem., .224 Valkyrie
Magazine: 3, 4 rounds
Features: Synthetic stock in Optifade camo; free-floating, heavy profile fluted barrel with muzzle brake in Midnight Bronze Cerakote; flush-fit magazine (¾ rounds) and one extended magazine (8 rounds); soft-touch overmolds on grip and cheekpiece; topside Picatinny rail
MSRP $999.00

FRANKLIN ARMORY BSFIII M4

Action: Semiautomatic
Stock: Synthetic
Barrel: 16 in.
Sights: None
Weight: N/A
Caliber: 5.56 NATO
Magazine: 20 rounds
Features: Franklin's Binary Firing System Gen III, a 3-position trigger: Position 1 is safe, position 2 is one shot per pull, and position 3 fires one round on pull and one on release; LTW contour barrel; 15-in. FST handguard; standard charging handle; mid-length gas system; low-profile gas block; A2 flash hider and grip; M4 stock
MSRP $1109.99

FRANKLIN ARMORY M4-HTF R3 XTD

FRANKLIN ARMORY REFORMATION RS7, RS11

FRANKLIN ARMORY XO-26 R3

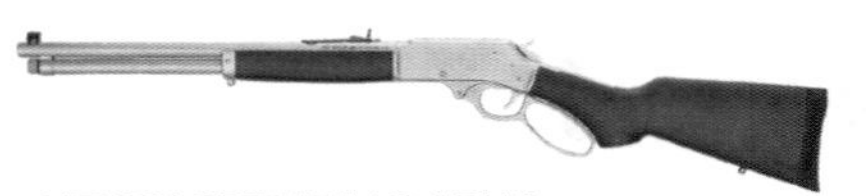

HENRY REPEATING ARMS ALL-WEATHER LEVER ACTION SIDE GATE

HENRY REPEATING ARMS BIG BOY ALL WEATHER SIDE GATE

HENRY REPEATING ARMS BIG BOY, BIG BOY CARBINE COLOR CASE HARDENED SIDE GATE

FRANKLIN ARMORY M4-HTF R3 XTD

Action: Semiautomatic
Stock: Synthetic
Barrel: 16 in.
Sights: None
Weight: N/A
Caliber: 5.56 NATO, .350 Legend
Magazine: 20 rounds
Features: Binary Firing System Gen III, a 3-position trigger: position 1 is safe, position 2 is one shot per pull, and position 3 fires one round on pull and one on release; LTW contour barrel; 15-in. FSR M-LOK handguard; mil-spec charging handle; mid-length gas system; low-profile gas block; Aura XTD muzzle device; B5 grip; B5 Bravo stock
MSRP $1369.99

FRANKLIN ARMORY REFORMATION RS7, RS11

Action: Semiautomatic
Stock: Synthetic
Barrel: 7.5 in., 11.5 in.
Sights: MBUS
Weight: N/A
Caliber: 5.56 NATO, .300 BLK
Magazine: 20 rounds
Features: The Reformation barrel does not impart spin on the projectile, so it does not meet the definition of 'rifling.' Franklin Armory has safely tested off-the-shelf ammunition in a Reformation barrel and routinely achieved 3.5 in. @100 yards with white box ammunition. .300 BLK has 11.5-in. barrel and choice of black or OD green receiver; 5.56 NATO has 7.5-in. barrel and is available in black; both calibers can option Franklin Armory's Binary Firing System Gen III trigger
RS7: . . . . $1254.99–$1429.99
RS-11: . . . . $1594.99–$1757.99

FRANKLIN ARMORY XO-26 R3

Action: Semiautomatic
Stock: Synthetic
Barrel: 12 in.
Sights: None
Weight: N/A
Caliber: 5.56 NATO, .350 Legend
Magazine: 10, 30 rounds
Features: Barrel has an LTW contour; 11.5-in. FST handguard; standard charging handle; pistol lower; BFSIII or custom-tuned trigger; carbine-length gas system; low-profile gas block; Triumvir muzzle device; Magpul SL grip; Magpul M-LOK MVG
MSRP . . . . $1369.99–$1519.99

HENRY REPEATING ARMS ALL-WEATHER LEVER ACTION SIDE GATE

Action: Lever
Stock: Hardwood
Barrel: 20 in.
Sights: Brass bead front, fully adjustable semi-buckhorn rear
Weight: 7 lb.
Caliber: .30-30 Win., .45-70 Gov't.
Magazine: 4, 5 rounds
Features: A side-loader for deer hunters, with a darkly stained hardwood stock; metalwork in an industrial hard chrome satin finish; drilled and tapped; swivel studs
MSRP $1141.00

HENRY REPEATING ARMS BIG BOY ALL WEATHER SIDE GATE

Action: Lever
Stock: Hardwood
Barrel: 20 in.
Sights: Brass bead front, fully adjustable semi-buckhorn rear
Weight: 7 lb.
Caliber: .38 Spl./.357 Mag., .44 Spl./.44 Mag., .45 LC
Magazine: 10 rounds
Features: Convenient side-gate loading; metalwork is hard-chrome plated and sealed to be moisture resistant; darkly stained hardwood stock; drilled and tapped; swivel studs included
MSRP $1141.00

HENRY REPEATING ARMS BIG BOY, BIG BOY CARBINE COLOR CASE HARDENED SIDE GATE

Action: Lever
Stock: American walnut
Barrel: 16.5 in. (carbine), 20 in. (standard)
Sights: Brass bead front, fully adjustable semi-buckhorn rear
Weight: 7 lb. 7 oz.–7 lb. 14 oz.
Caliber: .38 Spl./.357 Mag., .44 Spl./.44 Mag., .45 LC
Magazine: 7 rounds (carbine), 10 rounds (standard)
Features: A side-loading gate; case-hardened frame finish; octagon barrel in blue; carbines have large loop lever; drilled and tapped
MSRP $1141.00

NEW Products: Rifles

HENRY REPEATING ARMS BIG BOY, BIG BOY CARBINE STEEL SIDE GATE

HENRY REPEATING ARMS COLOR CASE HARDENED LEVER ACTION SIDE GATE

HENRY REPEATING ARMS NEW ORIGINAL B.T. HENRY 200TH ANNIVERSARY EDITION

HENRY REPEATING ARMS STEEL LEVER ACTION SIDE GATE

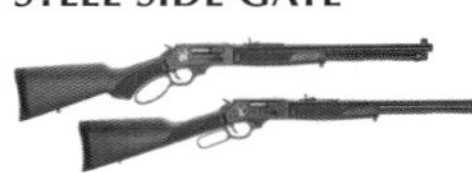

HENRY REPEATING ARMS STEEL WILDLIFE EDITION SIDE GATE

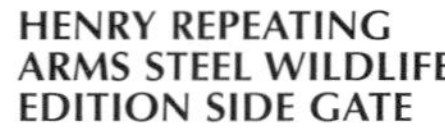

HERITAGE MANUFACTURING ROUGH RIDER RANCHER CARBINE

H-S PRECISION PLC (PROFESSIONAL LONG-RANGE CARBON FIBER)

HENRY REPEATING ARMS BIG BOY, BIG BOY CARBINE STEEL SIDE GATE

Action: Lever
Stock: American walnut
Barrel: 16.5 in., 20 in.
Sights: Brass bead front, fully adjustable semi-buckhorn rear
Weight: 6 lb. 9 oz.–7 lb.
Caliber: .38 Spl./.357 Mag., .44 Spl./.44 Mag., .45 LC
Magazine: 7 rounds (carbine), 10 rounds (standard)
Features: This variant wears a steel frame instead of brass; full-length version also available with a large loop lever; drilled and tapped; swivel studs
Standard lever: $969.00
Large loop lever: $986.00

HENRY REPEATING ARMS COLOR CASE HARDENED LEVER ACTION SIDE GATE

Action: Lever
Stock: American walnut
Barrel: 20 in., 22 in.
Sights: Brass bead front, fully adjustable semi-buckhorn rear
Weight: 8 lb. 2 oz.–8 lb. 8 oz.
Caliber: .30-30 Win., .45-70 Gov't.
Magazine: 4, 5 rounds
Features: Workhorse levers with side-gate loading wearing octagon barrels and rich color case-hardened steel receivers; .30-30 gets a straight grip and standard lever, .45-70 gets a pistol grip stock and large loop lever
MSRP $1141.00

HENRY REPEATING ARMS NEW ORIGINAL B.T. HENRY 200TH ANNIVERSARY EDITION

Action: Lever
Stock: American walnut
Barrel: 24.5 in.
Sights: Blade front, folding ladder rear
Weight: 9 lb.
Caliber: .44-40 WCF
Magazine: 13 rounds
Features: Commemorates the inventor of the first successful repeating rifle, Benjamin Tyler Henry; toggle-link lever action; steel octagon barrel in blue; upgraded walnut stock; half-cock safety; brass receiver with full-coverage leaf/vine scroll and anniversary engravings; limited production of 200
MSRP $4286.00

HENRY REPEATING ARMS STEEL LEVER ACTION SIDE GATE

Action: Lever
Stock: American walnut
Barrel: 18.43 in.
Sights: Brass bead front, fully adjustable semi-buckhorn rear
Weight: 7 lb. 1 oz.
Caliber: .30-30 Win., .45-70 Gov't.
Magazine: 4 rounds
Features: A traditional lever with side-gate loading; pistol grip stock with checkering; ventilated rubber recoil pad; drilled and tapped; swivel studs; .30-30 gets a straight grip and choice of standard or large loop lever, .45-70 gets a pistol grip stock and large loop lever
MSRP $969.00

HENRY REPEATING ARMS STEEL WILDLIFE EDITION SIDE GATE

Action: Lever
Stock: American walnut
Barrel: 18.43 in., 20 in.
Sights: Brass bead front, fully adjustable semi-buckhorn rear
Weight: 7 lb.–7 lb. 1 oz.
Caliber: .30-30 Win., .45-70 Gov't.
Magazine: 4, 5 rounds
Features: Two models in upgraded wood: the .30-30 has 20-in. barrel, whitetail deer in gold with gold highlights on engraved receiver, straight stock, and standard loop; the .45-70 has an 18.43-in. barrel, moose engraved in gold with gold highlights on the receiver, pistol grip stock, and large loop lever
MSRP $1618.00

HERITAGE MANUFACTURING ROUGH RIDER RANCHER CARBINE

Action: Revolver
Stock: Wood
Barrel: 16 in.
Sights: Blade front, adjustable buckhorn rear
Weight: 4 lb. 2 oz.
Caliber: .22 LR
Magazine: 6 rounds
Features: A different take on the PCC, with a straight wood shoulder stock; six-round cylinder; black oxide finish; single-action only; leather sling included
MSRP $297.00

H-S PRECISION PLC (PROFESSIONAL LONG-RANGE CARBON FIBER)

Action: Bolt
Stock: Synthetic
Barrel: Varies with caliber
Sights: None
Weight: Varies
Caliber: More than 50 calibers from .17 Rem. to .338 Win.
Magazine: 3, 4, 5 rounds
Features: A rifle of nearly unending customization, from barrel length, caliber, and left- or right-hand setups to length of pull, trigger, and dozens of accessories and scopes; features a carbon fiber barrel; completely redesigned stock
MSRP . . . . Starting at $4750.00

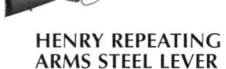

ISRAEL WEAPON INDUSTRIES TAVOR 7

ISRAEL WEAPON INDUSTRIES ZION-15

J.P. SAUER & SOHN S101 HIGHLAND XTC

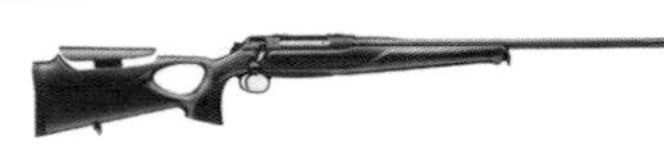
J.P. SAUER & SOHN S404 SYNCHRO XTC

KEL-TEC RDB

KEL-TEC SUB CQB

KIMBER OPEN RANGE PRO CARBON GRANITE

ISRAEL WEAPON INDUSTRIES TAVOR 7

Action: Semiautomatic
Stock: Polymer
Barrel: 16.5 in.
Sights: None
Weight: 9 lb.
Caliber: 7.62 NATO
Magazine: 20 rounds
Features: A bullpup to drive the 7.62 NATO round, with a 9-lb. weight to help control recoil; closed rotating bolt operating system has a short-stroke four-piston gas regulator; SR25 pattern magazines; M-LOK forend; Picatinny rails at 6 and 12 o'clock; ambidextrous safety, magazine release, bolt catch, ejection side, and charging handle; in black, flat dark earth, and olive drab
MSRP $2099.00

ISRAEL WEAPON INDUSTRIES ZION-15

Action: Semiautomatic
Stock: Synthetic
Barrel: 16 in.
Sights: None
Weight: 6 lb. 8 oz.
Caliber: 5.56 NATO
Magazine: 30 rounds
Features: A direct impingement MSR with an adjustable B5 Systems stock; B5 Systems grip; 4150 chrome-moly vanadium barrel; 12.5-in. SBR version also available
MSRP $899.99

J.P. SAUER & SOHN S101 HIGHLAND XTC

Action: Bolt
Stock: Carbon fiber
Barrel: 20 in., 22 in.
Sights: None
Weight: 5 lb. 8 oz.–5 lb. 10 oz.
Caliber: .243 Win., .270 Win., 6.5x55 SE, 7x64, .308 Win., .30-06 Spfd., 8x57 IS, 9.3x62, .300 Win. Mag., 7mm Rem. Mag.
Magazine: 4, 5 rounds
Features: Super lightweight, this rifle has a hand-laid carbon-fiber stock; fluted and threaded barrel; fluted bolt; Diamond-like Carbon surface treatment on metalwork; DURA SAFE firing pin safety; EVER REST bedding system; cold hammer-forged barrel; match rifle-shaped single-stage trigger
MSRP $3000.00

J.P. SAUER & SOHN S404 SYNCHRO XTC

Action: Bolt
Stock: Carbon fiber
Barrel: 22 in.
Sights: None
Weight: 6 lb. 2 oz.–6 lb. 5 oz.
Caliber: .223 Rem., .243 Win., 6.5x55 Swedish, 6.5 Creedmoor, .270 Win., 7x64, .308 Win., .30-06 Spfd., 8x57 IS, 9.3x62, 7mm Rem. Mag., .300 Win. Mag., 8x68 S, 10.3x60R
Magazine: 2, 3, 4 rounds
Features: Hand-laid carbon-fiber thumbhole stock of unique and trim design that's also modular, allowing the user to change stocks and barrel speedily with a Sauer SUS universal key integrated into the detachable forend swivel; adjustable cheekpiece; two-step bolt head from bolt body separation to render the gun instantly inoperable as needed; push-button manual cocking system; adjustable trigger pull weight and trigger blade position; cold hammer-forged threaded barrel
MSRP $8199.00

KEL-TEC RDB

Action: Semiautomatic
Stock: Synthetic
Barrel: 17.3 in.
Sights: None
Weight: 7 lb.
Caliber: 5.56 NATO
Magazine: 20, 30 rounds
Features: A bullpup that features downward ejection; high impact-resistant Zytel forend; completely ambidextrous; top and bottom Picatinny rails
MSRP $999.99

KEL-TEC SUB CQB

Action: Semiautomatic
Stock: Synthetic
Barrel: 16.2 in.
Sights: None
Weight: 9 lb. 8 oz.
Caliber: 9mm
Magazine: 10, 15, 17, 30 rounds
Features: Super interesting entry in the self-defense genre, an integrally suppressed 9mm (one NFA stamp—this is not an SBR) that folds in half and tales Glock magazines; lots of rail for lights and lasers; only 4.25 inches of rifling in a 16-in. baffled barrel
MSRP $995.00

KIMBER OPEN RANGE PRO CARBON GRANITE

Action: Bolt
Stock: Carbon fiber
Barrel: 24 in.
Sights: None
Weight: 6 lb. 3 oz.
Caliber: 6.5 Creedmoor
Magazine: 4 rounds
Features: With both a carbon fiber stock and barrel, this lightweight rifle also features a threaded muzzle with muzzle brake; metalwork finish in black KimPro II; medium-heavy barrel contour; stainless steel action; pillar-bedded stock in textured granite
MSRP $3236.00

KIMBER OPEN RANGE PRO CARBON OPEN COUNTRY

KRISS USA DMK22C LVOA

LAZZERONI M2012 SHORT-MAG HEAVY BARREL DANGEROUS GAME

LAZZERONI M2012 SHORT-MAG MOUNTAIN-LITE LONG-RANGE

LIVE Q OR DIE HONEY BADGER SD

LIVE Q OR DIE HONEY BADGER SBR

LIVE Q OR DIE THE FIX

KIMBER OPEN RANGE PRO CARBON OPEN COUNTRY

Action: Bolt
Stock: Carbon fiber
Barrel: 24 in.
Sights: None
Weight: 6 lb. 3 oz.
Caliber: 6.5 Creedmoor
Magazine: 4 rounds
Features: With both a carbon fiber stock and barrel, this lightweight rifle also features a threaded muzzle with muzzle brake; metalwork finish in black KimPro II; medium heavy barrel contour; stainless steel action finished in KimPro II gray; pillar-bedded stock in Tru Timber O2 Octane camo
MSRP $3236.00

KRISS USA DMK22C LVOA

Action: Semiautomatic
Stock: Synthetic
Barrel: 16 in.
Sights: None
Weight: 7 lb. 1 oz.
Caliber: .22 LR
Magazine: 15 rounds
Features: Licensed reproduction of War Sport Manufacturing's Low Visibility Operations Application rifle, this rimfire has an adaptor that allows for the installation of aftermarket Ruger 10/22 barrels; patented bolt lock keeps action open when magazine is removed; compatible with most AR-15 furniture and accessories; LVOA free-floating rail; low-profile flip-up sights; mil-spec buffer tube; six-position adjustable stock; direct blowback action; single-stage trigger; in black, flat dark earth, or alpine white
MSRP $825.00

LAZZERONI M2012 SHORT-MAG HEAVY BARREL DANGEROUS GAME

Action: Bolt
Stock: Composite
Barrel: 22 in.
Sights: None
Weight: 7 lb. 3 oz.
Caliber: 9.53 Hellcat, 10.57 Maverick, 12.04 Lilmufu
Magazine: 3 rounds
Features: Designed around Lazzeroni's short magnums, but for the larger calibers in this group; stainless steel match-grade button-rifled barrel; Timney trigger; High-tech Vais muzzle brake; barrel band with sling eye
MSRP $7499.99

LAZZERONI M2012 SHORT-MAG MOUNTAIN-LITE LONG-RANGE

Action: Bolt
Stock: Composite
Barrel: 24 in.
Sights: None
Weight: 6 lb. 9 oz.
Caliber: 7.21 Tomahawk, 7.82 Patriot, 8.59 Galaxy
Magazine: 4 rounds
Features: Specifically designed for Lazzeroni's short-mag calibers; stainless steel match-grade button-rifled barrel; Timney trigger; High-tech Vais muzzle brake Limbsaver recoil pad; custom molded, hand-bedded stock
MSRP $5999.99

LIVE Q OR DIE HONEY BADGER SBR

Action: Semiautomatic
Stock: Synthetic
Barrel: 7 in.
Sights: None
Weight: 4 lb. 8 oz.
Caliber: .300 BLK
Magazine: 20 rounds
Features: This is an NFA short-barreled rifle (no suppressor), so paperwork/tax stamps apply; adjustable low-profile gas block; two-position collapsible PDW stock; free-floating 6-inch M-LOK handguard; Cherry Bomb muzzle brake threaded at 5/8x24
MSRP $2999.00

LIVE Q OR DIE HONEY BADGER SD

Action: Semiautomatic
Stock: Synthetic
Barrel: 7 in.
Sights: None
Weight: 5 lb. 6 oz.
Caliber: .300 BLK
Magazine: 20 rounds
Features: This an NFA short-barrel rifle with silencer, so all paperwork/ tax stamps apply; free-floating 6061 aluminum M-LOK handguard; tapered muzzle threaded 5/8x24; AR-type controls; two-stage trigger; finished in clear hard coat anodized over tan; company's own Honey Badger silencer
MSRP $3499.00

LIVE Q OR DIE THE FIX

Action: Bolt
Stock: Synthetic
Barrel: 16 in.
Sights: None
Weight: 6 lb. 4 oz.–6 lb. 6 oz.
Caliber: 6.5 Creedmoor, .308 Win.
Magazine: 20 rounds
Features: 45-degree short-throw bolt; fully adjustable folding stock; free-floating Q-sert handguard; 5/8X24 threaded tapered muzzle with Cherry Bomb muzzle brake; two-stage match trigger; one-piece receiver; SR-25 magazine compatible; AR-type controls
MSRP $3299.00

MAGNUM RESEARCH SWITCHBOLT

MASTERPIECE ARMS MPA AR9 PCC

MASTERPIECE ARMS MPA PORK CHOP RIFLE

PATRIOT ORDNANCE FACTORY PRESCOTT

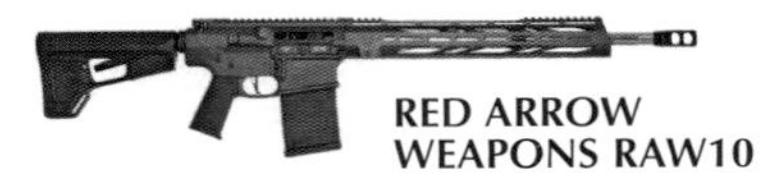
RED ARROW WEAPONS RAW10

RED ARROW WEAPONS RAW15

MAGNUM RESEARCH SWITCHBOLT

Action: Semiautomatic
Stock: Laminate, synthetic
Barrel: 17 in.
Sights: None
Weight: 4 lb. 8 oz.
Caliber: .22 LR
Magazine: 10 rounds
Features: Designed for rimfire speed competitions; operating bolt handle on the left side of the right-handed bolt, so that right-handed shooters never have to release their trigger hand grip to charge after a gone-dry reload or otherwise manipulate the bolt; skeletonized hardwood laminate (red, blue, black pepper, or forest camo) or black synthetic thumbhole stock; carbon barrel; gas-assisted blowback operation; Ruger 10/22 magazines
MSRP . . . . $638.00–$849.00

MASTERPIECE ARMS MPA AR9 PCC

Action: Semiautomatic
Stock: Aluminum
Barrel: 16 in.
Sights: None
Weight: 6 lb. 4 oz.
Caliber: 9mm
Magazine: 10, 15, 17, 30 rounds
Features: Closed-bolt blowback operating system; aluminum receiver that takes standard AR accessories and furniture; proprietary bolt carrier group; heavy duty claw extractor; suppressor compatibility; Glock magazine compatibility; multi-port steel Cerakoted compensator; adjustable buttstock; cool colors
MSRP $1499.00

MASTERPIECE ARMS MPA PORK CHOP RIFLE

Action: Bolt
Stock: Chassis
Barrel: 18 in., 20 in., 22 in., 24 in., 26 in.
Sights: None
Weight: 8 lb. 6 oz.
Caliber: .22 Creedmoor, .223 Wylde, 6 GT, 6mm Creedmoor, 6.5 Creedmoor, 6.5 PRC
Magazine: N/A
Features: Customer choice of barrel length, left-/right-hand setup, and stock type; MPA RAT rail (Arca Swiss Rail); adjustable cheekpiece and length of pull; EVG—enhanced vertical grip; inclinometer level; V4 spigot mount; length of pull ranging from 11.75 to 13.25 in.; one-piece spiral-fluted bolt; carbon fiber barrel hand-lapped, stress relieved, and threaded in choice of Sendero or Sendero Lite profiles; V bedding system with clearance glass bedding; thumb notch; bag rider; Trigger Tech Special trigger; choice of Cerakote finish
MSRP . . . . $3575.00–$3725.00

PATRIOT ORDNANCE FACTORY PRESCOTT

Action: Semiautomatic
Stock: Synthetic
Barrel: 20 in.
Sights: None
Weight: 7 lb.
Caliber: 6.5 Creedmoor
Magazine: 10 rounds
Features: Nitride heat-treated single port muzzle brake; rifle-length gas block; match-grade stainless steel barrel; E2 dual extraction; Renegade handguard and heat sink barrel nut; multiple quick-detach points; direct impingement operation; match-grade straight drop-in trigger with anti-walk pins; ambidextrous safety and quick-detach end plate; anti-tilt extension tube with Luth-AR MBA-4 stock; in black or burnt bronze
MSRP . . . . $1866.00–$1996.00

RED ARROW WEAPONS RAW10

Action: Semiautomatic
Stock: Synthetic
Barrel: 18 in.
Sights: None
Weight: 8 lb. 7.5 oz.
Caliber: .308 Win., 6.5 Creedmoor
Magazine: 20 rounds
Features: A heavier AR-10–type for action shooting, with stainless fluted barrel; rifle-length gas system; high-pressure firing pin; 15-in. M-LOK S rail; Magpul ACS-L carbine stock; DB10 threaded on muzzle brake; Magpul K grip; CMC 2.5-lb. single-stage trigger; dressed in midnight bronze
MSRP . . . . $1250.00–$1500.00

RED ARROW WEAPONS RAW15

Action: Semiautomatic
Stock: Synthetic
Barrel: 16 in.
Sights: None
Weight: 6 lb. 9 oz.
Caliber: .223 Rem/5.56 NATO, .300 BLK
Magazine: 30 rounds
Features: Melonite-coated 4150 chromoly barrel; mid-length gas system on .223, pistol-length system on .300 BLK; CMC 3.5-lb. single-stage trigger; A3 flattop upper and lower of 7075 T-6 forged aluminum; 15-in. M-LOK handguard; Magpul K2+ grip; Magpul P-Mag magazine; DB15 556 threaded-on muzzle brake; Magpul CTR stock; in black with red highlights or in midnight bronze
MSRP . . . . $1030.00–$1060.00

ROCK RIVER ARMS LAR-BT3

ROCK RIVER ARMS LAR-BT6

ROCK RIVER ARMS LAR-BT9G

RUGER 10/22 COLLECTOR'S SERIES NO. 4

RUGER CUSTOM SHOP PRECISION RIFLE

RUGER 10/22 TAKEDOWN WITH MAGPUL BACKPACKER STOCK

ROCK RIVER ARMS LAR-BT3

Action: Semiautomatic
Stock: Synthetic
Barrel: 16 in., 18 in., 20 in.
Sights: None
Weight: 8 lb. 3 oz.–9 lb. 14 oz.
Caliber: .308 Win.
Magazine: 20 rounds
Features: Four configurations in this series, all with Hogue grip and two-stage trigger: enhanced Mid-Length A4 with billet A4 upper and lower, 13-in. M-LOK free-floating rail, threaded-on A2 flash hider, mid-length gas system, six-position stock, and fluted, stainless, cryogenically treated heavy barrel; 18-in. Precision Rifle with fluted stainless steel barrel, 17-in. M-LOK extended rail, mid-length gas system, six-position stock; 20-in. Varmint Rifle with stainless steel bull barrel, rifle-length gas system, six-position stock; 20-in. Select Target with fluted heavy stainless steel barrel, Magpul Gen3 Precision Rifle stock, rifle-length gas system
MSRP . . . . $1575.00–$1895.00

ROCK RIVER ARMS LAR-BT6

Action: Semiautomatic
Stock: Synthetic
Barrel: 24 in.
Sights: None
Weight: 13 lb. 8 oz.
Caliber: .338 Lapua Mag.
Magazine: 10 rounds
Features: Takedown design; RRA Ultra-Match two-stage trigger; four-port muzzle brake; stainless steel barrel in a black nitride finish; billet aluminum upper and lower; Magpul Gen3 Precision Rifle stock; RRA overmolded A2 grip; RRA 17-in. quick-detach, lightweight, free-floating handguard with M-LOK compatibility; adjustable low-profile gas block; supplied with two magazines
MSRP $5310.00

ROCK RIVER ARMS LAR-BT9G

Action: Semiautomatic
Stock: Synthetic
Barrel: 16 in.
Sights: None
Weight: 6 lb. 14 oz.–7 lb. 1 oz.
Caliber: 9mm
Magazine: 10, 15, 17 rounds
Features: Two configurations that take Glock 9mm magazines and have six-position CAR stock: CAR A4 carbine with a 16-in. barrel, gas block with receiver-height sight base, single-stage trigger, R-4 handguard, winter trigger guard, and Hogue rubber grip; R9 Competition with a 16-in. chromoly barrel, threaded-on mini brake, two-stage trigger, 15-in. free-floating M-LOK-compatible rail
MSRP . . . . $1000.00–$1315.00

RUGER 10/22 COLLECTOR'S SERIES NO. 4

Action: Semiautomatic
Stock: Synthetic
Barrel: 18.5 in.
Sights: Blade front, adjustable ghost ring rear
Weight: 4 lb. 14 oz.
Caliber: .22 LR
Magazine: 10 rounds
Features: The fourth in the 10/22 Collector's Series, the long-lived 10/22 gets dressed up in the American flag from forend to buttstock
MSRP $369.00

RUGER 10/22 TAKEDOWN WITH MAGPUL BACKPACKER STOCK

Action: Semiautomatic
Stock: Synthetic
Barrel: 16.4 in.
Sights: Fiber optic front and rear
Weight: 4 lb. 3 oz.
Caliber: .22 LR
Magazine: 10 rounds
Features: A new configuration in the 10/22 breakdown family that wears a Magpul X-22 Backpacker stock in Stealth Gray; threaded stainless barrel
MSRP $529.00

RUGER CUSTOM SHOP PRECISION RIFLE

Action: Bolt
Stock: Synthetic
Barrel: 26 in.
Sights: None
Weight: 12 lb. 14 oz.
Caliber: 6mm Creedmoor
Magazine: 10 rounds
Features: Custom heavy-contour barrel that's free-floating, cold hammer-forged, and has R5 rifling; threaded muzzle with an APA muzzle brake; free-floating M-LOK handguard with slots on four sides and is flat-bottomed and compatible with RRS S.O.A.R. and other quick-detach systems; Magpul MOE K2 grip; Sorbothane cheek pad; Trigger Tech trigger; folding stock adjustable at cheekpiece and for length of pull; gray Cerakote finish
MSRP $2399.00

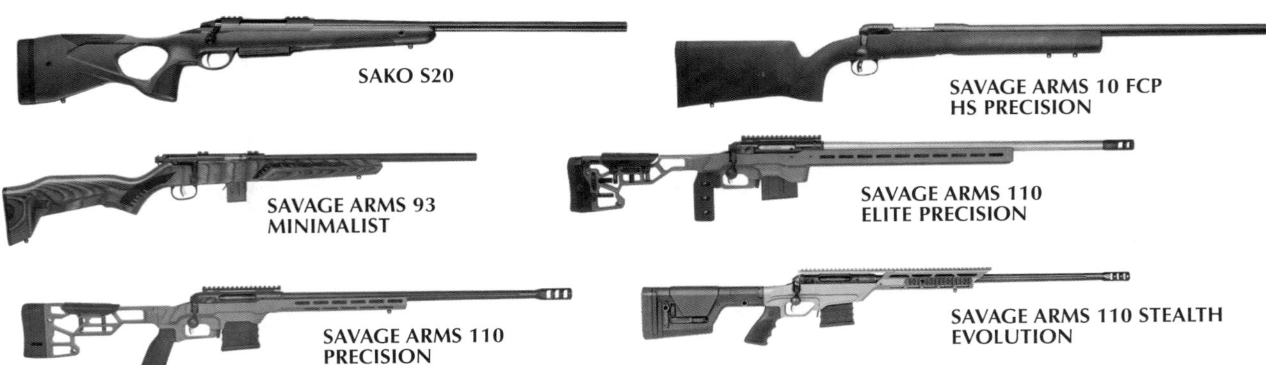

SAKO S20

Action: Bolt
Stock: Synthetic
Barrel: 20 in., 24 in.
Sights: None
Weight: N/A
Caliber: 6.5 Creedmoor, .308 Win., .243 Win., .30-06 Spfd., .270 Win., 6.5 PRC, 7mm Rem. Mag., .300 Win. Mag.
Magazine: 3, 4 rounds
Features: A modular configuration offers a semi-custom fit, with buyers able to choose from interchangeable stocks, barrel lengths and styles, and numerous accessories; full aluminum chassis; adjustable stock; cold hammer-forged barrels; adjustable trigger; double-stack magazines designed to prevent bullet damage; interchangeable bolt handle face; three-lug stainless steel bolt; receiver with integrated Picatinny rails; full aluminum bedding
MSRP . . . . $1599.00–$1699.00

SAVAGE ARMS 10 FCP HS PRECISION

Action: Bolt
Stock: Fiberglass
Barrel: 24 in.
Sights: None
Weight: 9 lb. 9 oz.
Caliber: .308 Win.
Magazine: 4 rounds
Features: Designed for law enforcement use; carbon steel receiver in matte black; matte black fiberglass stock with V-block by HS Precision; carbon steel barrel in a heavy profile; flush-fit detachable box magazine; floating bolt head; oversized bolt handle; AccuTrigger
MSRP $1339.00

SAVAGE ARMS 93 MINIMALIST

Action: Bolt
Stock: Laminate
Barrel: 18 in.
Sights: None
Weight: 5 lb. 7 oz.
Caliber: .22 WMR, .17 HMR
Magazine: 10 rounds
Features: With an adult-average length of pull, this little rimfire is ideal for rimfire steel competition, riding in a truck for pest dispatch and, yes, even just target fun. Features include a threaded barrel; 2.56-lb. adjustable AccuTrigger; two-piece Weaver scope base; detachable box magazine; in green or brown laminate
MSRP $350.00

SAVAGE ARMS 110 ELITE PRECISION

Action: Bolt
Stock: Aluminum
Barrel: 26 in., 30 in.
Sights: None
Weight: 12 lb. 9 oz.
Caliber: .300 PRC, .223 Rem., .300 Win. Mag., .338 Lapua, 6.5 Creedmoor, 6mm Creedmoor
Magazine: 5, 10 rounds
Features: Adjustable Core Competition aluminum chassis from Modular Driven Technologies; Savage blueprinted action; stainless steel flash nitride target receiver; titanium nitride bolt body; 1.4 to 4 lb. adjustable Accutrigger; vertical grip by Modular Driven Technologies; AICS detachable box magazine; self-timing taper-aligned muzzle brake in short-action calibers; full-length ARCA rail; Cerakote stock in gray; available left-hand
MSRP $2199.00

SAVAGE ARMS 110 PRECISION

Action: Bolt
Stock: Aluminum
Barrel: 20 in., 24 in.
Sights: None
Weight: 9 lb. 8 oz.–11 lb. 4 oz.
Caliber: .308 Win., .300 PRC, .300 Win. Mag., .338 Lapua, 6.5 Creedmoor
Magazine: 5, 10 rounds
Features: An affordable long-range entry featuring an XL aluminum chassis stock by Modular Driven Technologies; fully adjustable skeletonized stock; AICS magazine; BA muzzle brake; heavy barrel in matte black threaded 5/8x24; 1.5- to 4-lb. adjustable AccuTrigger; stock in flat dark earth; available left-hand
MSRP $1549.00

SAVAGE ARMS 110 STEALTH EVOLUTION

Action: Bolt
Stock: Aluminum
Barrel: 24 in.
Sights: None
Weight: 11 lb. 2 oz.
Caliber: .300 Win. Mag., .338 Lapua
Magazine: 5, 10 rounds
Features: A monolithic aluminum chassis in bronze Cerakote gets paired up with a heavy fluted barrel with 5R rifling; muzzle brake; Savage blueprinted action; Magpul PRS Gen 3 adjustable stock in flat dark earth; detachable box magazine; adjustable AccuTrigger; available left hand
MSRP $2199.00

SAVAGE ARMS 110 TIMBERLINE

SAVAGE ARMS 110 ULTRALITE

SAVAGE ARMS A22 BNS-SR

SAVAGE ARMS A22 PRECISION

SAVAGE ARMS B17 BNS-SR

SAVAGE ARMS B17 PRECISION

SAVAGE ARMS 110 TIMBERLINE

Action: Bolt
Stock: Synthetic
Barrel: 22 in., 24 in.
Sights: None
Weight: 8 lb. 2 oz.–8 lb. 8 oz.
Caliber: 6.5 Creedmoor, .243 Win., .270 Win., .30-06 Spfd., .300 Win. Mag., .300 WSM, 7mm Rem. Mag., 7mm-08 Rem.
Magazine: 2, 3, 4 rounds
Features: AccuFit AccuStock in Realtree Escape camo with overmolded touch surfaces; fluted barrel with a target crown, medium contour, and threaded on muzzle brake; metalwork in Cerakote OD green; detachable box magazine; 1.5- to 4-lb. adjustable AccuTrigger; drilled and tapped receiver; available left-hand
MSRP $1165.00

SAVAGE ARMS 110 ULTRALITE

Action: Bolt
Stock: Synthetic
Barrel: 22 in., 24 in.
Sights: None
Weight: 5 lb. 14 oz.–6 lb.
Caliber: .308 Win., .270 Win., .28 Nosler, .280 Ackley Improved, .30-06 Spfd., .300 WSM, 6.5 Creedmoor, 6.5 PRC
Magazine: 2, 4 rounds
Features: Proof Research carbon fiber-wrapped stainless steel barrel with cut rifling and a 5/8x24 threaded muzzle; gray or Kuiu Verde 2.0 camo AccuFit stock with overmolded touch surfaces; spiral-fluted bolt; drilled and tapped; lightweight stainless steel receiver with Melonite finish; detachable box magazine; adjustable AccuTrigger
Gray stock: $1545.00
Camo stock: $1589.00

SAVAGE ARMS A22 BNS-SR

Action: Semiautomatic
Stock: Laminate
Barrel: 18 in.
Sights: None
Weight: 6 lb. 9 oz.
Caliber: .22 LR
Magazine: 10 rounds
Features: Snazzy rimfire in a Timber hardwood laminate stock and with a rotary magazine; adjustable AccuTrigger; two-piece Weaver bases; matte-finished carbon steel barrel, sporter contour and threaded ½x28; straight blowback action
MSRP $495.00

SAVAGE ARMS A22 PRECISION

Action: Semiautomatic
Stock: Aluminum
Barrel: 18 in.
Sights: None
Weight: 7 lb. 3 oz.
Caliber: .22 LR
Magazine: 10 rounds
Features: Custom one-piece aluminum chassis by Modular Driven Technologies; heavy threaded barrel; adjustable AccuTrigger; oversized charging handle; one-piece Picatinny rail; adjustable stock for length of pull and cheekpiece; detachable magazine
MSRP $619.00

SAVAGE ARMS B17 BNS-SR

Action: Bolt
Stock: Laminate
Barrel: 18 in.
Sights: None
Weight: 6 lb. 9 oz.
Caliber: .17 HMR
Magazine: 10 rounds
Features: Laminate stock in Timber hardwood; adjustable AccuTrigger; two-piece Weaver bases; threaded-in headspacing; threaded muzzle ½x28; sporter-profile barrel in matte finish
MSRP $519.00

SAVAGE ARMS B17 PRECISION

Action: Bolt
Stock: Synthetic
Barrel: 18 in.
Sights: None
Weight: 7 lb. 4 oz.
Caliber: .17 HMR
Magazine: 10 rounds
Features: An aluminum chassis from Modular Driven Technologies gets topped with a heavy threaded barrel; adjustable AccuTrigger; adjustable length of pull and comb height; detachable magazine; one-piece Picatinny rail
MSRP $619.00

SAVAGE ARMS B22 BNS-SR

Action: Bolt
Stock: Laminate
Barrel: 18 in.
Sights: None
Weight: 6 lb. 8 oz.
Caliber: .22 LR
Magazine: 10 rounds
Features: A handy, good-looking rimfire with a Timber hardwood laminate stock; adjustable AccuTrigger; threaded-in headspacing; sporter barrel in matte black and threaded ½x28; two-piece Weaver bases; detachable magazine
MSRP. $499.00

SAVAGE ARMS B22 MAGNUM BNS-SR

Action: Bolt
Stock: Laminate
Barrel: 18 in.
Sights: None
Weight: 6 lb. 8 oz.
Caliber: .22 WMR
Magazine: 10 rounds
Features: Identical to the B22 BNS-SR, but chambered in .22 WM
MSRP. $519.00

SAVAGE ARMS B22 MAGNUM PRECISION

Action: Bolt
Stock: Synthetic
Barrel: 18 in.
Sights: None
Weight: 7 lb. 4 oz.
Caliber: .22 WMR
Magazine: 10 rounds
Features: An aluminum chassis from Modular Driven Technologies gets topped with a heavy threaded barrel; adjustable AccuTrigger; adjustable length of pull and comb height; detachable magazine; one-piece Picatinny rail
MSRP. $619.00

SAVAGE ARMS B22 PRECISION

Action: Bolt
Stock: Synthetic
Barrel: 18 in.
Sights: None
Weight: 7 lb. 4 oz.
Caliber: .22 LR
Magazine: 10 rounds
Features: Nearly identical to the B22 Magnum Precision model, but chambered in .22 LR
MSRP. $619.00

SAVAGE ARMS IMPULSE BIG GAME

Action: Bolt
Stock: Synthetic
Barrel: 22 in., 24 in.
Sights: None
Weight: 8 lb. 14 oz.–8 lb. 15 oz.
Caliber: 6.5 Creedmoor, .243 Win., .30-06 Spfd., .300 Win. Mag., .300 WSM, .308 Win.
Magazine: 3, 4 rounds
Features: A straight-pull bolt speeds things up for this big-game gun that also features an adjustable AccuTrigger; aluminum receiver and carbon steel barrel in Cerakote Hazel Green; AccuStock in Kuiu Verde 2.0 camo; fluted, threaded, medium-contour barrel; flush-fit detachable magazine; one-piece 20 MOA rail machined into receiver
MSRP. $1449.00

SAVAGE ARMS IMPULSE HOG HUNTER

Action: Bolt
Stock: Synthetic
Barrel: 18 in., 20 in., 24 in.
Sights: None
Weight: 8 lb. 8 oz.–9 lb. 1 oz.
Caliber: .308 Win., .30-06 Spfd., .300 Win. Mag., 6.5 Creedmoor
Magazine: 3, 4 rounds
Features: A fast-handling straight-pull bolt made for wild boar hunting and featuring an AccuFit AccuStock in OD green; aluminum receiver and carbon steel barrel in matte black; heavy-contour barrel threaded 5/8x24; flush-fit detachable magazine; one-piece 20 MOA rail machined into receiver
MSRP. $1379.00

SAVAGE ARMS IMPULSE PREDATOR

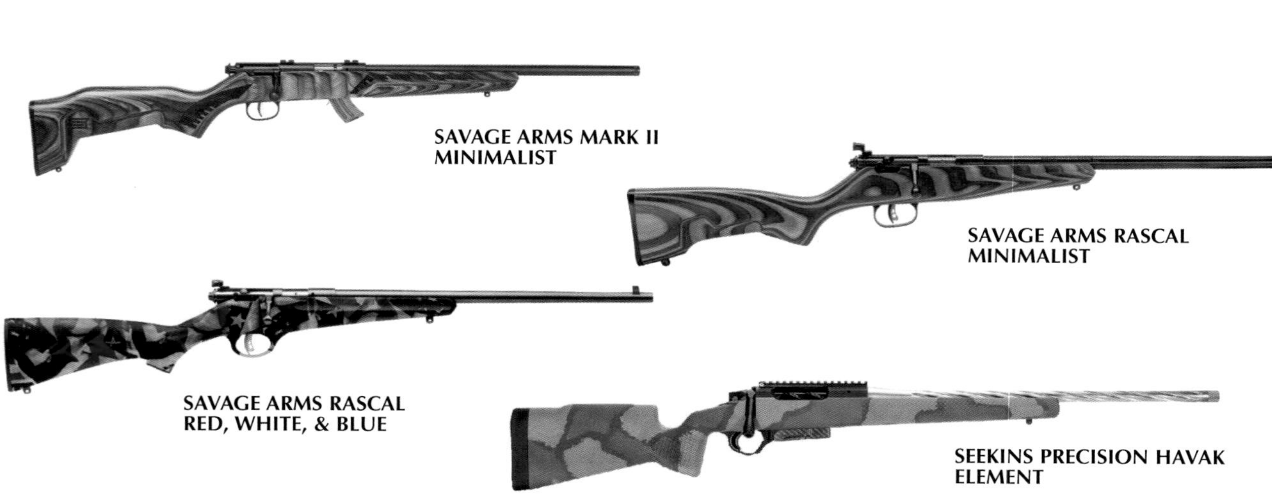

SAVAGE ARMS MARK II MINIMALIST

SAVAGE ARMS RASCAL MINIMALIST

SAVAGE ARMS RASCAL RED, WHITE, & BLUE

SEEKINS PRECISION HAVAK ELEMENT

SAVAGE ARMS IMPULSE PREDATOR

Action: Bolt
Stock: Synthetic
Barrel: 20 in.
Sights: None
Weight: 8 lb. 12 oz.
Caliber: .22-250 Rem., .243 Win., .308 Win., 6.5 Creedmoor
Magazine: 10 rounds
Features: Straight-pull bolt design; matte black aluminum receiver; matte black carbon steel barrel, threaded, in a medium contour; detachable AICS magazine with ambidextrous release; 20 MOA rail machined into receiver; user-adjustable AccuTrigger; adjustable AccuFit stock in Mossy Oak Terra Gila camo
MSRP $1379.00

SAVAGE ARMS MARK II MINIMALIST

Action: Bolt
Stock: Laminate
Barrel: 18 in.
Sights: None
Weight: 5 lb. 9 oz.
Caliber: .22 LR
Magazine: 10 rounds
Features: A futuristic looking rimfire with a Boyd's laminate hardwood stock in choice of green or brown tones; carbon steel barrel in matte finish and threaded ½x28; adjustable AccuTrigger; detachable magazine; two-piece Weaver bases
MSRP $350.00

SAVAGE ARMS RASCAL MINIMALIST

Action: Bolt
Stock: Laminate
Barrel: 16.125 in.
Sights: Blade front, peep rear
Weight: 3 lb. 8 oz.
Caliber: .22 LR
Magazine: 1 round
Features: Single-shot; Boyd's Minimalist stock of laminated hardwood in gray/teal or pink/purple; 11.25-in. length of pull; barrel has target crown and is threaded ½x28; can be unloaded without pulling the trigger; adjustable AccuTrigger; comes with firearm lock and eye and ear plugs
MSRP $289.00

SAVAGE ARMS RASCAL RED, WHITE, & BLUE

Action: Bolt
Stock: Synthetic
Barrel: 16.125 in.
Sights: Blade front, peep rear
Weight: 2 lb. 13 oz.
Caliber: .22 LR
Magazine: 1 round
Features: A Rascal with a classic stock swathed in American flag graphics; 11.25-in. length of pull; adjustable AccuTrigger; carbon steel sporter barrel
MSRP $235.00

SEEKINS PRECISION HAVAK ELEMENT

Action: Bolt
Stock: Carbon composite
Barrel: 21 in., 22 in.
Sights: None
Weight: 5 lb. 8 oz.–6 lb.
Caliber: 6mm Creedmoor, 6.5 Creedmoor, 6.5 PRC, .308 Win., .28 Nosler, .300 Win. Mag., .300 PRC
Magazine: 3, 5 rounds
Features: Seekins calls this a "hybrid" hunting rifle; Mountain Hunter contoured fluted barrel in stainless steel; integrated recoil lug; 20 MOA rail; bubble level; M16-style extractor; 90-degree bolt throw; removable bolt head; 2.5-lb. Timney Elite Hunter trigger; muzzle threaded 5/8X24; stock finished in Element camo; short-actions have 21-in. barrel and five-round Magpul PMag magazines (except 6.5 PRC), long-actions have 22-in. barrel and three-round detachable carbon fiber magazine (6.5 PRC also has the carbon fiber three-round mag)
MSRP $2795.00

SHAW CUSTOM RIFLES MK. VII GEN II
SHILOH SHARPS 1874 MILITARY CARBINE
SIG SAUER SIG716I TREAD
SIG SAUER SIGM400 TREAD COIL
SIG SAUER SIG MCX RATTLER CANEBRAKE

SHAW CUSTOM RIFLES MK. VII GEN II

Action: Bolt
Stock: Laminate, walnut
Barrel: Customer choice
Sights: None
Weight: 7 lb. 8 oz.–8 lb. 8 oz.
Caliber: Customer choice
Magazine: 2, 3, 4, 5 rounds
Features: Choice of #2.5 heavy sporter or #3 light varmint barrel contour with button rifling, choice of helical fluting, straight fluting, or no fluting, and 11-degree target crown; Shaw-tuned AccuTrigger; teardrop bolt handle; walnut stock or laminate stock in nutmeg or pepper, glass bedded and steel pillar bedded; drilled and tapped for Savage round-action scope bases; Pachmayr recoil pad
MSRP . . . . . . Contact manufacturer

SHILOH SHARPS 1874 MILITARY CARBINE

Action: Hammer
Stock: Wood
Barrel: 22 in., 24 in.
Sights: Blade front, Lawrence ladder buckhorn rear
Weight: 7 lb. 8 oz.
Caliber: .30-40 Krag, .38-55, .40-65, .45-70, .40-50 Sharps Straight
Magazine: 1 round
Features: We're slotting this in centerfire rifles based solely on the fact that .30-40 Krag was never a blackpowder cartridge, and all the other cartridges can be loaded with modern smokeless powders; tons of features and upgrades include color case-hardened finish as standard or pack harden and various levels of antique metal finish upgrades, patchbox, ebony pistol grip, barrel finish, saddle bar and ring, upgraded wood and finishes, brass escutcheons, custom bedding, various sling swivels, forearm designs, rear barrel sights, vernier tang sights, drilling and tapping, and checkering upgrades
MSRP . . . . Starting at $2007.00

SIG SAUER SIG716I TREAD

Action: Semiautomatic
Stock: Synthetic
Barrel: 16 in.
Sights: None
Weight: 8 lb. 8 oz.
Caliber: 7.62 NATO
Magazine: 20 rounds
Features: A direct impingement MSR with a telescoping stock; two-stage Matchlite Duo trigger; hard-coat anodized receiver; alloy forend; polymer grip; barrel threaded 5/8x24; M-LOK accessory rail
MSRP $1599.00

SIG SAUER SIGM400 TREAD COIL

Action: Semiautomatic
Stock: Synthetic
Barrel: 16 in.
Sights: Flip-up rear
Weight: 7 lb.
Caliber: 5.56 NATO
Magazine: 30 rounds
Features: A direct impingement MSR with a telescoping stock; two-stage Matchlite Duo trigger; hard-coat anodized receiver; alloy forend; polymer grip; barrel threaded ½x28; M-LOK accessory rail with lightning cuts, choice of 13- or 15-inch lengths; ambidextrous charging handle of aircraft-grade aluminum; M-LOK front sight adapter with co-witness height; upgraded flat-blade single-stage trigger; three-chamber compensator; ROMEO5 electro optic with 2 MOA dot
MSRP . . . . N/A

SIG SAUER SIG MCX RATTLER CANEBRAKE

Action: Semiautomatic
Stock: Synthetic
Barrel: 5.5 in.
Sights: None
Weight: 6 lb. 8 oz.
Caliber: .300 BLK
Magazine: 30 rounds
Features: Gas-piston SBR (NFA regs apply) with a receiver in Cerakote E190 (aka bronze); two-stage flat-blade trigger; folding PCB brace; Magpul magazine; inert training device factory installed so buyer can train while waiting for NFA paperwork to clear
MSRP . . . . N/A

SIG SAUER SIG MCX VIRTUS SBR

SPRINGFIELD ARMORY MODEL 2020 WAYPOINT

STANDARD MANUFACTURING MODEL 16721

S.W.O.R.D. INTERNATIONAL MK-17 MOD 1 GUNGNIR

TAYLOR'S & CO. FIREARMS ALASKAN THREADED

ULTIMATE ARMS WARRIOR LITE TACTICAL LONG RANGE RIFLE

SIG SAUER SIG MCX VIRTUS SBR

Action: Semiautomatic
Stock: Synthetic
Barrel: 5 in., 9 in., 11.5 in.
Sights: None
Weight: 7 lb.–5 lb. 11 oz.
Caliber: 5.56 NATO, .300 BLK
Magazine: 30 rounds
Features: Gas-piston SBR (NFA regs apply) with a Matchlite Duo trigger; M-LOK handguard; cold hammer-forged barrel; 5.56 NATO available in 11-in. barrel, five-position telescoping/folding stock, and choice of gray or hard-coat anodized receiver finish; .300 BLK available in a 9-in. barrel with a five-position folding/telescoping stock, and flat dark earth receiver or in a 5.5-in. barrel with a folding Minimalist stock and hard-coat anodized receiver
MSRP. N/A

SPRINGFIELD ARMORY MODEL 2020 WAYPOINT

Action: Bolt
Stock: Carbon fiber
Barrel: 20 in., 22 in., 24 in.
Sights: None
Weight: 6 lb. 15 oz.–7 lb. 5 oz.
Caliber: .308 Win., 6mm Creedmoor, 6.5 Creedmoor, 6.5 PRC
Magazine: 3 rounds
Features: Fluted bolt with dual locking lugs and removable bolt knob; enlarged ejection port; hybrid dual-plane feed ramp; AG Composites carbon-fiber stock in choice of fixed or adjustable cheekpiece configurations and in Evergreen or Ridgeline camo; TriggerTech adjustable trigger; five quick-detach mount inserts; removable Springfield Armory radial muzzle brake; AICS pattern magazine; Pachmayr Decelerator recoil pad; BSF barrel in a carbon-fiber sleeve or fluted stainless steel and free-floated
MSRP. . . . . $1699.00–$2399.00

STANDARD MANUFACTURING MODEL 16721

Action: Semiautomatic
Stock: Synthetic
Barrel: 16 in.
Sights: None
Weight: 6 lb. 7 oz.
Caliber: 5.56 NATO
Magazine: 30 rounds
Features: Direct impingement carbine-length gas system; A2 flash hider; A3 upper and lower of aluminum with mil-spec hard-anodized finish; standard charging handle; Rogers Super Stock; 13-in. M-LOK handguard; heavy-profile barrel with M4 feed ramp; two magazines
MSRP. $999.00

S.W.O.R.D. INTERNATIONAL MK-17 MOD 1 GUNGNIR

Action: Semiautomatic
Stock: Synthetic
Barrel: 20 in.
Sights: None
Weight: 8 lb. 15 oz.
Caliber: 6.5 Creedmoor
Magazine: 10, 20 rounds
Features: Gungnir is the name of the mighty spear that belongs to Odin, the leader of the Norse Gods, and is said to have had the most accurate and deadly aim; tuned compensator on a single-point-cut rifled barrel with a black nitride coating; self-regulating gas system; free-floating M-LOK rail system; ambidextrous bolt catch, bolt release pad, and magazine release; tungsten-filled heavy buffer; retractable stock; piston-rated heavy-duty action spring; in coyote brown Cerakote or mil-spec type 3 hardcoat anodized black
MSRP. $4295.00

TAYLOR'S & CO. FIREARMS ALASKAN THREADED

Action: Lever
Stock: Wood
Barrel: 16.5 in.
Sights: Fiber optic front, peep rear
Weight: 5 lb. 15 oz.
Caliber: .357 Mag., .44 Mag.
Magazine: 5 rounds
Features: Handy takedown rifle with a wood stock wearing a coverage of soft-touch finish in black; matte chrome finish metalwork; rear peep sight sits at back of topside Picatinny rail
MSRP. $1581.58

ULTIMATE ARMS WARRIOR LITE TACTICAL LONG RANGE RIFLE

Action: Bolt
Stock: Carbon Kevlar
Barrel: 26 in.
Sights: None
Weight: 10 lb. 8 oz.
Caliber: 7.82 Lazzeroni Warbird
Magazine: 5 rounds
Features: 416 stainless steel fluted barrel and action dressed in a ceramic coat finish; one-piece helical cut bolt; button rifling; removable muzzle brake; carbon Kevlar stock
MSRP. $6999.95

WEATHERBY MARK V COWPOKE EDITION

Action: Bolt
Stock: Fiberglass
Barrel: 24 in., 26 in.
Sights: None
Weight: 8 lb. 6 oz.
Caliber: .257 Wby. Mag., .30-378 Wby. Mag., .300 Wby. Mag., 6.5 Wby. RPM, 6.5-300 Wby. Mag.
Magazine: 3, 4 rounds
Features: This is a pretty fancy rifle to be dubbed the "Cowpoke," but surely the folks at Weatherby had a vision (okay, really, it's a Wyoming thing); receiver and #3 contour barrel in Cerakote brown but with its flutes in Cerakote gold; handlaid fiberglass stock mimics the color mix; TriggerTech trigger; Accubrake ST; 54-degree bolt
MSRP $2499.00

WEATHERBY MARK V WEATHERMARK LIMITED

Action: Bolt
Stock: Composite
Barrel: 22 in., 24 in., 26 in.
Sights: None
Weight: 7 lb. 3 oz.
Caliber: .257 Wby. Mag., .300 Wby. Mag., 6.5 Creedmoor, 6.5 Wby. RPM, 6.5-300 Wby. Mag.
Magazine: 3, 4 rounds
Features: Weatherby's first spiral-fluted barrel on a Mark V rifle; fluted bolt knob; flat-faced TriggerTech trigger; combination of black and burnt bronze Cerakote on the metal; black based composite stock with grey and brown accents; Accubrake ST
MSRP $2299.00

WEATHERBY VANGUARD HIGH COUNTRY

Action: Bolt
Stock: Composite
Barrel: 24 in., 26 in.
Sights: None
Weight: 7 lb. 4 oz.
Caliber: .257 Wby. Mag., .270 Win., .30-06 Spfd., .300 Wby. Mag., .300 Win. Mag., .308 Win., 6.5 Creedmoor, 6.5 PRC, 6.5-300 Wby. Mag.
Magazine: 3, 4, 5 rounds
Features: Monte Carlo stock with a right-hand palm swell; black base with green and tan accents; textured forearm and grip; adjustable two-stage trigger; fluted bolt body; Accubrake ST; metalwork in flat dark earth Cerakote
MSRP $949.00

WEATHERBY VANGUARD HUSH EDITION

Action: Bolt
Stock: Composite
Barrel: 24 in., 26 in.
Sights: None
Weight: 7 lb. 4 oz.
Caliber: .257 Wby. Mag., .300 Wby. Mag., 6.5 Creedmoor, 6.5-300 Wby. Mag.
Magazine: 3, 4 rounds
Features: A collaborative effort between Weatherby and HUSH, this rifle's receiver is in full graphite black Cerakote with a fluted bolt to match; straight-flute #2 contour barrel; stock in cement gray with black webbing, textured grip areas, and right-hand palm swell; threaded barrel with Accubrake ST
MSRP $999.00

WEATHERBY VANGUARD MEATEATER EDITION

Action: Bolt
Stock: Composite
Barrel: 24 in., 26 in.
Sights: None
Weight: 7 lb. 2 oz.
Caliber: .300 Wby. Mag., .300 Win. Mag., .308 Win., 6.5 Creedmoor, 6.5-300 Wby. Mag., 7mm Rem. Mag.
Magazine: 3, 4 rounds
Features: A collaborative effort with the MeatEater brand, this rifle's receiver and #2 contour spiral-fluted barrel are in tungsten Cerakote; fluted bolt is in black Cerakote; black-based stock has gray and brown accents, right palmswell, and textured grip areas; barrel is threaded but does not come with Accubrake
MSRP $999.00

WEATHERBY VANGUARD SELECT

Action: Bolt
Stock: Composite
Barrel: 24 in., 26 in.
Sights: None
Weight: 7 lb. 8 oz.
Caliber: .243 Win., .270 Win., .30-06 Spfd., .300 Win. Mag., .308 Win., 6.5 Creedmoor, 7mm Rem. Mag.
Magazine: 3, 4 rounds
Features: #2 contour barrel in a matte, bead-blasted blued finish; fluted bolt body; two-stage trigger; black Monte Carlo stock with textured grip areas and a right-hand palm swell
MSRP $549.00

WEATHERBY VANGUARD SYNTHETIC COMPACT

Action: Bolt
Stock: Composite
Barrel: 20 in.
Sights: None
Weight: 6 lb. 8 oz.
Caliber: .243 Win., .308 Win., 6.5 Creedmoor, 7mm-08 Rem.
Magazine: 4, 5 rounds
Features: Handy rifle for backcountry hunters or ranch work; injection-molded composite stock that includes a spacer for length-of-pull adjustment; #1 contour barrel in matte, bead-blasted blued finish; base model has the stock in black, while the blue model has splashes of gray and neon blue
Standard: $549.00
Blue: $629.00

WINCHESTER REPEATING ARMS MODEL 70 EXTREME TRUETIMBER VSX MB

Action: Bolt
Stock: Composite
Barrel: 22 in., 24 in., 26 in.
Sights: None
Weight: 6 lb. 12 oz.–7 lb. 4 oz.
Caliber: .243 Win., 6.5 Creedmoor, 7mm-08 Rem., .308 Win., 6.5 PRC, 6.8 Western, .270 WSM, .300 WSM, .25-06 Rem., .270 Win., .30-06 Spfd., .264 Win. Mag., 7mm Rem. Mag., .300 Win. Mag.
Magazine: 3, 4, 5 rounds
Features: Receiver and barrel finished in tungsten Cerakote; Bell & Carlson stock has sculpted cheekpiece and TrueTimber VSX camo; jeweled bolt body; MOA trigger system
MSRP $1649.99

WINCHESTER REPEATING ARMS MODEL 70 EXTREME TUNGSTEN MB

Action: Bolt
Stock: Composite
Barrel: 22 in., 24 in., 26 in.
Sights: None
Weight: 6 lb. 12 oz.–7 lb. 4 oz.
Caliber: .243 Win., 6.5 Creedmoor, 7mm-08 Rem., .308 Win., 6.5 PRC, 6.8 Western, .270 WSM, .300 WSM, .25-06 Rem., .270 Win., .30-06 Spfd., .264 Win. Mag., 7mm Rem. Mag., .300 Win. Mag.
Magazine: 3, 4, 5 rounds
Features: Receiver and barrel finished in tungsten Cerakote; Bell & Carlson lay-up stock has sculpted cheekpiece and charcoal grey textured finish; jeweled bolt body; MOA trigger system
MSRP $1549.99

WINCHESTER REPEATING ARMS MODEL 70 EXTREME WEATHER MB

Action: Bolt
Stock: Composite
Barrel: 22 in., 24 in., 26 in.
Sights: None
Weight: 6 lb. 12 oz.–7 lb. 4 oz.
Caliber: .243 Win., 6.5 Creedmoor, 7mm-08 Rem., .308 Win., 6.5 PRC, 6.8 Western, .270 WSM, .300 WSM, .25-06 Rem., .270 Win., .30-06 Spfd., .264 Win. Mag., 7mm Rem. Mag., .300 Win. Mag.
Magazine: 3, 4, 5 rounds
Features: Receiver and sporter contour barrel are finished in matte stainless finish; Bell & Carlson lay-up composite stock has sculpted cheekpiece and is in TrueTimber VSX camo; aluminum bedding block; MOA trigger system
MSRP $1609.99

WINCHESTER REPEATING ARMS MODEL 70 LONG RANGE MB

Action: Bolt
Stock: Composite
Barrel: 24 in.
Sights: None
Weight: 7 lb. 8 oz.
Caliber: .22-250 Rem., .243 Win., 6.5 Creedmoor, .308 Win., 6.5 PRC, .270 WSM, .300 WSM, 6.8 Western
Magazine: 3, 4 rounds
Features: Hand-laid Bell & Carlson stock is in tan with black spider webbing and a flat forend; aluminum bedding blocks; fluted barrel in a light varmint contour has muzzle brake; MOA trigger system; Pachmayr Decelerator pad
MSRP $1549.99

WINCHESTER REPEATING ARMS MODEL 94 DELUXE SPORTING

Action: Lever
Stock: Walnut
Barrel: 24 in.
Sights: Gold bead front, semi-buckhorn rear
Weight: 7 lb. 8 oz.
Caliber: .30-30 Win., .38-55 Win.
Magazine: 8 rounds
Features: Very attractive upgrade on a classic, with a steel receiver in a color case-hardened finish; button-rifled semi-gloss blue barrel; Grade V/VI walnut stock with crescent buttplate; hammer spur extension; Marble Arms sights
MSRP $2109.99

WINCHESTER REPEATING ARMS MODEL 1873 COMPETITION CARBINE HIGH GRADE

Action: Lever
Stock: Walnut
Barrel: 20 in.
Sights: Blade front, carbine ladder-style rear
Weight: 7 lb. 4 oz.
Caliber: .357 Mag., .45 Colt
Magazine: 10 rounds
Features: SASS ready and has a polished blue round barrel with barrel band; Grade III/IV walnut stock; color case-hardened carbine buttplate and steel receiver; top tang drilled for peep sight; saddle ring
MSRP $1789.99

WINCHESTER REPEATING ARMS MODEL 1885 LOW WALL HUNTER HIGH GRADE

Action: Lever
Stock: Walnut
Barrel: 24 in.
Sights: None
Weight: 7 lb. 8 oz.
Caliber: .22 Hornet, .222 Rem., .223 Rem., .243 Win., 6mm Creedmoor, 6.5 Creedmoor, 6.5x55 Swedish Mauser
Magazine: 1 rounds
Features: One of the prettiest single-shots around; full octagon barrel; Pachmayr Decelerator recoil pad; 22 lpi checkering; upgraded black walnut stock; drilled and tapped
MSRP $1719.99

WINCHESTER REPEATING ARMS MODEL 1886 SADDLE RING CARBINE

Action: Lever
Stock: Walnut
Barrel: 22 in.
Sights: Blade front, carbine ladder-style rear
Weight: 8 lb.
Caliber: .45-70 Gov't., .45-90 Win.
Magazine: 7 rounds
Features: A lever with some heft to soak up recoil; Grade I walnut stock; straight grip stock; carbine-style forend; round barrel in polished blue with barrel band; full-length magazine tube; saddle ring; drilled and tapped
MSRP $1509.99

WINCHESTER REPEATING ARMS MODEL 1892 DELUXE OCTAGON TAKEDOWN

WINCHESTER REPEATING ARMS MODEL 1895 HIGH GRADE

WINCHESTER REPEATING ARMS WILDCAT 22 COMBO

WINCHESTER REPEATING ARMS WILDCAT SR

WINCHESTER REPEATING ARMS XPR COMPACT SCOPE COMBO

WINCHESTER REPEATING ARMS MODEL 1892 DELUXE OCTAGON TAKEDOWN

Action: Lever
Stock: Walnut
Barrel: 24 in.
Sights: Gold bead front, semi-buckhorn rear
Weight: 7 lb.
Caliber: .357 Mag., .44 Rem. Mag., .44-40 Win., .45 Colt
Magazine: 11 rounds
Features: Color case-hardened steel receiver; full octagon barrel in a polished blue finish; Grade V/VI walnut stock with steel shotgun buttplate; Marble Arms sights; top tang drilled for peep sight
MSRP $2129.99

WINCHESTER REPEATING ARMS MODEL 1895 HIGH GRADE

Action: Lever
Stock: Walnut
Barrel: 24 in.
Sights: Gold bead front, buckhorn rear
Weight: 8 lb.
Caliber: .30-06 Spfd., .30-40 Krag, .405 Win.
Magazine: 4 rounds
Features: A classic lever with a box magazine; Grade III/IV in an oil finish with a straight grip and metal buttplate; Marble Arms sights; polished blue metalwork; schnabel forend; drilled and tapped for side-mount sight; traditional checkering
MSRP $1649.99

WINCHESTER REPEATING ARMS WILDCAT 22 COMBO

Action: Semiautomatic
Stock: Composite
Barrel: 18 in.
Sights: Ramped post front, adjustable ghost ring rear
Weight: 4 lb.
Caliber: .22 LR
Magazine: 10 rounds
Features: Budget-friendly rimfire; reflex-style red-dot sight factory mounted on it composite receiver, stock, and integrated sling swivels; sporter contour barrel in matte blue; detachable magazine with dual ambidextrous releases and spring-assisted ejection; reversible manual safety; integral Picatinny rail
MSRP $309.99

WINCHESTER REPEATING ARMS WILDCAT SR

Action: Semiautomatic
Stock: Composite
Barrel: 16.5 in.
Sights: Ramped post front, adjustable ghost ring rear
Weight: 4 lb.
Caliber: .22 LR
Magazine: 10 rounds
Features: The "SR" stands for suppressor ready; rimfire; composite receiver, stock, and integrated sling swivels; sporter contour barrel in matte blue; detachable magazine with dual ambidextrous releases and spring-assisted ejection; reversible manual safety; muzzle threaded ½x28; integral Picatinny rail
MSRP $299.99

WINCHESTER REPEATING ARMS XPR COMPACT SCOPE COMBO

Action: Bolt
Stock: Composite
Barrel: 20 in.
Sights: None
Weight: 6 lb. 12 oz.–7 lb.
Caliber: .243 Win., 6.5 Creedmoor, 7mm-08 Rem., .308 Win., .300 WSM, .270 WSM, .350 Legend, 6.5 PRC, 6.8 Western
Magazine: 3 rounds
Features: A smartly priced package that includes a rifle with a steel receiver in black Perma-Cote; free-floating barrel with a recessed crown in black Perma-Cote; 13-in. length of pull; Vortex Crossfire II 3–9x40 scope with BDC reticle; sling swivels; MOA trigger system; matte black stock
MSRP $729.99

WINCHESTER REPEATING ARMS XPR EXTREME HUNTER TRUETIMBER MIDNIGHT MB

WINCHESTER REPEATING ARMS XPR HUNTER MOSSY OAK DNA

WINCHESTER REPEATING ARMS XPR HUNTER SCOPE COMBO TRUE TIMBER STRATA

WINCHESTER REPEATING ARMS XPR TRUE TIMBER STRATA MB

WINCHESTER REPEATING ARMS XPR EXTREME HUNTER TRUETIMBER MIDNIGHT MB

Action: Bolt
Stock: Composite
Barrel: 22 in., 24 in., 26 in.
Sights: None
Weight: 6 lb. 12 oz.–7 lb.
Caliber: .223 Rem., .243 Win., 6.5 Creedmoor, 7mm-08 Rem., .308 Win., .350 Legend, 6.5 PRC, 6.8 Western, .270 WSM, .300 WSM, .270 Win., .30-06 Spfd., 7mm Rem. Mag., .300 Win. Mag.
Magazine: 3, 4, 5 rounds
Features: Steel receiver is drilled and tapped and appears in tungsten Cerakote; barrel is in tungsten Cerakote, free-floating, has a recessed crown, is threaded 9/16x24, and has a muzzle brake; MOA trigger system; Inflex Technology recoil pad; detachable box magazine; stock is dressed in TrueTimber Midnight camo
MSRP $749.99

WINCHESTER REPEATING ARMS XPR HUNTER MOSSY OAK DNA

Action: Bolt
Stock: Composite
Barrel: 22 in., 24 in., 26 in.
Sights: None
Weight: 6 lb. 12 oz.–7 lb. 4 oz.
Caliber: .223 Rem., .243 Win., 6.5 Creedmoor, 7mm-08 Rem., .308 Win., .350 Legend, 6.5 PRC, 6.8 Western, .270 WSM, .300 WSM, .270 Win., .30-06 Spfd., 7mm Rem. Mag., .300 Win. Mag., .338 Win. Mag.
Magazine: 3, 4, 5 rounds
Features: Steel receiver is drilled and tapped and appears in matte black Perma-Cote; barrel is in matte black Perma-Cote, free-floating, and has a recessed crown; MOA trigger system; Inflex Technology recoil pad; detachable box magazine; stock is dressed in Mossy Oak DNA camo
MSRP $629.99

WINCHESTER REPEATING ARMS XPR HUNTER SCOPE COMBO TRUE TIMBER STRATA

Action: Bolt
Stock: Composite
Barrel: 20 in., 22 in.
Sights: None
Weight: 6 lb. 12 oz.–7 lb.
Caliber: .270 WSM. .243 Win., 6.5 Creedmoor, 7mm-08 Rem., .300 WSM, .308 Win.
Magazine: 3 rounds
Features: Steel receiver is drilled and tapped and appears in flat dark earth Perma-Cote; barrel is in flat dark earth Perma-Cote, free-floating, has a recessed crown and muzzle brake; MOA trigger system; Inflex Technology recoil pad; 13-in length of pull stock is dressed in TrueTimber Strata camo; comes mounted with a Vortex Crossfire II 3–9x40 scope with BDC reticle; sling swivel studs
MSRP $799.99

WINCHESTER REPEATING ARMS XPR TRUE TIMBER STRATA MB

Action: Bolt
Stock: Composite
Barrel: 22 in., 24 in., 26 in.
Sights: None
Weight: 6 lb. 12 oz.–7 lb.
Caliber: .223 Rem., .243 Win., 6.5 Creedmoor, 7mm-08 Rem., .308 Win., .350 Legend, 6.5 PRC, 6.8 Western, .270 WSM, .300 WSM, .270 Win., .30-06 Spfd., 7mm Rem. Mag., .300 Win. Mag.
Magazine: 3, 4, 5 rounds
Features: Steel receiver is drilled and tapped and appears in flat dark earth Perma-Cote; barrel is in flat dark earth Perma-Cote, threaded 9/16x24, free-floating, has a recessed crown and muzzle brake; MOA trigger system; Inflex Technology recoil pad; stock is dressed in TrueTimber Strata camo
MSRP $719.99

NEW Products: Airguns

AIRFORCE AIRGUNS COMETA LYNX V10

Action: PCP
Stock: Wood
Barrel: 18.5 in.
Sights: None
Weight: 7 lb. 14 oz.
Caliber: .177
Magazine: 1 shot
Features: Single-shot loading tray; 11mm dovetail grooves; adjustable power; two-stage adjustable trigger; ambidextrous stock with dual-raised cheekpieces; checkered grip and forearm; built-in manometer; manual safety
MSRP $699.99

AIRFORCE AIRGUNS COMETA ORION

Action: PCP
Stock: Wood
Barrel: 18.5 in.
Sights: None
Weight: 7 lb. 4 oz.
Caliber: .177, .22, .25
Magazine: 17, 13, 11 shots
Features: A bolt-action PCP with a checkered hardwood stock; adjustable trigger; hammer-forged barrel; high-efficiency barrel shroud; integrated gauge; quick-fill port; adjustable cheekpiece
MSRP $499.99

AIRFORCE AIRGUNS TEXAN .50 CARBINE

Action: PCP
Stock: Synthetic
Barrel: 25 in.
Sights: None
Weight: 6 lb.
Caliber: .457
Magazine: 1 shot
Features: Intended for deer and hog hunters and the like, this one has an adjustable buttplate, adjustable power; extended optics rail; carbon fiber tank; Lothar Walther barrel; sidelever
MSRP $1229.95

AIR VENTURI DIANA STORMRIDER

Action: PCP
Stock: Wood
Barrel: 19 in.
Sights: Blade front, adjustable leaf rear
Weight: 5 lb.
Caliber: .177, .22
Magazine: 7, 9 shots
Features: Bolt-action repeater with a checkered beech stock; two-stage adjustable trigger; integrated pressure gauge; 11mm dovetail; rotary magazine and single-shot tray; Air Venturi G9 pump; barrel shroud
MSRP $299.99

AIR VENTURI V10 TARGET AIR PISTOL

Action: Single-stroke pneumatic
Stock: Wood
Barrel: 8.26 in.
Sights: Blade ramp front, adjustable rear
Weight: 1 lb. 17 oz.
Caliber: .177
Magazine: 1 shot
Features: Competition-ready air pistol with a two-stage adjustable trigger; single-stroke pneumatic power plant; recoil and vibration free
MSRP $341.99

BEEMAN PRECISION AIRGUNS 2027

Action: PCP
Stock: Wood
Barrel: N/A
Sights: Fiber optic front and rear
Weight: 3 lb. 12 oz.
Caliber: .177
Magazine: 12 shots
Features: Adjustable velocity target pistol with ergonomic wood stock; adjustable trigger; capable of 60 shots at 600 fps
MSRP $170.00

BEEMAN PRECISION AIRGUNS 10616, 10616GP

Action: Spring piston
Stock: Synthetic
Barrel: N/A
Sights: Fiber optic front and rear
Weight: 8 lb. 8 oz.
Caliber: .177
Magazine: 1 shot
Features: A break-barrel air rifle that includes a 4x32 scope; automatic gas safety; available in gas ram; velocity of 1,200 fps with lead pellets; single cocking stroke
MSRP $189.99

BEEMAN PRECISION AIRGUNS CHIEF

Action: PCP
Stock: Wood
Barrel: 21.5 in.
Sights: Fiber optic front and rear
Weight: 6 lb. 14 oz.
Caliber: .177, .22
Magazine: 1 shot
Features: A bolt-action with a rifled barrel; two-stage adjustable trigger; rubber buttplate; 50 shots per fill
MSRP $199.99

BEEMAN PRECISION AIRGUNS CHIEF II

Action: PCP
Stock: Wood
Barrel: 21.5 in.
Sights: Fiber optic front and rear
Weight: 6 lb. 14 oz.
Caliber: .177, .22
Magazine: 10 shots
Features: Similar to the Chief, but as a 10-shot repeating model; max velocity 1,000 fps; 50 shots per fill
MSRP $268.80

BEEMAN PRECISION AIRGUNS COMMANDER

Action: PCP
Stock: Wood
Barrel: 24.5 in.
Sights: Fiber optic front and rear
Weight: 10 lb. 1 oz.
Caliber: .177, .22
Magazine: 10 shots
Features: A more serious target rifle; bolt-action; rubber buttpad; 100 shots per fill max; max velocity 1,100 fps; integrated sound suppressor; ambidextrous hardwood thumbhole stock; include Beeman 5013 4x32mm scope and mounts
MSRP $249.99

BEEMAN PRECISION AIRGUNS COMPETITION 1380

Action: PCP
Stock: Wood
Barrel: N/A
Sights: None
Weight: 9 lb.
Caliber: .177
Magazine: 1 shot
Features: Designed for regulation competition; fully adjustable two-stage trigger with dry-fire option; adjustable cheekpiece, buttstock, forearm, and grip; 200 shots per fill; side lever; integral manometer; meets ISSF requirements
MSRP $959.99

BEEMAN PRECISION AIRGUNS MARKSMAN 1018

Action: Spring piston
Stock: Synthetic
Barrel: N/A
Sights: Fiber optic front and rear
Weight: 1 lb. 5 oz.
Caliber: .177, BB
Magazine: 18 shots
Features: Slide-cocking plinking air pistol with a smooth bore; 18-shot BB reservoir; fiber optic sights; a single shot with .177 pellets and bolts
MSRP $22.40

BEEMAN PRECISION AIRGUNS MARKSMAN 2066

Action: Spring piston
Stock: Wood
Barrel: 18.5 in.
Sights: Fiber optic front and rear
Weight: 6 lb. 4 oz.
Caliber: .177, .22
Magazine: 1 shot
Features: A break-barrel single-shot that includes a noise suppressor; 4x32 scope with mounts; automatic safety
MSRP $109.00

BEEMAN PRECISION AIRGUNS PCP UNDERLEVER 1378

Action: PCP
Stock: Wood
Barrel: N/A
Sights: Fiber optic front and rear
Weight: 7 lb. 4.5 oz.
Caliber: .177, .22
Magazine: 1 shot
Features: A unique underlever cocking design makes for faster shot-to-shot transition; supplied with scope
MSRP $370.00

BENJAMIN (BY CROSMAN) TRAIL XL MAGNUM

Action: Nitro Piston
Stock: Synthetic
Barrel: N/A
Sights: None
Weight: 9 lb. 2 oz.
Caliber: .177, .22, .25
Magazine: 1 shot
Features: Velocity up to 1,200 fps; traditionally styled wood stock with thumbhole; break-barrel action; supplied with 3–9x40 CenterPoint scope
MSRP . . . . $309.99–$339.99

NEW Products: Airguns

BO MANUFACTURE/ THE BLACK OPS SOUL LANGLEY

BO MANUFACTURE/ THE BLACK OPS SOUL PENDLETON

CHIAPPA AG92

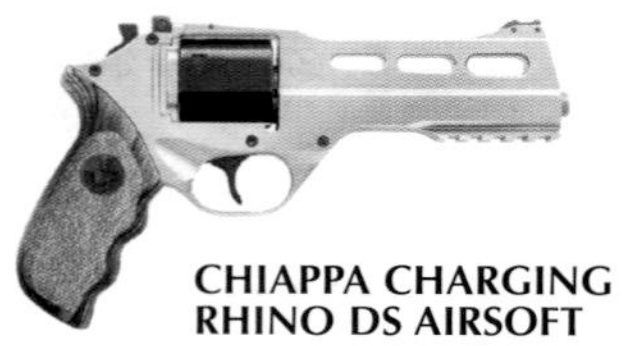

CHIAPPA CHARGING RHINO DS AIRSOFT

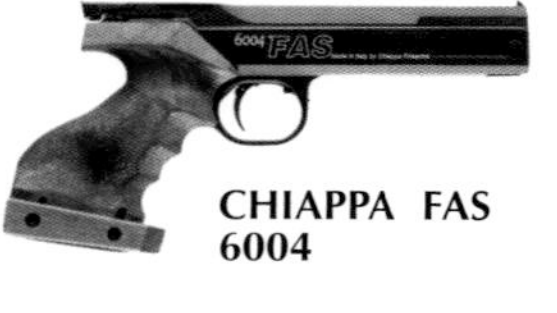

CHIAPPA FAS 6004

CROSMAN FULL AUTO R1

CROSMAN MAG-FIRE ULTRA

BO MANUFACTURE/THE BLACK OPS SOUL LANGLEY

Action: Spring piston
Stock: Synthetic
Barrel: 14.5 in.
Sights: Fiber optic front and rear
Weight: 3 lb. 15 oz.
Caliber: .177, .22
Magazine: 1 shot
Features: A lightweight break-barrel with fiber optic sights (adjustable rear); 21mm Picatinny rail; shrouded barrel; detachable polymer stock transforms the air rifle to an air pistol
MSRP $132.00

BO MANUFACTURE/THE BLACK OPS SOUL PENDLETON

Action: Break barrel
Stock: Synthetic
Barrel: 18.8 in.
Sights: Fiber optic front and rear
Weight: 6 lb. 14 oz.
Caliber: .177
Magazine: 1 shot
Features: A break-barrel with an adjustable high-density polymer stock; acres of topside, side, and bottom rails for optics and accessories; three sets of grip replacement modules
MSRP $241.00

CHIAPPA AG92

Action: CO2
Stock: Polymer
Barrel: 4.8 in.
Sights: Fixed front, windage adjustable rear
Weight: 1 lb. 4 oz.
Caliber: .177
Magazine: 14 shots
Features: A true double-/single-action air pistol replica of Beretta's iconic Model 92; automatic feed; pellets fed via seven-round cylinders
MSRP $139.00

CHIAPPA CHARGING RHINO DS AIRSOFT

Action: CO2
Stock: Imitation wood
Barrel: 5 in.
Sights: Fixed fiber optic front, adjustable rear
Weight: 2 lb. 5 oz.
Caliber: 6mm
Magazine: 6 shots
Features: An airsoft revolver that arms via an active pedal; metal barrel and body; double-/single-action; active safety flag; active barrel lock pedal; in a black frame/white grip as a standard selection, or a white frame/black grip as a limited edition
MSRP . . . . Black/white: $229.00
White/black: $239.00

CHIAPPA FAS 6004

Action: Break barrel
Stock: Wood
Barrel: 7.5 in.
Sights: Fixed front, adjustable rear
Weight: 2 lb.
Caliber: .177
Magazine: 1 shot
Features: A single-shot pneumatic air pistol for target shooters, with an ambidextrous walnut grip in non-target design or right-hand adjustable target grip; adjustable trigger; aluminum receiver; steel barrel in anodized black
MSRP . . . . Adjustable grip: $443.00
Target grip: $569.00

CROSMAN FULL AUTO R1

Action: C02
Stock: Nylon fiber
Barrel: N/A
Sights: Reflex red-dot
Weight: 6 lb.
Caliber: .177
Magazine: 25 shots
Features: This "MSR" utilizes two 12-gram CO2 cartridges to empty the 25-round magazine of its BBs in no time at all--1,400 rounds per minute, in fact; six-position adjustable buttstock; rails for light and laser add-ons; smooth bore
MSRP $169.99

CROSMAN MAG-FIRE ULTRA

Action: Break barrel
Stock: Synthetic
Barrel: N/A
Sights: Blade front, adjustable rear
Weight: 9 lb. 14 oz.
Caliber: .177, .22
Magazine: 12 shots
Features: Rifled/overmolded barrel; Quietfire sound suppression technology; 3–9x40 adjustable objective scope; Picatinny rail
MSRP $199.99

FX AIRGUNS CROWN MKII

FX AIRGUNS DREAMLINE CLASSIC

FX AIRGUNS DREAMLINE LITE

FX AIRGUNS DREAMLINE LITE COMPACT

FX AIRGUNS DREAMLINE TACTICAL

FX AIRGUNS DREAMLINE TACTICAL COMPACT

FX AIRGUNS IMPACT X MKII

FX AIRGUNS CROWN MKII

Action: PCP
Stock: Wood, laminate, synthetic
Barrel: 14.96 in., 19.69 in., 23.62 in., 27.56 in.
Sights: None
Weight: 6 lb. 3 oz.–9 lb. 9 oz.
Caliber: .177, .22, .25, .30
Magazine: 22, 18, 16, 13 shots
Features: Ambidextrous thumbhole stock paired with a fully-shrouded barrel; interchangeable calibers via barrel liners; rigid breech block; externally adjustable AMP; adjustable hammer spring; three-step transfer port adjustment; 480cc carbon fiber air cylinder; dual pressure gauges; STX fully barrel with built-in shroud; switch-style safety; Picatinny optics rail with 20 MOA angle; two-stage adjustable match trigger; adjustable buttpad; multiple stock/barrel/caliber choices
MSRP . . . . $1549.99–$2549.99

FX AIRGUNS DREAMLINE CLASSIC

Action: PCP
Stock: Walnut
Barrel: 19.69 in., 23.62 in.
Sights: None
Weight: 6 lb. 4 oz.
Caliber: .177, .22, .25, .30
Magazine: 22, 18, 16, 13 shots
Features: Removable rotary magazine; ambidextrous stock; match-grade free-floating Twist X barrel; 11mm dovetail optics mount; interchangeable caliber barrel liner system; externally adjustable AMP regulator; fixed DonnyFL moderator; adjustable hammer weight; two-stage adjustable trigger
MSRP $1399.99

FX AIRGUNS DREAMLINE LITE

Action: PCP
Stock: Synthetic
Barrel: 19.69 in., 23.62 in.
Sights: None
Weight: 5 lb. 8 oz.
Caliber: .177, .22, .25, .30
Magazine: 22, 18, 16, 13 shots
Features: Skeletonized buttstock; lightweight trigger guard with integrated rail; threaded FX Smooth Twist X match-grade, free-floating barrel; interchangeable barrel liner system; externally adjustable AMP regulator; adjustable match trigger; side-lever cocking system; 11mm dovetail scope mount; Hogue AR grip; DonnyFL and Huggett moderators, hard case, and bottle upgrades available
MSRP . . . . $1099.99–$1564.99

FX AIRGUNS DREAMLINE LITE COMPACT

Action: PCP
Stock: Synthetic
Barrel: 15.75 in., 19.29 in.
Sights: None
Weight: 5 lb. 1 oz.
Caliber: .177, .22, .25
Magazine: 22, 18, 16 shots
Features: Similar to the standard lite, but without the .30-caliber option and with shorter barrel options; side-lever cocking action; DonnyFL moderator and bottle options available
MSRP . . . . $1149.99–$1404.97

FX AIRGUNS DREAMLINE TACTICAL

Action: PCP
Stock: Synthetic
Barrel: 19.69 in., 23.62 in.
Sights: None
Weight: 6 lb.–7 lb. 15 oz.
Caliber: .177, .22, .25, .30
Magazine: 22, 18, 16, 13 shots
Features: Similar to the Dreamline Lite, but with a Hogue mil-spec buttstock, Hogue grip; bottle, stock color, six-position buffer tube, DonnyFL moderator and hard case upgrades available
MSRP . . . . $1149.99–$1764.99

FX AIRGUNS DREAMLINE TACTICAL COMPACT

Action: PCP
Stock: Synthetic
Barrel: 15.75 in., 19.29 in.
Sights: None
Weight: 6 lb.–7 lb. 7 oz.
Caliber: .177, .22, .25
Magazine: 22, 18, 16 shots
Features: Similar to the standard Tactical, but without the .30-caliber option and with shorter barrel options; DonnyFL moderator, buffer tube/stock, and bottle options available
MSRP . . . . $1249.99–$1684.99

FX AIRGUNS IMPACT X MKII

Action: PCP
Stock: Synthetic
Barrel: 19.69 in., 23.62 in., 31.50 in.
Sights: None
Weight: 6 lb. 9 oz.
Caliber: .177, .22, .25, .30, .35
Magazine: 38, 28, 28, 23, 18 shots
Features: Completely adjustable including hammer spring tension and air valve control; FX Smooth Twist X barrel with interchangeable liner system; side-cocking lever; power upgrade with FX Power Plenum; in a 9mm (.35) with 500cc bottle and 800mm barrel; Sniper with 700mm barrel; Compact with a 300cc bottle and shorter barrel; choice of black or bronze receiver
MSRP . . . . $2099.99–$2299.99

FX AIRGUNS MAVERICK SNIPER

FX AIRGUNS ROYALE 400

FX AIRGUNS ROYALE 500

FX AIRGUNS WILDCAT MKIII COMPACT

FX AIRGUNS WILDCAT MKIII SNIPER

GAMO USA P-430

GAMO USA SWARM MAGNUM 10X GEN2

GAMO USA SWARM MAXXIM 10X GEN2

FX AIRGUNS MAVERICK SNIPER

Action: PCP
Stock: Synthetic
Barrel: 27.56 in.
Sights: None
Weight: 7 lb. 3 oz.
Caliber: .22, .25, .30
Magazine: 18, 16, 13 shots
Features: A side-lever repeater that utilizes side-shot magazines; ½-in. UNF threaded Superior STX barrel; adjustable match trigger; Picatinny optics; textured AR-style grip; dual pressure gauges; 580cc carbon fiber air cylinder; dual AMP regulators
MSRP $1999.99

FX AIRGUNS ROYALE 400

Action: PCP
Stock: Synthetic, walnut, laminate
Barrel: 19.69 in.
Sights: None
Weight: 7 lb.–7 lb. 7 oz.
Caliber: .177, .22
Magazine: 16, 14 shots
Features: Side-lever repeater; thumbhole stock in choice of synthetic (adjustable recoil pad), laminate, or walnut (adjustable recoil pad and ambidextrous); adjustable match trigger; 11mm dovetail scope mount; shrouded muzzle; match-grade free-floating FX Smooth Twist barrel; manual safety
MSRP . . . . $1599.99–$1899.99

FX AIRGUNS ROYALE 500

Action: PCP
Stock: Synthetic, walnut, laminate
Barrel: 23.62 in.
Sights: None
Weight: 7 lb.–7 lb. 7 oz.
Caliber: .25
Magazine: 11 shots
Features: Similar to the 400, but in .25 caliber and with a longer barrel
MSRP . . . . $1599.99–$1899.99

FX AIRGUNS WILDCAT MKIII COMPACT

Action: PCP
Stock: Synthetic
Barrel: 19.69 in.
Sights: None
Weight: 6 lb.
Caliber: .177, .22, .25, .30
Magazine: 22, 18, 16, 13 shots
Features: A compact side-lever bullpup with a 230cc aluminum air cylinder; manual safety; Picatinny scope rail; moderator-ready ½-in. UNF threaded muzzle; Twist X barrel; externally adjustable AMP regulator; dual manometers; seven-position macro hammer spring tension adjustment
MSRP $1599.99

FX AIRGUNS WILDCAT MKIII SNIPER

Action: PCP
Stock: Synthetic
Barrel: 27.56 in.
Sights: None
Weight: 6 lb. 11 oz.
Caliber: .22, .25, .30
Magazine: 18, 16, 13 shots
Features: A sweet bullpup side-lever with a seven-position macro hammer spring tension adjustment; Twist X barrel; 300cc aluminum air cylinder; manual safety; Picatinny optics rail; dual manometers; externally adjustable AMP regulator
MSRP $1699.99

GAMO USA P-430

Action: CO2
Stock: Polymer
Barrel: N/A
Sights: Fixed front and rear
Weight: 15.5 oz.
Caliber: .177
Magazine: 16 shots
Features: Non-blowback air pistol with single-/double-action; smoothbore barrel; tactical accessory rail; aggressive slide, grip and trigger guard serrations
MSRP $49.99

GAMO USA SWARM MAGNUM 10X GEN2

Action: Inert gas
Stock: Glass-filled nylon
Barrel: N/A
Sights: Fiber optic front and rear
Weight: 6 lb. 14 oz.
Caliber: .177, .22
Magazine: 10 shots
Features: Break-action air rifle with a two-stage adjustable trigger; automatic cocking safety system; RRR-recoil reducing rail; inertia-fed technology; thumbhole stock of glass-filled nylon; Gamo 3–9x40 scope; jacketed rifled steel barrel; Whisper Fusion noise dampening
MSRP $329.99

GAMO USA SWARM MAXXIM 10X GEN2

Action: Inert gas
Stock: Glass-filled nylon
Barrel: N/A
Sights: Fiber optic front and rear
Weight: 5 lb. 10 oz.
Caliber: .177, .22
Magazine: 10 shots
Features: Similar to the Swarm Magnum 10X Gen2, but with a lighter weight; inertia-fed technology; fluted polymer jacketed rifled steel barrel with Whisper Maxxim noise reduction technology; stock with magazine compartment; Gamo 3–9x40 scope
MSRP $219.99

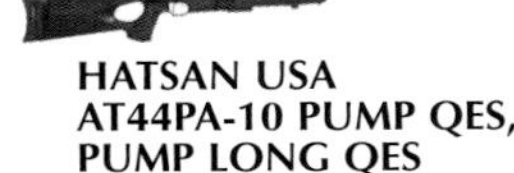
HATSAN USA AT44PA-10 PUMP QES, PUMP LONG QES

HATSAN USA FLASHPUP QE, SYN QE

HATSAN USA MOD 130S QE

HATSAN USA NEUTRONSTAR

HATSAN USA NOVASTAR

HATSAN USA SORTIE, SORTIE TACT

SIG AIR MCX AIR RIFLE

SIG AIR MCX AIR RIFLE RED DOT

HATSAN USA AT44PA-10 PUMP QES, PUMP LONG QES

Action: PCP
Stock: Synthetic
Barrel: 19.4 in., 23 in.
Sights: None
Weight: 9 lb. 10 oz.–9 lb. 15 oz.
Caliber: .177, .22, .25
Magazine: 10, 9 shots
Features: This repeater features a two-stage adjustable trigger; pump action; 11mm/22mm combo scope rail; TruGlo sights; Quiet Energy fully shrouded barrel with integrated sound moderator; Monte Carlo thumbhole stock with adjustable buttpad; long version sports the 23-in. barrel for added velocity
MSRP . . . . Standard: $449.99
Long: $499.99

HATSAN USA FLASHPUP QE, SYN QE

Action: PCP
Stock: Wood, synthetic
Barrel: 19.4 in.
Sights: None
Weight: 6 lb. 1 oz.
Caliber: .177, .22, .25
Magazine: 14, 12, 10 shots
Features: A bolt-action repeater in either wood or synthetic stock of bullpup style; Quattro trigger; QuietEnergy fully shrouded barrel; two indexing magazines and a single-shot tray included; combo 11mm/22mm rail; adjustable cheekpiece on via adjustment wheel; anti-knock system prevents gas waste
MSRP . . . . Synthetic: $359.99
Wood: $399.99

HATSAN USA MOD 130S QE

Action: Gas piston
Stock: Synthetic
Barrel: 10.6 in.
Sights: Fiber optic front and rear
Weight: 9 lb. 9 oz.
Caliber: .30
Magazine: 1 shot
Features: A single-shot break-action with a two-stage adjustable trigger; Vortex gas piston; anti-bear trap safety; TruGlo sights; SaS Shock Absorber System; QuietEnergy integrated suppressor; automatic safety; sling swivels
MSRP $239.99

HATSAN USA NEUTRONSTAR

Action: PCP
Stock: Wood
Barrel: 23 in.
Sights: None
Weight: 8 lb. 7 oz.
Caliber: .177, .22, .25
Magazine: 14, 12, 10 shots
Features: A repeater with a shrouded barrel and threaded muzzle cap; Turkish walnut thumbhole stock with adjustable comb; two-stage adjustable Quattro trigger; Picatinny rail; combo optics rail; spare magazine storage in stock; comes with two magazines and single-shot tray; anti-knock system prevents wasted gas
MSRP $889.99

HATSAN USA NOVASTAR

Action: PCP
Stock: Wood
Barrel: 23 in.
Sights: None
Weight: 8 lb. 7 oz.
Caliber: .177, .22, .25
Magazine: 14, 12, 10 shots
Features: A repeater with a side-lever action; two-stage adjustable Quattro trigger; Turkish walnut stock with adjustable comb and magazine storage; barrel shroud; anti-knock system to prevent gas waste; combo optics rail
MSRP $889.99

HATSAN USA SORTIE, SORTIE TACT

Action: PCP
Stock: Synthetic
Barrel: 7.9 in.
Sights: Fiber optic front and rear
Weight: 4 lb. 7 oz.
Caliber: .177, .22, .25
Magazine: 14, 12, 10 shots
Features: Hatsan's first PCP air pistol with a 62cc cylinder; detachable sights; ergonomic all-weather grip; Tact version has a removable folding rear stock; includes three magazines and hard case
MSRP $599.99

SIG AIR MCX AIR RIFLE

Action: CO2
Stock: Synthetic
Barrel: 18 in.
Sights: Flip-up front and rear
Weight: 7 lb. 4 oz.
Caliber: .177
Magazine: 39 shots
Features: An MSR-style air rifle; synthetic handguard; Picatinny rail; tactical front grip; in black or flat dark earth
MSRP $219.99

SIG AIR MCX AIR RIFLE RED DOT

Action: CO2
Stock: Synthetic
Barrel: 18 in.
Sights: Flip-up front and rear
Weight: 7 lb. 13 oz.
Caliber: .177
Magazine: 30 shots
Features: An MSR-style air rifle with rifled steel barrel; synthetic handguard; Picatinny rail; tactical front grip; micro red-dot optic; in black or flat dark earth
MSRP $269.99

NEW Products: Airguns

SIG AIR MCX AIR RIFLE SCOPED
SIG AIR MPX AIR RIFLE
SIG AIR MPX AIR RIFLE RED DOT
SIG AIR P226 AIR PISTOL

SIG AIR P365 AIR PISTOL

UMAREX A-REX

UMAREX HAMMER

SIG AIR MCX AIR RIFLE SCOPED

Action: CO2
Stock: Synthetic
Barrel: 18 in.
Sights: Flip-up front and rear
Weight: 7 lb. 14 oz.
Caliber: .177
Magazine: 30 shots
Features: An MSR-style air rifle with rifled steel barrel; synthetic handguard; Picatinny rail; tactical front grip; 1–4x24mm scope; in black or flat dark earth
MSRP $269.99

SIG AIR MPX AIR RIFLE

Action: CO2
Stock: Synthetic
Barrel: 8 in.
Sights: Flip-up front and rear
Weight: 6 lb. 3 oz.
Caliber: .177
Magazine: 30 shots
Features: Compact and light, this SBR air rifle has a metal housing; integral Picatinny rail; side rails; flip-up adjustable front and rear sights; muzzle velocity up to 498 fps; available in black
MSRP $199.99

SIG AIR MPX AIR RIFLE RED DOT

Action: CO2
Stock: Synthetic
Barrel: 8 in.
Sights: Flip-up front and rear
Weight: 6 lb. 9 oz.
Caliber: .177
Magazine: 30 shots
Features: Same as the standard MPX Air Rifle, but with the addition of a factory mounted micro red-dot sight; available in black or flat dark earth
MSRP $249.99

SIG AIR P226 AIR PISTOL

Action: CO2
Stock: Metal
Barrel: 4.75 in.
Sights: Fixed front and rear
Weight: 2 lb. 5 oz.
Caliber: .177
Magazine: 16 shots
Features: Metal frame; 8x2 rotary magazine; rifled steel barrel; Picatinny rail mount; can also use BBs; white dot fixed sights
MSRP $109.99

SIG AIR P365 AIR PISTOL

Action: CO2
Stock: Polymer
Barrel: 3.2 in.
Sights: Fixed front and rear
Weight: 13 oz.
Caliber: .177 BB
Magazine: 12 shots
Features: High visibility green dot fixed sights; similar in weight, feel, and action to its 9mm counterpart; full blowback metal slide that locks back on last shot fired; manual safety
MSRP $99.99

UMAREX A-REX

Action: TNT gas system
Stock: Synthetic
Barrel: 14.7 in.
Sights: Fiber optic front and rear
Weight: 7 lb. 14 oz.
Caliber: .177
Magazine: 1 shot
Features: A break-barrel single-shot with velocity up to 1,000 fps; SilencAir muzzle device; 3–9x32 adjustable objective scope included
MSRP $179.99

UMAREX LEGENDS M3 GREASE GUN

UMAREX HAMMER

Action: PCP
Stock: Synthetic
Barrel: 29.5 in.
Sights: None
Weight: 8 lb. 8 oz.
Caliber: .510
Magazine: 2 shots
Features: Intended for big-game hunting with a straight-pull speed bolt action; shrouded rifled barrel; manual safety; two-round magazine; built in manometer; Picatinny optics rail; PolyOne stock; three M-LOK forend slots
MSRP $849.99

UMAREX LEGENDS M3 GREASE GUN

Action: CO2
Stock: Metal
Barrel: N/A
Sights: Blade front, peep rear
Weight: 7 lb. 10 oz.
Caliber: .177
Magazine: 30 shots
Features: A full-auto replica of the iconic WWII gun with open-bolt action; drop-free magazine; collapsible wire stock
MSRP $219.99

UMAREX M1A1

UMAREX RUGER 10/22

UMAREX RUGER TARGIS HUNTER MAX

UMAREX RUGER TARGIS MAX

UMAREX SMITH & WESSON M29

UMAREX STEEL FORCE

UMAREX STEEL STRIKE

UMAREX SURGEMAX ELITE

UMAREX M1A1

Action: CO2
Stock: Wood
Barrel: 12 in.
Sights: Fixed front and rear
Weight: 7 lb. 13 oz.
Caliber: .177 BB
Magazine: 30 shots
Features: A full-auto replica of the Thompson M1A1, including its open-bolt functionality; sling mounts; drop-free magazine that also houses the CO2 cartridge; full metal frame
MSRP $229.99

UMAREX RUGER 10/22

Action: CO2
Stock: Synthetic
Barrel: 18 in.
Sights: Blade front, adjustable rear
Weight: 4 lb. 8 oz.
Caliber: .177
Magazine: 10 shots
Features: Faithful replica of Rugers rimfire autoloader; semiautomatic functionality; rifled barrel; rubber buttpad
MSRP $139.99

UMAREX RUGER TARGIS HUNTER MAX

Action: Gas piston
Stock: Synthetic
Barrel: 14 in.
Sights: Fiber optic front and rear
Weight: 8 lb. 8 oz.
Caliber: .22
Magazine: 1 shot
Features: A single-shot break-barrel with adjustable rear sight; all-weather stock; automatic safety; SilencAir muzzle device; 3–9x42 adjustable objective scope; sling and swivels
MSRP $199.99

UMAREX RUGER TARGIS MAX

Action: Spring piston
Stock: Synthetic
Barrel: 18.7 in.
Sights: Fiber optic front and rear
Weight: N/A
Caliber: .177
Magazine: 1 shot
Features: A single-shot break-barrel with fiber optics sights (adjustable rear); all-weather stock; automatic safety; SilencAir muzzle device; 3–9x42 adjustable objective scope on an integral scope rail
MSRP $179.99

UMAREX SMITH & WESSON M29

Action: CO2
Stock: Wood
Barrel: 8.375 in.
Sights: Ramp blade front, adjustable rear
Weight: N/A
Caliber: .177 BB
Magazine: 6 shots
Features: True to the firearm, this is a CO2 six-shot revolver; single-/double-action
MSRP . . . . N/A

UMAREX STEEL FORCE

Action: CO2
Stock: Synthetic
Barrel: 7.5 in.
Sights: Flip-up front and rear
Weight: 3 lb. 5 oz.
Caliber: .177 BB
Magazine: 30 shots
Features: Full-auto with a 300 BB reservoir above the handguard; fires in six-shot bursts; collapsible stock; dual C02 compartment in false vertical magazine; can also be fired in semiauto
MSRP $128.35

UMAREX STEEL STRIKE

Action: CO2
Stock: Synthetic
Barrel: 9 in.
Sights: Flip-up front and rear
Weight: N/A
Caliber: .177 BB
Magazine: 30 shots
Features: Full-auto with a 900 BB reservoir above the handguard; fires in six-shot bursts; CO2 housed in collapsible stock; integrated railing; can also be fired in semiauto
MSRP $114.99

UMAREX SURGEMAX ELITE

Action: Gas piston
Stock: Synthetic
Barrel: N/A
Sights: Fiber optic front and rear
Weight: N/A
Caliber: .177
Magazine: 1 shot
Features: A single-shot break-barrel with an all-weather stock featuring an ambidextrous cheekpiece; adjustable rear sight; two-stage adjustable trigger; integrated Nucleus rail system that absorbs and minimizes noise and vibration; automatic safety; muzzle brake; 4x32 adjustable objective scope; Turbo Nitrogen Technology (TNT) gas piston action
MSRP $149.99

NEW Products: Airguns

NEW PRODUCTS

UMAREX SYNERGIS

UMAREX T4E P2P HDX 68 SHOTGUN

UMAREX SYNERGIS

Action: Gas piston
Stock: Synthetic
Barrel: 18.5 in.
Sights: None
Weight: 8 lb.
Caliber: .177, .22
Magazine: 12 shots
Features: A gas-piston underlever repeater with a two-stage adjustable trigger; Picatinny top rail; Airflow Boost Technology auto-indexing pellet probe; RapidMag cartridge system; 3–9x40 scope included
MSRP . . . . $174.99–$189.99

UMAREX T4E P2P HDX 68 SHOTGUN

Action: CO2
Stock: Synthetic
Barrel: N/A
Sights: Fiber optic front and rear
Weight: N/A
Caliber: .68
Magazine: 10 shots
Features: Developed by Umarex and made by T4E, this P2P (Prepared 2 Protect) "shotgun" is a less-lethal option for home-defense practitioners that fires rubber rounds or pepper rounds; can be powered by a single 12g CO2, two 12g CO2 with an adaptor, or an 88g CO2 capsule
MSRP $350.00

NEW Products: Shotguns

AMERICAN TACTICAL CAVALRY

AMERICAN TACTICAL CAVALRY SV YOUTH

ARMSCOR/ROCK ISLAND ARMORY ALL GENERATIONS

ARMSCOR/ROCK ISLAND ARMORY MERIVA

AMERICAN TACTICAL CAVALRY, CAVALRY SPORT

Action: Over/under
Stock: Walnut
Barrel: 26 in., 28 in.
Chokes: 5
Sights: Brass bead front
Weight: 4 lb. 1 oz.–5 lb. 15 oz.
Bore/Gauge: 12, 20, 28, .410
Capacity: 2 shells
Features: An economically priced group of lightweight shotguns with Turkish walnut stocks; 3-in. chambers (2¾-in. 28-ga.); all but the .410 threaded for Benelli choke tubes; extractors; single selective trigger; long length of pull at 14.23 in. on the 12-ga.; Sport model has engraved receiver, between barrel venting
MSRP . . . . $599.95–$669.95

AMERICAN TACTICAL CAVALRY SV YOUTH

Action: Over/under
Stock: Walnut
Barrel: 26 in.
Chokes: 5
Sights: Brass bead front
Weight: N/A
Bore/Gauge: 20
Capacity: 2 shells
Features: Similar to the standard Cavalry, but with a much shorter length of pull at 12.47 in.; extractors only
MSRP $659.99

ARMSCOR/ROCK ISLAND ARMORY ALL GENERATIONS

Action: Pump
Stock: Synthetic
Barrel: 18.5 in., 26 in., 28 in.
Chokes: F, M
Sights: Bead front
Weight: 7 lb. 1 oz.–8 lb. 14 oz.
Bore/Gauge: 12, 20, .410
Capacity: 5 shells
Features: Modernized, affordable pump with an ergonomic synthetic stock and forend; 3-in. chamber; aluminum receiver; unique adjustable cheekpiece; stock spacers; 12-ga. available in a 28-in. barrel and in a self-defense 18.5-in. length, 20-ga. and .410-bore in 26-in. barrels
MSRP $299.00

ARMSCOR/ROCK ISLAND ARMORY MERIVA

Action: Pump
Stock: Synthetic
Barrel: 18.5 in.
Chokes: None
Sights: Fixed blade/ramp front
Weight: 5 lb. 15 oz.
Bore/Gauge: 12
Capacity: 5 shells
Features: A no-frills pump for self-defense
MSRP $232.00

ARMSCOR/ROCK ISLAND ARMORY VR82

Action: Semiautomatic
Stock: Synthetic
Barrel: 18 in.
Chokes: 3
Sights: Flip-up front, rear
Weight: 7 lb. 8 oz.
Bore/Gauge: 20
Capacity: 5 shells
Features: Contoured barrel with lightning cuts; thumbhole stock; black anodized finish; barrel shroud and forend compatible with aftermarket accessories; ambidextrous controls; aluminum frame
MSRP $729.00

BENELLI ETHOS CORDOBA BE.S.T.

Action: Semiautomatic
Stock: Synthetic
Barrel: 28 in., 30 in.
Chokes: 5
Sights: Fiber optic front
Weight: 5 lb. 7 oz.–7 lb.
Bore/Gauge: 12, 20, 28
Capacity: 2, 4 shells
Features: Semiauto with a ported barrel; ComforTech recoil system; inertia-driven operating system; Benelli Surface Treatment (BE.S.T.) aids in rust/corrosion resistance; Broadway rib; Shell View magazine; Crio choke set; right-hand only; recommended minimum load is 3-dram 1 1/8-oz.; 28-ga. magazine holds only two shells
MSRP $2349.00

BENELLI ETHOS SUPERSPORT

Action: Semiautomatic
Stock: Carbon fiber
Barrel: 28 in., 30 in.
Chokes: 5
Sights: Fiber optic front
Weight: 5 lb. 7 oz.–7 lb.
Bore/Gauge: 12, 20, 28
Capacity: 2, 4 shells
Features: Semiauto with a ported barrel; ComforTech 3 stock system; Shell View magazine; flush Crio choke set; right-hand only.; 28-ga. magazine holds only two shells
MSRP $2299.00

BERETTA 687 SILVER PIGEON III

Action: Over/under
Stock: Wood
Barrel: 26 in., 26.5 in., 28 in., 30 in.
Chokes: 3
Sights: White front bead
Weight: N/A
Bore/Gauge: 12, 20, 28, .410
Capacity: 2 shells
Features: Several improvements over earlier models, including 5-axis laser engraving on the receiver with game scenes and floral motifs; class 2.5 walnut with a high-gloss finish; Steelium Optima Bore HP tri-alloy barrels; 20mm MicroCore buttpad; 6x6 windowed top rib with anti-reflective checkering
MSRP $2699.00

BROWNING A5 CAMO REALTREE MAX-5, REALTREE TIMBER, MO BOTTOMLAND, MO ORIGINAL BOTTOMLAND, MO SHADOW GRASS HABITAT

Action: Semiautomatic
Stock: Synthetic
Barrel: 26 in., 28 in., 30 in.
Chokes: 3
Sights: Fiber optic front sight
Weight: 7 lb. 3 oz.–7 lb. 7 oz.
Bore/Gauge: 12
Capacity: 4 shells
Features: The A5 goes all things camo with three coverages to choose from; 3½-in. chamber; textured grip panels; aluminum alloy receiver; back-bored; VectorPro lengthened forcing cones; Invector DS chokes; nickel-Teflon coating on operating controls; stock shims; Speed Load Plus design; TurnKey magazine plug; Kinematic Drive action; Ergo Balanced design
MSRP . . . . $1799.99–$1859.99

BROWNING A5 CAMO VINTAGE TAN

Action: Semiautomatic
Stock: Synthetic
Barrel: 26 in., 28 in.
Chokes: 3
Sights: Fiber optic front sight
Weight: 7 lb. 3 oz.–7 lb. 5 oz.
Bore/Gauge: 12
Capacity: 4 shells
Features: Vintage is in with an old duck hunter's type of camo; 3½-in. chamber; textured grip panels; aluminum alloy receiver; back-bored; VectorPro lengthened forcing cones; Invector DS chokes; nickel-Teflon coating on operating controls; stock shims; Speed Load Plus design; TurnKey magazine plug; Kinematic Drive action; Ergo Balanced design
MSRP $1799.99

BROWNING A5 HIGH GRADE HUNTER MAPLE

Action: Semiautomatic
Stock: Maple
Barrel: 26 in., 28 in.
Chokes: 3
Sights: Fiber optic front sight, ivory mid-bead
Weight: 6 lb. 11 oz.–6 lb. 13 oz.
Bore/Gauge: 12
Capacity: 4 shells
Features: AAA-grade maple stock in a high-gloss finish; high-gloss blued barrel; 3-in. chamber; aluminum alloy receiver in a polished black finish with engraved pheasants on the left side, mallards on the right; back-bored; VectorPro lengthened forcing cones; Invector DS chokes; nickel-Teflon coating on operating controls; stock shims; Kinematic Drive action; Ergo Balanced design; ABS case included
MSRP $1999.99

BROWNING A5 HIGH GRADE HUNTER MAPLE SWEET 16

Action: Semiautomatic
Stock: Maple
Barrel: 26 in., 28 in.
Chokes: 3
Sights: Fiber optic front sight, ivory mid-bead
Weight: 5 lb. 12 oz.–5 lb. 13 oz.
Bore/Gauge: 16
Capacity: 4 shells
Features: AAA-grade maple stock in a high-gloss finish; high-gloss blued barrel; 2¾-in. chamber; aluminum alloy receiver in a polished black finish with engraved pheasants on the left side, mallards on the right; back-bored; VectorPro lengthened forcing cones; Invector DS chokes; nickel-Teflon coating on operating controls; stock shims; Kinematic Drive action; Ergo Balanced design; ABS case included
MSRP $1999.99

BROWNING A5 LIGHTNING SWEET 16

Action: Semiautomatic
Stock: Walnut
Barrel: 26 in., 28 in.
Chokes: 3
Sights: Fiber optic front sight, ivory mid-bead
Weight: 5 lb. 12 oz.–5 lb. 13 oz.
Bore/Gauge: 16
Capacity: 4 shells
Features: Turkish walnut stock in gloss finish; Prince of Wales grip; high-gloss blued barrel; 2¾-in. chamber; aluminum alloy receiver in a gloss black anodized finish; back-bored; VectorPro lengthened forcing cones; Invector DS chokes; nickel-Teflon coating on operating controls; stock shims; Kinematic Drive action; SpeedLoad Plus design; TurnKey magazine plug; Ergo Balanced design; ABS case included
MSRP $1739.99

BROWNING A5 ULTIMATE MAPLE

Action: Semiautomatic
Stock: Maple
Barrel: 26 in., 28 in.
Chokes: 3
Sights: Fiber optic front sight, ivory mid-bead
Weight: 6 lb. 11 oz.–6 lb. 13 oz.
Bore/Gauge: 12
Capacity: 4 shells
Features: AAAA-grade maple stock in gloss finish; high-gloss blued barrel; 3-in. chamber; aluminum alloy receiver in a satin nickel finish with engraved pheasants on the left side, mallards on the right; back-bored; VectorPro lengthened forcing cones; Invector DS chokes; nickel-Teflon coating on operating controls; stock shims; Speed Load Plus design; TurnKey magazine plug; Kinematic Drive action; Ergo Balanced design; ABS case included
MSRP $2139.99

BROWNING A5 WICKED WING VINTAGE TAN

BROWNING CITORI 725 SPORTING MAPLE

BROWNING BPS FIELD MICRO MIDAS

BROWNING CITORI 725 SPORTING PARALLEL COMB, PARALLEL COMB ADJUSTABLE COMB

BROWNING CITORI 725 SPORTING LEFT-HAND, LEFT-HAND ADJUSTABLE COMB

BROWNING CITORI 725 TRAP LEFT-HAND, LEFT-HAND ADJUSTABLE COMB

BROWNING A5 WICKED WING VINTAGE TAN

Action: Semiautomatic
Stock: Synthetic
Barrel: 26 in., 28 in.
Chokes: 3
Sights: Fiber optic front sight
Weight: 7 lb. 3 oz.–7 lb. 5 oz.
Bore/Gauge: 12
Capacity: 4 shells
Features: Wearing full-coverage old duck hunter's type of camo; 3½-in. chamber; textured grip panels; aluminum alloy receiver; back-bored; VectorPro lengthened forcing cones; Invector DS chokes; nickel-Teflon coating on operating controls; stock shims; Speed Load Plus design; TurnKey magazine plug; Kinematic Drive action; Ergo Balanced design
MSRP $1999.99

BROWNING BPS FIELD MICRO MIDAS

Action: Pump
Stock: Walnut
Barrel: 24 in., 26 in.
Chokes: 3
Sights: Silver bead front
Weight: 6 lb. 12 oz.–7 lb.
Bore/Gauge: 20, .410
Capacity: 4 shells
Features: Scaled-down pump with redesigned stock to deliver a faster, more natural swing; floating rib; Grade I walnut stock in a satin finished and with a 13-in. length of pull; matte blued receiver and barrel; 20-ga. available only in 24-in. barrel; 3-in. chambers both bore sizes
MSRP $699.99

BROWNING CITORI 725 SPORTING LEFT-HAND, LEFT-HAND ADJUSTABLE COMB

Action: Over/under
Stock: Walnut
Barrel: 30 in., 32 in.
Chokes: 5
Sights: HiViz Pro Comp fiber optic front
Weight: 7 lb. 8 oz.–7 lb. 13 oz.
Bore/Gauge: 12
Capacity: 2 shells
Features: Browning's Fire Lite mechanical trigger with three shoes; Invector-DS chokes; Ergo balance design; Inflex II recoil pad; gloss oil-finished Grade III/IV walnut stock; true left-hand top lever; wide floating rib and between barrel venting; ported barrels; optional adjustable comb model
Standard: $3199.99
Adjustable Comb: $3599.99

BROWNING CITORI 725 SPORTING MAPLE

Action: Over/under
Stock: Maple
Barrel: 30 in., 32 in.
Chokes: 5
Sights: HiViz Pro Comp fiber optic front
Weight: 7 lb. 6 oz.–7 lb. 8 oz.
Bore/Gauge: 12
Capacity: 2 shells
Features: AAAA-grade maple stock; Fire Lite mechanical trigger with three shoes; Invector-DS chokes; Ergo balance design; Inflex II recoil pad; low post floating rib and between barrel venting; ported barrels; gold-enhanced engraving
MSRP $3339.00

BROWNING CITORI 725 SPORTING PARALLEL COMB, PARALLEL COMB ADJUSTABLE COMB

Action: Over/under
Stock: Walnut
Barrel: 30 in., 32 in.
Chokes: 5
Sights: HiViz Pro Comp fiber optic front
Weight: 7 lb. 6 oz.–7 lb. 8 oz.
Bore/Gauge: 12
Capacity: 2 shells
Features: Fire Lite mechanical trigger with three shoes; Invector-DS chokes; Ergo balance design; Inflex II recoil pad; gloss oil-finished Grade III/IV walnut stock; low-post floating rib and between barrel venting; ported barrels; parallel comb stock; optional adjustable comb model; silver nitride receiver with gold-enhanced engraving; point of aim 50/50
Standard: $3199.99
Adjustable Comb: $3599.99

BROWNING CITORI 725 TRAP LEFT-HAND, LEFT-HAND ADJUSTABLE COMB

Action: Over/under
Stock: Walnut
Barrel: 30 in., 32 in.
Chokes: 3
Sights: HiViz Pro Comp fiber optic front, ivory mid bead
Weight: 8 lb. 10 oz.–9 lb. 1 oz.
Bore/Gauge: 12
Capacity: 2 shells
Features: Fire Lite mechanical trigger with three shoes; Invector-DS chokes; Ergo balance design; gloss oil-finished Grade III/IV walnut stock; true left-hand top lever; high post floating rib and between barrel venting; ported barrels; steel receiver in silver nitride finish with gold-enhanced engraving; supplied with three extended Invector-DS chokes; 2¾-chamber; optional adjustable comb model
MSRP $3399.99

NEW Products: Shotguns

BROWNING CITORI 725 TRAP MAPLE

BROWNING CITORI GRAN LIGHTNING 16-GA.

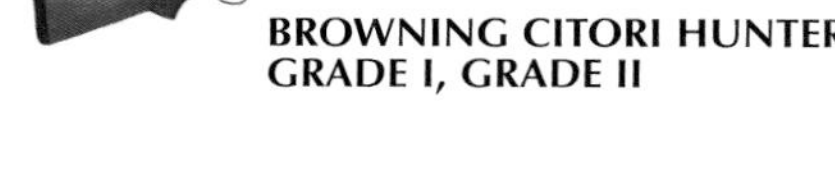
BROWNING CITORI HUNTER GRADE I, GRADE II

BROWNING CITORI WHITE LIGHTNING 16-GA.

BROWNING CYNERGY CX FEATHER

BROWNING CYNERGY WICKED WING VINTAGE TAN

BROWNING GOLD 10-GA. FIELD MO SHADOW GRASS HABITAT

BROWNING CITORI 725 TRAP MAPLE

Action: Over/under
Stock: Maple
Barrel: 30 in., 32 in.
Chokes: 3
Sights: HiViz Pro Comp fiber optic front
Weight: 8 lb. 2 oz.–8 lb. 4 oz.
Bore/Gauge: 12
Capacity: 2 shells
Features: AAAA-grade maple; Fire Lite mechanical trigger with three shoes; Invector-DS extended chokes; Ergo balance design; ventilated trap-style recoil pad; Monte Carlo comb; semi-beavertail forend; high post floating rib and between barrel venting; ported barrels; gold-enhanced engraving; point of impact 70/30
MSRP $3399.00

BROWNING CITORI GRAN LIGHTNING 16-GA.

Action: Over/under
Stock: Walnut
Barrel: 26 in., 28 in.
Chokes: 3
Sights: Ivory bead front, mid bead
Weight: 6 lb. 14 oz.–7 lb.
Bore/Gauge: 16
Capacity: 2 shells
Features: A very pretty 16-ga. with a gloss oil-finished Lightning-style stock; Prince of Wales grip; Grade V/VI walnut; Inflex 2 recoil pad; blued receiver with unique broad-coverage engraving and gold accents; three-set of extended Invector Plus Midas chokes
MSRP $3399.99

BROWNING CITORI HUNTER GRADE I, GRADE II

Action: Over/under
Stock: Walnut
Barrel: 26 in., 28 in.
Chokes: 3
Sights: Silver bead
Weight: 6 lb. 15 oz.–7 lb. 11 oz.
Bore/Gauge: 12, 16, 20, 28, .410
Capacity: 2 shells
Features: One for the hunters in every gauge available; Invector-Plus flush chokes; Grade I black walnut stock; Inflex 2 recoil pad; polished blue barrels and receiver with gold enhancements; 50/50 point of impact; Grade II has Grade II/III American walnut stock
Grade I: . . . . $1999.99–$2069.99
Grade II: . . . . . . $2199.99–$2269.99

BROWNING CITORI WHITE LIGHTNING 16-GA.

Action: Over/under
Stock: Walnut
Barrel: 26 in., 28 in.
Chokes: 3
Sights: Ivory bead front, mid bead
Weight: 6 lb. 14 oz.–7 lb.
Bore/Gauge: 16
Capacity: 2 shells
Features: Similar to the Gran Lightning 16-ga.; Grade III/IV walnut stock; silver nitride receiver with engraving and gold accents; extended black Invector Plus Midas chokes
MSRP $2739.00

BROWNING CYNERGY CX FEATHER

Action: Over/under
Stock: Walnut
Barrel: 28 in., 30 in.
Chokes: 3
Sights: Ivory bead front, mid bead
Weight: 6 lb. 13 oz.–6 lb. 15 oz.
Bore/Gauge: 12
Capacity: 2 shells
Features: Grade I walnut stock; stock spacer; three-position trigger with one shoe; Invector Plus Midas extended choke tubes; Inflex recoil pad; 3-in. chamber; silver nitride receiver; 60/40 point of impact
MSRP $2139.99

BROWNING CYNERGY WICKED WING VINTAGE TAN

Action: Over/under
Stock: Synthetic
Barrel: 26 in., 28 in., 30 in.
Chokes: 3
Sights: Ivory bead front
Weight: 7 lb. 6 oz.–7 lb. 10 oz.
Bore/Gauge: 12
Capacity: 2 shells
Features: Retro meets modern with a vintage tan camo pattern; burnt bronze Cerakote barrels and receiver; hard-chromed chambers and bores; Invector Plus Goose Band extended chokes; adjustable comb and stock spacer; textured grip surfaces
MSRP $2399.99

BROWNING GOLD 10-GA. FIELD MO SHADOW GRASS HABITAT

Action: Semiautomatic
Stock: Synthetic
Barrel: 26 in., 28 in.
Chokes: 3
Sights: Silver bead front
Weight: 9 lb. 9 oz.–9 lb. 11 oz.
Bore/Gauge: 10
Capacity: 4 shells
Features: With a 3½-in. chamber in 10-ga., this shotgun is in full-coverage camo; flush Invector chokes; Inflex 2 recoil pad; textured gripping areas; sling swivel studs; gas-operated action
MSRP $1859.99

BROWNING MAXUS II CAMO REALTREE MAX-5

BROWNING MAXUS II CAMO VINTAGE TAN

BROWNING MAXUS II HUNTER

BROWNING MAXUS II RIFLED DEER

BROWNING MAXUS II SPORTING CARBON FIBER

BROWNING MAXUS II STALKER

BROWNING MAXUS II CAMO REALTREE MAX-5, REALTREE TIMBER, MO BOTTOMLAND, MO ORIGINAL BOTTOMLAND, MO SHADOW GRASS HABITAT

Action: Semiautomatic
Stock: Synthetic
Barrel: 26 in., 28 in.
Chokes: 3
Sights: Fiber optic front, ivory mid bead
Weight: 7 lb.–7 lb. 2 oz.
Bore/Gauge: 12
Capacity: 4 shells
Features: Full-coverage camo in a wide variety of patterns make this Power Drive gas-operated semiauto the tool for every hunter; SoftFlex cheekpiece; oversized bolt and bolt handle; shims for cast, drop, and length of pull adjustment; ramped trigger guard for improved loading; reduced weight magazine tube; chrome chamber and bore; back-bored barrels; Lightning trigger; Speed Load Plus design; magazine cut-off and TurnKey magazine plug; extended Invector Plus choke tubes; hard case
MSRP . . . . $1789.99–$1899.99

BROWNING MAXUS II CAMO VINTAGE TAN

Action: Semiautomatic
Stock: Synthetic
Barrel: 26 in., 28 in.
Chokes: 3
Sights: Fiber optic front, ivory mid bead
Weight: 7 lb.–7 lb. 2 oz.
Bore/Gauge: 12
Capacity: 4 shells
Features: Power Drive gas-operated repeater; stock can be trimmed, dressed in a vintage "old duck hunters" tan splotch camo; over-molded grip panels; SoftFlex cheekpiece; oversized bolt and bolt handle; shims for cast, drop, and length of pull adjustment; ramped trigger guard for improved loading; reduced weight magazine tube; chrome chamber and bore; Lightning trigger; Speed Load Plus design; magazine cut-off and TurnKey magazine plug; extended Invector Plus choke tubes; hard case
MSRP $1829.99

BROWNING MAXUS II HUNTER

Action: Semiautomatic
Stock: Walnut
Barrel: 26 in., 28 in.
Chokes: 3
Sights: Fiber optic front, ivory mid bead
Weight: 7 lb.–7 lb. 2 oz.
Bore/Gauge: 12
Capacity: 4 shells
Features: Turkish walnut stock in a satin finish; oversized bolt and bolt handle; shims for cast, drop, and length of pull adjustment; matte black anodized receiver; ramped trigger guard for improved loading; reduced weight magazine tube; chrome chamber and bore; Lightning trigger; Speed Load Plus design; magazine cut-off and TurnKey magazine plug; Invector Plus choke tubes; hard case
MSRP $1599.99

BROWNING MAXUS II RIFLED DEER

Action: Semiautomatic
Stock: Synthetic
Barrel: 22 in.
Chokes: None
Sights: None
Weight: 7 lb. 3 oz.
Bore/Gauge: 12
Capacity: 4 shells
Features: With a 3-in. chamber, this gun for deer hunters has a topside Picatinny rail cantilever scope mount; full-coverage MO Break-Up Country; Lightning trigger; Speed Load Plus design; TurnKey magazine plug; rubber overmolding on grip areas; Power Drive gas operating system; SoftFlex cheekpad; oversized controls
MSRP $1739.99

BROWNING MAXUS II SPORTING CARBON FIBER

Action: Semiautomatic
Stock: Synthetic
Barrel: 28 in., 30 in.
Chokes: 5
Sights: HiViz TriComp front, ivory mid bead
Weight: 7 lb. 2 oz.
Bore/Gauge: 12
Capacity: 4 shells
Features: Stock, receiver, and barrel are carbon fiber-dipped; receiver has satin-finished flats; oversized controls; reduced weight magazine tube; Invector Plus Midas extended choke tubes; ramped trigger guard for easier loading; SoftFlex cheekpiece; rubber overmolding on grip areas; Lightning trigger; Speed Load Plus; chrome chamber and bore; ABS hard case
MSRP $1859.99

BROWNING MAXUS II STALKER

Action: Semiautomatic
Stock: Synthetic
Barrel: 26 in., 28 in.
Chokes: 3
Sights: HiViz TriComp front, ivory mid bead
Weight: 6 lb. 14 oz.–6 lb. 15 oz.
Bore/Gauge: 12
Capacity: 4 shells
Features: A deer or turkey hunter's friend, with a durable, all-black finish on stock and metal; oversized controls; reduced weight magazine tube; Invector Plus flush choke tubes; ramped trigger guard for easier loading; SoftFlex cheekpiece; rubber overmolding on grip areas; Lightning trigger; Speed Load Plus; chrome chamber and bore; ABS hard case included; 3½- or 3-in. chamber
MSRP . . . . $1589.99–$1779.99

NEW Products: Shotguns

BROWNING MAXUS II WICKED WING

CAESAR GUERINI ESSEX LIMITED GOLD SPORTING

BROWNING SILVER FIELD CAMO FDE VINTAGE TAN

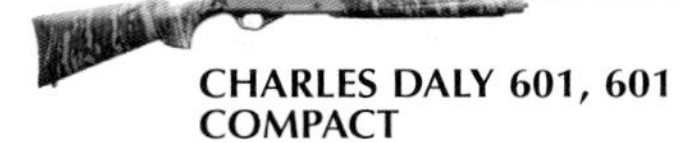

CHARLES DALY 601, 601 COMPACT

BROWNING SILVER FIELD CAMO VINTAGE TAN

CHARLES DALY 601 DPS

CHARLES DALY AR-12A, 12T

BROWNING MAXUS II WICKED WING REALTREE TIMBER, MO BOTTOMLAND, MO ORIGINAL BOTTOMLAND, MO SHADOW GRASS HABITAT

Action: Semiautomatic
Stock: Synthetic
Barrel: 26 in., 28 in.
Chokes: 3
Sights: Fiber optic front, ivory mid bead
Weight: 7 lb.–7 lb. 2 oz.
Bore/Gauge: 12
Capacity: 4 shells
Features: Barrels and receivers treated with burnt bronze Cerakote; oversized controls; reduced weight magazine tube; Invector Plus Midas extended choke tubes; ramped trigger guard for easier loading; SoftFlex cheekpiece; rubber overmolding on grip areas; Lightning trigger; Speed Load Plus; chrome chamber and bore; ABS hard case included; 3½-in. chambers on all, MO Shadow Grass Habitat also available with 3-in. chamber
MSRP . . . . $1939.99–$2069.99

BROWNING SILVER FIELD CAMO FDE VINTAGE TAN

Action: Semiautomatic
Stock: Synthetic
Barrel: 26 in., 28 in.
Chokes: 3
Sights: Brass bead front
Weight: 7 lb. 8 oz.–7 lb. 10 oz.
Bore/Gauge: 12
Capacity: 4 shells
Features: Identical to the other Silver Field Cerakote/camo shotguns, but with a stock in the duck hunter's camo of yesteryear for an almost-Vintage look
MSRP $1229.99

BROWNING SILVER FIELD CAMO VINTAGE TAN

Action: Semiautomatic
Stock: Synthetic
Barrel: 26 in., 28 in.
Chokes: 3
Sights: Brass bead front
Weight: 7 lb. 8 oz.–7 lb. 10 oz.
Bore/Gauge: 12
Capacity: 4 shells
Features: Identical to the other Silver Field non-Cerakote camo shotguns, but with a stock in the duck hunter's camo of yesteryear for an almost-Vintage look; aluminum alloy receiver in a combo black/charcoal finish
MSRP $1179.99

CAESAR GUERINI ESSEX LIMITED GOLD SPORTING

Action: Over/under
Stock: Walnut
Barrel: 30 in., 32 in.
Chokes: 6
Sights: White bead front, silver mid-bead
Weight: 7 lb. 14 oz.–8 lb.
Bore/Gauge: 12
Capacity: 2 shells
Features: Turkish walnut stock; case-colored receiver enhanced with white, yellow, and rose gold points and scroll engraving; receiver has Invisalloy protective finish; stock has hand-rubbed oil finish; 2¾-in. chamber; rib is parallel and ventilated, 6mm high and 10mm wide; 5-in. DuoCon forcing cones; DTS adjustable trigger system; add $245 for left-hand stock, $395 for adjustable comb
MSRP $8350.00

CHARLES DALY 601, 601 COMPACT

Action: Semiautomatic
Stock: Synthetic
Barrel: 22 in., 28 in.
Chokes: 3
Sights: Fiber optic front
Weight: 7 lb.–7 lb. 3 oz.
Bore/Gauge: 12, 20
Capacity: 4 shells
Features: An affordable shotgun for the hunter with a stock dressed in MO Bottomland; receiver and barrel finished in flat dark earth; Beretta/Benelli Mobil chokes (thread MC-3); Compact model is the 20-ga. with the 22-in. barrel
MSRP . . . . $354.00–$398.00

CHARLES DALY 601 DPS

Action: Semiautomatic
Stock: Synthetic
Barrel: 18.5 in.
Chokes: 1
Sights: Hooded front, ghost-ring rear
Weight: 8 lb. 1 oz.
Bore/Gauge: 12
Capacity: 5 shells
Features: The short barrel makes this a smart choice for home defense; topside rail for optics; pistol grip has finger grooves; Modified Beretta/Benelli Mobil choke
MSRP $649.00

CHARLES DALY AR-12A, 12T

Action: Semiautomatic
Stock: Synthetic
Barrel: 18.5 in.
Chokes: 1
Sights: Flip-up front, rear
Weight: 8 lb. 3 oz.
Bore/Gauge: 12
Capacity: 5 shells
Features: Scattergun AR with bells and whistles; stock with an adjustable cheekpiece; lots of top-side rail; handguard with M-LOK slots; 12T version has additional rail sections at 3, 6, and 9 o'clock
MSRP AR-12A: $458.00
AR-12T: $529.00

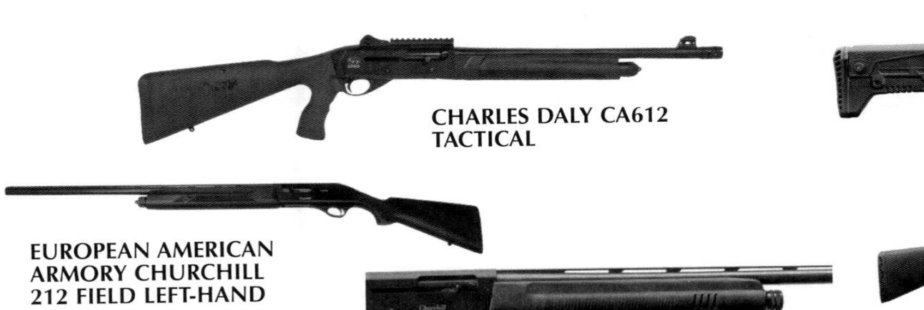

CHARLES DALY CA612 TACTICAL

EUROPEAN AMERICAN ARMORY CHURCHILL 212 FIELD LEFT-HAND

CHARLES DALY N4S BULLPUP G2

EUROPEAN AMERICAN ARMORY CHURCHILL 220

EUROPEAN AMERICAN ARMORY CHURCHILL 220 FIELD

EUROPEAN AMERICAN ARMORY CHURCHILL 220 GOBBLER

EUROPEAN AMERICAN ARMORY CHURCHILL 220 PISTOL GRIP

CHARLES DALY CA612 TACTICAL

Action: Semiautomatic
Stock: Synthetic
Barrel: 22 in.
Chokes: 5
Sights: Hooded front, ghost-ring rear
Weight: 6 lb. 11 oz.
Bore/Gauge: 12
Capacity: 4 shells
Features: Nice choice for home defense or 3-gun games; Beretta/ Benelli Mobil chokes that include two breaching chokes; 3-in. chamber; aluminum receiver; topside Picatinny rail
MSRP $473.00

CHARLES DALY N4S BULLPUP G2

Action: Semiautomatic
Stock: Synthetic
Barrel: 18.5 in.
Chokes: 1
Sights: None
Weight: 8 lb. 3 oz.
Bore/Gauge: 12, 20, .410
Capacity: 5 shells
Features: The only thing more fun than an AR-type shotgun is one in a bullpup configuration; solid weight to take up recoil; reversible bolt handle; carry handle; ambidextrous safety; 3-in. chamber; Modified Beretta/ Benelli Mobil choke
MSRP $529.00

EUROPEAN AMERICAN ARMORY CHURCHILL 212 FIELD LEFT-HAND

Action: Semiautomatic
Stock: Synthetic
Barrel: 28 in.
Chokes: 1
Sights: Fiber optic front
Weight: 6 lb. 4 oz.
Bore/Gauge: 12
Capacity: 3 shells
Features: A no-nonsense, lightweight, easy swinging autoloader for left-hand shooters; left-side bolt, ejection, and controls; vent rib barrel; blued metalwork; aluminum receiver
MSRP $451.00

EUROPEAN AMERICAN ARMORY CHURCHILL 220

Action: Semiautomatic
Stock: Synthetic
Barrel: 18.5 in.
Chokes: 1
Sights: Bead front
Weight: 5 lb.
Bore/Gauge: 20
Capacity: 5 shells
Features: Intended for home defense, with a lightweight 18.5-in. barrel
MSRP $376.00

EUROPEAN AMERICAN ARMORY CHURCHILL 220 FIELD

Action: Semiautomatic
Stock: Synthetic
Barrel: 24 in., 26 in., 28 in.
Chokes: 1
Sights: Bead front
Weight: 5 lb. 14 oz.
Bore/Gauge: 20
Capacity: 3 shells
Features: Similar to the home-defense 220, but with a longer barrel and reduced magazine capacity
MSRP $419.00

EUROPEAN AMERICAN ARMORY CHURCHILL 220 GOBBLER

Action: Semiautomatic
Stock: Synthetic
Barrel: 24 in.
Chokes: 1
Sights: Fiber optic front
Weight: 5 lb. 14 oz.
Bore/Gauge: 20
Capacity: 3 shells
Features: Burnt bronze Cerakote receiver and vent rib barrel; camo stock; receiver is optics ready and includes red-dot sight; length of pull stock spacers
MSRP $621.00

EUROPEAN AMERICAN ARMORY CHURCHILL 220 PISTOL GRIP

Action: Semiautomatic
Stock: Synthetic
Barrel: 18.5 in.
Chokes: 1
Sights: Fiber optic red-dot front
Weight: 5 lb.
Bore/Gauge: 20
Capacity: 5 shells
Features: A lightweight tactical gun for home defense; breaching type choke; extended magazine tube; optics-ready receiver; pistol grip
MSRP $561.00

EUROPEAN AMERICAN ARMORY CHURCHILL 228 FIELD

Action: Semiautomatic
Stock: Synthetic
Barrel: 24 in., 26 in., 28 in.
Chokes: 1
Sights: Bead front
Weight: 5 lb. 14 oz.
Bore/Gauge: 28
Capacity: 3 shells
Features: A lightweight 28-gauge for the field with vent rib barrel
MSRP $419.00

EUROPEAN AMERICAN ARMORY CHURCHILL 612, 612 PISTOL GRIP, 612 TACTICAL

Action: Pump
Stock: Synthetic
Barrel: 18.5 in.
Chokes: 1
Sights: Blade front
Weight: 5 lb. 8 oz.
Bore/Gauge: 12
Capacity: 5 shells
Features: A home-defense pump; Tactical pistol grip stock option; Picatinny optics rail; breaching-type choke tube
Standard: $233.00
Pistol Grip: $243.00
Tactical: $303.00

EUROPEAN AMERICAN ARMORY CHURCHILL 612 HUNTER

Action: Pump
Stock: Synthetic
Barrel: 28 in.
Chokes: 3
Sights: Bead front
Weight: 5 lb. 8 oz.
Bore/Gauge: 12
Capacity: 5 shells
Features: You can carry this one all day at under six pounds; full vent rib
MSRP $296.00

EUROPEAN AMERICAN ARMORY CHURCHILL 620, 620 PISTOL GRIP

Action: Pump
Stock: Synthetic
Barrel: 18.5 in.
Chokes: 1
Sights: Blade front, fiber optic
Weight: 5 lb.
Bore/Gauge: 20
Capacity: 5 shells
Features: Aggressively ribbed forearm for a sure grip; pistol grip model has breaching-type choke tube; Picatinny rail
MSRP . . . . Standard: $253.00
Tactical: $332.00

EUROPEAN AMERICAN ARMORY GIRSAN MC312 GOBBLER

Action: Semiautomatic
Stock: Synthetic
Barrel: 24 in.
Chokes: 1
Sights: Fiber optic front, red-dot optic
Weight: 6 lb. 12 oz.
Bore/Gauge: 12
Capacity: 5 shells
Features: Totally ready for the turkey woods with a barrel and receiver in burnt bronze Cerakote; camo stock; red-dot optic included; enhanced loading port and controls
MSRP $613.00

EUROPEAN AMERICAN ARMORY GIRSAN MC312 SPORT

Action: Semiautomatic
Stock: Synthetic
Barrel: 24 in.
Chokes: 5
Sights: Fiber optic front, red-dot optic
Weight: 6 lb. 12 oz.
Bore/Gauge: 12
Capacity: 5 shells
Features: Ready for 3-gun or other target games; low-profile accessory rail; stock in black; fully machined receiver in choice of blue, black, or red; pistol grip stock optional; red-dot optic included
MSRP $634.00

EUROPEAN AMERICAN ARMORY GIRSAN MC312 TACTICAL

Action: Semiautomatic
Stock: Synthetic
Barrel: 18.5 in.
Chokes: 1
Sights: Fiber optic front
Weight: 6 lb. 12 oz.
Bore/Gauge: 12
Capacity: 5 shells
Features: A home-defense 12-ga. with a breaching-type choke tube; black synthetic pistol grip stock; red-dot optic included
MSRP $634.00

FABARM AUTUMN

Action: Side-by-side
Stock: Wood
Barrel: 28 in., 30 in.
Chokes: 5
Sights: White bead front
Weight: 5 lb. 9 oz.–6 lb. 2 oz.
Bore/Gauge: 20
Capacity: 2 shells
Features: A beautiful first side-by-side; stock of deluxe Turkish walnut; color case-hardened receiver with full-coverage engraving; four-lug locking system; "swamped" rib textured to reduce glare; Tribore HP barrels; choice of straight English stock with splinter forend or pistol-grip stock with semi-beavertail forend; add $160 for left-hand stock
MSRP $4095.00

FRANCHI AFFINITY 3 ELITE TURKEY

Action: Semiautomatic
Stock: Synthetic
Barrel: 24 in.
Chokes: 2
Sights: Hooded dual-color fiber optic front
Weight: 6 lb. 14 oz.–7 lb. 10 oz.
Bore/Gauge: 12, 20
Capacity: 4 shells
Features: The Affinity 3 line gains a turkey gun; pistol grip stock in Optifade Subalpine; metalwork in midnight bronze Cerakote; Exteded Turkey and Exteneded Turkey XF chokes included
MSRP $1249.00

FRANCHI AFFINITY 3 TURKEY 20-GA.

Action: Semiautomatic
Stock: Synthetic
Barrel: 24 in.
Chokes: 2
Sights: Hooded dual-color fiber optic front
Weight: 6 lb. 10 oz.
Bore/Gauge: 20
Capacity: 4 shells
Features: Not everyone feels the need to throw a super-magnum 12-ga. load at a turkey; dual-color front sight; Extended Turkey and Extended Turkey XF chokes; Steadygrip pistol-grip stock and metalwork in full-coverage MO Bottomland
MSRP $959.00

FRANCHI AFFINITY 3.5 CERAKOTE

Action: Semiautomatic
Stock: Synthetic
Barrel: 26 in., 28 in.
Chokes: 3
Sights: Fiber optic red bar front
Weight: 6 lb. 15 oz.–7 lb.
Bore/Gauge: 12
Capacity: 4 shells
Features: Lots of power with a 3½-in. chamber; receiver drilled and tapped; stock is adjustable for drop; stepped ventilated rib; 28-in. model has stock in Realtree Max-5 and metalwork in Midnight Bronze Cerakote; 26-in. model has stock in MO Bottomland and metalwork in Patriot Bronze Cerakote
MSRP $1249.00

FRANCHI AFFINITY 3.5 TURKEY

Action: Semiautomatic
Stock: Synthetic
Barrel: 24 in.
Chokes: 2
Sights: Hooded dual-color fiber optic front
Weight: 7 lb. 8 oz.
Bore/Gauge: 12
Capacity: 4 shells
Features: Powerhouse turkey gun; Extended Turkey and Extended Turkey XF chokes; receiver drilled and tapped; Steadygrip pistol grip stock and metalwork in full-coverage MO Bottomland
MSRP $1129.00

FRANCHI INSTINCT L CATALYST, SL CATALYST

Action: Over/under
Stock: Wood
Barrel: 26 in.
Chokes: 3
Sights: Fiber optic front
Weight: 5 lb. 7 oz.–6 lb. 14 oz.
Bore/Gauge: 20
Capacity: 2 shells
Features: These field-grade 20-gauges have walnut stocks in a satin finish designed to better fit women shooters; auto ejectors; L wears a red fiber optic front bead, while the SL has a red fiber optic front bar; automatic safety; color case-hardened receiver and matte blue barrels on the L; brushed aluminum receiver and gloss blue barrels for the lighter SL model; SL model has extended choke tubes
L Catalyst: $1469.00
SL Catalyst: $1699.00

HENRY REPEATING ARMS SINGLE-SHOT SLUG BARREL

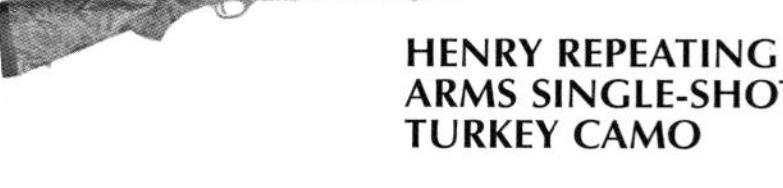
HENRY REPEATING ARMS SINGLE-SHOT TURKEY CAMO

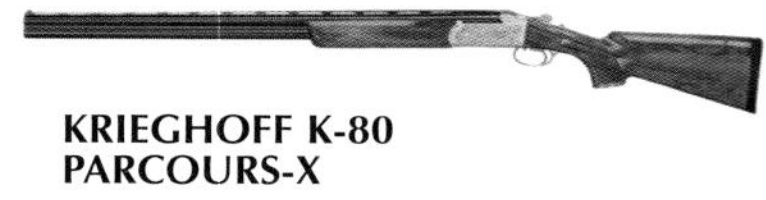
KRIEGHOFF K-80 PARCOURS-X

MOSSBERG 940 JM PRO 5-SHOT

MOSSBERG INTERNATIONAL GOLD RESERVE

MOSSBERG INTERNATIONAL GOLD RESERVE BLACK LABEL

MOSSBERG INTERNATIONAL GOLD RESERVE SUPER SPORT

HENRY REPEATING ARMS SINGLE-SHOT SLUG BARREL

Action: Single-shot
Stock: Walnut
Barrel: 24 in.
Chokes: None
Sights: Fiber optic front, rear
Weight: 6 lb. 14 oz.
Bore/Gauge: 12
Capacity: 1 shell
Features: American walnut stock topped with a round blued-steel rifled barrel with a 1:35 twist; rebounding hammer; dual-direction pivoting locking lever mechanism; 3-in. chamber
MSRP $560.00

HENRY REPEATING ARMS SINGLE-SHOT TURKEY CAMO

Action: Single-shot
Stock: Walnut
Barrel: 24 in.
Chokes: 1
Sights: Fiber optic front, rear
Weight: 6 lb. 11 oz.
Bore/Gauge: 12
Capacity: 1 shell
Features: Sporting a 3½-inch chamber, this single-shot break-action has metalwork dressed in full-coverage MO Obsession; Turkey choke; threaded for Remington-style chokes; solid rubber buttpad
MSRP $687.00

KRIEGHOFF K-80 PARCOURS-X

Action: Over/under
Stock: Walnut
Barrel: 32 in.
Chokes: 2
Sights: White pearl front, metal mid-bead
Weight: 8 lb. 8 oz.
Bore/Gauge: 12
Capacity: 2 shells
Features: A new gun specifically for sporting clays and FITASC competitors; Turkish walnut stock, checkered and with a satin epoxy finish; top-tang safety can be locked in "off" position; soldered 10mm-8mm tapered Parcours-X rib; M and IM Krieghoff Thin Wall chokes; nickel-plated steel receiver in a satin grey finish; right- or left-hand stock with adjustable comb and palm swell; 3-in. chambers
MSRP $13,695.00

MOSSBERG 940 JM PRO 5-SHOT

Action: Semiautomatic
Stock: Synthetic
Barrel: 24 in.
Chokes: 3
Sights: Fiber optic front
Weight: 7 lb. 12 oz.
Bore/Gauge: 12
Capacity: 4 shells
Features: With champion shooter Jerry Miculek's name on it, this one is surely meant for 3-gun games; stock adjustable for length of pull, drop, and cast; Briley extended choke set; oversized gold controls; extended magazine tube holds four with the crimped plug; 3-in. chamber
MSRP $1078.00

MOSSBERG INTERNATIONAL GOLD RESERVE

Action: Over/under
Stock: Walnut
Barrel: 28 in., 30 in.
Chokes: 5
Sights: Fiber optic front
Weight: 6 lb. 8 oz.–7 lb. 8 oz.
Bore/Gauge: 12, 20, .410 bore
Capacity: 2 shells
Features: Grade-A black walnut stocks; ejectors; silver-finish receiver with scroll engraving and gold inlays; 24K gold inlay "M" in a circle on bottom of receiver; extended sport chokes; 10mm rib; between barrel ventilation
MSRP $983.00

MOSSBERG INTERNATIONAL GOLD RESERVE BLACK LABEL

Action: Over/under
Stock: Walnut
Barrel: 30 in.
Chokes: 5
Sights: Fiber optic front
Weight: 7 lb. 8 oz.
Bore/Gauge: 12
Capacity: 2 shells
Features: Same as the International Gold Reserve standard model but with the receiver finished in polished black
MSRP $983.00

MOSSBERG INTERNATIONAL GOLD RESERVE SUPER SPORT

Action: Over/under
Stock: Walnut
Barrel: 30 in.
Chokes: 5
Sights: Fiber optic front
Weight: 7 lb. 8 oz.
Bore/Gauge: 12
Capacity: 2 shells
Features: Based on the standard International Gold Reserve, this model upgrades with an adjustable cheekpiece, fully adjustable buttstock, and a higher-profile rib
MSRP $1221.00

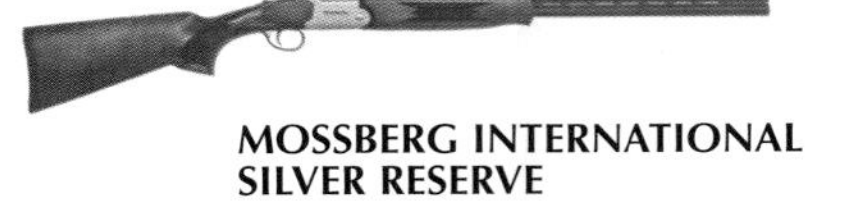

MOSSBERG INTERNATIONAL SILVER RESERVE

MOSSBERG INTERNATIONAL SILVER RESERVE EVENTIDE

MOSSBERG INTERNATIONAL SILVER RESERVE YOUTH BANTAM

POINTER BY LEGACY SPORTS ACRIUS

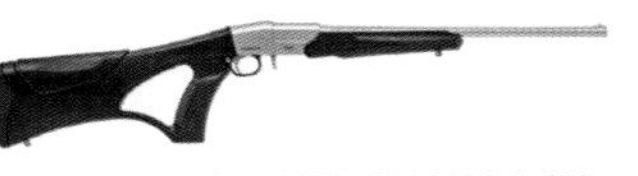

POINTER BY LEGACY SPORTS SINGLE-SHOT PUP THUMBHOLE

RETAY USA GPS DEFENSE

RETAY USA MASAI MARA WATERFOWL EXTRA BLACK

MOSSBERG INTERNATIONAL SILVER RESERVE

Action: Over/under
Stock: Walnut
Barrel: 26 in., 28 in.
Chokes: 5
Sights: Bead front
Weight: 6 lb. 8 oz.–7 lb. 8 oz.
Bore/Gauge: 12, 20, 28, .410
Capacity: 2 shells
Features: If you can live without ejectors, then this shotgun will serve you well for field or range; extractors only; field chokes; select black walnut stocks; satin finished receiver unadorned except for the laser-engraved Mossberg name; matte blue barrels; vet rib and between barrel venting
MSRP $692.00

MOSSBERG INTERNATIONAL SILVER RESERVE EVENTIDE

Action: Over/under
Stock: Synthetic
Barrel: 28 in.
Chokes: 5
Sights: Fiber optic front
Weight: 7 lb.
Bore/Gauge: 12
Capacity: 2 shells
Features: A great choice for hunting (or shooting skeet or trap in the pouring rain), with a synthetic stock; matte blue metalwork; field chokes
MSRP $636.00

MOSSBERG INTERNATIONAL SILVER RESERVE YOUTH BANTAM

Action: Over/under
Stock: Walnut
Barrel: 26 in.
Chokes: 5
Sights: Bead front
Weight: 7 lb.
Bore/Gauge: 20
Capacity: 2 shells
Features: Nice choice for a youth or smaller-statured person getting serious about competing or hunting; 13.25-in. length of pull; satin silver receiver; matte blue barrels
MSRP $692.00

POINTER BY LEGACY SPORTS ACRIUS

Action: Over/under
Stock: Walnut
Barrel: 28 in.
Chokes: 5
Sights: Fiber optic front
Weight: 6 lb. 10 oz.
Bore/Gauge: 12
Capacity: 2 shells
Features: Turkish walnut stock; coin-finished receiver with light floral laser-etching; vent rib and between barrel venting; chrome-lined barrels; supplied with extended chokes
MSRP $589.00

POINTER BY LEGACY SPORTS SINGLE-SHOT PUP THUMBHOLE

Action: Single-shot
Stock: Synthetic
Barrel: 18 in.
Chokes: None
Sights: Bead front
Weight: N/A
Bore/Gauge: .410
Capacity: 1 shell
Features: A sort of bullpup configuration for a single-shot, with a short barrel; compact thumbhole stock; matte blue or nickel receiver
MSRP $179.00

RETAY USA GPS DEFENSE

Action: Pump
Stock: Synthetic
Barrel: 18.5 in.
Chokes: 3
Sights: Blade front
Weight: N/A
Bore/Gauge: 12
Capacity: 5 shells
Features: Geometric Pump Shotgun (GPS)—what that really means is Retay used computer-enhanced geometry to produce a gun that required shorter pump strokes and made loading easier; 3-in. chamber; matte anodized receiver; matte black chrome-lined barrel; MaraPro chokes in C, M, and F included
MSRP $349.00

RETAY USA MASAI MARA WATERFOWL EXTRA BLACK

Action: Semiautomatic
Stock: Synthetic
Barrel: 24 in., 26 in., 28 in., 30 in.
Chokes: 5
Sights: Red TruGlo fiber optic front
Weight: N/A
Bore/Gauge: 12, 20
Capacity: 4 shells
Features: A waterfowler's friend with all-weather synthetic stock; oversized controls; Inertia Plus bolt system; MaraPro barrel; 12-ga. available in both 3- and 3½-in. chambers, 20-ga. In 3-in. only and only in 26- and 29-in. barrel lengths; supplied with a hard case
MSRP . . . . $1099.00–$1275.00

RETAY USA MASAI MARA WATERFOWL GREY LIGHTV

RETAY USA MASAI MARA REALTREE MAX-5, REALTREE TIMBER, MO NEW BOTTOMLAND

SAVAGE RENEGAUGE COMPETITION

SAVAGE RENEGAUGE PRAIRIE

SAVAGE STEVENS 301 TURKEY OBSESSION, 301 TURKEY XP OBSESSION

SAVAGE STEVENS 301 TURKEY THUMBHOLE

RETAY USA MASAI MARA WATERFOWL GREY LIGHT

Action: Semiautomatic
Stock: Synthetic
Barrel: 26 in., 28 in.
Chokes: 5
Sights: Fiber optic front
Weight: N/A
Bore/Gauge: 12
Capacity: 4 shells
Features: Slightly different take on the standard Masai Mara Waterfowl model with a receiver in grey Cerakote
MSRP $1275.00

RETAY USA MASAI MARA REALTREE MAX-5, REALTREE TIMBER, MO NEW BOTTOMLAND

Action: Semiautomatic
Stock: Synthetic
Barrel: 24 in., 26 in., 28 in., 30 in.
Chokes: 5
Sights: Fiber optic front
Weight: N/A
Bore/Gauge: 12, 20
Capacity: 4 shells
Features: Same as the Waterfowl Extra Black model, but in full-coverage camo patterns from Realtree and Mossy Oak
MSRP . . . . $1225.00–$1399.00

SAVAGE RENEGAUGE COMPETITION

Action: Semiautomatic
Stock: Synthetic
Barrel: 24 in.
Chokes: 3
Sights: Fiber optic front
Weight: 8 lb. 3 oz.
Bore/Gauge: 12
Capacity: 9 shells
Features: Ready for 3-gun out of the box; competition-ready easy-load magazine port; extended Skeet 2/Light Mod Beretta/Benelli Mobil-type choke; aluminum receiver, magazine tube, and choke extension in red Cerakote; carbon-steel vent rib; Hi-Viz Tri-Comp fiber optic sight; stock rod buffer to reduce recoil; stock adjustable for length of pull, cast, and drop; D.R.I.V. dual-regulating inline valve gas system
MSRP $1959.00

SAVAGE RENEGAUGE PRAIRIE

Action: Semiautomatic
Stock: Synthetic
Barrel: 28 in.
Chokes: 3
Sights: Fiber optic front
Weight: 7 lb. 15 oz.
Bore/Gauge: 12
Capacity: 4 shells
Features: Desert turkeys, predators, javelina, and the like are fair game for this shotgun; stock in TrueTimber Prairie camo; receiver and barrel in Brown Sand Cerakote; D.R.I.V. gas system; aluminum receiver; carbon steel barrel; vent rib; stock rod buffer to reduce recoil; oversized controls; easy-load magazine port; I, M, and F flush-mount Beretta/Benelli Mobil-type chokes and hard case included
MSRP $1599.00

SAVAGE STEVENS 301 TURKEY OBSESSION, 301 TURKEY XP OBSESSION

Action: Single-shot
Stock: Synthetic
Barrel: 26 in.
Chokes: 1
Sights: Bead front, 1x3 red-dot optic
Weight: 5 lb. 1 oz.
Bore/Gauge: 20, .410
Capacity: 1 shell
Features: Beware the turkey hunter who trusts in a single-shot; barrel optimized for Federal Premium Heavyweight TSS Turkey loads; removable rail; stock and forend in MO Obsession; matte black barrel and receiver; standard model has 3-in. chamber, XP is chambered for 3½-in.; includes Extra-Full choke tube in a Winchester ½x32UN thread pattern
Standard: $209.00
XP: $249.00

SAVAGE STEVENS 301 TURKEY THUMBHOLE

Action: Single-shot
Stock: Synthetic
Barrel: 26 in.
Chokes: 1
Sights: Bead front
Weight: 5 lb. 1 oz.
Bore/Gauge: .410
Capacity: 1 shell
Features: Handy thumbhole stock in an olive drab green keeps a turkey hunter steady; carbon steel receiver and chrome alloy steel barrel in matte black; ambidextrous cheek riser; removable topside rail; Extra Full choke Winchester-type ½x32UN threads; barrel optimized for use with Federal Premium Heavyweight TSS Turkey ammunition; swivel studs on forend and stock
MSRP $229.00

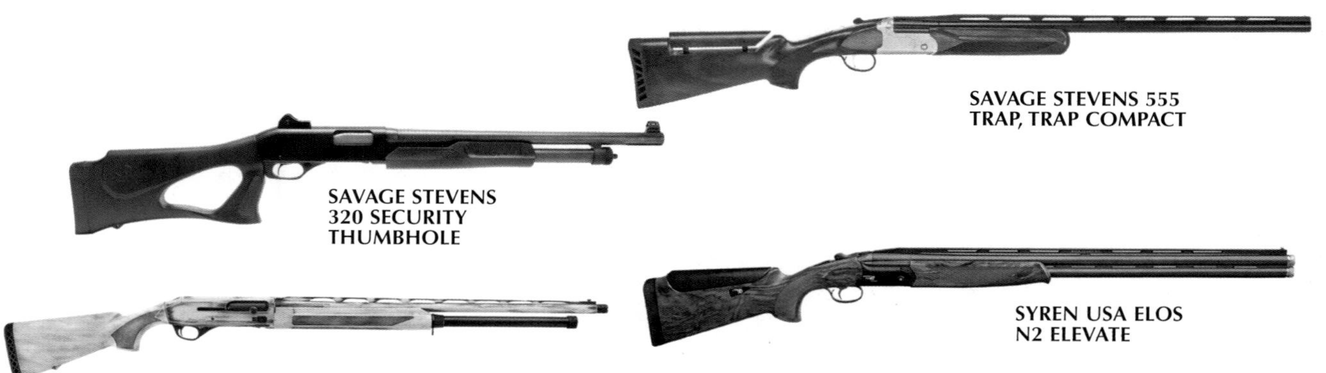

SAVAGE STEVENS 555 TRAP, TRAP COMPACT

SAVAGE STEVENS 320 SECURITY THUMBHOLE

SYREN USA ELOS N2 ELEVATE

STOEGER INDUSTRIES M3500 SNOW GOOSE

SYREN USA JULIA SPORTING

SAVAGE STEVENS 320 SECURITY THUMBHOLE

Action: Pump
Stock: Synthetic
Barrel: 18.5 in.
Chokes: None
Sights: Bead front, ghost ring
Weight: 7 lb.–7 lb. 3 oz.
Bore/Gauge: 12, 20
Capacity: 5 shells
Features: This is a smart choice for home defense with its shorter than average 13.75-in. length of pull; thumbhole stock has ambidextrous cheek riser; textured grip areas; 3-in. chamber; bottom-loading magazine tube; all-over matte black appearance; choice of front bead or front/rear ghost ring sights
Bead: $275.00
Ghost ring: $305.00

SAVAGE STEVENS 555 TRAP, TRAP COMPACT

Action: Single-shot
Stock: Walnut
Barrel: 30 in.
Chokes: 3
Sights: Bead front
Weight: 6 lb. 9 oz.–7 lb. 8 oz.
Bore/Gauge: 12, 20
Capacity: 1 shell
Features: Oil-finished Turkish walnut stock with adjustable cheekpiece; raised vent rib; aluminum alloy receiver in a semi-gloss finish; carbon steel barrel in a semi-gloss finish; 3-in. chamber; F, M, and I chokes; standard model has 14.75-in. length of pull, Compact is 13.75 in.
MSRP $709.00

STOEGER INDUSTRIES M3500 SNOW GOOSE

Action: Semiautomatic
Stock: Synthetic
Barrel: 28 in.
Chokes: 5
Sights: Red fiber optic front
Weight: 8 lb. 3 oz.
Bore/Gauge: 12
Capacity: 10 shells
Features: Designed for high-volume, extreme weather shooting with oversized controls; full-coverage distressed white Cerakote; huge magazine capacity; Close-Range, Mid-Range, Modified, Improved, and XFT extended choke tubes; drilled and tapped receiver; paracord sling
MSRP $899.00

SYREN USA ELOS N2 ELEVATE

Action: Over/under
Stock: Walnut
Barrel: 30 in.
Chokes: 5
Sights: White bead front, brass mid-bead
Weight: 7 lb. 10 oz.
Bore/Gauge: 12
Capacity: 2 shells
Features: Turkish walnut stock having a TRIWOOD finish and an adjustable stock; 10mm-8mm tapered vet rib and set of two quick-detach ribs, one pointing 50/50, the other 65/35; ventilated center rib; black satin finish receiver; microcell 22mm soft black rubber buttpad; TRIBORE HP bores; schnabel forend; trigger adjustable for length of pull; EXIS HP extended competition choke tubes; overall geometry designed for a more upright shooting stance; add $160 for left-hand configuration
MSRP $3195.00

SYREN USA JULIA SPORTING

Action: Over/under
Stock: Walnut
Barrel: 30 in.
Chokes: 6
Sights: White bead front, silver mid-bead
Weight: 7 lb. 15 oz.
Bore/Gauge: 12
Capacity: 2 shells
Features: Beautiful hand-rubbed oil stock with a rounded forend; tapered 10mm-8mm rib; MAXIS competition chokes; ventilated center rib; receiver is case colored and bears a fantasy engraving of syren Julia, Caesar's daughter, that portrait emerging from floral engraving that begins as her flowing hair; add $260 for left-hand option, $410 for adjustable stock, available only on right-hand models
MSRP $6050.00

TRISTAR ARMS BRISTOL

Action: Side-by-side
Stock: Walnut
Barrel: 28 in.
Chokes: 5
Sights: Bead front
Weight: 5 lb. 1 oz.–6 lb. 11 oz.
Bore/Gauge: 12, 20, 28, .410
Capacity: 2 shells
Features: Straight English stock of select Turkish walnut; splinter forend; checkering; case-colored, single-selective trigger; ejectors; Beretta Mobil flush-fit choke tubes
MSRP . . . . $1065.00–$1100.00

TRISTAR ARMS BRISTOL SILVER

Action: Side-by-side
Stock: Walnut
Barrel: 28 in.
Chokes: 5
Sights: Bead front
Weight: 5 lb. 1 oz.–6 lb. 11 oz.
Bore/Gauge: 12, 20, 28, .410
Capacity: 2 shells
Features: An upgrade from the standard Bristol, with improved wood; nickel-finished receiver with scroll engraving and gold inlays
MSRP . . . . $1000.00–$1040.00

TRISTAR ARMS COBRA III FORCE

Action: Pump
Stock: Synthetic
Barrel: 18.5 in.
Chokes: 2
Sights: Fiber optic bridge front, ghost ring rear
Weight: 6 lb. 8 oz.
Bore/Gauge: 12
Capacity: 5 shells
Features: Spring-loaded forearm; Picatinny under rail and top rail; pistol grip stock has soft rubber grip; Cylinder Beretta/Benelli Mobil choke plus a muzzle brake
MSRP $345.00

TRISTAR ARMS COBRA III MARINE

Action: Pump
Stock: Synthetic
Barrel: 18.5 in.
Chokes: 1
Sights: Blade front
Weight: 6 lb. 3 oz.
Bore/Gauge: 12
Capacity: 5 shells
Features: Spring-loaded forearm speeds cycling; underside forearm rail; matte stainless metalwork with black synthetic stock
MSRP $315.00

TRISTAR ARMS COBRA III TACTICAL

Action: Pump
Stock: Synthetic
Barrel: 18.5 in.
Chokes: 1
Sights: Blade front
Weight: 6 lb. 3 oz.
Bore/Gauge: 12
Capacity: 5 shells
Features: Similar to the Cobra III Marine, but all metalwork is in matte black
MSRP $300.00

WEATHERBY ELEMENT TUNGSTEN SYNTHETIC

WEATHERBY ELEMENT WATERFOWLER MAX-5

WINCHESTER REPEATING ARMS MODEL 101 DELUXE FIELD MAPLE

WINCHESTER REPEATING ARMS SUPER X PUMP HYBRID HUNTER

WINCHESTER REPEATING ARMS SUPER X PUMP UNIVERSAL HUNTER MO DNA

WEATHERBY ELEMENT TUNGSTEN SYNTHETIC

Action: Semiautomatic
Stock: Synthetic
Barrel: 26 in., 28 in.
Chokes: 3, 4
Sights: Fiber optic front
Weight: 6 lb. 4 oz.–6 lb. 12 oz.
Bore/Gauge: 12, 20
Capacity: 4 shells
Features: Black synthetic stock; all metalwork in tungsten Cerakote; inertia action; chrome-lined bore; Griptonite stock has textured grip inserts; 3-in. chamber; F, M, and I chokes; 12-ga. also comes with a Long Range Steel choke; stock shims
MSRP $599.00

WEATHERBY ELEMENT WATERFOWLER MAX-5

Action: Semiautomatic
Stock: Synthetic
Barrel: 26 in., 28 in.
Chokes: 3, 4
Sights: Fiber optic front
Weight: 6 lb. 4 oz.–6 lb. 12 oz.
Bore/Gauge: 12, 20
Capacity: 4 shells
Features: Full-coverage Realtree Max-5 camo; dual-purpose bolt release; inertia action; chrome-lined bore; Griptonite stock has textured grip inserts; 3-in. chamber; F, M, and I chokes; 12-ga. also comes with a Long Range Steel choke; stock shims
MSRP $699.00

WINCHESTER REPEATING ARMS MODEL 101 DELUXE FIELD MAPLE

Action: Over/under
Stock: Maple
Barrel: 26 in., 28 in.
Chokes: 3
Sights: Brass bead front, white mid bead
Weight: 6 lb. 12 oz.–6 lb. 14 oz.
Bore/Gauge: 12
Capacity: 2 shells
Features: Identical to the walnut-stocked Model 101 Deluxe Field, but with a stock and forearm in AAA maple
MSRP $2069.99

WINCHESTER REPEATING ARMS SUPER X PUMP HYBRID HUNTER MO BOTTOMLAND, REALTREE MAX-5, REALTREE TIMBER, TRUETIMBER PRAIRIE

Action: Pump
Stock: Synthetic
Barrel: 26 in., 28 in.
Chokes: 3
Sights: TruGlo fiber optic front
Weight: 6 lb. 8 oz.–7 lb.
Bore/Gauge: 12, 20
Capacity: 4 shells
Features: Aluminum alloy receiver and chrome-lined steel barrel in flat dark earth Permacote finish; Invector-Plus choke tubes; 12-ga. available in 3½- or 3-in. chambers, 20-ga. in 3-in.
MSRP $449.99

WINCHESTER REPEATING ARMS SUPER X PUMP UNIVERSAL HUNTER MO DNA

Action: Pump
Stock: Synthetic
Barrel: 24 in., 26 in., 28 in.
Chokes: 3
Sights: TruGlo fiber optic front
Weight: 6 lb. 8 oz.–7 lb.
Bore/Gauge: 12, 20
Capacity: 4 shells
Features: Full-coverage camo; Inflex recoil pad; aluminum alloy receiver; larger trigger guard opening; reversible safety; 12-ga. available in 3½- or 3-in. chamber, 20-ga. has a 3-in. chamber; flush Invector Plus chokes
MSRP $509.99

WINCHESTER REPEATING ARMS SUPER X PUMP WATERFOWL HUNTER MO BOTTOMLAND, REALTREE MAX-5, REALTREE TIMBER, TRUETIMBER PRAIRIE

Action: Pump
Stock: Synthetic
Barrel: 26 in., 28 in.
Chokes: 3
Sights: TruGlo fiber optic front
Weight: 6 lb. 12 oz.–7 lb. 2 oz.
Bore/Gauge: 12, 20
Capacity: 4 shells
Features: Full-coverage camo; Inflex recoil pad; aluminum alloy receiver; larger trigger guard opening; reversible safety; 12-ga. available in 3½- or 3-in. chamber, 20-ga. has a 3-in. chamber; flush Invector Plus chokes
MSRP $499.99

WINCHESTER REPEATING ARMS SX4 HYBRID HUNTER MO BOTTOMLAND, REALTREE MAX-5, TRUETIMBER PRAIRIE, WOODLAND, REALTREE TIMBER

Action: Semiautomatic
Stock: Synthetic
Barrel: 26 in., 28 in.
Chokes: 3
Sights: TruGlo fiber optic front
Weight: 6 lb. 10 oz.–7 lb. 2 oz.
Bore/Gauge: 12, 20
Capacity: 4 shells
Features: Aluminum alloy receiver and chrome-lined steel barrel in flat dark earth Cerakote finish; Invector-Plus choke tubes; 12-ga. available in 3½- or 3-in. chambers, 20-ga. in 3-in.; stock in choice of premium full-coverage camo patterns; Inflex recoil pad; oversized operating controls and trigger guard opening; Active Valve gas operating system
MSRP $1079.99

WINCHESTER REPEATING ARMS SX4 UNIVERSAL HUNTER MO DNA

Action: Semiautomatic
Stock: Synthetic
Barrel: 24 in., 26 in., 28 in.
Chokes: 3
Sights: Fiber optic front
Weight: 6 lb. 8 oz.–7 lb.
Bore/Gauge: 12, 20
Capacity: 4 shells
Features: Drop-out trigger group; Quadra-Vent ported and back-bored barrel; stock with new ergonomics, spacers, and dressed in MO DNA pattern; drilled and tapped receiver; ambidextrous safety; oversized bolt handle and release; Inflex recoil pad; Invector Plush flush choke tubes
MSRP $1099.99

WINCHESTER REPEATING ARMS SX4 WATERFOWL HUNTER MO BOTTOMLAND, REALTREE MAX-5, REALTREE TIMBER, TRUETIMBER PRAIRIE, WOODLAND

Action: Semiautomatic
Stock: Synthetic
Barrel: 26 in., 28 in.
Chokes: 3
Sights: TruGlo Long Bead fiber optic front
Weight: 6 lb. 10 oz.–7 lb. 2 oz.
Bore/Gauge: 12, 20
Capacity: 4 shells
Features: With an aluminum alloy receiver and chrome-lined steel barrel in flat dark earth Cerakote finish; Invector-Plus choke tubes; TruGlo fiber optic front sight; 12-ga. available in 3½- or 3-in. chambers, 20-ga. In 3-in.; stock and barrel in a full-coverage "Army Woodland" vintage camo pattern; Inflex recoil pad; oversized operating controls and trigger guard opening; Active Valve gas operating system
MSRP $1099.99

ANGSTADT ARMS UDP-9 WITH MAXIM CQB BRACE

ANGSTADT ARMS UDP-9 WITH SBA3 BRACE

ANGSTADT ARMS UDP-45 WITH SBA3 BRACE

AREX (FIME GROUP) REX ZERO 1 TACTICAL

ARMSCOR/ROCK ISLAND ARMORY AL3.0, AL3.1

ARMSCOR/ROCK ISLAND ARMORY AL9.0

ANGSTADT ARMS UDP-9 WITH MAXIM CQB BRACE

Action: Semiautomatic
Grips: Synthetic
Barrel: 4.5 in.
Sights: None
Weight: 5 lb.
Caliber: 9mm
Capacity: 10, 15, 17, 30 rounds
Features: Takes all Glock aftermarket mags; threaded barrel ½x28; billet aluminum lower and slick-side upper in black hardcoat anodized ; assembly uses standard AR-15 hammer; Maxim Defense CQB pistol stabilizing brace with PCC pistol buffer; Magpul K2 pistol grip; Angstadt Arms 4-in. free-floating M-LOK handguard; topside mil-spec Picatinny rail
MSRP $1849.00

ANGSTADT ARMS UDP-9 WITH SBA3 BRACE

Action: Semiautomatic
Grips: Synthetic
Barrel: 5.5 in.
Sights: None
Weight: < 5 lb.
Caliber: 9mm
Capacity: 10, 15, 17, 30 rounds
Features: Oversized trigger guard; flared magwell; SBTactical SBA3 five-position adjustable stabilizing brace; Magpul K2 or B5 Systems pistol grip; bolt assembly uses standard AR-15 hammer; billet aluminum lower and slick-side upper in hard-coat anodized matte black or Cerakote Tactical Grey or flat dark earth; barrel threaded ½x28; mil-spec topside Picatinny rail; Angstadt Arms 5.5-in. free-floating M-LOK handguard with seven-side design
Black: $1499.00
Cerakote: $1599.00

ANGSTADT ARMS UDP-45 WITH SBA3 BRACE

Action: Semiautomatic
Grips: Synthetic
Barrel: 6 in.
Sights: None
Weight: 5 lb.
Caliber: .45 ACP
Capacity: 13 rounds
Features: Accepts aftermarket Glock double-stack mags; oversized trigger guard; flared magwell; SBTactical SBA3 five-position adjustable stabilizing brace; B5 Systems pistol grip; bolt assembly uses standard AR-15 hammer; billet aluminum lower and slick-side upper in hardcoat anodized mattel black; barrel threaded .578x28; mil-spec topside Picatinny rail; Angstadt Arms 5.5-in. free-floating M-LOK handguard with seven-side design; SB Tactical SBA3 five-position stabilizing brace
MSRP $1599.00

AREX (FIME GROUP) REX ZERO 1 TACTICAL, TACTICAL COMPACT

Action: Semiautomatic
Grips: Synthetic
Barrel: 4.9 in., 4.5 In.
Sights: Blade front, drift-adjustable rear
Weight: 30 oz., 28 oz.
Caliber: 9mm
Capacity: 20, 17 rounds
Features: This aluminum-framed pistol has generous capacity; DA/SA with an exposed hammer; frame in black, flat dark earth, or grey
MSRP $699.99

ARMSCOR/ROCK ISLAND ARMORY AL3.0, AL3.1

Action: Revolver
Grips: Rubber
Barrel: 2 in.
Sights: Ramp front, notch rear
Weight: 24 oz.
Caliber: .357 Mag.
Capacity: 6 rounds
Features: There's a lot of power in a snubby in .357; exposed hammer for DA/SA; blued finish on 3.0, stainless on 3.1; drop safety
Blued: $549.99
Stainless: $656.99

ARMSCOR/ROCK ISLAND ARMORY AL9.0

Action: Revolver
Grips: Rubber
Barrel: 4 in.
Sights: Ramp front, adjustable rear
Weight: 24 oz.
Caliber: 9mm
Capacity: 6 rounds
Features: Fun to have a revolver in 9mm and keeps ammo simple when you have a semiautomatic of the same caliber; exposed hammer; DA/SA; blued finish; no moon clips needed
MSRP $599.00

ARMSCOR/ROCK ISLAND ARMORY AL22

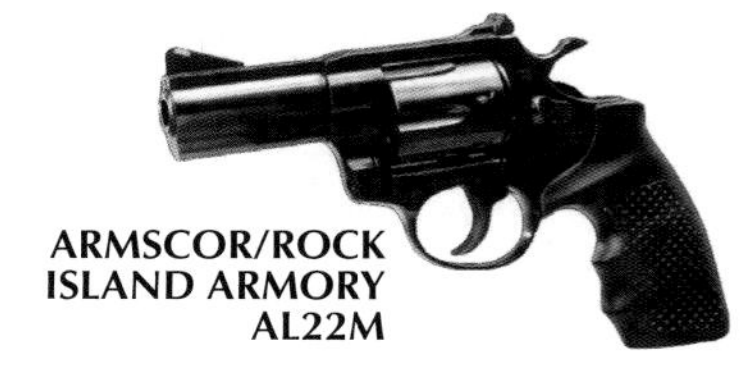

ARMSCOR/ROCK ISLAND ARMORY AL22M

ARMSCOR/ROCK ISLAND ARMORY BBR 3.10

ARMSCOR/ROCK ISLAND ARMORY TCM STANDARD FS

ARMSCOR/ROCK ISLAND ARMORY XT MAGNUM PRO

ARMSCOR/ROCK ISLAND ARMORY TCM STANDARD MS

ARMSCOR/ROCK ISLAND ARMORY TCM PREMIUM FS

ARMSCOR/ROCK ISLAND ARMORY AL22

Action: Revolver
Grips: Rubber
Barrel: 4 in.
Sights: Ramp front, adjustable rear
Weight: 39 oz.
Caliber: .22 LR
Capacity: 9 rounds
Features: Fully shrouded barrel; in all blue or a blue frame with stainless cylinder, barrel and shroud
Blued: $549.00
Stainless: $749.00

ARMSCOR/ROCK ISLAND ARMORY AL22M

Action: Revolver
Grips: Rubber
Barrel: 4 in.
Sights: Ramp front, adjustable rear
Weight: 39 oz.
Caliber: .22 WMR
Capacity: 8 rounds
Features: Same as the AL22, but chambered in the .22 WMR round
Blued: $589.00
Stainless: $799.00

ARMSCOR/ROCK ISLAND ARMORY BBR 3.10

Action: Semiautomatic
Grips: G10
Barrel: 3.1 in.
Sights: Fiber optic front, adjustable rear
Weight: 32 oz.
Caliber: .45 ACP
Capacity: 10 rounds
Features: G10 grips; parkerized finish; snag-free sights; beavertail grip safety
MSRP $699.00

ARMSCOR/ROCK ISLAND ARMORY TCM PREMIUM FS

Action: Semiautomatic
Grips: G10
Barrel: 5 in.
Sights: Fiber optic front, TRT1 adjustable rear
Weight: 40 oz.
Caliber: .22 TCM
Capacity: 17 rounds
Features: Combat-style hammer; G10 grips; parkerized frame; accessory underrail; skeletonized trigger; slide grooves front and rear
MSRP $873.99

ARMSCOR/ROCK ISLAND ARMORY TCM STANDARD FS

Action: Semiautomatic
Grips: Polymer
Barrel: 5 in.
Sights: Fiber optic front, adjustable rear
Weight: 40 oz.
Caliber: .22 TCM
Capacity: 17 rounds
Features: A standard government-sized 1911-style pistol; double-stack magazine; skeletonized hammer and trigger; parkerized finish
MSRP $629.99

ARMSCOR/ROCK ISLAND ARMORY TCM STANDARD MS

Action: Semiautomatic
Grips: Polymer
Barrel: 4.5 in.
Sights: Fiber optic front, adjustable rear
Weight: 40 oz.
Caliber: .22 TCM
Capacity: 17 rounds
Features: Similar to the TCM Standard FS, but with a slightly shorter, commander-length barrel; parkerized finish; skeletonized trigger and hammer
MSRP $609.00

ARMSCOR/ROCK ISLAND ARMORY XT MAGNUM PRO

Action: Semiautomatic
Grips: G10
Barrel: 5 in.
Sights: None
Weight: 40 oz.
Caliber: .22 WMR
Capacity: 14 rounds
Features: Full-length top rail; bull barrel; parkerized finish
MSRP $749.00

BERETTA APX TARGET

BIG HORN ARMORY AR500 .500 AUTO MAX PISTOL

BOND ARMS BLACKJACK

BROWNING 1911-22 BLACK LABEL SUPPRESSOR READY MUZZLE BRAKE LASER

BROWNING 1911-22 BLACK LABEL TUNGSTEN

BROWNING 1911-22 GRAY FULL-SIZE, COMPACT

BERETTA APX TARGET

Action: Semiautomatic
Grips: Polymer
Barrel: 4.76 in.
Sights: Fiber optic front, adjustable rear
Weight: 31 oz.
Caliber: 9mm
Capacity: 17 rounds
Features: Great capacity in a striker-fire designed for competition, featuring four mounting plates that accommodate four headlining red-dot reflex sights; interchangeable backstrap set; full-length slide serrations; 5-lb. trigger break
MSRP $699.00

BIG HORN ARMORY AR500 .500 AUTO MAX PISTOL

Action: Semiautomatic
Grips: Synthetic
Barrel: 10 in.
Sights: None
Weight: 8 lb. 1 oz.
Caliber: .500 Auto Max
Capacity: 5, 9 rounds
Features: A big round in a fast-handling pistol package; threaded barrel; M-LOK forearm with brace, Picatinny rail and sling swivels; hard-anodized aluminum action
MSRP $2199.00

BOND ARMS BLACKJACK

Action: Derringer
Grips: Wood
Barrel: 3.5 in.
Sights: Blade front, fixe rear
Weight: 22 oz.
Caliber: .45 LC/.410-bore
Capacity: 2 rounds
Features: A sleek matte black finish on the metalwork is complemented by the dark wood grips of black ash that wear an inletted ace of spades design
MSRP $689.00

BROWNING 1911-22 BLACK LABEL SUPPRESSOR READY MUZZLE BRAKE LASER

Action: Semiautomatic
Grips: Composite
Barrel: 4.87 in., 4.25 in.
Sights: Combat white dot
Weight: 13 oz., 14 oz.
Caliber: .22 LR
Capacity: 10 rounds
Features: Pistol has all-over black matte finish; grips with Buck Mark logo; muzzle brake threaded at ½x28; under-barrel accessory rail with Crimson Trace laser; comes with two magazines and pistol rug
MSRP $829.99

BROWNING 1911-22 BLACK LABEL TUNGSTEN

Action: Semiautomatic
Grips: Composite
Barrel: 4.25 in., 3.625 in.
Sights: Combat white dot
Weight: 15 oz., 14 oz.
Caliber: .22 LR
Capacity: 10 rounds
Features: Composite frame with alloy subframe in matte black; slide is in tungsten Cerakote; textured grip panels; steel three-dot sights; comes with two magazines and pistol rug; available with a rail on the dust cover for optics mounting
MSRP $619.99

BROWNING 1911-22 GRAY FULL-SIZE, COMPACT

Action: Semiautomatic
Grips: Walnut
Barrel: 4.25 in., 3.625 in.
Sights: A1 front and rear
Weight: 15 oz., 14 oz.
Caliber: .22 LR
Capacity: 10 rounds
Features: Blue alloy frame with gray anodized alloy slide; walnut grips with diamond pattern; comes with one magazine and hard case
MSRP $639.99

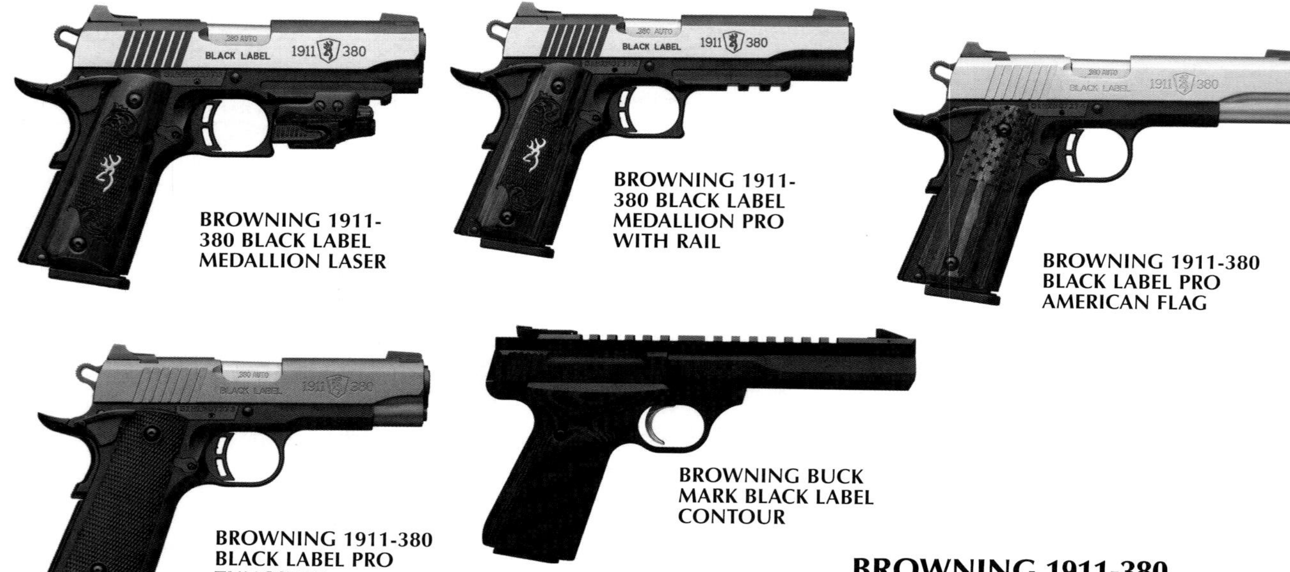

BROWNING 1911-380 BLACK LABEL MEDALLION LASER

BROWNING 1911-380 BLACK LABEL MEDALLION PRO WITH RAIL

BROWNING 1911-380 BLACK LABEL PRO AMERICAN FLAG

BROWNING 1911-380 BLACK LABEL PRO TUNGSTEN

BROWNING BUCK MARK BLACK LABEL CONTOUR

BROWNING 1911-380 BLACK LABEL MEDALLION LASER

Action: Semiautomatic
Grips: Wood
Barrel: 4.25 in., 3.625 in.
Sights: Combat white dot
Weight: 18 oz., 16 oz.
Caliber: .380 ACP
Capacity: 8 rounds
Features: Matte black frame; blackened slide with stainless steel finished flats; rosewood grips with checkering and gold Buck Mark logo; under-barrel Picatinny rail with Crimson Trace laser; with two magazines and a pistol rug
MSRP $979.99

BROWNING 1911-380 BLACK LABEL MEDALLION PRO WITH RAIL

Action: Semiautomatic
Grips: Wood
Barrel: 4.25 in., 3.625 in.
Sights: Combat white dot
Weight: 18 oz., 16 oz.
Caliber: .380 ACP
Capacity: 8 rounds
Features: Matte black frame; blackened slide with stainless steel finished flats; rosewood grips with checkering and gold Buck Mark logo; under-barrel Picatinny rail; extended ambidextrous thumb safety; extended slide release; Commander-style hammer; optional night sights; with two magazines and ABS case
MSRP . . . . $839.99–$919.99

BROWNING 1911-380 BLACK LABEL PRO AMERICAN FLAG

Action: Semiautomatic
Grips: Laminate
Barrel: 4.25 in., 3.625 in.
Sights: Combat white dot
Weight: 18 oz., 16 oz.
Caliber: .380 ACP
Capacity: 8 rounds
Features: Matte black frame; stainless steel finished slide; checkered frontstrap; optional night sights; grips have US flag pattern; extended ambidextrous thumb safety; extended slide release; Commander-style hammer; two magazines and an ABS case
MSRP . . . . $829.99–$939.99

BROWNING 1911-380 BLACK LABEL PRO TUNGSTEN

Action: Semiautomatic
Grips: Composite
Barrel: 4.25 in., 3.625 in.
Sights: Combat white dot
Weight: 18 oz., 16 oz.
Caliber: .380 ACP
Capacity: 8 rounds
Features: Matte black frame; slide in tungsten Cerakote; checkered frontstrap; textured grips; extended ambidextrous thumb safety; extended slide release; Commander-style hammer; two magazines and an ABS case; optional under-barrel Picatinny rail
MSRP . . . . $819.99–$839.99

BROWNING BUCK MARK BLACK LABEL CONTOUR

Action: Semiautomatic
Grips: G10
Barrel: 5.5 in.
Sights: Patridge front, Pro Target adjustable rear
Weight: 36 oz.
Caliber: .22 LR
Capacity: 10 rounds
Features: Special contour barrel has matte black finish to match the frame and full-length topside rail; grips in black with a blue swirl and stippling; comes with a pistol rug
MSRP $579.99

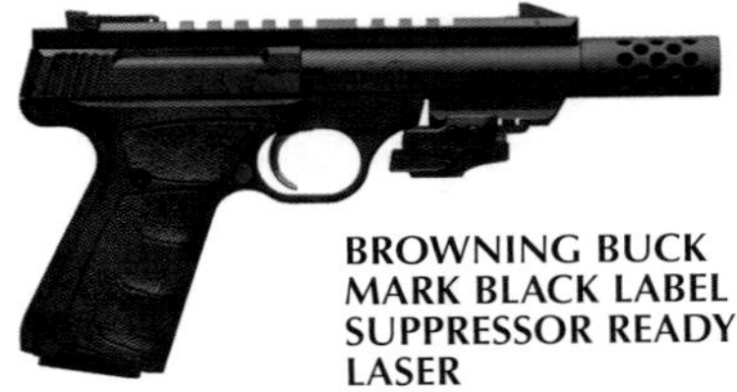
BROWNING BUCK MARK BLACK LABEL SUPPRESSOR READY LASER

BROWNING BUCK MARK CONTOUR GRAY URX

BROWNING BUCK MARK FIELD/ TARGET MICRO TUNGSTEN SUPPRESSOR READY

BROWNING BUCK MARK FIELD/TARGET SUPPRESSOR READY RED DOT

BROWNING BUCK MARK MICRO BULL SUPPRESSOR READY

BROWNING BUCK MARK PLUS PRACTICAL RED DOT

BROWNING BUCK MARK BLACK LABEL SUPPRESSOR READY LASER

Action: Semiautomatic
Grips: UFX overmolded
Barrel: 4.25 in.
Sights: Pro Target front and rear
Weight: 33 oz.
Caliber: .22 LR
Capacity: 10 rounds
Features: Bull barrel is threaded ½x28 and has muzzle brake; under-barrel rail holds a Crimson Trace laser; all over mattte black finish, including full-length top rail; comes with two magazines and pistol rug
MSRP $719.99

BROWNING BUCK MARK CONTOUR GRAY URX

Action: Semiautomatic
Grips: Ultragrip RX
Barrel: 5.5 in.
Sights: Patridge front, adjustable rear
Weight: 36 oz.
Caliber: .22 LR
Capacity: 10 rounds
Features: Contoured steel barrel in matte black; anodized gray full-length top rail; gray anodized frame; URX grips with finger molds; 16-click adjustable Pro Target rear sight; one magazine and pistol rug
MSRP $599.99

BROWNING BUCK MARK FIELD/TARGET MICRO TUNGSTEN SUPPRESSOR READY

Action: Semiautomatic
Grips: UFX overmolded
Barrel: 4.25 in.
Sights: Patridge front, Pro Target adjustable rear
Weight: 32 oz.
Caliber: .22 LR
Capacity: 10 rounds
Features: The bull barrel is threaded ½x28 and comes with a muzzle brake; slide and barrel finished in tungsten Cerakote; frame is matte black; includes a pistol rug
MSRP $599.99

BROWNING BUCK MARK FIELD/TARGET SUPPRESSOR READY RED DOT

Action: Semiautomatic
Grips: Laminate
Barrel: 5.9 in.
Sights: Patridge front, adjustable rear
Weight: 38 oz.
Caliber: .22 LR
Capacity: 10 rounds
Features: Matte blue bull barrel threaded ½x28 and comes with thread protector; full-length top rail with factory mounted Crimson Trace reflex red-dot sight; laminate grips made to look like cocobolo; matte blue frame; pistol rug
MSRP $699.99

BROWNING BUCK MARK MICRO BULL SUPPRESSOR READY

Action: Semiautomatic
Grips: UFX overmolded
Barrel: 4 in.
Sights: Pro Target front and rear
Weight: 29 oz.
Caliber: .22 LR
Capacity: 10 rounds
Features: Shorter blue barrel threaded ½x28 and comes with thread protector; frame and barrel in matte finish; comes with pistol rug
MSRP $469.99

BROWNING BUCK MARK PLUS PRACTICAL RED DOT

Action: Semiautomatic
Grips: Ultragrip RX
Barrel: 5.5 in.
Sights: Fiber optic front, adjustable rear
Weight: 35 oz.
Caliber: .22 LR
Capacity: 10 rounds
Features: Tapered bull barrel in matte blue; frame in matte gray; soft rubber URX grips with finger grooves; TruGlo/Marble Arms front sight, Pro Target rear; half-length top rail comes with factory-mounted Crimson Trace reflex red-dot sight; pistol rug
MSRP $579.99

BROWNING BUCK MARK PLUS VISION AMERICAN SUPPRESSOR READY

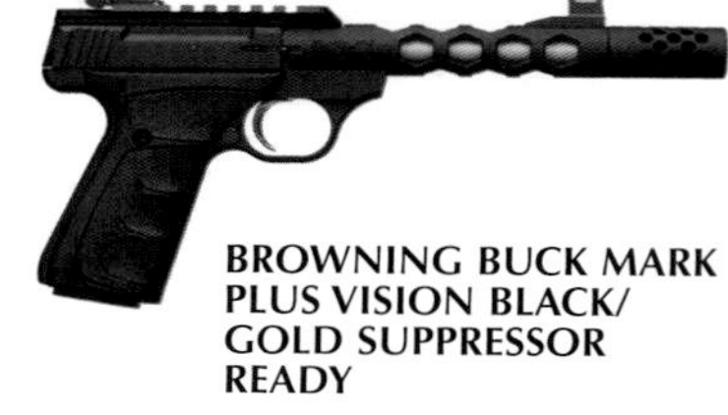
BROWNING BUCK MARK PLUS VISION BLACK/ GOLD SUPPRESSOR READY

BROWNING BUCK MARK PLUS VISION MOUNTAIN SUPPRESSOR READY

BROWNING BUCK MARK PLUS VISION ROUND SUPPRESSOR READY

BROWNING BUCK MARK PLUS VISION UFX BLACK, BLUE, RED

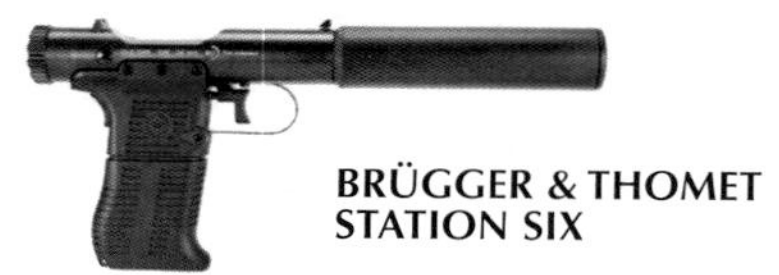
BRÜGGER & THOMET STATION SIX

BROWNING BUCK MARK PLUS VISION AMERICAN SUPPRESSOR READY

Action: Semiautomatic
Grips: UFX overmolded
Barrel: 5.9 in.
Sights: Fiber optic front, adjustable rear
Weight: 27 oz.
Caliber: .22 LR
Capacity: 10 rounds
Features: Vision barrel of an inner steel tube surrounded by a tensioned aluminum sleeve of anodized blue that has white stars and cutouts to reveal red underneath; anodized blue frame; barrel threaded ½x28 and has a muzzle brake; TruGlo/Marble Arms front sight, Pro Target rear; half-length topside optics rail; pistol rug
MSRP. $749.99

BROWNING BUCK MARK PLUS VISION BLACK/GOLD SUPPRESSOR READY

Action: Semiautomatic
Grips: UFX overmolded
Barrel: 5.9 in.
Sights: Fiber optic front, adjustable rear
Weight: 27 oz.
Caliber: .22 LR
Capacity: 10 rounds
Features: Similar to the Americana, but with aggressive diamond cutouts in the outer barrel sleeve that reveal gold underneath; all over matte black finish; pistol rug
MSRP. $719.99

BROWNING BUCK MARK PLUS VISION MOUNTAIN SUPPRESSOR READY

Action: Semiautomatic
Grips: G10
Barrel: 5.9 in.
Sights: Fiber optic front, adjustable rear
Weight: 27 oz.
Caliber: .22 LR
Capacity: 10 rounds
Features: Similar to the Americana, but with "snow-capped mountain" cutouts in the sleeve to reveal Robin's Egg Blue Cerakoting underneath; G10 grips carry the mountain theme; pistol rug
MSRP. $749.99

BROWNING BUCK MARK PLUS VISION ROUND SUPPRESSOR READY

Action: Semiautomatic
Grips: UFX overmolded
Barrel: 5.9 in.
Sights: Fiber optic front, adjustable rear
Weight: 27 oz.
Caliber: .22 LR
Capacity: 10 rounds
Features: Similar to other suppressor-ready Vison barrel models; outer barrel sleeve with bevy of round cutouts; all-over matte black finish; two magazines and a pistol rug
MSRP. $699.99

BROWNING BUCK MARK PLUS VISION UFX BLACK, BLUE, RED

Action: Semiautomatic
Grips: UFX overmolded
Barrel: 5.9 in.
Sights: Fiber optic front, adjustable rear
Weight: 27 oz.
Caliber: .22 LR
Capacity: 10 rounds
Features: Vision barrel; steel inner barrel wrapped in aluminum sleeve with sawtooth cuts; barrel threaded ½x28 with removable muzzle brake; Picatinny optics rail; TruGlo/Marble Arms front sight; 16-click Pro Target rear sight with white outline; pistol rug; matte black frame; sleeve colors in black, red, or blue
MSRP. $739.99

BRÜGGER & THOMET STATION SIX

Action: Bolt
Grips: Polymer
Barrel: 5.1 in.
Sights: Blade front, notch rear
Weight: 31 oz.
Caliber: 9mm, .45 ACP
Capacity: 5 rounds
Features: An integrally suppressed take on the WWII-era Welrod pistol; rotating bolt action; manually operated bolt to eliminate the sounds associated with semiautomatic actions; suppressor utilizes rubber wipes instead of metal baffles; left-side thumb safety and grip safety; training suppressor available for additional $400
MSRP. $2250.00

CABOT GUNS APOCALYPSE

CABOT GUNS REBELLION

CABOT GUNS THE NATIONAL STANDARD

CANIK USA TP9 ELITE SC, SC WITH SHIELD SMS2 OPTIC

CHARLES DALY 1911 FIELD GRADE

CHARLES DALY PAK-9

CABOT GUNS APOCALYPSE

Action: Semiautomatic
Grips: G10
Barrel: 4.25 in., 5 in.
Sights: Tritium front, ledge rear
Weight: N/A
Caliber: 9mm, .45 ACP
Capacity: 9, 8 rounds
Features: Full-size Government or Commander barrel lengths; slide of Damascus stainless steel in a long tongue pattern, deep etched, VC heritage finish; 13-degree front and rear slide serrations; rhombus cut frontstrap and mainspring housing checkering; one-piece extended magwell and mainspring housing; scalloped "idiot-proof" slide stop; one-piece full-length guide rod; integral rail; machined in place Perfect Fit ejector; aluminum tristar trigger; trigger in Tri Star, flat serrated, or ICON; optional accessory rail; barrel in either flush cut and crowned or threaded; optional Surefire X300 light
MSRP . . . . $7495.00–$9280.00

CABOT GUNS REBELLION

Action: Semiautomatic
Grips: G10, choice of wood
Barrel: 4.25 in.
Sights: Customer choice
Weight: N/A
Caliber: 9mm
Capacity: 9 rounds
Features: Aircraft-grade aluminum frame; speed-cut rails; match-grade bull barrel; front and rear slide serrations; carry cut; lowered ejection port; rhombus-cut checkering on frontstrap and mainspring housing; "idiot-proof" scratch-proof slide stop; standard or extended magwell; two-tone or black finish; trigger in Cabot flat, flat serrated, Cabot Tri Star, or ICON; right-hand or ambidextrous safety
MSRP . . . . $4295.00–$5860.00

CABOT GUNS THE NATIONAL STANDARD

Action: Semiautomatic
Grips: G10, choice of wood
Barrel: 4.25 in., 5 in.
Sights: Customer choice
Weight: N/A
Caliber: 9mm, .45 ACP
Capacity: 9, 8 rounds
Features: Hand-polished satin slide flats; steel billet Cabot frame and slide; rhombus cut frontstrap and mainspring housing; machined in place Perfect Fit ejector; aluminum tristar trigger; flats in stainless matte, black diamond-like-carbon vapor deposition finish (with or w/o polished flats); rear sight in Cabot ledge, low-mount adjustable rear, fixed tritium, or low-mount adjustable tritium; front sight in white dot, gold bead, fiber optic, or tritium; magwell in standard or extended; trigger in Cabot Tri Star, flat serrated, or ICON; optional accessory rail; barrel in either flush cut and crowned or threaded; right hand or ambidextrous setup
MSRP . . . . $3995.00–$6805.00

CANIK USA TP9 ELITE SC, SC WITH SHIELD SMS2 OPTIC

Action: Semiautomatic
Grips: Synthetic
Barrel: 3.6 in.
Sights: Phosphorous white dot front, blackout rear
Weight: 24 oz.
Caliber: 9mm
Capacity: 12, 15 rounds
Features: Two interchangeable backstraps; micro red-dot interface with cowitness feature; reversible magazine release; under-barrel rail; match-grade barrel; tungsten Cerakote finish over a nitride slide; 12-round magazine has finger rest, 15-round magazine is extended; optional SMS Shield red-dot sight factory mounted
MSRP . . . . Standard: $439.99
Red-dot: $699.99

CHARLES DALY 1911 FIELD GRADE

Action: Semiautomatic
Grips: Wood
Barrel: 5 in.
Sights: Blade front, notch rear
Weight: 38 oz.
Caliber: .45 ACP
Capacity: 8 rounds
Features: Standard Colt Government fare; matte blue finish; beavertail grip safety; diamond-pattern walnut grips
MSRP $499.00

CHARLES DALY PAK-9

Action: Semiautomatic
Grips: Synthetic
Barrel: 6.3 in.
Sights: Flip-up front, rear
Weight: 96 oz.
Caliber: 9mm
Capacity: 10, 30 rounds
Features: Pistol take on an AK-47 with a slim grip and integrated trigger guard; standard model takes Beretta magazines; interchangeable magazine adaptor upgrade allows for use of Glock magazines and comes with both a 10-round Beretta-style mag and a 30-round Glock-type magazine
Standard: $649.00
With Glock magazine adaptor: $679.00

CHIAPPA FIREARMS CHARGING RHINO GEN II 60DS

CHRISTENSEN ARMS C4-TI

CHRISTENSEN ARMS CA9MM PISTOL

CHRISTENSEN ARMS G5-TI

CIMARRON FIREARMS ANGEL EYES

CIMARRON FIREARMS MODEL 3 1ST MODEL AMERICAN

CHIAPPA FIREARMS CHARGING RHINO GEN II 60DS

Action: Revolver
Grips: Laminate
Barrel: 6 in.
Sights: Fiber optic front, adjustable rear
Weight: 32 oz.
Caliber: 9mm
Capacity: 6 rounds
Features: The Gen II is a DAO revolver with gray laminate grips with textured blue side inserts; Cerakote slate finish; comes with 10 moon clips; hammer spring and trigger return springs are separated for individual tuning; top-side and under-barrel rails; California-compliant version available
MSRP $1624.00

CHRISTENSEN ARMS C4-TI

Action: Semiautomatic
Grips: Carbon fiber
Barrel: 4.25 in.
Sights: Raised night sights
Weight: 33 oz.
Caliber: 9mm, .45 ACP
Capacity: 9, 7 rounds
Features: Very nice semi-custom handgun in a Commander size with a bobtail cut titanium frame; match-grade barrel; Damascus steel slide; checkered front-strap; full-length guide rod; adjustable overtravel
MSRP $5095.00

CHRISTENSEN ARMS CA9MM PISTOL

Action: Semiautomatic
Grips: Synthetic
Barrel: 7.5 in., 10 in.
Sights: None
Weight: 88 oz.
Caliber: 9mm
Capacity: 10, 15, 17 rounds
Features: 7075 forged aluminum upper and lower; nitride finished 416R stainless steel barrel carbon-fiber wrapped, button rifled, and ½x28 threaded; three-prong flash hider; 6.25- or 9.25-in. handguard M-LOK compatible, full aluminum rail, and with two quick detach mounts; SBA3 pistol brace; flared magwell; Gen4 Glock magazine compatible
MSRP $1495.00

CHRISTENSEN ARMS G5-TI

Action: Semiautomatic
Grips: Carbon fiber
Barrel: 5 in.
Sights: Raised night sights
Weight: 35 oz.
Caliber: 9mm, .45 ACP
Capacity: 9, 7 rounds
Features: Semi-custom handgun in a Government size; titanium frame; match-grade barrel; Damascus steel slide; checkered front-strap; full-length guide rod; adjustable overtravel
MSRP $4795.00

CIMARRON FIREARMS ANGEL EYES

Action: Revolver
Grips: Wood
Barrel: 8 in.
Sights: Blade front, integral rear
Weight: N/A
Caliber: .45 LC
Capacity: 6 rounds
Features: Part of the Hollywood The Good, the Bad, and the Ugly series, this revolver is named after that movie's Angel Eyes character, played by Lee Van Cleef, and this gun replicates the one that character carried in the movie; 1858 Remington-style, single-action; cold case-hardened barrel with a brass trigger guard and grip frame; smooth wood grip; "Angel Eyes" engraving on the frame
MSRP $607.10

CIMARRON FIREARMS MODEL 3 1ST MODEL AMERICAN

Action: Revolver
Grips: Wood
Barrel: 8 in.
Sights: Blade front, integral rear
Weight: 49 oz.
Caliber: .45 LC, .44-40, .44 S&W Russian, .44 Spec.
Capacity: 6 rounds
Features: A break-barrel replica of the original S&W model; single-action; smooth walnut grips; all-over blued finish
MSRP $1198.41

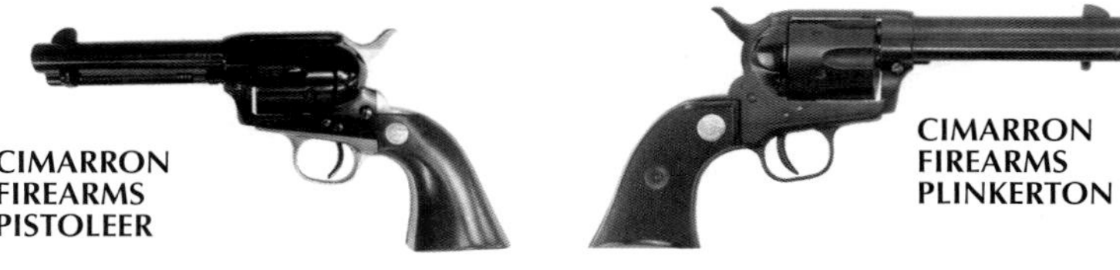
CIMARRON FIREARMS PISTOLEER

CIMARRON FIREARMS PLINKERTON

CIMARRON FIREARMS TUCO

CMMG BANSHEE 100 MK4 .22 PISTOL

CMMG BANSHEE 200 MK4 .22 PISTOL

CMMG BANSHEE 300 MK4 .22 PISTOL

CZ-USA ECP

CIMARRON FIREARMS PISTOLEER

Action: Revolver
Grips: Wood
Barrel: 4.75 in.
Sights: Blade front, integral rear
Weight: 40 oz.
Caliber: .45 LC, .357 Mag.
Capacity: 6 rounds
Features: Traditionally styled single-action; smooth walnut grips; steel frame; blued frame, cylinder, and barrel; stainless or nickel-plated backstrap and trigger guard; designed by Cimarron founder and CEO Mike Harvey, made by Uberti
MSRP $518.70

CIMARRON FIREARMS PLINKERTON

Action: Revolver
Grips: Plastic
Barrel: 4.75 in.
Sights: Blade front, integral rear
Weight: 34 oz.
Caliber: .22 LR/.22 Mag.
Capacity: 6 rounds
Features: Dual-cylinder single-action in all-over matte black finish; black plastic grips are checkered and have gold Cimarron medallion inset; manufactured by Chiappa
MSRP $218.01

CIMARRON FIREARMS TUCO

Action: Revolver
Grips: Wood
Barrel: 7.5 in.
Sights: Blade front, integral rear
Weight: N/A
Caliber: .45 LC
Capacity: 6 rounds
Features: Part of the Hollywood The Good, the Bad, and the Ugly series, this revolver is named after that movie's Tuco character, played by Eli Wallach, and this gun replicates the one that character created in the movie from various parts; this is a conversion revolver with a leech and Rigdon-style barrel and loading lever; color case-hardened blue; smooth wood grips; lanyard ring
MSRP $610.13

CMMG BANSHEE 100 MK4 .22 PISTOL

Action: Semiautomatic
Grips: Synthetic
Barrel: 9 in.
Sights: None
Weight: 59 oz.
Caliber: .22 LR
Capacity: 25 rounds
Features: Forged M4-type upper; forged AR-15–type lower; hard-coat anodized receiver and handguard; RML7 M-LOK handguard; A2 pistol grip; mil-spec single-stage trigger, trigger guard, and safety selector; anti-jam charging handle; medium taper barrel threaded ½x28 and with an A2 compensator; no buffer tube; logo end cap; NFA regs may apply
MSRP $799.95

CMMG BANSHEE 200 MK4 .22 PISTOL

Action: Semiautomatic
Grips: Synthetic
Barrel: 9 in.
Sights: None
Weight: 68 oz.
Caliber: .22 LR
Capacity: 25 rounds
Features: Similar to the 100, but weighing a few ounces more and wearing a quick-detach end cap; Magpul MOE grip and trigger guard; NFA regs may apply
MSRP $874.95

CMMG BANSHEE 300 MK4 .22 PISTOL

Action: Semiautomatic
Grips: Synthetic
Barrel: 4.5 in.
Sights: None
Weight: 57 oz.
Caliber: .22 LR
Capacity: 25 rounds
Features: Similar to the Banshee 100 and 200, but with a much shorter barrel; KAK Slim Flash Can threaded on ½x28; Cerakote finish; Magpul MOE pistol grip and trigger guard; ambidextrous safety selector; oversized ambidextrous charging handle; NFA regs may apply
MSRP $1024.95

CZ-USA ECP

Action: Semiautomatic
Grips: G10
Barrel: 4 in.
Sights: Brass front, U-notch rear
Weight: 29 oz.
Caliber: 9mm, .45 ACP
Capacity: 9, 8 rounds
Features: Forged aluminum frame; duty finish; single-action; match-grade bull barrel; bobbed mainspring housing; tri-topped slide with aggressive serrations and top rib to reduce glare
9mm: $1575.00
.45 ACP: $1600.00

NEW Products: Handguns

CZ-USA P-10 S FDE, OD GREEN

DAN WESSON RAZORBACK

CZ-USA TS2

DAN WESSON V-BOB, V-BOB TWO-TONE

DAN WESSON VIGIL

DAN WESSON VIGIL CCO

DAN WESSON VIGIL COMMANDER

CZ-USA P-10 S FDE, OD GREEN

Action: Semiautomatic
Grips: Polymer
Barrel: 3.5 in.
Sights: Fixed tritium night sights
Weight: 24.4 oz.
Caliber: 9mm
Capacity: 10, 12 rounds
Features: A lightweight striker-fire carry gun with a fiber-reinforced polymer frame; ambidextrous slide release; reversible magazine release; choice of flat dark earth or OD green frames, both with black slides; slide serrations fore and aft
MSRP. $619.00

CZ-USA TS2

Action: Semiautomatic
Grips: Aluminum
Barrel: 5.28 in.
Sights: Serrated fiber optic front, serrated fixed rear
Weight: 48.5 oz.
Caliber: 9mm
Capacity: 20 rounds
Features: Competition pistol sports thin aluminum grip panels; double-stack magazine; ambidextrous safety; SAO; aggressive stippling on front- and backstrap; evolved from the Tactical Sport with the slide profile of the Shadow 2 and a redesigned frame to reduce muzzle flip
MSRP. $1699.00

DAN WESSON RAZORBACK

Action: Semiautomatic
Grips: Cocobolo
Barrel: 5 in.
Sights: Serrated front, fixed rear
Weight: 40 oz.
Caliber: 10mm
Capacity: 8 rounds
Features: Reintroduction of a model that has been in the DW stable off and on; serrated Clark-style target rib machined into the top of the slide; forged frame with undercut trigger guard; slide has polished flats; cocobolo grips have double-diamond checkering; match-grade ramped barrel
MSRP. $1586.00

DAN WESSON V-BOB, V-BOB TWO-TONE

Action: Semiautomatic
Grips: G10
Barrel: 4.25 in.
Sights: Fixed night sight front, U-notch rear
Weight: 36.5 oz.
Caliber: .45 ACP
Capacity: 8 rounds
Features: A Commander-sized 1911 with a bobbed mainspring housing; recessed slide stop to better accommodate laser grips; match-grade barrel; ambidextrous safety; tapered grips; inset serrations at rear of slide to reduce glare; front night sight is a a large orange ring; in bead-blasted duty black or stainless or available as a two-tone with a duty black slide and bead-blasted stainless frame
Two-tone: $1864.00
Stainless: $1851.00
Duty black: $2103.00

DAN WESSON VIGIL

Action: Semiautomatic
Grips: Wood
Barrel: 5 in.
Sights: Fixed night sight front, tactical night sight rear
Weight: 32.8 oz.
Caliber: 9mm, .45 ACP
Capacity: 9, 8 rounds
Features: Government-sized frame of forged aluminum; rounded top slide; checkered frontstrap; rounded butt
MSRP. $1298.00

DAN WESSON VIGIL CCO

Action: Semiautomatic
Grips: Wood
Barrel: 4.25 in.
Sights: Fixed night sight front, tactical night sight rear
Weight: 29.5 oz.
Caliber: 9mm, .45 ACP
Capacity: 9, 8 rounds
Features: Same as the full-size Vigil, but with a Officer's-sized frame and Officer's-length slide
MSRP. $1298.00

DAN WESSON VIGIL COMMANDER

Action: Semiautomatic
Grips: Wood
Barrel: 4.25 in.
Sights: Fixed night sight front, tactical night sight rear
Weight: 30.5 oz.
Caliber: 9mm, .45 ACP
Capacity: 8 rounds
Features: Identical to the other Vigil models in configuration but in a true Commander profile
MSRP. $1298.00

ED BROWN PRODUCTS EVO KC9 G4 VTX

EUROPEAN AMERICAN ARMORY GIRSAN MC9 MATCH TV

EUROPEAN AMERICAN ARMORY GIRSAN MC9 STANDARD

EUROPEAN AMERICAN ARMORY GIRSAN MC9 STANDARD TV

EUROPEAN AMERICAN ARMORY GIRSAN MC1911S HUNTER

EUROPEAN AMERICAN ARMORY GIRSAN REGARD MC

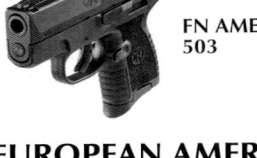

FN AMERICA FN 503

ED BROWN PRODUCTS EVO KC9 G4 VTX

Action: Semiautomatic
Grips: Wood
Barrel: 4 in.
Sights: Blade front, red-dot rear
Weight: 35 oz.
Caliber: 9mm
Capacity: 9 rounds
Features: The popular EVO line gets an upgrade with a factory-mounted Vortex Venom red-dot sight; Black Gen4 finish; thinned and shortened slide with 7-top custom cuts and front and rear slide serrations; "snakeskin" treatment to forestrap and bobtail housing; bull barrel
MSRP . . . . $2245.00–$2495.00

EUROPEAN AMERICAN ARMORY GIRSAN MC9 MATCH TV

Action: Semiautomatic
Grips: Polymer
Barrel: 4.63 in.
Sights: Dot front, red-dot optic rear
Weight: 25 oz.
Caliber: 9mm
Capacity: 17 rounds
Features: Sports slide cuts to keep the barrel cool; porting; rear slide serrations; accessory rail; distinctive red magazine well and trigger; interchangeable backstraps; FAR-DOT (Fast Acquisition Red Dot) system
MSRP $661.00

EUROPEAN AMERICAN ARMORY GIRSAN MC9 STANDARD

Action: Semiautomatic
Grips: Polymer
Barrel: 4.2 in.
Sights: White dot front, rear
Weight: 22.4 oz.
Caliber: 9mm
Capacity: 17 rounds
Features: No-frills striker-fire with generous capacity; accessory rail; not compatible with EAA's FAR-DOT system
MSRP $430.00

EUROPEAN AMERICAN ARMORY GIRSAN MC9 STANDARD TV

Action: Semiautomatic
Grips: Polymer
Barrel: 4.2 in.
Sights: Red dot front, rear
Weight: 22.4 oz.
Caliber: 9mm
Capacity: 17 rounds
Features: Identical to the Standard, but with EAA's FAR-DOT red-dot
MSRP $568.00

EUROPEAN AMERICAN ARMORY GIRSAN MC1911S HUNTER

Action: Semiautomatic
Grips: Polymer
Barrel: 6 in.
Sights: White dot front, adjustable rear
Weight: 51.2 oz.
Caliber: 10mm
Capacity: 8 rounds
Features: Another entry into the "return of the 10mm" trend, this one with an appropriately long barrel; weight to take the bite out of the recoil; long-hole hammer; rear slide serrations; target barrel; extended beavertail safety; checkered frame
MSRP $699.00

EUROPEAN AMERICAN ARMORY GIRSAN REGARD MC

Action: Semiautomatic
Grips: Polymer
Barrel: 4.9 in.
Sights: White dot front and rear
Weight: 34.4 oz.
Caliber: 9mm
Capacity: 18 rounds
Features: Modeled after the Beretta 92FS, this one has big capacity; accessory rail; website says this is a single-action, but with a decocker on the slide, we're going with DA/SA; in all black, flat dark earth frame with black grip panels, barrel and touchpoints, or silver frame with black grip panels, barrel and operating controls
MSRP $477.00

FN AMERICA FN 503

Action: Semiautomatic
Grips: Polymer
Barrel: 3.1 in.
Sights: Low-profile drift-adjustable front, rear
Weight: 21 oz.
Caliber: 9mm
Capacity: 6, 8 rounds
Features: A sweet CCW gun; striker-fired; low-profile iron sights; metal trigger; loaded chamber indicator; rear cocking serrations; barrel with recessed target crown; oversized controls; with one 6-round flush-fit magazine and one 8-round extended
MSRP $549.00

FN AMERICA FN 509 COMPACT

FN AMERICA FN 509 COMPACT TACTICAL

FN AMERICA FN 509 LS EDGE

GLOCK G43X, G43X MOS

GLOCK G48, G48 MOS

HECKLER & KOCH HK416 .22LR

FN AMERICA FN 509 COMPACT, COMPACT MRD

Action: Semiautomatic
Grips: Polymer
Barrel: 3.7 in.
Sights: Low-profile HiViz front, rear
Weight: 25.5 oz.
Caliber: 9mm
Capacity: 10, 12, 15 rounds
Features: Nice mid-size carry option with aggressive texturing on the frontstrap, grip sides, and interchangeable backstraps; external extractor; loaded chamber indicator; ambidextrous controls; accessory rail; flat-faced trigger; compatible with FN 509 24-round magazines; comes with two 10-round magazines or a 12-/15-round duo; MRD is optics ready
Compact:. $679.00
Compact MRD: $799.00

FN AMERICA FN 509 COMPACT TACTICAL

Action: Semiautomatic
Grips: Polymer
Barrel: 4.32 in.
Sights: Trijicon night sights front, rear
Weight: 26.2 oz.
Caliber: 9mm
Capacity: 10, 12, 24 rounds
Features: All the features of the other 509 Compact models, but this one comes with a threaded barrel; suppressor-height Trijicon three-dot green night sights; comes with three 10-round magazines or a 12-/24-round duo; in black or flat dark earth
MSRP $1049.00

FN AMERICA FN 509 LS EDGE

Action: Semiautomatic
Grips: Polymer
Barrel: 5 in.
Sights: Fiber optic front, MRD blackout notch rear
Weight: 31 oz.
Caliber: 9mm
Capacity: 10, 17 rounds
Features: Long-slide with lightning cuts and rear slide serrations; accessory rail; aggressively textured grip, frontstrap, and interchangeable backstraps; target-crowned hammer-forged barrel; flat-face facet-edge trigger; conical striker reduces trigger weight; low-profile optics mounting system accommodates most name brand red-dot reflex optics; compatible with FN 24-round FN 509 magazines; flared graphite anodized aluminum magwell
MSRP $1499.00

GLOCK G43X, G43X MOS

Action: Semiautomatic
Grips: Polymer
Barrel: 3.41 in.
Sights: White dot front, rear
Weight: 16.4 oz.
Caliber: 9mm
Capacity: 10 rounds
Features: A slim, light gun for concealed carry, featuring Glock's Slimline frame; nDLC finish; reversible magazine release; Glock Marksman Barrel; MOS version has accessory rail and the Glock Modular Optic System to allow for mounting micro red-dot sights
Standard:. $538.00
MOS:. $582.00

GLOCK G48, G48 MOS

Action: Semiautomatic
Grips: Polymer
Barrel: 4.17 in.
Sights: White dot front, rear
Weight: 18.48 oz.
Caliber: 9mm
Capacity: 10 rounds
Features: Slightly larger than the 43X but still in the Slimline family; Gen5 features; nDLC finish; Glock Marksman Barrel; Modular Optic System (MOS) version accommodates various micro red-dot sights
Standard:. $538.00
MOS:. $582.00

HECKLER & KOCH HK416 .22LR

Action: Semiautomatic
Grips: Synthetic
Barrel: 8.5 in.
Sights: Flip-up front, rear
Weight: 72 oz.
Caliber: .22 LR
Capacity: 10, 20, 30 rounds
Features: The looks of the real-deal HK416 but in a semiauto rimfire; last-round bolt hold-open; pistol grip with storage compartment; RIS rail interface with M-LOK; functional dust cover; aluminum receiver
MSRP $479.00

HECKLER & KOCH SP5K PDW

HECKLER & KOCH VP9 TACTICAL OR

HERITAGE MANUFACTURING ACE IN THE HOLE

HERITAGE MANUFACTURING BARKEEP

HERITAGE MANUFACTURING CORAL SNAKE

HERITAGE MANUFACTURING HONOR BETSY ROSS

HERITAGE MANUFACTURING MISS B. HAVIN'

HERITAGE MANUFACTURING MY BELLE

HECKLER & KOCH SP5K PDW

Action: Semiautomatic
Grips: Synthetic
Barrel: 5.83 in.
Sights: Ghost ring front, adjustable rear
Weight: 67.2 oz.
Caliber: 9mm
Capacity: 10, 15, 30 rounds
Features: A semiauto version of the famed MP5K with many of the same features, including a Navy-style threaded tri-lug adaptor; paddle magazine release; fluted chamber; "K" designation indicates shorter barrel and receiver
MSRP $2949.00

HECKLER & KOCH VP9 TACTICAL OR

Action: Semiautomatic
Grips: Polymer
Barrel: 4.7 in.
Sights: Night sights front, rear
Weight: 26.8 oz.
Caliber: 9mm
Capacity: 10, 17 rounds
Features: Suppressor- and optics-ready; threaded barrel; suppressor-height night sights; optics slide cut with five mounting plates; supplied with three 10- or three 17-round magazines
MSRP $999.00

HERITAGE MANUFACTURING ACE IN THE HOLE

Action: Revolver
Grips: N/A
Barrel: 4.75 in., 6.5 in.
Sights: Blade front, integral notch rear
Weight: 30.1 oz., 33.4 oz.
Caliber: .22 LR
Capacity: 6 rounds
Features: Blue finish metalwork on this single-action rimfire; special Ace in the Hole grips have a gray/green "rivet" background with a WWII-era pinup girl petting a shark-toothed bomb
MSRP $200.00

HERITAGE MANUFACTURING BARKEEP

Action: Revolver
Grips: Pearl, wood
Barrel: 2.68 in.
Sights: Blade front, integral notch rear
Weight: 35.5 oz.
Caliber: .22 LR
Capacity: 6 rounds
Features: A snubby .22 single-action that can option a compatible .22 WMR cylinder; in a black oxide finish with gray pearl handle or in a simulated case-hardened frame with blue barrel/cylinder with scrollwork wood grips
Wood grips: $180.30
Pearl grips: $189.39

HERITAGE MANUFACTURING CORAL SNAKE

Action: Revolver
Grips: N/A
Barrel: 4.75 in., 6.5 in.
Sights: Blade front, integral notch rear
Weight: 30.1 oz., 33.4 oz.
Caliber: .22 LR
Capacity: 6 rounds
Features: All-over blue finish on the metalwork is paired with grips wearing the distinctive scales and colors of a coral snake
MSRP $150.00

HERITAGE MANUFACTURING HONOR BETSY ROSS

Action: Revolver
Grips: Wood
Barrel: 4.75 in., 16 in.
Sights: Blade front, integral notch rear
Weight: 30.1 oz., 45.2 oz.
Caliber: .22 LR
Capacity: 6 rounds
Features: A very special revolver with a carbine rifle-length barrel; special grips with the original Betsy Ross flag star configuration
4.75-in.: $154.00
16-in.: $188.00

HERITAGE MANUFACTURING MISS B. HAVIN'

Action: Revolver
Grips: N/A
Barrel: 4.75 in., 6.5 in.
Sights: Blade front, integral notch rear
Weight: 30.1 oz., 33.4 oz.
Caliber: .22 LR
Capacity: 6 rounds
Features: All-over blue finish metalwork paired with grips that boast a raven-haired pinup girl on a gray background
MSRP $200.00

HERITAGE MANUFACTURING MY BELLE

Action: Revolver
Grips: N/A
Barrel: 4.75 in., 6.5 in.
Sights: Blade front, integral notch rear
Weight: 30.1 oz., 33.4 oz.
Caliber: .22 LR
Capacity: 6 rounds
Features: All-over blue finish metalwork is paired with grips that boast a fair-haired pinup girl posing with an American flag and the Liberty Bell on a light gray background with a rivet theme
MSRP $200.00

NEW Products: Handguns

HERITAGE MANUFACTURING USA FLAG

HI-POINT FIREARMS C9

HI-POINT FIREARMS C9 CAMO

HI-POINT FIREARMS C9 LLTGM

HI-POINT FIREARMS YEET CANNON G1

KEL-TEC P50

LIVE Q OR DIE HONEY BADGER PISTOL

LIVE Q OR DIE MINI FIX

HERITAGE MANUFACTURING USA FLAG

Action: Revolver
Grips: N/A
Barrel: 4.75 in., 6.5 in.
Sights: Blade front, integral notch rear
Weight: 30.1 oz., 33.4 oz.
Caliber: .22 LR
Capacity: 6 rounds
Features: Several variants in the USA Flag series of all blue-finished revolvers: USA Flag has grips that highlight both the stars and the stripes; Gold USA Flag has same stars and stripes grips, but with a vintage golden look; USA Flag 01 has grips of white stars on a blue background with just a bit of the red stripes at the heel; and USA Flag 02 has a bigger stars and stripes representation in a "wavy" presentation
MSRP . . . . $147.00–$209.00

HI-POINT FIREARMS C9

Action: Semiautomatic
Grips: Polymer
Barrel: 3.5 in.
Sights: Three dot, adjustable rear
Weight: 29 oz.
Caliber: 9mm
Capacity: 8, 10 rounds
Features: A compact CCW pistol rated +P; last round hold-open; black powdercoat finish; high-impact grips with easy-grip finish; magazine disconnect safety; manual thumb safety
MSRP $249.99

HI-POINT FIREARMS C9 CAMO

Action: Semiautomatic
Grips: Polymer
Barrel: 3.5 in.
Sights: Three dot, adjustable rear
Weight: 29 oz.
Caliber: 9mm
Capacity: 8, 10 rounds
Features: Compact CCW pistol rated +P; last round hold-open; black powdercoat finish; high-impact grips with easy-grip finish; magazine disconnect safety; manual thumb safety; available in what looks to be Muddy Girl purple camo, a woodland camo, or a tan/cream digital camo
MSRP $269.99

HI-POINT FIREARMS C9 LLTGM

Action: Semiautomatic
Grips: Polymer
Barrel: 3.5 in.
Sights: Three dot, adjustable rear
Weight: 29 oz.
Caliber: 9mm
Capacity: 8, 10 rounds
Features: Compact CCW pistol rated +P; last round hold-open; black powdercoat finish; high-impact grips with easy-grip finish; magazine disconnect safety; manual thumb safety; with a factory-installed trigger guard-mounted laser
MSRP $275.00

HI-POINT FIREARMS YEET CANNON G1

Action: Semiautomatic
Grips: Polymer
Barrel: 3.5 in.
Sights: Three dot, adjustable rear
Weight: 29 oz.
Caliber: 9mm
Capacity: 8, 10 rounds
Features: As the story goes, Hi-Point held a contest to name this gun, then threw away the votes to the consternation of just about everyone, and then, under advisement of H&K to listen to their customers, the company did, and voila, the YEET Cannon G1. Yeet means, more or less, to throw forcefully.
MSRP $212.00

KEL-TEC P50

Action: Semiautomatic
Grips: Synthetic
Barrel: 9.5 in.
Sights: None
Weight: 51.2 oz.
Caliber: 5.7x28mm
Capacity: 50 rounds
Features: The highlight of this gun may be its two—TWO—50-round magazines; abundant Picatinny rails; quick-detach mounts; under rail; magazine lies on top of the grip/frame
MSRP $995.00

LIVE Q OR DIE HONEY BADGER PISTOL

Action: Semiautomatic
Grips: Synthetic
Barrel: 7 in.
Sights: None
Weight: 4 lb. 8 oz.
Caliber: .300 BLK
Capacity: 20 rounds
Features: Clear-coat hard anodized aluminum receiver in tan; free-floating M-LOK handguard; AR-type controls; 5/8x24 threaded tapered muzzle with Cherry Bomb muzzle brake; two-stage match trigger; two-position telescopic brace; adjustable low-profile gas block
MSRP $2999.00

LIVE Q OR DIE MINI FIX

Action: Bolt
Grips: Synthetic
Barrel: 8 in.
Sights: None
Weight: 4 lb. 7 oz.
Caliber: .300 BLK
Capacity: 20 rounds
Features: Based on the company's rifle The Fix, the Mini Fix is a bolt-action pistol with a one-piece receiver; stabilizing brace; 45-degree short-throw bolt; full-length topside rail; free-floating Q-sert handguard; 5/8x24 threaded tapered muzzle with Cherry Bomb muzzle brake; two-stage match trigger
MSRP $3299.00

LIVE Q OR DIE SUGAR WEASEL

MASTERPIECE ARMS 35DMG

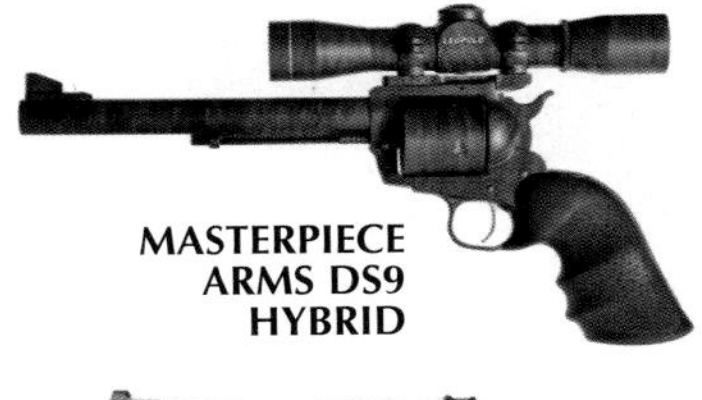
MASTERPIECE ARMS DS9 HYBRID

MG ARMS DRAGONFLY

MG ARMS DRAGONSLAYER

NIGHTHAWK CUSTOM AGENT 2 COMMANDER

LIVE Q OR DIE SUGAR WEASEL

Action: Semiautomatic
Grips: Synthetic
Barrel: 7 in.
Sights: None
Weight: 4 lb. 10 oz.
Caliber: .300 BLK
Capacity: 20 rounds
Features: A semiauto AR-type pistol an M16 spec receiver; direct impingement design in a pistol length gas system with adjustable gas block; single-stage trigger; six-position SBA3 pistol stabilizing brace; six-inch M-LOK handguard; 5/8x24 threaded muzzle with Cherry Bomb muzzle brake
MSRP $1999.00

MASTERPIECE ARMS 35DMG

Action: Semiautomatic
Grips: Synthetic
Barrel: 5.5 in.
Sights: Adjustable front, rear
Weight: N/A
Caliber: 9mm
Capacity: 17, 33 rounds
Features: Compatible with 17- and 30-round Glock magazines only, this unique pistol sports a barrel threaded ½x28; side cocker; scope mount; lower Picatinny rail; Ergo grip; MPA short handguard; side folding KAK Shockwave 2.0 arm brace; decal grip panels; barrel extension; no tax stamp required with the KAK arm brace; black or multiple Cerakote colors to choose from
Black: $799.00
Cerakote: $925.00

MASTERPIECE ARMS DS9 HYBRID

Action: Semiautomatic
Grips: Aluminum
Barrel: 5 in.
Sights: Accuracy X Shot base, Kensight
Weight: N/A
Caliber: 9mm
Capacity: 17, 20 rounds
Features: Hand-lapped frame to slide fit; full-length light rail frame; machined aluminum grip; Koenig hammer, sear, and disconnector; custom machined aluminum trigger shoe; FGW slide machining; slide lightning cuts; Wolff springs; MPA magwell; one-piece tool-less guide rod; iron sights or a slide-cut option with customer choice of mounting plates that accommodate a wide variety of reflex red-dot sights; in a hybrid black/stainless; hybrid stainless/blue; hybrid black/blue
MSRP $2999.00

MG ARMS DRAGONFLY

Action: Revolver
Grips: Customer choice
Barrel: 4 in.
Sights: Blade front, adjustable rear
Weight: 21 oz.
Caliber: .32 H&R Mag., .38 Spec. +P, .44 Spec.
Capacity: 6 rounds
Features: MG says this is the world's lightest single-action; colors in PTFE or Cerakote; titanium cylinder; titanium sleeved barrel; customer choice of grips; half-cock loading; limited product of 25 per year
MSRP $1295.00

MG ARMS DRAGONSLAYER

Action: Revolver
Grips: Customer choice
Barrel: Customer choice 4.5 in.–10 in.
Sights: Ramp front, adjustable rear
Weight: 36 oz.
Caliber: .45 LC +P, .454 Casull, .475 Linebaugh, .500 Linebaugh
Capacity: 5 rounds
Features: A big-bore for the hunters with multiple custom options including barrel length, metal finish colors, ceramic or Teflon finishes, barrel porting, and grips; limited production to 25 per year
MSRP $1895.00

NIGHTHAWK CUSTOM AGENT 2 COMMANDER

Action: Semiautomatic
Grips: G10
Barrel: 4.25 in.
Sights: Fiber optic front, Heinie ledge rear
Weight: 38.6 oz.
Caliber: 9mm, .45 ACP
Capacity: 10 rounds
Features: Jointly designed by Nighthawk and Agency Arms, this smart-looking pistol has cuts at the front-strap, mainspring housing, and controls to match the custom Railscales grips; red Nighthawk front sight with serrated Heinie ledge rear; extended, faceted, and angled magazine release; crowned, flush-cut match-grade barrel; smoke Cerakote finish; Agency front and rear slide serrations; light rail
MSRP $4499.00

NIGHTHAWK CUSTOM KORTH NXA

NIGHTHAWK CUSTOM KORTH NXR

NIGHTHAWK CUSTOM KORTH NXS

NIGHTHAWK CUSTOM THE BULL OFFICER

NIGHTHAWK CUSTOM THUNDER RANCH COMBAT SPECIAL

NIGHTHAWK CUSTOM TRS COMMANDER

NIGHTHAWK CUSTOM TRS COMP

NIGHTHAWK CUSTOM KORTH NXR

Action: Revolver
Grips: Walnut
Barrel: 4 in., 6 in.
Sights: Ramp front, adjustable rear
Weight: 55.3 oz.
Caliber: .44 Mag.
Capacity: 6 rounds
Features: A super choice for a hunting tool, this revolver sports an integral Picatinny rail on top for optics and under barrel for weights; ventilated barrel housing; nDLC coating; Turkish walnut grips with finger grooves; 416R hammer-forged barrel; front side has removable side panels for fast change-out
MSRP $5299.00

NIGHTHAWK CUSTOM KORTH NXS

Action: Revolver
Grips: Walnut
Barrel: 4 in., 6 in.
Sights: Ramp front, adjustable rear
Weight: 50.7 oz.
Caliber: .357 Mag.
Capacity: 8 rounds
Features: Complexly ventilated barrel shroud; wide swing-out cylinder cut for use with moon clips; Jim Wilson walnut grips with finger grooves; nDLC finish on metalwork; dual top-side Picatinny rails; under-barrel rail for lights or weights; optional 9mm cylinder with moon clips cuts
MSRP $5299.00

NIGHTHAWK CUSTOM THE BULL OFFICER

Action: Semiautomatic
Grips: Carbon fiber
Barrel: 3.8 in.
Sights: Tritium front, Heinie ledge rear
Weight: 32 oz.
Caliber: 9mm
Capacity: 8 rounds
Features: A single-stack 9mm in an Officer's foundation with a black nitride finish forged frame; bull-nose slide front; bow-tie plug; French border; shortened slide stop; beveled frame; rear slide serrations; completely dehorned
MSRP $3799.00

NIGHTHAWK CUSTOM THUNDER RANCH COMBAT SPECIAL

Action: Semiautomatic
Grips: Linen/Micarta
Barrel: 5 in.
Sights: Gold bead front, Heinie ledge rear
Weight: 41.3 oz.
Caliber: 9mm, .45 ACP
Capacity: 8 rounds
Features: Created by Nighthawk with cooperation from the Thunder Ranch firearm training facility, this special full-size build has front and rear slide serrations; GI numb-style thumb safety; 25 lpi checkering on frontstrap and mainspring housing; lanyard loop; linen/Micarta grips; smoked nitride finish; slide has Thunder Ranch logo
MSRP $3499.00

NIGHTHAWK CUSTOM TRS COMMANDER

Action: Semiautomatic
Grips: Polymer
Barrel: 4.25 in.
Sights: Tritium front, Heinie ledge rear
Weight: 36.7 oz.
Caliber: 9mm
Capacity: 17 rounds
Features: A double-stack on a Commander build with a match-grade barrel; full-length dust cover; unique dimpling on slide matches pattern on grip; ultra high-cut frontstrap; solid aluminum trigger with flat serrated face; complete dehorning
MSRP $3999.00

NIGHTHAWK CUSTOM TRS COMP

Action: Semiautomatic
Grips: Polymer
Barrel: 5 in.
Sights: Gold bead front, Heinie ledge rear
Weight: 39.6 oz.
Caliber: 9mm
Capacity: 17 rounds
Features: A double-stack Government frame build with precision ported compensator; monolithic slide; full-length dust cover; aluminum trigger with flat serrated face; dimpling pattern at rear of slide matches pattern on the grip; ultra high-cut frontstrap; complete dehorning
MSRP $4599.00

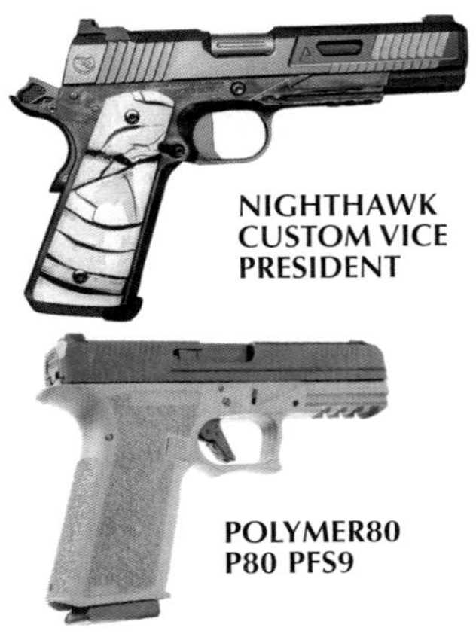

NIGHTHAWK CUSTOM VICE PRESIDENT

POLYMER80 P80 PFS9

NIGHTHAWK CUSTOM VIP AGENT 2

RED ARROW WEAPONS RAW15 300 BLACKOUT PISTOL

POLYMER80 P80 PFC9

ROCK RIVER ARMS LAR-BT9G

NIGHTHAWK CUSTOM VICE PRESIDENT

Action: Semiautomatic
Grips: G10
Barrel: 5 in.
Sights: Gold bead front, Heinie ledge rear
Weight: 38.2 oz.
Caliber: 9mm
Capacity: 10 rounds
Features: Part of Nighthawk's Boardroom Series, this custom build gets a Commander foundation stainless steel slide with nDLC finish, aggressive rear serrations and muzzle-end windows that show off the gold titanium nitride barrel with crown; custom Ascend scaled G10 grips from Railscales; aluminum Nighthawk tri-cavity trigger; 25 lpi checkering on frontstrap and one-piece mainspring housing; completely dehorned
MSRP $4199.00

NIGHTHAWK CUSTOM VIP AGENT 2

Action: Semiautomatic
Grips: Mammoth ivory
Barrel: 5 in.
Sights: Gold bead front, Heinie ledge rear
Weight: 39.6 oz.
Caliber: .45 ACP
Capacity: 10 rounds
Features: Mammoth ivory G10 grips by Railscales; polished charcoal blue slide; color case-hardened frame; crowned flush-cut match-grade barrel; slide is faceted and has side windows; forged frame with lightened Recon rail; Nighthawk/Agency custom trigger; pistol is a join creation of Nighthawk, Agency Arms, and Turnbull restoration
MSRP $8499.00

POLYMER80 P80 PFC9

Action: Semiautomatic
Grips: Polymer
Barrel: 4.02 in.
Sights: White dot front, serrated rear
Weight: 21.16 oz.
Caliber: 9mm
Capacity: 10, 15 rounds
Features: The smaller of two guns produced by a company best known for its slides, frames, and 80% kits, this striker-fire pistol takes Glock 17 magazines and features an underside Picatinny rail; front and rear slide serrations; textured grip surface
MSRP $550.00

POLYMER80 P80 PFS9

Action: Semiautomatic
Grips: Polymer
Barrel: 4.49 in.
Sights: White dot front, serrated rear
Weight: 24 oz.
Caliber: 9mm
Capacity: 10, 15, 17 rounds
Features: Utilizing Glock 17 mags, this full-size pistol has an improved grip angle; undercut trigger guard; extended beavertail; flared magwell; under rail; serrated slide
MSRP $550.00

RED ARROW WEAPONS RAW15 300 BLACKOUT PISTOL

Action: Semiautomatic
Grips: Synthetic
Barrel: 10.5 in.
Sights: None
Weight: 88 oz.
Caliber: .300 BLK
Capacity: 30 rounds
Features: This might stretch the definition of pistol, but it's not alone in the crowd of MSR legal pistols; Diamondback barrel that's melonite coated; pistol-length gas system; CMC 3.5-lb. single-stage trigger; forged aluminum lower; forged aluminum A3 upper, flattop and T-marked; Magpul P-Mag magazine; Tailhook Mod 2 brace; A2-style flash hider; ATI pistol buffer tube; 9-in. M-LOK S-rail handguard; in midnight bronze or in all-over black with flash red highlights
MSRP . . . . $1025.00–$1045.00

ROCK RIVER ARMS LAR-BT9G

Action: Semiautomatic
Grips: Rubber
Barrel: 4.5 in., 7 in., 10 in.
Sights: None, flip-up front, rear
Weight: 6 lb.
Caliber: 9mm
Capacity: 10, 15, 17, 30 rounds
Features: Glock magazine-compatible, the three guns in this series feature billet aluminum lowers with extruded aluminum uppers; RRA two-stage trigger; free-floating M-LOK handguard; A2 flash hider; Hogue rubber grip; low Pro M-LOK compatible handstop and NPS flip-up sights on 4.5-in. model; flared magwell; integral winter trigger guard; adjustable SB Tactical SBA3 stabilizing arm brace
MSRP . . . . $1315.00–$1420.00

RUGER AMERICAN PISTOL COMPACT

RUGER LCP II .22 LR

RUGER PC CHARGER

SAR USA B6, B6C

SAR USA K2 45

SAR USA K12 SPORT

SAR USA MODEL 2000

SAR USA P8L, P8S

RUGER AMERICAN PISTOL COMPACT

Action: Semiautomatic
Grips: Glass-filled nylon
Barrel: 3.55 in.
Sights: Novak low-mount carry three-dot
Weight: 29.2 oz.
Caliber: 9mm
Capacity: 17 rounds
Features: Generous capacity makes this a great carry choice; ergonomic wrap-around grip module; gray Cerakote finish; approved for +P use; grip frame texturing; slide serrations; ambidextrous slide stop and magazine release; mil-spec Picatinny rail; tool-less takedown
MSRP $579.00

RUGER LCP II .22 LR

Action: Semiautomatic
Grips: Glass-filled nylon
Barrel: 2.75 in.
Sights: Integral front, rear
Weight: 11.4 oz.
Caliber: .22 LR
Capacity: 10 rounds
Features: Designed for self-protection; Lite Rack system; Hogue HandALL slip-on sleeve; black oxide finish
MSRP $369.00

RUGER PC CHARGER

Action: Semiautomatic
Grips: Glass-filled polymer
Barrel: 6.5 in.
Sights: None
Weight: 5 lb. 3 oz.
Caliber: 9mm
Capacity: 17 rounds
Features: A chassis-built pistol that takes standard AR grips; integral aluminum Picatinny rails; flared interchangeable magwells to accommodate Ruger or Glock magazines; integrated rear quick-detach cups; six-position CNC-milled handguard with a handstop and Type III hardcoat anodized aluminum and M-LOK slots at 3, 6, and 9 o'clock; Dead Blow action; reversible magazine release and charging handle; threaded heavy-contour barrel
MSRP $799.00

SAR USA B6, B6C

Action: Semiautomatic
Grips: Polymer
Barrel: 4.5 in., 3.8 in.
Sights: Three dot combat
Weight: 28.2 oz., 25.2 oz.
Caliber: 9mm
Capacity: 17, 13 rounds
Features: A full-size and compact pair of pistols practical for target shooting or self-defense; low-profile combat sights; DA/SA; textured grip frame; blue or stainless slide; frame available in different colors including black and OD green
Full-size: $333.00
Compact: $311.10

SAR USA K2 45, K2 45C

Action: Semiautomatic
Grips: Polymer
Barrel: 4.7 in.
Sights: Three dot with adjustable target rear
Weight: 40.2 oz.
Caliber: .45 ACP
Capacity: 14 rounds
Features: A full-size and compact pair of double-stack .45s, designed as licensed copies of the CZ-75 from what we've read; underside Picatinny rail; forged alloy steel frame; two-position frame safety; DA/SA; in all blue or all stainless finish
Full-size: $533.32
Compact: $477.99

SAR USA K12 SPORT

Action: Semiautomatic
Grips: Polymer
Barrel: 4.7 in.
Sights: Three dot with adjustable target rear
Weight: 46.9 oz.
Caliber: 9mm
Capacity: 17 rounds
Features: Crowned barrel; SA firing system; checkered front- and back-strap; front and rear slide serrations; allover stainless metalwork with grey polymer grips; supplied with two magazines
MSRP $799.99

SAR USA MODEL 2000

Action: Semiautomatic
Grips: Polymer
Barrel: 4.5 in.
Sights: Three dot front, rear
Weight: 35.2 oz.
Caliber: 9mm
Capacity: 17 rounds
Features: Good for target or carry; forged steel frame; DA/SA; low-drag combat sights; crowned barrel; in all blue or all stainless metalwork
MSRP . . . . $477.77–$499.99

SAR USA P8L, P8S

Action: Semiautomatic
Grips: Polymer
Barrel: 4.6 in., 3.8 in.
Sights: Three dot low-profile combat, adjustable rear
Weight: 37.9 oz., 35.8 oz.
Caliber: 9mm
Capacity: 17 rounds
Features: A great one for target competition; ported slide for heat dissipation; crowned and ported barrel; forged alloy steel frame; S model has slightly shorter barrel; metalwork in all black or all stainless
MSRP . . . . $511.10–$533.32

SAR USA SAR9, SAR9 COMPACT

SAR USA SAR9 OPTICS READY

SAR USA SAR9-X PLATINUM

SHADOW SYSTEMS DR920 COMBAT

SHADOW SYSTEMS DR920 ELITE

SHADOW SYSTEMS MR920 COMBAT

SHADOW SYSTEMS MR920 ELITE, ELITE LONG SLIDE

SAR USA SAR9, SAR9 COMPACT

Action: Semiautomatic
Grips: Polymer
Barrel: 4.4 in., 4.0 in.
Sights: Three dot low-profile combat
Weight: 27.1 oz., 26.8 oz.
Caliber: 9mm
Capacity: 17 rounds
Features: A lightweight carry gun with double-stack capacity; striker-fire; polymer frame; low barrel axis; 20-degree grip angle; safety trigger
MSRP $799.99

SAR USA SAR9 OPTICS READY

Action: Semiautomatic
Grips: Polymer
Barrel: 4.4 in.
Sights: Three dot low-profile combat
Weight: 27.1 oz.
Caliber: 9mm
Capacity: 17 rounds
Features: Identical to the original SAR9 model, but with an optics-ready slide cut
MSRP $799.99

SAR USA SAR9-X PLATINUM

Action: Semiautomatic
Grips: Polymer
Barrel: 4.4 in.
Sights: Three dot low-profile combat
Weight: 27.5 oz.
Caliber: 9mm
Capacity: 15, 17 rounds
Features: Supplied with one flush-fit 15-round and an extended 17-round magazine, this lightweight CCW/ target pistol has a striker-fire mechanism; Picatinny rail; Cerakote gray finish; slide venting to reduce heat build-up; front and rear slide serrations; one source says this comes with the weapon light pictured, but most make no mention of it so we're going without
MSRP $499.99

SHADOW SYSTEMS DR920 COMBAT

Action: Semiautomatic
Grips: Polymer
Barrel: 4.5 in., 5 in.
Sights: Green tritium night sight front, black serrated rear
Weight: 23 oz.
Caliber: 9mm
Capacity: 17 rounds
Features: This full-size striker-fire pistol has a 416R stainless steel barrel; textured polymer frame; front and rear slide serrations; option of a threaded barrel; black or flat dark earth frame choices; interchangeable backstraps; extended beavertail; recoil control ledge on frame; optional magwell; spiral-fluted match barrel gives a unique look
MSRP . . . . Starting at $889.00

SHADOW SYSTEMS DR920 ELITE

Action: Semiautomatic
Grips: Polymer
Barrel: 4.5 in., 5 in.
Sights: Green tritium night sight front, black serrated rear
Weight: 22.5 oz.
Caliber: 9mm
Capacity: 17 rounds
Features: Identical to the Combat full-size version, but with additional slide enhancements that include topside serrations and lightning windows for weight reduction
MSRP . . . . Starting at $989.00

SHADOW SYSTEMS MR920 COMBAT

Action: Semiautomatic
Grips: Polymer
Barrel: 4 in., 4.5 in., 5 in.
Sights: Green tritium night sight front, black serrated rear
Weight: 21.5 oz.
Caliber: 9mm
Capacity: 15 rounds
Features: A compact striker-fire pistol with an aggressively textured frame; aluminum flat-faced trigger; spiral-fluted match-grade barrel available standard or threaded and finished in choice of bronze TiCN or black nitride; interchangeable backstraps; optional magwell; frame has recoil ledge; extended beavertail for a higher grip
MSRP . . . . Starting at $799.00

SHADOW SYSTEMS MR920 ELITE, ELITE LONG SLIDE

Action: Semiautomatic
Grips: Polymer
Barrel: 4 in., 4.5 in., 5 in.
Sights: Green tritium night sight front, black serrated rear
Weight: 20.9 oz.
Caliber: 9mm
Capacity: 15 rounds
Features: Both models are identical to the Combat version in most features, but the slides feature topside serrations in addition to the side serrations front and rear, and they also boast lightning cuts for weight reduction; long slide version is ½-in. longer at 4.5-in. unthreaded, 5-in. threaded
Elite: . . . . starting at $969.00
Elite Long Slide: . starting at $999.00

SIG SAUER M18 COMMEMORATIVE

SIG SAUER P220 NIGHTMARE FULL-SIZE

SIG SAUER P226 EQUINOX FULL-SIZE

SIG SAUER P226 NIGHTMARE FULL-SIZE

SIG SAUER P229 EQUINOX COMPACT

SIG SAUER P229 NIGHTMARE COMPACT

SIG SAUER P320 AXG SCORPION

SMITH & WESSON M&P9 M2.0 COMPACT OR

SIG SAUER M18 COMMEMORATIVE

Action: Semiautomatic
Grips: Polymer
Barrel: 3.9 in.
Sights: SIGLITE front, rear
Weight: 28.1 oz.
Caliber: 9mm
Capacity: 17, 21 rounds
Features: A limited release run of SIG's commemorative take on the official US service pistol; striker-fired; slide cut for optic plate/mounting; ambidextrous safety; grip modules; all-over coyote tan; ships with two 21-round magazine and one 17-round
MSRP $1499.99

SIG SAUER P220 NIGHTMARE FULL-SIZE

Action: Semiautomatic
Grips: G10
Barrel: 4.4 in.
Sights: X-RAY3 day/night sights
Weight: 30.4 oz.
Caliber: .45 ACP
Capacity: 8 rounds
Features: From the SIG Custom Works shop the full-size single-stack with a blacked-out frame; contrasting nickel-plated controls; Hogue Classic Contour SL G10 grips; under rail; Negrini case and two magazines
MSRP $1299.99

SIG SAUER P226 EQUINOX FULL-SIZE

Action: Semiautomatic
Grips: G10
Barrel: 4.4 in.
Sights: X-RAY3 day/night sights
Weight: 34 oz.
Caliber: 9mm
Capacity: 15 rounds
Features: From SIG Custom Works, this special P226 has an Equinox slide; contrasting nickel-plated controls; Hogue SL G10 grips; SRT trigger; two steel magazines and Custom Works Negrini case
MSRP $1349.99

SIG SAUER P226 NIGHTMARE FULL-SIZE

Action: Semiautomatic
Grips: G10
Barrel: 4.4 in.
Sights: X-RAY3 day/night sights
Weight: 34 oz.
Caliber: 9mm
Capacity: 15 rounds
Features: Similar to the .45 ACP P220 Nightmare, but in a double-stack 9mm
MSRP $1299.99

SIG SAUER P229 EQUINOX COMPACT

Action: Semiautomatic
Grips: G10
Barrel: 3.9 in.
Sights: X-RAY3 day/night sights
Weight: 34 oz.
Caliber: 9mm
Capacity: 15 rounds
Features: Similar to the P226 Equinox Full-Size, but with a shorter barrel
MSRP $1299.99

SIG SAUER P229 NIGHTMARE COMPACT

Action: Semiautomatic
Grips: G10
Barrel: 3.9 in.
Sights: X-RAY3 day/night sights
Weight: 34 oz.
Caliber: 9mm
Capacity: 15 rounds
Features: Much like the Custom Works P226 Nightmare, but with a shorter barrel
MSRP $1299.99

SIG SAUER P320 AXG SCORPION

Action: Semiautomatic
Grips: G10
Barrel: 3.9 in.
Sights: X-RAY3 day/night sights
Weight: 31.3 oz.
Caliber: 9mm
Capacity: 10, 17 rounds
Features: Utilizes SIG's new AXG--Alloy X Series Grip, a metal grip module with deep undercuts; Scorpion G10 grips; Cerakote Elite coating in flat dark earth; LEGION skeletonized flat-faced trigger; under-barrel accessory rail; ships with three 10- or 17-round magazines
MSRP $1162.99

SMITH & WESSON M&P9 M2.0 COMPACT OR

Action: Semiautomatic
Grips: Polymer
Barrel: 4 in.
Sights: Three dot front, rear
Weight: 27 oz.
Caliber: 9mm
Capacity: 15 rounds
Features: This compact in the M&P line gets a slide cut to be optic ready (OR) as well as an underside Picatinny rail; modular grip; front and rear slide "wave" serrations; steel three-dot sights
MSRP $616.00

SMITH & WESSON PERFORMANCE CENTER M&P SHIELD EZ

SPRINGFIELD ARMORY XD-S MOD.2 OSP

STACCATO 2011 C2 DPO CARRY, C2 DPO TACTICAL

STACCATO 2011 P, P DPO

STOEGER INDUSTRIES STR-9 OPTIC READY

STOEGER INDUSTRIES STR-9C COMPACT

STOEGER INDUSTRIES STR-9S COMBAT

SMITH & WESSON PERFORMANCE CENTER M&P SHIELD EZ

Action: Semiautomatic
Grips: Polymer
Barrel: 3.8 in.
Sights: Hi-Viz Litewave tritium/ Litepipe
Weight: 23.02 oz.
Caliber: .380 ACP, 9mm
Capacity: 8 rounds
Features: A micro-compact loaded with premium tritium/fiber optic sights; a slide with lightning cuts; ported barrel; Performance Center action; loaded chamber indicator; aluminum grip safety; Picatinny rail; two magazines; choice of manual or no thumb safety; black, silver, or gold accents
.380 ACP: $532.00
9mm: $606.00

SPRINGFIELD ARMORY XD-S MOD.2 OSP

Action: Semiautomatic
Grips: Polymer
Barrel: 3.3 in.
Sights: Three dot low-profile front, rear
Weight: 21.5 oz.–22.5 oz.
Caliber: 9mm
Capacity: 7, 9 rounds
Features: This small footprint, slim, single-stack has a slide cutout for reflex/micro red-dot optics mounting; comes with one 7-round flush and one 9-round extended magazine; available with factory installed Crimson Trace red-dot sight
Standard: $425.00
Crimson Trace: $549.00

STACCATO 2011 C2 DPO CARRY, C2 DPO TACTICAL

Action: Semiautomatic
Grips: G2
Barrel: 3.9 in.
Sights: Fiber optic front, drift adjustable rear
Weight: 25.7 oz.
Caliber: 9mm
Capacity: 16 rounds
Features: A very svelte, optics-ready double-stack for home-defense, with a Dawson Universal Optic System rear optics mounting plate cutout (plates sold separately); flush-fit 11-degree crown barrel; 3.9 Recoil Master Light recoil system; alloy frame; accessory rail; ambidextrous safety; black diamond-like-carbon finish
MSRP $2299.00

STACCATO 2011 P, P DPO

Action: Semiautomatic
Grips: G2
Barrel: 4.4 in.
Sights: Fiber optic front, T.A.S.II rear
Weight: 33 oz.
Caliber: 9mm
Capacity: 17, 20 rounds
Features: Actually designed for and utilized by a wide range of law enforcement agencies, you get a full-size frame with a shorter slide; bull barrel; Dawson 4.4 adaptive tool-less recoil system; billet frame with accessory rail; DPO version has Dawson Universal Optic System slide cut for optics mounting plates (plates sold separately); ships with two 17-round and one 20-round mags
P: $2099.00
P DPO: $2399.00

STOEGER INDUSTRIES STR-9 OPTIC READY

Action: Semiautomatic
Grips: Polymer
Barrel: 4.17 oz.
Sights: Three dot front, rear
Weight: 26 oz.
Caliber: 9mm
Capacity: 10, 15 rounds
Features: Optics-ready, double-stack pistol; four optics mounting plates included; choice of 10- or 15-round magazine
MSRP $379.00

STOEGER INDUSTRIES STR-9C COMPACT

Action: Semiautomatic
Grips: Polymer
Barrel: 3.8 in.
Sights: Tritium
Weight: 24 oz.
Caliber: 9mm
Capacity: 10, 13 rounds
Features: A smartly priced option for CCW or target practice; 10- or 13-round magazine option; striker-fired; slide serrations
MSRP $399.00

STOEGER INDUSTRIES STR-9S COMBAT

Action: Semiautomatic
Grips: Polymer
Barrel: 4.67 in.
Sights: Three dot front, adjustable rear
Weight: 28.8 oz.
Caliber: 9mm
Capacity: 10, 20 rounds
Features: Combat striker-fired model; threaded barrel; slide cut for mounting optics and four mounting plates; three interchangeable backstraps; in nitride hardened black with three 20-round magazines; optic not included
MSRP $549.00

TAURUS G3C

Action: Semiautomatic
Grips: Polymer
Barrel: 3.2 in.
Sights: Fixed front, drift adjustable rear
Weight: 22 oz.
Caliber: 9mm
Capacity: 10, 12 rounds
Features: A small, lightweight, and affordable double-stack carry option with a striker-fire action; stainless steel barrel; Tennifer finish in black; accessory rail; three magazines included in choice of 10- or 12-round
MSRP $308.77

TAURUS TX-22 COMPETITION

Action: Semiautomatic
Grips: Polymer
Barrel: 5.25 in.
Sights: White dot front, fully adjustable rear
Weight: 23 oz.
Caliber: .22 LR
Capacity: 10, 16 rounds
Features: A very lightweight rimfire designed for more serious target shooting, with a striker-fire action; threaded barrel; aggressive serrations on the aluminum slide; full-size polymer frame; four optics mounting plates; with three magazines
MSRP $484.85

TAYLOR'S & CO. FIREARMS 1860 ARMY LONG CYLINDER

Action: Revolver
Grips: Walnut
Barrel: 8 in.
Sights: Blade front, integral rear
Weight: 41.6 oz.
Caliber: .45 LC
Capacity: 6 rounds
Features: Originally a cap-n-ball blackpowder design, this one takes modern .45 LC rounds; forged steel frame; longer Army-sized walnut grips; case-hardened frame; blued cylinder, backstrap, barrel, and loading lever; brass trigger guard
MSRP $643.48

TAYLOR'S & CO. FIREARMS GUNFIGHTER DEFENDER

Action: Revolver
Grips: Walnut
Barrel: 4.75 in., 5.5 in.
Sights: Blade front, integral rear
Weight: 39.2 oz., 40 oz.
Caliber: .357 Mag., .45 LC
Capacity: 6 rounds
Features: This single-action wears extra-long smooth walnut grips; forged steel frame; a low, flat hammer-spur makes this a good choice for competition
MSRP $654.62

TROY INDUSTRIES A4 PISTOL

Action: Semiautomatic
Grips: Synthetic
Barrel: 10 in.
Sights: Flip-up front, rear
Weight: 67.2 oz.
Caliber: 5.56 NATO
Capacity: 30 rounds
Features: Gas-operated MSR pistol with features by the maker that include a standard trigger; SOCC92 BattleRail forend; control group; M4 front and rear folding BattleSight; 30-round BattleMag; Medieval muzzle brake; SBA3 pistol brace
MSRP $1149.00

UBERTI FIREARMS 1873 CATTLEMAN TEDDY

Action: Revolver
Grips: Simulated ivory
Barrel: 5.5 in.
Sights: Blade front, integral rear
Weight: 36.8 oz.
Caliber: .45 LC
Capacity: 6 rounds
Features: Sporting full laser engraving mimicking that of Roosevelt's Colt, this revolver is in full nickel-plated steel; fluted cylinder
MSRP $1249.00

UBERTI FIREARMS 1875 NO. 3 2ND MODEL TOP-BREAK HARDIN

Action: Revolver
Grips: Simulated buffalo horn
Barrel: 7 in.
Sights: Blade front, integral rear
Weight: 41.6 oz.
Caliber: .45 LC
Capacity: 6 rounds
Features: This top-break revolver comes with a case-hardened frame and blue barrel/cylinder for an eye-catching combination; fluted cylinder
MSRP $1479.00

VOLQUARTSEN FIREARMS MAMBA-TF

VOLQUARTSEN FIREARMS MAMBA-X

VOLQUARTSEN FIREARMS MINI-MAMBA

WALTHER CCP M2

WALTHER Q4 TAC M1, M2

WALTHER Q5 MATCH M1, M2

VOLQUARTSEN FIREARMS MAMBA-TF

Action: Semiautomatic
Grips: Polymer
Barrel: 4.5 in., 6 in.
Sights: Fiber optic front, target rear
Weight: 35 oz.
Caliber: .22 LR
Capacity: 10 rounds
Features: Push-button takedown for simple disassembly; Volquartsen LLV Competition upper; stainless steel barrel; laser-hardened stainless steel breech; integral top and underside Picatinny rails; aluminum frame retrofitted with Volquartsen Accurizing Kit; textured grip with pronounced finger grooves; metal in black, Arctic, or Battleworn finishes
MSRP . . . . $1554.00–$1804.00

VOLQUARTSEN FIREARMS MAMBA-X

Action: Semiautomatic
Grips: Polymer
Barrel: 4.5 in.
Sights: None
Weight: 28 oz.
Caliber: .22 LR
Capacity: 10 rounds
Features: Volquartsen takes a cue from the centerfire crowd, with its LLV Competition Upper configured with a slide cut for red-dot sight mounting; DLC-coated competition bolt; single-port compensator; ½x28 threaded barrel; black anodized aluminum frame with Volquartsen Accurizing Kit; Hogue grips; compatible with a wide range of name-brand red-dots
MSRP $1342.00

VOLQUARTSEN FIREARMS MINI-MAMBA

Action: Semiautomatic
Grips: Rubber
Barrel: 3 in.
Sights: Fiber optic front, adjustable rear
Weight: 25 oz.
Caliber: .22 LR
Capacity: 10 rounds
Features: This is Volquartsen's smallest Mamba package and it features a black anodized aluminum Ruger Mk IV 22/45 frame; Hogue grips; barrel threaded ½x28; DLC-coated competition bolt; LLV Competition upper; integral topside Picatinny rail
MSRP $1369.00

WALTHER CCP M2

Action: Semiautomatic
Grips: Polymer
Barrel: 3.54 in.
Sights: White three dot
Weight: 20 oz.
Caliber: 9mm, .380 ACP
Capacity: 8 rounds
Features: CCW pistol with a visible red cocking indicator at the back of the slide; front and rear slide serrations; underside Picatinny rail; grip with fingergrooves; Softcoil gas technology; tool-less takedown; fixed barrel; all-over Viridian black, black frame/matte stainless slide, blue titanium frame/black slide, or tungsten gray frame/black slide options; .380 available in black frame/matte stainless slide, angel blue frame/matte gray slide, or angle blue frame/ brushed stainless slide
MSRP . . . . Starting at $439.00

WALTHER Q4 TAC M1, M2

Action: Semiautomatic
Grips: Polymer
Barrel: 4.6 in.
Sights: Fiber optic front, adjustable rear
Weight: 25 oz.
Caliber: 9mm
Capacity: 15, 17 rounds
Features: A full-size but lightweight striker-fire; ambidextrous slide stop; paddle-style magazine release on M1, reversible button-style on M2; magazine with pinky rest; textured grip area with finger grooves; threaded barrel; underside rail; Quick-Defense trigger
MSRP $699.99

WALTHER Q5 MATCH M1, M2

Action: Semiautomatic
Grips: Polymer
Barrel: 5 in.
Sights: Fiber optic front, adjustable rear
Weight: 27.9 oz.
Caliber: 9mm
Capacity: 15 rounds
Features: Competition-ready full-size pistol; polygonal rifling; stepped chamber; interchangeable backstraps; ambidextrous slide stop; ported barrel; optic ready; LPA sights; slide is serrated and has lightning cuts; underside rail; M1 has paddle-style magazine release; M2 has reversible button-style magazine release
MSRP $799.99

NEW Products: Handguns

NEW PRODUCTS

WALTHER Q5 MATCH STEEL FRAME, STEEL FRAME PRO

ZEV TECHNOLOGIES OZ9 COMBAT

ZEV TECHNOLOGIES OZ9 ELITE COMPETITION

ZEV TECHNOLOGIES OZ9 ELITE STANDARD, OZ9C ELITE COMPACT

ZEV TECHNOLOGIES OZ9 ELITE X GRIP

ZEV TECHNOLOGIES OZ9C HYPERCOMP

ZEV TECHNOLOGIES Z365, Z365XL

WALTHER Q5 MATCH STEEL FRAME, STEEL FRAME PRO

Action: Semiautomatic
Grips: Polymer
Barrel: 5 in.
Sights: Fiber optic front, adjustable rear
Weight: 41.6 oz.
Caliber: 9mm
Capacity: 15 rounds
Features: USPSA approved for Production and Carry Optics; IDPA approved for Stock Service Pistol and Carry Optics; wrap-around grip panel; extended beavertail; underside Picatinny rail; polygonal rifling; stepped chamber; ported barrel; slide has serrations and lightning cuts; optic ready; low-profile magwell; Tenifer finish; Pro version includes Carl Walther Performance magwell and two aluminum baseplates that increase capacity to 17
Standard:. $1499.99
Pro: $1650.00

ZEV TECHNOLOGIES OZ9 COMBAT

Action: Semiautomatic
Grips: Polymer
Barrel: 4.5 in.
Sights: Fiber optic front, battle sight rear
Weight: 28 oz.
Caliber: 9mm
Capacity: 17 rounds
Features: Double-stack high-end striker fire with ZEV's windowless Citadel slide; PRO match barrel; PRO curved-face trigger; optic-ready slide cut; steeper grip angle for straighter pointing; full-length solid steel frame; accessory rail; slide has serrations front and rear and is serrated across the top to reduce glare
MSRP $1368.00

ZEV TECHNOLOGIES OZ9 ELITE COMPETITION

Action: Semiautomatic
Grips: Polymer
Barrel: 5.3 in.
Sights: Fiber optic front, battle sight rear
Weight: 26.25 oz.
Caliber: 9mm
Capacity: 15 rounds
Features: A double-stack striker-fire with a full-length solid steel frame; ZEV's RMR optics cut in slide; PRO flat-face trigger; match-grade barrel in bronze; KC Eusebio signature slide; PRO Plus magwell; SKB case
MSRP $1799.00

ZEV TECHNOLOGIES OZ9 ELITE STANDARD, OZ9C ELITE COMPACT

Action: Semiautomatic
Grips: Polymer
Barrel: 4.49 in., 4 in.
Sights: Fiber optic front, battle sight rear
Weight: 28 oz., 26.25 oz.
Caliber: 9mm
Capacity: 15 rounds
Features: Similar to other OZ9 models, this one has a top slide cutout behind the front sight; optics mounting plate cutout; threaded barrel; underside rail; in all black, black frame/slide with bronze barrel, or flat dark earth frame/slide with black barrel
MSRP $1729.00

ZEV TECHNOLOGIES OZ9 ELITE X GRIP

Action: Semiautomatic
Grips: Polymer
Barrel: 4 in.
Sights: Fiber optic front, battle sight rear
Weight: 27 oz.
Caliber: 9mm
Capacity: 17 rounds
Features: A hybrid OZ9, with the slide of the OZ9c compact model and the longer grip of the standard OZ9; optics ready; PRO magwell
MSRP $1679.00

ZEV TECHNOLOGIES OZ9C HYPERCOMP

Action: Semiautomatic
Grips: Polymer
Barrel: 4 in.
Sights: Three dot front, rear
Weight: 28 oz.
Caliber: 9mm
Capacity: 15 rounds
Features: Ready for trophy winning with a bronze Cerakote barrel ported across the top instead of the sides; slide serrations fore and aft; underside rail; textured grip; wide magwell; optics ready; fully integrated locking block on full-length steel frame; PRO flat-faced trigger
MSRP $1789.00

ZEV TECHNOLOGIES Z365, Z365XL

Action: Semiautomatic
Grips: Polymer
Barrel: 3.1 in., 3.7 in.
Sights: Fiber optic front, battle sight rear
Weight: 18 oz., 20 oz.
Caliber: 9mm
Capacity: 12 rounds
Features: A collaboration between SIG Sauer and Zev, this takes SIG's P365 foundation and adds a ZEV Octane slide in titanium gray, with an optics cut, front and rear slide serrations, and horizontal top slide serrations to reduce glare; PRO barrel; SIG P365 grip with ZEV diamond-pattern laser stippling; SIG P365 flat-faced trigger
Standard:. $1199.00
XL: $1299.00

CVA ACCURA X-TREME LR-X

CVA ACCURA X-TREME MR-X

CVA PARAMOUNT HTR

DAVIDE PEDERSOLI 1850 UNDERHAMMER COOK PISTOL

GUNWERKS MUZZLELOADER RIFLE SYSTEM .45-CAL.

GUNWERKS MUZZLELOADER RIFLE SYSTEM .50-CAL.

LYMAN GREAT PLAINS SIGNATURE SERIES

SHILOH SHARPS 1863 MILITARY CARBINE

CVA ACCURA X-TREME LR-X

Lock: Break-action
Stock: Synthetic
Barrel: 30 in.
Sights: None
Weight: 7 lb. 4 oz.
Bore/Caliber: .45, .50
Features: This is considered a long-range muzzleloader, featuring a QRBP quick-release breech plug; DuraSight rail; Quake Claw sling; fluted premium Bergara threaded barrel; stock in Veil Wildland with flat dark earth Cerakote metalwork or Realtree Hillside camo stock with Patriot Brown Cerakote metalwork; .50-cal available with Williams rear peep and fiber optic front sights
MSRP $675.00

CVA ACCURA X-TREME MR-X

Lock: Break-action
Stock: Synthetic
Barrel: 26 in.
Sights: None
Weight: 7 lb. 1 oz.
Bore/Caliber: .45, .50
Features: Similar to the LR-X, but with a more manageable barrel length, featuring a QRBP quick-release breech plug; DuraSight rail; Quake Claw sling; fluted premium Bergara threaded barrel; stock in Veil Alpine or Realtree Rockslide camo, both with Sniper Grey Cerakote metalwork; .50-cal available with Williams rear peep and fiber optic front sights
MSRP $670.00

CVA PARAMOUNT HTR

Lock: Bolt
Stock: Synthetic
Barrel: 26 in.
Sights: None
Weight: 9 Lb. 9.6 oz.
Bore/Caliber: .40, .45
Features: Internal aluminum chassis and adjustable cheek riser; free-floating barrel threaded for CVA muzzle brake; designed to use .40-cal. 225-gr. PowerBelt ELR or .45-cal. 285-gr. PowerBelt ELR projectiles and magnum loads of Blackhorn 209
MSRP $1225.00

DAVIDE PEDERSOLI 1850 UNDERHAMMER COOK PISTOL

Lock: Percussion
Stock: Walnut
Barrel: 7.8 in.
Sights: Blade front, notch rear
Weight: 2 lb. 2 oz.
Bore/Caliber: .36
Features: A target shooting pistol that will be coveted by MLAIC competitors; front sight adjustable for windage, rear sight adjustable for elevation; walnut grip in a rather inverted teardrop design; match-grade barrel
MSRP $975.00

GUNWERKS MUZZLELOADER RIFLE SYSTEM .45-CAL.

Lock: Bolt
Stock: Carbon fiber
Barrel: 26 in.
Sights: Revic EXO open sights
Weight: N/A
Bore/Caliber: .45
Features: Truly a custom build; an example build: carbon fiber stock in carbon black; factory-mounted Kahles K318i Max scope; Gunwerks Picatinny scope rings; Low Pro two-piece 20 MOA scope bases; underside Picatinny rail; adjustable recoil pad; TT Primary adjustable trigger; GLR action; G8-profile barrel in a graphite finish and with a directional muzzle brake
MSRP $12,699.00

GUNWERKS MUZZLELOADER RIFLE SYSTEM .50-CAL.

Lock: Bolt
Stock: Carbon fiber
Barrel: 26 in.
Sights: None
Weight: N/A
Bore/Caliber: .50
Features: Less intense (and expensive) custom build; carbon gray carbon fiber stock; GRB right-hand action; Leupold 5–25x56 RH1 MOA scope; stainless steel barrel in tungsten finish and with a radial muzzle brake; Gunwerks Unity baseless scope rings; laser-etched turret long-range package; underside Picatinny rail
MSRP $8539.99

LYMAN GREAT PLAINS SIGNATURE SERIES

Lock: Flintlock, percussion
Stock: Walnut
Barrel: 30 in., 32 in.
Sights: Silver blade front, semi-buckhorn rear
Weight: 9 lb. 7 oz.–9 lb. 11 oz.
Bore/Caliber: .50, .54
Features: Replaces the previous Great Plains rifle with a standard model with a 32-in. barrel or a hunter model with a 30-in. barrel; designed and produced in conjunction with Davide Pedersoli; double-set triggers; smooth-operating vintage-type flat mainspring lock; drilled and tapped receiver; standard model also available as a kit; hunter model has a bead front sight paired with a fiber optic rear
MSRP . . . . $1045.00–$1240.95

SHILOH SHARPS 1863 MILITARY CARBINE

Lock: Percussion
Stock: Wood
Barrel: 22 in.
Sights: Iron block front sight, Lawrence ladder rear
Weight: 7 lb. 8 oz.
Bore/Caliber: .45, .50, .54
Features: This round barrel model has a forearm barrel band; single trigger; lever catch; color case-hardened finish; numerous upgrades including pack harden and various levels of antique metal finishes, patchbox, ebony pistol grip, saddle bar and ring, upgraded wood and finishes, brass escutcheons, and custom bedding, various sling swivels, and checkering upgrades
MSRP . . . . Starting at $2007.00

NEW Products: Black Powder

SHILOH SHARPS 1863 SPORTING RIFLE

TAYLOR'S & CO. THE ACE

TRADITIONS FIREARMS BUCKSTALKER XT

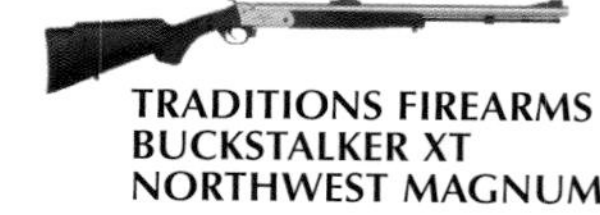
TRADITIONS FIREARMS BUCKSTALKER XT NORTHWEST MAGNUM

TRADITIONS FIREARMS PURSUIT XT

TRADITIONS FIREARMS PURSUIT XT NORTHWEST MAGNUM, PURSUIT XT LDR NORTHWEST MAGNUM

TRADITIONS FIREARMS VORTEK STRIKERFIRE LDR

SHILOH SHARPS 1863 SPORTING RIFLE

Lock: Percussion
Stock: Wood
Barrel: 26 in., 28 in., 30 in., 32 in., 34 in.
Sights: Blade front, buckhorn rear
Weight: N/A
Bore/Caliber: .45, .50, .54
Features: One for blackpowder cartridge metallic silhouette; optional color case-hardened finish; numerous upgrades including pack harden and various levels of antique metal finishes, patchbox, ebony pistol grip, barrel finish, upgraded wood and finishes, brass escutcheons, custom bedding, various sling swivels, forearm designs, rear barrel sights, vernier tang sights, drilling and tapping, and checkering upgrades
MSRP . . . . Starting at $2007.00

TAYLOR'S & CO. THE ACE

Lock: Caplock
Stock: PVC
Barrel: 3 in.
Sights: Blade front, integral notch rear
Weight: 2 lb. 7oz.
Bore/Caliber: .44/.45 LC
Features: An 1850 snubby for the caplock crowd that can also use a conversion cylinder in .45 LC; octagon barrel; brass trigger guard
MSRP $358.57

TRADITIONS FIREARMS BUCKSTALKER XT

Lock: Hinged breach
Stock: Synthetic
Barrel: 24 in.
Sights: None
Weight: 6 lb. 6 oz.
Bore/Caliber: .50
Features: This upgrades the current Buckstalker line with a premium-grade chromoly steel barrel; Elite XT trigger system; rebounding hammer; Accelerator breech plug; Speed Load system; accuracy to the 200-yard mark; various packages include: Vista camo stock with silver Cerakote barrel, with or without 3–9x40 scope and with or without case; black stock with silver Cerakote barrel, with or without 3-9x40 scope and with or without case; black stock with blued barrel, scope, and with or without case; Youth model in all black
MSRP . . . . $219.00–$403.00

TRADITIONS FIREARMS BUCKSTALKER XT NORTHWEST MAGNUM

Lock: Hinged breech
Stock: Synthetic
Barrel: 24 in.
Sights: Fiber optic front, adjustable rear
Weight: 6 lb. 6 oz.
Bore/Caliber: .50
Features: Similar to the Buckstalker XT, but designed specifically for hunters in Idaho and Oregon who need an open breech, open sights, and musket ignition
MSRP $279.00

TRADITIONS FIREARMS PURSUIT XT

Lock: Hinged breech
Stock: Synthetic
Barrel: 26 in.
Sights: None
Weight: 5 lb. 12 oz.
Bore/Caliber: .50
Features: An upgrade to the current Pursuit G4 Ultralight series; VAPR Twist barrel; Elite XT trigger; chromoly barrel; 209 primer ignition; 200-plus yard accuracy; numerous stock and metal finish combinations, including Cerakote metalwork, wood stocks, and full-coverage camo, available with and without 3–9x40 factory mounted scope and with or without cases
MSRP . . . . $349.00–$553.00

TRADITIONS FIREARMS PURSUIT XT NORTHWEST MAGNUM, PURSUIT XT LDR NORTHWEST MAGNUM

Lock: Hinged breech
Stock: Synthetic
Barrel: 26 in., 30 in.
Sights: Fiber optic front, adjustable rear
Weight: 5 lb. 12 oz.
Bore/Caliber: .50
Features: Similar to the Pursuit XT, but designed specifically for hunters in Idaho and Oregon who need an open breech, open sights, and musket ignition; available in black or Realtree Edge stocks with gray Cerakote metalwork; LDR has a 30-in. barrel and comes with a black stock and grey Cerakote metalwork
MSRP . . . . $354.00–$399.00

TRADITIONS FIREARMS VORTEK STRIKERFIRE LDR

Lock: Strikerfire
Stock: Synthetic
Barrel: 30 in.
Sights: None
Weight: 6 lb. 8 oz.
Bore/Caliber: .50
Features: Made for long-distance muzzleloader shooting, out to 300 yards; TAC2 two-stage competition-type trigger; 3–9x40 scope; nitride finish on metalwork; Hogue overmolded grip panels; recoil-reducing buttstock and buttpad; chromoly tapered and fluted barrel; recessed decocking button; stock in Realtree Edge; available with or without case and scope
MSRP . . . . $524.00–$629.00

SCOPES

ACCUFIRE TECHNOLOGY INCENDIS THERMAL

ACCUFIRE TECHNOLOGY NOCTIS TR1

ACCUFIRE TECHNOLOGY PROSPECTIS ATRO-8

ACCUFIRE TECHNOLOGY PROSPECTIS ATRO-20

ACCUFIRE TECHNOLOGY PROSPECTIS EVRO-6

ACCUFIRE TECHNOLOGY PROSPECTIS EVRO-12

ARMAMENT TECHNOLOGY ELCAN SPECTERDR 1X/4X DUAL ROLE OPTIC

ACCUFIRE TECHNOLOGY INCENDIS THERMAL

Available in: 1–4X
Weight: 14.8 oz.
Length: 5.9 in.
Obj. Dia.: 30mm
Main Dia.: N/A
Exit Pupil: 20–15mm
Field of View: N/A
Eye Relief: N/A
Features: A thermal imaging scope with 1X, 2X, and 4X magnification; heat display in white hot, black hot, red accent, and green hot; focus-adjustable objective lens; can be used as a standalone scope, a handheld unit, and as a forward mounted aid
MSRP $2899.00

ACCUFIRE TECHNOLOGY NOCTIS TR1

Available in: 1–16x60mm
Weight: 36.4 oz.
Length: 14.7 in.
Obj. Dia.: 60mm
Main Dia.: N/A
Exit Pupil: N/A
Field of View: 31.2m@100m
Eye Relief: 2.4 in.
Features: A night vision scope in a traditional presentation; can be used with quick-detach and return-to-zero mounts; on-board ballistics calcuator; Wi-Fi streaming and gallery sends to Android and iOS devices; Accufire Smart Range Finder; HD recording and streaming; color correction technology; rechargeable lithium batteries; built-in microphone; multi-band coatings; multiple reticles and color schemes
MSRP $999.00

ACCUFIRE TECHNOLOGY PROSPECTIS ATRO-8

Available in: 1–8x24mm
Weight: 19.4 oz.
Length: 10.31 in.
Obj. Dia.: 24mm
Main Dia.: 30mm
Exit Pupil: N/A
Field of View: 105–14.3 ft.@100 yd.
Eye Relief: 3.21–3.3 in.
Features: Accufire CQB-Comp illuminated reticle in the first focal plane; locking turrets
MSRP $939.00

ACCUFIRE TECHNOLOGY PROSPECTIS ATRO-20

Available in: 2.5–29x50mm
Weight: 27.51 oz.
Length: 14.56 in.
Obj. Dia.: 50mm
Main Dia.: 34mm
Exit Pupil: N/A
Field of View: 40–6.2 ft.@100 yd.
Eye Relief: 3.22 in.
Features: Illuminated Tango-20 reticle in the first focal plane that appears as a simple crosshair at the lowest magnification; fast-mag lever; ZRT locking turrets
MSRP $1199.00

ACCUFIRE TECHNOLOGY PROSPECTIS EVRO-6

Available in: 1–6x24mm
Weight: 15.34 oz.
Length: 10.31 in.
Obj. Dia.: 24mm
Main Dia.: 30mm
Exit Pupil: N/A
Field of View: 112–19 ft.@100 yd.
Eye Relief: 3.85–5.35 in.
Features: Second focal plane illuminated reticle with 12 adjustment points; locking turrets; .5-MRAD clicks
MSRP $649.00

ACCUFIRE TECHNOLOGY PROSPECTIS EVRO-12

Available in: 3–12x50mm
Weight: 23.98 oz.
Length: 13.97 in.
Obj. Dia.: 50mm
Main Dia.: 30mm
Exit Pupil: N/A
Field of View: 30.53–8.13 ft.@100 yd.
Eye Relief: 2.83–3.54 in.
Features: Uncomplicated, non-illuminated mil-spec reticle in the first focal plane that offers precise shot placement; green glass coatings; fast-mag lever; locking turrets; intended for hunting applications
MSRP $479.00

ARMAMENT TECHNOLOGY ELCAN SPECTERDR 1X/4X DUAL ROLE OPTIC

Available in: 1X/4X
Weight: 23.2 oz.
Length: 6.02 in.
Obj. Dia.: N/A
Main Dia.: N/A
Exit Pupil: 8mm
Field of View: 48.8–11.4m@100m
Eye Relief: 2.75 in.
Features: Throw lever changes the optic from a 4X magnified sight to a 1X CQB sight—this is not a zoom and eye relief is identical between the two; choice of setup between 5.56 and 7.62 ballistic reticles, user-selected illumination for both crosshairs and the red dot; mounts on a Picatinny rail
MSRP $1925.00

ARMAMENT TECHNOLOGY ELCAN SPECTERDR 1.5X/6X

ARMAMENT TECHNOLOGY ELCAN SPECTERTR 1X/3X/9X

ARMAMENT TECHNOLOGY TANGENT THETA 3–15X50MM LONG RANGE HUNTER

ATHLON ARES ETR UHD

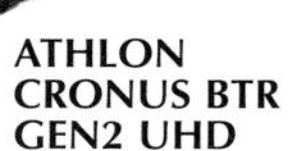
ATHLON CRONUS BTR GEN2 UHD

ATHLON HELOS BTR GEN2

ATHLON MIDAS TSP1

ARMAMENT TECHNOLOGY ELCAN SPECTERDR 1.5X/6X

Available in: 1.5X/6X
Weight: 24.86 oz.
Length: 7.2 in.
Obj. Dia.: N/A
Main Dia.: N/A
Exit Pupil: 7mm
Field of View: 28.7–7m@100m
Eye Relief: 2.75 in.
Features: Similar to the 1X/4X SpecterDR, but with larger magnification on both the low and high end; not a zoom, but two separate magnification levels accessed by the throw of a lever; choice of illuminated reticles calibrated for 5.56 or 7.62 NATO
MSRP $2250.00

ARMAMENT TECHNOLOGY ELCAN SPECTERTR 1X/3X/9X

Available in: 1X/3X/9X
Weight: 29.98 oz.
Length: 10.43 in.
Obj. Dia.: N/A
Main Dia.: N/A
Exit Pupil: 11.7mm
Field of View: 28.7m@100m
Eye Relief: 3 in.
Features: One more step up from the 1X/4X SpecterDR with three throw-lever magnification levels; 1X can provide both-eyes-open shooting; five illumination levels each for both the reticle and the red dot; Picatinny rail mounting; reticles available for either 5.56 or 7.62 NATO
MSRP $2049.00

ARMAMENT TECHNOLOGY TANGENT THETA 3–15X50MM LONG RANGE HUNTER

Available in: 3–15x50mm
Weight: 26.98 oz.
Length: 13.7 in.
Obj. Dia.: 50mm
Main Dia.: 30mm
Exit Pupil: N/A
Field of View: N/A
Eye Relief: N/A
Features: Illuminated reticle of a crosshair and auxiliary stadia lines in the first focal plane; no field of view occlusion in the shooting position; locking diopter; one-piece tube
MSRP $3729.00

ATHLON ARES ETR UHD

Available in: 1–10x24mm, 3–18x50mm, 4.5–30x56mm
Weight: 26.9 oz., 31.4 oz., 36.5 oz.
Length: 10 in., 14.2 in., 15.3 in.
Obj. Dia.: 24mm, 50mm, 56mm
Main Dia.: 34mm
Exit Pupil: N/A
Field of View: 117.3–11.7 ft.@100 yd., 39.2–6.65 ft.@100 yd., 24.5–3.75 ft.@100 yd.
Eye Relief: 3.7 in., 3.74 in., 3.9 in.
Features: These are first focal plane scopes with high-precision erector systems; extra-low dispersion glass; precision zero-stop turrets; locking windage turret; illuminated reticles in ATMR2 MOA, ATMR3 MIL, APLR2 MOA, APLR5 MOA, APRS1 MIL, and APRS6 MIL
MSRP . . . . $1139.99–$1499.99

ATHLON CRONUS BTR GEN2 UHD

Available in: 1–6x24mm, 4.5–29x56mm
Weight: 18.8 oz., 35.8 oz.
Length: 10.6 in., 14.4 in.
Obj. Dia.: 24mm, 56mm
Main Dia.: 34mm
Exit Pupil: 11.4–4mm, 8.8–1.9mm
Field of View: 106.9–17.7 ft.@100 yd., 24.8–3.83 ft.@100 yd.
Eye Relief: 3.6–4 in., 3.6–3.8 in.
Features: Extra-low dispersion glass; internal stainless steel-component turrets produce sharp, loud, and tactile clicks; true zero stop; reticles for both models are illuminated; XPL-coated exterior lenses
1–6X: $1249.99
4.5–29X: $1999.99

ATHLON HELOS BTR GEN2

Available in: 1–10x28mm, 2–12x42mm, 4–20x50mm, 6–24x56mm
Weight: 18.3 oz.–34.5 oz.
Length: 10.3 in., 11.8 in., 13.3 in., 14.3 in.
Obj. Dia.: 28mm, 42mm, 50mm, 56mm
Main Dia.: 30mm, 34mm
Exit Pupil: N/A
Field of View: 110–10 ft.@100 yd., 55.7–9.6 ft.@100 yd., 27.9–5.6 ft.@100 yd., 19.9–5.12 ft.@100 yd.
Eye Relief: 3.2 in., 3.6 in., 3.6 in., 3.7 in.
Features: Lenses with XPL external coatings; locking turrets; precision zero stop; heat-treated one-piece tube construction; all reticles are illuminated
MSRP . . . . $624.99–$749.99

ATHLON MIDAS TSP1

Available in: 1X
Weight: 6.25 oz.
Length: 2.7 in.
Obj. Dia.: 21mm
Main Dia.: N/A
Exit Pupil: N/A
Field of View: 66 ft.@100 yd.
Eye Relief: 3.2 in.
Features: Prism red-dot optic; can be used even when the batteries are dead and the etched-glass reticle unilluminated; when the TSP1 reticle is illuminated choice of red or green; Picatinny rail mount
MSRP $312.49

ATHLON MIDAS TSP3

Available in: 3X
Weight: 16 oz.
Length: 5.1 in.
Obj. Dia.: 28mm
Main Dia.: N/A
Exit Pupil: N/A
Field of View: 32.5 ft.@100 yd.
Eye Relief: 3.2 in.
Features: Prism optic of 3X with a TSP3 etched-glass reticle illuminated in selectable red or green; reticle is usable without illumination being activated
MSRP $324.99

ATHLON MIDAS TSP4

Available in: 3.9X
Weight: 16.8 oz.
Length: 5.7 in.
Obj. Dia.: 30mm
Main Dia.: N/A
Exit Pupil: N/A
Field of View: 24.9 ft.@100 yd.
Eye Relief: 3.1 in.
Features: Prism optic with a fixed 3.9X; etched-glass TSP4 reticle in selectable red or green illumination; Smart Power Management System
MSRP $337.49

ATN CORP. X-SIGHT LTV

Available in: 3–9X, 5–15X
Weight: 26.2 oz.–27.5 oz.
Length: 12.2 in., 13 in.
Obj. Dia.: N/A
Main Dia.: 30mm
Exit Pupil: N/A
Field of View: N/A
Eye Relief: 90mm
Features: A day/night scope with a One Shot Zero reticle; recoil-resistant hardened aluminum alloy construction; ATN Obsidian LT Core for ultra low-power consumption (10+ hours continuous use); 720P HD video recording; HD night vision mode; multiple reticle patterns to choose from
3–9X: $599.00
5–15X: $679.00

BURRIS THERMAL RIFLESCOPE

Available in: 1.7–6.8x35mm, 2.9–9.2x50mm
Weight: N/A
Length: N/A
Obj. Dia.: 35mm, 50mm
Main Dia.: N/A
Exit Pupil: N/A
Field of View: N/A
Eye Relief: N/A
Features: Thermal scope for rifle work with 10 reticle options; 7 color pallette settings; stadiametric ranging; adjustable brightness and contrast; hot track feature; one-hand operation; 400x300 resolution; manual focus
MSRP . . . . $3899.00–$4199.00

BUSHNELL AR OPTICS 1–6X24

Available in: 1–6x24mm
Weight: 16.5 oz.
Length: 10.2 in.
Obj. Dia.: 24mm
Main Dia.: 30mm
Exit Pupil: N/A
Field of View: 100–16 ft.@100 yd.
Eye Relief: 3.6 in.
Features: Illuminated BTR-1 reticle in the second focal plane; throw-down power lever for quick changes; capped turrets; IPX7 waterproof construction
MSRP $279.99

BUSHNELL BANNER 2

Available in: 3–9x40mm, 4–12x40mm, 3–9x50mm, 6–18x50mm
Weight: 16.5 oz.–21.6 oz.
Length: 12.3 in., 13.4 in., 13.5 in., 13 in.
Obj. Dia.: 40mm, 50mm
Main Dia.: 1 in.
Exit Pupil: N/A
Field of View: 37–12.2 ft.@100 yd., 27–9 ft.@100 yd., 33.6–10.4 ft.@100 yd., 17.3–6 ft.@100 yd.
Eye Relief: 3.5 in., 3.3 in., 3.5 in., 3.9 in.
Features: Second focal plane DOA QBR reticle; capped, non-locking turrets with 60 MOA windage/elevation adjustment; multicoated and ultra wideband coatings; EXO Barrier; IPX7 waterproofing; adjustable objective; aluminum body
MSRP . . . . $89.99–$139.99

BUSHNELL ELITE TACTICAL HDMR-II CR

Available in: 3.5–21x50mm
Weight: 37 oz.
Length: 13.2 in.
Obj. Dia.: 50mm
Main Dia.: 34mm
Exit Pupil: N/A
Field of View: 25–5 ft.@100 yd.
Eye Relief: 4 in.
Features: A close-range tactical scope with 33.5 Mils elevation travel; Horus H59 reticle in the first focal plane; 25-yd. parallax side focus; turrets with whole and half-Mil markings
MSRP $1299.99

BUSHNELL ENGAGE 1–4X24 ILLUMINATED GERMAN RETICLE

Available in: 1–4x24mm
Weight: 15.7 oz.
Length: 11.3 in.
Obj. Dia.: 24mm
Main Dia.: 30mm
Exit Pupil: N/A
Field of View: 84–24 ft.@100 yd.
Eye Relief: 3.9 in.
Features: One for close-quarters work with a second focal plane German No. 4 reticle with an illuminated center dot; generous 120 MOA windage/elevation adjustment; RevLimiter zero stop; Ultra Wideband coatings; EXO Barrier; IPX4 waterproofing; HDOS fully multicoated optic
MSRP $169.99

BUSHNELL ENGAGE 3–12X56 ILLUMINATED GERMAN RETICLE

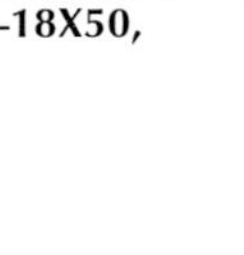

BUSHNELL LEGEND 3–9X40, 6–18X50, 4–12X40

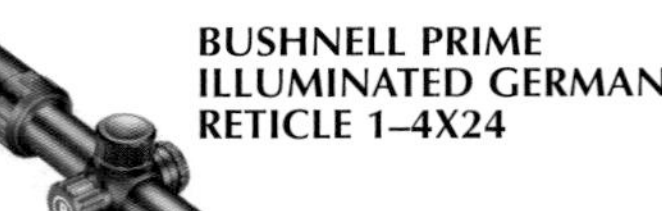

BUSHNELL PRIME ILLUMINATED GERMAN RETICLE 1–4X24

CRIMSON TRACE BRUSHLINE PRO

CRIMSON TRACE HARDLINE PRO

GPO SPECTRA 4X

GPO SPECTRA 5X

BUSHNELL ENGAGE 3–12X56 ILLUMINATED GERMAN RETICLE

Available in: 3–12x56mm
Weight: 25.8 oz.
Length: 15.5 in.
Obj. Dia.: 56mm
Main Dia.: 30mm
Exit Pupil: N/A
Field of View: 32.–8.5 ft.@100 yd.
Eye Relief: 3.9 in.
Features: German No. 4 reticle in the second focal plane has an illuminated centerpoint with 6 brightness levels; EXO Barrier; wide-band lens coatings; fast-focus eyepiece; capped turrets; 60 MOA elevation/windage adjustment
MSRP $199.99

BUSHNELL LEGEND 3–9X40, 6–18X50, 4–12X40

Available in: 3–9x40mm, 6–18x50mm, 4–12x40mm
Weight: 14.8 oz., 18.4 oz., 17.3 oz.
Length: 15.1 in., 12 in., 14.4 in.
Obj. Dia.: 40mm, 50mm, 40mm
Main Dia.: 1 in.
Exit Pupil: N/A
Field of View: N/A
Eye Relief: 3.5 in., 3.9 in., 3.9 in.
Features: Rainguard HD coating; choice of DOA QBR second focal plane reticle or illuminated Multi-X reticle second focal plane; aluminum body
MSRP . . . . $129.99–$224.95

BUSHNELL PRIME ILLUMINATED GERMAN RETICLE 1–4X24

Available in: 1–4x24mm
Weight: 16.5 oz.
Length: 9.2 in.
Obj. Dia.: 24mm
Main Dia.: 30mm
Exit Pupil: N/A
Field of View: 94.2–23.5 ft.@100 yd.
Eye Relief: 3.9 in.
Features: Illuminated German No. 4 reticle with an illuminated center dot in the second focal plane; CM-based, capped, non-locking turrets; 120 MOA of elevation/windage adjustment; IPX7 waterproofing; EXO. Barrier; ED Prime glass
MSRP $180.05

CRIMSON TRACE BRUSHLINE PRO

Available in: 2–7x32mm, 2.5–10x42mm, 3–9x40mm, 3–9x50mm, 3–12x42mm, 4–16x42mm, 4–16x50mm, 6–24x50mm
Weight: N/A
Length: N/A
Obj. Dia.: N/A
Main Dia.: 1 in., 30mm
Exit Pupil: N/A
Field of View: N/A
Eye Relief: N/A
Features: Designed for hunters, line has 24 models with second focal plane reticles (Plex, BDC, BDC Legend, BDC Rimfire, BDC Predator, BDC Muzzleloader); nitrogen purged; waterproof; lifetime guarantee
MSRP . . . . $199.99–$689.99

CRIMSON TRACE HARDLINE PRO

Available in: 1–6x24mm, 2–7x32mm, 3–9x40mm, 3–12x42mm, 4–12x40mm, 4–12x42mm, 4–16x50mm, 5–20x50mm, 6–24x50mm
Weight: N/A
Length: N/A
Obj. Dia.: N/A
Main Dia.: 30mm
Exit Pupil: N/A
Field of View: N/A
Eye Relief: N/A
Features: 23 variations in this new line, most with second focal plane reticles (MOA ILL, MIL ILL, BDC Comp, MR1-MOA, MR1-MIL, BDC Long-Range, BDC Carbine, BDC Blackout, Mildot) and a couple in the first focal plane (illuminated MOA ILL and MIL ILL); intended for target and tactical shooters; fully multicoated; nitrogen purged; lifetime warranty
MSRP . . . . $229.99–$899.99

GPO SPECTRA 4X

Available in: 2.5–10x44mm, 4–16x50mm
Weight: 21.9 oz.–24 oz.
Length: 13.3 in., 14.7 in.
Obj. Dia.: 44mm, 50mm
Main Dia.: 30mm
Exit Pupil: N/A
Field of View: 49.3 ft.@100 yd., 32.8 ft.@100 yd.
Eye Relief: 3.75mm
Features: Traditional G4 plex reticle; PASSIONtrac reset turrets; GPOBright lens coatings; DoubleHD objective lens technology; 2.5-10X available in standard or illuminated reticle, 4–12X with G4 illuminated or G4-Drop illuminated ballistic reticle; .1 MRAD turret clicks
MSRP . . . . $549.99–$749.99

GPO SPECTRA 5X

Available in: 3–15x56mm
Weight: 29.3 oz.
Length: 14.6 in.
Obj. Dia.: 56mm
Main Dia.: 30mm
Exit Pupil: N/A
Field of View: 34.7 ft.@100 yd.
Eye Relief: 3.75mm
Features: iControl illuminated G4 reticle; PASSIONtrac reset turrets; GPObright lens coatings; DoubleHD objective lens technology; removable magnification throw lever
MSRP $999.99

GPO SPECTRA 6X

GPO SPECTRA 8X

HAWKE SPORT OPTICS SIDEWINDER 30 SF

HAWKE SPORT OPTICS SIDEWINDER 30 FFP

HI-LUX PRECISION OPTICS WM. MALCOLM 6X TWO-TONE SHORT RIFLE TELESCOPE

KAHLES K521I DLR

KONUS EMPIRE

GPO SPECTRA 6X

Available in: 1–6x24mm, 1.5–9x32mm, 1.5–9x44mm, 2–12x44mm, 2–12x50mm, 3–18x56mm
Weight: 16.9 oz.–29.3 oz.
Length: 11.4 in.–14.6 in.
Obj. Dia.: 24mm, 32mm, 44mm, 50mm, 56mm
Main Dia.: 30mm
Exit Pupil: N/A
Field of View: 128–22 ft.@100 yd., 86–14 ft.@100 yd., 86–14 ft.@100 yd., 65–11 ft.@100 yd., 65–11 ft.@100 yd., 34–6 ft.@100 yd.
Eye Relief: 4mm, 3.75mm
Features: Illuminated G4-Drop reticle; PASSIONtrac reset turrets; GPObright lens coatings; DoubleHD objective lens technology; .1 MRAD clicks
MSRP . . . . $799.99–$1099.99

GPO SPECTRA 8X

Available in: 1–8x24mm, 2–16x44mm, 2.5–20x50mm
Weight: 17.8 oz.–25.3 oz.
Length: 10.1 in.–14.8 in.
Obj. Dia.: 24mm, 44mm, 50mm
Main Dia.: 30mm
Exit Pupil: N/A
Field of View: 123–15 ft.@100 yd., 59–8 ft.@100 yd., 48–6 ft.@100 yd.
Eye Relief: 3.5mm
Features: G4 illuminated reticles, and the 2–16X is also available in an illuminated BR reticle; PASSIONtrac reset turrets; GPObright lens coatings; DoubleHD objective lens technology; .1 MRAD
MSRP . . . . $1199.99–$1349.99

HAWKE SPORT OPTICS SIDEWINDER 30 SF

Available in: 4.5–14x44mm, 6.5–20x44mm, 4–16x50mm, 6–24x56mm, 8–32x56mm
Weight: 24 oz.–27.3 oz.
Length: 13.3 in.–15.5 in.
Obj. Dia.: 44mm, 50mm, 56mm
Main Dia.: 30mm
Exit Pupil: N/A
Field of View: 28.2–9ft.@100 yd., 19.5–6.3 ft.@100 yd., 31.8–8.1 ft.@100 yd., 21.3–5.4 ft.@100 yd., 15.9–3.9ft.@100 yd.
Eye Relief: 4 in.
Features: Second focal plane scopes; dual LED reticle illumination; mono-tube chassis; distortion-free low-dispersion crown glass; fully multicoated lenses (18 layers, ion-assisted); fast-focus eyebell with locking ring; side focus with removable index-matched side wheel; zoom magnification throw lever; exposed locking turrets with witness window
MSRP . . . . $619.00–$689.00

HAWKE SPORT OPTICS SIDEWINDER 30 FFP

Available in: 4–16x50mm, 6–24x56mm
Weight: 25.6 oz., 27.3 oz.
Length: 13.3 in., 14.3 in.
Obj. Dia.: 50mm, 56mm
Main Dia.: 30mm
Exit Pupil: N/A
Field of View: 31.8–8.1ft.@100 yd., 21.3–5.4 ft.@100 yd.
Eye Relief: 4 in.
Features: Dual LED reticle illumination; mono-tube chassis; distortion-free low-dispersion crown glass; fully multicoated lenses (18 layers, ion-assisted); fast-focus eyebell with locking ring; side focus with removable index-matched side wheel; zoom magnification throw lever; exposed locking turrets with witness window
MSRP . . . . $799.00–$819.00

HI-LUX PRECISION OPTICS WM. MALCOLM 6X TWO-TONE SHORT RIFLE TELESCOPE

Available in: 6X
Weight: 18 oz.
Length: 18 in.
Obj. Dia.: 17mm
Main Dia.: .75 in.
Exit Pupil: N/A
Field of View: 12 ft.@100 yd.
Eye Relief: 4 in.
Features: Gloss black and brass scope for a deserving vintage gun; clickless micrometer adjustment rear mount; fine cross reticle; sliding lock ring mitigates the impact of recoil to the scope and needs to be "reset to battery" after each shot
MSRP $450.00

KAHLES K521I DLR

Available in: 5–25x56mm
Weight: 35 oz.
Length: 14.8 in.
Obj. Dia.: 56mm
Main Dia.: 34mm
Exit Pupil: 9.5–2.3mm
Field of View: 7.7–1.6m@100m
Eye Relief: 3.7 in.
Features: Dynamic Long Range; extra-long throw lever; parallax spinner; illuminated SKMR4 reticle in the first focal plane; turrets with extra-large lettering and 100 clicks per rotation; optional left or right Twist Guard windage
MSRP $3549.00

KONUS EMPIRE

Available in: 3–18x50mm, 5–30x56mm
Weight: 26.8 oz., 34 oz.
Length: 14.68 in., 14.96 in.
Obj. Dia.: 50mm, 56mm
Main Dia.: 30mm
Exit Pupil: 8–3mm, 13–2mm
Field of View: 35–6.1 ft.@100 yd., 20.9–3 ft.@100 yd.
Eye Relief: 4 in.
Features: Lockable, zero-reset turrets, dual-color illuminated reticle; locking fast-focus eyepiece; 1/4-MOA clicks; level bubble; side knob has both parallax and illumination controls
MSRP $679.99

KONUS EVENT

KONUS GLORY

KONUS KONUSFIRE

LEICA AMPLUS 6

LEICA PRS

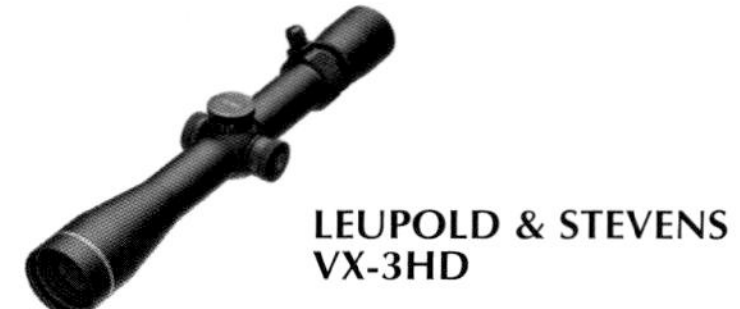
LEUPOLD & STEVENS VX-3HD

MARCH SCOPES MARCH 1.5–15X42MM SFF

KONUS EVENT

Available in: 1–10x24mm
Weight: 19.2 oz.
Length: 10.45 in.
Obj. Dia.: 24mm
Main Dia.: 30mm
Exit Pupil: 24–2.4mm
Field of View: 121.2–11.5 ft.@100 yd.
Eye Relief: 3.5–3.7 in.
Features: Removable zoom lever; lockable tactical turrets with zero reset; ½-MOA clicks; two-color illuminated reticle in a circle/dot configuration in the second focal plane; fully multi-coated lenses; fast-focus eyepiece
MSRP $649.99

KONUS GLORY

Available in: 3–24x56mm
Weight: 25.69 oz.
Length: 15 in.
Obj. Dia.: 56mm
Main Dia.: 30mm
Exit Pupil: 7.8–2.3mm
Field of View: 37.6–4.8 ft.@100 yd.
Eye Relief: 3.27–3.77 in.
Features: Constant long eye relief across the magnification spectrum; zero-reset locking turrets; removable zoom lever; redesigned erector system takes heavy recoil; side parallax wheel; illuminated reticle
MSRP $674.99

KONUS KONUSFIRE

Available in: 3–9x32mm
Weight: 12.6 oz.
Length: 12 in.
Obj. Dia.: 32mm
Main Dia.: 1 in.
Exit Pupil: 10.6–3.5mm
Field of View: 36.7–13.1 ft.@100 yd.
Eye Relief: 2.9 in.
Features: Scope for rimfire use with ¼-MOA clicks; coated optics; 30/30 reticle; .22 dovetail mounting rings included
MSRP $50.99

LEICA AMPLUS 6

Available in: 1–6x24mm, 2.5–15x50mm, 2.5–15x56mm
Weight: 16.9 oz., 24.7 oz., 28.7 oz.
Length: 10.7 in., 14.9 in.
Obj. Dia.: 24mm, 50mm, 56mm
Main Dia.: 30mm
Exit Pupil: 12.2–4.2mm, 11.6–3.4mm, 11.6–3.7mm
Field of View: 38–6.3m@100m, 15–2.8m@100m, 14.8–2.5m@100m
Eye Relief: 3.5 in.
Features: Leica says the 6X zoom is ideal when shots at running game are a probability; wide field of view and exit pupil; extra-fine illuminated dot L4-a reticle in the secondfocal plane; BDC option
MSRP . . . . $1199.00–$1599.00

LEICA PRS

Available in: 5–30x56mm
Weight: 36.3 oz.
Length: 14.37 in.
Obj. Dia.: 56mm
Main Dia.: 34mm
Exit Pupil: 9–2mm
Field of View: 8.2–1.3m@100m
Eye Relief: 3.5 in.
Features: Big heavy scope for long-range applications; L-4a, L-Ballistic, or L-PRB illuminated reticles in the first focal plane; sun shade, throw lever
MSRP $2699.00

LEUPOLD & STEVENS VX-3HD

Available in: 1.5–5x20mm, 2.5–8x36mm, 3.5–10x40mm, 3.5–10x50mm, 4.5–14x40mm, 4.5–14x50mm
Weight: 9.7 oz.–16.9 oz.
Length: N/A
Obj. Dia.: 20mm, 36mm, 40mm, 50mm
Main Dia.: 1 in., 30mm
Exit Pupil: N/A
Field of View: 19.9–7.4 ft.@100 yd., 37.5–13.7 ft.@100 yd., 29–11 ft.@100 yd., 29.7–11 ft.@100 yd., 19.9–7.4 ft.@100 yd., 20.5–7.6 ft.@100 yd.
Eye Relief: 3.6–4.4 in.
Features: CDS ZeroLock dial; Guard-Ion lens coating; Elite Optical System; removable throw lever; scratch-resistant lenses; second focal plane CDS-ZL Duplex reticle available in all models, CDS-ZL Boone & Crockett available in 4.5–14x40, and CDS-ZL Wind-Plex available in 4.5–14x40 Side Focus
MSRP . . . . $499.99–$749.99

MARCH SCOPES MARCH 1.5–15X42MM SFF

Available in: 1.5–15x42mm
Weight: 22 oz.
Length: 10.6 in.
Obj. Dia.: 42mm
Main Dia.: 30mm
Exit Pupil: 8.7–2.8mm
Field of View: 23.4–2.3m@100m
Eye Relief: 2.9–3.8 in.
Features: 10X zoom with a generous light-gathering objective; choice of MTR-3, MTR-4, or MTR-5 illuminated reticles in the second focal plane; ¼-MOA clicks; zero-reset turrets; fast-focus eyepiece; waterproof to 4 meters; designed for NRA's mid-range tactical rifle competitions
MSRP $2580.00

MARCH SCOPES MARCH-F 1–10X24MM SHORTY FFP

MARCH SCOPES MARCH-FX 4.5–28X52MM FFP WIDE ANGLE

MINOX 5–25X56MM LR

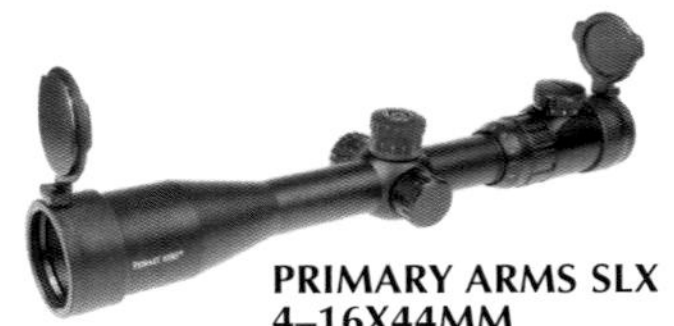
PRIMARY ARMS SLX 4–16X44MM

PULSAR DIGISIGHT ULTRA LRF N450, N455

PULSAR THERMION XM30

MARCH SCOPES MARCH-F 1–10X24MM SHORTY FFP

Available in: 1–10x24mm
Weight: 17.8 oz.
Length: 8.4 in.
Obj. Dia.: 24mm
Main Dia.: 30mm
Exit Pupil: 8.6–2.4mm
Field of View: 34–3.4m@100m
Eye Relief: 2.8–4 in.
Features: .1-Mil clicks; six illumination levels; capped tactical turrets; dual-reticle--both first and second focal plane reticles put together to produce the visible pattern; fast-focus eyepiece
MSRP $2650.00

MARCH SCOPES MARCH-FX 4.5–28X52MM FFP WIDE ANGLE

Available in: 4.5–28x52mm
Weight: 28.7 oz.–29.8 oz.
Length: 12.5 in.
Obj. Dia.: 52mm
Main Dia.: 34mm
Exit Pupil: 1.9mm
Field of View: 9.7–1.56m@100m
Eye Relief: 3.5–2.7 in.
Features: Super ED lenses with Anti-Temperature Drift lets the lens system naturally adapt to temperature change and maintain focus for the user; 25° wide-angle ocular; illuminated first focal plane reticles include FML-TR1 and FML-3 with six illumination levels; non-illuminated first focal plane reticles include FML-PDK and FML-LDK; throw lever; middle focus wheel; .1-Mil clicks
Non-illuminated: $3290.00
Illuminated: $3590.00

MINOX 5–25X56MM LR

Available in: 5–25x56mm
Weight: N/A
Length: 16.6 in.
Obj. Dia.: 56mm
Main Dia.: 34mm
Exit Pupil: 10.6–2.3mm
Field of View: 7.2–1.6m@100m
Eye Relief: 3.5 in.
Features: This is a big scope for long-range applications (thus the LR in the model name); M* multicoating; first focal plane LR illuminated reticle with 11 settings; IPX7 waterproof
MSRP $1999.00

PRIMARY ARMS SLX 4–16X44MM

Available in: 4–16x44mm
Weight: 25.4 oz.
Length: 14.3 in.
Obj. Dia.: 44mm
Main Dia.: 30mm
Exit Pupil: 11.2–3.3mm
Field of View: 27.2–7.85 ft.@100 yd.
Eye Relief: 3.22–3.14 in.
Features: HUD-308, RGRID, ARC-2-MOA, and Apollo illuminated reticles to choose from; first focal plane; side-adjustable parallax; fast-focus eyepiece
MSRP $159.99

PULSAR DIGISIGHT ULTRA LRF N450, N455

Available in: 4.5–18X
Weight: 38.8 oz.
Length: 14.56 in.
Obj. Dia.: N/A
Main Dia.: N/A
Exit Pupil: N/A
Field of View: N/A
Eye Relief: 1.96 in.
Features: Thermal imaging riflescope with 10 reticle shapes and 6 color choices; scalable ballistic reticles; zoom zeroing; 5 shooting profiles and 50 distance savings; can utilize the Stream Vision app for iOS and Android; extreme operating conditions from -25°C to +50°C; side incline and elevation angle sensor; long-range 850nm infrared illuminator wavelength for improved nighttime sensitivity on N450 model with a detection range of 550m; N455 has 940nm invisible infrared illumination wavelength with 500m detection; picture-in-picture; IPX7 waterproof; wide-angle eyepiece; Weaver rail mount; integrated video recorder
N450: $1599.99
N455: $1799.99

PULSAR THERMION XM30

Available in: 3.5–14x25mm
Weight: 26.5 oz.
Length: 15.2 in.
Obj. Dia.: 25mm
Main Dia.: N/A
Exit Pupil: N/A
Field of View: 45.9 ft.@100 yd.
Eye Relief: 2 in.
Features: Thermal imaging riflescope with 320x420 resolution; 1,400-yd. detection range; 8X digital zoom; picture-in-picture zoom; built-in recording with sound; one-shot zeroing with freeze function; 13 reticles; choice of identification modes; choice of viewing modes, including color; five hours of battery life; holds five rifle profiles and 50 zero points; stadiametric rangefinder
MSRP $2529.99

PULSAR TRAIL 2 LRF XP50, XQ50

RITON OPTICS PATRIOPTIC

SIGHTMARK CORE HX 3–9X40 VHR

SIGHTMARK WRAITHE 4K MAX 3–24X50MM

SIGHTMARK WRAITHE HD 2–16X28MM

SIGHTRON S-TAC 3–16X42FFP

PULSAR TRAIL 2 LRF XP50, XQ50

Available in: 2–16X, 3.5–14X
Weight: 28.21 oz.
Length: 13.6 in.
Obj. Dia.: N/A
Main Dia.: N/A
Exit Pupil: N/A
Field of View: N/A
Eye Relief: 1.96 in.
Features: A thermal imaging riflescope with a wide-angle six-lens eyepiece; AMOLED display; photo and video recorder with 16GB internal memory; 1,800m detection range; eight reticles customizable for color and scalable ballistic style; .03-second instant startup; recoil-rated up to .375 H&H/12-ga./9.3X64; stores five zeroing profiles; picture in picture display; Wi-Fi Stream Vision connectivity with iOS and Android smart devices; IPX7 waterproof; integrated laser rangefinder
XP50: $5999.97
XQ50: $4229.97

RITON OPTICS PATRIOPTIC

Available in: 1–8x28mm
Weight: 25 oz.
Length: 10.9 in.
Obj. Dia.: 28mm
Main Dia.: 34mm
Exit Pupil: 7.5–2.9mm
Field of View: 105.8–13.1 ft@100 yd.
Eye Relief: 3.5 in.
Features: An impressive field of view is complemented by zero-reset capped turrets; 175 MOA of adjustment; fully multi-coated, full wide-band and waterproof coatings; removable throw lever; first focal plane illuminated CM1 reticle in daylight green; fast-focus eyepiece
MSRP $1776.00

SIGHTMARK CORE HX 3–9X40 VHR

Available in: 3–9x40mm
Weight: 14.2 oz.
Length: 12.26 in.
Obj. Dia.: 40mm
Main Dia.: 1 in.
Exit Pupil: 13.3–4.4mm
Field of View: 11.8–4.07m@100m
Eye Relief: 4–3.7mm
Features: VHR stands for Venison Hunter Riflescope; rangefinding BDC reticle in the second focal plane; resettable capped turrets; hard anodized finish; 70 MOA of adjustment; also available with a .350 Legend 150-gr. BDC reticle or .450 Bushmaster 250-gr. BDC reticle
MSRP $159.99

SIGHTMARK WRAITHE 4K MAX 3–24X50MM

Available in: 3–24x50mm
Weight: 34.6 oz.
Length: 12 in.
Obj. Dia.: 50mm
Main Dia.: N/A
Exit Pupil: N/A
Field of View: 31.5 ft.@100 yd.
Eye Relief: 2.7 in.
Features: Ultra high-definition digital riflescope with a 4000x3000 CMOS sensor that picks up objects out to 300 yards at night; detachable 850nm infrared illuminator has a run time of 90 minutes on max; UHD 4K video recording with audio; 10 reticle options in nine colors; IPX5 water-resistant rating; rechargeable battery with eight-hour life
MSRP $999.96

SIGHTMARK WRAITHE HD 2–16X28MM

Available in: 2–16x28mm
Weight: 33.3 oz.
Length: 10 in.
Obj. Dia.: 28mm
Main Dia.: N/A
Exit Pupil: N/A
Field of View: 42 ft.@100 yd.
Eye Relief: 2.4 in.
Features: A night/day digital riflescope with an 850nm infrared illuminator; detection of objects out to 200 yards at night; black-and-white, green, or night and day color modes; aluminum body; 1080p HD video recording; 10 reticle options in nine colors; five firearm profile saves; IP55 water-resistant rating; 20ºF–122ºF operating range; includes fixed Picatinny mount and additional Weaver rail
MSRP $599.99

SIGHTRON S-TAC 3–16X42FFP

Available in: 3–16x42mm
Weight: 24.8 oz.
Length: 13.3 in.
Obj. Dia.: 42mm
Main Dia.: 30mm
Exit Pupil: N/A
Field of View: 29.2–6.1 ft.@100 yd.
Eye Relief: 4.1–3.6 in.
Features: Fast-focus eyepiece; resettable zero-stop turrets in ExacTrack .1 MRAD or MOA adjustment; pop-up zoom ring lever; Zact-7 Revcoat multicoating; illuminated MOA-5 or Mil-Hash-2 reticle in the first focal plane
MSRP $604.27

U.S. OPTICS TS SERIES

VORTEX OPTICS SPITFIRE HD GEN II 3X, 5X

U.S. OPTICS TS SERIES

Available in: 1–6x24mm, 1–8x24mm, 3–12x44mm, 2.5–20x50mm
Weight: 17.9 oz.–28.7 oz.
Length: 10.75 in., 10.5 in., 9.6 in., 14.64 in., 14.17 in.
Obj. Dia.: 24mm, 24mm, 44mm, 50mm, 50mm
Main Dia.: 30mm
Exit Pupil: 4mm, 3mm, 3mm, 2.5mm, 2mm
Field of View: N/A
Eye Relief: 2 in.
Features: First or second focal plane illuminated and non-illuminated reticles
MSRP. . . . . $545.00–$1595.00

VORTEX OPTICS SPITFIRE HD GEN II 3X, 5X

Available in: 3X, 5X
Weight: 9 oz., 10.3 oz.
Length: 3 in., 3.6 in.
Obj. Dia.: 21mm, 25mm
Main Dia.: N/A
Exit Pupil: N/A
Field of View: 37.9 ft.@100 yd., 23.3 ft.@100 yd.
Eye Relief: 2.6 in., 2.7 in.
Features: Small magnified optic intended for use with most 5.56 cartridges thanks to the illuminated AR-BDC4 reticle that includes holdovers to 600 yards; 12 brightness settings include two night vision settings; includes multi-height mounting system
3X: $549.99
5X: $649.99

RED-DOTS, REFLEX SIGHTS, AND RANGEFINDERS

AIMPOINT ACRO P-1

AIMPOINT COMPM5B

ARMAMENT TECHNOLOGY XOPTEK

ATHLON MIDAS LE

ATHLON MIDAS TSR1

AIMPOINT ACRO P-1

Type: Red-dot/reflex red-dot
Weight: 2.1 oz.
Length: 1.9 in.
Power: 1X
Obj. Dia.: N/A
Field of View: Unlimited
Eye Relief: Unlimited
Features: Reflex collimator sight with a 3.5 MOA red dot; lithium CR1225 battery; four night vision and six daylight settings; optimized for pistol use
MSRP. $599.99

AIMPOINT COMPM5B

Type: Red-dot/reflex red-dot
Weight: 9 oz.
Length: 3.3 in.
Power: 1X
Obj. Dia.: N/A
Field of View: N/A
Eye Relief: Unlimited
Features: Reflex dot for MSR-use with a 2 MOA red-dot; AAA battery; four night vision and six daylight illumination settings; 39mm spacer and LRP Lever Release Picatinny mount; flip-up lens covers; hard anodized non-reflective finish
MSRP. $1124.00

ARMAMENT TECHNOLOGY XOPTEK

Type: Red-dot/reflex red-dot
Weight: 1.3 oz.
Length: 1.8 in.
Power: 1X
Obj. Dia.: N/A
Field of View: N/A
Eye Relief: N/A
Features: With a 4 MOA red-dot, this super-micro reflex 60 MOA of adjustment; five illumination settings; Picatinny rail mount or Elcan SpecterDR mount; choice of 4 or 6 MOA with either mount option
MSRP. $399.00

ATHLON MIDAS LE

Type: Red-dot/reflex red-dot
Weight: 2.8 oz.
Length: 3.55 in.
Power: 1X
Obj. Dia.: 28x36mm
Field of View: N/A
Eye Relief: N/A
Features: Intended for close-range engagements; LE reticle of an illuminated circle and dot
MSRP. $312.49

ATHLON MIDAS TSR1

Type: Red-dot/reflex red-dot
Weight: 2.8 oz.
Length: 1.88 in.
Power: 1X
Obj. Dia.: 24x17mm
Field of View: N/A
Eye Relief: Unlimited
Features: 3 MOA dot; can be used on guns with slide cuts and mounting plates by removing the Picatinny rail mount
MSRP. $287.49

ATHLON MIDAS TSR2

ATHLON MIDAS TSR3

BLASER RD20

BUSHNELL BONE COLLECTOR 850 LRF REALTREE EDGE

BUSHNELL RXS-100

BUSHNELL RXS-250

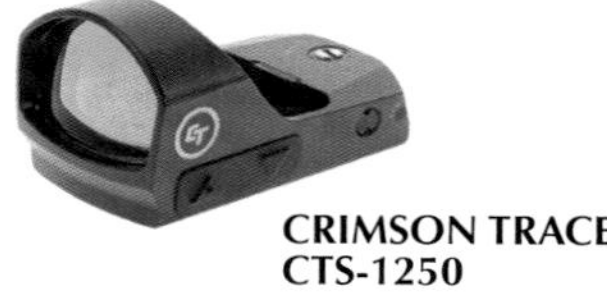

CRIMSON TRACE CTS-1250

CRIMSON TRACE CTS-1550

ATHLON MIDAS TSR2

Type: Red-dot/reflex red-dot
Weight: 6.7 oz.
Length: 2.8 in.
Power: 1X
Obj. Dia.: 20mm
Field of View: N/A
Eye Relief: Unlimited
Features: 2 MOA red dot in a more conventional tubed body; fully multicoated glass; Smart Power Management System sends the unit to sleep after five minutes of no activity
MSRP $212.49

ATHLON MIDAS TSR3

Type: Red-dot/reflex red-dot
Weight: 10.6 oz.
Length: 3.7 in.
Power: 1X
Obj. Dia.: 36mm
Field of View: N/A
Eye Relief: Unlimited
Features: A good choice for PPC competition or game and predator hunting, with a 2 MOA red dot that has 10 daylight settings and three night vision settings; motion activation sensor
MSRP $249.99

BLASER RD20

Type: Red-dot/reflex red-dot
Weight: 6.8 oz.
Length: 3.85 in.
Power: 1X
Obj. Dia.: 36mm
Field of View: N/A
Eye Relief: Unlimited
Features: Developed for Blaser's own rifles, this red-dot optic has scratch-resistant lenses; Intelligent Illumination Control with 30 settings; power-saving mode; Blaser saddle mount; 2 MOA dot
MSRP $873.89

BUSHNELL BONE COLLECTOR 850 LRF REALTREE EDGE

Type: Rangefinder
Weight: 6.34 oz.
Length: 4.3 in.
Power: 6X24mm
Obj. Dia.: 24mm
Field of View: N/A
Eye Relief: N/A
Features: Range up to 850 yards or meters; 3-volt CR2 battery; ARC mode; IPX4 water resistance; all-glass optical system; fast-ranging scan mode; includes leather lanyard and battery
MSRP $139.99

BUSHNELL RXS-100

Type: Red-dot/reflex red-dot
Weight: 1.3 oz.
Length: 1.8 in.
Power: 1X
Obj. Dia.: N/A
Field of View: N/A
Eye Relief: Unlimited
Features: Ultralight micro reflex with a 4 MOA dot and eight brightness settings; side battery door; CR2032 battery; Weaver-style low-rise mount included; can be used on pistols, MSRs, and shotguns
MSRP $99.99

BUSHNELL RXS-250

Type: Red-dot/reflex red-dot
Weight: 1.4 oz.
Length: 1.8 oz.
Power: 1X
Obj. Dia.: N/A
Field of View: N/A
Eye Relief: Unlimited
Features: 4 MOA red-dot reflex has 10 brightness settings; CR2032 battery; 12-hour auto-shutoff with no button pressed; IPX7 water resistant; Weaver-style mount included and will mount to a Deltapoint Pro standard plate; 1 MOA clicks; chamfered hood edges help prevent snags
MSRP $249.99

CRIMSON TRACE CTS-1250

Type: Red-dot/reflex red-dot
Weight: 1 oz.
Length: 1.8 in.
Power: 1X
Obj. Dia.: N/A
Field of View: N/A
Eye Relief: Unlimited
Features: With a bigger 3.25 MOA red dot; seven daylight and three night settings; 1 MOA clicks; fully multi-coated lens; industry standard mounting interface for pistols
MSRP $199.99

CRIMSON TRACE CTS-1550

Type: Red-dot/reflex red-dot
Weight: N/A
Length: N/A
Power: 1X
Obj. Dia.: N/A
Field of View: N/A
Eye Relief: Unlimited
Features: 3 MOA red dot; underside battery compartment allows for co-witnessing iron sights; industry-standard mounting interface; ambient light sensor automatically adjusts dot brightness; coated lenses; designed for compact and subcompact pistols
MSRP $139.99

CRIMSON TRACE RAD MAX, RAD MAX PRO

CRIMSON TRACE RAD MICRO

CRIMSON TRACE RAD MICRO PRO

CRIMSON TRACE RAD PRO

EOTECH HWS 300

EOTECH HWS 518

EOTECH HWS 552

EOTECH HWS 558

EOTECH HWS EXPS2

CRIMSON TRACE RAD MAX, RAD MAX PRO

Type: Red-dot/reflex red-dot
Weight: 0.5 oz.
Length: N/A
Power: 1X
Obj. Dia.: N/A
Field of View: N/A
Eye Relief: Unlimited
Features: 3.25 MOA red dot; utilizes Picatinny rail mount; 10 brightness levels
RAD Max: $329.99
RAD Max Pro: $449.99

CRIMSON TRACE RAD MICRO

Type: Red-dot/reflex red-dot
Weight: N/A
Length: N/A
Power: 1X
Obj. Dia.: N/A
Field of View: N/A
Eye Relief: Unlimited
Features: Rapid Aiming Dot; super-compact reflex sight with 3 MOA red dot; aerograde aluminum construction; ambient light sensor; high efficiency LED battery; bottom positioned battery access
MSRP $229.99

CRIMSON TRACE RAD MICRO PRO

Type: Red-dot/reflex red-dot
Weight: 0.3 oz.
Length: N/A
Power: 1X
Obj. Dia.: N/A
Field of View: N/A
Eye Relief: Unlimited
Features: 3 MOA red dot
MSRP $279.99

CRIMSON TRACE RAD PRO

Type: Red-dot/reflex red-dot
Weight: N/A
Length: N/A
Power: 1X
Obj. Dia.: N/A
Field of View: N/A
Eye Relief: Unlimited
Features: Top-accessible battery compartment; CR1632 battery; shake-to-wake function; sleep function; large operating buttons for brightness; includes low-mount Picatinny; snag-free design
MSRP $349.99

EOTECH HWS 300

Type: Red-dot/reflex red-dot
Weight: 9 oz.
Length: 3.8 in.
Power: 1X
Obj. Dia.: N/A
Field of View: N/A
Eye Relief: Unlimited
Features: Holographic sight employs a 2-dot ballistic drop reticle in red; 20 brightness settings; designed for .300 BLK use
MSRP $585.00

EOTECH HWS 518

Type: Red-dot/reflex red-dot
Weight: 11.5 oz.
Length: 5.6 in.
Power: 1X
Obj. Dia.: N/A
Field of View: N/A
Eye Relief: Unlimited
Features: Uses two AA batteries; one- or two-dot 68 MOA reticle models available, both in red
MSRP $575.00

EOTECH HWS 552

Type: Red-dot/reflex red-dot
Weight: 11.5 oz.
Length: 5.6 in.
Power: 1X
Obj. Dia.: N/A
Field of View: N/A
Eye Relief: Unlimited
Features: EoTech calls this an "operator grade" sight, and it's night-vision compatible; uses two AA batteries; 20 daylight settings with 10 additional settings for Gen1-Gen3 night vision devices; utilizes the 68 MOA 1-dot reticle in red
MSRP $605.00

EOTECH HWS 558

Type: Red-dot/reflex red-dot
Weight: 13.8 oz.
Length: 5.6 in.
Power: 1X
Obj. Dia.: N/A
Field of View: N/A
Eye Relief: Unlimited
Features: A night-vision compatible holographic sight with a quick-release locking mount; compatible with Gen1-Gen3 night vision devices; 20 daylight settings and 10 nighttime; uses 2 AA batteries
MSRP $675.00

EOTECH HWS EXPS2

Type: Red-dot/reflex red-dot
Weight: 11.2 oz.
Length: 3.8 in.
Power: 1X
Obj. Dia.: N/A
Field of View: N/A
Eye Relief: Unlimited
Features: Allows for cowitnessing of iron sights; locking, quick-detach lever; side buttons allow addition of magnifier; two-dot 68 MOA reticle has a center dot for 50- and 200-yard use, a second dot below that for 500-yard use, and the bottom post for 7 yards, while the 68 MOA reticle design with a 1 MOA dot is useful at 7, 50, and 200 yards, both designed for use with a 62-gr. .223 round at 2,900 fps; both reticles are red, have 20 brightness settings
MSRP $619.00

EOTECH HWS EXPS2 GREEN

EOTECH HWS XPS2

EOTECH HWS XPS3

FIREFIELD IMPACT MINI

HAWKE SPORT OPTICS ENDURANCE

HAWKE SPORT OPTICS MICRO REFLEX

HAWKE SPORT OPTICS REFLEX WIDE VIEW

HAWKE SPORT OPTICS VANTAGE

EOTECH HWS EXPS2 GREEN

Type: Red-dot/reflex red-dot
Weight: 9 oz.
Length: 3.8 in.
Power: 1X
Obj. Dia.: N/A
Field of View: N/A
Eye Relief: Unlimited
Features: 68 MOA reticle design, with a 1 MOA dot useful at 7, 50, and 200 yards with a 62-gr. .223 round at 2,900 fps; CR123 battery; 20 daylight settings; .5 MOA adjustments
MSRP $685.00

EOTECH HWS XPS2

Type: Red-dot/reflex red-dot
Weight: 9 oz.
Length: 3.8 in.
Power: 1X
Obj. Dia.: N/A
Field of View: N/A
Eye Relief: Unlimited
Features: 68 MOA reticle design, with a 1 MOA dot useful at 7, 50, and 200 yards with a 62-gr. .223 round at 2,900 fps; CR123 battery; 20 daylight settings; .5 MOA adjustments
MSRP $685.00

EOTECH HWS XPS3

Type: Red-dot/reflex red-dot
Weight: 9 oz.
Length: 3.8 in.
Power: 1X
Obj. Dia.: N/A
Field of View: N/A
Eye Relief: Unlimited
Features: Night-vision compatible holographic sight; works with Gen1-Gen3 night vision devices; CR123 battery; 20 daylight settings and 10 nighttime; offered in one- or two-dot 68 MOA reticle in red
MSRP $675.00

FIREFIELD IMPACT MINI

Type: Red-dot/reflex red-dot
Weight: 1 oz.
Length: 1.9 in.
Power: 1X
Obj. Dia.: 16x21mm
Field of View: N/A
Eye Relief: Unlimited
Features: Very small reflex red-dot mounts to Weaver or Picatinny rail; generous 120 MOA windage/elevation adjustment; aluminum housing; AR Red lens coating; CR1632 battery; 5 MOA dot
MSRP $46.97

HAWKE SPORT OPTICS ENDURANCE

Type: Red-dot/reflex red-dot
Weight: 6.5 oz., 8.5 oz.
Length: 2.8 in., 3.5 in.
Power: 1X
Obj. Dia.: 25mm, 30mm
Field of View: N/A
Eye Relief: Unlimited
Features: "Old-school" style tubular red-dot optics; 25-layer multicoated glass; 3 MOA dot in red with eight brightness settings; high quick-release and low Weaver mounts; standby mode after five minutes of no movement; in 1X25 and 1X30
MSRP $189.00

HAWKE SPORT OPTICS MICRO REFLEX

Type: Red-dot/reflex red-dot
Weight: 2.5 oz.
Length: 1.9 in.
Power: 1X
Obj. Dia.: N/A
Field of View: N/A
Eye Relief: Unlimited
Features: Reflex red-dot sight available in 3 MOA or 5 MOA dot; 1 MOA clicks; Weaver rail mount; standby mode after five minutes of no movement; 25 layers of multicoating
3 MOA: $139.00
5 MOA: $249.00

HAWKE SPORT OPTICS REFLEX WIDE VIEW

Type: Red-dot/reflex red-dot
Weight: 3 oz.
Length: 2.3 in.
Power: 1X
Obj. Dia.: N/A
Field of View: N/A
Eye Relief: Unlimited
Features: 25-layer multicoated glass; 3 MOA dot in red with eight brightness settings; Weaver mounts; standby mode after five minutes of no movement
MSRP $159.00

HAWKE SPORT OPTICS VANTAGE

Type: Rangefinder
Weight: 6 oz.
Length: 3.8 in.
Power: 6X21mm
Obj. Dia.: 21mm
Field of View: 420 ft.@100 yd.
Eye Relief: .7 in.
Features: Wide-angle optical system; fully multi-coated glass/BK-7 prism; adjustable diopter; LCD displays distance, horizontal distance, angle compensation, rain, and hunt modes; auto shut-off mode; three models range 400m, 600m, or 900m
400m: $219.00
600m: $239.00
900m: $259.00

HI-LUX PRECISION OPTICS MAX TAC DOT (MTD-30)

HI-LUX PRECISION OPTICS MM-2

HI-LUX PRECISION OPTICS TD-3

HOLOSUN HE407C-GR X2

HOLOSUN HE507C-GR X2, HS507C X2

HOLOSUN HE508T-GR X2, HE508T-RD X2

HOLOSUN HE509T-RD

HOLOSUN HE512C-GD, HS512C

HI-LUX PRECISION OPTICS MAX TAC DOT (MTD-30)

Type: Red-dot/reflex red-dot
Weight: 8.9 oz.
Length: 3.9 in.
Power: 1X
Obj. Dia.: 30mm
Field of View: N/A
Eye Relief: Unlimited
Features: A slim and super-rugged tubular red dot; 4 MOA red dot; fully multi-coated lenses; Picatinny mount is machined into the housing
MSRP $120.00

HI-LUX PRECISION OPTICS MM-2

Type: Red-dot/reflex red-dot
Weight: 3.8 oz.
Length: 2.5 in.
Power: 1X
Obj. Dia.: 20mm
Field of View: N/A
Eye Relief: Unlimited
Features: Collimator reflex red-dot sight that comes with a low mount; glass coatings reduce glare; co-witness lower 1/3 or AR riser is included; 2 MOA dot
MSRP $229.00

HI-LUX PRECISION OPTICS TD-3

Type: Red-dot/reflex red-dot
Weight: 2 oz.
Length: 1.78 in.
Power: 1X
Obj. Dia.: 28x19mm
Field of View: N/A
Eye Relief: Unlimited
Features: Reflex sight intended for mounting on optics-ready slide cuts; 1 MOA clicks; lowest two brightness settings are night-vision compatible
MSRP $239.00

HOLOSUN HE407C-GR X2

Type: Red-dot/reflex red-dot
Weight: 1.5 oz.
Length: 1.78 in.
Power: 1X
Obj. Dia.: .63x.91 in.
Field of View: N/A
Eye Relief: Unlimited
Features: Same as the HS407C X2, but with a green 2 MOA dot
MSRP $299.99

HOLOSUN HE507C-GR X2, HS507C X2

Type: Red-dot/reflex red-dot
Weight: 1.5 oz.
Length: 1.78 in.
Power: 1X
Obj. Dia.: .63x.91 in.
Field of View: N/A
Eye Relief: Unlimited
Features: Open reflex with a lock mode that prevents the activation buttons from changing settings if accidentally depressed; Solar Failsafe design; Shake Awake function; Multi-reticle system of a 32 MOA circle with a 2 MOA dot that can be used together or separately; Super LED display; model with GR in the name is green, the other is red
Red: $364.69
Green: $399.00

HOLOSUN HE508T-GR X2, HE508T-RD X2

Type: Red-dot/reflex red-dot
Weight: 2 oz.
Length: 1.78 in.
Power: 1X
Obj. Dia.: .63x.91 in.
Field of View: N/A
Eye Relief: Unlimited
Features: Reflex with titanium housing instead of aluminum; Solar Failsafe function; Shake Awake function, Super Led 2 MOA dot in a 32 MOA circle in choice of green or red, and the Multiple Reticle System allows the user to use circle and dot together or separately
Red: $435.28
Green: $470.58

HOLOSUN HE509T-RD

Type: Red-dot/reflex red-dot
Weight: 1.72 oz.
Length: 1.6 in.
Power: 1X
Obj. Dia.: .63x.91 in.
Field of View: N/A
Eye Relief: Unlimited
Features: Enclosed reflex sight with titanium housing; Solar Failsafe feature; Shake Awake feature; Super LED Multiple Reticle System with a 32 MOA circle and 2 MOA dot, all in red, that can be used together or individually
MSRP $506.00

HOLOSUN HE512C-GD, HS512C

Type: Red-dot/reflex red-dot
Weight: 8.1 oz.
Length: 3.35 in.
Power: 1X
Obj. Dia.: .91x1.26 in.
Field of View: N/A
Eye Relief: Unlimited
Features: Intended for carbine and rifle applications; enclosed reflex sight; Holosun's Gold Super LED display; Shake Awake function; Solar Failsafe function; Multiple reticle system with a 65 MOA circle and a 2 MOA dot, choice of gold or red, that can be used together or each element separately; Gold model number ends in "GD"
Red: $423.52
Gold: $458.81

HOLOSUN HE512T-RD, HE512T-GR

HOLOSUN HS407C X2, HS407CO X2

HOLOSUN HS407K X2

HOLOSUN HS507K X2

LEAPERS UTG OP3 SL, SLS

LEUPOLD & STEVENS DELTAPOINT MICRO

LEUPOLD & STEVENS DELTAPOINT PRO 6 MOA

LEUPOLD & STEVENS RX-1400I TBR/W

HOLOSUN HE512T-RD, HE512T-GR

Type: Red-dot/reflex red-dot
Weight: 9.1 oz.
Length: 3.35 in.
Power: 1X
Obj. Dia.: .91x1.26 in.
Field of View: N/A
Eye Relief: Unlimited
Features: Enclosed reflex has a titanium housing; Solar Failsafe function; Shake Awake function; Super LED display; Multiple Reticle System with a 65 MOA circle and a 2 MOA dot, available in choice of red or green; that can be used together or each element separately; multilayer reflective glass; RD model is red, GR model is green
Red:. $588.22
Green:. $623.52

HOLOSUN HS407C X2, HS407CO X2

Type: Red-dot/reflex red-dot
Weight: 1.5 oz.
Length: 1.78 in.
Power: 1X
Obj. Dia.: .63x.91 in.
Field of View: N/A
Eye Relief: Unlimited
Features: A reflex sight with multilayer glass coatings; shake-awake feature; Solar Failsafe; red 2 MOA dot; 10 daylight settings and two nighttime; 1 MOA clicks; CO X2 model has a an 8 MOA open circle red dot
HS407C X2: $282.34
HS407CO X2:. $317.64

HOLOSUN HS407K X2

Type: Red-dot/reflex red-dot
Weight: 1 oz.
Length: 1.6 in.
Power: 1X
Obj. Dia.: .58x.77 in.
Field of View: N/A
Eye Relief: Unlimited
Features: 6 MOA red dot; Shake Awake; Super LED; multilayer reflective glass; 10 daylight and two nighttime brightness settings
MSRP $258.81

HOLOSUN HS507K X2

Type: Red-dot/reflex red-dot
Weight: 1 oz.
Length: 1.6 in.
Power: 1X
Obj. Dia.: .58x.77 in.
Field of View: N/A
Eye Relief: Unlimited
Features: Super small reflex with Shake Awake function; multi-reticle system has red 32 MOA circle with a 2 MOA dot, both in red only, that can be used together or each element separately
MSRP $341.16

LEAPERS UTG OP3 SL, SLS

Type: Red-dot/reflex red-dot
Weight: 1.81 oz.
Length: 1.89 in.
Power: 1X
Obj. Dia.: N/A
Field of View: N/A
Eye Relief: Unlimited
Features: An IPSX7 waterproof-rated reflex red-dot with an aluminum housing; 1 MOA clicks; removable low-profile Picatinny base; can co-witness with suppressor-height iron sights; side-loading battery compartment; 4 MOA dot with eight brightness settings; compatible with most optics-ready pistols; SLS model has additional Surrounding Light Sensor that can automatically brighten/dampen dot intensity
SL: $159.97
SLS: $169.97

LEUPOLD & STEVENS DELTAPOINT MICRO

Type: Red-dot/reflex red-dot
Weight: 1.1 oz.
Length: N/A
Power: 1X
Obj. Dia.: N/A
Field of View: N/A
Eye Relief: Unlimited
Features: A very low-profile and concealable red-dot that's the same height as most factory iron sights; fully enclosed design; 3 MOA dot; CR1632 battery; eight illumination settings with night vision-compatible illumination; currently available for Glock and S&W M&P pistols
MSRP $399.99

LEUPOLD & STEVENS DELTAPOINT PRO 6 MOA

Type: Red-dot/reflex red-dot
Weight: 2 oz.
Length: N/A
Power: 1X
Obj. Dia.: N/A
Field of View: N/A
Eye Relief: Unlimited
Features: Designed for competitors and personal-defense, the large 6 MOA red dot is appropriate for close-quarters engagements; motion sensor technology; in black or flat dark earth; daylight bright illumination with eight settings
Black:. $399.99
Flat Dark Earth: $449.99

LEUPOLD & STEVENS RX-1400I TBR/W

Type: Rangefinder
Weight: 5.1 oz.
Length: 4 in.
Power: 5X21mm
Obj. Dia.: 21mm
Field of View: 368 ft.@1000 yd.
Eye Relief: 18.3 mm
Features: True Ballistic Range/Wind (TBR/W) for firearm use; bow mode; line of sight; last target mode; TOLED display; max ranging capability 1400 yds.
MSRP $199.99

NEWCON OPTIK LRM 3500M 35BT, 35C

NEWCON OPTIK NC 4X32

NEWCON OPTIK NC 6X50

NEWCON OPTIK NC BURD

PRIMARY ARMS SLX ADVANCED PUSH-BUTTON MICRO RED DOT GENII

PRIMARY ARMS SLX MD-25

RITON OPTICS X3 TACTIX MPRD

SIGHTMARK ELEMENT MINI SOLAR RED-DOT

NEWCON OPTIK LRM 3500M 35BT, 35C

Type: Rangefinder
Weight: 16.2 oz.
Length: 4.6 in.
Power: 6.5X
Obj. Dia.: 30mm
Field of View: N/A
Eye Relief: .78 in.
Features: Usable to 6,000m; viewable in yards or meters; compass; inclinometer; scan mode; last 10 readings recall; distance and horizontal distance between targets; height difference between targets; inclination difference between targets; target GPS coordinates (35BT only); customized Matrix Red OLED display; USB and Bluetooth ports; communication with Newcon's NC Cronus app; Kestral ballistics calculator
MSRP $6235.00

NEWCON OPTIK NC 4X32

Type: Red-dot/reflex red-dot
Weight: 16.47 oz.
Length: 5.39 in.
Power: 4X
Obj. Dia.: 32mm
Field of View: N/A
Eye Relief: 2.83 in.
Features: Holographic sight with illuminated reticle in user-selectable red or green; Picatinny mount and topside rail; night vision/thermal compatible
MSRP $565.00

NEWCON OPTIK NC 6X50

Type: Red-dot/reflex red-dot
Weight: 20.56 oz.
Length: 6.61 in.
Power: 6X
Obj. Dia.: 50mm
Field of View: N/A
Eye Relief: 2.83 in.
Features: Holographic sight with illuminated BDC rangefinding reticle in user-selectable red or green; Designed to take heavy recoil; Picatinny mount and topside rail
MSRP $767.00

NEWCON OPTIK NC BURD

Type: Red-dot/reflex red-dot
Weight: 2.2 oz.
Length: 1.8 in.
Power: 1X
Obj. Dia.: N/A
Field of View: N/A
Eye Relief: Unlimited
Features: Intended as back-up red-dot for CQB engagements; can be used on rifles, shotguns, and optics-ready pistols; side-loading battery compartment; integrates with Newcon's NC 4X32 and 6X50 optics; infrared compatible; adjustable LED; Picatinny mount
MSRP $403.00

PRIMARY ARMS SLX ADVANCED PUSH-BUTTON MICRO RED DOT GENII

Type: Red-dot/reflex red-dot
Weight: 3.8 oz.
Length: N/A
Power: 1X
Obj. Dia.: N/A
Field of View: N/A
Eye Relief: Unlimited
Features: Redesigned body has low-profile shield adjustment turrets; night-vision compatible; true daylight bright settings; 12 illumination settings; ½ MOA clicks; 2 MOA red dot
MSRP $149.99

PRIMARY ARMS SLX MD-25

Type: Red-dot/reflex red-dot
Weight: 6.5 oz.
Length: N/A
Power: 1X
Obj. Dia.: N/A
Field of View: N/A
Eye Relief: Unlimited
Features: Super-compact tubular-designed red-dot with 12 brightness settings; night-vision compatible; aluminum housing; 2 MOA dot; ½ MOA clicks
MSRP $169.99

RITON OPTICS X3 TACTIX MPRD

Type: Red-dot/reflex red-dot
Weight: 0.6 oz.
Length: 1.6 in.
Power: 1X
Obj. Dia.: N/A
Field of View: N/A
Eye Relief: Unlimited
Features: 10 levels of illumination, night-vision compatible on levels 1 and 2; water/fog/shock proof; CR2032 battery; 3 MOA red dot; 1 MOA clicks; optics ready footprint is S&W Shield RMSc-type
MSRP $299.99

SIGHTMARK ELEMENT MINI SOLAR RED-DOT

Type: Red-dot/reflex red-dot
Weight: 5.5 oz.
Length: 2.96 in.
Power: 1X
Obj. Dia.: 22mm
Field of View: N/A
Eye Relief: Unlimited
Features: Solar power or CR2032 battery; recoil rated to .338 Win. Mag.; AR Red lens coating; IP67 waterproof rating; 120 MOA elevation, 160 windage adjustable; 1 MOA click; adjustable mounting height; Eclipse light management system; 3 MOA dot; hinged battery door
MSRP $239.99

NEW Products: Optics

SIGHTMARK MINI SHOT A-SPEC M1 GREEN, RED

SIGHTMARK ULTRA SHOT M-SPEC FMS, LDS

TRIJICON MRO HD

TRIJICON RMRCC RED-DOT

VORTEX OPTICS RAZOR HD 4000

VORTEX OPTICS SPARC SOLAR

CRIMSON TRACE CMR-301 RAIL MASTER PRO

HIVIZ LITEWAVE H3 COMPSIGHT

SIGHTMARK MINI SHOT A-SPEC M1 GREEN, RED

Type: Red-dot/reflex red-dot
Weight: 2.3 oz.
Length: 1.85 in.
Power: 1X
Obj. Dia.: 22x17mm
Field of View: N/A
Eye Relief: Unlimited
Features: Green or red 2 MOA illuminated dot; aluminum alloy housing; parallax free; 10 brightness levels; 110 MOA adjustment
MSRP $119.99

SIGHTMARK ULTRA SHOT M-SPEC FMS, LDS

Type: Red-dot/reflex red-dot
Weight: 9.6 oz.
Length: 4.01 in.
Power: 1X
Obj. Dia.: 33x24mm
Field of View: N/A
Eye Relief: Unlimited
Features: 12-hour auto shut-off; 10 brightness settings with two night vision settings at the lower end; fixed Picatinny mount on FMS model, quick-detach locking Picatinny mount on the LQD model; integrated sunshade; magnesium housing; parallax free; scratch-resistant lens coating; 120 MOA adjustment; AR Red lens coating
FMS: $239.99
LQD: $299.99

TRIJICON MRO HD

Type: Red-dot/reflex red-dot
Weight: 4.6 oz.
Length: 2.9 in.
Power: 1X
Obj. Dia.: N/A
Field of View: N/A
Eye Relief: Unlimited
Features: Miniature Rifle Optic; can be used on rifles, carbines, and shotguns; both-eyes-open application; ambidextrous brightness controls; advanced lens coatings; fully sealed and waterproof; sub-flush adjusters; 70 MOA of adjustment; 16 illumination settings on the 68 MOA reticle with 2 MOA red dot; available as a standalone optic/no mount, with low mount, with full co-witness mount, with lower 1/3 co-witness mount, and as a combo unit with a full co-witness mount with a 3X magnifier and quick-release side mount
MSRP . . . . $919.00–$1428.00

TRIJICON RMRCC RED-DOT

Type: Red-dot/reflex red-dot
Weight: 1 oz.
Length: 1.8 in.
Power: 1X
Obj. Dia.: N/A
Field of View: N/A
Eye Relief: Unlimited
Features: 3.25 or 6.5 MOA red dot; eight illumination settings include two for night vision; forged aluminum housing; lock-in and lock-out modes; CR2032 battery; multi-coated lenses; waterproof to 20m/66 ft.; snag-free design
MSRP $699.00

VORTEX OPTICS RAZOR HD 4000

Type: Rangefinder
Weight: 9.9 oz.
Length: 4.49 in.
Power: 7X
Obj. Dia.: 25mm
Field of View: 341.25 ft.@1000 yd.
Eye Relief: .62 in.
Features: Reflective range of up to 2,400 yards; ELR mode to 4,000 yards; scan mode; line of sight mode; anti-reflective coatings on all air to surface glass; rubber armor; magnesium chassis; angle compensated ranging
MSRP $729.99

VORTEX OPTICS SPARC SOLAR

Type: Red-dot/reflex red-dot
Weight: 5.9 oz.
Length: 2.6 in.
Power: 1X
Obj. Dia.: N/A
Field of View: N/A
Eye Relief: Unlimited
Features: Red-dot sight with a 2 MOA dot; parallax free; 1 MOA clicks; power source auto-switches from sun to battery depending on amount of sun; CR2032 battery; includes low mount and lower 1/3 co-witness mounts
MSRP $399.99

SIGHTS/LASERS

CRIMSON TRACE CMR-301 RAIL MASTER PRO

Features: A two-for-one package for just about any MSR/AR-type rifle, with a green laser paired with 1,000-lumen tactical light; needs M1913 Picatinny rail or similar rail at least 2 ¾-in. to mount
MSRP $279.99

HIVIZ LITEWAVE H3 COMPSIGHT

Features: For shotgunners, this sight combines tritium with HIVIZ's LightPipe technology; all-steel construction; green pipe
MSRP $55.00

HOLOSUN LE11, LS11 SERIES LASERS

LEAPERS, INC. UTG PRO FLIP-UP SIGHTS, PICATINNY

NIGHT FISION ACCUR8

NIGHT FISION COSTA

NIGHT FISION OEM REPLACEMENT

NIGHT FISION OPTICS READY STEALTH

NIGHT FISION PERFECT DOT

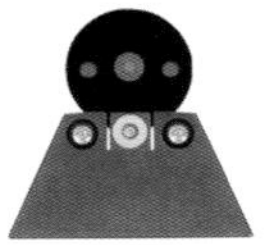
NIGHT FISION SUPPRESSOR HEIGHT

STEINER TOR FUSION

STEINER TOR MINI

TRIJICON DI NIGHT SIGHTS

XS SIGHTS XT12

HOLOSUN LE11, LS11 SERIES LASERS

Features: Pistol lasers in this series are available in a wide range of configurations, from polymer housings vs. titanium housings; dual red/infrared; single green, red, or infrared; ambidextrous controls
MSRP . . . . $111.75–$258.81

LEAPERS, INC. UTG PRO FLIP-UP SIGHTS, PICATINNY

Features: Aircraft-grade aluminum construction with reinforced steel components; matte black anodized finish; fits most Picatinny rails; locks upon flipping up, push-button spring lowers sights; front sight is standard elevation for AR-15 A2 front sight post
MSRP . . . . Front: $42.97
Rear: $42.97

NIGHT FISION ACCUR8

Features: Night sights with a black circle rear and front circle in choice of blue, orange, red, white, or yellow; for Glock, CZ-USA, S&W
MSRP $110.00

NIGHT FISION COSTA

Features: Serrated matte black rear, circle night sight front in choice of orange, white, or yellow; for Glock
MSRP $110.00

NIGHT FISION OEM REPLACEMENT

Features: Replaces factory sights; injection molded sleeve holds tritium vial tightly in place; available in square notch or u-notch rear with a night sight front circle sight in white orange, white, blue, or red, and with orange and yellow available in Glow Dome glowing ring; front sight also available as a standalone; available for Glock, CZ-USA, SIG Sauer, S&W, Walther
MSRP . . . . $48.00–$119.00

NIGHT FISION OPTICS READY STEALTH

Features: Works in conjunction with slide-mounted reflex sights; front ring in orange, yellow, or black dots; rear square-notch sight in serrated matte black or serrated matte black with two black dots; for Glock, CZ-USA, SIG Sauer
MSRP . . . . $101.00–$119.00

NIGHT FISION PERFECT DOT

Features: Night sights with choice of square-notch rear, u-notch rear, front sight only, and suppressor height; front ring available in white, orange, red, yellow, and blue; rear available in white or black dot; available for Canik, H&K, Springfield Armory, Novak 1911
MSRP . . . . $48.00–$121.75

NIGHT FISION SUPPRESSOR HEIGHT

Features: Flat matte black rear with a night sight circle front in white, yellow, orange, red, or blue, and orange and yellow are also available with Night Fision's Dome Glow glowing ring; for Glock, Canik, SIG Sauer, S&W
MSRP . . . . $48.00–$129.00

STEINER TOR FUSION

Features: At 2.7 inches long, this laser is available in choice of red or green; waterproof; 500 lumen white light wavelength; universal rail mount; light only, laser only, or laser/light modes; auto-on function; adjustable for windage and elevation; fits Surefire X300 holster
MSRP $401.99

STEINER TOR MINI

Features: Similar to the Fusion, but in a smaller package and without the added white light; waterproof; choice of red or green laser; aluminum housing; adjustable laser power levels; auto-on function; universal rail mount; ambidextrous operation
MSRP $286.99

TRIJICON DI NIGHT SIGHTS

Features: Uses both tritium and fiber optics with an interchangeable fiber optic pipe; tritium lamp is capped with a sapphire jewel; serrated notch/two-dot rear; available for Glock, SIG Sauer, S&W, and Springfield Armory pistols
MSRP $150.00

XS SIGHTS XT12

Features: Pistol sight designed to be secondary or backup sights for use during CQB engagements and also useful for 3-gun competition; front sight is orange ember glow; taller bases than in previous generations; fully ambidextrous for left-/right-hand shooting on top rail installations
MSRP $137.99

NEW Products: Ammunition

BERGER EXTREME OUTER LIMITS ELITE HUNTER

BERGER LONG RANGE HYBRID HUNTER

BLACK HILLS MK 262 MOD 1-C, MIL PACK

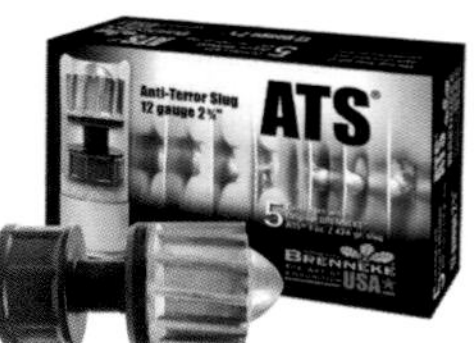

BRENNEKE ATS

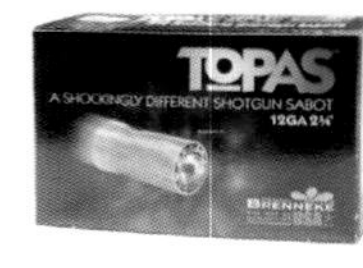

BRENNEKE TOPAS

BROWNING WICKED BLEND

BROWNING X-POINT DEFENSE

BUFFALO BORE .32 WINCHESTER SPECIAL

CCI CLEAN-22 REALTREE

BERGER EXTREME OUTER LIMITS ELITE HUNTER

Description: Long-nosed bullet that has a hybrid ogive that minimizes wind drift; J4 Precision jacket promotes rapid expansion after just two to three inches of penetration

Available in: 6.5 Creedmoor (156 gr.)

Box of 20.0: $41.99

BERGER LONG RANGE HYBRID HUNTER

Description: High ballistic coefficient and a jump-tolerant ogive; Berger says these bullets have been Doppler Radar-verified to have less than a 1% variation in BC

Available in: 6mm Creedmoor (109 gr.), 6.5 Creedmoor (144 gr., 153.5 gr.)

Box of 20.0: $42.99

BLACK HILLS MK 262 MOD 1-C, MIL PACK

Description: The result of a 1999 request from the US Navy to develop a 5.56 NATO precision round; no lot ships if it doesn't shoot sub-2-in. groups; 2750 fps, 1293 ft.-lbs.

Available in: 5.56 NATO (77 gr.)

Box of 460: $524.37

BRENNEKE ATS

Description: ATS stands for Anti-Terror Slug; super-hard slug; can be used with any shotgun barrel type; patented rear slides into the slug point after impact; 1680 fps, 2639 ft.-lbs.

Available in: 12-ga. (2 ¾ in., 424 gr.)

Box of 5: $19.38

BRENNEKE TOPAS

Description: New sabot design with cup deploys a sub-caliber slug; barrel-friendly; 2/3-oz. slug at 1673 fps, 1919 ft-lbs.

Available in: 12-ga. (2 ¾ in.)

Box of 5: $5.83

BROWNING LONG RANGE PRO HUNTER

Description: Designed for long-range hunting with a Sierra Tipped GameKing bullet

Available in: 6.5 Creedmoor, .270 Win., .300 Win. Mag., .308 Win., .300 WSM, .30-06 Spfd., 6.5 PRC, 6.8 Western

Box of 20: . . . . N/A

BROWNING WICKED BLEND

Description: Holds Browning's Wicked Wad with rear stabilizing pellets that provide a straighter shot and decrease shot slinging; slotted sidewalls improve choke responsiveness; stacked payloads of 12 ga. In BB/No. 1, No.2/No. 4 Bismuth, 20-ga. in No. 2/No. 4 Bismuth

Available in: 12 ga. (3 ½ in., 3 in.), 20 ga. (3 in.)

Box of 25: . . . . N/A

BROWNING X-POINT DEFENSE

Description: X-Point technology bullet front guards the hollowpoint from becoming obstructed

Available in: .380 ACP, 9mm, .40 S&W, .45 ACP, 10mm Auto

Box of 20: . . . . N/A

BUFFALO BORE .32 WINCHESTER SPECIAL

Description: Available in a 170-gr. jacketed flat-nose and a 200-gr. hard-cast gas-checked

ELEY ACTION

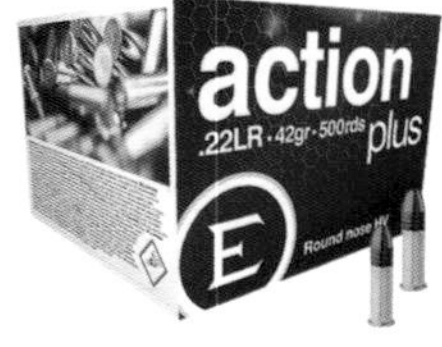

ELEY ACTION PLUS

Available in: .32 Win. Spec.

Box of 20: $46.00

CCI CLEAN-22 REALTREE

Description: Special Realtree bottle holds 400 rounds of its Clean-22 wearing a green, tan, and black polymer bullet coating that reduces copper fouling

Available in: .22 LR

Box of 400: $43.99

ELEY ACTION

Description: A subsonic round with reduced recoil; 1060 fps; designed specifically for use in semiautomatics, especially those high-end guns for competition; boxes of 50 and 500

Available in: .22 LR (42 gr.)

Box of 500: $50.00

ELEY ACTION PLUS

Description: A supersonic round traveling at 1150 fps; designed for high-end semiautomatic competition rifles; boxes of 50 and 500

Available in: .22 LR (46 gr.)

Box of 500: $50.00

FEDERAL PUNCH .22 LR

FEDERAL PUNCH 10MM AUTO

FEDERAL SWIFT A-FRAME .327 FEDERAL, 10MM

FEDERAL SWIFT SCIROCCO II

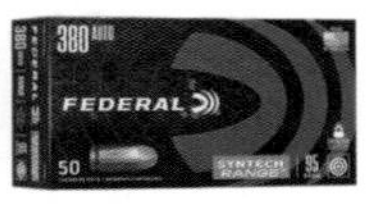
FEDERAL SYNTECH RANGE TSJ

HORNADY 6MM ARC PRECISION HUNTER

NORMA SAFEGUARD

SIERRA OUTDOOR MASTER

WINCHESTER AMMUNITION DEER SEASON COPPER IMPACT XP

SIG SAUER ELITE COPPER HUNTING

SIG SAUER MATCH ELITE COMPETITION

SIG SAUER SBR SOLID COPPER BLACK CASE

FEDERAL PUNCH .22 LR

Description: Intended for self-defense with a max velocity of 1,070 fps from a 2-in. barreled handgun, 1650 fps from a 24-in. barreled rifle; nickel-plated case; lead-core bullet
Available in: .22 LR (29 gr.)
Box of 50:. $9.99

FEDERAL PUNCH 10MM AUTO

Description: Another round adding to the Punch line, this 10mm has a jacketed hollow point moving at 1,100 fps
Available in: 10mm Auto (200 gr.)
Box of 20:. $30.99

FEDERAL SWIFT A-FRAME .327 FEDERAL, 10MM

Description: New calibers in 2021; jacketed hollowpoint; A-frame design aids expansion; nickel-plated case;
Available in: .327 Federal (100 gr.), 10mm Auto (200 gr.)
Box of 20:. . . . .$48.99–$54.99

FEDERAL SWIFT SCIROCCO II

Description: Bullet has a proprietary polymer tip; advanced secant ogive; bonded tapered copper jacket
Available in: .243 Win., 6.5 Creedmoor, .270 Win., .270 WSM, 7mm Rem. Mag., .308 Win., .30-06 Spfd., .300 Win. Mag., .300 WSM
Box of 20:. . . . .$54.99–$65.99

FEDERAL SYNTECH RANGE TSJ

Description: Clean ammunition wears a TSJ (Total Synthetic Jacket) to reduce fouling and barrel damage; Catalyst primer is lead-free
Available in: .380 Auto, .38 Spec., 10mm Auto
Box of 50:. . . . .$30.99–$36.99

HORNADY 6MM ARC PRECISION HUNTER

Description: Designed for a US DoD multipurpose combat rifle program; ELD-X bullet flying at 2,800 fps and with 1793 ft.-lbs. at the muzzle
Available in: 6mm ARC (103 gr.)
Box of 20:. $29.99

NORMA SAFEGUARD

Description: A jacketed hollowpoint line intended for self-defense use
Available in: .38 Spec., 9mm, .357 Mag., .45 ACP
Box of 50:. . . . .$32.49–$48.99

SIERRA OUTDOOR MASTER

Description: A full line of handgun cartridges with a Power Jacket topped with a Sports Master jacketed hollowpoint; skives in the jacket control expansion; brass casings can be reloaded
Available in: .380 Auto (115 gr.), 9mm (115 gr., 124 gr.), .40 S&W (180 gr.), .45 ACP (185 gr.)
Box of 20:. $18.99

SIG SAUER ELITE COPPER HUNTING

Description: A precision cartridge for hunters
Available in: .30-06 (150 gr.), .308 Win. (150 gr.), .300 Win. Mag. (165 gr.), .300 BLK (120 gr.)
Box of 20:. . . . .$31.95–$58.95

SIG SAUER MATCH ELITE COMPETITION

Description: Designed with input from Max Michel and Lena Miculek, jacketed hollowpoint with reduced charge weight to lower recoil; 880 fps, 254 ft.-lbs.
Available in: 9mm (147 gr.)
Box of 50:. $31.95

SIG SAUER SBR SOLID COPPER BLACK CASE

Description: A supersonic duty round for short barreled rifles, wearing a distinctive black oxide case; solid copper projectile; 1897 fps, 959 ft.-lbs. of energy out of a 6.75-in. barrel
Available in: .300 BLK (120 gr.)
Box of 20:. $31.95

WINCHESTER AMMUNITION DEER SEASON COPPER IMPACT XP

Description: Wears a huge polymer tip, Winchester's Extreme Point, over a copper-solid boattail bullet for extreme weight retention and big wound channels
Available in: .270 WSM (130 gr.), .300 WSM (150 gr.), .350 Legend (150 gr.), 6.5 Creedmoor (125 gr.), .243 Win. (85 gr.), .30-06 Spfd. (150 gr.), .308 Win. (150 gr.)
Box of 20:. . . . . N/A

NEW Products: Ammunition

WINCHESTER AMMUNITION DEFENDER RIFLE

WINCHESTER AMMUNITION DEFENDER SHOTGUN

WINCHESTER AMMUNITION DOUBLE X DIAMOND GRADE

WINCHESTER AMMUNITION EXPEDITION LONG RANGE

WINCHESTER AMMUNITION WILDCAT

WINCHESTER AMMUNITION DEFENDER RIFLE

Description: A protected holllowpoint with Split Core technology and a tapered copper alloy jacket provides quick shock, deep penetration, and 1.5X expansion

Available in: .350 Legend (160 gr.), 5.56 NATO (64 gr.), .223 Rem. (60 gr., 77 gr.), .308 Win. (120 gr.), 7.62x39 NATO (120 gr.)

Box of 20:. . . . . N/A

WINCHESTER AMMUNITION DEFENDER SHOTGUN

Description: Intended to deliver massive shock with plated 00 buckshot backed by a 1-oz. rifled slug; grex buffering improves patterns; 12- and 20-ga. in this line also available with a segmenting slug; .410-bore in both 3- and 2 ½-in. offered with a Defensive Disc load backed by BBs

Available in: 12 ga., 20 ga., .410 bore

Box of 10, 20: . . . . N/A

WINCHESTER AMMUNITION DOUBLE X DIAMOND GRADE

Description: Designed specifically for turkey hunting with a ¾-oz. payload of 8% antimony copper-plated pellets; 1100 fps

Available in: .410 bore

Box of 10:. . . . . N/A

WINCHESTER AMMUNITION EXPEDITION LONG RANGE

Description: Boattail bullets wear a polymer tip, have extended ogive, a bonded alloy core, and a jacket designed for maximum expansion at both close and long ranges

Available in: .308 Win. (168 gr.), 6.5 PRC (142 gr.), 6.8 Western (165 gr.), .270 Win. (150 gr.), .300 Win. Mag. (190 gr.), .300 WSM (190 gr.), .30-06 Spfd. (190 gr.), 6.5 Creedmoor (142 gr.), 7mm Rem. Mag. (168 gr.)

Box of 20:. . . . . N/A

WINCHESTER AMMUNITION WILDCAT

Description: A valued-priced round for target shooting and small game; available in a 500-count box with a Dynapoint bullet or a 50-count box with a lead round nose

Available in: .22 LR (40 gr.)

Box of 50, 500: . . . . N/A

NEW Products: Bullets

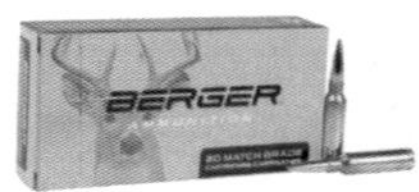

BERGER EXTREME OUTER LIMITS ELITE HUNTER

BERGER LONG RANGE HYBRID TARGET

BERGER ELITE HUNTER

Features: Heavy-for-caliber bullets for hunting applications in a 133-gr. .25 cal., 108-gr. 6mm, 205-gr. .30 cal.

Box of 100:. $53.99

BERGER EXTREME OUTER LIMITS ELITE HUNTER

Features: Designed for very long-range hunting applications with a hybrid ogive that reduces wind drift; a J4 Precision jacket for rapid expansion; available in a 240-gr. .30 cal

Box of 100:. $56.99

BERGER LONG RANGE HYBRID TARGET

Features: With a high ballistic coefficient and a jump-tolerant ogive, Berger says these bullets have been Doppler Radar-verified to have less than a 1% variation in BC. Available in .22 cal. 85.5-gr., 6mm 109-gr., 6.5mm 144-gr., 7mm 190-gr., .30 cal. 208-, 220-gr.

Box of 100:. $56.99

SIERRA BLITZKING

Features: Developed for Sierra's Prairie Enemy ammo line, this bullet is now available in component form for th 6.5 crowd in a 105-gr.

Box of 100, 500: . . . . $42.71–$201.12

SIERRA SPORTSMASTER

Features: A 9mm 124-gr. Jacketed hollowpoint for target, competition, self-defense and even small game

Box of 100:. $24.87

SIERRA TIPPED GAMEKING

Features: New in 2021 are a 140-gr. 7mm, 175-gr. .270, 140-gr. 6.5mm, .25 cal. 110-gr.

Box of 100, 500: . . . . $49.57–$269.06

SIG SAUER V-CROWN

Features: SIG's proprietary V-Crown bullet now available for handloaders in 9mm (115 gr., 124 gr., 147 gr.)

Box of 100:. . . . .$37.95–$39.95

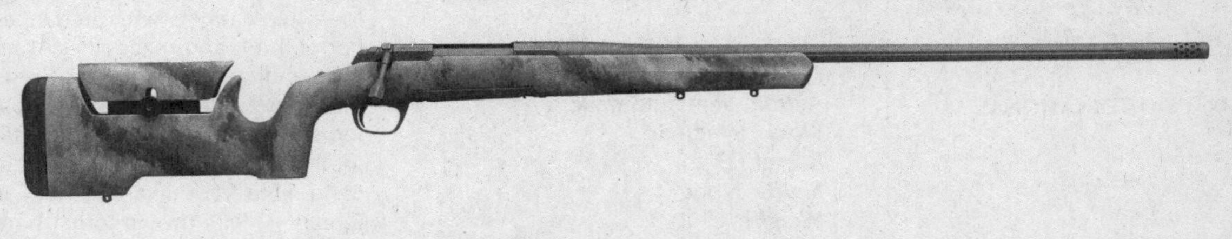

Accuracy International

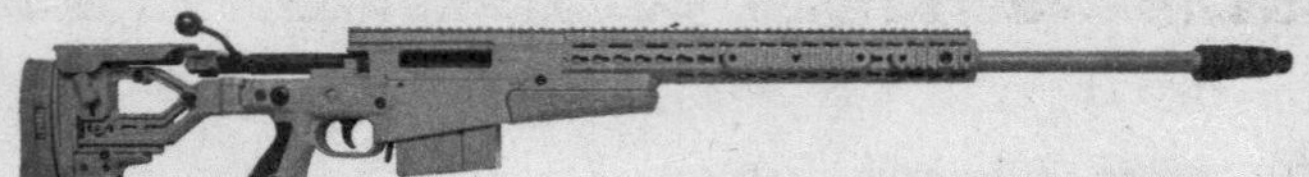

ACCURACY INTERNATIONAL AXMC

AXMC

Action: Semiautomatic
Stock: Synthetic
Barrel: 27 in.
Sights: None
Weight: 15 lb.
Caliber: .300 Win. Mag., .308 Win., .338 Lapua
Magazine: 10 rounds
Features: Multi-caliber, allowing users to switch calibers with a change of barrel, bolt, and magazine; AI's patent-pending Quicklok quick-release barrel; detachable magazine has a left-side cutout that eases insertion into the rifle; Cerakote finishes in Elite Sand, Elite Midnight, AI Dark Earth, AI Green, AI Pale Brown; other barrel lengths available on request; custom options available
MSRP . . . . .starting at $8687.00

Adcor Defense

ADCOR DEFENSE ELITE

ADCOR DEFENSE ELITE GI

ELITE

Action: Semiautomatic
Stock: Synthetic
Barrel: 16 in.
Sights: None
Weight: 10 lb.
Caliber: 7.62x39, .300 BLK
Magazine: 30 rounds
Features: Gas piston action, billet upper and lower, free-floating chrome-lined barrel and forward charging handle are standard. Choice of Quad or Key Mod rails; black, Flat Dark Earth, Olive Drab Green, or Patriot Brown
MSRP . . . .$2295.00–$2545.00

ELITE GI

Action: Semiautomatic
Stock: Synthetic
Barrel: 16 in., 18 in.
Sights: None
Weight: 6 lb. 13 oz.–6 lb. 15 oz.
Caliber: .223
Magazine: 31 rounds
Features: A gas impingement version of Adcor's popular gas pistol Elite; billet upper and lower; two barrel lengths to choose from, either length available with or without a forward-charging handle; choice of quad or Key-Mod rail; finishes in black, Flat Dark Earth, Olive Drab Green, and Patriot Brown
Black:. $1995.00
Colors:. $2245.00

American Tactical

AMERICAN TACTICAL GALEO

AMERICAN TACTICAL OMNI HYBRID MAXX

GALEO

Action: Semiautomatic
Stock: Synthetic
Barrel: 18.5 in.
Sights: Flip-up front, rear
Weight: N/A
Caliber: 5.56 NATO
Magazine: 30 rounds
Features: Completely assembled in Summerville, SC, with a combination of US-made parts and Israeli military Galil parts; available with wood or polymer handguard; side-folding stock
MSRP $1299.99

OMNI HYBRID MAXX

Action: Semiautomatic
Stock: Synthetic
Barrel: 16 in.
Sights: None
Weight: 6 lb. 4 oz., 6 lb. 8 oz.
Caliber: .223 Rem./5.56 NATO, .22 LR, .300 BLK
Magazine: Detachable box, 30 round
Features: Retractable stock; metal-reinforced polymer lower and upper receiver; Picatinny rail
.22 LR: $429.95
.223 Rem./5.56 NATO: . . . . $449.95–$669.95
.300 BLK: . . . . $489.95–$519.95

Anschütz (J.G. Anschütz)

ANSCHÜTZ 1416 AMERICAN VARMINTER

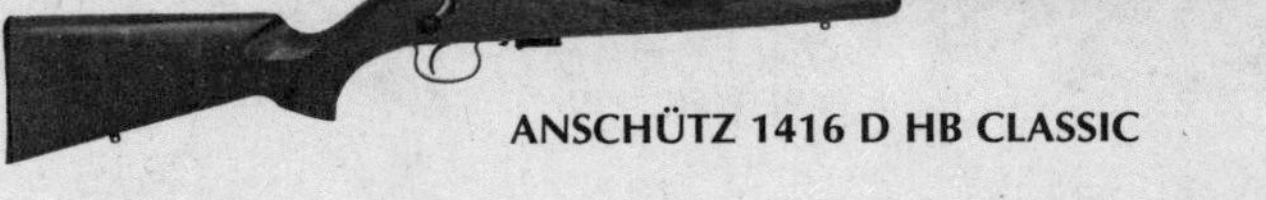
ANSCHÜTZ 1416 D HB CLASSIC

J.G. ANSCHÜTZ 1761, 1761 AV THREADED

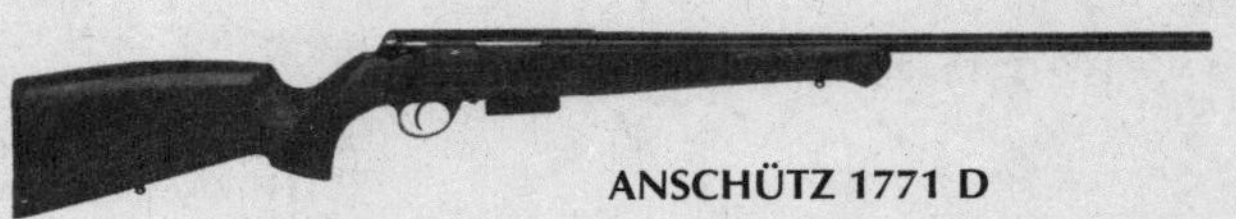
ANSCHÜTZ 1771 D

ANSCHÜTZ 1771 D GRS

ANSCHÜTZ 1780 D FL CLASSIC

J.G. ANSCHÜTZ 1782D

1416 AMERICAN VARMINTER

Action: Bolt
Stock: Thumbhole walnut
Barrel: 18 in.
Sights: None
Weight: 5 lb. 10 oz.
Caliber: .22 LR
Magazine: 5 rounds
Features: 64 bolt-action repeater; 5098 two-stage trigger; blued finish; hex-key bolts; medium-weight barrel threaded ½ in. x 28 tpi; no iron sight provision; counter-bored crown
MSRP $1749.00

1416 D HB CLASSIC

Action: Bolt
Stock: Walnut
Barrel: 23 in.
Sights: None
Weight: 6 lb. 7 oz.
Caliber: .22 LR
Magazine: Detachable box, 5 rounds
Features: Heavy barrel; lacquered walnut wood stock (optional beavertail); pistol grip; black buttplate; studs for sling swivel; lateral sliding safety
MSRP $1199.00

1761 D HB, HB, AV THREADED

Action: Bolt
Stock: Walnut
Barrel: 18 in., 20 in.
Sights: None
Weight: 6 lb. 6 oz.
Caliber: .22 LR, .17 HMR
Magazine: 5 rounds
Features: Simple target .22 LR with a Classic Anschütz stock; single-stage trigger; large bolt knob; AV model has an 18-in. heavy barrel with a threaded muzzle
D HB, HB: . . . . . $1775.00–$2095.00
AV Threaded: $1850.00

1771 D

Action: Bolt
Stock: Germany-styled walnut
Barrel: 21.5 in.
Sights: None
Weight: 7 lb. 7 oz.
Caliber: .22 Hornet, .222 Rem., .223 Rem., .204 Ruger
Magazine: 4 rounds
Features: 1771 bolt action repeater; six front locking lugs; blued finish; heavy barrel; no iron sight provision
MSRP $2549.00

1771 D GRS

Action: Bolt
Stock: Laminated birch
Barrel: 22 in.
Sights: None
Weight: 8 lb. 6 oz.
Caliber: .204 Ruger, .222 Rem., .223 Rem., .300 BLK
Magazine: Detachable box, 4 rounds
Features: Butt plate speed lock adjustment; GRS-rubber butt plate; cheek piece speed lock adjustment; ergonomical and gripping forend; precision barrel
MSRP $3300.00

1780 D FL CLASSIC

Action: Bolt
Stock: Walnut
Barrel: 23 in.
Sights: Drilled and tapped for scopes
Weight: 7 lb. 2 oz.
Caliber: .308 Win., .30-06 Spfd., 8x57 IS, 9.3x62 Mauser
Magazine: Detachable box, 5 rounds
Features: Single-stage trigger; fast acquisition sight; sliding safety catch; available in a variety of stock options, including wood Monte Carlo, German, thumbhole and classic stocks, and classic stocks in soft grip wood orange camo, wood green camo, and black
MSRP $1793.57

1782 D

Action: Bolt
Stock: Walnut
Barrel: 20.5 in., 22.8 in.
Sights: None
Weight:
Caliber: .243 Win., 6.5 Creedmoor, .308 Win., .30-06 Spfd., 8x57 IS, 9.3x62
Magazine: 3 rounds
Features: Classic or German-style walnut stocks in an oil finish; single-stage match-grade trigger with adjustable blade and ability to be changed to a two-stage; silent safety catch operation; 60-degree bolt throw; integrated recoil lug; V bedding; double Picatinny rails; Fast Release magazine; choice of threaded barrel or barrel with recessed crown
MSRP . . . . $2795.00–$2995.00

Anschütz (J.G. Anschütz)

ANSCHÜTZ 1827 FORTNER SPRINT

ANSCHÜTZ 1903 TARGET

ANSCHÜTZ 1907 IN 1914 STOCK

J.G. ANSCHÜTZ 1927 CISM WALNUT

ANSCHÜTZ MATCH 54.30

ANSCHÜTZ 2013/690 WITH 2018 PRECISE STOCK

1827 FORTNER SPRINT

Action: Bolt
Stock: Biathlon, walnut
Barrel: 22 in.
Sights: None
Weight: 8 lb. 2 oz.
Caliber: .22 LR
Magazine: Detachable box, 5 rounds
Features: Combination of an extra light 1827 Fortner barreled action with the stock of the 1827 model; lacquered walnut stock with stippled checkering; heavy, cylindrical match barrel; match stage two or single trigger
MSRP $3950.00

1903 TARGET

Action: Bolt
Stock: Hardwood
Barrel: 26 in., heavy
Sights: None
Weight: 9 lb. 11 oz.
Caliber: .22 LR
Magazine: None
Features: A match rifle for small bore shooters; anatomically perfect walnut stock with vertically adjustable cheek piece; optional aluminum, hook, or rubber buttplate; aluminum accessories rail
MSRP $1450.00

1907 IN 1914 STOCK

Action: Bolt
Stock: Walnut
Barrel: 32.28 in.
Sights: None
Weight: 10 lb. 12 oz.
Caliber: .22 LR
Magazine: None
Features: Match 54 action; heavy, cylindrical barrel; match two-stage or single-stage trigger; safety signal pin
MSRP $3650.00

1927 CISM WALNUT

Action: Bolt
Stock: Walnut
Barrel: 26 in.
Sights: None
Weight: 10 lb. 1 oz.
Caliber: .22 LR
Magazine: 10 rounds
Features: Top-end fast-fire (CISM) rimfire competition rifle; hefty walnut stock, lacquered finish and stippled checkering; sliding safety catch; 1927 action (similar to biathlon 1827 F) with a Match 54 Fortner straight-pull bolt; heavy-weight tapered barrel
MSRP $4995.00

2013/690 WITH 2018 PRECISE STOCK

Action: Bolt
Stock: Aluminum
Barrel: 27.17 in.
Sights: None
Weight: 13 lb.
Caliber: .22 LR
Magazine: None
Features: Single loader; two-stage trigger; optional buttplate; new backend offers large range of adjustment for small shooters
MSRP $4995.00

MATCH 54.30

Action: Barreled
Stock: Aluminum or walnut
Barrel: 26 in.
Sights: None
Weight: 11 lb. 3 oz.
Caliber: .22 LR
Magazine: 8 rounds
Features: Improved ergonomics; reduced weight of firing pin for increase in velocity and shorter lock time; newly designed target chamber for better accuracy; threaded receiver and barrel connection; available in aluminum or walnut stock
MSRP . . . . $3775.00–$5135.00

ArmaLite

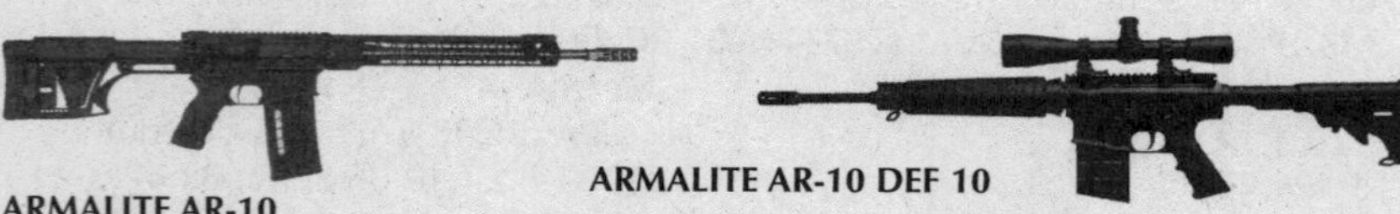

ARMALITE AR-10 COMPETITION RIFLE

ARMALITE AR-10 DEF 10

AR-10 COMPETITION RIFLE

Action: Semiautomatic
Stock: Synthetic
Barrel: 13 in., 18 in.
Sights: None
Weight: 8 lb. 3 oz.–8 lb. 14 oz.
Caliber: .308 Win./7.62 NATO
Magazine: Detachable box, 25 rounds
Features: Picatinny rail; Armalite tunable brake pinned and welded; 12-in. free-floating handguard; stock adjustable for length-of-pull and comb height; ambidextrous safety and charging handle
MSRP $2231.00

AR-10 DEF 10

Action: Semiautomatic
Stock: Synthetic
Barrel: 16 in.
Sights: Front
Weight: 7 lb. 14 oz.
Caliber: 7.62 NATO, .308 Win.
Magazine: 10, 20 rounds
Features: No-frills rifle built for sporting or defensive use; mid-length gas system, six-position collapsible stock, forged flat top with Mil-Std 1913 rail, 7075 forged aluminum lower and receiver, standard charging handle, single-stage trigger are standard; supplied with one 20-round Magpul Pmag; Colorado-compliant version comes with 10-round Magpul Pmag
MSRP $1126.00

ArmaLite

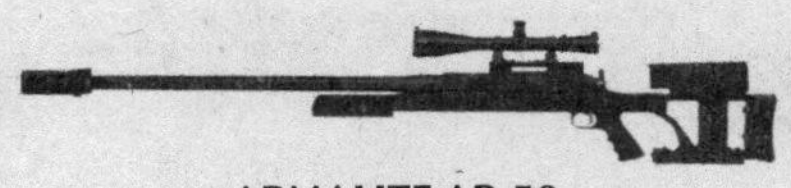

ARMALITE AR-50 .50 BMG PRECISION BOLT-ACTION RIFLE

AR-50 .50 BMG BOLT-ACTION RIFLE

Action: Bolt
Stock: Synthetic
Barrel: 33 in.
Sights: None
Weight: 33 lb. 3 oz.
Caliber: .50 BMG
Magazine: None
Features: Chromoly barrel; muzzle-brake; 15 minute rail; single-stage trigger
MSRP $3985.00

Arsenal, Inc.

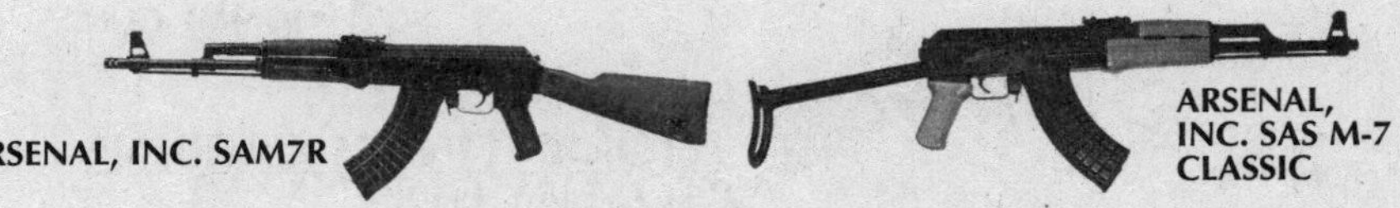

ARSENAL, INC. SAM7R

ARSENAL, INC. SAS M-7 CLASSIC

ARSENAL, INC. SLR-107R

SAM7R

Action: Semiautomatic
Stock: Polymer
Barrel: 16.25 in.
Sights: Scope rail
Weight: 8 lb.
Caliber: 7.62x39 Warsaw
Magazine: Detachable box, 10 rounds
Features: Milled receiver; chrome-lined, hammer-forged barrel; muzzle brake; cleaning rod; intermediate length US-made 10 in. trapdoor butt-stock
MSRP $1399.99

SAS M-7 CLASSIC

Action: Semiautomatic
Stock: Metal
Barrel: 16.25 in.
Sights: A-4-type front, 800m adjustable rear
Weight: 7 lb. 8 oz.
Caliber: 7.62X39mm
Magazine: 30 rounds
Features: Built in Nevada, a classic AK-47 design with under-folding stock; chrome-lined heavy barrel; left-hand threaded muzzle
MSRP $1999.00

SLR-107R

Action: Semiautomatic
Stock: Polymer
Barrel: 16.25 in.
Sights: Front sight, 800m rear
Weight: 7 lb. 5 oz.
Caliber: 7.62x39mm
Magazine: 5 rounds
Features: Manufactured in Las Vegas with a Bulgarian-made stamped receiver; anti-slap double-stage trigger; Warsaw-length buttstock with a cleaning kit compartment; stainless steel heat shield, side rail, and slings; available in black, Plum, Desert Sand, or OD Green
MSRP . . . . $1499.99–$1519.99

RIFLES

Auto-Ordnance

AUTO-ORDNANCE AOM150

AUTO-ORDNANCE IWO JIMA M1 CARBINE

AUTO-ORDNANCE IWO JIMA THOMPSON

AOM150

Action: Semiautomatic
Stock: Walnut; handguard
Barrel: 18 in.
Sights: Blade front; flip style rear
Weight: 5 lb. 6 oz.
Caliber: .30
Magazine: Detachable stick, 15 rounds
Features: Folding stock; Parkerized finish
MSRP $1253.00

IWO JIMA M1 CARBINE

Action: Semiautomatic
Stock: Wood
Barrel: 18 in.
Sights: Blade front, flip-style rear
Weight: 5 lb. 6 oz.
Caliber: .30 Carbine
Magazine: 15 rounds
Features: Honors the 75th anniversary of the Battle of Iwo Jima with grips emblazoned with "Among the men who fought on Iwo Jima, uncommon valor was a common virtue" (engraving by Outlaw Ordnance); finished in Cerakote OD green and Distressed Copper
MSRP $1391.00

IWO JIMA THOMPSON

Action: Semiautomatic
Stock: Wood
Barrel: 16.5 in.
Sights: Pinned front blade, open adjustable rear
Weight: 11 lb. 8 oz.
Caliber: .45 ACP
Magazine: 20, 30 rounds
Features: Honors the 75th anniversary of the Battle of Iwo Jima with grips emblazoned with "Among the men who fought on Iwo Jima, uncommon valor was a common virtue" (engraving by Outlaw Ordnance); finished in Cerakote OD green and Distressed Copper
MSRP $1886.00

Auto-Ordnance

AUTO-ORDNANCE TANKER THOMPSON

AUTO-ORDNANCE THOMPSON 1927 A-1 "COMMANDO" CARBINE

AUTO-ORDNANCE THOMPSON 1927 A-1 DELUXE CARBINE

AUTO-ORDNANCE THOMPSON 1927 A-1 DELUXE CARBINE HARD CHROME PLATED

AUTO-ORDNANCE THOMPSON 1927 A-1C LIGHTWEIGHT DELUXE SEMI-AUTO

AUTO-ORDNANCE THOMPSON M1 CARBINE "TOMMY GUN"

AUTO-ORDNANCE THOMPSON M1SB

AUTO-ORDNANCE TRUMP THOMPSON

RIFLES

TANKER THOMPSON

Action: Semiautomatic
Stock: Walnut
Barrel: 16.5 in.
Sights: Blade front, fixed battle rear
Weight: 11 lb. 8 oz.
Caliber: .45 ACP
Magazine: 20, 30 rounds
Features: Commemorative firearm dedicated to soldiers who fought in M4 Sherman tanks; Cerakoted in Army O.D. green; Sherman tank white star engraved in front of the mag well; U.S. logo on buttstock; stick magazines
MSRP $1749.00

THOMPSON 1927 A-1 "COMMANDO" CARBINE .45-CALIBER

Action: Semiautomatic
Stock: Black finish stock and forend
Barrel: 16.5 in.
Sights: Blade front, open rear adjustable
Weight: 13 lb.
Caliber: .45 ACP
Magazine: Detachable stick, 30 rounds
Features: Frame and receiver made from solid steel; compensator; black nylon sling
MSRP $1479.00

THOMPSON 1927 A-1 DELUXE CARBINE .45-CALIBER

Action: Semiautomatic
Stock: Walnut, vertical foregrip
Barrel: 10.5 in., 16.5 in.
Sights: Blade front, open rear adjustable
Weight: 13 lb.
Caliber: .45 ACP
Magazine: 20 rounds
Features: Finned barrel with compensator; blued steel or color case-hardened; magazine options range from 10- and 20-round sticks to 50- and 100-round drums; horizontal fore-grip option; detachable stock option; SBR 10.5-in. barrel option
MSRP . . . .$1618.00–$2027.00

THOMPSON 1927 A-1 DELUXE CARBINE .45-CALIBER HARD CHROME PLATED, GOLD PLATED

Action: Semiautomatic
Stock: Walnut
Barrel: 16.5 in.
Sights: Blade front, open rear adjustable
Weight: 13 lb.
Caliber: .45 ACP
Magazine: One each round 50 drum and 20 stick magazines
Features: Finned barrel; fixed stock with vertical foregrip; tiger strip detailing option available on both chrome and gold models
Standard: $3431.00
Tiger Stripe: $4173.00

THOMPSON 1927A-1C LIGHTWEIGHT DELUXE SEMI-AUTO 9MM

Action: Semiautomatic
Stock: Walnut
Barrel: 16.5 in.
Sights: Blade front, adjustable open rear
Weight: 13 lb.
Caliber: 9mm
Magazine: 20 rounds
Features: The famous 1927 in a pistol caliber; aluminum frame; finned barrel with compensator; comes with one 20-round magazine
MSRP $1403.00

THOMPSON M1 CARBINE "TOMMY GUN" .45-CALIBER

Action: Semiautomatic
Stock: Walnut, vertical foregrip
Barrel: 10.5 in., 16.5 in.
Sights: Blade front, fixed battle rear
Weight: 11 lb. 8 oz.
Caliber: .45 ACP
Magazine: 10, 30 rounds
Features: Choice of steel or aluminum receiver; 10- or 30-round stick magazines; no vertical fore-grip; SBR version has 10.5-in. barrel
Standard: $1457.00
SBR: $2234.00

THOMPSON M1SB

Action: Semiautomatic
Stock: Walnut, vertical foregrip
Barrel: 10.5 in.
Sights: Blade front, fixed battle rear
Weight: 10 lb. 8 oz.
Caliber: .45 ACP
Magazine: Detachable stick, 30 rounds
Features: Will not accept drum magazines; frame and receiver made from solid steel
MSRP $2234.00

TRUMP THOMPSON

Action: Semiautomatic
Stock: Wood
Barrel: 16.5 in.
Sights: Pinned front blade, open adjustable rear
Weight: 11 lb. 8 oz.
Caliber: .45 ACP
Magazine: 20, 50 rounds
Features: Left side of the receiver engraved with "Make America Great Again"; Trump's name and "45" engraved on right side; stock engraved with Presidential Seal, the White House, and the American Flag; finished in Cerakote Armor Black with Cerakote Clear over high-polished flats
MSRP $2794.00

Barrett

BARRETT M107A1

BARRETT 82A1

BARRETT 95

BARRETT MRAD

BARRETT 99

BARRETT REC7

BARRETT REC7 D1

M107A1

Action: Semiautomatic
Stock: Synthetic
Barrel: 20 in., 29 in.
Sights: Flip-up iron sights
Weight: 30 lb. 14 oz.
Caliber: .50 BMG
Magazine: Detachable box, 10 rounds
Features: Chrome-lined barrel, Flat Dark Earth stock finish; suppressor-ready muzzlebrake; pelican case; M1913 optics rail; detachable adjustable lightweight bipod legs; lightweight monopod; black, Flat Dark Earth, OD Green, or Tungsten Grey Cerakote receiver finishes
MSRP . . . . . . $11,914.00–$13,999.00

MODEL 82A1

Action: Semiautomatic
Stock: Synthetic
Barrel: 20 in., 29 in.
Sights: Flip-up iron sights or Leupold scope
Weight: 30 lb. 14 oz.
Caliber: .416 Barrett, .50 BMG
Magazine: Detachable box, 10 rounds
Features: Pelican case; detachable adjustable bipod legs; cleaning kit; carry handle; muzzlebrake; Picatinny rail; chrome-lined barrel; manganese phosphate finish or Cerakote receiver finishes in Flat Dark Earth, Burnt Bronze, Tungsten Grey, or OD Green
MSRP . . . . $7873.00–$10,999.00

MODEL 95

Action: Semiautomatic
Stock: Synthetic
Barrel: 29 in.
Sights: Flip-up iron sights
Weight: 25 lb.
Caliber: .50 BMG
Magazine: Detachable box, 5 rounds
Features: Pelican case; detachable adjustable bipod legs; cleaning kit; Picatinny rail
MSRP $6671.00

MODEL 99

Action: Bolt
Stock: Synthetic
Barrel: 29 in., 32 in.
Sights: None
Weight: 25 lb.
Caliber: .416 Barrett, .50 BMG
Magazine: None
Features: Picatinny rail; pelican case; detachable adjustable bipod; cleaning kit; available in black anodized or Cerakote Flat Dark Earth receiver
MSRP . . . . $4560.00–$4730.00

MRAD

Action: Bolt action repeater
Stock: Synthetic
Barrel: 17 in., 20 in., 22 in., 24 in., 26 in.
Sights: None
Weight: 12 lb. 15 oz.–14 lb. 8 oz.
Caliber: .338 Lapua Magnum, .338 Norma Magnum, .300 Norma Magnum, .300 PRC, .300 Win. Mag., .309 Win., 6.5 Creedmoor
Magazine: Detachable box, 10 rounds
Features: Fluted, carbon fiber, or heavy barrel; multi-role brown finish stock; folding stock; adjustable cheek-piece and buttplate; includes two 10-round magazines, two sling loops, and three adjustable accessory rails; receivers in black anodized or in Cerakote Tungsten Grey, Flat Dark Earth, OD Green, or Burnt Bronze
MSRP . . . . $4060.00–$5970.00

REC7

Action: Semiautomatic
Stock: Synthetic
Barrel: 11.5 in., 16 in., 18 in.
Sights: Flip up front and rear
Weight: 6 lb. 2 oz.–7 lb. 15 oz.
Caliber: 5.56 NATO
Magazine: 10, 20, 30 rounds
Features: Gas piston semi-auto with enhanced KeyMod rail, Magup MOE six-position buttstock, two-position gas plug, one-piece piston, and oversized trigger guard; 6.8 SPC only available in 16-inch carbine-profile barrel; 5.56 has all barrel profiles, with 16-inch in either a carbine- or flyweight profile; 18-inch is DMR profile; 11.5 is NFA regulated; Cerakote receivers in Black, Flat Dark Earth, OD Green, Tungsten Grey, or Burnt Bronze
MSRP . . . . $2349.00–$2899.00

REC7 D1

Action: Semiautomatic
Stock: Synthetic
Barrel: 10.25 in., 16 in., 18 in.
Sights: None
Weight: 5 lb. 8 oz.–6 lb. 3 oz.
Caliber: 5.56 NATO
Magazine: 10, 20, 30 rounds
Features: Hand-built, lightweight, direct impingement; Magpul MOE six-position stock, Barrett designed 15-in. KeyMod handguard, Bravo Company Gunfighter charging handle, and ALG Defense ACT trigger; bolt carrier group plated in nickel boron finish; Black, Flat Dark Earth, OD Green, Tungsten Grey, or Burnt Bronze Cerakote.
MSRP . . . . $1499.00–$2699.00

Benelli USA

BENELLI LUPO

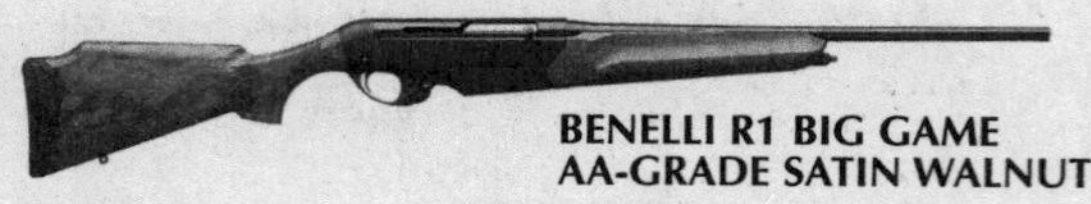
BENELLI R1 BIG GAME
AA-GRADE SATIN WALNUT

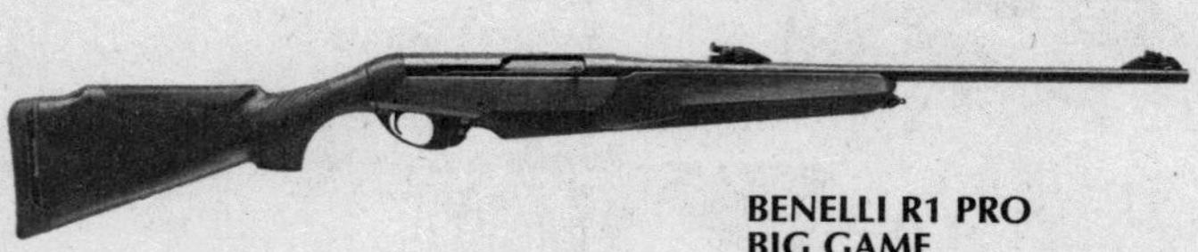
BENELLI R1 PRO
BIG GAME

LUPO

Action: Bolt
Stock: Synthetic
Barrel: 22 in., 24 in.
Sights: None
Weight: 7 lb.–7 lb. 2 oz.
Caliber: .30-06 Spfd., .300 Win. Mag., .270 Win., 6.5 Creedmoor, .308 Win., .243 Win.
Magazine: 3 rounds
Features: Benelli's first bolt-action rifle with a streamlined synthetic stock; Crio-treated free-floating barrel; alloy receiver; built-in Progressive Comfort combined with Combtech cheek pad reduce felt recoil
MSRP $1699.00

R1 BIG GAME

Action: Semiautomatic
Stock: AA-grade satin walnut, synthetic or Realtree APG
Barrel: 22 in., 24 in.
Sights: None
Weight: 7 lb. 2 oz.–7 lb. 5 oz.
Caliber: .30-06 Spfd., .300 Win. Mag., .338 Win. Mag.
Magazine: Detachable box, 3+1 or 4+1 rounds
Features: Picatinny rail; synthetic and APG finish come with GripTight coating; raised comb; auto-regulating gas-operated system
Walnut: $1149.00
ComforTech: $1349.00

R1 PRO BIG GAME

Action: Semiautomatic
Stock: Walnut
Barrel: 22 in.
Sights: Fiber optic front, adjustable rear
Weight: 7 lb. 3.2 oz.
Caliber: .30-06 Spfd.
Magazine: 4 rounds
Features: Includes Benelli's Progressive Comfort technology; AA walnut satin finish stock; receiver drilled and tapped for scope mount, Picatinny rail and shim kit included; CRIO treated barrel
MSRP $1499.00

Beretta USA

BERETTA USA
ARX100

BERETTA CX4 STORM

ARX100

Action: Semiautomatic
Stock: Telescopic folding
Barrel: 16 in.
Sights: Removable back-up sights
Weight: 6 lb. 13 oz.
Caliber: 5.56 NATO (other barrels available)
Magazine: 30 rounds
Features: Cold hammer forged barrel can be replaced with barrels in different lengths and calibers; case ejection switches from right to left at a button push; completely ambidextrous; technopolymer receiver; contains no pins and can be disassembled without the use of tools; optional .300 Black Out kit available
MSRP $1950.00

CX4 STORM

Action: Single-action
Stock: Synthetic
Barrel: 16.6 in.
Sights: Front sight post
Weight: 5 lb. 12 oz.
Caliber: 9mm
Magazine: 10, 15 rounds
Features: Picatinny rail; allows for reverse ejection and extraction; ideal for left-handed shooters; adjustable length-of-pull; easy to accessorize; takes Beretta series 92 pistol magazines
MSRP $799.00

Bergara

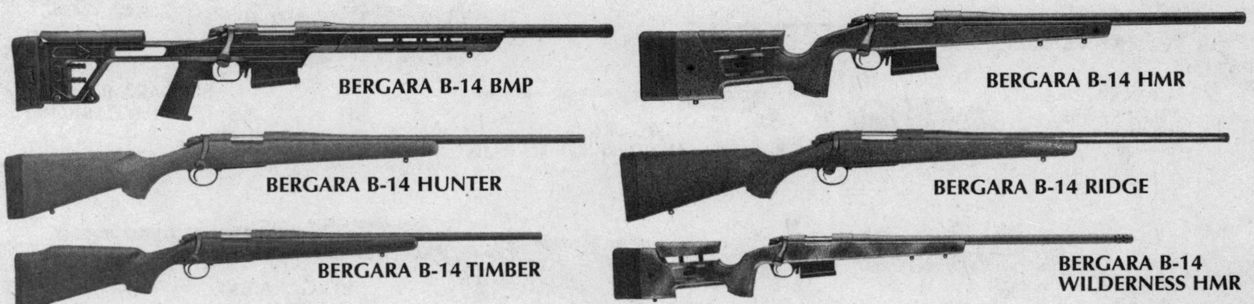

BERGARA B-14
WILDERNESS HUNTER

B-14 BMP

Action: Bolt
Stock: Bergara BMP chassis (machined aluminum)
Barrel: 24 in. (6.5 Creedmoor); 20 in. (.308 Win.)
Sights: None
Weight: 10 lb. 2 oz.–11 lb.
Caliber: 6.5 Creedmoor, .308 Win.
Magazine: 5 rounds
Features: Drilled and tapped for Remington 700 scope mounts; removable buttstock adjustable for cheekpiece and LOP, allowing for a standard AR-style stock and buffer tube to be installed; detachable magazine, threaded muzzle
MSRP $1265.00

B-14 HMR

Action: Bolt
Stock: Bergara BMP HMR molded with mini-chassis
Barrel: 20 in. (.308 Win.), 22 in. (6.5 Creedmoor)
Sights: None
Weight: 9 lb. 2.4 oz.–9 lb. 4 oz.
Caliber: 6.5 Creedmoor, 6.5 PRC, .308 Win., .22-250 Rem., .450 Bushmaster, .300 Win. Mag., .300 PRC
Magazine: 5 rounds
Features: Field or competition use; buttstock has adjustable cheekpiece, and LOP spacers, integrated minichassis; one-piece Bergara B-14 action, Bergara Performance trigger, AICS detachable magazine, threaded muzzle and thread protector; left-hand available in 6.5 Creedmoor, .308 Win., .22-250 Rem., and .300 Win. Mag.
MSRP . . . . $1150.00–$1230.00

B-14 HUNTER

Action: Bolt
Stock: Glass fiber-reinforced polymer
Barrel: 22 in. (short actions), 24 in. (long actions)
Sights: None
Weight: 7 lb.–7 lb. 2 oz.
Caliber: .30-06 Spfd., .300 Win. Mag., .270 Win., .308 Win., 6.5 Creedmoor, 7mm Rem. Mag., .243 Win., .22-250 Rem., 7mm-08 Rem.
Magazine: 3, 4 rounds
Features: Stock has Soft Touch coating for better purchase; drilled and tapped for Remington 700-style bases; barrel is matte blue
MSRP $825.00

B-14 RIDGE

Action: Bolt
Stock: Glass fiber-reinforced polymer
Barrel: 18, 22, 24 in.
Sights: None
Weight: 7 lb. 3 oz.–7 lb. 15 oz.
Caliber: 6.5 Creedmoor, 6.5 PRC, .308 Win., .243 Win., .22-250 Rem., 7mm-08 Rem., .450 Bushmaster, .270 Win., .30-06 Spfd., 7mm Rem. Mag., .300 Win. Mag., .300 PRC
Magazine: 3, 4 rounds
Features: Stock has Soft Touch coating for better purchase; drilled and tapped for Remington 700-style bases; barrel is a #5 profile of 4140 CrMo steel in matte blue and threaded for suppressor or muzzle brake use; choice of hinged floor plate or detachable magazine; .308 and 6.5 Creedmoor available in an 18-inch Special Purpose Short Barrel
MSRP . . . . $865.00–$945.00

B-14 TIMBER

Action: Bolt
Stock: Walnut
Barrel: 22 in. (short actions), 24 in. (long actions)
Sights: None
Weight: 7 lb. 5 oz.–7 lb. 9 oz.
Caliber: 6.5 Creedmoor, .308 Win., .30-06 Spfd., .270 Win., .300 Win. Mag., .243 Win.
Features: Monte Carlo cheekpiece; drilled and tapped for Remington 700-style bases; barrel is a #3 profile of 4140 CrMo steel in matte blue; integral epoxy resin pillars surround the action screws in the stock
MSRP $945.00

B-14 WILDERNESS HMR

Action: Bolt
Stock: Molded mini-chassis
Barrel: 20 in., 24 in., 26 in.
Sights: None
Weight: 9 lb. 8 oz.–9 lb. 15 oz.
Caliber: 6.5 Creedmoor, 6.5 PRC, .308 Win., 7mm Rem. Mag., .28 Nosler, .300 Win. Mag., .300 PRC
Magazine: 3, 5 rounds
Features: HMR is Hunting-Match Rifle; two-lug B-14 action; AICS detachable magazine; mini-chassis stock in hand-painted camo; multiport muzzle brake; free-floated #6 barrel; metalwork in Cerakote Sniper Grey
MSRP . . . .$1260.00–$1340.00

B-14 WILDERNESS HUNTER

Action: Bolt
Stock: Synthetic
Barrel: 22 in., 24 in., 26 in.
Sights: None
Weight: 7 lb. 2 oz.–7 lb. 8 oz.
Caliber: 6.5 Creedmoor, .308 Win., .28 Nosler, 7mm Rem. Mag., .300 Win. Mag.
Magazine: 2, 3, 4 rounds
Features: Two-lug B-14 action in a traditionally styled stock having soft-touch features; hinged floorplate magazine; free-floated #3 barrel; metalwork in Cerakote Sniper Grey
MSRP . . . . $899.00–$965.00

Bergara

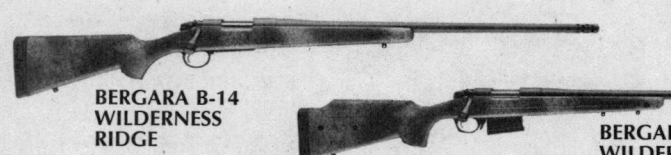

BERGARA B-14 WILDERNESS RIDGE

BERGARA B-14 WILDERNESS TERRAIN

BERGARA B-14R TRAINER CARBON

BERGARA B-14R TRAINER STEEL

BERGARA BXR CARBON

BERGARA BXR STEEL

BERGARA PREMIER APPROACH

B-14 WILDERNESS RIDGE

Action: Bolt
Stock: Synthetic
Barrel: 18 in., 20 in., 22 in., 24 in., 26 in.
Sights: None
Weight: 7 lb. 3 oz.–7 lb. 15 oz.
Caliber: 6.5 Creedmoor, 6.5 PRC, .308 Win., 7mm Rem. Mag., .28 Nosler, .300 Win. Mag., .300 PRC
Magazine: 2, 3, 4 rounds
Features: Two-lug B-14 action in a traditionally styled stock having soft-touch features; hinged floorplate magazine; free-floated #5 barrel with Omni muzzle brake; Bergara Performance Trigger; metalwork in Cerakote Sniper Grey
MSRP . . . . $975.00–$1055.00

B-14 WILDERNESS TERRAIN

Action: Bolt
Stock: Molded mini-chassis
Barrel: 20 in., 24 in., 26 in.
Sights: None
Weight: 8 lb. 15 oz.–10 lb. 2 oz.
Caliber: 6.5 Creedmoor, 6.5 PRC, .308 Win., 7mm Rem. Mag., .28 Nosler, .300 Win. Mag., .300 PRC
Magazine: 3, 5 rounds
Features: Two-lug B-14 action in a Bergara Terrain molded mini-chassis stock with adjustable cheekpiece; free-floated #5.5 barrel with Omni muzzle brake; Bergara Performance Trigger; metalwork in Cerakote Sniper Grey
MSRP . . . . $1199.00–$1279.00

B-14R TRAINER CARBON

Action: Bolt
Stock: Molded mini-chassis
Barrel: 18 in.
Sights: None
Weight: 8 lb. 2 oz.
Caliber: .22 LR
Magazine: 10 rounds
Features: A training rifle with some heft and a threaded #6 carbon-fiber barrel; AICS-style detachable magazine; Bergara Performance Trigger; Bergara HMR molded mini-chassis stock with adjustable cheekpiece and adjustable length of pull; QD flush cup sling mounts and swivels
MSRP $1245.00

B-14R TRAINER STEEL

Action: Bolt
Stock: Molded mini-chassis
Barrel: 18 in.
Sights: None
Weight: 9 lb. 3 oz.
Caliber: .22 LR
Magazine: 10 rounds
Features: Similar to the Trainer Carbon, but with a threaded steel barrel in #6 taper
MSRP $1150.00

BXR CARBON

Action: Bolt
Stock: Synthetic
Barrel: 16.5 in.
Sights: None
Weight: 4 lb. 12 oz.
Caliber: .22 LR
Magazine: 10 rounds
Features: Similar to the BXR base model, but with a carbon-fiber barrel for reduced weight; gray-flecked black stock
MSRP $659.00

BXR STEEL

Action: Bolt
Stock: Synthetic
Barrel: 16.5 in.
Sights: None
Weight: 6 lb. 2 oz.
Caliber: .22 LR
Magazine: 10 rounds
Features: Feature-rich rimfire for competitors with a black-flecked green stock adjustable for length of pull; threaded fluted steel barrel; 30 MOA Picatinny rail; Cerakote ceramic coating on metalwork; rotary magazine (Ruger 10/22 mag compatible)
MSRP $565.00

PREMIER APPROACH

Action: Bolt
Stock: Synthetic
Barrel: 20, 22, 24, 26 in.
Sights: None
Weight: 8 lb. 3 oz.–8 lb. 10 oz.
Caliber: 6.5 Creedmoor, .308 Win., .22-250 Rem., 6.5 PRC, 7mm Rem. Mag., .300 PRC, .300 Win. Mag., .28 Nosler
Features: Hand-laid fiberglass stock in a mottled gray and tan; barrel is threaded; a #5 taper profile; bronze Cerakote finish; TriggerTech Frictionless Release Technology; integral QD cup sling; swivel mounts
MSRP . . . . $1960.00–$2060.00

Bergara

BERGARA PREMIER HIGHLANDER

BERGARA PREMIER HMR PRO

BERGARA LRP 2.0

BERGARA MOUNTAIN 2.0

BERGARA PREMIER RIDGEBACK

PREMIER HIGHLANDER

Action: Bolt
Stock: Fiberglass
Barrel: 20 in., 24 in.
Sights: None
Weight: 7 lb. 3 oz.–7 lb. 11 oz.
Caliber: 6.5 Creedmoor, 6.5 PRC, .28 Nosler, .308 Win., 7mm Rem. Mag., .300 Win. Mag., .300 PRC
Magazine: 3, 4 rounds
Features: For the hunter looking for reach, a rifle featuring Graphite Black Cerakote-finished metalwork; No. 5.5 tapered barrel with threads; TriggerTech Friction Release Technology trigger
MSRP . . . . $1885.00–$1985.00

PREMIER HMR PRO

Action: Bolt
Stock: Synthetic
Barrel: 20, 22, 24, 26 in.
Sights: None
Weight: 9 lb. 5 oz.–9 lb. 13 oz.
Caliber: 6.5 Creedmoor, .308 Win., .22-250 Rem., 6mm Creedmoor, 6.5 PRC, .28 Nosler, 7mm Rem. Mag., .300 Win. Mag., .300 PRC
Magazine: 5, 7 rounds
Features: Stainless one-piece bolt with a cone-shaped nose and a spring-loaded sliding plate extractor; bolt shroud is fully nitrided and self-lubricating; free-floating #5 taper barrel in gray Cerakote; full-length mini chassis; stock adjustable for comb height and length of pull; threaded barrel; detachable AICS-style magazine
MSRP . . . . $1715.00–$1815.00

PREMIER LRP 2.0

Action: Bolt
Stock: Synthetic
Barrel: 24 in., 26 in.
Sights: None
Weight: 9 lb. 10 oz.–9 lb. 13 oz.
Caliber: 6.5 Creedmoor, 6.5 PRC, .300 Win. Mag., .300 PRC
Magazine: 5, 7 rounds
Features: LRP is Long-Range Precision and that's the game this one's built for with an XLR Element 3.0 stock; TriggerTech trigger; AICS-style detachable magazine; threaded muzzle; Cerakote finish in Graphite Black
MSRP . . . . $2000.00–$2100.00

PREMIER MOUNTAIN 2.0

Action: Bolt
Stock: Carbon fiber composite
Barrel: 22 in., 24 in.
Sights: None
Weight: 6 lb. 3 oz.–6 lb. 6 oz.
Caliber: 6.5 Creedmoor, 6.5 PRC, .308 Win., .300 Win. Mag., .300 PRC, .28 Nosler
Magazine: 2, 3, 4 rounds
Features: Part of Bergara's Premier Series with a 100-percent carbon-fiber stock; TriggerTech trigger; No. 3 taper barrel; hinged floor-plate magazine
MSRP . . . . $2150.00–$2250.00

PREMIER RIDGEBACK

Action: Bolt
Stock: Fiberglass
Barrel: 20 in., 24 in., 26 in.
Sights: None
Weight: 10 lb.–10 lb. 9 oz.
Caliber: 6mm Creedmoor, 6.5 Creedmoor, 6.5 PRC, .308 Win., .300 Win. Mag., .300 PRC, .28 Nosler
Magazine: 5, 7 rounds
Features: Dedicated long-range games rifle in all the latest cartridges. Features include: Cerakote black metalwork; medium Palma barrel profile; adjustable cheekpiece with M-LOK compatibility; AICS-type detachable magazine; TriggerTech Frictionless Release Technology trigger
MSRP . . . . $2000.00–$2100.00

Big Horn Armory

BIG HORN ARMORY AR500

AR500

Action: Semiautomatic
Stock: Synthetic
Barrel: 18 in.
Sights: None
Weight: 9 lb. 8 oz.
Caliber: .500 Auto Max
Magazine: 10 rounds
Features: Adjustable gas block; Picatinny rail; flash suppressor; adjustable buttstock; includes a hard case
MSRP $1999.00

Blaser USA

BLASER K95 STUTZEN

BLASER K95 ULTIMATE CARBON

BLASER R8 INTUITION

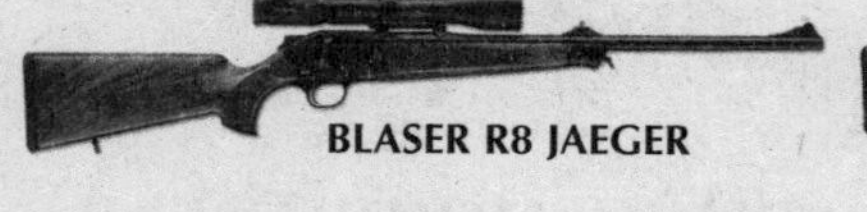

BLASER R8 JAEGER

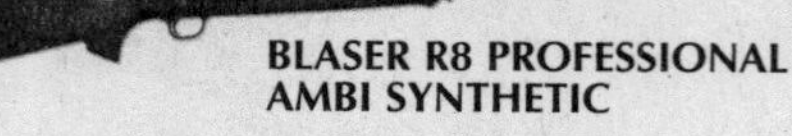

BLASER R8 PROFESSIONAL AMBI SYNTHETIC

BLASER R8 PROFESSIONAL SUCCESS

BLASER R8 ULTIMATE

K95 STUTZEN

Action: Single shot
Stock: Walnut
Barrel: 19.75 in.
Sights: None
Weight: 5 lb. 11 oz.
Caliber: .243 Win., 6.5x57R, 6.5x55 SE, .270 Win., 7x65R, 7x57 R, .308 Win., .30-06 Spfd., 8x57 IRS
Magazine: None
Features: Octagonal barrel standard, barrels are interchangeable; available grades, in order of least to most expensive, are Luxus, Attache, Super Luxus, Baronesse, Exclusive, Super Exclusive, and Imperial; split forearm for continuous precision even in extreme weather; black forearm tip; range of ornamentation and game engravings
MSRP . . . . starting at $10,444.00

K95 ULTIMATE CARBON

Action: Break-action
Stock: Carbon fiber
Barrel: 19.5 in., 23.6 in., 25.5 in., 27.5 in.
Sights: None
Weight: N/A
Caliber: More than 25 cartridges ranging from .22 Hornet to .338 Blaser Mag., plus 10.3X60R
Magazine: 1 round
Features: Featuring a unique, two-piece thumbhole stock with an adjustable comb option; special recoil absorption system or optional adjustable recoil pad; Blaser's cocking slide automatically illuminates the dot in Blaser illuminated riflescopes
MSRP $14,477.00

R8 INTUITION

Action: Bolt
Stock: Wood (various grades)
Barrel: Varies
Sights: Varies
Weight: N/A
Caliber: All common short-action, long-action, and magnum centerfire calibers from .204 Ruger to .338 Lapua.
Magazine: 1, 2, 3, 4, 5 rounds by caliber
Features: Designed specifically for women with a shorter length of pull and a buttstock designed to fit a woman's unique anatomy, including a higher comb, slimmer pistol grip, and a reduction of distance between the trigger and the grip; available in all R8 wood stock configurations
MSRP $5998.00

R8 JAEGER

Action: Straight-pull bolt-action
Stock: Walnut, pistol grip
Barrel: 20.5 in., 23 in., 25.75 in.
Sights: None
Weight: 6 lb. 6 oz.
Caliber: .222 Rem. to .338 Win. Mag.
Magazine: Detachable box, 3 rounds with lock
Features: Cold-hammer-forged barrels and chambers; black forearm tip; synthetic stock in dark green or walnut, straight comb; manual cocking system; integrated trigger/magazine unit; original Blaser saddle mount
MSRP $5545.00

R8 PROFESSIONAL AMBI SYNTHETIC

Action: Straight-pull bolt-action
Stock: Matte dark green synthetic stock, pistol grip
Barrel: 20.5 in., 23 in., 25.75 in.
Sights: None
Weight: 6 lb. 6 oz.
Caliber: .222 Rem. to .338 Win. Mag.
Magazine: Detachable box, 3 rounds with lock
Features: Shatter-proof synthetic stock in dark green brown/black, Savannah or camo with elastomere inlay; detachable magazine/trigger unit; single-stage trigger; quick-release scope mount; ergonomically optimized pistol grip; kickstop optional; precision trigger; black forearm tip; integrated receiver
Single color: $4292.00
Camo: $5195.00

R8 PROFESSIONAL SUCCESS

Action: Bolt
Stock: Synthetic
Barrel: 22.8 in., 25.6 in.
Sights: Open
Weight: 7 lb.
Caliber: .222 Rem., .204 Ruger, .223 Rem., .22–250 Rem., .243 Win., 6XC, 6.5x55 Swedish, 6.5x57, 6.5x65 RWS, .270 Win., 7x64 Brenneke, .308 Win., .30-06 Spfd., 8x57 IS, 8.5x63, 9.3x57, 9.3x62 Mauser, 6.5x68, 7.5x55 Suisse, 8x68 S, .257 Wby. Mag., .270 Wby. Mag., .270 WSM, 7mm Blaser Mag., 7mm Rem. Mag., .300 Blaser Mag., .300 Win. Mag., .300 Wby. Mag., .300 WSM, .338 Blaser Mag., .338 Win. Mag., .375 Blaser Mag., .375 H&H
Magazine: 3+1, 4+1, 5+1 rounds
Features: Blaser precision trigger; radial locking system; ergonomically optimized stock in dark green or dark brown and elastomer grips; double loading option; leather model available
Single color: . . . $4875.00–$6147.00
Monza: $6783.00
Black edition: $6995.00
Ruthenium: $7843.00
Carbon: $10,789.00
Stutzen: . . . . $5405.00–$6498.00

R8 ULTIMATE

Action: Bolt
Stock: Carbon fiber
Barrel: 19.5 in., 22 in., 25.5 in., 23.6 in., 27.5 in.
Sights: None
Weight: N/A
Caliber: More than 40 cartridges ranging from .204 Ruger to .500 Jeffery, plus 10.3X60R
Magazine: 2, 3, 4 rounds
Features: Similar to the K95 break-action Ultimate Carbon, but in the renowned switch-barrel, box magazine R8 configuration; optional leather or elastomer stock inserts
MSRP . . . . $4875.00–$6783.00

Blaser USA

BLASER R8 ULTIMATE SILENCE

R8 ULTIMATE SILENCE

Action: Bolt
Stock: Synthetic
Barrel: varies with caliber
Sights: None
Weight: N/A
Caliber: .308 Win., 8x57 IS, 9.3x62, .30-06 Spfd., .300 Win. Mag., .300 Blaser Mag., 8.5x55 Blaser
Magazine: N/A
Features: Similar to the Ultimate and Ultimate Leather models, but with a limited number of calibers that benefit from the noise reduction provided by the integral silencer; optional leather stock inlays
MSRP . . . . N/A

Brownells

BROWNELLS BRN-10B

BROWNELLS BRN-605

BROWNELLS XBRN-177E2

BROWNELLS BRN-16A1

BROWNELLS BRN-PROTO

BROWNELLS BRN-601

BROWNELLS XBRN16E1

BRN-10B

Acti***on***: Semiautomatic
Stock: Synthetic
Barrel: 20 in.
Sights: Standard AR-15-style front, period-style rear
Weight: 8 lb.
Caliber: .308 Win.
Magazine: 20 rounds
Features: Based on the Stoner rifle in use from 1955-1960; closed-prong Portuguese flash hider; trigger-style charging handle; 7075-T6 aluminum receiver; black retro stock and forearm; aluminum magazine included
MSRP $1899.99

BRN-16A1

Acti***on***: Semiautomatic
Stock: Synthetic
Barrel: 20 in.
Sights: Standard AR-15-style front, period-style rear
Weight: 6 lb. 13 oz.
Caliber: 5.56 NATO
Magazine: 20 rounds
Features: Direct impingement rifle; matte gray anodized; three-prong A1 flash hider, 1:12 chrome bore barrel; based off the original in use from 1967-1982
MSRP $1299.99

BRN-601

Action: Semiautomatic
Stock: Synthetic
Barrel: 20 in.
Sights: Standard AR-15-style front, period-style rear
Weight: 6 lb. 11 oz.
Caliber: 5.56 NATO
Magazine: 20 rounds
Features: Based on 1959–1964 model; slickside upper; 1:12 chrome-bore barrel; a three-prong "duckbill" flash hider; green stock and pistol grip; waffle magazine
MSRP $1299.99

BRN-605

Action: Semiautomatic
Stock: Synthetic
Barrel: 15.5 in.
Sights: Fixed front, adjustable rear
Weight: 6 lb. 11 oz.
Caliber: 5.56 NATO
Magazine: 20 rounds
Features: A copy of Colt's prototype 605 carbine, a firearm that never saw issue, featuring a pinned and welded three-prong flash hider; XM16E1 lower with partial magazine fence; XM16E1 upper; chrome bolt carrier group; forward assist; matte gray anodized metal; black stock
MSRP $1398.99

BRN-PROTO

Action: Semiautomatic
Stock: Synthetic
Barrel: 20 in.
Sights: Fixed front, adjustable rear
Weight: 6 llb. 11 oz.
Caliber: 5.56 NATO
Magazine: 25 rounds
Features: Faithful reproduction of Stoner's original AR prototype, featuring a three-prong duckbill flash hider; brown stock; matt gray anodized finish; rifle-length gas tube; trigger-type charging handle located on top of the receiver; 1:12 twist; slab-side lower
MSRP $1633.99

XBRN16E1

Acti***on***: Semiautomatic
Stock: Synthetic
Barrel: 20 in.
Sights: Standard AR-15-style front, period-style rear
Weight: 6 lb. 11 oz.
Caliber: 5.56 NATO
Magazine: 20 rounds
Features: Based on 1964–1967 model; chrome bolt carrier group with forward assist; anodized matte gray finish; black stock and forend; three-prong flash hider; lower receiver has a partial "magazine fence"
MSRP $1399.99

XBRN-177E2

Action: Semiautomatic
Stock: Synthetic
Barrel: 12.7 in.
Sights: Standard AR-15-style front, period-style rear
Weight: 5 lb. 11 oz.
Caliber: 5.56 NATO
Magazine: 20 rounds
Features: Based on model used from 1967–1982; adjustable buttstock and short, maneuverable barrel; Mil-Spec phosphate/chrome bolt carrier group; AXM177 three-prong flash hider with a grenade ring; full "magazine fence"
MSRP $1397.99

Browning

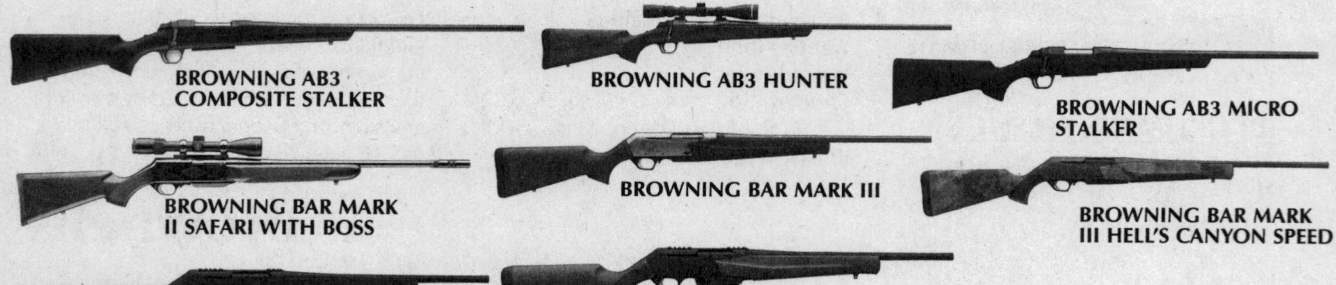

BROWNING AB3 COMPOSITE STALKER

BROWNING AB3 HUNTER

BROWNING AB3 MICRO STALKER

BROWNING BAR MARK II SAFARI WITH BOSS

BROWNING BAR MARK III

BROWNING BAR MARK III HELL'S CANYON SPEED

BROWNING BAR MARK III DBM, WOOD

BROWNING BAR MARK III DBM

RIFLES

AB3 COMPOSITE STALKER

Action: Bolt
Stock: Synthetic
Barrel: 22 in., 26 in.
Sights: None
Weight: 6 lb. 9 oz.–7 lb. 3 oz.
Caliber: .243 Win., .270 Win., .270 WSM, .30-06 Spfd., .300 Win. Mag., .300 WSM, .308 Win., 6.5 Creedmoor, 7mm Rem. Mag., 7mm-08 Rem.
Magazine: Detachable box, 4 rounds
Features: Inflex Technology recoil pad; top tang safety; blued barrel and action
MSRP. $629.99

AB3 HUNTER

Action: Bolt
Stock: Satin
Barrel: 22 in.
Sights: Drilled and tapped for sights
Weight: 6 lb. 11 oz.–7 lb. 6 oz.
Caliber: .243 Win., .270 Win., .270 WSM, .30-06 Spfd., .300 Win. Mag., .300 WSM, .308 Win., 6.5 Creedmoor, 7mm Rem. Mag., 7mm-08 Rem.
Magazine: Detachable box
Features: 5-round mag capacity; steel barrel; polished finish
MSRP. $719.99

AB3 MICRO STALKER

Action: Bolt
Stock: Composite
Barrel: 20 in.
Sights: None
Weight: 6 lb. 6 oz.–6 lb. 8 oz.
Caliber: .243 Win., 6.5 Creedmoor, 7mm-08 Rem., .308 Win.
Magazine: 5 rounds
Features: Intended for smaller-statured hunters; 13 in. length of pull; Pachmayr Decelerator recoil pad; drilled and tapped for scope mounts
MSRP. $629.99

BAR MARK II SAFARI WITH BOSS

Action: Gas-operated semiautomatic
Stock: Walnut
Barrel: 22 in., 24 in.
Sights: None
Weight: 8 lb. 1.6 oz.–8 lb. 3 oz.
Caliber: .270 Win., .30-06 Spfd., .300 Win. Mag., .338 Win. Mag.
Magazine: Detachable box
Features: Checkered, select gloss finish walnut stock; steel receiver with blued finish and scroll engraving; drilled and tapped for scope mounts; multi-lug rotary bolt; recoil pad sling swivel studs installed
MSRP. . . . . $1499.99–$1639.99

BAR MARK III

Action: Semiautomatic
Stock: Walnut
Barrel: 22 in., 23 in., 24 in.
Sights: None
Weight: 7 lb. 2 oz.–7 lb. 11 oz.
Caliber: .243 Win., .270 Win., .270 WSM, .30-06 Spfd., .300 Win. Mag., .300 WSM, .308 Win., 7mm Rem. Mag., 7mm-08 Rem.
Magazine: Detachable rotary, 3 or 4 rounds
Features: Completely new styling; fine oil-finished walnut; precision alloy receiver; hammer-forged barrel; drilled and tapped for scope; gold trigger guard engraving; left-hand version available
MSRP. . . . . $1339.99–$1479.99

BAR MARK III DBM

Action: Semiautomatic
Stock: Composite
Barrel: 18 in.
Sights: None
Weight: 6 lb. 10 oz.
Caliber: .308 Win.
Magazine: 10 rounds
Features: Detachable box magazine with a magwell instead of the standard hinged floor plate design; QD swivel cups (QD sling swivels included); 1913 Picatinny rail scope bases; hammer-forged barrel
MSRP. $1559.99

BAR MARK III DBM, WOOD

Action: Semiautomatic
Stock: Wood
Barrel: 18 in.
Sights: None
Weight: 6 lb. 10 oz.
Caliber: .308 Win.
Magazine: 10 rounds
Features: With a hybrid military/European hunting look, this lightweight and fast-handling .308 has detachable box magazine; two top-side scope mount rails; sling swivel studs; matte-finish metal; composite trigger guard; multi-lug rotary bolt; gas-piston functionality
MSRP. $1589.99

BAR MARK III HELL'S CANYON SPEED

Action: Semiautomatic
Stock: Composite
Barrel: 22 in., 23 in., 24 in.
Sights: None
Weight: 6 lb. 10 oz.–7 lb. 8 oz.
Caliber: .243 Win., 7mm-08 Rem., .308 Win., .270 WSM, .300 WSM, .270 Win., .30–06 Spfd., 7mm Rem. Mag., .300 Win. Mag.
Magazine: 4 rounds
Features: Eye-catching gun for the big-game hunter with: Burnt Bronze Cerakote-finish metal; composite stock with grip overmolds in A-TACS AU camo; shim-adjustable stock; Inflex recoil pad; detachable box magazine with hinged floor plate; hammer-forged barrel
MSRP. . . . . $1659.99–$1749.99

Browning

BROWNING BAR MARK III STALKER

BROWNING BLR LIGHTWEIGHT '81

BROWNING BLR LIGHTWEIGHT '81 STAINLESS TAKEDOWN

BROWNING BLR LIGHTWEIGHT STAINLESS WITH PISTOL GRIP

BROWNING SEMI-AUTO GRADE II OCTAGON

BROWNING T-BOLT COMPOSITE TARGET/VARMINT

BROWNING T-BOLT GRAY LAMINATED TARGET/VARMINT STAINLESS, SUPPRESSOR READY

BAR MARK III STALKER

Action: Semiautomatic
Stock: Composite
Barrel: 22 in., 23 in., 24 in.
Sights: None
Weight: 6 lb. 10 oz.–7 lb. 8 oz.
Caliber: .243 Win., 7mm-08 Rem., .308 Win., .270 Win., .30-06 Spfd., 7mm Rem. Mag., .300 Win. Mag., .300 WSM, .270 WSM
Magazine: 3, 4 rounds
Features: Composite stock with contemporary design; shim-adjustable for cast and drop at comb; gas-piston operation; lightweight aluminum alloy receiver drilled and tapped for scope mounts; hinged floor plate with detachable box magazine
Standard Stalker: $1339.99–$1439.99
Mossy Oak: . . . . $1459.99–$1589.99

BLR LIGHTWEIGHT '81

Action: Lever
Stock: Walnut, straight grip
Barrel: 20 in., 22 in., 24 in.
Sights: None
Weight: 6 lb. 8 oz.–7 lb. 12 oz.
Caliber: .22-250 Rem., .223 Rem., .243 Win., .270 Win., .270 WSM, .30-06 Spfd., .300 Win. Mag., .300 WSM, .308 Win., .325 WSM, .358 Win., .450 Marlin, 7mm Rem. Mag., 7mm WSM, 7mm-08 Rem., .222 Rem., 6.5 Creedmoor
Magazine: Detachable box
Features: Aircraft-grade alloy receiver; drilled and tapped for scope mounts; crowned muzzle; adjustable sights; gloss finish walnut stock; recoil pad
MSRP . . . . $959.99–$1019.99

BLR LIGHTWEIGHT '81 STAINLESS TAKEDOWN

Action: Lever-action
Stock: Laminate, straight grip
Barrel: 20 in., 22 in., 24 in.
Sights: Open
Weight: 6 lb. 8 oz.–7 lb. 12 oz.
Caliber: .223 Rem. .22-250 Rem., 6.5 Creedmoor, .243 Win., 7mm-08 Rem., .308 Win., .358 Win., .450 Marlin, .270 WSM, 7mm WSM, .270 Win., .30-06 Spfd., 7mm Rem. Mag., .300 WSM, .300 Win. Mag.
Magazine: Detachable box
Features: Aircraft-grade alloy receiver; drilled and tapped for scope mounts; stainless steel barrel with matte finish; gray laminate wood stock in satin finish; recoil pad; separates for storage or transportation; optional Scout-style scope mount; TRUGLO/Marble's fiber optic front sight
MSRP . . . . $1259.99–$1339.99

BLR LIGHTWEIGHT STAINLESS WITH PISTOL GRIP

Action: Lever-action
Stock: Walnut, pistol grip
Barrel: 20 in., 22 in., 24 in.
Sights: None
Weight: 6 lb. 8 oz.–7 lb. 12 oz.
Caliber: .450 Marlin, .22-250 Rem., .223 Rem., .243 Win., 6.5 Creedmoor, .270 Win., .270 WSM, .30-06 Spfd., .300 Win. Mag., .300 WSM, .308 Win., .325 WSM, .358 Win., 7mm Rem. Mag., 7mm-08 Rem., 7mm WSM
Magazine: Detachable box
Features: Aircraft-grade alloy receiver; drilled and tapped for scope mounts; steel barrel with matte finish; crowned muzzle; adjustable sights; gloss finish walnut stock with pistol grip; sling swivel studs installed; recoil pad
MSRP . . . . $1159.99–$1239.99

SEMI-AUTO GRADE II OCTAGON

Action: Semiautomatic
Stock: Grade II/III black walnut
Barrel: 19.4 in.
Sights: Blade front, notch rear
Weight: 5 lb. 3 oz.
Caliber: .22 LR
Magazine: 10 rounds
Features: A John Browning original gets a gloss-finish black walnut stock; takedown design; octagon barrel; metal buttplate; satin nickel receiver with scroll engraving; steel trigger guard; drilled and tapped for optic mounting
MSRP $1039.99

T-BOLT COMPOSITE TARGET/VARMINT

Action: T-bolt
Stock: Synthetic
Barrel: 22 in.
Sights: None
Weight: 5 lb. 13 oz.
Caliber: .22 LR, .22 WMR, .17 HMR
Magazine: 10 rounds
Features: Medium-contour varmint profile barrel; rimfire; stock with extra magazine storage; adjustable trigger; double helix rotary magazine (two included); satin blue metalwork
MSRP . . . . $779.99–$799.99

T-BOLT GRAY LAMINATED TARGET/VARMINT STAINLESS, SUPPRESSOR READY

Action: T-bolt
Stock: Laminate
Barrel: 22 in.
Sights: None
Weight: 5 lb. 10 oz.
Caliber: .22 LR, .22 WMR, .17 HMR
Magazine: 10 rounds
Features: Gray laminate stock with a Monte Carlo comb; a free-floating barrel with a medium target profile and recessed crown; semi-match grade chamber; adjustable trigger; installed sling swivels; threaded for suppressor use; thread protector included
MSRP . . . . $959.99–$1019.99

Browning

BROWNING T-BOLT SPORTER LEFT-HAND

BROWNING X-BOLT ECLIPSE HUNTER

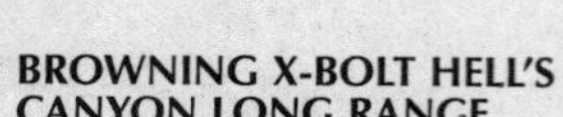

BROWNING X-BOLT HELL'S CANYON LONG RANGE

BROWNING X-BOLT HELL'S CANYON LONG RANGE MCMILLAN

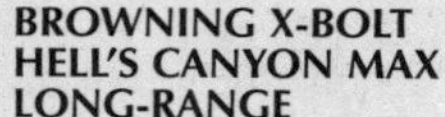

BROWNING X-BOLT HELL'S CANYON MAX LONG-RANGE

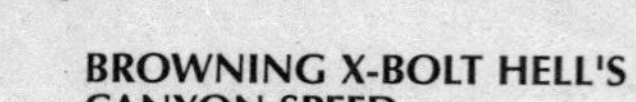

BROWNING X-BOLT HELL'S CANYON SPEED

T-BOLT SPORTER LEFT-HAND

Action: T-bolt
Stock: Walnut
Barrel: 22 in.
Sights: None
Weight: 4 lb. 14 oz.
Caliber: .22 LR, .22 WMR, .17 HMR
Magazine: 10 rounds
Features: With right-hand ejection, this lefty gun has a left-side bolt; medium-contour sporter barrel, free-floating and with a semi-match chamber and recessed crown
MSRP . . . . $749.99–$799.99

X-BOLT ECLIPSE HUNTER

Action: Bolt
Stock: Wood laminate
Barrel: 22 in., 23 in., 24 in., 26 in.
Sights: None
Weight: 6 lb. 7 oz.–7 lb. 8 oz.
Caliber: .243 Win., 6mm Creedmoor, 6.5 Creedmoor, 7mm-08 Rem., .308 Win., .270 WSM, .300 WSM, .25-06 Rem., .270 Win., .30-06 Spfd., 7mm Rem. Mag., .300 Win. Mag.
Magazine: Detachable box, 4 rounds
Features: Inflex Technology recoil pad
MSRP . . . . $1229.99–$1339.99

X-BOLT HELL'S CANYON LONG RANGE

Action: Bolt
Stock: Composite
Barrel: 26 in.
Sights: None
Weight: 7 lb. 3 oz.–7 lb. 8 oz.
Caliber: 6mm Creedmoor, 6.5 Creedmoor, .270 WSM, .300 WSM, 7mm Rem. Mag., .28 Nosler, .280 Ackley Improved, .300 Win. Mag., 6.5 PRC, .30 Nosler, .300 RUM, .300 PRC, 6.5 Western
Magazine: 4 rounds
Features: Heavy sporter contour barrel for increased long-range accuracy; exclusive A-TACS AU camouflage with DuraTouch Armor Coating; free-floated, fluted barrel and receiver metal are in burnt bronze Cerakote; barrel is threaded for suppressor use; bolt unlock button, Inflex recoil pad 60-degree short bolt lift, and detachable rotary magazine
MSRP . . . . $1279.99–$1389.99

X-BOLT HELL'S CANYON LONG RANGE MCMILLAN

Action: Bolt
Stock: Composite
Barrel: 26 in.
Sights: None
Weight: 7 lb. 7 oz.–7 lb. 12 oz.
Caliber: 6mm Creedmoor, 6.5 Creedmoor, .300 WSM, .26 Nosler, 7mm Rem. Mag., .28 Nosler, 7mm Rem. Mag., .28 Nosler, .280 Ackley Improved, .300 Win. Mag., 6.5 PRC, .30 Nosler, .300 RUM, .300 PRC, 6.8 Western
Magazine: 3, 4 rounds
Features: The McMillan Game Scout stock (high comb, vertical pistol grip) has a palm swell and textured grip panels, in Browning's A-TACS AU (arid/urban) camo; free-floating, hand-chambered barrel has a threaded muzzle brake mounted on suppressor-ready threads and wears a target crown; receiver is glass-bedded; magazine is detachable; top-side optics rail; adjustable Feather trigger; available left-hand
MSRP . . . . $2229.99–$2389.99

X-BOLT HELL'S CANYON MAX LONG-RANGE

Action: Bolt
Stock: Composite
Barrel: 26 in.
Sights: None
Weight: 8 lb.–8 lb. 3 oz.
Caliber: 6.5 Creedmoor, 6.5 PRC, 7mm Rem. Mag., .28 Nosler, .280 Ackley Improved, .300 Win. Mag., .30 Nosler, .300 RUM, .300 PRC, 6.8 Western
Magazine: 3, 4 rounds
Features: Target-ready Max stock has a deep vertical pistol grip, adjustable comb, and stock spacers; heavy sporter contour barrel is fluted and threaded, muzzle brake included; metalwork in burnt bronze Cerakote; stock in A-TACS TD-X camo
MSRP . . . . $1429.99–$1559.99

X-BOLT HELL'S CANYON SPEED

Action: Bolt
Stock: Composite
Barrel: 22 in., 23, in. 26 in.
Sights: None
Weight: 6 lb. 5 oz.–6 lb. 13 oz.
Caliber: .243 Win., 6mm Creedmoor, 6.5 Creedmoor, 7mm-08 Rem., .308 Win., .270 Win., .30-06 Spfd., .270 WSM, .300 WSM, 7mm Rem. Mag., .28 Nosler, .280 Ackley Improved, .300 Win. Mag., 6.5 PRC, .30 Nosler, .300 RUM, .300 PRC, 6.8 Western
Magazine: Detachable rotary, 3 or 4 rounds
Features: A-TACS AU (Arid/Urban) camouflage; Dura-Touch finish; composite stock; Cerakote finish; fluted; sporter barrel with threaded muzzle brake; detachable rotary magazine; short throw bolt; adjustable trigger; Inflex Technology recoil pad; also available in A-TACS TD-X in a narrower selection of calibers
MSRP . . . . $1259.99–$1359.99

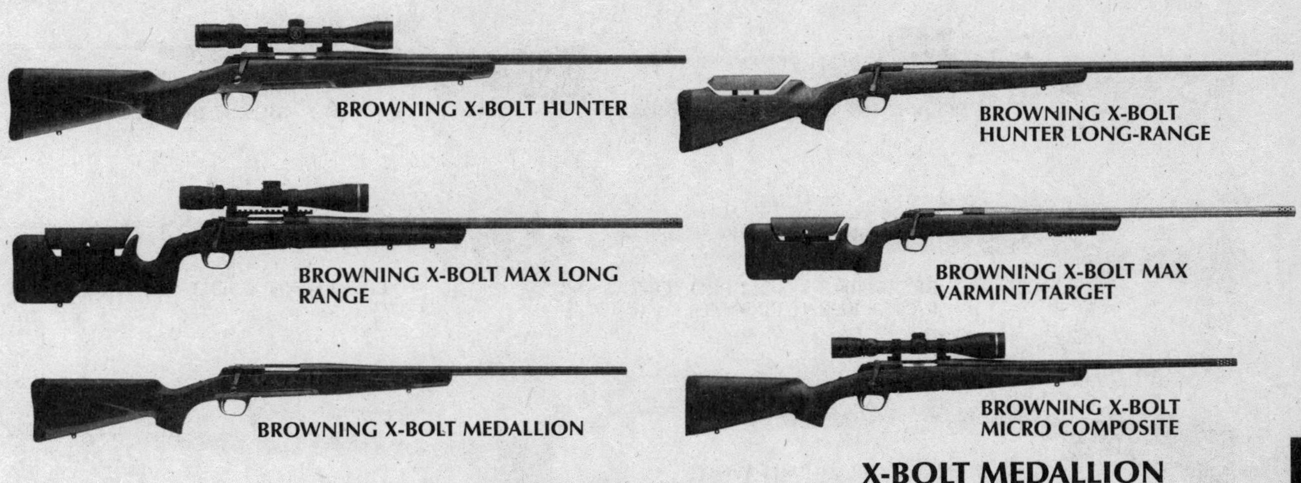

X-BOLT HUNTER

Action: Bolt
Stock: Satin finish walnut stock
Barrel: 22 in., 23 in., 24 in., 26 in.
Sights: None
Weight: 6 lb. 13 oz.–7 lb.
Caliber: 6.5 Creedmoor, 6mm Creedmoor, .223 Rem., .22-250 Rem., .243 Win., 7mm-08 Rem., .308 Win., .270 WSM, .300 WSM, .25-06 Rem., .270 Win., .280 Rem., .30-06 Spfd., 7mm Rem. Mag., .375 H&H Mag., 338 Win. Mag., .300 Win. Mag.
Magazine: Detachable rotary box
Features: Adjustable feather trigger; top-tang safety with bolt unlock button; sling swivel studs installed; Inflex technology recoil pad
MSRP . . . . $999.99–$1039.99

X-BOLT HUNTER LONG-RANGE

Action: Bolt
Stock: Black walnut
Barrel: 22 in., 24 in., 26 in.
Sights: None
Weight: 7 lb. 11 oz.–8 lb. 6 oz.
Caliber: 6.5 Creedmoor, 6.5 PRC, .308 Win., .270 Win., .30-06 Spfd., 7mm Rem. Mag., .300 Win. Mag., 6.8 Western, .280 Ackley Improved
Magazine: 3, 4 rounds
Features: Adjustable cheekpiece on traditionally styled rifle; removeable muzzle brake; heavy sporter contour barrel; matte blue metalwork; satin-finished stock with checkering
MSRP . . . . $1299.99–$1379.99

X-BOLT MAX LONG RANGE

Action: Bolt
Stock: Composite
Barrel: 26 in.
Sights: None
Weight: 8 lb. 3 oz.–8 lb. 7 oz.
Caliber: 6mm Creedmoor, 6.5 Creedmoor, .308 Win., .300 WSM, 7mm Rem. Mag., .28 Nosler, .300 Win. Mag., .300 RUM, 6.5 PRC, .30 Nosler, .300 PRC, 6.8 Western
Magazine: 3, 4 rounds
Features: Viable entry for those looking to get into the long-range game, featuring Composite Max stock with adjustable comb and a black-and-gray textured finish; fluted, stainless steel, heavy contour barrel; TPI threaded muzzle brake and thread protector; length of pull spacers; three swivel studs
MSRP . . . . $1339.99–$1399.99

X-BOLT MAX VARMINT/ TARGET

Action: Bolt
Stock: Composite
Barrel: 26 in.
Sights: None
Weight: 9 lb.–9 lb. 10 oz.
Caliber: .204 Ruger, .223 Rem., .22-250 Rem., 6.5 Creedmoor, .308 Win., .28 Nosler, .300 Win. Mag.
Magazine: 3, 4, 5 rounds
Features: Prairie dogs, coyotes, and other varmints are no match for this rifle with its adjustable scope; stainless fluted heavy bull barrel with removeable muzzle brake; forearm bipod rail; textured grip panels
MSRP . . . .$1379.99–$1459.99

X-BOLT MEDALLION

Action: Bolt
Stock: Walnut
Barrel: 22 in., 23 in., 24 in., 26 in.
Sights: Open
Weight: 6 lb. 6 oz.–7 lb.
Caliber: .223 Rem., .22-250 Rem., .243 Win., .270 Win., .308 Win., .25-06 Rem., .280 Rem., .30-06 Spfd., 7mm Rem. Mag., .300 Win. Mag., .300 WSM, .270 WSM, .325 WSM, .338 Win. Mag., .375 H&H Mag., 6.5 Creedmoor, 6mm Creedmoor
Magazine: Detachable rotary box
Features: Gloss finish walnut stock, rosewood forend grip and pistol cap; Inflex technology recoil pad; adjustable feather trigger; drilled and tapped for scope mounts; left-hand option
MSRP . . . . $1039.99–$1179.99

X-BOLT MICRO COMPOSITE

Action: Bolt
Stock: Composite
Barrel: 20 in.
Sights: None
Weight: 6 lb. 5 oz.
Caliber: .243 Win., 6mm Creedmoor, 6.5 Creedmoor, 7mm-08 Rem., .308 Rem.
Magazine: 4 rounds
Features: Shorter length of pull at 13 in.; stock is a non-glare composite in black and with textured gripping surfaces and a palm swell; free-floating barrel features a threaded muzzle brake, thread protector, target crown, and light sporter contour; sling swivel studs; Pachmayr Decelerator recoil pad
MSRP . . . . $999.99–$1029.99

Browning

BROWNING X-BOLT MICRO MIDAS

BROWNING X-BOLT PRO BURNT BRONZE

BROWNING X-BOLT PRO LONG RANGE BURNT BRONZE

BROWNING X-BOLT PRO TUNGSTEN

BROWNING X-BOLT RMEF WHITE GOLD MEDALLION

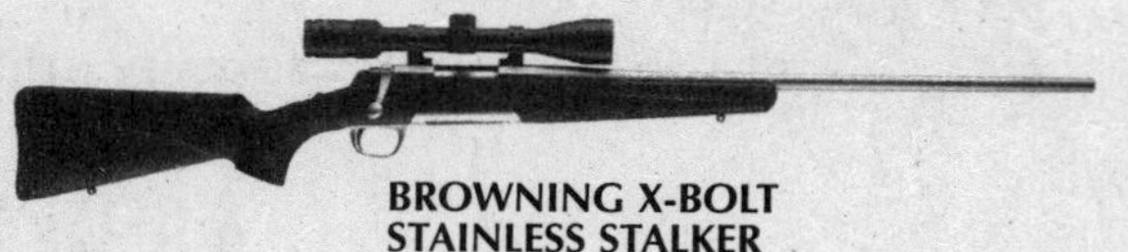
BROWNING X-BOLT STAINLESS STALKER

X-BOLT MICRO MIDAS

Action: Bolt
Stock: Walnut
Barrel: 20 in.
Sights: None
Weight: 6 lb. 1 oz–6 lb. 6 oz.
Caliber: .22-250 Rem., .243 Win., 6mm Creedmoor, 7mm-08 Rem., .308 Win., 6.5 Creedmoor, .270 WSM, .300 WSM
Magazine: Detachable rotary magazine
Features: Drilled and tapped for scope mounts, low-luster blued finish, free-floating barrel; adjustable feather trigger; top-tang safety; left-hand option
MSRP . . . . $859.99–$939.99

X-BOLT PRO BURNT BRONZE

Action: Bolt
Stock: Carbon fiber wrap
Barrel: 22 in., 23 in., 26 in.
Sights: None
Weight: 6 lb. 1 oz.–6 lb. 10 oz.
Caliber: 6.5 Creedmoor, .308 Win., .30-06 Spfd., .300 Win. Mag., .28 Nosler, .300 WSM, 7mm Rem. Mag., .270 Win., 6mm Creedmoor, 6.5 PRC, .30 Nosler, .300 RUM, .300 PRC
Magazine: 3, 4 rounds
Features: "Semi-custom" rifle; stock has a compressed foam core wrapped 360-degrees with carbon fiber; barrel is a lightweight sporter profile; threaded muzzle brake; spiral-fluted bolt with an oversized knob; Burnt Bronze Cerakote finish
MSRP . . . .$2099.99–$2389.99

X-BOLT PRO LONG RANGE BURNT BRONZE

Action: Bolt
Stock: Carbon fiber wrap
Barrel: 26 in.
Sights: None
Weight: 6 lb. 1 oz.–6 lb. 10 oz.
Caliber: 6.5 Creedmoor, .270 WSM, .300 WSM, 7mm Rem. Mag., .28 Nosler, .300 Win. Mag., 6.5 PRC, .30 Nosler, .300 RUM, .300 PRC
Magazine: 3, 4 rounds
Features: Pro Long Range barrel with heavy sporter contour, fluted, free-floating, and threaded muzzle brake; Burnt Bronze Cerakote finish
MSRP . . . . $2189.99–$2429.99

X-BOLT PRO TUNGSTEN

Action: Bolt
Stock: Carbon fiber
Barrel: 22 in., 26 in.
Sights: None
Weight: 6 lb. 1 oz.–6 lb. 10 oz.
Caliber: 6.5 Creedmoor, .308 Win., .300 WSM, .270 Win., .30–06 Spfd., 7mm Rem. Mag., .28 Nosler, .300 Win. Mag., 6.5 PRC, .30 Nosler, .300 RUM
Magazine: 3, 4 rounds
Features: Hunter or target master, this sleek rifle features a Tungsten Cerakote finish on the metalwork; full carbon-fiber-wrapped stock; spiral-fluted bolt; threaded on muzzle brake; oversized bolt knob; fluted barrel in lightweight sporter contour
MSRP . . . . $2279.99–$2389.99

X-BOLT RMEF WHITE GOLD MEDALLION

Action: Bolt
Stock: Walnut
Barrel: 26 in.
Sights: None
Weight: 7 lb.
Caliber: .300 Win. Mag.
Magazine: Detachable rotary box
Features: Monte Carlo stock; stainless steel barrel and receiver, receiver etched in gold; raised cheekpiece; Inflex technology recoil pad; adjustable feather trigger; top-tang safety
MSRP $1669.99

X-BOLT STAINLESS STALKER

Action: Bolt
Stock: Composite
Barrel: 22 in., 23 in., 24 in., 26 in.
Sights: None
Weight: 6 lb. 3 oz.–6 lb. 13 oz.
Caliber: .243 Win., 6.5 Creedmoor, 7mm-08 Rem., .308 Win., .270 WSM, .300 WSM, .25-06 Rem., .270 Win., .30-06 Spfd., 7mm Rem. Mag., .300 Win. Mag., .338 Win. Mag., .375 H&H Mag.
Magazine: Detachable rotary box
Features: Composite stock in matte black with textured gripping surfaces; Dura-Touch armor coating; adjustable feather trigger; top-tang safety; bolt unlock button; palm swell
MSRP . . . . $1189.99–$1269.99

Browning

BROWNING X-BOLT TARGET MCMILLAN A3-5 AMBUSH

BROWNING X-BOLT WESTERN HUNTER FIBER FUSION

X-BOLT TARGET MCMILLAN A3-5 AMBUSH

Action: Bolt
Stock: Composite
Barrel: 26 in.
Sights: None
Weight: 10 lb.–10 lb. 4 oz.
Caliber: 6.5 Creedmoor, .308 Win., 7mm Rem. Mag., .28 Nosler, .300 Win. Mag., 6.5 PRC
Magazine: 3, 4 rounds
Features: A serious long-range contender in enough calibers to satisfy most and featuring: McMillan's A3-5 adjustable comb composite stock in Urban Carbon Ambush camo; Pachmyr Decelerator recoil pad; TPI suppressor-threaded muzzle brake; over-length bolt handle; 20 MOA Picatinny rail; fluted bull barrel; swivel studs; bipod rail
MSRP . . . . $3069.99–$3309.99

X-BOLT WESTERN HUNTER FIBER FUSION

Action: Bolt
Stock: Carbon fiber
Barrel: 24 in., 26
Sights: None
Weight: 7 lb.–8 lb.
Caliber: 6.5 Creedmoor, 6.5 PRC, .270 Win., .30-06 Spfd., 7mm Rem. Mag., .28 Nosler, .300 Win. Mag., .30 Nosler, .300 RUM, .300 PRC
Magazine: 3, 4 rounds
Features: Hard-Core Fiber Fusion adjustable stock dressed in flat dark earth Cerakote with black spider-webbing; sporter contour (standard) or heavy sporter contour (Long-Range) barrel, fluted and threaded and with muzzle brake, dressed in a matte gray finish; receiver in matte blue
MSRP . . . .$2039.99–$2119.99

Caracal USA

CARACAL USA CAR814 A2 MOE

CARACAL USA CAR816 A2

CARACAL USA VERSUS COMPETITION

CAR814 A2 MOE

Action: Semiautomatic
Stock: Synthetic
Barrel: 11.5, 14.5, 15 in.
Sights: A2 front sight, flip-up rear
Weight: 7 lb.
Caliber: 5.56 NATO
Magazine: 30 rounds
Features: Direct impingement gas-operated system; Magpul MOE M-LOK handguard; Magpul CTR mil-spec carbine stock; Caracal grip
MSRP . . . . $655.00–$999.00

CAR816 A2

Action: Semiautomatic
Stock: Synthetic
Barrel: 11.5, 14.5, 16 in.
Sights: Flip-up front and rear
Weight: 7 lb. 6.4 oz.
Caliber: 5.56 NATO
Magazine: 30 rounds
Features: Short-stroke push rod gas piston system; three-position adjustable gas valve; Caracal handguard; full-length 1913 Picatinny rail; Modified M4 barrel contour; Magpul STR Carbine stock or SBA3 Pistol Brace stock; A2-style flash hider; select-fire option available; EDT Sharp Shooter trigger
MSRP . . . . $1254.00–$1929.00

VERSUS COMPETITION

Action: Semiautomatic
Stock: Synthetic
Barrel: 18 in.
Sights: None
Weight: 6 lb. 3 oz.
Caliber: .223 Wylde
Magazine: 10, 30 rounds
Features: A lightweight nimble gun for the 3-Gun crowd in an outside-the-box caliber. Features include carbon fiber-wrapped 416R stainless barrel; two-port, self-timing muzzle brake; 15-inch Caracal free-floating handguard with MLOK and QD attachment points; Caracal grip; direct impingement gas system
MSRP $1799.00

Century Arms

CENTURY ARMS VSKA

VSKA

Action: Semiautomatic
Stock: American maple
Barrel: 16.3 in.
Sights: A2-style front, ladder-type adjustable rear
Weight: N/A
Caliber: 7.62X39
Magazine: 30 rounds
Features: An upscale, heavy-duty AK-47-style rifle with American maple stock; heat-treated S7 tool steel bolt carrier, front trunnion, and feed ramp; chrome moly 4150 barrel; RAK-1 Enhanced Trigger Group; manganese-phosphate finish; available in synthetic stock and California-compliant versions
MSRP . . . . $799.99–$899.99

Chiappa Firearms

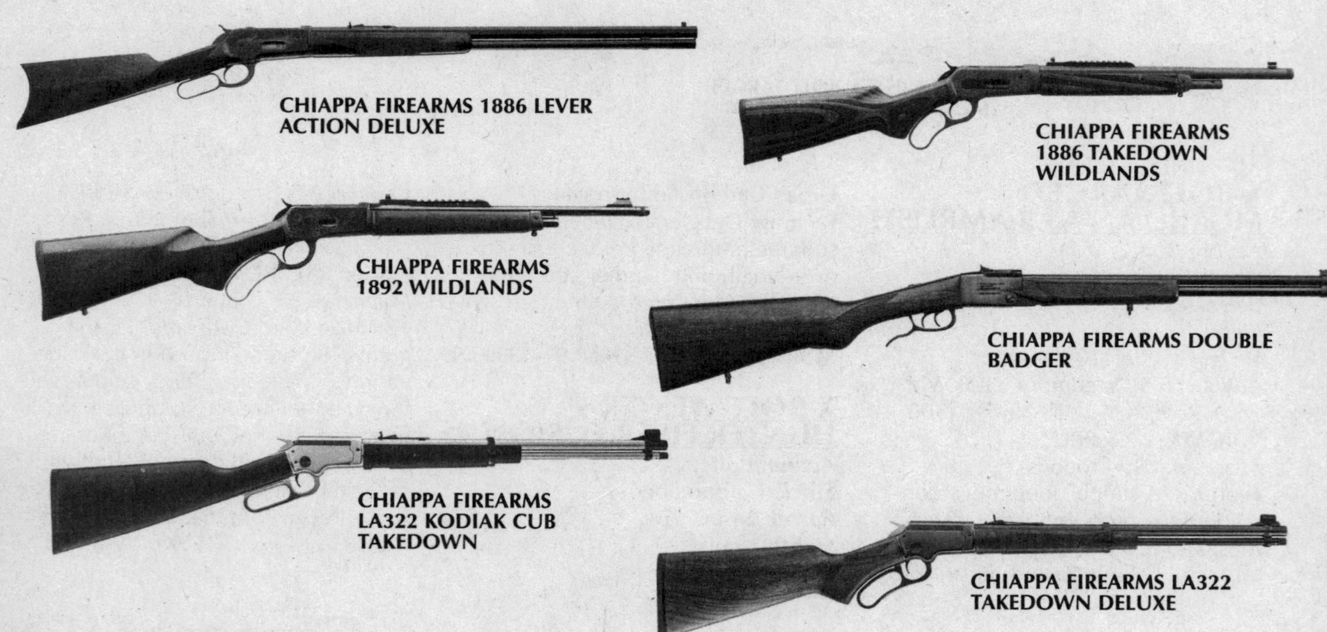

CHIAPPA FIREARMS 1886 LEVER ACTION DELUXE

CHIAPPA FIREARMS 1886 TAKEDOWN WILDLANDS

CHIAPPA FIREARMS 1892 WILDLANDS

CHIAPPA FIREARMS DOUBLE BADGER

CHIAPPA FIREARMS LA322 KODIAK CUB TAKEDOWN

CHIAPPA FIREARMS LA322 TAKEDOWN DELUXE

RIFLES

1886 LEVER ACTION DELUXE

Action: Lever
Stock: Walnut
Barrel: 26 in.
Sights: Dovetail front, buckhorn rear
Weight: 9 lb.
Caliber: .45-70 Govt.
Magazine: 8 rounds
Features: High-grade current production of Browning's classic 1886 rifle; color case finished receiver; select walnut; checkering at wrist and forend; octagonal barrel
MSRP $1880.00

1886 TAKEDOWN WILDLANDS

Action: Lever
Stock: Laminate
Barrel: 18.5 in.
Sights: Fiber optic front, Skinner peep rear
Weight: 9 lb. 8 oz.
Caliber: .45-70 Govt.
Magazine: 4 rounds
Features: A super takedown lever-action for backpacking in bear country, with heft to take up the .45-70 punch; threaded barrel; dark gray Cerakote finish
MSRP $2205.00

1892 WILDLANDS

Action: Lever
Stock: Laminate, walnut
Barrel: 16.5 in.
Sights: Fiber optic front, Skinner peep rear
Weight: 6 lb. 3 oz.–6 lb. 15 oz.
Caliber: .44 Mag.
Magazine: 5 rounds
Features: A classic lever-action in three versions: solid frame in laminate stock with Cerakote dark gray metalwork; takedown in laminate stock with Cerakote dark gray metalwork; solid frame in hand-oiled walnut stock with blued barrel and color-case receiver; all have threaded barrels, topside Picatinny rails
MSRP . . . . $1579.00–$1746.00

DOUBLE BADGER

Action: Break-open
Stock: Beech
Barrel: 19 in., 20 in.
Sights: Fixed red fiber optic front, Williams green fiber optic rear
Weight: 5 lb. 13 oz.
Caliber: .22 LR/.410-bore, .243 Win./.410-bore, .22 LR/20-gauge, .22 WMR/.410-bore
Magazine: 2 rounds
Features: A folding combo gun with double triggers; firearm folds by lowering the trigger guard; all shotgun bores are 3-inch chambers; blued finish metalwork; beech stocks
MSRP . . . . $441.00–$647.00

LA322 KODIAK CUB TAKEDOWN

Action: Lever action
Stock: English-style black soft touch
Barrel: 18.5 in.
Sights: Hooded front, adjustable rear
Weight: 5 lb. 8 oz.
Caliber: .22 LR
Magazine: 15 rounds
Features: Matte hard chrome finish that is durable and corrosion-resistant; black soft touch coating makes the stock easier to grip and protects from the elements; easy take down
MSRP $754.00

LA322 TAKEDOWN DELUXE

Action: Lever action
Stock: Walnut
Barrel: 18.5 in.
Sights: Hooded front, adjustable rear
Weight: 5 lb. 8 oz.
Caliber: .22 LR
Magazine: 15 rounds
Features: A takedown lever-action rimfire with a dovetail groove for scope mounting; pistol grip wood stock; blacked chrome receiver; blued barrel
MSRP $576.00

Chiappa Firearms

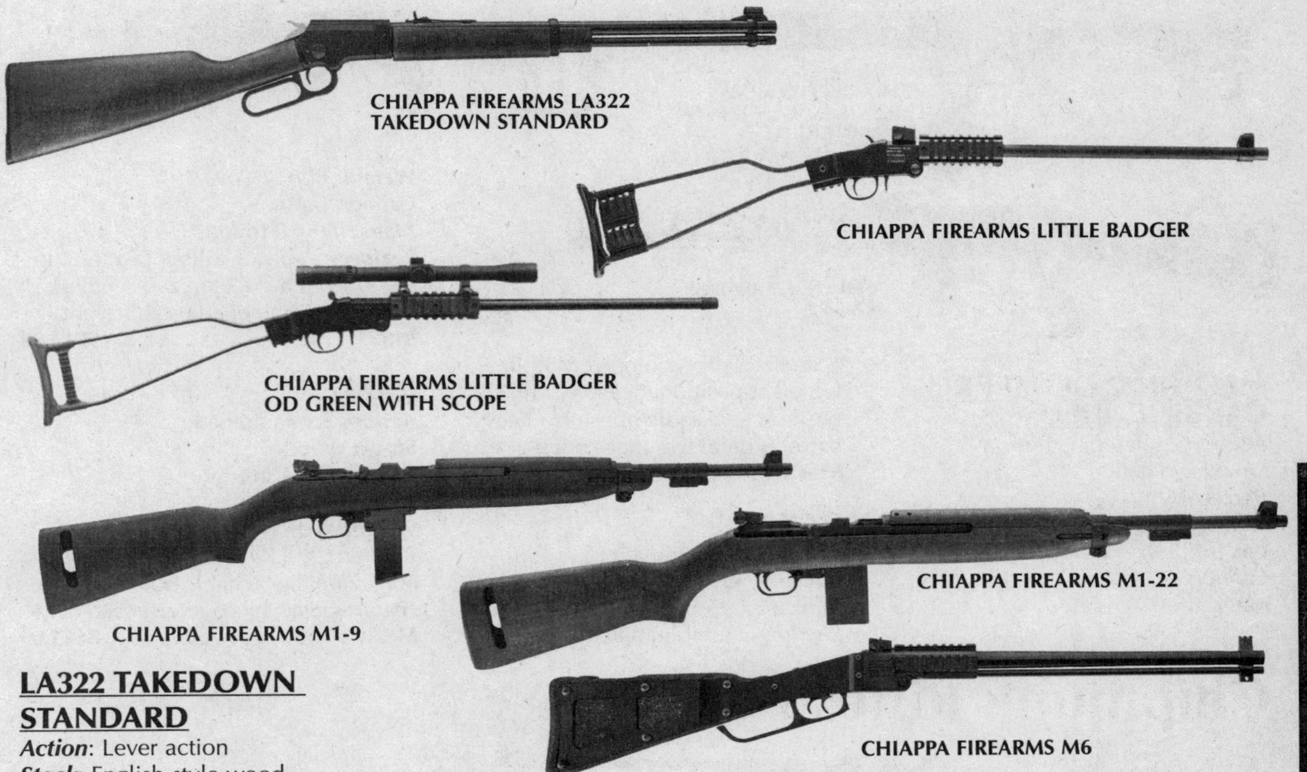

CHIAPPA FIREARMS LA322 TAKEDOWN STANDARD

CHIAPPA FIREARMS LITTLE BADGER

CHIAPPA FIREARMS LITTLE BADGER OD GREEN WITH SCOPE

CHIAPPA FIREARMS M1-9

CHIAPPA FIREARMS M1-22

CHIAPPA FIREARMS M6

RIFLES

LA322 TAKEDOWN STANDARD

Action: Lever action
Stock: English-style wood
Barrel: 18.5 in.
Sights: Hooded front, adjustable rear
Weight: 5 lb. 8 oz.
Caliber: .22 LR
Magazine: 15 rounds
Features: 3/8-inch dovetail on top of receiver for scope mounting; takedown design; straight wood stock; blued or matte black metalwork
MSRP . . . . $389.00–$399.00

LITTLE BADGER

Action: Single shot
Stock: Metal foldable
Barrel: 16.5 in.
Sights: Adjustable rear
Weight: 3 lb. 8 oz.
Caliber: .22 LR, .22WMR, .17 HMR
Magazine: None
Features: Single barrel; foldable rifle; extremely light for comfortable carry; folds to 16.5 in. total length; nylon carry bag and special cartridge holder available
MSRP . . . . $228.00–$243.00

LITTLE BADGER OD GREEN WITH SCOPE

Action: Break-open single-shot
Stock: Wire steel
Barrel: 16.5 in.
Sights: None
Weight: 3 lb. 10 oz.
Caliber: .22 LR
Magazine: 1 round
Features: Chiappa's handy folding survival rifle gets a makeover in all-over OD Green; four-sided Picatinny rail for optics and accessories
MSRP $233.00

M1-9

Action: Semiautomatic
Stock: Polymer, wood
Barrel: 18 in.
Sights: Winged front, sliding rear
Weight: 5 lb. 14.4 oz.–6 lb. 4.8 oz.
Caliber: 9mm
Magazine: 10 rounds
Features: Classic M1 carbine taking Beretta 9mm magazines; metals matte blue; two magazines included
Polymer: $597.32
Wood: $676.12

M1-22

Action: Semiautomatic
Stock: Polymer
Barrel: 18 in.
Sights: Adjustable rear
Weight: 5 lb. 8 oz.
Caliber: .22 LR
Magazine: Detachable box, 10 rounds
Features: The M1 carbine is a lightweight, easy-to-use semiautomatic carbine that became a standard firearm for the U.S. military during World War II, the Korean War, and the Vietnam War, and was produced in several variants
Polymer: $332.93
Wood: $460.37

M6

Action: Lever
Stock: Polypropylene closed cell foam
Barrel: 18.5 in.
Sights: Fiber optic front, military adjustable rear
Weight: 5 lb. 12.8 oz.–6 lb.
Caliber: 12 ga./.22 LR, 20 ga./.22 LR, 12 ga./.22 WMR, 20 ga./.22 WMR
Magazine: 2 rounds
Features: Combo gun, shotgun barrel top, .22 rimfire barrel bottom; folding stock, interchangeable choke tubes, and dedicated triggers for each barrel; cleaning kit and 4–8 additional rounds stored in the stock
MSRP . . . . $729.00–$999.00

Chiappa Firearms

CHIAPPA FIREARMS MFOUR-22 GEN II PRO CARBINE, RIFLE

CHIAPPA FIREARMS RAK-22

CHIAPPA FIREARMS RAK-9

MFOUR-22 GEN II PRO CARBINE, RIFLE

Action: Semiautomatic
Stock: Synthetic
Barrel: 16 in.
Sights: None
Weight: 5 lb. 11.2 oz.
Caliber: .22 LR
Magazine: 28 rounds
Features: Fully equipped MSR in .22 LR; eight-position Picatinny rail; six-position adjustable buttstock; heavy barrel profile; two magazines
MSRP . . . . $473.00–$569.00

RAK-9

Action: Semiautomatic
Stock: Synthetic
Barrel: 17.25 in.
Sights: Adjustable military-style
Weight: 6 lb. 10 oz.
Caliber: 9mm
Magazine: 10 rounds
Features: A pistol-caliber take on the AK-47 with a skeletonized synthetic stock; steel frame; adjustable sights
MSRP $719.00

RAK-22

Action: Semiautomatic
Stock: Wood
Barrel: 17.25 in.
Sights: Adjustable
Weight: 6 lb.
Caliber: .22 LR
Magazine: Detachable box, 10 rounds
Features: Steel blued receiver and barrel
MSRP $665.00

Chipmunk Rifles

CHIPMUNK RIFLES CHIPMUNK

CHIPMUNK

Action: Bolt
Stock: Walnut, laminated
Barrel: 16.125 in.
Sights: Target
Weight: 2 lb. 8 oz.
Caliber: .22 LR
Magazine: None
Features: Designed with younger shooters in mind; single-shot; manual-cocking action; receiver-mounted rear sights; metal with blued finish or stainless steel; post sight on ramp front, fully adjustable peep rear; adjustable trigger; extendable butt-plate and front rail; available in black, walnut, deluxe walnut, camo laminate, and brown laminate
Standard: . . . . $239.00–$379.00
Standard left-hand: $249.00
Barracuda: . . . . $289.00–$315.00

Christensen Arms

CHRISTENSEN ARMS BA TACTICAL

CHRISTENSEN ARMS CA-10 DMR

BA TACTICAL

Action: Bolt
Stock: Hand-laid fiberglass
Barrel: 16 in., 20 in., 22 in., 24 in., 26 in., 27 in.
Sights: None
Weight: 7 lb. 11 oz.–8 lb. 2 oz.
Caliber: .223 Rem., 6mm Creedmoor, 6.5 Creedmoor, 6.5 PRC, .308 Win., .300 Win. Mag., .338 Lapua Mag., .300 PRC
Magazine: Detachable box, 5 rounds
Features: Integral full-length rail incorporates a 20 MOA taper; front stud with five flush cups; adjustable cheek piece via inserts; stainless steel side-port muzzle brake
MSRP $2795.00

CA-10 DMR

Action: Semiautomatic
Stock: Synthetic
Barrel: 18 in., 20 in., 22 in., 24 in.
Sights: None
Weight: 7 lb. 13 oz.–8 lb. 3 oz.
Caliber: 6.5 Creedmoor, .308 Win.
Magazine: Detachable box
Features: Picatinny rail; OSS suppressor; ambidextrous magazine release; Magpul stock; various finishes available
MSRP $3245.00

Christensen Arms

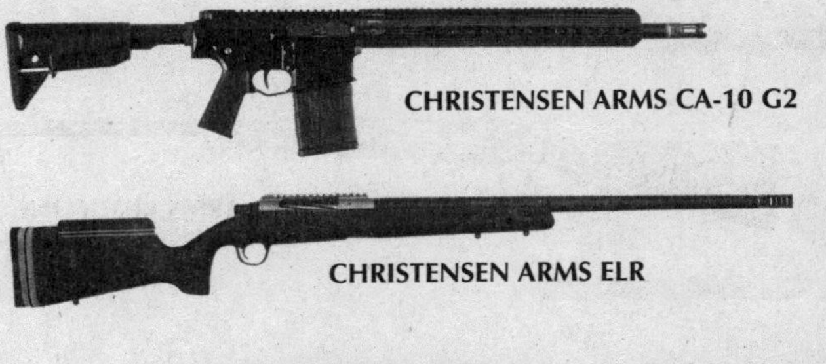

CHRISTENSEN ARMS CA-10 G2

CHRISTENSEN ARMS ELR

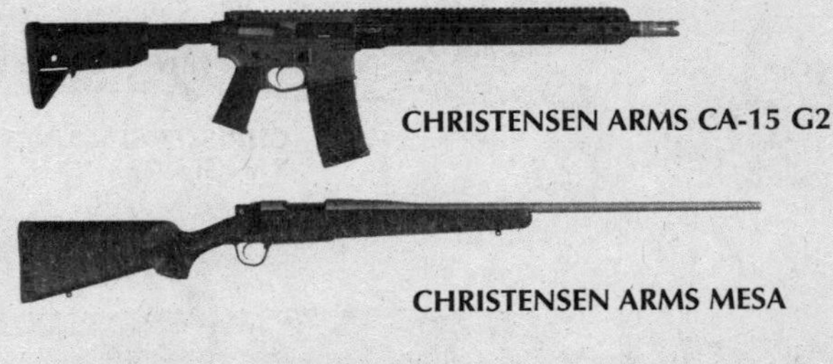

CHRISTENSEN ARMS CA-15 G2

CHRISTENSEN ARMS MESA

CHRISTENSEN ARMS MESA TITANIUM

CHRISTENSEN ARMS MODERN PRECISION RIFLE

CA-10 G2

Action: Semiautomatic
Stock: Synthetic
Barrel: 18 in., 20 in.
Sights: None
Weight: 7 lb. 12.8 oz.–8 lb. 3.2 oz.
Caliber: 6.5 Creedmoor, .308 Win.
Magazine: N/A
Features: Upper and lower of billet 7075 aluminum; integrated undercut trigger guard on lower, aerograde carbon fiber handguard on an upper with KeyMod or M-Lok configurations; match chamber and trigger; direct impingement system; Magpul adjustable STR stock; 416R stainless barrel wrapped in steel aerograde carbon fiber; Titanium side baffle brake; choice of stainless steel or carbon-fiber-wrapped stainless steel barrel
SS: $2595.00
Carbon-fiber-wrapped: . . . $2995.00

CA-15 G2

Action: Semiautomatic
Stock: Synthetic
Barrel: 16 in.
Sights: None
Weight: 5 lb. 12.8 oz.
Caliber: .223 Wylde
Magazine: N/A
Features: Custom-built AR optimized for weight and accuracy; newly designed matched receiver with a contour-matching carbon fiber handguard; single-stage match trigger; match chamber; flared magwell; button rifled, threaded, and carbon fiber-wrapped barrel; BCM Gunfighter adjustable stock; stainless steel flash hider; in stainless steel or carbon fiber
Stainless steel: $1749.00
Carbon fiber: $2295.00

ELR

Action: Bolt
Stock: Hand-laid carbon fiber
Barrel: 26 in.–27 in.
Sights: None
Weight: 7 lb. 8 oz.
Caliber: 6.5 Creedmoor, 6.5 PRC, .28 Nosler, 7mm Rem. Mag., .300 Win. Mag., .300 PRC, .338 Lapua Mag.
Magazine: 4 rounds
Features: Machined aluminum hinged floorplate; dual front studs with flush cups; adjustable cheek piece via inserts; titanium side-port muzzle brake
MSRP $2795.00

MESA

Action: Bolt
Stock: Carbon fiber composite
Barrel: 20 in., 22 in., 24 in., 26 in.
Sights: None
Weight: 6 lb. 8 oz.–6 lb. 11.2 oz.
Caliber: .450 Bushmaster, 6.5 Creedmoor, 6.5 PRC, 7mm-08 Rem., 7mm Rem. Mag., .308 Win., .28 Nosler, .300 Win. Mag., .300 PRC
Magazine: 3 (magnum), 4 rounds
Features: Featherweight contour barrel with removable stainless radial muzzle brake and tungsten Cerakote finish; skeletonized bolt handle; Limbsaver recoil pad; Invar pillars and spot bedding; match chamber and trigger; and button rifled, free-floating barrel
MSRP $1295.00

MESA TITANIUM

Action: Bolt
Stock: Carbon fiber composite
Barrel: 22 in., 24 in.
Sights: None
Weight: 6 lb. 2 oz.
Caliber: 6.5 Creedmoor, 6.5 PRC, .308 Win., .300 Win. Mag., .28 Nosler, .300 PRC, 7mm Rem. Mag.
Magazine: 3, 4 rounds
Features: An upgraded Mesa with a titanium receiver; hand-lapped, free-floating, button-rifled, and threaded barrel with a featherweight contour, bead-blasted finish, and radial brake; match chamber; match-grade trigger; stock in gray metallic with black webbing
MSRP $1795.00

MODERN PRECISION RIFLE

Action: Bolt
Stock: Billet aluminum
Barrel: 16 in., 20 in., 22 in., 24 in., 26 in., 27 in.
Sights: None
Weight: 6 lb. 14 oz.–8 lb. 2 oz.
Caliber: .223 Rem., 6mm Creedmoor, 6.5 PRC, 6.5 Creedmoor, .308 Win., .300 Win. Mag., .300 PRC, .338 Lapua Mag.
Magazine: N/A
Features: 416 stainless steel barrel is carbon fiber wrapped; removable stainless side-baffle brake in a black nitride finish; barrel is hand lapped, button rifled and free floating; chassis is 7075 billet aluminum with an adjustable carbon fiber cheek riser and adjustable length of pull; six Q/D flush cup mounts; carbon fiber handguard with M-LOK; V-Block bedding; monopod mount ready via Picatinny rail; match chamber; skeletonized bolt handle; twin lug spiral fluted bolt; flat match-grade trigger; 20 MOA of rail
Short action: $2295.00
Long action: $2395.00

Christensen Arms

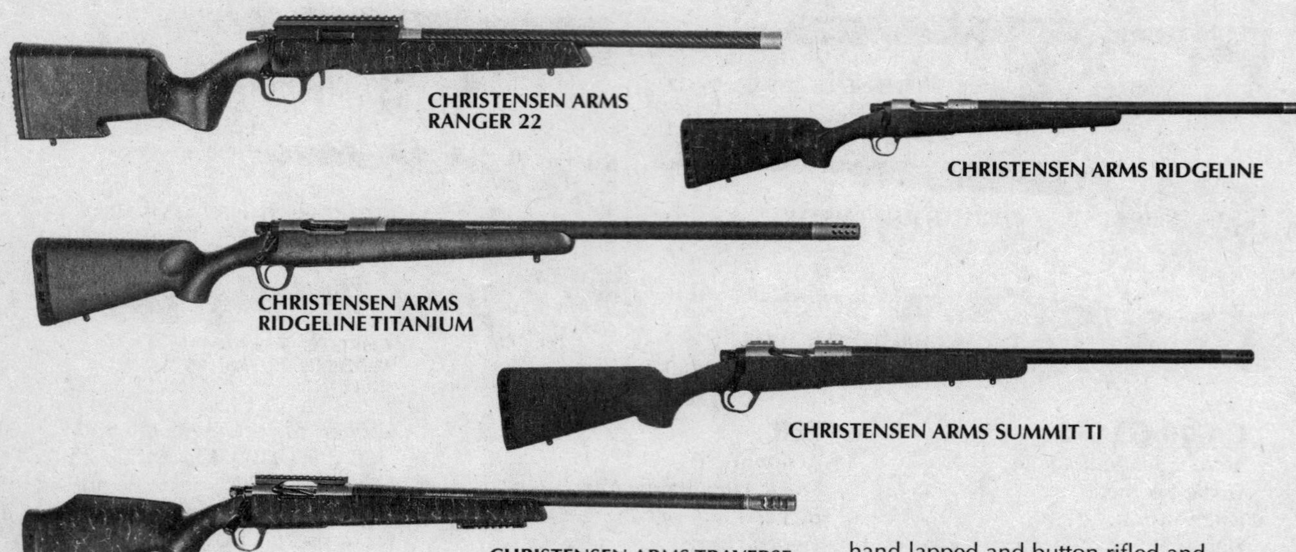

CHRISTENSEN ARMS RANGER 22

CHRISTENSEN ARMS RIDGELINE

CHRISTENSEN ARMS RIDGELINE TITANIUM

CHRISTENSEN ARMS SUMMIT TI

CHRISTENSEN ARMS TRAVERSE

RIFLES

RANGER 22

Action: Bolt
Stock: Carbon fiber composite
Barrel: 18 in.
Sights: None
Weight: 5 lb. 2 oz.
Caliber: .22 LR
Magazine: 10 rounds
Features: An above-average rimfire with upgraded features such as Christensen Arms's own hand-lapped, threaded, carbon fiber tension barrel; Bentz match chamber; dual ejectors; stock in choice of black with gray webbing or tan with black webbing
MSRP $795.00

RIDGELINE

Action: Bolt
Stock: Hand-laid fiberglass with carbon fiber reinforced stock
Barrel: 20 in., 24 in., 26 in.
Sights: None
Weight: 6 lb. 5 oz.–6 lb. 11 oz.
Caliber: .22-250 Rem., 6.5 Creedmoor, 6.5 PRC, 6.5-284 Norma, .26 Nosler, .270 Win., .270 WSM, 7mm-08 Rem, .28 Nosler, .280 Ackley Improved, 7mm Rem. Mag., .308 Win., .30 Nosler, .30-06 Spfd., .300 RUM, .300 Win. Mag., .300 WSM, .300 PRC, .450 Bushmaster
Magazine: 4 rounds
Features: Carbon fiber–wrapped barrel; a spiral fluted bolt; scalloped bolt knob; dual front studs; SUB MOA accuracy; bedded recoil lug and invar pillar inserts; machined aluminum hinged floorplate
MSRP $1995.00

RIDGELINE TITANIUM

Action: Bolt
Stock: Carbon fiber composite
Barrel: 22 in., 24 in.
Sights: None
Weight: 5 lb. 13 oz.
Caliber: 6.5 Creedmoor, 6.5 PRC, .308 Win., .300 Win. Mag., .28 Nosler, .300 PRC, 7mm Rem. Mag.
Magazine: 3, 4 rounds
Features: The hot feature on this premium rifle is its aerograde carbon fiber–wrapped, button-rifled barrel with a titanium radial brake; stock in metallic gray with black webbing
MSRP $2495.00

SUMMIT TI

Action: Bolt
Stock: Aerograde carbon fiber
Barrel: 24 in.–27 in.
Sights: None
Weight: 5 lb. 8 oz.–6 lb.
Caliber: .25-06 Rem., 6.5 Creedmoor, 6.5 PRC, 6.5-284 Norma, .26 Nosler, .270 Win., .270 WSM, .28 Nosler, .280 Ackley Improved, 7mm Rem. Mag., .30-06 Spfd., .308 Win., .30 Nosler, .300 Win. Mag.
Magazine: 3 rounds
Features: 416R stainless steel, aerograde carbon fiber-wrapped barrel is hand lapped and button rifled and sports a removable radial titanium muzzle brake; trued receiver has integrated Picatinny rail; fully adjustable match trigger, Nitride-treated bolt with fluted knob, enlarged ejection port, full-length bedding with carbon fiber pillars are standard; sporter or thumbhole stock
MSRP $5495.00

TRAVERSE

Action: Bolt
Stock: Carbon fiber composite
Barrel: 24 in., 26 in.
Sights: None
Weight: 7 lb. 5 oz.–7 lb. 11 oz.
Caliber: .22–250 Rem., .243 Win., 6.5 Creedmoor, 6.5 PRC, 6.5–284, .26 Nosler, .270 Win., .270 WSM, 7mm-08 Rem., .280 Ackley Improved, .28 Nosler, 7mm Rem. Mag., .308 Win., .30-06 Spfd., .30 Nosler, .300 WSM, .300 Win. Mag., .300 RUM, .30 PRC, .338 Lapua Mag.
Magazine: 3 rounds
Features: Classically styled and thoroughly modern backcountry rifle with a carbon fiber composite stock with Monte Carlo profile; full palm swell; light target contour, hand-lapped, carbon fiber-wrapped, free-floating threaded barrel with match chamber and 4-inch bottom rail; skeletonized bolt with fluted bolt knob; 0 MOA top rail; Invar pillars; spot bedding; Limbsaver recoil pad; black/gray or green/black spiderweb finish on stock
MSRP $2395.00

Cimarron Firearms Co.

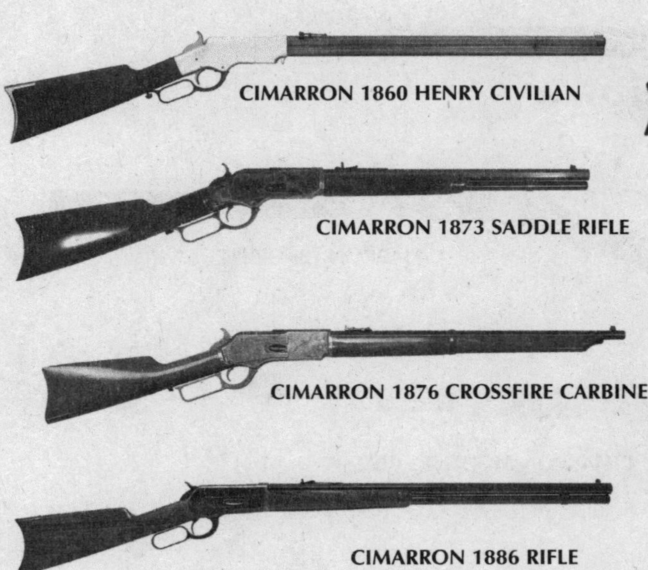

CIMARRON 1860 HENRY CIVILIAN

CIMARRON 1873 SADDLE RIFLE

CIMARRON 1876 CROSSFIRE CARBINE

CIMARRON 1886 RIFLE

CIMARRON 1860 IRON FRAME HENRY

CIMARRON 1876 CENTENNIAL

CIMARRON 1885 HIGH WALL SPORTING RIFLE

1860 HENRY CIVILIAN

Action: Lever
Stock: Walnut
Barrel: 24 in.
Sights: Open
Weight: 9 lb. 2 oz.
Caliber: .44 WCF, .45 LC
Magazine: Under-barrel tube, 12 rounds
Features: Reproduction of 1860 Civil War Henry rifle; includes military sling swivels; frame comes in charcoal blue or original finish
MSRP $1575.98

1860 IRON FRAME HENRY

Action: Lever
Stock: Walnut
Barrel: 24 in.
Sights: Ivory front blade, adjustable rear
Weight: 9 lb. 3 oz.
Caliber: .44 WCF, .45 LC
Magazine: 12 rounds
Features: An authentic reproduction any collector would be proud of, featuring case hardened frame; walnut stock; octagon barrel
MSRP $1661.95

1873 SADDLE RIFLE

Action: Lever
Stock: Wood
Barrel: 18 in.
Sights: Open
Weight: 8 lb.
Caliber: .357 Mag., .45 Colt, .44 WCF
Magazine: Fixed tube
Features: Full octagon barrel; straight stock with checkered forearm and stock
MSRP $1479.69

1876 CENTENNIAL

Action: Lever
Stock: Walnut
Barrel: 28 in.
Sights: Open
Weight: 9 lb. 15 oz.–10 lb. 2 oz.
Caliber: .45-60, .45-75, .40-60, .50-95
Magazine: Under-barrel tube, 12 rounds
Features: Originally dubbed the "Centennial Model" because of its introduction during America's 100th anniversary of the Declaration of Independence from British rule, and featured at Philadelphia's Centennial Exposition, this enlarged version of the famed 1873 Winchester was designed to handle stronger loads than its predecessor; finished in a standard blue octagonal barrel, tubular magazine, barrel band and fore-end, with a color case hardened receiver, lever, trigger, hammer and butt plate
MSRP . . . . $1782.85–$1836.59

1876 CROSSFIRE CARBINE

Action: Lever
Stock: Walnut
Barrel: 22 in.
Sights: None
Weight: 8 lb. 15 oz.
Caliber: .45-60, .45-75
Magazine: Under-barrel tube, 8 rounds
Features: Gun was glorified in the movie *Crossfire Trail;* case-hardened stock with standard blued finish
MSRP $2013.99

1885 HIGH WALL SPORTING RIFLE

Action: Dropping block
Stock: Walnut, pistol grip
Barrel: 30 in.
Sights: Open
Weight: 9 lb. 4 oz.–10 lb. 6 oz.
Caliber: .38-55, .45-70
Magazine: None
Features: Reproduction of the Winchester single-shot hunting rifle popular in 1880s; standard blued finish on octagonal barrel; single- or double-set triggers
MSRP . . . . $1160.00–$1186.00

1886 RIFLE

Action: Lever
Stock: Walnut
Barrel: 26 in.
Sights: None
Weight: 8 lb.–9 lb.
Caliber: .45-70 Govt.
Magazine: Under-barrel tube, 7+1, 8+1 rounds
Features: Made by Armi Sport in Italy; color case-hardened receiver and buttplate; octagonal barrel; standard blued finish
MSRP $1610.70

Cimarron Firearms Co.

CIMARRON 1894 CARBINE

CIMARRON 1894 RIFLE

CIMARRON MODEL 71 CLASSIC

RIFLES

1894 CARBINE

Action: Lever
Stock: Walnut
Barrel: 20 in.
Sights: Blade front, adjustable rear
Weight: N/A
Caliber: .30-30 Win., .38-55 Win.
Magazine: N/A
Features: Faithful to John Browning's original, with both calibers available in case-colored frame
MSRP $1324.70

1894 RIFLE

Action: Lever
Stock: Walnut
Barrel: 24.25 in., 26 in.
Sights: Blade front, adjustable rear
Weight: N/A
Caliber: .30-30 Win., .38-55 Win.
Magazine: N/A
Features: Identical to Cimarron's 1894 Carbine, though with a more pronounced crescent shape to the buttstock and with an appropriately longer barrel; .30-30 also available in all blue instead of case-hardened
MSRP . . . .$1324.70–$1393.90

MODEL 71 CLASSIC

Action: Lever
Stock: Walnut
Barrel: 24 in.
Sights: Open
Weight: 8 lb. 11 oz.
Caliber: .45-70 Gov't.
Magazine: Fixed tube
Features: Blued receiver; pistol grip stock
Standard: $1715.10
Deluxe: $2011.25

Citadel by Legacy Sports

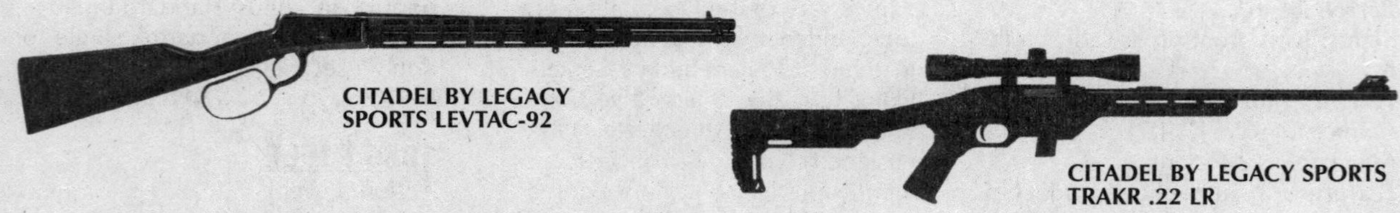

CITADEL BY LEGACY SPORTS LEVTAC-92

CITADEL BY LEGACY SPORTS TRAKR .22 LR

LEVTAC-92

Action: Lever
Stock: Synthetic
Barrel: 18 in.
Sights: Blade front, peep rear
Weight: N/A
Caliber: .357 Mag., .44 Mag., .454 Casull
Magazine: 3, 4 rounds
Features: Super-handy and tough lever-action with an M-LOK handguard; topside Picatinny rail; oversized lever for gloved hands
MSRP $799.00

TRAKR .22 LR

Action: Semiautomatic
Stock: Synthetic
Barrel: 18 in.
Sights: Fiber optic front
Weight: N/A
Caliber: .22 LR
Magazine: 10 rounds
Features: Economical choice for plinking, fun competition, and even small game, this rifle gets a lightweight MSR-style stock and pistol grip
MSRP $199.00

CMMG, Inc.

ENDEAVOR 100 SERIES

Action: Semiautomatic
Stock: Synthetic
Barrel: 18 in., 20 in.
Sights: None
Weight: 6 lb. 15 oz.–8 lb. 15 oz.
Caliber: 5.56 NATO, .22 Nosler, .224 Valkyrie, 6mm ARC, 6.5 Grendel, 6.5 Creedmoor, .308 Win.
Magazine: 10, 20, 30 rounds
Features: A full-length direct impingement MSR platform with the long-range game in mind. Features include Type III hard coat anodizing; A2 pistol grip and compensator; A1 buttstock; free-floating CMMG M-LOK handguard
MSRP . . . . $1049.95–$1749.95

ENDEAVOR 200 SERIES

Action: Semiautomatic
Stock: Synthetic
Barrel: 18 in., 20 in.
Sights: None
Weight: 7 lb. 2 oz.–9 lb. 2 oz.
Caliber: 5.56 NATO, .22 Nosler, .224 Valkyrie, 6mm ARC, 6.5 Grendel, 6.5 Creedmoor, .308 Win.
Magazine: 10, 20, 30 rounds
Features: The 100 Series with added features such as CMMG SV muzzle brake; Magpul MOE stock and pistol grip
MSRP . . . . $1149.95–$1849.95

ENDEAVOR 300 SERIES

Action: Semiautomatic
Stock: Synthetic
Barrel: 22 in., 24 in.
Sights: None
Weight: 8 lb. 10 oz.–11 lb. 5 oz.
Caliber: 5.56 NATO, .22 Nosler, .224 Valkyrie, 6mm ARC, 6.5 Grendel, 6.5 Creedmoor, .308 Win.
Magazine: 10, 20, 30 rounds
Features: The top end of the Endeavor Series with upgraded features such as: Geissele two-stage trigger; Magpul MOE pistol grip, PRS stock; CMMG ambidextrous safety selector and charging handle; 10 Premier Cerakote color options
MSRP . . . . $1695.95–$2349.95

RESOLUTE 100 SERIES

Action: Semiautomatic
Stock: Synthetic
Barrel: 16.1 in., 17 in.
Sights: None
Weight: 6 lb. 1 oz.–7 lb. 2 oz.
Caliber: 5.56 NATO, 6mm ARC, 6.5 Grendel, .300 BLK, .350 Legend, 5.7X28mm, 9mm, .308 Win., 7.62 NATO, .458 SOCOM, .40 S&W
Magazine: 10, 20, 30 rounds
Features: Carbine-length rifle with an interesting selection of calibers. Features include M4-type buttstock; M-Lok free-float handguards; Type III hard coat anodize; A2 pistol grip and compensator
MSRP . . . . $1099.99–$1899.95

RESOLUTE 200 SERIES

Action: Semiautomatic
Stock: Synthetic
Barrel: 16.1 in.
Sights: None
Weight: 6 lb. 6 oz.–7 lb. 4 oz.
Caliber: 5.56 NATO, 6mm ARC, 6.5 Grendel, .300 BLK, .350 Legend, 5.7X28mm, 9mm, .308 Win., 7.62 NATO, .458 SOCOM, .40 S&W, .45 ACP, .22 LR
Magazine: 10, 20, 30 rounds
Features: A set-up from the 100 series with the addition of CMMG Ripstock and SV muzzle brake
MSRP . . . . $1124.95–$2024.95

RESOLUTE 300 SERIES

Action: Semiautomatic
Stock: Synthetic
Barrel: 16.1 in.
Sights: None
Weight: 6 lb. 2 oz.–8 lb. 4 oz.
Caliber: 5.56 NATO, 6mm ARC, 6.5 Grendel, .300 BLK, .350 Legend, 5.7X28mm, 9mm, .308 Win., 7.62 NATO, .458 SOCOM, .40 S&W, .45 ACP, .22 LR
Magazine: 10, 20, 30 rounds
Features: The fanciest of the Resolute series, with: 10 Premier Cerakote color options; Geissele two-stage trigger; Magpul MOE pistol grip; "Resolute" engraved on lower receiver
MSRP . . . . $1649.95–$2349.95

Colt's Manufacturing Company

COLT M4 MONOLITHIC

COLT M4 TROOPER

M4 MONOLITHIC

Action: Semiautomatic
Stock: Combat-style, synthetic
Barrel: 16.1 in.
Sights: Flip-up front flip-up rear
Weight: 6 lb. 11 oz.
Caliber: 5.56 NATO
Magazine: Detachable box, 20, 30 rounds
Features: Incorporates a continuous Picatinny rail from the rear of the upper receiver to the front sight, free-floating chrome-line barrel, folding locking front sight, Magpul MBUS rear sight, integrated quad-rail; single-stage trigger, direct gas impingement system are standard
MSRP $1399.00

M4 TROOPER

Action: Semiautomatic
Stock: Synthetic
Barrel: 16.1 in.
Sights: None
Weight: 6 lb. 7 oz.
Caliber: 5.56 NATO
Magazine: 30 rounds
Features: Centurion free-floating fore-end M-Lok capable; 12 o'clock Picatinny rail; black M4 buttstock; black A2 pistol grip; Magpul P-Mag 30-round magazine
MSRP $1049.00

Connecticut Valley Arms (CVA)

CVA CASCADE

CVA SCOUT

CASCADE

Action: Bolt
Stock: Synthetic
Barrel: 18 in., 22 in.
Sights: None
Weight: N/A
Caliber: .243 Win., 6.5 Creedmoor, 7mm-08 Rem., .308 Win., .450 Bushmaster, .350 Legend, .22-250 Rem., 6.5 PRC, 7mm Rem. Mag., .300 Win. Mag., .300 BLK
Magazine: 3 roumds
Features: CVA's first centerfire bolt-action featuring a fiberglass-reinforced CVA stock in Veil Camo with Cascade Cerakote metalwork, in Veil Tac Black with Graphite Black Cerakote (short-barrel) or in charcoal gray with blued metalwork; 70-degree bolt throw; 4140 carbon steel barrel; flush-fit detachable box magazine; spacers for adjustable length of pull; dual front swivel studs; short-barrel model available in 6.5 Creedmoor, .308 Win., .300 BLK only
MSRP . . . . $566.95–$670.00

SCOUT, SCOUT COMPACT

Action: Break-open single-shot
Stock: Synthetic
Barrel: 20 in., 25 in.
Sights: None
Weight: 5 lb. 13 oz.
Caliber: .444 Marlin, .44 Mag., .45-70 Gov't., .450 Bushmaster, .35 Whelen, .243 Win., .300 BLK, 7mm-09 Rem., 6.5 Creedmoor, .350 Legend
Magazine: N/A
Features: Fluted stainless steel barrel; ambidextrous stock; reversible hammer spur; CrushZone recoil pad; black stock with stainless steel barrel; some models available with factory-mounted Konus 3–9x40mm scope; DF muzzlebrake on unscoped model, scoped model available with or without muzzlebrake
MSRP . . . . $348.95–$418.95

Cooper Firearms of Montana

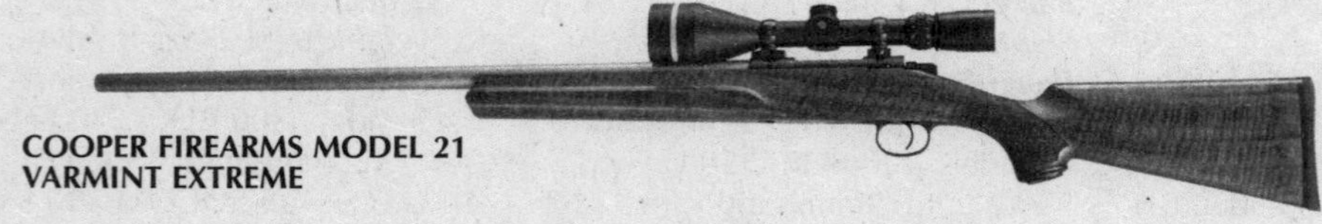

COOPER FIREARMS MODEL 21 VARMINT EXTREME

MODEL 21 CLASSIC

Action: Bolt
Stock: AA Claro Walnut
Barrel: 24 in.
Sights: None
Weight: 6 lb.–7 lb. 12 oz.
Caliber: .17 Fireball, .17 Rem., .20 VarTag, .20 Tactical, .204 Ruger, .221 Fireball, .22 Rem., .222 Rem. Mag., .222 Rem., .223 Rem. AI,.300 BLK
Features: Hand-rubbed oil-finished stock with four-panel hand checkering, Pachmayer recoil pad, chrome-moly premium match grade Wilson Arms barrel, steel grip cap are standard
Right-hand: $2795.00
Left-hand: $3045.00

Cooper Firearms of Montana

COOPER FIREARMS MODEL 21 VARMINTER (LAMINATE STOCK)

COOPER FIREARMS MODEL 51

COOPER FIREARMS MODEL 52 WESTERN CLASSIC

COOPER FIREARMS MODEL 57-M CLASSIC

COOPER FIREARMS MODEL 52 TIMBERLINE

RIFLES

MODEL 22 CLASSIC

Action: Bolt
Stock: AA Claro Walnut
Barrel: N/A
Sights: None
Weight: N/A
Caliber: .More than 30 calibers available, from .22 BR to .338 Federal
Magazine: None
Features: Hand-rubbed oil-finished stock with four-panel hand checkering, Pachmayer recoil pad, chrome-moly premium match grade Wilson Arms barrel, steel grip cap are standard
Right-hand: $2795.00
Left-hand: $3045.00

MODEL 51

Action: Bolt
Stock: AA Claro Walnut
Barrel: 24 in.
Sights: None
Weight: 6 lb. –7 lb. 12 oz.
Caliber: .17 Rem., .20 Tactical, .204 Ruger, .222 Rem., .223 Rem., .223 Rem. AI
Magazine: None
Features: Longer barrel standard on all varmint models; fully adjustable single-stage trigger; Sako style extraction machined from solid bar stock
Right-hand: $2795.00
Left-hand: $3045.00

MODEL 52 TIMBERLINE

Action: Bolt
Stock: Composite
Barrel: N/A
Sights: None
Weight: 7 lb.
Caliber: Thirty-five calibrs available ranging from .240 Wby. Mag. to .340 Wby. Mag.
Magazine: N/A
Features: Cooper's own carbon-fiber and Kevlar reinforced composite stock in black with tan webbing; semi-vertical grip; palm swell; raised comb; adjustable single-stage trigger; spiral-fluted three-lug bolt; muzzle brake
Right-hand: $2695.00
Left-hand: $2945.00

MODEL 52 WESTERN CLASSIC

Action: Bolt
Stock: AAA+ Claro Walnut
Barrel: 24 in.
Sights: None
Weight: 6 lb. 12 oz.–8 lb.
Caliber: More than 30 calibers available from .257 Wtby. Mag. to .375 H&H
Magazine: 3 rounds
Features: Stock has shadowline beaded cheekpiece, African ebony tip, and western fleur wraparound checkering. Steel grip cap, sling swivels, and case coloring on selected metal work are standard
Right-hand: $4595.00
Left-hand: $4845.00

MODEL 54 CLASSIC

Action: Bolt
Stock: AA Claro Walnut
Barrel: 24 in.
Sights: None
Weight: 6 lb.–7 lb. 12 oz.
Caliber: .22-250 Rem., .22-250 AI, .220 Swift, .243 Win., .243 Win. AI, 6mm Rem., 6mm Creedmoor, .250 Savage, .250 Savage AI, .257 Roberts, .257 Roberts AI, 6.5 Creedmoor, 6.5x47 Lapua, .260 Rem., 7mm-08, .308 Win., .338 Federal, .358 Win.
Magazine: 3 rounds
Features: Three-rear locking lug bolt action magazine fed repeater; centerfire action, also available in stainless steel; Sako style extraction machined from solid bar stock; plunger style ejector machined form solid bar; fully adjustable single-stage trigger
Right-hand: $2795.00
Left-hand: $3045.00

MODEL 57-M CLASSIC

Action: Bolt
Stock: AA Claro walnut
Barrel: 24 in,
Sights: None
Weight: 6 lb.–7 lb. 12 oz.
Caliber: .17 HMR, .22 LR, .22 WMR
Magazine: 4, 5 rounds
Features: Hand-rubbed oil-finished stock with four-panel hand checkering, Pachmayer recoil pad, chrome-moly premium match grade Wilson Arms barrel, steel grip cap are standard
Right-hand: $2795.00
Left-hand: $3045.00

Cooper Firearms of Montana

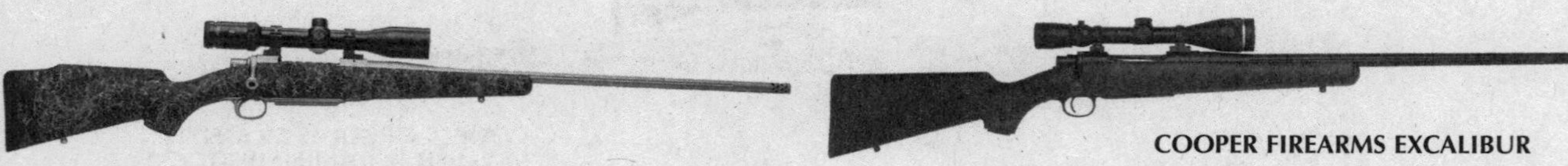

COOPER FIREARMS EXCALIBUR

COOPER FIREARMS MODEL 92 BACKCOUNTRY

MODEL 92 BACKCOUNTRY

Action: Bolt
Stock: Composite
Barrel: 24 in.
Sights: None
Weight: 5 lb. 12 oz.
Caliber: All standard long-action calibers and magnums up to .340 Wby. Mag.
Magazine: 3 rounds
Features: Lightweight Cooper Model 92 all-stainless steel action (Chromoly available on request); detachable magazine; Jewell trigger; Wilson Arms fluted barrel with muzzle brake; guaranteed ½-MOA accuracy
Right-hand: $3295.00
Left-hand: $3545.00

MODEL TRP-3

Action: Bolt
Stock: Wood; synthetic
Barrel: 26 in.
Sights: None
Weight: 8 lb.
Magazine: N/A
Caliber: A wide variety of calibers across three Cooper platforms
Features: Available in the Model 21, Model 22, and Model 57-M platforms; choice of wood or synthetic stock; adjustable single-stage trigger; matte stainless steel barrel with straight taper
Model 21: $3395.00
Model 22: $3395.00
Model 57-M: $2695.00

"VARIATIONS"

1. Classic

AA Claro walnut; steel grip; four-panel hand checkering; oil finish; matte metal finish; no options; available in all Cooper models

2. Custom Classic

AAA Claro walnut stock, shadowline beaded cheekpiece, African ebony tip, and western fleur wraparound checkering; sling swivel studs and chorome-moly premium match-grade Wilson Arms barrel are standard; all metal work has high gloss finish; available in all models

3. Excalibur

Hand-laid synthetics with Kevlar reinforcing material surrounding an aircraft-grade aluminum bedding block. Spiral fluted bolt, chrome-moly premium match grade Wilson Arms fluted barrel are standard; all metal work is matte finish; available for models 51, 52, and 54

4. Jackson Game

AA+ Claro walnut stock, rollover cheekpiece, semi-beavertail forearm. VE hand checkered grip in crossover multi-point pattern; stainless steel premium match grade Wilson Arms barrel; laminate version available; available for Models 51, 52, and 54

5. Jackson Hunter

Hand-laid synthetics with Kevlar reinforcing material surrounding an aircraft-grade aluminum bedding block; stainless steel premium match grade Wilson Arms barrel is standard; all metal work is matte finish; available for models 51, 52, 54, and 57-M

6. Jackson Squirrel

AA+ Claro walnut stock with rollover cheekpiece and semi-beavertail forearm. Grip has VE hand checkering in a crossover multi-point pattern; stainless steel premium match Wilson Arms barrel; also available in laminate; all metal work is matte finish; available in Model 57-M only

7. Mannlicher

AAA+ Claro walnut, shadowline beaded cheekpiece, African ebony tip, western fleur wraparound hand checking, chrome-moly premium match grade Wilson Arms octagonal barrel; all metal work is high gloss finish; available in all models

8. Montana Varminter

AA+ Claro walnut stock, hand-checkered grip, stainless steel straight taper premium match grade Wilson Arms barrel; all metal work is matte finish; available in models 21, 22, 38, 51, 52, 54, and 57-M

9. Phoenix

Hand-laid synthetics with Kevlar reinforcing material surrounding an aircraft-grade aluminum bedding block; spiral fluted bolt, chrome-moly premium match grade Wilson Arms fluted barrel are standard; all metal work is matte finish; available for models 21, 22, 38, 51, 54; left-hand options only in models 21 and 38

10. Schnabel

Available in models 52, 54, 56, and 57; AA+ Claro walnut; raised comb; slim taper forearm; multi-point two panel hand checkering; oil finish; standard grade sling swivel studs; Pachmayr pad; steel grip cap; chromoly premium match grade barrel; metal work is matte finished; available in Models 51, 52, 54, 57-M, 58, and muzzleloader

11. Varminter

AA Claro walnut stock, hand checkered grip, stainless steel straight taper premium match grade Wilson Arms barrel; all metal work is matte finish; available in Models 21, 22, 38, 51, 52, 54, and 57-M

12. Varmint Extreme

AAA Claro walnut stock, hand checkered grip in a crossover western fleur pattern; stainless steel straight taper matte finish premium match grade Wilson Arms barrel; all blued steel is high gloss finish; available in models 21, 22, 38, 51, 52, 54, and 57-M

13. Western Classic

AAA+ Claro walnut, shadowline beaded cheekpiece, African ebony tip, western fleur wraparound hand checking, chrome-moly premium match grade Wilson Arms octagonal barrel; all metal work is high gloss finish, selected metal work is highlighted with case coloring

CZ-USA (Ceska Zbrojovka)

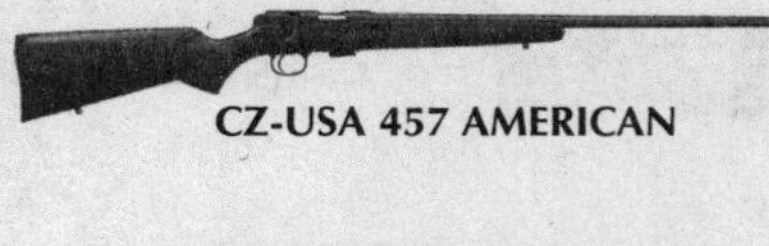
CZ-USA 457 AMERICAN

CZ-USA 457 AMERICAN COMBO

CZ-USA 457 JAGUAR

CZ-USA 457 LUX

CZ-USA 457 PREMIUM

CZ-USA 457 PRO VARMINT SUPPRESSOR-READY

CZ-USA 457 ROYAL

CZ-USA 457 SCOUT

CZ-USA 457 TRAINING RIFLE

457 AMERICAN

Action: Bolt
Stock: Turkish walnut
Barrel: 24.8 in.
Sights: None
Weight: 6 lb. 3 oz.
Caliber: .22 LR, .17 HMR, .22 WMR
Magazine: 5 rounds
Features: Classically styled, walnut-stocked rimfire with a cold hammer-forged barrel; integral 11mm dovetail scope mount cutouts; detachable magazine
MSRP $515.00

457 AMERICAN COMBO

Action: Bolt
Stock: Turkish walnut
Barrel: 24.8 in.
Sights: None
Weight: 6 lb. 2 oz.
Caliber: .22 LR/.17 HMR
Magazine: 5 rounds
Features: A nimble, pretty rimfire in two-caliber combo featuring a Turkish walnut stock; detachable magazine; cold hammer forged barrel; adjustable trigger; 60-degree bolt rotation
MSRP $655.00

457 JAGUAR

Action: Bolt
Stock: Beechwood
Barrel: 28.6 in.
Sights: Adjustable iron
Weight: 6 lb. 6 oz.
Caliber: .22 LR
Magazine: 10 rounds
Features: Wearing a stock in the European style, this rimfire features a fully adjustable trigger
MSRP $585.00

457 LUX

Action: Bolt
Stock: Turkish walnut
Barrel: 24.8 in.
Sights: Hooded front, tangent adjustable rear
Weight: 6 lb. 3 oz.
Caliber: .22 LR, .17 HMR, .22 WMR
Magazine: 5 rounds
Features: A rimfire with a European flair; detachable box magazine; fully adjustable trigger; 60-degree bolt rotation for easier scope use; swappable barrel system
MSRP $549.00

457 PREMIUM

Action: Bolt
Stock: Turkish walnut
Barrel: 24.8 in.
Sights: Adjustable tangent
Weight: 6 lb. 6 oz.
Caliber: .22 LR
Magazine: 5 rounds
Features: With a European-styled stock in Turkish walnut, this rimfire features adjustable tangent sights; adjustable trigger; detachable magazine; 60-degree bolt rotation; threaded muzzle
MSRP $799.00

457 PRO VARMINT SUPPRESSOR-READY

Action: Bolt
Stock: Laminate
Barrel: 16.5 in.
Sights: None
Weight: 7 lb. 4 oz.
Caliber: .22 LR
Magazine: 5 rounds
Features: A short-barreled, suppressor-ready rifle for small varmints: detachable box magazine; laminate stock with black paint; fully adjustable trigger; barrel threaded ½X28
MSRP $615.00

457 ROYAL

Action: Bolt
Stock: Turkish walnut
Barrel: 16.5 in., 20.5 in.
Sights: None
Weight: 5 lb. 15 oz.–6 lb. 2 oz.
Caliber: .22 LR
Magazine: 5 rounds
Features: Specifically designed for scope use, this rimfire has an adjustable trigger
MSRP $769.00

457 SCOUT

Action: Bolt
Stock: Beechwood
Barrel: 16.5 in.
Sights: Skeletonized hooded blade front, leaf rear
Weight: 5 lb.
Caliber: .22 LR
Magazine: 1 round
Features: A youth rifle with a 12-inch length of pull; ½X28 threaded muzzle for suppressor use; modular 457 platform; single-shot adaptor, but accepts all 457/455 magazines; American style beechwood stock; adjustable trigger
MSRP $475.00

457 TRAINING RIFLE

Action: Bolt
Stock: Beechwood
Barrel: 24.8 in.
Sights: Hooded front, tangent adjustable rear
Weight: 6 lb. 3 oz.
Caliber: .22 LR
Magazine: 5 rounds
Features: A serious practice and small-game rifle with: fully adjustable trigger; distance adjustable tangent rear sight, hooded front; slab-sided
MSRP $475.00

CZ-USA (Ceska Zbrojovka)

CZ-USA 457 VARMINT

CZ-USA 457 VARMINT AT-ONE

CZ-USA 457 VARMINT MTR

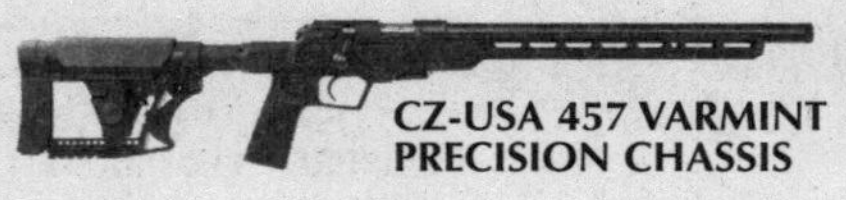

CZ-USA 457 VARMINT PRECISION CHASSIS

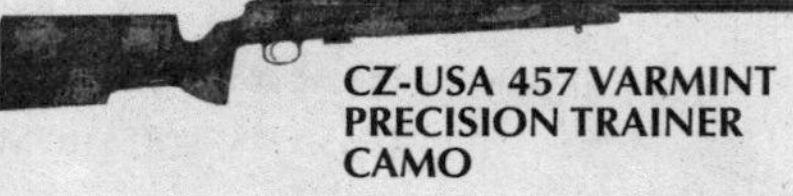

CZ-USA 457 VARMINT PRECISION TRAINER CAMO

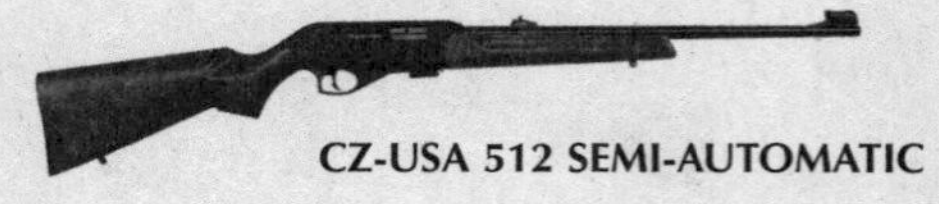

CZ-USA 512 SEMI-AUTOMATIC

CZ-USA 527 VARMINT

CZ-USA CZ 527 AMERICAN SYNTHETIC SUPPRESSOR-READY

457 VARMINT

Action: Bolt
Stock: Turkish walnut
Barrel: 20.5 in.
Sights: None
Weight: 7 lb. 1 oz.
Caliber: .22 LR, .17 HMR, .22 WMR
Magazine: 5 rounds
Features: A maneuverable varmint rifle with: heavy barrel profile; detachable box magazine; swappable barrel system; 60-degree bolt rotation for easier use with optics; laser-cut stippling
MSRP $565.00

457 VARMINT AT-ONE

Action: Bolt
Stock: Laminate
Barrel: 16.5 in., 24 in.
Sights: None
Weight: 7 lb. 12 oz.
Caliber: .22 LR
Magazine: 5 rounds
Features: A varmint-getter made to fit with a Boyd's AT-ONE laminate stock adjustable at cheekpiece and for length of pull; swappable barrel system; fully adjustable trigger
MSRP $689.00

457 VARMINT MTR

Action: Bolt
Stock: Turkish walnut
Barrel: 20.5 in.
Sights: None
Weight: 7 lb. 1 oz.
Caliber: .22 LR
Magazine: 5 rounds
Features: A rock-steady small-varmint or paper-puncher gun- (MTR = Match Target Rifle) with a handsome target-style stock of Turkish walnut; fully adjustable trigger; detachable box magazine; match chamber; heavy barrel profile; flat fore-end; dual QD studs front, single rear
MSRP $785.00

457 VARMINT PRECISION CHASSIS

Action: Bolt
Stock: Aluminum chassis
Barrel: 16.5 in., 24 in.
Sights: None
Weight: 7 lb.
Caliber: .22 LR
Magazine: 5 rounds
Features: A suppressor-ready rimfire with a chassis foundation for serious competition; fully adjustable trigger; heavy cold hammer forged barrel; adjustable Luth-AR stock; AR-style grip; multiple M-LOK slots; QD sling pockets
MSRP $1039.00

457 VARMINT PRECISION TRAINER CAMO

Action: Bolt
Stock: Composite
Barrel: 16.5, 20.5 in., 24 in.
Sights: None
Weight: 7 lb. 2 oz.–7 lb. 9 oz.
Caliber: .22 LR
Magazine: 5 rounda
Features: A dedicated rimfire training rifle or small-game getter with a Manners carbon-fiber/fiberglass composite stock in a three-color camo; ½X28 threaded barrel; swappable barrel system
MSRP $1449.00

512 SEMI-AUTOMATIC

Action: Semiautomatic
Stock: Lacquered beech wood
Barrel: 20.7 in.
Sights: Adjustable
Weight: 5 lb. 14 oz.
Caliber: .22 WMR
Magazine: Detachable box, 5 rounds
Features: Aluminum alloy upper receiver and fiberglass reinforced polymer lower half; dual guide rods; hammer-forged CZ barrel; integral 11mm dovetail for mounting optics
MSRP $549.00

527 SERIES

Action: Bolt
Stock: Walnut
Barrel: 18.5 in.–24 in.
Sights: Open
Weight: 5 lb. 14 oz.–7 lb. 13 oz.
Caliber: .223 Rem., .204 Ruger, 7.62x39, 6.5 Grendel, .222 Rem., .22 Hornet, .17 Hornet; Carbine .223 Rem., 7.62x39; FS .223 Rem.; Lux .223 Rem., .22 Hornet, .222 Rem.; Lux left-hand .223 Rem.; Varmint .223 Rem., .204 Ruger, .17 Hornet
Magazine: Detachable box, 5 rounds
Features: Hammer-forged barrel; controlled round feed; single-set trigger; each model comes in a variety of calibers and a different stock
MSRP . . . . $779.00–$925.00

527 AMERICAN SYNTHETIC SUPPRESSOR-READY

Action: Bolt
Stock: Synthetic
Barrel: 16.5 in.
Sights: None
Weight: 5 lb. 14 oz.
Caliber: .223 Rem., 6.5 Grendel, 7.62x39
Magazine: 5 rounds
Features: Threaded 5/8×24 for a suppressor; 13.5 in. length of pull; cold hammer-forged barrel; two-position safety; single set trigger; detachable magazine; integral 16mm scope bases
MSRP . . . . $779.00–$799.00

CZ-USA (Ceska Zbrojovka)

CZ-USA 527 VARMINT MTR
CZ-USA 527 VARMINT SUPPRESSOR-READY
CZ-USA 557 LEFT HAND
CZ-USA BREN 2 MS CARBINE
CZ-USA SCORPION BULLPUP CARBINE KIT
CZ–USA SCORPION EVO 3 S1 CARBINE

527 VARMINT MTR

Action: Bolt
Stock: Turkish walnut
Barrel: 25.6 in.
Sights: None
Weight: 8 lb. 11 oz.
Caliber: .223 Rem., 6.5 Grendel
Magazine: 5 rounds
Features: Nicely priced varmint or paper-punching rifle (MTR = Match Target Rifle) with choice of an American pattern heavy target stock; flat fore-end; longer barrel; fully adjustable trigger; .866-inch heavy profile barrel
MSRP **$925.00**

527 VARMINT SUPPRESSOR-READY

Action: Bolt
Stock: Turkish walnut
Barrel: 24 in.
Sights: None
Weight: 7 lb. 13 oz.
Caliber: 6.5 Grendel
Magazine: 5 rounds
Features: Chambered only for the 6.5 Grendel, this varmint rifle features: single set trigger; controlled round feed; claw extractor; 5/8X24 muzzle threads
MSRP **$815.00**

557 LEFT HAND

Action: Bolt
Stock: Turkish walnut
Barrel: 24 in.
Sights: None
Weight: 7 lb. 14 oz.
Caliber: .30-06 Spfd., .308 Win.
Magazine: 4 rounds
Features: Integrated dovetail mounts; hinged floorplate; fully adjustable trigger; unique checking on the forend
MSRP **$899.00**

BREN 2 MS CARBINE

Action: Semiautomatic
Stock: Synthetic
Barrel: 26.5 in.
Sights: None
Weight: 7 lb. 5 oz.
Caliber: .223 Rem.
Magazine: 30 rounds
Features: Based off the original select-fire Bren 2, this semiautomatic has a manual safety; folding adjustable stock; aluminum upper; carbon-fiber composite lower; Ms designation stands for modular forearm
MSRP **$2255.00**

SCORPION BULLPUP CARBINE KIT

Action: Semiautomatic
Stock: Synthetic
Barrel: Less than 16 in.
Sights: None
Weight: N/A
Caliber: 9mm
Magazine: N/A
Features: Fun bullpup in you-build-it kit form; short-barreled firearm requires appropriate tax stamps and Class III paperwork
MSRP **$399.00**

SCORPION EVO 3 S1 CARBINE

Action: Semiautomatic
Stock: Synthetic
Barrel: 16.2 in.
Sights: Low-profile fully adjustable aperture and post, 4 rear aperture sizes
Weight: 7 lb.
Caliber: 9mm
Magazine: 10 or 30 rounds
Features: 16.2 in. barrel fitted with either a compensating muzzle brake or a faux suppressor built specifically for CZ-USA by SilencerCo; newly designed forend covered in M-LOK attachment points to keep the profile slim while still being big enough to swallow most pistol-caliber suppressors; top Picatinny rail; low-profile aluminum adjustable sights; ambidextrous controls; swappable non-reciprocating charging handle; adjustable trigger
MSRP . . . . **$1209.00–$1285.00**

Dakota Arms

DAKOTA MODEL 10

DAKOTA MODEL 76 CLASSIC

DAKOTA MODEL 97 OUTFITTER

DAKOTA SHARPS

DAKOTA VARMINTER

MODEL 10

Action: Falling block
Stock: Walnut
Barrel: 23 in.
Sights: None
Weight: 6 lb.–7 lb.
Caliber: .22 LR to .300 Win., .338 to .375 H&H Mag.
Magazine: None
Features: Point wrap checkering; scope ring bases installed; custom length of pull; barrel break in
Classic: $5395.00
Deluxe: $6995.00
Mannlicher: $6595.00

MODEL 76

Action: Bolt
Stock: Walnut
Barrel: 23 in.
Sights: None
Weight: 6 lb. 8 oz.–9 lb. 8 oz.
Caliber: Classic: .257 Roberts, .260 Rem., .270 Win., .280 Rem., .30-06 Spfd., .300 Dakota, .300 Win. Mag., .300 WSM, .308 Win., .330 Dakota, .416 Rem., 7mm Rem. Mag., 7mm-08 Rem.; Safari: .300 H&H, .375 Dakota, .416 Rem., 7mm Dakota; African: .338 Win. Mag., .375 H&H, .416 Rem., .404 Jeffery, .416 Rigby, .450 Dakota, .458 Lott
Magazine: Box, 4 rounds
Features: Barrel break in; custom length of pull; optional engraving; point panel checkering; Dakota swivel studs; 1-inch recoil pad; straddle floor plate; right- or left-hand configurations; Safari model has front island sight with flip-up night sight; African model has quarter rib sights with banded front sights and flip-up night sights
Classic: $6295.00
Deluxe: $8995.00
Alpine: $6995.00
Mannlicher: $7595.00
Safari: $8995.00
African: $9995.00
Professional Hunter: $6995.00
Traveler: $9995.00

MODEL 97

Action: Bolt
Stock: Fiberglass, composite, walnut
Barrel: 22 in. (short action), 25 in. (long action)
Sights: None
Weight: 7 lb.
Caliber: Numerous calibers from .22-250 Rem. to .375 H&H Mag.
Magazine: Blind box
Features: Round-body configuration; stainless action and barrel; deluxe recoil pad; island front and rear sights; pillar and glass bedded; adjustable Model 76 trigger; match-grade barrel. Outfitter has a wide variety of Cerakote colors to choose from with a splatter stock to match the Cerakote choice; Classic has a black synthetic stock and blued metalwork; Stainless has black synthetic stock and stainless finish metalwork; left- and right-hand available all versions
Classic: $4295.00
Stainless: $4695.00
Outfitter: $5495.00

SHARPS

Action: Falling block
Stock: Walnut
Barrel: 26 in.
Sights: Open
Weight: 8 lb. 4 oz.
Caliber: Rimmed cartridges from .17 HMR to .444 Marlin
Magazine: None
Features: Scaled to 80% of the original model; blueprinted action; front bead sight combinations; tang rear sight; steel buttplate; XX-grade walnut standard; matte blue metalwork standard, rust blue, French gray, case-colored, high-polish blue, and Cerakote are upgrade options; extensive list of stock, barrel, sight, and engraving options
MSRP . . . . from $4995.00

VARMINTER

Action: Bolt
Stock: Walnut
Barrel: 22 in.
Sights: None
Weight: 8 lb. 4 oz.
Caliber: small calibers
Magazine: None
Features: Standard features include XX Claro walnut stock, blueprinted action, Talley scope rings and bases, benchrest tolerances, box-style match trigger, free-floated barrel, plunger ejector, matte bead-blast finish, recessed target crown; Deluxe model gets an upgraded stock in XXX walnut or a Bastogne XX sporter configuration and a checkered fore-end; Heavy Barrel has a stock in XX walnut with a semi-beavertail fore-end, heavy straight taper match barrel; HB All-Weather gets a composite stock in OD green with black webbing, heavy straight taper match-grade barrel; numerous stock, barrel, finish, and engraving upgrades available for all versions
MSRP . . . . from $2495.00

DAMKO

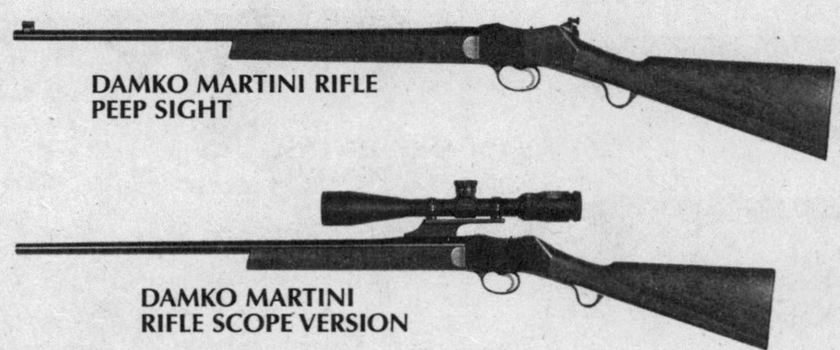
DAMKO MARTINI RIFLE PEEP SIGHT

DAMKO MARTINI RIFLE SCOPE VERSION

DAMKO MARTINI RIFLE STANDARD

MARTINI RIFLE PEEP SIGHT

Action: Single-shot Martini falling block
Stock: Walnut
Barrel: 20 in., 24 in.
Sights: Hooded bead front, threaded rear peep
Weight: N/A
Caliber: .25–35 Win., .30–30 Win., .30–40 Krag, .44 Rem. Mag.
Magazine: 1 round
Features: All the features of the standard Martini, with the addition of DAMKO's own peep sight with a 12–40 thread
MSRP $1956.99

MARTINI RIFLE SCOPE VERSION

Action: Single-shot Martini falling block
Stock: Walnut
Barrel: 20 in., 26 in.
Sights: None
Weight: N/A
Caliber: .25–35 Win., .30–30 Win., .30–40 Krag, .44 Rem. Mag.
Magazine: 1 round
Features: An original take on the Martini rifle with a flat-top PAC-NOR barrel mounted with DAMKO's own cantilever scope mount base
MSRP $2059.99

MARTINI RIFLE STANDARD

Action: Single-shot Martini falling block
Stock: Walnut
Barrel: 20 in., 24 in.
Sights: Hooded bead front, tangent-adjustable flat-top rear
Weight: N/A
Caliber: .25–35 Win., .30–30 Win., .30–40 Krag, .44 Rem. Mag.
Magazine: 1 round
Features: An updated take on a classic Martini falling block action in four popular calibers; .44 Rem. Mag with 20-inch barrel, all others 24 inches; steel butt plate; Chromoly Pac-Nor barrel
MSRP $1853.99

Daniel Defense

DANIEL DEFENSE DDM4ISR

DANIEL DEFENSE DDM4 PDW SBR

DANIEL DEFENSE DD5 V3

DDM4ISR

Acti***o**n*: Semiautomatic
Stock: Synthetic
Barrel: 9 in.
Sights: None
Weight: 7 lb. 9 oz.
Caliber: .300 BLK
Magazine: DD magazine
Features: Integrally suppressed weapon system optimized for the .300 BLK cartridge; cold-hammer-forged barrel is fluted, has a target crown; standard pistol length gas system; direct impingement; MFR XL 15.0 rail with KeyMod attachments on sides and bottom; Mil-Spec with enhanced flared magwell; rear receiver QD swivel attachment point; available in black, Deep Woods, or Mil Spec+
MSRP $3260.00

DDM4 PDW SBR

Action: Semiautomatic
Stock: Synthetic
Barrel: 7 in.
Sights: None
Weight: 5 lb. 11 oz.
Caliber: .300 BLK
Magazine: 30 rounds
Features: Super-compact SBR—short-barreled rifle—featuring a Maxim Defense CQB Gen 7 stock; 6-in. MFR flat front rail; carbine-length gas system
MSRP $2012.00

DD5 V3

Action: Semiautomatic
Stock: Synthetic
Barrel: 16 in.
Sights: None
Weight: 8 lb. 5 oz.
Caliber: .308 Win.
Magazine: 20 rounds
Features: Ample .308 power in a nimble configuration that includes dual ejectors; super-finished DLC-coated bolt carrier group; proprietary chrome-lined barrel; four-bolt connection system; GRIP-N-RIP independent and ambidextrous charging handle; adjustable gas block in an intermediate-length gas system
MSRP $2499.00

Daniel Defense

DD5 V4

Action: Semiautomatic
Stock: Synthetic
Barrel: 18 in.
Sights: None
Weight: 8 lb. 10 oz.
Caliber: 6.5 Creedmoor, .308 Win.
Magazine: 20 rounds
Features: Similar to the DD5 V3, but with a slightly longer barrel, a couple more ounces, and a rifle-length gas system; in black or Mil Spec+ choice of finishes
MSRP . . . .$2499.00–$2672.00

DD5 V5

Action: Semiautomatic
Stock: Synthetic
Barrel: 18 in.
Sights: None
Weight: 8 lb. 10 oz.
Caliber: 6.5 Creedmoor, .260 Rem.
Magazine: 20 rounds
Features: Super-finished DLC-coated bolt carrier group; dual ejectors; proprietary chrome-lined barrel; four-bolt connection system; GRIP-N-RIP independent and ambidextrous charging handle; threaded muzzle; both calibers available in black, 6.5 Creedmoor also available in Mil Spec+ finish
MSRP . . . .$2499.00–$2672.00

DDM4V4S

Action: Semiautomatic
Stock: Synthetic
Barrel: 11.5 in.
Sights: None
Weight: 5 lb. 14 oz.
Caliber: 5.56 NATO
Magazine: Detachable box, 30 rounds
Features: Lightweight, ergonomic rail system affords ample room for securely mounting multiple accessories and offers the longest possible sight radius with iron sights; three removable high-temperature-resistant Daniel Defense Rail Panels for a secure, comfortable grip while also protecting the support hand from heat; compatibility with a wide variety of muzzle devices and sound suppressors; free-floating, cold hammer-forged barrel
MSRP $1826.00

DDM4V7

Action: Semiautomatic
Stock: Synthetic
Barrel: 16 in.
Sights: None
Weight: 6 lb. 3 oz.
Caliber: 5.56 NATO
Magazine: Detachable box, 30 rounds
Features: M-LOK attachment technology with Daniel Defense MFR XS 15.0 rail; DD improved flash suppressor; mid-length gas system; uninterrupted 1913 Picatinny rail; black, Deep Woods, Daniel Defense Tornado or Mil Spec+ choice of finishes
MSRP . . . . $1798.00–$1978.00

DDM4V7 LW

Action: Semiautomatic
Stock: Synthetic
Barrel: 16 in.
Sights: None
Weight: 6 lb. 1 oz.
Caliber: 5.56 NATO
Magazine: Detachable box, 30 rounds
Features: M-LOK attachment technology with Daniel Defense MFR XS 15.0 rail; DD improved flash suppressor; mid-length gas system; uninterrupted 1913 Picatinny rail; available in black or hybrid paint scheme called Rattlecan
MSRP . . . . $1798.00–$1978.00

DDM4V7 PRO

Action: Semiautomatic
Stock: Synthetic
Barrel: 18 in.
Sights: None
Weight: 7 lb. 6.4 oz.
Caliber: 5.56 NATO
Magazine: DD magazine
Features: Designed for multi-gun competitors; 18-in. Strength-to-Weight (S2W), cold-hammer-forged barrel; rifle-length direct impingement gas system; Muzzle Climb Mitigator; Geissele Automatics Super Dynamic 3 Gun trigger; MFR XS 15.0 rail with M-LOK attachment system; Grip-N-Rip charging handle; DD buttstock and pistol grip; glass-filled polymer stock with soft-touch overmolding; in black or Rattlecan finish
MSRP . . . . $2079.00–$2259.00

DDM4V7 S

Action: Semiautomatic
Stock: Synthetic
Barrel: 11.5 in.
Sights: None
Weight: 5 lb. 9.6 oz.
Caliber: 5.56 NATO
Magazine: DD magazine
Features: Short-barreled rifle featuring M-LOK attachment technology; free-floating, cold-hammer-forged barrel; carbine-length gas system; free-floating MFR XS 10.0 rail; M-LOK attachment points that run along seven positions; uninterrupted 1913 Picatinny rail on top
MSRP $1798.00

Daniel Defense

DDM4V9

Action: Semiautomatic
Stock: Synthetic
Barrel: 16 in.
Sights: None
Weight: 6 lb. 10 oz.
Caliber: 5.56 NATO
Magazine: Detachable box, 30 rounds
Features: Daniel Defense glass-filled polymer stock, pistol and vertical grips; rail panels of Santoprene heat-resistant to 300-degrees; flash suppressor; H buffer; mid-length direct impingement system; M4 rail; Grip-N-Rip charging handle; adjustable six-position buttstock; upper and lower Type III hard-coat anodized
MSRP $1899.00

DDM4V11 PRO

Action: Semiautomatic
Stock: Synthetic
Barrel: 18 in.
Sights: None
Weight: 7 lb. 8 oz.
Caliber: 5.56 NATO
Magazine: Detachable box, 30 rounds
Features: Picatinny rails; muzzle climb mitigator; freefloat rail; Geissele automatics super dynamic 3-gun trigger; flared magazine well
MSRP $2079.00

DELTA 5

Action: Bolt
Stock: Synthetic
Barrel: 20 in., 24 in.
Sights: None
Weight: 8 lb. 15 oz.–9 lb. 8 oz.
Caliber: .308 Win., 6.5 Creedmoor
Magazine: 5 rounds
Features: DD's first bolt-action featuring a user-interchangeable stainless steel barrel; bedded stainless steel action with integral recoil lug; removeable bolt knob; carbon fiber-reinforced stock adjustable for length of pull and height; 11 M-LOK points on the fore-end, one on the buttstock, and three M-LOK sling points; AICS single-feed mag compatible; adjustable Timney Elite Hunter trigger, single-stage with two-position safety
MSRP $1799.00

DELTA 5 ACCURACY PACKAGE

Action: Bolt
Stock: Synthetic
Barrel: 24 in.
Sights: None
Weight: 11 lb. 13 oz.
Caliber: 6.5 Creedmoor
Magazine: 5 rounds
Features: Daniel Defense builds on the success of the Delta 5 with an upgraded package that includes a Nightforce SHV 4-14X50 scope; Atlas bipod; heavy Palma barrel profile
MSRP $3395.00

Dark Storm Industries

DARK STORM INDUSTRIES DS1 VARIANT 1 FEATURELESS

DARK STORM INDUSTRIES DS1 VARIANT 1 FIXED MAGAZINE RIFLE

DS1 VARIANT 1 FEATURELESS

Action: Semiautomatic
Stock: Synthetic
Barrel: 16 in.
Sights: None
Weight: N/A
Caliber: 5.56 NATO
Magazine: 10 rounds
Features: Featureless version fits the bill with a weird but workable stock; 7075 aluminum billet receiver set; deburred edges; M4 feed ramp extensions; winter trigger guard; 90-degree ambidextrous safety selector; 9-in. narrow-profile M-LOK forearm; in black or tungsten finishes
Black: $1595.00
Tungsten: $1695.00

DS1 VARIANT 1 FIXED MAGAZINE RIFLE

Action: Semiautomatic
Stock: Synthetic
Barrel: 16 in.
Sights: None
Weight: N/A
Caliber: 5.56 NATO
Magazine: 10 rounds
Features: Similar to the Featureless model, but with a Magpul CTR adjustable stock and a fixed magazine; Dark Storm says this rifle is legal to own in all 50 states; in a tungsten or black finish
Black: $1595.00
Tungsten: $1695.00

Dark Storm Industries

DARK STORM INDUSTRIES DS1 VARIANT 1 NON-NFA FIREARM

DARK STORM INDUSTRIES DS1 VARIANT 1 POST-BAN

DARK STORM INDUSTRIES DS1 VARIANT 1 RIFLE

DS1 VARIANT 1 NON-NFA FIREARM

Action: Semiautomatic
Stock: Synthetic
Barrel: 12.5 in.
Sights: None
Weight: N/A
Caliber: 5.56 NATO
Magazine: 10, 30 rounds
Features: Dark Storm says this is not a rifle, not a pistol, and not an AOW—any other weapon. It also says it fails to qualify as an "assault weapon" under CT and NJ law, but it is not currently legal to own this firearm in MA, NY, CA, or MD.; in black or tungsten finishes
Black:. $1595.00
Tungsten:. $1695.00

DS1 VARIANT 1 POST-BAN

Action: Semiautomatic
Stock: Synthetic
Barrel: 16 in.
Sights: None
Weight: N/A
Caliber: 5.56 NATO
Magazine: 10 rounds
Features: Similar to the Featureless model, but with a Magpul fixed carbine stock; DSI Competition Compensator; carbine gas system; steel micro gas block; optics ready; in black or tungsten finishes
Black:. $1595.00
Tungsten:. $1695.00

DS1 VARIANT 1 RIFLE

Action: Semiautomatic
Stock: Synthetic
Barrel: 16 in.
Sights: None
Weight: N/A
Caliber: 5.56 NATO
Magazine: 30 rounds
Features: No AR restrictions to worry about? Then this is the Dark Storm rifle for you with a carbine gas system; threaded barrel; DSI competition compensator; Magpul CTR adjustable stock; optic ready design; ambidextrous sling; ambidextrous 90-degree safety selector; ambidextrous charging handle; winter trigger guar; in black or tungsten finishes; HBAR variant available
Black:. $1595.00
Tungsten:. $1695.00

RIFLES

Davide Pedersoli & C.

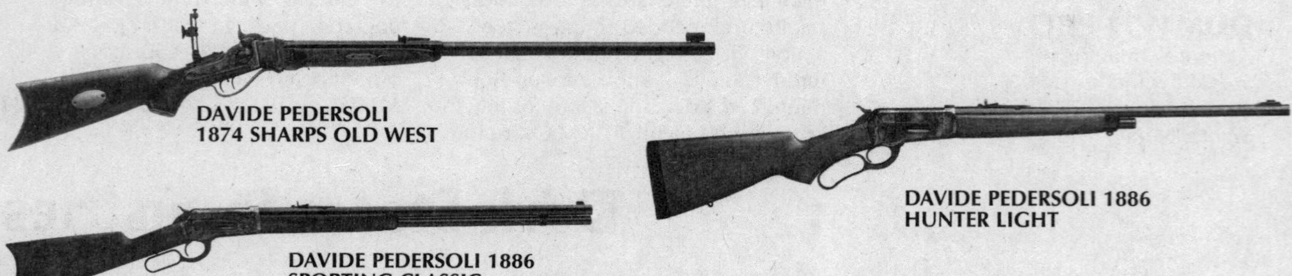

DAVIDE PEDERSOLI 1874 SHARPS OLD WEST

DAVIDE PEDERSOLI 1886 HUNTER LIGHT

DAVIDE PEDERSOLI 1886 SPORTING CLASSIC

1874 SHARPS OLD WEST MAPLE

Action: Dropping block
Stock: Maple
Barrel: 30 in.
Sights: None
Weight: 11 lb. 7 oz.
Caliber: .45-70 Govt.
Magazine: None
Features: Optional Creedmoor and tunnel sights; brass plate on right side of butt stock can be personalized; forend has wedge plates; pistol grip cap is made of hardened steel
MSRP $2560.00

1886 HUNTER LIGHT

Action: Lever
Stock: Walnut
Barrel: 22 in.
Sights: Ramped front, buckhorn rear
Weight: 7 lb. 2 oz.
Caliber: .45-70 Govt., .444 Marlin
Magazine: 3 rounds
Features: Lighter, shorter version of standard 1886 lever-action; designed to accommodate a left side-mounted Creedmoor sight; barrel is broach rifled; sling swivels included
.45-70: $1885.00
.444 Marlin: $1935.00

1886 SPORTING CLASSIC

Action: Lever
Stock: American walnut
Barrel: 26 in.
Sights: Blade front sight, semi-buckhorn rear
Weight: 9 lb. 4 oz.
Caliber: .45-70 Gov't.
Magazine: 8 rounds
Features: Straight English stock of American walnut; case hardened receiver; blued round barrel; crescent buttplate; receiver can accept a peep sight
MSRP $2110.00

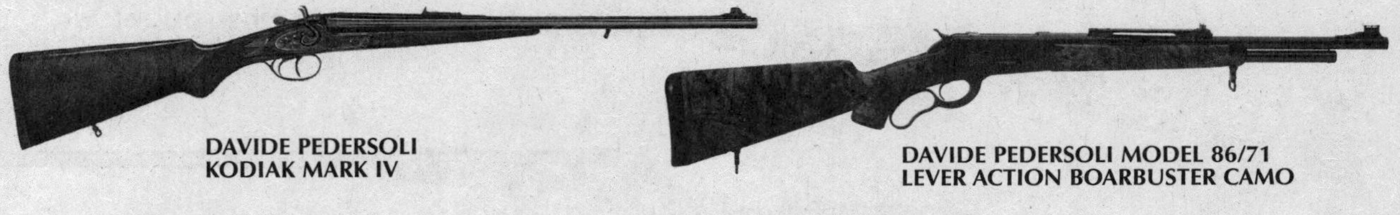

DAVIDE PEDERSOLI KODIAK MARK IV

DAVIDE PEDERSOLI MODEL 86/71 LEVER ACTION BOARBUSTER CAMO

DAVIDE PEDERSOLI MODEL 86/71 BOARBUSTER MARK II

DAVIDE PEDERSOLI MODEL 86/71 LEVER ACTION CLASSIC

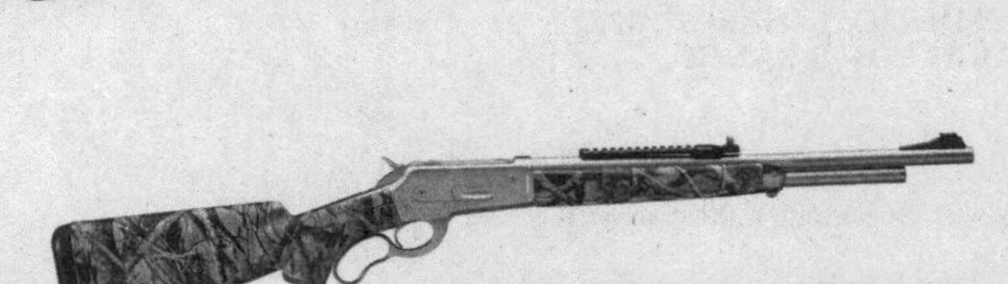

DAVIDE PEDERSOLI MODEL 86/71 LEVER ACTION STAINLESS STEEL

DAVIDE PEDERSOLI MODEL 86/71 LEVER ACTION WILDBUSTER

KODIAK MARK IV

Action: Breech loading
Stock: Walnut
Barrel: 22 in., 24 in.
Sights: Open
Weight: 9 lb. 11 oz.–10 lb. 5 oz.
Caliber: .450 NE, .45-70 Govt. 8x57JRS, 9.3x74R
Magazine: None
Features: Double-leave rear sight in a dovetail; tapered round barrels made of blued steel; select walnut stock with checkering and oil finish; available with an interchangeable 20-gauge barrel in all calibers except the .450 NE
Rifle calibers only:........ $6665.00–$8935.00
With 20-gauge barrel: ...... $9050.00–$9115.00

MODEL 86/71 LEVER ACTION BOARBUSTER

Action: Lever
Stock: Walnut
Barrel: 19 in.
Sights: Drilled and tapped for scopes
Weight: 7 lb. 4 oz.
Caliber: .444 Marlin, .45-70 Govt.
Magazine: 5 rounds
Features: Barrel equipped with European Picatinny style base with integral rear sight; half cock safety on hammer; safety slide catch at the rear of the frame; checkered pistol grip stock and forend are made from walnut; also available in soft touch orange camo color; metal parts are blued; drilled and tapped for sights
MSRP......... $2085.00–$2125.00

MODEL 86/71 LEVER ACTION BOARBUSTER MARK II

Action: Lever
Stock: Synthetic
Barrel: 19 in.
Sights: Superluminova front and rear
Weight: 7 lb. 4 oz.
Caliber: .444 Marlin, .45-70
Magazine: 5 rounds
Features: Adjustable comb synthetic stock Cerakoted metalwork in bronze; ample rail for optics
MSRP.................$2645.00

MODEL 86/71 LEVER ACTION CLASSIC

Action: Lever
Stock: Walnut
Barrel: 24 in.
Sights: Drilled and tapped for scopes
Weight: 8 lb. 3 oz.
Caliber: .348 Win., .45-70 Govt.
Magazine: 5 rounds
Features: Last "big frame" rifle for Winchester; drilled and tapped for scopes; broach rifled barrel and magazine are blued finished; checkered walnut pistol grip; frame is forged and CNC-machined, with a blued finish on the standard version and case-hardened frame and buttcap on the Premium model with select walnut stock and forend
Standard:...... $1945.00–$1980.00
Premium:..............$2100.00

MODEL 86/71 LEVER ACTION STAINLESS STEEL

Action: Lever
Stock: Synthetic
Barrel: 19 in.
Sights: Adjustable rear, fixed front
Weight: 7 lb. 15 oz.
Caliber: .45-70 Govt.
Magazine: N/A
Features: PMG barrel, broach rifled; fiber optic front sight and Weaver/ Picatinny base with integrated rear sight; stock is made of American walnut covered with a camouflage film; microcell thick butt plate and swivel stud
MSRP................$2640.00

MODEL 86/71 LEVER ACTION WILDBUSTER

Action: Lever
Stock: Walnut
Barrel: 24 in.
Sights: Drilled and tapped for scopes
Weight: 8 lb. 3 oz.
Caliber: .45-70 Govt.
Magazine: 5 rounds
Features: Ramp rear sight; walnut forend and pistol grip stock with checkered buttplate; blued finish on metal parts; drilled and tapped for scopes
MSRP................$1900.00

Davide Pedersoli & C.

RIFLES

ROLLING BLOCK MISSISSIPPI CLASSIC

Action: N/A
Stock: Wood
Barrel: 26 in.
Sights: Adjustable rear, fixed front
Weight: 7 lb. 8 oz.
Caliber: .357 Mag, .38-55, .45 Colt
Magazine: N/A
Features: High carbon steel barrel is broach rifled; alloy frame is embellished with a engraving; old silver colour finishing; equipped with a blade front sight and an adjustable rear sight, drilled to assemble the Creedmoor sight; stock and forend are made of American walnut with brass fittings
MSRP $1120.00

ROLLING BLOCK TARGET

Action: Dropping block
Stock: Walnut
Barrel: 30 in.
Sights: Open
Weight: 10 lb. 9 oz.
Caliber: .357 Mag., .45–70 Govt.
Magazine: None
Features: Octagonal, conical blued barrel; case-hardened color frame is equipped with ramp rear sight adjustable in elevation; steel buttplate and trigger guard; straight stock and forend made of walnut with oil finish; Deluxe grade also available
Standard: $1360.00
Deluxe: $2815.00

SHARPS 1877 OVERBAUGH LONG RANGE

Action: Sharps
Stock: Walnut
Barrel: 30 in.
Sights: Blade front, military-style rear
Weight: 8 lb. 4.8 oz.
Caliber: .45-70 Govt.
Magazine: N/A
Features: Designed to meet the 10-lb. weight limitations in NRA competition; forged frame and parts; oil-finished American walnut stock with checkering; double set triggers are standard; rifle is drilled and tapped for Creedmoor sights
MSRP $2350.00

SHARPS LITTLE BETSY

Action: N/A
Stock: Wood
Barrel: 24 in.
Sights: Creedmoor
Weight: 7 lb. 10 oz.
Caliber: .17 HRM, .22LR, .22 Hornet, .357 Mag, .30-30 Win.
Magazine: N/A
Features: Forged and CNC machined frame features a floral engraving; stock is made of American walnut; barrel PMG quality features a matt blue finish; sights includes a tunnel front sight and the folding Creedmoor sight; with double set trigger
MSRP . . . . $1930.00–$2105.00

SHARPS SMALL GAME

Action: Sharps
Stock: Walnut
Barrel: 24 in.
Sights: Brass bead front, buckhorn rear
Weight: 7 lb. 9.6 oz.
Caliber: .22 LR, .22 Hornet
Magazine: N/A
Features: Lighter, slimmer version of standard 1874 Sharps; half-octagon, half-round barrel styling; overall length is under 42 in.; match barrel and double-set triggers
.22 LR: $1675.00
.22 Hornet: $1700.00

Del-Ton

DTI EXTREME DUTY 316

Action: Semiautomatic
Stock: M4 reinforced fiber
Barrel: 16 in.
Sights: Samson quick flip dual aperture rear sight
Weight: 6 lb. 6.4 oz.
Caliber: 5.56 NATO
Magazine: Detachable box
Features: Hammer forged CMV chrome-lined barrel; H-buffer
MSRP $1119.05

ECHO 7.62X39

Action: Semiautomatic
Stock: Synthetic
Barrel: 16 in.
Sights: Adjustable front sight
Weight: 6 lb. 10 oz.
Caliber: 7.62x39
Magazine: Detachable box, 30 rounds
Features: Carbine gas system; phosphated under F-marked front sight base; chrome-lined carrier interior; carbine-length hand guards; aluminum delta ring; single heat shield
MSRP $753.42

ECHO 316H OR

Action: Semiautomatic
Stock: M4 five-position
Barrel: 16 in.
Sights: None
Weight: 6 lb. 10 oz.
Caliber: 5.56 NATO
Magazine: Detachable box, 30 rounds
Features: Single rail gas block; CAR handguards with single heat shields; A2 flash hider; forged 7075 T6 aluminum upper and lower receivers
MSRP $816.44

RIFLES

Devil Dog Arms

DDA KRP-15

Action: Semiautomatic
Stock: Synthetic
Barrel: 16 in.
Sights: None
Weight: 7 lb.
Caliber: .223 Rem./5.56 NATO
Magazine: N/A
Features: KRP is Keymod Rifle Package, an AR platform with miles of rail on its 15-inch free-floating Keymod handguard; billet machined upper and lower; gas impingement system; Type III hard coat anodized receiver finish; nitride finish 1:7 twist barrel; Devil Dog Arms tactical muzzle brake; Magpul six-position MOE buttstock and MOE+ grip
MSRP $1499.00

HOG

Action: Bolt
Stock: Carbon fiber
Barrel: N/A
Sights: None
Weight: 13 lb. 6 oz.–14 lb.
Caliber: 6.5 Creedmoor, .308 Win., .338 Lapua
Magazine: N/A
Features: This is a premium rifle for the long-range crowd, featuring a Kelby Model KTS stock, hand laid with three-way buttplate and adjustable cheekpiece; black nitride action; Calvin Elite two-stage trigger; match-grade M24 Krieger barrel; hand-polished chamber; 5/8X24 threaded muzzle; detachable box magazine
MSRP $3000.00

DoubleStar Corp.

DOUBLESTAR 3GR 2.0 GO-FAST RED

DOUBLESTAR STAR10-B

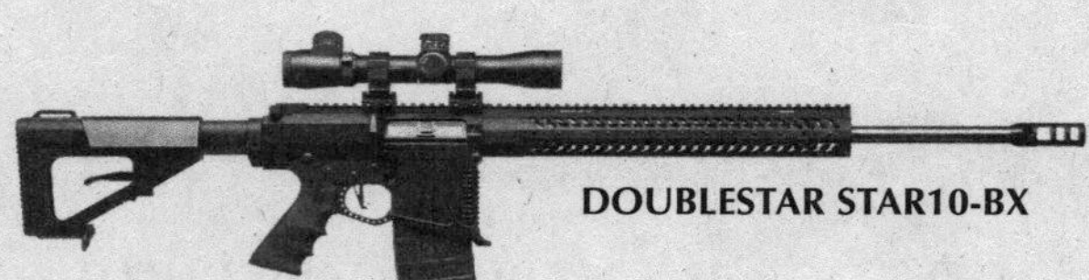
DOUBLESTAR STAR10-BX

DOUBLESTAR ZERO CARBINE RIFLE

3GR 2.0 GO-FAST RED

Action: Semiautomatic
Stock: Synthetic
Barrel: 16 in.
Sights: None
Weight: N/A
Caliber: 5.56 NATO
Magazine: 30 rounds
Features: The Go-Fast title and bright red cosmetics tell you this is one for the 3-Gun game; direct impingement gas system; ACE ARFX stock; low-profile steel gas block; billet backbone charging handle; billet winter trigger guard; forged aircraft 7075 upper and lower
MSRP $1469.99

STAR10-B

Action: Semiautomatic
Stock: Synthetic
Barrel: 18 in.
Sights: None
Weight: 9 lb. 13 oz.
Caliber: .308 cal
Magazine: 20 rounds
Features: Hogue pistol grip; Wilson air gauged stainless steel barrel (fluted); Samson Evolution handguard; brass deflector and dust cover; integrated trigger guard
MSRP $2549.99

STAR10-BX

Action: Semiautomatic
Stock: Synthetic
Barrel: 22 in.
Sights: None
Weight: 10 lb.
Caliber: .260 Rem.
Magazine: 20 rounds
Features: Direct impingement; stainless steel free-floating barrel; Bullseye muzzle brake; 15-in. Samson .309 Evolution handguard; brass deflector; dust cover; enhanced magazine well; CMC flat trigger group set to 3.5 pounds; ACE Hammer stock
MSRP $2549.99

ZERO CARBINE RIFLE

Action: Semiautomatic
Stock: Synthetic
Barrel: 16 in.
Sights: None
Weight: N/A
Caliber: 5.56 NATO
Magazine: 30 rounds
Features: A premium accuracy rifle with a 1:8 twist Wilson Air Gauge heavy barrel; low-profile gas block; Cloak 15 ½-inch M-LOK handguard; Alpha AR Comp compensator; flattop receiver; billet winter triggerguard and backbone charging handle; forward assist; ACE SOCOM stock; Ergo Ambi Sure Grip; direct gas impingement action
MSRP $1479.99

Drake Associates

DRAKE ASSOCIATES ATHENA PRECISION CHASSIS TACTICAL RIFLE

ATHENA PRECISION CHASSIS TACTICAL RIFLE

Action: Semiautomatic
Stock: Aluminum chassis
Barrel: 16 in., 18 in., 20 in.
Sights: None
Weight: 9 lb.
Caliber: 5.56 NATO
Magazine: 20, 30 rounds
Features: Military design made semiautomatic for the civilian market and loaded with features like a SATERN match barrel; A2 birdcage flash hider; threaded muzzle with 11-degree target crown; 11 o'clock M-LOK-compatible rail system; 12 o'clock Picatinny rail; anodized colors in flat dark earth, OD green, or black
MSRP $1776.00

DRD Tactical

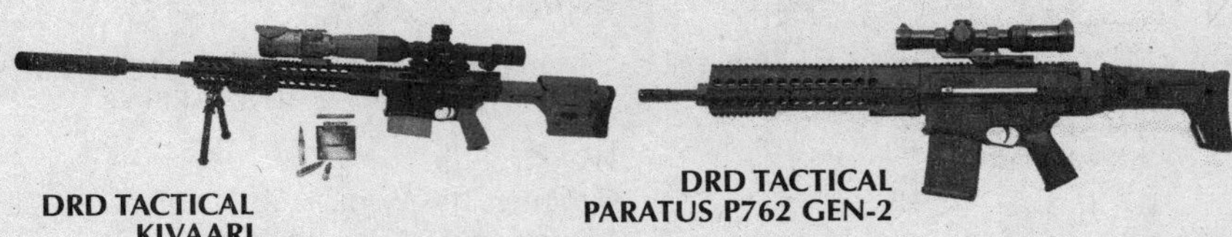
DRD TACTICAL KIVAARI

DRD TACTICAL PARATUS P762 GEN-2

KIVAARI

Action: Semiautomatic
Stock: Synthetic
Barrel: 24 in.
Sights: None
Weight: 13 lb. 9 oz.
Caliber: .338 Lapua, .300 Norma Mag.
Magazine: 10 rounds
Features: Billet aircraft aluminum receiver; direct gas operated action; fully adjustable Magpul PRS stock is mated with 17-in. QD Magpul M-LOK rail; SilencerCo QD muzzle brake; ambidextrous safety; Wilson Combat two-stage match trigger; choice of hard case or Tactical-Tailor Trekker backpack; available in anodized black, Cerakote Flat Dark Earth, or NiB Battle Worn finishes
MSRP . . . . $5500.00–$6250.00

PARATUS P762 GEN-2

Action: Semiautomatic
Stock: Synthetic
Barrel: 16 in.
Sights: None
Weight: 9 lb. 3 oz.
Caliber: 7.62x51 NATO, 6.5 Creedmoor
Magazine: 20 rounds
Features: Compact enough when disassembled to be stowed in a briefcase or backpack; adjustable Magpul folding stock; Mil-Std 1913 rail; direct gas operated; rifle may be fired with the stock in the folded position; in black or NiB Battle Worn finishes.
MSRP . . . . $3700.00–$4300.00

Excel Arms

EXCEL ARMS ACCELERATOR RIFLE

EXCEL ARMS X-5.7R

ACCELERATOR RIFLE MR-22, MR-5.7

Action: Semiautomatic
Stock: Polymer composite, pistol grip
Barrel: 18 in.
Sights: Standard includes Red/Green dot optic
Weight: 8 lb.
Caliber: .22 WMR, 5.7X28mm
Magaine: 9 rounds
Features: Corrosion-resistant 17-4 stainless steel, including its fluted barrel; manual and firing pin safeties; last-round-fired hold-open bolt; flattop accessory rail; choice of black or silver shroud. Basic model is supplied with one magazine; Package P-2 comes with a sling, two magazines, and a 3–9X40mm scope; Package P-5 is available only in .22 WMR and comes with a red dot optic, tactical rails, flashlight, bipod, detachable iron sights, and two magazines
Basic MR-22: $605.00
Basic MR 5.7: $755.00
Package P-2 MR-22: $788.00
Package P-2 MR 5.7: $942.00
Package P-5 MR-22: $1109.00

X-5.7R

Action: Semiautomatic
Stock: Synthetic
Barrel: 18 in.
Sights: None
Weight: 6 lb. 4 oz.
Caliber: 5.7X28mm, 9mm
Magazine: 10, 17, 20 rounds
Features: CNC-machined aluminum; Picatinny rail; tactical AR styling; collapsible stock; tapped holes in the handguard for mounting accessory rails; 5.7x28mm takes FN Five-SeveN magazines; 9mm takes Glock magazines; 10-round models are California-compliant featureless rifles
MSRP . . . . $837.00–$852.00

FN America

FN AMERICA FN 15 TACTICAL II

FN AMERICA FN M249S PARA

FN AMERICA FN SCAR 17S CARBINE

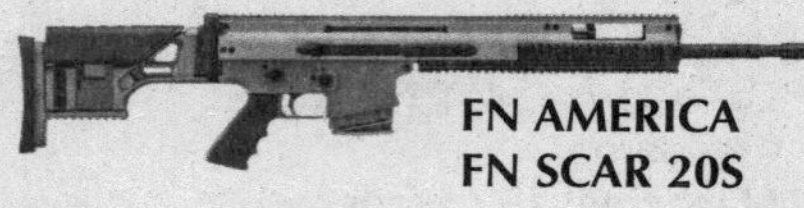

FN AMERICA FN SCAR 20S

FN 15 TACTICAL II

Action: Semiautomatic
Stock: Synthetic
Barrel: 16 in.
Sights: None
Weight: 6 lb. 14.5 oz.
Caliber: 5.56 NATO
Magazine: 30 rounds
Features: Direct impingement; FN Rail System with M-LOK that allows accessories to be mounted without any shift to zero; cold-hammer-forged, chrome lined, and free floating barrel; FN Combat trigger; hard anodized aluminum flat-top receiver; Magpul MOE grip; MOE SL buttstock; Surefire ProComp 762 muzzle brake
MSRP $1599.00

FN M249S PARA

Action: Semiautomatic
Stock: Metal
Barrel: 16.1 in.
Sights: Graduated 1000-meter front and rear combo
Weight: 17 lb.
Caliber: 5.56 NATO
Magazine: 30, 200 rounds
Features: Semiauto version of the full-auto M249 Para light machine gun; originally developed by FN Herstal as the FN MINIMI and adopted by the U.S. military in 1988; features signature 16-in. FN cold-hammer-forged, chrome-lined barrel in a quick-change configuration; formed steel frame receiver with claw extractor and fixed, pivoting ejector that ejects to the side; rotating, telescoping stock assembly with a hydraulic recoil buffer system; operates from a closed bolt and will accept both magazine and linked ammunition belts; Picatinny top rail and integral Mil-Std bipod
Black:. $8799.00
Flat Dark Earth: $9199.00

FN SCAR 16S, 17S

Action: Gas-operated semiautomatic
Stock: Polymer
Barrel: 16.25 in.
Sights: Adjustable, folding, removable
Weight: 8 lb.
Caliber: .308 Win., 7.62 NATO
Magazine: Detachable box, 10, 20 rounds
Features: Fully adjustable stock; Picatinny rail plus three accessory rails for attaching a variety of sights and lasers; free-floating, cold-hammer-forged barrel; available in black or Flat Dark Earth tactical, telescoping, side-folding polymer stock
16S: $3399.00
17S: $3569.00

FN SCAR 20S

Action: Semiautomatic
Stock: Synthetic
Barrel: 20 in.
Sights: None
Weight: 11 lb. 3 oz.
Caliber: 7.62x51mm, 6.5 Creedmoor
Magazine: 10 rounds
Features: Slick, short-stroke gas piston semiauto with miles of rail; two-stage match Geissele "Super SCAR" trigger; stock adjustable for length of pull and comb height; Hogue finger-groove pistol grip; monolithic aluminum receiver; left- or right-hand charging handle mounting; polymer trigger module; adjustable cheekpiece
MSRP $4499.00

Franchi

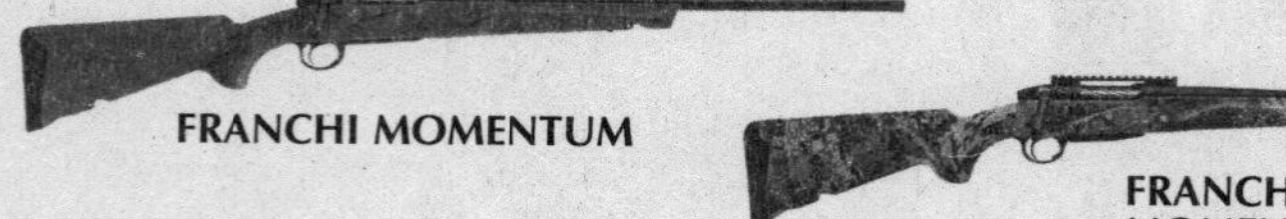

FRANCHI MOMENTUM

FRANCHI MOMENTUM ELITE

MOMENTUM

Action: Bolt
Stock: Synthetic
Barrel: 22 in., 24 in.
Sights: None
Weight: 6 lb. 11 oz.–7 lb. 13 oz.
Caliber: 6.5 Creedmoor, .308 Win., .300 Win. Mag., .350 Legend
Magazine: 3, 4 rounds
Features: Franchi's first ever rifle; synthetic stocks in flat dark earth or hunter gray; free-floating barrels; 60-degree bolt throws; adjustable triggers; barrels are available plain or threaded for suppressor use
MSRP $609.00

MOMENTUM ELITE

Action: Bolt
Stock: Synthetic
Barrel: 22 in., 24 in.
Sights: None
Weight: 7 lb. 2 oz.–7 lb. 8 oz.
Caliber: 6.5 Creedmoor, .308 Win., 6.5 PRC, .300 Win. Mag., .350 Legend, .223 Rem., 22-250 Rem., .224 Valkyrie
Magazine: 3, 4 rounds
Features: Trim, ergonomic stock; muzzle brake; topside Picatinny scope rail; TrueTimber Strata/Midnight Bronze Cerakote and Realtree Excape/Burnt Bronze Cerakote available in 6.5 Creedmoor, .308 Win., 6.5 PRC, and .300 Win. Mag.; Optifade Elevated II/Cobalt Cerakote available for 6.5 Creedmoor, .308 Win., and .350 Legend; Optifade Subalpine/Midnight Bronze Cerakote available in .223 Rem., .22-250 Rem., .224 Valkyrie
MSRP . . . . $899.00–$999.00

Heckler & Koch

HECKLER & KOCH MR556A1

HECKLER & KOCH MR762A1

HECKLER & KOCH MR762A1 LONG RIFLE PACKAGE II

MR556A1

Action: Semiautomatic
Stock: Synthetic
Barrel: 14 in., 16.5 in.
Sights: Troy microsights
Weight: 8 lb. 10 oz.
Caliber: 5.56 NATO
Magazine: Detachable box, 30 rounds
Features: Free-floating Picatinny rail; gas operated piston system
MSRP $3499.00

MR762A1

Action: Semiautomatic
Stock: Synthetic
Barrel: 16.5 in.
Sights: None
Weight: 9 lb. 15 oz.
Caliber: 7.62 NATO
Magazine: Detachable box, 10, 20 rounds
Features: Match rifle features; direct descendant of HK416/417 series, but made for civilians; uses a piston and a solid operating "pusher" rod in place of the common gas tube normally used in AR-style rifles; cold-hammer-forged barrel; adjustable stock
MSRP $3999.00

MR762A1 LONG RIFLE PACKAGE II

Action: Semiautomatic
Stock: Synthetic
Barrel: 16.5 in.
Sights: 3–9x40mm scope
Weight: 10 lb. 7 oz.
Caliber: 7.62 NATO
Magazine: Detachable box, 10, 20 rounds
Features: Rifle; Leupold 3–9 VX-R Patrol scope and mount; HK G28 buttstock; LaRue Tactical BRM-S bipod; ERGO Pistol Grip; Blue Force Gear sling; Manta rail covers; OTIS cleaning kit; a 10- and 20-round magazine; Model 1720 Pelican case
MSRP $7199.00

RIFLES

Henry Repeating Arms

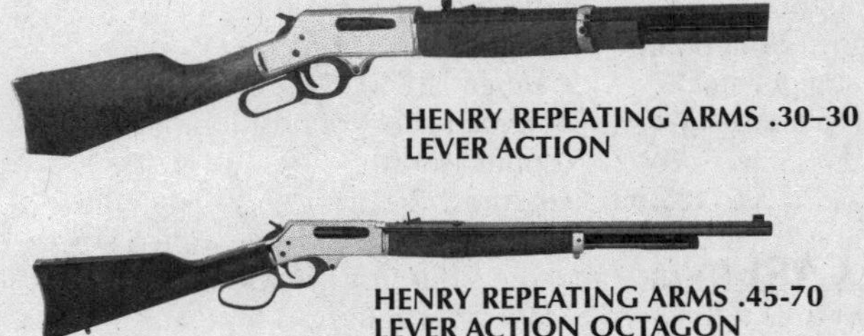
HENRY REPEATING ARMS .30–30 LEVER ACTION

HENRY REPEATING ARMS .45-70 LEVER ACTION OCTAGON

HENRY REPEATING ARMS .45-70 LEVER ACTION

.30-30 LEVER ACTION

Action: Lever
Stock: Walnut
Barrel: 20 in.
Sights: Open
Weight: 7 lb.
Caliber: .30-30 Win.
Magazine: Under-barrel tube, 5 rounds
Features: Steel round barrel: deluxe checkered American walnut with rubber buttpad; XS Ghost Rings sights; blued steel receiver, drilled and tapped for easy scope mounting. Brass octagon barrel: straight-grip American walnut with buttplate; marble fully adjustable semi-buckhorn rear sight, with diamond insert, beaded front sight; brass receiver, drilled and tapped for easy scope mounting
Steel: $986.00
Brass: $1036.00

.45-70 LEVER ACTION

Action: Lever
Stock: Walnut
Barrel: 18.43 in.
Sights: Closed rear, blade front
Weight: 7 lb. 1 oz.
Caliber: .45-70 Govt.
Magazine: Under-barrel tube, 4 rounds
Features: Pistol-grip American walnut with buttplate; blued steel drilled and tapped for easy scope mounting; fully adjustable semi-buckhorn rear sight with diamond insert paired with a brass bed front sight
MSRP $969.00

.45-70 LEVER ACTION OCTAGON

Action: Lever
Stock: Wood
Barrel: 22 in.
Sights: Adjustable
Weight: 8 lb. 2 oz.
Caliber: .45-70 Govt.
Magazine: 4 rounds
Features: Straight-grip American Walnut stock with brass buttplate; fully adjustable semi-buckhorn rear, and brass beaded front sight; brass drilled and tapped for a Weaver 63B mount
MSRP $1036.00

Henry Repeating Arms

HENRY REPEATING ARMS AMERICAN EAGLE

HENRY REPEATING ARMS BIG BOY CLASSIC

HENRY REPEATING ARMS BIG BOY SILVER

HENRY REPEATING ARMS BIG BOY STEEL CARBINE

HENRY REPEATING ARMS BIG BOY X-MODEL

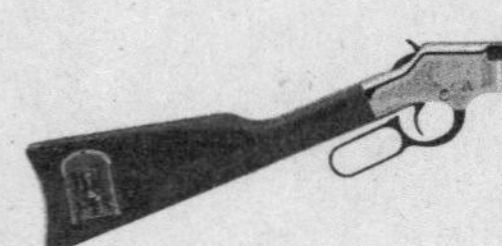

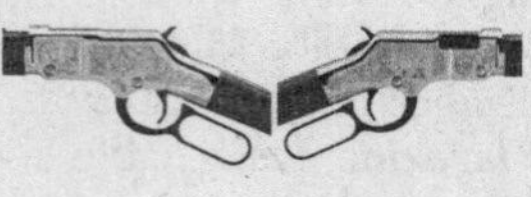

HENRY REPEATING ARMS FREEMASONS TRIBUTE EDITION

HENRY REPEATING ARMS FRONTIER MODEL LONG BARREL 24"

AMERICAN EAGLE

Action: Lever
Stock: Walnut
Barrel: 20 in.
Sights: Brass bead front, adjustable buckhorn rear with diamond insert
Weight: 6 lb. 12 oz.
Caliber: .22 LR
Magazine: 16 rounds
Features: A unique salute to America with a ivory-washed walnut stock engraved with border patterns, an American eagle head, and aggressive, distinctive checkering; blued octagon barrel
MSRP $1020.00

BIG BOY CLASSIC

Action: Lever
Stock: Walnut
Barrel: 20 in.
Sights: Open
Weight: 8.68 lb.
Caliber: .41 Mag., .327 Fed. Mag., .44 Mag., .45 Colt, .357 Mag.
Magazine: Under-barrel tube, 10 rounds
Features: Adjustable marble semi-buckhorn rear with white diamond insert and brass beaded front sight; solid top brass receiver, brass butt-plate and brass barrel band; straight-grip American walnut stock; octagonal barrel
MSRP $1001.00

BIG BOY SILVER

Action: Lever
Stock: Walnut
Barrel: 20 in.
Sights: Semi-buckhorn rear, brass bead front
Weight: 8 lb. 11 oz.
Caliber: .44 Magnum, .45 Colt, .357 Mag/.38 Spl.
Magazine: Under-barrel tube, 10 rounds
Features: Nickel plating; octagon barrel; buckhorn/bead sights; drilled and tapped scope option; straight stock wrist; carbine-style buttplate; okay for left-handed shooters
MSRP $1105.00

BIG BOY STEEL CARBINE

Action: Lever
Stock: Checkered walnut
Barrel: 16.5 in.
Sights: Adjustable semi-buckhorn rear with adjustable white diamond insert, brass bead front
Weight: 6 lb. 9 oz.
Caliber: .44 Magnum, .45 Colt, .357 Mag/.38 Spl., .327 Fed., .41 Mag.
Magazine: Under-barrel tube, 7 rounds
Features: Sliding transfer bar safety system in its hammer; lighter steel frame; ventilated rubber recoil pad; sling swivel studs; rifle-style fore-end cap; glove-friendly oversized lever
MSRP $950.00

BIG BOY X-MODEL

Action: Lever
Stock: Synthetic
Barrel: 17.4 in.
Sights: Fiber optic front, adjustable fiber optic rear
Weight: 7 lb. 5 oz.
Caliber: .45 Colt, .357 Mag., .44 Mag.
Magazine: 7 rounds
Features: Who knew you could modernize a lever-action to this extent? Henry did, adding features like a tough synthetic stock and forend with an ergonomic design
MSRP $1000.00

FREEMASONS TRIBUTE EDITION

Action: Lever
Stock: Walnut
Barrel: 20 in.
Sights: Adjustable semi-buckhorn rear with adjustable white diamond insert, brass bead front
Weight: 6 lb. 12 oz.
Caliber: .22 S/L/LR
Magazine: 16 rounds (long range), 21 rounds (short)
Features: Receiver engraving with 24K gold plating; engraved/painted stock; depicts our first president in full Masonic regalia
MSRP $1122.00

FRONTIER MODEL LONG BARREL 24"

Action: Lever
Stock: Walnut
Barrel: 24 in.
Sights: Brass bead front, fully adjustable semi-buckhorn rear with adjustable white diamond insert
Weight: 7 lb.
Caliber: .22 LR, .22 Mag.
Magazine: 12, 16, 21 rounds by caliber
Features: Merge of Henry's Lever Octagon and Frontier models; octagonal barrel adds weight, rigidity, and stability; grooved receiver for scope mounting
.22 LR: $527.00
.22 Mag.: $629.00

Henry Repeating Arms

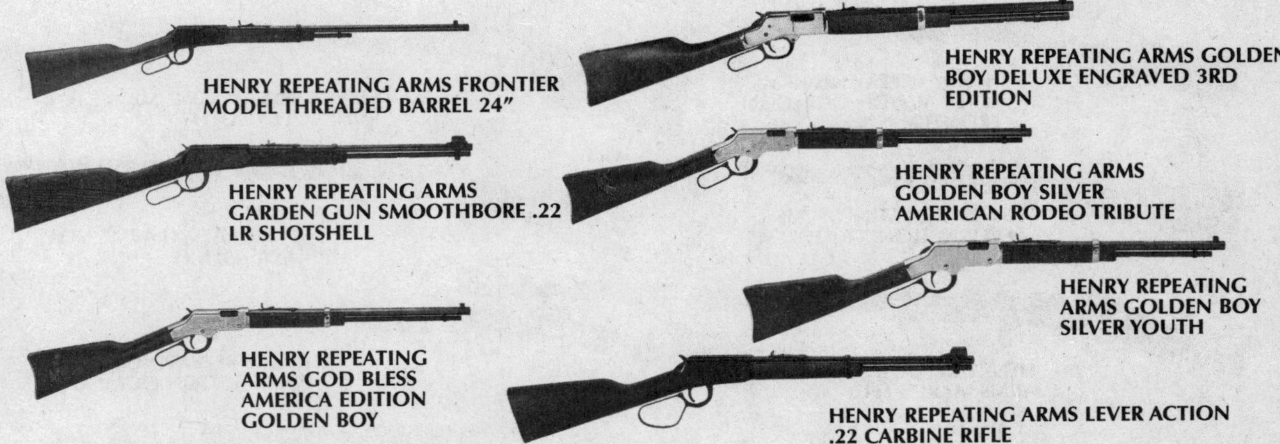

FRONTIER MODEL THREADED BARREL 24"

Action: Lever
Stock: Walnut
Barrel: 24 in.
Sights: Brass bead front, fully adjustable semi-buckhorn rear with adjustable white diamond insert
Weight: 7 lb.
Caliber: .22 LR, .22 Mag.
Magazine: 12, 16, 21 rounds by caliber
Features: Similar to the standard Frontier Long Barrel 24-in. model but with a ½x28 threads for suppressor use
.22 LR: $552.00
.22 Mag.: $656.00

GARDEN GUN SMOOTHBORE .22 LR SHOTSHELL

Action: Lever
Stock: Black ash
Barrel: 18.5 in.
Sights: Hooded blade front, adjustable rear
Weight: 5 lb. 4 oz.
Caliber: .22 LR shotshell
Magazine: 15 rounds
Features: Designed to rid your vegetable garden of undesirable four-legged critters
MSRP $446.00

GOD BLESS AMERICA EDITION GOLDEN BOY

Action: Lever
Stock: American walnut
Barrel: 20 in.
Sights: Brass bead front, fully adjustable semi-buckhorn rear with diamond insert
Weight: 6 lb. 12 oz.
Caliber: .22 LR
Magazine: 16 rounds
Features: Nickel receiver is engraved on both sides with floral scrollwork; right side features 24k gold banner reading "Home of the Free Because of the Brave" and gold American flag; left side features the Liberty Bell and a bald eagle in gold; the right side of the stock has a painted rendition of the Statue of Liberty's raised arm and torch; the forend has painted engraving that reads "God Bless America"
MSRP $1296.00

GOLDEN BOY DELUXE ENGRAVED 3RD EDITION

Action: Lever
Stock: Walnut
Barrel: 20 in.
Sights: Fully adjustable rear, brass-beaded front
Weight: 6 lb. 12 oz.
Caliber: .22 LR, .22 WMR, .17 HMR
Magazine: Under-barrel tube, 16 rounds (LR), 12 rounds (Short)
Features: American walnut stock; adjustable buckhorn rear sight, beaded front sight; brasslite receiver, brass buttplate, and blued barrel
.22 LR: $1641.00
.22 Mag.: $1693.00
.17 HMR: $1717.00

GOLDEN BOY SILVER AMERICAN RODEO TRIBUTE

Action: Lever
Stock: Walnut
Barrel: 20 in.
Sights: Brass bead front, adjustable rear
Weight: 6 lb. 12 oz.
Caliber: .22 LR
Magazine: 16 rounds
Features: A tribute to the sport and cowboys of American rodeo, featuring a blued octagon barrel; engraved stock with 24K gold highlights; bucking bull rider engraved in color on stock
MSRP $1296.00

GOLDEN BOY SILVER YOUTH

Action: Lever
Stock: Walnut
Barrel: 17 in.
Sights: Brass bead front, adjustable semi-buckhorn rear
Weight: 6 lb.
Caliber: .22 LR
Magazine: 12 rounds
Features: An easy shooting lever .22 (short, long, and long rifle) with a high-shine nickel-plated receiver and butt plate; quarter-cock safety; blued octagon barrel; drilled and tapped for scope mounting; 13-in. length of pull
MSRP $663.00

LEVER ACTION .22 CARBINE RIFLE

Action: Lever
Stock: Walnut
Barrel: 16.13 in.
Sights: Open
Weight: 4 lb. 8 oz.
Caliber: .22 LR
Magazine: 15 rounds (.22 LR), 17 rounds (.22 L), 18 rounds (.22 S), 21 rounds (.22)
Features: Straight-grip American walnut stock; adjustable rear, hooded front sight; blued round barrel; large loop lever
MSRP $415.00

Henry Repeating Arms

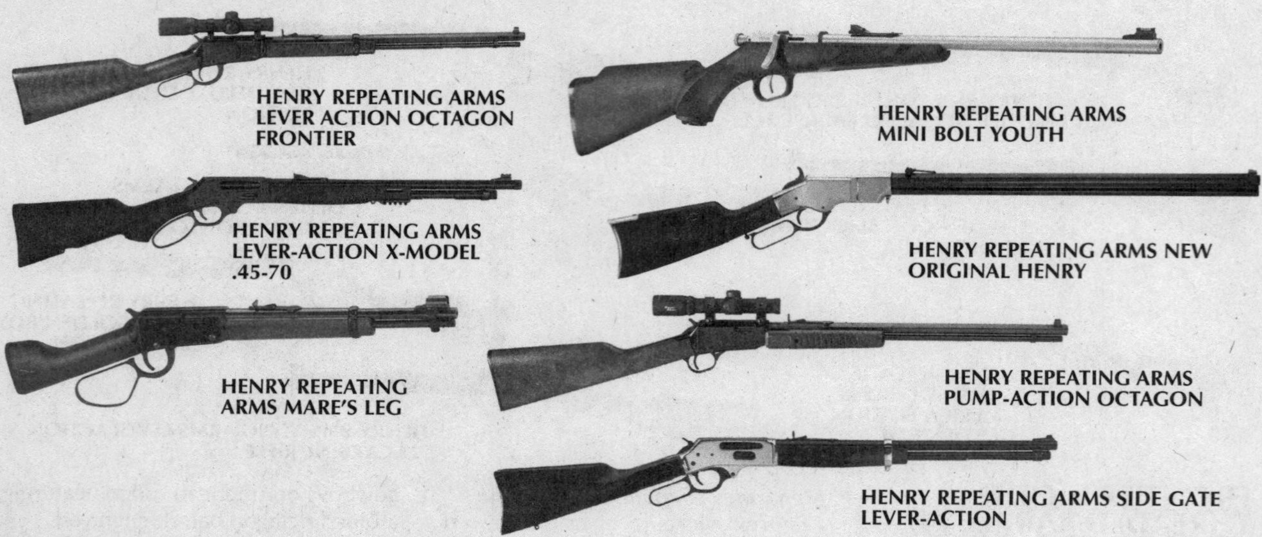

RIFLES

LEVER-ACTION OCTAGON FRONTIER

Action: Lever
Stock: Walnut
Barrel: 20 in.
Sights: Open
Weight: 6 lb. 4 oz.
Caliber: .22 LR, .22 WMR, .17 HMR
Magazine: Under-barrel tube, 21 rounds (.22 S), 16 rounds (.22 LR); 12 rounds (.22 Mag.); 11 rounds (.17 HMR)
Features: American walnut; marble fully adjustable semi-buckhorn rear with reversible white diamond insert and brass beaded front sight; blued barrel and lever
.22 LR: $501.00
.22 Mag.: $605.00
.17 HMR: $605.00

LEVER-ACTION X-MODEL .45-70

Action: Lever
Stock: Synthetic
Barrel: 19.8 in.
Sights: Fiber optic front, adjustable fiber optic rear
Weight: 7 lb. 6 oz.
Caliber: .45-70 Govt.
Magazine: 4 rounds
Features: Similar to the Big Boy X-Model, but in a longer barrel to accommodate the fat .45-70 round
MSRP $1000.00

MARE'S LEG

Action: Lever
Stock: Walnut
Barrel: 12.5 in.–12.9 in.
Sights: Open
Weight: 4 lb. 7 oz.–5 lb. 13 oz.
Caliber: .22 LR, .22 WMR, .357 Mag., .44 Mag., .45 Colt
Magazine: 5–10 rounds depending on caliber
Features: Centerfire: American walnut; Marble fully adjustable semi-buckhorn rear with reversible white diamond insert and brass beaded front sights; brasslite receiver, brass buttplate, and blued barrel; .22 S/L/LR: American walnut; fully adjustable rear, with hooded front sight; blued metal barrel and lever
.22 LR: $484.00
.22 Mag.: $501.00
Centerfire: $1079.00

MINI BOLT YOUTH

Action: Bolt
Stock: Synthetic
Barrel: 16.25 in.
Sights: Open
Weight: 3 lb. 4 oz.
Caliber: .22 LR
Magazine: None
Features: Single-shot; one-piece fiberglass synthetic stock; Williams fire sights; stainless steel receiver and barrel; black, Muddy Girl Camo, or Instant Orange stock finishes; right-hand only
MSRP $304.00

NEW ORIGINAL HENRY

Action: Lever
Stock: Walnut
Barrel: 24.5
Sights: Folding ladder rear
Weight: 9 lb.
Caliber: .44-40, .45 Colt
Magazine: Under-barrel tube, 13+1 rounds
Features: True to original 1860 specifications; fancy American walnut stock; blade front sight with a folding ladder rear; half-cock safety hammer notch
MSRP $2590.00

PUMP-ACTION OCTAGON

Action: Pump
Stock: Walnut
Barrel: 19.75 in.
Sights: Open
Weight: 6 lb.
Caliber: .22 LR, .22 WMR
Magazine: Under-barrel tube, 15 rounds (.22 LR), 12 rounds (.22 WMR)
Features: American walnut stock; adjustable rear, beaded front sight; blued octagonal barrel
.22 LR: $605.00
.22 Mag.: $648.00

SIDE GATE LEVER-ACTION

Action: Lever
Stock: American walnut
Barrel: 20 in.
Sights: Ramp front, adjustable semi-buckhorn rear
Weight: 7 lb. 8 oz.
Caliber: .38-55, .30-30 Win., .45-70 Govt., .35 Rem.
Magazine: 4, 5 rounds
Features: Henry says this is SASS-approved, with a brass receiver; deep checkering; ramp front sight with ivory bead; round barrel
MSRP $1100.00

Henry Repeating Arms

HENRY REPEATING ARMS SINGLE-SHOT RIFLE IN STEEL & BRASS

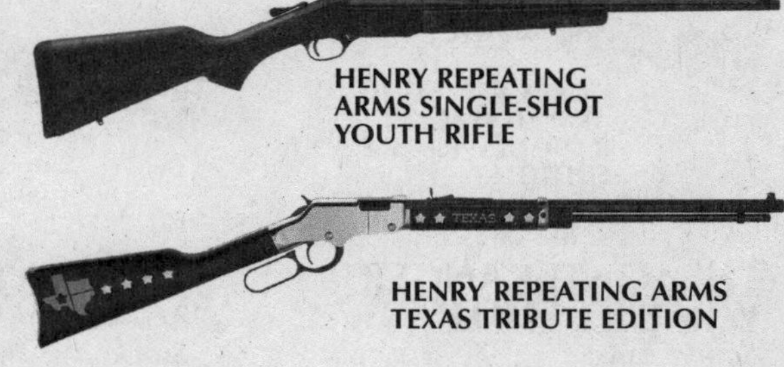

HENRY REPEATING ARMS SINGLE-SHOT YOUTH RIFLE

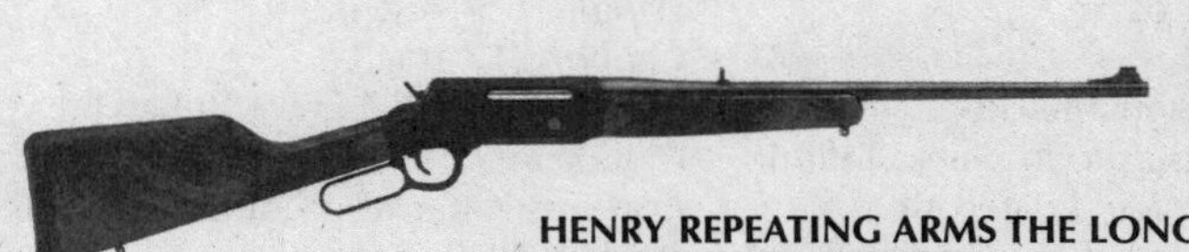

HENRY REPEATING ARMS STAND FOR THE FLAG EDITION GOLDEN BOY

HENRY REPEATING ARMS TEXAS TRIBUTE EDITION

HENRY REPEATING ARMS THE LONG RANGER WITH SIGHTS

HENRY REPEATING ARMS THE LONG RANGER DELUXE ENGRAVED

SINGLE-SHOT RIFLE IN STEEL & BRASS

Action: Break-open single-shot
Stock: Walnut
Barrel: 22 in.
Sights: Brass bead front, fully adjustable folding leaf rear
Weight: 6 lb. 15 oz.
Caliber: .223 Rem., .243 Win., .308 Win., .44 Mag., .45-70 Govt. (brass version .44 Mag./.45-70 Govt. only).
Magazine: N/A
Features: Centerfire top-lever rifle; matte finish on steel frame or a high-polished finish on hardened brass frame; steel models get curved pistol grip and rubber recoil pad; brass version have straight English grip and and brass buttplate; top lever is ambidextrous
Brass:..................$646.00
Steel:..................$525.00

SINGLE-SHOT YOUTH RIFLE

Action: Break-open
Stock: Walnut
Barrel: 22 in.
Sights: Folding fully adjustable leaf rear, brass bead front
Weight: 6 lb. 15 oz.
Caliber: .243 Win.
Magazine: 1 round
Features: The first time Henry's single-shot youth rifle offered in a caliber other than .22. Features include solid rubber recoil pad; blued steel receiver; round blued steel barrel with 1:10 twist
MSRP..................$525.00

STAND FOR THE FLAG EDITION GOLDEN BOY

Action: Lever
Stock: American walnut
Barrel: 20 in.
Sights: Brass bead front, fully adjustable semi-buckhorn rear with diamond insert
Weight: 6 lb. 12 oz.
Caliber: .22 LR
Magazine: 16 rounds
Features: Bright nickel receiver 90 percent covered with a Cerakote American flag; on the stock's right side, a man pays homage to the flag with his hand over his heart, surrounded by a circle bearing the opening line from the National Anthem
MSRP..................$1296.00

TEXAS TRIBUTE EDITION

Action: Lever
Stock: American walnut
Barrel: 20 in.
Sights: Brass bead front, adjustable semi-buckhorn rear
Weight: 6 lb. 12 oz.
Caliber: .22 LR
Magazine: 16 rounds
Features: This one certainly screams Texas—literally—with the state's name and shape in 24K, plus a number of brass stars, highlighting the dark walnut stock, an ode to Texas's "black gold" history
MSRP..................$1020.00

THE LONG RANGER

Action: Lever
Stock: Walnut
Barrel: 20 in.
Sights: Ramp ivory bead front, fully adjustable folding rear
Weight: 7 lb.
Caliber: .223 Rem.. .243 Win., .308 Win. 6.5 Creedmoor
Magazine: 4 rounds
Features: Henry's first long-range hunting rifle; exposed hammer and forged steel lever; geared action that drives a machined and chromed steel bolt with a six-lug rotary head into a rear extension of the barrel; side-ejection from alloy receiver; drilled and tapped for scope mounts; laser-cut checkering
MSRP..................$1138.00

THE LONG RANGER DELUXE ENGRAVED

Action: Lever
Stock: Walnut
Barrel: 20 in.
Sights: Folding fully adjustable rear, ramp front with ivory bead
Weight: 7 lb.
Caliber: .223 Rem./5.56 NATO, .243 Win., .308 Win.
Magazine: 5, 4 rounds
Features: Freshly updated versions of Henry's popular hunting rifle. All have checkered American walnut straight-wrist stocks; solid rubber recoil pads; sling swivels; detachable steel magazines; high-polished nickel receivers with gold-inlay enhanced scroll engraving
MSRP..................$1973.00

Henry Repeating Arms

HENRY REPEATING ARMS THE LONG RANGER WILDLIFE EDITION

HENRY REPEATING ARMS U.S. SURVIVAL AR-7

HENRY REPEATING ARMS VARMINT EXPRESS

THE LONG RANGER WILDLIFE EDITION

Action: Lever
Stock: Walnut
Barrel: 20 in.
Sights: Folding fully adjustable rear, ramp front with ivory bead
Weight: 7 lb.
Caliber: .223 Rem./5.56 NATO, .243 Win., .308 Win.
Magazine: 5, 4 rounds
Features: Similar to the Long Ranger Deluxe Engraved, but each caliber is dedicated to a specific game animal with appropriate portrait engravings highlighted in 24K gold: the Coyote in .223/5.56 NATO; the Antelope in .243; and the Elk in .308
MSRP $1973.00

US SURVIVAL AR-7

Action: Semiautomatic
Stock: ABS Plastic
Barrel: 16 in.
Sights: Adjustable rear, blade front
Weight: 3 lb. 8 oz.
Caliber: .22 LR
Magazine: Detachable box, 8 rounds
Features: ABS plastic in black; Teflon coated receiver and coated steel barrel; in black or choice of True Timber-Kanati or Viper Western full-coverage camo
Black: $319.00
Camo: $388.00

VARMINT EXPRESS

Action: Lever
Stock: Walnut
Barrel: 20 in.
Sights: Open
Weight: 5 lb. 12 oz.
Caliber: .17 HMR
Magazine: Under-barrel tube, 11 rounds
Features: Checkered American walnut stock; Williams fire sights; blued round barrel and lever
MSRP $605.00

RIFLES

Hi-Point Firearms

HI-POINT FIREARMS MODEL 995

HI-POINT FIREARMS 1095

HI-POINT FIREARMS 4095

995

Action: Blow-back semiautomatic
Stock: Black, skeleton-style, all-weather molded polymer
Barrel: 16.5 in.
Sights: Adjustable
Weight: 7 lb.
Caliber: 9mm
Magazine: Detachable box, 10 rounds
Features: Sling, swivels, and base mount included; last round lock-open latch; multiple Picatinny rails; internal recoil buffer; also available in digital tan, pink, and woodland camos
MSRP . . . . $315.00–$481.00

1095

Action: Semiautomatic
Stock: Synthetic
Barrel: 17.5 in.
Sights: Fully adjustable front, rear
Weight: 7 lb.
Caliber: 10mm
Magazine: 10 rounds
Features: Skeletonized stock; fully adjustable front and rear sights; a raised soft-rubber cheekpiece; sling swivels; scope base; accessory rails; threaded barrel; available in black, flat dark earth, and Realtree Edge, Kryptek Yeti, and Mothwing Winter Mimicry camo patterns
Black: $389.99
Realtree Edge: $439.00
Flat Dark Earth: $445.00
Kryptek Yeti: $449.00
Mothwing Winter Mimicry: . . $449.00

4095

Action: Semiautomatic
Stock: Polymer
Barrel: 17.5 in.
Sights: Adjustable
Weight: 7 lb.
Caliber: .40 S&W
Magazine: 9 rounds
Features: All-weather; black polymer skeletonized stock sling; swivels and scope base internal recoil buffer in stock weaver style rails; fully adjustable sights ("ghost ring" rear peep and post front); quick on/off thumb safety; grip-mounted clip release; also available in digital tan, pink, and woodland camos
MSRP . . . . $325.00–$495.00

HM Defense

HM DEFENSE AVENGER M308 TUNGSTEN

AVENGER M308 TUNGSTEN

Action: Semiautomatic
Stock: Synthetic
Barrel: 18 in.
Sights: None
Weight: 8 lb. 15 oz.
Caliber: .308 Win.
Magazine: 10 rounds
Features: Rifle-length gas system; Chrome-moly steel barrel threaded; 15-inch free-floating Picatinny rail with Magpul's M-LOK mounting system; three-pound Velocity trigger; custom charging handle; available in tungsten Cerakote finishes
MSRP $1995.00

Howa by Legacy Sports

HOWA BY LEGACY SPORTS APC FLAG CHASSIS

HOWA BY LEGACY SPORTS HOGUE GAMEPRO 2

HOWA BY LEGACY SPORTS HOGUE RIFLE

HOWA BY LEGACY SPORTS HS PRECISION RIFLE

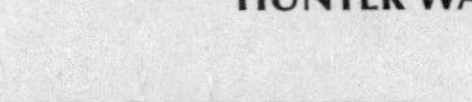
HOWA BY LEGACY SPORTS HUNTER WALNUT

HOWA BY LEGACY SPORTS KUIU RIFLE

APC FLAG CHASSIS

Action: Bolt
Stock: Aluminum
Barrel: 16.25 in., 24 in.
Sights: Nikko Sterling Diamond 4–16X50 Long Range scope
Weight: 11 lb. 8 oz.–12 lb. 5 oz.
Caliber: .223 Rem., 6mm Creedmoor, 6.5mm Creedmoor, .308 Win.
Magazine: 10 rounds
Features: Chassis rifle Cerakoted in red-white-and-blue or a gray-scale American flag graphics; Nikko Sterling Diamond 4–16X50 Long Range scope; heavy barrel with muzzle three-chamber Midwest Industries muzzle brake (semi-heavy barrel option does not include brake); Hogue finger groove pistol grip; adjustable bipod
MSRP $1549.00

HOGUE GAMEPRO 2

Action: Bolt
Stock: Synthetic
Barrel: 22 in., 24 in.
Sights: Nikko Stirling Gamepro scope
Weight: 7 lb. 13 oz.–8 lb.
Caliber: .22-250 Rem., .243 Win., 6.5 Creedmoor, 7mm-08 Rem., .308 Win., .270 Win., .30-06 Spfd., 7mm Rem. Mag., .300 Win. Mag., .300 PRC, 6.5 PRC
Magazine: N/A
Features: Users of this rifle get a Hogue pillar-bedded stock; suppressor-ready threaded barrel
MSRP $769.00

HOGUE RIFLE

Action: Bolt
Stock: Synthetic
Barrel: 22 in., 24 in.
Sights: None
Weight: 7 lb. 12 oz.–8 lb.
Caliber: .22-250 Rem., .243 Win., 6.5 Creedmoor, 7mm-08 Rem., .308 Win., .270 Win., .30-06 Spfd., 7mm Rem. Mag., .300 Win. Mag., .300 PRC, 6.5 PRC
Magazine: Internal box
Features: Blue metalwork; Hogue overmolded stock with pillar bedding; hinged floor plate; sling; swivel studs; threaded barrel
MSRP $699.00

HS PRECISION RIFLE

Action: Bolt
Stock: HS precision
Barrel: 22 in., 24 in.
Sights: None
Weight: 7 lb. 9 oz.–7 lb. 12 oz.
Caliber: .22-250 Rem., .243 Win., 6.5 Creedmoor, .308 Win., .270 Win., .30-06 Spfd., 7mm Rem. Mag., .300 Win. Mag., .300 PRC, 6.5 PRC
Magazine: 3, 4 rounds
Features: HOWA 1500 barreled action set in an aluminum bedding block with hand-laminated stock of Kevlar, fiberglass, carbon fiber molded around it; two-stage HACT trigger; stocks in gray, tan, or OD green with black webbing
MSRP $1099.00

HUNTER WALNUT

Action: Bolt
Stock: Walnut
Barrel: 22 in.
Sights: N/A
Weight: 7 lb. 3 oz.
Caliber: 6.5 Creedmoor, .308 Win.
Magazine: N/A
Features: A traditionally styled rifle for the hunter with a pretty walnut stock and stainless hardware, in two of today's best all-around cartridges
MSRP $699.00

KUIU RIFLE

Action: Bolt
Stock: Synthetic
Barrel: 22 in., 24 in.
Sights: None
Weight: 7 lb. 12 oz.–8 lb.
Caliber: .22-250 Rem., .243 Win., 6.5 Creedmoor, 7mm-08 Rem., .308 Win., .270 Win., .30-06 Spfd., 7mm Rem. Mag., .300 Win. Mag.
Magazine: 5 rounds
Features: KUIU camo on Hogue pillar-bedded stock and recoil pad; Cerakote Gun Metal finish on barrel and action; KUIU Vias or Verde camo finishes
MSRP $759.00

Howa by Legacy Sports

HOWA BY LEGACY SPORTS MINI ACTION

HOWA BY LEGACY SPORTS MINI EXCL LITE CHASSIS

HOWA BY LEGACY SPORTS ORYX

HOWA BY LEGACY SPORTS ORYX MINI-ACTION

HOWA BY LEGACY SPORTS RIMFIRE GAMEPRO PACKAGE

HOWA BY LEGACY SPORTS TSP X FOLDING CHASSIS

MINI ACTION

Action: Bolt
Stock: Synthetic
Barrel: 16.25 in., 20 in., 22 in.
Sights: None
Weight: 5 lb. 11 oz.–6 lb. 10 oz.
Caliber: .223 Rem., 7.62X39, 6.5 Grendel, .350 Legend
Magazine: Detachable box, 10 rounds
Features: HOWA's Mini Action is only 6 in. long and weighs just 10.2 oz., 3 oz. and almost a full inch less than a standard short action and two ounces nearly 1.5 in. less than a long-action; barrels in lightweight (#1), standard (#2), and heavy (#6) options, as well as stocks in black, OD Green, Kryptek Highlander, Multicam and Yote camo finishes; package includes Nikko Stirling 3-9x40mm scope and one-piece base and rings
MSRP . . . . $521.00–$899.00

MINI EXCL LITE CHASSIS

Action: Bolt
Stock: Synthetic
Barrel: 16.25 in., 20 in.
Sights: None
Weight: N/A
Caliber: .223 Rem., .300 BLK, 7.62X39, 6.5 Grendel, .350 Legend
Magazine: 5, 10 rounds
Features: An ultra-compact lightweight chassis rifle with threaded barrel; detachable box magazine; adjustable length of pull from 12.75 to 15.75 in.
MSRP $639.00

ORYX

Action: Bolt
Stock: Aluminum
Barrel: 20 in., 24 in., 26 in.
Sights: None
Weight: 10 lb. 13 oz.–11 lb. 4 oz
Caliber: 6.5 PRC, .300 PRC, 6.5 Creedmoor, .308 Win.
Magazine: N/A
Features: A full monolithic aluminum chassis with a back end adjustable for length of pull and comb height; heavy barrel; available in grey, green, or flat dark earth; barrel threaded 5/8X24
MSRP . . . . $1189.00–$1299.00

ORYX MINI-ACTION

Action: Bolt
Stock: Aluminum
Barrel: 16 in..25 in., 20 in.
Sights: None
Weight: 8 lb. 3 oz.–8 lb. 23 oz.
Caliber: .300 BLK, .223 Rem., 7.62X39, 6.5 Grendel
Magazine: N/A
Features: The compact chassis footprint of the full-size Oryx and with a different set of caliber offerings
MSRP $1299.00

RIMFIRE GAMEPRO PACKAGE

Action: Bolt
Stock: Synthetic
Barrel: 18 in.
Sights: Nikko Stirling Gamepro scope
Weight: 6 lb. 5 oz.
Caliber: .22 LR, .22 WMR, .17 HMR
Magazine: N/A
Features: Great rifle for the aspiring rimfire competitor; comes with 3.5–10x44mm Nikko Stirling Gamepro scope; available in green, black, or Kratos camo stocks
MSRP $699.00

TSP X FOLDING CHASSIS

Action: Bolt
Stock: Aluminum
Barrel: 24 in.
Sights: N/A
Weight: 13 lb. 8 oz.
Caliber: 6.5 Creedmoor, .300 PRC, 6.5 PRC
Magazine: N/A
Features: A dedicated rifle for the long-range game made more portable with a folding stock design; available in black or in a Cerakoted American flag graphic overlay; muzzle brake; top-side optics rail
MSRP $1189.00

H-S Precision

H-S PRECISION HTR

H-S PRECISION PHR

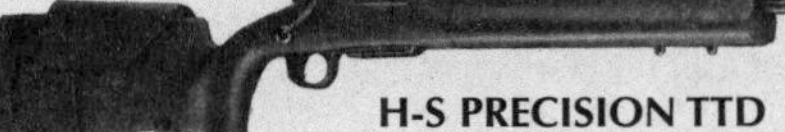
H-S PRECISION TTD

HTR (HEAVY TACTICAL RIFLE)

Action: Bolt
Stock: Synthetic
Barrel: 20 in., 22 in., 24 in., 26 in., 28 in.
Sights: None
Weight: 10 lb. 12 oz.–11 lb. 4 oz.
Caliber: Any standard SAAMI, LR calibers
Magazine: Detachable box, 3, 10 rounds
Features: Pro-Series 2000; fully adjustable synthetic stock comes in sand, black, olive, gray, and spruce green; heavy fluted barrel
MSRP $3999.00

PHR (PROFESSIONAL HUNTER RIFLE)

Action: Bolt
Stock: Synthetic
Barrel: 20 in., 22 in., 24 in., 26 in., 28 in.
Sights: None
Weight: 7 lb. 12 oz.–8 lb. 4 oz.
Caliber: All popular magnum calibers up to .458 Lott
Magazine: Detachable box, 3, 4 rounds
Features: Pro-Series 2000; cheekpiece and built-in recoil reduction system; steel barrel; optional muzzlebrake; synthetic stock comes in sand, black, olive, gray, and spruce green
MSRP $3799.00

TTD (TACTICAL TAKE-DOWN RIFLE)

Action: Bolt
Stock: Composite
Barrel: 22 in., 24 in.
Sights: None
Weight: 11 lb. 4 oz.–11 lb. 12 oz.
Caliber: Available in all standard SA SAAMI and LR calibers
Magazine: Detachable box, 3, rounds
Features: Stainless steel barrel and floor plate; synthetic stock with full length bedding block chassis system; metal parts are finished in matte black Teflon; stock colors include sand, black, olive, gray, and spruce green
MSRP $6499.00

Israel Weapons Industry (IWI)

ISRAEL WEAPON INDUSTRIES TAVOR X95

TAVOR X95

Action: Semiautomatic
Stock: Polymer
Barrel: 16.5 in.
Sights: Folding front blade with tritium insert, aperture rear
Weight: 7 lb. 15 oz.
Caliber: .300 BLK, .223 Rem., 9mm
Magazine: 30 rounds
Features: Bullpup with a long-stroke gas-piston action and a closed rotating bolt; ambidextrous mag release; Picatinny rail; pistol grip is modular; in black or Flat Dark Earth; conversion kits for 9mm and 5.56 NATO available
MSRP . . . . $1999.00–$2049.00

Iver Johnson

IVER JOHNSON 1911A1 CARBINE

1911A1 CARBINE

Action: Semiautomatic
Stock: Walnut
Barrel: 16.125 in.
Sights: Blade front, notch rear
Weight: 4 lb.
Caliber: .45 ACP
Magazine: 8, 28 rounds
Features: Detachable walnut stock; barrel has a black oxide finish; walnut pistol grips with checkering and the Iver Johnson logo; 28-round drum magazine is available; includes one eight-round magazine
MSRP $881.00

Jarrett Rifles

JARRETT BEANFIELD

JARRETT PROFESSIONAL HUNTER

JARRETT SHIKAR SERIES

JARRETT WIND WALKER

RIFLES

BEANFIELD

Action: Bolt
Stock: Synthetic
Barrel: Various lengths available
Sights: None
Weight: Varies depending on options
Caliber: Any popular standard or magnum chambering
Magazine: Comes with 20 rounds
Features: Can build rifle on any receiver provided; optional caliber, stock style, color, muzzlebrake, barrel size, and taper; includes load data and 20 rounds of custom ammo
MSRP . . . . .starting at $6050.00

PROFESSIONAL HUNTER

Action: Bolt
Stock: Synthetic or walnut
Barrel: Various lengths available
Sights: None
Weight: Varies depending on options
Caliber: .375 H&H, .416 Rem., .416 Rigby, .450 Rigby
Magazine: Comes with 40 rounds
Features: Includes 40 rounds of soft pointed bullets and solids created custom for each gun; ballistics printout and last three targets the gun shot also provided; optional scopes; .416 Rem. comes with Jarrett Tri-Lock receiver
MSRP . . . . . . .starting at $11,700.00

SHIKAR SERIES

Action: Bolt
Stock: Wood
Barrel: N/A
Sights: None
Weight: 8 lb.
Caliber: Any long action, standard or magnum caliber
Magazine: N/A
Features: Muzzle brake; decelerator pad; hand checkering; trap door plate; Shilen or Jewell trigger; aged American black walnut stock; Jarrett Tri-Lock left or right hand receiver
MSRP . . . . starting at $10,320.00

WIND WALKER

Action: Bolt
Stock: Synthetic
Barrel: Up to 24 in.
Sights: None
Weight: 7 lb. 8 oz.
Caliber: Any popular short-action
Magazine: Comes with 20 rounds
Features: Jarrett Tri-Lock action; muzzlebrake; Tally scope mounting system; phenolic resin metal finish with choice of stock colors; ballistic print out included
MSRP . . . . starting at $8320.00

J.P. Sauer & Sohn

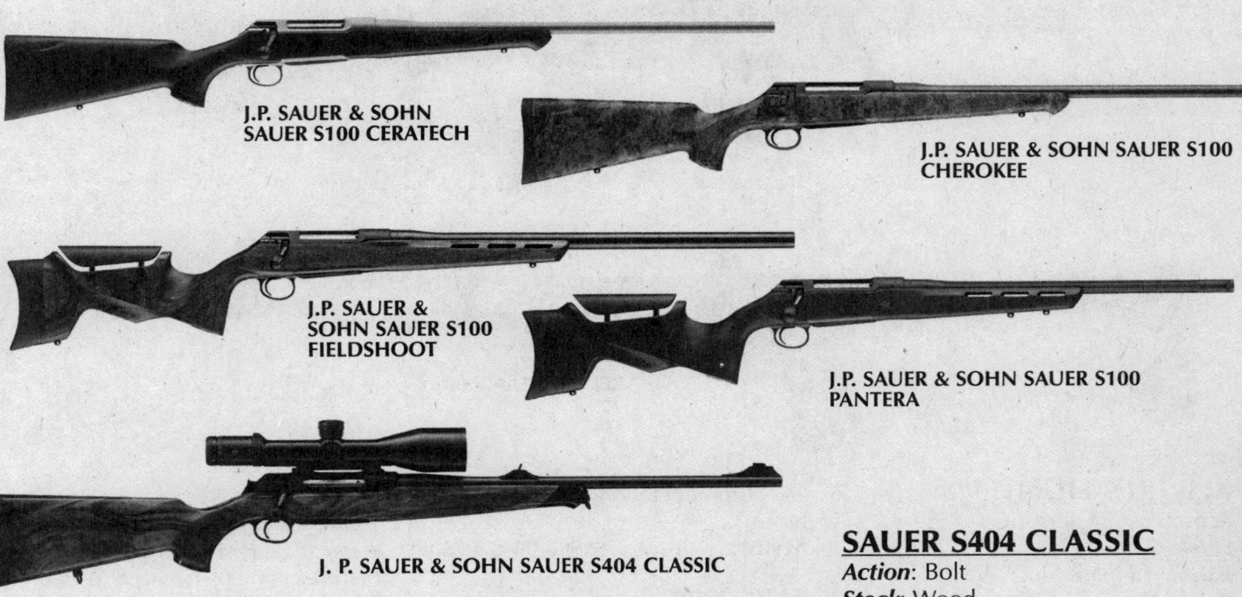

J.P. SAUER & SOHN SAUER S100 CERATECH

J.P. SAUER & SOHN SAUER S100 CHEROKEE

J.P. SAUER & SOHN SAUER S100 FIELDSHOOT

J.P. SAUER & SOHN SAUER S100 PANTERA

J. P. SAUER & SOHN SAUER S404 CLASSIC

SAUER S100 CERATECH

Action: Bolt
Stock: Synthetic
Barrel: 22 in., 24 in.
Sights: None
Weight: N/A
Caliber: .223 Rem., .243 Win. .270 Win., 7mm-08 Rem., 6.5x55 SE, 6.5 Creedmoor, 6.5 PRC, .308 Win., .30-06 Spfd., 8x57 IS, 9.3x62, 7mm Rem. Mag., .300 Win Mag.
Magazine: N/A
Features: Adjustable trigger; detachable magazine; ERGO MAX Stock; cold hammer forged barrel; receiver and barrel are in Cerakote Grey Ice
MSRP $949.00

SAUER S100 CHEROKEE

Action: Bolt
Stock: Synthetic
Barrel: 22 in., 24 in.
Sights: None
Weight: N/A
Caliber: .270 Win., .300 Win. Mag., .308 Win., 6.5 Creedmoor, 7mm Rem. Mag., 7mm-08 Rem., 6.5 PRC
Magazine: N/A
Features: Schnabel forend in soft-touch green/gold Digi-Camo; bolt, steel receiver, and barrel are in Cerakote Tundra Green; adjustable trigger; optional threaded muzzle
MSRP $1100.00

SAUER S100 FIELDSHOOT

Action: Bolt
Stock: Wood
Barrel: 24 in.
Sights: None
Weight: N/A
Caliber: .223 Rem., .243 Win., .308 Win., 6.5x55 SE, 6.5 Creedmoor, 6.5 PRC
Magazine: N/A
Features: Oiled wood stock is adjustable for vertical height and length of pull; adjustable cheekpiece; vented forend is trim and has a bipod adaptor; barrel has a varmint match profile; bolt knob is an oversized cone design; threaded muzzle
MSRP $1649.99

SAUER S100 PANTERA

Action: Bolt
Stock: Laminated wood
Barrel: 20 in., 22 in.
Sights: None
Weight: N/A
Caliber: .223 Rem., .243 Win., .300 Win. Mag., .30-06 Spfd., .308 Win., 6.5 Creedmoor, 6.5 PRC
Magazine: N/A
Features: Threaded fluted barrel treated in Cerakote Black Recon; adjustable cheek piece; vented forend is trim and has a bipod adaptor; threaded muzzle
MSRP $1649.99

SAUER S404 CLASSIC

Action: Bolt
Stock: Wood
Barrel: 20–24.4 in.
Sights: Adjustable
Weight: 7 lb.–7 lb. 3 oz.
Caliber: .243 Win., 6.5x55 Swedish, .270 Win., 7x64 Brenneke, .308 Win., .30-06 Spfd., 8x57IS, 9.3x62 Mauser, 7mm Rem. Mag., .300 Win. Mag., 8x68 S, .338 Win. Mag., .375 H&H Mag.
Magazine: 2–3 rounds
Features: ERGO LUX stock in grade-5 figured walnut; aviation-grade high-alloy aluminum receiver; perfectly placed ergonomic manual cocking slide on the bolt shroud; easily replaceable bolt head makes switching from standard to magnum calibers a snap; twin ejectors for a precisely perpendicular ejection pattern; 6-lug bolt locks directly into the barrel; jeweled bolt body; SAUER Quattro trigger with choice of four trigger pull weights: 550 g (1.2 lbs), 750 g (1.7 lbs), 1000 g (2.2 lbs) and 1250 g (2.7 lbs); infinitely adjustable trigger blade with 8 mm (0.3 in) adjustment range for length of pull and a left-to-right swivel range of 5 degrees; SAUER Universal Mount (SUM) integral to with receiver for an extremely low build height; SAUER universal key (SUS) integrated into the front sling swivel for forend and buttstock removal, barrel removal or replacement, and selection of trigger pull weight; MagLock magazine safety
MSRP $5299.00

Kel-Tec

KEL-TEC RFB

KEL-TEC SUB-2000

RIFLES

RFB, RFB HUNTER

Action: Semiautomatic
Stock: Synthetic
Barrel: 18 in., 24 in.
Sights: None
Weight: 8 lb.–8 lb. 11 oz.
Caliber: .308 Win.
Magazine: Detachable box, 10 or 20 rounds
Features: Picatinny rail; short-stroke gas piston operation; A2-style flash hider
MSRP . . . . $1800.00–$2000.00

SUB-2000

Action: Semiautomatic
Stock: Polymer
Barrel: 16.1 in.
Sights: Target
Weight: 4 lb.
Caliber: 9mm, .40 S&W
Magazine: 10+1 rounds
Features: Accepts Smith & Wesson M&P an SIG P226 magazines in 9mm or .40 S&W, Beretta 92 and 96 magazines, and Glock 17, 19, 22, and 23 magazines; folds away for storage and transportation
MSRP . . . . $578.00–$621.00

Kimber

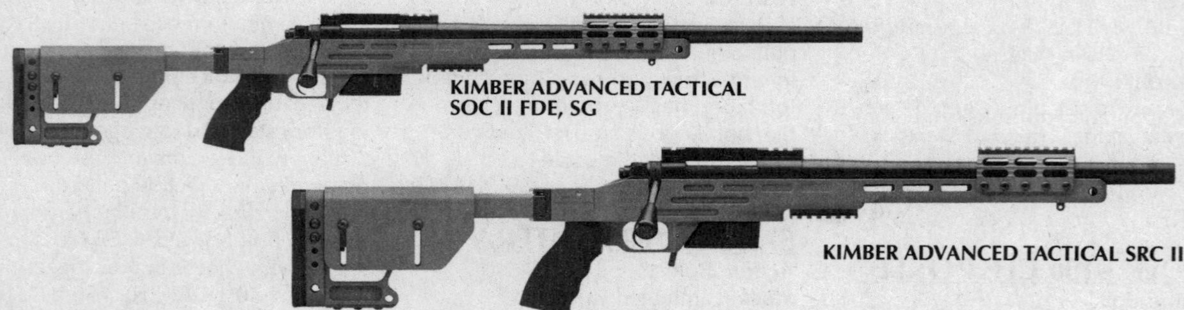
KIMBER ADVANCED TACTICAL SOC II FDE, SG

KIMBER ADVANCED TACTICAL SRC II

ADVANCED TACTICAL SOC II FDE, SG

Action: Bolt
Stock: Aluminum
Barrel: 22 in.
Sights: None
Weight: 11 lb.
Caliber: 6.5 Creedmoor, .308 Win.
Magazine: 5 rounds
Features: Sub .5-MOA accuracy guarantee; match grade chamber; threaded barrel; side-folding stock adjustable for length and comb height; night vision mount; M-LOK rail; 1913 Mil-Spec tripod mount; Mauser claw extractor; in Flat Dark Earth (FDE) or anodized black (SG) stocks; barrels and action are finished in matte black Kim Pro II; SOC stands for Special Operations Capable
MSRP $2556.00

ADVANCED TACTICAL SRC II

Action: Bolt
Stock: Aluminum
Barrel: 16 in.
Sights: None
Weight: 10 lb.
Caliber: .308 Win.
Magazine: 5 rounds
Features: Similar to the SOC II, but with a shorter, suppressor-ready barrel; SRC stands for Suppressor Ready Compact
MSRP $2556.00

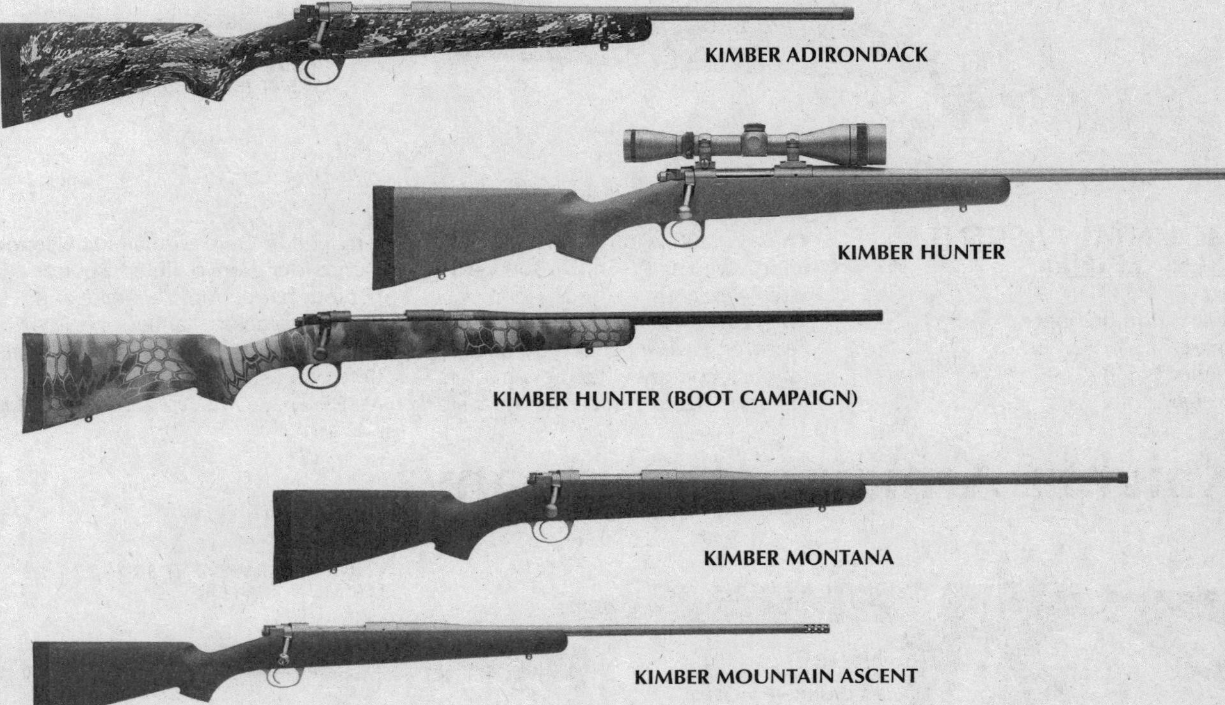

ADIRONDACK

Action: Bolt
Stock: Synthetic
Barrel: 18 in.
Sights: None
Weight: 4 lb. 13 oz.
Caliber: .308 Win., 7mm-08 Rem., 6.5 Creedmoor
Magazine: Internal, 4 rounds
Features: Kevlar/carbon fiber stock with Optifade Forrest finish; recoil pad; fluted barrel threaded for muzzle break/suppressor
MSRP $1883.00

HUNTER

Action: Bolt
Stock: FDE composite
Barrel: 22 in., 24 in.
Sights: None
Weight: 5 lb. 10 oz.
Caliber: .243 Win., .257 Roberts, 6.5 Creedmoor, .270 Win., .280 Ackley Imp., 7mm-08 Rem., .308 Win., .30-06 Spfd.
Magazine: 3 rounds
Features: Lightweight stock; match-grade adjustable trigger; match-grade chamber; sporter contour stainless barrel; removable box magazine; available in Flat Dark Earth stocks with either blue or stainless hardware
MSRP $891.00

HUNTER (BOOT CAMPAIGN)

Action: Bolt
Stock: Composite
Barrel: 22 in., 24 in.
Sights: None
Weight: 5 lb. 11 oz.
Caliber: .308 Win., .270 Win., .280 Ackley Improved, .30-06 Spfd., 6.5 Creedmoor
Magazine: 3
Features: Similar to the Hunter (Black) model; additional caliber options; a stock wearing Kryptek Highlander camo
MSRP $1046.00

MONTANA

Action: Bolt
Stock: Reinforced carbon fiber
Barrel: 22 in., 24 in., 26 in.
Sights: None
Weight: 5 lb. 2 oz.–6 lb. 13 oz.
Caliber: .300 Win. Mag., .300 WSM, .30-06 Spfd., .280 Ackley Improved, .308 Win., 7mm-08 Rem., 6.5 Creedmoor
Magazine: 4, 5 rounds
Features: A Montana rifle with Kimber enhancements; match-grade chamber; threaded barrel; sling swivel studs; pillar bedding; sporter contour stainless barrel with satin finish; adjustable trigger; green stock; stainless hardware
MSRP $1522.00

MOUNTAIN ASCENT

Action: Bolt
Stock: Reinforced carbon fiber
Barrel: 22 in., 24 in., 26 in.
Sights: None
Weight: 4 lb. 13 oz.–6 lb. 7 oz.
Caliber: .280 Ackley Improved, .270 Win., .30-06 Spfd., .308 Win., .300 WSM, .270 WSM, .300 Win. Mag., 7mm Rem. Mag., 7mm-08 Rem., 6.5 Creedmoor
Magazine: 4 rounds
Features: Stainless fluted barrel with muzzle brake and thread protector; adjustable trigger; 1-inch Pachmayr Decelerator pad; three-position M70-type safety; Mauser claw extractor; match-grade chamber; 84M action; Moss Green stock
MSRP $2175.00

Kimber

KIMBER MOUNTAIN ASCENT (SUBALPINE)

MOUNTAIN ASCENT (SUBALPINE)

Action: Bolt
Stock: Carbon fiber
Barrel: 22 in., 24 in.
Sights: None
Weight: 5 lb. 6 oz.
Caliber: .308 Win., .280 Ackley Improved, .30–06 Spfd., .300 WSM, .300 Win. Mag.
Magazine: 4 rounds
Features: A very lightweight offering for back-country wilderness hunters featuring reinforced carbon fiber stock wrapped in Gore Optifade SubAlpine camo; four-groove, fluted, sporter-contour barrel; muzzle brake and thread protector; stainless steel 84M action; Mauser claw extractor; spiral-fluted bolt
MSRP $2175.00

RIFLES

Knight's Armament Company

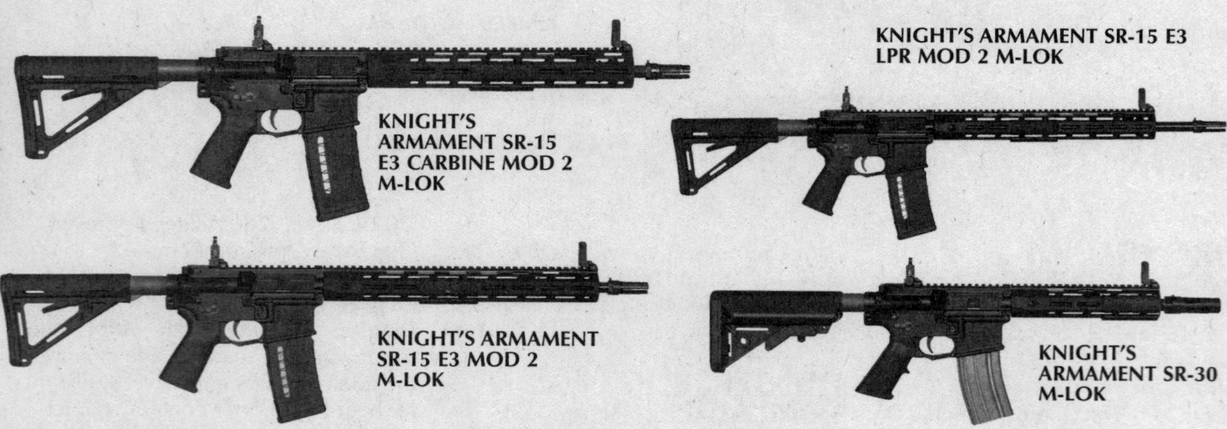

KNIGHT'S ARMAMENT SR-15 E3 CARBINE MOD 2 M-LOK

KNIGHT'S ARMAMENT SR-15 E3 LPR MOD 2 M-LOK

KNIGHT'S ARMAMENT SR-15 E3 MOD 2 M-LOK

KNIGHT'S ARMAMENT SR-30 M-LOK

SR-15 E3 CARBINE MOD 2 M-LOK

Action: Semiautomatic
Stock: Synthetic
Barrel: 14.5 in.
Sights: Adjustable
Weight: 6 lb. 6.4 oz.
Caliber: 5.56mm NATO
Magazine: 30 rounds
Features: Free-floated barrel inside a URX4 M-LOK handguard; improved E3 round-lug bolt design; ambidextrous bolt release, selector lever, and magazine release; drop-in two-stage trigger; 3-prong flash eliminator
MSRP $2596.16

SR-15 E3 LPR MOD 2 M-LOK

Action: Semiautomatic
Stock: Synthetic
Barrel: 18 in.
Sights: Adjustable
Weight: 7 lb. 6.4 oz.
Caliber: 5.56mm NATO
Magazine: 30 rounds
Features: Free-floated barrel inside a URX4 M-LOK handguard; improved E3 round-lug bolt design; ambidextrous bolt release, selector lever, and magazine release; drop-in two-stage trigger; 3-prong flash eliminator
MSRP $2883.99

SR-15 E3 MOD 2 M-LOK

Action: Semiautomatic
Stock: Synthetic
Barrel: 16 in.
Sights: Adjustable
Weight: 6 lb. 9 oz.
Caliber: 5.56mm NATO
Magazine: 30 rounds
Features: Free-floated barrel inside a URX4 M-LOK handguard; improved E3 round-lug bolt design; ambidextrous bolt release, selector lever, and magazine release; drop-in two-stage trigger; 3-prong flash eliminator
MSRP $2699.99

SR-30 M-LOK

Action: Semiautomatic
Stock: Synthetic
Barrel: 9.5 in.
Sights: Adjustable
Weight: 6 lb. 3 oz.
Caliber: .300 BLK (7.62x35mm)
Magazine: 30 rounds
Features: QDC-compatible flash hider will mount any of the KAC 7.62mm QDC suppressors; ambidextrous controls; two-stage match trigger; M-Lok accessory mounting system
MSRP $2653.00

Krieghoff

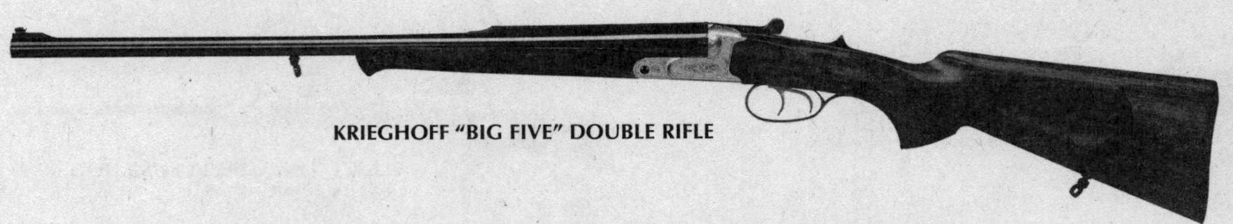

KRIEGHOFF "BIG FIVE" DOUBLE RIFLE

"BIG FIVE" DOUBLE RIFLE

Action: Hinged breech
Stock: Walnut
Barrel: 23.5 in.
Sights: Open
Weight: 9 lb. 8 oz.–10 lb. 8 oz.
Caliber: .375 H&H Mag., .375 Flanged Magnum N.E., .450/.400 NE, .500/.416 N.E., .470 N.E., .500 N.E.
Magazine: None
Features: Double triggers; V-shaped rear sight with a white, vertical middle line and a pearl front sight; optional Super-Express sight; Monte Carlo style cheekpiece; European walnut stock with small game scene engraving; steel trigger and floor plate; straight comb and large recoil pad
MSRP . . . . starting at $15,395.00

Kriss USA

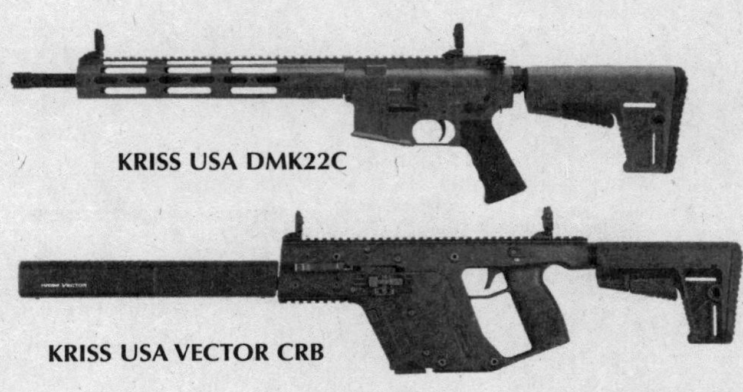

KRISS USA DMK22C

KRISS USA VECTOR CRB

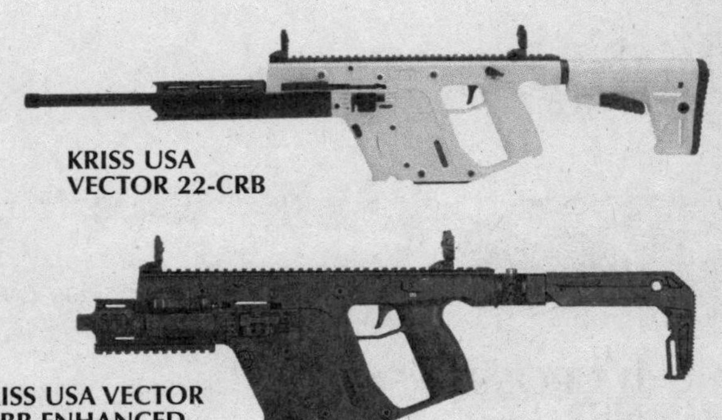

KRISS USA VECTOR 22-CRB

KRISS USA VECTOR SBR ENHANCED

DMK22C

Action: Semiautomatic
Stock: Synthetic
Barrel: 16 in.
Sights: Adjustable
Weight: N/A
Caliber: .22 LR
Magazine: 10 or 15 rounds
Features: Full metal construction; mil-spec buffer tube; free-floating modular handguard; bolt stays open when magazine is pulled; compatible with most AR-15 parts; six-position adjustable stock; black nitride finish on barrel; direct blowback action; in black, flat dark earth, Alpine, camo black, camo Alpine
MSRP . . . . $725.00–$985.00

VECTOR 22-CRB, 22-CRB ENHANCED

Action: Semiautomatic
Stock: Synthetic
Barrel: 16 in.
Sights: Flip-up front, rear
Weight: 7 lb. 6 oz.
Caliber: .22 LR
Magazine: 10 rounds
Features: A very sophisticated rimfire in the Kriss bull-pup style with an ambidextrous safety; six-position adjustable stock; direct blowback action with last round bolt hold-open; aluminum M-LOK handguard; enhanced gets a free-floating M-LOK handguard; standard model in black, Alpine, or flat dark earth Nitride finish; Enhanced model in camo black or camo white
22-CRB: . . . . $675.00–$695.00
Enhanced: $895.00

VECTOR CRB

Action: Semiautomatic
Barrel: 16 in.
Sights: Low-profile folding front and rear
Weight: 8 lb.
Caliber: 9mm,.45 ACP, 10mm, .40 S&W
Magazine: Glock magazines
Features: Patented Kriss Super V recoil mitigation system; closed bolt/delayed blowback action; six-position adjustable stock; full-length top rail; low-profile flip-up sights; compatible with Glock magazines; in black, flat dark earth or Alpine white; California, Maryland, Massachusetts, New Jersey and Canada compliant variants available
MSRP . . . .$1575.00–$1695.00

VECTOR SBR, SBR ENHANCED

Barrel: 5.5 in., 6.5 in.
Sights: Custom flip-up iron
Weight: 7 lb.–7 lb. 4 oz.
Caliber: .45 ACP, 9mm, 10mm, .40 S&W
Magazine: Glock magazines
Features: Kriss's Super V recoil management system; topside and under muzzle rails; Glock magazine compatibility; threaded barrel; Enhanced has slightly longer barrel and additional rail space; both versions available in black, flat dark earth, or Alpine white
SBR: . . . .$1625.00–$1645.00
Enhanced: . . . . . .$1825.00–$1845.00

Lazzeroni Arms, Inc.

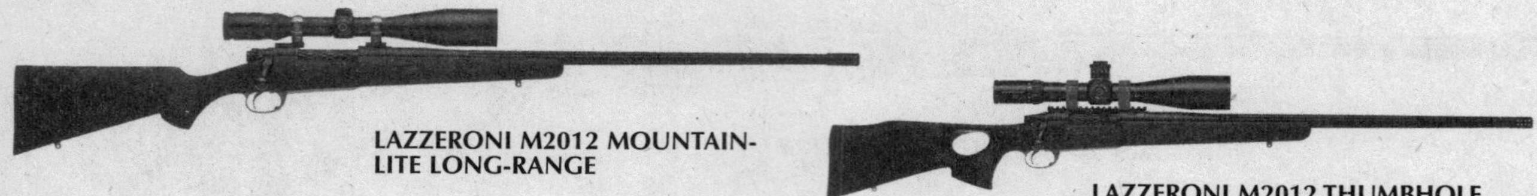

LAZZERONI M2012 MOUNTAIN-LITE LONG-RANGE

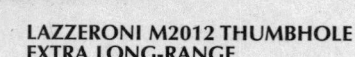

LAZZERONI M2012 THUMBHOLE EXTRA LONG-RANGE

M2012 MOUNTAIN-LITE LONG-RANGE

Action: Bolt
Stock: Graphite/composite
Barrel: 26 in.
Sights: None
Weight: 7 lb. 5 oz.
Caliber: 6.53 Scramjet, 7.21 Firebird, 7.82 Firebird
Magazine: 4 rounds
Features: All new precision CNC-machined chromoly receiver; one-piece diamond-fluted bolt shaft; stainless steel match-grade button-barrel; custom molded hand-bedded graphite/composite stock designs; precision-machined aluminum alloy floor plate/trigger guard assembly; jewel competition trigger; Vais muzzlebrake; Limbsaver recoil pad
MSRP $5999.99

M2012 THUMBHOLE EXTRA LONG-RANGE

Action: Bolt
Stock: Graphite/composite
Barrel: 25 in.
Sights: None
Weight: 7 lb. 11 oz.
Caliber: 7.21 Warbird, 7.82 Warbird, 8.59 Titan, 9.53 Saturn
Magazine: 4 rounds
Features: 20 MOA Picatinny style rail; 34mm or 30mm ring sets; right hand only
MSRP $6999.99

Lithgow Arms

LITHGOW ARMS LA101 CROSSOVER RIMFIRE

LITHGOW ARMS LA105 WOOMERA

LA101 CROSSOVER RIMFIRE

Action: Bolt
Stock: Synthetic, laminate
Barrel: 20.9 in.
Sights: None
Weight: 6 lb. 9.6 oz.–7 lb. 3.2 oz.
Caliber: .22 LR, .22 WMR, .17 HMR
Magazine: N/A
Features: Free-floating barrel; integral molded trigger guard; length of pull adjustment spacers; Cerakote-finished barrel; receiver, bolt handle, and integral scope bases; black synthetic and laminate stock options
MSRP . . . . $1199.00–$1299.00

LA105 WOOMERA

Action: Bolt
Stock: Polymer
Barrel: 24 in.
Sights: None
Weight: 11 lb.
Caliber: 6.5 Creedmoor, .308 Win.
Magazine: 10 rounds
Features: Adjustable KRG tactical rifle stock; muzzle brake; Cerakote finish; threaded muzzle; 20 MOA Picatinny rail; in black or Flat Dark Earth finishes
MSRP $2199.00

LWRC International

LWRCI IC A5

IC A5

Action: Semiautomatic
Stock: Composite
Barrel: 10.5 in., 14.7 in., 16.1 in.
Sights: Skirmish back up iron sights
Weight: 6 lb. 8 oz.–7 lb. 5 oz.
Caliber: .5.56 NATO
Magazine: 10 or 30 rounds
Features: Enhanced Fire Control Group; dual-control fully ambidextrous lower receiver; Magpul MOE grip; NiCorr treated cold hammer-forged barrel; ambidextrous charging handle; Monoforge upper receiver with modular rail system; adjustable two-position gas block; A2 birdcage flash hider
MSRP $2704.02

LWRC International

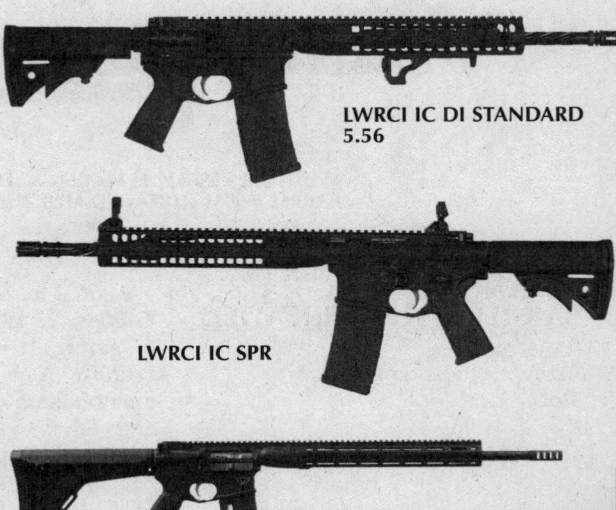

IC DI COMPETITION

Action: Semiautomatic
Stock: Polymer
Barrel: 16.1 in.
Sights: None
Weight: 7 lb.
Caliber: 5.56 NATO
Magazine: 10, 30 rounds
Features: A shorter-barreled direct impingement AR platform; fully ambidextrous controls; sling mount; charging handle; LWRCI's new four-port Ultra Brake and M-LOK free-float handguard; Timney 6675 straight competition trigger; short-throw selector; in black, Flat Dark Earth, OD Green, Patriot Brown, or Tungsten Grey
MSRP $2180.00

IC DI STANDARD 5.56

Action: Semiautomatic
Stock: Synthetic
Barrel: 16.1 in., 18.1 in.
Sights: None
Weight: 6 lb. 10 oz.
Caliber: 5.56 NATO, .300 Blackout
Magazine: Detachable box
Features: Direct impingement system; modular, one-piece free-float rail; angled ergonomic fore grip with QD sling point; fully ambidextrous lower controls; A2 birdcade flash hider
MSRP $1649.44

IC DI STANDARD .300 BLK

Action: Semiautomatic
Stock: Polymer
Barrel: 16.1 in.
Sights: None
Weight: 6 lb. 10 oz.
Caliber: .300 Blackout
Magazine: 30 rounds
Features: Direct impingement AR platform; A2 flash hider; ambidextrous controls; six-position Mil-Spec buffer tube; NiCorr-treated barrel; gas block; gas tube; in black, Patriot Brown, or Gun Metal Gray
MSRP $1649.44

IC SPR

Action: Semiautomatic
Stock: Composite
Barrel: 14.7 in., 16.1 in.
Sights: Skirmish back up iron sights
Weight: 7 lb.–7 lb. 5 oz.
Caliber: 5.56 NATO
Magazine: 10 or 30 rounds
Features: Monoforge upper receiver with user-configurable 12-inch rail system; cold hammer-forged spiral fluted barrel that is 20 percent lighter; Enhanced Fire Control Group; advanced trigger guard; adjustable compact stock; compact high-efficiency flash hider; patented short-stroke gas piston system; Magpul MOE grip
MSRP $2443.92

R.E.P.R. MK II, MK II ELITE

Action: Semiautomatic
Stock: Synthetic
Barrel: 12.7 in., 16.1 in., 20 in.
Sights: None
Weight: 9 lb. 4.8 oz.
Caliber: 6.5 Creedmoor, 7.62x39
Magazine: N/A
Features: Rapid Engagement Precision Rifle utilizes patented Short Stroke Gas Piston System; billet 7075 aluminum upper and lower; 12.5-in. modular rail system; gas system normal and suppressed settings; side-mounted non-reciprocating charging handle; NiCorr-treated cold-hammer-forged heavy barrel; Patriot Brown, OD Green, Flat Dark Earth, and black anodized finishes available, plus many custom options
Standard: $4233.00
Elite: $4763.00

VALKYRIE 224 DI

Action: Semiautomatic
Stock: Polymer
Barrel: 20.1 in.
Sights: None
Weight: 8 lb. 2 oz.
Caliber: .224 Valkyrie
Magazine: N/A
Features: Direct impingement, Rifle+1-length system with LWRCI fire control group; LWRCI's news four-port Ultra Brake; NiCorr-treated gas block; cold hammer-forged non-fluted NiCorr-treated barrel; Magpul MOE stock; LWRCI's all-new SnakeSkin Pistol grip provides for sight tool and battery storage; in black, Flat Dark Earth, Olive Drab, Patriot Brown, and Tungsten Grey
MSRP . . . . $2034.00–$2178.00

Magnum Research

MAGNUM RESEARCH MAGNUMLITE ULTRA BARREL WITH THREADED MUZZLE

MAGNUMLITE ULTRA BARREL WITH THREADED MUZZLE

Action: Semiatuomatic
Stock: Synthetic
Barrel: 17 in.
Sights: None
Weight: 4 lb. 4 oz.
Caliber: .22 LR
Magazine: 10+1
Features: Ambidextrous lightweight thumbhole stock made of polypropylene with fiber additives; semi palm swell on both sides of the pistol grip; molded-to-fit hard rubber buttplate attached with screws; graphite bull barrel with uni-directional graphite fibers parallel to the bore axis; full floating barrel; French gray anodized finish
MSRP $596.00

MasterPiece Arms

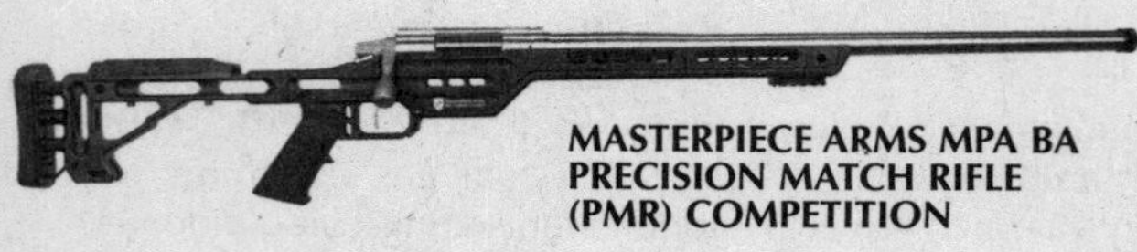

MASTERPIECE ARMS MPA BA PRECISION MATCH RIFLE (PMR) COMPETITION

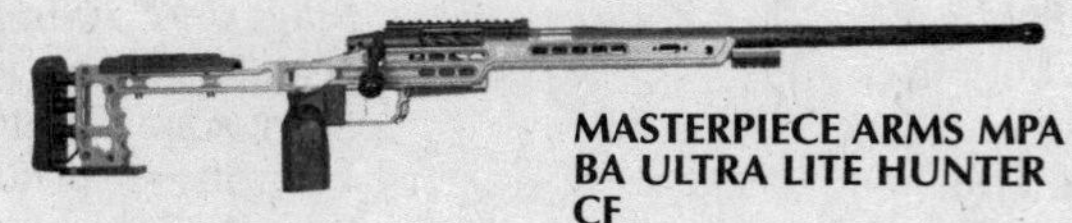

MASTERPIECE ARMS MPA BA ULTRA LITE HUNTER CF

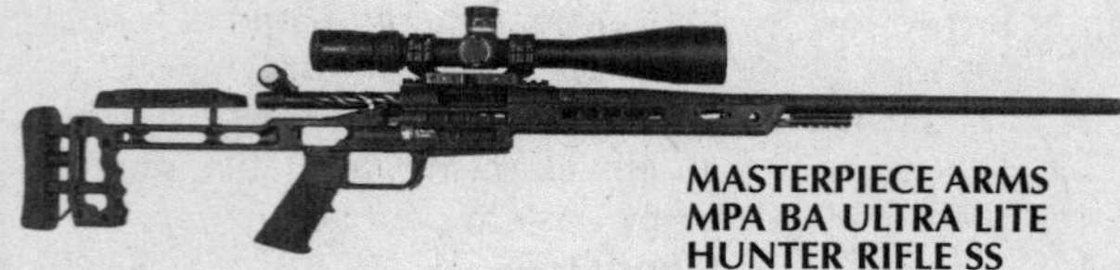

MASTERPIECE ARMS MPA BA ULTRA LITE HUNTER RIFLE SS

MPA BA PRECISION MATCH RIFLE (PMR) COMPETITION

Action: Bolt
Stock: Aluminum
Barrel: 26 in.
Sights: None
Weight: 11 lb. 8 oz.
Caliber: 6mm Creedmoor, 6.5 Creedmor, .308 Win.
Magazine: 10 rounds
Features: Developed specifically for the Production Class in formal Precision Rifle Series competition, this rifle sport's MPA's BA Hybrid Chassis in Cerakote with v-bedding, built-in inclinometer, thumb notch, and lower rail; MPA/Curtis short action; X-Caliber hand-lapped barrel with a #7 profile threaded 5/8X24; TriggerTech Special trigger; Magpul AICS-type magazine
MSRP $1999.99

MPA BA ULTRA LITE HUNTER CF (CARBON FIBER)

Action: Bolt
Stock: Aluminum
Barrel: customer determined
Sights: None
Weight: 7 lb. 8 oz.
Caliber: 6.5 Creedmoor, 6.5 PRC, .300 PRC, .28 Nosler
Magazine: 3 rounds
Features: Nearly 2 pounds lighter than the Hybrid Hunter, this chassis rifle features a Proof carbon fiber barrel in a Sendero light contour and threaded 5/8X25; Curtis Axiom action; MPA's Ultra-Light Chassis with V-bedding system; vertical grip; built-in inclinometer; TriggerTech trigger; Cerakote finish
MSRP . . . . $3575.00–$3725.00

MPA BA ULTRA LITE HUNTER RIFLE SS

Action: Bolt
Stock: Aluminum
Barrel: Customer choice
Sights: N/A
Weight: 7 lb. 8 oz.
Caliber: .300 Win. Mag., .300 WSM, 7mm SAUM, .243 Win., .28 Nosler, 6.5 PRC, .300 PRC, .308 Win., 6.5 Creedmoor, 6mm Creedmoor
Magazine: 3 rounds
Features: Curtis Custom Axiom bolt action in a Remington 700 configuration; stainless hand-lapped, pull-button-rifled barrel in a sendero profile and threaded 5/8-24
MSRP . . . . $2999.00–$3600.00

Mauser

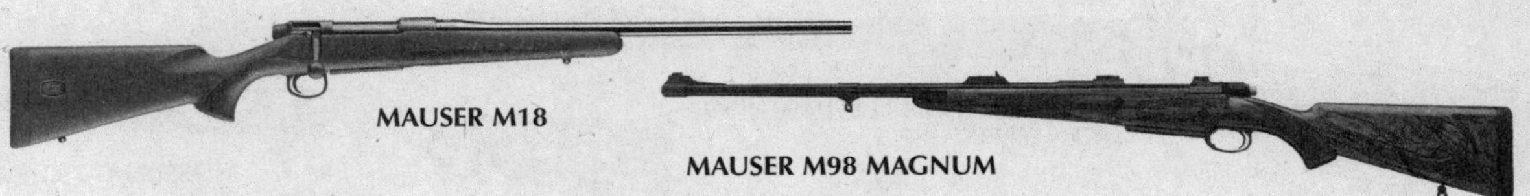

MAUSER M18

MAUSER M98 MAGNUM

M18

Action: Bolt
Stock: Polymer
Barrel: 22 in., 24 in.
Sights: None
Weight: 6 lb. 6 oz.–6 lb. 10 oz.
Caliber: .243 Win., .270 Win., .300 Win. Mag., .30-06 Spfd., .308 Win., 6.5 Creedmoor, 6.5 PRC, 7mm Rem. Mag.
Magazine: 5 rounds
Features: All-steel receiver; an all-weather polymer stock with soft-grip inserts; three-position safety; cold-hammer-forged barrel; adjustable trigger; buttstock has a removable cap for small-tool or compact cleaning kit storage
MSRP $749.00

M98 MAGNUM

Action: Bolt
Stock: Wood
Barrel: 24.4 in.
Sights: Windage and elevation adjustable two-leaf express sights.
Weight: 9 lb. 7 oz.–10 lb. 1.6 oz.
Caliber: .375 H&H Mag., .416 Rigby, .450 Rigby
Magazine: 4, 5 rounds
Features: Premium steel construction with plasma nitriding; long extractor; controlled round feed; double recoil lugs; pillar bedding; newly designed horizontal safety; double square bridge system designed for swing-off scope mounts; heavy barrel contour option for .416 and .450 Rigby calibers. Two variants: Expert has noble walnut root WG5 grade, while Diplomat has upgraded WG7 grade; both have M98 Classic Sporter stock profile, ebony fore-end caps; hinged floorplate steel magazine, M98 express open sights
Expert: $13,797.00
Diplomat: $14,772.00

McMillan Firearms

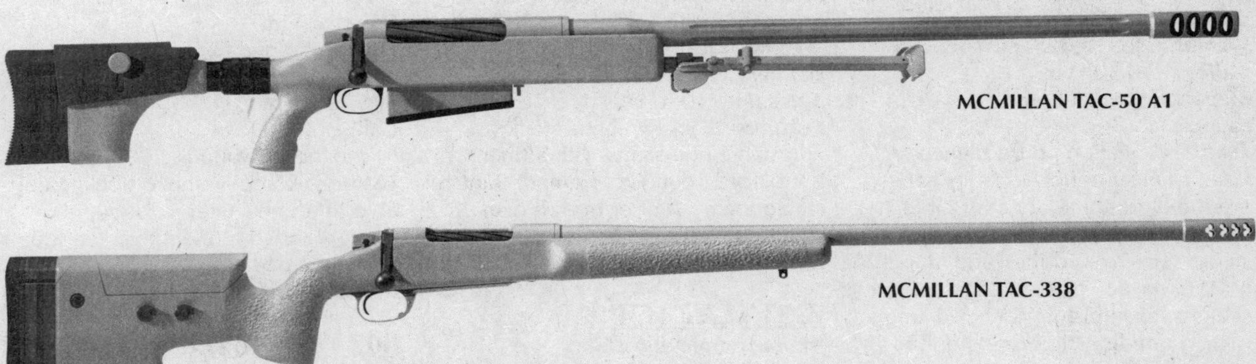

MCMILLAN TAC-50 A1

MCMILLAN TAC-338

TAC-50 A1

Action: Semiautomatic
Stock: Synthetic
Barrel: 29 in.
Sights: Drilled and tapped for scopes
Weight: 26 lb.
Caliber: .50 BMG
Magazine: Detachable box, 5 rounds
Features: McMillan's TAC-50A1 features the company's TAC-50A1 removable stock with an adjustable cheekpiece, Decelerator recoil pad, bipod, and four flush-mount cups with 1.25-in. sling loops; barrel is a 29-in. Navy contour 1:15 twist, free-floating, match grade, hand-lapped, and fluted with a threaded muzzle and threaded McMillan muzzle brake; metal finish made to match stock color, available in black, olive, gray, tan, and Dark Earth
MSRP $10,000.00

TAC-338

Action: Bolt
Stock: Composite
Barrel: 27 in.
Sights: None
Weight: 11 lb.
Caliber: .338 Alpha Mag.
Magazine: Detachable box, 1 to 5 rounds
Features: Featuring McMillan's own TAC-338 action designed for the .338 Lapua; the 27-in. barrel has a medium-heavy contour, is match grade and stainless steel, and has a muzzle brake with ¾-24 threads; McMIllan's Tactical stock with adjustable cheekpiece, length-of-pull spacers, one stud, and six flush-mount cups with ¼-in. sling loops; 20 MOA 1913 Mil-Std rail is standard; metalwork finished to match the stock, available in black, OD Green, and Flat Dark Earth
MSRP $6250.00

Mossberg (O. F. Mossberg & Sons)

MOSSBERG 464 LEVER-ACTION CENTERFIRE RIFLE

MOSSBERG 702 PLINKSTER

MOSSBERG 702 YOUTH BANTAM PLINKSTER

MOSSBERG 715T FLAT TOP

MOSSBERG 802 PLINKSTER

MOSSBERG 802 PLINKSTER SCOPED COMBO

RIFLES

464 LEVER-ACTION CENTERFIRE RIFLE

Action: Lever
Stock: Walnut
Barrel: 20 in.
Sights: Adjustable rifle sights or three-dot adjustable fiber optic
Weight: 6 lb. 12 oz.
Caliber: .30-30 Win.
Magazine: Under-barrel tube, 7–14 rounds
Features: Ejection port designed for cases to clear optics, top tang safety are standard; three-dot adjustable fiber optic sights or adjustable rifle sights; receiver is drilled and tapped for Weaver #403 bases; pistol grip or straight stock; pistol grip has diamond pattern fine-line checkering on the grip and wrapped around edge-to-edge on the forearm
Straight grip: $568.00
Pistol grip: $610.00

702 PLINKSTER

Action: Semiautomatic
Stock: Synthetic
Barrel: 18 in.
Sights: Hooded fiber optic front, adjustable rear
Weight: 4 lb.
Caliber: .22 LR
Magazine: 10, 25 rounds
Features: A handy, economical youth rimfire; black synthetic stock; rounded fore-end; vented rubber recoil pad
MSRP . . . . $143.00–$245.00

702 YOUTH BANTAM PLINKSTER

Action: Semiautomatic
Stock: Synthetic
Barrel: 18 in.
Sights: Hooded fiber optic front, adjustable rear
Weight: 4 lb.
Caliber: .22 LR
Magazine: 10 rounds
Features: Black synthetic stock; adjustable rifle sights with a fiber optic front; rounded fore-end; Bantam is two inches shorter overall than standard Plinkster
MSRP $204.00

715T FLAT TOP

Action: Semiautomatic
Stock: Synthetic
Barrel: 16.25 in.
Sights: Mounted front, adjustable rear; rail mount and adjustable front and rear; 30mm red-dot
Weight: 5 lb. 8 oz.
Caliber: .22 LR
Magazine: Detachable box, 11 or 26 rounds
Features: Adjustable stock; 10-round magazine or 25-round magazine/loader; FLEX Pad; standard model has rail mount adjustable sights and is available with choice of black or Muddy Girl Serenity synthetic stock; red-dot combo has black synthetic stock; green-dot combo has flat dark earth stock
Sights only: $358.00
Red-/Green-dot sight: $409.00

802 PLINKSTER

Action: Bolt
Stock: Synthetic
Barrel: 18 in.
Sights: Hooded fiber optic front, adjustable rear
Weight: 4 lb.
Caliber: .22 LR
Magazine: 10 rounds
Features: Black synthetic stock; adjustable rifle sights with a fiber optic front; rounded fore-end; vented rubber recoil pad
MSRP $204.00

802 PLINKSTER SCOPED COMBO

Action: Bolt
Stock: Synthetic
Barrel: 18 in.
Sights: Hooded fiber optic front, adjustable rear/4X scope
Weight: 4 lb. 8 oz.
Caliber: .22 LR
Magazine: 10 rounds
Features: Black synthetic stock; adjustable rifle sights with a fiber optic front; factory mounted 4X scope; rounded fore-end; vented rubber recoil pad
MSRP $216.00

Mossberg (O. F. Mossberg & Sons)

RIFLES

817

Action: Bolt
Stock: Synthetic or wood
Barrel: 21 in.
Sights: None
Weight: 4 lb. 8 oz.–5 lb.
Caliber: .17 HMR
Magazine: Detachable box, 6 rounds
Features: Factory-mounted Weaver-style scope bases; cross-bolt safety and magazine release buttons; free gun lock included
MSRP $237.00

BLAZE

Action: Semiautomatic
Stock: Synthetic
Barrel: 16.5 in.
Sights: Fixed
Weight: 3 lb. 8 oz.
Caliber: .22 LR
Magazine: 10, 25 rounds
Features: Free-floating 16.5-inch barrel with 1:16 twist rate; 3/8-inch dovetail for scope mounting; blue metal finish; black synthetic stock; adjustable rear sight with adjustable fiber optic front
MSRP $224.00

MMR CARBINE

Action: Semiautomatic
Stock: Synthetic
Barrel: 16.25 in.
Sights: Rail-mounted adjustable
Weight: 6 lb. 12 oz.
Caliber: 5.56mm NATO/.223 Rem.
Magazine: 10 or 30 rounds
Features: Direct-impingement gas system; 13 in. handguard that combines a comfortable, slim profile with the versatile Magpul M-LOK system and a full-length top rail; Magpul MOE polymer trigger guard; 6-position adjustable or optional fixed length-of-pull stock; free-floating, button-rifled, carbon steel barrel; black phosphate/anodized metal finishes for enhanced durability; CA-compliant versions available
MSRP $997.00

MMR PRO

Action: Semiautomatic
Stock: Synthetic
Barrel: 18 in.
Sights: None
Weight: 7 lb.
Caliber: .223 Rem./5.56 NATO, .224 Valkyrie
Magazine: 30 rounds
Features: Designed for 3-Gun competition; full-length direct impingement gas system; 18-in. free floating stainless barrel with M-LOK 15-in. forend; forward assist; ejection port dust cover; six-position stock; interchangeable FLEX pad
MSRP $1478.00

MVP LC (LIGHT CHASSIS) SERIES

Action: Bolt
Stock: Synthetic
Barrel: 16.25 in., 18.5 in., 22 in.
Sights: None
Weight: 8 lb.–10 lb.
Caliber: 5.56 NATO, 6.5 Creedmoor, 7.62 NATO
Magazine: Detachable box, 11 rounds
Features: Housed in an aluminum, tan-finished, light chassis stock designed by MDT that provides a modular, ergonomic base; free-floating, medium bull barrel is threaded and comes with a SilencerCo Saker muzzle brake, utilizing the Trifecta quick-detach mounting system (thread cap included); the barrels, constructed of carbon steel, are button-rifled with 16.25-inch length and 1:7 twist rate in the 5.56 NATO (.223 Rem.) chambering and the 7.62 NATO (.308 Win.) sports an 18.5-inch barrel with a 1:10 twist rate; both barrels feature a matte blue finish on all metalwork; Mossberg's Lightning Bolt Action (LBA) Trigger System is user-adjustable from 3 to 7 pounds and is machined from aircraft-grade aluminum and hard-coat anodized to military spec; spiral fluted bolt; oversized tactical-style bolt handle; Picatinny top rail; adjustable bipod; Magpul P-Mag 10-round magazines standard; tan-colored chassis with Magpul accessories added in 2018
MSRP $1082.00

Mossberg (O. F. Mossberg & Sons)

RIFLES

MVP LR

Action: Bolt
Stock: Synthetic
Barrel: 20 in.
Sights: None
Weight: 8 lb.
Caliber: 7.62 NATO, 6.5 Creedmoor
Magazine: 10 rounds
Features: Features include a textured OD green stock with adjustable cheekpiece; detachable box magazine; fluted and threaded barrel; top-side optics rail; dual swivels front, single rear
MSRP $938.00

MVP PATROL

Action: Bolt
Stock: Synthetic
Barrel: 16.25 in.
Sights: Adjustable
Weight: 7 lb.–7 lb. 8 oz.
Caliber: 5.56 NATO, 7.62 NATO
Magazine: Detachable box, 10+1 rounds
Features: Picatinny rail; threaded barrel for flash suppressor; Lightning Bolt action adjustable trigger system; Standard Patrol rifles have 16.25-in. barrels and come in black
MSRP. $613.00

MVP PRECISION RIFLE

Action: Bolt
Stock: Aluminum
Barrel: 20 in., 24 in.
Sights: None
Weight: 9 lb. 4 oz. (7.62 NATO), 10 lb. (6.5 Creedmoor)
Caliber: 7.62 NATO, 6.5 Creedmoor
Magazine: 11 rounds
Features: Mossberg chassis; UTH-AR MBA-3 adjustable stock; Magpul MOE grip; accepts both M1A/M14 and AR10-SR25 magazines; Magpul M-LOK modular mounting system; medium bull barrel is free-floating and threaded; the Mossberg Lightning Trigger System adjusts from three to seven pounds; oversized bolt and trigger guard; 20 MOA Picatinny rail
MSRP $1450.00

MVP SCOUT

Action: Bolt
Stock: Synthetic
Barrel: 16.25 in.
Sights: Fiber optic front ghost ring
Weight: 6 lb. 12 oz.
Caliber: 7.62 NATO
Magazine: Detachable box, 11 rounds
Features: Has an 11-inch receiver/barrel-mounted Picatinny rail; an integrated, rail-mounted, Ghost Ring rear sight is paired with a barrel-mounted, fiber optic front sight; two Picatinny side rails, located near the front of the forend; a compact 16 ¼-inch medium bull, carbon steel button-rifled, threaded barrel with an A2-style suppressor, with a 1:10 twist rate; a protective thread cap is provided; an adjustable rifle sling; scoped package includes Vortex 2-7x32 rifle scope
Sights only: $643.00
With scope: $804.00

PATRIOT NIGHT TRAIN

Action: Bolt
Stock: Synthetic
Barrel: 24 in.
Sights: 6–24X50mm scope
Weight: N/A
Caliber: .308 Win., 6.5 Creedmoor, .300 Win. Mag.
Magazine: 5 rounds
Features: A long-range rifle, complete with factory-mounted scope, that won't break the bank; matte finished fluted barrel; OD green in .308, flat dark earth stock in 6.5 Creedmoor, O.D. green stock in .300 Win. Mag.
MSRP $871.00

PATRIOT PREDATOR

Action: Bolt
Stock: Synthetic
Barrel: 16.25 in.
Sights: None
Weight: 6 lb. 4 oz.
Caliber: .243 Win., .308 Win., 6.5 Creedmoor, .450 Bushmaster, 6.5 PRC
Magazine: 4, 5 rounds
Features: Threaded fluted barrel and Picatinny rail on all calibers, and the .450 Bushmaster also gets adjustable sights; flat dark earth stock with matte blued metalwork
MSRP . . . . $484.00–$514.00

Mossberg (O. F. Mossberg & Sons)

PATRIOT PREDATOR CERAKOTE/STRATA CAMO

Action: Bolt
Stock: Synthetic
Barrel: 22 in.
Sights: None
Weight: 6 lb. 8 oz.
Caliber: .22-250 Rem., .243 Win., .3008 Win. 6.5 Creedmoor, 6.5 PRC
Magazine: 4, 5 rounds
Features: Synthetic stock in Strata camo; metalwork in Cerakote Patriot Brown; fluted threaded barrel
MSRP $574.00

PATRIOT SYNTHETIC

Action: Bolt
Stock: Synthetic
Barrel: 20 in.
Sights: None
Weight: 6 lb. 8 oz.
Caliber: .243 Win., .22-250 Rem., 7mm-08 Rem., .308 Win., .25-06 Rem., .270 Win., .30-06 Spfd., 6.5 Creedmoor, .450 Bushmaster, .350 Legend, .300 Win. Mag., 7mm Rem. Mag.
Magazine: 3, 4, 5 rounds
Features: Utilitarian hunting rifle in the straight-wall .450 Bushmaster round; threaded barrel; Weaver-type bases
MSRP . . . . $421.00–$437.00

PATRIOT SYNTHETIC CERAKOTE

Action: Bolt
Stock: Synthetic
Barrel: 22 in.
Sights: None; adjustable
Weight: 6 lb. 8 oz.
Caliber: 6.5 Creedmoor, .243 Win., .308 Win., 7mm-08 Rem., .270 Win., .30-06 Spfd., .22-250 Rem., .25-06 Rem., 7mm Rem. Mag., .300 Win. Mag., .338 Win. Mag., .375 Ruger
Magazine: 3, 5 rounds
Features: Cerakote Stainless with black synthetic stocks; button-rifled, carbon steel, free-floating fluted barrel; Weaver-style optics bases; spiral-fluted bolts; the Lightning Bolt Action Trigger System
MSRP . . . . $483.00–$519.00

PATRIOT SYNTHETIC VORTEX SCOPED COMBO

Action: Bolt
Stock: Synthetic
Barrel: 22 in.
Sights: Vortex Crossfire II 3–9X40mm scope
Weight: 7 lb. 8 oz.
Caliber: .243 Win., .308 Win., .270 Win., .30-06 Spfd., 6.5 Creedmoor, .22-250 Rem., 7mm-08 Rem., .25-06 Rem., .300 Win. Mag., 7mm Rem. Mag.
Magazine: 3, 5 rounds
Features: Utilitarian hunting rifle featuring a fluted barrel; Vortex scope; matte blue metalwork
MSRP . . . . $570.00–$585.00

PATRIOT WALNUT

Action: Bolt
Stock: Walnut
Barrel: 20 in.
Sights: None
Weight: 7 lb.
Caliber: .243 Win., .308 Win., .270 Win., .30-06 Spfd., 6.5 Creedmoor, .22-250 Rem., 7mm-08 Rem., .25-06 Rem., .300 Win. Mag., 7mm Rem. Mag., .350 Legend, .450 Bushmaster
Magazine: 4 rounds
Features: A traditionally styled rifle for the straight-wall .450 Bushmaster with walnut stock; matte blue metalwork; vented rubber recoil pad; threaded barrel; Weaver-style bases
MSRP . . . . $594.00–$609.00

PATRIOT WALNUT VORTEX SCOPED COMBO

Action: Bolt
Stock: Walnut
Barrel: 22 in.
Sights: Vortex Crossfire II 3–9X40mm scope
Weight: 8 lb.
Caliber: .243 Win., .308 Win., .270 Win., .30-06 Spfd., 6.5 Creedmoor, .22-250 Rem., 7mm-08 Rem., .25-06 Rem., .300 Win. Mag., 7mm Rem. Mag.
Magazine: 3, 5 rounds
Features: The walnut-stocked Patriot in a variety of common calibers; factory-mounted Vortex scope; fluted barrel; vented recoil pad
MSRP . . . . $752.00–$766.00

PATRIOT YOUTH SUPER BANTAM SCOPED COMBO

Action: Bolt
Stock: Synthetic
Barrel: 20 in.
Sights: 3-9x40mm scope
Weight: 7 lb. 8 oz.
Caliber: .243 Win., 6.5 Creedmoor, 7mm-08 Rem., .308 Win., .243 Win., .350 Legend
Magazine: 5 rounds
Features: Adjustable stock; fluted matte blue barrel; stock in black or choice of Muddy Girl Wild or Strata camo
MSRP . . . . $463.00–$519.00

Nesika

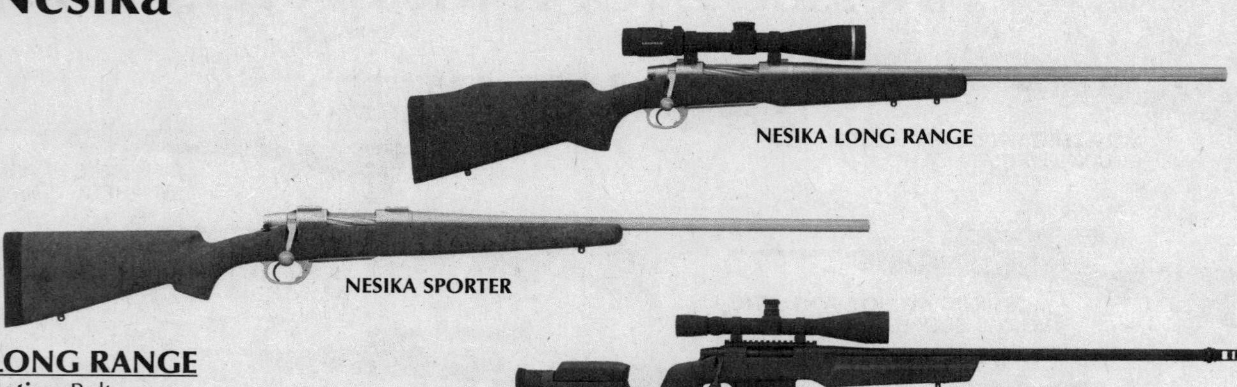
NESIKA LONG RANGE

NESIKA SPORTER

NESIKA TACTICAL

LONG RANGE

Action: Bolt
Stock: Synthetic
Barrel: 26 in.
Sights: None
Weight: 9 lb. 12 oz.
Caliber: .300 Win. Mag., 6.5x284, 7mm Rem. Mag.
Magazine: Internal
Features: Nesika stainless Hunter action; receiver made from 15-5 stainless steel; one-piece bolt from 4340 CM steel; Douglas air-gauged stainless steel barrel; fluted Varmint contour; Timney trigger set at a 3 lbs.; Leupold QRW bases
MSRP $3999.00

SPORTER

Action: Bolt
Stock: Synthetic
Barrel: 24 in., 26 in.
Sights: None
Weight: 8 lb.
Caliber: .260 Rem., 7mm-08 Rem., .308 Win., .30-06 Spfd., .280 Rem., 7mm Rem. Mag., .300 Win. Mag., 6.5x284
Magazine: Internal
Features: Nesika stainless Hunter action; receiver made from 15-5 stainless steel; one-piece bolt from 4340 CM steel; Douglas air-gauged stainless steel barrel; fluted Varmint contour; Timney trigger set at a 3 lbs.; Leupold QRW bases
MSRP $3499.00

TACTICAL

Action: Bolt
Stock: Synthetic
Barrel: 26 in., 28 in.
Sights: None
Weight: 13 lb. 12 oz.
Caliber: .300 Win. Mag., .338 Lapua
Magazine: Detachable box, 5 rounds
Features: Picatinny rail; all metal coated with Cerakoted matte black finish; tactical hand laid-up composite stock with aluminum bedding block, spacer adjuster system, and adjustable cheekpiece; Timney trigger set at 3 lbs.
MSRP $4499.00

New Ultra Light Arms

NEW ULTRA LIGHT ARMS MODEL 20 RIMFIRE

NEW ULTRA LIGHT ARMS MODEL 20 ULTIMATE MOUNTAIN RIFLE

MODEL 20 RIMFIRE

Action: Bolt
Stock: Kevlar/graphite composite
Barrel: 22 in.
Sights: None
Weight: 5 lb. 4 oz.
Caliber: .22 LR
Magazine: None or detachable box, 5 rounds
Features: Single-shot or repeater; drilled and tapped for scope; recoil pad; sling swivels; color stock options; left-hand models available for no extra charge
Single shot: $1800.00
Repeater: $1850.00

MODEL 20 ULTIMATE MOUNTAIN RIFLE

Action: Bolt
Stock: Kevlar/graphite composite
Barrel: 22 in.
Sights: None
Weight: 5 lb.
Caliber: .308 Win., .243 Win., 6mm Rem., .257 Roberts, 7mm-08, .284 Win.
Magazine: Detachable box
Features: Available in left-hand; choice of stock colors; 20-oz. action; two-position safety
MSRP $3500.00
Left-hand: $3600.00

NOSLER M48 CUSTOM RIFLE

NOSLER M48 HERITAGE

NOSLER M48 LONG-RANGE CARBON

NOSLER M48 MOUNTAIN CARBON

M48 CUSTOM RIFLE

Action: Bolt
Stock: Walnut
Barrel: 24 in., 24.75 in.
Sights: Open
Weight: 8 lb. 4 oz.–8 lb. 12 oz.
Caliber: 26 choices ranging from .22 Nosler to .458 Win. Mag.
Magazine: Internal, 3, 4 rounds
Features: Leupold Custom Shop; match-grade stainless, fully free-floated hand lapped barrel; three-stage safety; glass pillar-bedded fancy walnut stock; custom case cruzer by Pelican; custom leather sling
MSRP . . . . .starting at $2595.00

M48 HERITAGE

Action: Bolt
Stock: Wood
Barrel: 24 in.–26 in.
Sights: None
Weight: 7 lb. 4 oz.–7 lb. 13 oz.
Caliber: .22 Nosler, .243 Win., 6mm Creedmoor, 6.5 Creedmoor, 6.5-284 Norma, .26 Nosler, .270 Win., .280 AI, 7mm Rem. Mag.
Magazine: N/A
Features: Nosler Model 48 Custom action; stainless match-grade barrel; fancy walnut stock with heckering; hinged floor-plate; two-position Rocker safety; Cerakote all-weather finish
MSRP $2035.00

M48 LONG-RANGE CARBON

Action: Bolt
Stock: Carbon Fiber
Barrel: 26 in.
Sights: None
Weight: 7 lb.
Caliber: 6.5 Creedmoor, .26 Nosler, .27 Nosler, .300 Win. Mag., .30 Nosler, .33 Nosler
Magazine: 3, 4 rounds
Features: Proof Research carbon-fiber-wrapped match-grade barrel; Manners MCS carbon-fiber stock in Elite Midnight Camo; action and bottom metal in Cerakote Sniper Grey; glass and aluminum pillar bedding; threaded muzzle; muzzle brake is available
MSRP $3190.00

M48 MOUNTAIN CARBON

Action: Bolt
Stock: Carbon fiber
Barrel: 24 in.
Sights: None
Weight: 6 lb.
Caliber: 6mm Creedmoor, 6.5 Creedmoor, 6.5 PRC, .26 Nosler, .27 Nosler, .280 Ackley Improved, .28 Nosler, .300 Win. Mag., .30 Nosler, .33 Nosler
Magazine: 3, 4 rounds
Features: Super-light hunter with a carbon-wrapped, Tungsten Grey Cerakote, free-floating barrel with Sendero profile; textured carbon fiber Aramid-reinforced, pillar-bedded Mountain Hunter stock; aluminum floorplate
MSRP $3140.00

Noveske

NOVESKE GEN I SERIES

NOVESKE GEN III HEAVY INFIDEL N6

NOVESKE GEN IV SERIES

NOVESKE GEN I SERIES

Action: Semiautomatic
Stock: Synthetic
Barrel: 10.5 in., 16 in., 18 in.
Sights: Open, none
Weight: N/A
Caliber: 5.56 NATO
Magazine: 30 rounds
Features: Gen I series of Noveske modern sporting rifles include cold hammer-forged barrels with extended feed ramps; forged flat-top receivers; Radian Raptor charging handles; hard coat Type III anodizing with Cerakote; ALG Defense ACT trigger; Magpul stocks and grips; Troy backup iron sights on some model. Current production includes Light Shorty Basic, Shorty, Light Recon Basic, Recon, and SPR models
MSRP . . . . $1775.00–$1825.00

GEN III SERIES

Action: Semiautomatic
Stock: Synthetic
Barrel: 7.5 in.–18 in.
Sights: Adjustable
Weight: N/A
Caliber: .300 BLK, 5.56 NATO, 6.5 Creedmoor, 6.5 Grendel; .22 Nosler, 7.62X51 NATO,
Magazine: Detachable box, 30 rounds
Features: Noveske's Gen III rifles come in a wide variety of barrel lengths, handguard and stock configurations, rails, and sight options. Current Gen III models includes OMW (One More Wave); Light Recce; Diplomat; Switchblock; 6.5 Grendel; Varmageddon; N6; Afghan; Infidel; Leonidas Switchblock N6; Leonidas Switchblock
MSRP . . . . $2725.00–$4075.00

GEN IV SERIES

Action: Semiautomatic
Stock: Synthetic
Barrel: 8.5 in., 10.5 in., 13.7 in., 16 in.
Sights: Open, none
Weight: N/A
Caliber: 5.56 NATO, .300 BLK, 9mm
Magazine: 30 rounds
Features: Gen I series of Noveske modern sporting rifles include cold hammer-forged barrels with extended feed ramps; Geissele Super Badass charging handle, Q-bolt, and carrier group; free-floating M-LOK or Keymod handguards; hard coat Type III anodizing with Cerakote; ALG Defense ACT trigger; Magpul stocks and grips; Magpul MBUS folding sights on some model. Current production includes Infidel, Space Invader SBR, Noveske9, and Shorty models
MSRP . . . . $2450.00–$2675.00

Patriot Ordnance Factory

PATRIOT ORDNANCE FACTORY MINUTEMAN

PATRIOT ORDNANCE FACTORY P415 EDGE

PATRIOT ORDNANCE FACTORY RENEGADE PLUS

MINUTEMAN

Action: Semiautomatic
Stock: Synthetic
Barrel: 16.5 in.
Sights: None
Weight: 6 lb. 3 oz.
Caliber: 5.56 NATO, .350 Legend
Magazine: N/A
Features: Direct impingement carbine with a straight, drop-in match-grade trigger; ambidextrous rear QD sling swivel plate; mid-length gas system; POF three-prong flash-hider; Renegade rail; in black or tungsten finishes; California-compliant versions offered in 5.56 NATO
MSRP . . . . $1466.00–$1661.00

P415 EDGE

Action: Semiautomatic
Stock: Synthetic
Barrel: 16.5 in.
Sights: None
Weight: 7 lb.
Caliber: 5.56 NATO, .300 Blackout
Magazine: N/A
Features: Short-stroke gas piston action; nitride heat-treated barrel; 14½-in. M-LOK rail; triple port muzzle break; six-position anti-tilt buffer tube; chrome-plated bolt; Mission First Tactical furniture; E2 Dual Extraction Technology chamber; POF drop-in trigger group; black, NP3, Burnt Bronze, and Tungsten finishes
MSRP . . . . $2019.00–$2175.00

RENEGADE PLUS

Action: Semiautomatic
Stock: Synthetic
Barrel: 16.5 in. (5.56 NATO), 18.5 in. (.223 Wylde)
Sights: None
Weight: 6 lb. 6 oz. (5.56 NATO), 7 lb. 11 oz. (.223 Wylde)
Caliber: 5.56 NATO, .300 Blackout
Magazine: Detachable box
Features: M-LOK compatible Renegade rail; heat sink barrel nut; Dictator 9-position adjustable gas block with straight gas tube; nitride heat-treated barrel; Gen 4 POF-USA ambidextrous billet lower receiver and POF-USA Ultimate Bolt Carrier Group; flat 3.5 lb match-grade trigger with KNS Precision anti-walk pins; NP3 coated for maximum protection and reliability; integrated gas key (no screws required)
MSRP . . . . $1887.00–$2043.00

Patriot Ordnance Factory

PATRIOT ORDNANCE FACTORY REVOLUTION

PATRIOT ORDNANCE FACTORY ROGUE

PATRIOT ORDNANCE FACTORY WONDER

REVOLUTION

Action: Semiautomatic
Stock: Synthetic
Barrel: 14.5, 16.5. 20 in.
Sights: None
Weight: 7 lb. 4 oz.–9 lb. 4 oz.
Caliber: .308 Win., 6.5 Creedmoor
Magazine: N/A
Features: A .308/6.5 Creedmoor that handles like a 5.56; Edge handguard with four built-in QD mounts; five-position gas operating system; single stage match grade trigger; 6.5 Creedmoor available in 20-inch barrel only; both calibers available in black or burnt bronze finishes; gas piston and direct impingement operating systems available
Gas Piston: .... $2730.00–$2860.00
Direct Impingement: ... $2639.00–$2769.00

ROGUE

Action: Semiautomatic
Stock: Synthetic
Barrel: 16.5 in.
Sights: None
Weight: 5 lb. 14 oz.
Caliber: .308 Win.
Magazine: N/A
Features: A direct impingement carbine .308 under six pounds and featuring an anti-tilt buffer tube; 11-in. Renegade forearm; key-lock DI bolt carrier group; multiple QD sling attachment points; Micro B muzzle brake
MSRP .... $1828.00–$1958.00

WONDER

Action: Semiautomatic
Stock: Synthetic
Barrel: 16.5 in.
Sights: None
Weight: 6 lb. 3 oz.
Caliber: 5.56 NATO
Magazine: 30 rounds
Features: A lightened up and eye-catching AR platform featuring an eye-catching titanium blue Cerakote receiver and 14.5-inch M-LOK Renegade handguard; match-grade Puritan barrel heat-treated and threaded ½X28; single-port Micro-B muzzle brake; carbine length low-profile gas block; direct impingement system
MSRP .... $1636.00–$1701.00

Primary Weapons Systems

PRIMARY WEAPONS SYSTEMS MK216 MOD-1 M

MK216 MOD-1 M

Action: Semiautomatic
Stock: Synthetic
Barrel: 16 in.
Sights: Adjustable
Weight: 8 lb. 10 oz.
Caliber: .308 Win., 7.62 NATO
Magazine: Detachable box, 10 or 20 rounds
Features: FSC muzzle brake and suppressor; Picatinny rail; adjustable stock
MSRP $2199.95

Proof Research

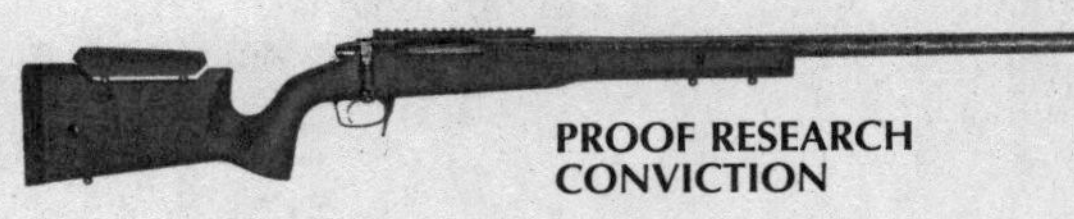

PROOF RESEARCH CONVICTION

PROOF RESEARCH ELEVATION

CONVICTION

Action: Bolt
Stock: Synthetic
Barrel: 20 in., 22 in., 24 in., 26 in., 28 in.
Sights: None
Weight: 6 lb. 13 oz.–8 lb. 8 oz.
Caliber: 6 Creedmoor, 6.5 Creedmoor, 6.5 PRC, .28 Nosler, .308 Win., 7mm Rem. Mag.,.300 Win. Mag., .300 WSM, .300 PRC, .300 RUM, .338 Lapua
Magazine: 3, 4 rounds
Features: A competition-ready long-range rifle built with PR's Conviction carbon-fiber stock; PR carbon-fiber wrapped match-grade barrel; tactical action; modified ball or tactical bolt knob; Triggertech trigger; Sendero contour barrel
MSRP .... $7699.00–$7899.00

ELEVATION

Action: Bolt
Stock: Synthetic
Barrel: 20 in., 22 in., 24 in.
Sights: None
Weight: 5 lb. 14 oz.–6 lb. 8 oz.
Caliber: 6mm Creedmoor, 6.5 Creedmoor, .308 Win., 7mm Rem. Mag., .300 Win. Mag.
Magazine: 3, 4 rounds
Features: A light rifle for backcountry hunters with PR's carbon fiber-wrapped match-grade barrel; PR's carbon fiber stock; TriggerTech trigger; Zermatt Arms Origin action
MSRP .... $2999.00–$3099.00

Proof Research

PROOF RESEARCH ELEVATION MTR

PROOF RESEARCH GLACIER TI

PROOF RESEARCH MPA CHASSIS RIFLE

PROOF RESEARCH TERMINUS

ELEVATION MTR

Action: Bolt
Stock: Synthetic
Barrel: 20 in., 22 in., 24 in.
Sights: None
Weight: 6 lb. 5 oz.–7 lb. 2 oz.
Caliber: .223 Rem., 6 ARC, 6mm Creedmoor, 6.5 Creedoor, 6.5 PRC, .308 Win., 7mm Rem. Mag., .300 Win. Mag.
Magazine: 3, 4 rounds
Features: MTR is for Mountain Tactical Rifle; it features PR's carbon fiber-wrapped match-grade barrel; PR's carbon fiber stock; TriggerTech trigger; Zermatt Arms Origin action; detachable box magazine or hinged floorplate; Sendero Light contour barrel; black metalwork finish; topside scope rail
MSRP . . . .$3199.00–$3299.00

GLACIER, GLACIER TI

Action: Bolt
Stock: Synthetic
Barrel: 20 in., 22 in., 24 in., 26 in.
Sights: None
Weight: 5 lb. 5 oz.–7 lb. 2 oz.
Caliber: 6 Creedmoor, 6.5 Creedmoor, 6.5 PRC,.308 Win., 7mm Rem. Mag., .28 Nosler, .300 WSM, .300 Win. Mag., .300 PRC
Magazine: 3, 4 rounds
Features: Superbly accurate rifle for the mountain hunter, featuring PR's carbon fiber-wrapped match-grade barrel; PR's carbon fiber stock; TriggerTech trigger; Lone Peak Arms Razor action; detachable BDL-type magazine; threaded Sendero or Sendero Light contour barrel; Cerakote metalwork in flat dark earth, olive drab, black, tungsten or Sniper Gray; topside scope rail; stock in several single colors and a wide range of multi-color and patterns; stock and barrel can be ordered in custom lengths; TI variant has titanium action
Glacier: . . . .$5699.00–$5899.00
Glacier Ti: . . . . . .$6499.00–$6699.00

MPA CHASSIS RIFLE

Action: Bolt
Stock: Synthetic
Barrel: 20 in., 22 in., 24 in., 26 in., 28 in.
Sights: None
Weight: 15 lb. 4 oz.
Caliber: 6 Dasher, 6 Creedmoor, 6.5 Creedmoor
Magazine: 12 rounds
Features: A competition-ready (and flashy!) rifle built on a Masterpiece Arms BA chassis; Triggertech Pro Curved Diamond adjustable trigger; Area 419 Hellfire muzzle brake; Zermatt Arms TL3 action; 20 MOA rail; steel Competition contour barrel; AICS steel magazine
MSRP $5000.00

TERMINUS

Action: Bolt
Stock: Synthetic
Barrel: 20 in., 22 in., 24 in., 26 in., 28 in.
Sights: None
Weight: 5 lb. 5 oz.–7 lb. 2 oz.
Caliber: 6 Creedmoor, 6.5 Creedmoor, 6.5 PRC, .308 Win., 7mm Rem. Mag., .28 Nosler, .300 Win. Mag., .300 PRC
Magazine: 3, 4 rounds
Features: One for the long-range hunter, featuring PR's carbon fiber-wrapped match-grade barrel; PR's carbon fiber Monte Carlo stock; TriggerTech trigger; Lone Peak Arms Razor action; hinged floor-plate magazine; threaded Sendero or Sendero Light contour barrel; Cerakote metalwork in flat dark earth, olive drab, black, tungsten or Sniper Gray; topside scope rail; stock in several single colors and a wide range of multi-color and patterns; stock and barrel can be ordered in custom lengths
MSRP . . . .$6999.00–$7199.00

PTR Industries

PTR INDUSTRIES 32 KFR PTR 200

32 KFR PTR 200

Action: Semiautomatic
Stock: Synthetic
Barrel: 16 in.
Sights: Fixed
Weight: 9 lb. 5 oz.
Caliber: 7.62X39
Magazine: 10, 30 rounds
Features: H&K Navy-type polymer trigger group housing, HK 91-length handguards, cocking tube, welded scope mount, paddle magazine release, delayed blowback roller lock system are standard; now with 5/8-24 barrel threading.
MSRP . . . . $1336.00–$1418.00

RIFLES

Rifles Inc.

RIFLES INC. CANYON

RIFLES INC. CLASSIC

RIFLES INC. LIGHTWEIGHT STRATA

RIFLES INC. MASTER'S SERIES

RIFLES INC. SAFARI

RIFLES

CANYON

Action: Bolt
Stock: McMillan HTG
Barrel: 24 in.
Sights: None
Weight: 10 lb.
Caliber: Most popular calibers
Magazine: Internal
Features: Blind or hinged floor plate; customer-supplied Rem. 700 action; match grade stainless steel Lilja number 6 barrel; optional muzzlebrake; matte stainless metal finish, optional black Teflon; adjustable cheekpiece; custom buttpad
MSRP $3500.00

CLASSIC

Action: Bolt
Stock: Laminated fiberglass
Barrel: 24 in.–26 in.
Sights: None
Weight: 6 lb. 8 oz.
Caliber: All popular chamberings up to .375 H&H
Magazine: Internal
Features: Customer-supplied Rem. 700 action; match grade stainless steel Lilja barrel; blind or hinged floor plate; matte stainless metal finish, optional Black Teflon finish; black laminated fiberglass, pillar glass bedded stock
MSRP $2900.00

LIGHTWEIGHT STRATA, LIGHTWEIGHT 70

Action: Bolt
Stock: Laminate
Barrel: 22 in.–26 in.
Sights: None
Weight: 4 lb. 8 oz.–5 lb. 12 oz.
Caliber: All popular chamberings up to .375 H&H
Magazine: Internal
Features: Customer-supplied Rem. 700 action; match grade stainless steel Lilja barrel; fluted bolt and hollowed-handle; blind or hinged floor plate; matte stainless metal finish, optional black Teflon finish; hand-laminated blend of Kevlar/graphite and boron, pillar glass bedded stock; Titanium Strata has hand-laminated graphite stock with pillar glass bedded; custom buttpad; Quiet Slimbrake II muzzlebrake
Lightweight Strata: $3200.00
Lightweight 70: $3100.00

MASTER'S SERIES

Action: Bolt
Stock: Laminated fiberglass
Barrel: 24 in.–27 in.
Sights: None
Weight: 7 lb. 12 oz.
Caliber: All popular chamberings up to .375 H&H
Magazine: Internal
Features: Customer-supplied Rem. 700 action; match grade stainless steel Lilja number 5 barrel; hinged floor plate; matte stainless metal finish, optional black Teflon finish; black laminated fiberglass, pillar glass bedded stock; optional muzzlebrake
MSRP $3200.00

SAFARI

Action: Bolt
Stock: Laminated fiberglass
Barrel: 23 in.–25 in.
Sights: Optional Express Sights
Weight: 8 lb. 8 oz.
Caliber: .375 H&H, .416 Rem. Mag., and other large game cartridges
Magazine: 4 rounds
Features: Customer-supplied Winchester Model 70 Classic action; lapped and face trued bolt; match grade stainless steel Lilja barrel; Quiet Slimbrake II muzzlebrake; hinged floor plate or optional drop box; matte stainless finish, optional black Teflon; double laminated fiberglass, pillar glass bedded stock; Pachmayr decelerator; optional barrel band
MSRP $3500.00

Rock River Arms

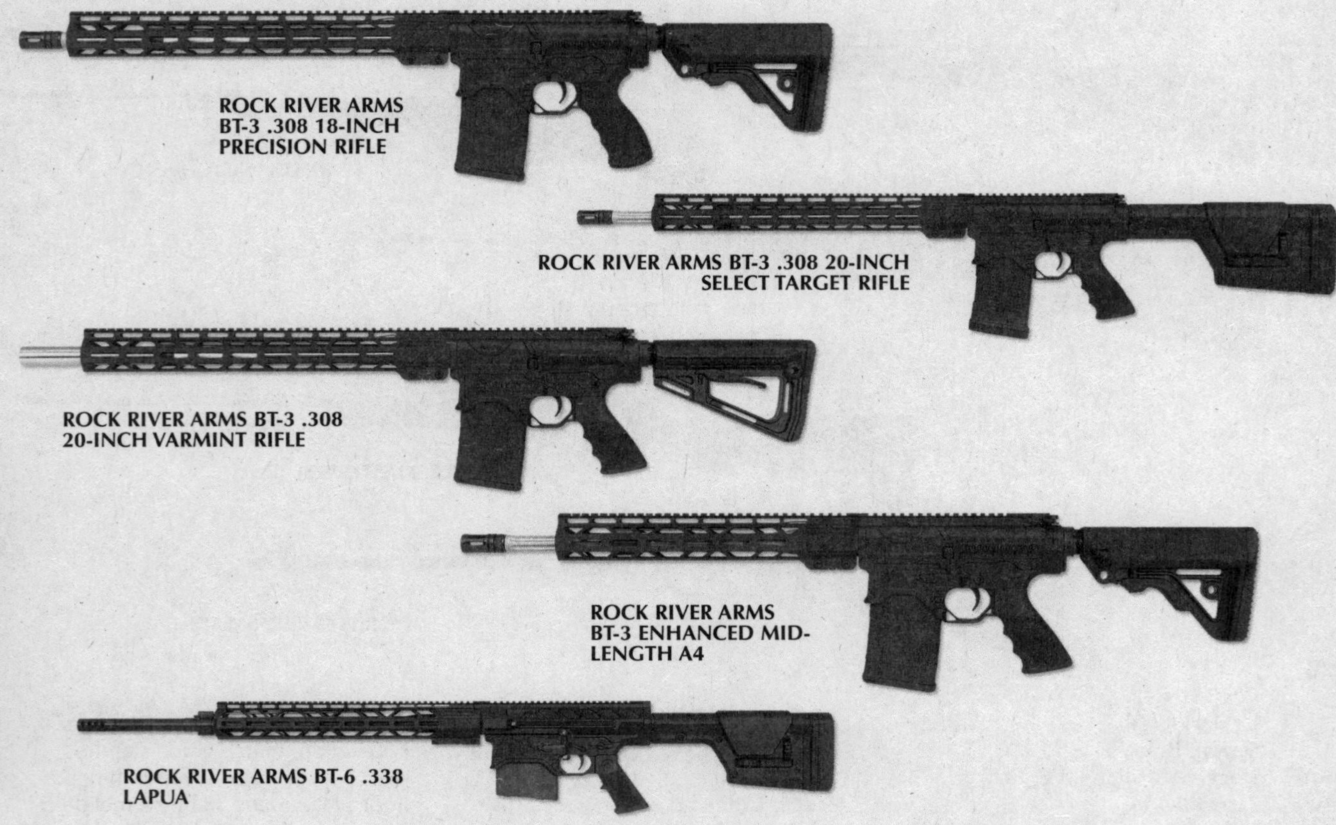

RIFLES

BT-3 .308 18-INCH PRECISION RIFLE

Action: Semiautomatic
Stock: Synthetic
Barrel: 18 in.
Sights: None
Weight: 8 lb. 3 oz.
Caliber: .308 Win.
Magazine: 10 rounds
Features: Features a six-position adjustable stock; cryogenically treated fluted stainless barrel; Rock River's BT-3 billet lower and billet A4 upper; two-stage trigger; low-profile gas block; mid-length gas block
MSRP $1635.00

BT-3 .308 20-INCH SELECT TARGET RIFLE

Action: Semiautomatic
Stock: Synthetic
Barrel: 20 in.
Sights: None
Weight: 8 lb. 10 oz.
Caliber: .308 Win.
Magazine: 10 rounds
Features: Features a Gen3 Precision Rifle stock; cryogenically treated fluted stainless barrel with heavy profile; Rock River's BT-3 billet lower and billet A4 upper; two-stage trigger
MSRP $1895.00

BT-3 .308 20-INCH VARMINT RIFLE

Action: Semiautomatic
Stock: Synthetic
Barrel: 20 in.
Sights: None
Weight: 9 lb. 13 oz.
Caliber: .308 Win.
Magazine: 10 rounds
Features: More than a pound over the other BT-3 models for steadiness on long-distance critters; six-position NSP-2 CAR stock; Rock River's BT-3 billet lower and billet A4 upper; two-stage trigger; low-profile gas block; rifle-length gas block; 17-in. M-LOK compatible free-floating handrail; Hogue rubber grip
MSRP $1575.00

BT-3 ENHANCED MID-LENGTH A4

Action: Semiautomatic
Stock: Synthetic
Barrel: 16 in.
Sights: None
Weight: 8 lb. 3 oz.
Caliber: .308 Win.
Magazine: 10 rounds
Features: Features a six-position Operator CAR stock; cryogenically treated fluted stainless barrel with heavy profile; Rock River's BT-3 billet lower and billet A4 upper; two-stage trigger; low-profile gas block
MSRP $1575.00

BT-6 .338 LAPUA

Action: Semiautomatic
Stock: Synthetic
Barrel: 24 in.
Sights: None
Weight: 13 lb. 8 oz.
Caliber: .338 Lapua
Magazine: 10 rounds
Features: Two-stage Ultra Match trigger; Magpul Gen Precision Rifle stock; Rock River overmolded A2 pistol grip; black nitride stainless steel barrel; adjustable low-profile gas block; four-port muzzle brake; quick takedown design
MSRP $5310.00

Rock River Arms

ROCK RIVER ARMS LAR-6.8 COYOTE CARBINE

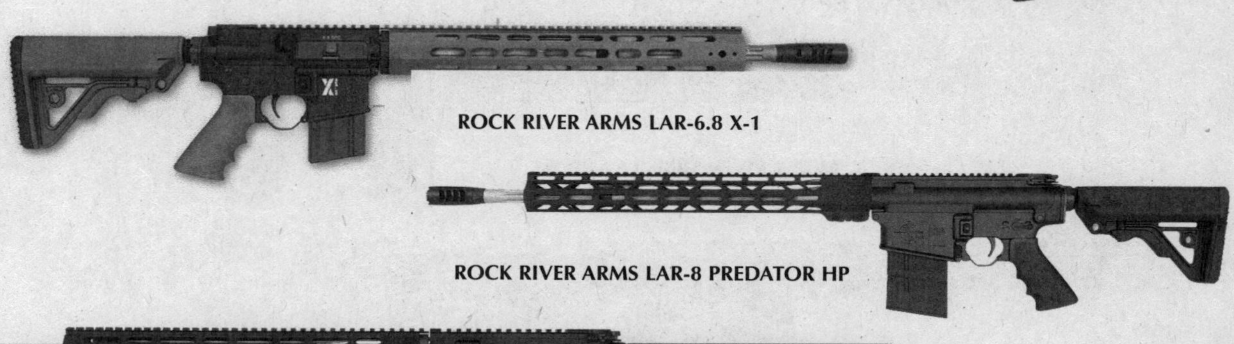
ROCK RIVER ARMS LAR-6.8 X-1

ROCK RIVER ARMS LAR-8 PREDATOR HP

ROCK RIVER ARMS LAR-8 PREDATOR HP MID-LENGTH

ROCK RIVER ARMS LAR-8 X-1

LAR-6.8 COYOTE CARBINE

Action: Semiautomatic
Stock: Synthetic
Barrel: 16 in.
Sights: None
Weight: 7 lb.
Caliber: 6.8 SPC II
Magazine: 1 round
Features: Smith Vortex flash hider; chromoly barrel; RRA two-stage match trigger
MSRP $1290.00

LAR-6.8 X-1

Action: Semiautomatic
Stock: Synthetic
Barrel: 18 in.
Sights: None
Weight: 7 lb. 13 oz.
Caliber: 6.8 SPC II
Magazine: Detachable box, 25 rounds
Features: RRA Beast of Hunter muzzle brake; available in black or tan; available with A2 or CAR stocks
MSRP . . . . $1490.00–$1520.00

LAR-8 PREDATOR HP

Action: Semiautomatic
Stock: Synthetic
Barrel: 20 in.
Sights: None
Weight: 8 lb. 10 oz.
Caliber: .243 Win., 6.5 Creedmoor
Magazine: Detachable box
Features: Forged A4 receiver with forward assist and port door; stainless steel barrel; gas block sight Base; two-stage trigger; Hogue rubber grip; RRA aluminum free-float tube; A2 buttstock or operator stock
MSRP $1575.00

LAR-8 PREDATOR HP MID-LENGTH

Action: Semiautomatic
Stock: Synthetic
Barrel: 16 in.
Sights: None
Weight: 8 lb. 14.4 oz.–9 lb. 3.2 oz.
Caliber: .308 Win.
Magazine: N/A
Features: Forged LAR-8 lower and A4 upper; stainless steel barrel has 1:10 twist, is fluted, bead-blasted, and cryogenically treated; available with or without muzzle brake; two-stage match trigger with winter trigger guard; RRA Operator CAR or A2 buttstock; RRA LAR-8 DLX rifle-length free-floating handguard with three short accessory rails; Hogue pistol grip
MSRP $1605.00

LAR-8 X-1

Action: Semiautomatic
Stock: Synthetic
Barrel: 18 in.
Sights: None
Weight: 9 lb. 8 oz.
Caliber: .308 Win., 7.62 NATO
Magazine: Detachable box, 20 rounds
Features: RRA Beast of Hunter muzzle brake; available in black or tan; available with A2 or CAR stocks
MSRP . . . . $1685.00–$1715.00

Rock River Arms

RIFLES

LAR-8M .243 PREDATOR HP

Action: Semiautomatic
Stock: Synthetic
Barrel: 20 in.
Sights: None
Weight: 9 lb. 3.2 oz.–9 lb. 8 oz.
Caliber: .243 Win.
Magazine: N/A
Features: Rifle features a forged, multi-caliber marked LAR-8M lower and a forged A4 upper; stainless steel barrel has 1:10 twist, is fluted, and cryogenically treated; Rock River's Operator muzzle brake available; low-profile gas block; two-stage match trigger with a winter trigger guard; RRA Operator A2 or CAR stock; RRA LAR-8 DLX free-floating rifle-length handrail with three short accessory rails; Hogue pistol grip
MSRP $1575.00

LAR-8M 6.5 CREEDMOOR PREDATOR HP

Action: Semiautomatic
Stock: Synthetic
Barrel: 20 in.
Sights: None
Weight: 9 lb. 3.2 oz.–9 lb. 6.4 oz.
Caliber: 6.5 Creedmoor
Magazine: N/A
Features: Rifle features a forged, multi-caliber marked LAR-8M lower and a forged A4 upper; barrel has 1:8 twist, is bead blasted, and cryogenically treated; Rock River's Operator muzzle break available; low-profile gas block; two-stage match trigger with a winter trigger guard; RRA Operator A2 stock; RRA LAR-8 DLX free-float handrail with three short accessory rails; Hogue pistol grip
MSRP . . . . $1575.00–$1605.00

LAR-9 R9 COMPETITION

Action: Semiautomatic
Stock: Synthetic
Barrel: 16 in.
Sights: None
Weight: 7 lb. 6.4 oz.
Caliber: 9mm
Magazine: N/A
Features: Forged LAR-9 lower with integral Magwell and a forged A4 upper; barrel has 1:10 twist, is chain-link fluted, and cryogenically treated; wears a 9mm Mini-Break; two-stage match trigger; RRA Operator CAR stock; RRA Lightweight Extended Mid-Length handguard; Hogue pistol grip
MSRP $1235.00

LAR-15 FES LIGHT PREDATOR2L

Action: Semiautomatic
Stock: Synthetic
Barrel: 16 in.
Sights: None
Weight: 6 lb. 14 oz.
Caliber: .223 Wylde
Magazine: 20 rounds
Features: Free-floating, extended length, top rail handguard; FES muzzle brake; lightweight fluted steel barrel; mid-length gas system with low-profile gas block; Rock River's Operator stock; two-stage trigger; Winter trigger guard; BCM GUNFIGHTER charging handle; furniture is black; receiver and lower can be upgraded to Rock River's ROCKote Gunmetal Gray
MSRP $1945.00
ROCKote Gunmetal Gray receiver: $2010.00

Rock River Arms

ROCK RIVER ARMS LAR-15 FES PREDATOR2 GHOST CAMO

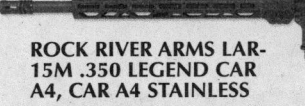

ROCK RIVER ARMS LAR-15LH LEF-T COYOTE RIFLE

ROCK RIVER ARMS LAR-15M .224 VALKYRIE

ROCK RIVER ARMS LAR-15M .350 LEGEND CAR A4, CAR A4 STAINLESS

ROCK RIVER ARMS LAR-15M .450 BUSHMASTER

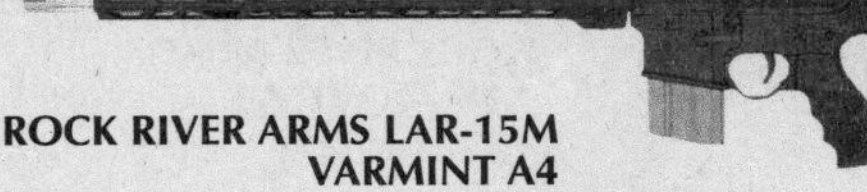

ROCK RIVER ARMS LAR-15M VARMINT A4

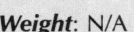

ROCK RIVER ARMS LAR-15 R3 COMPETITION RIFLE

LAR-15 FES PREDATOR2 GHOST CAMO

Action: Semiautomatic
Stock: Synthetic
Barrel: 16 in.
Sights: None
Weight: 7 lb. 10 oz.
Caliber: .223 Wylde
Magazine: 20 rounds
Features: FES stands for Fred Eichler Series; Ghost Camo stock; handguard emblazoned with paw prints; Rock River's FES muzzle brake; Operator CAR stock; chrome two-stage trigger; FES extended free-floating handguard with full-length rail; Cryo-treated fluted barrel; Hogue rubber pistol grip; Rock River's Winter trigger guard; BCM GUNFIGHTER charging handle
MSRP $2100.00

LAR-15LH LEF-T COYOTE RIFLE & CARBINE

Action: Semiautomatic
Stock: Synthetic A2
Barrel: 16 in., 20 in.
Sights: None
Weight: 7 lb.-8 lb. 6.4 oz.
Caliber: 5.56 NATO, .223 Rem., .223 Wylde
Magazine: Detachable box, 20 rounds
Features: Smith Vortex Flash Hider; Hogue free float tube; Hogue grip; two stage trigger
MSRP $1290.00

LAR-15M .224 VALKYRIE

Action: Semiautomatic
Stock: Synthetic
Barrel: 24 in.
Sights: None
Weight: N/A
Caliber: .224 Valkyrie
Magazine: 10 rounds
Features: Air-gauged, cryogenically threaded stainless steel barrel; low-profile gas block; two-stage trigger and winter trigger guard
MSRP $1235.00

LAR-15M .350 LEGEND CAR A4, CAR A4 STAINLESS

Action: Semiautomatic
Stock: Synthetic
Barrel: 16 in.
Sights: None
Weight: 6 lb. 13 oz.
Caliber: .350 Legend
Magazine: 10 rounds
Features: Operator CAR stock, over-molded A2 grip, two-stage trigger, and winter trigger guard; low-profile gas block; carbine-length gas system; chrome-moly barrel; forged upper and lower; 13-inch free-floating M-LOK compatible rail
Standard: $1160.00
Stainless: $1210.00

LAR-15M .450 BUSHMASTER

Action: Semiautomatic
Stock: Synthetic
Barrel: 16 in.
Sights: None
Weight: 6 lb. 13 oz.
Caliber: .450 Bushmaster
Magazine: N/A
Features: One for the new straight-wall cartridge, featuring cryo-treated 1:14 twist barrel; RRA's Operator muzzle brake with 5/8X24 threads; mid-length gas system; 13-inch free-floating M-LOK rail; two-stage trigger; winter trigger guard
MSRP $1160.00

LAR-15M VARMINT A4

Action: Semiautomatic
Stock: Synthetic
Barrel: 20 in.
Sights: None
Weight: 9 lb. 1.6 oz.
Caliber: .204 Ruger
Magazine: N/A
Features: Forged, multi-caliber marked LAR-15M lower and A4 upper; stainless steel bull barrel has 1:12 twist, is fluted, air gauged, and cryogenically treated; low-profile gas block; two-stage match trigger with a winter trigger guard; A2 buttstock; RRA TRO-STD free-floating handrail with octagonal top rail providing one STD and two short accessory rails; Hogue pistol grip
MSRP $1260.00

LAR-15 R3 COMPETITION RIFLE

Action: Semiautomatic
Stock: Synthetic A2 or CAR
Barrel: 18 in.
Sights: None
Weight: 7 lb. 9.6 oz.
Caliber: .223 Wylde
Magazine: Detachable box, 30 rounds
Features: RRA tuned and ported muzzle brake; low profile gas block; two stage trigger; Hogue Rubber grip
MSRP $1315.00

Rock River Arms

LAR-15 RRAGE 3G

Action: Semiautomatic
Stock: Synthetic
Barrel: 16 in.
Sights: None
Weight: 6 lb. 3 oz.
Caliber: 5.56mm NATO/.223 Rem.
Magazine: 30 rounds
Features: For the 3-Gun crowd, a carbine featuring a low-profile carbine-length gas block; single-stage trigger; forged lower; 15-inch RRA 3G handguard; A2 grip; adjustable stock; no forward assist
MSRP $860.00

LAR-15 RRAGE CARBINE

Action: Semiautomatic
Stock: Synthetic
Barrel: 16 in.
Sights: None
Weight: 5 lb. 11 oz.
Caliber: 5.56mm NATO/.223 Rem.
Magazine: 30 rounds
Features: Feature-rich AR carbine with an extruded aluminum A4 upper with port door; A2 flash hider; single-stage trigger; six-position tactical CAR stock; CAR-length free-floating aluminum handguard with M1913 top rail and M-LOK compatible;
MSRP $800.00

LAR-22 MID A4

Action: Semiautomatic
Stock: Synthetic
Barrel: 16 in.
Sights: None
Weight: 5 lb. 6 oz.
Caliber: .22 LR
Magazine: N/A
Features: A classic look in a .22 LR featuring single-stage trigger; six-position tactical CAR stock; mid-length handguard with heat shield; choice of poly or forged aluminum A4 upper
Aluminum: $560.00
Poly: $465.00

LAR-22 NM A4 RIFLE

Action: Semiautomatic
Stock: Synthetic
Barrel: 20 in.
Sights: None
Weight: 8 lb. 14 oz.
Caliber: .22 LR
Magazine: 30 rounds
Features: A vintage look with modern features like a free-floating, high-temp thermo-molded handguard with NM barrel sleeve; stainless steel HBAR barrel; two-stage match chrome trigger group
MSRP $875.00

LAR-22 NM CMP TRAINER

Action: Semiautomatic
Stock: Synthetic
Barrel: 20 in.
Sights: None
Weight: 8 lb. 13 oz.
Caliber: .22 LR
Magazine: N/A
Features: One for serious small-bore competition with added weight; two-stage chrome match trigger group; stainless steel HBAR barrel with 1:16 twist; NM CMP TRO free-floating rifle-length handguard with rail and swivel; A2 pistol grip; forged aluminum upper and lower
MSRP $930.00

LAR-22 TACTICAL CARBINE

Action: Semiautomatic
Stock: Synthetic
Barrel: 16 in.
Sights: None
Weight: N/A
Caliber: .22 LR
Magazine: 30 rounds
Features: AR plinking fun or serious rimfire competition thanks to features such as a two-stage trigger; winter trigger guard; six-position stock; A2 flash hider; Hogue rubber grip; 11-inch free-floating M-LOK handguard; choice of aluminum or poly receiver construction
Aluminum: $665.00
Poly: $580.00

Rock River Arms

ROCK RIVER ARMS LAR-47 CAR A4

ROCK RIVER ARMS LAR-47 X-1

ROCK RIVER ARMS LAR-300 X-1

ROCK RIVER ARMS LAR-458 CAR A4

ROCK RIVER ARMS LAR-PDS CARBINE

ROCK RIVER ARMS RBG BOLT GUN

LAR-47 CAR A4

Action: Semiautomatic
Stock: Synthetic
Barrel: 16 in.
Sights: None
Weight: 6 lb. 6 oz.
Caliber: 7.62x39
Magazine: Detachable box, 30 rounds, standard AK-47 mag
Features: RRA 6-postion tactical CAR stock; A2 pistol grip; CAR handguards; RRA two-stage trigger; A2 flash hider; ambidextrous mag release
MSRP $1080.00

LAR-47 X-1

Action: Semiautomatic
Stock: Synthetic
Barrel: 18 in.
Sights: None
Weight: 8 lb. 3 oz.
Caliber: 7.62 Warsaw
Magazine: Detachable box
Features: Available in black or tan; RRA Operator A2 Stock; RRA Beast muzzle brake
MSRP . . . .$1490.00–$1520.00

LAR-300 X-1

Action: Semiautomatic
Stock: Synthetic
Barrel: 18 in.
Sights: None
Weight: 7 lb. 14 oz.
Caliber: .300 BLK
Magazine: Detachable box
Features: Stainless steal cryo treated barrel; RRA two stage trigger; RRA beast muzzle break; A2 or CAR stock
MSRP . . . . $1490.00–$1520.00

LAR-458 CAR A4

Action: Semiautomatic
Stock: Synthetic
Barrel: 16 in.
Sights: None
Weight: 7 lb. 10 oz.
Caliber: .458 SOCOM
Magazine: Detachable box
Features: Forged A4 receiver; A2 flash hider; chromoly bull barrel; varmint gas block with sight rail; RRA two-stage trigger; RRA aluminum free-float tube; A2 pistol grip; A2 buttstock
MSRP $1160.00

LAR PDS CARBINE RIBBED, TRI-RAIL

Action: Semiautomatic
Stock: Synthetic
Barrel: 16 in.
Sights: None
Weight: 7 lb. 6 oz.
Caliber: .223 Rem.
Magazine: Detachable box
Features: Ambidextrous non-reciprocating charging handle; A2 flash hider; RRA two-stage trigger; Hogue rubber grip; tri-rail handguard available
Ribbed: $1420.00
Tri-Rail: $1500.00

RBG BOLT GUN

Action: Bolt
Stock: Synthetic
Barrel: 20 in.
Sights: None
Weight: 10 lb. 3 oz.
Caliber: .308 Win., 6.5 Creedmoor
Magazine: 10 rounds
Features: Serious competitors will appreciate the KRG chassis foundation; air-gauged, cryogenically-treated fluted stainless barrel; Triggertech trigger
MSRP $4235.00

RIFLES

Rossi

ROSSI RB22LR

RB22LR, RB22WMR, RB17HMR

Action: Semiautomatic
Stock: Bolt
Barrel: 18 in., 21 in.
Sights: Fiber optic
Weight: 5 lb. 4 oz.–5 lb. 7 oz.
Caliber: .22 LR, .22 WMR, .17 HMR
Magazine: 5, 10 rounds
Features: Super-economical choice in a bolt-action rimfire for new shooters with; fiber optic sights on the .22 LR with dovetail scope bases; .22 WMR and .17 HMR have scope bases and five-round magazines; cross-bolt safety
MSRP . . . . $171.83–$201.05

Rossi

RS22LR, RS22WMR
Action: Semiautomatic
Stock: Synthetic
Barrel: 18 in., 21 in.
Sights: Fiber optic
Weight: 5 lb. 4 oz.–5 lb. 7 oz.
Caliber: .22 LR, .22 WMR
Magazine: 10 rounds
Features: A wallet-friendly rimfire to start new shooters with; fiber optic sights on the .22 LR, topside rail on .22 WMR, dovetail scope bases on both; cross-bolt safety on both, .22 WMR also gets a trigger safety
.22 LR: $171.83
.22 WMR: $312.18

Ruger (Sturm, Ruger & Co.)

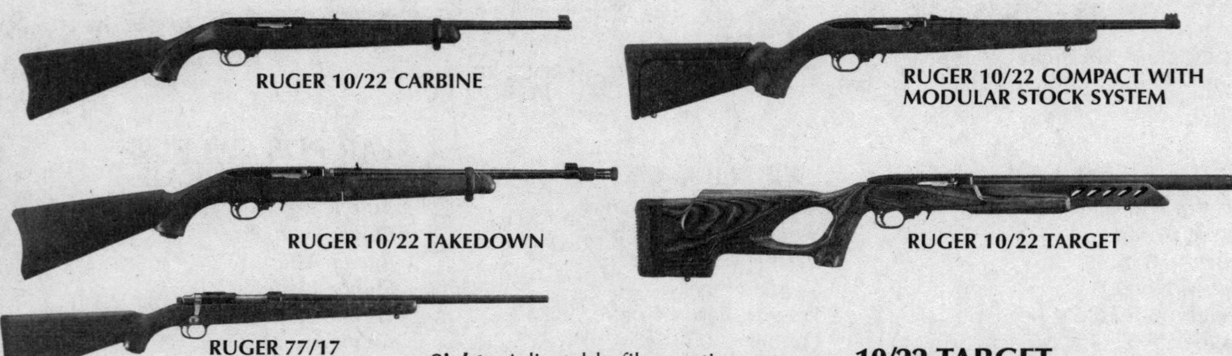

10/22 CARBINE
Action: Semiautomatic
Stock: Synthetic or hardwood
Barrel: 18.5 in.
Sights: Gold bead front sight, adjustable rear
Weight: 5 lb.
Caliber: .22 LR
Magazine: Detachable rotary, 10 rounds
Features: Available versions come in wood, black, gray or Go Wild Rock Star camo synthetic stocks with blue metalwork or a black synthetic stock with stainless steel hardware; extended magazine release; hammer-forged barrel; polymer trigger housing; aluminum receiver; contoured buttpad; barrel band; modular stock version has topside Picatinny rail
Wood, black or gray synthetic: $309.00
Black synthetic/ stainless: $339.00
Black synthetic with scope: . . . $399.00
Go Wild Rock Star camo: . . $399.00

10/22 COMPACT WITH MODULAR STOCK SYSTEM
Action: Semiautomatic
Stock: Synthetic
Barrel: 16.12 in.
Sights: Adjustable fiber optic rear, fiber optic front
Weight: 4 lb. 9 oz.
Caliber: .22 LR
Magazine: 10 rounds
Features: The rugged, reliable 10/22 now with a Modular Stock System; low comb and short length of pull
MSRP $309.00

10/22 TAKEDOWN
Action: Semiautomatic
Stock: Black synthetic
Barrel: 16.12 in.–18.5 in.
Sights: Gold bead front, adjustable rear
Weight: 4 lb. 9.6 oz.–5 lb. 5 oz.
Caliber: .22 LR
Magazine: Detachable rotary, 10 rounds
Features: Built of alloy steel with satin black finish; easy takedown and reassembly; detachable rotary magazine; extended magazine release; available in three configurations: black synthetic stock with 18.5-in. stainless barrel; black synthetic stock with 16.4-in. threaded barrel with flash suppressor in blue; black synthetic Ruger modular stock with 16.12-in. satin black threaded, fluted target barrel
Stainless: $439.00
Blued with flash suppressor: $459.00
Blued threaded/fluted: $629.00

10/22 TARGET
Action: Semiautomatic
Stock: Laminate
Barrel: 16.13 in.
Sights: None
Weight: 5 lb.
Caliber: .22 LR
Magazine: 10 rounds
Features: Laminated thumbhole stock adjustable for length of pull; vented forearm; cold hammer-forge barrel; scope base adapter that works with Weaver-style and .22 tip-off mounts; metal has a satin blue finish
MSRP $649.00

77/17
Action: Bolt
Stock: Walnut
Barrel: 20 in.
Sights: None
Weight: 5 lb. 11 oz.
Caliber: .17 WSM, .17 Hornet
Magazine: 6 rounds
Features: Traditionally styled smallbore for varmint or target work with: detachable rotary magazine; sling swivel studs; integral scope mounts; three-position safety; both calibers available in Green Mountain laminate stock, .17 WSM also available in American walnut
MSRP . . . . $999.00–$1069.00

Ruger (Sturm, Ruger & Co.)

RUGER AMERICAN RIFLE

RUGER AMERICAN RIFLE HUNTER

RUGER AMERICAN RIFLE PREDATOR

RUGER AMERICAN RIFLE RANCH

RUGER AMERICAN RIFLE WITH GO WILD CAMO

RUGER AMERICAN RIFLE WITH VORTEX RIFLESCOPE

RIFLES

AMERICAN RIFLE

Action: Bolt
Stock: Synthetic
Barrel: 22 in.
Sights: Drilled and tapped for scopes
Weight: 6 lb. 2 oz.–6 lb. 4 oz.
Caliber: .22-250 Rem., .223 Rem., 6.5 Creedmoor, 7mm-08 Rem., .243 Win., .270 Win., .30-06 Spfd., .308 Win.
Magazine: Detachable rotary, 4 rounds
Features: Ruger Marksman adjustable trigger; ergonomic, lightweight stock; soft rubber recoil pad; three-lug 70 degree bolt; Power Bedding positively locates the receiver and free-floats the barrel; hammer-forged barrel; tang safety; round rotary magazine
MSRP $489.00

AMERICAN RIFLE HUNTER

Action: Bolt
Stock: Synthetic
Barrel: 20 in.
Sights: None
Weight: 9 lb. 3 oz.
Caliber: 6.5 Creedmoor, .308 Win.
Magazine: 5 rounds
Features: This long-range-game rifle gets a Magpul Hunter American short-action adjustable stock; Ruger Marksman Adjustable trigger
MSRP $799.00

AMERICAN RIFLE PREDATOR

Action: Bolt
Stock: Synthetic
Barrel: 22 in.
Sights: None
Weight: 6 lb. 9 oz.
Caliber: .22-250 Rem., 6.5 Creedmoor, .308 Win., .243 Win., 7mm-08 Rem., 6.5 Grendel, .223 Rem., 6mm Creedmoor, .204 Ruger
Magazine: 10 rounds
Features: Moss Green synthetic stock; Ruger Marksman Adjustable Trigger and Power Bedding; threaded barrel; unscoped model has installed Picatinny rail; scoped model comes with a Vortex Crossfire II 4-12x44mm scope factory mounted and the Dead-Hold BDC reticle; left-hand version available
Rifle only: . . . . $529.00–$569.00

AMERICAN RIFLE RANCH

Action: Bolt
Stock: Synthetic
Barrel: 16.1 in.
Sights: None
Weight: 6 lb.–6 lb. 8 oz.
Caliber: 5.56 NATO, .300 BLK, .450 Bushmaster, 7.62x39, .350 Legend, 6.5 Grendel
Magazine: Detachable rotary, 3–5 rounds
Features: Ruger Marksman Adjustable trigger offers a pull weight that is adjustable between 3 and 5 pounds; ergonomic, lightweight flat dark earth composite stock with modern forend contouring and grip serrations and swivel studs; soft rubber recoil pad; Power Bedding positively locates the receiver and free-floats the barrel for outstanding accuracy; threaded barrel is cold hammer-forged; tang safety; rotary magazine; factory installed one-piece aluminum scope rail
MSRP $549.00

AMERICAN RIFLE WITH GO WILD CAMO

Action: Bolt
Stock: Synthetic
Barrel: 22 in.
Sights: None
Weight: 6 lb. 9 oz.
Caliber: 7mm-08 Rem., .243 Win., 6.5 Creedmoor, .308 Win., .30-06 Spfd., .450 Bushmaster, .300 Win. Mag., .350 Legend, .25-06 Rem., 6.5 PRC
Magazine: 3 rounds
Features: Go Wild I-M Brush camo; action and barrel in Bronze Cerakote; Picatinny rail; muzzle brake; Ruger's Marksman Adjustable Trigger and Power Bedding
MSRP $629.00

AMERICAN RIFLE WITH VORTEX SCOPE

Action: Bolt
Stock: Synthetic
Barrel: 22 in.
Sights: None
Weight: 7 lb. 3 oz.
Caliber: .223 Rem., .243 Win., .270 Win., .30-06 Spfd., 6.5 Creedmoor, .204 Ruger
Magazine: 5 rounds
Features: Vortex 3–9x40mm or 4–12x44mm Crossfire II scope (Dead-Head BDC reticle) already mounted; Ruger Marksman Adjustable Trigger and Power Bedding; a cold hammer forged barrel
MSRP . . . . $639.00–$699.00

Ruger (Sturm, Ruger & Co.)

RUGER AMERICAN RIMFIRE TARGET

RUGER AMERICAN RIMFIRE TARGET STAINLESS

RUGER AMERICAN RIMFIRE WITH WOOD STOCK

RUGER AR-556

RUGER AR-556 MPR

AMERICAN RIMFIRE TARGET

Action: Bolt
Stock: Laminate
Barrel: 18 in.
Sights: None
Weight: 6 lb. 8 oz.–6 lb. 11 oz.
Caliber: .17 HMR, .22 LR, .22 WMR
Magazine: 9, 10 rounds
Features: Ruger Marksman Adjustable trigger; aluminum Picatinny rail; cold hamme-forged threaded bull barrel; Power Bedding; flush-fit BX-1 magazines. Variants include GO Wild Camo I-M stocks with burnt bronze Cerakote or black synthetic stocks, some with adjustable stock modules, and blue or stainless metalwork
MSRP . . . . $389.00–$469.00

AMERICAN RIMFIRE TARGET STAINLESS

Action: Bolt
Stock: Laminate
Barrel: 18 in.
Sights: None
Weight: 6 lb. 11 oz.
Caliber: .22 LR, .22 WMR, .17 HMR
Magazine: 9, 10 rounds
Features: The durability and rust-resistance of a stainless receiver and barrel meet the Ruger American rimfire; flush-mount BX-1 magazine; Ruger Marksman Adjustable trigger; Power Bedding bedding block system
MSRP . . . . $529.00–$579.00

AMERICAN RIMFIRE WOOD STOCK

Action: Bolt
Stock: Wood
Barrel: 22 in.
Sights: Fiber optic front, adjustable rear
Weight: 6 lb. 2 oz.
Caliber: .22 LR
Magazine: 10 rounds
Features: Extended magazine release; patent-pending Power Bedding integral bedding block system; Ruger Marksman Adjustable trigger offers a crisp release with a pull weight that is user adjustable between 3 and 5 lb.; wood stock with checkering on the grip and forend and a rubber buttpad for a comfortable length of pull; cold hammer-forged barrel
MSRP $509.00

AR-556

Action: Semiautomatic
Stock: Synthetic
Barrel: 16.1 in.
Sights: Adjustable
Weight: 6 lb. 8 oz.
Caliber: .223 Rem./5.56 NATO
Magazine: Detachable box, 30 rounds
Features: The milled gas block is located at a carbine length (M4) position; multiple attachment points include a QD socket and bayonet lug; front sight post is elevation adjustable, and a front sight tool is included; A-2 Style F-Height allows co-witness with many optics; Ruger Rapid Deploy folding rear sight provides windage adjustability; six-position telescoping M4-style buttstock and Mil-Spec buffer tube; barrel is cold hammer-forged; Ruger flash suppressor; matte black oxide finish on the exterior of the bolt carrier
MSRP . . . . $799.00–$849.00

AR-556 MPR

Action: Semiautomatic
Stock: Synthetic
Barrel: 18 in.
Sights: Adjustable post front, adjustable Ruger rapid deploy rear
Weight: 6 lb. 8 oz.
Caliber: 5.56 NATO, .450 Bushmaster, .350 Legend
Magazine: 5, 10, 30 rounds
Features: M-LOK accessory-compatible 15-in. free-floating handguard; Ruger's Elite 452 AR trigger; rifle-length gas system; contoured barrel that reduces overall weight; low-profile gas block; stock is adjustable; long topside Picatinny rail; variants include a model with Magpul furniture, and state-compliant models that have either a non-threaded barrel or a fixed magazine
MSRP . . . . $899.00–$1099.00

Ruger (Sturm, Ruger & Co.)

RUGER AR-556 MPR FLAG SERIES

RUGER CUSTOM SHOP 10/22 COMPETITION

RUGER CUSTOM SHOP 10/22 COMPETITION WITH SKELETONIZED GREEN MOUNTAIN STOCK

RUGER HAWKEYE ALASKAN

RUGER HAWKEYE HUNTER

RUGER HAWKEYE LONG-RANGE TARGET

RUGER HAWKEYE PREDATOR

AR-556 MPR FLAG SERIES

Action: Semiautomatic
Stock: Synthetic
Barrel: 18 in.
Sights: None
Weight: 6 lb. 13 oz.
Caliber: 5.56 NATO
Magazine: 30 rounds
Features: A subtle if somewhat battle-worn American flag graphic is overlaid on the upper, lower, and handguard of this MSR; rifle-length gas system; Magpul MOE grip; Magpul MOE SL collapsible stock
MSRP $949.00

CUSTOM SHOP 10/22 COMPETITION

Action: Semiautomatic
Stock: Laminate
Barrel: 16.12 in.
Sights: None
Weight: 6 lb.
Caliber: .22 LR
Magazine: 10 rounds
Features: A next-level .22 for the serious rimfire competitor with features that include: heat-treated and stress-relieved aluminum receiver; 30mm Picatinny rail for optics mounting; adjustable cheekpiece; free-floating barrel with rear cleaning port; extended ambidextrous magazine release; match-grade bolt release; BX Trigger; choice of traditional speckled black/gray laminate stock with satin black metalwork, natural brown laminate traditional stock with stainless steel hardware, or a Green Mountain skeletonized laminate thumbhole stock with angled forend, hard-coat anodized black receiver, and satin stainless barrel with black Cerakote accents
MSRP $899.00

CUSTOM SHOP 10/22 COMPETITION WITH SKELETONIZED GREEN MOUNTAIN STOCK

Action: Semiautomatic
Stock: Laminate
Barrel: 16.12 in.
Sights: None
Weight: 5 lb. 8 oz.
Caliber: .22 LR
Magazine: 10 rounds
Features: Skeletonized laminate stock from Green Mountain; free-floating stainless steel barrel with black Cerakote highlights; 30 MOA topside Picatinny rail; black hard-coat anodized receiver with rear cleaning port; dual bedding system; BX-Trigger; match bolt release; includes Ruger hard case, Custom Shop letter of authenticity, and challenge coin
MSRP $899.00

HAWKEYE ALASKAN

Action: Bolt
Stock: Hogue synthetic
Barrel: 20 in.
Sights: Bead front, adjustable rear
Weight: 8 lb. 2 oz.
Caliber: .375 Ruger, .338 Win. Mag., .300 Win. Mag.
Magazine: 3 rounds
Features: Ruger brings back the Alaskan in three bear/moose/wolf-stopping cartridges and with enough weight to sop up some of the recoil; Hogue overmolded stock; Hawkeye Matte durable metal finish; non-rotating, Mauser-type controlled round feed extractor; LC6 trigger
MSRP $1279.00

HAWKEYE HUNTER

Action: Bolt
Stock: American walnut
Barrel: 20 in., 22 in., 24 in.
Sights: None
Weight: 7 lb.–8 lb. 2 oz.
Caliber: 6.5 Creedmoor, 6.5 PRC, .308 Win., .30-06 Spfd., .300 Win. Mag., 7mm Rem. Mag., .204 Ruger
Magazine: 3, 4 rounds
Features: American walnut stock; satin stainless hardware; non-rotating, Mauser-type controlled round feed extractor; 20 MOA topside Picatinny rail; free-floating cold hammer-forged barrel with 5R rifling
MSRP $1099.00

HAWKEYE LONG-RANGE TARGET

Action: Bolt
Stock: Laminate
Barrel: 24 in.
Sights: None
Weight: 10 lb. 11 oz.
Caliber: .300 Win. Mag., 6.5 Creedmoor, 6.5 PRC, .204 Ruger, .308 Win.
Magazine: 5 rounds
Features: Heavy contour barrel; Ruger's Precision Rifle Muzzle Brake; two-stage target trigger; controlled round feed; fixed-blade ejecto;, a 20 MOA rail that screws down on top of Ruger's own integral mounts; adjustable laminate stock
MSRP $1279.000

HAWKEYE PREDATOR

Action: Bolt
Stock: Laminate
Barrel: 22 in., 24 in.
Sights: None
Weight: 7 lb. 11 oz.–8 lb. 2 oz.
Caliber: .22-250 Rem., .223 Rem., .204 Ruger, .6.5 Creedmor
Magazine: 4 rounds
Features: Non-rotating, Mauser-type controlled round feed extractor; hinged solid-steel floorplate; cold hammer-forged barrel; patented integral scope mounts
MSRP . . . . $1139.00–$1159.00

Ruger (Sturm, Ruger & Co.)

RUGER MINI-14 RANCH RIFLE

RUGER MINI-14 TACTICAL

RUGER MINI-14 TACTICAL WOOD STOCK

RUGER NO. 1

RUGER PC CARBINE

RUGER PC CARBINE CHASSIS

RUGER PC CARBINE FLAG SERIES

MINI-14 RANCH RIFLE

Action: Semiautomatic
Stock: Hardwood, synthetic
Barrel: 18.5 in.
Sights: Blade front sight, adjustable rear
Weight: 6 lb. 12 oz.–7 lb.
Caliber: 5.56 NATO, .223 Rem.
Magazine: 5 rounds, or detachable box, 20 rounds
Features: Stock comes in hardwood or black synthetic; Garand style action; hammer-forged barrel; sighting system; integral scope mounts; flat buttpad; integral sling swivels on hardwood or black synthetic stocks
MSRP . . . . $999.00–$1139.00

MINI-14 TACTICAL

Action: Semiautomatic
Stock: Synthetic
Barrel: 16.1 in.
Sights: Adjustable
Weight: 6 lb. 12 oz.–7 lb. 4 oz.
Caliber: 5.56 NATO, .223 Rem., .300 BLK
Magazine: Detachable box, 5, 20 rounds
Features: Standard features include Garand-style action; flash suppressor; adjustable ghost ring rear sight, non-glare protected-post front sight; drilled and tapped receiver; Picatinny rail; scope rings; two magazines. Variants include black synthetic stock with stainless or blued hardware; ATI six-position collapsible/folding stock with blued hardware; speckled black/brown hardwood stock with blued hardware
MSRP . . . . $1069.00–$1169.00

MINI-14 TACTICAL WOOD STOCK

Action: Semiautomatic
Stock: Hardwood
Barrel: 16.12 in.
Sights: Blade front, adjustable rear
Weight: 7 lb. 3 oz.
Caliber: 5.56 NATO
Magazine: 20 rounds
Features: The Mini-14 gets a new look and improved gripping surface with a speckled black-and-brown hardwood stock while retaining standard features such as its Garand-style, breech-bolt locking action
MSRP $1069.00

NO. 1

Action: Single-shot
Stock: American walnut
Barrel: 20 in.
Sights: Blade front and rear
Weight: 7 lb. 1 oz.
Caliber: .450 Marlin, .308 Win., .450 Bushmaster
Magazine: 1 round
Features: Falling-block breech mechanism rifle includes a sliding tang safety; Ruger's patented scope mounting system; ejector that can be adjusted to perform as an extractor only; caliber changes from year to year and rifle is available in limited quantities; for 2021, this model is available through Lipseys Distributors in: American walnut/satin blue in .475 Linebaugh, 6.5 Creedmoor, or .480 Ruger; in American walnut/stainless steel in .30-30 Win.; American walnut mannlicher/stainless steel in .257 Roberts
MSRP . . . . N/A

PC CARBINE

Action: Semiautomatic
Stock: Synthetic
Barrel: 16.12 in.
Sights: Protected blade front, adjustable ghost ring rear
Weight: 6 lb. 12 oz.
Caliber: 9mm
Magazine: 10, 17 rounds
Features: Interchangeable magwell that lets the operator use a variety of Ruger or Glock magazines; buttstock is adjustable for length of pull via included spacers; magazine release and charging handle are both reversible; dead blow action with a tungsten weight both shortens the overall bolt trave, reduces felt recoil and muzzle rise
MSRP $649.00

PC CARBINE CHASSIS

Action: Semiautomatic
Stock: Glass-filled polymer
Barrel: 16.12 in.
Sights: None
Weight: 7 lb. 5 oz.
Caliber: 9mm
Magazine: 10, 17 rounds
Features: A favorite carbine gets a technology upgrade; glass-filled polymer chassis foundation; aluminum free-floating handguard; threaded and fluted heavy-contour barrel; telescopic, six-position Magpul MOE buttstock; SR series magazine
MSRP $799.00

PC CARBINE FLAG SERIES

Action: Semiautomatic
Stock: Glass-filled nylon
Barrel: 16.12 in.
Sights: Blade front, adjustable ghost ring rear
Weight: 7 lb.
Caliber: 9mm
Magazine: 17 rounds
Features: Quick-handling and visibly startling, you'll have loads of fun in PCC competitions thanks to the rifle's free-floating aluminum handguard; reversible magazine release and charging handle; heavy contour barrel; Type III hard coat anodizing
MSRP $779.00

Ruger (Sturm, Ruger & Co.)

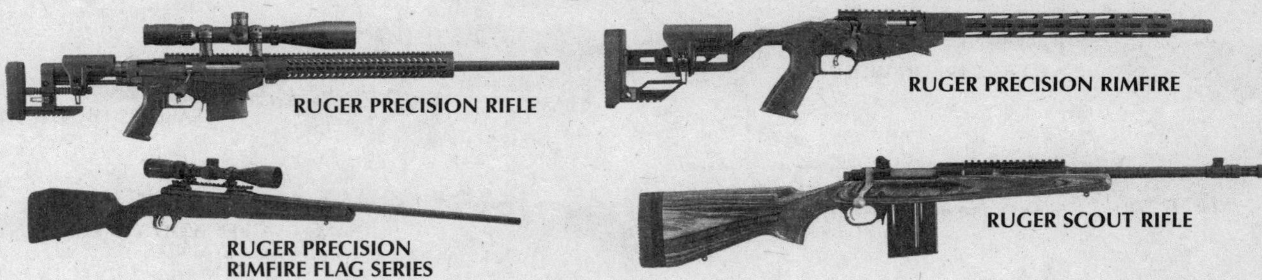

RUGER PRECISION RIFLE

RUGER PRECISION RIMFIRE

RUGER PRECISION RIMFIRE FLAG SERIES

RUGER SCOUT RIFLE

PRECISION RIFLE

Action: Bolt
Stock: Synthetic
Barrel: 20 in., 24 in.
Sights: None
Weight: 9 lb. 12 oz.–10 lb. 12 oz.
Caliber: .308 Win., 6.5 Creedmoor, 6mm Creedmoor, ,338 Lapua, .300 Win. Mag., 6.5 PRC, .300 PRC, 6mm Creedmoor
Magazine: 10 rounds
Features: Cold hammer-forged chrome-moly steel barrel with 5R rifling at minimum bore and groove dimensions, minimum, headspace and centralized chamber; Samson Evolution KeyMod handguard; 20 MOA Picatinny rail; in-line recoil path manages recoil directly from the rear of the receiver to the buttstock; patent-pending multi-magazine interface functions interchangeably with M110, SR25, DPMS, and Magpul-style magazines and AICS magazines (works with some M14 magazines); Ruger Marksman Adjustable trigger
MSRP . . . . $1599.00–$2099.00

PRECISION RIMFIRE

Action: Bolt
Stock: Synthetic
Barrel: 18 in.
Sights: None
Weight: 6 lb. 12 oz.
Caliber: .22 LR, .22 WMR, .17HMR
Magazine: 10, 15 rounds
Features: One-piece molded chassis is mated with an oversized bolt; adjustable bolt throw to prevent short stroking; Ruger's Marksman Adjustable trigger; reversible safety; glass-filled nylon buttstock is fully adjustable; Picatinny rail bag rider for monopod use; a molded in window allows squeeze bag attachment; variant with full-coverage American flag graphics
MSRP . . . . $529.00–$579.00

PRECISION RIMFIRE FLAG SERIES

Action: Bolt
Stock: Glass-filled nylon chassis
Barrel: 18 in.
Sights: None
Weight: 6 lb. 13 oz.
Caliber: .22 LR
Magazine: 15 rounds
Features: Competition-ready rimfire features a one-piece chassis and Quick-Fit adjustable buttstock, both of glass-filled nylon; Ruger Marksman Adjustable trigger
MSRP $579.00

SCOUT RIFLE

Action: Bolt
Stock: Laminate; synthetic; wood
Barrel: 16.50 in.
Sights: Post front sight, adjustable rear
Weight: 7 lb.
Caliber: .308 Win., .350 Legend,.450 Bushmaster
Magazine: Detachable box, 10 rounds
Features: Flash suppressor, Picatinny rail; recoil pad; integral scope mounts; Mauser-type extractor; detachable magazine; stainless finish bolt. Variants include black laminate stock with matte blue barrel/receiver and 10-round magazine; black laminate stock with stainless barrel/receiver and 10-round magazine; black synthetic stock with matte black barrel/receiver and five-round magazine; black synthetic stock with stainless barrel/receiver and 10-round magazine; wood stock in .450 Bushmaster only with Ruger Precision Rifle Hybrid Muzzle Brake, blued barrel/receiver, four-round magazine
MSRP . . . .$1139.00–$1199.00

Sako

SAKO 85 BAVARIAN CARBINE

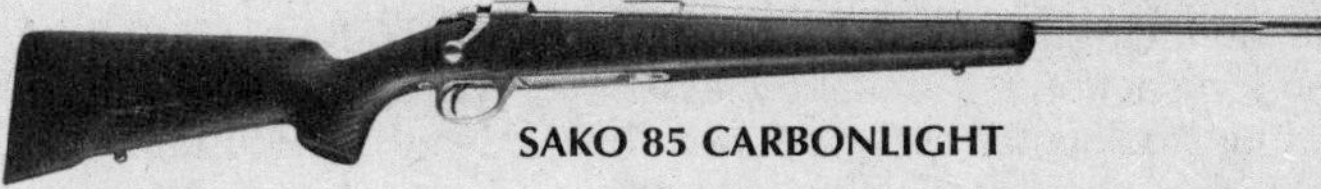

SAKO 85 CARBONLIGHT

85 BAVARIAN CARBINE

Action: Bolt
Stock: Walnut
Barrel: 22.5, 24.3 in.
Sights: Rifled sights
Weight: N/A
Caliber: .308 Win., .270 Win., .30-06 Spfd., .300 Win. Mag., 6.5 Creedmoor
Features: Featuring a full Mannlicher stock with Schnabel fore-tip and Bavarian cheekpiece/comb; iron sights; sling swivel studs; single set trigger
MSRP: $2225.00

85 CARBONLIGHT

Action:Bolt
Stock: Carbon fiber
Barrel: 20 in.
Sights: None
Weight: 5 lb. 5 oz.
Caliber: .308 Win., .260 Rem., 7mm-08 Rem.
Magazine: Detachable box, 5 rounds
Features: Fluted barrel; stainless steel action; stainless steel barrel; single stage trigger; single set trigger available
MSRP $3175.00

Sako

85 CARBON WOLF

Action: Bolt
Stock: Carbon fiber
Barrel: 24 in.
Sights: None
Weight: 7 lb. 4 oz.–7 lb. 11 oz.
Caliber: .308 Win., .30-06 Spfd., .300 Win. Mag., 7mm Rem. Mag., 6.5 Creedmoor
Magazine: 5, 6
Features: Carbon fiber stock with a RTM technology and a soft-touch coating; stock is adjustable for length of pull and cheek-piece height
MSRP $3600.00

85 CLASSIC

Action: Bolt
Stock: Walnut
Barrel: 22.4 in., 24.4 in.
Sights: Open
Weight: 7 lb.–7 lb. 12 oz.
Caliber: .308 Win., .25-06 Rem., .270 Win., .30-06 Spfd., .300 Win. Mag., .338 Win. Mag., .375 H&H, .270 WSM, .300 WSM, 7mm Rem. Mag.
Magazine: Detachable box, S/M 6 rounds, SM/L 5 rounds
Features: Comes in short actions Extra Short (XS), Short (S) and Short Magnum (SM), medium action (M), and long action (L); straight, classic walnut stock with rosewood forend tip and pistol grip cap; integral rails for scope mounts; free-floating barrel is cold-hammer-forged; adjustable single-stage trigger
MSRP . . . . $2275.00–$2325.00

85 FINNLIGHT

Action: Bolt
Stock: Synthetic
Barrel: 20.25, 22.4, 24.3 in.
Sights: None
Weight: 6 lb. 3 oz.–6 lb. 13 oz.
Caliber: (Short): .22-250 Rem., .243 Win., .260 Rem., .7mm-08 Rem., .308 Win.; (SM) .270 Win. Short Mag., .300 Win. Short Mag.; (Medium): .25-06 Rem., 6.5x55 Swedish, .270 Win., .30-06 Spfd.; (Long) 7mm Rem. Mag., .300 Win. Mag.
Magazine: Detachable box, S/M 6 rounds, SM/L 5 rounds
Features: Comes in short actions Short (S) and Short magnum (SM), Medium action (M), and Long action (L); single-stage trigger; two-way Sako safety locks both trigger and bolt handle; black synthetic stock with soft gray grip areas; pistol grip stock; integral rails for scope mounts; free-floating barrel is cold-hammer-forged of stainless steel
MSRP . . . . $1800.00–$1850.00

85 FINNLIGHT II

Action: Bolt
Stock: Fiberglass
Barrel: 20 in., 23 in., 24 in.
Sights: None
Weight: 6 lb. 3 oz.–6 lb. 13 oz.
Caliber: .22-250 Rem., .243 Win., .308 Win., .25-96 Rem., .270 Win., .30-06 Spfd., .260 Rem., .300 Win. Mag., .270 WSM, .300 WSM, 6.5x55 Swedish Mauser, 7mm-08 Rem., 7mm Rem. Mag., 6.5 Creedmoor
Magazine: 4, 5 rounds
Features: Fiberglass stock with RTM technology; fully adjustable cheekpiece; improved gripping surfaces; barrel finished in Cerakote
MSRP $2475.00

85 GREY WOLF

Action: Bolt
Stock: Laminated
Barrel: 23 in., 24 in.
Sights: None
Weight: 6 lb. 6 oz.–7 lb. 8 oz.
Caliber: .270 Win., .30-06 Spfd., .300 Win. Mag., .270 WSM, .300 WSM, 7mm Rem. Mag.
Magazine: 4, 5 rounds
Features: Gray matte-lacquered laminate stock; stainless hardware throughout; single stage trigger is standard, single set trigger optional; detachable magazine
MSRP . . . . $1725.00–$1775.00

85 KODIAK

Action: Bolt
Stock: Laminated hardwood
Barrel: 12.25 in.
Sights: Open
Weight: 7 lb. 15 oz.
Caliber: .375 H&H
Magazine: Detachable box, 5 rounds
Features: Adjustable single-stage trigger; barrel band for front swivel; integral dovetail rails for secure scope mounting; straight stock made of gray matte-lacquered laminated hardwood and reinforced with two cross-bolts; free-floating "bull" barrel
MSRP $1950.00

85 LONG RANGE

Action: Bolt
Stock: Wood
Barrel: 26 in.
Sights: None
Weight: 9 lb. 12 oz.
Caliber: .300 Win. Mag., .338 Lapua Mag.
Magazine: Detachable box, 4+1 rounds
Features: Flush design muzzle brake; designed for long range hunting
MSRP $2875.00

Sako

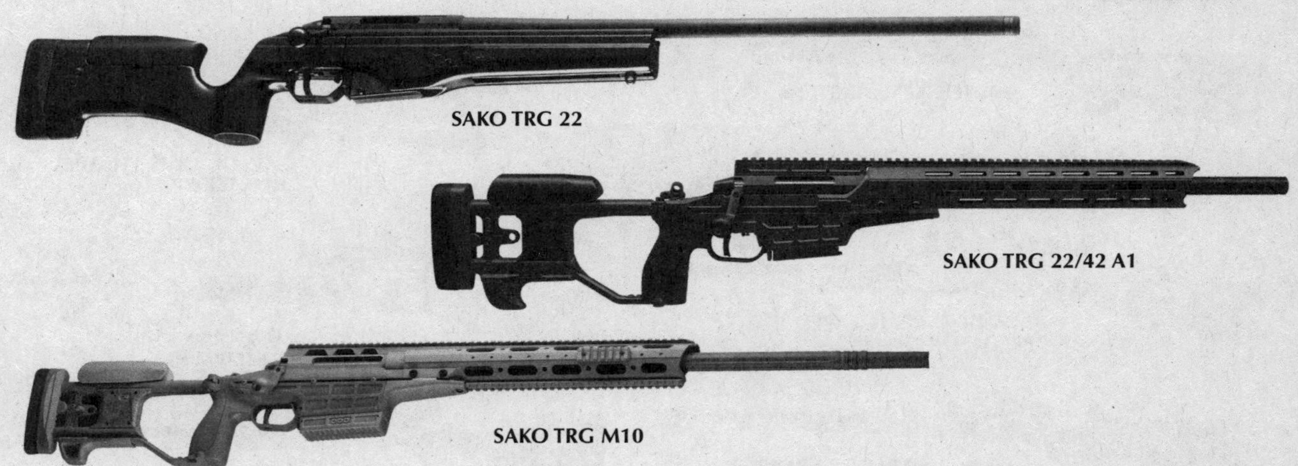
SAKO TRG 22

SAKO TRG 22/42 A1

SAKO TRG M10

TRG 22
Action: Bolt
Stock: Synthetic
Barrel: 20 in., 26 in., 27.1 in.
Sights: None
Weight: 10 lb. 4 oz.–10 lb. 12 oz.
Caliber: .308 Win., 6.5 Creedmoor
Magazine: Detachable box, 5, 7, 10 rounds
Features: Double-stage trigger; two-way Sako safety locks both trigger and bolt handle; base of stock is made of polyurethane with aluminum skeleton; adjustable cheekpiece and buttplate; Ambidextrous stock in green or desert tan color; includes integral dovetail on receiver and is drilled and tapped for Picatinny rail mounting
MSRP $3500.00

TRG 22/42 A1
Action: Bolt
Stock: Aluminum
Barrel: 26 in., 27 in.
Sights: None
Weight: 11 lb. 11 oz.–13 lb. 3 oz.
Caliber: .308 Win., .260 Rem., 6.5 Creedmoor, .300 Win. Mag., .338 Lapua
Magazine: 5, 7, 10 rounds
Features: Adjustable folding stock with two hinge points that eliminate wobble; M-LOK forend for accessory attachments; threaded muzzles; phosphatized steel parts; detachable magazine; muzzle brake and Picatinny or Weaver rail is standard on some models, optional on others
MSRP . . . . $6400.00–$7400.00

TRG M10
Action: Bolt
Stock: Synthetic
Barrel: 20–27 in.
Sights: None
Weight: 13 lb. 4 oz.–14 lb. 5 oz.
Caliber: .308 Win., .300 Win. Mag., .338 Lapua
Magazine: Detachable box, 8 or 11 rounds
Features: Threaded muzzle; muzzle break available; phosphatized steel parts; stainless steel barrel; double stage trigger; Picatinny or Weaver rail; fully adjustable rear stock; ambidextrous controls
MSRP $11,275.00

Savage Arms

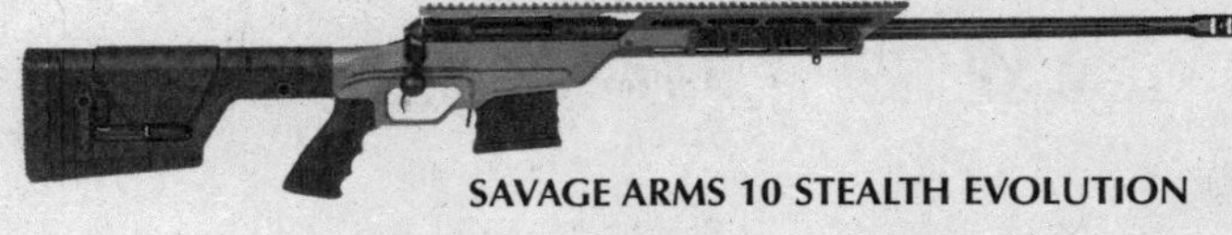
SAVAGE ARMS 10 STEALTH EVOLUTION

SAVAGE ARMS 10 GRS

10 GRS
Action: Bolt
Stock: Synthetic
Barrel: 26 in.
Sights: None
Weight: 9 lb. 8 oz.
Caliber: 6.5 Creedmoor, 6mm Creedmoor, .308 Win., 6.5 PRC
Magazine: 4 rounds
Features: Long-range bolt rifle with a GRS adjustable stock that's fiberglass reinforced synthetic; threaded muzzle; fluted heavy barrel; Savage's AccuTrigger
MSRP $1449.00

10 STEALTH EVOLUTION
Action: Bolt
Stock: Synthetic
Barrel: 20 in., 24 in., 26 in.
Sights: None
Weight: 10 lb. 12 oz.–11 lb. 2 oz.
Caliber: .223 Rem., 6mm Creedmoor, 6.5 Creedmoor, .308 Win.
Magazine: 10 rounds, 5 rounds magnum calibers
Features: Heavy fluted barrel; bronze Cerakote finish; Savage's zero-tolerance headspacing; AccuTrigger; 5R barrel rifling across six calibers all designed for long-range work; Magpul's PRS Gen3 adjustable buttstock allows for precise user fit; full-length top rail has room for optics, lights, other sights, and accessories
MSRP $1819.00

Savage Arms

RIFLES

12BTCSS

Action: Bolt
Stock: Laminate
Barrel: 26 in.
Sights: None
Weight: 10 lb.
Caliber: .204 Ruger, .223 Rem., .22-250 Rem.
Magazine: Detachable box, 4 rounds
Features: Drilled and tapped for scope mounts; stainless steel barrel with high luster finish; AccuTrigger; wood laminate with thumbhole and satin finish
MSRP $1369.00

110 APEX HUNTER XP

Action: Bolt
Stock: Synthetic
Barrel: 20 in., 22 in., 24 in.
Sights: Vortex Crossfire II 3–9X40mm scope
Weight: 7 lb. 11 oz.–8 lb. 2 oz.
Caliber: .223 Rem., .204 Ruger, .22–250 Rem., .243 Win., 6.5 Creedmoor, .260 Rem., .308 Win., .270 WSM, .300 WSM, .25–06 Rem., 6.5x284 Norma, .270 Win., .270 WSM, .30–06 Spfd., 7mm Rem. Mag., .300 Win. Mag., .338 Win. Mag., 7mm-08 Rem., .350 Legend, .450 Bushmaster, 6.5 PRC
Magazine: 3, 4 rounds
Features: With a caliber for every hunting pursuit except the most dangerous; adjustable AccuTrigger; detachable box magazine; matte black metalwork; stock with adjustable length of pull; left and right-hand configurations in black synthetic stock; right-hand stock in Muddy Girl camo in limited calibers
MSRP. . . . . $665.00–$759.00

110 APEX PREDATOR XP

Action: Bolt
Stock: Synthetic
Barrel: 20 in., 24 in.
Sights: Vortex Crossfire II 4–12X44mm scope
Weight: 8 lb. 7 oz.
Caliber: .223 Rem., .22–250 Rem., .204 Ruger, .243 Win., 6.5 Creedmoor, .308 Win.
Magazine: 3, 4 rounds
Features: A package rifle with a factory-mounted and bore-sighted Vortex scope; AccuTrigger; button-rifled heavy barrel; adjustable length of pull; matte blue metalwork; Mossy Oak camo coverage on stock; detachable box magazine
MSRP $785.00

110 APEX STORM XP

Action: Bolt
Stock: Synthetic
Barrel: 20 in., 22 in., 24 in.
Sights: Vortex Crossfire II 3–9X40mm scope
Weight: 7 lb. 11 oz.–8 lb. 2 oz.
Caliber: .223 Rem., .204 Ruger, .22–250 Rem., .243 Win., 6.5 Creedmoor, .260 Rem., .308 Win., .270 WSM, .25–06 Rem., 6.5x284 Norma, .270 Win., .270 WSM, .30–06 Spfd., 7mm Rem. Mag., .300 Win. Mag., .338 Win. Mag., 7mm-08 Rem., .350 Legend, 6.5 PRC
Magazine: 3, 4 rounds
Features: Similar to the 110 Apex Hunter XP, but with matte stainless metalwork
MSRP $769.00

110 BEAR HUNTER

Action: Bolt
Stock: Synthetic
Barrel: 23 in.
Sights: None
Weight: 8 lb. 6 oz.
Caliber: .300 Win. Mag., .300 WSM, .338 Federal, .338 Win. Mag., .375 Ruger
Magazine: 2 rounds
Features: AccuFit System Accustock; four ¼-in. length-of-pull spacers and five 1/8-in. comb risers, all easily swappable; stainless steel finish; hinged floorplate magazine; straight fluted barrel; stock in Mossy Oak Breakup Country.
MSRP . . . . $1099.00–$1055.00

110 CLASSIC

Action: Bolt
Stock: Walnut
Barrel: 22 in.
Sights: None
Weight: 8 lb.
Caliber: .243 Win., .270 Win., .30-06 Spfd., .300 Win. Mag., .308 Win., 6.5 Creedmoor, 7mm Rem. Mag., 7mm-08 Rem.
Magazine: 3, 4 rounds
Features: Classic indeed! Totally retro look from the grain and color of the hardwood stock to the funky slashed checkering, but you also get modern upgrades like an adjustable AccuTrigger
MSRP $1059.00

SAVAGE ARMS 110 ENGAGE HUNTER XP

SAVAGE ARMS 110 HIGH COUNTRY

SAVAGE ARMS 110 HOG HUNTER

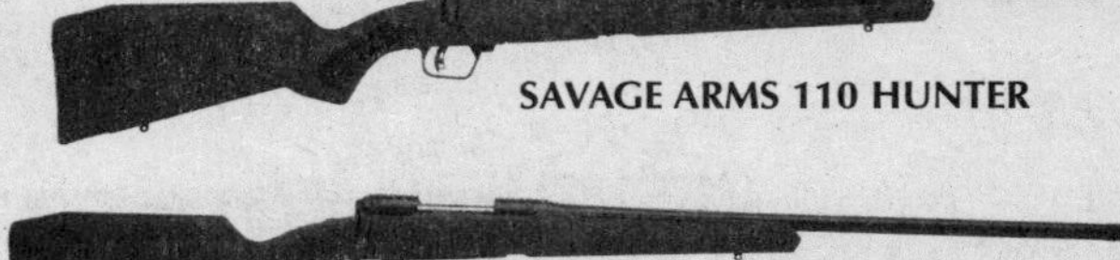

SAVAGE ARMS 110 HUNTER

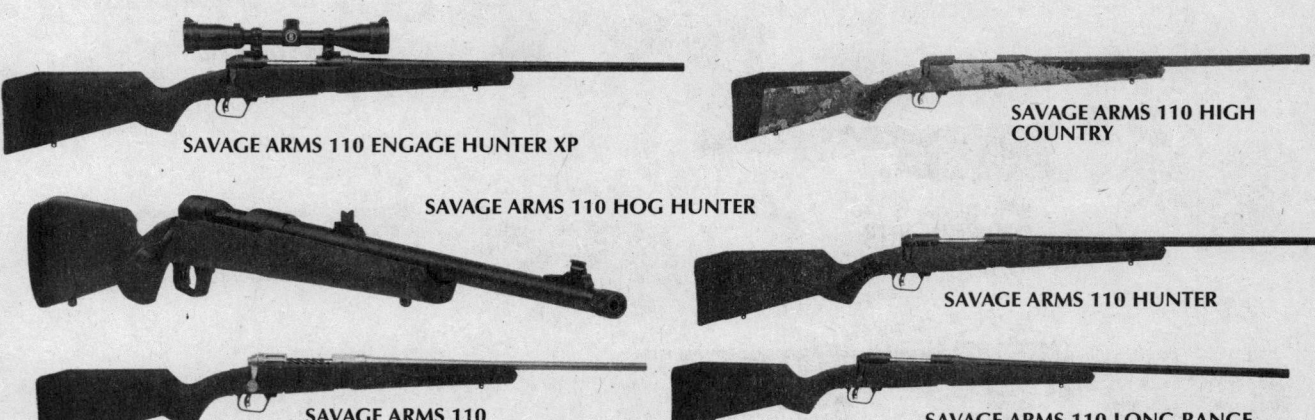

SAVAGE ARMS 110 LIGHTWEIGHT STORM WITH ADJUSTABLE LENGTH OF PULL

SAVAGE ARMS 110 LONG RANGE HUNTER

110 ENGAGE HUNTER XP

Action: Bolt
Stock: Synthetic
Barrel: 22 in.
Sights: None
Weight: 7 lb. 4 oz.
Caliber: .243 Win., 6.5 Creedmoor, 7mm-08 Rem., .308 Win., .260 Rem., .270 WSM, .300 WSM, .338 Win. Mag., .25-06 Rem., .270 Win., 6.5x284 Norma, .30-06 Spfd., 7mm Rem. Mag., .300 Win. Mag., .280 Ackley Improved, .350 Legend, .450 Bushmaster, 6.5 PRC
Magazine: 4 rounds
Features: Adjustable stock for length of pull; user-adjustable AccuTrigger; detachable box magazine; Weaver Grand Slam bases and rings; Bushnell Engage 3–9x40mm drop-compensating reticle scope mounted and bore sighted
MSRP . . . . $625.00–$725.00

110 HIGH COUNTRY

Action: Bolt
Stock: Synthetic
Barrel: 22 in., 24 in.
Sights: None
Weight: 8 lb. 1 oz.
Caliber: .243 Win., 6.5 Creedmoor, 6.5 PRC, .270 Win., .280 Ackley Improved, 7mm-08 Rem., 7mm Rem. Mag., .308 Win., .30–06 Spfd., .300 Win. Mag., .300 WSM
Magazine: 3, 4, 5 rounds
Features: One for the backcountry hunters featuring Accufit stock with overmold gripping surfaces and full-coverage TrueTimber Strata camo; PVD-coated stainless action; spiral-0fluted bolt and barrel in bronze; threaded barrel (magnum barrels include taplock-interface muzzle brake); detachable box magazine; AccuTrigger; Accufit adjustable stock
MSRP $1165.00

110 HOG HUNTER

Action: Bolt
Stock: Synthetic
Barrel: 20 in.
Sights: Adjustable iron
Weight: 7 lb. 4 oz.
Caliber: .223 Rem., .308 Win., .350 Legend
Magazine: 4 rounds
Features: A responsive gun for today's growing legions of wild boar hunters with a medium contour, threaded, carbon steel barrel; oversize bolt handle; olive drab stock; detachable box magazine; adjustable length of pull; AccuTrigger
MSRP $629.00

110 HUNTER

Action: Bolt
Stock: Synthetic
Barrel: 22 in., 24 in.
Sights: None
Weight: 7 lb. 2 oz.–7 lb. 5 oz.
Caliber: .204 Ruger, .22-250 Rem., .223 Rem., .243 Win., .25-06 Rem., .270 Win., .280 Ackley Imp., .30-06 Spfd., .300 Win Mag., .308 Win., 7mm Rem. Mag., 7mm-08 Rem., 6.5 Creedmoor
Magazine: 3, 4 rounds
Features: AccuFit System Accustock; four ¼-inch length-of-pull spacers and five 1/8-inch comb risers, all easily swappable; black matte finish; detachable box magazine
MSRP $795.00

110 LIGHTWEIGHT STORM WITH ADJUSTABLE LENGTH OF PULL

Action: Bolt
Stock: Synthetic
Barrel: 20 in.
Sights: None
Weight: 5 lb. 9 oz.–5 lb. 13 oz.
Caliber: .270 Win., .223 Win., 7mm-08 Rem., .308 Win., .243 Win., 6.5 Creedmoor
Magazine: 4 rounds
Features: Savage takes its popular Storm model and shaves off more than a pound with a light-contour barrel that gets spiral fluting. Other features include: detachable box magazine; AccuTrigger; adjustable length of pull; skeletonized receiver
MSRP $795.00

110 LONG RANGE HUNTER

Action: Bolt
Stock: Synthetic
Barrel: 26 in.
Sights: None
Weight: 8 lb.
Caliber: .280 Ackley Imp., .300 Win. Mag., .300 WSM, .308 Win., 6.5 Creedmoor, 6.5x284 Norma, 7mm Rem. Mag., .28 Nosler
Magazine: 3, 4 rounds
Features: AccuFit System Accustock; four ¼-inch length-of-pull spacers and five ⅛-inch comb risers, all easily swappable; black matte finish barrel; hinged floorplate magazine; muzzle brake
MSRP $1169.00

Savage Arms

SAVAGE ARMS 110 LONG RANGE HUNTER .338 LAPUA

SAVAGE ARMS 110 PRAIRIE HUNTER

SAVAGE ARMS 110 PREDATOR

SAVAGE ARMS 110 RIDGE WARRIOR

SAVAGE ARMS 110 STORM

SAVAGE ARMS 110 SCOUT

110 LONG RANGE HUNTER .338 LAPUA

Action: Bolt
Stock: Synthetic
Barrel: 26 in.
Sights: None
Weight: 8 lb. 14 oz.
Caliber: .338 Lapua
Magazine: 5 rounds
Features: AccuFit System Accustock; four ¼-inch length-of-pull spacers and five ⅛-inch comb risers, all easily swappable; black matte finish barrel; detachable box magazine; muzzle brake
MSRP $1379.00

110 PRAIRIE HUNTER

Action: Bolt
Stock: Synthetic
Barrel: 22 in.
Sights: None
Weight: 8 lb. 12 oz.
Caliber: .224 Valkyrie
Magazine: 3 rounds
Features: Features an adjustable AccuTrigger; threaded and capped carbon steel barrel; topside optics rail
MSRP $759.00

110 PREDATOR

Action: Bolt
Stock: Synthetic
Barrel: 22 in., 24 in.
Sights: None
Weight: 8 lb. 4 oz.–8 lb. 11 oz.
Caliber: .204 Ruger, .22-250 Rem., .223 Rem., .243 Win., .260 Rem., 6.5 Creedmoor, .308 Win.
Magazine: 4 rounds
Features: AccuFit System Accustock; four ¼-inch length-of-pull spacers and five ⅛-inch comb risers, all easily swappable; black matte finish barrel; detachable box magazine; stock in Realtree Max-1 camo stock; two-piece Weaver-style bases
MSRP $945.00

110 RIDGE WARRIOR

Action: Bolt
Stock: Synthetic
Barrel: 24 in.
Sights: None
Weight: 8 lb. 13 oz.
Caliber: 6.5 Creedmoor, .308 Win.
Magazine: 10 rounds
Features: AccuFit AccuStock and an adjustable AccuTrigger; Mossy Oak Overwatch camo on the stock; Gunsmoke gray receiver with PVD coating; fluted, threaded heavy barrel
MSRP $949.00

110 SCOUT

Action: Bolt
Stock: Synthetic
Barrel: 16.5 in.
Sights: Adjustable iron
Weight: 7 lb. 11 oz.
Caliber: .223 Rem., .308 Win., .450 Bushmaster
Magazine: 10 rounds
Features: AccuFit System Accustock; four ¼-inch length-of-pull spacers and five ⅛-inch comb risers, all easily swappable; black matte finish barrel; detachable Magpul AICS box magazine; Flat Dark Earth stock; adjustable iron sights; forward-mounted accessory/optic rail
MSRP $865.00

110 STORM

Action: Bolt
Stock: Synthetic
Barrel: 22 in., 24 in.
Sights: None
Weight: 7 lb. 2 oz.–7 lb. 5 oz.
Caliber: .22-250 Rem., .223 Rem., .243 Rem., .25-06 Rem., .270 Win., .270 WSM, .280 Ackley Imp., .30-06 Spfd., 300 Win. Mag., .300 WSM, .308 Win., 6.5 Creedmoor, 6.5x284 Norma, 7mm Rem., Mag., 7mm-08 Rem., .338 Win. Mag.
Magazine: 3, 4 rounds
Features: AccuFit System Accustock; four ¼-inch length-of-pull spacers and five 1/8-inch comb risers, all easily swappable; matte stainless steel barrel finish; detachable box magazine; left-hand versions available
MSRP . . . . $865.00–$900.00

Savage Arms

SAVAGE ARMS 110 TACTICAL

SAVAGE ARMS 110 TACTICAL DESERT

SAVAGE ARMS 110 TACTICAL LEFT-HAND

SAVAGE ARMS 110 VARMINT

SAVAGE ARMS A SERIES A17

SAVAGE ARMS A17 HM2

RIFLES

110 TACTICAL

Action: Bolt
Stock: Synthetic
Barrel: 20 in., 24 in.
Sights: None
Weight: 8 lb. 11 oz.–8 lb. 14 oz.
Caliber: .308 Win., .300 Win. Mag., 6.5 Creedmoor, 6.5 PRC, 6mm ARC
Magazine: 10 rounds
Features: AccuFit System Accustock; four ¼-inch length-of-pull spacers and five 1/8-inch comb risers, all easily swappable; matte black barrel finish; detachable box magazine; threaded heavy barrel with end cap; an oversized bolt; a 20 MOA EGW accessory/optic rail; left-hand available in .308 Win. and 6.5 Creedmoor
MSRP $830.00

110 TACTICAL DESERT

Action: Bolt
Stock: Synthetic
Barrel: 24 in., 26 in.
Sights: None
Weight: 8 lb. 14 oz.–9 lb.
Caliber: 6.5 Creedmoor, .300 Win. Mag., 6.5 PRC, 6mm Creedmoor
Magazine: 10 rounds
Features: AccuFit System Accustock; four-inch length-of-pull spacers and five 1/8-inch comb risers, all easily swappable; a matte black barrel finish; detachable box magazine; Flat Dark Earth stock; threaded heavy barrel with end cap; oversized bolt; 20 MOA EGW accessory/optic rail; left-hand available in 6.5 Creedmoor
MSRP $815.00

110 TACTICAL LEFT-HAND, 110 TACTICAL DESERT LEFT-HAND

Action: Bolt
Stock: Synthetic
Barrel: 24 in.
Sights: None
Weight: 8 lb. 13 oz.
Caliber: 6.5 Creedmoor
Magazine: 10 rounds
Features: A true tactical for lefties in a matte gray or a spiffy desert tan stock with detachable Magpul AICS magazine; adjustable AccuTrigger; oversize bolt knob; soft-grip surfaces; AccuFit stock; threaded heavy barrel
MSRP $815.00

110 VARMINT

Action: Bolt
Stock: Synthetic
Barrel: 26 in.
Sights: None
Weight: N/A
Caliber: .204 Ruger, .22-250 Rem., .223 Rem.,
Magazine: 4 rounds
Features: AccuFit System Accustock; four ¼-inch length-of-pull spacers and five 1/8-inch comb risers, all easily swappable; matte black barrel finish; detachable box magazine
MSRP $795.00

A SERIES A17

Action: Semiautomatic
Stock: Synthetic
Barrel: 22 in.
Sights: Drilled and tapped for scope mounts
Weight: 5 lb. 7 oz.
Caliber: .17 HMR
Magazine: Detachable rotary
Features: Carbon steel barrel; high luster barrel finish; Delayed Blowback Action, Hard Chromed Bolt with Dual Controlled Round Feed, Case Hardened Receiver, Button-Rifled Barrel
MSRP $505.00

A SERIES A17 HM2

Action: Semiautomatic
Stock: Synthetic
Barrel: 20 in.
Sights: None
Weight: 5 lb. 8 oz.
Caliber: .17 HMR
Magazine: 10 rounds
Features: This varmint-getter is easy on the wallet and has a sporter-profile carbon steel barrel, free-floating and with button rifling
MSRP $389.00

Savage Arms

SAVAGE ARMS A SERIES A17 OVERWATCH

SAVAGE ARMS A SERIES A17 TARGET SPORTER LAMINATE

SAVAGE ARMS A17 TARGET THUMBHOLE

SAVAGE ARMS A SERIES A22

SAVAGE ARMS A SERIES A22 FV-SR, FV-SR OVERWATCH

SAVAGE ARMS A SERIES A22 MAGNUM

RIFLES

A SERIES A17 OVERWATCH

Action: Semiautomatic
Stock: Synthetic
Barrel: 22 in.
Sights: None
Weight: 5 lb. 13 oz.
Caliber: .17 HMR
Magazine: 10 rounds
Features: Neat-looking .17 HMR rimfire semiautomatic dressed in Mossy Oak Overwatch camo; rotary magazine; adjustable AccuTrigger; carbon steel barrel in heavy profile
MSRP $559.00

A SERIES A17 TARGET SPORTER LAMINATE

Action: Semiautomatic
Stock: Wood laminate
Barrel: 22 in.
Sights: None
Weight: 6 lb. 15 oz.
Caliber: .17 HMR
Magazine: Detachable rotary, 10 rounds
Features: Delayed blowback action; hard chromed bolt with dual controlled round feed; case hardened receiver; button-rifled barrel
MSRP $605.00

A SERIES A17 TARGET THUMBHOLE

Action: Semiautomatic
Stock: Wood laminate
Barrel: 22 in.
Sights: None
Weight: 7 lb. 1 oz.
Caliber: .17 HMR
Magazine: Detachable rotary, 10 rounds
Features: Grey laminate thumbhole stock; delayed blowback action; hard chromed bolt with dual controlled round feed; case hardened receiver; button-rifled barrel
MSRP $669.00

A SERIES A22

Action: Semiautomatic
Stock: Synthetic
Barrel: 21 in.
Sights: Adjustable
Weight: 5 lb. 10 oz.
Caliber: .22 LR
Magazine: 10 rounds
Features: Modeled after the A17, but chambered for .22 LR; straight blowback action; steel billet receiver; user-adjustable AccuTrigger
MSRP $295.00

A SERIES A22 FV-SR, FV-SR OVERWATCH

Action: Semiautomatic
Stock: Synthetic
Barrel: 16.5 in.
Sights: None
Weight: 5 lb. 4 oz.
Caliber: .22 LR
Magazine: 10 rounds
Features: This rimfire wears a shorter, medium-contour button-rifled barrel of carbon steel; carbon steel receiver; rotary magazine; one-piece Picatinny rail topside; adjustable AccuTrigger
Black stock: $365.00
Camo stock: $399.00

A SERIES A22 MAGNUM

Action: Semiautomatic
Stock: Synthetic
Barrel: 21 in.
Sights: None
Weight: 5 lb. 9 oz.
Caliber: .22 WMR
Magazine: Detachable rotary, 10 rounds
Features: Delayed blowback action; hard chromed bolt with dual controlled round feed; case hardened receiver; button-rifled barrel
MSRP $505.00

Savage Arms

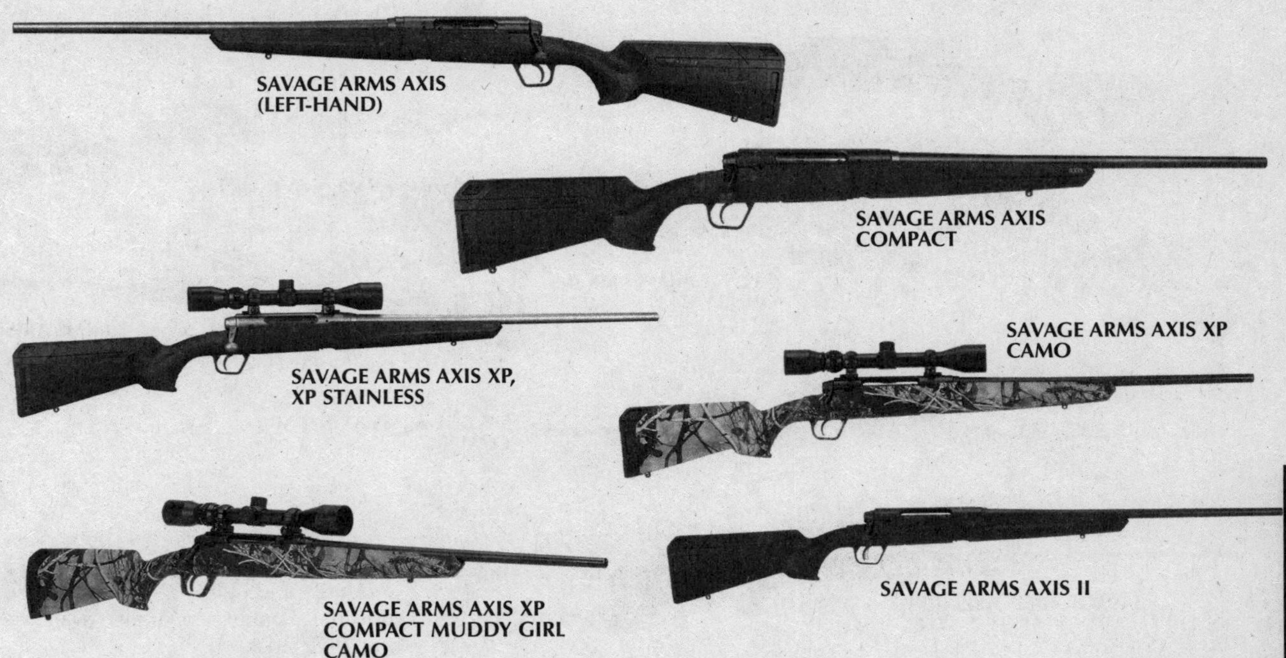

RIFLES

AXIS

Action: Bolt
Stock: Synthetic
Barrel: 18 in., 22 in.
Sights: None
Weight: 6 lb. 5 oz.
Caliber: .223 Rem., .22-250 Rem., .243 Win., .25-06 Rem., .270 Win., .308 Win., .30-06 Spfd., .350 Legend, 6.5 Creedmoor, 7mm-08 Rem.
Magazine: 4 rounds
Features: Budget-friendly, lightweight hunting rifle great for treestand use and featuring a detachable magazine; button-rifled carbon steel barrel
MSRP $389.00

AXIS COMPACT

Action: Bolt
Stock: Synthetic
Barrel: 20 in.
Sights: None
Weight: 6 lb. 4 oz.
Caliber: .223 Rem., .243 Win., 6.5 Creedmoor, 7mm-08 Rem.
Magazine: 4 rounds
Features: Identical to the Axis, but with a shorter 12.75-in. length of pull and shorter barrel; left-hand available in .243 Win. and 7mm -08 Rem. only
MSRP $389.00

AXIS XP, XP STAINLESS

Action: Bolt
Stock: Synthetic
Barrel: 22 in.
Sights: Weaver 3–9X40mm scope
Weight: 7 lb. 5 oz.
Caliber: .223 Rem., .22–250 Rem., .243 Win., .25–06 Rem., 6.5 Creedmoor, .270 Win., 7mm-08 Rem., .308 Win., .30–06 Spfd., .350 Legend
Magazine: 5 rounds
Features: A package rifles with a factory-mounted and boresighted Weaver scope; detachable box magazine; sporter-contour barrel
XP: $430.00
Stainless: $539.00

AXIS XP CAMO

Action: Bolt
Stock: Synthetic
Barrel: 22 in.
Sights: Weaver 3–9X40mm scope
Weight: 7 lb. 5 oz.
Caliber: .223 Rem., .22–250 Rem., .243 Win., .25–06 Rem., 6.5, .350 Legend
Magazine: 5 rounds
Features: The popular, no-frills, scope-packaged rifle available in Muddy Girl or Mossy Oak Break-Up Country full-coverage stocks; sporter barrel contour; carbon steel barreled action
MSRP $515.00

AXIS XP COMPACT

Action: Bolt
Stock: Synthetic
Barrel: 20 in.
Sights: None
Weight: 7 lb. 5 oz.
Caliber: 6.5 Creedmoor
Magazine: 4 rounds
Features: The popular 6.5 Creedmoor in an ergonomic stock with a 12.75-in. length of pull; factory mounted 3–9x40mm Weaver scope; carbon-steel barrel; detachable box magazine; stock available in black, camo, and Muddy Girl camo
Black stock: $430.00
Camo stock: $515.00

AXIS II

Action: Bolt
Stock: Synthetic
Barrel: 22 in.
Sights: None
Weight: 6 lb. 4 oz.
Caliber: .223 Rem., .22–250 Rem., .243 Win., .25–06 Rem., 6.5 Creedmoor, .270 Win., 7mm-08 Rem., .280 Ackley Improved, .308 Win., .30–06 Spfd., .350 Legend
Magazine: 5 rounds
Features: Improved ergonomics with a redesigned stock; adjustable AccuTrigger; four-round detachable box magazine; button-rifled sporter barrel
MSRP $449.00

Savage Arms

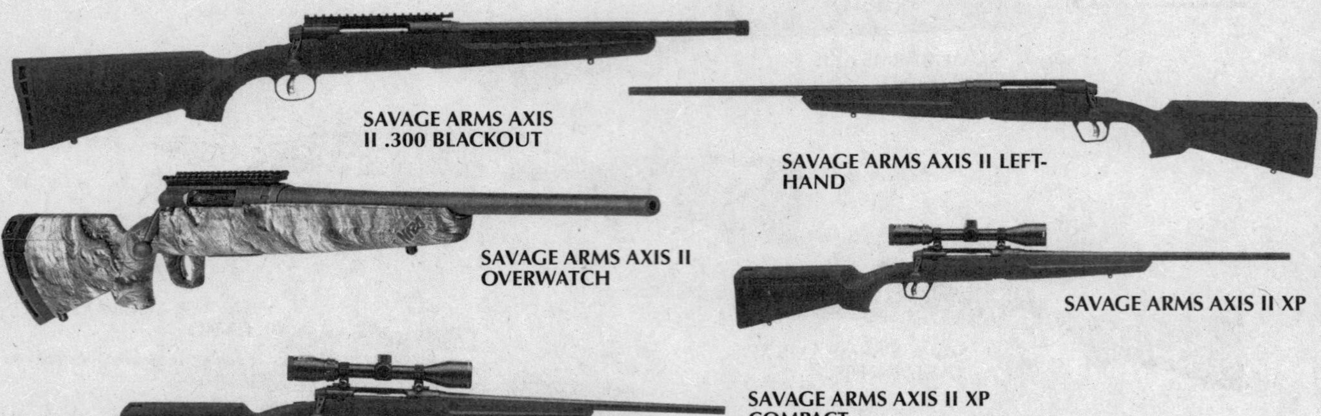

SAVAGE ARMS AXIS II .300 BLACKOUT

SAVAGE ARMS AXIS II LEFT-HAND

SAVAGE ARMS AXIS II OVERWATCH

SAVAGE ARMS AXIS II XP

SAVAGE ARMS AXIS II XP COMPACT

SAVAGE ARMS AXIS II XP STAINLESS STEEL

AXIS II .300 BLACKOUT

Action: Bolt
Stock: Synthetic
Barrel: 16.125 in.
Sights: None
Weight: 6 lb. 10 oz.
Caliber: .300 BLK
Magazine: 4 rounds
Features: This shorty rifle has a threaded carbon-steel barrel with a heavy profile; adjustable AccuTrigger; detachable box magazine; topside optics rail; ergonomic stock with textured grip areas
MSRP **$449.00**

AXIS II LEFT-HAND

Action: Bolt
Stock: Synthetic
Barrel: 22 in.
Sights: None
Weight: 6 lb. 5 oz.
Caliber: .223 Rem., .22-250 Rem., .243 Win., .25-06 Rem., .270 Win., .308 Win., .30-06 Spfd., 6.5 Creedmoor, 7mm-08 Rem.
Magazine: 4 rounds
Features: A great, budget-friendly choice for southpaws; adjustable AccuTrigger; detachable box magazine; button-rifled carbon steel barrel in a sporter contour; thread-in barrel headspacing
MSRP **$449.00**

AXIS II OVERWATCH

Action: Bolt
Stock: Synthetic
Barrel: 20 in.
Sights: None
Weight: 6 lb. 8 oz.
Caliber: .223 Rem., .22-250 Rem., .243 Win., .25-06 Rem., .270 Win., .280 Ackley Improved, .20-06 Spfd., .308 Win., 6.5 Creedmoor, 7mm-08 Rem.
Magazine: 4 rounds
Features: Stainless steel receiver and sporter-profile barrel in PVD-coated Gunsmoke gray; detachable box magazine; EGW one-piece optics rail; adjustable AccuTrigger; stock in Mossy Oak Overwatch camo
MSRP **$549.00**

AXIS II XP

Action: Bolt
Stock: Synthetic
Barrel: 22 in.
Sights: None
Weight: 6 lb. 8 oz.
Caliber: .22-250 Rem., .223 Rem., .243 Win., .25-06 Rem., .270 Win., .280 Ackley Improved, .30-06 Spfd., .308 Win., 6.5 Creedmoor, 7mm-08 Rem., .350 Legend
Magazine: 4 rounds
Features: Carbon steel, button-rifled barrel; user-adjustable AccuTrigger; detachable box magazine; factory-mounted and bore-sighted 3–9x40mm Bushnell Banner scope; also available in a FDE stock
MSRP **$499.00**

AXIS II XP COMPACT

Action: Bolt
Stock: Synthetic
Barrel: 20 in.
Sights: None
Weight: 6 lb. 3 oz.
Caliber: .243 Win., .350 Legend, 6.5 Creedmoor
Magazine: 4 rounds
Features: Shorter length of pull; carbon steel, button-rifled barrel; user-adjustable AccuTrigger; detachable box magazine; factory-mounted and bore-sighted 3–9x40mm Bushnell Banner scope
MSRP **$499.00**

AXIS II XP STAINLESS

Action: Bolt
Stock: Synthetic
Barrel: 22 in.
Sights: None
Weight: 6 lb. 8 oz.
Caliber: .223 Rem., .22-250 Rem., 6.5 Creedmoor, .243 Win., .25-06 Rem., .280 Ackley Improved, 7mm-08 Rem., .308 Win., .30-06 Spfd., .270 Win., .350 Legend
Magazine: 4 rounds
Features: Carbon steel, button-rifled barrel; user-adjustable AccuTrigger; detachable box magazine; factory-mounted and bore-sighted 3–9x40mm Bushnell Banner scope; stainless-finish barrel, receiver, and bolt
MSRP **$589.00**

Savage Arms

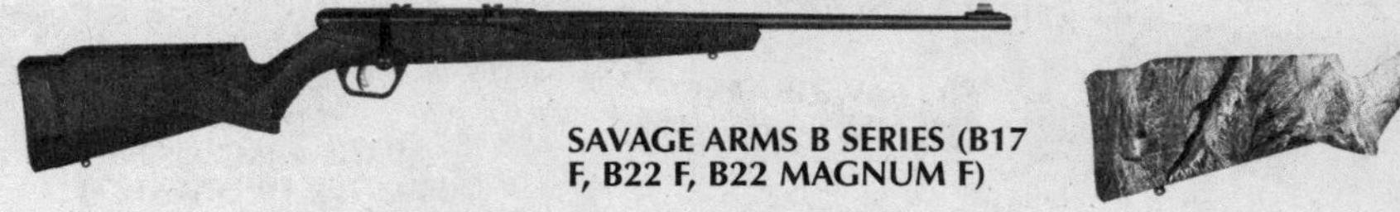
SAVAGE ARMS B SERIES (B17 F, B22 F, B22 MAGNUM F)

SAVAGE ARMS B SERIES B17 FV-SR OVERWATCH

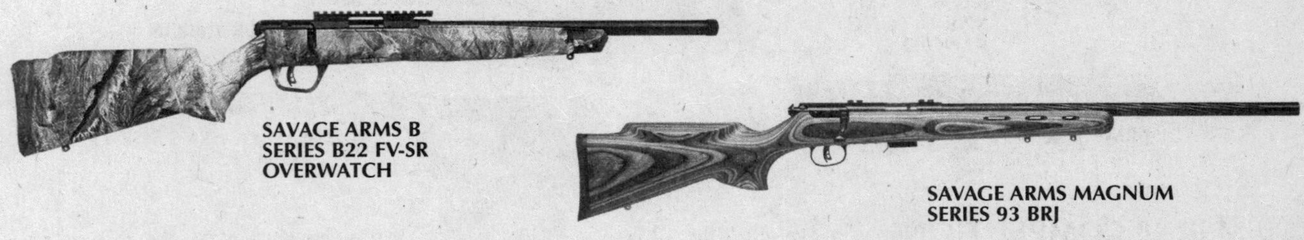
SAVAGE ARMS B SERIES B22 FV-SR OVERWATCH

SAVAGE ARMS MAGNUM SERIES 93 BRJ

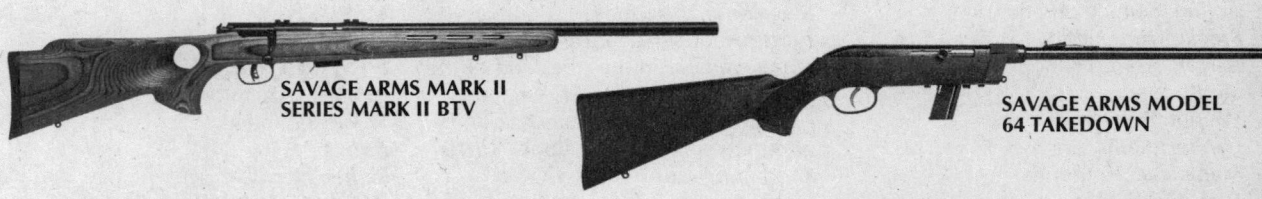

SAVAGE ARMS MARK II SERIES MARK II BTV

SAVAGE ARMS MODEL 64 TAKEDOWN

B SERIES

Action: Bolt
Stock: Synthetic
Barrel: 16.25 in., 21 in.
Sights: None
Weight: 5 lb. 8 oz.–6 lb.
Caliber: .17 HMR, .22 LR, .22 WMR
Magazine: 10 rounds
Features: In 2021, this series boasts nearly 30 models; three available calibers; wood and synthetic stocks; some left-hand models; G models get a raised cheekpiece and vertical pistol grip on a hardwood stock and a fore-end with grooves; compact models has 12.5-inch length of pull
MSRP . . . . $319.00–$619.00

B SERIES B17 FV-SR OVERWATCH

Action: Bolt
Stock: Synthetic
Barrel: 16.5 in.
Sights: None
Weight: 5 lb. 10 oz.
Caliber: .17 HMR
Magazine: 10 rounds
Features: Handy .17 HMR rimfire with a carbine-length threaded barrel of carbon steel in a heavy profile and with a target crown; rotary magazine; adjustable AccuTrigger; stock with raised comb and vertical target grip in Mossy Oak Overwatch camo; topside optics rail; sling swivel studs
MSRP $419.00

B SERIES B22 FV-SR OVERWATCH

Action: Bolt
Stock: Synthetic
Barrel: 16.5 in.
Sights: None
Weight: 5 lb. 10 oz.
Caliber: .22 LR
Magazine: 10 rounds
Features: A .22 LR with a carbine-length threaded barrel of carbon steel in a heavy profile and with a target crown; rotary magazine; adjustable AccuTrigger; stock with raised comb and vertical target grip in Mossy Oak Overwatch camo; topside optics rail; sling swivel studs
MSRP $369.00

MAGNUM SERIES 93 BRJ

Action: Bolt
Stock: Wood laminate
Barrel: 21 in.
Sights: None
Weight: 7 lb.
Caliber: .22 WMR
Magazine: Detachable box, 5 rounds
Features: Carbon steel barrel in blued satin finish; wood laminate stock; AccuTrigger
MSRP $575.00

MARK II SERIES MARK II BTV

Action: Bolt
Stock: Wood laminate
Barrel: 21 in.
Sights: None
Weight: 6 lb. 8 oz.
Caliber: .22 LR
Magazine: Detachable box, 5 rounds
Features: Carbon steel barrel with blued satin finish; wood laminate stock with thumbhole; AccuTrigger
MSRP $415.00

MODEL 64 TAKEDOWN

Action: Semiautomatic
Stock: Synthetic
Barrel: 16.5 in.
Sights: Front post, ladder-type leaf rear
Weight: 5 lb.
Caliber: .22 LR
Magazine: 10 rounds
Features: A portable, tear-apart rimfire that comes with an Uncle Mike's Bug-Out Bag; detachable box magazine; available left or right hand; drilled and tapped for scope mount; sling swivel studs
MSRP $249.00

Savage Arms

SAVAGE ARMS MSR 10 COMPETITION HD

SAVAGE ARMS MSR 10 HUNTER

SAVAGE ARMS MSR 10 HUNTER OVERWATCH CAMO

SAVAGE ARMS MSR 10 LONG RANGE

SAVAGE ARMS MSR 10 PRECISION

SAVAGE ARMS MSR 15 COMPETITION

SAVAGE ARMS MSR 15 LONG RANGE

MSR 10 COMPETITION HD

Action: Semiautomatic
Stock: Synthetic
Barrel: 18 in.
Sights: None
Weight: 9 lb.
Caliber: .308 Win.
Magazine: 20 rounds
Features: For the 3-Gunner shooting outside the .223 class, a souped up rig in .308 with features that include two-stage trigger; non-glare, free-floating rigid hand guard MLOK-ready; ambidextrous selector and mag release; tunable Savage muzzle brake; Hogue pistol grip; Magpul CTR buttstock; aluminum receiver with matte finish; custom-forged upper and lower; custom-length gas system; PROOF Research/Savage carbon-fiber wrapped stainless barrel
MSRP $3735.00

MSR 10 HUNTER

Action: Semiautomatic
Stock: Synthetic
Barrel: 16.125 in.
Sights: None
Weight: 7 lb. 13 oz.–8 lb.
Caliber: .308 Win., 6.5 Creedmoor
Magazine: 20 rounds
Features: Light, compact sporting platform with 5R rifled upgraded barrel; target chamber; BLACKHAWK! AR Blaze trigger; Melonite QPQ finish
MSRP $1615.00

MSR 10 HUNTER OVERWATCH

Action: Semiautomatic
Stock: Synthetic
Barrel: 16.125 in.
Sights: None
Weight: 7 lb. 13 oz.
Caliber: .308 Win., 6.5 Creedmoor
Magazine: 20 rounds
Features: Super deer rifle and maneuverable in the treestand or the blind; free-floating M-LOK handguard; Magpul MOE buttstock and grip; two-stage trigger; upper, lower, and handguard in Mossy Oak Overwatch camo
MSRP $1715.00

MSR 10 LONG RANGE

Action: Semiautomatic
Stock: Synthetic
Barrel: 20 in.
Sights: None
Weight: 9 lb. 12 oz.
Caliber: .308 Win., 6.5 Creedmoor, 6mm Creedmoor
Magazine: 10 rounds
Features: Long distance capabilities built on a compact frame; non-reciprocating side-charging handle; fluted heavy barrel; BLACKHAWK! two-stage target trigger; Magpul PRS adjustable stock; target chamber
MSRP $2490.00

MSR 10 PRECISION

Action: Semiautomatic
Stock: Synthetic
Barrel: 22.5 in.
Sights: None
Weight: 11 lb. 6 oz.
Caliber: .308 Win., 6.5 Creedmoor, 6mm Creedmoor
Magazine: 20 rounds
Features: An MSR for the long-range crowd with weight to steady the shot; stainless steel heavy barrel; direct-impingement functionality; adjustable gas block with lock nut; TangoDown Battlegrip Flip Grip; non-reciprocating side-charging upper; Arca 18-inch handguard
MSRP $2655.00

MSR 15 COMPETITION

Action: Semiautomatic
Stock: Synthetic
Barrel: 18 in.
Sights: None
Weight: 5 lb. 13 oz.–7 lb. 14 oz.
Caliber: .223 Rem., .224 Valkyrie
Magazine: 30 rounds
Features: This should be a top pick for 3-Gunners with features like non-glare, free-floating rigid hand guard MLOK-ready; ambidextrous selector and mag release; tunable Savage muzzle brake; Hogue pistol grip; Magpul CTR buttstock; aluminum receiver with matte finish; custom-forged upper and lower; custom-length gas system; PROOF Research/Savage carbon-fiber wrapped stainless barrel; flashy red highlights
MSRP $3115.00

MSR 15 LONG RANGE

Action: Semiautomatic
Stock: Synthetic
Barrel: 22 in.
Sights: None
Weight: 10 lb. 8 oz.
Caliber: .224 Valkyrie
Magazine: 11 rounds
Features: Savage adds weight and stability for the long range crowd. Features include two-port muzzle brake; Hogue pistol grip; free-floating MLOK-capable handguard; low-profile adjustable gas block; Magpul Gen 3 PRS adjustable stock; custom-forged upper and lower; custom length gas system; non-reciprocating side charging handle
MSRP $1859.00

MSR 15 PATROL

Action: Semiautomatic
Stock: Synthetic
Barrel: 16.125 in.
Sights: Custom gas block front, BLACKHAWK! flip-up rear
Weight: 6 lb. 8 oz.
Caliber: .223 Rem.
Magazine: 30 rounds
Features: BLACKHAWK! pistol grip, forend, and buttstock; .223 Wylde target chamber; 5R rifling
MSRP $910.00

MSR 15 RECON 2.0

Action: Semiautomatic
Stock: Synthetic
Barrel: 16.125 in.
Sights: None
Weight: 7 lb. 5 oz.
Caliber: .223 Rem.
Magazine: 30 rounds
Features: Compact MSR with a nickel-boron-coated trigger; custom-forged lower; Melonite QPQ finish; Magpul buttstock and pistol grip; lots of rail for optics and accessories
MSRP $1085.00

MSR 15 RECON 2.0 OVERWATCH

Action: Semiautomatic
Stock: Synthetic
Barrel: 16.125 in.
Sights: None
Weight: 7 lb. 5 oz.
Caliber: .223 Rem.
Magazine: 30 rounds
Features: Compact MSR with forward assist; custom-forged lower; Magpul MOE pistol grip and buttstock; Savage gas block nut and straight gas tube; flatwire recoil spring; upper, lower, and handgun in Mossy Oak Overwatch camo
MSRP $1179.00

MSR 15 RECON LRP

Action: Semiautomatic
Stock: Synthetic
Barrel: 18 in.
Sights: None
Weight: 7 lb. 14 oz.
Caliber: .22 Nosler, .224 Valkyrie, 6.8 SPC
Magazine: 25 rounds
Features: Fast-handling MSR with an adjustable gas block; two-stage trigger; Melonite QPQ finish; Magpul CTR stock; tunable muzzle brake
MSRP $1355.00

MSR 15 VALKYRIE

Action: Semiautomatic
Stock: Aluminum
Barrel: 18 in.
Sights: None
Weight: 7 lb. 12 oz.
Caliber: .224 Valkyrie
Magazine: 30 rounds
Features: Aluminum UBR Gen 2 buttstock; Hogue pistol grip; two-stage trigger; adjustable gas block with mid-length system; muzzle brake with a Class 3 thread; Elite Series Cerakote on the upper and lower
MSRP $1625.00

RASCAL FV-SR

Action: Bolt
Stock: Synthetic
Barrel: 16.125 in.
Sights: None
Weight: 2 lb. 11 oz.
Caliber: .22 LR
Magazine: 1 round
Features: A bolt-cocking single-shot for youths, but one with "big gun" features like a heavy barrel with threaded muzzle and AccuTrigger; pink or black synthetic stock; left- or right-handed
MSRP $230.00

RASCAL SYNTHETIC LEFT-HAND

Action: Bolt
Stock: Synthetic
Barrel: 16.125 in.
Sights: Peep sights
Weight: 2 lb. 11 oz.
Caliber: .22 LR
Magazine: 1 round
Features: The popular youth rifle in a lightweight synthetic stock for left-handers; available in black or pink
MSRP $195.00

Savage Arms

RIFLES

RASCAL TARGET

Action: Bolt
Stock: Hardwood
Barrel: 16.125 in.
Sights: None
Weight: 4 lb. 8 oz.
Caliber: .22 LR
Magazine: 1 round
Features: A wood-stocked Rascal for the youth shooter ready to improve on the basics, with a rifle two pounds heavier than its synthetic-stocked cousins; a threaded barrel; and top-side Picatinny rail for optics mounting.
MSRP $330.00

RASCAL TARGET XP

Action: Bolt
Stock: Hardwood
Barrel: 16.125 in.
Sights: 4X32mm scope
Weight: 5 lb. 14 oz.
Caliber: .22 LR
Magazine: 1 round
Features: For the youth shooter getting serious about improving skills and target acquisition with a single-shot .22 LR that includes a factory-installed and sighted 4X32mm scope; heavy barrel; threaded muzzle; AccuTrigger; bipod; swivel mounts; left-hand available
MSRP $420.00

SPECIALTY SERIES MODEL 42 TAKEDOWN, COMPACT

Action: Over/under
Stock: Synthetic
Barrel: 20 in.
Sights: Adjustable
Weight: 6 lb.
Caliber: .22 LR/.410-bore, .22 WMR/.410-bore
Magazine: 2 rounds
Features: Carbon steel barrel; matte barrel finish; break-open combination gun, .22 LR over .410
MSRP $529.00

TARGET SERIES 12 BENCHREST

Action: Bolt, single shot
Stock: Wood laminate
Barrel: 29 in.
Sights: None
Weight: 12 lb. 12 oz.
Caliber: .308 Win., 6 Norma BR
Magazine: None
Features: Drilled and tapped for scope mounts; stainless steel barrel with high luster finish; wood laminate stock with satin finish; AccuTrigger
MSRP $1775.00

TARGET SERIES 112 MAGNUM TARGET

Action: Bolt
Stock: Wood laminate
Barrel: 26 in.
Sights: None
Weight: 12 lb.
Caliber: .338 Lapua Mag.
Magazine: Single shot
Features: Carbon steel barrel; matte barrel finish
MSRP $1039.00

Savage Arms

SAVAGE ARMS VARMINT SERIES 25 LIGHTWEIGHT VARMINTER

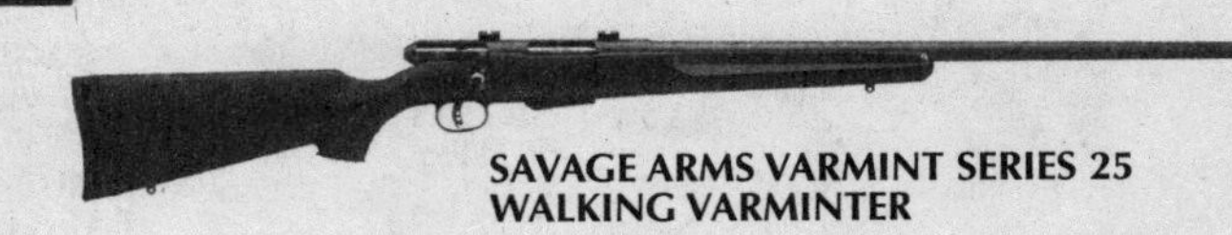

SAVAGE ARMS VARMINT SERIES 25 WALKING VARMINTER

VARMINT SERIES 25 LIGHTWEIGHT VARMINTER

Action: Bolt
Stock: Wood laminate
Barrel: 24 in.
Sights: None
Weight: 8 lb. 4 oz.
Caliber: .17 Hornet, .204 Ruger, .22 Hornet, .223 Rem.
Magazine: Detachable box, 4 rounds
Features: Drilled and tapped for scope mounts; carbon steel barrel with blued satin finish; wood laminate stock with satin finish
MSRP $819.00

VARMINT SERIES 25 WALKING VARMINTER

Action: Bolt
Stock: Synthetic
Barrel: 22 in.
Sights: None
Weight: 6 lb. 14 oz.
Caliber: .17 Hornet, .204 Ruger, .22 Hornet, .222 Rem., .223 Rem.
Magazine: Detachable box, 4 rounds
Features: Matte black synthetic stock; matte black carbon steel barrel; AccuTrigger; camo version has stock in Realtree Max-1
Black stock: $659.00
Camo stock: $715.00

RIFLES

Sero International

SERO INTERNATIONAL GM6 LYNX

GM6 LYNX

Action: Semiautomatic
Stock: N/A
Barrel: 28.7 in.
Sights: None
Weight: 25 lb. 6 oz.
Caliber: .50 BMG
Magazine: 5 rounds
Features: Hungarian-made .50 BMG bullpup; "unique barrel recoil technology" knocks the punch down to half of any other comparable rifle; a match-grade Lothar Walther barrel; long-recoil action; an effective range of 1500 meters
MSRP $14,750.00

Shaw Barrels Custom Rifles

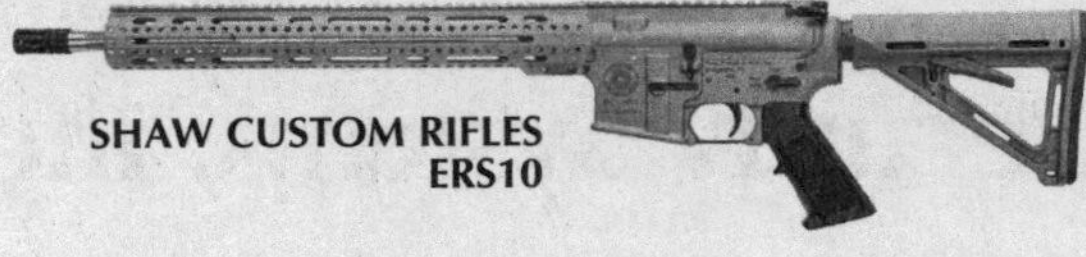

SHAW CUSTOM RIFLES ERS10

SHAW CUSTOM RIFLES MARK X

ERS10

Action: Semiautomatic
Stock: Synthetic
Barrel: 16 in., 18 in., 20 in. (ERS15), 20 in. (ERS10)
Sights: None
Weight: Varies
Caliber: 5.56 NATO, .308, .300 Blackout (ERS15).308, 6.5 Creedmoor (ERS10)
Magazine: N/A
Features: Barrels have continuous twist fluted profiles and can be matte or polished finish; the handguard is either a Magpul MOE or a T-Mod rail heat shield; 7075-T6 forged aluminum upper/lowers; uppers with an M4 feed ramp and finished in black anodized, dry film lube, or Cerakote; lowers in anodized black or Cerakote; button-rifled barrel with an H-bar profile, one-piece hard anodized T-Mod heat shield
MSRP . . . . starting at $1200.00

MARK X

Action: Bolt
Stock: Walnut
Barrel: Varies
Sights: None
Weight: Varies
Caliber: Customer choice
Magazine: Varies
Features: Customizable in thousands of combinations; choice of two barrel profiles; more than 80 caliber choices; Grade 5 walnut stocks; integral scope mount bases machined into the receiver; hybrid push/controlled-round feeding; Savage's AccuTrigger; numerous upgrades offered
MSRP . . . . starting at $1400.00

SIG Sauer

SIG SAUER CROSS RIFLE

SIG SAUER MCX RATTLER SBR

SIG SAUER MCX VIRTUS PATROL

SIG SAUER SIGM400 TREAD 16-INCH

SIG SAUER MPX PCC

CROSS RIFLE

Action: Bolt
Stock: Synthetic
Barrel: 16 in., 18 in.
Sights: None
Weight: 6 lb. 8 oz.–6 lb. 13 oz.
Caliber: .277 Fury, .308 Win., 6.5 Creedmoor
Magazine: 5 rounds
Features: SIG's own fully adjustable folding Precision Stock; a one-piece receiver of aluminum ; M-LOK rail; AICS mags; alloy forend; threaded stainless steel barrel
MSRP . . . . $1649.99–$1879.99

MCX RATTLER SBR

Action: Semiautomatic
Stock: Aluminum
Barrel: 5.5 in.
Sights: None
Weight: 5 lb. 11 oz.
Caliber: .300 Blackout
Magazine: 30 rounds
Features: Takes AR mags; PDW upper and Ultra Thin Folding Aluminum Stock; M-LOK handguard is free-floating; action is gas piston
MSRP $2749.99

MCX VIRTUS PATROL

Action: Semiautomatic
Stock: Synthetic
Barrel: 16 in.
Sights: None
Weight: 7 lb. 15 oz.
Caliber: 5.56 NATO, .300 BLK
Magazine: 30 rounds
Features: An AR platform designed for patrol use and featuring user-changeable barrels; free-floating M-LOK handguard in four lengths; ambidextrous controls; adjustable folding stock; available in Stealth Grey or Flat Dark Earth
MSRP $2199.00

MPX PCC

Action: Semiautomatic
Stock: Synthetic
Barrel: 16 in.
Sights: None
Weight: 6 lb. 9 oz.
Caliber: 9mm
Magazine: 30 rounds
Features: Jumping into the trendy pistol-caliber carbine game with an AR platform featuring a gas piston operating system; free-floating M-LOK handguard; folding, telescoping stock; three-chamber compensator; MPX magazine; 1:10 twist barrel; Timney single-stage MPX trigger
MSRP $2099.99

SIGM400 TREAD 16-INCH

Action: Semiautomatic
Stock: Synthetic
Barrel: 16 in.
Sights: None
Weight: 7 lb.
Caliber: 5.56 NATO
Magazine: 30 rounds
Features: An AR for on-the-go, featuring: reduced weigh MLOK handguard; direct impingement mid-length gas system functionality; aluminum frame; ambidextrous controls; single-stage trigger; Magpul SL-K6 telescoping buttstock
MSRP . . . . $949.99–$1129.99

Silver Shadow Advanced Security Systems, Inc.

SILVER SHADOW GILBOA DBR SNAKE

SILVER SHADOW GILBOA M43 CARBINE

GILBOA DBR SNAKE

Action: Semiautomatic
Stock: Synthetic
Barrel: 11.5 in.
Sights: Flip-up
Weight: 10 lb. 13 oz.
Caliber: 5.56 NATO
Magazine: 40 rounds
Features: Double the fun with a two-barrel, two-magazine, two-trigger gas impingement semiauto that fires two shots at the same time; made in Israel
MSRP $2319.00

GILBOA M43 CARBINE

Action: Semiautomatic
Stock: Synthetic
Barrel: 16 in.
Sights: Flip-up
Weight: 6 lb. 7 oz.
Caliber: 7.62X39mm NATO
Magazine: 30 rounds
Features: Lightweight, Israeli-made; gas impingement system; hard anodized billet aircraft aluminum alloy upper and lower; ample rail; accepts standard AK-47 magazines; free-floating key-mod handguard; Gilboa compensator
MSRP $1599.00

SMITH & WESSON M&P10 6.5 CREEDMOOR

SMITH & WESSON M&P10 SPORT OPTICS READY

SMITH & WESSON M&P15

SMITH & WESSON M&P15 COMPETITION

M&P10 6.5 CREEDMOOR

Action: Semiautomatic
Stock: Synthetic
Barrel: 20 in.
Sights: None
Weight: 9 lb.
Caliber: 6.5 Creedmoor
Magazine: 10 rounds
Features: MSR flattop platform; threaded muzzle with thread protector; two-stage match trigger; 15-in. free-floating Troy Alpha M-LOK handguard; 2-in. aluminum M-LOK accessory rail; Magpul MOE stock; gas-operated
MSRP $2055.00

M&P10 SPORT OPTICS READY

Action: Semiautomatic
Stock: Synthetic
Barrel: 16. in.
Sights: None
Weight: 8 lb.
Caliber: .308 Win.
Magazine: 20 rounds
Features: Mid-length gas system; ambidextrous safety; bolt and magazine releases; mid-length handguard; A2 suppressor; chromed firing pin; six-position telescoping stock; gas block with Picatinny rail; barrel is finished inside and out with Armornite
MSRP . . . . $1089.00–$1639.00

M&P15

Action: Semiautomatic
Stock: Synthetic
Barrel: 16 in.
Sights: Troy adjustable front post, folding rear battle sight
Weight: 6 lb. 12 oz.
Caliber: 5.56 NATO, .223 Rem.
Magazine: Detachable box, 30 rounds
Features: Six-position telescopic black stock; chrome-lined gas key and bolt carrier; flash suppressor compensator; two-position safety lever
MSRP $1189.00

M&P15 COMPETITION

Action: Semiautomatic
Stock: Synthetic
Barrel: 18 in.
Sights: None
Weight: 7 lb. 6 oz.
Caliber: 5.56 NATO
Magazine: 30 rounds
Features: Performance Center muzzle brake; two-stage match trigger; 15-in. free-floating Troy Alpha M-LOK handguard; 2-in. aluminum M-Lok rail; VLTOR I-Mod stock; Hogue pistol grip; aluminum frame; gas-operated
MSRP $1599.00

Smith & Wesson

SMITH & WESSON M&P15 SPORT II

SMITH & WESSON M&P15-22 SPORT, SPORT M-LOK

SMITH & WESSON M&P15-22 SPORT ROBIN'S EGG BLUE PLATINUM FINISH

SMITH & WESSON PERFORMANCE CENTER T/C LRR

M&P15 SPORT II

Action: Semiautomatic
Stock: Synthetic
Barrel: 16 in.
Sights: Adjustable front, Magpul MBUS rear
Weight: 6 lb. 7 oz.
Caliber: 5.56 NATO
Magazine: 10, 30 rounds
Features: Forged, integral trigger guard; Armornite finish (durable corrosion-resistant finish); chromed firing pin; forward assist; dust cover; available in Colorado- and California-compliant versions, MOE M-LOK, and as Optics Ready variant with or without M-LOK handguard
MSRP . . . . $772.00–$814.00

M&P15-22 SPORT

Stock: Synthetic
Barrel: 16.5 in.
Sights: Folding Magpul MBUS front and rear
Weight: 4 lb. 12 oz.
Caliber: .22 LR
Capacity: 10, 25 rounds
Features: Updated version of the original M&P 15-22, with a slightly shorter barrel; six-position collapsible stock, 10-in. slim handguard, M-LOK compatible, functioning charging handle, shell deflector, two-position receiver-mounted safety, and Armonite barrel finish are standard; available in black, Kryptek, and Muddy Girl finishes; California-compliant version available in black only
MSRP . . . . $461.00–$521.00

M&P15-22 SPORT ROBIN'S EGG BLUE PLATINUM FINISH

Action: Semiautomatic
Stock: Synthetic
Barrel: 16.5 in.
Sights: MBUS folding front and rear
Weight: 5 lb.
Caliber: .22 LR
Magazine: 25 rounds
Features: carbon steel barrel; folding sights; six-position CAR stock; 2-in. M-LOK rail panel; M&P handguard with Magpul's M-LOKTM
MSRP $521.00

PERFORMANCE CENTER T/C LRR, T/C LRR SCOPED

Action: Bolt
Stock: Synthetic
Barrel: 20 in.
Sights: None
Weight: 11 lb.
Caliber: .308 Win., 6.5 Creedmoor, .243 Win.
Magazine: 10 rounds
Features: LRR is Long Range Rifle, loaded with features such as adjustable stock and cheekpiece; numerous Magpul M-LOK cuts; 20 MOA of rail; adjustable Performance Center trigger; Caldwell bipod; threaded barrel; muzzle brake; aluminum chassis; available in black or Flat Dark Earth; scoped models have Vortex Diamondback 4–12X40mm; carrying bag included
Rifle only: $1231.00
Scoped package: $1523.00

Springfield Armory

RIFLES

M1A LOADED

Action: Semiautomatic
Stock: Synthetic
Barrel: 22 in.
Sights: Adjustable
Weight: 11 lb. 4 oz.
Caliber: 7.62 NATO, 6.5 Creedmoor
Magazine: 10 rounds
Features: 1:11 inch barrel twist; match grade aperture with ½ MOA adjustment for windage and 1 MOA for elevation; FDE precision adjustable stock
MSRP . . . . $1884.00–$2088.00

M1A NATIONAL MATCH

Action: Semiautomatic
Stock: Walnut
Barrel: 22 in.
Sights: National Match front military post sight; rear National Match hooded aperture
Weight: 9 lb. 13 oz.
Caliber: 7.62 NATO, .308 Win.
Magazine: Detachable box, 10 rounds
Features: Glass bedded; NM gas cylinder; NM recoil spring guide; NM flash suppressor; walnut stock; stainless steel or carbon barrel; two-stage military trigger
MSRP . . . . $2485.00–$2542.00

M1A SCOUT SQUAD

Action: Semiautomatic
Stock: Walnut, composite
Barrel: 18 in.
Sights: National Match front military post sight; rear military aperture
Weight: 9 lb. 5 oz.
Caliber: 7.62 NATO, .308 Win.
Magazine: Detachable box, 10 rounds
Features: Mounted optical sight base; muzzle stabilizers; black or green fiberglass composite, American walnut stock or Mossy Oak camo stock; two-stage military trigger
MSRP . . . . $1886.00–$2026.00

M1A SOCOM 16

Action: Semiautomatic
Stock: Composite
Barrel: 16.25 in.
Sights: Tritium front sight
Weight: 8 lb. 13 oz.
Caliber: 7.62 NATO, .308 Win
Magazine: Detachable box, 10 rounds
Features: Muzzlebrake; forward mounted scope base; two-stage military trigger; composite black or green stock
MSRP $2026.00

M1A SOCOM 16 CQB

Action: Semiautomatic
Stock: Synthetic
Barrel: 16.25 in.
Sights: XS Post with tritium insert front, adjustable rear
Weight: 9 lb. 3 oz.
Caliber: .308 Win., 7.62x51mm NATO
Magazine: 10 or 20 rounds
Features: Adjustable buttstock; five-position length and two-position adjustable cheek piece; standard AR-type commercial buffer tube; AK-style pistol grip; accepts any standard AK-style replacement; M-Lok compatible system; fixed top rail
Standard: $2188.00
With Vortex Venom Red-Dot: $2470.00

M1A STANDARD ISSUE

Action: Semiautomatic
Stock: Composite or walnut
Barrel: 22 in.
Sights: National Match military front post, adjustable rear aperture sight
Weight: 9 lb. 5 oz.
Caliber: 7.62 NATO, .308 Win.
Magazine: Detachable box, 10 rounds
Features: Stocks available in Highlander camo, solid Flat Dark Earth, walnut, or black composite; parkerized carbon steel barrels; two-stage military trigger
MSRP . . . . $1720.00–$1823.00

M1A TANKER

Action: Semiautomatic
Stock: Walnut
Barrel: 16.25 in.
Sights: XS post with tritium insert front, ghost ring rear
Weight: 8 lb. 12 oz.
Caliber: .308 Win.
Magazine: 10 rounds
Features: A throwback to WWII's Tanker Garands, with a carbine-length barrel; Parkerized metalwork; detachable magazine; carbon steel barrel
MSRP $2026.00

Springfield Armory

SPRINGFIELD ARMORY SAINT EDGE

SPRINGFIELD ARMORY SAINT VICTOR

SPRINGFIELD ARMORY SAINT M-LOK

SPRINGFIELD ARMORY SAINT VICTOR SBR

SAINT EDGE

Action: Semiautomatic
Stock: Synthetic
Barrel: 16 in.
Sights: Flip-up front and rear
Weight: 6 lb. 3 oz.
Caliber: 5.56 NATO
Magazine: 30 rounds
Features: Mid-length multi-mode adjustable gas block; Bravo Company M3 pistol grip; Mod 0 SOPMOD buttstock; Springfield mid-size charging handle; free-floating full-length aluminum handguard; Tungsten Carbine H heavy buffer; flip-up sights are Springfield Armory's low-profile, dual-aperture rear; Springfield multiport muzzle brake
MSRP $1350.00

SAINT M-LOK

Action: Semiautomatic
Stock: Synthetic
Barrel: 16 in.
Sights: Standard post front, Springfield Armory low profile flip-up dual aperture rear
Weight: 6 lb. 11 oz.
Caliber: 5.56 NATO
Magazine: 30 rounds
Features: Type III aircraft-grade 7075 T6 aluminum upper and lower receivers are joined using the Accu-Tite system; 16-inch chrome moly vanadium barrel treated with Melonite; 1:8-inch twist; mid-length gas system paired with a heavier carbine "H" heavy tungsten buffer; Bravo Company Mod 0 pistol grip and Bravo Company buttstock; QD and fixed sling swivels; Bravo PKMT two-piece handguard; aluminum heat shields; black or Flat Dark Earth; California-compliant in black only
MSRP $995.00

SAINT VICTOR

Action: Semiautomatic
Stock: Synthetic
Barrel: 16 in.
Sights: Flip-up
Weight: 6 lb. 9 oz.
Caliber: 5.56 NATO, .308 Win., .350 Legend
Magazine: 30 rounds
Features: Game-ready AR-platform with direct impingement mid-length gas system; Bravo Company six-position buttstock and Mod.3 grip; carbine H heavy tungsten buffer; forged Type III aluminum upper, Accu-Tite lower, both hard anodized; GI-type charging handle; 15-inch M-LOK handguard; spring-loaded flip-up sights; soft rifle case
MSRP . . . . $1125.00–$1452.00

SAINT VICTOR SBR

Action: Semiautomatic
Stock: Synthetic
Barrel: 11.5 in.
Sights: None
Weight: 5 lb. 9 oz.
Caliber: 5.56 NATO
Magazine: 30 rounds
Features: A loaded SBR with features that include a forged lower with Accu-Tite tension system; ambidextrous safety; Type III hard coat anodized upper and lower; low-profile, adjustable carbine-length gas block; forward assist; Bravo Company Gunfighter buttstock; Carbine "H" heavy tungsten buffer; Melonite finish on barrel and bolt-carrier group; nickel-boron coated GI-style trigger; Magpul PMAG; full-length, free-floating handguard M-LOK compatible
MSRP $1125.00

Stag Arms

STAG ARMS MODEL 3GUN ELITE

MODEL 3GUN ELITE

Action: Semiautomatic
Stock: Synthetic
Barrel: 18 in.
Sights: None
Weight: N/A
Caliber: 5.56 NATO, .223 Rem.
Features: A2 flash hider; Picatinny rail; Magpul ACS buttstock; aluminum enhanced trigger guard; manganese phosphate-coated chrome-lined bolt carrier group; Stag 3G compensator; Geissele Super 3-Gun trigger; New York-, New Jersey-, California, and 10-round-compliant models available in left and right hand
Firearm: . . . . $1599.99–$1649.99
Kit: $1299.99

Steyr Arms

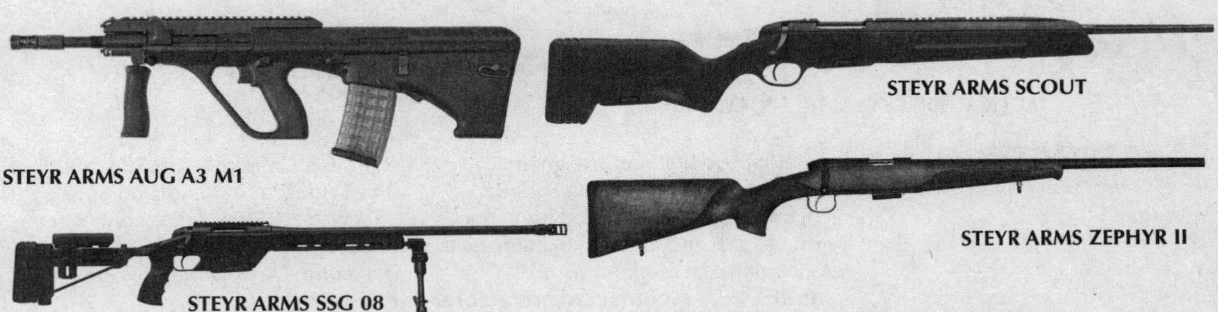

STEYR ARMS AUG A3 M1

STEYR ARMS SCOUT

STEYR ARMS SSG 08

STEYR ARMS ZEPHYR II

AUG A3 M1

Action: Semiautomatic
Stock: Synthetic
Barrel: 16 in.
Sights: None
Weight: 7 lb. 11 oz.–8 lb. 13. oz.
Caliber: 5.56 NATO, .223 Rem.
Magazine: Detachable box, 30 rounds
Features: Bullpup rifle has adjustable short-stroke gas piston, hard Eloxalcoated aircraft aluminum receiver, chrome-lined CHF barrel with muzzle brake, two-position trigger-blocking safety; short rail, high rail, and optics configurations; available in white/ black, OD Green, or MUD; choice of short, long, or extended rails; choice of 1.5X or 3X optic
MSRP $2050.00

SCOUT

Action: Bolt
Stock: Synthetic
Barrel: 19 in.
Sights: None
Weight: 6 lb. 10 oz.
Caliber: .308 Win., 7mm-08 Rem.
Magazine: Detachable box, 5 rounds (optional 10 round magazine)
Features: Weaver scope mounting rail; set trigger or direct trigger; synthetic stock in black or gray wood imitation; optional bipod integrated into forearm; matte black or stainless steel finish on barrel
MSRP $1749.00

SSG 08

Action: Bolt
Stock: Synthetic
Barrel: 20, 23.6, 25.6 in.
Sights: None
Weight: 5 lb. 8 oz.–5 lb. 11 oz.
Caliber: .300 Win. Mag., .308 Win., .338 Lapua
Magazine: Detachable box, 10 rounds
Features: Direct trigger; Mannox TM system; high grade aluminum folding stock; adjustable cheekpiece and buttplate with height marking; ergonomic exchangeable pistol grip; UIT rail and Picatinny rail; muzzlebrake; Versa-Pod
MSRP . . . . $4999.00–$6999.00

ZEPHYR II

Action: Bolt
Stock: Walnut
Barrel: 19.7 in.
Sights: None
Weight: 5 lb. 13 oz.
Caliber: .17 HMR, .22 LR, .22 WMR
Magazine: 5 rounds
Features: Trim, European walnut stock; fish scale checkering; tang safety; detachable magazine; available with threaded barrel
MSRP $1099.00

S.W.O.R.D. International

S.W.O.R.D. INTERNATIONAL MK-17 MOD O TYRANT 22

S .W .O .R .D . INTERNATIONAL MK-18 MOD 1 MJÖLNIR

MK-17 MOD O TYRANT 22

Action: Semiautomatic
Stock: Synthetic
Barrel: 16 in., 20 in.
Sights: None
Weight: 9 lb. 5 oz.
Caliber: 6.5 Creedmoor, .308 Win.
Magazine: 20 rounds
Features: Built for medium-range applications, this rifle features a tuned compensator; black nitride-coated barrel with cut rifling (20-in. 6.5 Creedmoor, 16 in. .308 Win.); self-regulating piston system
MSRP $4150.00

MK-18 MOD 1 MJÖLNIR

Action: Semiautomatic
Stock: Synthetic
Barrel: 20 in., 24 in.
Sights: None
Weight: 12 lb. 4 oz.
Caliber: .338 Lapua, .338 Norma, .300 Norma
Magazine: 10 rounds
Features: It's all long-distance business with the MK-18, featuring a proprietary self-regulating short-stroke gas piston system; mil-spec Type 3 hard anodized coating in Coyote Brown; single-point cut-rifled barrel with nitride coating; free-floating M-LOK rail; ambidextrous mag release; tungsten-filled heavy buffer; tuned compensator to reduce muzzle rise
MSRP $6995.00

Tactical Rifles

TACTICAL RIFLES CLASSIC SPORTER

TACTICAL RIFLES TACTICAL LONG RANGE

CLASSIC SPORTER

Action: Chimera bolt
Stock: Walnut
Barrel: 22 in.
Sights: None
Weight: 8 lb. 14 oz.
Caliber: .308 Win., .260 Rem., 6.5 Creedmoor and Lapua, .243 Win., 7mm-08 Rem. (short action), .25-06,.30-06 Spfd., .270 Win., .300 Win. Mag., 7mm Rem. Mag. (long action)
Magazine: 4+1 rounds
Features: Chimera action is constructed from stainless steel with a hand-fitted spiral-groove bolt and "Magnum" extractor; Picatinny rail; XXX grade English walnut stock with 22 lpi checkering at grip and forearm; extreme environment matte black finish
MSRP . . . . . . .contact manufacturer

TACTICAL LONG RANGE

Action: Bolt, 700 Rem.
Stock: Synthetic
Barrel: 18 in.-26 in.
Sights: None
Weight: 12 lb.–13 lb. 6 oz.
Caliber: 7.62 NATO, .308 Win., .260 Rem., 6.5 Creedmoor, 6.5 Lapua, .243 Win., 7mm-08, .30-06 Spfd., .270 Win., .25-06; other calibers can be custom ordered
Magazine: Detachable box, 5 or 10 rounds
Features: Ergonomic thumbhole stock comes in black or green; raised cheekpiece; free-floating chromoly match grade barrel; ambidextrous sling swivel studs; soft rubber recoil pad; Picatinny rail; aluminum block chassis stock system; optional bipod
MSRP . . . . . . .contact manufacturer

RIFLES

Tactical Solutions

TACTICAL SOLUTIONS OWYHEE TAKEDOWN RIFLE

TACTICAL SOLUTIONS X-RING TD VR

TACTICAL SOLUTIONS X-RING TSS INTEGRALLY SUPPRESSED RIFLE

OWYHEE TAKEDOWN RIFLE

Action: Bolt
Stock: Synthetic
Barrel: 16.5 in.
Sights: Fiber optic front, adjustable rear
Weight: 3 lb. 14 oz.
Caliber: .22 LR
Magazine: N/A
Features: For hikers, new shooters, ranchers, and home-defense; aluminum receiver; extended mag release; fluted, threaded barrel with chromoly bore; modified Magpul X-22 Backpacker stock
MSRP $1065.00

X-RING TD VR

Action: Semiautomatic
Stock: Synthetic
Barrel: 16.5 in.
Sights: Adjustable rear, fiber-optic front
Weight: 3 lb. 11 oz.–4 lb. 10 oz.
Caliber: .22 LR
Magazine: 1 round, 10 rounds
Features: With a Ruger 10/22 as its backbone, hikers, ranch workers and survivalists get an ultralightweight, packable, takedown (TD) rifle in choice of a variety of metal and stock colors
MSRP . . . .$1155.00–$1255.00

X-RING TSS INTEGRALLY SUPPRESSED RIFLE

Action: Bolt
Stock: Synthetic
Barrel: 16.75 in.
Sights: None
Weight: 4 lb. 14 oz.
Caliber: .22 LR
Magazine: N/A
Features: Integrally suppressed for the .22 LR with a lightweight aluminum barrel, interlocking titanium baffles, and a stainless steel split tube; Magpul X-22 Hunter stock; topside 15 MOA Picatinny rail; Ruger BX trigger; receiver adjustable for right- or left-hand charging; black, flat dark earth, OD green and Stealth Gray stock options
MSRP $1465.00

Tactical Solutions

TACTICAL SOLUTIONS X-RING VR HOGUE STOCK OPEN SIGHTS

TACTICAL SOLUTIONS X-RING VR MAGPUL HUNTER X-22 STOCK

TACTICAL SOLUTIONS X-RING VR VANTAGE RS STOCK

X-RING VR HOGUE STOCK

Action: Semiautomatic
Stock: Synthetic
Barrel: 16.5 in.
Sights: None
Weight: 4 lb. 5 oz.
Caliber: .22 LR
Magazine: 10 rounds
Features: Features an ambidextrous bolt; 15 MOA rail; Ruger BX-Trigger; variety of stock color; threaded barrel options; various metal/stock finish options
MSRP $985.00

X-RING VR MAGPUL HUNTER X-22 STOCK

Action: Semiautomatic
Stock: Synthetic
Barrel: 16.5 in.
Sights: None, open
Weight: 5 lb. 2 oz.
Caliber: .22 LR
Magazine: 10 rounds
Features: Similar in features to the other VRs, but with Magpul's Hunter X-22 chassis stock designed specifically for Ruger 10/22 actions and with M-LOK slots and adjustable length of pull; variety of stock/metal finishes
MSRP . . . . $1110.00–$1190.00

X-RING VR VANTAGE RS STOCK

Action: Semiautomatic
Stock: Laminate
Barrel: 16.5 in.
Sights: None
Weight: 5 lb. 2 oz.
Caliber: .22 LR
Magazine: 10 rounds
Features: Similar in features to the other VRs, but with a heavier, laminate, one-piece thumbhole stock/forearm; variety of stock/metal finishes; sling swivel studs
MSRP $1100.00

Taylor's & Co. Firearms

TAYLOR'S & CO. 1860 HENRY LEVER ACTION RIFLE

TAYLOR'S & CO. 1873 RIFLE - CHECKERED STRAIGHT STOCK

1860 HENRY LEVER ACTION RIFLE

Action: Lever
Stock: Walnut
Barrel: 24.25 in.
Sights: Open
Weight: 9 lb. 3 oz.
Caliber: .44-40 Win., .45 LC
Magazine: Under-barrel tube, 9–13 rounds
Features: Brass frame; octagonal barrel with blued finish; includes sling swivels
MSRP . . . . $1463.00–$1811.00

1873 RIFLE - CHECKERED STRAIGHT STOCK

Action: Lever
Stock: Walnut
Barrel: 20 in.
Sights: Open
Weight: 8 lb. 8 oz.
Caliber: .357 Mag., .45 LC
Magazine: Under-barrel tube, 10+1 rounds
Features: Case-hardened frame; straight stock with checkering; available with full octagon barrel
MSRP $1383.00

Taylor's & Co. Firearms

TAYLOR'S & CO. 1886 RIDGE RUNNER

TAYLOR'S & CO. LIGHTNING SLIDE ACTION RIFLE

1886 RIDGE RUNNER

Action: Lever
Stock: Wood or synthetic
Barrel: 18.5 in.
Sights: Skinner rear peep sight, fiber optic front
Weight: 7 lb. 13 oz.
Caliber: .45-70 Govt.
Magazine: 4, 8 rounds
Features: Available in matte blue metal work. Stock is wood with soft-touch rubber overmold; Integrated Skinner rear peep sight, Weaver rail, front fiber optic sight, D-shaped lever, muzzle brake, and half-octagonal barrel are standard
MSRP . . . .$1818.18–$1923.21

LIGHTNING SLIDE ACTION RIFLE

Action: Slide
Stock: Walnut
Barrel: 20 in., 24 in.
Sights: Open
Weight: 6 lb. 6 oz.–6 lb. 14 oz.
Caliber: .357 Mag., .45 LC
Magazine: 10 rounds
Features: Case-hardened steel receiver; fancy walnut stock; octagonal barrel; made by Pedersoli
MSRP $1836.00

RIFLES

Thompson/Center Arms

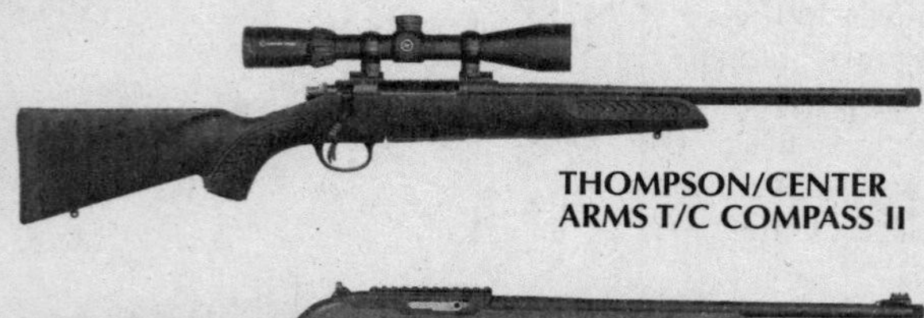

THOMPSON/CENTER ARMS T/C COMPASS II

THOMPSON/CENTER ARMS T/C COMPASS UTILITY

THOMPSON/CENTER ARMS T/CR22

THOMPSON/CENTER ARMS T/C VENTURE II

T/C COMPASS II

Action: Bolt
Stock: Synthetic
Barrel: 16.5 in., 21.6 in., 24 in.
Sights: None
Weight: 6 lb. 8 oz.–7 lb.
Caliber: .243 Win., .270 Win., .308 Win., .223 Rem., .30-06 Spfd., 6.5 Creedmoor, .300 Win. Mag., 7mm Rem. Mag.
Magazine: 4, 5 rounds
Features: A step up from the Compass Utility with a Gen 2 trigger; threaded muzzle; available with no sights or with Crimson Trace scope (7mm Rem. Mag. unscoped only); Compact version available in .243 Win., 6.5 Creedmoor, and .308 Win. only, 16.5-in barrel only, and has a 12.5-in. length of pull
Standard: $417.00
Scoped: $595.00

T/C COMPASS UTILITY

Action: Bolt
Stock: Synthetic
Barrel: 21.6 in.
Sights: None
Weight: 7 lb.
Caliber: .243 Win., .270 Win., .308 Win., .223 Rem., .30-06 Spfd., 6.5 Creedmoor
Magazine: 5 rounds
Features: Great entry-level rifle in several common cartridges; flush-fit rotary magazine; 60-degree bolt throw; 5R rifling; three-position safety; available as a scoped package
Standard: $370.00
Scoped: $459.00

T/CR22

Action: Semiautomatic
Stock: Synthetic
Barrel: 17 in.
Sights: Fiber optic front, adjustable rear
Weight: 4 lb. 6 oz.
Caliber: .22 LR
Magazine: 10 rounds
Features: Handy small-game, varmint, or target rimfire with both sights and a topside rail; detachable magazine; blued metalwork with stock in choice of green, Realtree Edge, or Mossy Oak Break-Up Country
Green: $399.00
Camo: $419.00

T/C VENTURE II

Action: Bolt
Stock: Synthetic
Barrel: 22 in., 24 in.
Sights: None
Weight: 7 lb. 8 oz.
Caliber: .243 Win., .270 Win., .308 Win., .223 Rem., .30-06 Spfd., 6.5 Creedmoor, .300 Win. Mag., 7mm Rem. Mag., .350 Legend
Magazine: 3 rounds
Features: With a Generation II trigger, this rifle also features a corrosion-resistant Weather Shield coating; 5R rifling; composite stock with Hogue panels at grip areas
MSRP $540.00

Tikka

RIFLES

T1X MTR

Action: Bolt
Stock: Synthetic
Barrel: 20 in.
Sights: None
Weight: 5 lb. 5 oz.
Caliber: .22 LR, .17 HMR
Magazine: 10 rounds
Features: Detachable magazine; threaded muzzle; modular stock with grip adjustable for angle
MSRP $529.99

T3X COMPACT TACTICAL

Action: Bolt
Stock: Synthetic
Barrel: 20 in.
Sights: None
Weight: 5 lb. 14.4 oz.
Caliber: .308 Win., .260 Rem., 6.5 Creedmoor
Magazine: 3, 4 rounds
Features: Designed specifically for low-recoiling centerfire rifle rounds; 30mm spacer and larger recoil pad to further improve fit and reduce felt recoil; black synthetic stock; stainless steel barrel; single-stage adjustable trigger; integral 17mm rail; drilled and tapped for scope mounts; blue or stainless metal finishes
MSRP $1029.99

T3X FOREST

Action: Bolt
Stock: Synthetic
Barrel: 20 in., 22.4 in., 24.4 in.
Sights: Optional open
Weight: 6 lb. 9.8 oz.–7 lb.
Caliber: .270 Win., .300 Win. Mag., .308 Win., .30-06 Spfd., 7mm Rem. Mag.
Magazine: 3, 4 rounds
Features: Designed for hunter using scopes with large variable optics that require higher mounting; modular synthetic stock has interchangeable pistol grip and optional attachment point that allows the user to change the width of the forend; asymmetrical grip pattern provides solid grip in adverse conditions; stocks without cheekpieces have foam insert that lowers stock-generated noise; widened ejection port improves cycling; extra top-side receiver screw permits Picatinny rail mounting; set and standard triggers available
MSRP $968.00

T3X HUNTER, HUNTER STAINLESS

Action: Bolt
Stock: Walnut
Barrel: 22.4 in.
Sights: None
Weight: 6 lb. 12.8 oz.
Caliber: .243 Win., 6.5x55mm, .270 Win., .308 Win., .30-06 Spfd., 7mm-08 Rem., 7mm Rem. Mag. 6.5 Creedmoor
Magazine: 3 rounds
Features: Classic walnut stock has improved checkering and enhanced recoil pad; stainless finish barrel is fluted and has hand-cut target crown; receiver has widened ejection port; integral 17mm rail drilled and tapped to accept standard scope mounts or Picatinny rail
Blue: $818.00
Stainless: $1018.00

T3X LAMINATED STAINLESS

Action: Bolt
Stock: Laminate
Barrel: 22.4 in., 24.3 in.
Sights: None
Weight: 6 lb. 9.6 oz.–7 lb.
Caliber: .243 Win., .260 Rem., .270 Rem., .270 WSM, .308 Win., .30-06 Spfd., 7mm Rem. Mag, .300 WSM, 6.5 Creedmoor
Magazine: N/A
Features: Weather-resistant gray laminate stock; cold-hammer-forged stainless steel free-floating barrel with hand-cut target crown; receiver has widened ejection port; integral 17mm rail drilled and tapped to accept standard scope mounts or Picatinny rail
MSRP . . . . $1018.00–$1049.00

Tikka

RIFLES

T3X LITE

Action: Bolt
Stock: Synthetic
Barrel: 22 in., 24 in.
Sights: None
Weight: 7 lb. 3 oz.
Caliber: .223 Rem., .22-250 Rem., .243 Win., .25-06 Rem., .270 Win., .270 WSM, .300 Win. Mag., .300 WSM, .30-06 Spfd., .308 Win., 7mm-08 Rem., 7mm Rem. Mag., 6.5 Creedmoor
Magazine: 3, 4 rounds
Features: Weather-resistant rifle; modular stock that allows for grip angle adjustment; new recoil pad; improved textured gripping surfaces; stock's foam insert reduces noise; left-hand models available
MSRP . . . . $649.99–$999.99

T3X LITE COMPACT

Action: Bolt
Stock: Synthetic
Barrel: 20 in.
Sights: None
Weight: 6 lb. 10 oz.
Caliber: .204 Ruger, .22-250 Rem., .223 Rem., .243 Win., .308 Win., 7mm-08 Rem., 6.5 Creedmoor
Magazine: 3, 4 rounds
Features: Stock comes with a 1-in. spacer and a thick recoil pad; length of pull is 12.5 in.; detachable magazine; textured grip panels; blued hardware
MSRP $678.00

T3X LITE ROUGHTECH

Action: Bolt
Stock: Synthetic
Barrel: 20 in., 22.4 in., 24.3 in.
Sights: None
Weight: 6 lb. 6 oz.
Caliber: 6.5 Creedmoor, .270 Win., .270 WSM, .300 Win. Mag., .300 WSM, .7mm Rem. Mag.
Magazine: 3 rounds
Features: Great for hunting in wet, inclement conditions thanks to the textured Roughtech stock; blued metalwork; fluted bolt with oversized bolt knob; integral rail; single-stage trigger; fluted barrel with threaded-on muzzle brake; modular stock in black or tan with black webbing
MSRP $999.99

T3X LITE VEIL ALPINE, VEIL WIDELAND

Action: Bolt
Stock: Synthetic
Barrel: 20 in., 22.4 in., 24.3 in.
Sights: None
Weight: 6 lb. 6 oz.
Caliber: .22-250 Rem., .223 Rem., .243 Win., .25-06 Rem., .270 Win., .270 WSM, .30-06 Spfd., .300 Win. Mag., .300 WSM, .308 Win., 6.5 Creedmoor, 7mm Rem. Mag., 7mm-08 Rem.
Magazine: 3 rounds
Features: A lightweight hunter with a fluted bolt and barrel; modular stock with interchangeable pistol grip; improved grip and recoil pad; stock designed for reduced noise; widened ejection port; barrel is Cerakoted; muzzle brake included; in Alpine or Wideland camo patterns from Veil Camo
MSRP $1199.00

T3X SUPERLITE

Action: Bolt
Stock: Synthetic
Barrel: 22.4 in.
Sights: None
Weight: 6 lb.
Caliber: .243 Win., .308 Win., .270 Win., .30-06 Spfd., 7mm Rem. Mag., 6.5 Creedmoor, .300 Win. Mag., 7mm-08 Rem.
Magazine: 3 rounds
Features: Enhanced gripping areas; new recoil pad; stock's foam insert reduces noise; black stock model is exclusive to Sportsmen's Warehouse; Camo model is available only through Cabela's; both models have a single-stage adjustable trigger, fluted barrels
MSRP . . . . $749.99–$829.99

Tikka

TIKKA T3X TAC A1

TIKKA T3X UPR

TIKKA T3X VARMINT

T3X TAC A1

Action: Bolt
Stock: Aluminum rear stock and middle chassis
Barrel: 16 in., 20 in., 24 in.
Sights: None
Weight: 10 lb. 5.7 oz.–11 lb. 4 oz.
Caliber: .260 Rem., 6.5 Creedmoor, .308 Win.
Magazine: 10 rounds
Features: Long-range chassis rifle; aluminum rear stock with height- and angle-adjustable cheekpiece; adjustable-height recoil pad; Picatinny rail for monopod attachment; aluminum middle chassis with modular, removable forend connector; AR-15 buffer tube-compatible interface; AR-15 pistol grip compatible slot; barrel is threaded and mid-contour; trigger is two-stage and adjustable; detachable magazine; two-way safety with bolt release lever; topside Picatinny rail
MSRP $1849.00

T3X UPR

Action: Bolt
Stock: Synthetic
Barrel: 20 in., 24.3 in.
Sights: None
Weight: 8 lb. oz.
Caliber: .260 Rem., .308 Win., 6.5 Creedmoor
Magazine: 10 rounds
Features: A long-range entry with an adjustable cheekpiece; choice of flat rail or 20 MOA inclined rail; modular stock with interchangeable pistol grip; improved grip and recoil pad; stock designed for reduced noise; Tikka website says the stock is an olive drab green, but the picture shows a light beige with black flecking
MSRP $1955.00

T3X VARMINT

Action: Bolt
Stock: Synthetic
Barrel: 23.7 in.
Sights: None
Weight: 7 lb. 8 oz.
Caliber: .223 Rem., .22-250 Rem. 6.5 Creedmoor
Magazine: 5, 6 rounds
Features: Raised Varmint cheekpiece aids in alignment with larger scopes; free-floating barrel; wide forend perfect for sandbag use
MSRP $898.00

TNW Firearms

TNW FIREARMS AERO SURVIVAL RIFLE

TNW FIREARMS AERO SURVIVAL RIFLE LTE

AERO SURVIVAL RIFLE

Action: Semiautomatic
Stock: Synthetic
Barrel: 16.25 in.
Sights: None
Weight: 5 lb.
Caliber: 9mm, 10mm, .45 ACP, .460 Rowland, .40 S&W, .357 SIG
Magazine: 10, 15, 24, 29, 31 rounds by caliber
Features: Specialty survival/home-defense rifle; removable barrel and collapsible AR stock; calibers can easily be converted; TNW offers barrel threading services for suppressor use; black, Tiger Green, Pink Attitude, Dark Earth, and OD Green finishes
MSRP $799.00

AERO SURVIVAL RIFLE LTE

Action: Semiautomatic
Stock: Synthetic
Barrel: 16.25 in.
Sights: None
Weight: 3 lb. 15 oz.
Caliber: 9mm
Magazine: 10, 15, 17 rounds
Features: Perhaps the lightest pistol-caliber carbine on the modern market; takes Glock magazines; hard anodized coating; direct blowback action; integrated child safety lock; rapid takedown design; in gray, black, dark earth, or OD green
MSRP $799.00

Troy Industries

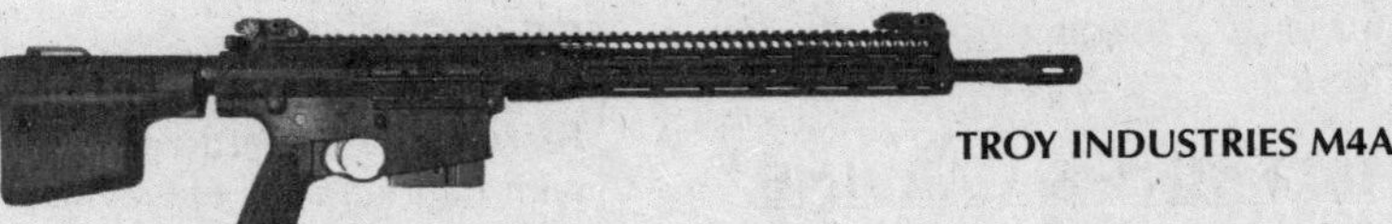

TROY INDUSTRIES M4A4

M4A4

Action: Semiautomatic
Stock: Synthetic
Barrel: 12 in., 16 in., 20 in.
Sights: Troy folding battle sights front, rear
Weight: N/A
Caliber: .308 Win., 6.5 Creedmoor
Magazine: 10 rounds
Features: A conventionally styled MSR with acres of top rail; CMC trigger; Magpul stock; Troy Control Grip; M-LOK forend; hard-coat anodized finish; 6.5 Creedmoor available only in 20-in. barrel
.308: $1499.00
6.5 Creedmoor: $1899.00

Troy Industries

TROY INDUSTRIES PUMP-ACTION RIFLE WITH FOLDING STOCK

PUMP-ACTION RIFLE WITH FOLDING STOCK

Action: Pump
Stock: Synthetic
Barrel: 16 in.
Sights: None
Weight: 6 lb.
Caliber: .223 Rem., .300 BLK
Magazine: 10 rounds
Features: An AR platform in a pump-action configuration; optic ready; TRX2-style handguard; full-length top rail; Troy SAR folding stock; uses brass-cased ammo only
MSRP . . . .$1169.00–$1189.00

Uberti

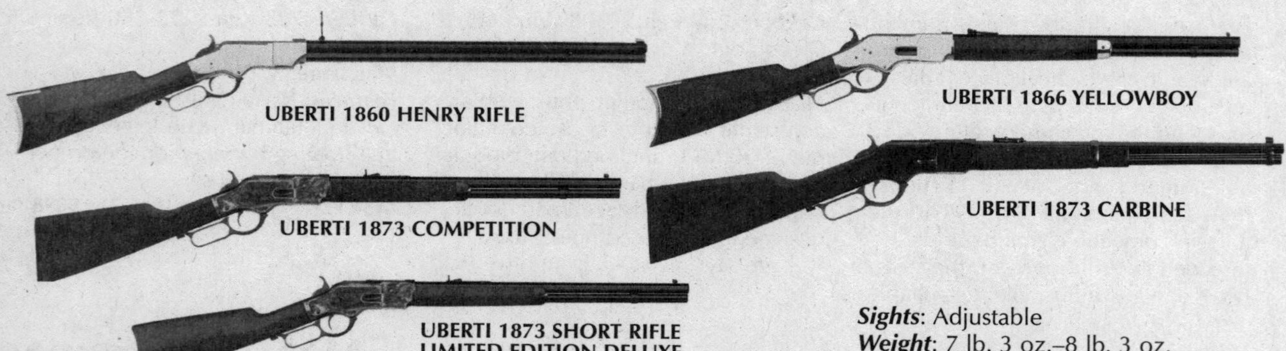

UBERTI 1860 HENRY RIFLE

UBERTI 1866 YELLOWBOY

UBERTI 1873 COMPETITION

UBERTI 1873 CARBINE

UBERTI 1873 SHORT RIFLE LIMITED EDITION DELUXE

1860 HENRY RIFLE

Action: Lever
Stock: Walnut
Barrel: 18.5 in., 24.5 in.
Sights: Adjustable
Weight: 9 lb.
Caliber: .45 Colt, .44-40 Win.
Magazine: Under-barrel tube, 8+1 or 13+1 rounds
Features: Several versions: Trapper has 18.5-in barrel, brass frame/buttplate, and case-hardened lever, Rifle has 24.5-in. barrel, brass frame/buttplate, and case-hardened receiver; Steel Rifle has 24.5-in. barrel, case-hardened frame/lever, blue buttplate
MSRP . . . . $1499.00–$1579.00

1866 YELLOWBOY

Action: Lever
Stock: Walnut
Barrel: 19 in., 20 in., 24.25 in.
Sights: Adjustable
Weight: 8 lb. 3 oz.
Caliber: .45 Colt, .44-40 Win., .38 Spl.
Magazine: Under barrel tube, 10+1 or 13+1 rounds
Features: Three versions, all calibers available in all three: Carbine, 19-in. barrel; Short Rifle, 20-in. barrel; Sporting Rifle, 24.25-in. barrel. All have brass frames and buttplates, case-hardened levers
MSRP . . . . $1239.00–$1269.00

1873 COMPETITION

Action: Lever
Stock: Wood
Barrel: 20 in.
Sights: Adjustable
Weight: 8 lb.
Caliber: .357 Mag., .45 Colt
Magazine: Under-barrel tube, 10+1 rounds
Features: Octagonal barrel; A-grade walnut; lever lock; side loading gate for ease of loading
MSRP $1499.00

1873 RIFLE & CARBINE

Action: Lever
Stock: Walnut
Barrel: 16.1 in., 18 in., 19 in., 20 in., 24.5 in.
Sights: Adjustable
Weight: 7 lb. 3 oz.–8 lb. 3 oz.
Caliber: .45 Colt, .357 Mag., .44-44
Magazine: Under-barrel tube, 9+1, 10+1 or 13+1 rounds
Features: Octagonal barrel on rifle; round barrel on carbine and trapper; A-grade walnut with checkered pistol grip and forend
Carbine: $1309.00
Half Octagon Rifle: $1379.00
Short Rifle: . . . . .$1339.00–$1349.00
Special Sporting: $1339.00
Special Sporting Short: . . .$1449.00
Sporting: . . . .$1339.00–$1349.00
Trapper: $1329.00

1873 SHORT RIFLE LIMITED EDITION DELUXE

Action: Lever
Stock: Walnut
Barrel: 20 in.
Sights: Rifle sights
Weight: 8 lb. 3 oz.
Caliber: .45 Colt
Magazine: 10 rounds
Features: Case-hardened steel receiver with hand-chased engraving; A-grade walnut; case-hardened loop; blue octagon barrel; side-loading gate; crescent buttplate
MSRP $1929.00

UBERTI 1874 SHARPS RIFLE

UBERTI 1876 CENTENNIAL

UBERTI 1885 COURTNEY STALKING RIFLE

UBERTI 1885 HIGH-WALL SPECIAL SPORTING MODEL

UBERTI SPRINGFIELD TRAPDOOR ARMY

UBERTI SPRINGFIELD TRAPDOOR CARBINE

1874 SHARPS RIFLE

Action: Falling block
Stock: Walnut
Barrel: 32 in., 34 in.
Sights: Creedmoor Sight
Weight: 10 lb. 4 oz.–11 lb.
Caliber: .45-70 Govt.
Magazine: None
Features: Blued octagonal barrel; checkered walnut stock; case-hardened; double-set trigger; pewter forend cap
Special: $2429.00
Deluxe: $3849.00
Down Under:. $3189.00
Buffalo Hunter: $3079.00

1876 CENTENNIAL

Action: Lever
Stock: Walnut
Barrel: 28 in.
Sights: Adjustable
Weight: 10 lb.
Caliber: .50-95
Magazine: Under-barrel tube, 11+1 rounds
Features: Case-hardened frame and lever; blued buttplate; octagonal barrel; straight stock
MSRP $1709.00

1885 COURTNEY STALKING RIFLE

Action: Single-shot
Stock: Walnut
Barrel: 24 in.
Sights: Blade front, adjustable rear
Weight: 7 lb. 2 oz.
Caliber: .303 British, .45-70 Gov't.
Magazine: 1 round
Features: A lovely rifle in a nearly forgotten cartridge, featuring a Grade A walnut stock with a Prince of Wales grip; color case receiver; round barrel in polished blue
MSRP $1689.00

1885 HIGH-WALL

Action: Falling block
Stock: Walnut
Barrel: 28 in., 30 in., 32 in.
Sights: Adjustable
Weight: 9 lb. 5 oz. (carbine), 10 lb.
Caliber: .45-70
Magazine: None
Features: Case-hardened frame and lever; blued buttplate; octagonal barrel; carbine model has round barrel; carbine and sporting rifle have straight stock
Special Sporting: $1349.00
Sporting Straight Stock:. . . $1149.00

SPRINGFIELD TRAPDOOR ARMY

Action: Hinged breech
Stock: Walnut
Barrel: 32.5 in.
Sights: Adjustable
Weight: 8 lb. 13 oz.
Caliber: .45-70 Govt.
Magazine: None
Features: Blued steel, case-hardened breechblock and buttplate
MSRP $2389.00

SPRINGFIELD TRAPDOOR CARBINE

Action: Hinged breech
Stock: Walnut
Barrel: 22 in.
Sights: Adjustable
Weight: 7 lb. 5 oz.
Caliber: .45-70 Govt.
Magazine: None
Features: Blued steel, case-hardened breechblock and buttplate; fitted with sliding ring and bar for cavalryman to carry it clipped to carbine sling
MSRP $2109.00

Ultimate Arms

ULTIMATE ARMS MOUNTAIN LITE RIFLE

MOUNTAIN LITE RIFLE

Action: Bolt
Stock: Synthetic
Barrel: 26 in.
Sights: None
Weight: N/A
Caliber: .308 Warbird (7.82 Lazzeroni)
Magazine: 3 rounds
Features: Housing a most powerful round, this custom-built rifle has a six-groove fluted medium-contour barrel with button rifling; removeable muzzle brake; proprietary Warrior Mountain Lite action; center feed
MSRP $5899.95

Vigilance Rifles, Inc.

VIGILANCE RIFLES, INC. M18 WINDRUNNER

M18 WINDRUNNER

Action: Bolt
Stock: Synthetic
Barrel: 29 in.
Sights: None
Weight: 29 lb. 8 oz.
Caliber: .50 BMG, 12.7x108mm Russian, .440 Vigilance
Magazine: 10 rounds
Features: Adjustable AR-style stock; fixed, screwed-in barrel; Chromoly upper; Windrunner bolt handle; oversized AR-style chromoly extractor; folding, pivoting bipod; aluminum lower; 1:15 twist chromoly bull barrel; 0 MOA rail
MSRP . . . . starting at $5299.00

Volquartsen Firearms

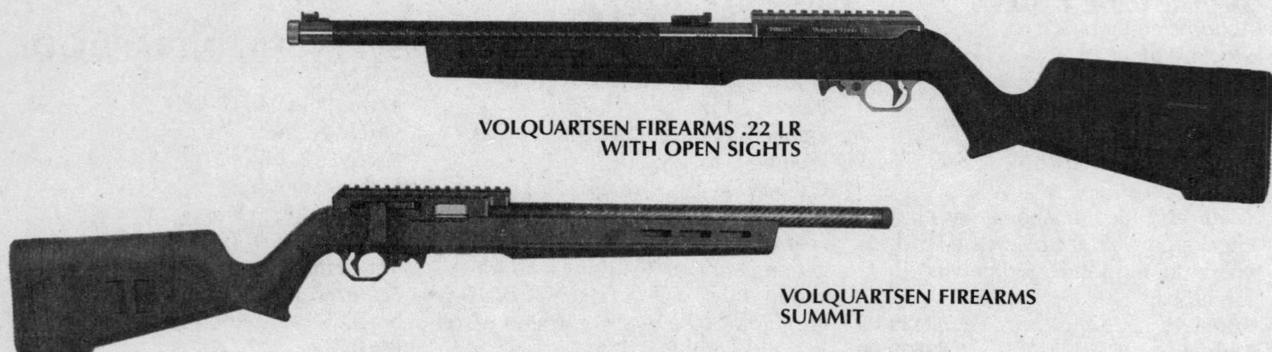

VOLQUARTSEN FIREARMS .22 LR WITH OPEN SIGHTS

VOLQUARTSEN FIREARMS SUMMIT

.22 LR WITH OPEN SIGHTS

Action: Semiautomatic
Stock: Synthetic
Barrel: 16.5 in.
Sights: HiViz fiber optic front, TL tritium rear
Weight: 6 lb.
Caliber: .22 LR
Magazine: 10 rounds
Features: CNC-machined stainless steel receiver; carbon fiber THM tension barrel; TG2000 trigger guard; Magpul X-22 Hunter stock; black, OD Green, or Flat Dark Earth stock colors
MSRP $1589.00

SUMMIT

Action: Bolt
Stock: Synthetic
Barrel: N/A
Sights: None
Weight: 5 lb. 13 oz.
Caliber: .22 LR, .17 Mach 2
Magazine: N/A
Features: Lightweight Magpul stock adjustable for length of pull; carbon fiber barrel; 1.75-pound trigger; ample rail on the top for optics; threaded barrel accommodates suppressor use; a variety of colored stocks from Magpul, a laminate thumbhole configuration, plus a Hogue stock option in .17 Mach; .22 LR available with Magpul stocks, lightweight thumbhole, or ambidextrous stocks/tapered barrel
Magpul stock: $1267.00
Ambidextrous laminate: . . $1515.00
Thumbhole laminate: $1500.00

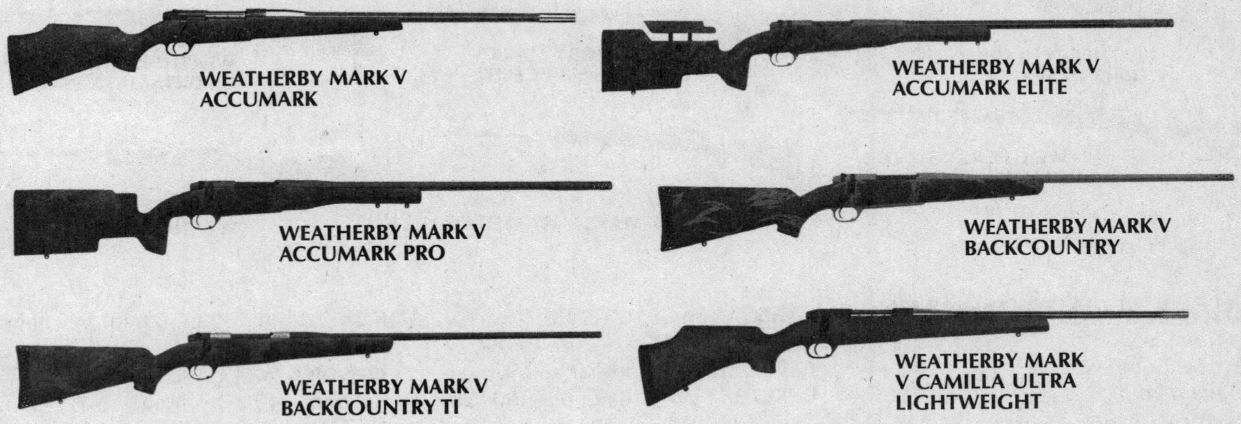

MARK V ACCUMARK

Action: Bolt
Stock: Composite
Barrel: 24 in., 26 in., 28 in. by caliber
Sights: None
Weight: 7 lb. 4 oz.–8 lb. 8 oz.
Caliber: .240 Wby. Mag., .257 Wby. Mag., .270 Wby. Mag., .30-378 Wby. Mag., .300 Wby. Mag., .300 Win. Mag., .338 Lapua, .338-378 Wby. Mag., .340 Wby Mag., 6.5 Creedmoor, 6.5-300 Wby. Mag. 6.5 Wby. RPM, 7mm Wby. Mag.
Magazine: 2, 3, 4, 5 rounds by caliber
Features: Overhauled Mark V line; enhanced ergonomic stock; reduced grip diameter with added palm swell; overall weight reduction; LXX Trigger; fluted #3 contour barrel; Accubrake available
MSRP . . . . $2049.00–$2249.00

MARK V ACCUMARK ELITE

Action: Bolt
Stock: Carbon fiber
Barrel: 24 in., 26 in.
Sights: None
Weight: 7 lb. 10 oz.–8 lb. 6 oz.
Caliber: .240 Wby. Mag., .257 Wby. Mag., 6.5 Creedmoor, 6.5 Wby. RPM, 6.5-300 Wby. Mag., .270 Wby. Mag., 7mm Wby. Mag., .300 Win. Mag., .300 Wby. Mag., .30-378 Wby. Mag., .340 Wby. Mag., .338 Lapua Mag., .338-378 Wby. Mag.
Magazine: 2, 3, 4 rounds
Features: Similar to the Accumark Pro, but with the fluted barrel, muzzle brake, trigger guard, and receiver in Elite Cerakote Coyote Tan; fluted bolt, bolt knob, and safety in Cerakote Graphite Black; adjustable stock is dark brown with tan splotching
MSRP . . . . $2799.00–$2999.00

MARK V ACCUMARK PRO

Action: Bolt
Stock: Carbon fiber
Barrel: 24 in., 26 in.
Sights: None
Weight: 7 lb. 2 oz.–7 lb. 14 oz.
Caliber: .240 Wby. Mag., .257 Wby. Mag., 6.5 Creedmoor, 6.5 Wby. RPM, 6.5-300 Wby. Mag., .270 Wby. Mag., 7mm Wby. Mag., .300 Win. Mag., .300 Wby. Mag., .30-378 Wby. Mag., .340 Wby. Mag., .338 Lapua Mag., .338-378 Wby. Mag.
Magazine: 2, 3, 4 rounds
Features: The carbon fiber stock appears in dark gray with lighter gray splotches; fluted barrel, muzzle brake, trigger guard, and receiver are in Tungsten Cerakote
MSRP . . . . $2499.00–$2699.00

MARK V BACKCOUNTRY

Action: Bolt
Stock: Carbon fiber
Barrel: 22 in., 24 in., 26 in.
Sights: None
Weight: 5 lb. 4 oz.–6 lb. 4 oz.
Caliber: 6mm Creedmoor, .240 Wby. Mag., .257 Wby. Mag., 6.5 Creedmoor, 6.5 Wby. Mag., 6.5-300 Wby. Mag., .270 Wby. Mag., .280 Ackley Improved, 7mm Wby. Mag., .300 Wby. Mag.
Magazine: 3, 4, 5 rounds
Features: Carbon fiber stock in a green and tan "sponge" pattern; bolt, bolt knob and safety in Graphite Black Cerakote; fluted, threaded barrel, trigger guard and receiver in McMillan Tan Cerakote
MSRP . . . . $2499.00–$2599.00

MARK V BACKCOUNTRY TI

Action: Bolt
Stock: Carbon fiber
Barrel: 22 in., 24 in., 26 in.
Sights: None
Weight: 4 lb. 14 oz.–5 lb. 14 oz.
Caliber: .240 Wby. Mag., .257 Wby. Mag., .270 Wby. Mag., .280 Ackley Improved, .300 Wby. Mag., 6.5 Creedmoor, 6.5 Wby. RPM, 6.5-300 Wby. Mag., 7mm Wby. Mag.
Magazine: 3, 4, 5 rounds
Features: Nearly identical to the standard Backcountry, but with a titanium receiver, all metalwork in Graphite Black Cerakote, and a dark gray stock with gray "sponge" gel coat and spiderwebbing accents
MSRP . . . . $3349.00–$3449.00

MARK V CAMILLA ULTRA LIGHTWEIGHT

Action: Bolt
Stock: Composite
Barrel: 22 in., 24 in.
Sights: None
Weight: 5 lb. 12 oz.
Caliber: .240 Wby. Mag., .243 Win., 6.5 Creedmoor, .280 Ackley Improved, 6.5 Wby. RPM
Magazine: 4, 5 rounds
Features: One for the hiker with a stock made to better fit a woman's physique; hand-laid composite stock with full-length aluminum bedding block and wearing a Forest Green/black web gel coating; fluted stainless barrel with #1 contour; fluted bolt body; LXX trigger with grooves
MSRP $1999.00

Weatherby

WEATHERBY MARK V CARBONMARK

WEATHERBY MARK V DELUXE

WEATHERBY MARK V CARBONMARK ELITE

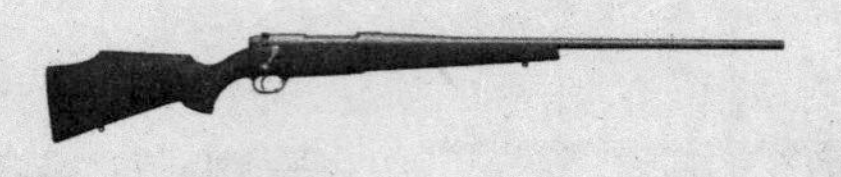
WEATHERBY MARK V WEATHERMARK

WEATHERBY MARK V CARBONMARK PRO

WEATHERBY MARK V WEATHERMARK LT

MARK V CARBONMARK

Action: Bolt
Stock: Composite
Barrel: 26 in.
Sights: None
Weight: 7 lb. 12 oz.
Caliber: .257 Wby. Mag., .300 Wby. Mag., 6.5 Creedmoor, 6.5 Wby. RPM, 6.5-300 Wby.
Magazine: 3 rounds
Features: A collaboration with Proof Research featuring a stock with a reduced grip diameter, right-hand palm swell, aluminum bedding block, and a dark gray/black matte gel finish; Proof Research carbon fiber barrel with a stainless steel core, #4 contour, cut-rifled, hand-lapped, and threaded 5/8X24; Tactical Grey Cerakote metalwork; magnum 9-lug action; fluted bolt body; LXX trigger
MSRP . . . . $2499.00–$2599.00

MARK V CARBONMARK ELITE

Action: Bolt
Stock: Carbon fiber
Barrel: 22 in., 24 in., 26 in.
Sights: None
Weight: 7 lb. 3 oz.–8 lb. 6 oz.
Caliber: 6.5 Creedmoor, 6.5 Wby. RPM, .257 Wby. Mag., 6.5-300 Wby. Mag., .300 Wby. Mag.
Magazine: 3, 4 rounds
Features: Similar to the Carbonmark Pro, but with an adjustable stock in dark gray with a tan sponge pattern; bolt, bolt knob, and safety in Graphite Black Cerakote; receiver, muzzle brake, and trigger guard in Elite Cerakote Coyote Tan
MSRP . . . . $3299.00–$3399.00

MARK V CARBONMARK PRO

Action: Bolt
Stock: Carbon fiber
Barrel: 22 in., 24 in., 26 in.
Sights: None
Weight: 6 lb. 11 oz.–7 lb. 8 oz.
Caliber: 6.5 Creedmoor, 6.5 Wby. RPM, .257 Wby. Mag., 6.5-300 Wby. Mag., .300 Wby. Mag.
Magazine: 3, 4 rounds
Features: Carbon fiber sleeve with a 416 stainless steel barrel; receiver, muzzle brake, and trigger guard in Tungsten Cerakote; fluted bolt, bolt knob, and safety in Cerakote Graphite Gray; charcoal stock
MSRP . . . . $2999.00–$3099.00

MARK V DELUXE, CAMILLA DELUXE

Action: Bolt
Stock: Walnut
Barrel: 24 in., 26 in., 28 in.
Sights: None
Weight: 6 lb. 12 oz.–10 lb.
Caliber: 240 Wby. Mag., .243 Win., .257 Wby. Mag., .270 Wby., .30-378 Wby. Mag., .300 Wby. Mag., .338-378 Wby. Mag., .340 Wby. Mag., .378 Wby. Mag., .416 Wby. Mag., .460 Wby. Mag., 6.5 Creedmoor, 6.5 Wby. RPM, 6.5-300 Wby. Mag., 7mm Wby. Mag.
Magazine: 2+1, 3+1, 5+1 rounds
Features: Weatherby overhauled the Mark V in 2018 with ergonomically enhanced stocks that include reduced grip diameter and lighter overall weight, an improved LXX trigger with a wider face, and the company's sub-MOA accuracy gurantee; also new to the Deluxe line is the addition of the Camilla Deluxe, the upgraded sister to the previous Vanguard Camilla, with a six-lug action and a stock designed to better fit the female form
Deluxe: . . . . $2399.00–$2799.00
Camilla Deluxe: $2399.00

MARK V WEATHERMARK, WEATHERMARK BRONZE

Action: Bolt
Stock: Composite
Barrel: 24 in., 26 in., 28 in. by caliber
Sights: None
Weight: 6 lb. 4 oz.–8 lb. 4 oz.
Caliber: .240 Wby. Mag., .243 Win., .257 Wby. Mag.,, .270 Wby. Mag., .300 Wby. Mag., .30-378 Wby. Mag., .340 Wby. Mag., .338-378 Wby. Mag., 6.5 Creedmoor, 6.5 Wby. RPM, 6.5-300 Wby. Mag., 7mm Wby. Mag.
Magazine: 2, 3, 5 rounds by caliber
Features: First Mark V to feature a Cerakote finish; #2 contour threaded barrels; hand-laid fiberglass stock with Monte Carlo cheekpiece; aluminum bedding block; spiral-fluted bolt body; standard Weathermark has barrel and receiver in Tac Gray Cerakote, Bronze model in Burnt Bronze Cerakote
MSRP . . . . $1549.00–$1749.00

MARK V WEATHERMARK LT

Action: Bolt
Stock: Fiberglass
Barrel: 22 in., 24 in., 26 in.
Sights: None
Weight: 5 lb. 14 oz.–7 lb. 3 oz.
Caliber: .240 Wby. Mag., .257 Wby. Mag., .270 Wby. Mag., 6.5 Creedmoor, 6.5 Wby. RPM, 6.5-300 Wby. Mag., 7mm Wby. Mag., .300 Wby. Mag.
Magazine: 3, 4 rounds
Features: Handlaid fiberglass stock in traditional Weatherby styling; raised comb, with a green base and flat dark earth flecking; fluted barrel, muzzle brake, receiver, and trigger guard in flat dark earth Cerakote; fluted bolt, bolt knob, and safety in Graphite Black Cerakote; 6mm Creedmoor, 6.5 Creedmoor, 6.5 Wby. RPM, and .240 Wby Mag. have six-lug actions and are the lightest of the lineup at 5 lb. 14 oz.; left-hand available in .257, 6.5-300, and .300 Wby. Mags.
MSRP . . . . $1999.00–$2099.00

WEATHERBY VANGUARD BADLANDS

WEATHERBY VANGUARD CAMILLA

WEATHERBY VANGUARD CAMILLA WILDERNESS

WEATHERBY VANGUARD FIRST LITE

WEATHERBY VANGUARD LAMINATE SPORTER

WEATHERBY VANGUARD MULTICAM

VANGUARD BADLANDS

Action: Bolt
Stock: Composite
Barrel: 25 in., 28 in.
Sights: None
Weight: 7 lb. 8 oz.
Caliber: .25-06 Rem., .257 Wby. Mag., .270 Win., .30-06 Spfd., .300 Wby. Mag., .300 Win. Mag., .308 Win., 6.5 Creedmoor, 6.5 PRC, 6.5-300 Wby. Mag., 7mm Rem. Mag., 7mm-08 Rem.
Magazine: 3, 4, 5 rounds
Features: Standard Vanguard features; #2 contour barrel; metalwork in Burnt Bronze Cerakote; polymer stock with textured gripping surfaces, all dressed in Badlands Approach camo; adjustable match-grade two-stage trigger; fluted, one-piece machined bolt body with fully enclosed bolt sleeve
MSRP $849.00

VANGUARD CAMILLA

Action: Bolt
Stock: Turkish walnut
Barrel: 20 in.
Sights: None
Weight: 6 lb. 4 oz.
Caliber: .22-250 Rem., .243 Win., .308 Win., 6.5 Creedmoor, 7mm-08 Rem.
Magazine: 4, 5 rounds
Features: SUB-MOA accuracy guarantee; "creep-free," match-quality, two-stage trigger; three-position safety; slimmer grip angle; shorter, slimmer forearm and grip with right side palm swell for better balance and fit; fleur de lis checkering pattern; recoil pad has been given a negative angle, reduced in size, and the toe canted away from the body to better fit a woman's shoulder
MSRP . . . . $749.00–$839.00

VANGUARD CAMILLA WILDERNESS

Action: Bolt
Stock: Fiberglass
Barrel: 20 in.
Sights: None
Weight: 7 lb.
Caliber: .243 Win., 6.5 Creedmoor, 7mm-08 Rem., .308 Win.
Magazine: 4, 5 rounds
Features: Known for its stock dimensions and balance best suited to female shooters, the Camilla lineup gains the Wilderness model with a green handlaid fiberglass stock with black webbing; #2 contour barrel; fluted bolt body; skeletonized aluminum bedding block
MSRP $899.00

VANGUARD FIRST LITE

Action: Bolt
Stock: Composite
Barrel: 26 in., 28 in.
Sights: None
Weight: 7 lb. 8 oz.
Caliber: .240 Wby. Mag., .25-06 Rem., .257 Wby. Mag., 6.5-3000 Wby. Mag., .270 Win., .308 Win., .30-06 Spfd., .300 Win. Mag. .300 Wby. Mag., 6.5 Creedmoor, 6.5 PRC
Magazine: 3, 5 rounds
Features: Stock finished in First Lite Fusion camo; stock has texturing at the grip and forearm; Flat Dark Earth Cerakote finish on the barrel and action; one-piece machined fluted bolt body; #2 contour fluted barrel with Accubrake; adjustable match-grade two-stage trigger
MSRP $1049.00

VANGUARD LAMINATE SPORTER

Action: Bolt
Stock: Laminate
Barrel: 24 in., 26 in.
Sights: None
Weight: 7 lb. 4 oz.–7 lb. 8 oz.
Caliber: .223 Rem., .22-250 Rem., .243 Win., .240 Wby. Mag., .25-06 Rem., .257 Wby. Mag., 6.5 Creedmoor, .270 Win., 7mm-08 Rem., 7mm Rem. Mag., .308 Win., .30-06 Spfd., .300 Win. Mag., .300 Wby. Mag.
Magazine: 3, 4, 5 rounds
Features: Handsome laminate stock in Nutmeg from Boyds; fluted bolt body; cold hammer-forged barrel in a #2 contour; matte blue metalwork
MSRP $849.00

VANGUARD MULTICAM

Action: Bolt
Stock: Polymer
Barrel: 24 in., 26 in.
Sights: None
Weight: 7 lb. 4 oz.–7 lb. 8 oz.
Caliber: .243 Win., .240 Wby. Mag., .25-06 Rem., .257 Wby. Mag., 6.5 Creedmoor, 6.5-300 Wby. Mag., .270 Win., 7mm-08 Rem., 7mm Rem. Mag., .308 Win., .30-06 Spfd., .300 Win. Mag., .300 Wby. Mag., 6.5 PRC
Magazine: 3, 4, 5 rounds
Features: The MultiCam finish on the stock lends a lot of versatility to this rifle, which also features metalwork with Cerakote flat dark earth finish; fluted bolt body; #2 contour barrel
MSRP $899.00

Weatherby

RIFLES

VANGUARD SPORTER

Action: Bolt
Stock: Walnut
Barrel: 24 in.
Sights: None
Weight: 7 lb. 4 oz.–7 lb. 8 oz.
Caliber: .223 Rem., .22-250 Rem., .243 Win., .25-06 Rem., .270 Win., 7mm-08 Rem., .308 Win., .30-06 Spfd., .257 Wby. Mag., 7mm Rem. Mag., .300 Win. Mag., .300 Wby. Mag., 6.5 Creedmoor, 6.5-300 Wby. Mag.
Magazine: 3+1, 5+1 rounds
Features: Two-stage trigger; raised comb, Monte Carlo stock with satin urethane finish; hand-selected A fancy grade Turkish walnut; rosewood forend; low luster, matte blued metalwork; fine line diamond point checkering; low density recoil pad
MSRP $849.00

VANGUARD SPORTER DBM

Action: Bolt
Stock: Walnut Monte Carlo
Barrel: 24 in.
Sights: None
Weight: 7 lb. 4 oz.
Caliber: .25-06 Rem., .270 Win., .30-06 Spfd.
Magazine: Detachable box, 3 rounds
Features: Rosewood forend; raised comb; satin urethane finish; matte blued metalwork; adjustable trigger
MSRP $849.00

VANGUARD SYNTHETIC

Action: Bolt
Stock: Synthetic
Barrel: 24 in.
Sights: None
Weight: 7 lb. 4 oz.
Caliber: .22-250 Rem., .223 Rem., .240 Wby. Mag., .243 Win., .25-06 Rem., .257 Wby. Mag., .270 Win., .30-06 Spfd., .300 Wby. Mag., .300 Win. Mag., .308 Win., 6.5 Creedmoor, 6.5 PRC, 6.5-300 Wby. Mag., 7mm Rem. Mag., 7mm-08 Rem.
Magazine: Internal, 6+1 rounds
Features: Lightweight, composite Monte Carlo Griptonite stock; matte bead blasted blued finish; three-position safety.
MSRP $649.00

VANGUARD SYNTHETIC DBM

Action: Bolt
Stock: Injection-molded Monte Carlo
Barrel: 24 in.
Sights: None
Weight: 7 lb. 4 oz.
Caliber: .240 Wby., .25-06 Rem., .270 Win., .30-06 Spfd.
Magazine: Detachable box, 3 rounds
Features: Matte bead blasted blued metalwork; low density recoil pad; two-stage trigger
MSRP $649.00

VANGUARD WEATHERGUARD, WEATHERGUARD BRONZE

Action: Bolt
Stock: Monte Carlo Griptonite
Barrel: 24 in.
Sights: None
Weight: 7 lb. 12 oz.
Caliber: .22-250 Rem., .223 Rem., .240 Wby. Mag., .243 Win., .25-06 Rem., .257 Wby. Mag., .270 Win., .30-06 Spfd., .300 Wby. Mag., .300 Win. Mag., .308 Win., 6.5 Creedmoor, 6.5 PRC, 7mm Rem. Mag., 7mm-08 Rem.
Magazine: 3+1 or 5+1 rounds
Features: Guaranteed SUB-MOA accuracy; Monte Carlo Griptonite stock features pistol grip, forend inserts, and right-side palm swell (aids shooter's comfort and control); Tactical Gray or Burnt Bronze Cerakoting on receiver and barrel for exceptional weather and corrosion resistance; fluted bolt body; three-position safety; hinged floorplate; cold hammer-forged barrel; match quality two-stage trigger
MSRP $699.00

Wilson Combat

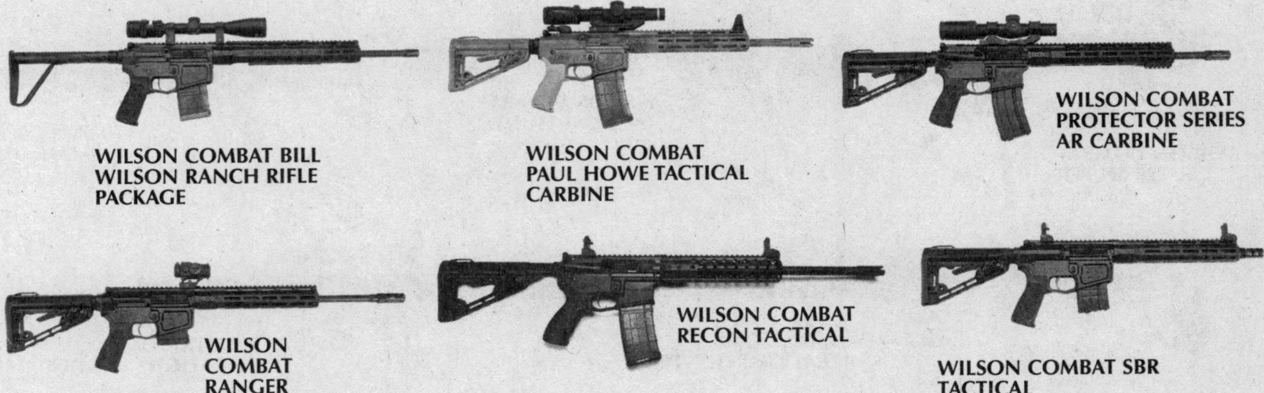

WILSON COMBAT BILL WILSON RANCH RIFLE PACKAGE

WILSON COMBAT PAUL HOWE TACTICAL CARBINE

WILSON COMBAT PROTECTOR SERIES AR CARBINE

WILSON COMBAT RANGER

WILSON COMBAT RECON TACTICAL

WILSON COMBAT SBR TACTICAL

BILL WILSON RANCH RIFLE PACKAGE

Action: Semiautomatic
Stock: Carbon fiber
Barrel: 18 in.
Sights: Trijicon 3–9x40mm green dot scope
Weight: 6 lb. 2 oz.
Caliber: .300 HAM'R
Magazine: 5, 10, 20, 30 rounds
Features: Bill Wilson Ranch Rifle Round threaded match-grade barrel with Circle WC Ranch logo; 12-in. M-LOK rail with three rail covers in green; 18-in. Ergo ladder top rail cover in black; smoke-colored composite carbon fiber buttstock with closed shoulder; Wilson Combat/BCM Starburst Gunfighter pistol grip; TTU M2 trigger; factory-mounted/zeroed Trijicon Accupoint green-dot scope in lightweight rings; Armor-Tuff finish over hard-anodized finish, green/black standard, Forest camo optional
MSRP . . . . .starting at $3350.00

PAUL HOWE TACTICAL CARBINE

Action: Semiautomatic
Stock: Synthetic
Barrel: 14.7 in.
Sights: Detachable fixed front, flip-up BUS rear, Leupold scope
Weight: 6 lb. 4 oz.
Caliber: .223 Rem.
Magazine: N/A
Features: Super-compact MSR; two-stage TTU trigger with heavy mil-spec springs; fluted Recon barrel with a permanent flash hider; M-LOK rail; Daniel Defense detachable fixed front sight; flip-up BUS rear sight with CSAT aperture; Leupold VX-6HD scope; Streamlight TLR-1 HL light; Wilson Combat/BCM Starburst Gunfighter grip; Vickers sling; Armor-Tuff camo finish; California magazine options available; multiple barrel options; kit version available
MSRP . . . . .starting at $2700.00

PROTECTOR SERIES AR CARBINE

Action: Semiautomatic
Stock: Synthetic
Barrel: 16.25 in.
Sights: None
Weight: 6 lb. 1 oz.
Caliber: .300 HAM'R, .223 Rem., .300 BLK
Magazine: 30 rounds
Features: Wilson Combat match-grade barrel; low-profile gas block; QComp muzzle brake; M-LOK handguard with 4-in. rail; direct impingement mid-length operation in 5.56 and .300 HAM'R, pistol length on .300 BLK; TTU M2 two-stage trigger; Rogers/Wilson Super Stoc stock; Wilson Combat/BCM Starburst Gunfighter pistol grip; oversized tactical trigger guard; in black or Coyote Tan Armor-Tuff finish; left-hand options available; no forward assist available
MSRP . . . . .starting at $1995.95

RANGER

Action: Semiautomatic
Stock: Synthetic
Barrel: 16 in., 16.2 in.
Sights: None
Weight: 8 lb.
Caliber: .300 BLK, 5.56 NATO, 6.8 SPC II, 7.62X40 WT, .350 Legend, .300 Ham'r
Magazine: N/A
Features: Match-grade WC Ranger barrel; Rogers/Wilson Super-Stoc stock; Wilson Combat/BCM Starburst Gunfighter grip; threaded muzzle with QComp brake; 1-in. M-LOK rail with three Falcon/Ergo rail covers
MSRP . . . . .starting at $2300.00

RECON TACTICAL

Action: Semiautomatic
Stock: Synthetic tactical
Barrel: 16 in.
Sights: Optional rail
Weight: 7 lb.
Caliber: .204 Ruger, .224 Valkyrie, .300 BLK, .458 SOCOM, 5.56 NATO, 6.5 Grendel, 6.8 SPC, 7.62X40 WT, .300 Ham'R, .350 Legend, .375 SOCOM, .450 Bushmaster
Magazine: Detachable box, 30 rounds
Features: Match grade medium weight stainnless steel barrel; forged 7075 upper (flat top) and lower receiver; mid-length gas system with low-profile gas block; Wilson Combat T.R.I.M. rail; ergo pistol grip
MSRP . . . . starting at $2350.00

SBR TACTICAL

Action: Semiautomatic
Stock: Synthetic
Barrel: 11.3 in.
Sights: Flip-up front, rear
Weight: 6 lb. 5 oz.
Caliber: .300 BLK, .300 HAM'R, 6.8 SPC II, .223 Rem.
Magazine: N/A
Features: SBR (short-barreled rifle) with BILLet upper and lower; match-grade SBR Tactical barrel with a threaded muzzle; choice of Accu-Tac or QComp flash hider; carbine-length gas system with low-profile gas block
MSRP . . . . .starting at $2225.00

Wilson Combat

SUPER SNIPER

Action: Semiautomatic
Stock: Synthetic, telescoping
Barrel: 20 in.
Sights: None
Weight: 10 lb. 11 oz.
Caliber: .260 Rem., 6mm Creedmoor, 6.5 Creedmoor, .308 Win.
Magazine: 10 rounds, 20 rounds
Features: Barrel is precision button rifled from 416-R stainless steel; 1:10 twist; Picatinny rail; BILLet-AR machined aluminum upper and lower receivers; 12 inch or 14 inch free-floating TRIM rail; available with a fluted or non-fluted barrel
MSRP . . . . starting at $2970.00

TACTICAL HUNTER

Action: Semiautomatic
Stock: Synthetic
Barrel: 18 in., 20 in.
Sights: None
Weight: 7 lb. 11 oz.
Caliber: 7mm-08 Rem., .308 Win., .338 Fed., 6mm Creedmoor, 6.5 Creedmoor, .260 Rem.
Magazine: N/A
Features: Ready for the predator and game fields; threaded match-grade Tactical Hunter barrel; rifle-length gas system; SLR Rifleworks adjustable gas block; Rogers/Wilson Super Stoc stock; 14.6-in. M-LOK rail with three three-section Magpul Type 1 rail covers; nickel-boron low-mass bolt carrier; small-latch BCM charging handle
MSRP . . . . starting at $3095.00

ULTIMATE HUNTER

Action: Semiautomatic
Stock: Synthetic
Barrel: 18 in.
Sights: None
Weight: 7 lb. 4 oz.
Caliber: .308 Win. .358 Win.
Magazine: 7, 9 rounds
Features: Smoke-colored composite carbon fiber closed-shoulder buttstock with Limbsaver recoil pad; Tactical Trigger Unit M2 #4; Armor-Tuff finish over hardcoat anodized, green/black is standard, other colors and camo optional
MSRP . . . . starting at $3310.00

ULTRALIGHT HUNTER

Action: Semiautomatic
Stock: Synthetic
Barrel: 16.2 in.
Sights: None
Weight: 7 lb.
Caliber: .300 Ham'r
Magazine: N/A
Features: Match-grade Ultralight Hunter barrel wearing a crowned muzzle; intermediate-length gas system; SLR Rifleworks adjustable gas block; smoke-colored composite carbon fiber buttstock with closed shoulder; 12.6-in. M-LOK rail with three three-section Magpul Type 1 rail covers; nickel-boron low-mass bolt carrier; small-latch BCM charging handle; Mission First tactical pistol grip; kit version available
MSRP . . . . starting at $2465.00

ULTRALIGHT RANGER

Action: Semiautomatic
Stock: Carbon fiber
Barrel: 16, 18 in.
Sights: None
Weight: 7 lb. 6 oz.
Caliber: .300 BLK, .223 Rem., 6.8 SPC, 7.62x40 WT, .300 HAM'R, .350 Legend
Magazine: N/A
Features: Composite carbon fiber stock in smoke and with a closed shoulder buttstock; match-grade Ranger barrel; SLR Rifleworks adjustable gas block; 10-in. M-LOK rail with three Falcon/Ergo rail covers; TTU M2 #4 trigger; Mission First tactical pistol grip; fluted barrel in .350 Legend (16-in.) and .30 HAM'R (18 in.); Armor-Tuff finish over hard anodize finish, standard in green/black with other color choices and camo available
MSRP . . . . starting at $2415.00

URBAN SUPER SNIPER

Action: Semiautomatic, mid-length gas system with low-profile gas block
Stock: Synthetic, telescoping
Barrel: 18 in.
Sights: None
Weight: 7 lb. 5 oz.
Caliber: 6.8 SPC, .223 Wylde, .300 Ham'R
Magazine: 10, 20, or 30 rounds
Features: Medium heavy-weight, fluted, stainless steel premium match-grade barrel; 1:8 twist; Picatinny rail; 10.4 inch free-floating TRIM rail
MSRP . . . . starting at $2300.00

Winchester Repeating Arms

MODEL 70 ALASKAN

Action: Bolt
Stock: Walnut
Barrel: 25 in.
Sights: Open
Weight: 8 lb. 8 oz.
Caliber: .30-06 Spfd., .300 Win. Mag. .338 Win. Mag., .375 HH Mag.
Magazine: None
Features: Satin finish Monte Carlo walnut stock with cut checkering; folding adjustable rear sight with hooded gold bead front sight; recessed target crown
MSRP . . . . $1439.99–$1489.99

MODEL 70 EXTREME TUNGSTEN

Action: Bolt
Stock: Synthetic
Barrel: 22 in., 24 in., 26 in.
Sights: None
Weight: 6 lb. 12 oz.–7 lb. 4 oz.
Caliber: .243 Win., 6.5 Creedmoor, 7mm-08 Rem., .308 Win., .270 WSM, .300 WSM, .25-06 Rem., 270 Win., .30-06 Spfd., .264 Win. Mag., 7mm Rem. Mag., .300 Win. Mag., 6.8 Western
Magazine: 3, 5 rounds
Features: Wearing a charcoal gray Bell & Carlson synthetic stock, this rifle has a free-floating barrel with a muzzle brake in Tungsten Cerakote; receiver in Tungsten Cerakote; Pachmayr Decelerator recoil pad MOA trigger system; pre-'64 action
MSRP . . . .$1549.99–$1589.99

MODEL 70 FEATHERWEIGHT COMPACT

Action: Bolt
Stock: Walnut
Barrel: 20 in.
Sights: None
Weight: 6 lb. 8 oz.
Caliber: 6.5 Creedmoor 7mm-08 Rem., .308 Win., 6.8 Western, 6.5 PRC
Magazine: 5 rounds
Features: Pachmayr decelerator recoil pad; action is drilled and tapped for optics
MSRP . . . . $1049.99–$1089.99

MODEL 70 FEATHERWEIGHT STAINLESS, FEATHERWEIGHT STAINLESS DARK MAPLE

Action: Bolt
Stock: Black walnut, maple
Barrel: 22 in., 24 in.
Sights: None
Weight: 6 lb. 12 oz.–7 lb. 4 oz.
Caliber: .243 Win., 6.5 Creedmoor, 7mm-08 Rem., .308 Win., .270 WSM, .300 WSM, .270 Win., .30-06 Spfd., .264 Win. Mag., 7mm Rem. Mag., .300 Win. Mag.
Magazine: 3, 5 rounds
Features: Matte-finish stainless steel barrel, free-floating and with a target crown; jeweled bolt body; knurled bolt knob; Pachmayr Decelerator pad; pre-'64 action with controlled round feed; controlled round ejection; Standard stainless has a satin-finish Grade I black walnut stock with cut checkering and a schnabel forearm; Dark Maple version has a stock in AAAA dark maple
Standard: . . . .$1249.99–$1299.99
Dark Maple: . . . . .$1589.99–$1629.99

MODEL 70 SAFARI EXPRESS

Action: Bolt
Stock: Satin-finished checkered walnut with deluxe cheekpiece
Barrel: 24 in.
Sights: Hooded-blade front and express-style rear
Weight: 9 lb.
Caliber: .375 H&H Mag., .416 Rem. Mag., .458 Win. Mag.
Magazine: 3 rounds
Features: Pre-'64 type claw extractor; Pachmayr decelerator recoil pad; barrel band front swivel base; dual recoil lugs and three-position safety; MOA trigger system; matte blued finish; two steel cross-bolts and one-piece steel trigger guard and hinged floor plate
MSRP $1609.99

MODEL 70 SUPER GRADE FRENCH WALNUT

Action: Bolt
Stock: French walnut
Barrel: 22 in., 24 in., 26 in.
Sights: None
Weight: 7 lb. 12 oz.–8 lb. 8 oz.
Caliber: .243 Win., 6.5 Creedmoor, .308 Win., .270 Win., .30-06 Spfd., .264 Win. Mag., 7mm Rem. Mag., .300 Win. Mag., 6.8 Western
Magazine: 3, 5 rounds
Features: Grade AAA French walnut stock that features an ebony forearm tip, Shadowline cheekpiece, and polished steel pistol grip cap; free-floating barrel with target crown is in a high-polished blue; M.O.A. trigger assembly; pre-'64 action
MSRP . . . .$2029.99–$2069.99

Winchester Repeating Arms

WINCHESTER MODEL 70 SUPER GRADE MAPLE

WINCHESTER MODEL 94 DELUXE SHORT RIFLE

WINCHESTER MODEL 70 SUPER GRADE STAINLESS

WINCHESTER MODEL 94 CARBINE

WINCHESTER MODEL 94 SHORT RIFLE

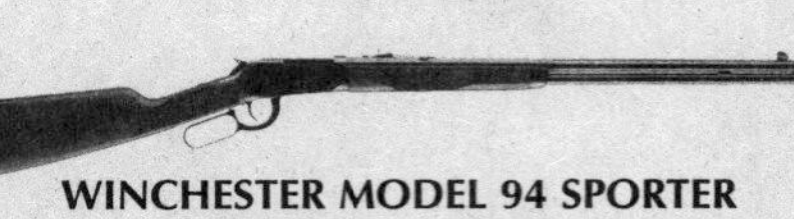

WINCHESTER MODEL 94 SPORTER

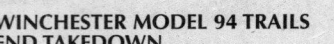

WINCHESTER MODEL 94 TRAILS END TAKEDOWN

WINCHESTER MODEL 1873 CARBINE

MODEL 70 SUPER GRADE MAPLE

Action: Bolt
Stock: Maple
Barrel: 24 in., 26 in.
Sights: None
Weight: 7 lb. 12 oz.–8 lb. 6 oz.
Caliber: .243 Win., .308 Win., .270 Win., .30-06 Spfd., .264 Win. Mag., 7mm Rem. Mag., .300 Win. Mag., 6.5 Creedmoor, 6.8 Western
Magazine: 3, 5 rounds
Features: Gloss-finished AAA maple stock with ebony forend tip; Shadowline cheekpiece; Super Grade engraved hinged floorplate; jeweled bolt body; knurled bolt handle; pre-64 action with MOA Trigger System; hammer-forged, free-floating steel barrel with target crown
MSRP. . . . . $1719.99–$1759.99

MODEL 70 SUPER GRADE STAINLESS

Action: Bolt
Stock: Walnut
Barrel: 22 in., 24 in., 26 in.
Sights: None
Weight: 7 lb. 12 oz.–8 lb. 8 oz.
Caliber: .243 Win., .308 Win., .270 Win., .30-06 Spfd., .264 Win. Mag., 7mm Rem. Mag., .300 Win. Mag.
Magazine: 3, 5 rounds
Features: Similar to the French Walnut and Maple Super Grades, but with a darkly pretty Grade IV/V walnut stock in a satin finish and barrel and receiver in matte stainless
MSRP. . . . . $1689.99–$1729.99

MODEL 94 CARBINE

Action: Lever
Stock: Walnut
Barrel: 20 in.
Sights: Adjustable semi-buckhorn rear, Marble Arms front
Weight: 6 lb. 8 oz.
Caliber: .30-30 Win., .38-55 Win.
Magazine: 7 rounds
Features: Triple-checked button rifled barrel; round locking bolt trunnions; top-tang safety; rebounding hammer; bolt relief cut; steel loading gate; articulated cartridge stop; available knurled hammer spur extension
MSRP. . . . . $1199.99–$1239.99

MODEL 94 DELUXE SHORT RIFLE

Action: Lever
Stock: Black walnut
Barrel: 20 in.
Sights: Hooded front, semi-buckhorn rear
Weight: 6 lb. 12 oz.
Caliber: .30-30 Win., .38-55 Win.
Magazine: 7 rounds
Features: Grade V/VI black walnut stock in an oil finish; color case-hardened frame, lever and fore-arm cap; drilled and tapped for hammer spur extension, which is included
MSRP. $1919.99

MODEL 94 SHORT RIFLE

Action: Lever
Stock: Walnut
Barrel: 20 in.
Sights: Front, adjustable rear
Weight: 6 lb. 12 oz.
Caliber: .30-30 Win., .450 Marlin, .38-55 Win.
Magazine: 7 rounds
Features: Straight grip; rifle-style forearm and black grip cap; semi-buckhorn rear sights, Marble Arms gold-bead front sight; drilled and tapped for optics
MSRP. $1269.99

MODEL 94 SPORTER

Action: Lever
Stock: Walnut
Barrel: 24 in.
Sights: Marble Arms front, adjustable rear
Weight: 7 lb. 8 oz.
Caliber: .30-30 Win., .38-55 Win.
Magazine: 8 rounds
Features: Half-round, half-octagon blued barrel; straight grip stock with a crescent butt and finely checkered blued-steel buttplate with double-line bordering; drilled and tapped for optics
MSRP. $1439.99

MODEL 94 TRAILS END TAKEDOWN

Action: Lever
Stock: Walnut
Barrel: 20 in.
Sights: Adjustable
Weight: 6 lb. 12 oz.
Caliber: .30-30 Win., .38-55 Win., .450 Marlin
Magazine: 6 rounds
Features: Walnut stock and forearm with satin finish and straight-grip styling; blued steel receiver and barrel; Marble Arms front sight with semi-buckhorn rear sight; Pachmayr Decelerator recoil pad (450 model)
MSRP. $1509.99

MODEL 1873 CARBINE

Action: Lever-action
Stock: Black walnut
Barrel: 20 in.
Sights: Marble Arms gold bead front, semi-buckhorn rear
Weight: 7 lb. 4 oz.
Caliber: .357-38, .44-40 Win., .45 Colt
Magazine: 10 rounds
Features: Blued carbine strap buttplate; round barrel; full-length magazine; receiver is drilled and tapped for a tang-mounted rear sight; saddle ring is also in blue
MSRP. $1349.99

Winchester Repeating Arms

MODEL 1873 DELUXE SPORTING

Action: Lever
Stock: Black walnut
Barrel: 24 in.
Sights: Hooded front, semi-buckhorn rear
Weight: 8 lb.
Caliber: .357-38, .44-40 Win., .45 Colt
Magazine: 14 rounds
Features: Grade V/VI black walnut stock with a metal "shotgun" buttplate; color case-hardened receiver, lever, forearm cap and buttplate; drilled and tapped for peep sights; barrel is half round/half octagon, button rifled, and has a gloss blue finish
MSRP $1849.99

MODEL 1873 SHORT RIFLE

Action: Lever
Stock: Wood
Barrel: 20 in.
Sights: Adjustable
Weight: 7 lb. 4 oz.
Caliber: .357 Mag., .45 Colt, .44-40 Win.
Magazine: Under-barrel tube, 10 rounds
Features: Walnut straight grip stock with satin oil finish; classic rifle style forearm with blued steel cap; semi-buckhorn rear sight with Marble Arms gold bead front sights; steel loading gate; receiver rear tang drilled and tapped for optional tang-mounted rear sight
MSRP $1349.99

MODEL 1873 SHORT RIFLE COLOR CASE HARDENED

Action: Lever
Stock: Wood
Barrel: 20 in.
Sights: Adjustable
Weight: 7 lb. 4 oz.
Caliber: .357 Mag., .38 Spl., .44-40 Win., .45 Colt
Magazine: 10–11 rounds
Features: Steel receiver, color case hardened; steel loading gate; rear tang is drilled and tapped for scope mount; steel barrel, polished blued finish; full-length magazine tube; grade II/III walnut stock; straight grip; classic rifle-style forearm; steel forend cap; semi-buckhorn rear sight; Marble's gold bead front sight; color case hardened crescent buttplate, lever, forend cap, and loading gate
MSRP $1629.99

MODEL 1873 SPORTER OCTAGON COLOR CASE HARDENED

Action: Lever
Stock: Walnut
Barrel: 24 in.
Sights: Marble Arms gold bead front, semi-buckhorn rear
Weight: 8 lb.
Caliber: .357 Mag., .44-40 Win., .45 Colt
Magazine: 14 rounds
Features: Classic lever has octagon barrel; pistol grip Grade II/III walnut stock; top tang drilled and tapped for tang-mounted rear sight; crescent buttplate; deep-polished blue finish
MSRP $1789.99

MODEL 1885 HIGH WALL HUNTER HIGH GRADE

Action: Single-shot
Stock: Black walnut
Barrel: 28 in.
Sights: None
Weight: 8 lb. 8 oz.
Caliber: .220 Swift, .22-250 Rem., .243 Win., 6mm Creedmoor, 6.5 Creedmoor, .308 Win., 6.5 PRC, .270 WSM, .300 WSM, .270 Win., .30-06 Spfd., .264 Win. Mag., .28 Nosler, .300 Win. Mag., .300 PRC
Magazine: 1 round
Features: Grade III/IV black walnut stock with 22 lines-per-inch checkering and a Pachmayr Decelerator pad; polished blue metalwork; full octagon barrel; drilled and tapped for scope mount, and a Talley one-piece base is included
MSRP . . . . $1729.99–$1789.99

MODEL 1886 DELUXE RIFLE CASE HARDENED

Action: Lever
Stock: Black walnut
Barrel: 24 in.
Sights: Hooded front, semi-buckhorn rear
Weight: 9 lb. 12 oz.
Caliber: .45-90 Win., .45-70 Gov't.
Magazine: 8 rounds
Features: Grade III/IV black walnut stock; color case-hardened receiver, crescent buttplate, forearm cap, lever, and lower tang; full octagon barrel in polished blue
MSRP $1789.99

MODEL 1886 SHORT RIFLE

Action: Lever
Stock: Walnut
Barrel: 20 in., 24 in.
Sights: Front with brass bead, adjustable rear
Weight: 8 lb. 6 oz.
Caliber: .45-70 Govt., .45-90 Win.
Magazine: Under-barrel, tube, 8 rounds
Features: Deeply blued receiver and lever; end cap and steel crescent buttplate; straight grip
MSRP $1369.99

Winchester Repeating Arms

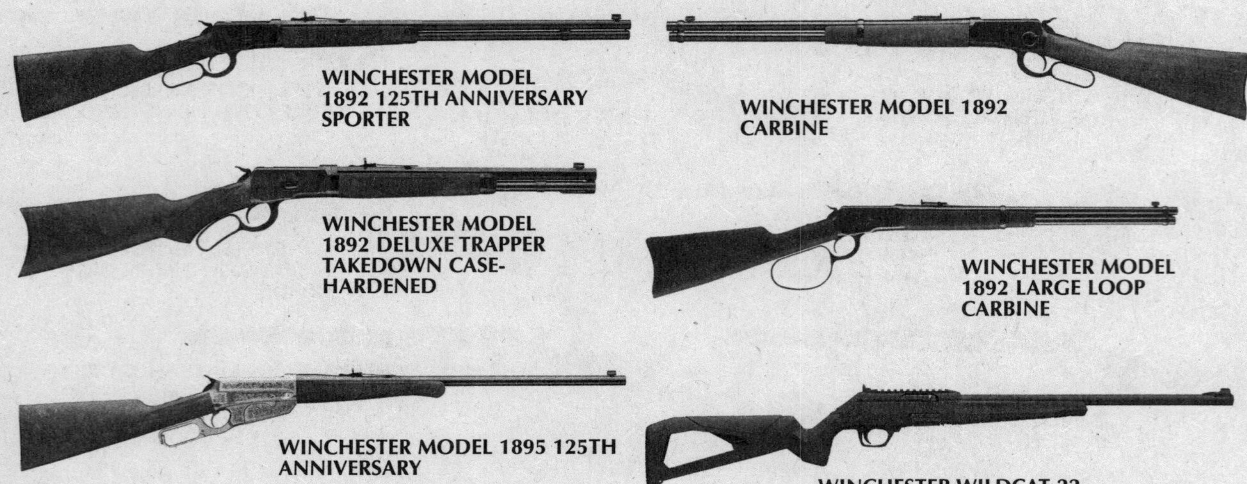

RIFLES

MODEL 1892 125TH ANNIVERSARY SPORTER

Action: Lever
Stock: Walnut
Barrel: 24 in.
Sights: Front post, folding leaf rear
Weight: 6 lb.
Caliber: .357 Mag., .44 Rem. Mag., .44-40 Win., .45 Colt
Magazine: 13 rounds
Features: Half-octagon/half-round button rifled barrel in gloss blue finish; grade IV/V walnut with top tang safety; scroll engraving on receiver; top tang is drilled and tapped for optional peep sight
MSRP $1799.99

MODEL 1892 CARBINE

Action: Lever-action
Stock: Black walnut
Barrel: 20 in.
Sights: Marble Arms gold bead front, semi-buckhorn rear
Weight: 6 lb.
Caliber: .357 Mag., .44 Rem. Mag., .44-40 Win., .45 Colt
Magazine: 10 rounds
Features: Blued carbine strap buttplate; barrel band; saddle ring; straight-grip stock; top tang is drilled and tapped to add a peep sight
MSRP $1109.99

MODEL 1892 DELUXE TRAPPER TAKEDOWN CASE-HARDENED

Action: Lever
Stock: Black walnut
Barrel: 16 in.
Sights: Hooded front, semi-buckhorn rear
Weight: 5 lb. 14 oz.
Caliber: .357 Mag., .44 Rem. Mag., .45 Colt
Magazine: 7 rounds
Features: Grade III/IV black walnut stock in an oil finish; full-octagon button-rifled barrel in polished blue; metal crescent buttplate, receiver, lever, and forearm cap in color case-hardened; drilled and tapped for peep sights
MSRP $1789.99

MODEL 1892 LARGE LOOP CARBINE

Action: Lever
Stock: Walnut
Barrel: 20 in.
Sights: Marble Arms brass bead front, adjustable rear
Weight: 6 lb.
Caliber: .357 Mag., .44 Rem. Mag., .44–40 Win., .45 Colt
Magazine: 10 rounds
Features: Classic saddle rifle with Grade I walnut; large loop with radiused edges; rebounding hammer, metal carbon buttplate; saddle ring; button rifled barrel with recessed crown
MSRP $1309.99

MODEL 1895 125TH ANNIVERSARY

Action: Lever
Stock: Black walnut
Barrel: 24 in.
Sights: Hooded front, semi-buckhorn rear
Weight: 8 lb.
Caliber: .405 Win., .30-40 Krag
Magazine: 4 rounds
Features: A super way to celebrate a grand gun's 125th anniversary with a button-rifled barrel in a gloss finish with special markings; Grade V/VI black walnut stock with a straight grip and traditional checkering
MSRP $2499.99

WILDCAT 22

Action: Semiautomatic
Stock: Polymer
Barrel: 18 in.
Sights: Ramped post front, adjustable ghost ring rear
Weight: 4 lb.
Caliber: .22 LR
Magazine: 10 rounds
Features: Super-fun plinker is super portable at just 4 pounds and has a number of innovative features such as a lower receiver that drops out at the push of a button; removeable rotary magazine; adjustable rear ghost sight; striker-fired mechanism; slide lock; top-side Picatinny rail and a second rail at fore-end tip; ambidextrous skeletonized stock in black or True Timber Strata camo
MSRP $269.99

Winchester Repeating Arms

WINCHESTER XPR

WINCHESTER XPR COMPACT

WINCHESTER XPR HUNTER MOSSY OAK BREAK-UP COUNTRY

WINCHESTER XPR HUNTER KRYPTIC HIGHLANDER

WINCHESTER XPR HUNTER KUIU VERDE 2.0

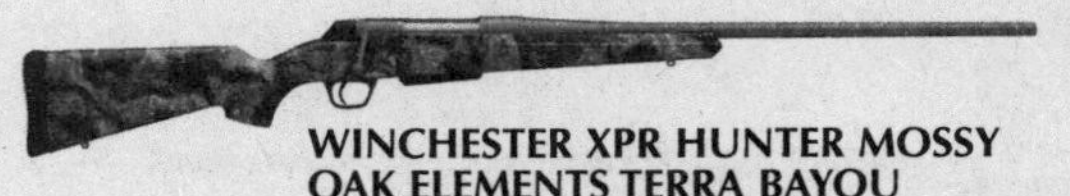

WINCHESTER XPR HUNTER MOSSY OAK ELEMENTS TERRA BAYOU

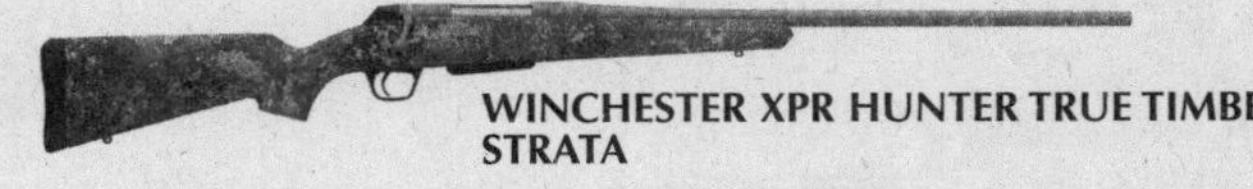

WINCHESTER XPR HUNTER TRUE TIMBER STRATA

XPR

Action: Bolt
Stock: Composite polymer
Barrel: 24 in., 26 in.
Sights: None
Weight: 7 lb.
Caliber: .243 Win., 7mm-08, .308 Win., .270 WSM, .300 WSM, .325 WSM, .270 Win., .30-06 Spfd., 7mm Rem. Mag., .300 Win. Mag., .338 Win. Mag., 6.5 Creedmoor, .350 Legend, .223 Rem., 6.5 PRC, 6.8 Western
Magazine: Detachable box, 3 rounds
Features: Chromoly steel barrel; matte blue finish; hardened steel components; recessed target-style crown; Inflex recoil pad
MSRP **$549.99**

XPR COMPACT

Action: Bolt
Stock: Composite
Barrel: 20 in., 22 in., 24 in.
Sights: None
Weight: 6 lb. 12 oz.–7 lb.
Caliber: .243 Win., 6.5 Creedmoor, 7mm-08 Rem., .308 Win., .270 WSM, .300 WSM, .325 WSM, .350 Legend, 6.5 PRC
Magazine: 3 rounds
Features: Shorter 13-in. length of pull; advanced polymer stock in black, matte blue metal finish; detachable box magazine
MSRP **$549.99**

XPR HUNTER, HUNTER COMPACT MOSSY OAK BREAK-UP COUNTRY

Action: Bolt
Stock: Composite
Barrel: 24 in.
Sights: None
Weight: 6 lb. 5.44 oz.
Caliber: .243 Win., 7mm-08 Rem., .308 Win., .270 WSM, .300 WSM, .325 WSM, .270 Win., .30-06 Spfd., 7mm Rem. Mag., .300 Win. Mag., .338 Win. Mag., 6.5 Creedmoor, .350 Legend, .223 Rem., 6.5 PRC
Magazine: 3 rounds
Features: Mossy Oak Break-Up Country with Perma-Cote matte black hardware on fullsize, matte gray on Compact; drilled and tapped for scope mounts; free-floating barrel; MOA trigger system; two- position thumb safety; Inflex technology recoil pad; swing swivel studs
MSRP **$629.99**

XPR HUNTER KRYPTIC HIGHLANDER

Action: Bolt
Stock: Composite
Barrel: 22 in., 24 in., 26 in.
Sights: None
Weight: 6 lb. 12 oz.–7 lb. 4 oz.
Caliber: 6.5 Creedmoor, 6.5 PRC
Magazine: 3 rounds
Features: The popular XPR bolt rifle with a stock dressed in Kryptik Highlander camo; Permacoat Gray metalwork finish; MOA trigger system
MSRP **$599.99**

XPR HUNTER KUIU VERDE 2.0, VIAS

Action: Bolt
Stock: Composite
Barrel: 22 in., 24 in., 26 in.
Sights: None
Weight: 6 lb. 12 oz.–7 lb. 4 oz.
Caliber: .350 Legend, 6.5 PRC
Magazine: 3 rounds
Features: XPR rifle featuring steel receiver and free-floating, button rifled barrel in Permacote gray finish; Kuiu's Vias macro or Verde composite patterns on stock; Highlander version has metal in Flat Dark Earth Permacote and wears Kryptek's Highlander camo
MSRP **$599.99**

XPR HUNTER MOSSY OAK ELEMENTS TERRA BAYOU

Action: Bolt
Stock: Composite
Barrel: 22 in., 24 in., 26 in.
Sights: None
Weight: 6 lb. 12 oz.–7 lb. 4 oz.
Caliber: .243 Win., 7mm-08 Rem., .308 Win., .350 Legend, 6.5 PRC, .270 WSM, .300 WSM, .270 Win., .30-06 Spfd., 7mm Rem. Mag., .300 Win. Mag., .338 Win. Mag.
Magazine: 3, 4, 5 rounds
Features: Receiver, barrel, and bolt in flat dark earth Perma-Cote; M.O.A. trigger system; stock in full-coverage Mossy Oak Elements Terra Bayou camo pattern and with textured grip panels; Inflex Technology recoil pad
MSRP **$629.99**

XPR HUNTER TRUE TIMBER STRATA

Action: Bolt
Stock: Composite
Barrel: 22 in., 24 in., 26 in.
Sights: None
Weight: 6 lb. 12 oz.–7 lb. 4 oz.
Caliber: ..223 Rem., 243 Win, 6.5 Creedmoor, 7mm-08 Rem., .308 Win., .270 Win., .30-06 Spfd., 7mm Rem. Mag., .300 Win. Mag., .338 Win. Mag., .300 WSM, .270 WSM, .325 WSM, .350 Legend, 6.5 PRC, 6.8 Western
Magazine: 3 rounds
Features: The popular XPR bolt rifle with a stock dressed in True Timber Strata camo; Permacoat Flat Dark Earth metalwork finish; MOA trigger system
MSRP **$629.99**

Winchester Repeating Arms

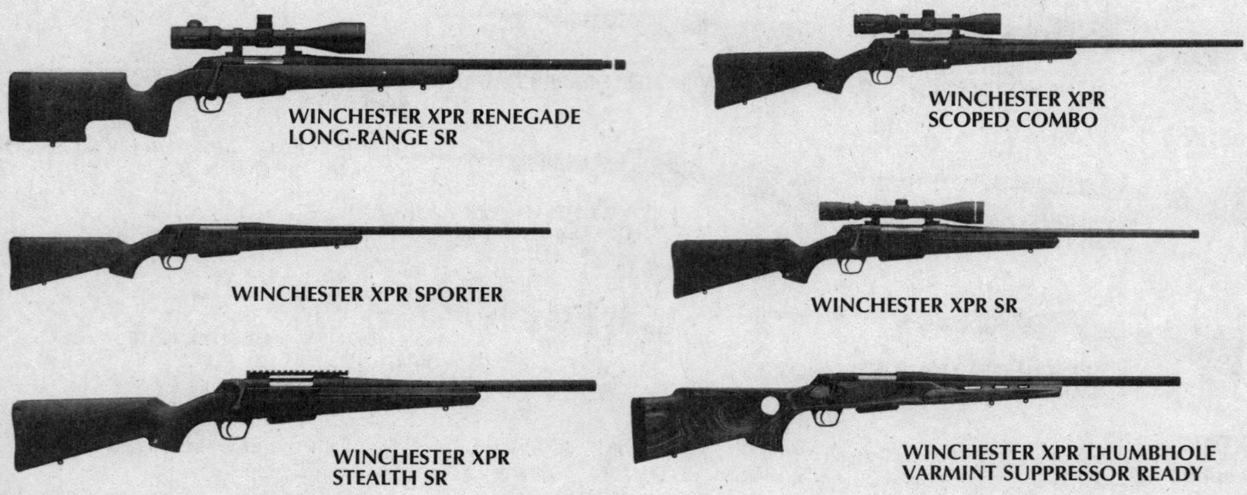

RIFLES

XPR RENEGADE LONG-RANGE SR

Action: Bolt
Stock: Composite
Barrel: 22 in., 24 in.
Sights: None
Weight: 8 lb. 8 oz.
Caliber: .243 Win., 6.5 Creedmoor, 7mm-08 Rem., .308 Win., .270 WSM, .300 WSM, 6.5 PRC, 6.8 Western
Magazine: 3 rounds
Features: Advance Grayboe Renegade Long-Range stock with an upright grip profile, flattened forend, and undercut butt for bench use, as well as length-of-pull spacers; a button-rifled, fluted, free-floating barrel threaded and with a recessed target crown
MSRP $1099.99

XPR SCOPED COMBO

Action: Bolt
Stock: Composite
Barrel: 22 in., 24 in., 26 in.
Sights: None
Weight: 6 lb. 12 oz.–8 lb. 8 oz.
Caliber: .243 Win., 7mm-08 Rem., .308 Win., .350 Legend, 6.5 PRC, .270 WSM, .300 WSM, .325 WSM, .270 Win., .30-06 Spfd., 7mm Rem. Mag., .300 Win. Mag., .338 Win. Mag., 6.5 Creedmoor, 6.8 Western
Magazine: 3, 4 rounds
Features: Vortex Crossfire II 3–9x4mm scope with BDC reticle; Weaver-style rings and bases; Inflex Technology recoil pad; MOA trigger assembly; matte blue metalwork; free-floating button-rifled barrel with target crown
MSRP $729.99

XPR SPORTER

Action: Bolt
Stock: Walnut
Barrel: 22 in., 24 in., 26 in.
Sights: None
Weight: 6 lb. 12 oz.–7 lb. 4 oz.
Caliber: .243 Win., 6.5 Creedmoor, 7mm-08 Rem., .308 Win., .270 Win., .30-06 Spfd., 7mm Rem. Mag., .300 Win. Mag., .338 Win. Mag., .300 WSM, .270 WSM, .325 WSM, .350 Legend 6.5 PRC, 6.8 Western
Magazine: 3 rounds
Features: Button-rifled free-floating barrel; M.O.A. Trigger System; detachable box magazine; Inflex Technology recoil pad; metal is finished in matte black Perma-Cote
MSRP $599.99

XPR SR

Action: Bolt
Stock: Composite
Barrel: 20 in.
Sights: None
Weight: 6 lb. 12 oz.
Caliber: 6.5 Creedmoor, .243 Win., .308 Win., .30-06 Spfd., .300 Win. Mag., .350 Legend, .223 Rem., 6.5 PRC, 6.8 Western
Magazine: 3, 4, 5 rounds
Features: A suppressor-ready rifle for hunters with a sporter-contour, button-rifled, free-floating barrel threaded and with a recessed target crown; M.O.A. trigger assembly; Inflex Technology recoil pad; matte blue metalwork
MSRP $669.99

XPR STEALTH SR

Action: Bolt
Stock: Composite
Barrel: 16.5 in.
Sights: None
Weight: 6 lb. 8 oz.
Caliber: .223 Rem., .243 Win., 6.5 Creedmoor, 7mm-08 Rem., .308 Win., .250 Legend, 6.5 PRC, .270 WSM, .300 WSM, 6.8 Western
Magazine: 3, 4, 5 rounds
Features: A suppressor-ready rifle in a handy barrel length with a button-rifled, free-floating, threaded barrel in a black Perma-Cote finish and with a recessed target crown; dark-green composite stock; swivel studs
MSRP $669.99

XPR THUMBHOLE VARMINT SUPPRESSOR READY

Action: Bolt
Stock: Laminate
Barrel: 24 in.
Sights: None
Weight: 6 lb. 12 oz.
Caliber: .243 Win., 6.5 Creedmoor, .308 Win., .270 Win., .30-06 Spfd., .350 Legend, .223 Rem., 6.5 PRC, 6.8 Western
Magazine: 3 rounds
Features: Laminate thumbhole stock; raised cheekpiece; vented forearm aids cooling; two front sling swivels accommodate sling and bipod simultaneously; metal is matte blue finished; barrel is threaded
MSRP $799.99

Windham Weaponry

WINDHAM WEAPONRY 6.5 CREEDMOOR

WINDHAM WEAPONRY 20-INCH WOOD GRAIN VEX

WINDHAM WEAPONRY .223 SUPERLIGHT

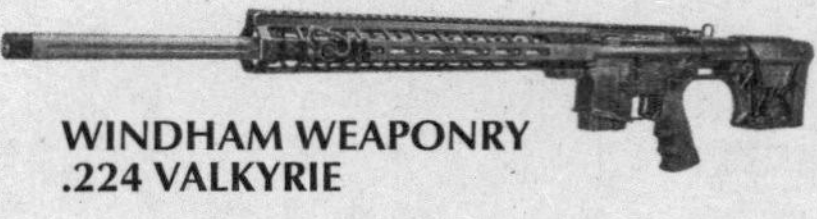
WINDHAM WEAPONRY .224 VALKYRIE

WINDHAM WEAPONRY .450 THUMPER

WINDHAM WEAPONRY RMCS-2 (MULTI-CALIBER SYSTEM) RIFLE KIT

WINDHAM WEAPONRY R20FFTM-308

6.5 CREEDMOOR

Action: Semiautomatic
Stock: Synthetic
Barrel: 20 in.
Sights: None
Weight: 9 lb. 2 oz.
Caliber: 6.5 Creedmoor
Magazine: 5 rounds
Features: Fluted barrel with threaded muzzle; Luth-AR adjustable buttstock; Windham Weaponry free-floating handguard; Hogue overmolded beavertail grip; acres of optics/accessory rail; Hiperfire EDT3 Trigger; gas impingement system
MSRP $2056.00

20-INCH WOOD GRAIN VEX

Action: Semiautomatic
Stock: Synthetic
Barrel: 20 in.
Sights: None
Weight: 8 lb. 5 oz.
Caliber: .223 Rem.
Magazine: 5 rounds
Features: Standard A4 stock gets a dipped wood grain finish, while the receiver gets a hardcoat anodized Coyote finish. Other features include a flattop upper with optic riser blocks; 15-in. M-LOK free-float handguard
MSRP $1544.00

.223 SUPERLIGHT

Action: Semiautomatic
Stock: Synthetic
Barrel: 16 in.
Sights: Flip-up front and rear
Weight: 6 lb.
Caliber: .223 Rem.
Magazine: 30 rounds
Features: Ultralight .223 MSR with a superlight barrel profile wearing a Melonite QPQ finish and A2 flash suppressor; Mission First Tactical Minimalist buttstock; mil-spec buffer tube; Mission First Tactical Engage pistol grip; Kriss flip-up sights
MSRP $1368.00

.224 VALKYRIE

Action: Semiautomatic
Stock: Synthetic
Barrel: 22 in.
Sights: None
Weight: 8 lb. 13 oz.
Caliber: .224 Valkyrie
Magazine: 5 rounds
Features: A gas impingement MSR designed specifically for the .224 Valkyrie round, with a fluted barrel threaded ½X28 and 1:7 right-hand twist; flat-top upper hard coat anodized; Luth-AR adjustable buttstock; 15-inch free-floating fore-end; Hogue overmolded beavertail pistol grip
MSRP $1800.00

.450 THUMPER

Action: Semiautomatic
Stock: Synthetic
Barrel: 16 in.
Sights: None
Weight: 7 lb. 3 oz.
Caliber: .450 Bushmaster
Magazine: 5 rounds
Features: Designed specifically for the straight-wall .450 Bushmaster, with Luth-AR adjustable buttstock; free-floating handguard with rail; Hogue overmolded beavertail pistol grip; chrome-lined barrel with A2 flash hider
MSRP $1608.00

R20FFTM-308

Action: Semiautomatic
Stock: Synthetic
Barrel: 20 in.
Sights: None
Weight: 9 lb. 0.8 oz.
Caliber: .308 Win.
Magazine: 5+1 rounds
Features: Magpul fixed length buttstock with multiple sling attachments; comfortable rubber recoil pad under which is a handy storage compartment; multiple attachment options for M-Lok accessory rails; internal heat shielding; Hogue overmolded rubber pistol grip; Mil Std 1913 Picatinny rails on both receiver and gas block
MSRP $1888.00

RMCS-2 (MULTI-CALIBER SYSTEM) RIFLE KIT

Action: Semiautomatic
Stock: Synthetic
Barrel: 16 in.
Sights: None
Weight: N/A
Caliber: .223 Rem./5.56 NATO–300 BLK
Magazine: 30 rounds
Features: Two calibers in the same AR platform by simply switching out the barrel; chrome-lined barrels; Mil Std 1913 railed gas block; receivers are CNC machined from forged 7075 T6 aircraft aluminum and finished in hardcoat black anodize; twist rates differ depending on barrel
MSRP $1738.00

Windham Weaponry

WINDHAM WEAPONRY RMCS-3 (MULTI-CALIBER SYSTEM) RIFLE KIT

WINDHAM WEAPONRY RMCS-4 (MULTI-CALIBER SYSTEM) RIFLE KIT

RIFLES

RMCS-3 (MULTI-CALIBER SYSTEM) RIFLE KIT

Action: Semiautomatic
Stock: Synthetic
Barrel: 16 in.
Sights: None
Weight: N/A
Caliber: .223 Rem./5.56 NATO–300 BLK–7.62x36mm
Magazine: Standard 30 rd. for .223 Rem./5.56 NATO; standard Magpul for 7.62x39mm; standard Colt type Mag for 9mm
Features: Two calibers in the same AR platform by simply switching out the barrels and magazine wells; chrome-lined barrels; Mil Std 1913 railed gas block; receivers are CNC machined from forged 7075 T6 aircraft aluminum and finished in hardcoat black anodize; twist rates differ depending on barrel
MSRP $2391.00

RMCS-4 (MULTI-CALIBER SYSTEM) RIFLE KIT

Action: Semiautomatic
Stock: Synthetic
Barrel: 16 in.
Sights: None
Weight: N/A
Caliber: .223 Rem./5.56 NATO–300 BLK–7.62x36mm–9mm
Magazine: Standard 30 rd. for .223 Rem./5.56 NATO; standard Magpul for 7.62x39mm; standard Colt type Mag for 9mm
Features: Two calibers in the same AR platform by simply switching out the barrels and magazine wells; chrome-lined barrels; Mil Std 1913 railed gas block; receivers are CNC machined from forged 7075 T6 aircraft aluminum and finished in hardcoat black anodize; twist rates differ depending on barrel
MSRP $2971.00

AIRGUNS

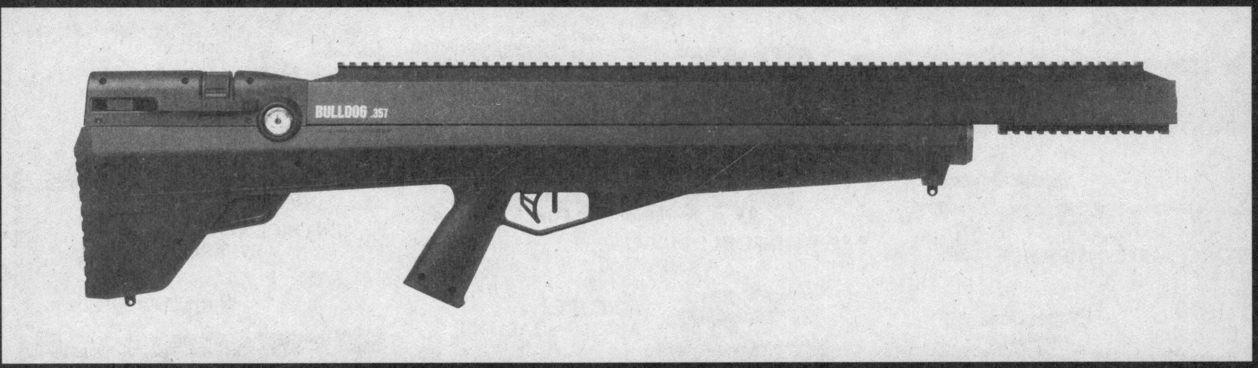

AirForce Airguns

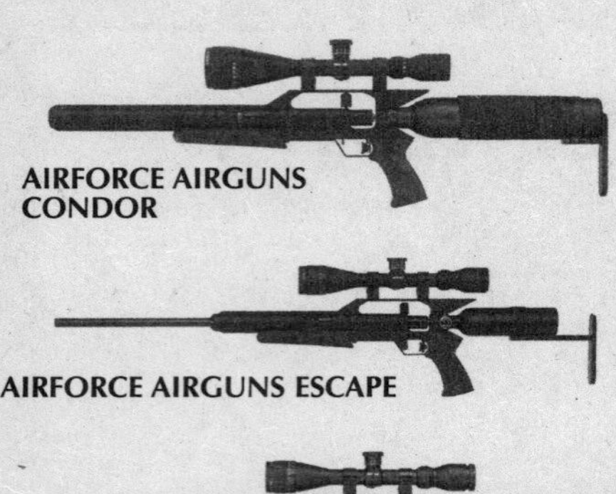

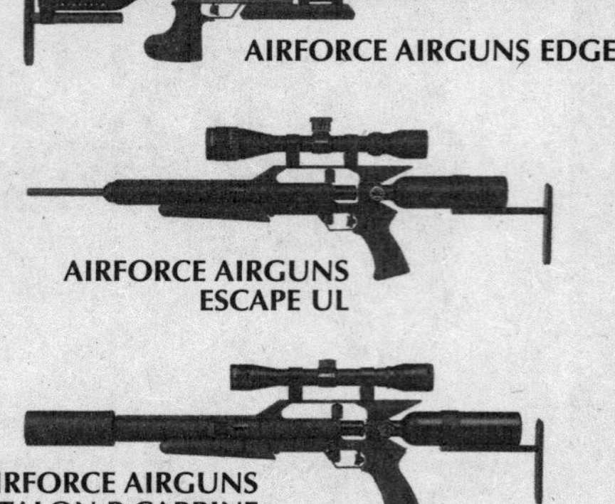

AIRFORCE AIRGUNS
ESCAPE SS

AIRFORCE
AIRGUNS TALON

AIRFORCE
AIRGUNS TALON P

AIRFORCE AIRGUNS
TALON P CARBINE

CONDOR

Power: Pre-charged pneumatic, user adjustable
Stock: Composite
Overall Length: 38.7 in.
Sights: None
Weight: 6 lb. 8 oz.
Caliber: .25, .22, .20, .177
Features: Black, red, or blue composite stock; integral extended scope rail; detachable air tank; Lothar Walther barrel; pressure relief device; adjustable power; scopes optional
Spin-Loc: $784.95

CONDOR SS

Power: Compressed air
Stock: Composite
Overall Length: 38.125 in.
Sights: Open or optical may be installed
Weight: 6 lb. 2 oz.
Caliber: .177, .20, .22, .25
Features: CondorSS combines the major attributes of the TalonSS's quiet operation and the Condor's high power levels; new sound reduction technology; 18-inch barrel blue, red, or original black; 600–1300 fps; two-stage trigger; single shot
MSRP $814.95

EDGE

Power: Pre-charged pneumatic
Stock: Composite
Overall Length: 35–40 in.
Sights: TS1 peep sight system
Weight: 6 lb. 2 oz.
Caliber: .177
Features: Ambidextrous cocking knob; regulated air system; adjustable length of pull; adjustable forend; hooded front sight only or front and rear sight available; two-stage adjustable trigger; composite stock in red or blue finish; scopes optional
Front sight only: $639.95
Front and rear sights: $799.95

ESCAPE

Power: Compressed air
Stock: Synthetic
Overall Length: 34.5 in.–39 in.
Sights: Open or optical
Weight: 5 lb. 4.8 oz
Caliber: .22, .25
Features: Lothar Walther Barrels; Quick-Detach or Spin-Loc air tanks; lightweight and compact; geared for survival situations; user adjustable length
MSRP $729.95

ESCAPE SS

Power: Compressed air
Stock: Synthetic
Overall Length: 27.75 in.–32.25 in.
Sights: Open or optical
Weight: 4 lb. 4.8 oz
Caliber: .22, .25
Features: Lothar Walther Barrels; Quick-Detach or Spin-Loc air tanks; lightweight and compact; geared for survival situations; user adjustable length; Sound-Loc sound reduction technology installed
MSRP $719.95

ESCAPE UL

Power: Compressed air
Stock: Synthetic
Overall Length: 28.5 in.–33 in.
Sights: Open or optical
Weight: 4 lb. 4 oz
Caliber: .22, .25
Features: Lothar Walther Barrels; Quick-Detach or Spin-Loc air tanks; lightweight and compact; geared for survival situations; user adjustable length
MSRP $674.95

TALON

Power: Compressed air
Stock: Composite
Overall Length: 32.6 in.
Sights: None
Weight: 5 lb. 8 oz.
Caliber: .25, .22, .20, .177
Features: Lothar Walther barrel; pressure relief device; adjustable power; detachable air tank; black composite stock; scopes optional
MSRP $639.95

TALON P

Power: Compressed air
Stock: Composite
Overall Length: 24 in.
Sights: None
Weight: 3 lb. 8 oz.
Caliber: .25
Features: Designed to deliver over 50 ft.-lbs. of energy with a .25-caliber hunting pellet; integral extended scope rail; Lothar Walther barrels; variant with buttstock and moderator
MSRP . . . . $504.95–$749.95

TALON P CARBINE

Action: PCP
Stock: Synthetic
Barrel: 12 in.
Sights: None
Weight: 4 lb. 5 oz.
Caliber: .25
Magazine: 1 shot
Features: A single-shot PCP with adjustable power; pressure relief valve; two-stage adjustable trigger; moderator similar to the one on Airforce's LSS air rifles, which helps mitigate sound
MSRP $749.95

AirForce Airguns

AIRFORCE AIRGUNS TALON SS

AIRFORCE AIRGUNS TEXAN LSS

AIRFORCE AIRGUNS TEXAN

AIRFORCE AIRGUNS TEXAN LSS-CF

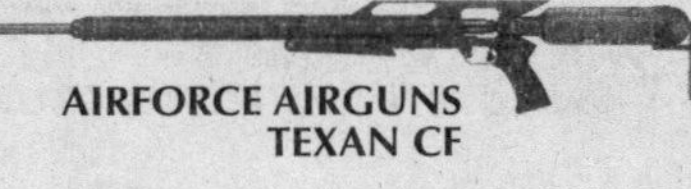
AIRFORCE AIRGUNS TEXAN CF

TALON SS

Power: Compressed air
Stock: Composite
Overall Length: 32.7 in.
Sights: None
Weight: 5 lb. 4 oz.
Caliber: .25, .22, .20, .177
Features: Improved sound reduction; Lothar Walther barrel; pressure relief device; adjustable power; detachable air tank; black, red, or blue composite stock; multiple mounting rails; two-stage trigger; innovative muzzle cap that strips away air turbulence and reduces discharge sound levels; scopes optional
MSRP $689.95

TEXAN

Power: Compressed air
Stock: Synthetic
Overall Length: 48 in.
Sights: Open or optical
Weight: 8 lb.
Caliber: .257, .308, .357, .457
Features: With the ability to launch .45 caliber projectiles at over 1000 feet per second and generating energy levels of over 500 foot pounds, the Texan takes its place as the world's most powerful production air rifle. Easy to load and simple to use, this Big Bore air rifle will let you focus on hunting with the knowledge you have enough power to get the job done.
MSRP $1084.95

TEXAN CF

Action: PCP
Stock: Synthetic
Barrel: 34 in.
Sights: None
Weight: 8 lb.
Caliber: .457, .50
Magazine: 1 shot
Features: Luthar Walther barrel; carbon fiber tank with pressure relief valve can be filled with compressed air or dried nitrogen to a max fill pressure of 3,625 psi; auto-safe upon cocking with side-lever
MSRP $1229.95

TEXAN LSS

Action: PCP
Stock: Synthetic
Barrel: 34 in.
Sights: None
Weight: 8 lb.
Caliber: .257, .308, .357, .457
Magazine: N/A
Features: Capable of taking medium-sized game animals, this suppresses big-bore rifle features adjustable power; pressure relief device; side-cocking lever; two-stage position-adjustable trigger; automatic safety on cocking
MSRP $1254.95

TEXAN LSS-CF

Action: PCP
Stock: Synthetic
Barrel: 34 in.
Sights: None
Weight: 9 lb. 5 oz.
Caliber: .457, .50
Magazine: 1 shot
Features: A big-bore air rifle with a carbon fiber tank; Lothar Walther barrel; side-lever cocking; auto-safe upon cocking; two-stage adjustable trigger; adjustable power; pressure relief valve; TX2 valve
MSRP $1399.95

Air Venturi

AIR VENTURI AVENGER

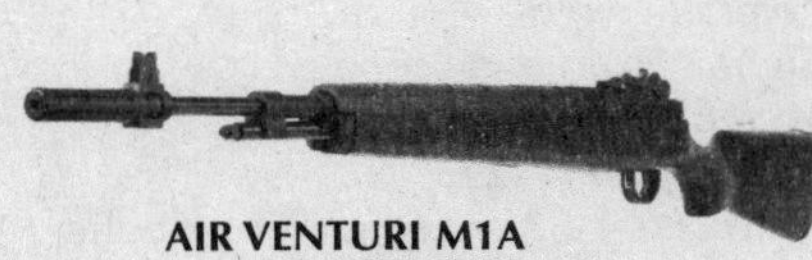
AIR VENTURI M1A UNDERLEVER

AVENGER

Action: PCP
Stock: Synthetic
Barrel: 22.75 in.
Sights: None
Weight: 6 lb.
Caliber: .177, .22, .25
Magazine: 10 shots
Features: Features a regulator that can be adjusted externally; adjustable two-stage trigger; regulated and fill pressure gauges; fully shrouded barrel; scope rail tp, accessory rail at underside of forearm; pre-drilled holes for stud installation
MSRP $349.99

M1A UNDERLEVER

Action: Spring piston
Stock: Wood
Barrel: N/A
Sights: M1A iron sights
Weight: N/A
Caliber: .177, .22
Magazine: 1 shot
Features: With nearly the heft and balance of the real thing, this single-shot spring-piston air rifle has a forward-cocking underlever
MSRP $219.99

Anschütz (J.G. Anschütz)

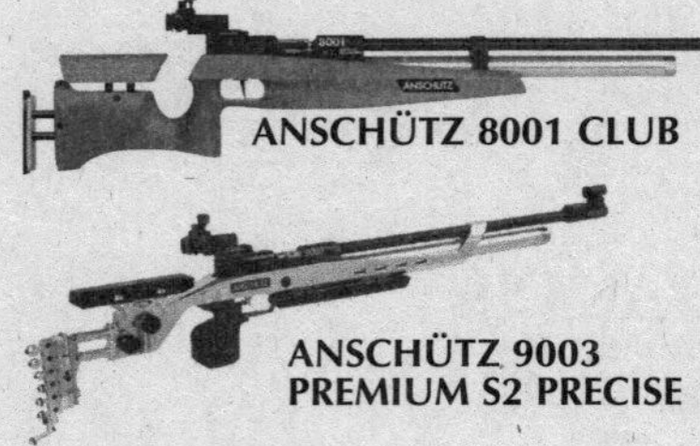
ANSCHÜTZ 8001 CLUB

ANSCHÜTZ 9003 PREMIUM S2 PRECISE

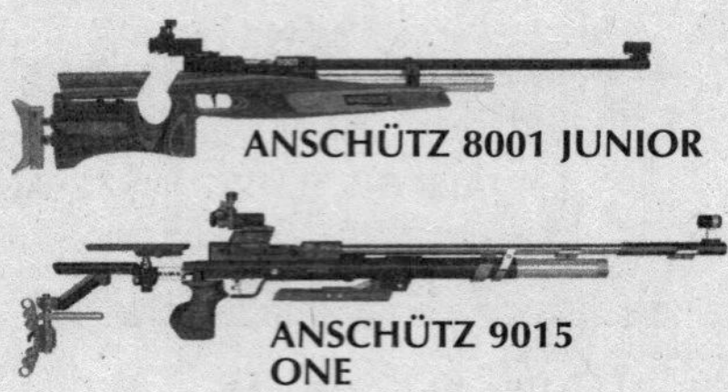
ANSCHÜTZ 8001 JUNIOR

ANSCHÜTZ 9015 ONE

ANSCHÜTZ 8002 S2

8001 CLUB

Power: Compressed air
Stock: Walnut
Overall Length: 42.1 in.
Sights: Open, includes sight set 6834
Weight: 8 lb. 6 oz.
Caliber: .177
Features: Walnut stock with stippled checkering and non-stained aluminum or rubber buttplate; adjustable trigger; match grade barrel
MSRP $1999.99

8001 JUNIOR

Power: Compressed air
Stock: Laminate
Overall Length: 37.4 in.
Sights: Open, includes sight set 6834
Weight: 8 lb. 2 oz.
Caliber: .177
Features: Laminated wood in blue and orange with aluminum buttplate stock; cylindrical match grade barrel; comes with accessory box
MSRP $1999.99

8002 S2

Power: Compressed air
Stock: Aluminum and synthetic pistol grip or laminated wood pistol grip
Overall Length: 42.1 in.
Sights: Open, includes sight set 6834
Weight: 10 lb. 2 oz.
Caliber: .177
Features: Aluminum stock in silver and blue with laminated wood or synthetic pistol grip; blue air cylinder; ProGrip cheekpiece and forend; includes accessory box; aluminum accessory rail
Wood: $2619.99

9003 PREMIUM S2 PRECISE

Power: Compressed air
Stock: Aluminum
Overall Length: 43.7 in.
Sights: Open, includes sight set 6834
Weight: 9 lb. 15 oz.
Caliber: .177
Features: Silver/black aluminum stock pistol grip; Soft Link shock absorber pads; adjustable forend stock, cheekpiece, and buttplate; includes plastic rifle case; steel match barrel; aluminum accessory rail on stock
MSRP $4345.00

9015 ONE

Power: Barreled action
Stock: Aluminum; stainless steel; carbon
Overall Length: 39 in.–47.2 in.
Sights: Adjustable
Weight: 10.1 lb.
Caliber: .177
Features: New patented 5065 4K trigger with ball bearings and versatile adjustable trigger blade; a stainless steel barrel unit; thin, special coated barrel extension; maintenance free stabilizer; air filter against pollutions; cocking lever mountable left and right; adjustable cheekpiece; scalloped grip
MSRP . . . . $3595.00–$4795.00

Beeman Precision Airguns

BEEMAN PRECISION AIRGUNS GRIZZLY X2 DUAL CALIBER

BEEMAN PRECISION AIRGUNS WOLVERINE CARBINE

BEEMAN PRECISION AIRGUNS SILVER KODIAK X2 DC

BEEMAN PRECISION AIRGUNS TETON

GRIZZLY X2 DUAL CALIBER

Power: Spring piston
Stock: Wood
Overall Length: 45.5 in.
Sights: Fixed and scope
Weight: 8 lb. 8 oz.
Caliber: .177, .22
Features: 4x32 scope and fiber optics sights; break barrel action; interchangeable barrels; available with case
MSRP $145.26

SILVER KODIAK X2 DC

Power: Break action, spring piston
Stock: All-weather synthetic
Overall Length: 47.5 in.
Sights: 3–9x32 or 4x32 scope
Weight: 8 lb. 12 oz.
Caliber: .177, .22
Features: Two airguns in one; satin nickel plated barrel and receiver; ported muzzle brake; 1000 fps max velocity
MSRP $179.99

TETON

Power: Spring piston
Stock: Wood
Overall Length: 44.5 in.
Sights: Fixed and scope
Weight: 9 lb.
Caliber: .177, .22
Features: 4x32 scope and fiber optic sights; break barrel action; rifled barrel
MSRP $199.99

WOLVERINE CARBINE

Power: Spring piston
Stock: Synthetic
Overall Length: 45.5 in.
Sights: Fixed and scope
Weight: 8 lb. 8 oz.
Caliber: .177, .22
Features: 4x32 scope and fiber optic sights; break barrel action; rifled barrel; rubber recoil pad
MSRP $129.95

Bo Manufacture/Black Ops Soul

BO MANUFACTURE BLACK OPS QUANTICO

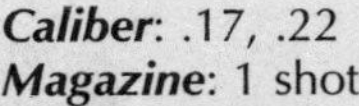

QUANTICO
Action: Spring piston
Stock: Synthetic
Barrel: 18.8 in.
Sights: Fiber optic front, rear
Weight: 7 lb. 3 oz.
Caliber: .17, .22
Magazine: 1 shot
Features: Features a super-adjustable buttstock; top-side Picatinny rail
MSRP $130.00

BSA Guns

BSA DEFIANT

BSA R-10 TH

DEFIANT
Action: PCP
Stock: Walnut, laminate
Barrel: 18.5 in.
Sights: N/A
Weight: 9 lb.
Caliber: .177, .22
Magazine: 10 shots
Features: Ambidextrous stock that is adjustable, soft-touch cheekpiece, and magazine housing; pressure gauge with quick-fill design; barrel with shroud and integrated silencer
MSRP . . . . $1599.00–$1699.00

R-10 TH
Action: PCP
Stock: Walnut, laminate
Barrel: 15 in.
Sights: N/A
Weight: 8 lb.
Caliber: .177, .22
Magazine: 10 shots
Features: Ambidextrous thumbhole stock in maple or black pepper laminate; adjustable cheekpiece and adjustable buttstock; rotary numbered magazine with last shot indicator; fully regulated
MSRP $1299.99

Chiappa Firearms

CHIAPPA RHINO 50DS

RHINO 50DS
Action: CO2
Stock: Synthetic
Barrel: 5 in.
Sights: Fixed front, adjustable rear
Weight: 38.4 oz.
Caliber: 6mm, 4.5BB
Magazine: 6 shots
Features: A 6mm airsoft or 4.5 BB revolver with underlug accessory rail; double-/single-action; metalwork available in black, nickel, black/white, white/black
MSRP . . . . $149.00–$239.00

AIRGUNS

Crosman

CROSMAN 760 PUMPMASTER KIT

CROSMAN 1911

760 PUMPMASTER, PUMPMASTER KIT
Action: Pump
Stock: Synthetic
Barrel: N/A
Sights: Ramp blade front, adjustable rear
Weight: N/A
Caliber: BB, .177
Magazine: 18 shots
Features: In 2019, a total revamp of this tried and true airgun, with all new stock, trigger design, 1,000-shot BB reservoir, and easier to access loading port; stocks in turquoise blue, pink and, both available with optional scope; earth brown stock available for Canadian market; kits include 4X scope, Copperhead BBs, Crosman pellets, safety glasses, and targets
MSRP $44.99
Kit: $64.99

1911
Power: CO2
Stock: Polymer
Overall Length: 8 in.
Sights: Fixed
Weight: 1 lb. 14 oz.
Caliber: .177
Magazine: 6 rounds
Features: In traditional Colt 1911 style; polymer frame; metal slide; accessory rail; removable metal magazine with two six-round rotary clips; available in blue or stainless finishes
MSRP $99.99

Crosman

CROSMAN AIRMASTER

CROSMAN BENJAMIN 392S

CROSMAN BENJAMIN 397S

CROSMAN BENJAMIN AKELA

CROSMAN BENJAMIN CAYDEN

CROSMAN BENJAMIN ARMADA

CROSMAN BENJAMIN BULLDOG .357

CROSMAN BENJAMIN DISCOVERY

CROSMAN BENJAMIN FORTITUDE GEN 2

AIRMASTER

Power: Variable pump
Stock: Synthetic
Overall length: 39.75 in.
Sights: Fiber optic front, adjustable rear
Weight: 4 lb. 12 oz.
Caliber: BB, .177
Features: Variable pump; rifled steel barrel; single-stage trigger; crossbolt safety; 4x15mm scope; optional kit includes metal swinging target, 500 pellets, 1,500 BBs, and safety glasses
MSRP $89.99

BENJAMIN 392S

Action: Variable pump
Stock: Synthetic
Barrel: 19.25 in.
Sights: Fixed front, adjustable rear
Weight: 5 lb. 8 oz.
Caliber: .22
Magazine: 1 shot
Features: Good for plinking or small game, this favorite in the Benjamin lineup gets a new all-weather synthetic stock; fully rifled brass barrel; easier-to-pump forearm
MSRP $199.99

BENJAMIN 397S

Action: Variable pump
Stock: Synthetic
Barrel: 19.25 in.
Sights: Fixed front, adjustable rear
Weight: 5 lb. 8 oz.
Caliber: .177
Magazine: 1`shot
Features: An old favorite gets a new look with an all-weather synthetic stock; fully rifled brass barrel; easier-to-pump forearm
MSRP $199.99

BENJAMIN AKELA

Action: PCP
Stock: Turkish walnut
Barrel: N/A
Sights: None
Weight: 7 lb. 11 oz.
Caliber: .22
Magazine: 12 shots
Features: Similar to the Cayden model, but with a slightly lighter and more compact bullpup stock with texturing at the grip area
MSRP $649.99

BENJAMIN ARMADA

Power:Multi-shot pneumatic, bolt
Stock: Synthetic
Overall Length: 42 in.
Sights: None
Weight: 7 lb. 5 oz.
Caliber: .177, .22, .25
Features: Modular, versatile design; backwards compatible with Mil-Spec AR-15 grips and stocks; machined receiver featuring 5 inches of Picatinny rail space; delivers over 30 consistent shots per fill (up to 16 in .25 cal); bolt action is reversible; integrated resonance dampener; 10-round magazine delivers fast follow up shots (8-rd magazine in .25 cal); rifled barrel, choked and shrouded; optics and bipod not included
MSRP . . . . $799.99–$819.99

BENJAMIN BULLDOG .357

Power:Multi-shot pneumatic, bolt
Stock: Synthetic
Overall Length: 36 in.
Sights: None
Weight: 7 lb. 11 oz.
Caliber: .357
Features: Bullpup configuration; 26 inches of picatinny rail; Baffle-less SoundTrap shroud for big bore sound suppression; sidelever bolt reversible for left hand shooters; intuitive, easy to load 5-shot magazine; reversible bolt; 10 shots per fill
Airgun only: $849.99
Value pack: $1099.99

BENJAMIN CAYDEN

Action: PCP
Stock: Turkish walnut
Barrel: N/A
Sights: None
Weight: 7 lb. 15 oz.
Caliber: .22
Magazine: 12 shots
Features: Bolt-action operation with a two-stage trigger; rotary magazine; rifled steel barrel; sling swivel studs; side cocking lever; adjustable trigger shoe; adjustable cheekpiece
MSRP $599.99

BENJAMIN DISCOVERY

Power: Dual fuel compressed air
Stock: Walnut
Overall Length: 39 in.
Sights: Fiber optic front, adjustable rear
Weight: 5 lb. 2 oz.–5 lb. 3 oz.
Caliber: .22, .177
Features: Rifled steel barrel; velocity up to 900 fps; cross-bolt safety; built-in pressure gauge; high pressure pump included
MSRP . . . . $269.95–$279.95

BENJAMIN FORTITUDE GEN 2

Action: PCP
Stock: Synthetic
Barrel: N/A
Sights: None
Weight: N/A
Caliber: .177, .22
Magazine: 10 shots
Features: Cocking force is light; rotary magazine; 3,000 psi regulated pressure gauge; shrouded barrel; suppressor; rifled barrel
MSRP $309.99

Crosman

CROSMAN BENJAMIN IRONHIDE

CROSMAN BENJAMIN KRATOS

CROSMAN BENJAMIN MARAUDER

CROSMAN BENJAMIN TITAN NP

CROSMAN BENJAMIN MARAUDER LOTHAR BARREL

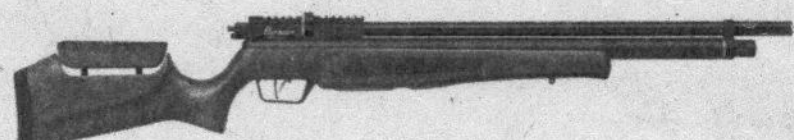
CROSMAN BENJAMIN MARAUDER SEMI-AUTOMATIC

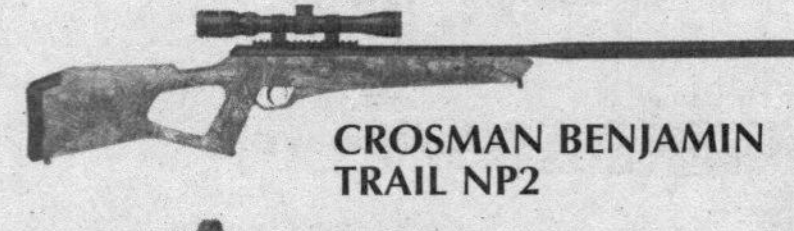
CROSMAN BENJAMIN TRAIL NP2

CROSMAN BENJAMIN VAPORIZER

CROSMAN BENJAMIN MPW

BENJAMIN IRONHIDE

Power: Gas piston
Stock: Synthetic
Overall Length: N/A
Sights: Fixed front, adjustable open rear
Weight: 10 lb.
Caliber: .177, .22
Magazine: 1 round
Features: Thumbhole-stocked break-barre; two-stage adjustable trigger; SBD Gold Sound Suppression; CenterPoint 3–9x40mm scope
MSRP $159.99

BENJAMIN KRATOS

Action: PCP
Stock: Turkish walnut
Barrel: N/A
Sights: None
Weight: 8 lb. 3 oz.
Caliber: .22, .25
Magazine: 10, 12 shots
Features: Similar to the Cayden model with a different powerplant arrangement and availability in .25
MSRP $699.99

BENJAMIN MARAUDER

Power: Compressed air
Stock: Wood
Overall Length: 42.8 in.
Sights: None
Weight: 8 lb. 3 oz.
Caliber: .177, .22, .25
Features: Bolt action; ten round magazine; reversable bolt; dovetail mounting rail; available in wood, black synthetic, and Realtree Max1, Realtree Xtra, and Muddy Girl camo stocks
MSRP . . . . $539.99–$599.99

BENJAMIN MARAUDER LOTHAR BARREL

Action: PCP
Stock: Wood
Barrel: N/A
Sights: None
Weight: N/A
Caliber: .177, .22
Magazine: 10 shots
Features: Adjustable cheekpiece; rifled barrel; reversible bolt handle; Picatinny breech; Lothar Walther barrel; multi-shot bolt-action
MSRP . . . . $599.99–$639.99

BENJAMIN MARAUDER SEMI-AUTOMATIC

Action: PCP
Stock: Hardwood
Barrel: N/A
Sights: None
Weight: 8 lb. 3 oz.
Caliber: .22
Magazine: 10 shots
Features: Semiautomatic air rifle; ambidextrous charging handle; shrouded rifled barrel with resonance damper; regulated for 60 shots per fill; adjustable cheekpiece on hardwood stock; auto-indexing magazine is backwards compatible
MSRP $729.99

BENJAMIN TITAN NP

Power: Nitro piston
Stock: Hardwood, synthetic
Length: 43 in., 44.5 in.
Sights: 4x32mm scope included
Weight: 6 lb. 10 oz.–6 lb. 14 oz.
Caliber: .177
Features: Powered by Nitro Piston technology; delivers velocities up to 1200 fps (.177) with alloy pellets; included 4x32mm scope; ambidextrous hardwood stock with thumbhole; two-stage adjustable trigger; ventilated rubber recoil pad; hardwood
MSRP $139.99

BENJAMIN TRAIL NP2

Power: NP2 nitro piston
Stock: Synthetic or wood
Overall Length: 46.25 in.
Sights: CenterPoint 3–9x32mm scope
Weight: 8 lb. 5 oz.
Caliber: .177
Features: Break barrel; first to feature new NP2 power system; enhanced Clean Break Trigger; integrated sound suppression system; shoots up to 1200 fps alloy, 900 fps pellet
MSRP $249.99

BENJAMIN VAPORIZER

Power: Gas piston
Stock: Synthetic
Overall Length: N/A
Sights: Fixed front sight, adjustable rear
Weight: 10 lb.
Caliber: .177, .22
Magazine: 1 round
Features: Crosman's SBD Gold Sound Suppression; synthetic stock with soft-touch inserts; Picatinny rail; CenterPoint 3–9x40mm scope
MSRP $259.99

BUSHMASTER MPW

Action: CO2
Stock: Synthetic
Barrel: N/A
Sights: Red dot
Weight: N/A
Caliber: BB
Magazine: 25 shots
Features: An AR-style CO2 BB gun with adjustable buttstock; quad rail forearm; red dot sight; full-auto and semiauto modes; 25-round drop magazine; can be customized with AR-compatible buffer tubes and grips; speedloader included
MSRP $199.99

Crosman

CHALLENGER PCP

Power: Pneumatic pump and CO2
Stock: Synthetic
Overall Length: 41.5 in.
Sights: Open
Weight: 7 lb. 2 oz.
Caliber: .177
Features: Two-stage match grade adjustable trigger; Lothar Walther barrel; adjustable cheekpiece and buttpiece; black synthetic stock; 11mm scope mount rails; ambidextrous
Without sights: $529.99
Sights: $629.99

CLASSIC 1911 PISTOL KIT

Action: CO2
Stock: Synthetic
Barrel: 5 in.
Sights: Low-profile blade front, notch rear
Weight: N/A
Caliber: BB
Magazine: N/A
Features: A full-size 1911-type BB pistol with textured grip; skeletonized trigger; under rail; tan frame with black slide and grips; comes with targets and 250 BBs
MSRP $29.99

CLASSIC 2100

Power: Pneumatic pump
Stock: Synthetic
Overall Length: 39.75 in.
Sights: Visible impact front, adjustable rear
Weight: 4 lb. 13 oz.
Caliber: .177
Features: Cross-bolt safety; BB up to 755 fps, pellet up to 725 fps
MSRP $69.99

COWBOY

Action: Lever
Stock: Wood
Barrel: N/A
Sights: Ramp blade front, adjustable rear
Weight: N/A
Caliber: BB
Magazine: 1 shot
Features: Have your kid watch a couple John Wayne movies, then buy them this fun lever BB gun with a ratcheted lever that locks to prevent pinched fingers during cocking; all-metal receiver; hardwood stock
MSRP $39.99

DIAMONDBACK

Power: Gas piston
Stock: Synthetic
Overall Length: N/A
Sights: Fixed front sight, adjustable rear
Weight: N/A
Caliber: .177, .22
Magazine: 1 round
Features: Sturdy pistol grip stock; rifled barrel; SBD Gold Sound Suppression; CenterPoint 4x32mm scope
MSRP $189.99

DPMS CLASSIC M4 NITRO PISTON

Power: Nitro Piston 2
Stock: Synthetic
Overall length: 40 in.
Sights: None
Weight: 5 lb. 12.8 oz.
Caliber: .177
Features: Break-barrel action modeled after DPMS A4 platform; two-stage adjustable trigger; Picatinny rail; CenterPoint 4x32mm scope included
MSRP $219.99

FURY NP

Power: Break action Nitro Piston
Stock: Synthetic all-weather
Overall Length: 45 in.
Sights: 4X32mm scope; rifled sights
Weight: 6 lb. 6 oz.
Caliber: .177
Features: Velocities up to 1200 fps; rifled steel barrel; adjustable two-stage trigger; Nitro Piston technology delivers smooth cocking, reduced vibration and shoots with 70 percent less noise
Scope: $139.99

M4-177

Power: Multi-pump pneumatic
Stock: Synthetic
Length: 34 in.
Sights: Adjustable front and rear
Weight: 3 lb. 9 oz.
Caliber: .177
Features: Rifled steel barrel; shoots both pellets and BBs; variable pump action easy to use for right- or lefthanded shooters; Picatinny rails; front and rear sights and stock are removable for upgrades; adjustable stock; velocities up to 660 fps with BBs and 625 fps with 7.9gr, .177 caliber pellets
MSRP $79.99

Crosman

CROSMAN MAKO

CROSMAN MAXIMUS

CROSMAN MK45

CROSMAN NIGHT STALKER

CROSMAN OPTIMUS

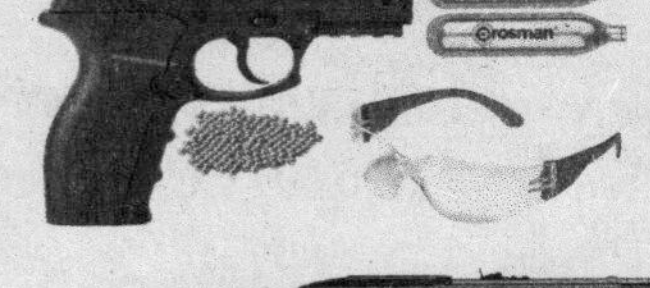

CROSMAN P10KT

CROSMAN REMINGTON 1875

CROSMAN REMINGTON R1100 PUMP RIFLE

CROSMAN REPEATAIR 1077

CROSMAN SILVER FOX NITRO PISTON

MAKO

Power: CO2
Stock: Synthetic
Overall Length: 8.56 in.
Sights: Fiber optic front and rear
Weight: 1 lb. 11 oz.
Caliber: BB
Magazine: 20 rounds
Features: Designed based on the Beretta Model 92; tri-color look; finger grips on the front strap; removable backstraps; accessory rail
MSRP $79.99

MAXIMUS

Power: Bolt
Stock: Synthetic
Overall Length: N/A
Sights: Fiber optic front and rear
Weight: N/A
Caliber: .22, .177
Features: Easy filling 2000 PSI reservoir; rifled barrel; up to 30 effective shots per fill
MSRP $219.99

MK45

Power: CO2
Stock: Synthetic
Overall Length: 7.5 in.
Sights: Fixed blade front, notch rear
Weight: N/A
Caliber: BB
Magazine: 20 rounds
Features: Removable grip makes CO2 cartridge loading easy; tan with a black grip; accessory rail
MSRP $34.95

NIGHT STALKER

Action: CO2
Stock: Synthetic
Barrel: N/A
Sights: Low-profile blade front, notch rear, laser
Weight: N/A
Caliber: BB
Magazine: 18 shots
Features: A Walther lookalike with a built-in red laser; 18-shot BB magazine; blowback action
MSRP $99.99

OPTIMUS

Power: Break action
Stock: Hardwood
Overall Length: 43 in.
Sights: 4x32mm CenterPoint scope
Weight: 6 lb. 8 oz.
Caliber: .177, .22
Features: Ambidextrous hardwood stock; relatively light cocking force and a two-stage adjustable trigger; barrel incorporates a micro-adjustable rear sight and fiber optic front sight; .177 also available without scope
MSRP . . . . $109.99–$139.99

P10KT

Power: CO2
Stock: Synthetic
Overall Length: 6.9 in.
Sights: Fixed blade front, notch rear
Weight: 1 lb. 1.6 oz.
Caliber: BB
Magazine: 20 rounds
Features: Steel barrel; grip removes for CO2 cartridge replacement; accessory rail
MSRP $59.99

REMINGTON 1875

Power: CO2
Stock: Faux ivory
Overall length: 13.125 in.
Sights: Fixed blade front, fixed notch rear
Weight: 2 lb. 4.8 oz.
Caliber: BB, .177
Features: Replica of Remington 1875 revolver; single-action; functional hammer, load gate, and extractor; nickel finish
MSRP $119.99

REMINGTON R1100 PUMP RIFLE

Action: Pump
Stock: Synthetic
Barrel: N/A
Sights: Blade front, adjustable rear
Weight: N/A
Caliber: BB, .177
Magazine: 1 shot
Features: A variable speed pump (more pumps equal more velocity) in a shotgun-style stock of youth proportions
MSRP $59.99

REPEATAIR 1077

Power: CO2
Stock: All-weather, synthetic, wood
Overall Length: 36.88 in.
Sight: Fiber optic front, adjustable rear
Weight: 3 lb. 11 oz.
Caliber: .177
Features: Exclusive 12-shot rotary pellet clip lets you shoot longer; maximum velocity 625 fps; cross-bolt safety
Synthetic: $79.99
Wood: $114.99

SILVER FOX NITRO PISTON

Power: Nitro Piston
Stock: Synthetic
Overall length: 43.5 in.
Sights: None
Weight: 6 lb.
Caliber: .177, .22
Features: Break-barrel action; dovetail mounting rail; two-stage trigger; CenterPoint 4x32mm scope
MSRP $199.99

Crosman

CROSMAN THRASHER

CROSMAN TRAIL MARK II NP PISTOL

CROSMAN TRIPLE THREAT

CROSMAN TYRO

CROSMAN VALIANT

CROSMAN VANTAGE NP

THRASHER

Power: Gas piston
Stock: Synthetic
Overall Length: 45.5 in.
Sights: Fixed front, adjustable rear
Weight: 8 lb. 5 oz.
Caliber: .22
Magazine: 1 round
Features: Skeleton stock; rifled barrel; two-stage adjustable trigger; CenterPoint 4x32mm scope
MSRP $184.99

TRAIL MARK II NP PISTOL

Power: Nitro Piston
Stock: Synthetic
Overall length: N/A
Sights: Fiber optic front, adjustable notch rear
Weight: 3 lb. 7 oz.
Caliber: .177
Features: Break-barrel action; rifled steel barrel; tactical frame; removable cocking aid
MSRP $99.99

TRIPLE THREAT

Action: CO2
Stock: Polymer
Barrel: 3 in., 6 in., 8 in.
Sights: Ramp front, adjustable rear
Weight: N/A
Caliber: BB, .177
Magazine: 6, 10 shots
Features: A fun CO2 revolver with three barrels, all with vent ribs and rifled; grips remove to replace CO2 cartridge; 10-shot pellet clip; 6-shot BB clip
MSRP $99.99

TYRO

Power: Spring
Stock: Synthetic
Overall Length: 30.5 in.–32.75 in.
Sights: Fiber optic front, adjustable rear
Weight: 5 lb.
Caliber: .177
Magazine: 1 round
Features: Designed for younger shooters; soft shooting; ambidextrous stock with a number of spacers to adjust for length of pull
MSRP $105.99

VALIANT

Power: Gas piston
Stock: Wood
Overall Length: N/A
Sights: Fixed front sight, adjustable rear
Weight: 6 lb. 4 oz.
Caliber: .177, .22
Magazine: 1 round
Features: Ambidextrous thumbhole stock of hardwood; two-stage adjustable trigger; CenterPoint 4x32mm scope
MSRP $219.99

VANTAGE NP

Power: Break action
Stock: Hardwood
Length: 45 in.
Sights: Fiber optic front, adjustable rear 4x32mm scope included
Weight: 7 lb. 2 oz.
Caliber: .177, .22
Features: Crosman's own version of the Bantage NP; hardwood stock; fiber optic front sight and fully adjustable rear sight; .177-caliber comes with scope; .22-caliber only with fiber optic sights and 11mm dovetail groove for optics mounting
.22-caliber: $104.99
.177-caliber: $159.99

Daisy

DAISY MATCH-GRADE MODEL 887 GOLD MEDALIST

DAISY MODEL 599 COMPETITION

MATCH-GRADE MODEL 887 GOLD MEDALIST

Power: CO2 single shot bolt
Stock: Laminated hardwood
Overall Length: 39.5 in.
Sights: Front globe with changeable aperture inserts, rear diopter with micrometer
Weight: 7 lb. 5 oz.
Caliber: .177
Features: Laminated hardwood stock; Lothar Walther rifled high-grade steel barrel; manual, cross-bolt trigger block; includes scope rail adapter
MSRP $499.99

MODEL 599 COMPETITION

Action: PCP
Stock: Beechwood
Barrel: N/A
Sights: Hooded front, diopter rear
Weight: N/A
Caliber: .177
Magazine: 1 shot
Features: Competition ready air rifle with integral dovetail scope rail; sling rail; pressure gauge; adjustable stock; position and weight adjustable trigger; cold hammer forged BSA barrel; straight-pull T handle
MSRP $595.00

Daisy

DAISY POWERLINE MODEL 880

DAISY POWERLINE MODEL 901

POWERLINE MODEL 880

Power: Multi-pump pneumatic
Stock: Molded wood grain
Overall Length: 37.6 in.
Sights: TruGlo fiber optic front, adjustable rear
Weight: 3 lb. 11 oz.
Caliber: .177
Features: Wood-grained, Monte Carlo stock and forearm; rifled steel barrel; cross-bolt trigger block; velocity up to 750 fps; engineering resin with dovetail mount for scope
MSRP **$49.99**

POWERLINE MODEL 901

Power: Multi-pump pneumatic
Stock: Composite
Overall Length: 37.5 in.
Sights: Fiber optic front, adjustable rear
Weight: 3 lb. 11 oz.
Caliber: .177
Features: Rifled steel barrel; black advanced composite stock; dovetail mounts for optics
MSRP **$69.99**

Gamo USA

GAMO USA COYOTE WHISPER FUSION

GAMO SWARM FUSION 10X GEN2

GAMO USA URBAN PCP

GAMO USA WHISPER FUSION MACH 1

COYOTE WHISPER FUSION

Power: PCP
Stock: Beechwood
Overall length: 42.9 in.
Sights: None
Weight: 7 lb. 13.6 oz.
Caliber: .177, .22
Features: An entry-level PCP-power plant bolt-action air rifle that boasts a 10-pellet rotary clip, hammer forged rifled barrel, selve-regulating valve, Custom Action Trigger, Shock Wave Absorber, double-sided molded cheekpiece, and Whisper Fusion technology
MSRP **$759.99**

SWARM FUSION 10X GEN2

Action: Gas piston
Stock: Synthetic
Barrel: 20.5 in.
Sights: None
Weight: 5 lb. 13 oz.
Caliber: .22
Magazine: 10 shots
Features: Already upgraded after just a year, with a new horizontal magazine design and fiber optic sights front and (adjustable) rear; two-stage adjustable trigger; recoil reducing rail; Inert Gas Technology piston; Gamo 3–9x40mm scope; fluted, rifled barrel with a polymer jacket, and Whisper Fusion noise suppression
MSRP **$289.99**

URBAN PCP

Power: PCP
Stock: Synthetic
Overall length: 42.9 in.
Sights: None
Weight: 6 lb. 11.2 oz.
Caliber: .22
Features: Bolt-action air rifle features Whisper Fusion technology multi-shot mechanism, Custom Action Trigger, hammer forged barrel, and thumbhole stock with double-sided molded cheekpiece
MSRP **$399.99**

WHISPER FUSION MACH 1

Power: IGT Mach 1
Stock: Synthetic
Overall length: 46.5 in.
Sights: Fiber optic front, adjustable rear
Weight: 8 lb.
Caliber: .177, .22
Features: Break-barrel, single-cocking action; single-shot; fluted polymer jacketed steel barrel; Custom Action Trigger; Recoil Reducing Rail; 3-9x40 air rifle scope
MSRP **$269.99**

Gletcher

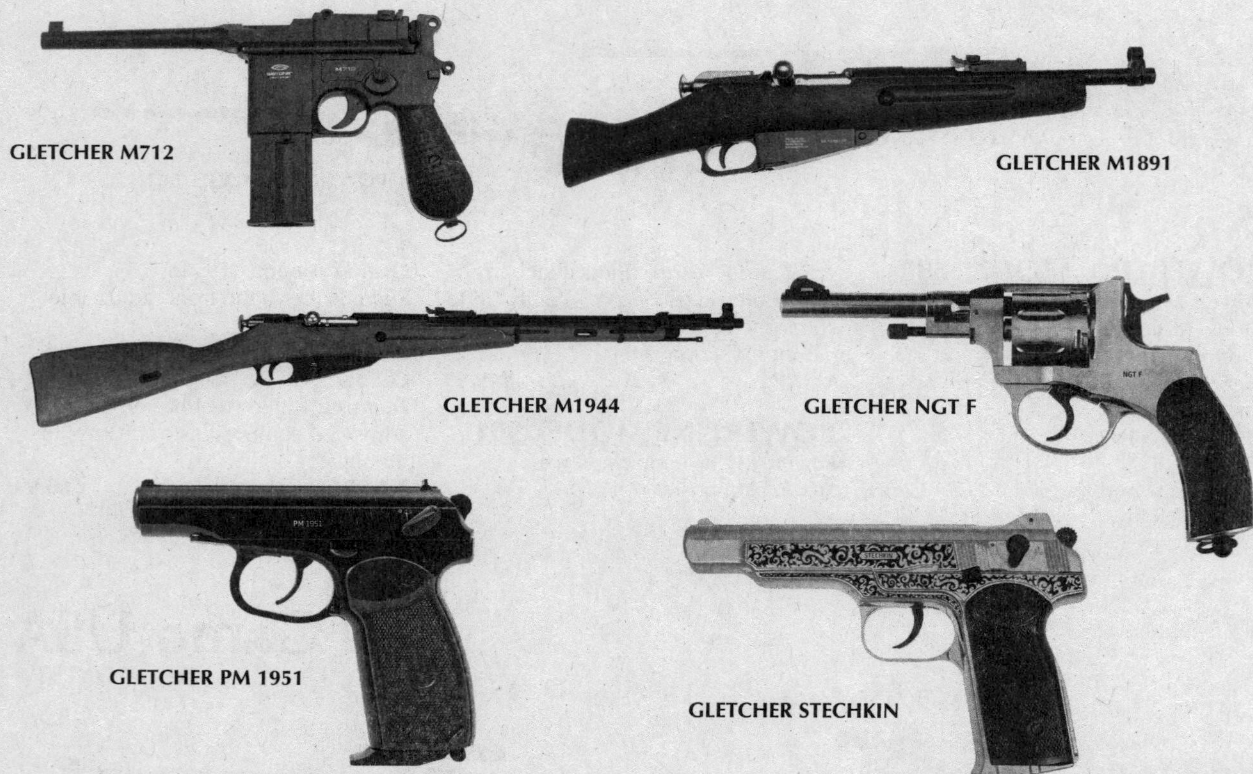
GLETCHER M712

GLETCHER M1891

GLETCHER M1944

GLETCHER NGT F

GLETCHER PM 1951

GLETCHER STECHKIN

M712

Power: CO2
Stock: Wood
Overall length: 23 in.
Sights: Post front, tangent rear
Weight: 3 lb.
Caliber: .177
Features: Reproduction of WWII 1932 broomhandle Mauser; breech mechanism moves when firing; full-auto functionality and blowback system
MSRP $149.95

M1891

Power: CO2
Stock: Imitation wood
Overall length: 22.43 in.
Sights: Hooded front post, tangent rear
Weight: 5 lb. 9.6 oz.
Caliber: .177
Features: Reproduction of Russian Civil War "Obrez" model, a sawed-off Mosin-Nagant; mechanism works as in the original; built-in hex key for CO2 cartridge installation
MSRP $199.99

M1944

Power: CO2
Stock: Imitation wood
Overall length: 52.75 in.
Sights: Post front, tangent rear
Weight: 8 lb. 3 oz.
Caliber: .177
Features: Reproduction of M44 Russian Mosin-Nagant carbine; barrel, bolt mechanism, and magazine are metal; action operates like the original firearm; integral folding bayonet; built-in hex wrench for CO2 cartridge installation
MSRP $329.99

NGT F

Power: CO2
Stock: Plastic
Overall length: 9 in.
Sights: Front post, cutout rear
Weight: 1 lb. 8 oz.
Caliber: .177
Features: Reproduction of the Belgian Nagant revolver; steel BBs fired through decorative snap cap "cartridges"; seven-shot true revolving action; blue or silver finishes
MSRP . . . . $134.99–$164.99

PM 1951

Power: CO2
Stock: Plastic
Overall length: 6.3 in.
Sights: Low-profile integral front and rear
Weight: 1 lb. 10 oz.
Caliber: .177
Features: Reproduction of Russian Makarov sidearm; metal body and slide; safety lever; magazine pinky finger extension
MSRP $99.99

STECHKIN

Power: CO2
Stock: Plastic
Overall length: 8.8 in.
Sights: Low-profile integral front, adjustable rear
Weight: 2 lb. 4.8 oz.
Caliber: .177
Features: Reproduction of Soviet Stretchkin pistol; weight is identical to the firearm version; double-action, with gold finish, engraving on slide and frame; comes in a presentation box
MSRP $259.99

AIRGUNS

HatsanUSA

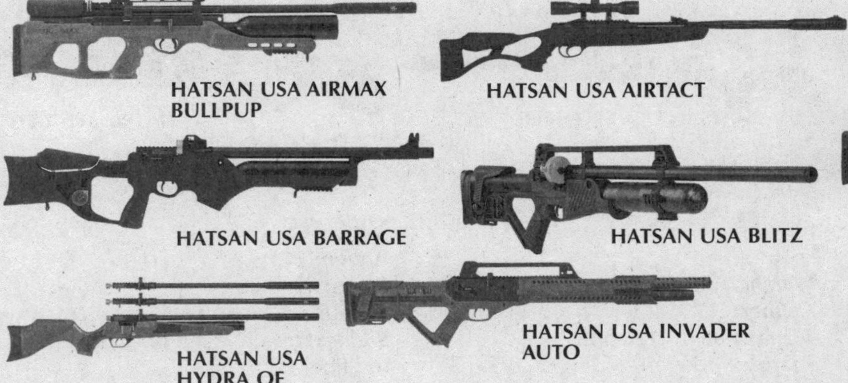

HATSAN USA AIRMAX BULLPUP

HATSAN USA AIRTACT

HATSAN USA ALPHA YOUTH QE

HATSAN USA BARRAGE

HATSAN USA BLITZ

HATSAN USA BULLMASTER

HATSAN USA HYDRA QE

HATSAN USA INVADER AUTO

AIRMAX

Action: PCP
Stock: Turkish walnut
Barrel: 23 in.
Sights: None
Weight: 10 lb. 14 oz.
Caliber: .177, .22, .25
Magazine: 9, 10 shots
Features: A bullpup design featuring the QuietEnergy fully shrouded barrel; ambidextrous thumbhole stock with adjustable cheekpiece; detachable magazine; Anti-Double Pellet Feed technology; under rail; sling swivels; Quattro adjustable two-stage match trigger
MSRP................. $629.99

AIRTACT

Action: Break-barrel
Stock: Synthetic
Barrel: 14.5 in.
Sights: Fiber optic front, adjustable rear, 4X32mm Optima scope
Weight: 5 lb. 11 oz.
Caliber: .177, .22, .25
Magazine: 1 shot
Features: Beginner's single-shot with a slim, skeletonized thumbhole stock; large muzzle break for easy cocking; steel rifled barrel with molded shroud; manual firing safety; automatic cocking safety; adjustable trigger; scope and sights provided
MSRP................. $109.99

ALPHA YOUTH QE

Action: Spring piston
Stock: Synthetic
Barrel: 15.4 in.
Sights: Red fiber optic front, green fiber optic rear
Weight: 5 lb. 4 oz.
Caliber: .177
Magazine: 1 shot
Features: Perhaps the perfect starter air rifle for your kids, with an ambidextrous stock; easy break-action cocking mechanism
MSRP..................$109.99

BARRAGE

Power: PCP
Stock: Synthetic
Overall length: 19.7 in.
Sights: Fiber optic front and rear
Weight: 10 lb. 1.6 oz.
Caliber: .177, .22
Features: Semiautomatic; fitted with a 500cc air bottle mounted to the forearm; barrel is precision rifled, choked, and fully shrouded; ambidextrous thumbhole stock; Picatinny rail on the forearm; includes magazines for both calibers (.177 mag holds 14 shots, .22 holds 12 shots); TruGlo sights; HatSan's patented anti-knock system that prevents gas discharge and waste if the rifle is knocked or bounced
MSRP..................$799.99

BLITZ

Action: PCP
Stock: Synthetic
Barrel: 23 in.
Sights: None
Weight: 8 lb. 13 oz.
Caliber: .22, .25, .30
Magazine: 16, 19, 21 shots
Features: A select-fire—semiauto or full-auto—air rifle with a rotary magazine; buttstock adjustable at buttpad and comb; three forearm accessory rails; quick-fill nozzle; anti-knock safety system prevents firing when the air rifle is knocked or bounced; fully shrouded barrel
MSRP..................$999.99

BULLMASTER

Power: PCP
Stock: Synthetic
Overall length: 19.7 in.
Sights: None
Weight: 10 lb. 4.8 oz.
Caliber: .177, .22
Features: Semiautomatic bullpup design; 500cc air bottle mounted to the forearm; barrel is precision rifled, choked, and fully shrouded; includes magazines for both calibers (.177 mag holds 14 shots, .22 holds 12 shots); topside and and under forearm Picatinny rails; elevation adjustable cheekpiece; HatSan's patented anti-knock system that prevents gas discharge and waste if the rifle is knocked or bounced
MSRP..................$799.99

HYDRA QE

Action: PCP
Stock: Turkish walnut
Barrel: 17.7 in.
Sights: None
Weight: 6 lb. 13 oz.
Caliber: .177, .22, .25
Magazine: 10, 12, 14 shots
Features: Features interchangeable barrel system; detachable magazine; aluminum receiver; built-in pressure gauge; ambidextrous, ergonomic stock with an adjustable cheekpiece and checkering at grip locations
MSRP..................$399.99

INVADER AUTO

Action: PCP
Stock: Synthetic
Barrel: 19.7 in.
Sights: Adjustable fiber optic
Weight: 8 lb. 2 oz.
Caliber: .177, .22, .25
Magazine: 10, 12, 14 shots
Features: Bolt-action; QuietEnergy shrouded rifled barrel; three Picatinny rails; detachable magazine; built-in pressure gauge; rotating dust cover; anti-knock system to prevent accidental discharges
Auto:..................$609.99

HatsanUSA

HATSAN USA PILEDRIVER

HATSAN USA SPEEDFIRE

HATSAN USA VECTIS

PILEDRIVER

Action: PCP
Stock: Synthetic
Barrel: 33 in.
Sights: Adjustable fiber optic
Weight: 10 lb.
Caliber: .45, .50
Magazine: 1 shot
Features: A big-bore air rifle in a compact bullpup package; gas piston hammer spring; rifled barrel; long optics rail; adjustable cheekrest
MSRP . . . . $1173.99–$1179.99

SPEEDFIRE

Action: Break-barrel
Stock: Synthetic
Barrel: 14.5 in.
Sights: Green fiber optic front, red fiber optic rear, Optima 3–9x32mm scope
Weight: 6 lb. 9 oz.
Caliber: .177, .22
Magazine: 10, 12 shots
Features: Modern-looing ergonomically designed stock with raised cheekpiece; removeable Rapid Performance Mag; front sight folds down for use with optics on the topside rail; rifled steel barrel with QuickEnergy synthetic shroud; Quattro two-stage adjustable trigger; manual, automatic cocking, and antibeartrap safeties; SAS shock absorber system
MSRP $189.99

VECTIS

Action: PCP
Stock: Synthetic
Barrel: 17.7 in.
Sights: Flip-up green fiber optic front, red fiber optic rear
Weight: 7 lb. 2 oz.
Caliber: .177, .22, .25
Magazine: 10, 12, 14 shots
Features: A lever-activated thoroughly modern PCP air rifle featuring the QuietEnergy barrel shroud; S/Roto magazines and single-shot tray; Quattro adjustable two-stage trigger; all-weather thumbhole stock with Monte Carlo cheekpiece; removeable fiber optic flip-up sights; acres of rail top and bottom; rifled and choked barrel
MSRP $369.99

Sig Air

SIG AIR 1911 SPARTAN CO2 BB GUN

SIG AIR 1911 WE THE PEOPLE BB PISTOL

SIG AIR ASP20 WOOD STOCK

SIG AIR MCX VIRTUS PCP

1911 SPARTAN CO2 BB GUN

Power: CO2
Stock: Custom Spartan
Overall length: 8.7 in.
Sights: White dot front and rear
Weight: 2 lb. 9.6 oz.
Caliber: BB (4.5mm)
Features: CO2-operated BB gun replication of SIG Spartan 1911 pistol; MOLON LABE engraved slide; custom Spartan grips; skeletonized trigger; cam-lever CO2 loading port; functional grip safety; full blowback metal slide; 16-round magazine; oil-rubbed bronze finish
MSRP $109.99

1911 WE THE PEOPLE BB PISTOL

Power: CO2
Stock: Aluminum
Overall Length: 8.5 in.
Sights: Fixed
Weight: 2 lb. 3 oz.
Caliber: BB
Magazine: 17 rounds
Features: Custom aluminum 50-star grips (25 each side); distressed finish slide and frame
MSRP $119.99

ASP20 SYNTHETIC STOCK, WOOD STOCK

Power: Gas piston
Stock: Synthetic, wood
Overall Length: 45.6 in.
Sights: None
Weight: N/A
Caliber: .177, .22
Magazine: 1 round
Features: Advanced Sport Pellet; suppressed break-barrel single-shot air rifle designed to reduce the force needed to cock the action to 33 pounds; ambidextrous safety located outside the trigger guard; rifled steel barrel; adjustable MatchLite trigger; factory-mounted scope
Synthetic: $399.99
Wood: $489.99

MCX VIRTUS PCP

Action: PCP
Stock: Synthetic
Barrel: 17.5 in.
Sights: Folding front and rear
Weight: 7 lb. 8 oz.
Caliber: .22
Magazine: 30 shots
Features: SIG's premium PCP pellet rifle sends .22-caliber pellets at velocities up to 700 fps; SIG Rapid Pellet Magazine
MSRP $349.99

Sig Air

SIG AIR P320 AIR PISTOL

SIG AIR P320 M17 AIR PISTOL

SIG AIR PROFORCE M17 AIRSOFT

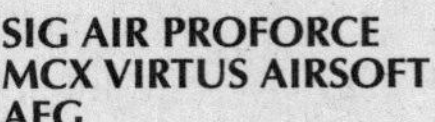
SIG AIR PROFORCE MCX VIRTUS AIRSOFT AEG

SIG AIR PROFORCE P229

SIG AIR X-FIVE

P320 AIR PISTOL, AIR PISTOL COYOTE TAN

Power: CO2
Stock: Polymer
Overall length: 7.9 in.
Sights: White dot front and rear
Weight: 1 lb. 11 oz.
Caliber: .177
Features: CO2-operated airgun model of SIG's P320 carry gun; rotary magazine holds 30 rounds; rifled steel barrel; manual safety; all-metal slide; black or Coyote Tan finishes
MSRP $119.99

P320 M17 AIR PISTOL

Action: CO2
Stock: Polymer
Barrel: N/A
Sights: Fixed
Weight: 34 oz.
Caliber: .177
Magazine: 20 shots
Features: Copy of the U.S. Army's M17 semiautomatic. Features full blowback action for realistic shooting
MSRP $139.99

PROFORCE M17 AIRSOFT, M18 AIRSOFT

Action: CO2; green gas
Stock: Synthetic
Barrel: N/A
Sights: Fixed front, optics-ready rear
Weight: 48 oz.
Caliber: 6mm BB
Magazine: 21 shots
Features: An airsoft pistol nearly identical to the US Army's M17 sidearm that can use both CO2 or green gas power supply (M18 is green gas only); metal slide with full blowback action
MSRP $179.99

PROFORCE MCX VIRTUS AIRSOFT AEG

Action: AEG
Stock: Synthetic
Barrel: 11.5 in.
Sights: None
Weight: 7 lb.
Caliber: 6mm BB
Magazine: 120 shots
Features: AEG (Auto Electric Gun) powered by an 11.1-volt LIPO battery and featuring a three-position telescoping stock; M-LOK accessory rail; muzzle velocity up to 370 fps
MSRP $459.99

PROFORCE P229

Action: Green gas
Stock: Metal
Barrel: 7 in.
Sights: Fixed front and rear
Weight: 29.6 oz.
Caliber: 6mm BB
Magazine: 25 shots
Features: A full-size metal-frame airsoft pistol with a generous 25-round capacity powered by green gas and featuring a full-metal slide with realistic blowback action
MSRP $169.99

X-FIVE

Power: CO2
Stock: Metal
Overall Length: 8.7 in.
Sights: Adjustable
Weight: 2 lb. 11.2 oz.
Caliber: .177
Magazine: 20 rounds
Features: Advanced Sport Pellet; full blowback, metal-framed CO2 air pistol; cam-lever CO2 housing; ambidextrous safety
MSRP $139.99

Stoeger Airguns

STOEGER S3000-C COMPACT COMBO

S3000-C COMPACT, COMPACT COMBO

Action: Spring piston
Stock: Synthetic, hardwood
Barrel: N/A
Sights: Fiber optic front, rear, scope
Weight: N/A
Caliber: .177
Magazine: N/A
Features: One for the younger or shorter-statured air rifle aficionado, with an ergonomic stock featuring ProAdaptive checkering; fully adjustable rear sight with a fiber optic front; 4x32mm scope
Synthetic sights only $99.00
Synthetic combo: $119.00
Hardwood combo: $149.00

Stoeger Airguns

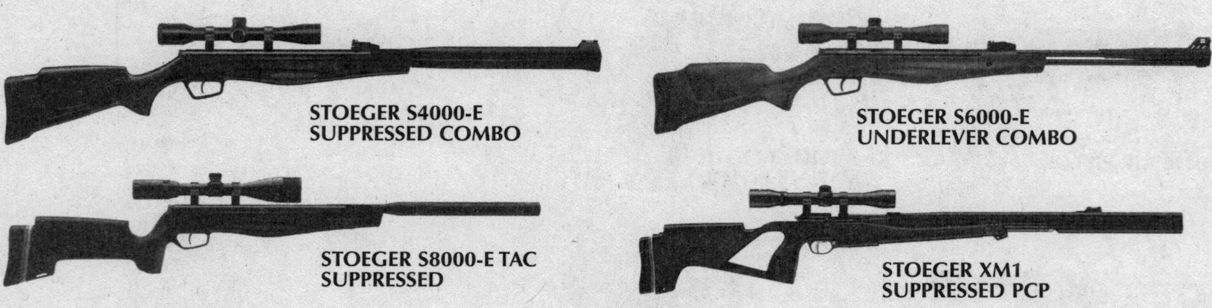

STOEGER S4000-E SUPPRESSED COMBO

STOEGER S6000-E UNDERLEVER COMBO

STOEGER S8000-E TAC SUPPRESSED

STOEGER XM1 SUPPRESSED PCP

S4000-E SUPPRESSED

Action: Break-barrel
Stock: Synthetic
Barrel: N/A
Sights: Interchangeable fiber optic front, adjustable fiber optic rear; 4X32 scope
Weight: N/A
Caliber: .177, .22
Magazine: 1 shot
Features: Employing the Gas Ram System break-action design; ProAdaptive stock texturing; adjustable two-stage trigger; integral S3 suppressor; MultiGrip system; comes with both the fiber optic sights and a 4x32 scope; sights-only variant; stock options include black synthetic, hardwood, synthetic OD green, and synthetic in Realtree Edge camo
MSRP. . . . . $149.00–$199.00

S6000-E UNDERLEVER COMBO

Action: Spring piston
Stock: Synthetic, hardwood
Barrel: N/A
Sights: Fiber optic front, rear, scope
Weight: N/A
Caliber: .177, .22
Magazine: N/A
Features: A well-balanced air rifle with the cocking lever placed under the barrel for better handling while aiming; hooded front sight with red fiber optic pipe; 4x32mm scope; black synthetic or hardwood stock
Synthetic: $199.00
Hardwood: $229.00

S8000-E TAC SUPPRESSED

Power: Gas ram
Stock: Synthetic
Overall Length: 42.5 in.
Sights: 3–9x40mm scope
Weight: 8 lb. 14 oz.
Caliber: .177, .22
Features: Airflow control technology and dual-stage noise reduction system; automatic ambidextrous safety; black tactical stock; up to 1200 fps with alloy pellets (.177); adjustable length of pull; integral Picatinny rails
MSRP. $249.00

XM1 SUPPRESSED PCP

Action: PCP
Stock: Synthetic
Barrel: N/A
Sights: Fiber optic front, rear, scope
Weight: 5 lb. 11 oz.
Caliber: .177, .22
Magazine: 7, 9 shots
Features: Interchangeable pistol grip inserts; cross-bolt safety; integral suppression; on-board air reservoir; two-stage adjustable trigger; also available in choice of black or Realtree Edge stock as a combo air rifle with a 4x32 scope
MSRP. . . . . $199.00–$249.00

UMAREX

UMAREX 850 M2

UMAREX BERETTA APX

850 M2

Action: CO2
Stock: Synthetic
Barrel: N/A
Sights: Fiber optic front, rear
Weight: 6 lb. 12 oz.
Caliber: .177, .22
Magazine: 8 shots
Features: A sweet little repeater with a threaded muzzle; three Picatinny rails; removeable additional cheekpiece for scope use; no energy loss shot to shot
MSRP. $349.99

BERETTA APX

Power: CO2
Stock: N/A
Overall length: 7.25 in.
Sights: Fixed front and rear
Weight: 1 lb. 12 oz.
Caliber: BB
Features: Semiautomatic; 20-shot; double-action repeater has realistic recoil action; CO2 cartridge housed in grip; drop-free steel BB magazine; integrated Picatinny rail
MSRP. $69.99

UMAREX

UMAREX DX17

UMAREX EMBARK

UMAREX FORGE

UMAREX FUSION 2

UMAREX GAUNTLET

UMAREX GLOCK 19X

UMAREX HECKLER & KOCH USP BLOWBACK

DX17

Power: Spring-powered
Stock: Synthetic
Overall length: 9.5 in.
Sights: Fixed fiber optic front, fixed rear
Weight: 1 lb.
Caliber: BB
Features: Single-action air pistol shoots steel BBs; built-in BB reservoir; integrated accessory rail; 15-shot capacity; includes 200 steel BBs
MSRP \$19.00

EMBARK

Power: Break-barrel spring piston
Stock: Synthetic
Overall Length: 40 in.
Sights: Fixed open blade front, micrometer adjustable rear
Weight: 4 lb. 7 oz.
Caliber: .177
Magazine: 1 round
Features: An electric-green, ambidextrous thumbhole stock; official air rifle of the Student Air Rifle Program; cocking poundage is 16.25 lbs
MSRP \$99.99

FORGE

Power: T.N.T. Turbo Nitrogen Technology gas piston
Stock: Wood
Overall length: 44.8 in.
Sights: 4x32mm scope
Weight: 7 lb. 13 oz.
Caliber: .177
Features: T.N.T. fast piston system; spring piston break barrel with a single-shot cocking mechanism and automatic safety; adjustable trigger; integrated rail platform; 4x32 airgun scope; rifled barrel; enhanced SilencAir noise dampener
MSRP \$179.99

FUSION 2

Action: CO2
Stock: Synthetic
Barrel: N/A
Sights: None
Weight: N/A
Caliber: .177
Magazine: 9 shots
Features: Topside optics rail; SilencAir noise suppression
MSRP \$139.99

GAUNTLET

Power: Pre-charged pneumatic
Stock: Synthetic
Overall length: 46.75 in.
Sights: N/A
Weight: 8 lb. 8 oz.
Caliber: .177, .22, .25
Features: Bolt-action repeater; removable 3000 psi 13 cubic in. tank; 1100 psi regulator; adjustable stock comb; pressure key release; rotary magazine; single-shot tray; stock in black or in "multi-purpose" camo pattern
MSRP . . . . \$289.99–\$329.99

GLOCK 19X

Action: CO2, green gas
Stock: Polymer
Barrel: 3.36 in.
Sights: Fixed front, rear
Weight: 1 lb. 10 oz.
Caliber: .177
Magazine: 18 shots
Features: Glock replica; realistic blowback action; double-action trigger; metal slide
MSRP \$104.99

HECKLER & KOCH USP BLOWBACK

Power: CO2
Stock: Synthetic
Overall Length: 7.75 in.
Sights: Fixed front blade, fixed rear
Weight: 2 lb. 2 oz.
Caliber: BB
Magazine: 16 rounds
Features: Replica of H&K's semiautomatic pistol; magazine houses both BBs and the CO2 capsule; blowback action
MSRP \$109.99

UMAREX

LEGENDS ACE IN THE HOLE

Power: CO2
Stock: Synthetic
Overall Length: 9 in.
Sights: Blade front, groove rear
Weight: 1 lb. 15 oz.
Caliber: .177
Magazine: 6 rounds
Features: Single-action CO2 revolver; weathered finish; black grips with an embossed spade; speed-draw thumb spur; by Umarex
MSRP. $120.95

LEGENDS MP

Power: CO2
Stock: Metal
Overall length: 33 in.
Sights: Fixed front, elevation adjustable rear
Weight: N/A
Caliber: .177
Features: Distinctive German replication; 10-in. barrel; folding stock; full-auto blowback action; 60-shot drop-free steel BB magazine; two CO2 cartridges housed in the magazine
MSRP. . . . . $199.99–$267.50

MCP KIT

Power: CO2
Stock: Synthetic
Overall Length: 7.75 in.
Sights: Fixed blade front, fixed rear
Weight: 14.4 oz.
Caliber: BB
Magazine: 19 rounds
Features: Safety glasses; packet of 250 BBs; pair of CO2 cartridges; CO2 is housed in the grip; accessory rail
MSRP. $39.99

OCTANE ELITE

Power: ReAxis gas-powered piston
Stock: Synthetic
Overall length: 48.6 in.
Sights: 3-9x40mm scope
Weight: 9 lb. 8 oz.
Caliber: .177, .22
Features: Lockdown rail mounting system; 3-9x40mm airgun scope with adjustable objective; Stopshox anti-recoil system; SilencAir 5 chamber noise dampener; all-weather stock; rifled barrel; single-shot cocking mechanism
.22: $279.99
.177: $249.99

RUGER YUKON MAGNUM

Power: Break-barrel gas piston
Stock: Wood
Overall Length: 48.25 in.
Sights: Fiber optic front, adjustable rear
Weight: 9 lb. 3 oz.
Caliber: .22
Magazine: 1 round
Features: Made by Umarex; ReAxis piston for improved velocities; equipped with a 3–9x42mm scoped premounted on the air rifle's Picatinny rail; two-stage adjustable trigger; SilencAir suppressor; cocking effort is 47 pounds
MSRP. $197.97

RWS MODEL 34

Power: Break action/spring piston
Stock: Hardwood, synthetic
Overall Length: 45 in.
Sights: 4x32mm scope
Weight: 7 lb. 8 oz.–8 lb.
Caliber: .177, .22
Features: Polished with blued metalwork; full-sized hardwood stock; two-stage adjustable trigger; automatic safety; finely rifled barrel; 34 Pro large muzzlebrake
.22 airgun only: $399.99
.22 with scope: $419.99
.177 with scope: $385.99

RWS MODEL 48

Power: Side lever/spring piston
Stock: Hardwood
Overall Length: 42.5 in.
Sights: Adjustable rear
Weight: 8 lb. 8 oz.
Caliber: .177
Features: Extended breech stock to reduce recoil; fixed barrel system; adjustable trigger; automatic safety; optional RWS 4x32mm scope and mounts
.22 airgun only: $589.99
.177 with scope: $599.99
.22 with scope: $599.99

UMAREX

UMAREX RWS MODEL 54

UMAREX RWS MODEL 350 MAGNUM

UMAREX TREVOX

UMAREX SA10

UMAREX STRIKE POINT

UMAREX WALTHER REIGN UXT

UMAREX WALTHER PPQ

UMAREX WALTHER PPS M2

RWS MODEL 54

Power: Side lever/spring piston
Stock: Hardwood
Overall Length: 43.75 in.
Sights: Adjustable rear
Weight: 9 lb.
Caliber: .177, .22
Features: Adjustable trigger; scope rail; Monte Carlo hardwood stock with cheekpiece and checkering; automatic safety; 1100 fps maximum velocity
.22 airgun only: $809.99
.22 with scope: $869.99
.177 with scope: $695.45

RWS MODEL 350 MAGNUM

Power: Break action/spring piston
Stock: Hardwood
Overall Length: 48.3 in.
Sights: 4x32mm scope
Weight: 8 lb. 3 oz.
Caliber: .177, .22
Features: Two-stage trigger; mounted scope rail
Sight Airgun only: $549.99
With scope: $569.99

SA10

Power: CO2
Stock: Synthetic
Overall length: 9.25 in.
Sights: None
Weight: 2 lb. 1 oz.
Caliber: BB, .177
Features: Dual-ammo air pistol accommodating both BBs and .177-caliber pellets; uses one CO2 cartridge; blowback action; DA/SA trigger; eight-round rotary magazine; integrated accessory rail; gold-colored barrel; includes 1 polymer and three metal bonus magazines
MSRP $89.99

STRIKE POINT

Power: Multi-pump pneumatic
Stock: Synthetic
Overall length: 14 in.
Sights: Fiber optic
Weight: 2 lb. 10 oz.
Caliber: .177, .22
Features: Variable pump power; easy grip pump-action; easy load bolt-action; SilencAir 3 chamber noise dampener
MSRP $55.99

TREVOX

Power: T.N.T. Turbo Nitrogen Technology gas piston
Stock: Synthetic
Overall length: 18.11 in.
Sights: Fiber optic
Weight: 3 lb. 2 oz.
Caliber: .177
Features: Rifled barrel accuracy with an easy-grip; single-stroke cocking mechanism; SilencAir 3 chamber noise dampener; 11mm dovetail cuts for optics mounting; blued finish
MSRP $89.99

WALTHER PPQ

Action: CO2
Stock: Synthetic
Barrel: N/A
Sights: Fixed front, adjustable rear
Weight: N/A
Caliber: .177
Magazine: 8 shots
Features: Fun BB pistol powered by a 12-gram CO2 cartridge; under-muzzle accessory rail
MSRP $72.00

WALTHER PPS M2

Power: CO2
Stock: Synthetic
Overall Length: 6.3 in.
Sights: Fixed blade front, fixed rear
Weight: 1 lb. 2 oz.
Caliber: BB
Magazine: 18 rounds
Features: Blowback design; metal parts for added weight; CO2 housing is hidden in the backstrap; from Umarex
MSRP $74.99

WALTHER REIGN UXT

Action: PCP
Stock: Synthetic
Barrel: N/A
Sights: None
Weight: 5 lb. 8 oz.
Caliber: .177, .22, .25
Magazine: 9 shots
Features: A bullpup stock houses high-grade aluminum components; cocking lever can be operated without coming off the stock; topside optics rail
MSRP $599.99

SHOTGUNS

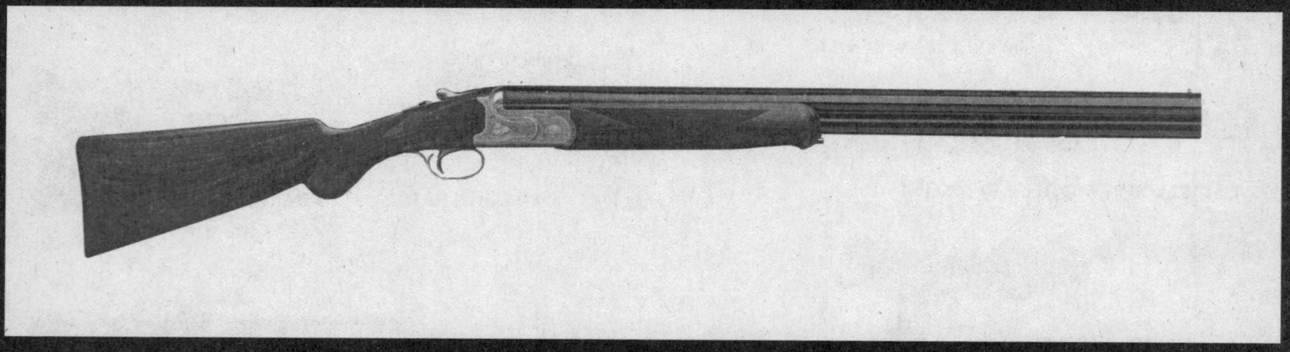

American Tactical

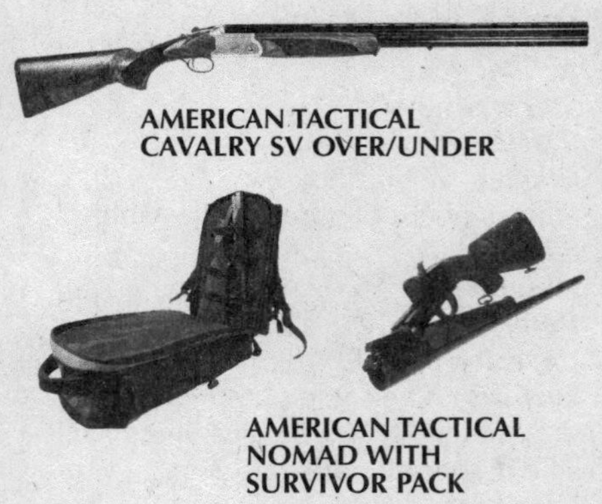
AMERICAN TACTICAL CAVALRY SV OVER/UNDER

AMERICAN TACTICAL NOMAD WITH SURVIVOR PACK

CAVALRY SV OVER/UNDER

Action: Over/under
Stock: Turkish walnut
Barrel: 26 in., 28 in.
Chokes: C, IC, M, IM, F
Weight: N/A
Bore/Gauge: 12, 20, 28, .410
Magazine: 2 shells
Features: Brass front bead sights, available with auto ejector, chambered for 3-in. Mag. shells, single selective trigger
Standard: $659.95
Extractors only: $599.95

NOMAD WITH SURVIVOR PACK

Action: Single-shot
Stock: Synthetic
Barrel: 18.5 in.
Chokes: None
Sights: Bead front
Weight: N/A
Bore/Gauge: .410, 20, 12
Capacity: 1 shell
Features: Break-action folder with a hardy, checkered, synthetic stock and schnabel forend; 3-in. chamber; combo pack comes with a water-resistant Rukx Gear Survivor backpack made for this shotgun and with a hidden handgun pocket, among other features
MSRP $209.95

Armscor/Rock Island Armory

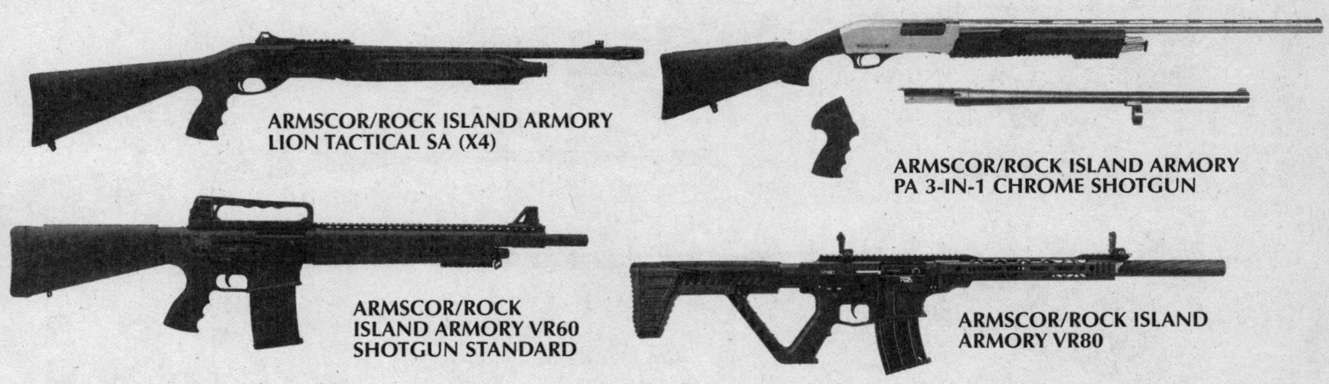
ARMSCOR/ROCK ISLAND ARMORY LION TACTICAL SA (X4)

ARMSCOR/ROCK ISLAND ARMORY PA 3-IN-1 CHROME SHOTGUN

ARMSCOR/ROCK ISLAND ARMORY VR60 SHOTGUN STANDARD

ARMSCOR/ROCK ISLAND ARMORY VR80

LION TACTICAL SA (X4)

Action: Semiautomatic
Stock: Polymer
Barrel: 18.5 in.
Chokes: F, M, IC
Weight: 7 lb.
Bore/Gauge: 12
Magazine: 4 shells
Features: Economical shotgun for home-defense or 3-Gun competition; flash hider at the muzzle; fiber optic front sight, rear sight; Picatinny rail; aluminum receiver in black chrome finish; polymer stock with pistol grip
MSRP $399.00

PA 3-IN-1 CHROME SHOTGUN

Action: Pump
Stock: Polymer
Barrel: 18.5 in., 28 in.
Chokes: S, F, M, IC
Weight: 6 lb. 2.7 oz.
Bore/Gauge: 12
Magazine: 4 shells
Features: 28-in. vent rib barrel with removable chokes; 18.5-in. cylinder bored barrel with front post sight; full polymer stock; add-on pistol grip; aluminum receiver; metalwork finished in Marine Chrome
MSRP $375.00

VR60 SHOTGUN STANDARD

Action: Semiautomatic
Stock: Polymer
Barrel: 20 in.
Chokes: F, M, IC
Weight: 7 lb. 6.2 oz.
Bore/Gauge: 12
Magazine: 5 shells
Features: AR-platform semiautomatic; conventional gas-operated action; removable carry handle; full-length Picatinny rail
MSRP $499.00

VR80

Action: Semiautomatic
Stock: Synthetic
Barrel: 20 in.
Chokes: Mobil Choke
Sights: Flip-up front and rear
Weight: 8 lb. 4 oz.
Bore/Gauge: 12
Capacity: 5 shells
Features: A gas-operated tactical shotgun with aluminum upper, lower, and forend; THS buffer tube stock; fluted barrel shroud
MSRP $699.00

Armscor/Rock Island Armory

ARMSCOR/ROCK ISLAND ARMORY VRBP100

ARMSCOR/ROCK ISLAND ARMORY VRPA40

VRBP100
Action: Semiautomatic
Stock: Synthetic
Barrel: 20 in.
Chokes: Mobil Choke
Sights: Flip-up front and rear
Weight: 7 lb. 15 oz.
Bore/Gauge: 12
Capacity: 5 shells
Features: A tactical shotgun in bullpup configuration featuring a spacer-adjustable buttstock with adjustable cheekpiece; detachable VR series magazine; side and top Picatinny rails; aluminum receiver
MSRP $774.00

VRPA40
Action: Pump
Stock: Synthetic
Barrel: 20 in.
Chokes: Mobil Choke
Sights: Fiber optic front, adjustable rear
Weight: 6 lb. 15 oz.
Bore/Gauge: 12
Capacity: 5 shells
Features: A versatile pump with a detachable VR series magazine; heat shield; topside optic rail; 3-in. chamber
MSRP $399.00

AYA (Aguirre y Aranzabal)

AYA CENTENARY

AYA IMPERIAL

AYA MODEL NO. 4/53

CENTENARY
Action: Side-by-side
Stock: Wood
Barrel: 28 in.
Chokes: N/A
Weight: 6 lb. 12 oz.
Bore/Gauge: 12, 16, 20, 28, .410
Magazine: 2 shells
Features: Forged steel action with double locking mechanism and gas vents; hardened steel intercepting safety sears; gold lined cocking indicators; double trigger with hinged front trigger; optional selective or non-selective single trigger; chopper lump steel barrels; concave rib; straight hand, finely chequered oil finished walnut stock; exhibition wood; custom Centenary engraving, gold inlays; initial oval; automatic safety
MSRP . . . . . . Contact manufacturer

IMPERIAL
Action: Side-by-side hammerless sidelock
Stock: Walnut
Barrel: 28 in., with other lengths to order
Chokes: Screw-in tubes
Weight: 6 lb. 12 oz.
Bore/Gauge: 12, 16, 20, 28, .410
Magazine: None
Features: Forged steel action with double locking mechanism and gas vents; gold washed internal lock parts; gold lined cocking indicators; optional selective or non-selective single trigger; concave rib; straight hand, finely checkered walnut stock; gold initial oval
MSRP . . . . . . Contact manufacturer

MODEL NO. 4/53
Action: Side-by-side hammerless boxlock ejector
Stock: Walnut
Barrel: 28 in., with other lengths to order
Chokes: Screw-in tubes
Weight: 6 lb. 10 oz.
Bore/Gauge: 12, 16, 20, 28, .410
Magazine: None
Features: Double locking mechanism with replaceable hinge pin; disk set firing pins; double trigger; chopper lump barrels with concave rib; light scroll engraving; metal finish available in hardened, old silver, or white finish; automatic safety
MSRP . . . . . . Contact manufacturer

AYA (Aguirre y Aranzabal)

AYA MODEL NO. 37

MODEL NO. 37

Action: Over/under sidelock
Stock: Walnut
Barrel: 28 in.
Chokes: Screw-in tubes
Weight: 7 lb. 8 oz.
Bore/Gauge: 12
Magazine: None
Features: Double underlocking lugs and double crossbolt; chopper lump chrome nickel steel barrels; hardened steel intercepting safety sears; gold line cocking indicators; gold washed internal lock parts; double trigger with hinged front trigger; fine rose and scroll, game scene, or bold relief engraving on action plates; full pistol grip walnut stock
MSRP . . . . . . Contact manufacturer

Benelli USA

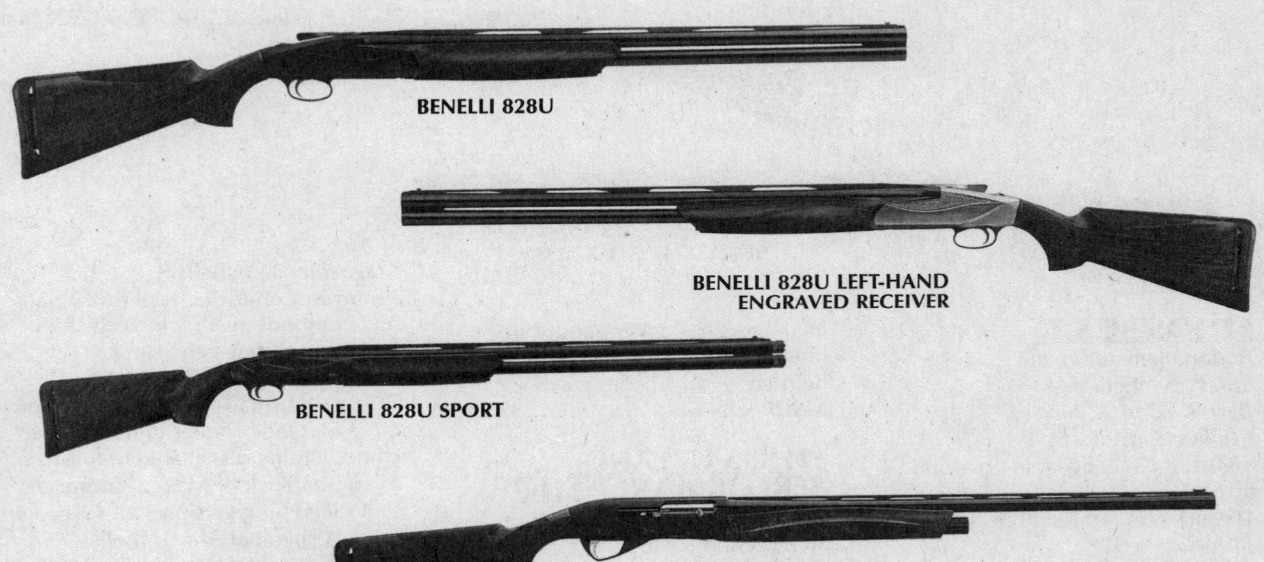
BENELLI 828U

BENELLI 828U LEFT-HAND ENGRAVED RECEIVER

BENELLI 828U SPORT

BENELLI ETHOS

828U

Action: Over/under
Stock: Wood
Barrel: 26 in., 28 in.
Chokes: C, IC, M, IM, F, wrench
Weight: 6 lb. 8 oz.
Bore/Gauge: 12, 20
Magazine: 2 shells
Features: Patented steel locking system and plate; easily removable trigger group receiver; adjustable drop and cast; ergonomic opening lever; impulse activated ejectors; available with the receiver in either black anodized finish or engraved nickel finish
MSRP . . . . $2699.00–$3199.00

828U LEFT-HAND ENGRAVED RECEIVER

Action: Over/under
Stock: Walnut
Barrel: 26 in., 28 in.
Chokes: Crio (C, IC, M, IM, F)
Weight: 6 lb. 8 oz.–6 lb. 9.6 oz.
Bore/Gauge: 12
Magazine: 2 shells
Features: Left-hand stock orientation with engraved nickel-plated receiver
MSRP $3199.00

828U SPORT

Action: Over/under
Stock: Walnut
Barrel: 30 in., 32 in.
Chokes: 5 (C, IC, M, IM, F)
Sights: White bead front
Weight: 8 lb.
Bore/Gauge: 12
Capacity: 2 shells
Features: For the sporting clays crowd, the 828U gets an adjustable trigger; automatic ejectors; AA-grade walnut stock; Crio barrel; shim plates for drop and cast adjustments; wide carbon fiber rib with sight channel; balancing weight system; custom hardshell case
MSRP $4399.00

ETHOS

Action: Inertia-operated semiautomatic
Stock: Walnut
Barrel: 26 in., 28 in.
Chokes: C, IC, M, IM, F
Weight: 5 lb.–6 lb. 5 oz.
Bore/Gauge: 12, 20, 28
Magazine: 4+1 shells
Features: Progressive Comfort recoil reduction system; two-part carrier latch for easy reloading; interchangerable fiber optic sights; available with engraved nickel-plated receiver
MSRP . . . . $1999.00–$2149.00

Benelli USA

ETHOS BE.S.T.

Action: Semiautomatic
Stock: Synthetic
Barrel: 26 in., 28 in.
Chokes: 5 (C, IC, M, IM, F)
Sights: Interchangeable fiber optic front
Weight: 6 lb. 10 oz.–6 lb. 11 oz.
Bore/Gauge: 12
Capacity: 4 shells
Features: BE.S.T. stands for Benelli Surface Treatment, a metal surface treatment that Benelli says is impenetrable and actually stops rust and corrosion with a twenty-five-year warranty.
MSRP $2199.00

ETHOS SPORT

Action: Semiautomatic
Stock: Walnut
Barrel: 28 in., 30 in.
Chokes: Five Extended Crio (C, IC, M, IM, F)
Sights: Interchangeable fiber optic front, mid-rib bead
Weight: 5 lb. 6 oz.–6 lb. 11 oz.
Bore/Gauge: 12, 20, 28
Magazine: 4 shells
Features: Cycles loads from featherweight to heavy without interruption; stocks are AA walnut satin finished; receivers are nickel-plated and anodized with light engraving; red, green, and yellow fiber optic sight inserts; stock shim kit; hard case
MSRP $2269.00

ETHOS UPLAND PERFORMANCE SHOP

Action: Semiautomatic
Stock: Walnut
Barrel: 26 in.
Chokes: 8 (C, IC, M, IM, F, T1, T2, T3)
Sights: Interchangeable fiber optic front
Weight: 5 lb. 10 oz.–6 lb. 10 oz.
Bore/Gauge: 20, 12
Capacity: 4 shells
Features: Performance gun for the bird fields with lengthened forcing cone; ported barrel; enlarged bolt release and bolt handle; 3-in. chamber; Progressive Comfort stock in AA-grade satin-finished walnut; nickel-plated receiver (20-ga. has alloy receiver); barrel in gloss blue
MSRP $2999.00

M2 FIELD 12 GA.

Action: Inertia operated semiautomatic
Stock: Synthetic, Realtree APG
Barrel: 21 in., 24 in., 26 in., 28 in.
Chokes: Crio Chokes (IC, M, F)
Weight: 6 lb. 14 oz.–7 lb. 3 oz.
Bore/Gauge: 12
Magazine: 3+1 shells
Features: ComforTech gel recoil pad and comb insert; ComforTech shim kit; red bar front sight; stock comes in black synthetic, Realtree MAX-5, Mossy Oak Shadow Grass Blades, or Gore Optifade Timber full-coverage camo; left-hand available in full-size model in black or Max-5; Compact and Rifled Slug versions; all 12-gauge models chamber 3-inch shells
Black: $1449.00
Realtree Max-5, Mossy Oak Shadow Grass Blades, Gore Optifade Timber: $1559.00
Compact: $1449.00
Rifled slug: . . . . $1449.00–$1559.00

M2 FIELD 20 GA.

Action: Inertia operated semiautomatic
Stock: Synthetic
Barrel: 24 in., 26 in.
Chokes: Crio Chokes (IC, M, F)
Weight: 5 lb. 13 oz.–6 lb. 8 oz.
Bore/Gauge: 20
Magazine: 3+1 shells
Features: ComforTech gel recoil pad and comb insert; ComforTech shim kit; red bar front sight; stock comes in black synthetic, Realtree MAX-5, Mossy Oak Shadow Grass Blades, or Gore Optifade Timber full-coverage camo; left-hand available in full-size model in black; Compact and Rifled Slug versions; all 12-gauge models chamber 3-inch shells
MSRP: . . . . $1449.00–$1559.00

Benelli USA

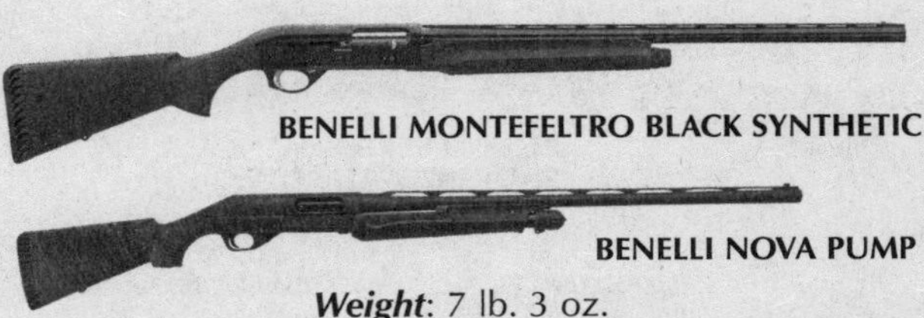

M4 TACTICAL

Action: Pump
Stock: Synthetic
Barrel: 18.5 in.
Chokes: M
Weight: 7 lb. 12.8 oz.
Bore/Gauge: 12
Magazine: 5 shells
Features: Titanium Cerakote finish on barrel, receiver, and magazine tube; black Cerakote on bolt; internal components receive corrosion-resistant coatings; ghost ring sights; Picatinny rail; standard or pistol grip stocks
MSRP . . . . $1999.00–$2269.00

MONTEFELTRO

Action: Semiautomatic
Stock: Synthetic, walnut
Barrel: 24 in., 26 in., 28 in., 30 in.
Chokes: IC, M, F
Weight: 5 lb. 5 oz.–5 lb. 10 oz. (20 ga.); 6 lb. 15 oz.–7 lb. 3 oz. (12 ga.)
Bore/ Gauge: 12, 20
Magazine: 4 +1 shells
Features: A traditionally styled semiauto field gun with a low-profile rib, slim fore-end, and a lightweight anodized receiver; Sporting 12-ga. has a 30-inch barrel and walnut stock; field 12-ga. has choice of 26- or 28-inch barrel with either walnut stock or black synthetic stock (non-Comfort Tech); left-hand 12-ga. choice of 26- or 28-inch barrel in walnut stock only; 20-ga. and Compact 20-ga. in walnut stock only with 24- or 26-inch barrel; all walnut stocks are satin-finished
MSRP: $1129.00

MONTEFELTRO SILVER FEATHERWEIGHT

Action: Semiautomatic
Stock: Walnut
Barrel: 26 in.
Chokes: Five
Sights: Red bar front
Weight: 6 lb. 3 oz.
Bore/Gauge: 12, 20
Capacity: 3 shells
Features: A lightweight field gun with a 26-inch barrel; AA-grade walnut stock; slim fore-end; low-profile vent rib; engraved nickel-plated alloy receiver; Inertia Driven system; full set of extended Crio chokes
MSRP $1999.00

NOVA PUMP

Action: Pump
Stock: Synthetic
Barrel: 28 in., 26 in.
Chokes: Three
Sights: Red bar front, mid bead
Weight: 8 lb. (12 ga.); 6 lb. 9 oz. (20 ga.)
Bore/Gauge: 12, 20
Capacity: 3 shells
Features: The Nova Pump now available in Mossy Oak Bottomland, Realtree Max-5 or black; 12-gauge chambered for 3 ½-inch and with 28- or 26-inch barrel; 20-gauge chambered for 3-inch, 26-inch barrel only
MSRP . . . . $449.00–$559.00

NOVA TACTICAL

Action: Pump
Stock: Synthetic
Barrel: 18.5 in.
Chokes: Fixed cylinder choke
Weight: 7 lb. 3 oz.
Bore/Gauge: 12
Magazine: 4+1 shells
Features: Available with ghost-ring or open rifle sights; push-button shell stop; grooved grip surface stocks in black synthetic stock; available with H2O technology, including a matte nickel-plated metal work
Standard rifled sights: $439.00
Standard ghost ring sights: . . $449.00
H2O: $669.00

PERFORMANCE SHOP 828U UPLAND

Action: Over/under
Stock: Walnut
Barrel: 24 in.
Chokes: Eight
Sights: Red fiber optic front
Weight: 6 lb. 6 oz.
Bore/Gauge: 12
Capacity: 2 shells
Features: A short-barreled upland gun with upgraded AA walnut stock in a satin finish; five flush-mount chokes plus three Rob Roberts Triple Threat chokes; carbon fiber stepped rib; drop and cast adjustment shims; no automatic ejectors; lengthened forcing cones; reduced 14.25-inch length of pull; 3-inch chambers; Dark Bronze anodized metalwork
MSRP $3499.00

PERFORMANCE SHOP M2 TURKEY 20-GAUGE

Action: Semiautomatic
Stock: Synthetic
Barrel: 24 in.
Chokes: Six
Sights: Burris Fast-Fire II red dot
Weight: 5 lb. 11 oz.
Bore/Gauge: 20
Capacity: 4 shells
Features: With custom enhancements from patterning expert Rob Roberts; five flush-fit Crio tubes in normal constrictions, plus one extended custom XFT choke; Burris Fast-Fire red dot factory installed; Mossy Oak Bottomland coverage on stock; Burnt Bronze metalwork; ComforTech stock
MSRP $2999.00

Benelli USA

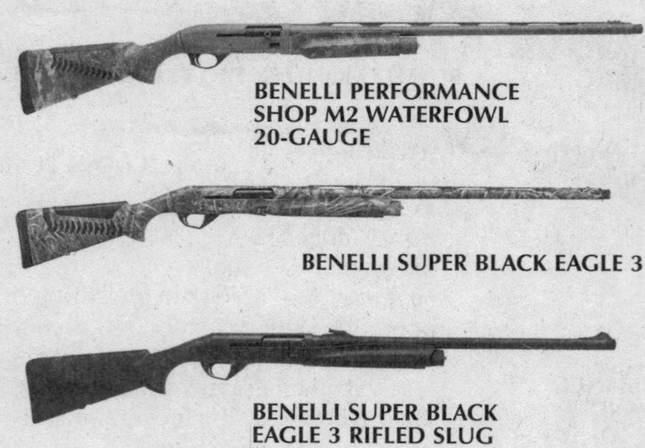

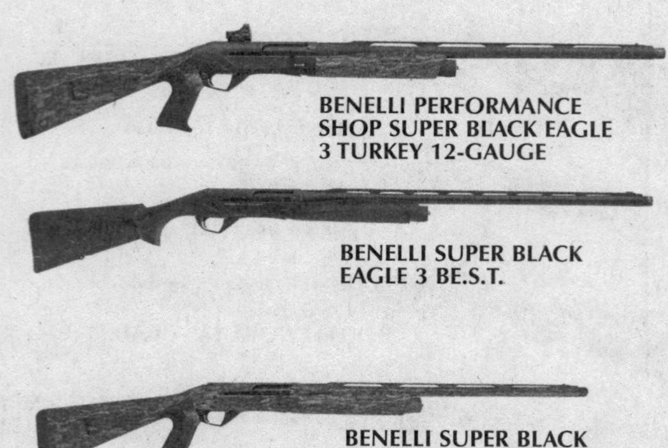

PERFORMANCE SHOP M2 WATERFOWL 20-GAUGE

Action: Semiautomatic
Stock: Synthetic
Barrel: 28 in.
Chokes: Three
Sights: Hi-Viz Comp front, metal mid-rib
Weight: 5 lb. 15 oz.
Bore/Gauge: 20
Capacity: 4 shells
Features: Honed and polished action; custom-tuned trigger group; oversized bolt handle; paracord survival sling; three Rob Roberts Triple Threat chokes; chambers 3-inch shells; Gore Optifade Marsh camo on stock; Burnt Bronze metalwork
MSRP $2699.00

PERFORMANCE SHOP SUPER BLACK EAGLE 3 TURKEY 12-GAUGE

Action: Semiautomatic
Stock: Synthetic
Barrel: 24 in.
Chokes: Six
Sights: Burris Fast-Fire II red dot
Weight: 6 lb. 13 oz.
Bore/Gauge: 12
Capacity: 4 shells
Features: With custom enhancements from patterning expert Rob Roberts; five flush-fit Crio tubes in normal constrictions, plus one extended custom XFT choke; Burris Fast-Fire red dot factory installed; Mossy Oak Bottomland coverage on stock; Burnt Bronze metalwork; ComforTech stock
MSRP $3099.00

SUPER BLACK EAGLE 3

Action: Semiautomatic
Stock: Synthetic
Barrel: 26 in., 28 in.
Chokes: Crio (C, IM, F), Extended Crio (IC, M)
Weight: 7 lb.–7 lb. 3 oz.
Bore/Gauge: 12, 20
Magazine: 2 shells
Features: Inertia-driven action with 3.5-in. chamber; Easy Locking System; oversized safety, bolt handle, and bolt release button; enlarged loading port; Easy Fitting System shim kit; ComforTech stock; Combtech cheek pad; Crio-treated barrel; stocks in black synthetic, A-Grade satin walnut, Realtree Max-5, GORE OPTIFADE Timber, GORE OPTIFADE Marsh, or Mossy Oak Bottomlands; red bar front sight, midbead; drilled and tapped for 93A Weaver scope mounts
MSRP . . . . $1699.00–$1999.00

SUPER BLACK EAGLE 3 BE.S.T.

Action: Semiautomatic
Stock: Synthetic
Barrel: 26 in., 28 in.
Chokes: 6 (IC, M, F–flush and extended)
Sights: Red bar front
Weight: 6 lb. 15 oz.–7 lb.
Bore/Gauge: 12
Capacity: 3 shells
Features: BE.S.T. stands for Benelli Surface Treatment, a metal surface treatment that Benelli says is impenetrable and stops rust and corrosion with a 25-year warranty. Other features include a 3.5-in. chamber; six Crio chokes (extended chokes get BE.S.T. treatment); drilled and tapped for scope mounts; minimum recommended load is 3 DE/1 1/8-oz. payload; black stock and black anodized receiver
MSRP $2199.00

SUPER BLACK EAGLE 3 RIFLED SLUG

Action: Semiautomatic
Stock: Synthetic
Barrel: 24 in.
Chokes: None
Sights: Adjustable rifle sights
Weight: 7 lb. 2 oz.
Bore/Gauge: 12
Capacity: 4 shells
Features: Dedicated rifled bore in an easy to manage 24-inch length; adjustable rifled sights; 3-inch chamber
MSRP $1999.00

SUPER BLACK EAGLE 3 WITH STEADY GRIP

Action: Semiautomatic
Stock: Synthetic
Barrel: 24 in.
Chokes: Five
Sights: Red bar front
Weight: 6 lb. 13 oz.
Bore/Gauge: 12
Capacity: 4 shells
Features: The SBE3 now with a Steady Grip and short barrel for turkey hunters; three flush and two extended Crio chokes; stock adjustment shim kit; ComfortTech3 and Combtech pads; Crio barrel; custom fitted hard case; full-coverage Mossy Oak Bottomlands
MSRP $1999.00

Benelli USA

SUPERNOVA PUMP SHOTGUN

Action: Pump
Stock: Synthetic
Barrel: 24 in., 26 in., 28 in.
Chokes: Standard choke (IC, M, F)
Weight: 7 lb. 13 oz.–8 lb.
Bore/Gauge: 12
Magazine: 4+1 shells
Features: Stock comes in black synthetic or Realtree Max-5 camo; receiver drilled and tapped for scope mounting; standard chokes; vented recoil pad; standard model chambers up to 3 ½-inch shells
MSRP: . . . . $559.00–$669.00

SUPERSPORT

Action: Inertia operated semiautomatic
Stock: Synthetic
Barrel: 28 in., 30 in.
Chokes: Extended Crio Chokes(C, IC, M, IM, F)
Weight: 6 lb. 5 oz.–7 lb. 5 oz.
Bore/Gauge: 12, 20
Magazine: 4+1 shells
Features: Stock comes in black SuperSport carbon fiber finish; red bar front sight and metal bead mid sight; Crio ported barrels; ComforTech gel recoil pad and comb insert
MSRP $2199.00

SUPER VINCI

Action: Inertia operated semiautomatic
Stock: Synthetic, Realtree APG
Barrel: 26 in., 28 in., 30 in.
Chokes: Crio Chokes (C, IC, M, IM, F)
Weight: 6 lb. 14 oz.–7 lb. 2 oz.
Bore/Gauge: 12
Magazine: 3+1 shells
Features: In-line inertia driven system; enlarged trigger and trigger guard for use with gloves; ComforTech Plus recoil pad; QuadraFit shim kit; drilled and tapped for scopes; available in black, Realtree Max-5. or Mossy Oak Shadow Grass Blades or Gore Optifade Concealment Marsh; all models chamber up to 3 ½-inch shells
MSRP . . . . $1599.00–$1699.00

ULTRA LIGHT

Action: Inertia operated semiautomatic
Stock: Walnut
Barrel: 24 in., 26 in.
Chokes: Crio Chokes (IC, M, F)
Weight: 5 lb. 3 oz.–6 lb. 2 oz.
Bore/Gauge: 12, 20, 28
Magazine: 2+1 shells
Features: Weather-coated walnut stock; red bar front sight and metal bead mid sight; gel recoil pad; option of checkered Montefeltro forend or ultra light forend
MSRP . . . . $1669.00–$1799.00

VINCI

Action: Inertia operated semiautomatic
Stock: Synthetic
Barrel: 26 in., 28 in.
Chokes: Crio Chokes (C, IC, M, IM, F)
Weight: 6 lb. 13 oz.–6 lb. 14 oz.
Bore/Gauge: 12
Magazine: 3+1 shells
Features: Stock in black, or Realtree MAX-5 camo; red bar front sight and metal bead mid sight; drilled and tapped for scope mounting; ComforTech Plus recoil pads
MSRP: . . . . $1349.00–$1449.00

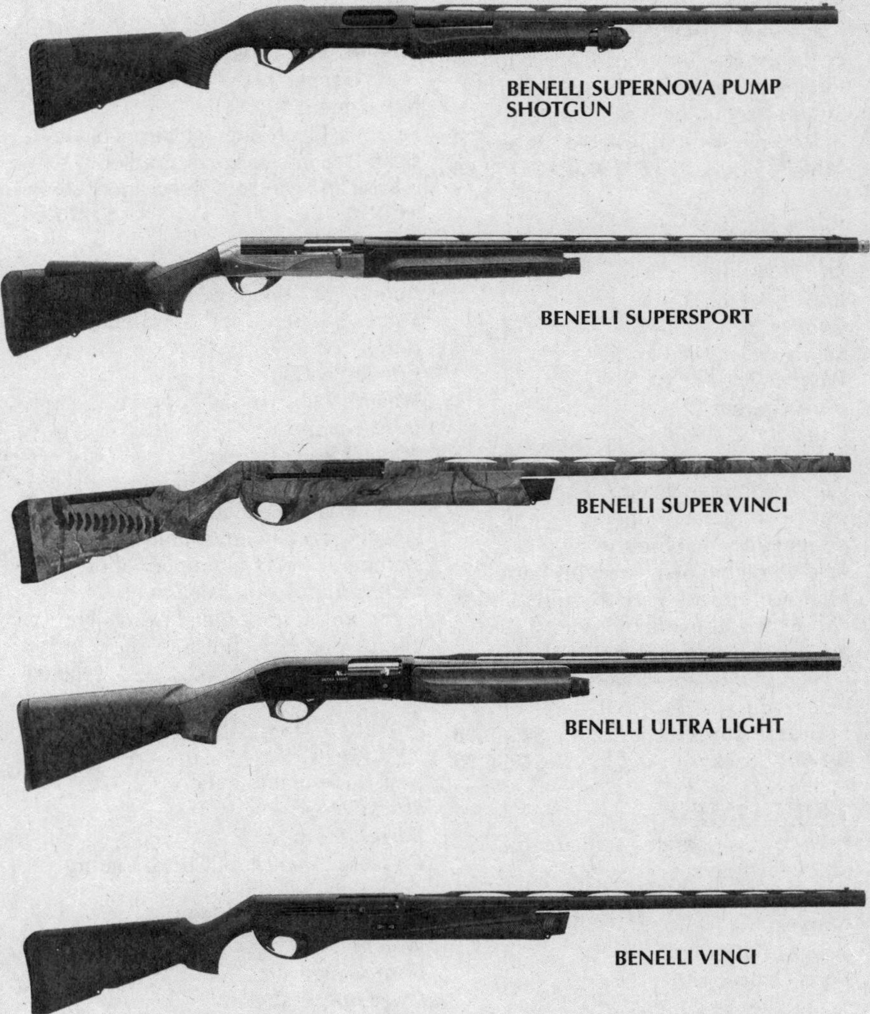

BENELLI SUPERNOVA PUMP SHOTGUN

BENELLI SUPERSPORT

BENELLI SUPER VINCI

BENELLI ULTRA LIGHT

BENELLI VINCI

Beretta USA

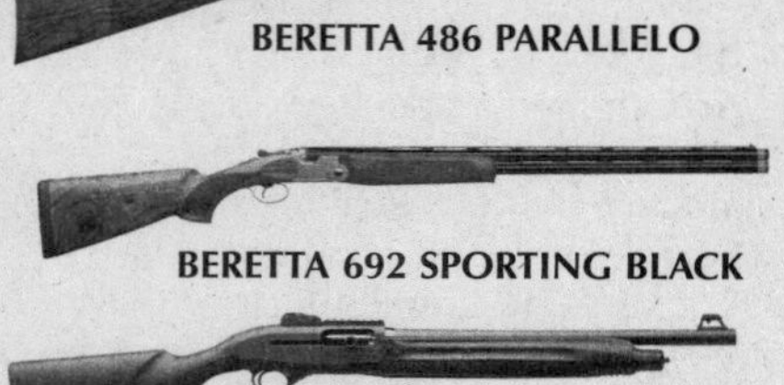

BERETTA 486 PARALLELO

BERETTA 692 SPORTING BLACK

BERETTA 1301 TACTICAL

BERETTA 686 SILVER PIGEON I

BERETTA 694

BERETTA A300 OUTLANDER

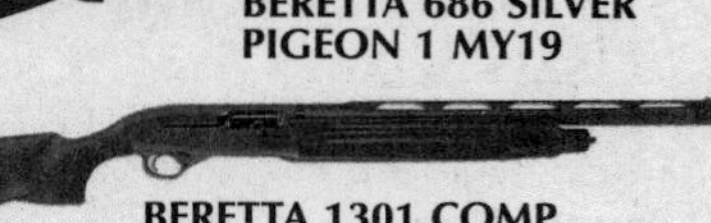

BERETTA 686 SILVER PIGEON 1 MY19

BERETTA 1301 COMP

BERETTA A300 OUTLANDER SPORTING

486 PARALLELO

Action: Side-by-side
Stock: Wood
Barrel: 28 in., 30 in.
Chokes: Fixed, Optima-Choke
Weight: 7 lb.
Bore/Gauge: 12
Magazine: 2 shells
Features: Round action with lavish scroll engraving; new leaf springs, trigger group, barrel technology
MSRP $5350.00

686 SILVER PIGEON I

Action: Over/under
Stock: Walnut
Barrel: 26 in., 28 in., 30 in.
Chokes: MC
Weight: 6 lb. 13 oz.
Bore/Gauge: 12, 20, 28, .410
Magazine: 2 shells
Features: Extensive but refined floral and scroll decoration on the frame; dual-conical locking mechanism; automatic safety; oil finish on checkered walnut stock and forend; metal bead sight
MSRP $2350.00

686 SILVER PIGEON 1 MY19

Action: Over/under
Stock: Walnut
Barrel: 26 in., 28 in., 30 in.
Chokes: 3
Sights: Steel bead front
Weight: N/A
Bore/Gauge: 12
Capacity: 2 shells
Features: Replaces the 686 Silver Pigeon 1 of many years, thanks to upgrades that include Steelium Optima Bore HP barrels; 80mm double forcing cones; 70mm-long Optima Choke HP chokes; 3-in. chamber; oil-finished stock
Standard: $2250.00
Sporting: $2350.0

692 SPORTING BLACK

Action: Over/under
Stock: Walnut
Barrel: 30 in., 32 in.
Chokes: 5 OCHP
Weight: 7 lb. 11 oz.
Bore/ Gauge: 12
Magazine: 2 shells
Features: Steelium Plus barrels; longer forcing cone; Beretta Fast Adjustment System Technology; Adjustable Balance System; adjustable trigger
MSRP . . . . $5250.00–$5750.00

694

Action: Over/under
Stock: Walnut
Barrel: 30 in., 32 in.
Chokes: 5
Sights: Steel bead front
Weight: 7 lb. 13 oz.
Bore/Gauge: 12
Capacity: 2 shells
Features: A slick offering for clay games with new action shape and stock configuration including grip designed to increase the shooter's field of vision; Steelium Plus barrels; MicroCore recoil pad; expanded pitch checkering at handhold points; steel action in Nistan gray finish; three-position adjustable trigger; new ejector design
Standard stock: $4500.00
B-FAST stock: $4850.00

1301 COMP

Action: Gas-operated semiautomatic
Stock: Synthetic
Barrel: 21 in., 24 in.
Chokes: IC
Weight: 7 lb. 2 oz.
Bore/Gauge: 12
Magazine: 5+1 shells
Features: Fiber optic sights; oversized bolt release and handle; Optima Bore HP interchangable choke system
MSRP $1275.00

1301 TACTICAL

Action: Gas-operated semiautomatic
Stock: Synthetic
Barrel: 18.5 in.
Chokes: F
Weight: 7 lb. 2 oz.
Bore/Gauge: 12
Magazine: 5+1 shells
Features: Ghost ring sight; front blade sight; Picatinny rail; oversized bolt release and handle; fixed cylinder choke
MSRP $1275.00

A300 OUTLANDER

Action: Gas-operated semiautomatic
Stock: Synthetic, camo, walnut
Barrel: 28 in.
Chokes: MC3
Weight: 7 lb. 10 oz.
Bore/Gauge: 12
Magazine: 3+1 shells
Features: Gas operation with compensating exhaust valve and self-cleaning piston; adjustable shim system on stock; aluminum alloy receiver; crossbolt safety with ergonomics; front metal bead sight; oiled wood stock finish
MSRP $900.00

A300 OUTLANDER SPORTING

Action: Semiautomatic
Stock: Wood
Barrel: 30 in.
Chokes: Three MobilChoke Victory (IC, M, F)
Sights: Front and mid-rib beads
Weight: N/A
Bore/Gauge: 12
Magazine: 3 shells
Features: High-grade wood with checkering pattern; gas-operated; valve with a self-cleaning cylinder and piston combination
MSRP $1100.00

A300 OUTLANDER TURKEY

Action: Semiautomatic
Stock: Synthetic
Barrel: 24 in.
Chokes: 3 chokes (F, M, IC)
Weight: 7 lb. 9 oz.
Bore/Gauge: 12
Magazine: 3+1 shells
Features: TRUGLO fiber optic sights; Realtree XTRA camo finish; adjustable drop cast; reliable/clean gas operating system; sling attachment
MSRP $900.00

A350 EXTREMA MAX-5

Action: Semiautomatic
Stock: Synthetic
Barrel: 28 in.
Chokes: Optima HP
Weight: 7 lb. 2 oz.
Bore/Gauge: 12
Magazine: N/A
Features: Adjustable shim system for drop and right-hand or left-hand configuration; 3.5 in. chamber; steelium barrel; fiber optic bead front sight; sling points; Micro Core recoil pad; Max-5 camo finish
MSRP $1150.00

A400 LITE SYNTHETIC

Action: Semiautomatic
Stock: Walnut and polymer
Barrel: 24 in., 26 in., 28 in., 30 in.
Chokes: OptimaChoke screw-in tube
Weight: 6 lb. 3 oz.–6 lb. 10 oz.
Bore/Gauge: 12, 20
Magazine: 3+1 or 2+1 shells
Features: Steelium barrel design, walnut stock with polymer forend insert, trigger guard and kick-off interface; 3-in. chamber; blink operating system; Micro-Core recoil pad; available with Kick-Off damper system; available in a standard-length 20-ga. and a Compact 20-ga., both with 3-inch chambers; Compact does not include the Kick-Off system
12-ga.: $1600.00
20-ga.: $1600.00
Compact 20-ga.: $1500.00

A400 XPLOR ACTION

Action: Gas-operated semiautomatic
Stock: Walnut
Barrel: 26 in., 28 in.
Chokes: F
Weight: 5 lb. 8 oz.
Bore/Gauge: 12, 20, 28
Magazine: 3+1 shells
Features: Fiber optic sights; Gun Pod shell counter, cartridge tester, and temperature display; Kick-Off recoil reduction system; Optima Bore interchangable bore system; left-hand available in 12-ga. 3-inch chamber with 28-inch barrel only
MSRP . . . .$1600.00–$1750.00

A400 XTREME PLUS CAMO

Action: Semiautomatic
Stock: Synthetic
Barrel: 26 in., 28 in.
Chokes: Five
Sights: Red bar front, integral mid bead
Weight: N/A
Bore/Gauge: 12
Capacity: 4 shells
Features: Improved stock features a soft-touch comb; barrels are Steelium Plus and reduce felt recoil; stepped rib with integral mid-rib bead; 3 ½-inch chamber; full-coverage Realtree Max-5, Kryptek Wraith, True Timber DTR, Realtree Timber, or MO Bottomland camo; five extended Black Edition choke tubes
MSRP $1900.00

A400 XTREME PLUS SYNTHETIC

Action: Semiautomatic
Stock: Synthetic
Barrel: 26 in., 28 in.
Chokes: Five
Sights: Red bar front, integral mid bead
Weight: N/A
Bore/Gauge: 12
Capacity: 4 shells
Features: Kick-Off Mega/Kick-Off3 stock features a soft-touch comb; barrels are Steelium Plus and reduce felt recoil; stepped rib with integral mid-rib bead; 3 ½-inch chamber; black synthetic stock with complementary dark-gray receiver finish; five extended Black Edition choke tubes
MSRP $1750.00

A400 XTREME UNICO SYNTHETIC

Action: Semiautomatic
Stock: Synthetic or camo
Barrel: 26 in., 28 in., 30 in.
Chokes: Optima Bore HP (C, Mod, Full)
Weight: 7 lb. 10 oz.
Bore/Gauge: 12
Magazine: 4+1 or 3+1 shells
Features: Adjustable buttstock shim kits, anti-corosion coatings on the barrel, Beretta's fast-cycling Blink technology, fast-assembly B-Lock fore-end cap, Kick-Off 3/Kick-Off Mega recoil reduction system, and Steelium Optma Bore HP barrels; chamber 3 ½-in. shells; left-hand available
MSRP: . . . . $1750.00–$1800.00

Beretta USA

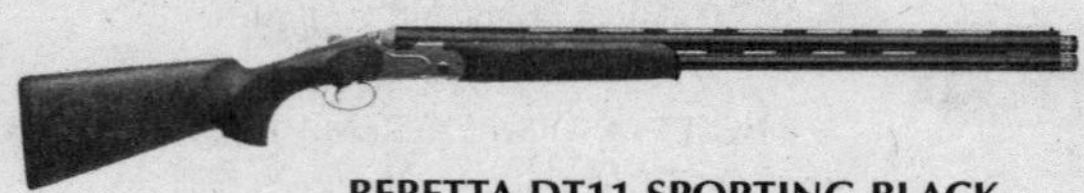
BERETTA DT11 SPORTING BLACK

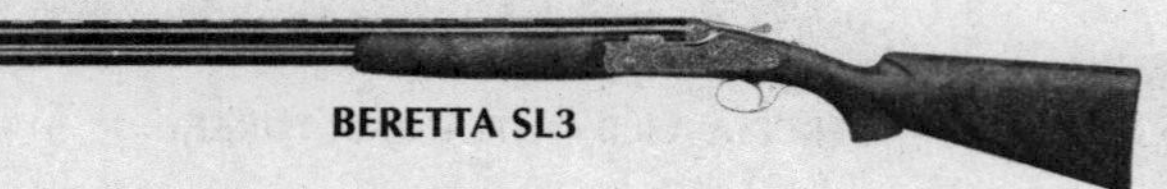
BERETTA SL3

DT11 SPORTING BLACK

Action: Over/under
Stock: Walnut
Barrel: 30 in., 32 in.
Chokes: OCHPe
Weight: 9 lb.
Bore/ Gauge: 12
Magazine: 2 shells
Features: Steelium Pro barrel; top rib with hollowed bridges; ergonomic top lever; safety selector switch; increased receiver side wall thickness; select high-quality walnut wood finished in oil; stock and forend can be fitted to customer's measurement; pistol grip and forend are hand-checkered; B-Fast adjustable stock available; left-hand model available in both barrel lengths, but without B-Fast stock option
MSRP . . . . . . $12,550.00–$12,950.00

SL3

Action: Over/under
Stock: Walnut
Barrel: 28 in., 30 in.
Chokes: N/A
Sights: Bead front
Weight: Fixed
Bore/Gauge: 12
Capacity: 2 shells
Features: A handmade boxlock with superior walnut stock; double triggers; Optima Bore HP barrels; rounded body design; light scroll, deep scroll, or game scene engravings, as well as a striking unengraved high-polish receiver option available
MSRP . . . . . . $21,100.00–$21,500.00

Blackwater/Iron Horse

IRON HORSE FIREARMS SENTRY 12

SENTRY 12

Action: Pump
Stock: Synthetic
Barrel: N/A
Chokes: N/A
Sights: None
Weight: N/A
Bore/Gauge: 12
Capacity: 5 shells
Features: An easy to take apart modular pump shotgun with plenty of rail on top for optics mounting; detachable box magazine; ambidextrous controls
MSRP $899.99

Blaser USA

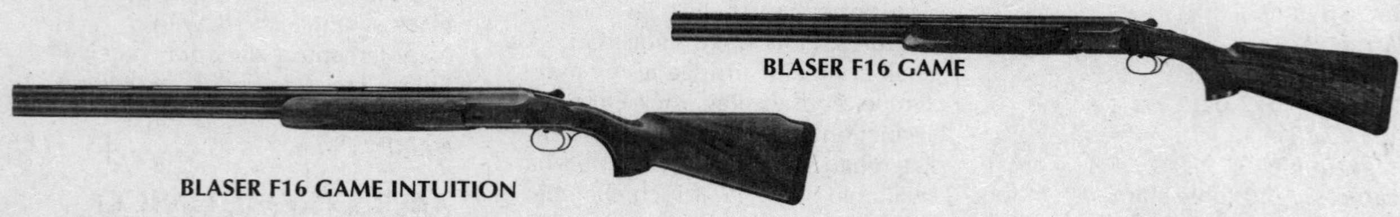
BLASER F16 GAME

BLASER F16 GAME INTUITION

F16 GAME

Action: Over/under
Stock: Walnut
Barrel: 28 in., 30 in.
Chokes: Blaser chokes flush to muzzle
Weight: 6 lb. 13 oz.
Bore/Gauge: 12
Magazine: 2 shells
Features: Sleak English-style forearm design; crisp trigger pull; Triplex bore design; tapered rib; proven Blaser ejection system; Inertial Block System (IBS) prevents an involuntary second shot or the unintentional triggering of a second shot while maintaining a superb trigger pull; many options available within three grades: Standard, Grande Luxe, and Heritage
Standard/wood grade 4: . . $4769.00
Grande Luxe/wood grade 6: $8479.00
Heritage/wood grade 8: . .$11,659.00

F16 GAME INTUITION

Action: Over/under
Stock: Wood grade II
Barrel: 28 in., 30 in.
Chokes: Three flush chokes (1/4, 1/2, 3/4)
Weight: 6 lb. 10 oz.
Bore/Gauge: 12
Magazine: 2 shells
Features: Designed specifically for women, with a specially designed buttstock tailored to the female anatomy, including a more slender pistol grip, higher comb, and reduced pitch; non-adjustable trigger; 13.8-in. length of pull; sling swivel (not mounted); silver F16 logo and silver front bead; many options available, including upgraded wood and weight balancer
Standard/wood grade 4: . . $4769.00
Grande Luxe/wood grade 6: $8479.00
Heritage/wood grade 8: . .$11,659.00

Blaser USA

BLASER F16 SPORTING

BLASER F16 SPORTING INTUITION

F16 SPORTING

Action: Over/under
Stock: Walnut
Barrel: 30 in., 32 in.
Chokes: Blaser chokes flush to muzzle
Weight: 7 lb. 8 oz.–8 lb. 6 oz.
Bore/Gauge: 12
Magazine: 2 shells
Features: Balancer system allows the adjustment of the weight distribution to shooter's personal needs; sleak English-style forearm design; crisp trigger pull; Triplex bore design; tapered rib; proven Blaser ejection system; Inertial Block System (IBS) prevents an involuntary second shot or the unintentional triggering of a second shot while maintaining a superb trigger pull; many options available within three grades: Standard, Grande Luxe, and Heritage
Standard/wood grade 4: . . $5299.00
Grande Luxe/wood grade 6: $8903.00
Heritage/wood grade 8: . . .$11,977.00

F16 SPORTING INTUITION

Action: Over/under
Stock: Wood grade II
Barrel: 30 in., 32 in.
Chokes: Three flush chokes (¼, ½, ¾)
Weight: 7 lb. 5 oz.–8 lb. 3 oz.
Bore/Gauge: 12
Magazine: 2 shells
Features: Designed specifically for women, with a specially designed buttstock tailored to the female anatomy, including a more slender pistol grip, higher comb, and reduced pitch; non-adjustable trigger; 13.8-in. length of pull; Blaser Comfort recoil pad; adjustable trigger length; prep for barrel balancer and stock balancer; red F16 logo and red fiber optic front bead; many options available, including upgraded wood and barrel balancer weights
Standard/wood grade 4: . . . $5299.00
Grande Luxe/wood grade 6: $8903.00
Heritage/wood grade 8: . . .$11,977.00

Browning

BROWNING A5 HUNTER

BROWNING A5 HUNTER HIGH GRADE

A5 MOSSY OAK BREAK-UP COUNTRY

BROWNING A5 STALKER

A5 HUNTER

Action: Semiautomatic
Stock: Walnut
Barrel: 26 in., 28 in.
Chokes: Invector-DS
Weight: 6 lb. 15 oz.
Bore/Gauge: 12
Magazine: None
Features: Strong, lightweight aluminum alloy; black anodized bi-tone finish; flat, ventilated rib; recoil operated Kinematic Drive cycles a wide range of loads; gloss finish walnut with close radius pistol grip; shim adjustable for length of pull, cast and drop; Vector Pro lengthened forcing cone; three invector-DS choke tubes; brass front bead sight; ivory mid-bead sight; included ABS case
3-inch: $1719.99
3½-inch: $1859.99

A5 HUNTER HIGH GRADE

Action: Semiautomatic
Stock: Walnut
Barrel: 26 in., 28 in.
Chokes: Invector-DS (F, M, IC)
Weight: 6 lb. 11 oz.–6 lb. 13 oz.
Bore/Gauge: 12
Magazine: 4 shells
Features: 3-in. chambered gun; gloss finished barrel; receiver with intricate scrollwork, pheasant and mallard engraving; grade 2.5 gloss varnish finish walnut stock with 22 lines-per-inch checkering; lightweight profile barrel; aluminum alloy receiver; recoil-operated Kinematic drive; Vector Pro lengthened forcing cones
MSRP $1959.99

A5 MOSSY OAK BREAK-UP COUNTRY

Action: Semiautomatic
Stock: Composite
Barrel: 26 in., 28 in.
Chokes: 3 (F, M, IC)
Sights: Fiber optic front
Weight: 7 lb. 3 oz.–7 lb. 7 oz.
Bore/Gauge: 12, 20
Capacity: 4 shells
Features: The "new" A5 with Kinetic Drive System; aluminum alloy receiver; Vector Pro lengthened forcing cones; Inflex recoil pad; stock spacers; length of pull/drop/cast shims; Invector DS chokes; 3.5-in. chamber; ABS case
MSRP . . . .$1719.99–$1859.99

A5 STALKER

Action: Semiautomatic
Stock: Composite
Barrel: 26 in., 28 in.
Chokes: Invector-DS
Weight: 7 lb. 3 oz.–7 lb. 7 oz.
Bore/Gauge: 12
Magazine: None
Features: Strong, lightweight aluminum alloy; flat, ventilated rib; recoil operated Kinematic Drive cycles a wide range of loads; composite with close radius pistol grip; textured gripping surfaces; shim adjustable for cast and drop; matte black finish; Dura-Touch armor coating; Vector Pro lengthened forcing cone; fiber-optic front sight; included ABS case
3-inch: $1589.99
3½-inch: $1719.99

Browning

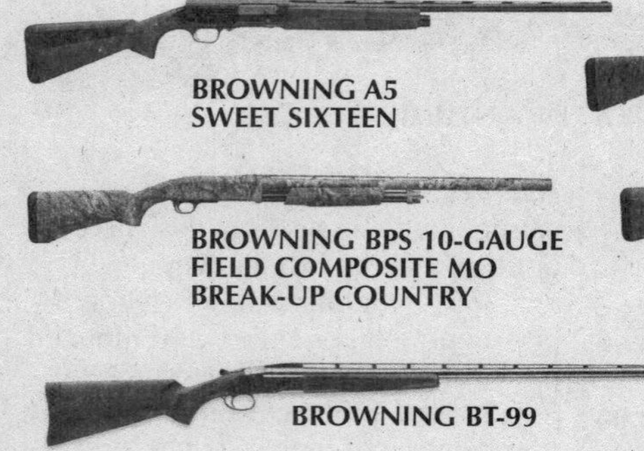

BROWNING A5 SWEET SIXTEEN

BROWNING BPS 10-GAUGE FIELD COMPOSITE MO BREAK-UP COUNTRY

BROWNING A5 WICKED WING

BROWNING BPS FIELD

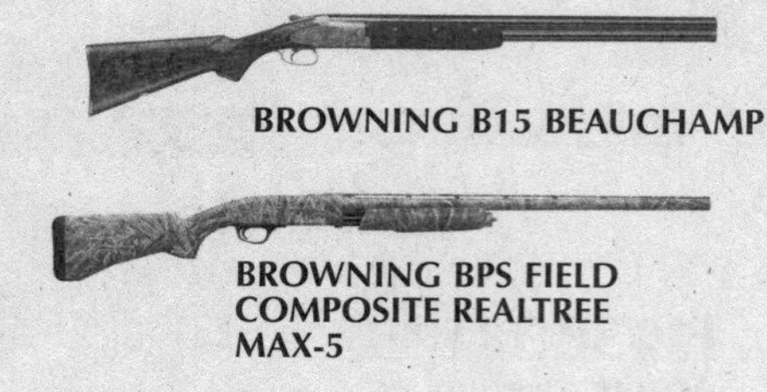

BROWNING B15 BEAUCHAMP

BROWNING BPS FIELD COMPOSITE REALTREE MAX-5

BROWNING BT-99 MAX HIGH-GRADE

BROWNING BT-99

A5 SWEET SIXTEEN

Action: Semiautomatic
Stock: Turkish walnut
Barrel: 28 in.
Chokes: Invector-DS flush
Weight: 5 lb. 13 oz.
Bore/Gauge: 16
Magazine: 4 shells
Features: Gloss walnut stock; brass bead front sight; humbpack receiver; short recoil-operated Kinematic Drive System; Invector-DS choke tubes; built on a smaller, lighter receiver for reduced weight
MSRP $1789.99

A5 WICKED WING

Action: Semiautomatic
Stock: Composite
Barrel: 26 in., 28 in.
Chokes: Extended Invector-DS Banded (F,M,IC)
Weight: 7 lb. 3 oz.–7 lb. 5 oz.
Bore/Gauge: 12
Magazine: 4 shells
Features: Chambered for 3.5-in. shells; Cerakote Burnt Bronze camo receiver and Burnt Bronze barrel with Mossy Oak Shadow Grass Blades stock; Briley extended bolt handle and oversize bolt release; fully chromed bore; recoil operated Kinematic Drive; Vector Pro lengthened forcing cone; fiber-optic front sight and ivory mid-bead
MSRP . . . . $1999.99–$2069.99

B15 BEAUCHAMP

Action: Over/under
Stock: Walnut
Barrel: 26 in., 28 in., 30 in.
Chokes: Five Invector DS
Sights: Front bead
Weight: 6 lb. 6 oz.
Bore/Gauge: 12
Magazine: 2 shells
Features: Part of Belgium-produced John M. Browning Collection; offered in four wood grades and three barrel lengths, with various forearms, buttplates and engraving levels; mechanical triggers; back-bored Vector Pro barrels; full flush-mounted choke set; leather case
MSRP $18,999.99

BPS 10-GAUGE FIELD COMPOSITE MO BREAK-UP COUNTRY

Action: Pump
Stock: Composite
Barrel: 26 in., 28 in.
Chokes: 3 (F, M, IC)
Sights: Silver bead front
Weight: 8 lb.
Bore/Gauge: 10
Capacity: 4 shells
Features: The BPS 10 was overhauled in 2020, with an upgraded stock and forend design; Inflex recoil pad; textured grip panels; enlarged trigger guard
MSRP $899.99

BPS FIELD

Action: Pump
Stock: Walnut
Barrel: 26 in., 28 in.
Chokes: 3 (F, M, IC)
Sights: Silver bead front
Weight: 7 lb.–7 lb. 10 oz.
Bore/Gauge: 12, 20, 28, .410
Capacity: 4 shells
Features: This long-standing pump was overhauled in 2020, with an upgraded stock and forend design in a satin-finish walnut; Inflex recoil pad; improved checkering at grip points; floating rib; classic bottom feed/ejection; flush Invector Plus chokes
MSRP: . . . . $739.99–$799.99

BPS FIELD COMPOSITE

Action: Pump
Stock: Composite
Barrel: 26 in., 28 in.
Chokes: 3 (F, M, IC)
Sights: Silver bead front
Weight: 7 lb.–8 lb. 1 oz.
Bore/Gauge: 10, 12, 20
Capacity: 4 shells
Features: A redesigned stock and forend for a faster feel, and other changes in 2020 include an Inflex recoil pad; textured grip points; floating rib; classic bottom feed/ejection; flush Invector Plus chokes
MSRP . . . . $699.99–$799.99

BT-99

Action: Pump
Stock: Walnut
Barrel: 32 in., 34 in.
Chokes: Screw-in tubes
Weight: 8 lb. 3 oz.–8 lb. 5 oz.
Bore/Gauge: 12
Magazine: None
Features: Satin finish walnut stock with beavertail forearm; steel receiver with blued finish; high-post ventilated rib
MSRP $1559.99

BT-99 MAX HIGH-GRADE

Action: Break-open
Stock: Grade V/VI walnut
Barrel: 32 in., 34 in.
Chokes: Three extended
Sights: Hi-Viz Pro Comp fiber optic front, mid-rib bead
Weight: 9 lb. 5 oz.
Bore/Gauge: 12
Capacity: 1 shell
Features: Top-of-the-line single-shot trap model with three extended Midas grade choke tubes; Pachmayr Decelerator XLT recoil pad; adjustable Graco buttpad, comb, and recoil reduction system; point of impact adjustable high rib; gloss oil stock finish; fitted Universal BT Trap case
MSRP $5619.99

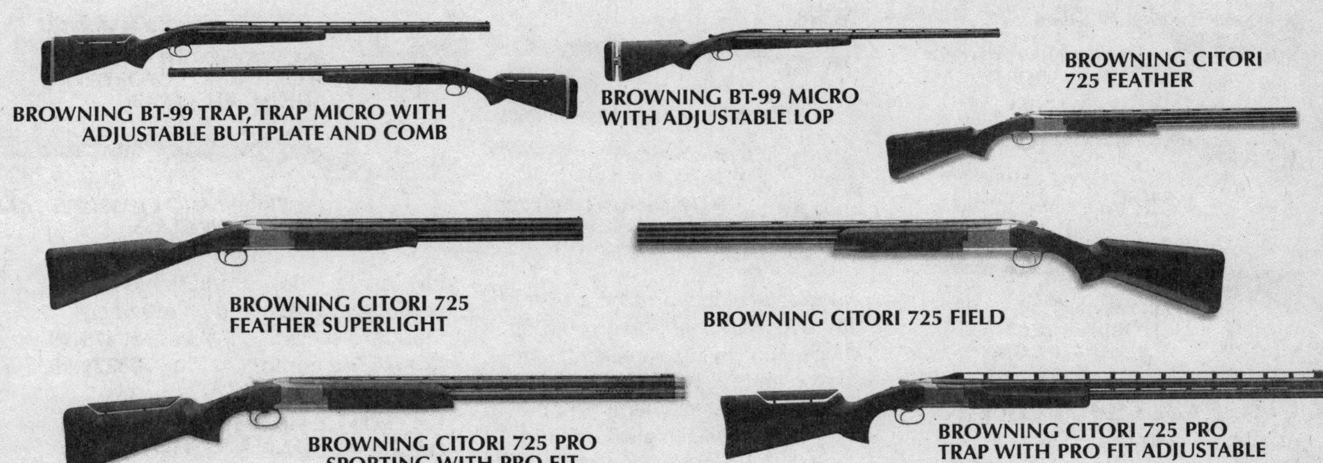
BROWNING BT-99 TRAP, TRAP MICRO WITH ADJUSTABLE BUTTPLATE AND COMB

BROWNING BT-99 MICRO WITH ADJUSTABLE LOP

BROWNING CITORI 725 FEATHER

BROWNING CITORI 725 FEATHER SUPERLIGHT

BROWNING CITORI 725 FIELD

BROWNING CITORI 725 PRO SPORTING WITH PRO FIT ADJUSTABLE COMB

BROWNING CITORI 725 PRO TRAP WITH PRO FIT ADJUSTABLE COMB

BT-99, BT-99 MICRO WITH ADJUSTABLE BUTTPLATE AND COMB

Action: Single-shot
Stock: Black walnut
Barrel: 30 in., 32 in., 34 in.
Chokes: One Invector-Plus flush
Sights: Ivory bead
Weight: 7 lb. 12 oz.–8 lb. 5 oz.
Bore/Gauge: 12
Magazine: 1 shell
Features: Graco Pro Fit adjustable buttpad plate and comb; barrels and receiver are satin blue; stock is in a satin finish; standard model (32-in., 34-in. barrel); Micro version (30-in., 32-i.n barrel) has shorter length of pull and is 12 ga., 2.75-in. chamber
MSRP. $1949.99

BT-99 MICRO WITH ADJUSTABLE LOP

Action: Single-shot
Stock: Black walnut
Barrel: 30 in.
Chokes: Invector Plus flush (F)
Sights: Ivory front sight, mid-bead
Weight: 7 lb. 12 oz.
Bore/Gauge: 12
Capacity: 1 shell
Features: A dedicated trap gun for smaller-statured shooters with an adjustable length of pull; Graco trap recoil pad; satin-finish stock; 2 ¾-in. chamber
MSRP. $1719.99

CITORI 725 FEATHER

Action: Over/under
Stock: Walnut
Barrel: 26 in., 28 in.
Chokes: 3 Invector-DS
Weight: 5 lb. 14 oz.–6 lb. 9 oz.
Bore/ Gauge: 12, 20
Magazine: 2 shells
Features: Lightweight alloy receiver; low-profile; silver nitride finish; ventilated top rib barrel; Fire Lite Mechanical Trigger system; hammer ejectors; ivory front and mid-bead sights
MSRP. $2829.99

CITORI 725 FEATHER SUPERLIGHT

Action: Over/under
Stock: Grade II/III walnut
Barrel: 26 in.
Chokes: Three (F, M, IC)
Sights: Ivory bead front
Weight: 6 lb. 2 oz. (12-ga.); 5 lb. 7 oz. (20-ga.)
Bore/Gauge: 12, 20
Capacity: 2 shells
Features: Super lightweight swinger for the upland hunter who goes all day, featuring: flush-mounted Invector DS chokes; aluminum alloy receiver with silver nitride receiver; gloss-finish straight-grip stock; 2¾-inch chrome-plated chambers
MSRP. $2749.99

CITORI 725 FIELD

Action: Over/under
Stock: Walnut
Barrel: 26, 28 in.
Chokes: Invector-DS
Weight: 6 lb. 7 oz.–7 lb. 8 oz.
Bore/Gauge: 12, 20, 28, .410
Magazine: 2 shells
Features: Steel receiver with silver nitride finish; accented, high-relief engraving; ventilated top rib action; mechanical trigger system; hammer ejectors; top-tang barrel selector/ safety; gloss oil finish Grade II/III walnut with close radius pistol grip; Vector Pro lengthened forcing cones; ivory front and mid-bead sights
MSRP. . . . . $2679.99–$2749.99

CITORI 725 PRO SPORTING WITH PRO FIT ADJUSTABLE COMB

Action: Over/under
Stock: Wood
Barrel: 30 in., 32 in.
Chokes: F, IM, M, IC, S
Weight: 7 lb. 5 oz.–7 lb. 13 oz.
Bore/Gauge: 12, 20
Magazine: 2 shells
Features: Polished blue barrel finish; grade III/IV black walnut stock with gloss oil finish; HiViz ProComp sights; vented ribs; drilled and tapped for scopes
MSRP. $4219.99

CITORI 725 PRO TRAP WITH PRO FIT ADJUSTABLE COMB

Action: Over/under
Stock: Wood
Barrel: 30 in., 32 in.
Chokes: F, LF, M, 2IM
Weight: 8 lb. 8 oz., 8 lb. 11 oz.
Bore/Gauge: 12
Magazine: 2 shells
Features: Polished blue barrel finish; grade III/IV black walnut stock with gloss oil finish; HiViz ProComp sights; vented ribs; drilled and tapped for scopes
MSRP. $4219.99

Browning

BROWNING CITORI 725 S3 SPORTING

BROWNING CITORI 725 SPORTING

BROWNING CITORI 725 SPORTING NON-PORTED ADJUSTABLE COMB

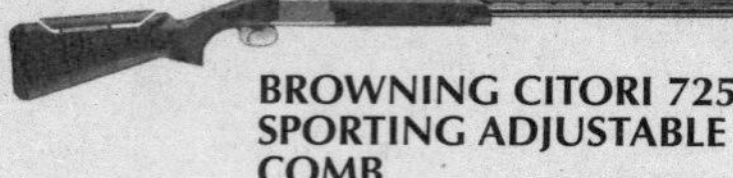

BROWNING CITORI 725 SPORTING ADJUSTABLE COMB

BROWNING CITORI 725 SPORTING GOLDEN CLAYS

BROWNING CITORI 725 TRAP GOLDEN CLAYS

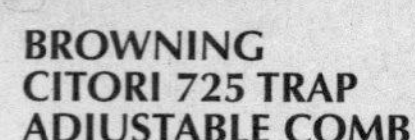

BROWNING CITORI 725 TRAP ADJUSTABLE COMB

CITORI 725 S3 SPORTING

Action: Over/under
Stock: Black walnut
Barrel: 30 in., 32 in.
Chokes: 5 (F, IM, M, IC, SK)
Sights: Ivory bead front
Weight: 8 lb. 2 oz.–8 lb. 4 oz.
Bore/Gauge: 12
Capacity: 2 shells
Features: A darkly handsome 725 clays gun with Grade V/VI black walnut stock; 20 lines-per-inch checkering; low-luster blue receiver with polished blue barrels
MSRP $3989.99

CITORI 725 SPORTING

Action: Over/under
Stock: Walnut
Barrel: 30, 32 in.
Chokes: Invector-DS
Weight: 6 lb. 4 oz.–7 lb. 10 oz.
Bore/Gauge: 12, 20, 28, .410
Magazine: 2 shells
Features: Steel receiver with silver nitride finish; gold accented engraving; ventilated top and side rib action; mechanical trigger system; hammer ejectors; top-tang barrel selector/safety; gloss oil finish Grade III/IV walnut with close radius pistol grip; Vector Pro lengthened forcing cones; five Invector-DS choke tubes; HiViz Pro-Comp sight and ivory mid-bead
MSRP . . . . $3309.99–$3379.99

CITORI 725 SPORTING ADJUSTABLE COMB

Action: Over/under
Stock: Wood
Barrel: 30 in., 32 in.
Chokes: F, IM, M, IC, S
Weight: 7 lb. 13 oz.
Bore/Gauge: 12
Magazine: 2 shells
Features: Steel low-profile receiver with silver nitride finish and gold accented engraving; ventilated barrel with top and side ribs; Fire Lite mechanical trigger system; top-tang barrel selector/safety; gloss oil finish Grade III/IV walnut stock with close radius pistol grip and adjustable comb; HiViz Pro-Comp sight and ivory mid-bead
MSRP $3709.99

CITORI 725 SPORTING GOLDEN CLAYS

Action: Over/under
Stock: Walnut
Barrel: 30 in., 32 in.
Chokes: Extended Invector-DS (F, IM, M, IC, Skeet)
Weight: 7 lb. 13 oz.
Bore/Gauge: 12
Magazine: 2 shells
Features: Unique "Golden Clays" accented gold engraving; Pro Fit adjustable comb; ported barrels with vented top and side ribs; HiViz Pro-Comp fiber optic front side and ivory mid-bead; grade V/VI walnut stock; low-profile silver nitride finish steel receiver; FireLite mechanical trigger
MSRP $5619.99

CITORI 725 SPORTING NON-PORTED

Action: Over/under
Stock: Black walnut
Barrel: 30 in., 32 in.
Chokes: 5 (F, IM, M, IC, SK)
Sights: Hi-Viz Pro Comp front, mid bead
Weight: 7 lb. 8 oz.–7 lb. 10 oz.
Bore/Gauge: 12
Capacity: 2 shells
Features: Not everyone sees the benefit in ported barrels, so Browning gives you this clays gun without the holes; Grade III/IV black walnut stock in a gloss oil finish; triple trigger system; silver nitride receiver with gold accents; 3-in. chamber; extended Invector DS chokes; adjustable comb version has right-hand palm swell
Standard stock: $3179.99
Adjustable comb: $3579.99

CITORI 725 TRAP ADJUSTABLE COMB

Action: Over/under
Stock: Wood
Barrel: 30 in., 32 in.
Chokes: F, IM, M
Weight: 8 lb. 8 oz.–8 lb. 11 oz.
Bore/Gauge: 12
Magazine: 2 shells
Features: Steel low-profile receiver with silver nitride finish and gold accented engraving; ventilated barrel with top and side ribs; Fire Lite mechanical trigger system; top-tang barrel selector/safety; gloss oil finish Grade III/IV walnut stock with close radius pistol grip and Monte Carlo or adjustable straight comb; HiViz Pro-Comp sight and ivory mid-bead
MSRP $3939.99

CITORI 725 TRAP GOLDEN CLAYS

Action: Over/under
Stock: Walnut
Barrel: 30 in., 32 in.
Chokes: Extended Invector-DS (F, LF, IM, IM, M)
Weight: 8 lb. 8 oz.–8 lb. 11 oz.
Bore/Gauge: 12
Magazine: 2 shells
Features: 2¾ in. chamber; hammer ejectors and top-tang barrel selector/safety; gloss grade V/VI walnut stock with close radius pistol grip and right-hand palm swell; receiver has a silver nitride finish and gold-accented engraving; adjustable Monte Carlo comb; Pachmayr Decelerator XLT Trap recoil pad; ventilated top and side ribs; Vector Pro lengthened forcing cones; GraCoil recoil reduction system; HiViz Pro-Comp front sight and ivory mid-bead
MSRP $6039.99

CITORI 725 TRAP MAX

Action: Over/under
Stock: Black walnut
Barrel: 30 in., 32 in.
Chokes: 5 (F, LF, M, IM x2)
Sights: Hi-Viz Pro Comp front, ivory mid bead
Weight: 9 lb.–9 lb. 2 oz.
Bore/Gauge: 12
Capacity: 2 shells
Features: You'll be aiming for gold with this trap gun featuring a Graco buttpad plate for cant/toe-in/toe-out adjusting; adjustable GraCoil Recoil Reduction System; Grade V/VI gloss-finished walnut stock; Triple Trigger System with three shoes; Pachmayr Decelerator XLT recoil pad; adjustable high trap rib changes POI from 50/50 up to 90/10; ported barrels
MSRP $6039.99

CITORI CX

Action: Over/under
Stock: Grade II American walnut
Barrel: 28 in., 30 in., 32 in.
Chokes: Three extended (F, M, IC)
Sights: Ivory bead front
Weight: 8 lb. 1 oz.–8 lb. 5 oz.
Bore/Gauge: 12
Capacity: 2 shells
Features: Browning calls this a "crossover" gun with a 60/40 point of impact to address targets or game and featuring: high-polished blued finish with CX logo in gold on the receiver; 3-inch chrome chambers; Vector Pro lengthened forcing cones; Inflex recoil pad; gloss-finish stock; Midas-grade extended chokes; ventilated high-post rib and vented barrel joint; Triple Trigger System with one trigger included
MSRP $2269.99

CITORI CX WHITE

Action: Over/under
Stock: Black walnut
Barrel: 28 in., 30 in., 32 in.
Chokes: Invector Plus Midas
Sights: Ivory front, mid-bead
Weight: 8 lb. 1 oz.–8 lb. 9 oz.
Bore/Gauge: 12
Capacity: 2 shells
Features: Similar to the standard CX, but with a receiver in a silver nitride finish
Standard stock: $2379.99
Adjustable comb: $2779.99

CITORI CXS 20-/28-GAUGE COMBO

Action: Over/under
Stock: Black walnut
Barrel: 30 in., 32 in.
Chokes: 6 (F, M, IC)
Sights: Ivory front, mid-bead
Weight: 7 lb. 2 oz.–7 lb. 15 oz.
Bore/Gauge: 20/28
Capacity: 2 shells
Features: A two-barrel set for sub-gauge competitors with a Grade II walnut stock with 18 lines-per-inch checkering and in a gloss finish; polished blue receiver and barrels; wide floating rib with 50/50 point of impact; Inflex 2 recoil pad; six extended Invector Plus Midas-grade chokes, three for each gauge
MSRP $3939.99

CITORI CXS, CXS WITH ADJUSTABLE COMB

Action: Over/under
Stock: Black walnut
Barrel: 28 in., 30 in., 32 in.
Chokes: Three Invector-Plus Midas (F, M, IC)
Sights: Ivory bead
Weight: 6 lb. 3 oz.–6 lb. 7 oz. (20-gauge); 7 lb. 10 oz.–7 lb. 14 oz. (12-gauge); 7 lb. 14 oz.–8 lb. 2 oz. (12-gauge with adjustable comb)
Bore/Gauge: 12, 20
Magazine: 2 shells
Features: Barrels with a lightweight profile, vented top and side; shoots 50/50 point of impact; Grade II American walnut with a gloss finish; Vector Pro lengthened forcing cones; Triple Trigger system (one trigger included); ivory mid-bead
CXS: $2319.99
Adjustable comb: $2749.99

CITORI CXS MICRO

Action: Over/under
Stock: Grade II/III American walnut
Barrel: 24 in., 26 in.
Chokes: Three extended (F, M, IC)
Sights: Ivory bead front and mid-rib
Weight: 6 lb. 7 oz.–7 lb. 8 oz.
Bore/Gauge: 12, 20
Capacity: 2 shells
Features: In Browning's "crossover" category of over/unders, this one with shorter barrels for nimble handling on the skeet field or in the grouse woods. Features include: 50/50 point of impact; Inflex recoil pad; shorter 13-inch length of pull; extended Midas-grade chokes; front and mid-rib beads; 3-inch chambers both gauges
MSRP $2269.99

Browning

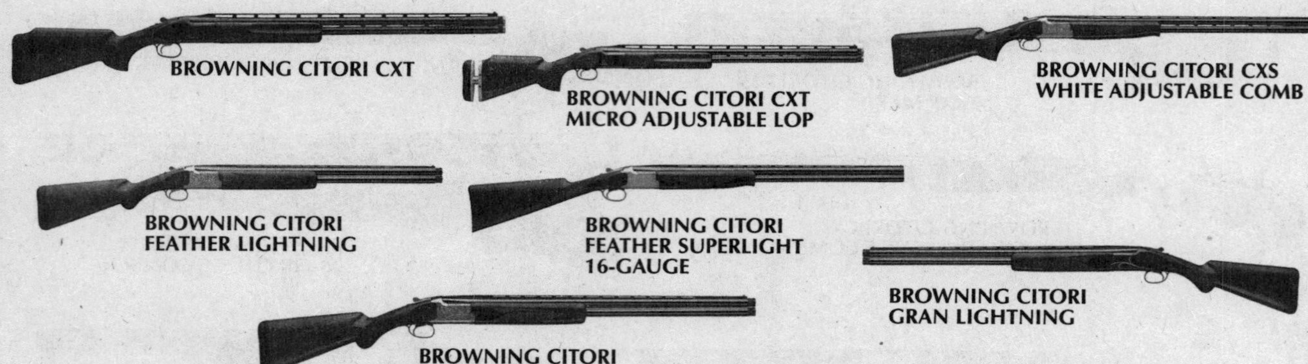

CITORI CXT, CXT WITH ADJUSTABLE COMB

Action: Over/under
Stock: Black walnut
Barrel: 30 in., 32 in.
Chokes: Three Invector-Plus Midas Extended (F, M, IC)
Sights: Ivory bead
Weight: 8 lb. 6 oz.–8 lb. 8 oz. (CXT); 8 lb. 10 oz.–8 lb. 12 oz. (CXT with adjustable comb)
Bore/Gauge: 12
Magazine: 2 shells
Features: Raised comb (in the non-adjustable model); high-post floating rib; point of impact is 70/30; 3-in. chamber
CXT: $2389.99
Adjustable comb: $2829.99

CITORI CXT MICRO ADJUSTABLE LOP

Action: Over/under
Stock: Black walnut
Barrel: 28 in., 30 in.
Chokes: 3 (F, M, IC)
Sights: Ivory front sight, mid-bead
Weight: 8 lb. 9 oz.–8 lb. 11 oz.
Bore/Gauge: 12
Capacity: 2 shells
Features: Stock adjustable for length of pull and with a Graco butt pad and Inflex recoil pad; Grade II American walnut stock with gloss finish; 70/30 point of impact; three-position trigger; 3-inch chambers; ported barrels; vented mid-rib
MSRP $2549.99

CITORI CXT WHITE

Action: Over/under
Stock: Black walnut
Barrel: 30 in., 32 in.
Chokes: 3 (F, IM, M)
Sights: Ivory front, mid-bead
Weight: 8 lb. 2 oz.–8 lb. 4 oz.
Bore/Gauge: 12
Capacity: 2 shells
Features: This member of the crossover CXT family is intended for Trap, with a Monte Carlo-type stock and a wide, floating higher-shooting rib designed for a 70/30 point of impact; silver nitride barrel; side venting; ported barrels; supplied with extended Invector-Plus Midas-grade chokes; adjustable comb model has Graco comb
Standard stock: $2499.00
Adjustable stock: $2939.00

CITORI FEATHER LIGHTNING

Action: Over/under
Stock: Grade III/IV walnut
Barrel: 26 in., 28 in.
Chokes: Three extended (F, M, IC)
Sights: Ivory bead front and mid-rib
Weight: 7 lb.–7 lb. 2 oz.
Bore/Gauge: 12, 20
Capacity: 2 shells
Features: A super-lightweight hunter's favorite returns to the Browning family with: three extended Invector Plus chokes; 3-inch chambers; upgraded wood; updated receiver engraving in a pronounced leaf pattern; rounded pistol grip
MSRP $2959.99

CITORI FEATHER SUPERLIGHT 16-GAUGE

Action: Over/under
Stock: Black walnut
Barrel: 26 in., 28 in.
Chokes: 3 (F, M, IC)
Sights: Ivory bead front
Weight: 6 lb. 2 oz.–6 lb. 4 oz.
Bore/Gauge: 16
Capacity: 2 shells
Features: Another entry in the 16-ga. revival field, and one with a British flare thanks to its Grade II/III straight-grip stock and hard, snag-free buttplate; 18 lines-per-inch checkering; low-profile vent rib; flush-fit Invector chokes; 2 ¾-in. chamber
MSRP $2469.99

CITORI GRAN LIGHTNING

Action: Over/under
Stock: Grade V/VI walnut
Barrel: 26 in., 28 in.
Chokes: Three extended (F, M, IC)
Sights: Ivory bead front and mid-rib
Weight: 6 lb. 13 oz.–8 lb. 2 oz.
Bore/Gauge: 12, 20, 28, .410
Capacity: 2 shells
Features: Top-grade wood; rounded pistol grip; all-new leaf-pattern engraving in polished blue with gold accents; Midas-grade extended choke tubes; 3-inch chambers on 12- and 20-gauge and .410 bore, 28-gauge has 2¾-inch chambers
MSRP . . . . $3439.99–$3509.99

CITORI WHITE LIGHTNING

Action: Over/under
Stock: Grade IIiI/IV walnut
Barrel: 26 in., 28 in.
Chokes: Three extended (F, M, IC)
Sights: Ivory bead front and mid-rib
Weight: 6 lb. 12 oz.–8 lb. 2 oz.
Bore/Gauge: 12, 20, 28, .410
Capacity: 2 shells
Features: Mid-grade wood paired with a silver nitride receiver left naturally "in the white" and polished blue barrels; chrome-plated 3-inch chambers; extended Invector Plus chokes; new engraving in a bold leaf pattern
MSRP . . . . $2749.99–$2829.99

BROWNING CYNERGY CLASSIC TRAP UNSINGLE COMBO WITH ADJUSTABLE COMB

BROWNING CYNERGY CX WITH ADJUSTABLE COMB

BROWNING CYNERGY WICKED WING REALTREE MAX-5

BROWNING GOLD 10-GAUGE FIELD MO BREAK-UP COUNTRY

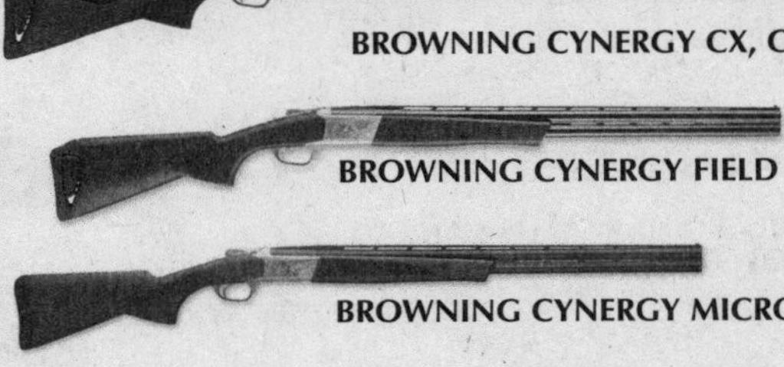

BROWNING CYNERGY CX, CX COMPOSITE

BROWNING CYNERGY FIELD

BROWNING CYNERGY MICRO MIDAS

CYNERGY CLASSIC TRAP UNSINGLE COMBO WITH ADJUSTABLE COMB

Action: Single shot and over/under
Stock: Walnut
Barrel: 32/34 in.
Chokes: Four Invector-Plus Midas Grade choke tubes
Weight: 8 lb. 13 oz.–8 lb. 15 oz.
Bore/Gauge: 12
Magazine: 1 or 2 shells
Features: Steel receiver with MonoLock hinge; double- and single-barrel sets included; reverse striker ignition system; impact ejectors; top-tang barrel selector/safety; gloss finish Monte Carlo grade III/IV walnut stock with right-hand palm swell
MSRP $4359.99

CYNERGY CX, CX COMPOSITE

Action: Over/under
Stock: Black walnut, composite
Barrel: 30 in., 32 in.
Chokes: Invector-Plus Midas Grade (F, M, IC)
Weight: 7 lb. 14 oz.–8.0 lb. (CX); 7 lb. 11 oz.–7 lb. 13 oz. (CX Composite)
Bore/Gauge: 12
Magazine: 2 shells
Features: Crossover barrel design with a 60/40 POI; ventilated top and side ribs; ivory front and mid-bead sights; steel ultra-low profile receiver with MonoLock Hinge engraved with a silver nitride finish; reverse striker ignition system; mechanical trigger design; Impact Ejectors; top-tang barrel selector/safety; 3-in. chamber; composite version features black rubber overmolding at grip points and adjustable comb
CX: $1899.99
Composite: $1819.99

CYNERGY CX WITH ADJUSTABLE COMB

Action: Over/under
Stock: Black walnut
Barrel: 30 in., 32 in.
Chokes: Three Invector-Plus Midas Extended (F, M, IC)
Sights: Ivory bead
Weight: 8 lb. 2 oz.–8 lb. 6 oz.
Bore/Gauge: 12
Magazine: 2 shells
Features: Shoots 60/40 point of impact; adjustable comb; trigger adjustable for length of pull; 0.25-in. stock spacer; reverse striker ignition system; mechanical trigger; impact ejectors; Grade 1 walnut in a satin finish; Vector Pro lengthened forcing cones
MSRP $2319.99

CYNERGY FIELD

Action: Over/under
Stock: Walnut
Barrel: 26 in., 28 in.
Chokes: Three Invector-Plus
Weight: 6 lb. 2 oz.–7 lb. 11 oz.
Bore/Gauge: 12, 20
Magazine: 2 shells
Features: Steel receiver with MonoLock hinge; reverse striker ignition system; impact ejectors; oil finish walnut stock; ivory front and mid-bead sights
MSRP . . . . $2039.99–$2109.99

CYNERGY MICRO MIDAS

Action: Over/under
Stock: Wood
Barrel: 24 in., 26 in.
Chokes: F, M, IC
Weight: 6 lb.–6 lb. 2 oz.
Bore/Gauge: 20
Magazine: 2 shells
Features: Matte blued barrel finish; grade I/II black walnut stock with satin finish; ivory bead front sight; Cynergy Inflex recoil pad
MSRP $2039.99

CYNERGY WICKED WING REALTREE MAX-5, MO SHADOW GRASS HABITAT, MO BOTTOMLAND

Action: Over/under
Stock: Composite
Barrel: 26 in., 28 in., 30 in.
Chokes: 3 (F, M, IC)
Sights: Ivory bead front
Weight: 7 lb. 6 oz.–7 lb. 10 oz.
Bore/Gauge: 12
Capacity: 2 shells
Features: A big one for geese or far away toms with 3.5-in. chamber; stock with adjustable comb and spacers; full chrome bore; receiver and barrels in burnt bronze Cerakote; with extended, banded Invector-Plus chokes
MSRP . . . . $2339.99–$2419.99

GOLD 10-GAUGE FIELD MO BREAK-UP COUNTRY

Action: Semiautomatic
Stock: Composite
Barrel: 26 in., 28 in.
Chokes: 3 (F, M, IC)
Sights: Silver front bead
Weight: 9 lb. 9 oz.–9 lb. 10 oz.
Bore/Gauge: 10
Capacity: 4 shells
Features: Browning remains dedicated to the 10-ga. with a new one for turkey hunters; dressed in Mossy Oak Break-Up Country; Inflex recoil pad; textured grip areas
MSRP $1859.99

Browning

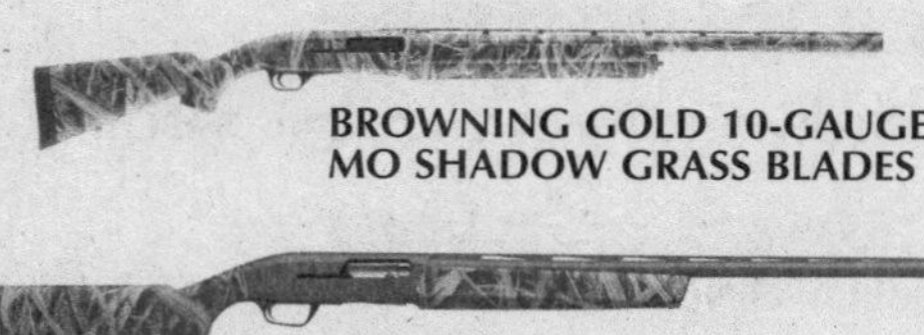
BROWNING GOLD 10-GAUGE MO SHADOW GRASS BLADES

BROWNING MAXUS MO BOTTOMLAND

BROWNING MAXUS HUNTER

BROWNING MAXUS SPORTING

BROWNING MAXUS SPORTING GOLDEN CLAYS

BROWNING MAXUS STALKER

BROWNING MAXUS ULTIMATE

GOLD 10-GAUGE FIELD MO SHADOW GRASS BLADES

Action: Semiautomatic
Stock: Composite
Barrel: 26 in., 28 in.
Chokes: 3 (F, M, IC)
Sights: Brass front bead
Weight: 9 lb. 9 oz.–9 lb. 10 oz.
Bore/Gauge: 10
Capacity: 4 shells
Features: This differs from the standard Gold 10-ga. with a vented recoil pad instead of the Inflex and a more traditionally styled buttstock; supplied with flush Invector chokes; 3.5-in. chamber; full-coverage camo
MSRP $1779.99

MAXUS HUNTER

Action: Gas-operated semiautomatic
Stock: Composite
Barrel: 26 in., 28 in., 30 in.
Chokes: Three Invector-Plus
Weight: 6 lb. 15 oz.–7 lb. 1 oz.
Bore/Gauge: 12
Magazine: None
Features: Aluminum alloy receiver with durable satin nickel finish; laser engraving of pheasant and mallard on receiver; Inflex technology recoil pad; ivory front bead sight
3-inch: $1589.99
3½-inch: $1739.99

MAXUS MO SHADOW GRASS HABITAT, MO BOTTOMLAND, REALTREE TIMBER, REALTREE MAX-5

Action: Semiautomatic
Stock: Composite
Barrel: 26 in., 28 in.
Chokes: 3 (F, M, IC)
Sights: Fiber optic front
Weight: 6 lb. 14 oz.–6 lb. 15 oz.
Bore/Gauge: 12
Capacity: 4 shells
Features: This is a light one in the 12-ga. 3.5-in. chamber game and features Browning's Power Drive Gas System; aluminum alloy receiver; Lightning trigger; Speed Lock forearm; full-coverage camo; Inflex recoil pad; flush Invector-Plus chokes
MSRP $1699.99

MAXUS SPORTING

Action: Gas-operated semiautomatic
Stock: Walnut
Barrel: 28 in., 30 in.
Chokes: Five Invector-Plus choke tubes
Weight: 7 lb.–7 lb. 1 oz.
Bore/Gauge: 12
Magazine: None
Features: Aluminum alloy receiver with durable satin nickel finish; laser engraving of game birds transforming into clay birds; speed lock forearm; ivory mid bead sight, HiVix Tri-Comp fiber optic front sight
MSRP $1799.99

MAXUS SPORTING GOLDEN CLAYS

Action: Gas-operated semiautomatic
Stock: Walnut
Barrel: 28 in., 30 in.
Chokes: 5 Invector-Plus
Weight: 7 lb. 3 oz.–7 lb. 4 oz.
Bore/ Gauge: 12
Magazine: None
Features: Gold-enhanced engraving; lightweight aluminum alloy; flat, ventilated rib; 3 in. chamber; Power Drive Gas System; Speed Lock Forearm; Vector Pro lengthened forcing cone; HiViz Pro-Comp fiber optic front sight
MSRP $2099.99

MAXUS STALKER

Action: Gas-operated semiautomatic
Stock: Composite
Barrel: 26 in., 28 in.
Chokes: Three Invector Plus choke tubes
Weight: 6 lb. 14 oz.–7 lb. 2.08 oz.
Bore/Gauge: 12
Magazine: None
Features: Magazine cut-off, matte black composite stock with pistol grip; speed lock forearm; textured gripping surfaces; Dura Touch armor coating; Inflex technology recoil pads; lightning trigger system; ventilated rib
3-inch: $1399.99
3 1/2-inch: $1589.99

MAXUS ULTIMATE

Action: Gas-operated semiautomatic
Stock: Walnut
Barrel: 26 in., 28 in., 30 in.
Chokes: Invector Plus (F, M, IC)
Weight: 7 lb. 1 oz.–7 lb. 4 oz.
Bore/Gauge: 12
Magazine: None
Features: Strong, lightweight aluminum alloy receiver; durable satin nickel finish; laser engraved (pintails on the left-hand side and pheasants on the right); gloss blued finish; ventilated rib; gloss oil finished grade III walnut with close radius pistol grip; speed lock forearm; shim adjustable for length of pull, cast, and drop; Inflex technology recoil pad; brass bead front sight; ABS case included
MSRP $1979.99

BROWNING MAXUS WICKED WING

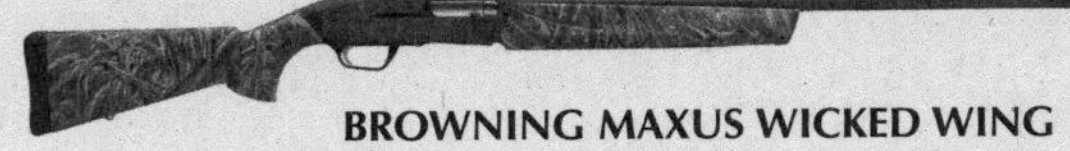

BROWNING MAXUS WICKED WING

BROWNING MAXUS WICKED WING TUNGSTEN MO SHADOW GRASS HABITAT

BROWNING SILVER BLACK LIGHTNING AND SILVER HUNTER MATTE

BROWNING SILVER FIELD COMPOSITE

BROWNING SILVER FIELD

BROWNING SILVER FIELD MICRO MIDAS

MAXUS WICKED WING

Action: Semiautomatic
Stock: Composite
Barrel: 26 in., 28 in.
Chokes: Banded Invector-Plus Extended
Weight: 7.0 lb.–7 lb. 2 oz.
Bore/Gauge: 12
Magazine: 4 shells
Features: 3.5-in. autoloader; MO Shadow Grass Blades stock; Browning's Dura-Touch Armor Coating and burnt bronze Cerakote finish on receiver and barrel; Briley extended bolt handles; oversized bolt release come
MSRP $1899.99

MAXUS WICKED WING MO SHADOW GRASS HABITAT, MO BOTTOMLAND, REALTREE TIMBER, REALTREE MAX-5

Action: Semiautomatic
Stock: Composite
Barrel: 26 in., 28 in.
Chokes: 3 (F, M, IC)
Sights: Fiber optic front
Weight: 7 lb.–7 lb. 2 oz.
Bore/Gauge: 12
Capacity: 4 shells
Features: An upgrade from the entry-grade camo Maxus, the Wicked Wings get a barrel and receiver in burnt bronze Cerakote; oversized bolt release; PowerDrive gas system; Lightning trigger; fully-chromed bore and chamber; extended Invector Plus Goose Band choke tubes
MSRP $1899.99

MAXUS WICKED WING TUNGSTEN MO SHADOW GRASS HABITAT, MO BOTTOMLAND, REALTREE TIMBER, REALTREE MAX-5

Action: Semiautomatic
Stock: Composite
Barrel: 26 in., 28 in.
Chokes: 3 (F, M, IC)
Sights: Fiber optic front
Weight: 7 lb.–7 lb. 2 oz.
Bore/Gauge: 12
Capacity: 4 shells
Features: Similar to the standard Wicked Wing, but with barrel and receiver in tungsten Cerakote; stock adjustable for cast, drop, and length of pull; Speed Load Plus feature; TurnKey magazine plug; Briley oversized bolt release
MSRP $1899.99

SILVER BLACK LIGHTNING

Action: Semiautomatic
Stock: Turkish walnut
Barrel: 26 in., 28 in.
Chokes: Invector-Plus (F, M, IC)
Weight: 7 lb. 4 oz.–7 lb. 6 oz.
Bore/Gauge: 12
Magazine: 4 shells
Features: Gloss black and deep blued metal with gloss finish walnut Lightweight aluminum alloy receiver; Active Valve System regulates light and heavy loads; semi-humpback receiver styling; brass front bead; back-bored barrel; matte version features satin finish stock and bi-tone matte black and silver finish on the receiver
MSRP $1179.99

SILVER FIELD

Action: Semiautomatic
Stock: Turkish walnut
Barrel: 26 in., 28 in.
Chokes: Three Invector-Plus flush (F, M, IC)
Sights: Brass bead
Weight: 7 lb. 4 oz.–7 lb. 5 oz. (12-gauge); 6 lb. 5 oz.–6 lb. 6 oz. (20-gauge)
Bore/Gauge: 12, 20
Magazine: 4 shells
Features: Aluminum receiver; matte blue barrel; satin-finished bi-tone receiver; 3-in. chamber; square pistol grip
MSRP . . . . $1139.99–$1199.99

SILVER FIELD COMPOSITE

Action: Semiautomatic
Stock: Composite
Barrel: 26 in., 28 in.
Chokes: Three Invector-Plus flush (F, M, IC)
Sights: Brass bead
Weight: 7 lb. 8 oz.–7 lb. 9 oz.
Bore/Gauge: 12
Magazine: 4 shells
Features: Active Valve system for reliable cycling across a variety of loads; stock in a matte black finish; two-tone gray/black receiver emblazoned with Buckmark logo; choice of 3-in. or 3.5-in. chamber
MSRP . . . . $1069.99–$1139.99

SILVER FIELD MICRO MIDAS

Action: Semiautomatic
Stock: Turkish walnut
Barrel: 24 in., 26 in.
Chokes: Three Invector-Plus flush (F, M, IC)
Sights: Brass bead
Weight: 6 lb. 2 oz.
Bore/Gauge: 20
Magazine: 4 shells
Features: A reduced stock version (13 in.) for young and shorter-statured hunters; two-tone silver and black receiver; Inflex 1 small buttpad with a hard heel insert; 3-in. chamber
MSRP $1199.99

Browning

BROWNING SILVER FIELD MO BOTTOMLAND/FDE

BROWNING SILVER FIELD REALTREE MAX-5

BROWNING SILVER RIFLED DEER MATTE

SILVER FIELD MO BOTTOMLAND, REALTREE MAX-5

Action: Semiautomatic
Stock: Composite
Barrel: 26 in., 28 in.
Chokes: 3 (F, M, IC)
Sights: Brass front bead
Weight: 7 lb. 8 oz.–7 lb. 9 oz.
Bore/Gauge: 12
Capacity: 4 shells
Features: One of Browning's more budget-friendly semiauto field guns with the company's Active Valve gas system; lightweight profile barrel; alloy receiver with semi-humpback design; barrel in matte black, receiver in bi-tone black/charcoal with a large Buck Mark logo in gray; flush Invector Plus chokes; 3.5-in. chamber
MSRP $1179.99

SILVER FIELD MO SHADOW GRASS HABITAT/FDE, MO BOTTOMLAND/FDE, REALTREE MAX-5/FDE

Action: Semiautomatic
Stock: Composite
Barrel: 26 in., 28 in.
Chokes: 3 (F, M, IC)
Sights: Brass front bead
Weight: 7 lb. 8 oz.–7 lb. 9 oz.
Bore/Gauge: 12
Capacity: 4 shells
Features: Similar to the standard Silver Field in camo, but with a receiver and barrel in flat dark earth Cerakote
MSRP $1229.99

SILVER RIFLED DEER MATTE

Action: Semiautomatic
Stock: Turkish walnut
Barrel: 22 in.
Chokes: N/A
Weight: 6 lb. 12 oz.
Bore/Gauge: 20
Magazine: 4 shells
Features: Fully rifled barrel for sabot slugs; top cantilever scope mount; gas operation; 3-in. chamber; satin finish stock
MSRP $1239.99

Caesar Guerini

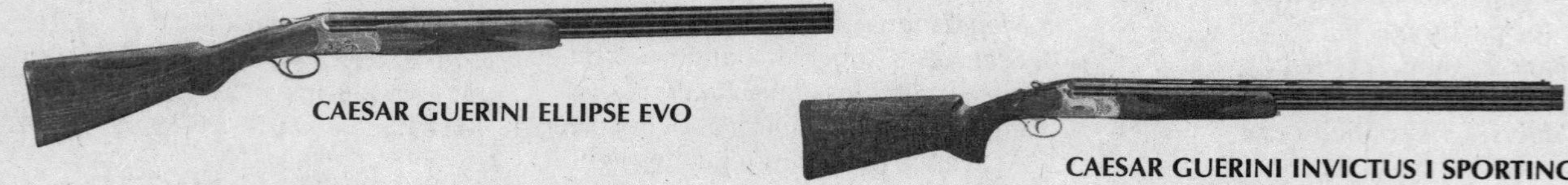

CAESAR GUERINI ELLIPSE EVO

CAESAR GUERINI INVICTUS I SPORTING

ELLIPSE CURVE, EVO, EVO LIGHT

Action: Round body
Stock: Hand-rubbed oil on walnut
Barrel: 28 in.
Chokes: 5 nickel plated, flush fitting
Weight: 6 lb. 1 oz.–7 lb. 4 oz.
Bore/ Gauge: 12, 20, 28
Magazine: 2 shells
Features: Engraving pattern coated with Invisalloy; brass front bead sight; single (selective optional) trigger; manual safety; tapered, solid top rib; three variants available: the Curve (rose scroll engraving with nude goddess on receiver bottom), Evo (tight scroll engraving with large oak leaf carvings, and Evo Light (a lighter Evo); left-hand and English stocks available
Curve: . . . . $7895.00–$8155.00
Curve 20/28 Combo: . . .$10,720.00–$10,900.00
Evo/Evo Light: . . $7225.00–$7485.00

INVICTUS I SPORTING

Action: Over/under
Stock: Wood
Barrel: 30 in., 32 in.
Chokes: 6 MAXIS competition chokes
Weight: 8 lb. 1 oz.–8 lb. 3 oz.
Bore/Gauge: 12
Magazine: 2 shells
Features: White Bradley style front silver center bead; manual safety (automatic optional); DTS-2 trigger system with two trigger pull weight options, take up, over travel and length of pull adjustments
MSRP $7775.00
Left-hand: . . . . add $260.00
Adjustable comb: . . . . add $410.00

Caesar Guerini

CAESAR GUERINI INVICTUS III SPORTING

CAESAR GUERINI INVICTUS III TRAP COMBO

CAESAR GUERINI INVICTUS V SPORTING

CAESAR GUERINI INVICTUS VII SPORTING

CAESAR GUERINI REVENANT

CAESAR GUERINI MAGNUS SPORTING

INVICTUS III SPORTING

Action: Over/under
Stock: Walnut
Barrel: 30 in., 32 in.
Chokes: Six
Sights: White Bradley-style front, silver mid-bead
Weight: 8 lb. 1 oz.–8 lb. 3 oz.
Bore/Gauge: 12
Capacity: 2 shells
Features: This one's a head-turner on the sporting clays course, with features like the receiver's hand-polished coin finish gold highlights; ventilated barrel joint; tapered 10mm–8mm top rib; chrome-line barrels; 5-inch DuoCon forcing cones; MAXIS competition chokes; available in left-hand option and with adjustable comb

MSRP $8915.00
Left-hand: . . . . add $260.00
Adjustable comb: . . . . add $410.00

INVICTUS III TRAP COMBO

Action: Unsingle, over/under
Stock: Walnut
Barrel: 32 in., 34 in.
Chokes: 3 unsingle (M, IM, Fl), 5 O/U (LM, M, IM, LF, F)
Sights: White bead front, silver mid-bead
Weight: 8 lb. 15 oz.–9 lb. 5 oz.
Bore/Gauge: 12
Capacity: 1, 2 shells
Features: Available as a 32-in. over/under with a 34-in Unsingle barrel, this high-grade trap-specific combo shotgun features a stock with a hand-rubbed oil finish and four-way adjustable DTS Monte Carlo comb; 5-in. DuoCon forcing cones; semi-beavertail forearm with finger grooves; 12mm tapered vent rib 25mm high, DTS adjustable 60/40–100 for over/under, 60/40–120 for Unsingle; ventilated center rib on over/under; manual safety (can option automatic); adjustable DPS trigger

MSRP $14,735.00
Left-hand . . . . add $260.00

INVICTUS V SPORTING

Action: Over/under
Stock: Wood
Barrel: 30 in., 32 in.
Chokes: 6 MAXIS competition chokes
Weight: 8 lb. 1 oz.–8 lb. 3 oz.
Bore/Gauge: 12
Magazine: 2 shells
Features: DPS2 trigger system; factory selective release triggers available in single and double release; contemporary Italian Ornato-style engraving with deep relief game scenes; white Bradley-style front silver center bead

MSRP $9895.00
Left-hand: . . . . add $260.00
Adjustable comb: . . . . add $410.00

INVICTUS VII SPORTING

Action: Over/under
Stock: Walnut
Barrel: 30 in., 32, in.
Chokes: Six
Sights: White Bradley-style front, silver mid-bead
Weight: 8 lb. 1 oz.–8 lb. 3 oz.
Bore/Gauge: 12
Capacity: 2 shells
Features: Similar to the Invictus III Sporting, but with additional gold engravings of five flushing quail on the right side panels, three quail on the rise on the left side, a pheasant and quail on the receiver's underside

MSRP $10,165.00
Left-hand: . . . . add $260.00
Adjustable comb: . . . . add $410.00

MAGNUS SPORTING

Action: Over/under
Stock: Hand-rubbed oil on walnut
Barrel: 30 in., 32 in., 34 in.
Chokes: 6 CCP competition chokes (6 MAXIS for 12 Ga. models)
Weight: 7 lb. 6 oz.–8 lb. 2 oz.
Bore/Gauge: 12, 20, 28, .410
Magazine: 2 shells
Features: Single selective trigger; manual safety; ventilated center rib; available 20/28 gauge combo and 20/28/.410 gauge combo

Standard right-hand: $6095.00
20/28-ga. combo: $8870.00
20/28/.410 combo: $11,800.00
Left-hand stock:. . . . . . add $260.00
Adjustable comb: . . . . add $410.00
Case-hardened receiver:. . . . . add $405.00

REVENANT

Action: Over/under
Stock: Walnut
Barrel: 28 in., 30 in.
Chokes: 5
Sights: Silver bead front
Weight: 6 lb. 6 oz.–6 lb. 11 oz.
Bore/Gauge: 20, 28
Capacity: 2 shells
Features: A beautiful round-body sub-gauge with an Ellipse rounded forend; radiused sideplates gorgeously engraved by master engravers Bottega C. Giovanelli and Dario Cortini and featuring an organic motif of maple leaves and branches in a hand-polished coin finish and gold game birds; solid 8–6mm tapered rib

MSRP $13,895.00
Left-hand . . . . add $400.00

Caesar Guerini

CAESAR GUERINI TEMPIO

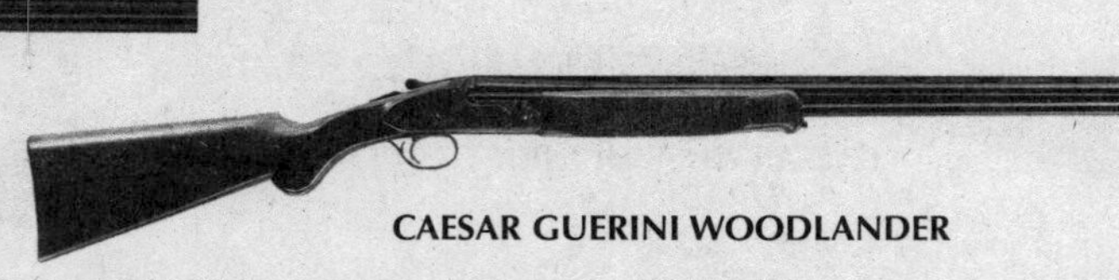

CAESAR GUERINI WOODLANDER

TEMPIO

Action: Over/under
Stock: Turkish walnut
Barrel: 26 in., 28 in., 30 in.
Chokes: 5 nickel plated, flush fitting chokes
Weight: 6 lb.–7 lb.
Bore/Gauge: 12, 20, 28, .410
Magazine: 2 shells
Features: Designed to be a sleek and fast pointing shotgun in the field; perfect companion for upland game hunters; low-profile receiver matched with a trim stock, classic Prince-of-Wales grip and schnabel forend make the gun a perfect match for fast game birds; contemporary style of "ornato" style scroll with tasteful gold accents; Invisalloy protective coating
Standard 12-, 20-, 28-ga.: . . . $4525.00
Standard .410-bore: $4725.00
20/28-ga. combo: $6810.00
20/28/.410 combo: $9290.00
Left-hand or English stock: . . . . add $260.00

WOODLANDER

Action: Over/under
Stock: English walnut
Barrel: 26 in., 28 in., 30 in.
Chokes: Five precision patterned flush chokes (CYL, IC, M, IM, F)
Weight: 6 lb.–7 lb.
Bore/Gauge: 12, 20, 28, .410
Magazine: 2 shells
Features: Gun reflects passion for fall coverts, autumn foliage, wet gun dogs, and the smell of wood; understated elegance of color case hardening and nicely figured, oil-finished English walnut that speaks of quality from a bygone era; a superior-handling upland game gun that's perfect for tight cover and fast-flushing birds
Standard 12-, 20-, 28-ga.: . . . $3995.00
20/28-ga. combo: $6275.00
20/28/.410 combo: $8760.00
Left-hand or English stock: . . . . add $260.00

Charles Daly/Chiappa Firearms

CHARLES DALY/CHIAPPA FIREARMS 204X

CHARLES DALY 512

CHARLES DALY 520

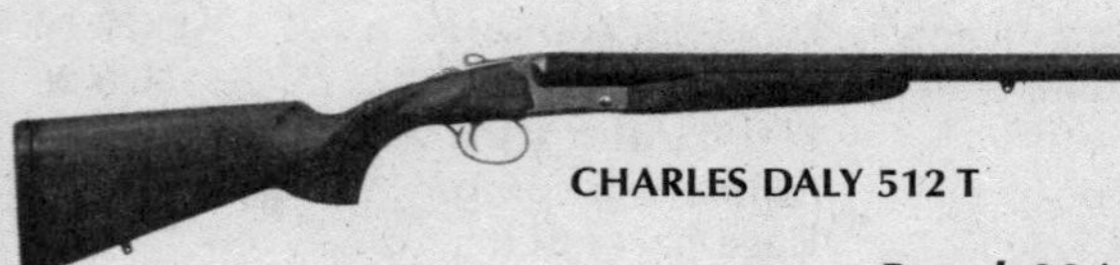

CHARLES DALY 512 T

204X

Action: Over/under
Stock: Synthetic
Barrel: 24 in.
Chokes: Skeet, IC, MOD, IM, F
Weight: 6 lb. 6 oz.–6 lb. 13 oz.
Bore/Gauge: 20, 12
Magazine: 2 shells
Features: Fiber optic sights; black receiver with full-coverage camo in Realtree APG or Mossy Oak Obsession; 3 ½-in. chamber; topside Picatinny rail for optics; Improved, Modified, Full, 2X and XF Rem Choke threaded chokes included
MSRP $899.00

512

Action: Side-by-side
Stock: Walnut
Barrel: 28 in.
Chokes: Five (F, IM, M, IC, Skeet)
Sights: Bead front
Weight: 5 lb. 10 oz.
Bore/Gauge: 12
Capacity: 2 shells
Features: A lightweight side-by-side with single selective trigger; extractors; Rem Choke threads; gloss blue barrels; receiver left in the white; one sling swivel stud only under barrel joint
MSRP $945.00

512 T

Action: Side-by-side
Stock: Walnut
Barrel: 20 in.
Chokes: Five
Sights: Bead front
Weight: 5 lb. 8 oz.
Bore/Gauge: 12
Capacity: 2 shells
Features: The coach gun version of the 512, with matte blue barrels; sling swivel studs under barrel joint and buttstock
MSRP $945.00

520

Action: Side-by-side
Stock: Walnut
Barrel: 26 in.
Chokes: Five (F, IM, M, IC, Skeet)
Sights: Bead front
Weight: 5 lb. 10 oz.
Bore/Gauge: 20
Capacity: 2 shells
Features: Single selective trigger; extractors; Rem Choke threads; gloss blue barrels; receiver left in the white; one sling swivel stud only under barrel joint
MSRP $945.00

Charles Daly/Chiappa Firearms

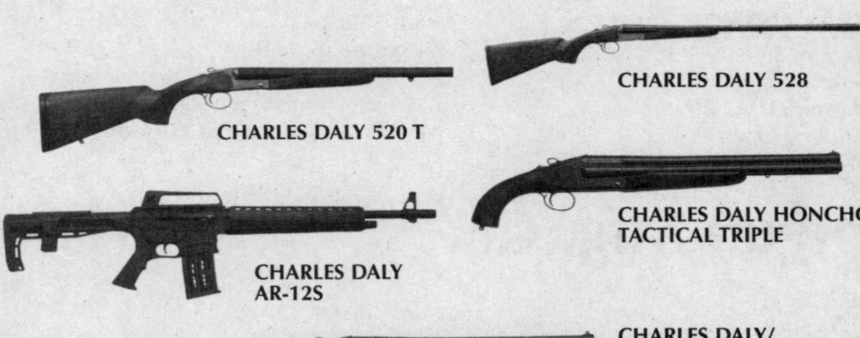

CHARLES DALY 520 T

CHARLES DALY 528

CHARLES DALY HONCHO TACTICAL TRIPLE

CHARLES DALY AR-12S

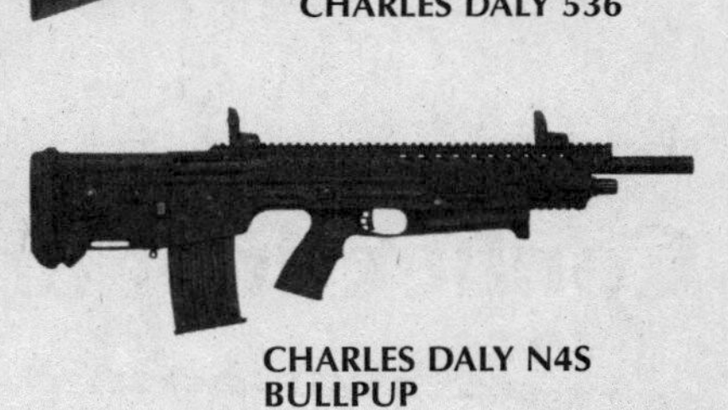

CHARLES DALY 536

CHARLES DALY N4S BULLPUP

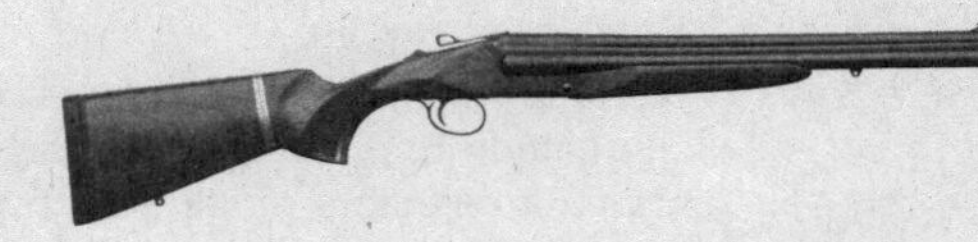

CHARLES DALY/ CHIAPPA FIREARMS TRIPLE THREAT

CHARLES DALY/CHIAPPA FIREARMS TRIPLE CROWN

520 T

Action: Side-by-side
Stock: Walnut
Barrel: 20 in.
Chokes: Five
Sights: Bead front
Weight: 5 lb. 4 oz.
Bore/Gauge: 20
Capacity: 2 shells
Features: The coach gun version of the 520, with matte blue barrels; sling swivel studs under barrel joint and buttstock
MSRP $945.00

528

Action: Side-by-side
Stock: Walnut
Barrel: 26 in.
Chokes: Five
Sights: Bead front
Weight: 5 lb. 8 oz.
Bore/Gauge: 28
Capacity: 2 shells
Features: Nice little grouse or quail gun with polished blue barrels; single trigger; receiver left in the white; extractors; one sling swivel stud only under barrel joint
MSRP $945.00

536

Action: Side-by-side
Stock: Walnut
Barrel: 26 in.
Chokes: Five
Sights: Bead front
Weight: 5 lb. 6 oz.
Bore/Gauge: .410
Capacity: 2 shells
Features: Properly scaled .410 with polished blue barrels with Rem Choke threads; receiver left in the white; single trigger; extractors; extended chokes; no sling swivel studs
MSRP $945.00

AR-12S

Action: Semiautomatic
Stock: Synthetic
Barrel: 20 in.
Chokes: One (M)
Sights: A4-style front, adjustable carry handle rear
Weight: 7 lb. 8 oz.
Bore/Gauge: 12
Capacity: 5 shells
Features: Proving the AR really is a do-it-all firearm, this one chambered for the 3-inch 12-gauge and featuring choke with Beretta/Benelli Mobil Choke threads; adjustable buttstock;
MSRP $413.00

HONCHO TACTICAL TRIPLE

Action: Over/under
Stock: Rubber-coated walnut
Barrel: 18.5 in.
Chokes: None
Sights: Bead front
Weight: 6 lb.
Bore/Gauge: 12
Capacity: 3 shells
Features: A single over double three-shot self-defense shotgun with rubber-coated walnut fore-end and pistol grip for added weight and improved grip; overall length 27 inches; top-tang safety; single trigger; sling swivels
MSRP $1329.00

N4S BULLPUP

Action: Semiautomatic
Stock: Synthetic
Barrel: 20 in.
Chokes: One
Sights: Flip-up
Weight: 9 lb. 5 oz.
Bore/Gauge: 12
Capacity: 5 shells
Features: A bullpup with a little weight for better handling; fixed Modified choke with Beretta/Benelli Mobil Choke thread; adjustable flip-up sights front and rear; detachable magazine
MSRP $529.00

TRIPLE CROWN

Action: Break-action
Stock: Wood
Barrel: 26 in., 28 in.
Chokes: Rem-choke in all barrels
Weight: 8 lb. 11 oz.
Bore/Gauge: 12, 20, 28, .410
Magazine: 3 shells
Features: Side-by-side and middle arrangement sporting model with three shotgun barrels; chokes in all three barrels; sling swivel studs
MSRP $1979.00

TRIPLE THREAT

Action: Break-action
Stock: Wood
Barrel: 18.5 in.
Chokes: Rem-choke in all barrels
Weight: 8 lb.
Bore/Gauge: 12, 20, .410
Magazine: 3 shells
Features: Side-by-side and middle arrangement defense model with three shotgun barrels; chokes in all three barrels; sling swivel studs; wooden stock can be partly disassembled
MSRP . . . . $1969.00–$2015.00

Cimarron Firearms Co.

CIMARRON 1878 COACH GUN

1878 COACH GUN

Action: Side-by-Side
Stock: Wood
Barrel: 20 in., 26 in.
Chokes: Open
Weight: 8 lb.–8 lb. 15 oz.
Bore/ Gauge: 12
Magazine: 2 shells
Features: 3 in. blue steel real working hammers; available in standard blue
MSRP . . . . $635.70–$648.70

Connecticut Shotgun Mfg. Co.

CONNECTICUT SHOTGUN MFG. CO. A-10

A-10

Action: Sidelock over/under
Stock: Checkered American black walnut
Barrel: 26 in.–32 in.
Chokes: 5 TruLock tubes
Weight: 6 lb. 8 oz.–7 lb. 8 oz.
Bore/Gauge: 12, 20, 28
Magazine: 2 shells
Features: Finely engraved, cut checkering; ventilated rib; pistol grip or straight grip; auto ejectors, single selective trigger; Galazan pad
MSRP . . . . . . Contact manufacturer

Connecticut Valley Arms (CVA)

CVA SCOUT .410 SHOTGUN COMPACT

SCOUT .410 SHOTGUN COMPACT

Action: Break-open single-shot
Stock: Synthetic
Barrel: 20 in.
Chokes: 1 Full turkey
Sights: None
Weight: 6 lb. 5 oz.
Bore/Gauge: .410
Capacity: 1 shell
Features: An affordable single-shot .410 for home-defense or close-range turkey hunting with a stock in Realtree Timber camo; optic rail
MSRP $397.95

CZ-USA (Ceska Zbrojovka)

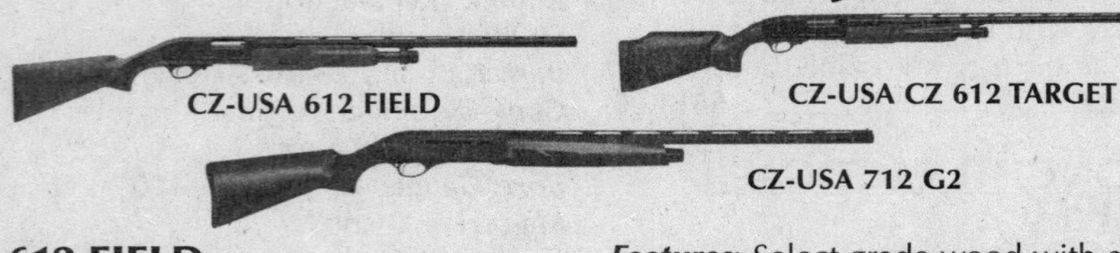

CZ-USA 612 FIELD

CZ-USA CZ 612 TARGET

CZ-USA 712 G2

CZ-USA CZ 620/628 FIELD SELECT

612 FIELD

Action: Pump
Stock: Walnut
Barrel: 28 in.
Chokes: 3 chokes
Weight: 6 lb. 3 oz.
Bore/Gauge: 12
Magazine: 4+1 shells
Features: Satin chrome finish; capable of shooting 2 ¾-in. and 3-in. shells; supplied with three chokes
MSRP $395.00

612 TARGET

Action: Pump
Stock: Turkish walnut
Barrel: 32 in.
Chokes: Extended knurled
Weight: 7 lb. 5 oz.
Bore/Gauge: 12
Magazine: 4 shells
Features: Select grade wood with a glossy oil finish; metal is a deep polished blue; tuned trigger system; raised rib; comfortable Monte Carlo stock; pair of Bradley-style white beads
MSRP $585.00

620/628 FIELD SELECT

Action: Pump
Stock: Turkish walnut
Barrel: 28 in.
Chokes: F, M, C
Weight: 5 lb. 6 oz.
Bore/Gauge: 28 (628); 20 (620)
Magazine: 4 shells
Features: Gauge-specific 7075 aluminum action; deep glossy blue finish; select grade Turkish Walnut; full forend
MSRP $445.00

712 G2

Action: Semiautomatic
Stock: Turkish walnut
Barrel: 26 in., 28 in.
Chokes: 5 included
Weight: 7 lb. 5 oz.–7 lb. 6 oz.
Bore/Gauge: 12
Magazine: 4+1 shells
Features: Accepting 2¾ and 3-inch shells, it is an all-arounder, a great choice for upland game, waterfowl, or clays; barrel is chrome-lined and has a matte black hard chrome exterior that will resist corrosion for many seasons in the field; G2 stock adds new laser-engraved checkering, right-hand palm swell as well as a barrel lock-ring to make assembly easier
MSRP $535.00

CZ-USA (Ceska Zbrojovka)

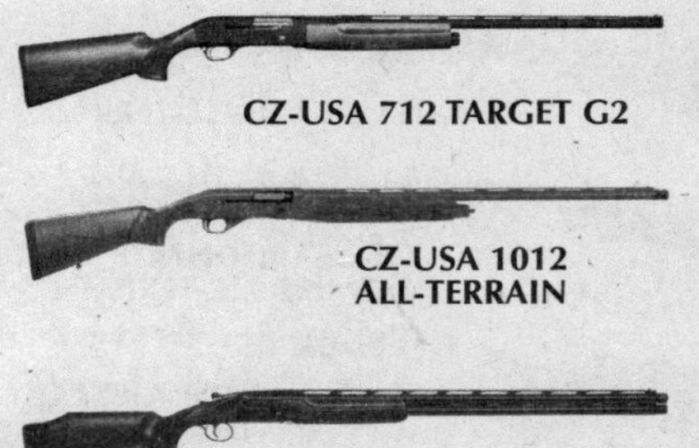

CZ-USA 712 TARGET G2

CZ-USA 1012 ALL-TERRAIN

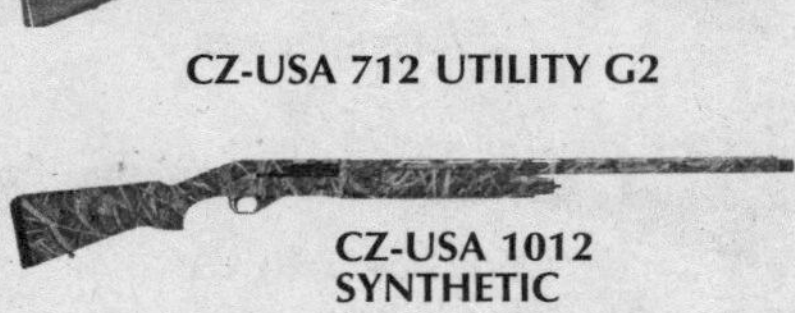

CZ-USA 712 UTILITY G2

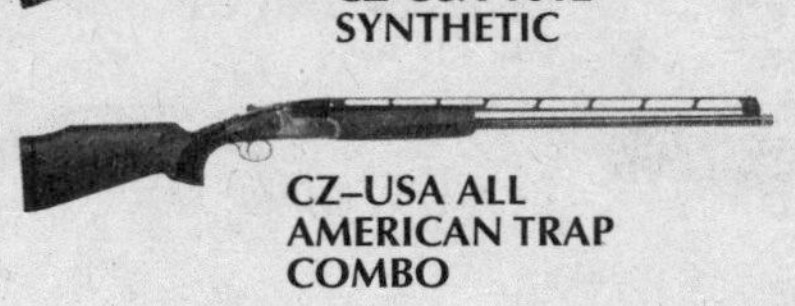

CZ-USA 1012 SYNTHETIC

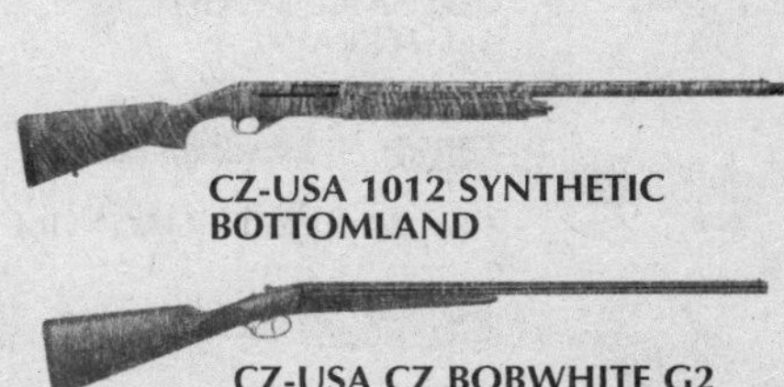

CZ-USA 1012

CZ-USA 1012 SYNTHETIC BOTTOMLAND

CZ-USA CZ ALL-AMERICAN

CZ–USA ALL AMERICAN TRAP COMBO

CZ-USA CZ BOBWHITE G2

712 TARGET G2

Action: Gas-operated semiautomatic
Stock: Walnut
Barrel: 30 in.
Chokes: Interchangeable chokes (F, M, IC)
Weight: 7 lb. 10 oz.
Bore/Gauge: 12
Magazine: 4+1 shells
Features: Gas operated aluminum alloy action with target-grade enhancements; chrome-lined barrel; fiber optic front sight on a 10mm stepped rib; Schnabel forend; smooth rounded heel; Monte Carlo buttstock
MSRP $725.00

712 UTILITY G2

Action: Semiautomatic
Stock: Synthetic
Barrel: 20 in.
Chokes: Screw-in chokes (F, IM, M, IC, C)
Weight: 6 lb. 10 oz.
Bore/Gauge: 12
Magazine: 4+1 shells
Features: 3-in. chamber cross-bolt safety; black synthetic stock; matte chrome black barrel
MSRP $535.00

1012

Action: Semiautomatic
Stock: Turkish walnut
Barrel: 28 in.
Chokes: Five (F, MIM, M, IC, C)
Sights: Bead front
Weight: 6 lb. 8 oz.
Bore/Gauge: 12
Capacity: 5 shells
Features: A unique gas-less inertia operating system that features the softest shooting 2 ¾ shells to the hottest 3-inch shells. Features include: 8mm flat vent rib; 14 ½-inch length of pull; choice of Bronze, Grey, or gloss black receiver finishes
MSRP $645.00

1012 ALL-TERRAIN

Action: Side-by-side
Stock: Turkish walnut
Barrel: 28 in.
Chokes: Extended black
Sights: Front bead
Weight: 6 lb. 8 oz.
Bore/Gauge: 12
Capacity: 4 shells
Features: A favorite semiauto gets a Turkish walnut stock paired with metalwork in Cerakote OD Green; flat 8mm vent rib; extended choke tubes provided; crossbolt safety
MSRP $715.00

1012 SYNTHETIC

Action: Semiautomatic
Stock: Synthetic
Barrel: 28 in.
Chokes: Five
Sights: Bead front
Weight: 6 lb. 8 oz.
Bore/Gauge: 12
Capacity: 5 shells
Features: Similar to the standard 1012, but in either a matte black or full-coverage camo
MSRP . . . . $645.00–$715.00

1012 SYNTHETIC BOTTOMLAND

Action: Semiautomatic
Stock: Synthetic
Barrel: 28 in.
Chokes: Extended black
Sights: Front bead
Weight: 6 lb. 8 oz.
Bore/Gauge: 12
Capacity: 4 shells
Features: A sturdy gun for waterfowl, especially geese at distance thanks to the 28-in. barrel; Mossy Oak Bottomland full-coverage camo; extended choke tubes
MSRP $715.00

ALL-AMERICAN

Action: Over/under
Stock: Turkish walnut
Barrel: 30 in., 32 in.
Chokes: Extended black
Weight: 8 lb. 8 oz.
Bore/Gauge: 12
Magazine: 2 shells
Features: CNCed throughout; drop-in replacement parts (including locking blocks for those who shoot tens of thousands of rounds a year); four-way comb; adjustable buttplate hardware; barrels have lengthened forcing cones and are ported; 3-in. chambers
MSRP $2649.00

ALL-AMERICAN TRAP COMBO

Action: Over/under
Stock: Turkish walnut
Barrel: 32 in.
Chokes: 1 Skeet, 1 IC, 2 M, 1 IM, 2 F
Weight: 8 lb. 8 oz.
Bore/Gauge: 12
Magazine: 2 shells
Features: Comes with a single-shot un-single with a dial-adjustable aluminum rib (adjustable from 50/50 up to 90/10 point of impact) and a standard set of barrels with stepped rib (50/50 point of impact); replaceable locking blocks; adjustable parallel comb; competition trigger; auto ejectors
MSRP $3575.00

BOBWHITE G2

Action: Side-by-side
Stock: Wood
Barrel: 28 in.
Chokes: Five (F, M, IM, IC, C)
Sights: Bead front
Weight: 5 lb 8 oz.–7 lb. 4 oz.
Bore/Gauge: 12, 20, 28
Capacity: 2 shells
Features: Features a straight, English-style stock; flush-mount choke tubes; double triggers; black chrome finish; gauge-specific frames
MSRP . . . . $675.00–$725.00

CZ-USA (Ceska Zbrojovka)

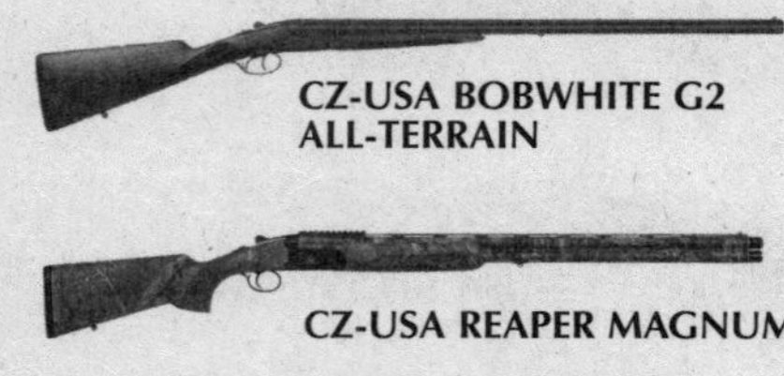

CZ-USA BOBWHITE G2 ALL-TERRAIN

CZ-USA REAPER MAGNUM

CZ–USA DRAKE

CZ–USA REDHEAD PREMIER

CZ–USA SHARP-TAIL

CZ-USA SCTP STERLING

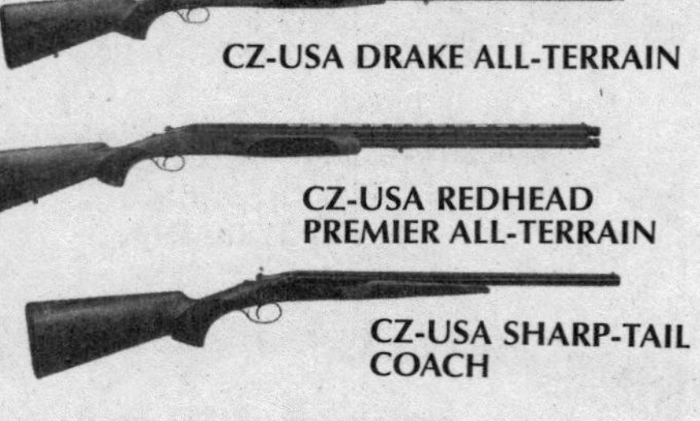

CZ-USA DRAKE ALL-TERRAIN

CZ-USA REDHEAD PREMIER ALL-TERRAIN

CZ-USA SHARP-TAIL COACH

BOBWHITE G2 ALL-TERRAIN

Action: Side-by-side
Stock: Turkish walnut
Barrel: 28 in.
Chokes: 5 (F, IM, M, IC, C)
Sights: Front bead
Weight: 6 lb.–7 lb. 5 oz.
Bore/Gauge: 20, 12
Capacity: 2 shells
Features: Wearing a straight English-style stock of walnut, the All-Terrain has barrels and receiver in Cerakote OD Green; dual triggers
MSRP $855.00

DRAKE

Action: Over/under
Stock: Turkish walnut
Barrel: 28 in.
Chokes: 5 chokes
Weight: 6 lb.–7 lb. 6 oz.
Bore/Gauge: 12, 20, 28, .410
Magazine: 2 shells
Features: CNC action; extractor operation; single selectable trigger; .410-bore has fixed Improved Cylinder/Modified chokes; left-hand Southpaw model available in 12- and 20-gauge.
MSRP . . . . $675.00–$702.00

DRAKE ALL-TERRAIN

Action: Over/under
Stock: Turkish walnut
Barrel: 28 in.
Chokes: Extended black
Sights: Front bead
Weight: 6 lb. 8 oz.–7 lb.
Bore/Gauge: 20, 12
Capacity: 2 shells
Features: A balanced over under with a pretty walnut stock paired with metalwork in Cerakote OD Green; single selectable trigger
MSRP $815.00

REAPER MAGNUM

Action: Over/under
Stock: Polymer
Barrel: 26 in.
Chokes: Five extended
Sights: Front bead
Weight: 7 lb.
Bore/Gauge: 12
Magazine: 2 shells
Features: Dressed in Realtree Xtra Green with a black receiver; topside Picatinny rail for optics mounting; mechanical trigger
MSRP $1025.00

REDHEAD PREMIER

Action: Over/under
Stock: Turkish walnut
Barrel: 26 in., 28 in.
Chokes: 5 flush-mount
Weight: 6 lb. 14 oz.
Bore/Gauge: 12, 20
Magazine: 2 shells
Features: The tried-and-true Redhead also gets CZ's new 1-piece CNCed receiver; laser-cut checkering, solid mid-ribs, pistol grip, and a classy white bead; silver receiver and ejectors that kick out the spent shells automatically, hard plastic case included
MSRP $1019.00

REDHEAD PREMIER ALL-TERRAIN

Action: Over/under
Stock: Turkish walnut
Barrel: 28 in., 30 in.
Chokes: Extended black
Sights: Front bead
Weight: 6 lb. 14 oz.–8 lb.
Bore/Gauge: 20, 12
Capacity: 2 shells
Features: Nice field gun with extended choke tubes; single selectable trigger; Turkish walnut stock; metalwork in Cerakote OD Green; 3-in. chamber; extended choke tubes provided; both gauges available in both barrel lengths
MSRP $1159.00

SCTP STERLING

Action: Over/under
Stock: Turkish walnut
Barrel: 28 in.
Chokes: Five flush chokes (C, IC, M, IM, F)
Sights: None
Weight: 7 lb. 8 oz.
Bore/Gauge: 12
Magazine: 2 shells
Features: Stock designed to fit female and young shooters; silver receiver is finished in two-tone satin and gloss chrome; the barrels are gloss black chrome; stock features laser stippling; 3-in. chambers; left-hand Southpaw model available
MSRP $1445.00

SHARP-TAIL

Action: Side-by-side
Stock: Wood
Barrel: 28 in.
Chokes: 5 flush interchangeable
Weight: 6 lb.– 7 lb. 5 oz.
Bore/Gauge: 12, 20, 28, .410
Magazine: 2 shells
Features: Black hard chrome barrel finish; color case hardened receiver finish; semi-beavertail forend; extractor; manual safety
MSRP . . . .$1105.00–$1329.00

SHARP-TAIL COACH

Action: Side-by-side
Stock: Turkish walnut
Barrel: 20 in.
Chokes: Fixed chokes (C/C)
Sights: Front bead
Weight: 6 lb. 11 oz.
Bore/Gauge: 12, 20
Magazine: 2 shells
Features: Semi-beavertail forearm for a solid grip; single selectable trigger; extractors
MSRP $1039.00

CZ-USA (Ceska Zbrojovka)

CZ-USA SUPREME FIELD

CZ-USA CZ SWAMP MAGNUM CAMO

CZ-USA UPLAND ULTRALIGHT

CZ–USA WINGSHOOTER ELITE

CZ-USA UPLAND ULTRALIGHT ALL-TERRAIN

SUPREME FIELD

Action: Over/under
Stock: Grade III Turkish walnut
Barrel: 28 in.
Chokes: Five extended
Sights: Front bead
Weight: 6 lb.–7 lb. 14 oz.
Bore/Gauge: 12, 20, 28
Magazine: 2 shells
Features: Grade III walnut; polished nickel chrome receiver with border engraving; ejectors; solid mid-rib; sharp checkering
MSRP $1839.00

SWAMP MAGNUM CAMO

Action: Over/under
Stock: Polymer
Barrel: 30 in.
Chokes: Extended black
Weight: 7 lb. 2 oz.
Bore/Gauge: 12
Magazine: 2 shells
Features: Only over/under in CZ's line with an automatic safety, which engages every time the action is opened; polymer stocks in camo; all metal work blacked out; chambered for 3 ½ in.
MSRP $1109.00

UPLAND ULTRALIGHT

Action: Over/under
Stock: Turkish walnut
Barrel: 26 in., 28 in.
Chokes: 5 (F, IM, M, IC, C)
Sights: Front bead
Weight: 5 lb. 3 oz.–6 lb.
Bore/Gauge: 12
Capacity: 2 shells
Features: Super upland choice with a mechanical trigger selectable for barrel; aluminum alloy frame with black anodized finish; matte black finish on barrels; flat 6mm vent rib; separated barrels; 3-in. chamber; extractors
MSRP $809.00

UPLAND ULTRALIGHT ALL-TERRAIN

Action: Over/under
Stock: Turkish walnut
Barrel: 28 in.
Chokes: Extended black
Sights: Front bead
Weight: 5 lb. 14 oz.–6 lb. 5 oz.
Bore/Gauge: 20, 12
Capacity: 2 shells
Features: Upland hunters putting in the miles will appreciate this lightweight over/under with its Turkish walnut stock; metalwork in Cerakote OD Green; separated barrels for reduced ounces
MSRP $919.00

WINGSHOOTER ELITE

Action: Over/under
Stock: Turkish walnut
Barrel: 28 in.
Chokes: 5 flush-mount
Weight: 7 lb. 6 oz.
Bore/Gauge: 12, 20
Magazine: 2 shells
Features: Replaces the Wingshooter; new CNCed 1-piece receiver; fully hand-engraved side-plates, reminiscent of custom-grade Super Scroll; single selectable trigger, solid mid-ribs, ejectors, and two-tone chromed finish; laser-cut checkering, solid mid-ribs, pistol grip stock, white bead; hard plastic case
MSRP $1139.00

European American Armory

EUROPEAN AMERICAN ARMORY CHURCHILL 512

EUROPEAN AMERICAN ARMORY CHURCHILL 812 FIELD

CHURCHILL 512

Action: Side-by-side
Stock: Walnut
Barrel: 26 in., 28 in.
Chokes: 3
Sights: Front bead
Weight: N/A
Bore/Gauge: .410, 28, 20, 12
Capacity: 2 shells
Features: A no-frills, well-made side-by-side by Turkish manufacturer Akkar Firearms; manual safety; extractors; standard grip profile; checkering; blued barrels with stainless receiver
MSRP . . . . $916.00–$978.00

CHURCHILL 812 FIELD

Action: Over/under
Stock: Walnut
Barrel: 26 in., 28 in.
Chokes: 3
Sights: Fiber optic front
Weight: N/A
Bore/Gauge: .410, 28, 20, 12
Capacity: 2 shells
Features: A no-frills, well-made over/under by Turkish manufacturer Akkar Firearms; automatic safety; extractors; standard grip profile; checkering; fiber optic front sight; blued barrels with stainless receiver
MSRP $870.00

European American Armory

CHURCHILL 812 SPORTING

Action: Over/under
Stock: Walnut
Barrel: 28 in., 30 in.
Chokes: 5
Sights: Fiber optic front, mid-bead
Weight: N/A
Bore/Gauge: 12
Capacity: 2 shells
Features: Similar to the Sporting 812 ORCAP, this clays gun has its receiver in stainless with light engraving
MSRP $1773.00

CHURCHILL 812 SPORTING ORCAP

Action: Over/under
Stock: Walnut
Barrel: 28 in., 30 in.
Chokes: 5
Sights: Fiber optic front, mid-bead
Weight: N/A
Bore/Gauge: 12
Capacity: 2 shells
Features: Akkar Firearms dedicated clays game gun with five extended choke tubes; auto ejectors; manual safety; 10mm-wide vent rib; back-bored barrels; between barrel venting; case-colored receiver; adjustable comb; adjustable trigger; upgraded walnut stock with hand-rubbed oil finish and standard grip profile
MSRP $1866.00

Fabarm

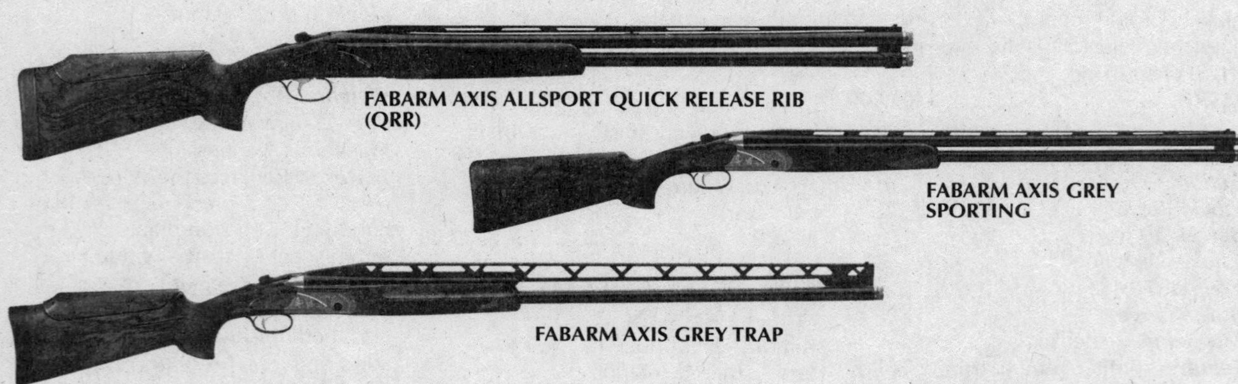

AXIS ALLSPORT QUICK RELEASE RIB (QRR)

Action: Over/under
Stock: Wood
Barrel: 30–32 in.
Chokes: 5 Exis HP
Weight: 8 lb. 6 oz.
Bore/Gauge: 12
Magazine: 2 shells
Features: Quick Release Rib design allows configuration for varying shooting styles and disciplines; standard offering includes two 10mm high ramp style ribs—one with a 50/50 percent point-of-impact and a second for a higher 65/35 percent; includes Tribore free floating barrels for improved balance and performance; 97mm Exis HP hyperbolic choke tubes; integrated recoil reducer; adjustable trigger; Triwood enhanced stock finish; Micro Metric adjustable stock comb
MSRP $4675.00
Left-hand: . . . . add $160.00

AXIS GREY SPORTING

Action: Over/under
Stock: Triwood
Barrel: 30 in., 32 in.
Chokes: Five EXIS HP Competition tubes
Sights: Front bead
Weight: 8 lb. 4 oz.
Bore/Gauge: 12
Magazine: 2 shells
Features: Protective Triwood finish; greyed receiver with scroll engraving and gold game bird scenes; vent rib; separated barrels; available with adjustable stock.
MSRP $3925.00
Left-hand: . . . . add $160.00
Adjustable stock: . . . . . add $380.00

AXIS GREY TRAP

Action: Over/under
Stock: Triwood
Barrel: 32 in., 34 in.
Chokes: Five EXIS HP Competition tubes
Sights: Front bead
Weight: 8 lb. 14 oz.
Bore/Gauge: 12
Magazine: 1, 2 shells
Features: High rib adjustable for point of impact; available in an over/under, as an single-shot configuration, or a combination
Over/under or unsingle: $5195.00
Combo: $6995.00
Left-hand stock: . . . . add $160.00

Fabarm

FABARM AXIS RS12 SPORTING

FABARM AXIS RS12 TRAP

FABARM ELOS D2

FABARM ELOS N2 ALLSPORT

FABARM ELOS N2 SPORTING

FABARM L4S SERIES

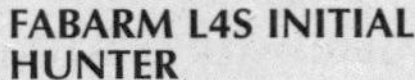
FABARM L4S INITIAL HUNTER

FABARM L4S SPORTING, GREY SPORTING, DELUXE SPORTING

AXIS RS12 SPORTING

Action: Over/under
Stock: Wood
Barrel: 30 in., 32 in.
Chokes: 5 Exis HP
Weight: 8 lb. 4 oz.
Bore/Gauge: 12
Magazine: 2 shells
Features: Axis free-floating barrels feature Tribore HP tapered bores that lower recoil and reduce the need for excessively long forcing cones; blued action; Fabarm Micro Metric adjustable comb and left hand stocks available
MSRP $3495.00
Left-hand: . . . . add $160.00
Adjustable stock: . . . . . add $380.00

AXIS RS12 TRAP

Action: Over/under
Stock: Wood
Barrel: 32 in., 34 in. (unsingle)
Chokes: 5 Exis HP
Weight: 8 lb. 14 oz.
Bore/Gauge: 12
Magazine: 1 or 2 shells
Features: Free-floating over-and-under barrels; adjustable ribs on all barrels; tapered bores; integrated recoil reducer; adjustable comb; optional release triggers; 97mm Exis HP hyperbolic choke tubes; adjustable trigger; Triwood enhanced stock finish
Over/under or unsingle: . . . $4675.00
Combo: $6575.00
Left-hand: . . . . add $160.00

ELOS D2

Action: Over/under
Stock: Wood
Barrel: 28 in.
Chokes: Five INNER HP chokes
Sights: Front bead
Weight: 5 lb. 8 oz.–6 lb. 8 oz.
Bore/Gauge: 12, 20, 28
Magazine: 2 shells
Features: A lightweight upland bird gun; stainless receiver with scroll and game birds engravings
MSRP $2825.00
Left-hand: . . . . add $160.00

ELOS N2 ALLSPORT

Action: Over/under
Stock: Turkish walnut
Barrel: 30 in., 32 in.
Chokes: 5
Sights: White front bead, silver mid-bead
Weight: 7 lb. 11 oz.
Bore/Gauge: 12
Capacity: 2 shells
Features: Truly meant to cover all the clay sports with an interchangeable rib system that includes one QRR (Quick Release Rib) at 50/50 and another at 65/35, as well as a Micro Metric adjustable stock; stock has Triwood finish; barrels are Tribore
MSRP $3195.00
Left-hand . . . . add $160.00

ELOS N2 SPORTING

Action: Over/under
Stock: Wood
Barrel: 30 in., 32 in.
Chokes: Five EXIS HP Competition tubes
Sights: Front bead
Weight: 7 lb. 7 oz.
Bore/Gauge: 12
Magazine: 2 shells
Features: Micro-meter adjustable comb; vented barrel separation; adjustable competition trigger
MSRP $2950.00
Left-hand: . . . . add $160.00

L4S DELUXE HUNTER, GREY HUNTER

Action: Semiautomatic
Stock: Wood
Barrel: 26 in., 28 in.
Chokes: 3 Inner HP
Weight: 6 lb. 5 oz.–6 lb. 13 oz.
Bore/Gauge: 12
Magazine: 4 shells
Features: Stock shim system for adjusting fit; Tribore HP tapered barrels; available in three grades: Initial Hunter (black action), Grey Hunter (silver action with game scene), and Deluxe Hunter (silver action with detailed game scene with gold inlays and upgraded wood); Initial Hunter available in left-hand
Deluxe: $2350.00
Grey: $1925.00

L4S INITIAL HUNTER

Action: Semiautomatic
Stock: Turkish walnut
Barrel: 26 in., 28 in.
Chokes: 3 inner HP
Weight: 6 lb. 5 oz.–6 lb. 13 oz
Bore/Gauge: 12
Magazine: 4 shells
Features: Pulse Piston system; TRIBORE HP tapered barrels; innovative new design that allows the fore-end to be removed without disassembling the shotgun; gas-operating system that significantly reduces recoil; stock shim system for adjusting fit; left-hand versions available in both barrel lengths; model chambers 3-in. shells
Right-hand: $1375.00
Left-hand: $1575.00

L4S SPORTING, GREY SPORTING, DELUXE SPORTING

Action: Semiautomatic
Stock: Walnut
Barrel: 28 in., 30 in., 32 in.
Chokes: Five EXIS HP Competition tubes
Sights: White bead
Weight: 7 lb. 3 oz.
Bore/Gauge: 12
Magazine: 4 shells
Features: Designed around the 2.75-in.,12 ga. shell; Fabarm's tapered Tribore that improves patterns and velocities; oversized bolt handle and bolt release; highlights in bright red; stock can accept Kinetik recoil reducer; available left-handed; Grey and Deluxe include engraving and gold inlays of game birds
Sporting: . . . . . . $2025.00–$2225.00
Grey: $2475.00
Deluxe: $2895.00

Fabarm

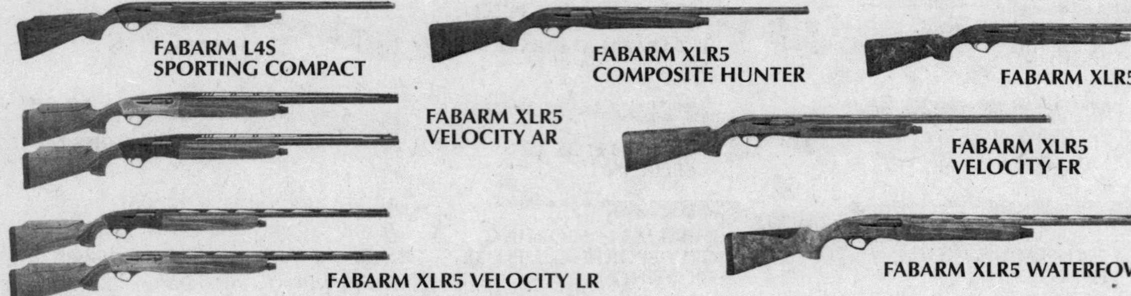

L4S SPORTING COMPACT

Action: Semiautomatic
Stock: Walnut
Barrel: 28 in.
Chokes: 5
Sights: White bead front
Weight: 6 lb. 12 oz.
Bore/Gauge: 12
Capacity: 4 shells
Features: With a lively swing at under 7 lbs. and a 13.75-in. length of pull, youth and small-statured shooters will appreciate this gun's Tribore HP barrel; stainless steel piston gas operation
Right-hand $2025.00
Left-hand $2225.00

XLR5 COMPOSITE HUNTER

Action: Semiautomatic
Stock: Synthetic
Barrel: 28 in.
Chokes: 5
Sights: Fiber optic front
Weight: 6 lb. 14 oz.
Bore/Gauge: 12
Capacity: 4 shells
Features: A relatively lightweight jack-of-all-trades hunter with a soft-touch finish synthetic stock; hard-anodized black finish on receiver; Tribore HP barrel with five flush INNER HP chokes; Pulse Piston gas action; hard case included; right-hand only
MSRP $1755.00

XLR5 GRYPHON

Action: Semiautomatic
Stock: Synthetic
Barrel: 30 in., 32 in.
Chokes: 5
Sights: White bead front
Weight: 7 lb. 5 oz.
Bore/Gauge: 12
Capacity: 4 shells
Features: A limited edition shotgun dressed in the flashy True Timber blue Viper camo with soft-touch finish; stainless steel piston gas operation; black hard anodized receiver; five Exis HP competition choke tubes; calibrated for use with only 2 ¾-in. target loads
MSRP $2475.00

XLR5 VELOCITY AR

Action: Semiautomatic
Stock: Walnut
Barrel: 30 in., 32 in.
Chokes: 5
Sights: White bead front
Weight: 7 lb. 9 oz.–7 lb. 12 oz.
Bore/Gauge: 12
Capacity: 4 shells
Features: Semiauto users get what over/under users have benefitted from for years: perfect weight and balance thanks to a magazine cap with adjustable weight; integrated recoil reducer; adjustable rib; Pulse Piston gas operation; receiver in black anodized or titanium silver finishes; matte-finish hand-oiled stock with adjustable cheekpiece; Tribore HP barrel
Right-hand . . . . . $3110.00–$3525.00
Left-hand . . . . . . $3310.00–$3725.00

XLR5 VELOCITY FR

Action: Semiautomatic
Stock: Walnut
Barrel: 30 in., 32 in.
Chokes: 5
Sights: White bead front
Weight: 7 lb. 9 oz.–7 lb. 12 oz.
Bore/Gauge: 12
Capacity: 4 shells
Features: A classy gun designed for sporting clays with a well-figured walnut stock; stainless steel piston gas operation; Tribore HP barrel; black hard anodized receiver; five extended Exis HP chokes; oversized bolt handle and release; calibrated only for 2 ¾-in. target loads; tapered top rib; hard case included; right- or left-hand
MSRP $2475.00

XLR5 VELOCITY LR

Action: Semiautomatic
Stock: Walnut
Barrel: 30 in., 32 in.
Chokes: 5
Sights: White bead front
Weight: 8 lb. 4 oz.
Bore/Gauge: 12
Capacity: 4 shells
Features: Slightly heavier than the other XLR5 models, the LR version features a long rib that starts at the back of the receiver, rather than the front; hand-oiled matte finish stock; Tibore HP barrel; receiver in black anodized or titanium silver finishes; adjustable cheekpiece
Right-hand . . . . . $2550.00–$2975.00
Left-hand . . . . . . $2750.00–$3175.00

XLR5 WATERFOWLER

Action: Semiautomatic
Stock: Synthetic
Barrel: 28 in., 30 in.
Chokes: 3 inner HP, 1 EXIS DK
Weight: 7 lb.
Bore/Gauge: 12
Magazine: 5 shells
Features: Pulse Piston system; TRIBORE HP barrel design for reduced recoil and improved pattern performance; special competition choke tube, the EXIS DK, tuned for non-toxic ammo in the most popular pellet sizes; a top rib increases the sighting plain by 4 in. and allows the shooter to see down the rib with a more comfortable head-up posture; chrome plated barrel extension and bores; left-hand versions available in both barrel lengths; model chambers 3-in. shells; in True Timber Viper camo stock with OD green receiver or a left-hand-only version in full-coverage Kryptec Banshee camo
Right-hand: $1895.00
Left-hand: $2095.00

Fausti USA

CALEDON

Action: Over/under
Stock: Walnut
Barrel: 26 in., 28 in., 30 in.
Chokes: Fixed or interchangeable choke tubes
Weight: 5 lb. 12 oz.–7 lb. 4 oz.
Bore/Gauge: 12, 16, 20, 28, .410
Magazine: 2 shells
Features: Single selectable trigger; A+ Turkish walnut stock with oil finish; laser-engraved lower receiver; automatic ejectors; metallic bead sight
MSRP . . . . $1999.00–$2569.00

CLASS

Action: Over/under
Stock: Walnut
Barrel: 26 in., 28 in., 30 in.
Chokes: Fixed or interchangeable choke tubes
Weight: 5 lb. 12 oz.–7 lb. 5 oz.
Bore/Gauge: 12, 16, 20, 28, .410
Magazine: 2 shells
Features: Features automatic ejectors; metallic bead; single-selectable trigger; 14–3/8-in. length of pull; timeless AA walnut oil-polished stock; Prince of Wales style stock; receiver laser-engraved with flushing quail
MSRP . . . . $2549.00–$3099.00

ITALYCO

Action: Over/under
Stock: Wood
Barrel: 23–32 in.
Chokes: Fixed
Weight: N/A
Bore/Gauge: 12 (2 ¾ in., 3 in.), 16 (2 ¾ in.), 20 (2 ¾ in., 3 in.), 28 (2 ¾ in.), .410 (3 in.)
Magazine: 2 shells
Features: Single selective trigger (double trigger available); automatic ejector (manual ejector available); box lock round body; pistol grip with steel grip cap or Prince of Wales or English
MSRP . . . . . . Contact manufacturer

MAGNIFICENT

Action: Over/under
Stock: Walnut
Barrel: 26 in., 28 in., 30 in.
Chokes: Fixed or interchangeable choke tubes
Weight: 5 lb. 12 oz.–7 lb. 6 oz.
Bore/Gauge: 12, 16, 20, 28, .410
Magazine: 2 shells
Features: AAA+ walnut stock with oil finish; precision scroll engraving accompanies Aphrodite, the Greek goddess of love and beauty, on the receiver; the Crest of the city of Brescia, Italy, where all Fausti shotguns are produced, is on the underside of the receiver; single selectable trigger; automatic ejectors; metallic bead sight
MSRP: . . . . $4999.00–$5559.00

Fox by Savage Arms

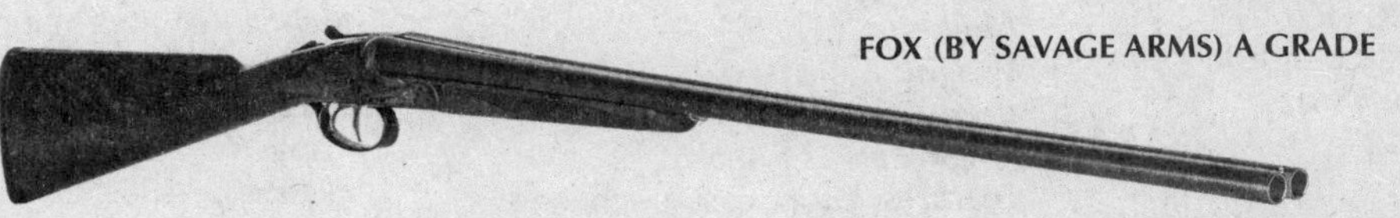

A GRADE

Action: Side-by-side
Stock: American black walnut
Barrel: 26 in., 28 in.
Chokes: IM, M, F
Sights: Front brass bead
Weight: N/A
Bore/Gauge: 12, 20
Magazine: 2 shells
Features: Splinter forend; checkered stock; straight grip; case-colored receiver; three interchangeable chokes; double triggers; 14.5-in. length of pull; hard polymer case
MSRP $4259.00

Franchi

FRANCHI AFFINITY 3 COMPACT

FRANCHI AFFINITY 3 ELITE UPLAND

FRANCHI AFFINITY 3.5

FRANCHI AFFINITY CATALYST

FRANCHI INSTINCT LX

FRANCHI INSTINCT L

AFFINITY 3

Action: Semiautomatic
Stock: Synthetic, walnut
Barrel: 26 in., 28 in.
Chokes: Three chokes (F, IC, M)
Sights: Fiber optic bar front sight
Weight: 5 lb. 15 oz.–6 lb. 15 oz.
Bore/Gauge: 12, 20
Magazine: 4 shells
Features: Drop at heel is adjustable; in black, Realtree Max-5, or Mossy Oak Bottomland synthetic stocks or A-grade satin-finished walnut; chambers 3-inch shells
MSRP . . . . $849.00–$959.00

AFFINITY 3 COMPACT

Action: Semiautomatic
Stock: Synthetic
Barrel: 24 in., 26 in.
Chokes: Three chokes (F, IC, M)
Sights: Fiber optic bar front sight
Weight: 5 lb. 15 oz.–6 lb. 11 oz.
Bore/Gauge: 12, 20
Magazine: 4 shells
Features: A hunting semiautomatic for youth, women, and shorter-statured shooters; length of pull and drop at heel are adjustable; chambers 3-inch shells; both gauges available in full-coverage Realtree Max-5; 20 ga. available in all-black
MSRP . . . . $899.00–$999.00

AFFINITY 3 ELITE UPLAND

Action: Semiautomatic
Stock: Walnut
Barrel: 26 in., 28 in.
Chokes: 3 (CR, MR, LR)
Sights: TruGlo dual-color front
Weight: 6 lb.–6 lb. 15 oz.
Bore/Gauge: 20, 12
Capacity: 4 shells
Features: Satin-finished Grade A walnut stock; gun metal-gray Cerakote metal finish; stock adjustable for drop at heel
MSRP $1249.00

AFFINITY 3 SPORTING

Action: Semiautomatic
Stock: Walnut
Barrel: 28 in., 30 in.
Chokes: 3 (IC, M, F)
Sights: Red fiber optic front
Weight: 6 lb. 3 oz.–7 lb. 2 oz.
Bore/Gauge: 20, 12
Capacity: 4 shells
Features: Neatly priced semiautomatic for the sporting clays crowd, with a red fiber optic front sight; A-grade satin-finished walnut stock adjustable for drop at heel; TSA recoil pad; extended chokes
MSRP $999.00

AFFINITY 3.5

Action: Semiautomatic
Stock: Synthetic
Barrel: 26 in., 28 in.
Chokes: Three chokes (F, IC, M)
Sights: Fiber optic bar front sight
Weight: 6 lb. 15 oz.–7 lb.
Bore/Gauge: 12
Magazine: 4 shells
Features: Chambers 3.5-in. shells; adjustable drop at heel; 26-in. barrel model available in black synthetic or Realtree Max-5; 28-in. barrel model available in Realtree Max-5 or Mossy Oak Bottomland
Black: $999.00
Camo: $1129.00

AFFINITY CATALYST

Action: Semiautomatic
Stock: Walnut
Barrel: 28 in.
Chokes: IC, M, F
Weight: 6 lb. 10 oz.
Bore/Gauge: 12
Magazine: 4+1 shells
Features: Drop, cast, pitch, and length-of-pull are all tailored to a woman's build; fiber optic red-bar front sight
MSRP $969.00

AFFINITY LEFT-HAND

Action: Semiautomatic
Stock: Synthetic
Barrel: 28 in.
Chokes: Three chokes (F, IC, M)
Sights: Fiber optic bar front sight
Weight: 6 lb. 15 oz.
Bore/Gauge: 12
Magazine: 4 shells
Features: Drop at heel is adjustable; in black, Realtree Max-5, or Mossy Oak Bottomland synthetic stocks or A-grade satin-finished walnut; chambers 3-inch shells
MSRP $849.00

INSTINCT L

Action: Over/under
Stock: Walnut
Barrel: 26 in., 28 in.
Chokes: Interchangeable (IC, M, F)
Weight: 6 lb. 2 oz.–6 lb. 6 oz.
Bore/Gauge: 12, 20, 28, .410
Magazine: 2 shells
Features: Ventilated raised rib; red fiber optic front sight; blued and color-case-hardened finish on the receiver, with gold inlay; A-grade walnut stock in Prince-of-Wales style with cut checkering on the forend and pistol grip; satin oil finish; single gold-plated trigger; chrome-lined barrels proofed for steel shot; hard-shell custom-fitted gun case included
MSRP $1369.00

INSTINCT LX

Action: Over/under
Stock: Walnut
Barrel: 28 in.
Chokes: 3 (IC, M, F)
Sights: Red fiber optic front
Weight: 6 lb. 10 oz.–7 lb.
Bore/Gauge: 12, 20, 28
Capacity: 2 shells
Features: A much fancier Instinct with AA-grade walnut in a satin finish and with fine line checkering, Prince of Wales grip, and schnabel forearm; deep color case-hardened receiver with gold inlays; barrel selector; extended chokes
MSRP . . . .$1699.00–$1799.00

Franchi

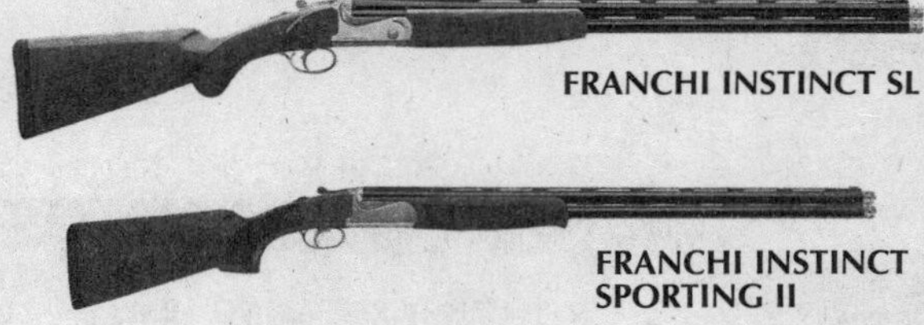

FRANCHI INSTINCT SL

FRANCHI INSTINCT SLX

FRANCHI INSTINCT SPORTING II

INSTINCT SL

Action: Over/under
Stock: Walnut
Barrel: 26 in., 28 in.
Chokes: Interchangeable (IC, M, F)
Weight: 5 lb. 2 oz.–6 lb. 2 oz.
Bore/Gauge: 12, 20, 16, 28, .410
Magazine: 2 shells
Features: Vent rib; red fiber optic front bead; aluminum alloy receiver; blued barrels; AA-grade satin walnut stock in Prince-of-Wales style with cut checkering and oil finish; tang-mounted automatic safety; custom-fitted, hard-shell gun case included
MSRP . . . . $1599.00–$1699.00

INSTINCT SLX

Action: Over/under
Stock: Walnut
Barrel: 28 in.
Chokes: 5 (C, IC, M, IM, F)
Sights: Red fiber optic front
Weight: 5 lb. 10 oz.–6 lb. 5 oz.
Bore/Gauge: 12, 16, 20, 28
Capacity: 2 shells
Features: AA-grade walnut stock in a satin finish and with a Prince of Wales grip and schnabel forearm; a satin stainless receiver with floral engraving; between barrel venting; auto ejectors; barrel select switch; extended chokes
MSRP . . . . $1999.00–$2099.00

INSTINCT SPORTING II

Action: Over/under
Stock: Walnut
Barrel: 30 in.
Chokes: 3 (IC, M, F)
Sights: Red fiber optic front
Weight: 7 lb. 7 oz.–7 lb. 13 oz.
Bore/Gauge: 20, 12
Capacity: 2 shells
Features: A-Grade walnut stock in a satin finish; between-barrel venting; matte stainless receiver; adjustable comb
MSRP $1999.00

Hatsan USA

HATSAN USA ESCORT DF12

HATSAN USA ESCORT DYNAMAX

HATSAN USA ESCORT SLUGGER, SLUGGER TACTICAL

ESCORT DF12

Action: Semiautomatic
Stock: Synthetic
Barrel: 18 in.
Chokes: Five (F, M, IM, IC, C)
Sights: A4-style front, adjustable rear, flip-up front and rear
Weight: 8 lb. 15 oz.
Bore/Gauge: 12
Capacity: 6 shells
Features: An AR-platform shotgun for the 3-Gun crowd; 3-inch chambers; oxidation-proof chrome-plated barrel; reversible cocking handle; ample rail acreage; elevation-adjustable comb
MSRP $699.99

ESCORT DYNAMAX

Action: Semiautomatic
Stock: Synthetic
Barrel: 28 in.
Chokes: Five (F, M, IM, IC, C)
Sights: Fiber optic front
Weight: 7 lb.
Bore/Gauge: 12
Capacity: 5 shells
Features: A fast-handling semiauto with three-inch chamber; DaSoft soft-touch stock finish; checkered anti-glare vent rib; Hi-Viz fiber optic front bead; detachable sling swivels; 11mm grooved receiver for optics mounting; steel-shot acceptable chokes
MSRP $699.99

ESCORT SLUGGER, SLUGGER TACTICAL

Action: Pump-action
Stock: Synthetic
Barrel: 18 in.
Chokes: None
Sights: Fixed blade front
Weight: 6 lb. 6 oz.–6 lb. 8 oz.
Bore/Gauge: 12
Capacity: 5 shells
Features: Sling swivel studs; aggressively textured forearms; Tactical version gets a pistol grip and a five-shot shellholder built into the skeletal buttstock, as well as a Picatinny rail in front of the forend or light mounting
Slugger. $179.00
Slugger Tactical $199.00

Henry Repeating Arms Co.

HENRY REPEATING ARMS LEVER-ACTION AXE .410

HENRY REPEATING ARMS LEVER-ACTION X-MODEL .410

HENRY REPEATING ARMS SIDE GATE LEVER-ACTION .410

HENRY REPEATING ARMS SINGLE SHOT SHOTGUN IN STEEL & BRASS

LEVER-ACTION AXE .410

Action: Lever
Stock: American walnut
Barrel: 15.14 in.
Chokes: Invector-style Full
Sights: Brass bead front
Weight: 5 lb. 12 oz.
Bore/Gauge: .410
Capacity: 5 shells
Features: Certainly a home-defense consideration with its five-round tube magazine; ergonomic pistol grip; swivel studs; 2.5-in. chamber
MSRP $1000.00

LEVER-ACTION X-MODEL .410

Action: Lever
Stock: Synthetic
Barrel: 19.8 in.
Chokes: Invector-style Full
Sights: Fiber optic front
Weight: 7 lb. 8 oz.
Bore/Gauge: .410
Capacity: 5 shells
Features: A very modernized lever-action with an ergonomically designed lever loop and tough synthetic stock; Picatinny rail and M-LOK slots; 2.5-in shells only
MSRP $1000.00

SIDE GATE LEVER-ACTION .410

Action: Lever
Stock: American walnut
Barrel: 19.75 in., 24 in.
Chokes: None
Sights: Ramp ivory bead, adjustable semi-buckhorn rear
Weight: 7 lb. 1 oz.
Bore/Gauge: .410
Capacity: 5 shells
Features: A handsome .410-bore with deep engraving at wrist and forend; Cylinder bore (no chokes); swivel studs; polished brass receiver and butt plate; 2.5-in. shells only
MSRP . . . . $969.00–$1012.00

SINGLE SHOT SHOTGUN IN STEEL & BRASS

Action: Break-open single-shot
Stock: Walnut
Barrel: 26 in., 28 in.
Chokes: 1 (varies with gauge)
Weight: 6 lb. 10 oz.–6 lb. 12 oz.
Bore/Gauge: 12, 20, .410
Magazine: 1 shell
Features: Sharing the same action as the single-shot rifle; front brass bead; steel models have pistol grip, brass models sport a straight grip; Rem-Choke style threaded chokes
Steel: $525.00
Brass: $646.00

Israel Weapon Industries (IWI)

ISRAEL WEAPON INDUSTRIES (IWI) TAVOR TS 12

TAVOR TS 12

Action: Semiautomatic
Stock: Synthetic
Barrel: 18.5 in.
Chokes: One
Sights: None
Weight: 8 lb.
Bore/Gauge: 12
Magazine: 15 shells
Features: Triple-magazine bullpup semiauto shotgun; each magazine can hold a maximum of four 3-in. or five 2.75-in. 12-ga. shells and can be both fed and unloaded from either side; available in black, Flat Dark Earth, and OD Green
MSRP $1399.00

Ithaca Gun Company

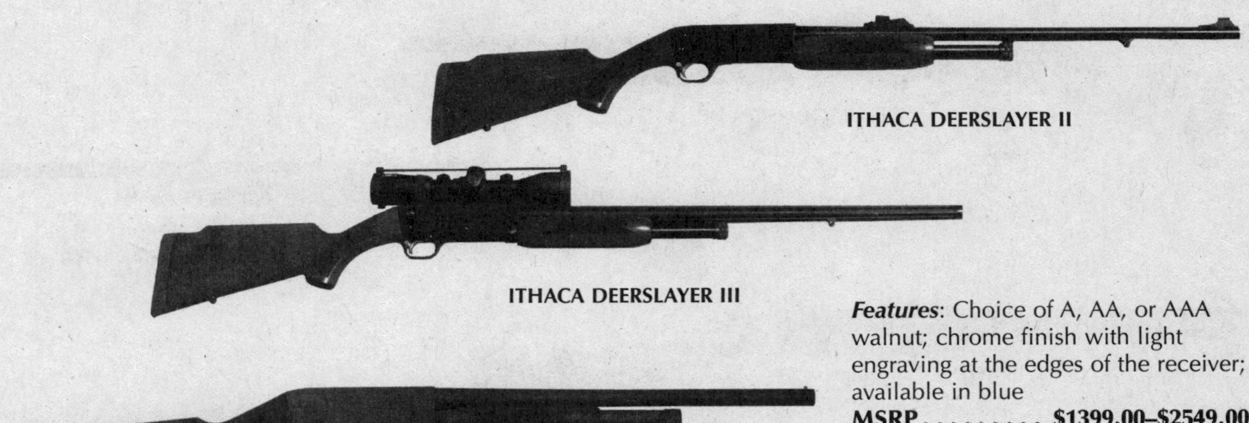

ITHACA DEERSLAYER II

ITHACA DEERSLAYER III

ITHACA MODEL 37 DEFENSE SYNTHETIC

ITHACA GUN CO. MODEL 37 28-GAUGE

ITHACA MODEL 37 FEATHERLIGHT

ITHACA MODEL 37 WATERFOWL

DEERSLAYER II

Action: Pump
Stock: Walnut
Barrel: 24 in.
Chokes: None
Weight: 6.8 lb.–8 lb. 6 oz.
Bore/Gauge: 12, 20
Magazine: 4+1 shells
Features: Solderless barrel system; thumbhole or standard black walnut Monte Carlo stock; fat deluxe checkered forend; sling swivel studs; Pachmayr 750 Decelerator recoil pad; matte blued finish on barrel; gold-plated trigger; Marble Arms rifle sights; drilled and tapped for Weaver #62 scope rail
MSRP . . . . $1199.00–$1749.00

DEERSLAYER III

Action: Pump
Stock: Walnut
Barrel: 20 in., 26 in., 28 in.
Chokes: None
Weight: 8.1 lb.–9 lb. 8 oz.
Bore/Gauge: 12, 20
Magazine: 4+1 shells
Features: Heavy-walled, fluted, fixed barrel in blue matted finish; walnut Monte Carlo stock with optional thumbhole; Pachmayr 750 Decelerator recoil pad; sling swivel studs; gold-plated trigger; Weaver #62 rail pre-installed on receiver
MSRP . . . . $1399.00–$1949.00

MODEL 37 28-GAUGE

Action: Pump
Stock: Walnut
Barrel: 24 in., 26 in., 28 in.
Chokes: N/A
Sights: Bead
Weight: N/A
Bore/Gauge: 28
Magazine: 4 shells
Features: Choice of A, AA, or AAA walnut; chrome finish with light engraving at the edges of the receiver; available in blue
MSRP . . . . $1399.00–$2549.00

MODEL 37 DEFENSE

Action: Pump
Stock: Walnut
Barrel: 18.5 in., 20 in.
Chokes: None
Weight: 6.5 lb.–7 lb. 2 oz.
Bore/Gauge: 12, 20
Magazine: 4+1 or 7+1 shells
Features: Choice of walnut or black synthetic stock; 3 in. chamber; matte blued finish barrel; Pachmayr decelerator recoil pad
MSRP . . . . $999.00–$1199.00

MODEL 37 FEATHERLIGHT

Action: Pump
Stock: Walnut
Barrel: 26 in., 28 in., 20 in.
Chokes: 3 Briley Choke tubes (F, M, IC, and wrench)
Weight: 6.1 lb.–7 lb. 10 oz.
Bore/Gauge: 12, 16, 20, 28
Magazine: 4+1 rounds
Features: Solderless shells system; classic game scene engraving; black walnut stock with semi-pistol butt stock; TruGlo red front sight; Pachmayr 752 Decelerator recoil pad
MSRP . . . . $1199.00–$2154.00

MODEL 37 WATERFOWL

Action: Pump
Stock: Camo, synthetic black
Barrel: 28 in., 30 in.
Chokes: Briley choke tubes
Weight: 7 lb. 3 oz.–7 lb. 6 oz.
Bore/ Gauge: 12, 20
Magazine: 4+1 shells
Features: 3 in. chamber; gold plated trigger; gamescene engraving; perma-guard protection
MSRP . . . . $1039.00–$1369.00

Iver Johnson Arms

IVER JOHNSON HP 18

IVER JOHNSON IJ500

IVER JOHNSON IJ600

IVER JOHNSON IJ700

IVER JOHNSON PAS12, PAS12-PG

HP 18

Action: Semiautomatic
Stock: Synthetic
Barrel: 18.5 in.
Chokes: N/A
Weight: 6 lb. 6 oz.
Bore/Gauge: 12, 20
Magazine: 5+1 shells
Features: High grade alloy receiver for reduced weight; two-piece detachable pistol grip stock; rubber buttpad on the stock to help reduce felt recoil; Picatinny rail on top of the receiver, with a fully adjustable white dot rear sight; fiber optic front sight; finger grooves on the forend to ensure a solid grip while firing; muzzle break externally threaded onto the barrel; 12-ga. available in black or Digital Tan, 20-ga. in black only
Black:. $379.00
Digital Tan 12-ga.: $486.00

IJ500

Action: Semiautomatic
Stock: Walnut
Barrel: 28 in.
Chokes: 3 internally threaded choke tubes (F, IM, M)
Weight: 7 lb. 2 oz.
Bore/Gauge: 12
Magazine: 5+1 shells
Features: Front brass bead sight; checkered stock and forend; chambered for 2 ¾" and 3" shotshells. —12-ga. now available in synthetic stock in Max-4 camo.
Wood stock: $385.00
Max-4 camo: $486.00

IJ600

Action: Over/under
Stock: Walnut
Barrel: 28 in.
Chokes: 5 internal (F, IM, M, IC, C)
Weight: 6 lb. 1 oz.–7 lb. 5 oz.
Bore/Gauge: 12, 20, .410
Magazine: N/A
Features: Vent rib on top and bottom barrel; extractors on both barrels; engraved receiver with birds accented in gold colored coating; selector switch located on the safety for choosing which barrel fires first; checkered stock and forend; sling swivel on barrel and stock; 20 gauge has a scaled down receiver, stock, and forend
MSRP $527.00

IJ700

Action: Break-open single-shot
Stock: Walnut
Barrel: 18 in., 26 in.
Chokes: None
Weight: 4 lb. 8 oz.–4 lb. 14 oz.
Bore/Gauge: .410
Magazine: 1 shell
Features: Silver receiver; blued barrel; single extractor; sling swivels
MSRP $180.00

PAS12, PAS12-PG

Action: Pump
Stock: Synthetic
Barrel: 18 in.
Chokes: N/A
Sights: Blade front
Weight: 6 lb.
Bore/Gauge: 12
Magazine: 4 shells
Features: Lightweight alloy frame; chambers 3-in. shells; forend is grooved and belled on the back end to ensure proper stroking of the action; PAS12 is available with or without a muzzle brake; PAS12 PG is equipped with a pistol grip; PAS12 standard barrel is available in all-over satin nickel
PAS12: . . . . $257.00–$297.00
PAS12-PG: . . . . $257.00–$338.00

Kalashnikov USA

KALASHNIKOV USA
KS-12, KS-12T

KS-12, KS-12T

Action: Semiautomatic
Stock: Polymer
Barrel: 18.25 in.
Chokes: None
Sights: Fixed
Weight: 8 lb. 8 oz.
Bore/Gauge: 12
Magazine: 5 shells
Features: Based on historical Kalashnikov rifle platform goes shotgun; threaded barrel; T–Tactical–version has a skeletonized collapsible stock, a 10-round magazine, and side accessory rails on the handguard; available in black or flat dark earth
KS-12: $805.00
KS-12T: . . . . $845.00–$885.00

Kel-Tec

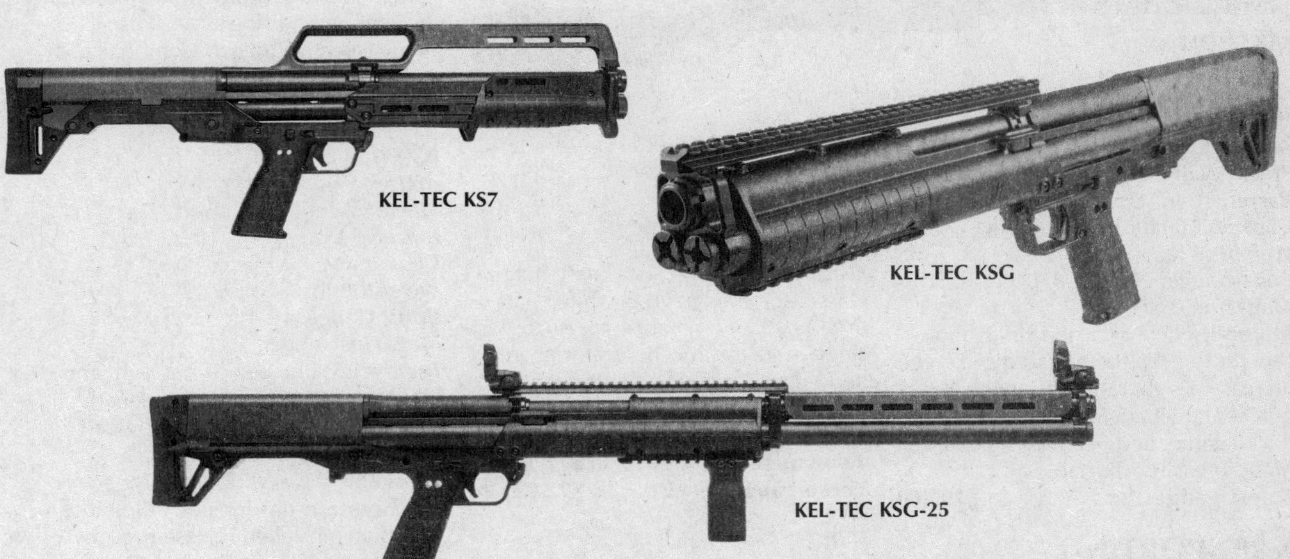

KEL-TEC KS7

KEL-TEC KSG

KEL-TEC KSG-25

KS7

Action: Pump
Stock: Synthetic
Barrel: 18.5 in.
Chokes: None
Sights: None
Weight: 5 lb. 15 oz.
Bore/Gauge: 12
Capacity: 8 shells
Features: A shotgun in compact bullpup design with a 13-inch length of pull; carry handle; ambidextrous adjustable stock
MSRP $580.00

KSG

Action: Pump
Stock: Glass reinforced nylon
Barrel: 18.5 in.
Chokes: Cylinder bore
Weight: 6 lb. 14.4 oz.-8 lb. 8 oz.
Bore/Gauge: 12 gauge (3 in.)
Magazine: 6+6+1
Features: KSG receiver is made from hardened steel and includes the magazine tubes which have been welded in place; pump action feeds from either the left or right tube
MSRP $900.00

KSG-25

Action: Pump
Stock: Synthetic
Barrel: 30 in.
Chokes: None
Weight: 9 lb. 4 oz.
Bore/Gauge: 12
Magazine: 21, 25 shells
Features: Magpul MBUS and an RVG vertical grip on the pump; 3-in. chambers; holds a full box of 2¾-in. or 3-in. shells
MSRP $1150.00

Krieghoff

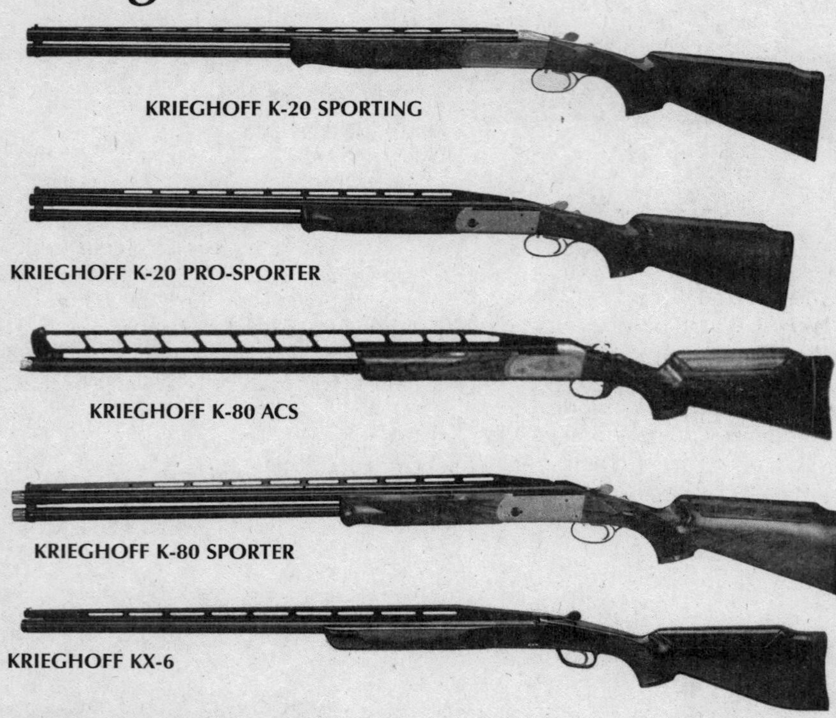

KRIEGHOFF K-20 SPORTING

KRIEGHOFF K-20 PRO-SPORTER

KRIEGHOFF K-80 ACS

KRIEGHOFF K-80 SPORTER

KRIEGHOFF KX-6

K-20 PRO-SPORTER

Action: Over/under
Stock: Walnut
Barrel: 30 in., 32 in.
Chokes: Titanium choke tubes
Weight: 8 lb.
Bore/Gauge: 20, 28, .410
Magazine: 2 shells
Features: Higher rib and stock allows shooter to keep their head more erect, increasing sight range, allowing for quicker target acquisition, reduced neck fatigue, and perceived recoil; high rib easily adjustable
Single gauge:. $12,795.00

K-20 SPORTING

Action: Over/under
Stock: Walnut
Barrel: 30 in., 32 in.
Chokes: 5 choke tubes (C, S, IC, LM, M, LIM, IM, F)
Weight: 7 lb. 8 oz.
Bore/Gauge: 20, 28, .410
Magazine: 2 shells
Features: Top-tang push safety button; classic scroll engraving; white pearl front bead and metal center bead; single-selective mechanical trigger; hand-checkered select European walnut stock with satin epoxy finish
Single gauge:. $12,395.00
Two-gauge set: $17,625.00
Three-gauge set: $22,820.00

K-80

Action: Over/under
Stock: Walnut
Barrel: 30 in., 32 in., 34 in.
Chokes: Steel or Titanium choke tubes (C, S, IC, LM, M, LIM, IM, F, SF)
Weight: 8 lb. 4 oz.
Bore/Gauge: 12
Magazine: 2 shells
Features: White pearl front sight and metal center bead; nickel-plated steel receiver with satin grey finish; single select trigger; top-tang push button safety; fine-checkered Turkish walnut
From:. . . . . . $11,795.00–$18,695.00

K-80 ACS COMBO

Action: Single barrel
Stock: Walnut
Barrel: 30 in., 32 in., 34 in.
Chokes: 8 factory steel choke tubes
Weight: 8 lb. 12 oz.
Bore/Gauge: 12
Magazine: 2 shells
Features: White pearl front bead and metal center bead sight; case-hardened action, nickel-plated steel receiver with nitride silver finish; single selective trigger; Combo is a an over/under and Unsingle.
From:. $18,695.00

KX-6

Action: Single-shot trap
Stock: Walnut
Barrel: 34 in.
Chokes: IM, LIM, F
Weight: 8 lb. 12 oz.
Bore/ Gauge: 12
Magazine: 1 shell
Features: White pearl front sight and metal center bead; case hardened, long lasting black nitro carbonized finish; semiautomatic ejector; adjustable tapered rib; readily available add-ons include adjustable butt-plate, installed release trigger, and upgraded titanium choke tubes
MSRP . . . . starting at $6695.00

K-Var

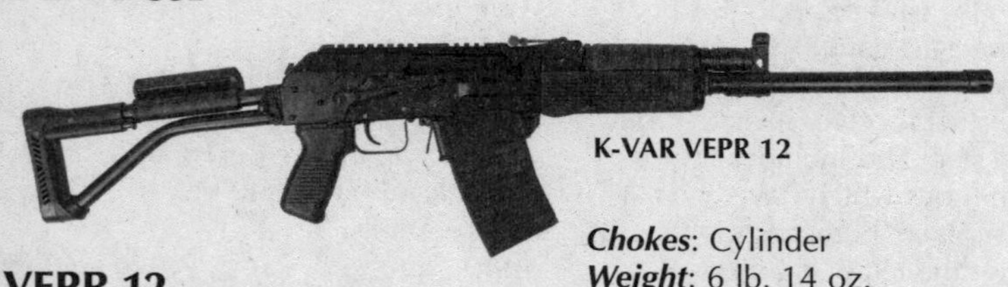

K-VAR VEPR 12

VEPR 12

Action: Semiautomatic
Stock: Synthetic
Barrel: 19 in.
Chokes: Cylinder
Weight: 6 lb. 14 oz.
Bore/Gauge: 12
Magazine: 5+1 shells
Features: AK safety selector with levers on both sides for easy operation; ability to insert magazines straight into the magazine well without canting; RPK-style windage adjustable rear sights; windage and elevation adjustable front sights integrated to the gas block; Picatinny rail incorporated into the hinged dust cover; left-side folding tubular buttstock with cheek rest and sling loop
MSRP $1999.99

Ljutic

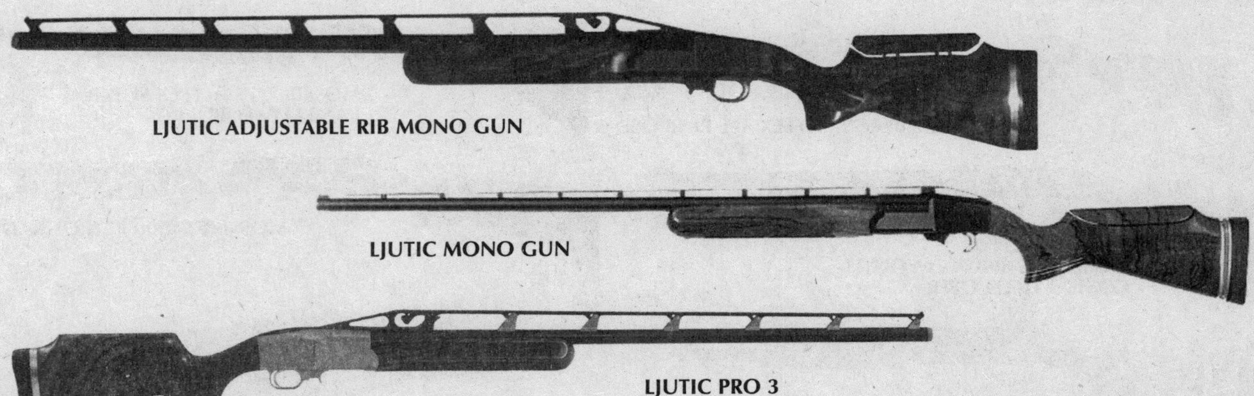

ADJUSTABLE RIB MONO GUN

Action: Single barrel
Stock: Walnut
Barrel: 34 in.
Chokes: Fixed or Ljutic SIC
Weight: 10 lb.
Bore/Gauge: .740, 12
Magazine: 1 shell
Features: "One Touch" adjustable rib allows you to change your point-of-impact; adjustable comb stock
MSRP: . . . . POR

MONO GUN

Action: Single barrel
Stock: Walnut
Barrel: 32 in.–34 in.
Chokes: Optional screw in chokes (Fixed, Ljutic SIC, Briley SIC)
Weight: 10 lb.
Bore/Gauge: .740, 12
Magazine: 1 shell
Features: Comes with American walnut wood; optional roll over combs and cheek pieces; various upgrades available
MSRP . . . . POR

PRO 3

Action: Single barrel
Stock: Walnut
Barrel: 34 in.
Chokes: 4 Briley Series 12 chokes
Weight: 9 lb.
Bore/Gauge: .740, 12
Magazine: 1 shell
Features: Aluminum baseplate; interchangeable two-pad system; adjustable comb; English or American walnut stock; screw in hinge pin; stainless or blued barrel
MSRP . . . . POR

Merkel

147EL

Action: Side-by-side
Stock: Wood
Barrel: 27 in., 28 in.
Chokes: Steel-shot proofed chokes
Weight: 6 lb. 3 oz.
Bore/Gauge: 12
Magazine: None
Features: English stock finished with fine hand-cut checkering at buttplate; silver monogram plate; steel action is gray nitrated; Anson & Deeley locks; Greener-style cross bolt and double bottom bite; double trigger; automatic safety
MSRP $8885.00

Mossberg (O. F. Mossberg & Sons)

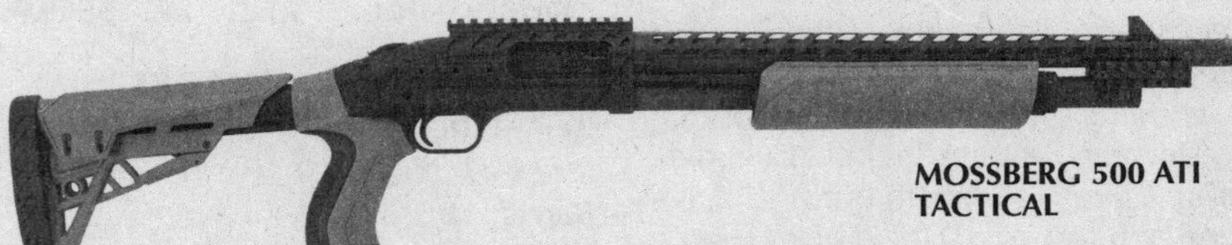

500 ATI TACTICAL

Action: Pump
Stock: Synthetic
Barrel: 18.5 in.
Chokes: Cylinder
Weight: 6 lb. 12 oz.
Bore/Gauge: 12
Magazine: 5 shells
Features: ATI TacLite six-position adjustable buttstock; Scorpion Recoil ATI Akita fore-end; heat shield; topside and muzzle-end rails; three-shell side-saddle; in Flat Dark Earth or Destroyer Gray
MSRP: $643.00

Mossberg (O. F. Mossberg & Sons)

MOSSBERG 500 FLEX ALL-PURPOSE

MOSSBERG 500 FLEX SUPER BANTAM ALL-PURPOSE

MOSSBERG 500 FLEX YOUTH COMBO FIELD/DEER

MOSSBERG 500 RETROGRADE

MOSSBERG 500 SUPER BANTAM TURKEY

MOSSBERG 500 TACTICAL JIC

MOSSBERG 500 TACTICAL JIC FLEX

500 FLEX ALL-PURPOSE

Action: Pump
Stock: Synthetic
Barrel: 28 in.
Chokes: Accu-Set
Weight: 7 lb. 8 oz.
Bore/Gauge: 12
Magazine: 5 shells
Features: Matte metal finishes; stock with medium recoil pad; stock and forend constructed of synthetic with black matte finish; twin bead sights
MSRP $536.00

500 FLEX SUPER BANTAM ALL-PURPOSE

Action: Pump
Stock: Synthetic
Barrel: 22 in.
Chokes: Accu-Set
Sights: Front and mid-rib beads
Weight: 6 lb. 8 oz.
Bore/Gauge: 20
Capacity: 6 shells
Features: A gun to grow with thanks to the FLEX stock system; vent rib; chokes; mid-rib and front beads; 12 ½-inch length of pull
MSRP $498.00

500 FLEX YOUTH COMBO FIELD/DEER

Action: Pump
Stock: Synthetic
Barrel: 22 in., 24 in.
Chokes: Accu-Set
Sights: Front and mid-rib beads/ adjustable rifle sights
Weight: 6 lb. 8 oz.–6 lb. 12 oz.
Bore/Gauge: 20
Capacity: 6 shells
Features: A combo youth gun with a 24-inch vent rib barrel with Accu-Set chokes and dual beads; 22-inch fully rifled slug barrel with adjustable sights; FLEX four-position adjustable stock; three-inch chamber
MSRP $582.00

500 RETROGRADE

Action: Pump
Stock: Walnut
Barrel: 18.5 in.
Chokes: None
Sights: Bead front
Weight: 6 lb. 4 oz.
Bore/Gauge: 12
Capacity: 6 shells
Features: Designed to celebrate Mossberg's 100th anniversary, buyers get a pump shotgun they revere for its technology with the retro look of yesteryear. Features include Cylinder-bore barrel; full-length buttstock; corncob fore-end; single brass bead; blued finish
MSRP $553.00

500 SUPER BANTAM TURKEY

Action: Pump
Stock: Synthetic
Barrel: 22 in.
Chokes: Interchangeable Accu-Choke (X-full and wrench)
Weight: 5 lb. 4 oz.
Bore/Gauge: 20
Magazine: 6 shells
Features: Adjustable synthetic stock in Mossy Oak Obsession; adjustable fiber optic sights; drilled and tapped for scopes; gun lock
MSRP $533.00

500 TACTICAL JIC

Action: Pump
Stock: Synthetic
Barrel: 18.5 in.
Chokes: Cylinder bore chokes
Weight: 5 lb. 8 oz.
Bore/Gauge: 12
Magazine: 6 shells
Features: Bead sight; Marinecote metal finish; comes with multi-tool, survival knife and cordura carrying case; gun lock; swivel studs; black synthetic stock; only pump-action shotguns to pass all U.S. Military Mil-Spec 3443 standards; available with matte blued metalwork
Blue: $515.00
Marinecoate: $666.00

500 TACTICAL JIC FLEX

Action: Pump
Stock: Synthetic
Barrel: 18.5 in.
Chokes: C
Weight: 5 lb. 8 oz.
Bore/Gauge: 12
Magazine: 6 shells
Features: Bead sights; FLEX pistol grip; 3-in. barrel with matte black finish
MSRP $556.00

Mossberg (O. F. Mossberg & Sons)

500 TURKEY

Action: Pump
Stock: Synthetic
Barrel: 20 in., 22 in., 26 in.
Chokes: X-Factor; none
Weight: 6 lb. 8 oz.–7 lb.
Bore/Gauge: 12, 20, .410
Magazine: 5, 6 shells
Features: 12-gauge has X-Factor ported choke tube, adjustable fiber optic sights, full-coverage Mossy Oak Obsession; 20-gauge has X-Factor choke, adjustable fiber optic sights, full-coverage Mossy Oak Obsession; .410-bore has fixed Full choke, front fiber optic sight, full-coverage Mossy Oak Bottomland
MSRP: $549.00

500 YOUTH SUPER BANTAM ALL-PURPOSE

Action: Pump
Stock: Synthetic
Barrel: 22 in.
Chokes: Accu-Set
Sights: Bead
Weight: 5 lb. 4 oz.
Bore/Gauge: 20
Magazine: 6 shells
Features: Designed for youth and people with a shorter length of pull; black or Muddy Girl Wild camo adjustable stock; Accu-Set chokes; vent rib
MSRP . . . . $459.00–$515.00

510 YOUTH MINI SUPER BANTAM ALL-PURPOSE

Action: Pump
Stock: Synthetic
Barrel: 18.5 in.
Chokes: None
Sights: Bead
Weight: 5 lb.
Bore/Gauge: 20, .410
Magazine: 4 shells
Features: Designed for youth and people with a shorter length of pull; stock in black, Muddy Girl Wild, or Mossy Oak Break-Up Country; adjustable stock; vent rib on the fixed-choke Modified barrel
MSRP . . . . $459.00–$517.00

590 7-SHOT

Action: Pump
Stock: Synthetic
Barrel: 18.5 in.
Chokes: None
Sights: Bead front
Weight: 5 lb. 12 oz.–7 lb.
Bore/Gauge: 20, 12, .410
Capacity: 6 shells
Features: Handy pump for self-defense and even 3-Gun games, with a FLEX stock adjustable for length of pull; FLEX pistol grip; Cylinder bore; matte blue finish
MSRP . . . . $500.00–$659.00

590 9-SHOT

Action: Pump
Stock: Synthetic
Barrel: 20 in.
Chokes: None
Sights: None; ghost ring
Weight: 5 lb. 12 oz.–7 lb. 12 oz.
Bore/Gauge: 20, 12
Capacity: 8 shells
Features: Three 12-ga. configurations include 1) ghost ring sights and a heat shield 2) no sights, with heat shield, with adjustable stock and pistol grip kit, and 3) ghost ring sights, no heat shield, and with the six-position Flex buttstock and Flex pistol grip; all models are fixed Cylinder bore
MSRP . . . . $519.00–$659.00

590 CHAINSAW

Action: Pump
Stock: Synthetic
Barrel: 18.5 in.
Chokes: None
Sights: White dot front
Weight: 6 lb.
Bore/Gauge: 12
Capacity: 5 shells
Features: A pistol-grip-only model with a removeable top handle for more secure hip-shooting technique; accessory rails on forend at 3, 6, and 9 o'clock; breaching "stand-off" barrel; matte blue finish
MSRP $601.00

590 CRUISER

Action: Pump
Stock: Synthetic
Barrel: 18.5 in.
Chokes: None
Sights: White dot front
Weight: 5 lb. 12 oz.
Bore/Gauge: 12
Capacity: 6 shells
Features: The reliable Cruiser in a pistol-grip configuration gets a breaching "stand-off" barrel; matte blue finish; forend hand strap
MSRP $500.00

590 M-LOK

Action: Pump
Stock: Synthetic
Barrel: 20 in.
Chokes: Accu Choke Cylinder
Sights: Ghost ring
Weight: 7 lb. 4 oz.
Bore/Gauge: 12
Capacity: 8 shells
Features: A great pump for ranch work or 3-Gun with a longer barrel; ghost ring sights; M-LOK forend
MSRP $603.00

Mossberg (O. F. Mossberg & Sons)

MOSSBERG 590 NIGHTSTICK

MOSSBERG 590 RETROGRADE

MOSSBERG 590 SHOCKWAVE

MOSSBERG 590 SHOCKWAVE 7-SHOT

MOSSBERG 590 SHOCKWAVE 20-GAUGE (NON-NFA)

MOSSBERG 590 SHOCKWAVE FLAT DARK EARTH CERAKOTE (NON-NFA)

MOSSBERG 590 JIC SHOCKWAVE

MOSSBERG 590 SHOCKWAVE LASER SADDLE

590 NIGHTSTICK

Action: Pump
Stock: Hardwood
Barrel: 14 in.
Chokes: None
Sights: Bead front
Weight: 5 lb. 3 oz.
Bore/Gauge: 12, 20
Capacity: 6 shells
Features: Five-round magazine; non-NFA (no ATF tax stamp required) fixed Cylinder choke barrel; hardwood bird's-head grip and corncob fore-end; matte blue finish; chambers 3-inch shells
MSRP. . . . . $555.00–$573.00

590 RETROGRADE

Action: Pump
Stock: Walnut
Barrel: 18.5 in., 20 in.
Chokes: None
Sights: Bead front
Weight: 7 lb.–7 lb. 4 oz.
Bore/Gauge: 12
Capacity: 6, 8 shells
Features: A 3-Gun or ranch work pump with a good-looking walnut stock in traditional styling; heat shield; fixed Cylinder bore; matte blue metalwork
MSRP. . . . . $594.00–$609.00

590 SHOCKWAVE

Action: Pump
Stock: Synthetic
Barrel: 14 in.
Chokes: None
Weight: 5 lb. 4.8 oz.
Bore/Gauge: 12
Magazine: 6 shells
Features: Features unique Raptor pistol grip
MSRP. $500.00

590 SHOCKWAVE 7-SHOT

Action: Pump
Stock: Synthetic
Barrel: 18.5 in.
Chokes: None
Sights: Bead front
Weight: N/A
Bore/Gauge: 12
Capacity: 7 shells
Features: The Shockwave with a higher-capacity magazine tube; Raptor grip; sling; corncob fore-end
MSRP. $500.00

590 SHOCKWAVE 20-GAUGE

Action: Pump
Stock: Synthetic
Barrel: 14.375 in.
Chokes: None
Sights: Front bead
Weight: 4 lb. 14 oz.
Bore/Gauge: 20
Magazine: 6 shells
Features: Bird's head Raptor pistol grip; strapped forend for additional stability; no NFA paperwork needed
MSRP. $500.00

590 SHOCKWAVE FLAT DARK EARTH CERAKOTE

Action: Pump
Stock: Synthetic
Barrel: 14.375 in.
Chokes: None
Sights: Bead
Weight: 5 lb. 5 oz.
Bore/Gauge: 12
Magazine: 6 shells
Features: Flat Dark Earth Cerakote treatment; Raptor pistol grip; corn-cob forend; forend hand strap; barrel is Cylinder bore; no NFA paperwork needed
MSRP. $553.00

590 SHOCKWAVE JIC

Action: Pump
Stock: Synthetic
Barrel: 14.375 in.
Chokes: None
Sights: Bead
Weight: 5 lb. 5 oz.
Bore/Gauge: 12
Magazine: 6 shells
Features: Mossberg's Shockwave in the Just in Case package; water-resistant carry tube; non-reflective Cerakote Stainless finish on the metal
MSRP. $708.00

590 SHOCKWAVE LASER SADDLE

Action: Pump
Stock: Synthetic
Barrel: 14 in.
Chokes: None
Sights: Front bead
Weight: N/A
Bore/Gauge: 12, 20
Capacity: 6 shells
Features: The Shockwave with the addition of a Crimson Trace Laser Saddle; Raptor grip, sling; corncob fore-end
MSRP. $652.00

Mossberg (O. F. Mossberg & Sons)

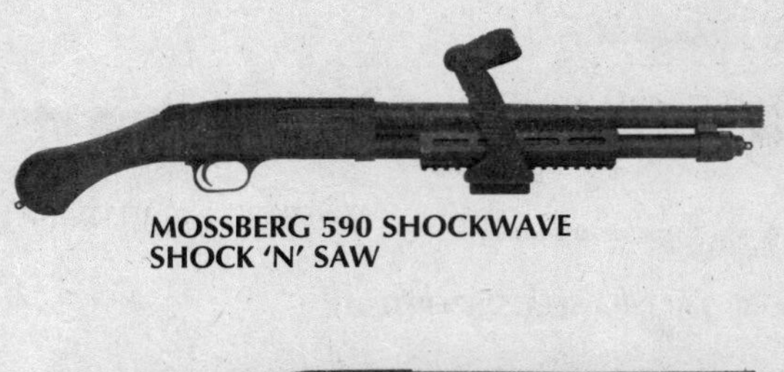

MOSSBERG 590 SHOCKWAVE SHOCK 'N' SAW

MOSSBERG 590 SHOCKWAVE SPX

MOSSBERG 590 SPX

MOSSBERG 590 TACTICAL 7-SHOT

MOSSBERG 5901A1 CLASS III PUMP-ACTION 6-SHOT

MOSSBERG 590 THUNDER RANCH

MOSSBERG 590A1 RETROGRADE

590 SHOCKWAVE SHOCK 'N' SAW

Action: Pump
Stock: Synthetic
Barrel: 14 in.
Chokes: None
Sights: Bead front
Weight: 6 lb.
Bore/Gauge: 12
Capacity: 6 shells
Features: This non-NFA (no ATF tax stamp required) shotgun features: fixed Cylinder choke barrel; Shockwave's polymer Raptor grip; aluminum MLOK fore-end with Mossberg's own Chainsaw grip; breacher muzzle; matte blue finish; chambers 3-inch shells
MSRP $613.00

590 SHOCKWAVE SPX

Action: Pump
Stock: Synthetic
Barrel: 14 in.
Chokes: None
Sights: Bead front
Weight: 5 lb. 12 oz.
Bore/Gauge: 12
Capacity: 6 shells
Features: This non-NFA (no ATF tax stamp required) shotgun features: fixed Cylinder choke barrel; Shockwave's polymer Raptor grip; corncob fore-end with strap; polymer seven-round side-saddle shell holder; heat shield; top-side Picatinny rail; matte blue finish; chambers 3-inch shells
MSRP $613.00

590 SPX

Action: Pump
Stock: Synthetic
Barrel: 18.5 in.
Chokes: None
Sights: Fiber optic front, ghost ring
Weight: 5 lb. 12 oz.–7 lb.
Bore/Gauge: 12
Capacity: 6 shells
Features: Lots of options with this scattergun thanks to its six-position Flex buttstock and Flex pistol grip; ghost ring rear sight paired with fiber optic front; topside Picatinny rail; forend hand strap
MSRP $802.00

590 TACTICAL 7-SHOT

Action: Pump
Stock: Synthetic
Barrel: 18.5 in.
Chokes: Cylinder
Weight: 5 lb. 12 oz.–6 lb. 12 oz.
Bore/Gauge: 12, 20, .410
Magazine: 7 shells
Features: Front bead sight; matte blue metal barrel with Heatshield; black synthetic stock; top-mounted safety for amidextrous operation; tri-rail forend
MSRP . . . . $500.00–$659.00

590 THUNDER RANCH

Action: Pump
Stock: Synthetic
Barrel: 18.5 in.
Chokes: None
Sights: Fiber optic front
Weight: 6 lb. 12 oz.
Bore/Gauge: 12
Capacity: 6 shells
Features: Dressed in Kuiu camo; muzzle sports a door breaching add-on; matte blue metalwork
MSRP $606.00

5901A1 CLASS III PUMP-ACTION 6-SHOT

Action: Pump
Stock: Synthetic
Barrel: 14 in.
Chokes: None
Sights: Bead, ghost ring
Weight: 6 lb. 12 oz.
Bore/Gauge: 12
Magazine: 6 shells
Features: fore-end with hand strap; Parkerized finish, 3-inch chamber; heavy-walled Cylinder barrel; Compact Synthetic has 13-in. length of pull and ghost ring sights; Parkerized finish; ghost ring sights; Plus-4 shell-holder stock
MSRP $783.00

590A1 RETROGRADE

Action: Pump
Stock: Walnut
Barrel: 20 in.
Chokes: None
Sights: Ghost ring
Weight: 7 lb 4 oz.
Bore/Gauge: 12
Capacity: 9 shells
Features: The sister companion to the 500 Persuader Retrograde, features on this MIL-SPEC pump include: Parkerized finish; metal trigger and safety button; heat shield; bayonet lug; full-length stock; corncob fore-end; heavy-wall barrel with Cylinder fixed choke
MSRP $987.00

Mossberg (O. F. Mossberg & Sons)

MOSSBERG 590M MAG-FED
MOSSBERG 590M SHOCKWAVE
MOSSBERG 835 ULTI-MAG
MOSSBERG 930 PRO SERIES SPORTING
MOSSBERG 930 HUNTING ALL PURPOSE FIELD
MOSSBERG 930, 935 MAGNUM PRO-SERIES WATERFOWL

590M MAGFED

Action: Pump
Stock: Synthetic
Barrel: 18.5 in.
Chokes: none; Accu-Choke
Sights: Bead; ghost ring
Weight: 7 lb. 12 oz.–8 lb.
Bore/Gauge: 12
Magazine: 10 shells
Features: Detachable double-stack magazine; magazine tube is inactive and serves as support for the pumping action of the fore-end and rails; basic version gets a fixed Cylinder bore with a front bead; heat-shield option gets heat shield, ghost ring sights, a Cylinder Accu-Choke only
Standard:.............. $599.00
Heat shield:............ $682.00

590M SHOCKWAVE

Action: Pump
Stock: Synthetic
Barrel: 15 in.
Chokes: None
Sights: Bead front
Weight: 6 lb. 8 oz.
Bore/Gauge: 12
Capacity: 11 shells
Features: This non-NFA (no ATF tax stamp required) shotgun features: fixed Cylinder choke barrel; Shockwave's polymer Raptor grip; corncob fore-end with strap; increased 11-round overall capacity with a 10-round double-stack removeable magazine; drilled and tapped for optics; chambers 3-inch shells
MSRP................. $599.00

835 ULTI-MAG

Action: Pump
Stock: Synthetic
Barrel: 20 in., 24 in., 28 in.
Chokes: Ulti-full tube chokes, Accu-Mag Set, or Modified Tube
Weight: 7 lb. 8 oz.–7 lb. 12 oz.
Bore/Gauge: 12
Magazine: 5 shells
Features: Features 3 ½-inch chambers; dual extractors; over-bored and ported barrels. Variations include Turkey/Waterfowl combo in MO Break-Up Country, fiber optic front sight; Turkey/Deer combo with dual combs, Ulti- Full barrel/fully rifled barrel with cantilever scope base in MO Break-Up Country; Field/Deer combo with wood stock, 28-inch vent rib/24-in. rifled barrel adjustable rifle sights; Turkey with Marble Arms Bullseye fiber optic sights, Ulti-Full choke, MO Obsession; Waterfowl with Accu-Set chokes, fiber optic front sight, MO Shadow Grass Blades; Tactical Turkey with six-position adjustable stock, fiber optic front sight, and full-coverage MO Obsession; All-Purpose Field with Accu-Mag chokes, X-Factor ported turkey choke, MO New Bottomland
All-Purpose Field Camo: . . .$568.00
Combo Field/Deer: $540.00
Combo Turkey/Deer:. $624.00
Combo Turkey/Waterfowl: . . .$624.00
Tactical Turkey: $714.00
Waterfowl:. $568.00
Turkey with Marble Arms sights: $594.00

930 HUNTING ALL PURPOSE FIELD

Action: Semiautomatic
Stock: Synthetic; walnut
Barrel: 28 in.
Chokes: Accu-Set (F, M, IC)
Sights: Fiber optic
Weight: 7 lb. 8 oz.–7 lb. 12 oz.
Bore/Gauge: 12
Magazine: 5 shells
Features: Black-stocked version with a 28-in. vent rib barrel; full-coverage Mossy Oak Bottomland shooter with a 26-in. vent rib barrel, plus a ported XX-Full Turkey X-Factor tube; sling swivel studs; drilled and tapped for optics mounting
Walnut: $766.00
Synthetic: $613.00

930 PRO SERIES SPORTING

Action: Semiautomatic
Stock: Walnut
Barrel: 28 in.
Chokes: 3 chokes (F, M, IC)
Weight: 7 lb. 12 oz.
Bore/Gauge: 12
Magazine: 5 shells
Features: Chambered in 2 ¾ in. and 3 in.; engraved Cerakote receiver; beveled loading gate; Briley extended chokes; vented rib ported barrel; boron nitride-coated gas piston, piston rings, magazine tube, hammer, and sear prevents corrosion and facilitates cleaning
MSRP. $1162.00

930, 935 MAGNUM PRO-SERIES WATERFOWL

Action: Semiautomatic
Stock: Synthetic
Barrel: 28 in.
Chokes: 3 chokes (F, M, IC)
Weight: 7 lb. 12 oz.
Bore/Gauge: 12
Magazine: 5 shells
Features: Synthetic stock covered in Mossy Oak Shadowgrass Blades; overbored vent rib barrel; Stock Drop System; 930 model has 3-in. chamber, 935 has 3.5-in chamber
930: $844.00
935: $958.00

Mossberg (O. F. Mossberg & Sons)

MOSSBERG 930 TACTICAL 8 SHOT

MOSSBERG 935 MAGNUM TURKEY

MOSSBERG MAVERICK 88 ALL-PURPOSE

MOSSBERG 930 THUNDER RANCH

MOSSBERG 940 JM PRO

MOSSBERG MAVERICK 88 CRUISER 6-SHOT, 8-SHOT

MOSSBERG MAVERICK 88-SECURITY WITH TOP FOLDING STOCK

930 TACTICAL 8-SHOT

Action: Semiautomatic
Stock: Synthetic
Barrel: 18.5 in.
Chokes: None
Weight: 6 lb. 12 oz.
Bore/Gauge: 12
Magazine: 8 shells
Features: The popular 930 tactical autoloader gets an extended eight-shot magazine
MSRP $671.00

930 THUNDER RANCH

Action: Semiautomatic
Stock: Synthetic
Barrel: 18.5 in.
Chokes: None
Sights: Fiber optic front
Weight: 6 lb. 12 oz.
Bore/Gauge: 12
Capacity: 5 shells
Features: Self-defense gun with a door-breeching muzzle accessory; Kuiu camo stock; matte blue metalwork; Cylinder bore
MSRP $766.00

935 MAGNUM TURKEY

Action: Semiautomatic
Stock: Synthetic
Barrel: 22 in.
Chokes: Vent rib. overbored
Weight: 7 lb. 8 oz.
Bore/Gauge: 12
Magazine: 5 shells
Features: Chambers 3 1/2-inch shells; over-bored barrels; dual vent system; Quick Empty magazine release button; stock spacer system; drilled and tapped receivers; X-Factor choke; adjustable fiber optic sights; standard stock option in MO Bottomland or pistol grip stock in MO Obsession
Standard stock: $829.00
Pistol-grip stock: $1012.00

940 JM PRO

Action: Semiautomatic
Stock: Synthetic
Barrel: 24 in.
Chokes: 3 (C, IC, M)
Sights: HiViz TriComp
Weight: 7 lb. 12 oz.
Bore/Gauge: 12
Capacity: 10 shells
Features: One for the 3-Gun crowd, developed by Jerry and Lena Miculek; newly designed gas system that cycles a wide variety of 2¾- and 3-in. shells reliably; loading port designed to quad-load the magazine tube; adjustable stock; interchangeable light tube HiViz sights; Briley extended chokes; base model in black stock, matte blue barrel, tungsten gray anodized receiver, and gold-highlighted parts accents
MSRP $1078.00

MAVERICK 88 ALL-PURPOSE

Action: Pump
Stock: Synthetic
Barrel: 26 in., 28 in.
Chokes: Modified
Sights: Bead front
Weight: 7 lb.
Bore/Gauge: 20, 12
Capacity: 5 shells
Features: Simple pump has vent rib; stock in Mossy Oak Treestand; 3-inch chamber; 28-in. barrel on 12 ga., 26-in. barrel on 20 ga.
MSRP . . . . $245.00–$274.00

MAVERICK 88 CRUISER 6-SHOT, 8-SHOT

Action: Pump
Stock: Synthetic
Barrel: 18.5 in.
Chokes: None
Sights: Bead front
Weight: 5 lb. 8 oz.–5 lb. 12 oz.
Bore/Gauge: 20, 12
Capacity: 5, 7 shells
Features: Pistol grip pump with a 5+1 or 7+1 capacity; fixed Cylinder bore
MSRP $245.00

MAVERICK 88-SECURITY WITH TOP FOLDING STOCK

Action: Pump
Stock: Glass-reinforced polymer
Barrel: 18.5 in.
Chokes: None
Sights: Bead
Weight: 6 lb.
Bore/Gauge: 12
Magazine: 6 shells
Features: Top-folding stock by Advanced Technology International; chambers 3-in. rounds
MSRP $274.00

Mossberg (O. F. Mossberg & Sons)

MOSSBERG MAVERICK 88 YOUTH ALL-PURPOSE

MOSSBERG SA-20 ALL-PURPOSE FIELD

MOSSBERG SA-20 YOUTH BANTAM WALNUT, SYNTHETIC

MOSSBERG INTERNATIONAL SA-28 ALL-PURPOSE FIELD

MOSSBERG SA-28 YOUTH BANTAM WALNUT, SYNTHETIC

MOSSBERG SA-410 FIELD

MOSSBERG SA-410 TURKEY

MAVERICK 88 YOUTH ALL-PURPOSE

Action: Pump
Stock: Synthetic
Barrel: 22 in.
Chokes: Modified
Sights: Bead front
Weight: 5 lb. 4 oz.
Bore/Gauge: 20
Capacity: 5 shells
Features: A great pump for new youth shooters with a shorter length of pull and barrel; stock in Mossy Oak Treestand
MSRP $274.00

SA-20 ALL-PURPOSE FIELD

Action: Semiautomatic
Stock: Walnut, synthetic
Barrel: 26 in.
Chokes: 5 chokes (C, IC, M, IM, F)
Weight: 5 lb. 12 oz.
Bore/Gauge: 20
Magazine: 5 shells
Features: Smooth cycling gas-operated system; bead sight; blue finish on barrel; available in walnut or synthetic stocked All-Purpose Field, pink Muddy Girl synthetic stock, a Turkey version in Mossy Oak Obsession, railed versions with and without pistol grips in black synthetic stock, and in a 13-in. length of pull Youth Bantam version with a black synthetic stock
Walnut: $717.00
Synthetic: $624.00

SA-20 YOUTH BANTAM WALNUT, SYNTHETIC

Action: Semiautomatic
Stock: Walnut, synthetic
Barrel: 24 in.
Chokes: Five tubes (F, IM, M, IC, C)
Sights: Bead
Weight: 5 lb. 8 oz. (synthetic), 6 lb. 4 oz. (walnut)
Bore/Gauge: 20
Magazine: 5 shells
Features: Easy recoiling, semiautomatic youth shotgun with shortened stock and barrel; chambers 3-in. shells; synthetic stock has metal with a matte blue finish; high-gloss walnut stock has polished blue metalwork
Walnut: $717.00
Synthetic: $624.00

SA-28 ALL-PURPOSE FIELD

Action: Semiautomatic
Stock: Walnut
Barrel: 26 in.
Chokes: Sport Set
Weight: 6 lb. 8 oz.
Bore/Gauge: 28
Magazine: 5 shells
Features: Lightweight field gun in 2¾-in.; front bead; high-polish blue metal; high-gloss walnut stock
MSRP $717.00

SA-28 YOUTH BANTAM ALL-PURPOSE FIELD

Action: Semiautomatic
Stock: Synthetic
Barrel: 24 in.
Chokes: Five tubes (F, IM, M, IC, C)
Sights: Bead
Weight: 5 lb. 8 oz.
Bore/Gauge: 28
Magazine: 5 shells
Features: Easy recoiling, semiautomatic youth shotgun with shortened stock and barrel; chambers 2¾-inch shells
MSRP: $624.00

SA-410 FIELD

Action: Semiautomatic
Stock: Synthetic
Barrel: 26 in.
Chokes: Sport set
Sights: Bead front
Weight: 6 lb. 8 oz.
Bore/Gauge: .410
Capacity: 4 shells
Features: A reliably functioning semiauto in .410-bore with a 3-in. chamber; gas-operation
MSRP $655.00

SA-410 TURKEY

Action: Semiautomatic
Stock: Synthetic
Barrel: 26 in.
Chokes: XX-Full turkey
Sights: FO ghost ring
Weight: 6 lb. 8 oz.
Bore/Gauge: .410
Capacity: 4 shells
Features: Same as the Field SA-410, but in full-coverage Mossy Oak Bottomland camo; FO ghost ring sights
MSRP $781.00

Nighthawk Custom

NIGHTHAWK OVERSEER MODEL 3

OVERSEER

Action: Pump
Stock: Synthetic
Barrel: 18 in.
Chokes: None
Sights: Fiber optic front
Weight: N/A
Bore/Gauge: 12
Capacity: 6 shells
Features: Based on a Remington 870 action, the standard-package Model 1 includes hand-honed action and rails, Nighthawk tactical ghost ring rear sight with a fiber optic rear, Picatinny receiver mount, six-round side saddle; Hogue overmolded stock and fore-end, and a black Cerakote finish on the metalwork; Model 2 adds an SGA Magpul fore-end and stock with adapter plates; Model 2.5 builds on Model 2 by adding a Vang Comp System barrel porting; Model 3 builds on Model 2 with a custom Shadow Tan finish on stock and fore-end; Model 4 builds on Model 2 with a custom Shadow Urban camo stock and fore-end, a Surefire Z2X combat light, a barrel clamp with swivel, and a Picatinny rail; Model 5 builds on Model 2 with a custom Battle-Worn Silver Patriot overall finish; Model 6 builds on Model 1 with a collapsible stock, Hogue pistol grip, SureFire DSF870 fore-end, ambidextrous and selectable light switch, three-shot mag extension, and breeching device
MSRP . . . . $1499.00–$2199.00

Perazzi

PERAZZI HIGH TECH

PERAZZI MX8 SPORTING CLAYS

HIGH TECH

Action: Over/under
Stock: Wood
Barrel: 27–31 in.
Chokes: Can be specified or made interchangeable
Weight: N/A
Bore/Gauge: 12
Magazine: 2 shells
Features:High Tech has a sporty and futuristic look; a large logo engraved in black smoke color on both sides of the receiver, under clear varnish, in contrast to the rest of the receiver; hinge pins are engraved with a checkered design; action is two-tone and varnished "in the white" only in the areas where the logo appears; frame has a greater weight than other Perazzi models and it is distributed within the median line between the grip of the hands, which both improves the fluidity of handling and further reduces recoil; divergent rib that goes from 7mm wide at the action to 10mm at the front end of the barrels allows you to greatly speed up your perception of the target and also expands your field of vision.
MSRP . . . Contact retailers for pricing

MX8 SPORTING CLAYS

Action: Over/under
Stock: Walnut
Barrel: 29 in., 30 in., 31 in.
Chokes: Interchangeable chokes
Weight: 7 lb. 5 oz.
Bore/Gauge: 12, 20
Magazine: 2 shells
Features: Custom walnut stock with beavertail forend; half-ventilated side ribs on barrel; removable trigger with flat or coil springs; blue or nickel plating; Sporting, Skeet and Trap models; 28 Ga. and .410 models also available
MSRP . . . . Contact retailers for pricing

Retay USA

RETAY USA GORDION UPLAND

GORDION UPLAND

Action: Semiautomatic
Stock: Turkish walnut
Barrel: 26 in., 28 in.
Chokes: 5 (IC, SK, M, IM, F)
Sights: TruGlo red front
Weight: N/A
Bore/Gauge: 12
Capacity: 4 shells
Features: Reasonably priced semiauto for upland bird work or clay games; Inertia-Plus bolt system; Mara bolt; hard case included
MSRP $899.00

Retay USA

RETAY USA GORDION WATERFOWL

RETAY USA MASAI MARA AIR KING WATERFOWL

RETAY USA MASAI MARA UPLAND

RETAY USA MASAI MARA WARDEN

GORDION WATERFOWL, TURKEY, TURKEY XT SMALL TOWN HUNTING

Action: Semiautomatic
Stock: Synthetic
Barrel: 22 in., 24 in., 26 in., 28 in.
Chokes: 5 (F, IM, M, IC, C), 6
Sights: TruGlo red front
Weight: N/A
Bore/Gauge: 12
Capacity: 4 shells
Features: Feature-loaded hunting guns with a Mara (Upland) or MaraPro (Turkey) barrel; oversized control; quick-unload design; Inertia Plus bolt system
Upland: . . . . $799.000–$899.00
Turkey:. $925.00
Turkey XT Small Town Hunting:. $1225.00

MASAI MARA AIR KING WATERFOWL

Action: Semiautomatic
Stock: Synthetic
Barrel: 26 in., 28 in.
Chokes: 5 (IC, SK, M, IM, F)
Sights: TruGlo red front
Weight: N/A
Bore/Gauge: 12
Capacity: 4 shells
Features: Waterfowler series; camo-covered or solid stocks and Cerakoted barrels and receivers; 3.5-in. chamber; MaraPro barrel; oversized controls; hard case included
MSRP $1600.00

MASAI MARA UPLAND

Action: Semiautomatic
Stock: Turkish walnut
Barrel: 24 in., 26 in., 28 in., 30 in.
Chokes: 5 (IC, SK, M, IM, F)
Sights: TruGlo red front
Weight: N/A
Bore/Gauge: 20, 12
Capacity: 4 shells
Features: An inertia-driven semiauto supplied with a MaraPro barrel, choice of Grade 2 or 4 Turkish walnut, in five receiver configurations
Grade 2 walnut stock: . . . . $1250.00–$1299.00
Grade 4 walnut stock: . . . . $1850.00–$2100.00

MASAI MARA WARDEN

Action: Semiautomatic
Stock: Synthetic
Barrel: 18.5 in.
Chokes: 5 (IC, SK, M, IM, F)
Sights: Blade front, ghost ring rear
Weight: N/A
Bore/Gauge: 12
Capacity: 4 shells
Features: Wearing a matte black anodized receiver and matte black chrome barrel, this handy tactical shotgun has a topside optics rail; 3-in. chamber; sling swivel studs; oversized controls; hard case
MSRP $1099.00

Savage Arms

SAVAGE ARMS 220 SLUG GUN

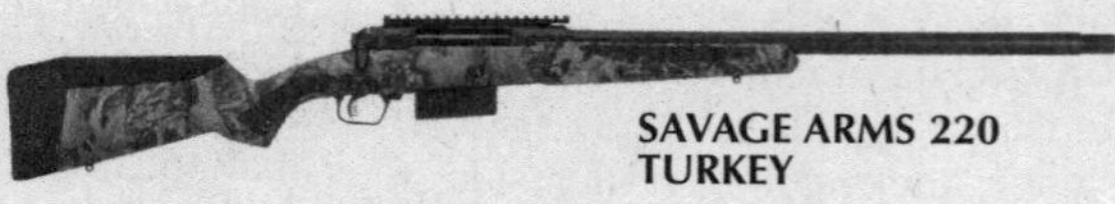

SAVAGE ARMS 220 TURKEY

220 SLUG GUN

Action: Bolt
Stock: Synthetic
Barrel: 22 in.
Sights: None
Weight: 7 lb. 8 oz.
Caliber: 20
Magazine: 2 shells
Features: Detachable box magazine; AccuTrigger; button-rifled barrels; left-hand in black synthetic stock and matte black metalwork; right-hand version in Mossy Oak Break-Up stock and matte stainless metalwork or Mossy Oak Break-Up Infinity with matte black metalwork
Black:. $655.00
Camo/black: $725.00
Camo/stainless: $835.00

220 TURKEY

Action: Bolt
Stock: Synthetic
Barrel: 22 in.
Chokes: Extra-full turkey
Sights: None
Weight: 7 lb.
Bore/Gauge: 20
Capacity: 3 shells
Features: A dedicated turkey gun on a bolt-action platform; Winchester-thread for chokes; adjustable AccuFit stock in Mossy Oak Obsession; matte black metal; topside optics rail; detachable two-round box magazine
MSRP $725.00

SHOTGUNS

Savage Arms

SAVAGE RENEGAUGE FIELD

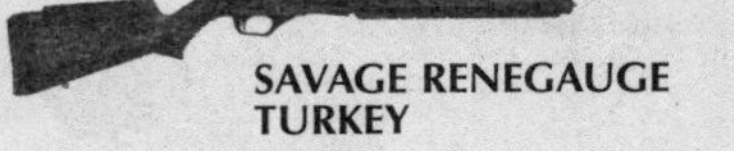
SAVAGE RENEGAUGE TURKEY

SAVAGE RENEGAUGE WATERFOWL

SAVAGE ARMS STEVENS 301 SINGLE-SHOT

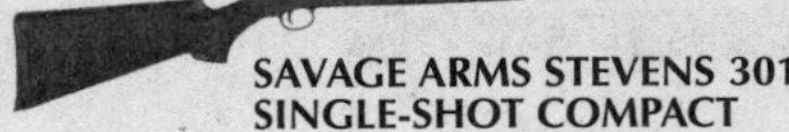
SAVAGE ARMS STEVENS 301 SINGLE-SHOT COMPACT

SAVAGE ARMS STEVENS 301 TURKEY

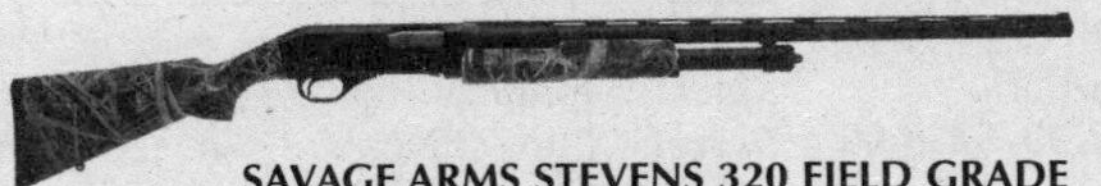
SAVAGE ARMS STEVENS 320 FIELD GRADE

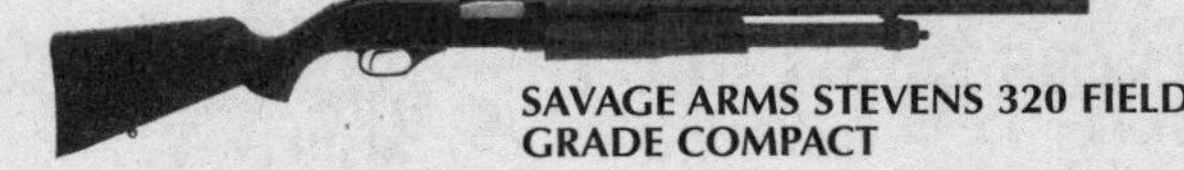
SAVAGE ARMS STEVENS 320 FIELD GRADE COMPACT

RENEGAUGE FIELD

Action: Semiautomatic
Stock: Synthetic
Barrel: 26 in., 28 in.
Chokes: 3 (IC, M, F)
Sights: Front fiber optic
Weight: 7 lb. 13.6 oz.–7 lb. 14.4 oz.
Bore/Gauge: 12
Capacity: 4 shells
Features: The first semiautomatic shotgun produced by Savage and featuring the new DRIV (Dual Regulating Inline Valve) system that speeds cycling while minimizing recoil across a spectrum of payloads; fluted vent-rib barrel with red fiber optic front sight; easy-load ejection port; oversized bolt handle and safety
MSRP $1489.00

RENEGAUGE TURKEY

Action: Semiautomatic
Stock: Synthetic
Barrel: 24 in.
Chokes: 4 (XF, IC, M, F)
Sights: Front fiber optic
Weight: 7 lb. 12 oz.
Bore/Gauge: 12
Capacity: 4 shells
Features: Similar to the Field but with a shorter barrel for tom hunting; Beretta/Benelli chokes; choice of Mossy Oak Bottomland or Obsession full-coverage camo
MSRP $1599.00

RENEGAUGE WATERFOWL

Action: Semiautomatic
Stock: Synthetic
Barrel: 26 in., 28 in.
Chokes: 3 (IC, M, F)
Sights: Front fiber optic
Weight: 7 lb. 13.6 oz.–7 lb. 14 oz.
Bore/Gauge: 12
Capacity: 4 shells
Features: Similar to the Field but in full-coverage Mossy Oak Shadow Grass Blades camo; melonite finish on barrel; Beretta/Benelli chokes
MSRP $1599.00

STEVENS 301 SINGLE-SHOT

Action: Single-shot
Stock: Synthetic
Barrel: 26 in. (12-ga.); 22, 24 in. (20-ga.); 22, 26 in. (.410-bore)
Chokes: None
Sights: Front bead
Weight: N/A
Bore/Gauge: 12, 20, .410
Magazine: 1 shell
Features: Break-action single-shot with a receiver-side safety; synthetic stock; carbon steel barrel
MSRP $189.00

STEVENS 301 SINGLE-SHOT COMPACT

Action: Single-shot
Stock: Synthetic
Barrel: 22 in. (Compact); 26 in. (Standard)
Chokes: Interchangeable
Sights: Bead
Weight: 5 lb. 4 oz. (Compact); 5 lb. 8 oz. (Standard)
Bore/Gauge: 12, 20, .410
Magazine: 1 shell
Features: Interchangeable chokes; two-position safety; 3-in. chambers; compact available only in the 20 ga. and .410-bore
MSRP $189.00

STEVENS 301 TURKEY

Action: Single-shot
Stock: Synthetic
Barrel: 26 in.
Chokes: Extra-full
Sights: Bead front, rear rail
Weight: 5 lb.
Bore/Gauge: 20, .410
Capacity: 1 shell
Features: Designed to be optimized in barrel length for Federal's HEAVYWEIGHT TSS turkey loads; available in Mossy Oak Bottomland or Obsession; sling swivel studs; removeable front sight can be replaced with TruGlo fiber optics; 3-inch chamber
MSRP $209.00

STEVENS 320 FIELD GRADE

Action: Pump
Stock: Synthetic
Barrel: 26 in., 28 in.
Chokes: M
Weight: 6 lb. 15.2 oz.–7 lb. 7.2 oz.
Bore/Gauge: 12, 20
Magazine: 5 shells
Features: Base model has black synthetic stock; camo options in MO Shadow Grass or Obsession and matte blue metalwork, mid-length fore-end and fiber-optic front sight;
Black: $259.00
Camo: . . . . $299.00–$309.00

STEVENS 320 FIELD GRADE COMPACT

Action: Pump
Stock: Synthetic
Barrel: 22 in.
Chokes: N/A
Weight: 7 lb.
Bore/Gauge: 20
Magazine: 2 shells
Features: Carbon steel barrel; compact size and light recoil make it the ideal shotgun for introducing young people to the shooting sports; in all-black, MO Shadow Grass Blades, or Muddy Girl camo
Black: $259.00
Camo: $299.00

Savage Arms

SAVAGE ARMS STEVENS 320 SECURITY

SAVAGE ARMS STEVENS 555

SAVAGE ARMS STEVENS 555 ENHANCED

STEVENS 320 SECURITY

Action: Pump
Stock: Synthetic
Barrel: 18.5 in.
Chokes: M
Weight: 6 lb. 13.6 oz.–7lb.
Bore/Gauge: 12, 20
Magazine: 5 shells
Features: Intended for home and personal defense, five versions available: heat shield with top-side optics rail; ghost ring with pistol grip stock; ergonomic stock with bead sight; ergonomic stock with ghost ring sights; bead sight and pistol grip
MSRP: . . . . $259.00–$299.00

STEVENS 555

Action: Over/under
Stock: Wood
Barrel: 28 in.
Chokes: 5 interchangeable chokes
Weight: 6 lb.
Bore/Gauge: 12, 20, 16, 28, .410
Magazine: 2 shells
Features: Lightweight alloy receiver, Turkish walnut stock & forearm, single selective trigger, mechanical triggers, extractors, manual safetys
MSRP $709.00

STEVENS 555 ENHANCED

Action: Over/under
Stock: Walnut
Barrel: 28 in. (12-ga.); 26 in. (20- and 28-ga, .410)
Chokes: SK, IC, M, IM, F
Weight: 5 lb. 8 oz.–6 lb.
Bore/Gauge: 12, 20, 16, 28, .410
Magazine: 2 shells
Features: Lightweight aluminum receiver is scaled to gauge; imperial walnut stock; automatic shell ejectors; laser-engraved filigree decoration on the receiver
MSRP $859.00

SRM Arms

SRM ARMS MODEL 1216

MODEL 1216

Action: Semiautomatic
Stock: Synthetic
Barrel: 18 in.
Chokes: N/A
Weight: 7 lb. 4 oz.
Bore/Gauge: 12
Magazine: 16 shells
Features: Picatinny rail combined with a three face handguard rail; ambidextrous receiver and controls; quad-tube, revolving detachable magazine
MSRP $1799.00

Standard Manufacturing Co.

STANDARD MANUFACTURING CO. SKO MINI

STANDARD MANUFACTURING CO. SKO MINI WORKS PACKAGE

SKO MINI

Action: Semiautomatic
Stock: Polymer, composite
Barrel: 14.75 in.
Chokes: N/A
Sights: None
Weight: 7 lb. 2 oz.
Bore/Gauge: 12
Capacity: 2, 5, 10 shells
Features: Overall length 27 inches; internal parts salt bath nitride coated; gas-operation; ready for user to add optics, accessories, and chokes, including specialty chokes such as breaking types; accepts most AR-type grips; 3-inch chamber
MSRP $750.00

SKO MINI WORKS PACKAGE

Action: Semiautomatic
Stock: Polymer, composite
Barrel: 14.75 in.
Chokes: One
Sights: Flip-up AR-style, reflex red dot
Weight: 7 lb. 2 oz.
Bore/Gauge: 12
Capacity: 2, 5, 10 shells
Features: An NFA "other" firearm featuring a 3-inch chamber; gas operation; aluminum receiver; composite fore-end with MOE slots; vertical forward grip; Tru-Choke threading; aluminum tactical grip
MSRP $1200.00

Stoeger Industries

STOEGER COACH GUN

STOEGER CONDOR

STOEGER CONDOR OUTBACK

STOEGER CONDOR COMPETITION

STOEGER DOUBLE DEFENSE

STOEGER DOUBLE DEFENSE OVER/UNDER

STOEGER M3000

STOEGER M3K 3-GUN

COACH GUN

Action: Side-by-side
Stock: Walnut, hardwood
Barrel: 20 in.
Chokes: Fixed chokes (IC, M)
Weight: 6 lb. 5 oz.–7 lb.
Bore/Gauge: 12, 20, .410
Magazine: 2 shells
Features: A-grade satin or black finished hardwood stock; brass bead sights; nickel or blued metal finish
MSRP . . . . $449.00–$549.00

CONDOR

Action: Over/under
Stock: Walnut
Barrel: 22 in., 24 in., 26 in., 28 in.
Chokes: Screw-in and fixed chokes on 12 Ga., 20 Ga., 28 Ga. (IC, M), 16 Ga. (M, F), .410 (F&F)
Weight: 5 lb. 8 oz.–7 lb. 6 oz.
Bore/Gauge: 12, 16, 20, 28, .410
Magazine: 2 shells
Features: Walnut stock; brass bead sight; single trigger; auto-ejectors
Field: . . . . $349.00–$449.00
Field 12-/20-Ga. Combo: . . . $649.00
Youth: $449.00
Skeet: $449.00
Supreme: $619.00
Longfowler: $449.00

CONDOR COMPETITION

Action: Over/under
Stock: Walnut
Barrel: 30 in.
Chokes: Screw-in (IC, M, F)
Weight: 7 lb. 5 oz.–7 lb. 13 oz.
Bore/Gauge: 12, 20
Magazine: 2 shells
Features: Walnut stock; brass bead with silver mid-bead sight; single selective trigger; automatic ejector; ported barrel
MSRP $669.00

CONDOR OUTBACK

Action: Over/under
Stock: Walnut, hardwood
Barrel: 20 in.
Chokes: Screw-in (IC, M)
Weight: 6 lb. 8 oz.–7 lb.
Bore/Gauge: 12, 20
Magazine: 2 shells
Features: Notched rear sight and fixed blade front sight; shell extractor; single trigger; A-grade satin walnut or black finished hardwood
MSRP . . . . $449.00–$499.00

DOUBLE DEFENSE OVER/ UNDER

Action: Over/under
Stock: Hardwood
Barrel: 20 in.
Chokes: Screw-in chokes (IC/IC fixed)
Weight: 6 lb. 3 oz.–6 lb. 8 oz.
Bore/Gauge: 12, 20
Magazine: 2 shells
Features: Black hardwood stock; green fiber optic front sight; ported barrels; two Picatinny rails; single trigger design; tang-mounted automatic safety
MSRP $449.00

DOUBLE DEFENSE SIDE-BY-SIDE

Action: Side-by-side
Stock: Hardwood
Barrel: 20 in.
Chokes: Screw-in chokes (IC/IC fixed)
Weight: 6 lb. 8 oz.
Bore/Gauge: 12, 20
Magazine: 2 shells
Features: Black hardwood stock; fiber optic front sight; ported barrels; two Picatinny rails; single trigger design; tang-mounted automatic safety
MSRP $489.00

M3K 3-GUN, FREEDOM SERIES 3-GUN

Action: Semiautomatic, inertia-driven
Stock: Synthetic
Barrel: 24 in.
Chokes: XC, IC, M
Weight: 7 lb. 5 oz.
Bore/Gauge: 12
Magazine: 4+1
Features: Fiber optic sights; based on the M3000 line of shotguns; 3-gun ready; oversized anodized aluminum bolt release, oversized safety, and extended tactical-style anodized aluminum bolt handle; elongated carrier and enlarged, beveled loading port for quicker and easier reloading
MSRP . . . . $669.00–$699.00

M3000

Action: Semiautomatic
Stock: Black synthetic, Realtree APG, Realtree APG SteadyGrip, Realtree Max-5
Barrel: 24 in.
Chokes: IC, M, XFT, wrench
Weight: 7 lb. 5 oz.
Bore/ Gauge: 12
Magazine: 4+1 shells
Features: Inertia driven; red-bar front sight; drilled and tapped; shim kit; 3-in. loads; available with stocks in A-grade satin walnut, black synthetic, Mossy Oak Bottomland or Realtree Max-5, all with blue metalwork
MSRP . . . . $559.00–$619.00

Stoeger Industries

STOEGER M3000 DEFENSE

STOEGER INDUSTRIES M3000 FREEDOM SERIES DEFENSE SHOTGUN

STOEGER M3000 SPORTING

STOEGER M3000 WALNUT/ BURNT BRONZE

STOEGER M3020 WALNUT/ BURNT BRONZE

STOEGER INDUSTRIES M3020 DEFENSE SHOTGUN 20-GAUGE

STOEGER INDUSTRIES M3020 UPLAND SPECIAL

M3000 DEFENSE

Action: Semiautomatic
Stock: Synthetic
Barrel: 18.5 in.
Chokes: Cylinder fixed
Weight: 7 lb.
Bore/Gauge: 12
Magazine: 4 shells
Features: 3-in. chamber; blade front sight; field or pistol grip stock
Pistol grip:. $619.00
Standard:. $559.00

M3000 FREEDOM SERIES DEFENSE

Action: Semiautomatic
Stock: Synthetic
Barrel: 18.5 in.
Chokes: None
Sights: Blade front sight
Weight: 6 lb. 10 oz.–7 lb.
Bore/Gauge: 12
Magazine: 7 shells
Features: A super self-defense shotgun with a seven-round magazine, blade front sight, fixed Cylinder choke. Includes a stock shim kit included. Available with a pistol grip stock.
MSRP $619.00
Pistol grip: $669.00

M3000 SPORTING

Action: Semiautomatic
Stock: Synthetic
Barrel: 30 in.
Chokes: SK1, SK2, IC
Weight: 7 lb. 8 oz.
Bore/Gauge: 12
Magazine: 4 shells
Features: Built for clay game competition; 3-in. chamber; fiber optic front sight; extended choke tubes
MSRP $669.00

M3000 WALNUT/BURNT BRONZE

Action: Semiautomatic
Stock: Walnut
Barrel: 28 in.
Chokes: Three
Sights: Red bar front
Weight: 7 lb. 6 oz.
Bore/Gauge: 12
Capacity: 4 shells
Features: Inertia Driven semiauto in a 3-inch 12-gauge; satin-finished walnut stock paired with Burnt Bronze Cerakote metalwork; also available with a Realtree Max-5 stock; stepped vent rib; drilled and tapped
MSRP $649.00

M3020 DEFENSE SHOTGUN 20-GAUGE

Action: Semiautomatic
Stock: Synthetic
Barrel: 18.5 in.
Chokes: None
Sights: Ghost ring sights
Weight: 5 lb. 8 oz.
Bore/Gauge: 20
Magazine: 4 shells
Features: Self-defense shotgun; fixed Cylinder choke; ghost ring sights; chambers 3-in. shells
MSRP $619.00

M3020 UPLAND SPECIAL

Action: Semiautomatic
Stock: Walnut
Barrel: 26 in.
Chokes: 3 (M, F, C)
Sights: Red bar front
Weight: 5 lb. 7 oz.
Bore/Gauge: 20
Capacity: 4 shells
Features: Nice upland semiauto with an anodized silver receiver; gloss-finished walnut stock; extended chokes; 3-in. chamber; Inertia-Driven system
MSRP $649.00

M3020 WALNUT/BURNT BRONZE

Action: Semiautomatic
Stock: Walnut
Barrel: 28 in.
Chokes: Three
Sights: Red bar front
Weight: 5 lb. 12 oz.
Bore/Gauge: 20
Capacity: 4 shells
Features: Who says you have to pay big bucks for today's upgraded finishes? Stoeger adds Burnt Bronze Cerakote metalwork to a satin-finished walnut stock, all within a working man's budget
MSRP $649.00

Stoeger Industries

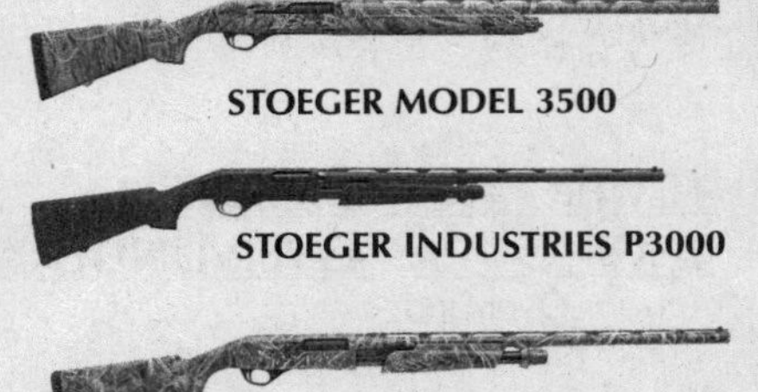

STOEGER MODEL 3500

STOEGER INDUSTRIES P3000

STOEGER P3500

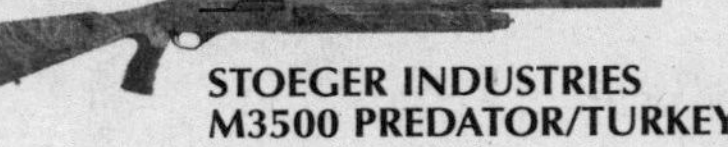

STOEGER INDUSTRIES M3500 PREDATOR/TURKEY

STOEGER P3000 DEFENSE

STOEGER UPLANDER

STOEGER M3500 WATERFOWL

STOEGER INDUSTRIES P3000 FREEDOM SERIES DEFENSE

STOEGER THE GRAND

M3500

Action: Semiautomatic
Stock: Synthetic
Barrel: 24 in., 26 in., 28 in.
Chokes: Screw-in choke tubes (C, IC, M, F, XFT) and wrench
Weight: 7 lb. 7 oz.–7 lb. 10 oz.
Bore/Gauge: 12
Magazine: 4+1 shells
Features: Synthetic stock comes in black or camo finish in Realtree Max-5 or Mossy Oak Bottomland; one Mossy Oak Bottomland version offered with Burnt Bronze Cerakote metalwork; satin walnut stock version available; inertia drive system; recoil reducer; red-bar front sight; Weaver scope base; includes shim kit
Black synthetic: $669.00
Camo or walnut stock: $769.00
Camo with Cerakote: $799.00

M3500 PREDATOR/TURKEY

Action: Semiautomatic
Stock: Synthetic
Barrel: 24 in.
Chokes: 5 (Predator, Turkey, M, IC, C)
Sights: Red bar front
Weight: 7 lb. 8 oz.
Bore/Gauge: 12
Capacity: 4 shells
Features: With a short, maneuverable barrel, this is a great choice for turkeys or coyotes, especially given it has enough weight to suck up some of the recoil from bigger 3-in. loads; drilled and tapped for optics mounting; full-coverage Mossy Oak Overwatch camo; pistol grip stock
MSRP $929.00

M3500 WATERFOWL

Action: Semiautomatic
Stock: Synthetic
Barrel: 28 in.
Chokes: Five
Sights: Red bar front
Weight: 7 lb. 13 oz.
Bore/Gauge: 12
Capacity: 4 shells
Features: Dressed in Realtree Max-5 on the stock and Flat Dark Earth metalwork, this one handles all waterfowl with a 3 ½-inch chamber; extended chokes in Close-Range, Mid-Range, Modified, Improved Cylinder, and XFT; paracord sling; drilled and tapped
MSRP $849.00

P3000

Action: Pump
Stock: Synthetic
Barrel: 18.5 in., 26 in., 28 in.
Chokes: M inner choke
Weight: 6 lb. 6 oz.–6 lb. 14 oz.
Bore/Gauge: 12
Magazine: 4+1 shells
Features: Chambered for 2 ¾- and 3-in. shells; in black or Realtree Max-5 camo in long barrel options; 18.5-in. barrel option only in black synthetic but with choice of pistol grip or standard buttstock
MSRP . . . . $289.00–$339.00

P3000 DEFENSE

Action: Pump
Stock: Synthetic, wood
Barrel: 18.5 in.
Chokes: Cylinder fixed
Weight: 6 lb. 8 oz.
Bore/Gauge: 12
Magazine: 4 shells
Features: Blade front sight; 3-in. chamber; field or pistol grip stock
MSRP . . . . $289.00–$339.00

P3000 FREEDOM SERIES DEFENSE

Action: Pump
Stock: Synthetic
Barrel: 18.5 in.
Chokes: None
Sights: Blade front sight
Weight: 6 lb. 4 oz.
Bore/Gauge: 12
Magazine: 7 shells
Features: A pump self-defense shotgun with added capacity; fixed Cylinder choke
MSRP $339.00

P3500

Action: Pump
Stock: Synthetic
Barrel: 26 in., 28 in.
Chokes: M
Weight: 6 lb. 14 oz.–7 lb.
Bore/Gauge: 12
Magazine: 4 shells
Features: Chambered for 2 ¾-, 3-, and 3 ½-in.; mechanical rotating bolt; dual action rails; red fiber optic front sight; chrome-lined steel barrel; black or Realtree Max-5
Black: $339.00
Camo: $389.00

THE GRAND

Action: Break-action
Stock: Wood
Barrel: 30 in.
Chokes: M, IM, F
Weight: 9 lb.
Bore/Gauge: 12
Magazine: 1 shell
Features: Single-barrel target gun designed for shooting trap; stepped ventilated rib and fiber optic front sight; automatic safety that engages when the lever is activated to open the action
MSRP $629.00

UPLANDER

Action: Side-by-side
Stock: Walnut
Barrel: 22 in. (youth), 26 in., 28 in., 28 in.
Chokes: Screw-in and fixed tubes
Weight: 6 lb. 8 oz.–7 lb. 8 oz.
Bore/Gauge: 12, 16, 20, 28, .410
Magazine: 2 shels
Features: Brass bead sights; A-grade satin walnut stock; tang-mounted safety; single or double triggers; extractors included
Uplander Field: $449.00
Uplander Supreme: $549.00
Uplander Youth: $449.00
Uplander Longfowler: $449.00

Syren USA

SYREN ELOS N2 SPORTING

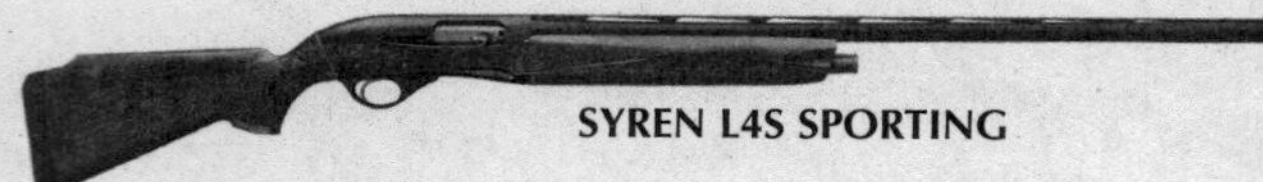

SYREN L4S SPORTING

SYREN TEMPIO TRAP UNSINGLE AND TEMPIO TRAP OVER/UNDER

ELOS N2 SPORTING

Action: Semiautomatic
Stock: Turkish walnut
Barrel: 30 in.
Chokes: 5 EXIS HP
Weight: 7 lb. 14 oz.
Bore/Gauge: 12
Magazine: 4+1 shells
Features: Turkish walnut stock enhanced by a proprietary TRIWOOD finish, which adds grain and water resistance; TRIBORE HP barrels for the ultimate in ballistic performance; adjustable trigger; lefthand option; 32-in. barrels can be optioned for additional charge
Standard:. $2950.00
Left-hand: . . . . add $160.00

L4S SPORTING

Action: Semiautomatic
Stock: Walnut
Barrel: 28 in., 30 in.
Chokes: N/A
Sights: Bead
Weight: N/A
Bore/Gauge: 12
Magazine: 4 shells
Features: Syren's firearms are designed for women shooters; Monte Carlo comb; slimmed pistol grip; drop and cast dimensions that are better suited to the female form; lefthand model available
Right-hand: $2025.00
Left-hand: $2225.00

TEMPIO TRAP UNSINGLE, TEMPIO TRAP OVER/UNDER

Action: Over/under
Stock: Turkish walnut
Barrel: 30 in., 32 in.
Chokes: 3 MAXIS (unsingle); 5 MAXIS (over/under)
Weight: 8 lb. 5 oz.–8 lb. 6 oz.
Bore/Gauge: 12
Magazine: 2 shells
Features: Stock designed to fit the female shooter with specialized dimensions, including length of pull, smaller grip, and increased pitch; calibrated barrel and stock weight; DTS trigger system with two trigger pull weight options, take up, over travel, and length of pull adjustments; hand-polished coin finish with Invisalloy protective finish; 30-in. barreled over/under, 32-in. barrel Unsingle, and combo with both barrel sets
Over/under or unsingle: . . $7275.00
Combo: $10,175.00
Left-hand: . . . . add $260.00

Taylor's & Co. Firearms

TAYLOR'S & CO. 1887 T-MODEL LEVER-ACTION SHOTGUN

TAYLOR'S & CO. WYATT EARP SHOTGUN

SHOTGUNS

1887 T-MODEL LEVER-ACTION SHOTGUN

Action: Lever
Stock: Synthetic
Barrel: 18.5 in.
Chokes: None
Weight: 7 lb.
Bore/Gauge: 12
Magazine: 5+1 shells
Features: Black soft touch stock, matte blued finish; Bootleg Model
MSRP $1496.71

WYATT EARP SHOTGUN

Action: Side-by-side
Stock: Walnut checkered pistol grip
Barrel: 20.06 in.
Chokes: N/A
Weight: 7 lb. 1 oz.
Bore/ Gauge: 12
Magazine: 2 shells
Features: Easily opened with one hand for fast shell loading; case-hardened frame stamped with 'Wyatt Earp'; chromed barrel bores with blued finish
MSRP $1535.00

Thompson/Center Arms

THOMPSON/CENTER ENCORE PRO HUNTER TURKEY

ENCORE PRO HUNTER TURKEY

Action: Hinged-breech single-shot
Stock: AP camo with Flextech
Barrel: 24 in. or 26 in.
Chokes: T/C extra full
Weight: 6 lb. 4 oz.–6 lb. 12 oz.
Bore/Gauge: 12, 20
Magazine: 1 shell
Features: Fiber optic sights; 14 in. length pull
MSRP $892.00

TriStar Arms

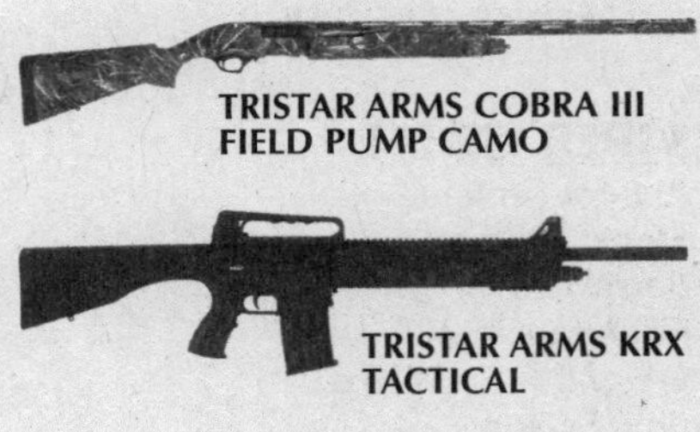
TRISTAR ARMS COBRA III FIELD PUMP CAMO

TRISTAR ARMS KRX TACTICAL

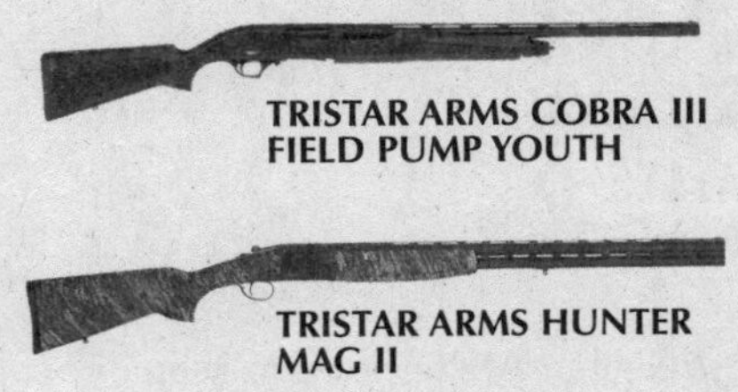
TRISTAR ARMS COBRA III FIELD PUMP YOUTH

TRISTAR ARMS HUNTER MAG II

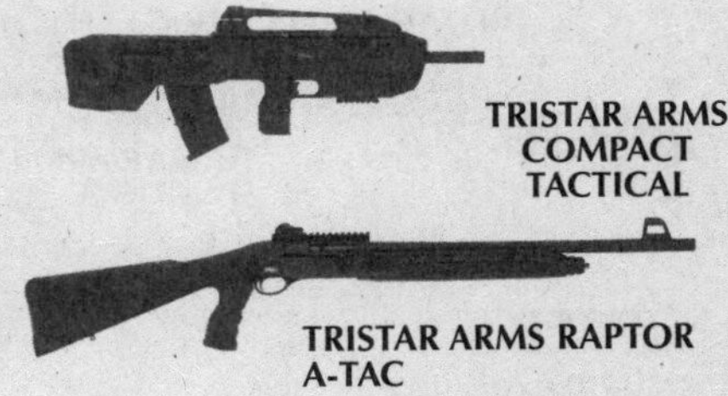
TRISTAR ARMS COMPACT TACTICAL

TRISTAR ARMS RAPTOR A-TAC

COBRA III FIELD PUMP

Action: Pump
Stock: Synthetic
Barrel: 24 in., 26 in., 28 in.
Chokes: 3 (IC, M, F)
Sights: Fiber optic front
Weight: 5 lb.–7 lb.
Bore/Gauge: 20, 12
Capacity: 5 shells
Features: 3-in. pump-action shotgun that allows you to shoot light target loads to heavy waterfowl loads; removable choke system uses Beretta/Benelli Mobil Threads; includes choke box and wrench; injection molded stock and forearm; camo available in Advantage Timber Turkey or Max-5
Black synthetic $345.00
Realtree Max-5, Advantage Timber . . . . $410.00–$450.00
Walnut . . . . $395.00–$415.00

COBRA III FIELD PUMP YOUTH

Action: Pump
Stock: Walnut, synthetic
Barrel: 24 in.
Chokes: 3 (IC, M, F)
Sights: Fiber optic front
Weight: 5 lb. 6 oz.–6 lb. 8 oz.
Bore/Gauge: 20
Capacity: 5 shells
Features: Extended forearm for superior fit and feel; vent rib with matted sight plane; fiber optic sight; five-round magazine, shot plug included; Quick Shot Plug Removal; chrome-lined chamber and barrel; youth stock LOP 13 in.
Black synthetic $345.00
Realtree Max-5 . . . . $410.00
Walnut . . . . $395.00–$410.00

COMPACT TACTICAL

Action: Semiautomatic
Stock: Synthetic
Barrel: 20 in.
Chokes: One
Sights: Flip-up front, rear
Weight: 8 lb.
Bore/Gauge: 12
Capacity: 5 shells
Features: A gas-operated bullpup design for action shooting games or home defense featuring a detachable magazine; forward grip; carry handle; 30-inch overall length
MSRP $760.00

HUNTER MAG II

Action: Over/under
Stock: Synthetic
Barrel: 26 in., 28 in., 30 in.
Chokes: 5 (SK, IC, M, IM, F)
Sights: Fiber optic front
Weight: 7 lb. 5 oz.–7 lb. 14 oz.
Bore/Gauge: 12
Capacity: 2 shells
Features: 3.5-in. chamber; sealed actions to keep dirt out; self-adjusting locking lugs; top tang barrel selector and safety; steel mono-block barrel construction; injection-molded stock and forearm; Beretta/Benelli Mobil style choke tubes with choke box and choke wrench; rubber recoil pad; swivel studs; four camo options
MSRP . . . . $790.00–$810.00

KRX TACTICAL

Action: Semiautomatic
Stock: Synthetic
Barrel: 20 in.
Chokes: Extended tactical choke
Weight: 7 lb. 6.4 oz.
Bore/Gauge: 12
Magazine: 5 shells
Features: AR-platform with a 3-in. chamber; controls similar to those of an actual AR; gas-operated; full-length Picatinny rail; removable carry handle; bridge front sight; injection-molded stock and forearm; two detachable magazines
Black: $540.00
Flat dark earth: $570.00

RAPTOR A-TAC

Action: Semiautomatic
Stock: Synthetic
Barrel: 20 in.
Chokes: N/A
Weight: 7 lb.
Bore/Gauge: 12
Magazine: 5 shells
Features: Gas-operated; bridge-front sight with fiber optic bead; Picatinny rail mounted on of the receiver with a ghost ring sight installed; fixed pistol grip stock, swivel studs, and a tactical style operating handle; comes with an Extended Tactical Beretta/Benelli style choke; available in Kryptec Typhon and digital camo finishes
MSRP $470.00

TriStar Arms

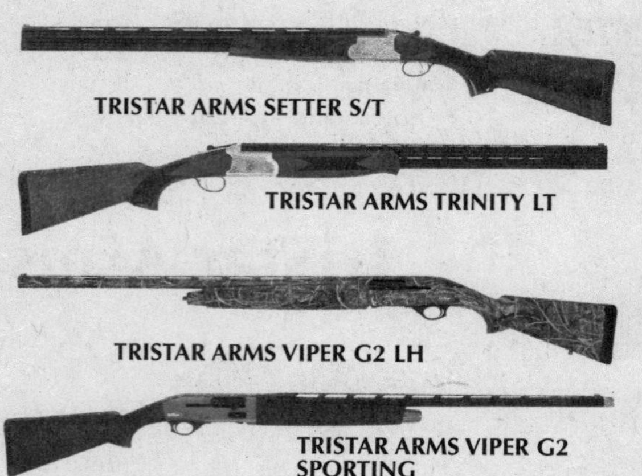

TRISTAR ARMS SETTER S/T

TRISTAR ARMS TRINITY LT

TRISTAR ARMS VIPER G2 LH

TRISTAR ARMS VIPER G2 SPORTING

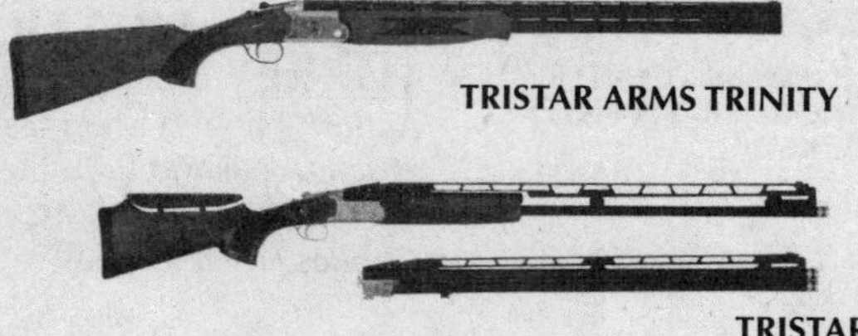

TRISTAR ARMS TRINITY

TRISTAR ARMS TT-15 FIELD

TRISTAR ARMS VIPER G2 BRONZE, G2 SILVER

SETTER S/T

Action: Over/under
Stock: Walnut
Barrel: 26 in., 28 in.
Chokes: 3-Beretta style tubes (IC, M, F)
Weight: 6 lb. 3 oz.–7 lb. 3 oz.
Bore/Gauge: 12, 20, 28, .410
Magazine: 2 shells
Features: Fiber optic front sight; high-gloss wood; single selective trigger; extractors; ventilated rib
12-, 20-gauge: $610.00
28-gauge, .410-bore: $640.00

TRINITY

Action: Over/under
Stock: Turkish walnut
Barrel: 26 in., 28 in.
Chokes: 5 (SK, IC, M, IM, F)
Sights: Fiber optic front
Weight: 6 lb. 5 oz.–6 lb. 14 oz.
Bore/Gauge: 20, 16, 12
Capacity: 2 shells
Features: Sealed actions to keep dirt out; self-adjusting locking lugs; top tang barrel selector and safety; steel mono-block barrel construction; Turkish walnut with semi-gloss finish; rubber recoil pad; 24k inlay on the receiver
MSRP $730.00

TRINITY LT

Action: Over/under
Stock: Turkish walnut
Barrel: 26 in., 28 in.
Chokes: 5 (SK, IC, M, IM, F)
Sights: Fiber optic front
Weight: 5 lb. 5 oz.–6 lb. 5 oz.
Bore/Gauge: .410, 28, 20, 12
Capacity: 2 shells
Features: 3-in. chamber; lightweight aluminum alloy frame with steel inserts at contact points for added strength; sealed actions to keep dirt out; self-adjusting locking lugs; top tang barrel selector and safety; steel mono-block barrel construction; Turkish Walnut with semi-gloss finish
MSRP . . . . $730.00–$750.00

TT-15 FIELD

Action: Over/under, top-single, top-unsingle, or combo
Stock: Turkish walnut
Barrel: 30 in., 32 in., 34 in.
Chokes: 3 or 5 extended Benelli/Beretta chokes
Weight: 7 lb. 13 oz.–8 lb. 14 oz.
Bore/Gauge: 12, 20, 28, .410
Magazine: 1 shell, 2 shells
Features: Monte Carlo stock; fully adjustable comb; elegant hand-engraved receiver with nickel finish; fitted with high-standing 3-point adjustable rib, auto-ejectors, and fiber optic front sight
12-, 20-gauge: $900.00
28-gauge, .410-bore: $930.00

VIPER G2 BRONZE

Action: Semiautomatic
Stock: Turkish walnut
Barrel: 26, 28 in.
Chokes: Three Beretta-style chokes
Sights: Fiber optic front sight
Weight: 5 lb. 3 oz.–6 lb. 13 oz.
Bore/Gauge: 12, 20, 28, .410
Magazine: 5 shells
Features: High-grade Turkish walnut stock and Cerakote Bronze receiver; tight checkering; shim kits; vent rib with a matte sighting plane; 20-ga. has a 26-in. barrel and chambers 2.75-in; other models have 28-in. barrels and 3-in. chambers.
12-, 20-gauge: $845.00
28-gauge, .410-bore: $900.00

VIPER G2 LH

Action: Semiautomatic
Stock: Synthetic
Barrel: 28 in.
Chokes: IC, M, F
Weight: 6 lb. 14.4 oz.
Bore/ Gauge: 12
Magazine: N/A
Features: Chrome-lined chambers; barrels threaded for Beretta/Benelli style choke tubes; 3 in. chambers
Black synthetic: $640.00
Realtree Max-5: $730.00

VIPER G2 SILVER

Action: Semiautomatic
Stock: Turkish walnut
Barrel: 26 in., 28 in.
Chokes: 3 (IC, M, F)
Sights: Fiber optic
Weight: 5 lb. 3 oz.–6 lb. 3 oz.
Bore/Gauge: .410, 28, 20, 12
Capacity: 5 shells
Features: A gas-operated semiauto vent rib that has a matte sight plane; stock shim kit; chrome-lined chamber and barrel; Quick Shot Plug removal; receiver in bronze or silver Cerakote
MSRP: . . . . $725.00–$770.00

VIPER G2 SPORTING

Action: Semiautomatic
Stock: Synthetic, walnut
Barrel: 30 in.
Chokes: 4 (SK, IC, M, F)
Sights: Middle bead, fiber optic
Weight: 7 lb. 3 oz.–7 lb. 6 oz.
Bore/Gauge: 12
Capacity: 5 shells
Features: Gas-operated semiauto; tubular magazine; manual E-Z Load magazine cutoff; wood stock has "TriStar Select" Turkish walnut stock and forearm with cut checkering and semi-gloss finish; synthetic stock comes with blue or red accents; adjustable comb; raised target rib
Synthetic $685.00
Walnut $885.00

TriStar Arms

TRISTAR ARMS VIPER G2 YOUTH

TRISTAR ARMS VIPER MAX

VIPER G2 YOUTH

Action: Semiautomatic, gas-operated
Stock: Synthetic
Barrel: 26 in.
Chokes: SK, IC, M, F
Weight: 5 lb. 11 oz.–6 lb. 3 oz.
Bore/Gauge: 12, 20
Magazine: 5 shells
Features: Manual E-Z Load magazine cut-off; raised target rib w/ matted sight plane; middle bead and fiber pptic sight; quick shot plug removal; chrome-lined chamber and barrel; adjustable comb; available in wood stock, black synthetic, Advantage Timber, black synthetic two-stock combo, and a black synthetic stock Sport model with red or blue metallic finish on receiver and magazine cap
MSRP . . . . $610.00–$740.00

VIPER MAX

Action: Semiautomatic
Stock: Synthetic
Barrel: 28 in., 30 in.
Chokes: Beretta Mobil (SK, IC, M, F)
Weight: 7 lb. 6.4 oz.
Bore/Gauge: 12
Magazine: 4 shells
Features: Gas-operated; 3 ó -in. chamber; heavy and light load pistons; extra piston can be stored in the forearm for instant in-the-field change-out; fiber optic front sight; sling swivel studs; magazine cut-off; Quick Shot plug removal; chrome-lined barrel and chamber; black synthetic stock with black metalwork, Mossy Oak Max-5 full-coverage camo, or Mossy Oak Shadow Grass Blades stock with bronze metalwork
Black: $700.00
Realtree Max-5: $765.00
Bronze Cerakote/MO Shadow Grass Blades: $780.00

Utas Defense

UTAS UTS-15 BLACK

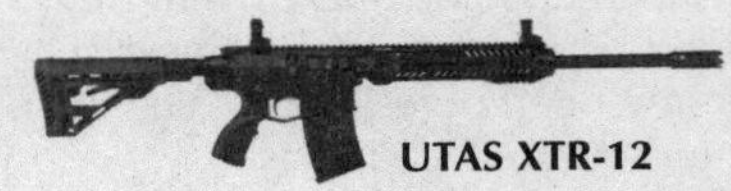

UTAS XTR-12

UTS-15

Action: Pump
Stock: Polymer
Barrel: 18.5 in.
Chokes: N/A
Weight: 6 lb. 15 oz.
Bore/ Gauge: 12
Magazine: 15 shells
Features: Unique pump action chambers up to 3-in. shells, features dual seven-round magazines with alternating or slectible feed, cartridge counter magazine followers, integrated top-side Picatinny rail, spring-assisted pin ejector, quick-removal fire control housing, fiber-reinforced buttplate, internally mounted point-and-shoot high-intensity lens focused LED spotlight, and adjustable laser sight; finishes in Flat Dark Earth, Burnt Bronze, Tungsten grey, OD Green, and Muddy Girl pink camo
MSRP . . . . $1099.00–$1299.00

XTR-12

Action: Semiautomatic
Stock: Synthetic
Barrel: 20 in.
Chokes: N/A
Weight: 8 lb. 8 oz.
Bore/Gauge: 12
Magazine: 5 shells
Features: Compact forend features a full-length top rail; machined from 7075 aluminum with standard mil-spec fire control parts; AR-style adjustable butt stock; available in matte black, burnt bronze, flat dark earth, OD green, or tungsten finishes
MSRP . . . . $899.99–$1199.00

Weatherby

WEATHERBY 18I DELUXE

18I DELUXE

Action: Semiautomatic
Stock: Walnut
Barrel: 26 in., 28 in.
Chokes: 5 (IC, IM, M, I, F)
Sights: LPA fiber optic
Weight: 6 lb.–7 lb.
Bore/Gauge: 20, 12
Capacity: 4 shells
Features: An inertia-operated shotgun with a matte-finished walnut stock; 3-in. chamber; four-round magazine tube; custom Lasertech engraving on the single-piece billet aluminum receiver in a matte silver; vent rib; includes choke tube wrench
MSRP $1899.00

Weatherby

WEATHERBY 18I SYNTHETIC

WEATHERBY ELEMENT SYNTHETIC

WEATHERBY ELEMENT UPLAND

WEATHERBY ORION I

WEATHERBY ORION SPORTING

WEATHERBY SA-08 SYNTHETIC, SYNTHETIC COMPACT

18I SYNTHETIC

Action: Semiautomatic
Stock: Synthetic
Barrel: 28 in.
Chokes: 5 (IC, IM, M, I, F)
Sights: LPA fiber optic
Weight: 7 lb.
Bore/Gauge: 12
Capacity: 4 shells
Features: An inertia-operated semiautomatic for turkeys or big geese with a 3.5-in. chamber; elastomer stock for reduced recoil despite the firearm's relatively light weight; matte finish all over
MSRP $1149.00

ELEMENT SYNTHETIC

Action: Semiautomatic
Stock: Synthetic
Barrel: 26 in., 28 in.
Chokes: 4 application specific chokes (IC, Mod, Full, Long Range Steel)
Weight: 6 lb. 4 oz.–6 lb. 12 oz.
Bore/Gauge: 12, 20
Magazine: 4+1 shells
Features: Griptonite stock features pistol grip and forend inserts gray/black design color; matte, bead blasted finish
MSRP $599.00

ELEMENT UPLAND

Action: Semiautomatic
Stock: Walnut
Barrel: 26 in., 28 in.
Chokes: Three (F, M, IM)
Sights: Fiber optic front
Weight: 6 lb. 9 oz.–6 lb. 12 oz.
Bore/Gauge: 12, 20
Capacity: 5 shells
Features: Inertia-operated semiauto made for the grouse woods and pheasant fields, featuring a chrome-line vent rib barrel; both gauges chamber 3-inch shells
MSRP $749.00

ORION I

Action: Over/under
Stock: Walnut
Barrel: 30 in.
Chokes: IC, M, F
Weight: 7 lb.
Bore/Gauge: 12
Magazine: 2 shells
Features: Brass front sights; ambidextrous top tang safety; automatic ejectors; low profile receiver; chrome-lined bores; matte ventilated top rib with brass bead; traditional boxlock action; integral multi choke system
MSRP $999.00

ORION SPORTING

Action: Over/under
Stock: Walnut
Barrel: 30 in.
Chokes: Five (F, M, IM, IC, S)
Sights: Fiber optic front
Weight: 7 lb. 8 oz.
Bore/Gauge: 12
Capacity: 2 shells
Features: A dedicated sporting clays gun featuring an "A"-grade stock with diamond point checkering and adjustable comb; tapered vent rib; ported barrels; automatic ejectors; chrome-lined bores; 3-inch chamber; knurled extended chokes
MSRP $1099.00

SA-08 SYNTHETIC COMPACT

Action: Semiautomatic
Stock: Synthetic
Barrel: 24 in.
Chokes: 3 (F, M, IC)
Sights: Brass bead
Weight: 5 lb. 12 oz.
Bore/Gauge: 20
Capacity: 5 shells
Features: An economical do-everything shotgun with a 3-in. chamber; low-profile vent rib; swivel studs front and rear; aircraft-grade alloy receiver; chrome-lined bore
MSRP $499.00

Wilkinson Tactical

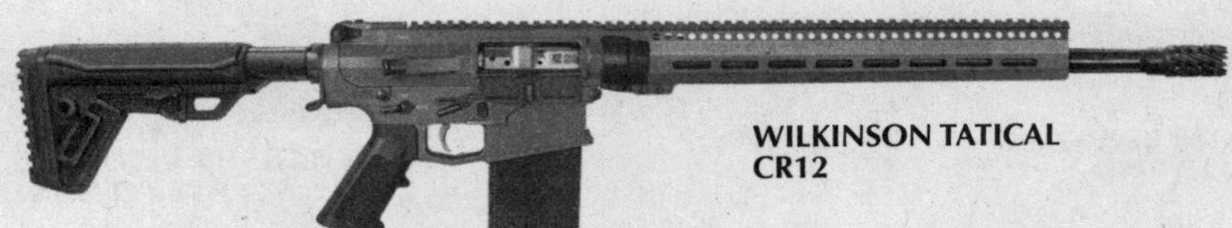

WILKINSON TATICAL CR12

CR12

Action: Semiautomatic
Stock: Synthetic
Barrel: 18 in.
Chokes: N/A
Sights: None
Weight: N/A
Bore/Gauge: 12
Capacity: 5, 10, 12 shells
Features: MAWS stands for Modular Advanced Weapons System; .308 AR lower pairs with an upper chambered for 12-ga.; upper can be exchanged for one in .308/7.62X39 NATO or the 6mm and 6.5 Creedmoors in seconds; direct impingement gas operation; smooth barrel threaded for Winchester chokes; FAILZERO EXO nickel boron-plated bolt carrier group; M4-type adjustable stock; black anodized finish; standard buffer on Basic model; Performance model gets Kynshot hydraulic buffer, Carlson breaching muzzle device, PDQ boly catch, and custom color upgrade
MSRP $1995.00

Winchester Repeating Arms

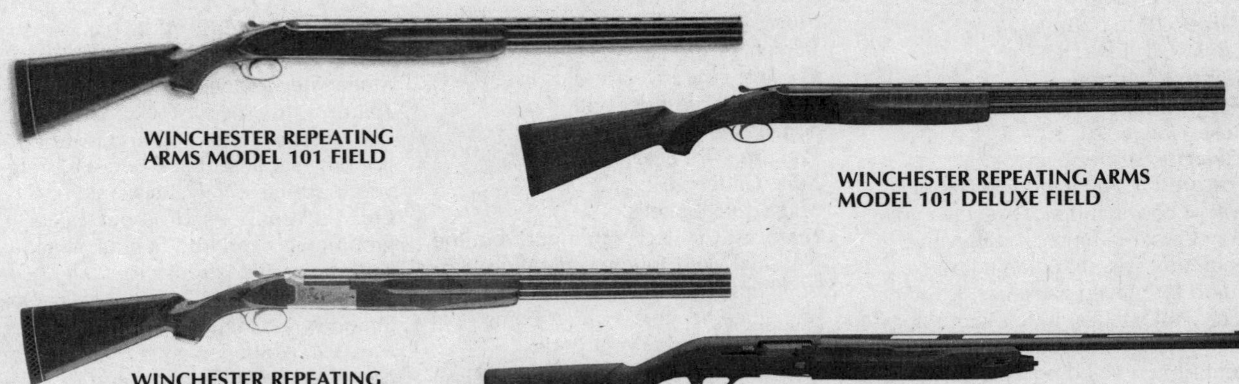

WINCHESTER REPEATING ARMS MODEL 101 FIELD

WINCHESTER REPEATING ARMS MODEL 101 DELUXE FIELD

WINCHESTER REPEATING ARMS MODEL 101 LIGHT

WINCHESTER REPEATING ARMS SX4 COMPACT

MODEL 101

Action: Over/under
Stock: Walnut
Barrel: 26 in., 28 in., 30 in., 32 in.
Chokes: Invector-Plus choke system, 3 tubes
Weight: 6 lb. 12 oz.–7 lb. 6 oz.
Bore/Gauge: 12
Magazine: 2 shells
Features: Solid brass bead front sight on Field; Truglo front sight on Sporting; deep relief receiver engraving; high-gloss grade II/III walnut stock; vented Pachmayr Decelerator pad with classic white line spacer
Field: $1959.99
Sporting: $2449.99

MODEL 101 DELUXE FIELD

Action: Over/under
Stock: Walnut
Barrel: 26 in., 28 in.
Chokes: Invector-Plus (F, M, IC)
Weight: 6 lb. 12 oz.
Bore/Gauge: 12
Magazine: 2 shells
Features: Grade III European walnut stock; detailed engraving on steel receiver; back-bored, hard-chromed barrels; front bead; 3-in. chambers
MSRP $2069.99

MODEL 101 LIGHT

Action: Over/under
Stock: Turkish walnut
Barrel: 26 in., 28 in.
Chokes: 3 (F, M, IC)
Sights: Brass bead
Weight: 6 lb.–6 lb. 4 oz.
Bore/Gauge: 12
Capacity: 2 shells
Features: This lightened classic has a Grade II/III Turkish walnut stock in a high-gloss finish; chrome-plated barrels in high-polished blue; aluminum alloy receiver engraved with game birds and in a nitride finish; 3-in. chamber
MSRP $1869.99

SX4 COMPACT

Action: Semiautomatic
Stock: Composite
Barrel: 24 in., 26 in., 28 in.
Chokes: Three (F, M, IC)
Sights: Fiber optic front
Weight: 6 lb. 8 oz.–6 lb. 12 oz.
Bore/Gauge: 12, 20
Capacity: 5 shells
Features: For youth or shorter-statured shooters with a 13-inch length of pull; all over matte black finish; aluminum alloy receiver; flush Invector-Plus chokes; 3-inch chamber
MSRP . . . . $829.99–$959.99

Winchester Repeating Arms

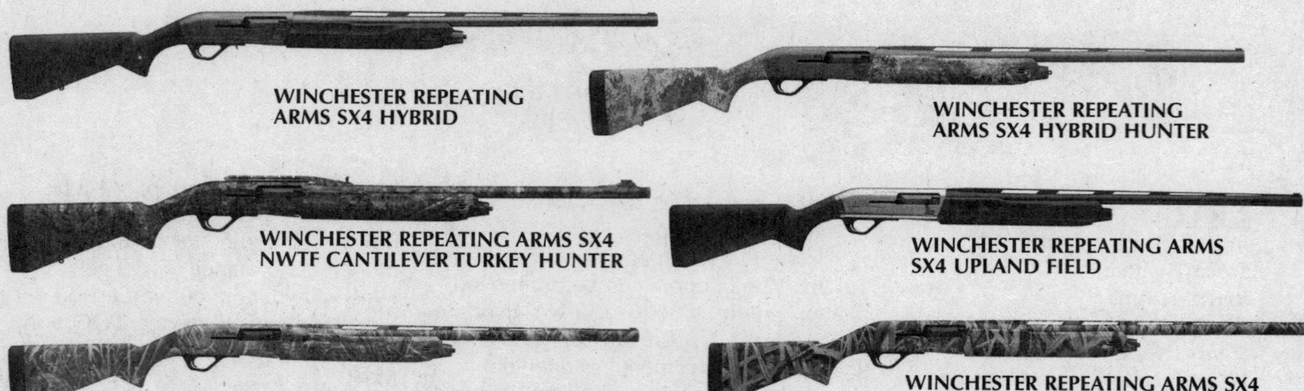

WINCHESTER REPEATING ARMS SX4 HYBRID

WINCHESTER REPEATING ARMS SX4 HYBRID HUNTER

WINCHESTER REPEATING ARMS SX4 NWTF CANTILEVER TURKEY HUNTER

WINCHESTER REPEATING ARMS SX4 UPLAND FIELD

WINCHESTER REPEATING ARMS SX4 WATERFOWL HUNTER

WINCHESTER REPEATING ARMS SX4 WATERFOWL HUNTER COMPACT

SX4 HYBRID

Action: Semiautomatic
Stock: Composite
Barrel: 26 in., 28 in.
Chokes: 3 (F, M, IC)
Sights: Fiber optic
Weight: 6 lb. 10 oz.–7 lb. 2 oz.
Bore/Gauge: 20, 12
Capacity: 4 shells
Features: An upgraded SX4 Hunter with a barrel and alloy receiver in gray Cerakote finish; Active Valve operating system; enlarged trigger guard for gloved hand use; Invector Plus choke tubes; Inflex Technology recoil pad; TruGlo fiber optic sight; vent rib; enlarged bolt handle; black synthetic stock with length of pull spacers

20 ga.: $1029.99
3-inch 12-ga.: $879.99
3.5-inch 12-ga.: $1029.99

SX4 HYBRID HUNTER

Action: Semiautomatic
Stock: Composite
Barrel: 26 in., 28 in.
Chokes: 3 (F, M, IC)
Sights: Fiber optic
Weight: 6 lb. 10 oz.–7 lb. 2 oz.
Bore/Gauge: 20, 12
Capacity: 4 shells
Features: An upgraded SX4 Hunter with a barrel and alloy receiver in FDE Cerakote finish; Active Valve operating system; enlarged trigger guard for gloved hand use; Invector Plus choke tubes; Inflex Technology recoil pad; TruGlo fiber optic sight; vent rib; six camo stock options

20 ga.: $1079.99
3-inch 12-ga.: $929.99
3.5-inch 12-ga.: $1079.99

SX4 NWTF CANTILEVER TURKEY HUNTER

Action: Semiautomatic
Stock: Composite
Barrel: 24 in.
Chokes: One Invector-Plus Extended
Sights: TruGlo fiber optic front, adjustable rear
Weight: 7 lb. 8 oz.
Bore/Gauge: 12
Magazine: 4 shells
Features: Created with input from the National Wild Turkey Federation; 3.5-in. chamber; back-bored barrels; reengineered stock with gripping surfaces; Quadra-Vent ports; cantilever optics mount; drop-out trigger group; stock spacers and one Extra-Full turkey choke are included; full-coverage Mossy Oak Obsession

MSRP $1099.99

SX4 UPLAND FIELD

Action: Semiautomatic
Stock: Walnut
Barrel: 26 in., 28 in.
Chokes: Three (F, M, IC)
Sights: Fiber optic front
Weight: 6 lb. 10 oz.
Bore/Gauge: 12, 20
Capacity: 5 shells
Features: Grade II/III walnut stock with a satin finish, 20 lines per inch checkering; aluminum alloy receiver with a matte nickel finish and engraved game bird scenes; length of pull spacers; 3-inch chamber; flush Invector-Plus chokes

MSRP . . . . $1149.99–$1279.99

SX4 WATERFOWL HUNTER

Action: Semiautomatic
Stock: Synthetic
Barrel: 26 in., 28 in.
Chokes: Invector-Plus (F, M, IC)
Weight: 6 lb. 10 oz.–7 lb. 2 oz.
Bore/Gauge: 12, 20
Magazine: 4 shells
Features: Improved stock ergonomics with smaller pistol grip and textured gripping surfaces; back-bored barrels; vent rib; Active Valve gas system; Quadra-Vent ports; drop-out trigger group; oversized bolt handle; stock spacers; ambidextrous crossbolt safety; True Timber Prairie, Mossy Oak Shadowgrass Habitat, Reeltree Timber, Mossy Oak Shadowgrass Blades, Mossy Oak Bottomlands, and Realtree Max-5 camo finishes; 3- and 3 ½-inch chambers in 12-gauge; 3-inch chamber 20-gauge

MSRP . . . . $959.99–$1099.99

SX4 WATERFOWL HUNTER COMPACT

Action: Semiautomatic
Stock: Composite
Barrel: 24 in., 26 in., 28 in.
Chokes: Three (F, M, IC)
Sights: Fiber optic front
Weight: 6 lb. 8 oz.–6 lb. 12 oz.
Bore/Gauge: 12, 20
Capacity: 5 shells
Features: For youth or shorter-statured hunters with a 13-inch length of pull; full-coverage Mossy Oak Shadow Grass Blades camo; Inflex-1 recoil pad with hard heel; flush Invector-Plus chokes; vent rib; 3-inch chamber

MSRP . . . . $939.99–$1069.99

Winchester Repeating Arms

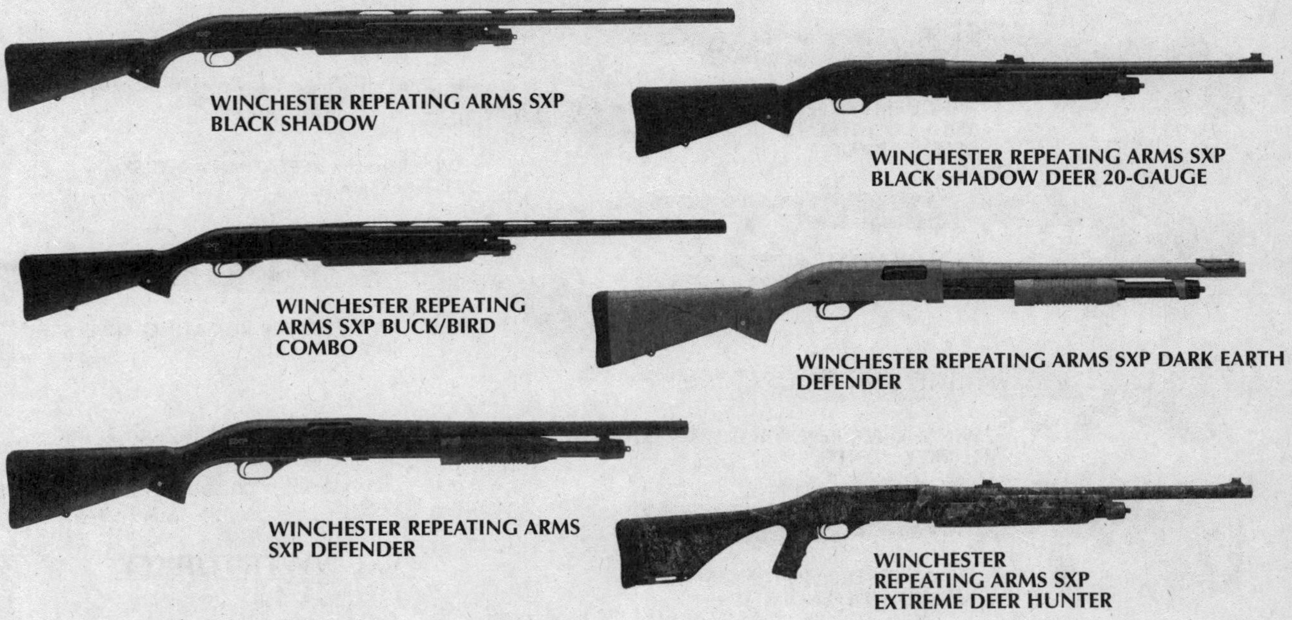

WINCHESTER REPEATING ARMS SXP BLACK SHADOW

WINCHESTER REPEATING ARMS SXP BLACK SHADOW DEER 20-GAUGE

WINCHESTER REPEATING ARMS SXP BUCK/BIRD COMBO

WINCHESTER REPEATING ARMS SXP DARK EARTH DEFENDER

WINCHESTER REPEATING ARMS SXP DEFENDER

WINCHESTER REPEATING ARMS SXP EXTREME DEER HUNTER

SXP BLACK SHADOW

Action: Pump
Stock: Synthetic
Barrel: 26 in., 28 in.
Chokes: Invector Plus
Weight: 6 lb. 12 oz.–7 lb.
Bore/Gauge: 12, 20
Magazine: 4 shells
Features: Hard chrome chamber and bores; drop-out trigger group for easy cleaning; synthetic stock with non-glare black matte finish on barrel and receiver
MSRP . . . . $389.99–$409.99

SXP BLACK SHADOW DEER

Action: Pump
Stock: Synthetic
Barrel: 22 in.
Chokes: None
Weight: 6 lb. 10 oz.
Bore/Gauge: 12, 20
Magazine: 4 shells
Features: Rotary-bolt pump; fully rifled barrel; alloy receiver; TruGlo fiber optic front sight; adjustable rear sight; three-shot Speed Plug adaptor; drop-out trigger; ambidextrous crossbolt safety; drilled and tapped for scope mounts
MSRP . . . . $529.99–$559.99

SXP BUCK/BIRD COMBO

Action: Pump
Stock: Composite
Barrel: 26 in., 28 in.
Chokes: 3 (F, M, IC)
Sights: Fiber optic, brass bead
Weight: 6 lb. 12 oz.–6 lb. 14 oz.
Bore/Gauge: 20, 12
Capacity: 4 shells
Features: A two-for-one pump with a vent rib barrel at 26 or 28 inches, as well as a shorter rifled deer barrel; Invector-Plus flush chokes; Inflex recoil pad; deer barrel has TruGlo fiber optic, field barrel has brass bead
20-ga.: $679.00
12-ga.: $649.99

SXP DARK EARTH DEFENDER

Action: Pump
Stock: Synthetic
Barrel: 18 in.
Chokes: Fixed cylinder
Weight: 6 lb. 4 oz.
Bore/Gauge: 12, 20
Magazine: 5 shells
Features: Aluminum alloy receiver; 3-in. chamber; front brass bead with removable TruGlo fiber optic sight; finished in Dark Earth
MSRP . . . . $389.99–$409.99

SXP DEFENDER

Action: Pump
Stock: Composite
Barrel: 18 in.
Chokes: Fixed cylinder choked barrel
Weight: 6 lb.–6 lb. 5 oz.
Bore/Gauge: 12, 20
Magazine: 5+1 shells
Features: Uses Foster-type slugs; non-glare metal surfaces with a tough black composite stock; deeply grooved forearm for control and stability
MSRP . . . . $359.99–$389.99

SXP EXTREME DEER

Action: Pump
Stock: Synthetic
Barrel: 22 in.
Chokes: None
Weight: 7 lb.
Bore/Gauge: 12
Magazine: 4 shells
Features: Rotary-bolt pump with fully rifled barrel; alloy receiver; TruGlo fiber optic front sight; adjustable rear sight; three-shot Speed Plug adaptor; drop-out trigger; ambidextrous crossbolt safety; drilled and tapped for scope mounts; 3-in. chamber; synthetic pistol grip stock has textured grip surfaces, two interchangeable cheek pieces, and two length-of-pull spacers
MSRP $569.99

Winchester Repeating Arms

WINCHESTER REPEATING ARMS SXP EXTREME DEFENDER FDE

WINCHESTER REPEATING ARMS SXP FIELD COMPACT

WINCHESTER REPEATING ARMS SXP HYBRID HUNTER

WINCHESTER REPEATING ARMS SXP LONG BEARD

WINCHESTER REPEATING ARMS SXP NWTF TURKEY HUNTER

WINCHESTER REPEATING ARMS SXP SHADOW DEFENDER

SXP EXTREME DEFENDER FDE

Action: Pump
Stock: Composite
Barrel: 18 in.
Chokes: 2
Sights: Steel blade front
Weight: 7 lb.
Bore/Gauge: 12
Capacity: 5 shells
Features: Nice choice for 3-Gun games or law enforcement with a stock that has two interchangeable comb pieces and two length of pull spacers; 3-in.chamber; aluminum alloy receiver with a topside Picatinny rail; finger-groove pistol grip; flat dark earth finish on barrel and most of stock; supplied with a flush Invector-Plus Cylinder choice and a door-breeching choke
MSRP $549.99

SXP FIELD COMPACT

Action: Pump
Stock: Satin finish
Barrel: 24 in., 26 in., 28 in.
Chokes: Three Invector-Plus chokes
Weight: 6 lb. 4 oz.–6 lb. 10 oz.
Bore/ Gauge: 12, 20
Magazine: None
Features: Aluminum alloy receiver; matte black finish; hard chrome chamber and bore; Speed plug system; brass bead front sight; Inflex technology recoil pad
MSRP . . . . $409.99–$439.99

SXP HYBRID HUNTER

Action: Pump
Stock: Composite
Barrel: 26 in., 28 in.
Chokes: 3 (F, M, IC)
Sights: Fiber optic
Weight: 6 lb. 8 oz.–7 lb.
Bore/Gauge: 20, 12
Capacity: 4 shells
Features: Barrel and receiver in FDE Perma-Cote; back-bored chrome-plated barrel; alloy receiver; Invector Plus choke tubes; Inflex Technology recoil pad; TruGlo fiber optic sight; vent rib; sling swivel studs; six dipped camo stock options
20-ga.: $449.99
3-inch 12-ga.: $429.99
3.5-inch 12-ga.: $449.99

SXP LONG BEARD

Action: Pump
Stock: Composite
Barrel: 24 in.
Chokes: Invector-Plus flush, extra full
Weight: 6 lb. 14 oz.–7 lb.
Bore/Gauge: 12, 20
Magazine: 4 shells
Features: TRUGLO fiber optic sights; two user-interchangeable combs and height adjust spacers; hard chromeplated chamber and bore; easily operated crossbolt safety; inflex technology recoil pad; in full-coverage Mossy Oak Obsession or Mossy Oak Break-Up Country; 12-gauge available in both 3- and 3½-inch chamber versions; 20-gauge chambers 3-inch shells
MSRP . . . . $549.99–$589.99

SXP NWTF TURKEY HUNTER

Action: Pump
Stock: Synthetic
Barrel: 24 in.
Chokes: Invector Plus
Weight: 6 lb. 4 oz.–6 lb. 10 oz.
Bore/Gauge: 12, 20
Magazine: 4 shells
Features: Hard chrome chamber and bores; drop-out trigger group for easy cleaning; Invector Plus Extra-Full Turkey Choke Tube; crossbolt safety; Inflex technology recoil pad; synthetic stock with textured gripping surfaces in Mossy Oak Break-Up Country or Mossy Oak Obsession; 12-gauge with 3 ½-inch chamber, 20-gauge with 3-inch chamber
MSRP $529.99

SXP SHADOW DEFENDER

Action: Pump
Stock: Synthetic
Barrel: 18 in.
Chokes: One Invector-Plus flush
Sights: TruGlo fiber optic
Weight: 7 lb. 8 oz.
Bore/Gauge: 12, 20
Magazine: 5 shells
Features: Pistol grip stock with textured gripping surfaces; two interchangeable comb modules; two length-of-pull spacers; ribbed forend; TruGlo fiber optic front sight; accessory rail; 3-in. chamber; one Cylinder choke tube
MSRP . . . . $449.99–$479.99

Winchester Repeating Arms

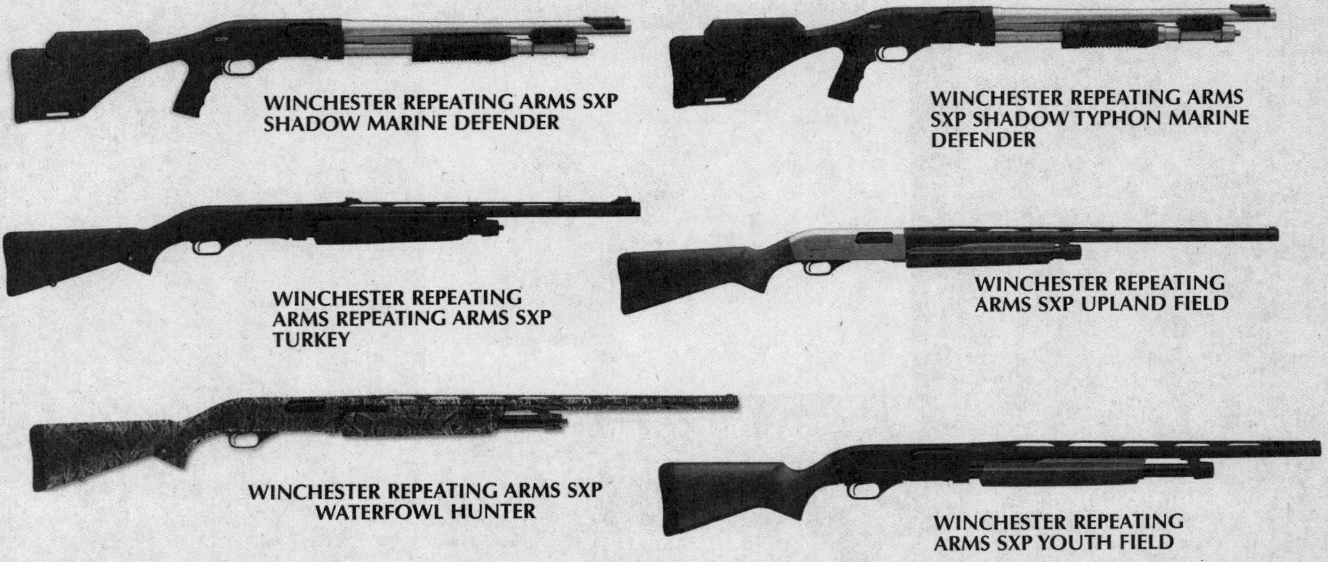

WINCHESTER REPEATING ARMS SXP SHADOW MARINE DEFENDER

WINCHESTER REPEATING ARMS SXP SHADOW TYPHON MARINE DEFENDER

WINCHESTER REPEATING ARMS REPEATING ARMS SXP TURKEY

WINCHESTER REPEATING ARMS SXP UPLAND FIELD

WINCHESTER REPEATING ARMS SXP WATERFOWL HUNTER

WINCHESTER REPEATING ARMS SXP YOUTH FIELD

SXP SHADOW MARINE DEFENDER

Action: Pump
Stock: Synthetic
Barrel: 18 in.
Chokes: Invector-Plus (C)
Weight: 7 lb. 8 oz.
Bore/Gauge: 12, 20
Magazine: 5 shells
Features: Hard chrome plating on most exterior metal surfaces and bore; alloy receiver is drilled and tapped for scope mounts; 3-in. chamber; synthetic pistol grip stock has textured grip surfaces; two interchangeable cheek pieces; two length-of-pull spacers
MSRP . . . . $499.99–$519.99

SXP SHADOW TYPHON MARINE DEFENDER

Action: Pump
Stock: Synthetic
Barrel: 18 in.
Chokes: Invector-Plus (C)
Weight: 7 lb. 8 oz.
Bore/Gauge: 12, 20
Magazine: 5 shells
Features: Hard chrome plating on most exterior metal surfaces and bore; alloy receiver is drilled and tapped for scope mounts; 3-in. chamber; synthetic pistol grip stock has textured grip surfaces; two interchangeable cheekpieces; two length-of-pull spacers; stock in dipped Kryptek Typhon camo
MSRP . . . . $519.99–$559.99

SXP TURKEY

Action: Pump
Stock: Synthetic
Barrel: 24 in.
Chokes: Invector-Plus Extra Full Turkey
Weight: 6 lb. 4 oz. (20-ga.), 6 lb. 10 oz. (12-ga.)
Bore/Gauge: 12, 20
Magazine: 4 shells
Features: Hard chrome plated chamber and bore; back-bore technology; TruGlo fiber optic adjustable sights; 12-ga. has 3½-in. chamber; 20-ga. has 3-in. chamber
MSRP $449.99

SXP UPLAND FIELD

Action: Pump
Stock: Turkish walnut
Barrel: 26 in., 28 in.
Chokes: 3 (F, M, IC)
Sights: Fiber optic
Weight: 6 lb. 12 oz.–7 lb. 2 oz.
Bore/Gauge: 20, 12
Capacity: 4 shells
Features: A very pretty pump with Grade II/III Turkish walnut stock; matte nickel receiver with game bird engravings on both sides; chrome-lined barrel in a matte finish; flush Invector-Plus chokes; Infex 1 recoil pad; 3-in chamber in both gauges
20-ga.: $529.99
12-ga.: $509.99

SXP WATERFOWL HUNTER

Action: Pump
Stock: Synthetic
Barrel: 26 in., 28 in.
Chokes: Invector Plus
Weight: 6 lb. 8 oz.–7 lb.
Bore/Gauge: 12, 20
Magazine: 4 shells
Features: Hard chrome chamber and bores; drop-out trigger group; synthetic stock with textured gripping surfaces; in full-coverage True Timber Prairie, Mossy Oak Shadow Grass Habitat, Mossy Oak Shadow Grass Blades, Mossy Oak Bottomlands, Realtree Max-5, Realtree Timber
MSRP . . . . $469.99–$499.99

SXP YOUTH FIELD

Action: Semiautomatic
Stock: Walnut
Barrel: 18 in., 20 in., 22 in., 24 in.
Chokes: Three (F, M, IC)
Sights: Brass bead front
Weight: 5 lb. 14 oz.–6 lb. 6 oz.
Bore/Gauge: 12, 20
Capacity: 5 shells
Features: A youth field shotgun in either 12- or 20-gauge, both with 3-inch chambers; flush Invector-Plus chokes; Grade I walnut stock with satin finish, laser-cut 18 lines per inch checkering; 12-inch length of pull
MSRP . . . . $409.99–$439.99

HANDGUNS

Accu-Tek

ACCU-TEK AT-380 II

ACCU-TEK HC-380

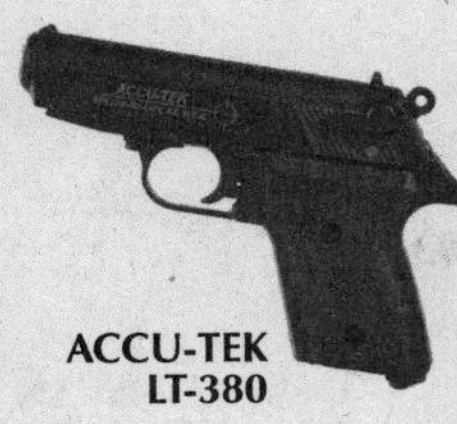

ACCU-TEK LT-380

AT-380 II

Action: Semiautomatic
Grips: Composite
Barrel: 2.8 in.
Sights: Target
Weight: 23.5 oz.
Caliber: .380 ACP
Capacity: 6+1 rounds
Features: Stainless steel construction; adjustable rear sight; one hand manual safety blocks; stainless steel magazine
MSRP $289.00

HC-380

Action: Semiautomatic
Grips: Composite
Barrel: 2.8 in.
Sights: Target
Weight: 26 oz.
Caliber: .380 ACP
Capacity: 13 rounds
Features: Adjustable rear sight; black checkered grip; one-hand manual safety block; includes two magazines and cable lock
MSRP $330.00

LT-380

Action: SA semiautomatic
Grips: Composite
Barrel: 2.8 in.
Sights: Adjustable rear sight
Weight: 15 oz.
Caliber: .380 ACP
Capacity: 6 rounds
Features: Aluminum frame; stainless steel slide; exposed hammer; manual safety; European type magazine release
MSRP $324.00

Altor Corp.

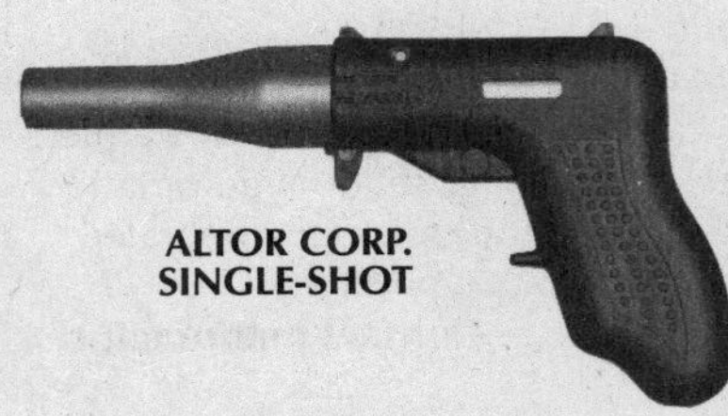
ALTOR CORP. SINGLE-SHOT

ALTOR SINGLE-SHOT

Action: Single-shot
Grips: Nylon
Barrel: 3 in.
Sights: Low-profile
Weight: 10 .5 oz.
Caliber: .380 ACP, 9mm
Capacity: 1 round
Features: There are just six parts—SIX!—to this detachable barrel, breech-loading single-shot pistol; all metal parts are stainless steel
.380 ACP: $119.00
9mm: $129.00

American Derringer

AMERICAN DERRINGER LM4 SIMMERLING

AMERICAN DERRINGER LM5

AMERICAN DERRINGER MODEL 1

LM4 SIMMERLING

Action: Hinged breech
Grips: Mesquite, Rosewood, custom
Barrel: 2 in.
Sights: Open, fixed
Weight: 24 oz.
Caliber: .45 ACP
Capacity: 5 rounds
Features: Vest pocket pistol; first round carried in the chamber; only 1in. thick; stainless steel
MSRP . . . . . . Contact manufacturer

LM5

Action: Hinged breech
Grips: Rosewood
Barrel: 2 in.
Sights: Open, fixed
Weight: 15 oz.
Caliber: .25 ACP
Capacity: 5
Features: Stainless steel; cam lock safety
MSRP . . . . . . Contact manufacturer

MODEL 1

Action: Hinged breech
Grips: Rosewood or stag
Barrel: 3 in.
Sights: Fixed, open
Weight: 15 oz.
Caliber: .45 Colt, .410, .45-70, .45 ACP, .45 Win. Mag., .44-40 Win., .44 Mag., .44 Spl., .41 Mag., .40 S&W, .380 ACP, .38 Spl., .38 Super, .357 Mag., .32-20, .32 Mag. S&W Long, .30-30 Win., .30 Carbine, .22 LR, .22 WMR, 10mm, 9mm, .223
Capacity: 2 rounds
Features: Single-action; automatic barrel selection; manually operated hammer-block safety
MSRP . . . . . . Contact manufacturer

American Derringer

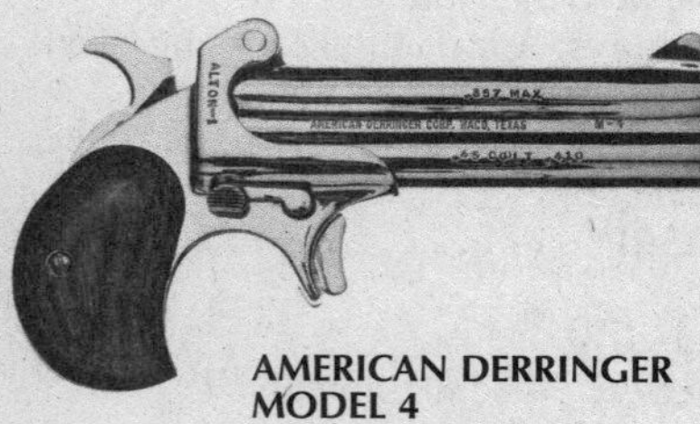
AMERICAN DERRINGER MODEL 4

AMERICAN DERRINGER MODEL 6

AMERICAN DERRINGER MODEL 7

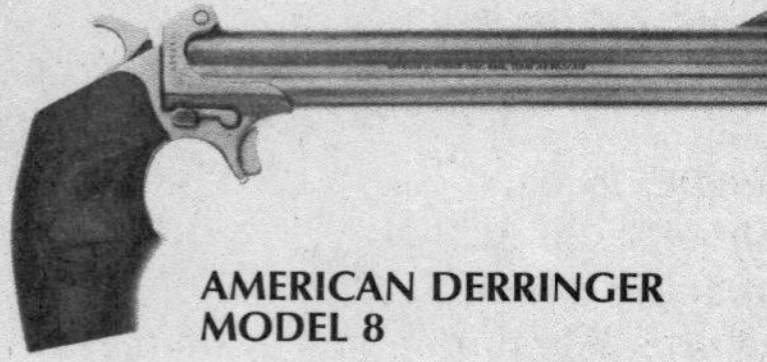
AMERICAN DERRINGER MODEL 8

MODEL 4

Action: Hinged breech
Grips: Rosewood
Barrel: 4.1 in
Sights: Fixed open
Weight: 16.5 oz.
Caliber: .375 Mag., 357 Max., .45-70 Govt.,
.45 Colt/.410, .44 Mag.
Capacity: 2 rounds
Features: Satin or high polish stainless steel finish; single-action; automatic barrel selection; manually operated hammer-block type safety
MSRP . . . . . . Contact manufacturer

MODEL 6

Action: Hinged breech
Grips: Rosewood, walnut, black
Barrel: 6 in.
Sights: Fixed open
Weight: 21 oz.
Caliber: .22 WMR, .357 Mag., .45 ACP, .45 Colt/.410
Capacity: 2 rounds
Features: Satin or high polish stainless steel finish; single-action; automatic barrel selection; manually operated hammer-block type safety
MSRP . . . . . . Contact manufacturer

MODEL 7 LIGHTWEIGHT & ULTRA LIGHTWEIGHT

Action: Hinged breech
Grips: Blackwood
Barrel: 3 in.
Sights: Fixed open
Weight: 7.5 oz.
Caliber: .44 Spl., .380 ACP, .38 Spl., .32 Mag./.32 S&W Long, .22 LR, .22 Mag.
Capacity: 2 rounds
Features: Grey matte finish; single-action; automatic barrel selection; manually operated hammer-block type safety
MSRP . . . . . . Contact manufacturer

MODEL 8

Action: Hinged breech
Grips: Rosewood, walnut, black
Barrel: 6 in.
Sights: Optional Adco red dot scope
Weight: 24 oz.
Caliber: .45 Colt/.410
Capacity: 2 rounds
Features: Satin or high polish stainless steel finish; single-action; automatic barrel selection; manually operated hammer-block type safety
MSRP . . . . . . Contact manufacturer

American Tactical Imports

AMERICAN TACTICAL IMPORTS FIREPOWER XTREME HYBRID 45ACP FXH-45 1911

AMERICAN TACTICAL IMPORTS FIREPOWER XTREME 45ACP G1 1911 (FX SERIES)

FIREPOWER XTREME HYBRID 45ACP FXH-45 1911 (FX SERIES)

Action: SA semiautomatic
Grips: Polymer
Barrel: 5 in.
Sights: Fixed
Weight: 27.5 oz.
Caliber: .45 ACP
Capacity: 8 rounds
Features: Polymer frame with 2 metal inserts for added stability and durability; steel match grade barrel and a custom designed steel slide; ergonomic frame with built-in finger grooves; accepts Glock front and rear sights, including aftermarket night sights
MSRP $599.95

FIREPOWER XTREME 45ACP G1 1911 (FX SERIES)

Action: Semiautomatic
Grips: Mahogany
Barrel: 4.25 in.
Sights: Fixed
Weight: 33.5 oz.
Caliber: .45 ACP
Capacity: 7+1 rounds
Features: Steel parts; black matte military-style fixed front and rear sights; military-style slide stop and thumb safety, solid mahogany grip panels
MSRP $479.95

American Tactical Imports

AMERICAN TACTICAL IMPORTS FX FIREPOWER XTREME 45ACP MILITARY 1911 (FX SERIES)

FIREPOWER XTREME 45ACP MILITARY 1911 (FX SERIES)

Action: Semiautomatic
Grips: Mahogany
Barrel: 5 in.
Sights: Fixed
Weight: 37 oz.
Caliber: .45 ACP
Capacity: 7+1 rounds
Features: Steel parts; black matte military-style fixed front and rear sights; military-style slide stop and thumb safety, solid mahogany grip panels
MSRP $479.95

Anderson Manufacturing

AM-15 EXT 5.56 7.5-INCH PISTOL

Action: Semiautomatic
Grips: Synthetic
Barrel: 7.5 in. extended barrel
Sights: None
Weight: 4 lb. 14 oz.
Caliber: 5.56 NATO, .300 BLK
Capacity: Detachable box, 30 rounds
Features: Picatinny rail; Anderson Knight Stalker flash hider; Magpul grip; available treated with proprietary no lube RF85 treatment
MSRP $678.09

ANDERSON MANUFACTURING AM-15 EXT 5.56 7.5-INCH PISTOL

Angstadt Arms

ANGSTADT ARMS MDP-9

MDP-9

Action: Semiautomatic
Grips: Synthetic
Barrel: 5.3 in.
Sights: None
Weight: 57.6 oz.
Caliber: 9mm
Capacity: 10, 15, 17 rounds
Features: Patent-pending roller-delayed action that the maker says "significantly reduces" both recoil and the overall weight of the gun; 15 inches long; rear 1913 rail with SB tactical braces in choice of telescoping or side-folding options; non-reciprocating left- or right-side charging handle; extended mag release; last round bolt hold-open
MSRP $2599.00

AREX (Fime Group)

AREX (FIME GROUP) REX ZERO 1CP

AREX (FIME GROUP) REX ZERO 1S

REX ZERO 1CP

Action: Semiautomatic
Grips: Polymer
Barrel: 3.85 in.
Sights: White dot
Weight: 25.2 oz.
Caliber: 9mm, 9x21
Capacity: 17 rounds
Features: Produced in Slovenia, this is the company's first entry into the U.S. market; DA/SA semiauto with a short-recoil, modified Browning linkless locking design; combo slide stop/ decocker; hard anodized T7075 aluminum frame; nitrocarburized steel slide and cold-hammer-forged barrel; ambidextrous safety and magazine release; loaded chamber indicator; Picatinny rail; oversized trigger guard for use with gloves
MSRP $589.99

REX ZERO 1S

Action: Semiautomatic
Grips: Polymer
Barrel: 4.3 in.
Sights: White dot
Weight: 29 oz.
Caliber: 9mm, 9x21
Capacity: 17 rounds
Features: Produced in Slovenia, this is the company's first entry into the U.S. market; DA/SA semiauto with short-recoil, modified Browning linkless locking design; combo slide stop/ decocker; hard anodized T7075 aluminum frame; nitrocarburized steel slide and cold-hammer-forged barrel; ambidextrous safety and magazine release; loaded chamber indicator; Picatinny rail; oversized trigger guard for use with gloves
MSRP $589.99

Armscor/Rock Island Armory

ARMSCOR/ ROCK ISLAND ARMORY BABY ROCK

ARMSCOR/ROCK ISLAND ARMORY GI STANDARD FS HC-45ACP

ARMSCOR/ ROCK ISLAND ARMORY GI STANDARD MS-45ACP

ARMSCOR/ROCK ISLAND ARMORY PRO MATCH ULTRA 6-IN-10MM

ARMSCOR/ROCK ISLAND ARMORY PRO MATCH ULTRA HC

ARMSCOR/ROCK ISLAND ARMORY ROCK ULTRA CS

ARMSCOR/ROCK ISLAND ARMORY TCM ROCK ULTRA CCO

ARMSCOR/ROCK ISLAND ARMORY XT 22 MAGNUM

BABY ROCK

Action: Semiautomatic
Grips: Rubber
Barrel: 4 in.
Sights: Fixed
Weight: 1 lb. 8 oz.
Caliber: .380 ACP
Capacity: 7 rounds
Features: Parkerized frame; front post, Novak-style rear sight
MSRP $460.00

GI STANDARD FS HC-45ACP

Action: Semiautomatic
Grips: Rubber
Barrel: 5 in.
Sights: Fixed
Weight: 2 lb. 9 oz.
Caliber: .45 ACP
Capacity: 10 rounds
Features: Parkerized frame; 1:16 in. twist; 4–6 lb. trigger pull
MSRP $608.00

GI STANDARD MS-45ACP

Action: Semiautomatic
Grips: Wood
Barrel: 4.25 in.
Sights: Fixed
Weight: 2 lb. 6 oz.
Caliber: .45 ACP
Capacity: 8 rounds
Features: Parkerized frame; 1:16 in. twist; 4–6 lb. trigger pull
MSRP $537.00

PRO MATCH ULTRA 6-IN. 10MM

Action: Semiautomatic
Grips: Rubber
Barrel: 6 in.
Sights: Dovetail mounted fiber optic front, LPA TRT1 adjustable rear
Weight: 2 lb. 8 oz.
Caliber: 10mm
Capacity: 8 rounds
Features: Parkerized frame; orange fiber-optic front sight, tactical adjustable rear sight; comes with 9mm conversion kit; 1:16 twist; 4–6 lb. trigger pull; ambidextrous safety; combat hammer; extended beavertail
MSRP $1168.00

PRO MATCH ULTRA HC-10MM, HC-40S&W

Action: Semiautomatic
Grips: G10
Barrel: 5 in., 6 in.
Sights: Dovetail mounted fiber-optic front, LPA TRT-type rear
Weight: 2 lb. 14 oz.
Caliber: .40 S&W, 10mm
Capacity: 17 rounds
Features: Parkerized frame; orange fiber-optic front sight, tactical adjustable rear sight; comes with 9mm conversion kit; 1:16 twist; 4–6 lb. trigger pull; ambidextrous safety; combat hammer; extended beavertail
.40 S&W: $1077.00
10mm: $1168.00

ROCK ULTRA CCO

Action: Semiautomatic
Grips: G10
Barrel: 4.25 in.
Sights: Dovetail fiber optic front, LPA MPS1-type adjustable rear
Weight: N/A
Caliber: .45 ACP
Capacity: 8 rounds
Features: Officer's grip; aluminum frame; Commander-length slide; full-length guide rod; button-rifled barrel; skeletonized hammer; trigger with overtravel; frame has black oxide finish; slide is parkerized
MSRP $760.00

ROCK ULTRA CS

Action: Semiautomatic
Grips: Rubber
Barrel: 3.62 in.
Sights: Dovetail standard front, low-profile, snag-free rear
Weight: 46.4 oz.
Caliber: .45 ACP
Capacity: 7 rounds
Features: Traditional 70-series 1911 design in a compact concealed carry package; snag-free features; checkered rubber grips; all-over parkerized matte finish
MSRP $731.00

XT 22 MAGNUM

Action: Semiautomatic
Grips: Rubber
Barrel: 5 in.
Sights: Fixed
Weight: 2 lb. 3 oz.
Caliber: .22 Mag.
Capacity: 22 rounds
Features: Parkerized frame; single action
MSRP $598.00

Arsenal, Inc.

ARSENAL, INC. SAM7K

SAM7K

Action: Semiautomatic
Grips: Black polymer
Barrel: 10.5 in.
Sights: Peep rear
Weight: 128 oz.
Caliber: 7.62x39 Warsaw
Capacity: 5 rounds
Features: Milled receiver; short gas system; front sight block; gas block system; chrome-lined hammer-forged barrel; ambidextrous safety lever; scope rail; sling included
MSRP . . . . $1799.99–$1899.99

Auto-Ordnance

AUTO-ORDNANCE 1911 9MM

AUTO-ORDNANCE 1911BKO

AUTO-ORDNANCE CUSTOM CASE HARDENED 1911

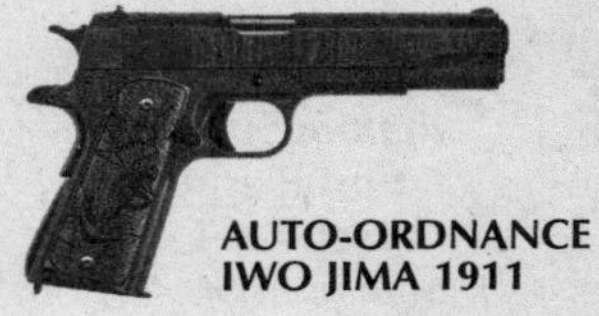

AUTO-ORDNANCE IWO JIMA 1911

AUTO-ORDNANCE LIBERTY 1911

AUTO-ORDNANCE REVOLUTION 1911

1911 9MM

Action: Semiautomatic
Grips: Plastic
Barrel: 5 in.
Sights: Low-profile blade front, notch rear
Weight: 39 oz.
Caliber: 9mm
Capacity: 9 rounds
Features: Faithful GI replica in 9mm; "Model 1911 U.S. Army" on left frame side; brown plastic checkered grips; matte finish
MSRP $861.00

1911BKO

Action: Semiautomatic
Grips: Brown checkered plastic, checkered wood grips
Barrel: 5 in.
Sights: Blade front, rear drift adjustable sight
Weight: 39 oz.
Caliber: .45 ACP
Capacity: 7+1 rounds
Features: Single-action 1911 Colt design; WWII parkerized; stainless steel or blued metal finish
MSRP $778.00

CUSTOM CASE HARDENED 1911

Action: Semiautomatic
Grips: Wood
Barrel: 5 in.
Sights: Low-profile blade front, notch rear
Weight: 39 oz.
Caliber: .45 ACP
Capacity: 7 rounds
Features: Gorgeous deep color case hardening on all metalwork; wood grips with raised military "U.S." logo
MSRP $1390.00

IWO JIMA 1911

Action: Semiautomatic
Grips: Wood
Barrel: 5 in.
Sights: GI
Weight: 36.8 oz.
Caliber: .45 ACP
Capacity: 7 rounds
Features: Honors the 75th anniversary of the Battle of Iwo Jima with grips emblazoned with "Among the men who fought on Iwo Jima, uncommon valor was a common virtue"; engraving by Outlaw Ordnance on both sides of slide and frame; finished in Cerakote OD green with copper highlights
MSRP $1247.00

LIBERTY 1911

Action: Semiautomatic
Grips: Goncalo wood
Barrel: 5 in.
Sights: GI
Weight: 36.8 oz.
Caliber: .45 ACP
Capacity: 7 rounds
Features: Left grip panel has "DTOM"—Don't Tread on Me; right grip panel has Liberty Bell in a circle of stars; left slide engraved with "Don't Tread"; right side engraved with "Liberty Death"; mixed Cerakote finish of brown and black
MSRP $1278.00

REVOLUTION 1911

Action: Semiautomatic
Grips: Copper
Barrel: 5 in.
Sights: GI
Weight: 36.8 oz.
Caliber: .45 ACP
Capacity: 7 rounds
Features: Solid copper grips with Liberty Bell design on right, Declaration of Independence on left; engravings of Benjamin Franklin, John Adams, George Washington, Paul Revere, and John Hancock by Outlaw Ordnance across the slide and frame
MSRP $1338.00

Auto-Ordnance

AUTO-ORDNANCE "SQUADRON" 1911

"SQUADRON" 1911

Action: Semiautomatic
Grips: Wood
Barrel: 5 in.
Sights: Low-profile blade front, notch rear
Weight: 39 oz.
Caliber: .45 ACP
Capacity: 7 rounds
Features: Custom graphics on slide/frame include the "shark mouth" of the P-40 warhawk fighter plane appearing at the muzzle; Army Air Corps insignia; "rivet" pattern; wood grips with raised military "U.S." logo
MSRP $1259.00

Beretta USA

92A1

Action: Semiautomatic
Grips: Plastic
Barrel: 4.9 in.
Sights: 3-Dot System
Weight: 34.4 oz.
Caliber: 9mm, .40 S&W
Capacity: 12 or 17 rounds, restricted capacity 10 rounds
Features: Removable front sight; Picatinny rail, internal recoil buffer; captive recoil spring assembly
MSRP . . . . $749.00–$775.00

92FS FUSION

Action: Semiautomatic
Grips: Carbon fiber and walnut
Barrel: 4.9 in.
Sights: Three-dot
Weight: N/A
Caliber: 9mm, 9x21
Capacity: 15 rounds
Features: A very limited edition with just 60 made in 9mm and 30 in 9x21; hand mirror-polished metal treatment; breech bolt, bolt release button, and trigger guard hand mirror-polished and checkered; short-barrel recoil operation; carbon fiber grips with a walnut insert inlaid with special silver plate bearing the PB and Fusion logos
MSRP . . . . price on request

92FSR_22 SNIPER GRAY

Action: Semiautomatic
Grips: Plastic
Barrel: 4.9 in.
Sights: Dovetailed front and rear
Weight: 26.08 oz.
Caliber: .22 LR
Capacity: 10, 15 rounds
Features: DA/SA .22 LR version of maker's famed 9mm; open slide design; reversible magazine release; ambidextrous decocker/safety; combat trigger guard; 1913 Picatinny rail; Sniper Gray frame finish
MSRP $450.00

92FSR_22 SUPPRESSOR READY KIT

Action: Semiautomatic
Grips: Plastic
Barrel: 4.9 in.
Sights: Suppressor-height front and rear
Weight: 26.08 oz.
Caliber: .22 LR
Capacity: 10, 15 rounds
Features: DA/SA .22 LR version of maker's famed 9mm; open slide design; reversible magazine release; ambidextrous decocker/safety; combat trigger guard; 1913 Picatinny rail; suppressor-height sights; extended threaded barrel with thread protector and mock suppressor
MSRP $449.00

92G ELITE LTT

Action: Semiautomatic
Grips: G10
Barrel: 4.7 in.
Sights: Red fiber optic front, blacked out notch rear
Weight: 33.3 oz.
Caliber: 9mm
Capacity: 15 rounds
Features: A collaboration with Landon Tactical that features the M9A1 frame; Vertec slide with added front serrations; exclusive radiused trigger guard; beveled mag well; ultra-thin VZ/LTT G10 grips; oversized mag release; no lanyard ring; solid steel guide rod; DA/SA with decocker; ships with three magazines
MSRP $1100.00

BERETTA 92A1

BERETTA 92FS FUSION

BERETTA 92FSR_22 SNIPER GRAY

BERETTA 92FSR_22 SUPPRESSOR READY KIT

BERETTA 92G ELITE LTT

Beretta USA

BERETTA 92X CENTURION

BERETTA 92X COMPACT, COMPACT WITH RAIL

BERETTA 92X FULL-SIZE

BERETTA 92X PERFORMANCE

BERETTA 3032 TOMCAT INOX

92X CENTURION

Action: Semiautomatic
Grips: Synthetic
Barrel: 4.25 in.
Sights: Orange-dot front, black-out notch rear
Weight: 28.5 oz.
Caliber: 9mm
Capacity: 10, 17 rounds
Features: A compact slide pairs with a Vertec full-length grip and a straight backstrap for maximum round count and hand accommodation; decocking safety that can be converted to a decocker only; high-visibility orange front sight against a blacked-out square-notch rear; oversized mag release; Gen 3 barrel locking block
MSRP $599.00

92X COMPACT, COMPACT WITH RAIL

Action: Semiautomatic
Grips: Synthetic
Barrel: 4.25 in.
Sights: Orange-dot front, black-out notch rear
Weight: 27.1 oz.
Caliber: 9mm
Capacity: 10, 13 rounds
Features: Smart double-stack carry choice with a decocking safety that can be converted to a decocker only; high-visibility orange front sight against a blacked-out square-notch rear; oversized mag release; Gen 3 barrel locking block; Vertec grip frame accommodates a wide variety of hand sizes; front- and backstrap checkering
MSRP $699.00

92X FULL-SIZE

Action: Semiautomatic
Grips: Synthetic
Barrel: 4.7 in.
Sights: Orange-dot front, black-out notch rear
Weight: 33.3 oz.
Caliber: 9mm
Capacity: 10, 15, 17 rounds
Features: This is a fine choice for a full-size carry, nightstand use, and lots of target practice with features such as a decocking safety that can be converted to a decocker only; high-visibility orange front sight against a blacked-out square-notch rear; oversized mag release; Gen 3 barrel locking block; 3-slot Picatinny accessory rail
MSRP $699.00

92X PERFORMANCE

Action: Semiautomatic
Grips: Synthetic
Barrel: 4.9 in.
Sights: Red fiber optic front, adjustable rear
Weight: 47.6 oz.
Caliber: 9mm, 9x21
Capacity: 15 rounds
Features: Open Brigadier slide that reduces weight and aids barrel cooling; Vertec steel frame with front and rear grip checkering and accessory rail fore of the trigger guard; front and rear slide serrations; oversized magazines with bumper pads; skeletonized hammer; oversized, reversible magazine release; raised frame profile for higher grip position
MSRP $1499.00

3032 TOMCAT INOX

Action: Semiautomatic
Grips: Plastic
Barrel: 2.5 in.
Sights: Fixed, open
Weight: 14.5 oz.
Caliber: .32 ACP, .380 ACP
Capacity: 7+1 round
Features: Double-action; tip-up barrel latch; Inox has stainless steel slide and barrel; titanium alloy frame in black or gray; double- or single-trigger
MSRP $529.00

Beretta USA

BERETTA APX CENTURION

BERETTA APX COMBAT

BERETTA APX COMPACT

BERETTA APX FDE

BERETTA APX RDO

BERETTA BU-9 NANO

BERETTA M9

BERETTA M9A1

APX CENTURION

Action: Semiautomatic
Grips: Polymer
Barrel: 3.7 in.
Sights: Drift adjustable three-dot front and rear
Weight: 27.7 oz.
Caliber: 9mm, .40 S&W
Capacity: 10, 13, 15 rounds
Features: A mid-size striker-fire suitable for concealed carry; doublestack magazine; aggressive slide serrations front and rear; 6-pound trigger with audible reset; under rail; standard model available in black or flat dark earth; RDO variant is red-dot-optic ready with slide cuts that take four different mounting plates; Combat is also RDO and has a threaded barrel
Black:..................$399.00
Flat dark earth: $419.00
RDO:..................$549.00
Combat: $579.00

APX COMBAT

Action: Semiautomatic
Grips: Polymer
Barrel: 4.9 in.
Sights: Drift-adjustable front and rear, optics plates
Weight: 33.3 oz.
Caliber: 9mm
Capacity: 10, 17 rounds
Features: Striker-fired DA/SA pistol; threaded barrel; slide cut out to accept four different optics mounting plates for reflex red dot sights from Burris, Trijicon, Leupold, and C-More; interchangeable backstraps
MSRP.................$579.00

APX COMPACT

Action: Semiautomatic
Grips: Polymer
Barrel: 3.7 in.
Sights: Drift adjustable three-dot front and rear
Weight: 26.4 oz.–27.2 oz.
Caliber: 9mm, .40 S&W
Capacity: 10, 13 rounds
Features: Short-gripped CCW version of the popular APX with flush-fit magazines; under rail; in black or FDE
Black:..................$399.00
FDE:..................$419.00

APX FDE

Action: Semiautomatic
Grips: Polymer
Barrel: 4.9 in.
Sights: Drift-adjustable
Weight: 33.3 oz.
Caliber: 9mm
Capacity: 10, 15, 17 rounds
Features: Developed for law enforcement and military personnel; easy-to-find controls; under frame accessory rail; three interchangeable backstraps; slide stop is ambidextrous; mag release is reversible
MSRP.................$419.00

APX RDO

Action: Semiautomatic
Grips: Polymer
Barrel: 4.9 in.
Sights: Drift-adjustable front and rear, optics plates
Weight: 33.3 oz.
Caliber: 9mm, .40 S&W
Capacity: 10, 15, 17 rounds
Features: Striker-fired DA/SA pistol; slide cut out to accept four different optics mounting plates for reflex red dot sights from Burris, Trijicon, Leupold, and C-More; interchangeable backstraps
MSRP................$549.00

BU-9 NANO

Action: Semiautomatic
Grips: Technopolymer
Barrel: 3.07 in.
Sights: 3-dot low profile
Weight: 17.67 oz.
Caliber: 9mm
Capacity: 6+1 rounds
Features: Interchangeable sights; ambidextrous magazine release button; serialized sub-chassis; patent-pending striker deactivator; technopolymer grip frame; three variations available include black, pink, Flat Dark Earth
MSRP $450.00

M9

Action: Semiautomatic
Grips: Plastic
Barrel: 4.9 in.
Sights: Dot-and-Post system
Weight: 33.3 oz.
Caliber: 9mm
Capacity: 15 rounds, restricted capacity 10+1 rounds
Features: Has distinctive military style markings; chrome-lined bore; double-action; automatic firing pin block; ambidextrous manual safety; lightweight forged aluminum alloy frame w/ combat-style trigger guard
MSRP..................$649.00

M9A1

Action: Semiautomatic
Grips: Plastic
Barrel: 4.9 in.
Sights: 3-Dot System
Weight: 33.9 oz.
Caliber: 9mm
Capacity: 15+1 rounds, restricted capacity 10+1 rounds
Features: Picatinny rail; magazine well bevel; sand-resistant magazine
MSRP..................$750.00

Beretta USA

BERETTA M9A3 BLACK

BERETTA NANO

BERETTA PICO

BERETTA PX4 COMPACT

BERETTA PX4 STORM COMPACT

BERETTA PX4 COMPACT CARRY

BERETTA PX4 STORM FULL SIZE

BERETTA U22 NEOS

M9A3

Action: Semiautomatic
Grips: Polymer
Barrel: 5 in.
Sights: Three-dot night sights
Weight: 33.4 oz.
Caliber: 9mm
Capacity: 10, 17 rounds
Features: An updated classic with night sights; under rail; textured grips; threaded barrel; decocker; lanyard ring; made in Italy; in black, flat dark earth, flat dark earth frame/black slide combo, black slide/green frame combo, black slide/grey frame combo, green slide/frame with black barrel and grips combo
MSRP . . . . $1099.00–$1100.00

NANO

Action: Semiautomatic
Grips: Polymer
Barrel: 3 in.
Sights: Three-dot white
Weight: 19.8 oz.
Caliber: 9mm
Capacity: 8 rounds
Features: Just a smidge bigger than the tiny Pico in order to take the smidge bigger 9mm, the Nano is available with a Robin's Egg Blue frame and matte stainless slide, Sniper Gray frame with matte black slide, Rosa (pink) frame with black slide, and flat dark earth frame with black slide
MSRP $450.00

PICO

Action: Semiautomatic
Grips: Technopolymer
Barrel: 2.7 in.
Sights: Front and rear adjustable
Weight: 11.5 oz.
Caliber: .380 ACP
Capacity: 6+1 rounds
Features: Stainless steel sub-chassis engraved with serial number; snag-free slide and frame; barrel can be replaced with a .32 ACP barrel; dovetail quick-change sights; frames available in flat dark earth, light aqua blue, black, or purple
MSRP $300.00

PX4 COMPACT

Action: Semiautomatic
Grips: Polymer
Barrel: 3.2 in.
Sights: Drift-adjustable white three dot
Weight: 27.3 oz.
Caliber: 9mm
Capacity: 15 rounds
Features: A super-concealable pistol with a full palm grip thanks to a double-stack magazine; under rail; front and rear slide serrations; DA/SA with decocker; with gray frame and black slide or in all-over Flat Dark Earth
MSRP $650.00

PX4 STORM COMPACT

Action: Semiautomatic
Grips: Plastic
Barrel: 3.2 in.
Sights: 3-Dot System
Weight: 27.3 oz.
Caliber: 9mm, .40 S&W
Capacity: 12 or 15 rounds; full size magazines 9mm: 17 or 20 rounds, .40 S&W: 14 or 17 rounds; restricted capacity 10 rounds
Features: Ambidextrous side stop lever; integral Picatinny rail; bruiton non-reflective black coating; visible automatic firing pin block
MSRP $650.00

PX4 STORM COMPACT CARRY

Action: DA/SA
Grips: Synthetic
Barrel: 3.2 in.
Sights: High-visibility night sights
Weight: 27.3 oz.
Caliber: 9mm
Capacity: 15 rounds
Features: Rotating barrel; grey Cerakote slide; Picatinny rail; competition trigger; double stack magazine; Talon grips; reversible magazine release; lightweight polymer frame; stealth levers decock only
MSRP $899.00

PX4 STORM FULL SIZE

Action: Semiautomatic
Grips: Plastic
Barrel: 4 in.
Sights: 3-Dot System
Weight: 27.7 oz.
Caliber: 9mm, .40 S&W
Capacity: 14 or 17 rounds, restricted capacity 10 rounds
Features: Picatinny rail; innovative locked-breech with a rotating barrel system; visible automatic firing pin block; ambidextrous safety; reversible magazine release; available in Inox finish; California-compliant model available with and without night sights
MSRP . . . . $599.00–$749.00

U22 NEOS

Action: Semiautomatic
Grips: Plastic
Barrel: 4.5 in., 6 in.
Sights: Target
Weight: 31.7–36.2 oz.
Caliber: .22 LR
Capacity: 10+1 rounds
Features: Single-action; removable colored grip inserts; deluxe model features adjustable trigger, replaceable sights; optional 7.5 in. barrel
MSRP . . . . $599.00–$749.00

Bersa

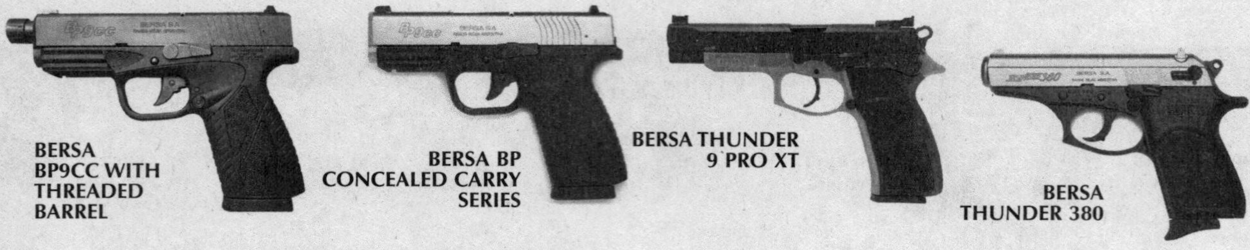

BERSA BP9CC WITH THREADED BARREL

BERSA BP CONCEALED CARRY SERIES

BERSA THUNDER 9 PRO XT

BERSA THUNDER 380

BERSA THUNDER 380 COMBAT PLUS

BERSA THUNDER 380 CONCEALED CARRY

BERSA THUNDER 380 WITH THREADED

BP9CC WITH THREADED BARREL

Action: Semiautomatic
Grips: Polymer
Barrel: 4 in.
Sights: Interchangeable front and rear
Weight: 22 oz.
Caliber: 9mm
Capacity: 8 rounds
Features: An everyday carry gun featuring a threaded barrel; short reset DAO; interchangeable Sig-type front, Glock-type rear sights; matte finish
MSRP. $353.99

BP CONCEALED CARRY SERIES

Action: Short reset DAO
Grips: Integral to frame
Barrel: 3.3 in.
Sights: Interchangeable front and rear
Weight: 21.5 oz.
Caliber: 9mm, .380 ACP, .40 S&W
Capacity: 6+1 or 8+1 rounds
Features: Bersa polymer concealed carry; high impact polymer frame; Picatinny rail, polygonal rifling, and loaded chamber indicator; ambidextrous magazine release; striker fired; micro-polished bore with sharp, deep rifling; 3-dot sight system; integral locking system; automatic firing pin safety
MSRP. . . . . starting at $311.00

THUNDER 9 PRO XT

Action: DA/SA
Grips: Checkered black polymer
Barrel: 4.96 in.
Sights: Fiber optic front sight, adjustable rear
Weight: 33.9 oz.
Caliber: 9mm
Capacity: 10–17 rounds
Features: Dovetailed front fiber optic sight; windage and elevation adjustable rear sights; ambidextrous controls for easy handling; 5-inch competition barrel fitted to slide for maximum precision; Cerakote finish to protect against abrasion, wear, and corrosion
MSRP. $835.00

THUNDER 380

Action: Semiautomatic
Grips: Black polymer
Barrel: 3.5 in.
Sights: 3-Dot system
Weight: 20 oz.
Caliber: .380 ACP
Capacity: 7+1 rounds
Features: Combat style trigger guard; extended slide release; micro-polished bore with sharp, deep rifling; integral locking system; available in matte, matte with pink rubber wraparound grips, duotone, or Cerakote nickel
MSRP. $307.00

THUNDER 380 COMBAT PLUS

Action: DA/SA
Grips: Olive rubber wrap-around
Barrel: 3.5 in.
Sights: Dovetail front, notched-bar dovetail rear
Weight: 20.5 oz.
Caliber: .380 ACP
Capacity: 8+1, 15+1
Features: Decocker for safer conceal carry; flat-bottom 8 shot magazine; integral locking system for the ultimate in safety; micro-polished bore with sharp, deep rifling for greater accuracy; slim side release for a lower profile; u-shaped combat rear sight for optimum sighting in low-light situations
MSRP. $353.99

THUNDER 380 CONCEALED CARRY

Action: Semiautomatic
Grips: Black polymer
Barrel: 3.2 in.
Sights: Blade front and notched-bar dovetailed rear
Weight: 16.4 oz.
Caliber: .380 ACP
Capacity: 8+1 rounds
Features: Extra low profile sights; combat style trigger guard; slim slide release; integral locking system; available with Crimson Trace laser
MSRP. $358.08

THUNDER 380 WITH THREADED BARREL, 22 WITH THREADED BARREL

Action: Semiautomatic
Grips: Polymer
Barrel: 4.3 in.
Sights: blade front, notch/bar rear
Weight: 19.4–20.5 oz.
Caliber: .22 LR, .380 ACP
Capacity: 10, 8 rounds
Features: Reminiscent of Walther's small handguns, features include checkered polymer grips; threaded barrel; magazine disconnect; .380 has a dovetail front sight, while the .22 has a low-profile integral blade
MSRP. $343.99

Bersa

BERSA TPR9C WITH THREADED BARREL

BERSA (BY EAGLE IMPORTS) TPR9C DUOTONE, MATTE

BERSA (BY EAGLE IMPORTS) TPR40C

BERSA (BY EAGLE IMPORTS) TPR45C DUOTONE, MATTE

TPR9, TPR9C WITH THREADED BARREL

Action: Semiautomatic
Grips: Polymer
Barrel: 5 in., 4.1 in.
Sights: Interchangeable Sig type front and rear
Weight: 31.2 oz., 23.5 oz.
Caliber: 9mm
Capacity: 17, 13 rounds
Features: Intended as a duty gun and perfectly serviceable as a carry or home-defense pistol, these threaded barrel models feature interchangeable Sig-type sights; matte finish; textured grips; alloy frames; steel slides; DA with manual safety; TPR9C is slightly shorter in both barrel and grip length
MSRP $479.00

TPR9C DUOTONE, MATTE

Action: Semiautomatic
Grips: Polymer
Barrel: 3.25 in.
Sights: Interchangeable Sig Sauer-type front and rear
Weight: 23 oz.
Caliber: 9mm
Capacity: 10, 13 rounds
Features: Compact DA/SA for concealed carry; Browning Petter locking action that enhances reliability
MSRP $413.00

TPR40C

Action: Semiautomatic
Grips: Polymer
Barrel: 3.6 in.
Sights: Interchangeable Sig Sauer-type front and rear
Weight: 23 oz.
Caliber: 40 S&W
Capacity: 10 rounds
Features: Compact DA/SA for concealed carry; Browning Petter locking action that enhances reliability; in all black only
MSRP $480.00

TPR45C DUOTONE, MATTE

Action: Semiautomatic
Grips: Polymer
Barrel: 3.6 in.
Sights: Interchangeable Sig Sauer-type front and rear
Weight: 27 oz.
Caliber: .45 ACP
Capacity: 10 rounds
Features: Compact DA/SA for concealed carry; Browning Petter locking action that enhances reliability; available in all black or as a Duotone with a stainless slide
MSRP $497.00

Bond Arms

BOND ARMS BACKUP

BOND ARMS, INC. BULLPUP 9

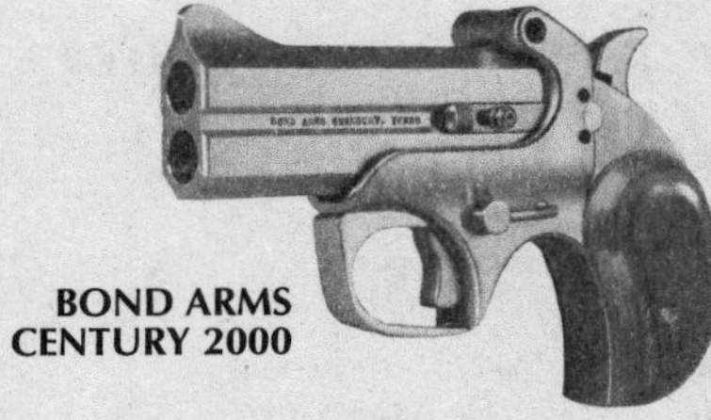
BOND ARMS CENTURY 2000

BACKUP

Action: SA semiautomatic
Grips: Rubber
Barrel: 2.5 in.
Sights: Blade front, fixed rear
Weight: 18.5 oz.
Caliber: .357 Mag., .38 Spl., .40 S&W, .45 ACP, .45 Colt
Capacity: 2 rounds
Features: Interchangable barrels; rebounding hammer; retracting firing pins; crossbolt safety
MSRP $540.00

BULLPUP 9

Action: Semiautomatic
Grips: Rosewood
Barrel: 3.35 in.
Sights: Dovetail drift-adjustable non-illuminated three-dot
Weight: 17.5 oz.
Caliber: 9mm Luger
Capacity: 7 rounds
Features: Based on the XR-9 by Boberg Arms; Bond Arms purchased the patents and rights to that gun in 2016, basing its new Bullpup on it
MSRP $1099.00

CENTURY 2000

Action: SA
Grips: Custom laminated black ash or rosewood
Barrel: 3.5 in.
Sights: Blade front, fixed rear
Weight: 21 oz.
Caliber: .357 Mag./.38 Spl., .410/.45 LC
Capacity: 2 rounds
Features: Interchangeable barrels; automatic extractor; rebounding hammer; retracting firing pins; crossbolt safety; spring-loaded cammed locking lever; trigger guard; stainless steel with satin polish finish
MSRP $567.00

Bond Arms

BOND ARMS MAMA BEAR

BOND ARMS MINI 45

BOND ARMS, INC. PT2A (PROTECT THE SECOND AMENDMENT)

BOND ARMS PATRIOT

BOND ARMS GIRL MINI

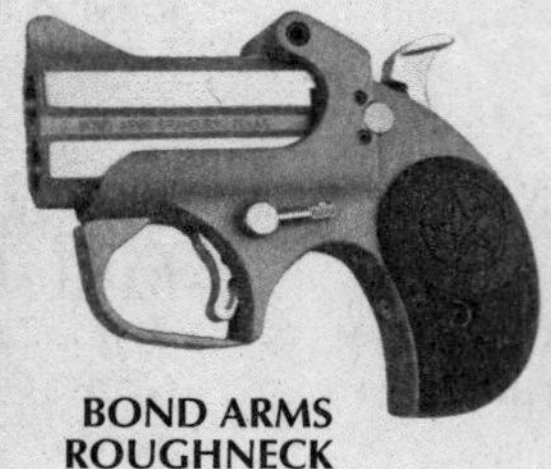
BOND ARMS ROUGHNECK

BOND ARMS ROWDY

BOND ARMS SNAKE SLAYER

MAMA BEAR

Action: SA
Grips: Pink wood
Barrel: 2.5 in.
Sights: Blade front, fixed rear
Weight: 18.5 oz.
Caliber: .357 Mag, .38 Spl.
Capacity: 2 rounds
Features: Stainless steel double barrel and frame; automatic spent casing extractor; rebounding hammer; retracting ring pins; crossbolt safety; spring-loaded, cammed locking lever; laser-carved American Flag and bald eagle grips
MSRP $541.00

MINI 45, GIRL MINI

Action: SA
Grips: Rosewood or pink
Barrel: 2.5 in.
Sights: Blade front, fixed rear
Weight: 18 oz.–19 oz.
Caliber: .45 Colt (Mini 45), .357 Mag. (Girl Mini)
Capacity: 2 rounds
Features: The Bond Mini was developed as a special edition gun that is even easier to conceal and carry, but still packs the same power Bond Arms guns are known for; comes in two models the Mini .45 and the Girl Mini; Girl Mini has slightly smaller barrel and pink grips
MSRP $534.00

PATRIOT

Action: SA
Grips: Rosewood
Barrel: 3 in.
Sights: Blade front, fixed rear
Weight: 21.5 oz.
Caliber: .45 Colt, .410
Capacity: 2 rounds
Features: Stainless steel double barrel and frame; automatic spent casing extractor; rebounding hammer; retracting ring pins; crossbolt safety; spring-loaded, cammed locking lever; laser-carved American Flag and bald eagle grips
MSRP $648.00

PT2A (PROTECT THE SECOND AMENDMENT)

Action: Break-top
Grips: Rosewood
Barrel: 4.25 in.
Sights: Front blade, fixed rear
Weight: 23.5 oz.
Caliber: .45 LC/.410-bore, .357 Mag.
Capacity: 2 rounds
Features: Custom extended rosewood grips; "The Right of the People to Keep and Bear Arms" is emblazoned on right side of top barrel; "shall not be infringed" on right side of bottom barrel; cross-bolt safety; stainless steel barrels; compatibility with all Bond barrels; automatic extractors; BAD premium leather driving holster
MSRP $887.00

ROUGHNECK

Action: Derringer
Grips: Rubber
Barrel: 2.5 in.
Sights: Integral
Weight: 19 oz.
Caliber: 9mm, .357 Mag., .45 ACP
Capacity: 2 rounds
Features: Designed to work with smooth-lined holsters, this two-shot has a bead-blasted stainless finish with polished barrel flats, trigger, and takedown mechanism
MSRP $269.00

ROWDY

Action: Derringer
Grips: Rubber
Barrel: 3 in.
Sights: Integral
Weight: 20 oz.
Caliber: .410-bore, .45 LC
Capacity: 2 rounds
Features: Similar to the Roughneck, but with a longer barrel and chambering for the .410 shotshell/.45 LC centerfire
MSRP $299.00

SNAKE SLAYER

Action: SA
Grips: Extended custom rosewood
Barrel: 3.5 in.
Sights: Blade front, fixed rear
Weight: 22 oz.
Caliber: .357 Mag./.38 Spl., .410/.45 LC
Capacity: 2 rounds
Features: Interchangeable barrels; automatic extractor; rebounding hammer; retracting firing pins; crossbolt safety; spring-loaded cammed locking lever; trigger guard; stainless steel with satin polish finish
MSRP $603.00

Bond Arms

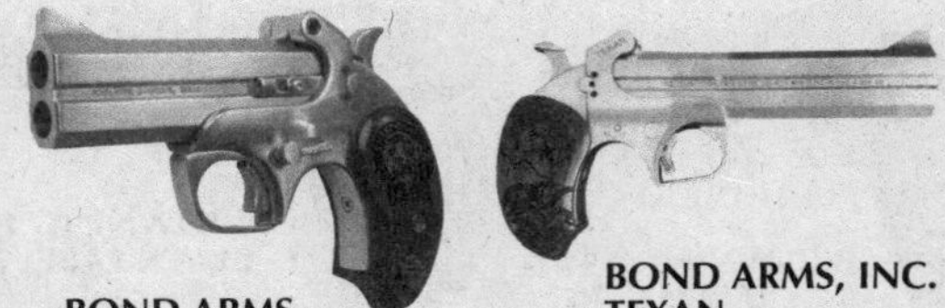

BOND ARMS SNAKE SLAYER IV

BOND ARMS, INC. TEXAN

BOND ARMS TEXAS DEFENDER

BOND TEXAS RANGER - SPECIAL EDITION

BOND ARMS Z SLAYER

SNAKE SLAYER IV

Action: SA
Grips: Extended custom rosewood
Barrel: 4.25 in.
Sights: Blade front, fixed rear
Weight: 23.5 oz.
Caliber: .357 Mag./.38 Spl., .410/.45 LC
Capacity: 2 rounds
Features: Automatic extractor; interchangeable barrels; rebounding hammer; retracting firing pins; crossbolt safety; spring-loaded cammed locking lever; trigger guard; stainless steel with satin polish finish
MSRP $648.00

TEXAN

Action: Break-top
Grips: Rosewood
Barrel: 6 in.
Sights: Front ramp
Weight: 23.5 oz.
Caliber: .45 LC/.410-bore
Capacity: 2 rounds
Features: Bond's first six-inch production model; patented rebounding hammer; cross-bolt safety; automatic spent casing extractor; spring-loaded cammed locking lever; compatible with all Bond Arms barrels; rosewood grips are extended and engraved
MSRP $700.00

TEXAS DEFENDER

Action: SA
Grips: Custom laminated black ash or rosewood
Barrel: 3 in.
Sights: Blade front and fixed rear
Weight: 20 oz.
Caliber: 45 Colt/.410
Capacity: 2 rounds
Features: Interchangeable barrels; automatic extractor; rebounding hammer; retracting firing pins; crossbolt safety; spring-loaded cammed locking lever; trigger guard; stainless steel with satin polish finish
MSRP $543.00

TEXAS RANGER - SPECIAL EDITION

Action: SA
Grips: Texas mesquite
Barrel: 3.5 in.
Sights: Blade front, fixed rear
Weight: 22 oz.
Caliber: .410/.45 LC
Capacity: 2 rounds
Features: Bond Arms has been chosen to represent the prestigious Texas Rangers in their historic 200th Anniversary; gun and knife grips are made from real Texas mesquite wood, the Texas Ranger Stars are handmade by Texas inmates in the Texas Department of Corrections, and it is gold engraved on the barrel; custom glass top display case included
MSRP $1355.00

Z SLAYER

Action: Derringer
Grips: Black ash
Barrel: 3.5 in.
Sights: Integral
Weight: 22 oz.
Caliber: .410-bore, .45 LC
Capacity: 2 rounds
Features: Zombie-green frame and barrels, the barrels sporting—yikes!—red "blood" splatter; trigger guard, hammer, and break-open mechanism in matte black; special black ash grips have a big "Z" emblazoned on them
MSRP $697.00

Browning

BROWNING 1911-22 A1 COMPACT

BROWNING 1911-22 A1 FULL SIZE

1911-22 A1 COMPACT

Action: Semiautomatic
Grips: Walnut
Barrel: 3.6 in.
Sights: A1 front, rear
Weight: 14 oz.
Caliber: .22 LR
Capacity: 10 rounds
Features: A flyweight rimfire in a compact frame; machined alloy slide with gray anodized finish; checkered walnut grips; hard case and one magazine included
MSRP $659.99

1911-22 A1 FULL SIZE

Action: Semiautomatic
Grips: Brown composite
Barrel: 4.25 in.
Sights: Fixed
Weight: 15 oz.
Caliber: 22 LR
Capacity: 10+1 rounds
Features: Alloy frame in matte blued finish; stainless steel barrel block with matte blued finish; blowback action; single-action trigger; detachable magazine; manual thumb safety; grip safety
MSRP $659.99

HANDGUNS

Browning

BROWNING 1911-22 BLACK LABEL MEDALLION

BROWNING 1911-22 SPEED, SPEED COMPACT

BROWNING 1911-380 BLACK LABEL MEDALLION PRO COMPACT

BROWNING 1911-380 BLACK LABEL PRO

BROWNING 1911-380 HIGH GRADE, HIGH GRADE COMPACT

BROWNING 1911-380 MEDALLION STAINLESS ENGRAVED, MEDALLION STAINLESS ENGRAVED COMPACT

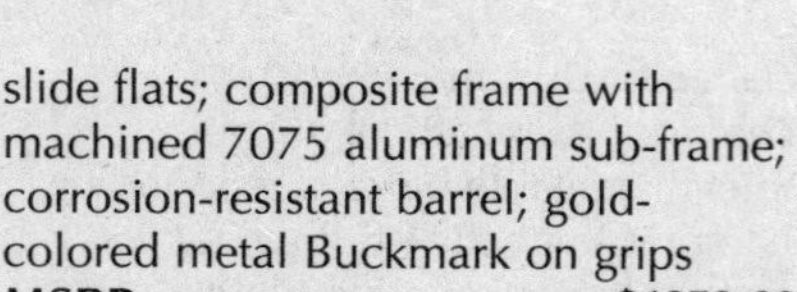
BROWNING 1911-380 SPEED, SPEED COMPACT

1911-22 BLACK LABEL MEDALLION

Action: Semiautomatic
Grips: Rosewood
Barrel: 3.625 in., 4.25 in.
Sights: Combat white dot
Weight: 13 oz., 15 oz.
Caliber: .22LR
Capacity: 10 rounds
Features: Available in full-size or compact 85-percent scale of 1911 package; checkered grips; extended slide release; machined aluminum slide; ambidextrous thumb safety; skeletonized trigger and hammer
MSRP $709.99

1911-22 SPEED, SPEED COMPACT

Action: Semiautomatic
Grips: Composite
Barrel: 3.6 in., 4.25 in.
Sights: Combat white dot
Weight: 14 oz.
Caliber: .22 LR
Capacity: 10 rounds
Features: Eye-catching rimfire with textured composite grip panels in A-TACS AU camo; composite frame over aluminum subframe in A-TACS AU camo; alloy slide in Cerakote burnt bronze
MSRP $639.99

1911-380 BLACK LABEL MEDALLION PRO COMPACT

Action: Semiautomatic
Grips: Laminate
Barrel: 3.625 in. (compact), 4.25 in. (full-size)
Sights: Steel three-dot combat or steel bar-dot combat night sights
Weight: 16 oz. (compact), 18 oz. (full-size)
Caliber: .380 ACP
Capacity: 8 rounds
Features: 85 percent-scale 1911; compact and full-size versions; stainless steel slide and rosewood laminate grips; ambidextrous manual thumb safety; extended slide release beavertail grip safety; two magazines; Commander hammer; target crown
Combat sights: $839.99
Night sights: $919.99

1911-380 BLACK LABEL PRO

Action: Semiautomatic
Grips: Synthetic
Barrel: 4.25 in.
Sights: Combat white three-dot, night sights
Weight: 18 oz.
Caliber: .380 ACP
Capacity: 8 rounds
Features: High strength/lightweight composite frame; machined steel slide; target crown; extended ambidextrous manual safety; skeletonized hammer
Combat sights: $839.99
Night sights: $919.99

1911-380 HIGH GRADE, HIGH GRADE COMPACT

Action: Semiautomatic
Grips: Black pearl
Barrel: 3.6 in., 4.25 in.
Sights: Steel 3-dot sights
Weight: 16 oz., 18 oz.
Caliber: .380
Capacity: 8 rounds
Features: Machined stainless steel slide with extensive engraving on the slide flats; composite frame with machined 7075 aluminum sub-frame; corrosion-resistant barrel; gold-colored metal Buckmark on grips
MSRP $1059.99

1911-380 MEDALLION STAINLESS ENGRAVED, MEDALLION STAINLESS ENGRAVED COMPACT

Action: Semiautomatic
Grips: White pearl
Barrel: 3.6 in., 4.25 in.
Sights: Steel 3-dot sights
Weight: 16 oz., 18 oz.
Caliber: .380
Capacity: 8 rounds
Features: High-strength, lightweight composite frame and alloy subframe; machined stainless steel slide with neo-classical American engraving, polished flats, and matte curves; corrosion-resistant barrel
MSRP $949.99

1911-380 SPEED, SPEED COMPACT

Action: Semiautomatic
Grips: Composite
Barrel: 4.25 in.
Sights: Steel 3-dot sights
Weight: 18 oz.
Caliber: .380
Capacity: 8 rounds
Features: High-strength, lightweight composite frame with A-TACS AU Camo finish and alloy subframe; stainless steel slide with Cerakote Burnt Bronze finish; corrosion-resistant barrel
MSRP $839.99

Browning

BROWNING BUCK MARK FIELD TARGET

BROWNING BUCK MARK MEDALLION ROSEWOOD

BROWNING BUCK MARK PLUS CAMPER UFX SR

BROWNING BUCK MARK PLUS PRACTICAL URX

BROWNING BUCK MARK PLUS STAINLESS UDX

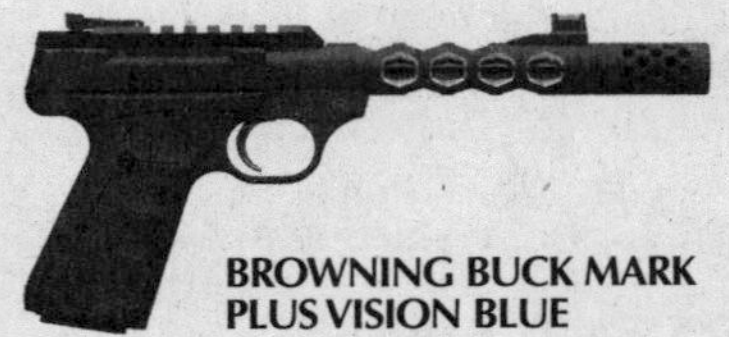
BROWNING BUCK MARK PLUS VISION BLUE

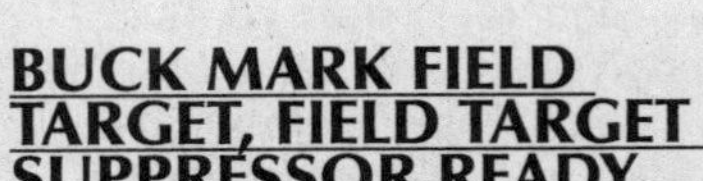

BUCK MARK FIELD TARGET, FIELD TARGET SUPPRESSOR READY

Action: Semiautomatic
Grips: Laminate cocobolo
Barrel: 5.5 in.
Sights: Pro Target adjustable
Weight: 38 oz.
Caliber: .22 LR
Capacity: 10 rounds
Features: Suppressor-ready; full-length Picatinny rail on top; barrel profile is heavy bull
Field Target: $619.99
Suppressor-ready: $639.99

BUCK MARK MEDALLION ROSEWOOD

Action: Semiautomatic
Grips: Laminated rosewood
Barrel: 5.5 in.
Sights: TRUGLO/Marble Arms fiber optic front, Pro Target adjustable rear
Weight: 34 oz.
Caliber: .22 LR
Capacity: 11 rounds
Features: A new look for the Buck Mark with blackened, polished-flats slab-sided barrel; adjustable rear sight and fiber optic front; textured grip panels
MSRP $549.99

BUCK MARK PLUS CAMPER UFX SR

Action: Semiautomatic
Grips: Ultragrip FX
Barrel: 6 in.
Sights: TruGlo/Marble Arms fiber optic front, white outline Pro Target rear
Weight: 34 oz.
Caliber: .22 LR
Capacity: 10 rounds
Features: Suppressor-ready; Browning ambidextrous Ultragrip FX grips; long tapered bull barrel with a matte finish; topside Picatinny rail for optics mounting; pistol rug
MSRP $549.99

BUCK MARK PLUS PRACTICAL URX

Action: Semiautomatic
Grips: Ultragrip RX ambidextrous
Barrel: 5.5 in.
Sights: Pro-target adjustable rear; Truglo/Marble's fiber-optic front
Weight: 34 oz.
Caliber: .22 LR
Capacity: 10+1 rounds
Features: Tapered bull barrel with matte blued finish; matte gray finish receiver
MSRP $499.99

BUCK MARK PLUS STAINLESS UDX, ROSEWOOD UDX

Action: Semiautomatic
Grips: Laminate
Barrel: 5.5 in.
Sights: TruGlo fiber optic front; white outline Pro-Target rear
Weight: 34 oz.
Caliber: .22 LR
Capacity: 10 rounds
Features: Wood laminate UDX grips (Utragrip Deluxe); stainless steel frame and slabside barrel with polished flats; SA trigger; Picatinny top rail for optics; grip frame machined with finger grooves that match up to textured wood grips; slab-side barrel has high-polished flats
Stainless: $639.99
Rosewood: $599.99

BUCK MARK PLUS VISION BLACK, RED, BLUE

Action: Semiautomatic
Grips: Rubber
Barrel: 5.875 in.
Sights: Fiber optic front, adjustable rear
Weight: 27 oz.
Caliber: .22 LR
Capacity: 10 rounds
Features: Lightweight alloy sleeved steel Vision barrel features a tensioned outer aluminum sleeve surrounding a strong steel inner barrel; cuts on barrel sleeve provide a dynamic look and reduce weight (black–sawtooth, blue–honeycomb, red–lateral); Picatinny optics rail; suppressor-ready threaded barrel; muzzle brake; UFX overmolded grips
MSRP $739.99

B&T (Brügger & Thomet)

B&T (BRÜGGER & THOMET) USWA1

USWA1

Action: Semiautomatic
Grips: Polymer
Barrel: 4.33 in.
Sights: Aimpoint NANO
Weight: 40.8 oz.
Caliber: 9mm
Capacity: 17, 19, 30 rounds
Features: Swiss-made with unique design; interchangeable grip panels; Aimpoint NANO red dot sight; APL tac light; sling; cleaning kit; hard case; optional stock kit is available with all the attendant NFA paperwork and taxes
MSRP $2350.00

Cabot Guns

CABOT GUNS GRAN TORINO SS

CABOT GUNS THE AMERICAN JOE COMMANDER

CABOT GUNS THE GENTLEMAN'S CARRY

CABOT GUNS THE ICON

CABOT GUNS VINTAGE CLASSIC

GRAN TORINO SS

Action: Semiautomatic
Grips: Carbon fiber
Barrel: 5 in.
Sights: Reverse dovetail front, low-mount fixed rear
Weight: N/A
Caliber: 9mm, .45 ACP
Capacity: 8, 9 rounds
Features: Complete stainless steel construction; chatoyant carbon fiber grips with luminescent silver flakes and inlaid Cabot medallion; Racing Vector rear slide serrations; top slide serrations; hand-fit match grade barrel with custom crown; front of guide rod has engraved star; aluminum Cabot Tristar trigger; machined in place ejector; Rhombus-textured front strap and mainspring housing
MSRP . . . . starting at $4495.00

THE AMERICAN JOE COMMANDER

Action: Semiautomatic
Grips: Aluminum
Barrel: 4.25 in.
Sights: Cabot reverse dovetail white-dot front, low-mount fixed rear
Weight: 33.5 oz.
Caliber: .45 ACP
Capacity: 8 rounds
Features: The original American Joe now in Commander-length slide; "Tire Tread" USA engraving at front of slide; wing and spiderweb engraving designed by Joe Faris covering the rest of the slide; special flag grips
MSRP . . . . starting at $4595.00

THE GENTLEMAN'S CARRY

Action: Semiautomatic
Grips: Walnut
Barrel: 4.25 in.
Sights: Reverse dovetail tritium front, Warren-style U-notch tritium rear
Weight: N/A
Caliber: .45 ACP, 9mm
Capacity: 8 rounds
Features: Rhombus-cut checkering on the frontstrap and mainspring housing; bobtail cut frame; Carry Cut slide and slide serrations; hand-polished ramp' Cabot's Idiot Scratch-Proof slide star; aluminum trigger skeletonized with a tristar pattern; checkered walnut grips with inlaid Cabot medallion
MSRP $4795.00

THE ICON

Action: Semiautomatic
Grips: Stainless steel
Barrel: 4.25 in., 5 in.
Sights: Reverse dovetail front, Cabot ACE fixed rear
Weight: N/A
Caliber: .45 ACP, 9mm
Capacity: 8 rounds
Features: Made from U.S. sourced stainless steel; choice of Government-length or Commander-length national match-grade barrels with reverse crowns; 24 lines-per-inch rhombus cut checkering on the mainspring housing and frontstrap; Cabot's beavertail safety grip; barrel bushing; mainspring housing with rhombus cuts; Idiot Scratch Proof takedown lever; full-length guide rod; stainless steel monochrome grips
MSRP . . . . starting at $4995.00

VINTAGE CLASSIC

Action: Semiautomatic
Grips: Walnut
Barrel: 5 in.
Sights: Gold bead Cabot reverse dovetail front, low-mount fixed rear
Weight: N/A
Caliber: .45 ACP
Capacity: 8 rounds
Features: Cabot frame and slide from 416 stainless steel billet; proprietary hardening and vintage "classic" finish; Cabot Trinity Stripes rear slide serrations; beveled magazine well; lowered and flared ejection port; Cabot aluminum TriStar trigger; match-grade hand-fit barrel; rhombus-cut front strap and mainspring housing checkering; sight and grip options
MSRP . . . . starting at $4295.00

Canik USA

CANIK USA TP9 ELITE COMBAT

TP9 ELITE COMBAT

Action: Semiautomatic
Grips: Polymer
Barrel: 4.73 in.
Sights: Fiber optic front, drift adjustable rear
Weight: 25.8 oz.
Caliber: 9mm
Capacity: 15, 18 rounds
Features: A sleek-looking striker-fired Canik pistol with a fluted, match-grade threaded barrel; aluminum Speed Funnel magwell; flat-faced aluminum trigger; optics-ready slide with adapter plates; extended mag release; retention holster with slide lock release; changeable backstraps; textured grip; Cerakote slide in flat dark earth (Combat) or black nitride (Combat Executive)
Combat: $849.99
Combat Executive: $779.99
Combat with Vortex Viper red-dot: $949.00

Canik USA

CANIK USA TP9 ELITE SC

CANIK USA TP9SFX

TP9 ELITE SC

Action: Semiautomatic
Grips: Polymer
Barrel: 3.6 in.
Sights: Phosphorous white front, black-out rear
Weight: 24.78 oz.
Caliber: 9mm
Capacity: 12, 15 rounds
Features: A nicely designed carry gun with striker-status and loaded chamber indicators; nitride-coated match-grade barrel; reversible magazine release and slide stop; red-dot optic mounting interface; interchangeable backstraps; tungsten Cerakote finish overnitride finish on slide; accessory rail
MSRP $439.99

TP9SFX

Action: SA
Grips: Plastic
Barrel: 5.2 in.
Sights: Industry-standard dovetail sight cuts & four red dot interface plates; removable red dot over
Weight: 29.92 oz.
Caliber: 9mm Luger
Capacity: 20+1 rounds
Features: Improved single action trigger with 3.5–4 lb. pull; lightening cuts on slide to reduce muzzle rise; reversible ambidextrous cocking lever; adjustable length reversible magazine catch; Picatinny rail; Tungsten grey Cerakote over phosphate
MSRP $549.99

Caracal USA

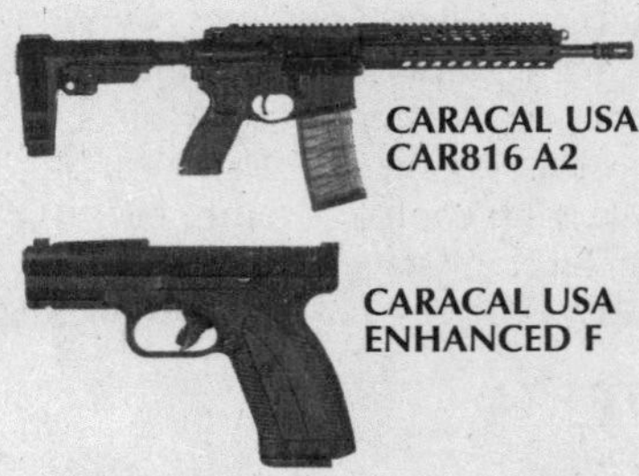
CARACAL USA CAR816 A2

CARACAL USA ENHANCED F

CAR816 A2

Action: Semiautomatic
Grips: Synthetic
Barrel: 11.5 in., 14.5 in., 16 in.
Sights: None
Weight: 6 lb. 15 oz.
Caliber: 5.56 NATO
Capacity: 10, 30 rounds
Features: Capitalizing on the AR pistol trend and featuring a short-stroke gas operated piston system; modified M4 barrel contour; black nitride finish; EDT Sharp Shooter trigger; SBA3 pistol brace; 9-inch key-lock M-LOK handguard; black or Flat Dark Earth
MSRP . . . . $1849.99–$1929.00

ENHANCED F

Action: Semiautomatic
Grips: Polymer
Barrel: 4 in.
Sights: Three-dot
Weight: 28 oz.
Caliber: 9mm
Capacity: 10, 18 rounds
Features: Striker-fired polymer frame; integrated trigger safety; firing pin safety; drop safety; rail interface for light and laser mounting; full-length steel slide guide; fully supported chamber; cold-hammer-forged barrel; Quick Sights, 3-dot night sights, and suppressor-height sights available
MSRP $699.99
Night Sights/Quick Sights: . .$773.00
Suppressor-Height 3-Dot: . .$799.00

Charter Arms

CHARTER ARMS BOOMER

CHARTER ARMS BULLDOG

BOOMER

Action: DAO revolver
Grips: Rubber
Barrel: 2 in. tapered
Sights: None
Weight: 20 oz.
Caliber: .44 Spl.
Capacity: 5 rounds
Features: Designed specifically for concealed carry; DAO hammer; full rubber combat grips; matte stainless finish; tapered barrel for reduced kick
MSRP $438.20

BULLDOG

Action: DA revolver
Grips: Rubber; Crimson Trace lasergrips
Barrel: 2.5 in., 3 in. or 5 in. in target model
Sights: Fixed, adjustable rear on Target model
Weight: 21 oz.
Caliber: .44 Spl.
Capacity: 5 rounds
Features: A larger concealed carry revolver, with DA/SA exposed hammer; available configurations include: Blue Standard; Tiger; Classic with 3-in. barrel, no underlug, exposed crane, and full wood grips; black Nitride; On Duty semi-concealed hammer in all stainless; Stainless Standard; Stainless DAO with concealed hammer; matte stainless with Crimson Trace laser grips; and Target with ramp front sight and adjustable rear
MSRP . . . . $425.60–$631.40

Charter Arms

CHARTER ARMS CHIC LADY DAO

CHARTER ARMS OFF DUTY

CHARTER ARMS MAG PUG

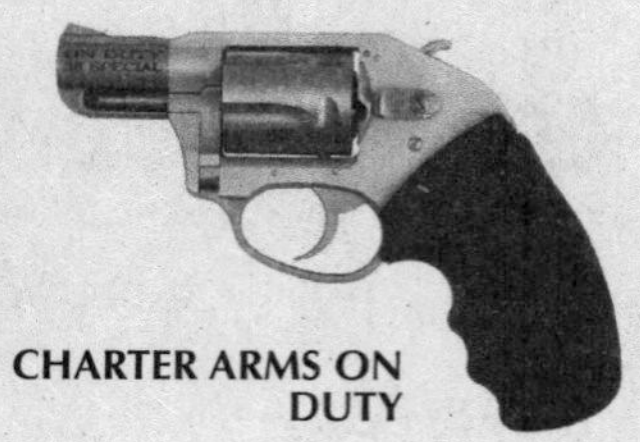
CHARTER ARMS ON DUTY

CHARTER ARMS PATHFINDER

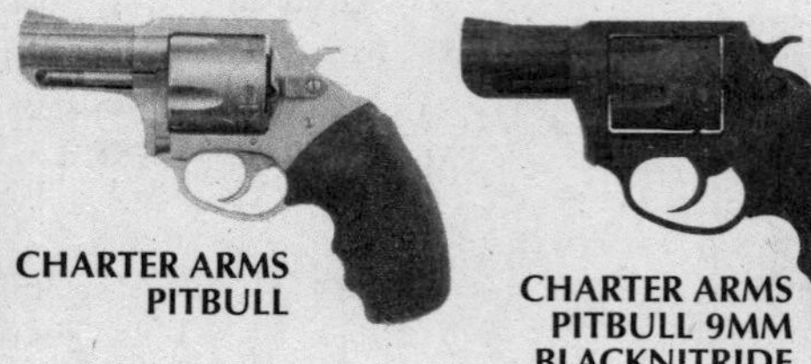
CHARTER ARMS PITBULL

CHARTER ARMS PITBULL 9MM BLACKNITRIDE

CHIC LADY

Action: DA/SA, DAO revolver
Grips: Rubber
Barrel: 2 in.
Sights: Fixed
Weight: 12 oz.
Caliber: .38 Spl.
Capacity: 5 rounds
Features: High-polish stainless-steel pink anodized aluminum frame; frame based on Undercover Lite models; DA/SA explosed hammer version also available with Crimson Trace laser grips
MSRP . . . . $491.40–$684.60

MAG PUG

Action: DA revolver
Grips: Rubber; Crimson Trace lasergrips
Barrel: 2.2 in., 4.2 in.
Sights: Fixed, adjustable rear on Target model
Weight: 23 oz.
Caliber: .357 Mag.
Capacity: 5 rounds
Features: Traditional spurred hammer and full-size grips; optional Crimson Trace grip; stainless steel frame; blued and stainless finish
MSRP . . . . $408.80–$600.60

OFF DUTY

Action: DA revolver
Grips: Crimson Trace lasergrip
Barrel: 2 in.
Sights: Serrated front, rear notch
Weight: 12 oz.
Caliber: .38 Spl. +P
Capacity: 5 rounds
Features: Lightweight, concealed hammer DAO concealed carry revolver of aircraft-grade aluminum and stainless steel; finishes include: black frame/high-polished stainless barrel and cylinder; black frame/matte stainless barrel and cylinder; matte aluminum frame/matte gray barrel and cylinder
MSRP . . . . $420.00–$452.20

ON DUTY

Action: DA revolver
Grips: Rubber; Crimson Trace lasergrips
Barrel: 2 in.
Sights: Fixed
Weight: 12 oz.
Caliber: .357 Mag., .38 Spl. +P
Capacity: 5 rounds
Features: Unique semi-concealed hammer design; constructed of heat-treated aluminum; allows single-action and double-action operations while minimizing the risk of snagging the hammer on clothing; standard or Crimson Trace grip
MSRP $418.60

PATHFINDER

Action: DA revolver
Grips: Rubber; Crimson Trace lasergrips
Barrel: 2 in., 4.2 in.
Sights: Fixed, adjustable rear on Target model
Weight: 12 oz.–24 oz.
Caliber: .22 LR, .22 Mag.
Capacity: 6 rounds
Features: Choice of stainless steel or aluminum frames, has exposed hammer for DA/SA operation; aluminum frame Lite models in .22 Mag only available in brushed silver frame with matte blue barrel and cylinder; pink frame with matte silver cylinder and barrel; lavender frame with matte silver barrel and cylinder; and matte black frame with matte stainless barrel and cylinder; steel frame models are in .22 LR and .22 WMR, with choice of barrel lengths, all in all stainless
MSRP . . . . $378.00–$429.80

PITBULL

Action: DA/SA
Grips: Rubber
Barrel: 2.5 in.
Sights: Fixed
Weight: 22 oz.
Caliber: .40 S&W, 9mm,.45 ACP
Capacity: 5 rounds
Features: Unique design provides a dual coil spring assembly located in the extractor which allows for the insertion and retention of rimless cartridges, so no moon clips are required
MSRP . . . . $506.80–$527.80

PITBULL 9MM BLACKNITRIDE

Action: DA/SA revolver
Grips: Rubber
Barrel: 2.2 in.
Sights: Fixed
Weight: 22 oz.
Caliber: 9mm
Capacity: 5 rounds
Features: Rimless cartridge extractor assembly system; dual coil spring assembly located in the extractor; nitride adds hardness to the finish and reduces friction and wear; scratch-resistant surface; extended life in the rifling and chambers
MSRP $522.00

Charter Arms

CHARTER ARMS PITBULL .40 S&W BLACKNITRIDE

CHARTER ARMS PITBULL .45 ACP BLACKNITRIDE

CHARTER ARMS PROFESSIONAL BLACKNITRIDE

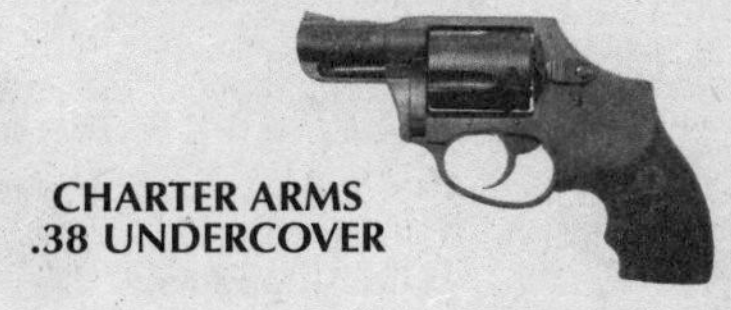

CHARTER ARMS .38 UNDERCOVER

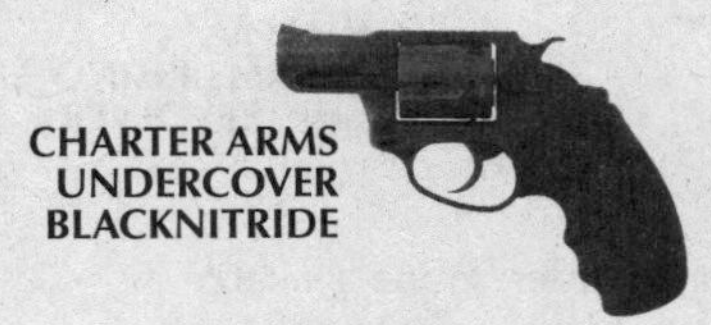

CHARTER ARMS UNDERCOVER BLACKNITRIDE

CHARTER ARMS UNDERCOVER LITE

PITBULL .40 S&W BLACKNITRIDE

Action: DA/SA revolver
Grips: Rubber
Barrel: 2.3 in.
Sights: Fixed
Weight: 20 oz.
Caliber: .40 caliber
Capacity: 5 rounds
Features: Dual coil spring assembly located in the extractor; nitride adds hardness to the finish and reduces friction and wear; scratch-resistant surface; extended life in the rifling and chambers
MSRP $527.80

PITBULL .45 ACP BLACKNITRIDE

Action: DA/SA revolver
Grips: Rubber
Barrel: 2.5 in.
Sights: Fixed
Weight: 22 oz.
Caliber: .45 ACP
Capacity: 5 rounds
Features: Rimless cartridge extractor assembly system; dual coil spring assembly located in the extractor; nitride adds hardness to the finish and reduces friction and wear; scratch-resistant surface
MSRP $527.80

PROFESSIONAL BLACKNITRIDE

Action: Revolver
Grips: Walnut
Barrel: 3 in.
Sights: Fiber optic front
Weight: N/A
Caliber: .32 H&R Mag.
Capacity: 7 rounds
Features: This undervalued round finds a home in a carry-ready revolver that has a full underlug; handsome black nitride finish
MSRP $438.00

UNDERCOVER

Action: DA revolver
Grips: Checkered compact rubber or Crimson Trace lasergrips
Barrel: 2 in.
Sights: Fixed
Weight: 16 oz.
Caliber: .38 Spl. +P
Capacity: 5 rounds
Features: Stainless steel frame; blued, stainless, tiger & black, DAO available; compact and lightweight, this revolver is ideal for concealed carry situations; 3-point cylinder lock-up
MSRP . . . . $358.40–$565.60

UNDERCOVER BLACKNITRIDE FINISH

Action: DA/SA revolver
Grips: Rubber
Barrel: 2 in.
Sights: Fixed
Weight: 16 oz.
Caliber: .38 Spl.
Capacity: 5 rounds
Features: Compact and lightweight; ideal for concealed carry due to 2 in. barrel and superior safety features; nitride adds hardness to the finish and reduces friction and wear; scratch-resistant surface
MSRP $533.40

UNDERCOVER LITE

Action: DA revolver
Grips: Rubber, compact
Barrel: 2 in.
Sights: Fixed
Weight: 12 oz.
Caliber: .38 Spl. +P
Capacity: 5 rounds
Features: Frame is constructed from aircraft-grade aluminum and steel; traditional spurred hammer; optional DAO (double action trigger); many finishes and special editions available
MSRP . . . . $411.60–$453.60

Chiappa Firearms

CHIAPPA FIREARMS 1873 REVOLVER S.A.A. REGULATOR CENTERFIRE

CHIAPPA FIREARMS CBR-9 BLACK RHINO PISTOL WITH ARM BRACE

1873 REVOLVER S.A.A. REGULATOR CENTERFIRE

Action: SA revolver
Grips: Black polymer
Barrel: 4.75 in.
Sights: Fixed front
Weight: 32 oz.
Caliber: .45 LC, .38 Spec.
Capacity: 6 rounds
Features: Centerfire cartridge; perfect for competition or plinking
MSRP $443.00

CBR-9 BLACK RHINO PISTOL WITH ARM BRACE

Action: Semiautomatic
Grips: Polymer
Barrel: 9 in.
Sights: Flip-up fiber optic front and rear
Weight: 76.8 oz.
Caliber: 9mm
Capacity: 18 rounds
Features: Designed as a personal defense weapon, but it's also likely a ball on the range with its arm brace
MSRP $2269.00

Chiappa Firearms

CHIAPPA FIREARMS FAS 6007

CHIAPPA FIREARMS RHINO REVOLVER MATCH MASTER

CHIAPPA FIREARMS RHINO 30 DS HUNTER, 60 DS HUNTER

CHIAPPA FIREARMS RHINO NEBULA

CHIAPPA FIREARMS RHINO REVOLVER 30DS X SPECIAL EDITION

CHIAPPA FIREARMS RHINO 200DS REVOLVER

FAS 6007

Action: Semiautomatic
Grips: Wood
Barrel: 5.63 in.
Sights: Two-position front, adjustable rear
Weight: 37.6 oz.
Caliber: .22 LR
Capacity: 5 rounds
Features: Developed in collaboration with Olympic shooters; adjustable palm rest; a rear sight with an adjustable window; adjustable grip; outside access set screws for hammer and hammer weight; modular weights; adjustable trigger; shock buffer
MSRP $1630.00

RHINO 30 DS HUNTER, 60 DS HUNTER

Action: Revolver
Grips: Walnut
Barrel: 3 in., 6 in.
Sights: Fiber optic front, adjustable rear
Weight: 28.8 oz.–32 oz.
Caliber: .357 Mag.
Capacity: 6 rounds
Features: Frame and barrel in "Hunter" OD Green Cerakote; barrels have vent ribs; stippled walnut grips with finger grooves; Rhino's distinct flat-sided cylinder; long-barrel version has accessory rail; includes three moon clips
30 DS Hunter: $1287.00
60 DS Hunter: $1379.00

RHINO 30DS X SPECIAL EDITION

Action: Revolver
Grips: G10
Barrel: 3 in.
Sights: Fiber optic front, adjustable rear
Weight: 44.8 oz.
Caliber: .357 Mag.
Capacity: 6 rounds
Features: The unique Rhino revolver in a nifty 3-inch barrel with upgraded G10 grips; brushed stainless steel finish
MSRP $1539.00

RHINO 200DS

Action: Revolver
Grips: Wood
Barrel: 6 in.
Sights: Front blade; adjustable rear
Weight: 37 oz.
Caliber: .357, .40 S&W, .357 Mag/9mm combo
Capacity: 6 rounds
Features: Rhino barrel is aligned with the bottom most chamber, which lowers the center of gravity and yields a centerline of the bore more in line with the shooter's arm allowing for the most natural "point ability" while engaging a target; reduces both recoil and muzzle flip which insures subsequent shots are on target faster; frame available in chrome, black, or gold finish
MSRP . . . . $1065.00–$1231.00

RHINO MATCH MASTER

Action: Revolver
Grips: Micarta
Barrel: 6 in.
Sights: Aristocrat front, adjustable rear
Weight: 46.6 oz.
Caliber: .38 Spec.
Capacity: 6 rounds
Features: Unique bottom-cylinder barrel alignment; Hogue Micarta grips; Ergal frame; steel barrel and breech shield; cylinder block, cylinder rotation, and hammer block safeties
MSRP $2990.00

RHINO NEBULA

Action: Revolver
Grips: Laminate
Barrel: 6 in.
Sights: Fiber optic front and rear
Weight: 33.6 oz.
Caliber: .357 Mag.
Capacity: 6 rounds
Features: The unique bottom chamber/barre alignment that is the Rhino now in a snazzy, mixed-color PVD metal finish and otherworldly blue laminate grips; top and bottom rails, fiber optics front and back with an adjustable rear; three moon clips provided; DA/SA or SA-only option
MSRP . . . . $1509.00–$1725.00

Christensen Arms

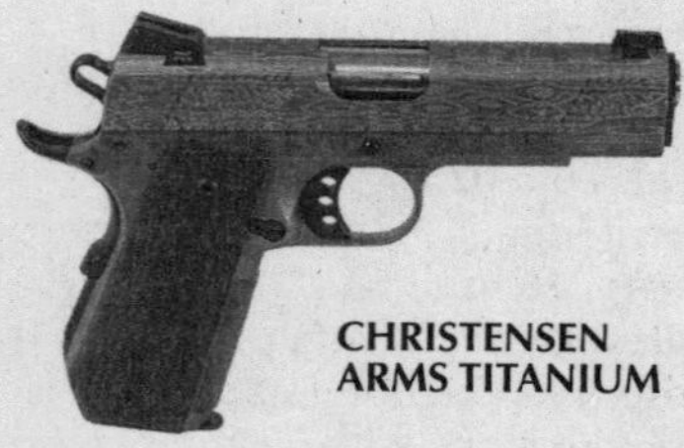

CHRISTENSEN ARMS TITANIUM

TITANIUM SERIES

Action: Semiautomatic
Grips: Carbon fiber
Barrel: 4.25 in., 5 in.
Sights: Raised night sights
Weight: N/A
Caliber: .45 ACP
Capacity: 7 rounds
Features: This is a step up, for sure, in the 1911 department, with a titanium frame; Damascus steel slide; match-grade barrel; carbon-fiber grips; checkered front strap and mainspring housing; full-length guide rod; skeletonized hammer; skeletonized trigger with adjustable overtravel; 4.25-in. model has bobtailcut
MSRP . . . . $4795.00–$5095.00

Cimarron Firearms Co.

CIMARRON 1872 OPEN TOP NAVY

CIMARRON 1911

CIMARRON 1911 WILD BUNCH COMBO

CIMARRON FIREARMS BAD BOY

CIMARRON FIREARMS EL MALO 2

CIMARRON FIREARMS EVIL ROY COMPETITION

CIMARRON FRONTIER

CIMARRON HOLY SMOKER

1872 OPEN TOP NAVY

Action: SA revolver
Grips: Walnut
Barrel: 4.75, 5.5, 7.5 in.
Sights: Fixed, open
Weight: 40 oz.
Caliber: .44 Spl.; .44 Colt, .44 Russian
Capacity: 6 rounds
Features: Forged, color case-hardened frame; Army or Navy grip; charcoal blued, standard blued, or original barrel finish
MSRP . . . . $518.70–$559.95

1911

Action: Semiautomatic
Grips: Walnut
Barrel: 5 in.
Sights: Open, fixed
Weight: 39.52 oz.
Caliber: .45 ACP
Capacity: 8+1 rounds
Features: Correct historical markings; diamond checkered walnut grips; nickel, polished blued, and parkerized finish; optional WWI-style lanyard magazine
MSRP . . . . $570.00–$799.50

1911 WILD BUNCH COMBO

Action: Semiautomatic
Grips: Diamond checkered walnut
Barrel: 5 in.
Sights: Fixed
Weight: 39.52 oz.
Caliber: .45 ACP
Capacity: 8+1 rounds
Features: Correct historical markings; the original 1911 frame with a Type 1 smooth mainspring housing; combo includes the 1911 in polished blue finish and the Tanker shoulder holster, a reproduction of the rig used by William Holden in the movie The Wild Bunch
MSRP $955.50

BAD BOY

Action: Revolver
Grips: Wood
Barrel: 6 in., 8 in.
Sights: Ramp front, adjustable rear
Weight: N/A
Caliber: .44 Mag., 10mm Auto
Capacity: 6 rounds
Features: Model P pre-war frame single action; octagonal barrel; flat top; adjustable rear sight
MSRP $742.39

EL MALO 2

Action: Revolver
Grips: Walnut
Barrel: 4.75 in.
Sights: Iron front
Weight: N/A
Caliber: .45 LC
Capacity: 6 rounds
Features: El Malo is Spanish for "The Bad" and this revolver is based on the 1873 Colt Single Action Army; octagon barrel; case-colored pre-war frame; low and wide competition hammer; one-piece walnut grip
MSRP $578.05

EVIL ROY COMPETITION

Action: Revolver
Grips: Walnut
Barrel: 4.75 in., 5.5 in.
Sights: Blade front, integral rear
Weight: 38 oz.–40.1 oz.
Caliber: .357 Mag., .44-40, .45 LC
Capacity: 6 rounds
Features: Competition-ready single-action with a tuned action; square notch rear sight paired with a wide front blade; slim walnut grip; some models available with a low, wide hammer
Blued: $840.62
Stainless: . . . . $1014.26–$1037.08

FRONTIER

Action: SA
Grips: Walnut
Barrel: 3.5 in., 4.75 in., 5.5 in., 7.5 in.
Sights: Fixed
Weight: 4 lb. 8 oz.
Caliber: .45 Colt
Capacity: N/A
Features: High-polished stainless finish; walnut grips; pre-war frame
MSRP $802.43

HOLY SMOKER

Action: SA revolver
Grips: Walnut
Barrel: 4.75 in.
Sights: Open, fixed
Weight: 36 oz.
Caliber: .45 Colt
Capacity: 6 rounds
Features: Revolver made famous in *3:10 to Yuma* film; standard blued finish; case-hardened pre-war frame; gold-plated sterling silver cross inlayed on both sides of one-piece walnut grip
MSRP $784.49

Cimarron Firearms Co.

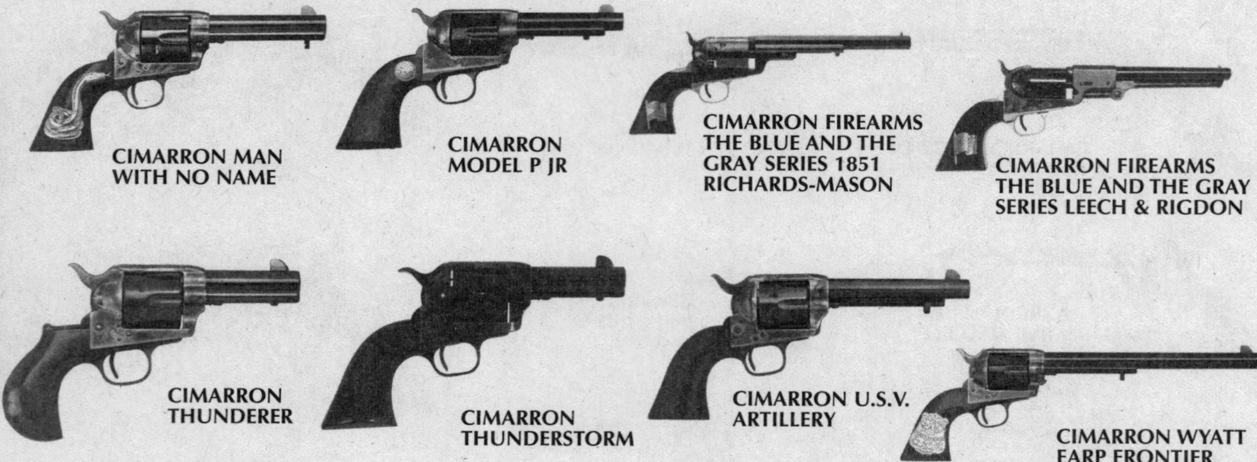

MAN WITH NO NAME

Action: SA revolver
Grips: Walnut
Barrel: 4.75 in., 5.5 in.
Sights: Open, fixed
Weight: 42.56 oz.–44.16 oz.
Caliber: .45 Colt
Capacity: 6 rounds
Features: Model P in .45 Colt; sterling silver snake on both sides of walnut grip
MSRP $798.53

MODEL P JR.

Action: SA revolver
Grips: Walnut
Barrel: 3.5 in., 4.75 in., 5.5 in.
Sights: Fixed, open
Weight: 35.2 oz.
Caliber: .38 Spl., .22 LR, .32-20 Win./.32 H&R Dual Cylinder
Capacity: 6 rounds
Features: Fashioned after the 1873 Colt SAA but on a smaller scale; color case-hardened frame
MSRP . . . . $506.45–$668.41

THE BLUE AND THE GRAY SERIES 1851 RICHARDS-MASON

Action: Cartridge conversion SAO
Grips: Walnut
Barrel: 7.5 in.
Sights: Post front
Weight: 45.2 oz.
Caliber: .38 Spec.
Capacity: 6 rounds
Features: Limited-edition run faithful to the original and featuring a lightly engraved unfluted cylinder; case-hardened frame with brass accents; pure silver CSA flag inlay in one-piece wooden grips
MSRP $790.50

THE BLUE AND THE GRAY SERIES LEECH & RIGDON

Action: Cartridge conversion SAO
Grips: Walnut
Barrel: 7.5 in.
Sights: Post front
Weight: 42.8 oz.
Caliber: .36
Capacity: 6 rounds
Features: Limited-edition run faithful to the original and featuring a charcoal blue unfluted cylinder and barrel; case-hardened frame with brass accents; pure silver CSA flag inlay in one-piece wooden grips
MSRP $740.31

THUNDERER

Action: SA revolver
Grips: Walnut, ivory, mother of pearl or black hard rubber
Barrel: 3.5 in. w/ ejector, 4.75 in., 5.5 in., 7.5 in.
Sights: Fixed, open
Weight: 38–43.60 oz.
Caliber: .45 LC, .44 Spl., .44 WCF, .357 Mag., .45 LC/.45 ACP Dual Cylinder
Capacity: 6 rounds
Features: Designed in 1990 by Cimarron founder & president "Texas Jack" Harvey; forged, stainless finish
Blued: . . . . $620.28–$634.32
Stainless: $818.88
Dual .45 ACP/.45 LC $736.76

THUNDERSTORM

Action: SA revolver
Grips: Walnut
Barrel: 3.5 in., 4.75 in.
Sights: Front, rear
Weight: 35.7 oz.–39.68 oz.
Caliber: .45 Colt, .357 Mag./.38 Spl.
Capacity: 6 rounds
Features: Checkered grips; stainless steel or standard blued finishes; wide front sights and deep rear notch; smooth action and hand-knurled hammer
Blued: $824.81
Stainless: $975.00

U.S.V. ARTILLERY

Action: SA revolver
Grips: Walnut
Barrel: 5.5 in.
Sights: Fixed, open
Weight: 40 oz.
Caliber: .45 LC
Capacity: 6 rounds
Features: Old model case-hardened with US Artillery markings; stock is a solid piece of walnut with RAC Cartouche; blued, charcoal blued, or original finish
MSRP . . . . $646.17–$666.00

WYATT EARP FRONTIER BUNTLINE

Action: SA revolver
Grips: Walnut
Barrel: 10 in.
Sights: Open, fixed
Weight: 43.04 oz.
Caliber: .45 LC
Capacity: 6 rounds
Features: Revolver made famous in the film *Tombstone*; one-piece walnut grips with silver inlaid medallion; choice of blue or case hardened finishes
MSRP . . . . $873.83–$931.79

Citadel by Legacy Sports

M-1911

Action: Semiautomatic
Grips: Cocobolo
Barrel: 3.5 in., 5 in.
Sights: Fixed
Weight: 33.6–37.6 oz.
Caliber: 9mm, .45 ACP
Capacity: 7 or 8 rounds
Features: Choice of Government or Officer models with a Series 70 firing system; extended slide stop, skeletonized hammer and trigger, matte blue finish; includes two magazines
MSRP $599.00

M1911 GOVERNMENT AMERICAN FLAG

Action: Semiautomatic
Grips: Wood
Barrel: 5 in.
Sights: Blade front, drift-adjustable rear
Weight: 36.8 oz.–38.8 oz.
Caliber: 9mm, .45 ACP
Capacity: 8, 10 rounds
Features: Citadel's 1911 Government wrapped in eye-catching red-white-and-blue or Grayscale American flag graphics; skeletonized trigger and hammer, extended beavertail grip safety; full-length guide rod; ambidextrous safety
MSRP $999.00

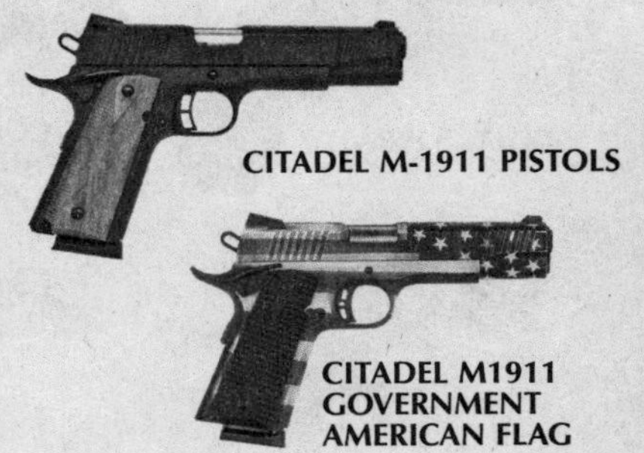

CITADEL M-1911 PISTOLS

CITADEL M1911 GOVERNMENT AMERICAN FLAG

CMMG, Inc.

CMMG INC . BANSHEE 100 SERIES PISTOL

CMMG INC . BANSHEE 300 SERIES PISTOL

CMMG INC. BANSHEE 200 SERIES PISTOL

BANSHEE 100 SERIES PISTOL

Action: Semiautomatic
Grips: Synthetic
Barrel: 8 in., 8.5 in., 9 in., 10 in., 12.5 in.
Sights: None
Weight: 4 lb. 8 oz.–6 lb. 4 oz.
Caliber: 9mm, .45 ACP, 5.7X28mm, .22 LR, 10mm, .458 SOCOM, .40 S&W, 5.56 NATO, 6.5 Grendel, .300 BLK, 7.62X39, .308 Win.,
Capacity: 10, 13, 20, 25, 30, 32, 33 rounds
Features: An interesting MSR pistol platform in a unique set of caliber offerings. Features include mil-spec trigger, charging handle; free-floating M-LOK handguard; 7075-T6 aluminum receivers; salt bath nitride finish; A2 compensator
MSRP . . . . $899.95–$1849.95

BANSHEE 200 SERIES PISTOL

Action: Semiautomatic
Grips: Synthetic
Barrel: 8 in., 8.5 in., 9 in., 10 in., 12.5 in.
Sights: None
Weight: 5 lb. 1 oz.–6 lb. 12 oz.
Caliber: 9mm, .45 ACP, 5.7X28mm, 7.62X39, .40 S&W, 5.56 NATO, .22 LR, .300 BLK, 10mm, 6.5 Grendel, .308 Win., .458 SOCOM
Capacity: 10, 13, 20, 25, 30, 32, 33 rounds
Features: A step up from the 100 Series with the addition of Magpul MOE pistol grip; CMMG Ripbrace (Ripstock NFA); Type III hard coat anodize; CMMG SV muzzle brake
MSRP . . . . $1049.95–$1949.95

BANSHEE 300 SERIES PISTOL

Action: Semiautomatic
Grips: Synthetic
Barrel: 8 in., 8.5 in., 9 in., 10 in., 12.5 in.
Sights: None
Weight: 4 lb. 5 oz.–6 lb. 3 oz.
Caliber: 9mm, 10mm, .45 ACP, 5.7X28mm, .300 BLK, 7.62X39, .22 LR, .40 S&W, 5.7X28mm
Capacity: 13, 20, 25, 30 rounds
Features: With fewer caliber offerings than the 100 and 200 series but with the addition of Magpul MOE pistol grip; Premier Cerakote finish in 10 color options; ambidextrous CMMG charging handle and safety; various muzzle brakes depending on caliber; "Banshee" engraved on lower receiver
MSRP . . . . $1199.95–$1799.95

Colt's Manufacturing Company

COBRA

Action: Revolver
Grips: Rubber
Barrel: 2 in.
Sights: Fiber optic front
Weight: 25 oz.
Caliber: .38 Spl.
Capacity: 6 rounds
Features: DA revolver with all-steel contruction; small frame and barrel ideal for concealed carry; Hogue Overmolded grip has been moved rearward to manage recoil on standard model; Classic version has medallion wood grips, brass front bead, and polished cylinder
Cobra: $699.00
Classic Cobra: $749.00
Night Cobra: $899.00
Bright Cobra: $1299.00
Cobra TT: $749.00

COMBAT UNIT RAIL GUN

Action: Semiautomatic
Grips: G10
Barrel: 5 in.
Sights: Novak night sight front, Novak Low Mount Carry rear
Weight: 40 oz.
Caliber: 9mm, .45 ACP
Capacity: 8 rounds (.45 ACP), 9 rounds (9mm)
Features: Upgraded duty-ready 1911 with 1913 Picatinny rail; checkered and scalloped gray G10 grips; designed with Special Forces trainers Daryl Holland and Ken Hackathorn
MSRP $1599.00

COMPETITION PISTOL

Action: SA
Grips: G10 grips
Barrel: 5 in.
Sights: Fiber optic front, Novak adjustable rear
Weight: 36 oz.
Caliber: .38 Super, .45 ACP, 9mm
Capacity: 8 or 9 rounds
Features: Dual spring recoil system; undercut trigger guard; upswept beavertail grip safety; National Match barrel
Standard: $899.00
SS 9mm, .45 ACP: $999.00
SS .38 Super: $1049.00
Titanium: $999.00
Competition Plus: $1199.00

CUSTOM COMPETITION PISTOL

Action: Semiautomatic
Grips: G10
Barrel: 5 in.
Sights: Novak fiber optic front, Bomar-style rear
Weight: N/A
Caliber: .45 ACP
Capacity: 8 rounds
Features: Hand-assembled by Colt's Custom Shop gunsmiths; blended magwell; frontstrap checkering; stainless steel slide and frame; wide slide serrations front and rear
MSRP $2299.00

DEFENDER

Action: Semiautomatic
Grips: Rubber finger-grooved
Barrel: 5 in.
Sights: White dot carry front and rear
Weight: 30 oz.
Caliber: .45 ACP, 9mm
Capacity: 7+1 rounds, 8+1 rounds
Features: Beveled magazine well; black skeletonized aluminum trigger; Series 80 firing system; beavertail grip and standard thumb safety; stainless steel slide, Teflon coated receiver; aluminum alloy frame
MSRP $999.00

GOLD CUP

Action: Semiautomatic
Grips: Black composite
Barrel: 5 in.
Sights: Dovetail front, adjustable rear
Weight: 39 oz.
Caliber: 9mm, .38 Super, .45 ACP
Capacity: 8+1 rounds
Features: Beveled magazine well; beavertail grip safety; Colt competition blue G10 grips; wide aluminum 3-Hole trigger adjustable for over travel; stainless steel frame finish and material; enhanced hammer. National Match version appears in blue and adds target sights, National Match barrel, wood grips with inset gold Colt medallion
Gold Cup: . . . . . . $1199.00–$1249.00
Trophy: . . . . $1699.00–$1749.00
National Match: $1299.00

KING COBRA

Action: Revolver
Grips: Hogue
Barrel: 3 in.
Sights: Brass bead front, groove rear
Weight: 28 oz.
Caliber: .357 Mag.
Capacity: 6 rounds
Features: Colt continues reintroductions of long-discontinued classics with the King Cobra .357 Mag.; a brushed stainless finish; Hogue overmolded grips; user-replaceable front sight; Linear Leaf (LL2) trigger; heavy frame; full lug
MSRP $899.00

Colt's Manufacturing Company

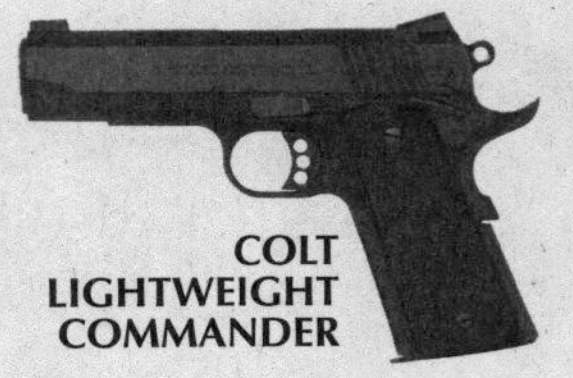
COLT LIGHTWEIGHT COMMANDER

COLT M45A1 MARINE PISTOL

COLT PYTHON

COLT SINGLE ACTION ARMY

LIGHTWEIGHT COMMANDER

Action: SA
Grips: G10 grips
Barrel: 4.25 in.
Sights: Novak sights
Weight: 29.4 oz.
Caliber: .45 ACP, 9mm
Capacity: 8 or 9 rounds
Features: Shorter profile and lower weight than a traditional full-size Government model; dual spring recoil system; undercut trigger guard; upswept beavertail grip safety
MSRP. $999.00

M45A1 MARINE PISTOL

Action: Semiautomatic
Grips: G10
Barrel: 5 in.
Sights: Novak night sights
Weight: 40 oz.
Caliber: .45 ACP
Capacity: 7 rounds
Features: Selected by the US Marine Corps as their Close Quarters Battle Pistol; available in Decobond Brown finish; checkered Desert Tan G10 grip panels; underside Picatinny rail
MSRP. $1699.00

PYTHON

Action: Revolver
Grips: Walnut
Barrel: 4.25 in., 6 in.
Sights: Orange insert ramp front, adjustable rear
Weight: 46 oz.
Caliber: .357 Mag.
Capacity: 6 rounds
Features: An oldie but a goodie returns to the fold with checkered target-style walnut grips; polished steel finish; redesigned guts have twelve fewer parts than original Python; metal under the rear sight has been made sturdier with 30% more steel
MSRP. $1499.00

SINGLE ACTION ARMY

Action: SA revolver
Grips: Black composite eagle
Barrel: 4.75 in., 5.5 in., 7.5 in.
Sights: Fixed
Weight: 46 oz.
Caliber: .357 Mag., .45 Colt
Capacity: 6 rounds
Features: Case-colored frame; transfer bar; second generation style cylinder bushing; blued or nickel finish
MSRP. $1799.00

Culper Precision

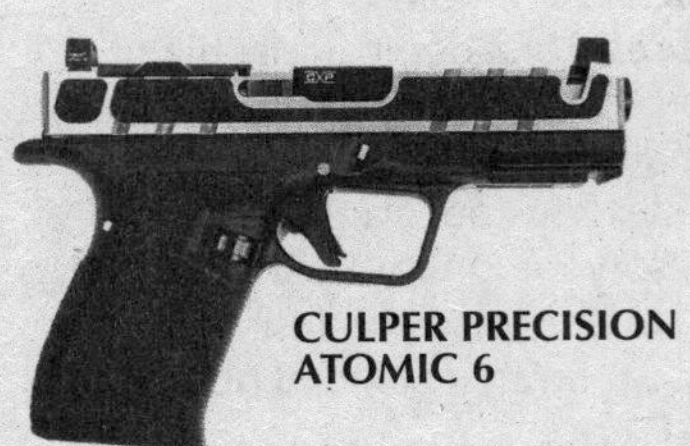
CULPER PRECISION ATOMIC 6

ATOMIC 6

Action: Semiautomatic
Grips: Polymer
Barrel: 4 in.
Sights: Trijicon night sights
Weight: 16.4 oz.
Caliber: 9mm
Capacity: 15 rounds
Features: CO-cured carbon fiber and steel slide based on the Glock Gen4 foundation; threaded or non-threaded, match-grade, DLC-coated barrel with box fluted target crown; custom SoftShoot recoil management system; installed Zev Pro upper parts kit; set of three grip sizing panels; enhanced trigger guard; Apex trigger
MSRP. . . . .$2499.00–$3035.00

CZ-USA (Ceska Zbrojovka)

CZ-USA 75 B

75 B

Action: Semiautomatic
Grips: Plastic
Barrel: 4.6 in.
Sights: Fixed, 3-dot system
Weight: 35.2 oz.
Caliber: 9mm
Capacity: 10, 16 rounds
Features: Steel frame; high-capacity double column magazines; hammer forged barrels; ergonomic grip and controls; DA/SA; firing pin block safety; black polycoat finish
MSRP. $699.00

CZ-USA (Ceska Zbrojovka)

CZ–USA 75 B Ω CONVERTIBLE

CZ–USA 75 B Ω URBAN GREY SUPPRESSOR-READY

CZ–USA 75 COMPACT

CZ–USA 75 P-01 Ω CONVERTIBLE

CZ–USA 75 P-01 Ω URBAN GREY SUPPRESSOR-READY

CZ-USA 75 SP-01

CZ–USA 75 SP-01 TACTICAL URBAN GREY SUPPRESSOR-READY

CZ–USA 75 TACTICAL SPORT ORANGE

75 B Ω CONVERTIBLE

Action: DA/SA
Grips: Plastic
Barrel: 4.6 in.
Sights: Fixed
Weight: 35.2 oz.
Caliber: 9mm Luger
Capacity: 10, 16 rounds
Features: Swappable safety/decocker; interlocking trigger design for easy disassembly and reassembly without tools
MSRP $699.00

75 B Ω URBAN GREY SUPPRESSOR-READY

Action: DA/SA
Grips: Plastic
Barrel: 5.2 in.
Sights: High titrium three dot
Weight: 42.1 oz.
Caliber: 9mm Luger
Capacity: 10, 18 rounds
Features: Threaded barrels; high suppressor sights with tritium lamps; swappable safety/decocker; interlocking trigger design for easy disassembly and reassembly without tools
MSRP $739.00

75 COMPACT

Action: Semiautomatic
Grips: Plastic
Barrel: 3.8 in.
Sights: Fixed, 3-dot system
Weight: 32.48 oz.
Caliber: 9mm Luger
Capacity: 10, 14 rounds
Features: Black polycoat, dual tone, satin nickel frame finishes; manual safety; steel frame; high capacity double column magazines; hammer forged barrels
MSRP $725.00

75 P-01 Ω CONVERTIBLE

Action: DA/SA
Grips: Rubber
Barrel: 3.8 in.
Sights: Fixed
Weight: 28 oz.
Caliber: 9mm Luger
Capacity: 10, 14 rounds
Features: Swappable safety/decocker; interlocking trigger design for easy disassembly and reassembly without tools; compact size and reduced weight ideal for discrete carry
MSRP $725.00

75 P-01 Ω URBAN GREY SUPPRESSOR-READY

Action: DA/SA
Grips: Rubber
Barrel: 4.5 in.
Sights: High titrium three dot
Weight: 30.1 oz.
Caliber: 9mm Luger
Capacity: 10, 16 rounds
Features: Swappable safety/decocker; threaded barrels; high suppressor sights with tritium lamps; extended capacity magazine; interlocking trigger design for easy disassembly and reassembly without tools; compact size
MSRP $769.00

75 SP-01

Action: Semiautomatic
Grips: Rubber
Barrel: 4.6 in.
Sights: 3-Dot tritium night
Weight: 38.4 oz.
Caliber: 9mm Luger
Capacity: 10, 18 rounds
Features: Based upon the Shadow Target; decocking lever; safety stop on hammer; firing pin safety; steel frame
MSRP $829.00

75 SP-01 TACTICAL URBAN GREY SUPPRESSOR-READY

Action: DA/SA
Grips: Rubber
Barrel: 5.2 in.
Sights: High titrium three dot
Weight: 42.1 oz.
Caliber: 9mm Luger
Capacity: 10, 18 rounds
Features: Threaded barrels; high suppressor sights with tritium lamps; extended capacity magazine; ambidextrous decocker; 1913 accessory rail on the dust cover; rubber grip panels; corrosion-resistant black polycoat finish; extended beavertail
MSRP $855.00

75 TACTICAL SPORT ORANGE

Action: SA
Grips: Thin aluminum
Barrel: 5.4 in.
Sights: Adjustable
Weight: 48 oz.
Caliber: 9mm Luger; .40 S&W
Capacity: 10, 16, 20 rounds
Features: Ambidextrous manual safety; slimmer trigger guard; improved grip geometry; thumb stop; long slide; full-length dust cover; light pull and short reset
MSRP $1949.00

CZ-USA (Ceska Zbrojovka)

CZ-USA 75 TS CZECHMATE

CZ-USA 97 B

CZ-USA ACCUSHADOW 2

CZ-USA BREN 2 MS

CZ-USA P-01

CZ–USA P-07

CZ-USA P-07 OD GREEN

CZ-USA P-07 SUPPRESSOR-READY

CZ–USA P-07 URBAN GREY SUPPRESSOR-READY

HANDGUNS

75 TS CZECHMATE

Action: Semiautomatic
Grips: Aluminum
Barrel: 5.4 in.
Sights: Fixed, C-more red dot
Weight: 48 oz.
Caliber: 9mm
Capacity: 20, 26 rounds
Features: Built upon a modified version of the CZ 75 TS frame; features a single-action trigger mechanism; red-dot sight; includes spare barrel; includes three 20-round magazines and one 26-round magazine; all-steel pistol is finished in black matte
MSRP $3659.00

97 B

Action: Semiautomatic
Grips: Plastic
Barrel: 4.8 in.
Sights: Fixed
Weight: 40 oz.
Caliber: .45 ACP
Capacity: 10 rounds
Features: Manual safety; cold hammer-forged barrel; single- or double-action
MSRP $819.00

ACCUSHADOW 2

Action: Semiautomatic
Grips: Polymer
Barrel: 4.89 in.
Sights: Fiber optic front, HAJO rear
Weight: 46.5 oz.
Caliber: 9mm
Capacity: 17 rounds
Features: Steel frame; new quarter-turn bushing; short-reset trigger; hand-fit disconnector; custom hammer; safety is ambidextrous
MSRP $2269.00

BREN 2 MS

Action: Semiautomatic
Grips: Synthetic
Barrel: 8 in., 9 in., 11 in., 14 in.
Sights: Folding adjustable
Weight: 5 lb. 6 oz.–5 lb. 14 oz.
Caliber: 5.56X45mm, 7.62X39mm
Capacity: 30 rounds
Features: Totally redesigned Bren replacing the 805 version. Features include trimmed aluminum receiver; carbon fiber-reinforced lower; forward-positioned swappable charging handle; AR-style bolt catch/release system; swappable barrels; designed for add-on buffer tube installation
MSRP $2075.00

P-01

Action: Semiautomatic
Grips: Rubber
Barrel: 3.8 in.
Sights: Fixed
Weight: 28.8 oz.
Caliber: 9mm Luger
Capacity: 10, 14 rounds
Features: Decocking lever; safety stop on hammer; firing pin safety; black polycoat frame finish; black or pink grips; single- or double-action
MSRP . . . . $646.00–$658.00

P-07

Action: DA/SA semiautomatic
Grips: Synthetic
Barrel: 3.8 in.
Sights: Fixed
Weight: 27 oz.
Caliber: 9mm
Capacity: 10, 15 rounds
Features: Ambidextrous safety or decocker; firing pin block
MSRP $535.00

P-07 OD GREEN

Action: Semiautomatic
Grips: Polymer
Barrel: 3.75 in.
Sights: Tritium night sights
Weight: 27.7 oz.
Caliber: 9mm
Capacity: 10, 15 rounds
Features: OD Green polymer frame; tritium nights sights; double-stack magazine
MSRP $559.00

P-07 SUPPRESSOR-READY

Action: Semiautomatic
Grips: Polymer
Barrel: 4.36 in.
Sights: High tritium thee-dot
Weight: 28.7 oz.
Caliber: 9mm
Capacity: 17 rounds
Features: Updated version of the CZ 75 P-07 Duty; interchangeable backstraps; nitrided finish on the slide; frame has been dehorned; interchangeable safety and decocker; muzzle is threaded ½×28 to accept suppressors
MSRP $559.00

P-07 URBAN GREY SUPPRESSOR-READY

Action: DA/SA
Grips: Stippled
Barrel: 4.5 in.
Sights: High titrium three dot
Weight: 28 oz.
Caliber: 9mm Luger
Capacity: 10, 17 rounds
Features: Swappable safety/decocker; threaded barrels; high suppressor sights with tritium lamps; extended capacity magazine; interlocking trigger design for easy disassembly and reassembly without tools; nitrated slide finish; increased corrosion resistance; small, medium, and large backstraps; integrated 1913 Picatinny rail on the dust cover; snag-free hammer; forward cocking serrations
MSRP $585.00

CZ-USA (Ceska Zbrojovka)

CZ–USA P-09

CZ-USA P-09 OD GREEN

CZ–USA P-09 URBAN GREY SUPPRESSOR-READY

CZ-USA P-10 C

CZ-USA P-10 C URBAN GREY SUPPRESSOR-READY

CZ–USA SCORPION EVO 3 S1 PISTOL

CZ-USA SCORPION EVO 3 S1 PISTOL WITH FLASH CAN AND FOLDING BRACE

CZ-USA CZ SCORPION EVO 3 S1 PISTOL W/ FLASH CAN

P-09

Action: DA/SA semiautomatic
Grips: Synthetic
Barrel: 4.53 in. or 5.23 in. (suppressor model)
Sights: Fixed
Weight: 30 oz.
Caliber: 9mm Luger
Capacity: 19 rounds
Features: Ambidextrous safety or decocker; firing pin block
MSRP **$555.00**

P-09 OD GREEN

Action: Semiautomatic
Grips: Polymer
Barrel: 4.54 in.
Sights: Tritium night sights
Weight: 31 oz.
Caliber: 9mm
Capacity: 10, 19 rounds
Features: OD Green polymer frame; night sights; ambidextrous decocker that can be converted to a manual safety; three backstrap sizes for a custom grip fit
MSRP **$629.00**

P-09 URBAN GREY SUPPRESSOR-READY

Action: DA/SA
Grips: Stippled
Barrel: 5.2 in.
Sights: High titrium three dot
Weight: 30.4 oz.
Caliber: 9mm Luger
Capacity: 21+1 rounds
Features: Threaded barrels; high suppressor sights with tritium lamps; Omega trigger system; swappable safety/decocker; 1913 Picatinny rail
MSRP **$655.00**

P-10 C

Action: Semiautomatic
Grips: Polymer
Barrel: 4.02 in.
Sights: Metal three-dot
Weight: 26 oz.
Caliber: 9mm
Capacity: 10, 12 rounds
Features: Striker-fired pistol; ergonomically designed with a mild palm swell, deep beavertail, and three interchangeable backstraps; trigger engineered to break at 4–4.5 lb. with a short reset; fiber-reinforced polymer frame with nitride finish
MSRP **$525.00**

P-10 C URBAN GREY SUPPRESSOR-READY

Action: Semiautomatic
Grips: Polymer
Barrel: 4.61 in.
Sights: High metal night sights
Weight: 26 oz.
Caliber: 9mm
Capacity: 10, 17 rounds
Features: Urban gray frame and darker gray slide; threaded barrel is suppressor-ready; high sights
MSRP **$585.00**

SCORPION EVO 3 S1 PISTOL

Action: SA
Grips: Polymer
Barrel: 7.72 in.
Sights: Low-profile fully adjustable aperture and post, 4 rear aperture sizes
Weight: 5 lb.
Caliber: 9mm Luger
Capacity: 10+1 rounds, 20+1 rounds
Features: Scorpion sub-gun, imported as a pistol; blowback-operated; 11-in. Picatinny rail; ambidextrous controls; non-reciprocating charging handle is swappable and reach to the trigger is adjustable; arm brace adapter adds an AR-style pistol buffer tube to the rear of the action; barrel threaded a 18x1 to accept the factory flash hider and also a ½x28 underneath flash hider for easy addition of suppressor or after market muzzle device
MSRP . . . . **$995.00–$1025.00**

SCORPION EVO 3 S1 PISTOL W/FLASH CAN

Action: Semiautomatic
Grips: Polymer
Barrel: 7.72 in.
Sights: Post front, low-profile fully adjustable aperture rear
Weight: 91.2 oz.
Caliber: 9mm
Capacity: 10, 20 rounds
Features: Extended forend; M-LOK attachment points; boosted the sight radius; dual threads of 18×1 and ½×28 provide options
MSRP **$1099.00**

SCORPION EVO 3 S1 PISTOL WITH FLASH CAN AND FOLDING BRACE

Action: Semiautomatic
Grips: Polymer
Barrel: 7.72 in.
Sights: Post front, low-profile fully adjustable rear
Weight: 104 oz.
Caliber: 9mm
Capacity: 10, 20 rounds
Features: ATF-legal pistol unless brace is attached; Adjustable grips; flash can is removable for suppressor installation; rail space for lights and optics
MSRP **$1175.00**

CZ-USA (Ceska Zbrojovka)

CZ-USA SCORPION EVO 3 S2 PISTOL MICRO WITH BRACE

CZ-USA SHADOW 2 BLACK & BLUE

CZ-USA SHADOW 2 SA

SCORPION EVO 3 S2 PISTOL MICRO WITH BRACE

Action: Semiautomatic
Grips: Polymer
Barrel: 4.12 in.
Sights: Post front, low-profile fully adjustable rear
Weight: 88 oz.
Caliber: 9mm
Capacity: 10, 20 rounds
Features: ATF-legal pistol unless brace is attached; NoOsprey false suppressor from SilencerCo
MSRP $1349.00

SHADOW 2 BLACK & BLUE, URBAN GREY

Action: Semiautomatic
Grips: Aluminum
Barrel: 4.89 in.
Sights: Fiber optic front, HAJO rear
Weight: 46.5 oz.
Caliber: 9mm
Capacity: 17 rounds
Features: Higher beavertail; undercut trigger guard; contoured slide; increased weight at the dust cover/rail helps keep muzzle down; steel frame with nitride finish; blue aluminum grips checkered to match front and backstraps; reversible mag release
MSRP $1359.00

SHADOW 2 SA

Action: Semiautomatic
Grips: Aluminum
Barrel: 4.89 in.
Sights: Fiber optic front, HAJO rear
Weight: 46.5 oz.
Caliber: 9mm
Capacity: 17 rounds
Features: A SAO target pistol with a steel frame; thin aluminum grips in sky blue; blue trigger; accessory rail; checkered front and backstraps
MSRP $1359.00

HANDGUNS

Dan Wesson Firearms

DAN WESSON BRUIN

DAN WESSON DWX

DAN WESSON DWX COMPACT

DAN WESSON GUARDIAN

BRUIN

Action: SA
Grips: Synthetic
Barrel: 6.3 in.
Sights: Adjustable titrium with titrium/ fiber optic front
Weight: 42.9 oz.
Caliber: 10mm Auto; .45 ACP
Capacity: 8 or 9 rounds
Features: Long slide for a long sight radius; 6.3 in. barrel allows full-power 10mm loads as much time as possible to use their powder charge; tritium/ fiber optic combo front sight to make sure the front glows day or night
MSRP $2235.00

DWX

Action: Semiautomatic
Grips: Aluminum
Barrel: 5 in.
Sights: Fiber optic front, adjustable rear
Weight: 43 oz.
Caliber: 9mm, .40 S&W
Capacity: 10, 15, 19 rounds
Features: A melding of Dan Wesson and CZ designs, with features that include single-action firing borrowed from DW's 1911; CZ-style takedown via the pistol's slidestop; bushingless match-grade barrel in a locked-breech system; double-stack magazine; grip contour borrowed from CZ 75; Black Duty finish; flashy red aluminum grips with coordinating red trigger
MSRP $1799.00

DWX COMPACT

Action: Semiautomatic
Grips: Aluminum
Barrel: 4 in.
Sights: Night sight front, U-notch rear
Weight: 28.5 oz.
Caliber: 9mm.
Capacity: 10, 15 rounds
Features: Similar to the full-size DWX; black aluminum grip panels with a raised square texturing that matches the texturing on the front and backstrap; bright red trigger
MSRP $1799.00

GUARDIAN

Action: SA semiautomatic
Grips: Wood
Barrel: 4.25 in.
Sights: Fixed
Weight: 29 oz.
Caliber: 9mm Luger, .38 Super, .45 ACP
Capacity: 8 (.45 ACP) or 9 rounds
Features: Ambidextrous thumb safety; grip safety; fixed night sights
MSRP . . . . $1586.00–$1649.00

Dan Wesson Firearms

HANDGUNS

KODIAK

Action: Semiautomatic
Grips: G10
Barrel: 6.03 in.
Sights: Fiber optic front, adjustable rear
Weight: 47.1 oz.
Caliber: 10mm
Capacity: 8 rounds
Features: Dan Wesson recommits to the 10mm with a long-barreled 1911 design in a choice of tri-tone with a stainless slide, black frame, and bronze controls, or an all Duty black frame/slide with bronze controls; textured tan and black G10 grips; dustcover rail; forged stainless frame
MSRP. . . . . $2299.00–$2349.00

RAZORBACK RZ-10

Action: SA semiautomatic
Grips: Diamond-checkered cocobolo
Barrel: 5 in.
Sights: Fixed
Weight: 38.4 oz.
Caliber: 10mm
Capacity: 9 rounds
Features: Razorback is back in 2012 in limited quantities; serrated Clark-style target rib; 1911 model; stainless steel frame; manual thumb safety, grip safety
MSRP. $1586.00

SPECIALIST

Action: SA semiautomatic
Grips: G10 VZ Operator II grips
Barrel: 5 in.
Sights: Fixed tritium
Weight: 37 oz.
Caliber: 9mm, 10mm, .45 ACP
Capacity: 8+1 or 10 rounds
Features: Full size single-stack pistol; matte stainless steel or black Duty finishes; forged slide and frame; Clark-style serrated rib with tritium dual-colored night sights stacked in a straight eight-type pattern; tactical ledge rear sight with single rear amber dot and green front with white target ring; Picatinny rail; undercut trigger guard with 25 lpi front strap checkering; ambidextrous thumb safety; two magazines with bumper pads included
Stainless: . . . . . . $1732.00–$1851.00
Black: . . . . $1984.00–$2115.00

TCP

Action: Semiautomatic
Grips: G10
Barrel: 4 in.
Sights: Brass blade front, notch rear
Weight: 32 oz.
Caliber: 9mm, .45 ACP
Capacity: 8 rounds
Features: TCP is Tactical Commander Pistol. Features aggressive slide serrations; ramped bull barrel with 30-degree crown; tapered grip profile; under barrel accessory rail; flat K-style trigger; top rib for reduced glare; one-piece magwell; square hammer
MSRP. . . . . $1700.00–$1725.00

VALOR

Action: Semiautomatic
Grips: G10
Barrel: 5 in.
Sights: Fixed night sight front, U-notch rear
Weight: 39.7 oz.
Caliber: .45 ACP
Capacity: 7 rounds
Features: A favorite model in the Dan Wesson lineage returns in 2020 in a choice of stainless bead-blasted or black Duty Coat finishes; inset rear slide serrations; recessed slide stop for use with laser grips; Stan Chen SI magwell; tactical ambidextrous safety; checkered front and backstrap
Stainless: $1864.00
Black Duty Coat: $2181.00

Daniel Defense

DDM4 PDW

Action: Semiautomatic
Grips: Synthetic
Barrel: 7 in.
Sights: None
Weight: 91.2 oz.
Caliber: .300 BLK
Capacity: 30 rounds
Features: Maxim Defense CQB pistol brace; multiple M-LOK slots; S2W "strength to weight" barrel profile; pistol-length gas system; SLR M-LOK MOD2 plain front handstop
MSRP. $1940.00

DDM4 V7P

Action: Semiautomatic
Grips: Synthetic
Barrel: 10.3 in.
Sights: None
Weight: 87 oz.
Caliber: 5.56 NATO
Capacity: N/A
Features: Chrome-moly vanadium steel barrel; carbine-length gas system; Daniel Defense flash suppressor; SB Tactical SBO pistol brace; MFR 9.0 rail
MSRP. $1798.00

Dark Storm Industries

DARK STORM INDUSTRIES DS1 VARIANT 1 PISTOL

DARK STORM INDUSTRIES DS-6TYPHOON PISTOL

DARK STORM INDUSTRIES DS-15 TYPHOON PISTOL

DS1 VARIANT 1 PISTOL, FIXED MAGAZINE

Action: Semiautomatic
Grips: Synthetic
Barrel: 12.5 in.
Sights: None
Weight: N/A
Caliber: 5.56 NATO
Capacity: 30 rounds
Features: SB Tactical SBA3 stabilizing brace; carbine gas system; DSI competition compensator; optic ready; ambidextrous sling plate, charging handle, and 90-degree safety selector
MSRP . . . . $1595.00–$1695.00

DS-9 TYPHOON PISTOL

Action: Semiautomatic
Grips: Synthetic
Barrel: 7.5 in.
Sights: None
Weight: N/A
Caliber: 9mm
Capacity: 17 rounds
Features: Similar to the DS-15 Typhoon Pistol but available only with the removeable magazine; choice of black or Flat Dark Earth furniture
MSRP . . . . $1395.00–$1495.00

DS-15 TYPHOON PISTOL

Action: Semiautomatic
Grips: Synthetic
Barrel: 7.5 in.
Sights: None
Weight: N/A
Caliber: 5.56 NATO, .300 Blackout
Capacity: 30 rounds
Features: Billet 7075 aluminum lower; forged upper with forward assist; 6-inch M-LOK forearm with ultra-narrow profile; threaded Nitrite barrel; choice of PMAG or fixed mag configurations; choice of black or FDE furniture; steel micro gas block; pistol gas system
MSRP . . . . $1295.00–$1395.00

Davide Pedersoli & C.

DAVIDE PEDERSOLI HOWDAH

HOWDAH

Action: Break-open side-by-side
Grips: Walnut
Barrel: 10 in.
Sights: Dovetail front
Weight: 63.5 oz.
Caliber: .45 LC/.410-bore
Capacity: 2 rounds
Features: Based on Ithaca's 1920 Auto & Burglar pistol; case hardened action; oil finished walnut stock; manual extractors; automatic safety on hammers; cartridge chamber allows interchangeable use of .45 LC or .410-bore
Standard: $1530.00
Deluxe: $1885.00
Alaskan: $1470.00
Vintage: $2095.00

Del-Ton

LIMA M-LOK PISTOL

Action: Semiautomatic
Grips: Synthetic
Barrel: 7.5 in.
Sights: None
Weight: 4 lb. 13 oz.
Caliber: 5.56x45mm
Capacity: 30 rounds
Features: Forged 7075 aluminum upper and lower hard-coat anodized; round forward assist; heavy-profile threaded barrel; low-profile gas block; 6.5-inch free-floating M-LOK handguard; full-length top rail
MSRP . . . . . $1148.00–$1547.00

DEL-TON LIMA M-LOK PISTOL

Devil Dog Arms

DDA 1911

Action: Semiautomatic
Grips: NBD
Barrel: 3.5 in., 4.25 in., 5 in.
Sights: Kensight DFS fixed white dot sights
Weight: N/A
Caliber: 9mm, .45 ACP
Capacity: 10 rounds (9mm), 8 rounds (.45 ACP)
Features: First 1911 offerings from this maker; available in full-size, Officer, and Commander versions; two caliber choices; black oxide, FDE Cerakote, or Boron nitride finish options; investment cast 4140 steel frames; 4140 billet steel machined slides with a custom flat-top design; button-rifled 416 stainless barrels with match-fit bushing; three-hole aluminum trigger; optional accessory rail; oversized slide serrations
MSRP . . . . $1148.00–$1547.00

DEVIL DOG ARMS DDA 1911

Diamondback Firearms

DIAMONDBACK FIREARMS DB9 4TH GENERATION

DIAMONDBACK FIREARMS DBAM29 (AM2)

DIAMONDBACK FIREARMS DBX57

DB9 4TH GENERATION

Action: Semiautomatic
Grips: Polymer
Barrel: 3.1 in.
Sights: White three-dot
Weight: 13.4 oz.
Caliber: 9mm
Capacity: 6 rounds
Features: Fabulously slim, lightweight, and affordable carry 9mm that features a striker-fire action; a short-reset non-safety trigger; deep front and rear slide serrations; Glock-compatible sights; enhanced grip texturing
MSRP $279.00

DBAM29 (AM2)

Action: Semiautomatic
Grips: Polymer
Barrel: 3.5 in.
Sights: White three-dot
Weight: 22 oz.
Caliber: 9mm
Capacity: 17 rounds
Features: Lots of folks think they can improve on a GLOCK, and some even do it successfully, like Diamondback Firearms with its new AM2 that features an all-steel captured recoil system; black nitride slide; safety trigger; creative grip texturing; accessory rail; Glock-compatible sights
Standard . . . . $339.00–$350.00
With laser. . . . . $506.00–$515.00

DBX57

Action: Semiautomatic
Grips: Aluminum
Barrel: 8 in.
Sights: None
Weight: 48 oz.–59.2 oz.
Caliber: 5.7x28mm
Capacity: 20 rounds
Features: Firing the unique 5.7x28mm, this dual gas piston pistol has a locked breech operating system; threaded barrel with DBX muzzle device; rear Picatinny rail for mounting the included side-folding brace; AR-15 mil-spec trigger; top-side full-length Picatinny rail
MSRP $1125.00

DoubleStar Corp.

DOUBLESTAR CORP. ARP7

ARP7

Action: Semiautomatic
Grips: Synthetic
Barrel: 7.5 in.
Sights: None
Weight: 5 lb. 6 oz.
Caliber: 5.56 NATO, .300 Blackout, 9mm
Capacity: 30 rounds
Features: An AR-style pistol featuring: free-floating barrel with M4 feed ramp; billet winter trigger guard; billet backbone charging handle; Ergo grip; direct gas impingement; Doublestar seven-inch Cloak M-LOK handguard
5.56 NATO: $1299.99
.300 Blackout: $1319.99
9mm: $1599.99

DoubleStar Corp.

PHD 1911

Action: SA
Grips: Magpul MOE 1911 grip panels
Barrel: 5 in.
Sights: XS Express titrium front sight, XS Express rear sight
Weight: 33 oz.
Caliber: .45 ACP
Capacity: 8 rounds
Features: Aggressive rear cocking serrations for a sure grip in the harshest of environments; flat-topped and serrated slide to reduce glare; round butt and Wilson combat high-ride beavertail grip safety
MSRP $1369.99

STAR10-P

Action: Semiautomatic
Grips: Synthetic
Barrel: 12.5 in.
Sights: None
Weight: N/A
Caliber: .308 Win.
Capacity: 20 rounds
Features: A big caliber in a compact handgun package with forged aluminum upper and lower; direct gas impingement action; low-profile gas block; heavy stainless steel barrel; flat trigger group; lots of rail
MSRP $2299.99

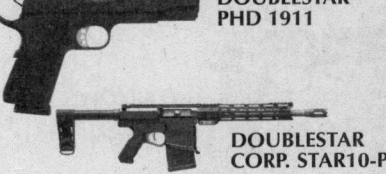

DOUBLESTAR PHD 1911

DOUBLESTAR CORP. STAR10-P

DoubleTap Defense LLC

DOUBLETAP

Action: DAO semiautomatic
Grips: Synthetic
Barrel: 3 in.
Sights: Front blade
Weight: 12 oz.–14 oz.
Caliber: .45 ACP, 9mm
Capacity: 2+2 rounds
Features: Titanium frame with a MIL-STD finish that resists corrosion; integral grips house additional two spare rounds; ported barrel reduces muzzle flip and recoil; ambidextrous thumb latch to eject spent rounds; quick-change interchangable barrels; comes with one barrel and you can purchase extra conversion kits; firearm and conversion kit available ported and non-ported
Aluminum: . . . . $499.00–$569.00
Conversion kits: . . . $199.00–$269.00

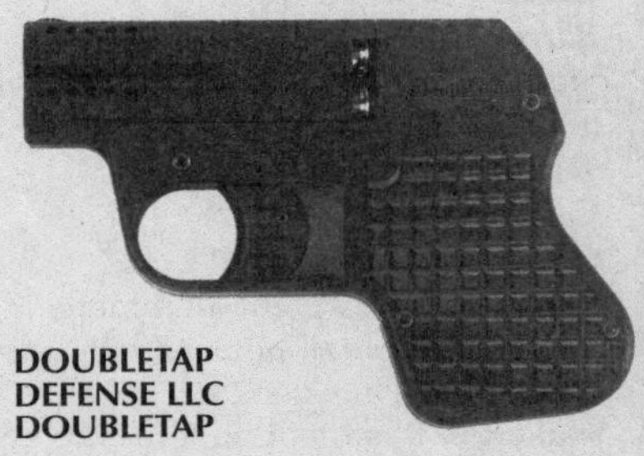

DOUBLETAP DEFENSE LLC DOUBLETAP

Eagle Imports

EAGLE IMPORTS MAC 1911 CLASSIC

MAC 1911 CLASSIC

Action: SA semiautomatic
Grips: Hardwood
Barrel: 5 in.
Sights: Adjustable rear, dovetail front
Weight: 40.56 oz.
Caliber: .45 ACP
Capacity: 8+1 rounds
Features: 4140 steel frame and hammer forged slide; fully adjustable bomar-type rear sight; dovetail front sight with fiber optic; flared and lowered ejection port; enhanced beavertail grip safety; skeletal hammer; combat trigger; checkered front strap serrations; ramped match grade bull barrel
MSRP . . . . .starting at $1045.00

Ed Brown Products

ED BROWN 18 CLASSIC CUSTOM

ED BROWN 18 EXECUTIVE ELITE

18 CLASSIC CUSTOM

Action: Semiautomatic
Grips: Cocobolo wood
Barrel: 5 in.
Sights: Adjustable rear, cross dovetail front
Weight: 40 oz.
Caliber: .45 ACP
Capacity: 7+1 rounds
Features: Single-action; single-stack government model frame; special mirror finished side; two-piece guide rod for smoother cycling and easier disassembly; stainless or blued finish
MSRP . . . . $3695.00–$3795.00

18 EXECUTIVE ELITE

Action: Semiautomatic
Grips: Checkered cocobolo wood
Barrel: 5 in.
Sights: Fixed, night
Weight: 38 oz.
Caliber: .45 ACP
Capacity: 7+1 rounds
Features: Single-stack government model frame; matte finished slide for low glare, with traditional square cut serrations on rear of slide only; blued or stainless finish
MSRP . . . . $3295.00–$3395.00

Ed Brown Products

ED BROWN BO 18 KOBRA CARRY LIGHTWEIGHT

ED BROWN PRODUCTS BO/EB ZEV 19 RMR

ED BROWN EVO KC9 G4, G4 AMBI

ED BROWN PRODUCTS FUELED SERIES MP-F1, MP-F2, MP-F3

ED BROWN SIGNATURE EDITION

BO 18 KOBRA CARRY LIGHTWEIGHT

Action: Semiautomatic
Grips: Cocobolo wood
Barrel: 4.25 in.
Sights: Fixed dovetail front night with high visibility white outlines
Weight: 27 oz.
Caliber: .45 ACP
Capacity: 7+1 rounds
Features: Lightweight aluminum frame and Bobtail housing; all other components are steel; exclusive snakeskin treatment on forestrap and housing; matte finished Gen III coated slide for low glare
MSRP . . . . $3410.00–$3510.00

BO/EB ZEV 19 RMR

Action: Semiautomatic
Grips: G10
Barrel: 4.25 in.
Sights: Tall night sights, Trijicon RMR reflex red dot
Weight: 40 oz.
Caliber: 9mm
Capacity: 8 rounds
Features: A joint venture with ZEV technologies; dimpled barrel; ported slide top and side; FX1 Snakeskin treatment to the frontstrap; threaded suppressor-ready barrel; VZ Alien G10 grips
MSRP . . . . $4995.00–$5295.00

EVO KC9 G4, G4 AMBI

Action: Semiautomatic
Grips: Ed Brown custom
Barrel: 4 in.
Sights: Orange HD XR night sight front, notch rear
Weight: 34 oz.
Caliber: 9mm
Capacity: 9 rounds
Features: EVO is for Evolution, Ed Brown's slimmed and lightened 9mm 1911 featuring Ed's snakeskin treatment to the front strap and his own Bobtail mainspring housing; 7-top custom slide with serrations; bull barrel; flat wire recoil system; two versions, a stainless finish with black textured grips, or a black Gen4 finish with textured brown ombre grips
Standard: $2195.00
Ambi: $2295.00

FUELED SERIES MP-F1, MP-F2, MP-F3

Action: Semiautomatic
Grips: Polymer
Barrel: N/A
Sights: Tritium front, black-out rear; Trijicon red-dot
Weight: N/A
Caliber: 9mm
Capacity: 17 rounds
Features: Ed Brown took a S&W M&P 2.0, stripped it down to just the frame, and built the rest from the ground up with all custom parts that include an accuracy rail, slide, tread-fluted and threaded barrel; extractor Ameriglo front sight and black-out rear that co-witness with Trijicon's RMR reflex sight, Apex tactical trigger, EB's own low-profile 360-degree magwell, slide backplate, magazine baseplates, and machined pins
MSRP $1995.00

SIGNATURE EDITION

Action: Semiautomatic
Grips: Buckeye burl
Barrel: 5 in.
Sights: Adjustable rear, cross dovetail front
Weight: 40 oz.
Caliber: .45 ACP
Capacity: 7+1 rounds
Features: Based on the timeless Classic Custom pistol, with hand relief engraving by our master engraver; single stack government model frame; special mirror finished slide; 50 lpi serrations on back of slide to match serrated adjustable sight; adjustable rear sight buried deep into slide; blued metal parts
MSRP . . . . $7095.00–$8095.00

EMF Company, Inc.

EMF 1873 GREAT WESTERN II ALCHIMISTA II

1873 GREAT WESTERN II ALCHIMISTA II, JR., DLX III

Action: SA revolver
Grips: Walnut
Barrel: 3.5 in., 4.75 in., 5.5 in., 7.5 in.
Sights: Fixed
Weight: 33.6 oz.
Caliber: .357 Mag., .44-40, .45 LC
Capacity: 6 rounds
Features: Standard case-hardening; stainless steel; three variations: Alchimista I has checkered walnut 1860 walnut grips, wide setback trigger, case hardened frame; Alchimista III is similar to II but with octagonal barrel; Jr. has a round barrel in the shortest configuration and engraved in Old Silver and Blue
II: $650.00
DLX III: $745.00
Jr.: $775.00

EMF Company, Inc.

EMF 1873 GREAT WESTERN II BUNTLINE

EMF 1873 GREAT WESTERN II CALIFORNIAN

EMF COMPANY, INC. 1873 GREAT WESTERN II DELUXE GRANDE CALIFORNIAN

EMF 1873 GREAT WESTERN II LIBERTY

EMF 1873 GREAT WESTERN II ALL BLUE PALADIN

EMF 1873 GREAT WESTERN II PONY EXPRESS

EMF COMPANY, INC. 1873 GREAT WESTERN II US MARSHAL

1873 GREAT WESTERN II BUNTLINE

Action: Revolver
Grips: Walnut or Ultra Ivory
Barrel: 12 in.
Sights: Fixed
Weight: N/A
Caliber: .45 LC
Capacity: 6 rounds
Features: Deep color case hardened finish; first version was designed by Colt for Ned Buntline
Walnut grips: $660.00
Ultra Ivory grips: $690.00

1873 GREAT WESTERN II CALIFORNIAN

Action: SA revolver
Grips: Walnut
Barrel: 4.75 in., 5.5 in., 7.5 in.
Sights: Fixed
Weight: 48 oz.
Caliber: .357 Mag., .44-40 Win., .45 LC
Capacity: 6 rounds
Features: Standard case-hardening; steel frame
MSRP $590.00

1873 GREAT WESTERN II DELUXE GRANDE CALIFORNIAN

Action: Revolver
Grips: Wood
Barrel: 4.75 in.
Sights: Blade front, integral notch rear
Weight: N/A
Caliber: .357 Mag., .45 LC
Capacity: 6 rounds
Features: Gorgeous single-action with a color-case-hardened frame; grips checkered in a pattern reminiscent of fleur-de-lis; Victorian scroll work and sunburst engraving on high-polished blue barrel and cylinder
MSRP $690.00

1873 GREAT WESTERN II LIBERTY

Action: Revolver
Grips: Ultra Ivory
Barrel: 4.75 in., 5.5 in.
Sights: Fixed
Weight: N/A
Caliber: .357 Mag., .45 LC
Capacity: 6 rounds
Features: Manufactured in Italy; all blued barrel, cylinder, and frame; factory laser engraved
MSRP $675.00

1873 GREAT WESTERN II PALADIN

Action: Revolver
Grips: Ultra Ivory
Barrel: 7.5 in.
Sights: Fixed
Weight: N/A
Caliber: .45 LC
Capacity: 6 rounds
Features: Single action; all blued barrel, cylinder, and frames as seen in Hollywood westerns
MSRP $640.00

1873 GREAT WESTERN II PONY EXPRESS

Action: SA revolver
Grips: Walnut express grips
Barrel: 3.5 in.
Sights: Fixed
Weight: 32 oz.
Caliber: .357 Mag., .45 LC
Capacity: 6 rounds
Features: Designed by Dave Anderson, one of the pioneering gunmakers in Cowboy Action Shooting and intended for mounted shooting competitors; available in an Express (bird's head) grip and turned-down hammer or a standard grip and Bisley hammer, both in bright stainless, or in a case hardened version with Express grip
MSRP . . . . $705.00–$945.00

1873 GREAT WESTERN II US MARSHAL

Action: Revolver
Grips: Walnut
Barrel: 4.75 in.
Sights: Blade front, integral notch rear
Weight: N/A
Caliber: .357 Mag., .45 LC
Capacity: 6 rounds
Features: Features a color case-hardened frame; blued barrel and cylinder; brass backstrap and trigger guard; walnut grips have "US Marshal" in its star logo
MSRP $560.00

European American Armory (EAA)

EUROPEAN AMERICAN ARMORY BOUNTY HUNTER

BOUNTY HUNTER

Action: SA revolver
Grips: Walnut
Barrel: 4.5 in., 6.75 in., 7.5 in.
Sights: Fixed, open
Weight: 39–41 oz.
Caliber: .357 Mag.,.44 Mag., .22 LR/.22 WMR, 45 LC
Capacity: 6 or 8 rounds
Features: Transfer bar safety; steel or alloy frame; in blued or nickel finishes
MSRP . . . . $416.99–$570.99

European American Armory (EAA)

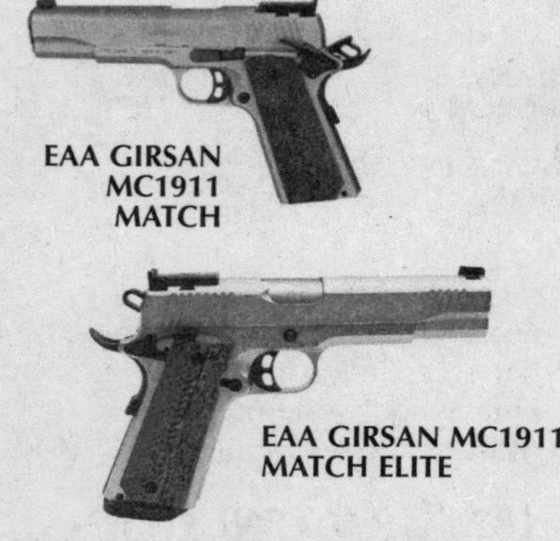

EAA GIRSAN MC1911 MATCH

EAA GIRSAN MC1911 MATCH ELITE

EUROPEAN AMERICAN ARMORY POLYMER FULL SIZE

EUROPEAN AMERICAN ARMORY WITNESS HUNTER

EUROPEAN AMERICAN ARMORY WITNESS STEEL COMPACT

GIRSAN MC1911 MATCH

Action: Semiautomatic
Grips: Laminate
Barrel: 5 in.
Sights: Fully adjustable target
Weight: 40 oz.
Caliber: .45 ACP
Capacity: 8 rounds
Features: A well-rounded full-size 1911 Govt. pistol built by GiRSAN for EAA and featuring an extended beavertail; steel slide and frame; extended ambidextrous safety; long-hole hammer; checkered frame
MSRP $753.00

GIRSAN MC1911 MATCH ELITE

Action: Semiautomatic
Grips: G10
Barrel: 5 in.
Sights: Fully adjustable target
Weight: 40 oz.
Caliber: .45 ACP
Capacity: 8 rounds
Features: Enhanced competition pistol based on the GiRSAN MC1911 Match but with the addition of a competition barrel, mag well and barrel; cone/barrel lock-up; aggressive slide serrations; in a matte hard chrome finish
MSRP $856.00

WITNESS HUNTER

Action: Semiautomatic
Grips: Rubber
Barrel: 6 in.
Sights: Dovetail front
Weight: 41 oz.
Caliber: 10mm, .45 ACP
Capacity: 10+1 or 15+1 rounds
Features: Single-action with over travel stop; extended manual safety; super sight; cone barrel, slide lockup; checkered non-slip frame; drilled and tapped for scope mount; auto-firing pin block
MSRP $1361.00

WITNESS POLYMER FULL SIZE

Action: Semiautomatic
Grips: Rubber
Barrel: 4.5 in.
Sights: 3-Dot
Weight: 33 oz.
Caliber: 9mm, 10mm, .40 S&W, .45 ACP
Capacity: 10+1, 14+1, or 17+1 rounds
Features: Windage adjustable sight; double- or single-action; polymer frame; integral accessory rail
MSRP $585.00

WITNESS STEEL COMPACT

Action: Semiautomatic
Grips: Rubber
Barrel: 3.6 in.
Sights: Adjustable
Weight: 30 oz.
Caliber: 9mm, .40 S&W, 10mm, .45 ACP
Capacity: 8+1, 12+1, or 14+1 rounds
Features: Wonder finish, windage adjustable sight; double- or single-action; polymer or steel frame; integral accessory rail; matte stainless finish
MSRP $693.00

Faxon Firearms

FAXON FIREARMS FX-19 HELLFIRE

FAXON FIREARMS FX-19 PATRIOT

FX-19 HELLFIRE

Action: Semiautomatic
Grips: Polymer
Barrel: 4.5 in.
Sights: Suppressor-height night sights
Weight: 18 oz.
Caliber: 9mm
Capacity: 15 rounds
Features: A semi-custom pistol based on the Glock frame--but with a 1911 grip angle--and taking Glock 19 magazines, featuring DLC Diamond-Like-Coating finish; deep slide serrations fore, aft, and top; optics mounting cuts; Overwatch trigger; extended magazine release; suppressor-height night sights; threaded muzzle
MSRP $1189.00

FX-19 PATRIOT

Action: Semiautomatic
Grips: Polymer
Barrel: 4 in.
Sights: Fiber optic front, blacked-out rear
Weight: 18 oz.
Caliber: 9mm
Capacity: 19 rounds
Features: Similar to the Hellfire, but with a fiber optic front/blacked-out rear sight combo and one standard Glock 19 magazine; unthreaded muzzle
MSRP $1049.00

Fightlite Industries

FIGHTLITE SCR M-LOK

SCR M-LOK

Action: Semiautomatic
Grips: Synthetic
Barrel: 7.25 in.
Sights: None
Weight: 63 oz.
Caliber: 5.56 NATO, .300 Blackout
Capacity: 10 rounds
Features: Short-barreled, grip stock rifle-caliber carbine pistol; overall length of about 20 inches;barrel of 4150 Vanadium that is gas-ferritic nitrocarbonized and threaded; hardcoat anodized finish on the aluminum receiver; choice of KeyMod or M-LOK handguards
MSRP **$865.00**

HANDGUNS

Fime Group, LLC

FIME GROUP/AREX D .O .O . REX ALPHA

FIME GROUP/ AREX D .O .O . REX DELTA

REX ALPHA

Action: Semiautomatic
Grips: Polymer
Barrel: 5 in.
Sights: Fiber optic front, adjustable rear
Weight: 39 oz.
Caliber: 9mm
Capacity: 17 rounds
Features: A hammer-fired competition handgun based on the Zero platform with ambidextrous controls; SA/DA; steel frame; competition-grade trigger; front and rear slide serrations; highly textured grip; under rail; grip panels available in choice of black, white, red, or blue
MSRP **$849.99**

REX DELTA

Action: Semiautomatic
Grips: Polymer
Barrel: 4 in.
Sights: Steel
Weight: 22.2 oz.
Caliber: 9mm
Capacity: N/A
Features: Arex's first striker-fired pistol featuring a two-stage trigger; angled edges for improved carry; double-stack magazine; front and rear slide serrations
MSRP **$425.00**

REX ZERO 1T

Action: Semiautomatic
Grips: N/A
Barrel: 4.9 in.
Sights: High-profile white three-dot
Weight: 30 oz.
Caliber: 9mm
Capacity: 20 rounds
Features: Adding features to the original Zero 1, including four optics mounting plates; ½X28 threaded barrel; DA/SA; bar stock barrel nitrocarburized; forward slide cocking serrations; ambidextrous mag release and safety; under-rail; decocker; hard anodized aluminum frame in black, gray, or Flat Dark Earth
MSRP **$699.99**

REX ZERO 1TC

Action: Semiautomatic
Grips: N/A
Barrel: 4.5 in.
Sights: High-profile white three-dot
Weight: 28.7 oz.
Caliber: 9mm
Capacity: 17 rounds
Features: Similar features the full-size Zero 1 Tactical, shaving a bit off barrel and grip length.
MSRP **$699.99**

FN America

FN AMERICA FN FIVE-SEVEN SERIES

FN FIVE-SEVEN SERIES

Action: SA semiautomatic
Grips: Plastic
Barrel: 4.8 in.
Sights: Adjustable 3-dot
Weight: 20.8 oz.
Caliber: 5.7x28mm
Capacity: 10 or 20 round magazines
Features: Integrated accessory rail for mounting tactical lights or lasers; reversible magazine button; ambidextrous manual safety levers; hammer-forged, chrome lined barrel; adjustable three-dot target sights available with matte or flat dark earth
MSRP **$1199.99**

FN America

FN AMERICA FNX-9

FN AMERICA FNX-45

FN AMERICA FNX-45 TACTICAL

FN AMERICA FN-509 TACTICAL

FN AMERICA FN-509 COMPACT MRD

FN AMERICA FN-509 MIDSIZE

FNX-9

Action: Semiautomatic
Grips: Interchangeable backstraps with lanyard eyelets
Barrel: 4 in.
Sights: 3-Dot system
Weight: 21.9 oz.
Caliber: 9mm, .40 S&W
Capacity: 17 rounds
Features: Ergonomic polymer black frame with low bore axis; checkered and ribbed grip panels; stainless steel slide and hammer-forged stainless barrel; DA/SA ambidextrous controls
MSRP $699.00

FNX-45

Action: DA/SA Semiautomatic
Grips: Interchangeable backstraps with lanyard eyelets
Barrel: 4.5 in.
Sights: Fixed 3-dot
Weight: 33.2 oz.
Caliber: .45 ACP
Capacity: 15 rounds
Features: Polymer frame with stainless steel barrel; external extractor with loaded chamber indicator; front and rear cocking serrations; Picatinny rail; manual, ambidextrous safety
MSRP $824.00

FNX-45 TACTICAL

Action: DA/SA semiautomatic
Grips: Textured polymer
Barrel: 5.3 in.
Sights: High-profile night sights
Weight: 33.6 oz.
Caliber: .45 ACP
Capacity: 15 rounds
Features: Stainless steel slide; external extractor with loaded chamber indicator; high-profile combat night sights; hammer-forged stainless steel barrel; flat dark earth or black polymer frame; Picatinny rail; fully ambidextrous
MSRP $1349.00

FN-509 COMPACT MRD

Action: Semiautomatic
Grips: Polymer
Barrel: 3.7 in.
Sights: Combat-style front and rear
Weight: 25.5 oz.
Caliber: 9mm
Capacity: 10, 12, 15 rounds
Features: FN grows its 509 series with a compact model for concealed carry. Features include DAO operation; aggressively textured grip, front and backstrap, and magazine finger rest
MSRP $799.00

FN-509 MIDSIZE

Action: Semiautomatic
Grips: Polymer
Barrel: 4 in.
Sights: Three-dot luminescent
Weight: 26.5 oz.
Caliber: 9mm
Capacity: 10, 15 rounds
Features: Designed for everyday carry with higher-profile combat-style sights that can make racking in stressed times easier; front and rear slide serrations; striker-fired double-action; loaded chamber indicator; ambidextrous controls; two textured backstraps; under rail
MSRP $799.00

FN-509 TACTICAL

Action: Semiautomatic
Grips: Polymer
Barrel: 4.5 in.
Sights: Three-dot night sights
Weight: 27.9 oz.
Caliber: 9mm
Capacity: 10, 17, 24 rounds
Features: Duty or competition ready with optics mounting plate; suppressor-height night sights, under rail; threaded barrel; interchangeable backstraps; ambidextrous slide stop and mag release; available in black or Flat Dark Earth
MSRP $1049.00

FoldAR

DOUBLE FOLDAR15 GEN3

Action: Semiautomatic
Grips: Polymer
Barrel: 9 in.
Sights: None
Weight: 94.4 oz.–97.6 oz.
Caliber: .223 Wylde, .300 BLK
Capacity: 10, 20 rounds
Features: The folding AR pistol features a fully adjustable gas block; Dead Foot Arms folding pistol brace; Aero Precision X15 lower; A2 compensator; shortened mil-spec bolt carrier group that's in black nitride; Magpul M-LOK rail; SHUT upper/lower locking hinge; folded length is 10.75 in.
MSRP $2399.00

FOLDAR DOUBLE FOLDAR15 GEN3

Freedom Arms

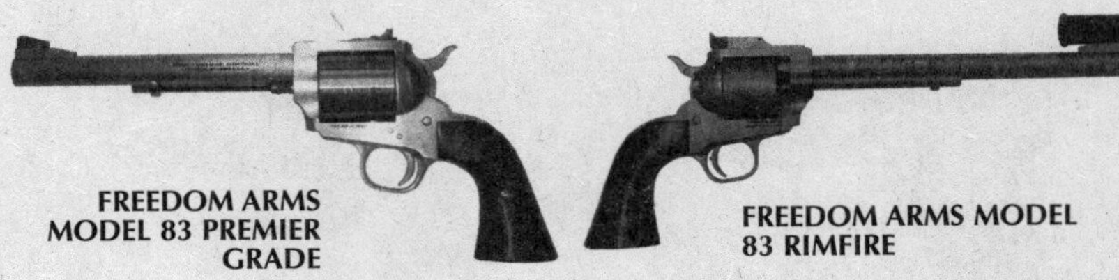
FREEDOM ARMS MODEL 83 PREMIER GRADE

FREEDOM ARMS MODEL 83 RIMFIRE

FREEDOM ARMS MODEL 97 PREMIER GRADE

MODEL 83 PREMIER GRADE

Action: SA revolver
Grips: Hardwood
Barrel: 4.75 in., 6 in., 7.5 in., 10 in.
Sights: Fixed or adjustable
Weight: 52.5 oz.
Caliber: .500 Wyoming Express, .475 Linebaugh, .454 Casull, .44 Rem. Mag., .41 Rem. Mag., .357 Mag.
Capacity: 5 rounds
Features: Adjustable sight models are drilled and tapped for scope mounts; stainless steel, brush finish and impregnated hardwood grips
MSRP . . . . $2830.00–$2939.00

MODEL 83 RIMFIRE

Action: SA revolver
Grips: Hardwood
Barrel: 10 in.
Sights: Adjustable
Weight: 55.5 oz.
Caliber: .22 LR
Capacity: 5 rounds
Features: Drilled and tapped for scope mounts; stainless steel frame; matte finish; match grade chambers
MSRP $2718.00

MODEL 97 PREMIER GRADE

Action: SA revolver
Grips: Laminated hardwood
Barrel: 4.5 in., 5.5 in., 7.5 in., or 10 in.
Sights: Adjustable or fixed
Weight: 39 oz.
Caliber: .45 Colt, .44 Spl., .41 Rem. Mag., .357 Mag., .327 Fed., .224-32 FA, .22 LR, .17 HMR,
Capacity: 5 or 6 rounds
Features: Impregnated hardwood grips; stainless steel frame; brush stainless finish
MSRP . . . .$2396.00–$2421.00

Glock

GLOCK G19 GEN5 MOS

GLOCK G19X

GLOCK G44

Glock Compact Models

G19 GEN5 MOS

Action: Semiautomatic
Grips: Polymer
Barrel: 4.02 in.
Sights: Drift adjustable rear, post front
Weight: 23.81 in.
Caliber: 9mm
Capacity: 15, 17, 24, 31, 33 rounds
Features: Fully updated with Gen5 technology, including the Modular Backstrap System, the GLOCK Marksman Barrel, nDLC finish, ambidextrous slide stop, flared mag well and now with the MOS Modular Optics System that allows mounting of multiple electronic red-dot and reflex sights
MSRP $745.00

G19X

Action: Semiautomatic
Grips: Polymer
Barrel: 4 in.
Sights: Fixed
Weight: 31.4 oz.
Caliber: 9mm
Capacity: 17 rounds
Features: GLOCK's first "crossover" pistol; originally developed for military; GLOCK's signature Coyote coloring, including on the factory-colored slide; GLOCK Marksman Barrel; tough nPVD slide coating; ambidextrous slide stop levers; a stock without finger grooves; lanyard loop; Coyote-colored hard case; two 17-round and two 17+2-round magazines unique to the 19X
MSRP $749.00

G38

Action: Semiautomatic
Grips: Polymer
Barrel: 4.01 in.
Sights: Fixed
Weight: 26.83 oz.
Caliber: .45 G.A.P.
Capacity: 8, 10 rounds
Features: Striker-fired, polymer framed pistol with safe action system, trigger safety, hexagonal barrel, DAO action
MSRP $614.00

G44

Action: Semiautomatic
Grips: Polymer
Barrel: 4.02 in.
Sights: White-dot front, white outline notch rear
Weight: 12.63 oz.
Caliber: .22 LR
Capacity: 10 rounds
Features: Glock's first rimfire with a hybrid steel/polymer slide; interchangeable backstraps; supplied with two load-assist magazines
MSRP $430.00

Glock

GLOCK G45

GLOCK G43X

GLOCK G48

GLOCK G34 GEN5 MODULAR OPTIC SYSTEM (MOS)

GLOCK G40 GEN4

G45

Action: Semiautomatic
Grips: Polymer
Barrel: 4.02 in.
Sights: Drift adjustable rear, post front
Weight: 30.34 oz.
Caliber: 9mm
Capacity: 17, 19, 24, 31, 33 rounds
Features: A second offering in what GLOCK is calling its Crossover pistols. Intended primarily for duty carry, this one combines the slide of the G19 with a full-size G17 frame and adds a non-reflective black hard surface finish
MSRP $699

Glock Compact Slimlines

G43X

Action: Semiautomatic
Grips: Polymer
Barrel: 3.41 in.
Sights: Drift adjustable rear, post front
Weight: 18.7 oz.
Caliber: 9mm
Capacity: 10 rounds
Features: The smaller of two new slimline GLOCK pistols for 2019 intended for CCW practitioners. Features a silver mPVD finish on the slide; forward slide serrations; Gen5 GLOCK Marksman Barrel
MSRP $538.00

G48

Action: Semiautomatic
Grips: Polymer
Barrel: 4.17 in.
Sights: Drift adjustable rear, post front
Weight: 20.74 oz.
Caliber: 9mm
Capacity: 10 rounds
Features: The larger of two new slimline GLOCK pistols for 2019 intended for CCW practitioners. Features a silver mPVD finish on the slide; forward slide serrations; Gen5 GLOCK Marksman Barrel
MSRP $538.00

Glock Competition Models

G34 GEN5 MODULAR OPTIC SYSTEM (MOS)

Action: Semiautomatic
Grips: Polymer
Barrel: 5.31 in.
Sights: Fixed
Weight: 25.7 oz.
Caliber: 9mm
Capacity: 17 rounds
Features: Glock's Modular Optics System (MOS), which allows the mounting of various red dot and reflex sights without the need to machine the slide for a custom mount; GLOCK's improved nDLC finish; GLOCK Marksman Barrel; improved barrel crown; grip frame without finger grooves
MSRP $899.00

G41 GEN4, G41 GEN4 MOS

Action: Semiautomatic
Grips: Polymer
Barrel: 5.31 in.
Sights: Fixed
Weight: 27 oz.
Caliber: .45 ACP
Capacity: 10, 13 rounds
Features: Striker-fired, polymer framed pistol with safe action system, trigger safety, hexagonal barrel, DAO action; Gen4 has modular backstrap design, rough-textured grip, enlarged and reversible magazine release, and is available in Glock's MOS—Modular Optic System—configuration, which simplifies mounting of many modern pistol red dot and reflex sight optics
G41 Gen4 MOS: $840.00
G41 Gen4: $729.00

Glock Long Slide Models

G40 GEN4 MOS

Action: Semiautomatic
Grips: Polymer
Barrel: 6.02 in.
Sights: Fixed
Weight: 28.15 oz.
Caliber: 10mm
Capacity: 15 rounds
Features: Striker-fired, polymer framed pistol with safe action system, trigger safety, hexagonal barrel, DAO action; Gen4 has modular backstrap design, rough-textured grip, enlarged and reversible magazine release, and is available in Glock's MOS—Modular Optic System—configuration, which simplifies mounting of many modern pistol red dot and reflex sight optics.
MSRP $840.00

GLOCK G17 GEN5 MOS

GLOCK STANDARD G17

GLOCK G20 GEN4

GLOCK G21 GEN4

GLOCK G26 GEN5

GLOCK G29 GEN4

Glock Standard Models

G17 GEN5 MOS

Action: Semiautomatic
Grips: Polymer
Barrel: 4.49 in
Sights: Drift adjustable rear, post front
Weight: 24.87 oz.
Caliber: 9mm
Capacity: 17, 19, 24, 31, 33 rounds
Features: Fully updated with Gen5 technology, including the Modular Backstrap System, the GLOCK Marksman Barrel, nDLC finish, ambidextrous slide stop, flared mag well and now with the MOS Modular Optics System that allows mounting of multiple electronic red-dot and reflex sights
MSRP $745.00

G20SF, G20 GEN4

Action: Semiautomatic
Grips: Polymer
Barrel: 4.6 in.
Sights: Fixed
Weight: 30.71 in.
Caliber: 10mm
Capacity: 10, 15 rounds
Features: Striker-fired, polymer framed pistol with safe action system, trigger safety, hexagonal barrel, DAO action; SF designation model has a reduced circumference backstrap. Gen4 has modular backstrap design, rough-textured grip, enlarged and reversible magazine release
G20 Gen4: $687.00
G20SF: $637.00

G21 SF, G21 GEN4

Action: Semiautomatic
Grips: Polymer
Barrel: 4.6 in.
Sights: Fixed
Weight: 29.30 in.
Caliber: .45 ACP
Capacity: 10, 13 rounds
Features: Striker-fired, polymer framed pistol with safe action system, trigger safety, hexagonal barrel, DAO action; SF designation model has a reduced circumference backstrap. Gen4 has modular backstrap design, rough-textured grip, enlarged and reversible magazine release
G21 Gen4: $687.00
G21 SF: $637.00

G31, G31 GEN4

Action: Semiautomatic
Grips: Polymer
Barrel: 4.48 in.
Sights: Fixed
Weight: 26.12 oz.
Caliber: .357 SIG
Capacity: 10, 15 round
Features: Striker-fired, polymer framed pistol with safe action system, trigger safety, hexagonal barrel, DAO action; Gen4 has modular backstrap design, rough-textured grip, enlarged and reversible magazine release
MSRP. $599.00

G37, G37 GEN4

Action: Semiautomatic
Grips: Polymer
Barrel: 4.48 in.
Sights: Fixed
Weight: 28.95 oz.
Caliber: .45 G.A.P.
Capacity: 10 rounds
Features: Striker-fired, polymer framed pistol with safe action system, trigger safety, hexagonal barrel, DAO action; Gen4 has modular backstrap design, rough-textured grip, enlarged and reversible magazine release
G37 Gen4: $664.00
G37:. $614.00

Glock Subcompact Models

G26 GEN5

Action: Semiautomatic
Grips: Polymer
Barrel: 3.42 in.
Sights: Fixed
Weight: 21.7 oz.
Caliber: 9mm
Capacity: 10 rounds
Features: GLOCK's improved nDLC finish; GLOCK Marksman Barrel; improved barrel crown; grip frame without finger grooves
MSRP $699.00

G29SF, G29 GEN4

Action: Semiautomatic
Grips: Polymer
Barrel: 3.77 in.
Sights: Fixed
Weight: 26.83 oz.
Caliber: 10mm
Capacity: 10, 15 rounds
Features: Striker-fired, polymer framed pistol with safe action system, trigger safety, hexagonal barrel, DAO action; SF designation model has a reduced circumference backstrap. Gen4 has modular backstrap design, rough-textured grip, enlarged and reversible magazine release
G29 Gen4: $687.00
G29SF: $637.00

G33, G33 GEN4

Action: Semiautomatic
Grips: Polymer
Barrel: 3.42 in.
Sights: Fixed
Weight: 21.89 oz.
Caliber: .357 SIG
Capacity: 9, 13, 15 rounds
Features: Striker-fired, polymer framed pistol with safe action system, trigger safety, hexagonal barrel, DAO action; Gen4 has modular backstrap design, rough-textured grip, enlarged and reversible magazine release
MSRP $599.00

Glock

GLOCK SUBCOMPACT G26

GLOCK G33 GEN4

GLOCK SUBCOMPACT SLIMLINE G36

GLOCK G42

G39
Action: Semiautomatic
Grips: Polymer
Barrel: 3.42 in.
Sights: Fixed
Weight: 24.18 oz.
Caliber: .45 G.A.P.
Capacity: 6, 8, 10 rounds
Features: Striker-fired, polymer framed pistol with safe action system, trigger safety, hexagonal barrel, DAO action
MSRP $614.00

Glock Subcompact Slimline Models

G36
Action: Semiautomatic
Grips: Polymer
Barrel: 3.77 in.
Sights: Fixed
Weight: 22.42 oz.
Caliber: .45 ACP
Capacity: 6 rounds
Features: Striker-fired, polymer framed pistol with safe action system, trigger safety, hexagonal barrel, DAO action, single-stack magazine
MSRP $637.00

G42
Action: Semiautomatic
Grips: Polymer
Barrel: 3.25 in.
Sights: Fixed
Weight: 13.76 oz.
Caliber: .380 ACP
Capacity: 6 rounds
Features: Striker-fired, polymer framed pistol with safe action system, trigger safety, hexagonal barrel, DAO action, single-stack magazine
MSRP $480.00

Hämmerli

HÄMMERLI MODEL X-ESSE LONG

MODEL X-ESSE
Action: Semiautomatic
Grips: Composite
Barrel: 4.5 in., 5.9 in.
Sights: Adjustable
Weight: 27.9–31 oz.
Caliber: .22 LR
Capacity: 10 rounds
Features: Single-action, two-stage trigger; universal hi-grip
MSRP $879.00

Heckler & Koch

HECKLER & KOCH HK45

HECKLER & KOCH HK45 COMPACT

HK45
Action: Semiautomatic
Grips: Polymer
Barrel: 4.53 in.
Sights: Fixed
Weight: 31 oz.
Caliber: .45 ACP
Capacity: 10 rounds
Features: DA/SA with control lever; integral Picatinny rail; ambidextrous controls with dual slide releases; modified Browning linkless recoil operating system; polygonal rifling; open square notch rear sight with contrast points; low profile drift adjustable three-dot sights; available in black, RAL8000 green brown, and olive finishes
MSRP . . . . $849.00–$949.00

HK45 COMPACT
Action: Semiautomatic
Grips: Synthetic
Barrel: 3.94 in.
Sights: Adjustable 3-dot
Weight: 28.48 oz.
Caliber: .45 ACP
Capacity: 8 or 10 rounds
Features: Picatinny rail molded into the polymer frame dust cover; slim-line grip profiles with user replaceable grip panels; ambidextrous controls with dual slide releases and enlarged magazine release; uses the proven modified Browning linkless recoil operating system; O-ring barrel; contoured and radiused slide with forward slide (grasping) grooves and anti-glare longitudinal ribs; polymer frame; available in black, RAL8000 green brown, and olive finishes
MSRP . . . . $849.00–$949.00

Heckler & Koch

HECKLER & KOCH HK45 COMPACT TACTICAL

HECKLER & KOCH HK45 TACTICAL

HECKLER & KOCH MARK 23

HECKLER & KOCH P30

HECKLER & KOCH P30 L

HECKLER & KOCH P30SK

HK45 COMPACT TACTICAL

Action: DA/SA semiautomatic
Grips: Textured polymer
Barrel: 4.57 in.
Sights: 3-dot
Weight: 29.12 oz.
Caliber: .45 ACP
Capacity: 10 rounds
Features: Proprietary internal mechanical recoil reduction system; O-ring barrel; cold-hammer-forged barrel; available in black, RAL8000 green brown, and olive finishes; supplied with one additional backstrap; night sights optional
MSRP $1029.00

HK45 TACTICAL

Action: Semiautomatic
Grips: Polymer with finger grooves
Barrel: 5.16 in.
Sights: 3-dot tritium night sights
Weight: 31.7 oz.
Caliber: .45 ACP
Capacity: 10 rounds
Features: Polymer frame; recoil-operated with modified Browning locking system; threaded barrel; Picatinny rail; key-based HK Lock-Out system; nine different trigger firing modes; available in black, RAL8000 green brown, and olive finishes; supplied with one additional backstrap; night sights optional
MSRP $1029.00

MARK 23

Action: Semiautomatic
Grips: Polymer
Barrel: 5.9 in.
Sights: 3-Dot
Weight: 39.4 oz.
Caliber: .45 ACP
Capacity: 12+1 rounds
Features: Threaded O-ring barrel with polygonal bore profile; match grade trigger; one piece machined steel slide; frame mounted decocking lever and separate ambidextrous safety lever; HK recoil reduction system; ambidextrous magazine release lever
MSRP $2499.00

P30

Action: Semiautomatic
Grips: Polymer
Barrel: 3.86 in.
Sights: Fixed
Weight: 26.08 oz.
Caliber: 9mm, .40 S&W
Capacity: 10, 15 rounds
Features: Corrosion proof fiber-reinforced polymer frame; multiple trigger firing modes; HK recoil reduction system; blued finish; Picatinny rail; ambidextrous magazine release levers and side release
MSRP . . . .$789.99–$899.00

P30 L

Action: Semiautomatic
Grips: Polymer
Barrel: 4.4 in.
Sights: Fixed
Weight: 27.5 oz.
Caliber: 9mm, .40 S&W
Capacity: 10, 13, or 15 rounds
Features: Interchangeable backstraps and side panel grips in small, medium, and large sizes; ambidextrous slide and magazine releases levers; integral Picatinny rail; modular design allows DA trigger or DA/SA system, with a decocking button
MSRP . . . .$789.99–$899.00

P30SK

Action: Semiautomatic
Grips: Rubber
Barrel: 3.27 in.
Sights: Fixed
Weight: 23.99 oz.
Caliber: 9mm
Capacity: 10 rounds
Features: Picatinny rail; interchangeable backstraps and lateral grip panels; available in multiple trigger firing modes including HK's enhanced double action only Law Enforcement Modification (LEM); trigger modes include conventional double action/single action (DA/SA)
MSRP . . . .$789.99–$899.00

Heckler & Koch

P2000, P2000 SK

Action: Semiautomatic
Grips: Polymer
Barrel: 3.26–3.66 in.
Sights: 3-Dot
Weight: 23.8–25.9 oz.
Caliber: 9mm, .40 S&W
Capacity: 9–13 rounds
Features: LEM trigger system; double-action; pre-cock hammer; ambidextrous magazine release and interchangeable grip straps; mounting rail
MSRP . . . . $879.00–$979.00

SP5

Action: Semiautomatic
Grips: Synthetic
Barrel: 8.86 in.
Sights: Post front, adjustable rear
Weight: 82 oz.
Caliber: 9mm
Capacity: 10, 15, 30 rounds
Features: If you've always yearned for an MP5, this is the next best thing in a super-compact 9mm that has a delayed blowback system; equipped with "bungee" sling
MSRP $2949.00

USP

Action: Semiautomatic
Grips: Polymer
Barrel: 4.25–4.41 in.
Sights: 3-Dot
Weight: 27.2–31.36 oz.
Caliber: 9mm, .40 S&W, .45 ACP
Capacity: 12, 13, 15 rounds
Features: Browning-type action with a patented recoil reduction system; double and single action modes; available in nine trigger/firing mode configurations; fiber-reinforced polymer frame; blued finish; ambidextrous magazine release trigger
MSRP . . . . $1059.00–$1259.00

USP COMPACT

Action: Semiautomatic
Grips: Polymer
Barrel: 3.58–3.80 in.
Sights: Fixed
Weight: 25.6–28.2 oz.
Caliber: 9mm, .40 S&W, .45 ACP
Capacity: 8, 12, 13 rounds
Features: Corrosion proof fiber-reinforced polymer frame; ambidextrous magazine release lever; grooved target triggers; nine trigger firing modes
MSRP . . . . $1089.00–$1309.00

HECKLER & KOCH P2000

HECKLER & KOCH SP5

HECKLER & KOCH USP COMPACT

HECKLER & KOCH USP

HECKLER & KOCH USP TACTICAL

HECKLER & KOCH VP9SK

HECKLER & KOCH VP40

USP TACTICAL

Action: Semiautomatic
Grips: Synthetic
Barrel: 4.86 in.
Sights: Adjustable
Weight: 28.16 oz.
Caliber: 9mm, .40 S&W
Capacity: 10 or 15 rounds
Features: High profile target sights; target sights with micrometer adjustment for windage and elevation; one piece machined, nitro-carburized steel slide; nine trigger firing modes; HK recoil reduction system; corrosion resistant "Hostile Environment" blued finish; corrosion proof fiber-reinforced polymer frame; oversized trigger guard for use with gloves; choice of flat and extended floorplate magazines; ambidextrous magazine release lever; extended slide release; extractor doubles as a loaded chamber indicator; patented Lock-Out Safety device
MSRP . . . . $1479.00–$1639.00

VP9, VP9 TACTICAL, VP40

Action: Semiautomatic
Grips: Rubber
Barrel: 4.09 in.
Sights: Fixed
Weight: 26.56 oz.
Caliber: .40 S&W, 9mm
Capacity: 10, 13, 15 rounds
Features: Ergonomic handgun grip design that includes three changeable backstraps and six grip side panels; ambidextrous controls; extended Picatinny rail molded into the polymer frame; captive flat recoil spring; supplied with two additional backstraps and two sets of lateral grip plates; night sights optional; specialty versions available with gray, OD Green, or Flat Dark Earth frames; tactical versions add threaded barrels and night sights; now available optics ready
MSRP . . . . $849.00–$1059.00

VP9SK

Action: Semiautomatic
Grips: Polymer
Barrel: 3.39 in.
Sights: Drift-adjustable front, rear
Weight: 23.07 oz.
Caliber: 9mm
Capacity: 10, 13, 15 rounds
Features: A light subcompact striker-fire with an adjustable grip; slide and magazine release are ambidextrous; grip is finger-grooved and textured; slide has serrations front and rear; accessory rail; magazines are available flush or with a finger rest extension; available in black, Flat Dark Earth, Gray, or OD Green frames
MSRP . . . . $789.00–$899.00

Heizer Defense

HEIZER DEFENSE PKO45

PKO45

Action: Semiautomatic
Grips: Stainless steel
Barrel: 2.75 in.
Sights: Low-profile three-dot
Weight: 28 oz.
Caliber: .45 ACP
Capacity: 5, 7 rounds
Features: Uses guide-rod-over-barrel configuration; front strap grip safety; one-groove accessory rail; loaded chamber indicator; available in Ghost Grey, Copperhead, and Tactical Black finishes; company plans to produce the gun in 9mm and .40 S&W
MSRP $899.00

HANDGUNS

Heritage Manufacturing

ROUGH RIDER BIG BORE

Action: SA revolver
Grips: Cocobolo wood
Barrel: 4.75 in., 5.5 in.
Sights: Fixed, open
Weight: 38 oz.
Caliber: .45 LC, .357 Mag.
Capacity: 6 rounds
Features: Patterned after 1873 Colt; blued, nickel, stainless and blued/color-case-hardened finishes are available; frame mounted inertia firing pin and transfer bar
MSRP $515.00

ROUGH RIDER SMALL BORE

Action: SA revolver
Grips: Cocobolo wood
Barrel: 3.5 in., 4.75 in., 6.5 in., 9 in., 16 in.
Sights: Fixed
Weight: 31 oz.
Caliber: .22 LR, .22 Mag.
Capacity: 6 rounds
Features: Machined barrel is micro-threaded; optional cocobolo grips include white mother of pearl, black mother of pearl, or green camo laminate grips; frame finish comes in smooth silver satin, deep matte black, low gloss black satin or case-hardened finish
Single caliber: . . . . $131.00–$285.00
Two-cylinder combo:. . . . . $184.00–$285.00

HERITAGE ROUGH RIDER BIG BORE

HERITAGE ROUGH RIDER SMALL BORE

Hi-Point Firearms

HI-POINT FIREARMS MODEL JHP45 ACP

HI-POINT FIREARMS MODEL CF-380

MODEL CF-380

Action: Semiautomatic
Grips: Polymer
Barrel: 3.5 in.
Sights: 3-Dots adjustable
Weight: 29 oz.
Caliber: .380 ACP
Capacity: 8 or 10 rounds
Features: High-impact polymer frame; black powder coat with chrome rail; durable, easy-grip finish; quick on-off thumb safety; free extra rear peep sight; in black with or without hard case or in hydro-dipped pink camo; available with a built-in Laserlyte laser or with an integral compensator
MSRP . . . . $179.00–$269.00

MODEL JHP45 ACP & JCP 40 S&W

Action: Semiautomatic
Grips: Polymer
Barrel: 4.5 in.
Sights: 3-Dots adjustable
Weight: 35 oz.
Caliber: .40 S&W, .45 ACP
Capacity: 10 rounds
Features: Polymer frame; quick on-off thumb safety; operations safety sheet; +P rated; free extra rear peep sight; free trigger lock; black finish available as standalone gun or with one of three package choices: with Laserlyte, with hard case, with Galco Kydex holster; camo versions (no packages) available in hydro-dipped Desert Digital, pink, or Woodlands
MSRP . . . . $219.00–$285.00

Ideal Conceal

IDEAL CONCEAL IC380

IC380

Action: Two-shot
Grips: Synthetic
Barrel: N/A
Sights: Ultra-low-profile front blade, raised groove rear
Weight: N/A
Caliber: .380 ACP
Capacity: 2 rounds
Features: A two-shot pistol that folds to look like a cell-phone; one side unfolds to become the grip and provide access to the trigger
MSRP $550.00

Israel Weapon Industries (IWI)

MASADA

Action: Semiautomatic
Grips: Polymer
Barrel: 4.1 in.
Sights: Combat-style
Weight: 22.9 oz.
Caliber: 9mm
Capacity: 17 rounds
Features: A striker-fired pistol with an interchangeable trigger system; tactile and visible loaded chamber indicator; polygonal rifled barrel; front and rear slide cocking serrations; visible round count magazines; underside accessory rail; ambidextrous control; optional night sights
MSRP $480.00

ISRAEL WEAPON INDUSTRIES (IWI) MASADA

Iver Johnson Arms, Inc.

IVER JOHNSON 1911 A1 CHROME

IVER JOHNSON EAGLE XL

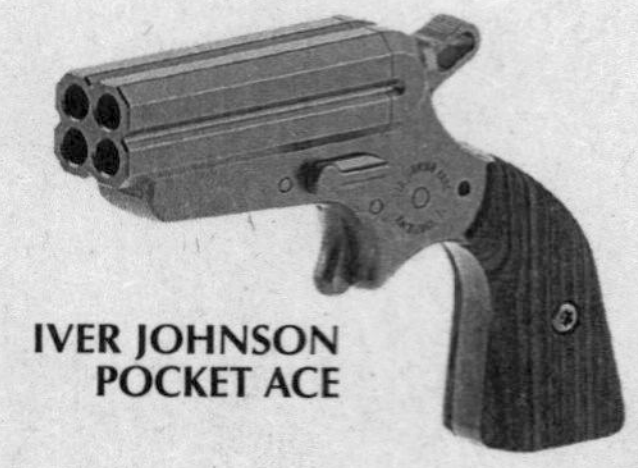
IVER JOHNSON POCKET ACE

1911A1 CHROME

Action: Semiautomatic
Grips: Black Dymondwood, black synthetic pearl
Barrel: 5 in.
Sights: GI fixed dovetail front and rear
Weight: 38 oz.
Caliber: .38 Super, .45 ACP
Capacity: 8 round
Features: Polished chrome finish; black Dymondwood grips or synthetic black pearl grips; slightly beveled magazine well; slide sports rear gripping serrations
MSRP . . . . $934.00–$956.00

EAGLE XL

Action: Semiautomatic
Grips: Dymondwood walnut
Barrel: 6 in.
Sights: Adjustable
Weight: 42 oz.
Caliber: .45 ACP, 10mm
Capacity: 8 rounds
Features: Front and rear serrations; extended thumb safety and slide stop; lowered and flared ejection port; beavertail grip safety; three-hole trigger; skeletonized hammer
MSRP . . . . $874.00–$964.00

POCKET ACE

Action: Revolver
Grips: Wood
Barrel: 2 in.
Sights: None
Weight: 7 oz.
Caliber: .22 LR
Capacity: 4 rounds
Features: Four-shot pepperbox; rotating firing pin; sighting grove; wood grips; ambidextrous release lever also functions as a safety
MSRP .N/A

Iver Johnson Arms, Inc.

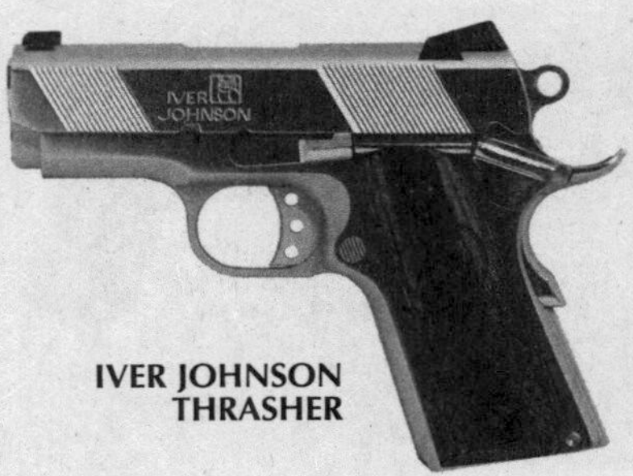

IVER JOHNSON THRASHER

THRASHER

Action: Semiautomatic
Grips: Wood
Barrel: 3.125 in.
Sights: Dovetail front, low-profile Novak-style rear
Weight: 30.4 oz.
Caliber: 9mm, .45 ACP
Capacity: 7, 8 rounds
Features: Officer-length slide, longer grip; tops and sides of slide are polished chrome; frame is satin finished; thin-line serrations at front and rear of slide; beveled magazine well; lowered and flared ejection port; available with Trijicon night sights
MSRP . . . . $713.00–$1023.00

Just Right Carbines

JUST RIGHT CARBINES 9MM QUADRAIL PISTOL

9MM QUADRAIL PISTOL

Action: Semiautomatic
Grips: Synthetic
Barrel: 6.5 in.
Sights: None
Weight: N/A
Caliber: 9mm
Capacity: 10, 15, 17 rounds
Features: Ambidextrous charging handle and ejection; one-piece machined aluminum receiver; M4 pistol buffer tube; threaded barrel; available as a smooth-fronted takedown model or equipped with an accessory quadrail
MSRP . . . . starting at $799.00

Kahr Arms

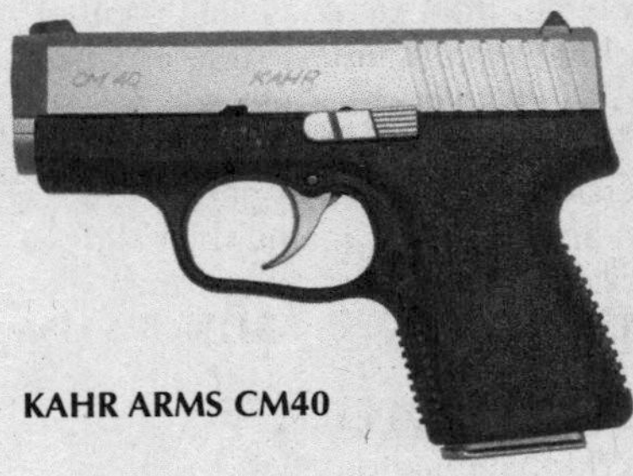

KAHR ARMS CM40

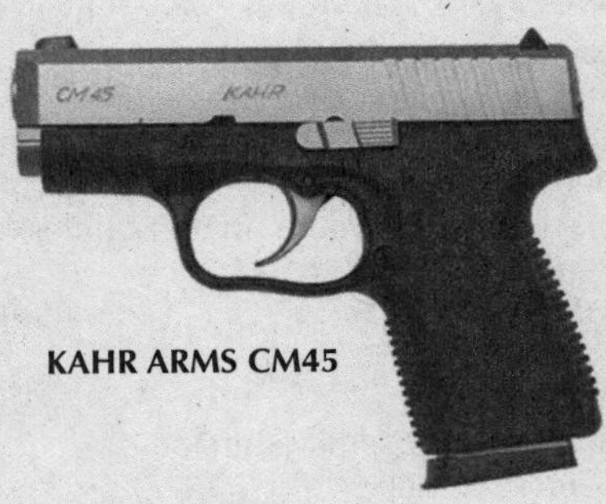

KAHR ARMS CM45

CM9

Action: Semiautomatic
Grips: Textured polymer
Barrel: 3 in.
Sights: Adjustable
Weight: 15.9 oz.
Caliber: 9mm
Capacity: 6+1 rounds
Features: Trigger cocking double-action; lock breech; Browning-type recoil lug; passive striker block; no magazine disconnect; drift adjustable, white bar-dot combat sights; available in Armor Black, Kryptek Camo, or matte stainless slide with front night sight
MSRP . . . . $499.00–$541.00

CM40

Action: Semiautomatic
Grips: Textured polymer
Barrel: 3 in.
Sights: Adjustable
Weight: 17.7 oz.
Caliber: .40 S&W
Capacity: 5+1 rounds
Features: Trigger cocking DAO; lock breech; "Browning-type" recoil lug; passive striker block; no magazine disconnect; black polymer frame, matte stainless steel slide
MSRP $460.00

CM45

Action: DAO semiautomatic
Grips: Synthetic
Barrel: 3.24 in.
Sights: Fixed
Weight: 17.3 oz.
Caliber: .45 ACP
Capacity: 5+1 rounds
Features: Trigger cocking DAO; lock breech; "Browning-type" recoil lug; passive striker block; no magazine disconnect; textured grips; drift adjustable white bar-dot combat rear sight; pinned in polymer front sight
MSRP $499.00

Kahr Arms

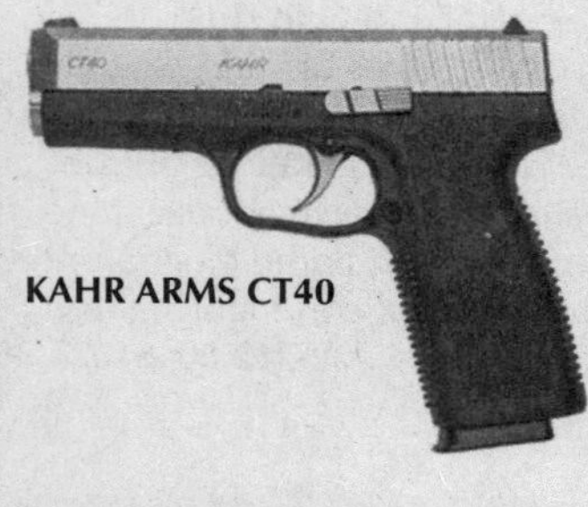
KAHR ARMS CT40

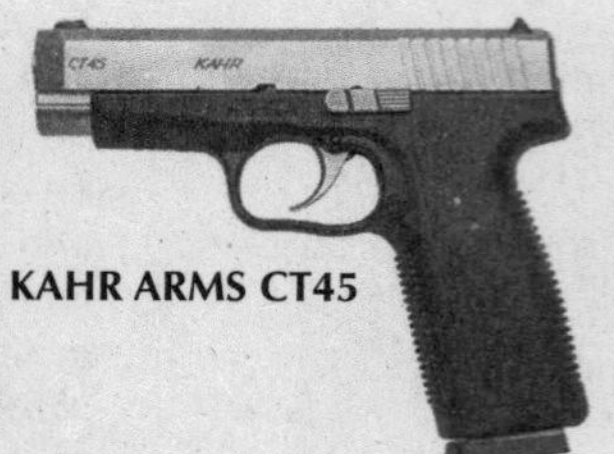
KAHR ARMS CT45

KAHR ARMS CT380

KAHR ARMS CT380, CW380 GOLD CERAKOTE LIMITED EDITION

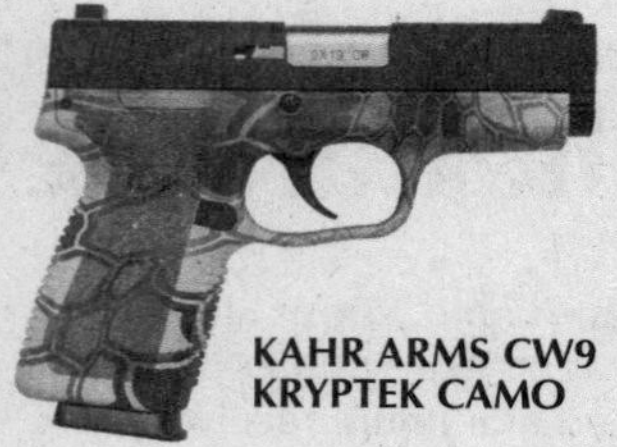
KAHR ARMS CW9 KRYPTEK CAMO

KAHR ARMS CW40 BURNT BRONZE

KAHR ARMS CW45

CT40

Action: DAO semiautomatic
Grips: Synthetic
Barrel: 4 in.
Sights: Fixed
Weight: 21.8 oz.
Caliber: .40 S&W
Capacity: 7+1 rounds
Features: Trigger cocking DAO; lock breech; "Browning-type" recoil lug; passive striker block; no magazine disconnect; textured grips; drift adjustable white bar-dot combat rear sight; pinned in polymer front sight; black polymer frame, matte stainless steel slide
MSRP $449.00

CT45

Action: DAO semiautomatic
Grips: Synthetic
Barrel: 4.04 in.
Sights: Fixed
Weight: 23.7 oz.
Caliber: .45 ACP
Capacity: 7+1 rounds
Features: Trigger cocking DAO; lock breech; "Browning-type" recoil lug; passive striker block; no magazine disconnect; textured grips; drift adjustable white bar-dot combat rear sight; pinned in polymer front sight; black polymer frame, matte stainless steel slide
MSRP $449.00

CT380

Action: Semiautomatic
Grips: Synthetic
Barrel: 3 in.
Sights: Fixed
Weight: 11.44 oz.
Caliber: .380 ACP
Capacity: 7+1 rounds
Features: Textured polymer grips; trigger cocking DAO; lock breech; Browning-type recoil lug; passive striker block; no magazine disconnect; drift adjustable white bar-dot combat rear sight; pinned in polymer front sight; available either with a matte stainless slide or with a Tungsten Cerakote slide with or without Grip Glove; matte stainless version also comes as package with an ambidextrous leather belt slide holster and an extra magazine
MSRP . . . . $419.00–$439.00

CT380 GOLD

Action: Semiautomatic
Grips: Textured polymer
Barrel: 3 in. (CT380), 2.58 in. (CW380)
Sights: Pinned polymer front, drift-adjustable white bar rear
Weight: 12.8 oz. (CT380), 11.5 oz (CW380)
Caliber: .380 ACP
Capacity: 7 rounds (CT380), 6 rounds (CW380)
Features: Concealed carry .380 ACP models in a limited edition featuring gold Cerakote coated stainless steel slide
MSRP $439.00

CW9 KRYPTEK CAMO

Action: Semiautomatic
Grips: Polymer
Barrel: 3.6 in.
Sights: Pinned polymer front dot, drift-adjustable two-dot rear
Weight: 15.8 oz.
Caliber: 9mm
Capacity: 7 rounds
Features: Lightweight and slim; Kryptek camo; Cerakote Black Armor slide
MSRP $523.00

CW40 BURNT BRONZE

Action: Semiautomatic
Grips: Polymer
Barrel: 3.6 in.
Sights: Pinned polymer front dot, drift-adjustable two-dot rear
Weight: 16.8 oz.
Caliber: .40 S&W
Capacity: 6 rounds
Features: Lightweight and slim; DAO action; Burnt Bronze Cerakote slide finish
MSRP $495.00

CW45

Action: Semiautomatic
Grips: Textured polymer
Barrel: 3.64 in.
Sights: Adjustable
Weight: 21.7 oz.
Caliber: .45 ACP
Capacity: 6+1 rounds
Features: Trigger cocking double-action; lock breech; Browning-type recoil lug; passive striker block; no magazine disconnect; drift adjustable, white bar-dot combat rear sight, pinned in polymer front sight; black frame; matte stainless steel slide
MSRP $449.00

Kahr Arms

KAHR ARMS CW380

KAHR ARMS P9 SERIES

KAHR ARMS P40 SERIES

KAHR ARMS P45 BLACK WITH NIGHT SIGHTS

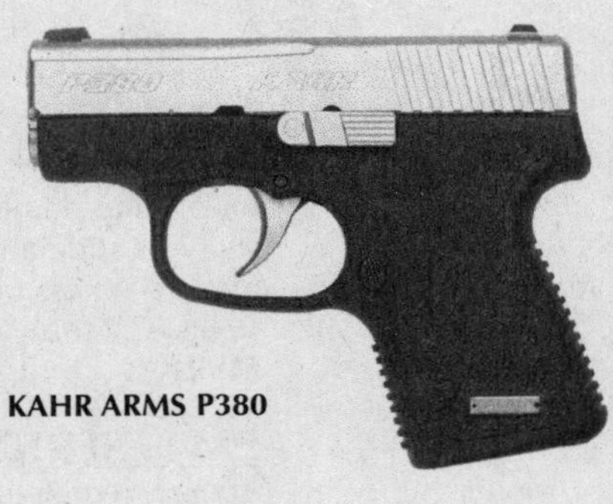
KAHR ARMS P380

CW380

Action: DAO semiautomatic
Grips: Black polymer
Barrel: 2.58 in.
Sights: Adjustable white bar-dot combat rear, pinned in polymer front
Weight: 10.2 oz.
Caliber: .380 ACP
Capacity: 6+1 rounds
Features: Lock breech; modified Browning type recoil lug; "safe cam" action; conventional rifled barrel; metal-injection-molded slide stop lever; slide lock after last round; available with front night sight; available configurations include black carbon fiber frame/matte stainless slide, Kryptec camo frame/black slide, black frame/matte stainless slide (also available with a front night sight)
MSRP . . . . $433.00–$475.00

P9 SERIES

Action: Semiautomatic
Grips: Textured polymer
Barrel: 3.6 in.
Sights: Adjustable
Weight: 16.9 oz.
Caliber: 9mm
Capacity: 7+1 rounds
Features: Trigger cocking DAO; lock breech; Browning-type recoil lug; passive striker block; no magazine disconnect; six versions available: Base P9 with matte stainless slide; with matte stainless slide and night sights; with matte stainless slide, night sights, external thumb safety, and loaded chamber indicator; with matte black slide; with matte black slide and night sights
MSRP . . . . $762.00–$996.00

P40 SERIES

Action: Semiautomatic
Grips: Textured polymer
Barrel: 3.6 in.
Sights: Adjustable
Weight: 18.7 oz.
Caliber: .40 S&W
Capacity: 6+1 rounds
Features: Trigger cocking DAO; lock breech; Browning-type recoil lug; passive striker block; no magazine disconnect; black polymer frame; six versions available: with matte stainless slide; with matte stainless slide and night sights; with matte black slide; with matte black slide and night sights; with matte stainless slide, external thumb safety, and loaded chamber indicator; and with matte stainless slide, external thumb safety, loaded chamber indicator, and night sights
MSRP $762.00

P45 SERIES

Action: Semiautomatic
Grips: Textured polymer
Barrel: 3.54 in.
Sights: Adjustable
Weight: 18.5 oz.
Caliber: .45 ACP
Capacity: 5+1 or 6+1 rounds
Features: Trigger cocking DAO; lock breech; Browning-type recoil lug; passive striker block; no magazine disconnect; black polymer frame
MSRP . . . . $762.00–$880.00

P380 SERIES

Action: Semiautomatic
Grips: Textured polymer
Barrel: 2.5 in.
Sights: Adjustable
Weight: 11.27 oz.
Caliber: .380 ACP
Capacity: 6+1 rounds
Features: Trigger cocking DAO; lock breech; Browning-type recoil lug; passive striker block; no magazine disconnect; eight versions available: with matte stainless slide; with matte stainless slide and night sights; with matte stainless or black slide; night sights; California-approved variant
MSRP . . . . $710.00–$762.00

Kahr Arms

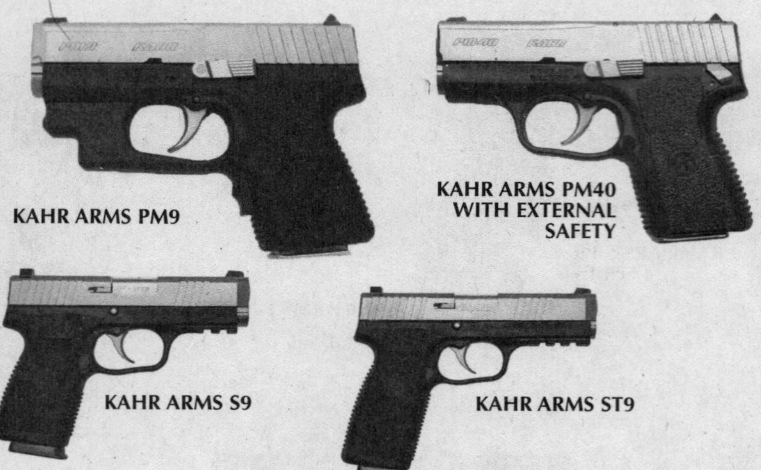
KAHR ARMS PM9

KAHR ARMS PM40 WITH EXTERNAL SAFETY

KAHR ARMS S9

KAHR ARMS ST9

KAHR ARMS PM45

PM9 SERIES
Action: Semiautomatic
Grips: Textured polymer
Barrel: 3 in.
Sights: Adjustable
Weight: 15.9 oz.
Caliber: 9mm
Capacity: 6+1 or 7+1 rounds
Features: Trigger cocking DAO; lock breech; Browning-type recoil lug; passive striker block; no magazine disconnect; eight versions available: with matte stainless slide; with matte stainless slide and night sights; with matte stainless or black slide; night sights; California-approved variant
MSRP $762.00

PM40 SERIES
Action: Semiautomatic
Grips: Textured polymer
Barrel: 3 in.
Sights: Adjustable
Weight: 17.7 oz.
Caliber: .40 S&W
Capacity: 5+1 or 6+1 rounds
Features: Trigger cocking DAO; lock breech; Browning-type recoil lug; passive striker block; no magazine disconnect; eight versions available: with matte stainless slide; with matte stainless slide and night sights; with matte stainless or black slide; night sights; California-approved variant
MSRP $762.00

PM45 SERIES
Action: Semiautomatic
Grips: Textured polymer
Barrel: 3.24 in.
Sights: Adjustable
Weight: 19.3 oz.
Caliber: .45 ACP
Capacity: 6+1 rounds
Features: Trigger cocking DAO; lock breech; Browning-type recoil lug; passive striker block; no magazine disconnect; eight versions available: with matte stainless slide; with matte stainless slide and night sights; with matte stainless or black slide; night sights
MSRP $762.00

S9
Action: Semiautomatic
Grips: Polymer
Barrel: 3.6 in.
Sights: Pinned polymer front dot, drift-adjustable two-dot rear
Weight: 15.8 oz.
Caliber: 9mm
Capacity: 7 rounds
Features: Intended primarily for concealed carry; stainless slide has grip serrations front and rear; accessory rail in front of the trigger guard; textured frame with ridges on the front and backstraps for improved purchase.; DAO pistol; Browning-type recoil lug; lock breech; passive striker block; no magazine disconnect; includes two magazines with a pinky rest
MSRP $477.00

ST9
Action: Semiautomatic
Grips: Polymer
Barrel: 4 in.
Sights: Pinned polymer front dot, drift-adjustable two-dot rear
Weight: 18.5 oz.
Caliber: 9mm
Capacity: 8 rounds
Features: Intended primarily for concealed carry; stainless slide has grip serrations front and rear; accessory rail in front of the trigger guard; textured frame with ridges on the front and backstraps for improved purchase.; DAO pistol; Browning-type recoil lug; lock breech; passive striker block; no magazine disconnect; includes two magazines with a pinky rest
MSRP $456.00

Kel-Tec

KEL-TEC CP33

CP33
Action: Semiautomatic
Grips: Polymer
Barrel: 5.5 in.
Sights: Adjustable fiber optic
Weight: 24 oz.
Caliber: .22 LR
Capacity: 33 rounds
Features: Loads of target fun with the 33-round double-double-stack magazine; fiber optic adjustable sights; full-length topside rail for optics
MSRP $475.00

Kel-Tec

KEL-TEC P-3AT

KEL-TEC P17

KEL-TEC P-32

KEL-TEC PF-9

KEL-TEC PMR-30

P-3AT

Action: Semiautomatic
Grips: Polymer
Barrel: 2.7 in.
Sights: Fixed
Weight: 8.3 oz.
Caliber: .380 ACP
Capacity: 6+1 rounds
Features: Double-action only; steel barrel and slide; aluminum frame; transfer bar
MSRP $340.00

P17

Action: Semiautomatic
Grips: Polymer
Barrel: 3.93 in.
Sights: Fiber optic front, adjustable rear
Weight: 12.8 oz.
Caliber: .22 LR
Capacity: 16 rounds
Features: A compact striker-fire rimfire with a textured grip; generous magazine capacity; accessory rail; threaded barrel; ambidextrous mag release and safety; three magazines included
MSRP $199.00

P-32

Action: Semiautomatic
Grips: Polymer
Barrel: 2.7 in.
Sights: Fixed
Weight: 6.6 oz.
Caliber: .32 ACP
Capacity: 7+1 rounds
Features: Steel barrel and slide; locked breech mechanism
MSRP $360.00

PF-9

Action: Semiautomatic
Grips: Polymer
Barrel: 3.1 in.
Sights: Adjustable
Weight: 12.7 oz.
Caliber: 9mm
Capacity: 7+1 rounds
Features: Firing mechanism is double-action only with an automatic hammer block safety; grips available in black, grey, and olive drab; rear sight is a new design and is adjustable for windage
MSRP $358.00

PMR-30

Action: SA Semiautomatic
Grips: Nylon
Barrel: 4.3 in.
Sights: Picatinny accessory rail under barrel
Weight: 13.6 oz.
Caliber: .22 WMR
Capacity: 30 rounds
Features: Blowback/locked breech system; lightweight but full sized; urethane recoil buffer; disassembles for cleaning with removal of one pin
MSRP $545.00

Kimber

KIMBER AEGIS ELITE CUSTOM, CUSTOM (OI)

KIMBER AEGIS ELITE PRO, PRO (OI)

KIMBER AEGIS ELITE ULTRA

AEGIS ELITE CUSTOM, CUSTOM (OI)

Action: Semiautomatic
Grips: G-10
Barrel: 5 in.
Sights: Venom reflex red dot sight
Weight: 38 oz.
Caliber: .45 ACP, 9mm
Capacity: 8, 9 rounds
Features: Full-size 1911; textured green/black/gray G-10 grips; full-length guide rod; 24 lines-per-inch frontstrap checkering; stainless steel frame in satin silver; matte black Kim Pro II finish on the stainless steel slide; cross-hatched slide serrations front and back; round heel frame; OI is Optics included
MSRP . . . .$1495.00–$1516.00

AEGIS ELITE PRO, PRO (OI)

Action: Semiautomatic
Grips: G-10
Barrel: 4 in.
Sights: Venom reflex red dot sight
Weight: 38 oz.
Caliber: .45 ACP, 9mm
Capacity: 7, 9 rounds
Features: Mid-size 1911; textured green/black/gray G-10 grips; full-length guide rod; 24 lines-per-inch frontstrap checkering; stainless steel frame in satin silver; stainless steel slide in matte black Kim Pro II finish; cross-hatch serrations at the rear of the slide; round heel frame; OI is Optics included
MSRP . . . .$1087.00–$1516.00

AEGIS ELITE ULTRA

Action: Semiautomatic
Grips: G-10
Barrel: 3 in.
Sights: Green and red fiber optic
Weight: 25 oz.
Caliber: .45 ACP, 9mm
Capacity: 7, 8 rounds
Features: Compact version in the Aegis Elite series; cross-hatch serrations only at the rear of the slide
MSRP . . . .$1087.00–$1108.00

Kimber

HANDGUNS

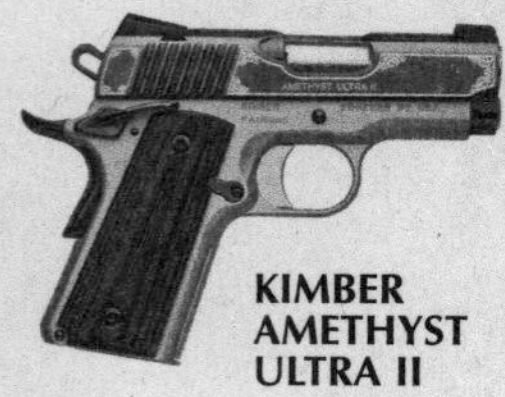
KIMBER AMETHYST ULTRA II

KIMBER CAMP GUARD 10

KIMBER CUSTOM II (TWO-TONE)

KIMBER CUSTOM II (TWO-TONE) (LG)

KIMBER CUSTOM TLE/RL II (TFS)

KIMBER EVO SP (CDP)

KIMBER EVO SP (CS)

KIMBER EVO SP SELECT (BLACK)

AMETHYST ULTRA II

Action: Semiautomatic
Grips: Micarta thin grips
Barrel: 3 in.
Sights: Fixed titrium night sights
Weight: 25 oz.
Caliber: .45 ACP, 9mm
Capacity: 7 or 8 rounds
Features: Ambidextrous thumb safety; full-length guide rod; amethyst purple PVD coating on small parts and fine engraving; front strap serrations and checkering; purple ball-milled Micarta thin grips
MSRP. . . . . $1754.00–$1774.00

CAMP GUARD 10

Action: Semiautomatic
Grips: Rosewood
Barrel: 5 in.
Sights: Tactical wedge
Weight: 38 oz.
Caliber: 10mm
Capacity: 8 rounds
Features: Designed in partnership with Rocky Mountain Elk Foundation for use in the backcountry; stainless steel frame, slide, and barrel; front strap checkering at 30 lines per inch
MSRP. $1298.00

CUSTOM II (TWO-TONE)

Action: Semiautomatic
Grips: Smooth/checkered rosewood
Barrel: 5 in.
Sights: Fixed, low profile
Weight: 38 oz.
Caliber: .45 ACP, 9mm
Capacity: 7 or 9 rounds
Features: Brushed polished carbon slide; stainless frame; full-length guide rod; sainless steel match-grade barrel
9mm: $904.00
.45 ACP: $883.00

CUSTOM II (TWO-TONE) (LG)

Action: Semiautomatic
Grips: Rosewood
Barrel: 5 in.
Sights: Fixed low-profile
Weight: 38 oz.
Caliber: .45 ACP
Capacity: 7 rounds
Features: A more robust Govt. model with match-grade stainless steel barrel and bushing; brush-polished black slide with front and rear serrations; brush-polished stainless steel frame
MSRP. $1136.00

CUSTOM TLE/RL II (TFS)

Action: Semiautomatic
Grips: G10
Barrel: 5 in.
Sights: Fixed
Weight: 39 oz.
Caliber: .45 ACP, 9mm
Capacity: 7 rounds
Features: Threaded for suppression; Meprolight Tritium 3-dot night sight; Picatinny rail
.45 ACP: $1175.00
9mm: $1195.00

EVO SP (CDP)

Action: Semiautomatic
Grips: G-10
Barrel: 3.16 in.
Sights: Tritium night sights
Weight: 19 oz.
Caliber: 9mm
Capacity: 7 rounds
Features: CDP is Custom Defense Package. Fancier take on the Two-Tone, with the aluminum frame in KimPro Charcoal Gray; FNC Black-finished stainless steel slide; Carry Melt treatment; red/black G10 grips and backstrap with checkering; front strap checkering
MSRP. $883.00

EVO SP (CS)

Action: Semiautomatic
Grips: G-10
Barrel: 3.16 in.
Sights: Tritium night sights
Weight: 18 oz.
Caliber: 9mm
Capacity: 7 rounds
Features: CS is the Custom Shop offering in the EVO line of carry guns, with Stiplex-inspired texturing on the slide, front strap, grips and backstrap; KimPro Charcoal Gray finish on the aluminum frame
MSRP. $965.00

EVO SP SELECT (BLACK)

Action: Semiautomatic
Grips: Nylon
Barrel: 3.16 in.
Sights: White three-dot
Weight: 19 oz.
Caliber: 9mm
Capacity: 7 rounds
Features: A smartly priced everyday carry gun with interchangeable grip system (side flats and backstrap) in checkered brown nylon; stainless steel slide in FNC black finish; aluminum frame in Kimpro II Black
MSRP. $638.00

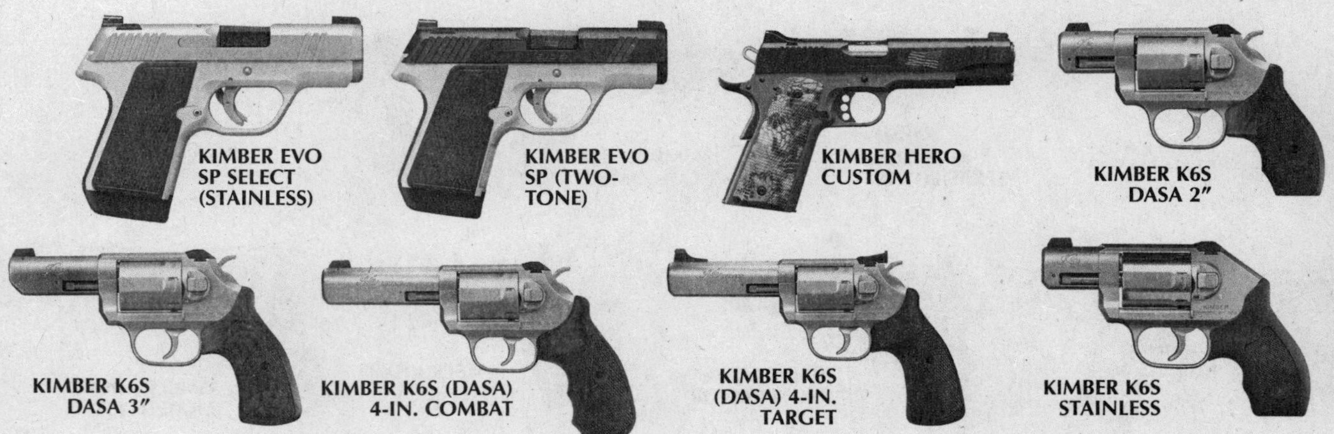

EVO SP SELECT (STAINLESS)

Action: Semiautomatic
Grips: Nylon
Barrel: 3.16 in.
Sights: White three-dot
Weight: 19 oz.
Caliber: 9mm
Capacity: 7 rounds
Features: Similar to the EVO SP Select (Black) model, but frame in Kimpro II Silver, slide in Kimpro Silver over FNC, and interchangeable checkered nylon grip/backstrap in black
MSRP. $638.00

EVO SP (TWO-TONE)

Action: Semiautomatic
Grips: Nylon
Barrel: 3.16 in.
Sights: Tritium night sights
Weight: 19 oz.
Caliber: 9mm
Capacity: 7 rounds
Features: Terrific striker-fired CCW pistol featuring an aluminum frame in KimPro Silver finish; stainless steel slide in FNC Black; diamond checkering on grips; bushing-less match-grade barrel; checkered nylon backstrap; front strap checkering
MSRP. $795.00

HERO CUSTOM

Action: Semiautomatic
Grips: Composite
Barrel: 5 in.
Sights: Green and red fiber optic
Weight: 38 oz.
Caliber: .45 ACP
Capacity: 7 rounds
Features: Full-size 1911; Desert Tan Kim Pro II finish on the frame; matte black Kim Pro II finish on the slide; composite checkered grips in Kryptek Highlander camo; match grade stainless steel barrel and bushing; aluminum three-hole trigger; the American flag is engraved in tan on the slide
MSRP. $1019.00

K6S DASA 2″

Action: Revolver
Grips: Walnut
Barrel: 2 in.
Sights: White three-dot
Weight: 23 oz.
Caliber: .357 Mag., .38 Spec.
Capacity: 6 rounds
Features: Compact powerhouse with Kimber's unique cylinder fluting; boot-style walnut grip; DA/SA exposed hammer; overbrushed stainless finish with minimal engraving; serrated backstrap
MSRP. $1033.00

K6S DASA 3″

Action: Revolver
Grips: Walnut
Barrel: 3 in.
Sights: White three-dot
Weight: 25.1 oz.
Caliber: .357 Mag.
Capacity: 6 rounds
Features: The extra inch of barrel also gets you enough grip for a three-finger hold; overbrushed stainless finish with minimal engraving; serrated backstrap
MSRP. $1033.00

K6S (DASA) 4-IN. COMBAT

Action: Revolver
Grips: Walnut
Barrel: 4 in.
Sights: White three-dot
Weight: 25.5 oz.
Caliber: .357 Mag.
Capacity: 6 rounds
Features: Great for competition or self-defense, this revolver has a non-stacking DA/SA trigger; three-finger-groove round butt combat grips with diamond checkering; flat-sided full underlug; serrated backstrap; brushed stainless finish
MSRP. $1046.00

K6S (DASA) 4-IN. TARGET

Action: Revolver
Grips: Walnut
Barrel: 4 in.
Sights: Adjustable combat target
Weight: 25.5 oz.
Caliber: .357 Mag.
Capacity: 6 rounds
Features: A solid full-size target revolver with adjustable sights; brushed stainless finish; diamond-checkered extended walnut grips; non-stacking DA/SA trigger; flat-sided full underlug
MSRP. $1046.00

K6S STAINLESS

Action: DAO
Grips: Rubber
Barrel: 2 in.
Sights: Low-profile removable dovetail sights
Weight: 23 oz.
Caliber: .357 Mag.
Capacity: 6 rounds
Features: Stainless steel barrel; low-profile removable front and rear dovetail sights; smooth no-stack double action trigger; superior ergonomic grip contour; serrated backstrap
MSRP. $938.00

Kimber

KIMBER K6S STAINLESS 3"

KIMBER K6S TEXAS EDITION

KIMBER KHX CUSTOM/RL (OI)

KIMBER KHX CUSTOM, CUSTOM (OR)

KIMBER KHX CUSTOM (OI)

KIMBER KHX PRO, PRO (OR)

KIMBER KHX ULTRA

KIMBER MICRO 9 AMETHYST

K6S STAINLESS 3"

Action: DA only
Grips: Walnut
Barrel: 3 in.
Sights: White dot
Weight: 25.1 oz.
Caliber: .357 Mag.
Capacity: 6 rounds
Features: Snub-nose small grip revolver; full crane shroud; longer barrel and grip than other K6s models; brushed stainless steel finish; smooth walnut grips
MSRP $965.00

K6S TEXAS EDITION

Action: Revolver
Grips: G10
Barrel: 2 in.
Sights: White three-dot
Weight: 23 oz.
Caliber: .357 Mag.
Capacity: 6 rounds
Features: A generous six-round cylinder on this special Texas Edition gets paired with smooth satin finish; serrated backstrap; ivory G10 grips with "Texas" and "Come and Take it" emblazoned in gold
MSRP $1454.00

KHX CUSTOM (OI)

Action: Semiautomatic
Grips: G-10
Barrel: 5 in.
Sights: Trijicon RMR red-dot, white-dot co-witness sights
Weight: 38 oz.
Caliber: 9mm, 10mm, .45 ACP
Capacity: 8 rounds
Features: A serious competition or even a home-defense gun, with full-length guide rod; match-grade barrel and bushing; Hogue Magrip G10 panels; aluminum trigger; Trijicon RMR Type 2 red-dot sight with 3.25 MOA dot; co-witness sights; KimPro II Gray finish on frame and slide
MSRP . . . . $1971.00–$1998.00

KHX CUSTOM, CUSTOM (OR)

Action: Semiautomatic
Grips: G-10
Barrel: 5 in.
Sights: Fiber optics
Weight: 38 oz.
Caliber: .45 ACP, 9mm
Capacity: 7, 9 rounds
Features: Full-size 1911; "snakeskin" textured Hogue Magrip G-10 grip panels; textured gripping areas on the slide; Stiplex front strap stippling; OR stands for "optics ready"; milled slide
Custom: . . . . $1325.00–$1373.00
Custom (OR): . . $1971.00–$1998.00

KHX CUSTOM/RL (OI)

Action: Semiautomatic
Grips: G-10
Barrel: 5 in.
Sights: Trijicon RMR red-dot, white-dot co-witness sights
Weight: 39 oz.
Caliber: 9mm, 10mm, .45 ACP
Capacity: 8 rounds
Features: Similar to the KHX Custom (OI), but with the addition of an under-barrel accessory rail
MSRP . . . . $2039.00–$2100.00

KHX PRO, PRO (OR)

Action: Semiautomatic
Grips: G-10
Barrel: 4 in.
Sights: Fiber optics
Weight: 38 oz.
Caliber: .45 ACP, 9mm
Capacity: 7, 9 rounds
Features: Hogue Magrip G-10 grip with a built-in red laser; G-10 mainspring housing; OR stands for "optics ready"; milled side
Pro: . . . . $1352.00–$1373.00
Pro (OR) (9mm only): $1182.00

KHX ULTRA

Action: Semiautomatic
Grips: G-10
Barrel: 3 in.
Sights: Fiber optics
Weight: 38 oz.
Caliber: .45 ACP, 9mm
Capacity: 7, 8 rounds
Features: G-10 mainspring housing; Hogue Enhanced Magrip G-10 grips with a built-in red laser; slide grip texturing appears only at the rear
MSRP . . . . $1352.00–$1373.00

MICRO 9 AMETHYST

Action: Semiautomatic
Grips: G10
Barrel: 3.15 in.
Sights: Standard night sights
Weight: 15.6 oz.
Caliber: 9mm
Capacity: 7 rounds
Features: Vertical serrations on the black/purple G10 grips, lower backside of the frame, and rear of the slide; aluminum frame in Kimpro II Silver finish; stainless steel slide gets a purple PVD finish on the flats as well as border scroll engraving; ramped barrel
MSRP $1114.00

Kimber

KIMBER MICRO 9 BEL AIR

KIMBER MICRO 9 DESERT NIGHT

KIMBER MICRO 9 DESERT TAN (LG)

KIMBER MICRO 9 ECLIPSE

KIMBER MICRO 9 ESV (BLACK)

KIMBER MICRO 9 KHX

KIMBER MICRO 9 NIGHTFALL (DN)

KIMBER MICRO 9 SAPPHIRE

MICRO 9 BEL AIR

Action: Semiautomatic
Grips: Ivory micarta
Barrel: 3.15 in.
Sights: Three-dot white
Weight: 15.6 oz.
Caliber: 9mm
Capacity: 6 rounds
Features: Kimber's unique Bel Air Blue finish on the aluminum frame; mirror-polished stainless slide; stainless steel barrel; bull-length guide rod; single-action
MSRP $904.00

MICRO 9 DESERT NIGHT (DN)

Action: Semiautomatic
Grips: Rubber
Barrel: 3.15 in.
Sights: TruGlo TFX Pro day/night sights
Weight: 15.6 oz.
Caliber: 9mm
Capacity: 7 rounds
Features: Desert Tan finish on an aluminum frame; Hogue wrap-around grips; matte black steel slide; full-length guide rod; matte black stainless slide; DN designates day/night sights
MSRP $795.00

MICRO 9 DESERT TAN (LG)

Action: Semiautomatic
Grips: Crimson Trace laser grips
Barrel: 3.15 in.
Sights: White-dot
Weight: 15.6 oz.
Caliber: 9mm
Capacity: 6 rounds
Features: Super slim, super lightweight concealed carry pistol; stainless barrel; bull-length guide rod; aluminum frame; single-action
MSRP $795.00

MICRO 9 ECLIPSE

Action: Semiautomatic
Grips: G-10
Barrel: 3.15 in.
Sights: Tritium night sights
Weight: 15.6 oz.
Caliber: 9mm
Capacity: 7 rounds
Features: Charcoal gray finish on an aluminum frame; stainless steel slide with polished flats; checkered gray G-10 grips; round-heel frame; 30 lines-per-inch front strap checkering; full-length guide rod; tritium night sights
MSRP $822.00

MICRO 9 ESV (BLACK)

Action: Semiautomatic
Grips: G-10
Barrel: 3.15 in.
Sights: Night sights
Weight: 15.35 oz.
Caliber: 9mm
Capacity: 7 rounds
Features: Shaving a couple ounces off the EVO line thanks to slide serrations. Two versions: (Black) has gold Titanium Nitride coating, black Altamont G-10 grips, KimPro II Black slide and frame; (Gray) has Rose Copper coated barrel, black Altamont G-10 grips, KimPro II Gray slide and frame
MSRP $856.00

MICRO 9 KHX

Action: Semiautomatic
Grips: G-10
Barrel: 3.15 in.
Sights: Red fiber optic front, green fiber optic rear
Weight: 15.6 oz.
Caliber: 9mm
Capacity: 7 rounds
Features: Outstanding features in the CCW pistol include hexagonal dot "serrations" fore and aft on the slide, that pattern repeated in part on the Hogue G-10 grips and backstrap; KimPro II Gray finish on slide and frame
MSRP $856.00

MICRO 9 NIGHTFALL

Action: Semiautomatic
Grips: Rubber
Barrel: 3.15 in.
Sights: TruGlo TFX Pro day/night sights
Weight: 15.6 oz.
Caliber: 9mm
Capacity: 7 rounds
Features: Satin silver finish on an aluminum frame; Hogue wrap-around grips; all-over matte black finish
MSRP $795.00

MICRO 9 SAPPHIRE

Action: Semiautomatic
Grips: G10
Barrel: 3.15 in.
Sights: Three-dot tritium night sights
Weight: 15.6 oz.
Caliber: 9mm
Capacity: 6 rounds
Features: Brilliant blue PVD finish on slide; coordinated blue and black G10 grips; slide has scroll engraving enhancements; aluminum frame; stainless steel barrel
MSRP $1114.00

Kimber

KIMBER MICRO 9 STAINLESS (DN)

KIMBER MICP 9 TRIARI

KIMBER MICRO 9 TWO-TONE (LG)

KIMBER MICRO AMETHYST

KIMBER MICRO DESERT NIGHT

KIMBER MICRO ECLIPSE

KIMBER MICRO STAINLESS ROSEWOOD

KIMBER MICRO TWO-TONE (LG) (NS)

MICRO 9 STAINLESS (DN)

Action: Semiautomatic
Grips: Rubber
Barrel: 3.15 in.
Sights: TruGlo TFX Pro day/night sights
Weight: 15.6 oz.
Caliber: 9mm
Capacity: 7 rounds
Features: Satin silver finish on an aluminum frame; Hogue wrap-around grips; full-length guide rod; satin silver finish on the stainless steel slide; DN designates day/night sights
MSRP $795.00

MICRO 9 TRIARI

Action: Semiautomatic
Grips: Micarta
Barrel: 3.15 in.
Sights: Red fiber optic front, green fiber optic rear
Weight: 15.6 oz.
Caliber: 9mm
Capacity: 7 rounds
Features: Black Linen Micarta grips with a stacked cube pattern; aluminum frame with Kimpro II Black finish; stainless slide in black oxide finish with stacked-cube serration patterning front and rear; rear sight has cocking ledge; solid aluminum trigger; match-grade barrel
MSRP $822.00

MICRO 9 TWO-TONE (LG)

Action: Semiautomatic
Grips: Rosewood
Barrel: 3.15 in.
Sights: White-dot
Weight: 15.6 oz.
Caliber: 9mm
Capacity: 7 rounds
Features: Excellent choice for CCW practitioners wanting a slim compact in 9mm; steel slide in matte black finish and with rear serrations; aluminum frame in brush silver finish with Crimson Trace laser grips
MSRP $822.00

MICRO AMETHYST

Action: Semiautomatic
Grips: G10
Barrel: 2.75 in.
Sights: Three-dot tritium night sights
Weight: 13.4 oz.
Caliber: .380 ACP
Capacity: 6 rounds
Features: Concealed carry gun in vibrant purple PVD finish; engraved scroll accents; aluminum frame; stainless steel barrel; bull-length guide rod; single-action
MSRP $1114.00

MICRO DESERT NIGHT

Action: Semiautomatic
Grips: G10
Barrel: 2.75 in.
Sights: Three-dot white
Weight: 13.4 oz.
Caliber: .380 ACP
Capacity: 6 rounds
Features: Concealed carry gun; Desert Tan KimPro finish; black-finished slide; stainless steel slide and barrel; bull-length guide rod
MSRP $659.00

MICRO ECLIPSE

Action: Semiautomatic
Grips: Rosewood
Barrel: 2.75 in.
Sights: Tactical wedge tritium night sights
Weight: 13.4 oz.
Caliber: .380 ACP
Capacity: 9 rounds
Features: Matte black finish on an aluminum frame; satin silver finish on the slide; Carry Melt treatment; thin ball-milled rosewood grips; round-heel frame; 30 lines-per-inch front strap checkering; full-length guide rod; tactical wedge night sights
MSRP $768.00

MICRO STAINLESS ROSEWOOD (NS)

Action: Semiautomatic
Grips: Rosewood
Barrel: 2.75 in.
Sights: Low-profile three-dot tritium night sights
Weight: 13.4 oz.
Caliber: .380 ACP
Capacity: 6 rounds
Features: Mild recoil; smooth trigger pulls; full-length guide rod; aluminum frame with anodized finish
MSRP $625.00

MICRO TWO-TONE (LG) (NS)

Action: Semiautomatic
Grips: Rosewood
Barrel: 2.75 in.
Sights: Tritium night sights
Weight: 13.4 oz.
Caliber: .380 ACP
Capacity: 7 rounds
Features: Super CCW choice with soft edges; checkered backstrap; Crimson Trace laser grips; aluminum frame in satin silver finish; matte black slide with rear serrations
MSRP $768.00

Kimber

KIMBER PRO COVERT

KIMBER PRO RAPTOR II

KIMBER RAPIDE (BLACK ICE)

KIMBER ROSE GOLD ULTRA II

KIMBER SAPPHIRE ULTRA II

KIMBER STAINLESS II

KIMBER STAINLESS TARGET (LS)

KIMBER SUPER JÄGARE

PRO COVERT

Action: Semiautomatic
Grips: Urban Camouflage Crimson Trace laser grips
Barrel: 4 in.
Sights: Tactical wedge tritium night sights
Weight: 28 oz.
Caliber: .45 ACP
Capacity: 7 rounds
Features: Carry Melt treatment; 30 lines per inch checkering on front strap; Charcoal Gray and KimPro II finish; aluminum frame
MSRP $1495.00

PRO RAPTOR II

Action: SA semiautomatic
Grips: Zebra wood, scale pattern
Barrel: 4 in.
Sights: Tactical wedge 3-dot
Weight: 35 oz.
Caliber: .45 ACP, 9mm
Capacity: 8 rounds
Features: Available in all stainless or all blue; match grade barrel; ambidextrous thumb safety; full-length guide rod; blue in .45 ACP only, stainless available in both calibers
Blue: $1257.00
Stainless: . . . . . . $1373.00–$1393.00

RAPIDE (BLACK ICE)

Action: Semiautomatic
Grips: G10
Barrel: 5 in.
Sights: TruGlo TFX Pro Day/Night
Weight: 38 oz.
Caliber: 9mm, 10mm, .45 ACP
Capacity: 8, 9 rounds
Features: A unique take on cosmetics with aggressively textured Black Rapide G10 grips; stainless steel slide in Kimpro II Silver/Gray with lightning cuts and front and rear cocking serrations; Kimber Stiplex frontstrap stippling; V-cut aluminum trigger
MSRP . . . . $1597.00–$1618.00

ROSE GOLD ULTRA II

Action: Semiautomatic
Grips: G10
Barrel: 3 in.
Sights: Tactical wedge
Weight: 25 oz.
Caliber: .45 ACP
Capacity: 7 rounds
Features: Personal defense gun; finished in Rose Gold PVD coating; solid aluminum trigger; aluminum round-heel frame; ambidextrous thumb safety; ball-milled front strap
MSRP $1774.00

SAPPHIRE ULTRA II

Action: SA semiautomatic
Grips: G-10 thin grips
Barrel: 3 in.
Sights: Tactical Wedge night sights
Weight: 25 oz.
Caliber: 9mm, .45 ACP
Capacity: 8 rounds
Features: Highly-polished stainless steel slide and small parts are finished with bright blue PVD finish accented with fine engraving; blue/black ball-milled G-10 thin grips and short trigger; ambidextrous thumb safety; Tactical Wedge night sights
MSRP $1774.00

STAINLESS II

Action: Semiautomatic
Grips: Synthetic
Barrel: 5 in.
Sights: Fixed, low profile
Weight: 38 oz.
Caliber: .45 ACP, 9mm
Capacity: 7 or 9 rounds
Features: Aluminum frame with satin silver finish; stainless stell slide; steel match-grade barrel; double-diamond textured grips ; blue in .45 ACP only, stainless available in both calibers
MSRP . . . . $938.00–$958.00

STAINLESS TARGET (LS)

Action: Semiautomatic
Grips: Rosewood
Barrel: 6 in.
Sights: Kimber adjustable
Weight: 42 oz.
Caliber: .45 ACP, 10mm
Capacity: 7, 8 rounds
Features: Full-size 1911 with a longer slide for bull's-eye or other precision competition; slide and frame are finished in a satin silver; LS stands for Long Slide
MSRP . . . . $1101.00–$1121.00

SUPER JÄGARE

Action: Semiautomatic
Grips: Micarta
Barrel: 6 in.
Sights: DeltaPoint Pro optic
Weight: 42 oz.
Caliber: 10mm
Capacity: 8 rounds
Features: Designed for close-range big-game and varmint hunting; stainless steel frame and slide; frame has round heel and high cut trigger guard; finished in KimPro and Charcoal Gray; slide has carbon coating and Super Carry pattern on its flat top; Carry Melt treatment; match-grade bushing; solid aluminum trigger
MSRP $2869.00

Kimber

KIMBER SUPER MATCH II

KIMBER TACTICAL ENTRY II

KIMBER ULTRA CARRY II

KIMBER ULTRA CARRY II (TWO-TONE) (LG)

KIMBER ULTRA CDP

SUPER MATCH II

Action: Semiautomatic
Grips: Walnut
Barrel: 5 in.
Sights: Adjustable
Weight: 38 oz.
Caliber: .45 ACP
Capacity: 8 rounds
Features: Ambidextrous thumb safety; full-length guide rod; stainless steel frame with satin silver finish; front strap checkering and checkering under trigger guard
MSRP $2420.00

TACTICAL ENTRY II

Action: SA semiautomatic
Grips: Laminated double diamond, Kimber logo
Barrel: 5 in.
Sights: Meprolight tritium 3-dot night, fixed
Weight: 40 oz.
Caliber: .45 ACP
Capacity: 7 rounds
Features: Ambidextrous thumb safety; full-length guide rod; stainless steel frame and slide; matte gray Kim Pro II frame finish
MSRP $1490.00

ULTRA CARRY II

Action: SA semiautomatic
Grips: Black synthetic double diamond
Barrel: 3 in.
Sights: Fixed, low profile
Weight: 25 oz.
Caliber: .45 ACP
Capacity: 7 rounds
Features: Black matte finish; aluminum frame; steel slide; full-length guide rod
MSRP $972.00

ULTRA CARRY II (TWO-TONE) (LG)

Action: Semiautomatic
Grips: Rosewood
Barrel: 3 in.
Sights: Fixed low-profile
Weight: 25 oz.
Caliber: .45 ACP
Capacity: 7 rounds
Features: Aluminum framed Officer's size pistol with Crimson Trace green laser grips; steel slide with matte black finish; aluminum frame in satin silver finish; match-grade trigger
MSRP . . . . $1189.00–$1210.00

ULTRA CDP

Action: Semiautomatic
Grips: Rosewood double diamond
Barrel: 3 in.
Sights: Meprolight tritium 3-dot night, fixed
Weight: 25 oz.
Caliber: 9mm, .45 ACP
Capacity: 7 rounds
Features: Ambidextrous thumb safety, Carry Melt treatment, aluminum frame with charcoal gray KimPro II finish, stainless slide is flat-topped with satin silver finish
MSRP . . . . $1230.00–$1250.00

Kriss USA

KRISS USA SPHINX SDP COMPACT

SPHINX SDP COMPACT

Action: DA/SA semiautomatic
Grips: Composite
Barrel: 3.7 in., 4.35 in.
Sights: Fiber optic/tritium front, tritium rear
Weight: 27.5 oz.
Caliber: 9mm
Capacity: 15+1 rounds
Features: Upper frame machined from aeronautic-grade hard-anodized aluminum; integral recoil buffer; Picatinny rail; polymer lower frame; Defiance fiber optic/tritium day-night green front sight with tritium two-dot red rear sight; internal firing pin safety, drop safety, hammer safety, and integrated slide-position safety; Cerakote finish
Standard: . . . . $999.00–$1049.00
Threaded: . . . . . $1049.00–$1099.00

Les Baer Custom

LES BAER 1911 BLACK BAER 9MM

1911 BLACK BAER 9MM

Action: SA
Grips: Black recon
Barrel: 4.25 in.
Sights: Fixed rear combat night sight, dovetail front night sight
Weight: N/A
Caliber: 9mm
Capacity: 9 rounds
Features: Compact concealed carry; slide fitted to frame; rear serrated slide; speed trigger with crisp 4 lb. pull; tactical extended combat safety; Dupont S coating on complete pistol for maximum corrosion resistance
MSRP $3070.00

Les Baer Custom

LES BAER CUSTOM AMERICAN HANDGUNNER SPECIAL EDITION 1911

LES BAER CUSTOM BAER 1911 GUNSITE

LES BAER CUSTOM BAER 1911 KENAI SPECIAL

LES BAER CUSTOM BAER 1911 PREMIER II HEAVYWEIGHT MONOLITH FRAME

AMERICAN HANDGUNNER SPECIAL EDITION 1911

Action: Semiautomatic
Grips: VZ
Barrel: 5 in.
Sights: Baer tritium adjustable
Weight: N/A
Caliber: .45 ACP
Capacity: 8 rounds
Features: A tribute to readers of the iconic *American Handgunner* magazine, with the pub's title engraved on the deep blue slide; stainless-finish frame; custom stainless bushing rod; Baer's low-mount Rolo adjustable rear sight and a dovetailed front with tritium inserts; extended ejector; speed trigger set to 4 lbs.; flat serrated mainspring housing; rounded corner Tactical package
MSRP $2995.00

BAER 1911 GUNSITE

Action: Semiautomatic
Grips: Wood
Barrel: 5 in.
Sights: Dovetail tritium front, fixed rear
Weight: N/A
Caliber: .45 ACP
Capacity: 8 rounds
Features: A tribute the legendary Gunsite Academy firearms training center with wood grips bearing the Gunsite logo; serial numbers starting with GAI-; solid match trigger; dehorned; Gunsite logo engraved on slide
MSRP $2323.00

BAER 1911 KENAI SPECIAL

Action: Semiautomatic
Grips: Baer Recon
Barrel: 5 in.
Sights: Fiber optic front, low-mount Baer adjustable with hidden leaf rear
Weight: N/A
Caliber: 10mm
Capacity: 9 rounds
Features: Baer jumps into the new-generation 10mm game with all-steel construction; 4-pound speed trigger; beveled mag well; tuned action; checkered high-cut front strap; flat serrated mainspring housing
MSRP $3739.00

BAER 1911 PREMIER II HEAVYWEIGHT MONOLITH FRAME

Action: Semiautomatic
Grips: Wood
Barrel: 5 in.
Sights: Dovetail front, low-mount Baer adjustable with hidden leaf rear
Weight: N/A
Caliber: .45 ACP
Capacity: 8 rounds
Features: Unique monolith frame with a flat underside adds 2.8 oz. to normal Government frame weights for steadier holds, reduced muzzle rise, and improved accuracy; brushed chrome finish; 4-pound Speed trigger; checkered wood Baer logo grips
MSRP $2545.00

Llama (by Eagle Imports)

LLAMA MAX-1

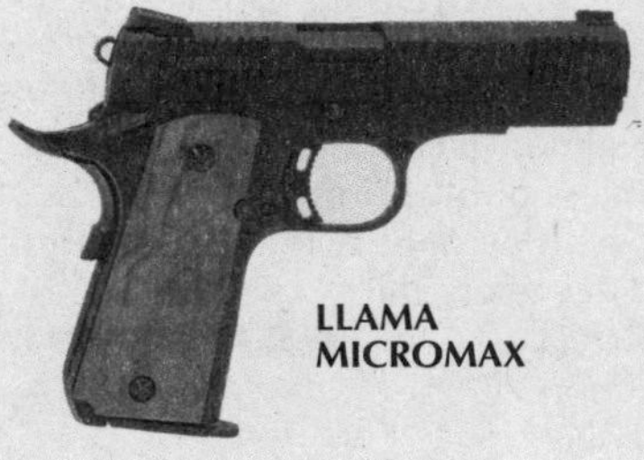
LLAMA MICROMAX

MAX-1

Action: Semiautomatic
Grips: G10
Barrel: 5.5 in.
Sights: Mil-Spec
Weight: 36.96 oz.
Caliber: .38 Super, .45 ACP
Capacity: 9 rounds
Features: 1911-type pistol; steel frame; blue or hard-chrome finishes for .38 Super; .45 ACP available only in blue
MSRP . . . . starting at $565.00

MICROMAX

Action: Semiautomatic
Grips: Polymer
Barrel: 3.75 in.
Sights: Dovetail fiber optic front, Novak-style rear
Weight: 22.9 oz.
Caliber: .380 ACP
Capacity: 7 rounds
Features: 1911-style frame; beavertail grip safety; lowered and flare ejection port; combat hammer and trigger that are both skeletonized; forged steel barrel; ambidextrous thumb safety; slide serrations
MSRP $468.00

Luxury Firearm/FK BRNO U.S.

7.5 FK FIELD PISTOL

7.5 FK FIELD PISTOL

Action: Semiautomatic
Grips: Aluminum G10
Barrel: 6 in.
Sights: Three-point butterfly
Weight: 44.8 oz.
Caliber: 7.5 FK
Capacity: 16 rounds
Features: Designed for long-distance silhouette with the proprietary 7.5 FK cartridge; proprietary recoil attenuating system; streamlined slide, frame, and grip; G10 grips; dark gray nitride finish; SA
MSRP $7500.00

LWRC International

LWRCI SMG-45

SMG-45

Action: Semiautomatic
Grips: Synthetic
Barrel: 8.5 in.
Sights: Magpul MBUS Pro
Weight: 94 oz.
Caliber: .45 ACP
Capacity: 25 rounds
Features: LWRCI dubs this a pistol-caliber "sub-gun" and it features a short recoil/delayed blowback action; LWRCI rail panels at 3, 6, and 9 o'clock; LWRCI Ultra Combat grip; anodized nitride nickel-boron metal surface treatment; chromoly steel barrel; ambidextrous lower controls; LWRCI Advanced Fire Control Group
MSRP $2995.00

Magnum Research

MAGNUM RESEARCH .429 DESERT EAGLE MARK XIX

MAGNUM RESEARCH BFR (BIGGEST FINEST REVOLVER)

MAGNUM RESEARCH DESERT EAGLE 1911

MAGNUM RESEARCH DESERT EAGLE 1911 C STAINLESS

MAGNUM RESEARCH DESERT EAGLE 1911 G STAINLESS

MAGNUM RESEARCH DESERT EAGLE 1911 U STAINLESS

.429 DESERT EAGLE MARK XIX

Action: Semiautomatic
Grips: Soft rubber
Barrel: 6 in.
Sights: Fixed combat type
Weight: 68.3 oz.
Caliber: .429 DE
Capacity: 7 rounds
Features: A new caliber from Magnum Research in a new gun featuring single-action; integral muzzle brake; Picatinny rails topside and under barrel; polygonal rifling with 1:18 twist; stainless finish
MSRP $2143.00

BFR (BIGGEST FINEST REVOLVER)

Action: SA revolver
Grips: Rubber, optional wood
Barrel: 5 in., 6.5 in., 7.5 in., 10 in.
Sights: Adjustable rear, fixed front
Weight: 57.6–85 oz.
Caliber: Long Cylinder: .30-30 Win., .444 Marlin, .45 LC/.410, .45-70 Govt., .450 Marlin, .44 Mag., .460 S&W Mag., .500 S&W Mag.; Short Cylinder: .22 Hornet, .454 Casull, .480 Ruger/.475 Linebaugh, .50AE, .500 JRH
Capacity: 5 rounds
Features: Both long and short-cylinder models are made of stainless steel; barrels are stress-relieved and cut rifled; rubber grips; Weaver style scope mount
MSRP . . . . $1219.00–$1391.00

DESERT EAGLE 1911 SERIES

Action: SA semiautomatic
Grips: Checkered wood
Barrel: 3 in., 5 in., 4.3 in.
Sights: Fixed
Weight: 36 oz. (5 in. barrel), 32 oz. (4.3 in. barrel), 25.8 oz. (3-in. barrel)
Caliber: .45 ACP
Capacity: 6, 8 rounds
Features: Seven variants comprise this series: C has 4.33-in. barrel, allover stainless or blue finish; G has 5.05-in. barrel, allover stainless or blue finish; U Stainless has a 3-in. barrel, allover stainless or blue finish; GR is in allover blue only, with 5.05-in barrel, and accessory rail
MSRP . . . . $831.00–$1019.00

Magnum Research

MAGNUM RESEARCH DESERT EAGLE BLACK TIGER STRIPE

MAGNUM RESEARCH DESERT EAGLE CASE HARDENED

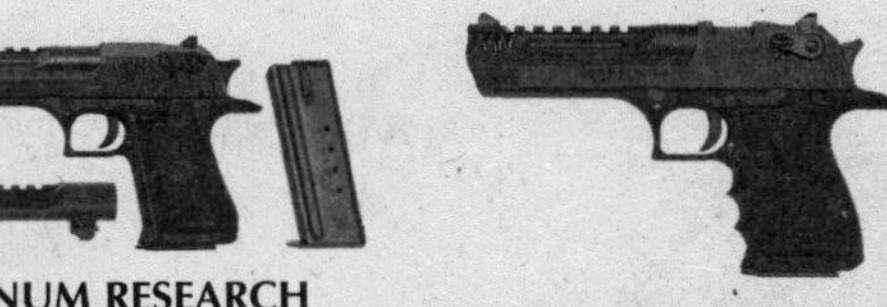
MAGNUM RESEARCH DESERT EAGLE COMBO CALIBER PACKAGE

MAGNUM RESEARCH DESERT EAGLE L5 5-INCH BARREL WITH MUZZLE BRAKE, NY-OKAY

MAGNUM RESEARCH DESERT EAGLE TUNGSTEN

MAGNUM RESEARCH DESERT EAGLE WHITE MATTE DISTRESSED

MAGNUM RESEARCH DESERT EAGLE WITH INTEGRAL MUZZLE BRAKE

DESERT EAGLE BLACK TIGER STRIPE

Action: Semiautomatic
Grips: Hard rubber
Barrel: 6 in.
Sights: Fixed combat style
Weight: 70 oz.–71 oz.
Caliber: .50 AE, .44 Mag.
Capacity: 8 rounds
Features: Desert Eagle in unique black tiger stripe finish
MSRP $1999.00

DESERT EAGLE CASE HARDENED

Action: Semiautomatic
Grips: Walnut, Hogue
Barrel: 6 in.
Sights: Fixed combat-type
Weight: 72.4 oz.
Caliber: .357 Mag., .44 Mag., .50 AE
Capacity: 7, 8, 9 rounds
Features: Gold trigger; walnut grips with the engraved Desert Eagle logo; includes a pair of Hogue grips
MSRP $2368.00

DESERT EAGLE COMBO CALIBER PACKAGE

Action: Semiautomatic
Grips: Polymer
Barrel: 6 in.
Sights: Fixed combat-type
Weight: 69.8 oz.–70.6 oz.
Caliber: .44 Mag./.50 AE
Capacity: 7, 8 rounds
Features: Comes assembled as a .44 Mag. with an 8-round magazine; .50 AE barrel with a .50 AE 7-round magazine included; both barrels have a Weaver-style rail on top
MSRP $1949.00

DESERT EAGLE L5 5-INCH BARREL WITH MUZZLE BRAKE, NY-OKAY

Action: SA semiautomatic
Grips: Plastic composite
Barrel: 5 in.
Sights: Fixed combat
Weight: 2 lb. 9 oz.
Caliber: .50 AE, .44 Mag., .357 Mag.
Capacity: 9 rounds
Features: Black aluminum frame; black slide/barrel with integral muzzle brake and full Weaver-style accessory rail
MSRP $1900.00

DESERT EAGLE TUNGSTEN

Action: SA semiautomatic
Grips: Plastic composite
Barrel: 6 in.
Sights: Fixed combat
Weight: 4 lb. 6.6 oz.
Caliber: .44 Magnum, .50 A.E.
Capacity: 8 rounds
Features: Tungsten Cerakote finish; high-quality carbon steel barrel; frame and slide with full Weaver-style accessory rail
MSRP $1782.00

DESERT EAGLE WHITE MATTE DISTRESSED

Action: Semiautomatic
Grips: Hard rubber
Barrel: 6 in.
Sights: Fixed combat style
Weight: 70 oz.–71 oz.
Caliber: .50 AE, .44 Mag.
Capacity: 8 rounds
Features: Desert Eagle in unique White Matte Distressed finish
MSRP $1999.00

DESERT EAGLE WITH INTEGRAL MUZZLE BRAKE

Action: Semiautomatic
Grips: Hard rubber
Barrel: 6 in.
Sights: Fixed combat style
Weight: 71 oz.–74 oz.
Caliber: .50 AE, .44 Mag., .357 Mag.
Capacity: 8 rounds
Features: Three-port integral muzzle brakel; Weaver-style accessory rail; black or stainless finish
MSRP . . . . $1708.00–$2143.00

Maxim Defense

MAXIM DEFENSE MDX:508

MDX:508

Action: Semiautomatic
Grips: Synthetic
Barrel: 8.5 in.
Sights: None
Weight: N/A
Caliber: 5.56 NATO, .300 BLK, 7.62x39mm
Capacity: 20 rounds
Features: A small-platform AR-type with a full-length top rail; HATEBRAKE muzzle brake; SCW stock or brace; in Arid or black; also available as an SBR
MSRP $2495.00

Maxim Defense

MAXIM DEFENSE PDX

PDX

Action: Semiautomatic
Grips: Aluminum
Barrel: 5.5 in.
Sights: None
Weight: 91 oz.
Caliber: 5.56 NATO, 7.62X29mm NATO
Capacity: N/A
Features: A CQC design featuring Maxim's all-new Heartbrake muzzle "booster"; MD's aluminum SCW stock system with 4-inch length; combo black and Arid tan color finishes; overall length just 18.75 inches
MSRP $2295.00

MG Arms

MG ARMS WRAITHE

WRAITHE

Action: Semiautomatic
Grips: Custom G10
Barrel: 4.5 in.
Sights: Night or fixed
Weight: 18 oz.–20 oz.
Caliber: .45 ACP, 9mm
Capacity: 8+1, 9+1 rounds
Features: Aluminum alloy bobtail frame; custom grip panels; high ride beavertail safety; two Wilson magazines included, available in olive drab, black or desert tan
MSRP $2895.00

Mossberg (O. F. Mossberg & Sons)

MOSSBERG MC1SC

MOSSBERG MC1SC CROSS-BOLT SAFETY

MOSSBERG MC1SC MASSACHUSETTS COMPLIANT

MOSSBERG MC1SC STAINLESS TWO-TONE

MC1SC

Action: Semiautomatic
Grips: Glass-reinforced polymer
Barrel: 3.4 in.
Sights: White three-dot
Weight: 19 oz.
Caliber: 9mm
Capacity: 6, 7 rounds
Features: Mossberg's first subcompact striker-fire pistol featuring a button-rifled barrel; front and rear slide serrations; flush-fit six-round magazine; extended seven-round magazine; trigger blade safety; DLC black or flat dark earth finishes
MSRP . . . .$435.00–$442.00

MC1SC CROSS-BOLT SAFETY

Action: Semiautomatic
Grips: Polymer
Barrel: 3.4 in.
Sights: White three-dot
Weight: 19 oz.
Caliber: 9mm
Capacity: 6, 7 rounds
Features: Same as the base MC1sc but with an additional manual crossbolt safety; in black or flat dark earth
MSRP . . . .$435.00–$442.00

MC1SC MASSACHUSETTS-COMPLIANT

Action: Semiautomatic
Grips: Glass-reinforced polymer
Barrel: 3.4 in.
Sights: White three-dot
Weight: 19 oz.
Caliber: 9mm
Capacity: 6, 7 rounds
Features: All-over matte black finish; MA-compliant with a loaded-chamber view port; stainless steel barrel with DLC (Diamond-Like Coating) finish; aggressive slide serrations; available in standard and cross-bolt safety frame options
MSRP $435.00

MC1SC STAINLESS TWO-TONE

Action: Semiautomatic
Grips: Glass-reinforced polymer
Barrel: 3.4 in.
Sights: White three-dot
Weight: 19 oz.
Caliber: 9mm
Capacity: 6, 7 rounds
Features: Features a stainless steel slide with bead-blasted finish over a matte black polymer frame; stainless steel barrel with DLC (Diamond-Like Coating) finish; aggressive slide serrations
MSRP $435.00

Mossberg (O. F. Mossberg & Sons)

MOSSBERG MC1SC TRUGLO TRITIUM PRO SIGHTS

MOSSBERG MC1SC VIRIDIAN LASER EQUIPPED

MOSSBERG MC2C

MOSSBERG MC2C STAINLESS TWO-TONE

MC1SC TRUGLO TRITIUM PRO SIGHTS

Action: Semiautomatic
Grips: Polymer
Barrel: 3.4 in.
Sights: TRUGLO Tritium sights
Weight: 19 oz.
Caliber: 9mm
Capacity: 6, 7 rounds
Features: Same as the base MC1sc but with TRUGLO tritium night sights replacing the standard white three-dot sights; in black or flat dark earth
MSRP . . . . $543.00–$550.00

MC1SC VIRIDIAN LASER EQUIPPED

Action: Semiautomatic
Grips: Polymer
Barrel: 3.4 in.
Sights:
Weight: 19 oz.
Caliber: 9mm
Capacity: 6, 7 rounds
Features: Same as the base MC1sc but with the addition of a VIRIDIAN E-Series red laser built into the trigger guard front; in black only
MSRP $531.00

MC2C

Action: Semiautomatic
Grips: Glass-reinforced polymer
Barrel: 3.9 in.
Sights: White three-dot
Weight: 21 oz.
Caliber: 9mm
Capacity: 13, 15 rounds
Features: Just two ounces more than the smaller MC1sc, but double the capacity. Features stainless steel barrel and slide; matte black finish; available with cross-bolt safety
Standard sights $505.00
TruGlog Pro sights $613.00

MC2C STAINLESS TWO-TONE

Action: Semiautomatic
Grips: Glass-reinforced polymer
Barrel: 3.9 in.
Sights: White three-dot
Weight: 21 oz.
Caliber: 9mm
Capacity: 13, 15 rounds
Features: Identical to the all-black base MC2c model, but with a matte stainless slide; available with cross-bolt safety
MSRP $505.00

Naroh Arms/Rainier Arms

NAROH ARMS N1

N1

Action: Semiautomatic
Grips: Polymer
Barrel: 3.13 in.
Sights: Low-profile blade front, low-profile drift adjustable rear
Weight: 16.1 oz.
Caliber: 9mm
Capacity: 8 rounds
Features: Despite its looks, this is a hammer-fired pistol, not a striker-fire. It has a beefy slide, slim body, and according to those R&Ding it, it fits neatly in places comparable Glocks and SIGs do not, performed admirably and maybe even exceptionally, and had nice features like wide slide serrations front and back, accessory rail, serial-numbered aluminum frame with a polymer housing
MSRP . . . . $359.00–$369.00

Nighthawk Custom

NIGHTHAWK CUSTOM AGENT2

NIGHTHAWK CUSTOM BOB MARVEL CUSTOM

AGENT2

Action: Semiautomatic
Grips: G10
Barrel: 5 in.
Sights: Fiber optic front, Heinie black ledge rear
Weight: 40.1 oz.
Caliber: 9mm, .45 ACP
Capacity: 8, 10 rounds
Features: Match-grade, crowned, flush-cut barrel; Nighthawk/Agency custom trigger; Ultra Hi-Cut front strap; one-piece magwell/mainspring housing; extended and angled magazine release; Agency slide serrations front and aft; Smoke Cerakote finish; Railscales G10 grip
MSRP $4499.00

BOB MARVEL CUSTOM

Action: Semiautomatic
Grips: Custom Mil Tac
Barrel: 4.25 in.
Sights: Novak tritium night sight front, tritium adjustable rear
Weight: 38 oz.
Caliber: 9mm, .45 ACP
Capacity: 8+1 rounds
Features: Incorporates new Nighthawk/Marvel Everlast Recoil System allowing for at least 10,000 rounds before a spring change is necessary and reduced recoil and muzzle flip
MSRP $4499.00

Nighthawk Custom

NIGHTHAWK CUSTOM BORDER SPECIAL

NIGHTHAWK CUSTOM CHAIRMAN

NIGHTHAWK CUSTOM COLT SERIES 70

NIGHTHAWK CUSTOM COMPLETE CUSTOM STIPPLE

NIGHTHAWK CUSTOM DOMINATOR

NIGHTHAWK CUSTOM ENFORCER

NIGHTHAWK CUSTOM FIREHAWK

BORDER SPECIAL

Action: Semiautomatic
Grips: Cocobolo
Barrel: 4.25 in.
Sights: Gold bead post front, Heinie Black Slant-Pro rear
Weight: 34.1 oz.
Caliber: .45 ACP
Capacity: 8 rounds
Features: Built on concealed carry cut; Commander-sized frame and slide; frame and mainspring housing dehorned for carry; match-grade barrel; ultra high-cut front strap; fluted barrel hood; Elite Midnight Cerakote finish; optional black, two-tone, or all-stainless upgrades available
MSRP $3799.00

CHAIRMAN

Action: Semiautomatic
Grips: G10
Barrel: 6 in.
Sights: Gold bead front, adjustable black rear
Weight: 40.9 oz.
Caliber: 9mm, .45 ACP
Capacity: 10 rounds
Features: Long-slide 9mm featuring Nighthawk's aluminum tri-cavity trigger; Ultra Hi-Cut front strap; match-grade crowned barrel; DLC frame/slide finish with cutouts revealing the gold titanium nitride barrel; heavy angle lightning slide cuts; Railscale G10 grips
MSRP $4199.00

COLT SERIES 70

Action: Semiautomatic
Grips: Wood
Barrel: 5 in.
Sights: Gold bead front, retro rear
Weight: 39 oz.
Caliber: .45 ACP
Capacity: 7 rounds
Features: Retro hammer; Nighthawk Custom beavertail, match barrel bushing, and mainspring housing; action and reliability enhancements; French border; dehorned frame and slide; match-grade trigger; ultra high-cut front strap
MSRP $2699.00

COMPLETE CUSTOM STIPPLE

Action: Semiautomatic
Grips: Cocobolo
Barrel: 5 in.
Sights: Nighthawk tritium front, Heinie 2-Dot Slant-Pro tritium rear
Weight: 38.8 oz.
Caliber: .45 ACP
Capacity: 8 rounds
Features: Aggressively stippled on top and rear of slide, front strap, mainspring housing, hammer top, slide stop, mag release, recoil spring plug, thumb safety, and grip safety pad; heavy French border; round butt mainspring housing; beveled frame; front and rear cocking serrations
MSRP $4299.00

DOMINATOR

Action: Semiautomatic
Grips: Cocobolo
Barrel: 5 in.
Sights: Nighthawk Custom adjustable two-dot tritium
Weight: 37.6 oz.
Caliber: 9mm, .45 ACP
Capacity: 8 rounds
Features: Half-smooth/half-checkered cocobolo grips; checkering at 25 lpi on the front strap and mainspring housing; slide serrations at 40 lpi; checkered recoil spring plug; fully dehorned; ultra-high front strap cut; two-piece magwell; black nitride slide; stainless frame and controls
MSRP $3799.00

ENFORCER

Action: Semiautomatic
Grips: G10
Barrel: 5 in.
Sights: Tritium front, Heinie Straight Eight Slant Edge rear
Weight: 38.6 oz.
Caliber: 9mm, .45 ACP
Capacity: 8 rounds
Features: A serrated slide top reduces glare, useful with the tritium Heinie Straight Eight sights; one-piece machined magwell and mainspring housing; rear slide serrations are handcut; slide stop is flush to frame
MSRP $3799.00

FIREHAWK

Action: Semiautomatic
Grips: Agent 1; G10
Barrel: 5 in.
Sights: Gold bead front, Heinie black slant pro rear
Weight: N/A
Caliber: 9mm, .45 ACP
Capacity: 8, 10 rounds
Features: Government-sized .45 featuring a French border; solid trigger; match-grade barrel; Ultra Hi-Cut front strap; compensator; rear slide serrations only; black finish with Agent 1 grips or stainless with G10 grips
MSRP $4399.00

NIGHTHAWK CUSTOM GLOBAL RESPONSE PISTOL

NIGHTHAWK CUSTOM HEINIE LADY HAWK 2.0

NIGHTHAWK CUSTOM HEINIE KESTREL

NIGHTHAWK CUSTOM/KORTH MONGOOSE .357

NIGHTHAWK CUSTOM/ KORTH SUPER SPORT .357

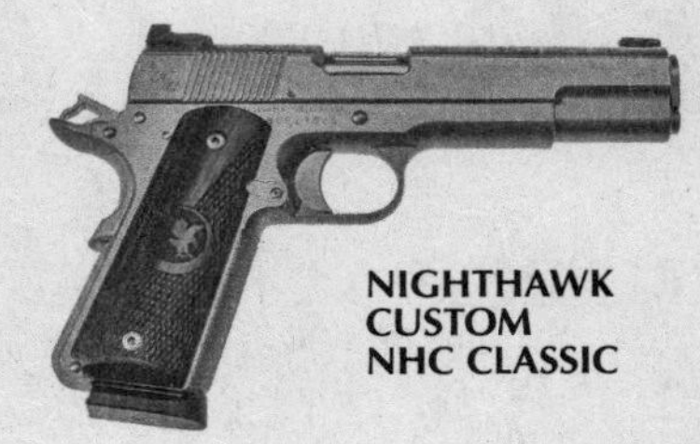

NIGHTHAWK CUSTOM NHC CLASSIC

GLOBAL RESPONSE PISTOL (GRP)

Action: SA Semiautomatic
Grips: Micarta gator grips
Barrel: 5 in.
Sights: Night
Weight: 39 oz.
Caliber: .45 ACP
Capacity: 8 rounds
Features: 1911 design; Lanyard loop integrated into the mainspring housing; forged slide stop axle is cut flush with the frame; Heinie Slant-Pro Night Sights, Novak Low Mount Night Sights, or Novak Extreme Duty Adjustable Night Sights are standard; Perma Kote finish in black, sniper gray, green, coyote tan, titanium blued, and hard chrome
MSRP $3199.00

HEINIE LADY HAWK 2.0

Action: Semiautomatic
Grips: Obsidian; abolone; zinc
Barrel: 4.25 in.
Sights: Tritium front, Heinie straight edge slant pro rear
Weight: 36 oz.
Caliber: 9mm, .45 ACP
Capacity: 8, 10 rounds
Features: Commander frame; match-grade barrel; scalloped front strap and mainspring housing; beveled frame; Nighthawk tri-cavity aluminum trigger; complete dehorning; DLC frame/slide finish with a rose gold TICN finish on barrel and controls
MSRP $4799.00

KESTREL

Action: Semiautomatic
Grips: Ultra-Thin Alumagrips
Barrel: 4.25 in.
Sights: Heinie Slant pro straight eight night sights
Weight: 34.25 oz.
Caliber: .45 ACP, 9mm
Capacity: 7-10 rounds
Features: Reduced overall frame circumference; magazine well beveled for insertion; hand serrated rear of slide; Heinie Signature scalloped front strap and mainspring housing; tactical checkered extended magazine release; standard black nitride finish with stainless controls and optional stainless steel upgrade
MSRP $3799.00

KORTH MONGOOSE .357

Action: Revolver
Grips: Hogue
Barrel: 3 in., 4 in., 5.25 in., 6 in.
Sights: Gold bead front post, adjustable rear
Weight: 37.6 oz.
Caliber: .357 Mag.
Capacity: 6 rounds
Features: Partnership with German manufacturer Korth; revolver has an AISI 4140 aluminum frame; skeletonized high-speed hammer; easy access cylinder release; optional 9mm cylinder designed for use without moon clips
MSRP $3699.00

KORTH SUPER SPORT .357

Action: Revolver
Grips: Hogue
Barrel: 6 in.
Sights: Fully adjustable front and rear
Weight: 58.24 oz.
Caliber: .357 Mag.
Capacity: 6 rounds
Features: Partnership with German manufacturer Korth; Lothar Walther cold-forged polygonal barrel; five-way adjustable DA mechanism; Roller Trigger; Picatinny rails; optional 9mm/.38 Spl. conversion cylinder available
MSRP $5199.00

NHC CLASSIC

Action: Semiautomatic
Grips: Cocobolo
Barrel: 5 in.
Sights: Gold bead front post, Heinie Black Ledge rear
Weight: 36.9 oz.
Caliber: .45 ACP
Capacity: 8 rounds
Features: Custom offering; slide top has been flattened and accented with arrow pattern and French border; curved slide stop; round butt mainspring housing; frame dehorning; ultra high-cut front strap; stainless finish with script engraving at slide rear; threaded barrel available
MSRP $3999.00

HANDGUNS

Nighthawk Custom

NIGHTHAWK CUSTOM PRESIDENT

NIGHTHAWK CUSTOM SILENT HAWK SUPPRESSOR READY

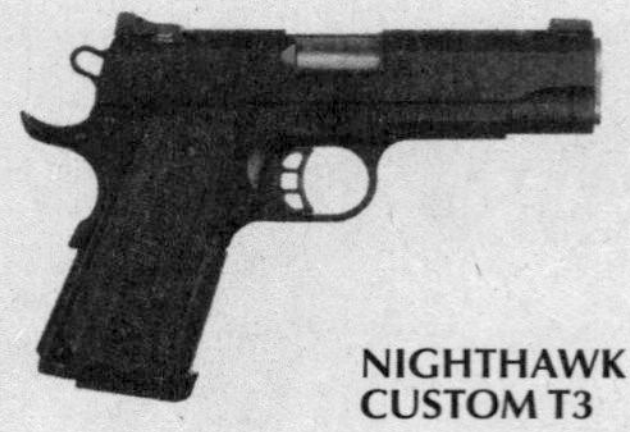
NIGHTHAWK CUSTOM T3

NIGHTHAWK CUSTOM T4

NIGHTHAWK CUSTOM THE BULL

NIGHTHAWK CUSTOM THE BULL COMMANDER

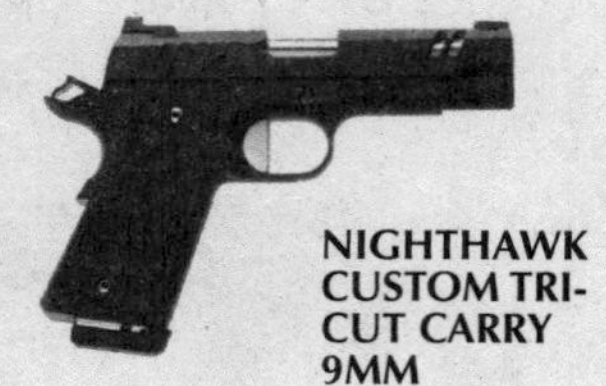
NIGHTHAWK CUSTOM TRI-CUT CARRY 9MM

PRESIDENT

Action: Semiautomatic
Grips: G10
Barrel: 5 in.
Sights: Gold bead front, Heinie black ledge rear
Weight: 38.2 oz.
Caliber: 9mm
Capacity: 10 rounds
Features: Government frame; Nighthawk tri-cavity trigger; complete dehorning; match-grade crowned barrel; DLC finish with gold titanium nitride barrel; heavy-angle lightning slide cuts; Railscale G10 grips
MSRP $4199.00

SILENT HAWK 9MM

Action: Semiautomatic
Grips: G10 grips
Barrel: 4.25 in.
Sights: Tritium tall suppressor night sights
Weight: 36.91 oz.
Caliber: 9mm
Capacity: 8 rounds
Features: Commander Recon frame and Commander slide; custom checkering on front strap of frame; one piece mainspring housing and magwell; hand serrated rear of the slide; custom slide cocking serrations to match Osprey silencer; nitride Blackout finish; G10 black and gray spiral cut grips; mag release cut-out
MSRP $4299.00

T3, T3 THIN

Action: SA semiautomatic
Grips: G10 grips
Barrel: 4.25 in.
Sights: Heinie Straight Eight Slant-Pro, night
Weight: 40 oz.
Caliber: .45 ACP, 9mm
Capacity: 7 rounds
Features: Frame based on Officer model; extended magazine well; Heinie Slant-Pro Straight Eights Night Sights are standard; mainspring housing and rear of slide are horizontally serrated to match; top of slide serrated to reduce glare; Nighthawk Custom lightweight aluminum trigger that has been blacked-out using Perma Kote; available in black, gun metal grey, green coyote tan, titanium blued, and hard chrome Perma Kote or stainless steel; T3 Thin model appears in two-tone with a blued slide and stainless frame
T3: $3599.00
T3 Stainless: $3799.00
T3 Thin: $3799.00

T4

Action: Semiautomatic
Grips: Slim
Barrel: 3.8 in.
Sights: Fixed
Weight: 34.3 oz.
Caliber: 9mm
Capacity: 9 or 10 rounds
Features: Thinned aluminum frame and mainspring housing
MSRP $3599.00

THE BULL

Action: Semiautomatic
Grips: Carbon fiber
Barrel: 5 in.
Sights: Nighthawk tritium front, Heinie Ledge Straight Eight tritium rear
Weight: 38.8 oz.
Caliber: .45 ACP
Capacity: 8 rounds
Features: Government frame with French border; bow tie plug; match-grade bull barrel; frame dehorning; Elite Smoke Cerakote finish
MSRP $3799.00

THE BULL COMMANDER

Action: Semiautomatic
Grips: Carbon fiber
Barrel: 4.25 in., 5 in.
Sights: Tritium front, Heinie Straight Eight tritium ledge rear
Weight: 36.7 oz.
Caliber: .45 ACP
Capacity: 8 rounds
Features: Choice of Government or Commander frames; Nighthawk curved slide stop; coarse rear slide serrations; beveled frame and slide bottom; Nighthawk Bow Tie plug and Bull Nose cut on the front of the slide; French border
MSRP $3799.00

TRI-CUT CARRY 9MM

Action: Semiautomatic
Grips: Aluminum
Barrel: 4.25 in.
Sights: Nighthawk tritium front, Heinie Ledge Straight Eight tritium rear
Weight: 34.7 oz.
Caliber: 9mm
Capacity: 10 rounds
Features: Commander-sized frame with custom tri-cut angled design; pneumatic stippling; slide ports; flat-faced Nighthawk Custom trigger; angled mag release
MSRP $4499.00

Nighthawk Custom

NIGHTHAWK CUSTOM TROOPER

NIGHTHAWK CUSTOM TURNBULL VIP 1

NIGHTHAWK CUSTOM VIP

NIGHTHAWK CUSTOM WAR HAWK GOVERNMENT

NIGHTHAWK CUSTOM VIP BLACK

NIGHTHAWK CUSTOM WAR HAWK CCO

TROOPER

Action: Semiautomatic
Grips: G10
Barrel: 5 in.
Sights: Tritium front, Heinie Straight Eight tritium ledge rear
Weight: 37.1 oz.
Caliber: .45 ACP
Capacity: 8 rounds
Features: Government frame; match-grade crowned barrel; Nighthawk tri-cavity trigger; complete dehorning; black nitride finish; Gator Back G10 grips
MSRP $3299.00

TURNBULL VIP 1, TURNBULL VIP 2

Action: Semiautomatic
Grips: Mastodon ivory
Barrel: 5 in.
Sights: Gold bead front, Heinie solid black Slant-Pro rear
Weight: 37.4 oz.
Caliber: .45 ACP
Capacity: 8 rounds
Features: Very Impressive Pistol is a collaboration between Nighthawk Custom and Doug Turnbull; mastodon ivory grips; custom display case; all-over charcoal blue finish; VIP II has case-hardened frame
VIP I: $7999.00
VIP II: $7499.00

VIP

Action: Semiautomatic
Grips: Giraffe bone
Barrel: 5 in.
Sights: Heinie black rear, 14k gold bead front
Weight: 39.78 oz.
Caliber: .45 ACP
Capacity: 8 rounds
Features: Custom vertical front strap and mainspring serrations; 14k plated gold bead front sight and crowned barrel; deep hand engraving featured throughout; antiqued nickel finish; custom cocobolo hardwood presentation case
MSRP $7999.00

VIP BLACK

Action: Semiautomatic
Grips: Girrafe bone
Barrel: 5 in.
Sights: Gold bead front, Heinie black slant pro rear
Weight: N/A
Caliber: .45 ACP
Capacity: 8 rounds
Features: Government frame; 14k solid gold front bead sight; giraffe bone grips; hand serrations at rear of slide and at ejection port match the Heinie sight; hand engraving; comes in custom walnut case
MSRP $7999.00

WAR HAWK CCO

Action: Semitautomatic
Grips: Synthetic
Barrel: 4.25 in.
Sights: Fixed
Weight: 34.7 oz.
Caliber: 9mm, .45 ACP
Capacity: N/A
Features: Unique tri-cut slide with bold angles; serrated arrow style slide top; heavy bevel on bottom of slide; hand serrated rear of slide; barrel is crowned and beveled with the bushing; one-piece fully machined 20 LPI checkered mainspring housing/magwell; high-cut front strap; hightweight solid aluminum match grade trigger; thin G10 in hyena brown; Heinie Slant Pro Straight Eight Tritium night sights; Nighthawk Custom/Marvel EVERLAST recoil system; War Hawk logo engraved on slide; stainless steel frame standard; black nitride finish
MSRP $3999.00

WAR HAWK GOVERNMENT

Action: Semitautomatic
Grips: Synthetic
Barrel: 5 in.
Sights: Fixed
Weight: 39.6 oz.
Caliber: 9mm, .45 ACP
Capacity: N/A
Features: Unique multi-faceted slide; serrated arrow style slide top; heavy bevel on bottom of slide; hand serrated rear of slide; barrel is crowned and beveled with the bushing; lightweight aluminum medium solid match trigger; aggressive G10 hyena brown grips; red fiber optic front sights; Tritium dot front sight upgrade available; Jardine Hook rear sight; tactical magazine catch; Nighthawk Custom/Marvel EVERLAST recoil system; War Hawk logo engraved on slide
MSRP $3999.00

North American Arms

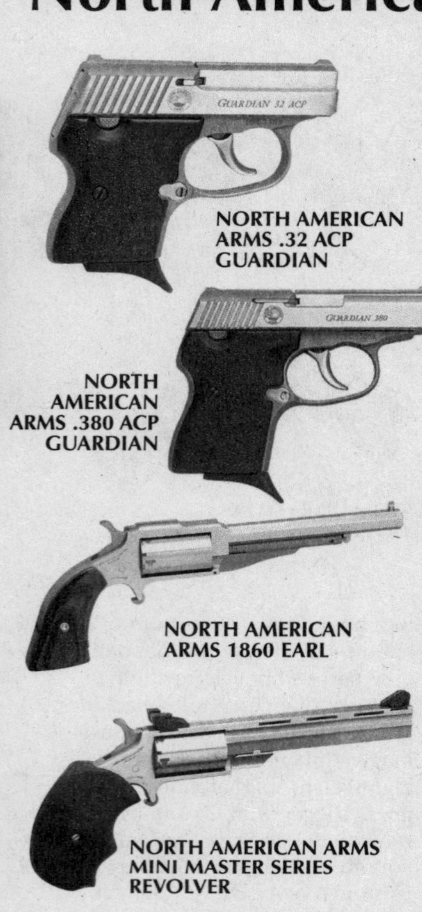

NORTH AMERICAN ARMS .32 ACP GUARDIAN

NORTH AMERICAN ARMS .380 ACP GUARDIAN

NORTH AMERICAN ARMS 1860 EARL

NORTH AMERICAN ARMS MINI MASTER SERIES REVOLVER

NORTH AMERICAN ARMS BLACK WIDOW

NORTH AMERICAN ARMS MINI-REVOLVER

NORTH AMERICAN ARMS RANGER II

.32 ACP/.25 NAA GUARDIAN

Action: DAO semiautomatic
Grips: Polymer
Barrel: 2.5 in.
Sights: Fixed, open
Weight: 13.5 oz.
Caliber: .32 ACP, .25 NAA
Capacity: 6+1 rounds
Features: Stainless steel; double action only; optional Integral Locking System (ILS)
Standard (either caliber):. . .$409.00
ILS (.32 ACP only): $437.00

.380 ACP/.32 NAA GUARDIAN

Action: DAO semiautomatic
Grips: Composite
Barrel: 2.49 in.
Sights: Fixed, open
Weight: 18.72 oz.
Caliber: .380 ACP, .32 NAA
Capacity: 6+1 rounds
Features: Stainless steel; double action only; optional Integral Locking System (ILS)
Standard (either caliber): $456.00
ILS (.380 ACP only): $486.00

1860 EARL

Action: SA revolver
Grips: Rosewood
Barrel: 3 in., 4 in.
Sights: Stainless steel post front sight
Weight: 9.7 oz.
Caliber: .22 Mag.
Capacity: 5 rounds
Features: Replica of 1860s Hogleg, with faux loading lever and pin, octagonal barrel, rosewood grips; available with .22 LR conversion cylinder
MSRP $298.00
With conversion cylinder: . .$332.00

BLACK WIDOW

Action: Revolver
Grips: Rubber
Barrel: 2 in.
Sights: Marble Arms fixed or adjustable
Weight: 8.9 oz.
Caliber: .22 Win. Mag.
Capacity: 5 rounds
Features: A short-barreled .22 Win. Mag. with oversized grips to hang onto; SA only; non-fluted cylinder; vent rib; stainless available with fixed or adjustable sights; PVD black and stainless versions available with .22 LR conversion cylinders
Stainless: . . . . $288.00–$312.00
PVD Black: $318.00
PVD Black w/conversion cylinder: $353.00
Stainless w/conversion cylinder: $323.00

MINI MASTER SERIES REVOLVER

Action: SA revolver
Grips: Rubber
Barrel: 4 in.
Sights: Fixed or adjustable
Weight: 10.7 oz.
Caliber: .22 LR, .22 Mag.
Capacity: 5 rounds
Features: Conversion cylinder or adjustable sights available
Fixed sights: $298.00
W/ conversion cylinder: . . . $332.00
W/ adjustable sights: $328.00
W/ conversion and adjustable sights: $363.00

MINI-REVOLVER

Action: SA revolver
Grips: Laminated rosewood
Barrel: 1.2 in., 1.625 in.
Sights: Fixed, open
Weight: 4 oz.–6.2 oz.
Caliber: .22 Short, .22 LR, .22 Mag.
Capacity: 5 rounds
Features: Features NAA's safety cylinder so mini-revolver can be carried fully loaded; .22 LR available with folding "holster grip." .22 Mag available ported or with folding "holster grip"
.22 Short: $226.00
.22 LR: . . . . $226.00–$256.00
.22 Mag: . . . . $236.00–$301.00

RANGER II

Action: Revolver
Grips: Rosewood
Barrel: 1.63 in.
Sights: Bead front
Weight: 6.9 oz.
Caliber: .22 Win. Mag.
Capacity: 5 rounds
Features: Tiny break-top revolver has rosewood boot grip; star ejector; fully ribbed barrel; bead-blast stainless finish on barrel and frame, polished finish on cylinder
MSRP $519.00
With conversion cylinder: $639.00

North American Arms

NORTH AMERICAN ARMS SIDEWINDER

NORTH AMERICAN ARMS THE PUG

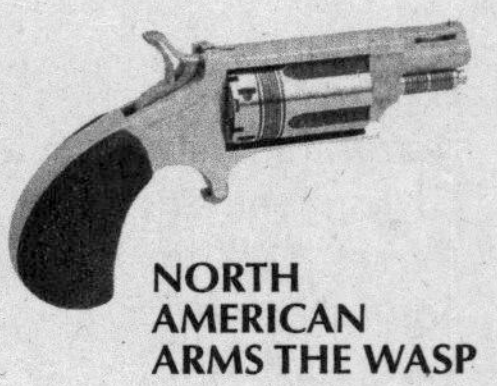
NORTH AMERICAN ARMS THE WASP

SIDEWINDER

Action: Revolver
Grips: Laminated rosewood
Barrel: 1 in., 2.5 in., 4. in.
Sights: Stainless steel post
Weight: 6.7 oz.
Caliber: .22 Mag.
Capacity: 5 rounds
Features: Features NAA's safety cylinder; stainless steel frame; available .22 LR conversion
MSRP . . . . $350.00–$508.00

THE PUG

Action: Revolver
Grips: Rubber
Barrel: 1 in.
Sights: Tritium and white dot
Weight: 6.4 oz.
Caliber: .22 Mag.
Capacity: 5 rounds
Features: Oversized pebble-textured rubber grips enable the handler to keep a firm grip
White dot sights: $328.00
White dot with conversion cylinder: $360.00
XS tritium sights: $347.00
XS tritium with conversion cylinder: $380.00

THE WASP

Action: SA revolver
Grips: Rubber pebble finish
Barrel: 1.125 in., 1.625 in.
Sights: Stainless post
Weight: 5.9 oz.–7.2 oz.
Caliber: .22 Mag.
Capacity: 5 rounds
Features: Stainless steel frame; vent rib barrel; skeleton hammer; .22 LR conversion cylinders available; brushed sides, matte contours, black inlay
MSRP . . . . $266.00–$301.00

Nosler, Inc.

NOSLER M48 NCH

M48 NCH

Action: Bolt
Grips: Synthetic
Barrel: 15 in.
Sights: None
Weight: N/A
Caliber: .22 Nosler, .24 Nosler, 6mm Creedmoor, 6.5 Creedmoor, 7mm-08 Rem., .308 Win.
Capacity: 1 round
Features: The bolt handgun comes back to life with a one-piece billet aluminum frame; Nosler's Model 58 short-action; Cerakoted metalwork; bedded action; free-floating barrel
MSRP $2495.00

Patriot Ordnance Factory, Inc.

PATRIOT ORDNANCE FACTORY MINUTEMAN

PATRIOT ORDNANCE FACTORY RENEGADE PLUS

MINUTEMAN

Action: Semiautomatic
Grips: Synthetic
Barrel: 9 in.
Sights: None
Weight: 88 oz.
Caliber: 5.56 NATO, .350 Legend
Capacity: N/A
Features: A direct impingement pistol with a straight, drop-in match-grade trigger; ambidextrous rear QD sling swivel plate; carbine-length gas system; POF three-prong flash-hider; Renegade rail; ambidextrous Strike Eagle charging handle; nitride heat-treated barrel; anti-tilt buffer tube
MSRP . . . . $1531.00–$1661.00

RENEGADE PLUS

Action: Semiautomatic
Grips: Synthetic
Barrel: 10.5 in.
Sights: None
Weight: 5 lb. 13 oz.
Caliber: 5.56 NATO, .300 Blackout
Capacity: 20, 30 rounds
Features: Identical to the company's now discontinued rifle configuration, but in pistol form featuring a nine-inch rail; five-position SB Tactical SBA3 arm brace; M-LOK compatibility; Dictator nine-position gas block; straight gas tube; in black or Burnt Bronze; Ultimate Bolt Carrier Group; match-grade trigger; ambidextrous receiver
MSRP . . . . $1887.00–$2017.00

Patriot Ordnance Factory, Inc.

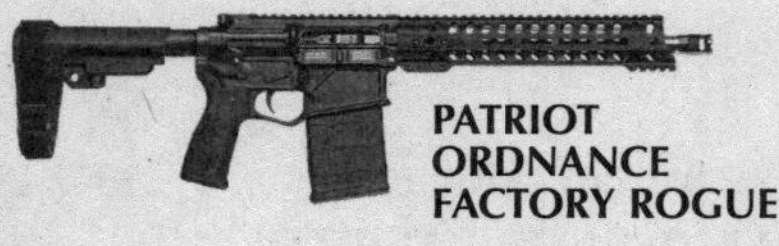
PATRIOT ORDNANCE FACTORY ROGUE

ROGUE

Action: Semiautomatic
Grips: Synthetic
Barrel: 12.5 in.
Sights: None
Weight: 89.6 oz.
Caliber: .308 Win.
Capacity: N/A
Features: A direct impingement pistol featuring an anti-tilt buffer tube; 11-in. Renegade forearm; key-lock DI bolt carrier group; multiple QD sling attachment points; Micro B muzzle brake
MSRP . . . .$1828.00–$1958.00

Rock River Arms

ROCK RIVER ARMS 1911 POLY

ROCK RIVER ARMS BT-9 WITH SBA3 ARM BRACE

ROCK RIVER ARMS LAR-9 7-INCH PISTOL WITH SBA3 ARM BRACE

ROCK RIVER ARMS LAR-15LH LEF-T

ROCK RIVER ARMS LAR-15 RRAGE 7-INCH PISTOL

1911 POLY

Action: SA semiautomatic
Grips: Polymer
Barrel: 5 in.
Sights: Dovetail front and rear
Weight: 32.6 oz.
Caliber: .45 ACP
Capacity: 7 rounds
Features: Chromoly barrel; polymer frame and mainspring housing; steel frame insert; steel slide; parkerized finish on metal; RRA overmolded grips; aluminum speed trigger; beavertail grip safety; RRA dovetail front and rear sights
MSRP $1025.00

BT-9 WITH SBA3 ARM BRACE

Action: Semiautomatic
Grips: Synthetic
Barrel: 4 in.
Sights: None
Weight: 82 oz., 86 oz.
Caliber: 9mm
Capacity: 10, 15, 17 rounds
Features: A Glock magazine-compatible pistol with extruded aluminum A4 upper; BT-9 billet aluminum lower; flared mag well; winter trigger guard; Rock River two-stage trigger; Smith Vortex flash suppressor, threaded ½x36; Rock River free-floating, aluminum, M-LOK compatible handguard; chrome-lined chromoly barrel
MSRP $1420.00

LAR-9 7-INCH PISTOL WITH SBA3 ARM BRACE

Action: Semiautomatic
Grips: Synthetic
Barrel: 7 in.
Sights: None
Weight: 5 lb. 6 oz.
Caliber: 9mm
Capacity: N/A
Features: Tons of 9mm fun in a rifle featuring an extruded aluminum upper; billet aluminum lower with integral winter trigger guard; flared mag well takes Glock magazines; SBA3 five-position arm brace; two-stage trigger; A2 flash hider with ½X28 threads
MSRP $1025.00

LAR-15LH LEF-T

Action: Semiautomatic
Grips: Synthetic
Barrel: 10.5 in.
Sights: None
Weight: 101 oz.
Caliber: 5.56 NATO
Capacity: 10 rounds
Features: This rifle-round pistol features a threaded A2 flash hider; SB Tactical SBA3 adjustable stabilizing arm brace; Hogue rubber grip; left-side operation/ejection; ambidextrous mag release; left-hand charging handle; forged upper/lower; low-profile gas block
MSRP $1075.00

LAR-15 RRAGE 7-INCH PISTOL

Action: Semiautomatic
Grips: Synthetic
Barrel: 7 in.
Sights: None
Weight: 4 lb. 13 oz.
Caliber: 5.56mm NATO/.223 Rem.
Capacity: 20 rounds
Features: Featuring a low-profile gas block; A2 pistol grip; A2 flash hider; single-stage trigger; free-floating aluminum M-LOK-compatible handguard; SBX-K stabilizing arm brace; long A2 flash hider
MSRP $940.00

Rock River Arms

ROCK RIVER ARMS LAR-22 7-INCH PISTOL

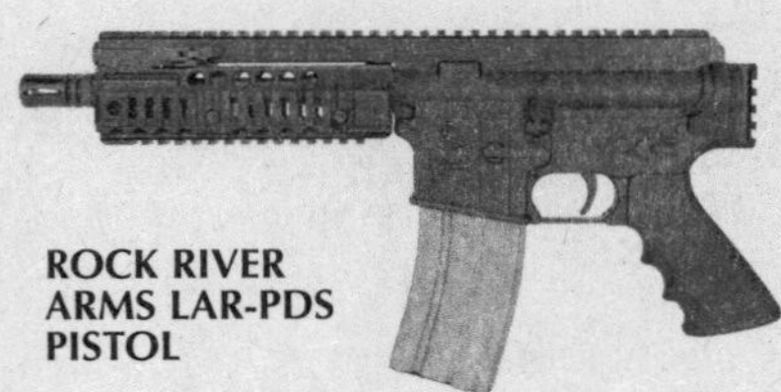

ROCK RIVER ARMS LAR-PDS PISTOL

LAR-22 7-INCH PISTOL

Action: Semiautomatic
Grips: Synthetic; poly
Barrel: 7 in.
Sights: None
Weight: 3 lb. 13 oz.
Caliber: .22 LR
Capacity: N/A
Features: Super-fun rimfire featuring an A2 flash hider with ½X28 threads; two-stage trigger; chrome-moly barrel; SBA3 arm brace; six-inch free-floating M-LOK handguard; choice of poly or forged aluminum receiver
Poly: $605.00
Aluminum: $695.00

LAR-PDS PISTOL

Action: Gas-operated semiautomatic
Grips: Hogue rubber
Barrel: 8 in. chromoly
Sights: Picatinny rail
Weight: 80 oz.
Caliber: 5.56 NATO
Capacity: 30 rounds
Features: Forged lower; Hogue rubber grip; A2 flash hider; two-position regulator; not compatible with suppressors; one version has injection-molded ribbed handguard, second version has an aluminum tri-rail handguard
Ribbed handguard: $1260.00
Tri-rail handguard: $1315.00

Ruger (Sturm, Ruger & Co.)

RUGER 22 CHARGER TAKEDOWN

RUGER 22 CHARGER LITE

RUGER 22/45 LITE

RUGER AMERICAN PISTOL

RUGER AR-556 PISTOL FLAG SERIES

22 CHARGER

Action: Semiautomatic
Grips: Synthetic
Barrel: 10 in.
Sights: None
Weight: 52 oz.
Caliber: .22 LR
Capacity: 15 rounds
Features: Cold hammer-forged barrel; threaded barrel; Picatinny rail; A2-style grip; adjustable bipod
Standard: $309.00
Takedown: $419.00

22 CHARGER LITE

Action: Semiautomatic
Grips: Polymer
Barrel: 10 in.
Sights: None
Weight: 57 oz.
Caliber: .22 LR
Capacity: 15 rounds
Features: This handy "tactical" pistol has a new Picatinny brace mount attachment point; A2-style grip; aluminum alloy barrel sleeve; threaded barrel with thread cap and compatible with Silent-SR suppressor
MSRP $599.00

22/45 LITE

Action: Semiautomatic
Grips: Synthetic
Barrel: 4.4 in.
Sights: Adjustable
Weight: 22.7 oz.
Caliber: .22 LR
Capacity: 6 rounds
Features: Zytel polymer grip frame; threaded barrel; ccontoured ejection port; loaded chamber indicator; available in black or bronze anodized finishes
MSRP $559.00

AMERICAN PISTOL

Action: Semiautomatic
Grips: Ergonomic wrap-around
Barrel: 4.2 in., 4.5 in.
Sights: Three dot
Weight: 30 oz.–31.5 oz.
Caliber: 9mm Luger, .45 ACP
Capacity: 10 or 17 rounds
Features: Trigger features a short takeup with positive reset; recoil-reducing barrel cam; low-mass slide; Novak LoMount Carry three-dot sights; modular wrap-around grip system for adjusting palm swell and trigger reach; ambidextrous slide stop and magazine release; safety features include internal, automatic sear block system, integrated trigger safety and no trigger pull required for takedown
MSRP $579.00

AR-556 PISTOL FLAG SERIES

Action: Semiautomatic
Grips: Polymer
Barrel: 10.5 in.
Sights: None
Weight: 99.2 oz.
Caliber: 5.56 NATO
Capacity: 30 rounds
Features: Ultra maneuverable and sharp-looking to boot, this handy rifle-cartridge pistol features an SB Tactical SBA3 stabilizing brace; free-floating handguard with Magpul M-LOK attachment slots at 3, 6, and 9 o'clock; carbine-length gas system; 1:8 twist rate to stabilize bullets from 35 to 77 grains; Ruger flash suppressor; staked gas key; American flag graphics
MSRP $949.00

Ruger (Sturm, Ruger & Co.)

RUGER BEARCAT

RUGER CUSTOM SHOP SR1911 COMPETITION

RUGER CUSTOM SHOP SUPER GP100 COMPETITION

RUGER EC9S

RUGER GP100

RUGER GP100 .22 LR

RUGER GP100 7-ROUND .357 MAG.

RUGER GP100 MATCH CHAMPION

BEARCAT

Action: SA revolver
Grips: Hardwood
Barrel: 4.2 in.
Sights: Blade front, integral notch
Weight: 24 oz.
Caliber: .22 LR
Capacity: 6 rounds
Features: Alloy steel with blued finish or stainless steel frame with satin stainless finish; decorative cylinder; transfer bar mechanism; features one piece frame
Alloy Steel: $639.00
SS: $689.00

CUSTOM SHOP SR1911 COMPETITION

Action: Semiautomatic
Grips: G10
Barrel: 5 in.
Sights: Fiber optic front, adjustable target rear
Weight: 40 oz.
Caliber: .45 ACP, 9mm
Capacity: 8 rounds
Features: Textured G10 grips; low-profile hammer; match trigger with flat-faced shoe; Cylinder & Slide disconnector and tuned sear spring; undercut trigger guard; ambidextrous slide stop and mag release; competition barrel with fitted lug, fitted bushing, and target crown; black-nitrided stainless steel frame paired with a stainless finish slide having black nitride-filled serrations
.45 ACP $2299.00
9mm. $2499.00

CUSTOM SHOP SUPER GP100 COMPETITION

Action: Revolver
Grips: Hogue hardwood
Barrel: 5.5 in.
Sights: Fiber optic front, adjustable rear
Weight: 47 oz.
Caliber: .357 Mag.
Capacity: 8 rounds
Features: Triple-locking cylinder with PVD finish; hand-finished hardwood grips by Hogue; Super Redhawk action; centering boss on trigger; centering shims on hammer; cylinder and extractor cut for moon clip use
MSRP $1549.00

EC9S

Action: Semiautomatic
Grips: Glass-filled nylon
Barrel: 3.12 in.
Sights: Integral
Weight: 17.2 oz.
Caliber: 9mm
Capacity: 7 rounds
Features: Striker-fired lightweight has checkered grip; alloy steel barrel; pinky floorplate that can be added to magazine; polymer IWB holster included
MSRP . . . . $299.00–$329.00

GP100

Action: DA revolver
Grips: Black hogue monogrip
Barrel: 3 in., 4.2 in., 6 in.
Sights: Ramp front, fixed or adjustable rear
Weight: 36 oz.–45 oz.
Caliber: .327 Fed Mag., .357 Mag., .44 Spl.
Capacity: 5, 6, 7 rounds
Features: Satin stainless or blued finish; stainless steel or alloy steel frame; cushioned rubber grip; transfer bar; triple-locking cylinder
MSRP . . . . $769.00–$829.00

GP100 .22 LR

Action: DA revolver
Grips: Cushioned rubber with wood insert
Barrel: 5.5 in.
Sights: Fiber optic front, adjustable rear
Weight: 42 oz
Caliber: .22 LR
Capacity: 10 rounds
Features: Triple-locking cylinder locked into the frame at the front, rear, and bottom; patented grip frame design easily accommodates a wide variety of custom grips; takedown of integrated subassemblies requires no special tools and allows for easy maintenance and assembly; patented transfer bar mechanism provides an unparalleled measure of security against accidental discharge
MSRP $829.00

GP100 7-ROUND .357 MAG.

Action: DA/SA
Grips: Rubber with hardwood inserts
Barrel: 2.5 in., 4.2 in., 6 in.
Sights: Fiber optic front, adjustable rear
Weight: 36 oz., 40 oz., 43.5 oz.
Caliber: .357 Mag.
Capacity: 7 rounds
Features: Cylinder locks into the frame at the front, rear and bottom, improving alignment and reliability; adjustable sights at the rear with a fiber optic front; three barrel lengths
MSRP $899.00

GP100 MATCH CHAMPION

Action: DA revolver
Grips: Wood
Barrel: 4.2 in.
Sights: Fixed or adjustable
Weight: 38 oz.
Caliber: .357 Mag., 10mm
Capacity: 6 rounds
Features: Hogue stippled hardwood; fiber optic front site; triple-locking cylinder; easy takedown; features a slab-sided, half-lug barrel
MSRP $969.00

Ruger (Sturm, Ruger & Co.)

RUGER LC380

RUGER LCP

RUGER LCP II

RUGER LCP II EXTENDED MAGAZINE

RUGER LCRX

RUGER LCRX 3-INCH .357 MAG.

RUGER LITE RACK LCP II

LC380

Action: Semiautomatic
Grips: Black, glass-filled nylon
Barrel: 3.12 in.
Sights: Adjustable 3-dot
Weight: 17.2 oz.
Caliber: .380 ACP
Capacity: 7+1 rounds
Features: Hardened alloy steel slide; checkered grip frame; finger grip extension floorplate; three safeties and loaded chamber indicator; blued finish; California-approved version available
MSRP $539.00

LCP

Action: Semiautomatic
Grips: Glass-filled nylon
Barrel: 2.75 in.
Sights: Integral, Viridian E-Series red laser
Weight: 9.9 oz.
Caliber: .380 ACP
Capacity: 6+1 rounds
Features: Alloy steel barrel and slide; blued finish; fixed/LaserMax CenterFire sights; black, glass-filled nylon grips; standard model is all black and is available with a built-in laser; Moon Shine camo frames in Harvest moon or Toxic patterns
Standard: . . . . $259.00–$299.00
With laser: $349.00

LCP II

Action: Semiautomatic
Grips: Glass-filled nylon
Barrel: 2.75 in.
Sights: Fixed front and rear
Weight: 10.6 oz.
Caliber: .380 ACP
Capacity: 6 rounds
Features: Updated from the original; improved sights and trigger; last round hold open; larger grip surface
Standard: $349.00
With laser: $439.00

LCP II EXTENDED MAGAZINE

Action: Semiautomatic
Grips: Glass-filled nylon
Barrel: 2.75 in.
Sights: Integral
Weight: 11 oz.
Caliber: .380 ACP
Capacity: 8 rounds
Features: This handy little CCW .380 keeps you in the game with a seven-round extended magazine that also offers a little extra grip purchase. Comes with a pocket holster. Note: Ruger states that 7-round LCP magazines are not compatible with this LCP II firearm.
MSRP $399.00

LCR

Action: DA/SA
Grips: Rubber
Barrel: 1.87 in.
Sights: Adjustable
Weight: 13.5 oz.–17.2 oz.
Caliber: .38 Spl. +P, 22 LR, 22 WMR, .327 Fed. Mag., .357 Mag., 9mm Luger
Capacity: 5–8 rounds
Features: Hogue Tamer monogrip; adjustable black blade rear sight; Ionbond Diamondblack cylinder finish
MSRP . . . . $579.00–$669.00

LCRX

Action: DA/SA revolver
Grips: Rubber
Barrel: 1.87 in.–3 in.
Sights: Fixed
Weight: 13.5 oz.
Caliber: .22 LR, .22 WMR, .38 Spec. +P, .327 Fed. Mag., .357 Mag., 9mm
Capacity: 5 rounds
Features: High-strength stainless steel cylinder features an Ionbond Diamondblack finish; Grip Peg allows a variety of grip styles to be installed; external hammer that allows for single-action mode; also available with Crimson Trace lasergrips
MSRP . . . . $579.00–$669.00

LCRX 3-INCH .357 MAG.

Action: Revolver
Grips: Hogue Tamer Monogrip
Barrel: 3 in..
Sights: Pinned front ramp, adjustable blade rear
Weight: 21.3 oz.
Caliber: .357 Mag.
Capacity: 5 rounds
Features: A little extra barrel and the longer Hogue Tamer grip make handling the .357 Mag. in a carry gun more manageable
MSRP $669.00

LITE RACK LCP II

Action: Semiautomatic
Grips: Glass-filled nylon
Barrel: 2.75 in.
Sights: Integral
Weight: 11.2 oz.
Caliber: .22 LR
Capacity: 10 rounds
Features: A featherweight rimfire with an all-new floorplate assembly that permits ten rounds in the mag while still minimizing the pistol's profile; lightened recoil spring; last shot hold-open; manual push-forward-off safety
MSRP $369.00

Ruger (Sturm, Ruger & Co.)

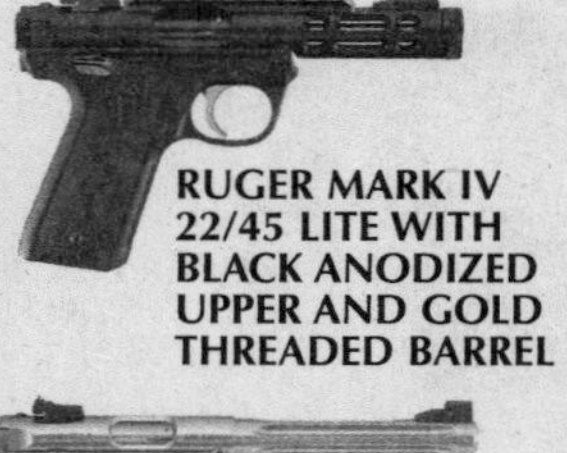
RUGER MARK IV 22/45 LITE WITH BLACK ANODIZED UPPER AND GOLD THREADED BARREL

RUGER MARK IV 22/45 LITE WITH DIAMOND GRAY ANODIZED FINISH, TARGET LAMINATE GRIPS

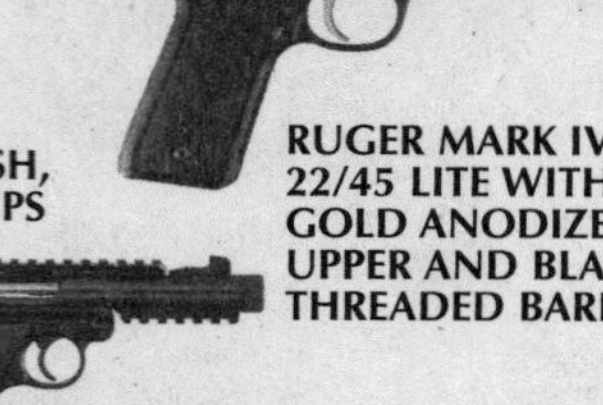
RUGER MARK IV 22/45 LITE WITH GOLD ANODIZED UPPER AND BLACK THREADED BARREL

RUGER MARK IV TARGET

RUGER MARK IV HUNTER

RUGER MARK IV STANDARD

RUGER MARK IV TACTICAL

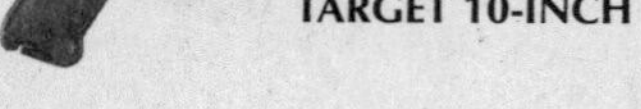
RUGER MARK IV TARGET 10-INCH

MARK IV 22/45 LITE WITH BLACK ANODIZED UPPER AND GOLD THREADED BARREL

Action: Semiautomatic
Grips: Checkered 1911-style
Barrel: 4.4 in.
Sights: Adjustable rear, fixed front
Weight: 25 oz.
Caliber: .22 LR
Capacity: 10 rounds
Features: A sleek black finish is complemented by the sight here and there of the gold-finished barrel threaded for suppressor; Picatinny topside rail is standard
MSRP $559.00

MARK IV 22/45 LITE WITH DIAMOND GRAY ANODIZED FINISH, TARGET LAMINATE GRIPS

Action: Semiautomatic
Grips: Laminate
Barrel: 4.4 in.
Sights: Adjustable rear, fixed front
Weight: 27 oz.
Caliber: .22 LR
Capacity: 10 rounds
Features: Updated take on a favorite target pistol with features that include: one-button takedown; polymer frame; laminate grips with target finger grooves; aluminum receiver; ambidextrous safety; drop-free magazine; magazine disconnect; Diamond Gray anodized finish
MSRP $599.00

MARK IV 22/45 LITE WITH GOLD ANODIZED UPPER AND BLACK THREADED BARREL

Action: Semiautomatic
Grips: Checkered 1911-style
Barrel: 4.4 in.
Sights: Adjustable rear, fixed front
Weight: 25 oz.
Caliber: .22 LR
Capacity: 10 rounds
Features: A flashy and fun target pistol with a Gold anodized aluminum receiver; polymer frame with black, checkered 1911-style grips; threaded barrel
MSRP $559.00

MARK IV HUNTER

Action: SA semiautomatic
Grips: Checkered laminate
Barrel 6.88 in.
Sights: Fiber optic front sight, adjustable rear
Weight: 44 oz.
Caliber: .22 LR
Capacity: 10 rounds
Features: Stainless steel frame with satin finish; fluted bull barrel; one-button takedown; drop-free magazine
MSRP . . . . $769.00–$799.00

MARK IV STANDARD

Action: Semiautomatic
Grips: Synthetic
Barrel: 4.75 in., 6 in.
Sights: Fixed blade front, fixed notch rear
Weight: 28.2–30.1 oz.
Caliber: .22 LR
Capacity: 10 rounds
Features: Tapered barrel; naturally pointing grip angle; ambidextrous safety; bolt stop; drop-free magazines; magazine disconnect; one-button takedown
MSRP $449.00

MARK IV TACTICAL

Action: Semiautomatic
Grips: Synthetic
Barrel: 4.4 in.
Sights: Fixed blade front, adjustable rear
Weight: 34.6 oz.
Caliber: .22 LR
Capacity: 10 rounds
Features: Threaded barrel; Picatinny rails both top and bottom; drop-free magazines; magazine disconnect
MSRP $569.00

MARK IV TARGET

Action: Semiautomatic
Grips: Laminate, synthetic
Barrel: 5.5 in.
Sights: Fixed front, adjustable rear
Weight: 35.6 oz.–42.8 oz.
Caliber: .22 LR
Capacity: 10 rounds
Features: Latest version of Ruger's esteemed .22-caliber SA handguns; one-piece CNC-machined frame; ambidextrous manual safety; drop-free mag design; magazine disconnect; one-button takedown; two magazines; blued or stainless steel options
Blued: . . . . $529.00–$569.00
Stainless steel: $689.00

MARK IV TARGET 10-INCH

Action: Semiautomatic
Grips: Synthetic
Barrel: 10 in.
Sights: Fixed front, adjustable rear
Weight: 46.3 oz.
Caliber: .22 LR
Capacity: 10 rounds
Features: A looooong-barreled one for the bull's-eye circuit with a cold hammer forged barrel; contoured ejection port; one-button takedown; in all-blue or all-stainless finish
Blue: $645.00
Stainless: $719.00

Ruger (Sturm, Ruger & Co.)

RUGER MARK IV TARGET WITH THREADED BULL BARREL

RUGER NEW MODEL SUPER BLACKHAWK

RUGER REDHAWK WITH SLEEVE AND SHROUD BARREL

RUGER RUGER-57

RUGER SECURITY-9 COMPACT WITH VIRIDIAN E-SERIES RED LASER

RUGER SECURITY-9

RUGER SECURITY-9 COMPACT PRO

RUGER SECURITY-9 COMPACT WITH HOGUE GRIP SLEEVE

RUGER SECURITY-9 PRO

MARK IV TARGET WITH THREADED BULL BARREL

Action: Semiautomatic
Grips: Synthetic
Barrel: 5.5 in.
Sights: Fixed front, adjustable rear
Weight: 42.8 oz.
Caliber: .22 LR
Capacity: 10 rounds
Features: Threaded bull barrel; includes two drop-free magazines
MSRP $699.00

NEW MODEL SUPER BLACKHAWK

Action: SA revolver
Grips: Hardwood, laminate
Barrel: 4.62 in., 5.5 in., 7.5 in., 10.5 in.
Sights: Ramp front, adjustable rear
Weight: 45–55 oz.
Caliber: .44 Rem. Mag.
Capacity: 6 rounds
Features: Alloy steel or stainless steel frame; blued or satin stainless finish; transfer bar mechanism; western-style grip; Bisley Hunter variation has 7.5-in. barrel, black laminate grips
Standard: . . . . $829.00–$859.00
Hunter: $959.00
Bisley Hunter: $959.00

REDHAWK WITH SLEEVE AND SHROUD BARREL

Action: DA/SA
Grips: Hardwood
Barrel: 4.2 in., 5.5 in.
Sights: Color insert front blade, white outline adjustable rear
Weight: 44 oz., 49 oz.
Caliber: .357 Mag., .45 ACP, .44 Mag.
Capacity: 8 rounds
Features: Two cold hammer-forged sleeve and shroud barrel models; satin stainless finish; colored front sight insert is easily replaced
MSRP $1079.00

RUGER-57

Action: Semiautomatic
Grips: Glass-filled nylon
Barrel: 4.94 in.
Sights: Fiber optic front, adjustable rear
Weight: 24.5 oz.
Caliber: 5.7x28mm
Capacity: 10, 20 rounds
Features: Suitable as a full-size carry or a competition gun, this new Secure Action fire-control pistol features an internal hammer; billet steel slide with front and rear serrations
MSRP $799.00

SECURITY-9

Action: Semiautomatic
Grips: Glass-filled nylon
Barrel: 4 in.
Sights: Drift-adjustable front and rear
Weight: 23.7 oz.
Caliber: 9mm
Capacity: 10, 15 rounds
Features: Aluminum chassis; full-length rails; blued alloy steel slide; Ruger's Secure Action found on the LCP II; textured grip frame
Standard: $379.00
With Viridian E-Series red laser: $439.00
With Hogue grip: $399.00

SECURITY-9 COMPACT PRO

Action: Semiautomatic
Grips: Glass-filled nylon
Barrel: 3.42 in.
Sights: Steel tritium
Weight: 21.9 oz.
Caliber: 9mm
Capacity: 10 rounds
Features: Through-hardened alloy steel slide; Secure Action system; textured grip frame
MSRP $549.00

SECURITY-9 COMPACT WITH HOGUE GRIP SLEEVE

Action: Semiautomatic
Grips: Glass-filled nylon
Barrel: 3.42 in.
Sights: Drift adjustable
Weight: 22.5 oz.
Caliber: 9mm
Capacity: 10 rounds
Features: A top choice for those who like a very compact handgun for everyday carry, but are frustrated with the lack of hand purchase many offer—the Hogue sleeve grip remedies that problem
MSRP $399.00

SECURITY-9 COMPACT WITH VIRIDIAN E-SERIES RED LASER

Action: Semiautomatic
Grips: Glass-filled nylon
Barrel: 3.42 in.
Sights: Drift adjustable
Weight: 22.4 oz.
Caliber: 9mm
Capacity: 10 rounds
Features: Similar to the Compact Pro, but with a factory-installed Viridian E-Series red laser
MSRP $439.00

SECURITY-9 PRO

Action: Semiautomatic
Grips: Glass-filled nylon
Barrel: 4 in.
Sights: Steel tritium
Weight: 23.8 oz.
Caliber: 9mm
Capacity: 15 rounds
Features: Slim feel but longer grip; hard-coat anodized aluminum chassis; full-length guide rod rails
MSRP $549.00

Ruger (Sturm, Ruger & Co.)

RUGER SINGLE-SIX .17 HMR

RUGER SP101

RUGER SP101 MATCH CHAMPION

RUGER SP101 WITH BLUED ALLOY STEEL FINISH

RUGER SR22 RIMFIRE PISTOL

RUGER SR1911

RUGER SR1911 LIGHTWEIGHT COMMANDER-STYLE 9MM

RUGER SR1911 OFFICER-STYLE

SINGLE-SIX

Action: SA revolver
Grips: Black checkered hard rubber
Barrel: 6.5, 7.5 in.
Sights: Ramp or front bead, adjustable rear
Weight: 35, 45 oz.
Caliber: .17 HMR, .22 LR
Capacity: 6 rounds
Features: Cold hammer-forged barrel; checkered hard-rubber grips; .17 HMR is in blue; .22 LR is in stainless and has integral scope mount grooves
.17 HMR: $629.00
.22 LR: $879.00

SP101

Action: DA/SA
Grips: Wood and rubber
Barrel: 2.25 in.–4.2 in.
Sights: Fixed
Weight: 25 oz.–30 oz.
Caliber: .22 LR, .38 Spl +P, .327 Fed. Mag., .357 Mag., 9mm
Capacity: 6 rounds
Features: Features a light-gathering front sight, windage and elevation adjustable rear sight; triple-locking cylinder; easy takedown
MSRP . . . . $719.00–$769.00

SP101 MATCH CHAMPION

Action: DA/SA
Grips: Hardwood
Barrel: 4.2 in.
Sights: Fiber optic front, adjustable rear
Weight: 30 oz.
Caliber: .357 Mag.
Capacity: 5 rounds
Features: Target crown barrel; checkered hardwood grips; full-lug barrel
MSRP $859.00

SP101 WITH BLUED ALLOY STEEL FINISH

Action: Revolver
Grips: Cushioned rubber, engraved wood
Barrel: 2.25 in.
Sights: Integral rear, black ramp front
Weight: 26 oz.
Caliber: .357 Mag.
Capacity: 5 rounds
Features: A lightweight CCW option in the powerful .357 Mag round; prominent feature is the unexposed backstrap, which improves shooter comfort.
MSRP $719.00

SR22

Action: DA semiautomatic
Grips: Polymer
Barrel: 3.5 in., 4.5 in.
Sights: Adjustable 3-dot
Weight: 17.5 oz.
Caliber: .22 LR
Capacity: 10 rounds
Features: 3-dot sight system has fixed front sight and adjustable rear sight; polymer frame and two interchangeable rubberized grips; underside Picatinny rail; aluminum slide; ambidextrous manual thumb safety/decocking lever; ambidextrous magazine release; Talo Distributor exclusives were offered in purple, black, flat dark earth, red titanium Cerakote, yellow Cerakote, and turquoise Cerakote finishes
MSRP $439.00
Silver: $469.00
Threaded Barrel: $479.00

SR1911

Action: Semiautomatic
Grips: G10, Wood
Barrel: 4.25 in., 5 in.
Sights: Fixed, adjustable
Weight: 29.3 oz.–39 oz.
Caliber: .45 ACP
Capacity: 7+1 rounds, 8+1 rounds
Features: Anodized aluminum frame; stainless steel barrel; standard recoil guide system and flat mainspring housing; rear slide serrations allow for positive grip; now available as a Target model with checkered G10 grips, low-glare stainless finish, and Bomar-style adjustable sights
MSRP $939.00

SR1911 LIGHTWEIGHT COMMANDER-STYLE

Action: Semiautomatic
Grips: G10
Barrel: 4.25 in.
Sights: Novak drift-adjustable three-dot
Weight: 29.3 oz.
Caliber: .45 ACP, 9mm
Capacity: 9 rounds
Features: Classic 1911 70-series style in Commander-length slide
MSRP $979.00

SR1911 OFFICER-STYLE

Action: Semiautomatic
Grips: G-10
Barrel: 3.6 in.
Sights: Novak three-dot
Weight: 31 oz.
Caliber: .45 ACP
Capacity: 8 rounds
Features: A sleek carry 1911-style pistol featuring: skeletonized hammer and trigger; round mainspring housing; oversized beavertail grip safety; oversized ejection port; comes with two seven-round magazines; accepts other 1911 magazines, parts and accessories
MSRP $979.00

Ruger (Sturm, Ruger & Co.)

RUGER SR1911 OFFICER-STYLE

RUGER SR1911 TARGET

RUGER SUPER GP100 9MM

RUGER SUPER REDHAWK

RUGER VAQUERO BISLEY

RUGER VAQUERO BLUED

RUGER WRANGLER

HANDGUNS

SR1911 OFFICER-STYLE, LIGHTWEIGHT OFFICER-STYLE

Action: Semiautomatic
Grips: G-10
Barrel: 3.6 in.
Sights: Drift-adjustable three-dot Novak
Weight: 27.2, 31 oz.
Caliber: 9mm
Capacity: 8 rounds
Features: 9mm is the lightweight version, .45 ACP in the standard; anodized aluminum frame; checkered G10 grips; low-glare stainless finish
MSRP $979.00

SR1911 TARGET

Action: Semiautomatic
Grips: G10
Barrel: 5 in.
Sights: Bomar-style adjustable
Weight: 39 oz.–40.4 oz.
Caliber: 9mm, 10mm, .45 ACP
Capacity: 8 rounds
Features: Classic 1911 70-series style; oversized ejection port; skeletonized aluminum trigger
MSRP $1019.00

SUPER GP100 9MM

Action: Revolver
Grips: Hardwood
Barrel: 6 in.
Sights: Fiber optic front, adjustable rear
Weight: 45.6 oz.
Caliber: 9mm
Capacity: 8 rounds
Features: Chamfered ejector and chamber mouths ease use of included moon clips; cold hammer-forged, vented shrouded barrel with half-lug; Super Redhawk action; stainless barrel shroud/frame finish; blue cylinder and barrel
MSRP $1549.00

SUPER REDHAWK

Action: DA revolver
Grips: Black Hogue Tamer monogrip
Barrel: 2.5 in., 7.5 in., 9.5 in.
Sights: Ramp front, adjustable rear
Weight: 53 oz.–58 oz.
Caliber: 10mm, .44 Mag., .454 Casull, .480 Ruger
Capacity: 6 rounds
Features: Satin stainless finish; triple-locking cylinder; integral scope system; corrosion-resistant; extended frame; dual chambering; transfer bar; Alaskan model has short 2.5-in. barrel
MSRP . . . . $1159.00–$1189.00

VAQUERO BISLEY

Action: SA revolver
Grips: Simulated ivory
Barrel: 5.5 in.
Sights: Fixed
Weight: 41 oz.–45 oz.
Caliber: .45 Colt, .357 Mag.
Capacity: 6 rounds
Features: Stainless steel frame with high-gloss stainless finish
MSRP $899.00

VAQUERO BLUED

Action: SA revolver
Grips: Hardwood
Barrel: 4.62 in., 5.5 in.
Sights: Fixed
Weight: 40 oz.–43 oz.
Caliber: .45 Colt, .357 Mag.
Capacity: 6 rounds
Features: Blued finish alloy steel; reverse Indexing Pawl; ejector rod head; transfer bar mechanism; internal lock
MSRP $829.00

WRANGLER

Action: Revolver
Grips: Synthetic
Barrel: 4.62 in.
Sights: Blade front, integral rear
Weight: 30 oz.
Caliber: .22 LR
Capacity: 6 rounds
Features: A fun plinker or a great tool for low-cost SASS practice, the Ruger Wrangler has an aluminum alloy frame; checkered synthetic grips; Cerakote finish in choice of black, silver, or burnt bronze
MSRP $249.00

HANDGUNS

SCCY Firearms

SCCY CPX-2RD

SCCY CPX-4RD

SCCY DVG-1

CPX-1RD, CPX-2RD

Action: Semiautomatic
Grips: Polymer
Barrel: 3.1 in.
Sights: Low-profile blade front, Crimson Trace red-dot
Weight: 17.5 oz.
Caliber: 9mm
Capacity: 10 rounds
Features: This CCW striker-fire has a heat-treated slide in natural stainless or black nitride finish; bar stock barrel; all-steel recoil system; aircraft-grade heat-treated aluminum alloy frame

CPX-1RD: $349.00
CPX-2RD: $339.00

CPX-3RD, CPX-4RD

Action: Semiautomatic
Grips: Polymer
Barrel: 3.1 in.
Sights: Low-profile blade front, Crimson Trace red-dot
Weight: 17.5 oz.
Caliber: 9mm
Capacity: 10 rounds
Features: Similar to the 1RD and 2RD models, this version gets a barrel with Quad-Lock technology that improves repeatable accuracy

CPX-4RD: $349.00
CPX-3RD: $339.00

DVG-1, DVG-1RD

Action: Semiautomatic
Grips: Polymer
Barrel: 3 in.
Sights: Low-profile front, rear
Weight: 15.5 oz.
Caliber: 9mm
Capacity: 10 rounds
Features: A refinement of SCCY's CPX series; a straight trigger with a 5.5-lb. trigger; black nitride coating; optional Crimson Trace red-dot

DVG-1 . . . . $299.99
DVG-1RD $399.99

SIG Sauer

SIG SAUER MCX RATTLER CANEBRAKE 5 .5-INCH

SIG SAUER MCX RATTLER PCB

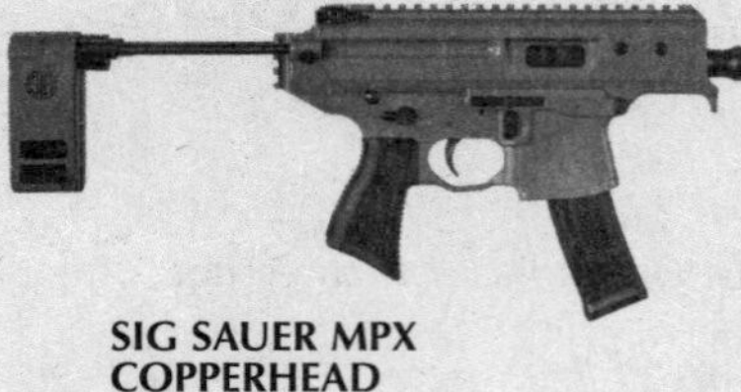
SIG SAUER MPX COPPERHEAD

SIG SAUER MPX K

MCX RATTLER CANEBRAKE 5.5-INCH

Action: Semiautomatic
Grips: PCB
Barrel: 5.5 in.
Sights: None
Weight: 6 lb. 8 oz.
Caliber: .300 Blackout
Capacity: 30 rounds
Features: NFA firearm comes with an inert training device so new owners can head to the range while paperwork clears the feds; suppressor ready; SD handguard; flat, two-stage match trigger; folding PCB brace in Coyote tan; upper and lower in Cerakote E190

MSRP $2699.99

MCX RATTLER PCB

Action: Semiautomatic
Grips: N/A
Barrel: 5.5 in.
Sights: None
Weight: 82 oz.
Caliber: .300 Blackout
Capacity: 30 rounds
Features: Pistol version of Sig's short-barreled rifle takes standard AR mags; sports PDW upper; three-position telescoping PSB pistol brace; M-LOK handguard is free-floating; action is gas piston

MSRP $2529.99

MPX COPPERHEAD

Action: Semiautomatic
Grips: Synthetic
Barrel: 3.5 in.
Sights: None
Weight: 72 oz.
Caliber: 9mm
Capacity: 30 rounds
Features: A barrel of fun in an uber-small package featuring a monolithic upper; barrel with flared flash hider; two-position Pivoting Contour Brace; completely ambidextrous controls; short-stroke gas piston; fully close bolt firing operation; Elite Series Cerakote finish in an eye-catching FDE

MSRP $1779.99

MPX K

Action: Semiautomatic
Grips: Synthetic
Barrel: 4.5 in.
Sights: None
Weight: 96 oz.
Caliber: 9mm
Capacity: 30 rounds
Features: Semiauto take on the submachine gun featuring a dual-side selector switch, magazine release, charging handle, and bolt; full-length Picatinny rail; free-floating eight-inch Keymod handguard; three-position telescoping brace; operation from a fully closed bolt

MSRP $2099.99

SIG Sauer

SIG SAUER P210 TARGET

SIG SAUER P226 LEGION FULL-SIZE

SIG SAUER P226 MK25

SIG SAUER P229 LEGION RX COMPACT

SIG SAUER P238

SIG SAUER P320 M17

SIG SAUER P320 NITRON COMPACT

P210 TARGET

Action: Semiautomatic
Grips: Walnut
Barrel: 4.8 in.
Sights: Adjustable
Weight: 36.9 oz.
Caliber: 9mm
Capacity: 8 rounds
Features: Ergonomic walnut grips; frontstrap stippling; sleek controls; target trigger; reversed rail design; single-action-only; the slide is Nitron-coated to reduce wear
MSRP $1649.99

P226 LEGION FULL-SIZE

Action: DA/SA
Grips: Checkered G10 grips
Barrel: 4.4 in.
Sights: X-ray blacked-out day/night rear
Weight: 34 oz.
Caliber: 9mm
Capacity: 10, 12, 15 rounds
Features: Legion gray PVD finish; enhanced action with SRT; low-profile slide catch and decocking levers; reduced and contoured beavertail
MSRP $1329.99

P226 MK25 FULL-SIZE

Action: SA/DA semiautomatic
Grips: Polymer
Barrel: 4.4 in.
Sights: SIGLITE night sights
Weight: 34 oz.–35 oz.
Caliber: 9mm
Capacity: 10 or 15 rounds
Features: New designation of the Navy's P226 9mm variant issued to U. S. Navy SEALs; still with phosphated internals; (three) 15 round magazines; classic two-piece polymer grips; anchor engraved on slide; Picatinny rail; actual UID scanable serial number label; packaged with FDE grip band and a certificate of authenticity; available in black Nitron or in Desert Tan Nitron; black version can be had with threaded barrel
MSRP $1099.99

P229

Action: Semiautomatic
Grips: FDE polymer
Barrel: 3.9 in.
Sights: Contrast, Siglite night optional
Weight: 34.4 oz.
Caliber: 9mm, .40 S&W, .357 SIG
Capacity: 9mm: 10, 13 rounds; .357 SIG: 10, 12 rounds, .40 S&W: 10, 12 rounds
Features: Mid-size 9mm double-stack pistol comes in several versions (note that all Legion models have Legion Gray finish): Legion Compact SAO is a single-action-only with accessory rail,P-SAIT trigger, XRAY3 day/night sights, X-Five undercut trigger guard; Legion Compact has X-Ray sights, SIG rail, P-SAIT trigger, black G10 grips, alloy frame, PVD finish, double-/single-action; Legion RXP Compact has all the other features of this line plus a ROMEO1 PRO sight; Legion Compact SAO RXP has same features as Compact SAO, but gets a ROMEO1 PRO sight; Nitron variant has black nitron finish, SIGlite sights, E2 grip
Compact/Compact SAO: . . . $1329.00
RXP Compact/Compact SAO: $1549.00

P238

Action: SA semiautomatic
Grips: Fluted polymer, Rosewood Tribal, Pearl, Tribal Engraved Aluminum, Hogue pink rubber
Barrel: 2.7 in.
Sights: Siglite night
Weight: 15.2 oz.
Caliber: .380 ACP (9mm Short)
Capacity: 6 rounds
Features: Ultra compact, single-action-only (miniature 1911 design) .380 carry pistol.
MSRP $649.99

P320

Action: DAO semiautomatic
Grips: Synthetic
Barrel: 3.6 in.–4.7 in.
Sights: Fixed
Weight: 25 oz.–29.4 oz.
Caliber: .40 S&W, 9mm, .357 SIG, .45 ACP
Capacity: 10–17 rounds
Features: Expansive line of subcompact, compact and full-size modular striker-fired pistols with three-point takedown and interchangeable grip sets. 2020 lineup includes eight full-size (all 9mm), two carry (both 9mm), and seven compact models (four in 9mm, as well as Nitron models in .357 SIG, .40 S&W, and .45 ACP)
Full-size: . . . . $549.99–$999.99
Carry: $679.99
Compact: . . . . $599.99–$870.99

P320 M17

Action: Semiautomatic
Grips: Polymer
Barrel: 4.7 in.
Sights: Night sight rear plate, SIGLITE front
Weight: 29.6 oz.
Caliber: 9mm
Capacity: 17 rounds
Features: Recently awarded the MHS--Modular Handgun Contract--from the U.S. Army, this striker-fired mil-spec pistol is now available to the public. Features include optics-ready PVD0-coated slide in Coyote tan; removeable night sight plate; available with or without manual safety; carry-length Coyote grip module
MSRP $679.99

SIG Sauer

SIG SAUER P320-M18

SIG SAUER P320 RXP COMPACT

SIG SAUER P320 RXP FULL-SIZE

SIG SAUER P320 RXP XCOMPACT

SIG SAUER P320 RXP XFULL

SIG SAUER P320 XCOMPACT

SIG SAUER P320 XFIVE LEGION

SIG SAUER P365 NITRON MICRO COMPACT

P320-M18

Action: Semiautomatic
Grips: Polymer
Barrel: 3.9 in.
Sights: SIGLITE front, rear
Weight: 28.1 oz.
Caliber: 9mm
Capacity: 10, 17 rounds
Features: Optic-ready striker-fired 9mm with a curved trigger; M1913 accessory rail; polymer medium carry grip module; stainless steel frame and slide in PVD-coated Coyote Tan
MSRP $679.99

P320 RXP COMPACT

Action: Semiautomatic
Grips: Polymer
Barrel: 3.9 in.
Sights: Contrast three-dot suppressor sights
Weight: 26.3 oz.
Caliber: 9mm
Capacity: 10, 15 rounds
Features: Factory-installed ROMEO1Pro dot optic; medium Compact polymer grip module; standard curved trigger; Nitron-finished stainless steel frame and slide; underside Picatinny rail
MSRP $879.99

P320 RXP FULL-SIZE

Action: Semiautomatic
Grips: Polymer
Barrel: 4.7 in.
Sights: Contrast three-dot suppressor sights
Weight: 30 oz.
Caliber: 9mm
Capacity: 10, 17 rounds
Features: Similar to the Xfull-Size, but with a medium Full-Size polymer grip module; underside Picatinny rail
MSRP $879.99

P320 RXP XCOMPACT

Action: Semiautomatic
Grips: Polymer
Barrel: 3.6 in.
Sights: XRAY3 suppressor sights
Weight: 25.8 oz.
Caliber: 9mm
Capacity: 10, 15 rounds
Features: Fitted with a ROMEO1Pro dot optic and suppressor height XRAY3 sights, this striker-fired 9mm has a medium XCompact polymer grip module; straight XSeries trigger
MSRP $999.99

P320 RXP XFULL

Action: Semiautomatic
Grips: Polymer
Barrel: 4.7 in.
Sights: XRAY3 suppressor sights
Weight: 30 oz.
Caliber: 9mm
Capacity: 10, 17 rounds
Features: Similar to the XCompact version but with a longer barrel, longer grip; underside Picatinny rail
MSRP $999.99

P320 XCOMPACT

Action: Semiautomatic
Grips: Polymer
Barrel: 3.6 in.
Sights: XRAY3 day/night sights
Weight: 25.3 oz.
Caliber: 9mm
Capacity: 15 rounds
Features: A concealable pistol with stainless steel frame and slide with a black Nitron finish; carbon steel barrel; striker-fired; modular grip panels; compatible with SIG's ROMEO1PRO reflex sight; M1913 rail
XRAY3 sights only: $679.99
With ROMEO1 Pro: $999.99

P320 XFIVE LEGION

Action: Semiautomatic
Grips: Polymer
Barrel: 5 in.
Sights: Dawson Precision adjustable
Weight: 43.5 oz.
Caliber: 9mm
Capacity: 10, 17 rounds
Features: TXG tungsten-infused heavy XGrip module; slide in Legion Gray with topside lightning cuts, optic plate, and rear serrations; carbon steel barrel; Xseries straight trigger; under-barrel accessory rail
MSRP $999.99

P365 NITRON MICRO COMPACT

Action: Semiautomatic
Grips: Polymer
Barrel: 3.1 in.
Sights: X-Ray3 day/night sights
Weight: 17.8 oz.
Caliber: 9mm
Capacity: 10 rounds
Features: This tiny 9mm manages to cram 10 rounds into its flush-fit magazine; Nitron-finished stainless steel slide; striker-fired; optional 12-round mag available.
MSRP $599.99

SIG Sauer

SIG SAUER P365 SAS

SIG SAUER P365 XL

SIG SAUER P365 XL ROMEOZERO

SIG SAUER P938 BLACKWOOD

SIG SAUER P938 LEGION

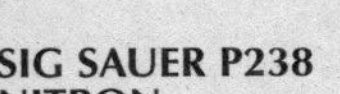

SIG SAUER P238 NITRON

SIG SAUER SP2022 NITRON FULL-SIZE

SIG SAUER SIGM400 TREAD PISTOL

P365 SAS

Action: Semiautomatic
Grips: Polymer
Barrel: 3.1 in.
Sights: FT Bullseye
Weight: 17.8 oz.
Caliber: 9mm
Capacity: 10 rounds
Features: SAS—SIG Anti-Snag—treatment of rounded edges; ported slide for reduced muzzle flip; flat controls; carbon steel barrel; stainless steel slide with Nitron finish
MSRP $679.99

P365 XL

Action: Semiautomatic
Grips: Polymer
Barrel: 3.7 in.
Sights: XRAY3 day/night sights
Weight: 20.7 oz.
Caliber: 9mm
Capacity: 12 rounds
Features: At home on the range, in the nightstand, or your everyday-carry holster with features like an extended beavertail; 365 Xseries grip module; integrated carry magwell; flat trigger; optics-ready slide that works with SIG's RomeoZero and RMSc optics
MSRP $679.99

P365 XL ROMEOZERO

Action: Semiautomatic
Grips: Polymer
Barrel: 3.7 in.
Sights: XRAY3 front sight, RomeoZero optic
Weight: 20.7 oz.
Caliber: 9mm
Capacity: 10, 12 rounds
Features: Lightweight striker-fired pistol; Xseries straight trigger; carbon steel barrel; stainless steel frame and slide; Nitron finish
MSRP $829.99

P938

Action: SA semiautomatic
Grips: Synthetic or wood
Barrel: 3 in.
Sights: Siglite, FT Bullseye
Weight: 16 oz.
Caliber: 9mm
Capacity: 6+1, 7+1 rounds
Features: 9mm version of the P238 family, with similar aesthetics; single-action-only; ambidextrous safety.
BRX: $699.99
SAS: $779.99

P938 LEGION

Action: Semiautomatic
Grips: Polymer
Barrel: 3 in.
Sights: XRAY3 day/night sights
Weight: 17 oz.
Caliber: 9mm
Capacity: 7 rounds
Features: The smallest of the smallest 9mms in a SAO platform with seven-round magazine; Legion Gray Cerakote finish; front and rear cocking serrations on slide; extended mag well
MSRP $779.99

SIGM400 TREAD PISTOL

Action: Semiautomatic
Grips: Synthetic
Barrel: 11.5 in.
Sights: None
Weight: 96 oz.
Caliber: 5.56 NATO
Capacity: 30 rounds
Features: A direct-impingement AR platform in a pistol configuration with single-stage trigger; FNC carbon steel barrel; M-LOK accessory rail; adjustable stabilizing brace
MSRP $949.99

SP2022

Action: Semiautomatic
Grips: Polymer
Barrel: 3.9 in.
Sights: Siglite
Weight: 29 oz.
Caliber: 9mm, .40 S&W
Capacity: 12, 15 rounds
Features: SIG's original full-size polymer pistol, available in Nitron black; DA/SA; contrast sights; polymer grip; steel magazine
MSRP $679.99

Smith & Wesson

SMITH & WESSON M&P BODYGUARD 38 CRIMSON TRACE LASER

REVOLVERS

M&P BODYGUARD 38 CRIMSON TRACE LASER

Action: Revolver
Grips: Polymer
Barrel: 1.875 in.
Sights: Black ramp front, groove rear
Weight: 14.4 oz.
Caliber: .38 Spec.
Capacity: 5 rounds
Features: Aluminum alloy frame; gray polymer grips; top-frame mounted red Crimson Trace laser; PVD coated stainless steel cylinder; ambidextrous cylinder release; DA only
MSRP $539.00

Smith & Wesson

SMITH & WESSON MODEL 10

SMITH & WESSON MODEL 19 CLASSIC

SMITH & WESSON MODEL 27 CLASSICS

SMITH & WESSON MODEL 29 CLASSICS

SMITH & WESSON MODEL 36 CLASSICS

SMITH & WESSON MODEL 57 CLASSICS

SMITH & WESSON MODEL 60

SMITH & WESSON MODEL 60 LADYSMITH

SMITH & WESSON MODEL 66

MODEL 10

Action: SA/DA revolver
Grips: Wood
Barrel: 4 in.
Sights: Black blade, fixed
Weight: 36 oz.
Caliber: .38 S&W Spl. +P
Capacity: 6 rounds
Features: Carbon steel frame; carbon steel cylinder; blued finish; medium size frame; exposed hammer
MSRP $772.00

MODEL 19 CLASSIC

Action: Revolver
Grips: Wood
Barrel: 4.25 in.
Sights: Red ramp front, adjustable black blade rear
Weight: 37.2 oz.
Caliber: .357 Mag.
Capacity: 6 rounds
Features: A true classic is back in S&W's lineup, featuring a high-polished blue finish; traditional thumbpiece; half-lug; carbon steel frame and cylinder; checkered custom wood grips with S&W silver medallion
MSRP $863.00

MODEL 27 CLASSICS

Action: SA/DA revolver
Grips: Checkered square butt walnut
Barrel: 4 in., 6.5 in.
Sights: Pinned serrated ramp front; Micro adjustable with cross serrations
Weight: 48.5 oz.
Caliber: .357 Mag., .38 S&W Spl. +P
Capacity: 6 rounds
Features: Carbon steel frame; bright blued finish
MSRP . . . . $1053.00–$1091.00

MODEL 29 CLASSICS

Action: Revolver
Grips: Checkered square butt walnut; 6 in. model features Altamont Service walnut grips
Barrel: 4 in., 6.5 in.
Sights: Red ramp, micro adjustable rear
Weight: 48.5 oz.
Caliber: .44 Mag., .44 S&W Spl.
Capacity: 6 rounds
Features: Carbon steel frame in blue; blued with machine engraving and grips with enhanced carvings also available in 4-inch barrel only
MSRP . . . . $1031.00–$1200.00

MODEL 36 CLASSICS

Action: Revolver
Grips: Wood
Barrel: 1.8 in.
Sights: Integral front, fixed rear
Weight: 19.5 oz.
Caliber: .38 S&W Spl. +P
Capacity: 5 rounds
Features: Small sized frame; exposed hammer; carbon steel frame and cylinder; blued finish; single or double action
MSRP $789.00

MODEL 57 CLASSICS

Action: DA N-frame revolver
Grips: Checkered square-butt walnut
Barrel: 6 in.
Sights: Pinned red ramp front, micro adjustable white outline rear;
Weight: 4.8 oz.
Caliber: .41 Mag.
Capacity: 6 rounds
Features: Bright blued finish; carbon steel frame; classic style thumbpiece; color case wide spur hammer; color case wide serrated target trigger
MSRP $1038.00

MODEL 60, MODEL 60 LADYSMITH

Action: Revolver
Grips: Synthetic, wood
Barrel: 2.125 in., 3 in.
Sights: Black blade front, adjustable rear
Weight: 21.4 oz.–23.2 oz.
Caliber: .357 Mag., .38 S&W Spl. +P
Capacity: 5 rounds
Features: Satin stainless finish; single- or double-action; stainless steel fame and cylinder. Lady Smith has finger-grooved wood grips designed for smaller hands, brushed stainless finish, and is engraved with "Lady Smith" on the frame.
2.125-in. barrel: $775.00
3-inch barrel: $786.00
Ladysmith: $786.00

MODEL 66

Action: DA/SA revolver
Grips: Synthetic
Barrel: 2.75 in., 4.25 in.
Sights: Adjustable
Weight: 36.9 oz.–37.4 oz.
Caliber: .38 S&W Spl. +P, .357 Mag.
Capacity: 6 rounds
Features: Full top strap and barrel serration; ball-detent lock-up; two-piece barrel; matte stainless finish
MSRP $874.00

SMITH & WESSON MODEL 66 COMBAT MAGNUM

SMITH & WESSON MODEL 69

SMITH & WESSON MODEL 69 COMBAT MAGNUM

SMITH & WESSON MODEL 442 ENGRAVED

SMITH & WESSON PERFORMANCE CENTER MODEL 460XVR 14-IN BARREL WITH BIPOD

SMITH & WESSON MODEL 586

SMITH & WESSON MODEL 617

MODEL 66 COMBAT MAGNUM

Action: Revolver
Grips: Synthetic
Barrel: 2.75 in., 4 in.
Sights: Red ramp front, white outline adjustable rear
Weight: 33.5 oz.
Caliber: .357 Mag., .38 Spl. +P
Capacity: 6 rounds
Features: K-frame revolver; full top strap and barrel serration; ball detent lockup; two-piece barrel; full-length extractor rod
MSRP $874.00

MODEL 69

Action: DA/SA revolver
Grips: Synthetic
Barrel: 2.75 in., 4.25 in.
Sights: Adjustable
Weight: 34.4 oz.–37.4 oz.
Caliber: .44 Mag., .44 Spl.
Capacity: 5 rounds
Features: Full top strap and barrel serration; ball-detent lock-up; two-piece barrel
MSRP $874.00

MODEL 69 COMBAT MAGNUM

Action: Revolver
Grips: Synthetic
Barrel: 2.75 in., 4.25 in.
Sights: Red ramp front, white outline adjustable rear
Weight: 34.4 oz.–37.4 oz.
Caliber: .44 Mag.
Capacity: 5 rounds
Features: Full top strap and barrel serration; ball detent lockup; two-piece barrel; full-length extractor rod
MSRP $874.00

MODEL 442 ENGRAVED

Action: DA revolver
Grips: Engraved wood
Barrel: 1.875 in.
Sights: Integral front, fixed rear
Weight: 14.2 oz.
Caliber: .38 S&W Spl. +P
Capacity: 5 rounds
Features: Aluminum alloy frame; stainless barrel/cylinder; matte black
MSRP $772.00

MODEL 460XVR, PERFORMANCE CENTER 460XVR, PERFORMANCE CENTER HIVIZ 460XVR

Action: SA/DA revolver
Grips: Synthetic
Barrel: 3.5 in., 7 in., 8.38-in., 10.5 in., 12 in., 14 in.
Sights: Vary with model
Weight: 72.02 oz.–79.3 oz.
Caliber: .460 S&W Mag., .45 LC, .454 Casull, .460 S&W Mag.
Capacity: 5 rounds
Features: Highest muzzle velocity revolver in the world, gain-twist rifling; HIVIZ gets muzzle brake, integral scope base, unfluted cylinder, HIVIZ fiber optic front sight and adjustable white outline rear, PC-tuned action, full underlug on 7.5-in. barrel; 14-in. Barrel with Bipod gets bipod, black ramp front sight, adjustable rear sight, muzzle brake, top and bottom accessory/optics rails, chrome hammer, chrome trigger with trigger stop, PC-tuned action (.460 S&W Mag); 12-inch barrel has sling swivels and integrated Picatinny topside rail, removeable Patridge front sight; 10.5-inch barrel has interchangeable fiber optic front sight, adjustable rear sight, muzzle brake, graduated underlug, sling swivels; 3.5-inch barrel has unfluted cylinder, HiViz green fiber optic front and adjustable rear sights; Model 460XVR has 8.38-inch barrel, removeable compensator, gain twist barrel, interchangeable front sight and adjustable rear, full underlug
460V: $1389.00
PC HiViz: . . . . . . $1598.00–$1799.00
PC XVR: . . . . $1598.00–$1799.00
PC XVR 14-in barrel/ bipod: . . . . . . $1598.00–$1799.00
XVR: $1389.00

MODEL 586

Action: SA/DA revolver
Grips: Wood
Barrel: 4 in., 6 in.
Sights: Adjustable
Weight: 46.3 oz.
Caliber: .357 Mag., .38 S&W Spl. +P
Capacity: 6 rounds
Features: Carbon steel frame and cylinder with blued finish; adjustable white outline rear sight and red ramp front sight; square-butt design; checkered wood grips
MSRP $871.00

MODEL 617

Action: SA/DA revolver
Grips: Synthetic
Barrel: 4 in., 6 in.
Sights: Partridge front, adjustable rear
Weight: 38.9 oz.–44.1 oz.
Caliber: .22 LR
Capacity: 10 rounds
Features: Stainless steel frame and cylinder with satin stainless finish; medium size frame with exposed hammer
MSRP $853.00

Smith & Wesson

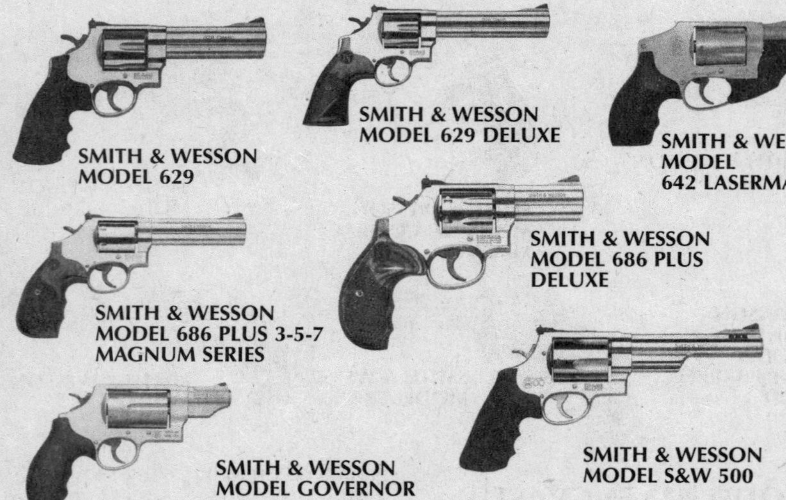

SMITH & WESSON MODEL 629

SMITH & WESSON MODEL 629 DELUXE

SMITH & WESSON MODEL 642 LASERMAX

SMITH & WESSON MODEL 686 PLUS DELUXE

SMITH & WESSON MODEL 686 PLUS 3-5-7 MAGNUM SERIES

SMITH & WESSON MODEL GOVERNOR

SMITH & WESSON MODEL S&W 500

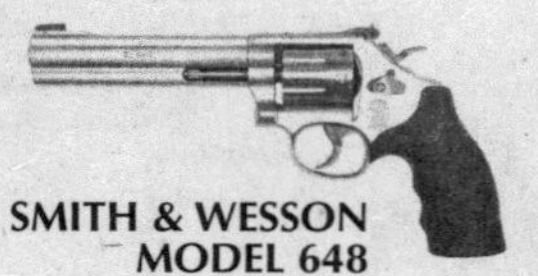

SMITH & WESSON MODEL 648

SMITH & WESSON MODEL 686

MODEL 629, 629 CLASSIC

Action: SA/DA revolver
Grips: Synthetic
Barrel: 3 in., 4.125 in., 5 in., 6 in., 6.5 in.
Sights: Red ramp, adjustable white outline
Weight: 39.6 oz.–50.7 oz.
Caliber: .44 Mag, .44 S&W Spl.
Capacity: 6 rounds
Features: Stainless steel frame and cylinder with satin stainless finish; exposed hammer
MSRP. . . . . $949.00–$1029.00

MODEL 629 DELUXE

Action: Revolver
Grips: Wood
Barrel: 3 in., 4.125 in., 5 in., 6 in., 6.5 in.
Sights: Red ramp front, white outline adjustable rear
Weight: 39.6 oz.–50.7 oz.
Caliber: .44 Mag., .44 S&W Spl.
Capacity: 6 rounds
Features: N-frame revolver; all-stainless construction; textured wood grips
MSRP. . . . . $949.00–$1029.00

MODEL 642 LASERMAX

Action: DAO
Grips: Synthetic
Barrel: 1.88 in.
Sights: Fixed front, integral rear
Weight: 15.5 oz.
Caliber: .38 S&W Special +P
Capacity: 5 rounds
Features: No-snag, hammerless design; rapid target acquisition of the LaserMax sighting system; matte silver finish
MSRP. $539.00

MODEL 648

Action: Revolver
Grips: Synthetic
Barrel: 6 in.
Sights: Partridge front, adjustable rear
Weight: 46.2 oz.
Caliber: .22 Mag.
Capacity: 8 rounds
Features: Double-/single-action in all stainless steel; K-frame; eight-round cylinder; full underlug
MSRP. $772.00

MODEL 686

Action: Revolver
Grips: Synthetic
Barrel: 4.125, 6 in.
Sights: Varies with model
Weight: 44.8 oz.
Caliber: .357 Mag.
Capacity: 6 rounds
New Features: L-frame six-shot revolver in satin stainless finish; red ramp front sight, adjustable white outline rear, synthetic grips, full underlug
MSRP. $853.00

MODEL 686 PLUS 3-5-7 MAGNUM SERIES

Action: Revolver
Grips: Wood
Barrel: 2.5 in., 3 in., 4.125 in., 5 in., 6 in., 7 in.
Sights: Red ramp front, white outline adjustable rear
Weight: 37.4 oz. (3-in. barrel), 37.4 oz. (5-in. barrel)
Caliber: .357 Mag.
Capacity: 7 rounds
Features: Collector's Model 686 L-frame; custom black/silver wood grips bearing "357"; cylinder is unfluted
MSRP. . . . . $874.00–$899.00

MODEL 686 PLUS DELUXE

Action: Revolver
Grips: Wood
Barrel: 2.5 in., 3 in., 4.125 in., 5 in., 6 in., 7 in.
Sights: Red ramp front, white outline adjustable rear
Weight: 34.1 oz.–51.2 oz.
Caliber: .357 Mag.
Capacity: 7 rounds
Features: S&W's classic 686 L-frame revolver; all stainless steel
MSRP. $899.00

MODEL GOVERNOR

Action: SA/DA revolver
Grips: Synthetic, Crimson Trace
Barrel: 2.75 in.
Sights: Tritium front, fixed rear
Weight: 30.3 oz.
Caliber: .45 Colt, .45 ACP, .410
Capacity: 6 rounds
Features: Patented heat-treated scandium frame; PVD coated cylinder; matte silver finish; furnished with two full moon clips and three two-shot moon clips for use with .45 ACP
MSRP. . . . . $825.00–$885.00

MODEL S&W 500

Action: SA/DA revolver
Grips: Synthetic
Barrel: 3.5 in., 4 in., 6.5 in., 7.5 in., 8.38-in., 10.5 in.
Sights: Vary with model
Weight 55.6 oz.–79.6 oz.
Caliber: .500 S&W Mag.
Capacity: 5 rounds
Features: First X-frame debuted in 2003; removable high-efficiency compensator; HIVIZ red dot interchangeable front sight
MSRP. . . . .$1319.00–$1636.00
Performance Center:. . . . . . .$1619.00–$1649.00

SMITH & WESSON PERFORMANCE CENTER MODEL 19 CARRY COMP

SMITH & WESSON PERFORMANCE CENTER MODEL 327

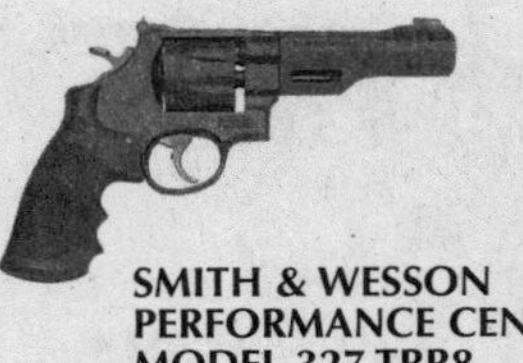

SMITH & WESSON PERFORMANCE CENTER MODEL 327 TRR8

SMITH & WESSON PERFORMANCE CENTER MODEL 442 CRIMSON TRACE LG 105

SMITH & WESSON PERFORMANCE CENTER MODEL 637 ENHANCED ACTION

SMITH & WESSON PERFORMANCE CENTER MODEL 642 ENHANCED ACTION

SMITH & WESSON PERFORMANCE CENTER MODEL 686

SMITH & WESSON PERFORMANCE PERFORMANCE CENTER MODEL 686 PLUS

PERFORMANCE CENTER MODEL 19 CARRY COMP

Action: Revolver
Grips: Wood/synthetic
Barrel: 3 in.
Sights: Tritium ramp front, adjustable black blade rear
Weight: 34.1 oz.
Caliber: .357 Mag.
Capacity: 6 rounds
Features: The return of the 19K Comp but in a Performance Center iteration featuring a carbon steel frame and cylinder; stainless steel Power Port vented barrel; tritium front sight; PC-tuned action; custom grips of wood and synthetic materials; trigger overtravel stop
MSRP $1132.00

PERFORMANCE CENTER MODEL 327

Action: Revolver
Grips: Wood
Barrel: 2 in.
Sights: Orange ramp front sight, integral "U" rear
Weight: 23.1 oz.
Caliber: .357 Mag., .38 S&W Spl. +P
Capacity: 8 rounds
Features: Color case with overtravel stop; color case tear drop with pinned sear; exposed hammer; matte black finish; scandium alloy frame and titanium alloy cylinder; smooth DA with Wolff Mainspring
MSRP $1344.00

PERFORMANCE CENTER MODEL 327 TRR8

Action: SA/DA revolver
Grips: Synthetic
Barrel: 5 in.
Sights: Interchangeable front; adjustable V-notch rear
Weight: 35.3 oz.
Caliber: .357 Mag., .38 S&W Spl. +P
Capacity: 8 rounds
Features: Scandium alloy frame; stainless steel cylinder; matte black; exposed hammer; equipment rails
MSRP $1360.00

PERFORMANCE CENTER MODEL 442 CRIMSON TRACE LG 105

Action: Revolver
Grips: Crimson Trace
Barrel: 1.875 in.
Sights: Ramp front, groove rear, Crimson Trace red laser
Weight: 15 oz.
Caliber: .38 Spec.
Capacity: 5 rounds
Features: Concealed hammer DA only revolver with high-polished parts, including cylinder flutes; carbon steel cylinder in stainless finish; aluminum alloy frame in matte black finish; Crimson Trace LG 105 red laser grips; +P rated; Performance Center tuned action; no internal lock
MSRP . . . . $531.00–$782.00

PERFORMANCE CENTER MODEL 637 ENHANCED ACTION

Action: Revolver
Grips: Wood
Barrel: 1.875 in.
Sights: Integral ramp front
Weight: 15 oz.
Caliber: .38 Spl. +P
Capacity: 5 rounds
Features: J-frame with Performance Center-tuned action; stainless steel barrel; aluminum alloy frame; matte silver finish; custom wood grips
MSRP $565.00

PERFORMANCE CENTER MODEL 642 ENHANCED ACTION

Action: Revolver
Grips: Wood
Barrel: 1.875 in.
Sights: Integral ramp front
Weight: 15 oz.
Caliber: .38 Spl. +P
Capacity: 5 rounds
Features: J-frame with Performance Center-tuned action; stainless steel barrel; aluminum alloy frame; matte silver finish; custom wood grips; DAO has concealed hammer
MSRP . . . . $531.00–$576.00

PERFORMANCE CENTER MODEL 686

Action: Revolver
Grips: Wood
Barrel: 2.5 in., 4 in., 5 in.
Sights: Red ramp front, ***adjustable rear***
Weight: 34.1 oz.
Caliber: .357 Mag.
Capacity: 7 rounds
Features: Unfluted cylinder; Performance Center-tuned action; custom teardrop hammer; precision crowned barrel; cylinder cut for moon
MSRP . . . . $1006.00–$1129.00

PERFORMANCE CENTER MODEL 686 PLUS

Action: Revolver
Grips: Synthetic
Barrel: 2.5 in., 4 in., 5 in.
Sights: Interchangeable blade front, adjustable rear
Weight: 38.4 oz.
Caliber: .357 Mag.
Capacity: 7 rounds
Features: Slanted half-underlug; unfluted cylinder; vent rib; Performance Center-tuned action; custom teardrop hammer; speed-release cylinder thumbpiece; includes an orange front blade, which can be subbed out for the user's choice
MSRP . . . . $1006.00–$1129.00

Smith & Wesson

SMITH & WESSON PERFORMANCE CENTER MODEL 929

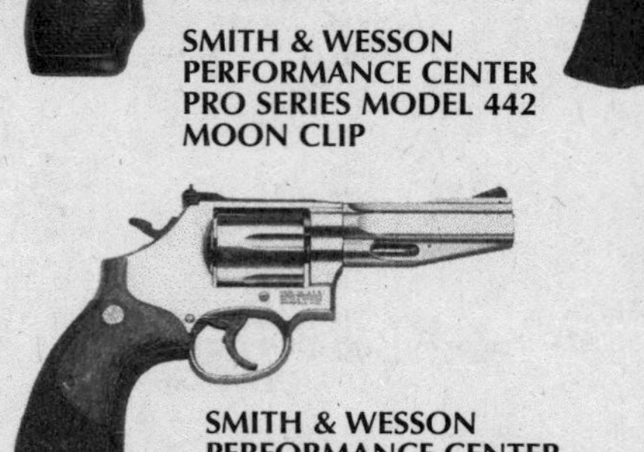

SMITH & WESSON PERFORMANCE CENTER PRO SERIES MODEL 442 MOON CLIP

SMITH & WESSON PERFORMANCE CENTER PRO SERIES MODEL 627

SMITH & WESSON PERFORMANCE CENTER PRO SERIES MODEL 986

SMITH & WESSON PERFORMANCE CENTER PRO SERIES MODEL 640

SMITH & WESSON PERFORMANCE CENTER PRO SERIES MODEL 686 SSR

PERFORMANCE CENTER MODEL 929

Action: DA/SA revolver
Grips: Synthetic
Barrel: 6.5 in.
Sights: Adjustable
Weight: 44.2 oz.
Caliber: 9mm
Capacity: 8 rounds
Features: Removable compensator; titanium cylinder; Jerry Miculek signature; chrome teardrop hammer; chrome trigger with stop
MSRP $1229.00

PERFORMANCE CENTER MODEL 986

Action: Revolver
Grips: Wood
Barrel: 2.5 in.
Sights: Red ramp front, adjustable rear
Weight: 31.7 oz.
Caliber: 9mm
Capacity: 7 rounds
Features: L-frame 9mm with unfluted cylinder; custom barrel with recessed crown; trigger overstop travel; bossed mainspring; Performance Center-tuned action; stainless steel barrel and frame; titanium cylinder; moon clips
MSRP . . . . $1129.00–$1189.00

PERFORMANCE CENTER PRO SERIES MODEL 442 MOON CLIP

Action: DA revolver
Grips: Synthetic
Barrel: 1.87 in.
Sights: Integral front, fixed rear
Weight: 15 oz.
Caliber: .38 S&W Spl. +P
Capacity: 5 rounds
Features: Aluminum alloy frame; stainless steel cylinder; matte black finish; internal hammer; cylinder cut for moon clips
MSRP . . . . $531.00–$782.00

PERFORMANCE CENTER PRO SERIES MODEL 627

Action: SA/DA revolver
Grips: Synthetic
Barrel: 2.625 in., 4 in., 5 in.
Sights: varies with model
Weight: 37.8 oz.–46.7 oz.
Caliber: .357 Mag.
Capacity: 8 rounds
Features: Performance Center Pro Series with 4-in. barrel has matte silver finish, chamfered charge holes, custom barrel with recessed precision crown, bossed mainspring, Hogue grips, interchangeable front sight, adjustable rear; Performance Center V-Comp variant has 5-in. barrel, removable compensator, two-tone black frame and barrel/matte stainless cylinder and controls, Hogue grips, adjustable orange dovetail front sight, adjustable rear sight, chrome hammer, chrome trigger with trigger stop; two variants known simply as Performance Center Model 627: 1) Has 2.625-in. barrel, unfluted cylinder, wood gripsdovetail red ramp front sight, adjustable white outline rear, ball detent lockup, chrome flashed custom tear drop hammer, chrome flashed trigger with stop, cylinder cut for moon clips; 2) Performance Center 5-in. barrel similar to Pro Series with tapering underlug, but with both wood and synthetic grips, gold bead front sight, adjustable rear sight, matte silver finish
MSRP . . . . $1024.00–$1598.00

PERFORMANCE CENTER PRO SERIES MODEL 640

Action: DA revolver
Grips: Synthetic
Barrel: 2.1 in.
Sights: Black blade front, fixed rear
Weight: 23 oz.
Caliber: .357 Mag.
Capacity: 5 rounds
Features: Stainless steel frame, barrel, and cylinder, front and rear dovetail tritium night sights, concealed hammer, cylinder cut for moon clips, satin stainless finish
MSRP $859.00

PERFORMANCE CENTER PRO SERIES MODEL 686 SSR

Action: Revolver
Grips: Wood
Barrel: 2.5 in., 4 in., 5 in.
Sights: Interchangeable front, adjustable rear
Weight: 38.3 oz.
Caliber: .357 Mag., .38 S&W Spl. +P
Capacity: 6 rounds
Features: Stainless steel frame and barrel with satin finish; exposed hammer; chamfered charge holes; bossed mainspring; ergonomic grip to force high-hand hold; custom barrel with recessed precision crown
MSRP . . . . $1006.00–$1129.00

PERFORMANCE CENTER PRO SERIES MODEL 986

Action: DA/SA revolver
Grips: Synthetic
Barrel: 5 in.
Sights: Adjustable
Weight: 34.9 oz.
Caliber: 9mm
Capacity: 7 rounds
Features: Titanium, fluted cylinder; precision crowned barrel; cylinder cut for moonclips
MSRP . . . . $1129.00–$1189.00

Smith & Wesson

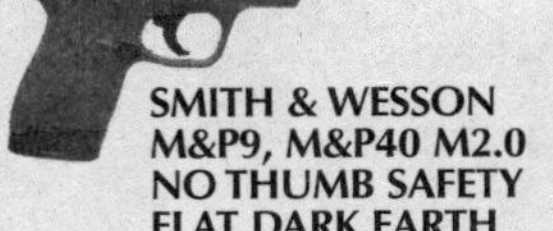
SMITH & WESSON M&P9, M&P40 M2.0 NO THUMB SAFETY FLAT DARK EARTH

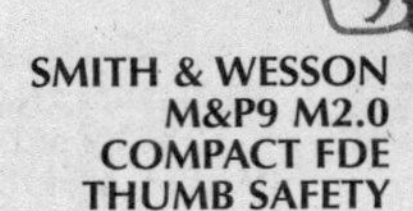
SMITH & WESSON M&P9 M2.0 COMPACT FDE THUMB SAFETY

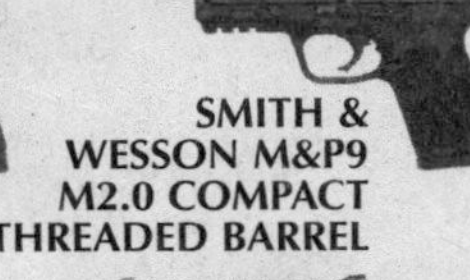
SMITH & WESSON M&P9 M2.0 COMPACT THREADED BARREL

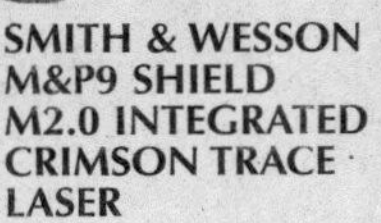
SMITH & WESSON M&P9 SHIELD M2.0 INTEGRATED CRIMSON TRACE LASER

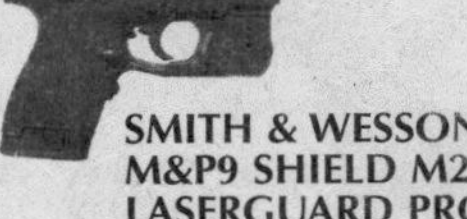
SMITH & WESSON M&P9 SHIELD M2.0 LASERGUARD PRO COMBO

SMITH & WESSON M&P9 SHIELD EZ WITH CRIMSON TRACE LASERGUARD

SMITH & WESSON M&P22 COMPACT CERAKOTE FLAT DARK EARTH THREADED

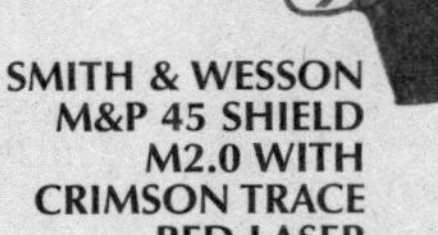
SMITH & WESSON M&P 45 SHIELD M2.0 WITH CRIMSON TRACE RED LASER

SMITH & WESSON M&P 380 SHIELD EZ

SEMIAUTOMATICS

M&P9, M&P40 M2.0 NO THUMB SAFETY FLAT DARK EARTH

Action: Semiautomatic
Grips: Polymer
Barrel: 5 in.
Sights: White three-dot
Weight: 26.9 oz.
Caliber: 9mm, .40 S&W
Capacity: 15, 17 rounds
Features: Armonite finish; unique rear slide serrations; improved M2.0 trigger; accessory rail; no loaded chamber indicator
MSRP $599.00

M&P9 M2.0 COMPACT FDE THUMB SAFETY

Action: Semiautomatic
Grips: Polymer
Barrel: 4 in.
Sights: White three-dot
Weight: 27 oz.
Caliber: 9mm
Capacity: 10, 15 rounds
Features: Striker-fired pistol with a manual thumb safety; stainless steel barrel finished in Armonite; stainless slide finished in Cerakote flat dark earth; four interchangeable palm swell size inserts; accessory rail
MSRP $569.00

M&P9 M2.0 COMPACT THREADED BARREL

Action: Semiautomatic
Grips: Polymer
Barrel: 4.625 in.
Sights: Suppressor-height white-dot front, rear
Weight: 27.4 oz.
Caliber: 9mm
Capacity: 10, 15 rounds
Features: Striker-fired pistol with a threaded stainless steel barrel finished in Armonite; stainless slide finished in Armonite; four interchangeable palm swell size inserts; accessory rail
MSRP $569.00

M&P9 SHIELD M2.0 INTEGRATED CRIMSON TRACE LASER

Action: Semiautomatic
Grips: Polymer
Barrel: 3.1 in.
Sights: Steel three-dot white
Weight: 18.8 oz.
Caliber: 9mm, .40 S&W
Capacity: 7, 8 rounds
Features: Super-compact striker-fired pistol; built-in Crimson Trace Laser in red
MSRP $524.00

M&P9 SHIELD M2.0 LASERGUARD PRO GREEN LASER/LIGHT COMBO

Action: Semiautomatic
Grips: Polymer
Barrel: 3.1 in.
Sights: Steel three-dot white
Weight: 22 oz.
Caliber: 9mm
Capacity: 7, 8 rounds
Features: An ultra-compact firearm; integrated combination Laserguard green laser; tactical light
MSRP $690.00

M&P9 SHIELD EZ

Action: Semiautomatic
Grips: Polymer
Barrel: 3.675 in.
Sights: White three-dot
Weight: 23.2 oz.–23.8 oz.
Caliber: 9mm
Capacity: 8 rounds
Features: Single-stack striker-fire with a stainless steel slide and barrel with Armornite finish; accessory rail; no-trigger-pull disassembly; EZ is for an easier to rack slide; grip safety; reversible magazine release
Gun only . . . . $490.00–$570.00
With laser. $591.00

M&P22 COMPACT CERAKOTE FLAT DARK EARTH THREADED

Action: Semiautomatic
Grips: Polymer
Barrel: 3.5 in.
Sights: White three-dot
Weight: 15.3 oz.
Caliber: .22 LR
Capacity: 10 rounds
Features: Reduced scale version of full-size M&P pistols; ambidextrous manual safety; reversible magazine release; Picatinny accessory rail; magazine safety; threaded barrel; two magazines
MSRP $429.00

M&P 45 SHIELD M2.0 WITH CRIMSON TRACE RED LASER

Action: Semiautomatic
Grips: Polymer
Barrel: 3.3 in.
Sights: Steel three dot
Weight: 23.1 oz.
Caliber: .45 ACP
Capacity: 6, 7 rounds
Features: A lightweight carry gun in .45 ACP featuring a built-in Crimson Trace laser in red; improved trigger; Armonite finish on metalwork; available with or without manual thumb safety
MSRP $524.00

M&P 380 SHIELD EZ

Action: Semiautomatic
Grips: Polymer
Barrel: 3.675 in.
Sights: Fixed white-dot front, adjustable white-dot rear
Weight: 18.5 o.
Caliber: .380 ACP
Capacity: 8 rounds
Features: An EDC pistol featuring a grip safety; drift adjustable rear sight; under rail; tactile loaded chamber indicator; metalwork including barrel Armonite finished; internal hammer fired; available with or without thumb safety
MSRP $428.00

Smith & Wesson

SMITH & WESSON M&P BODYGUARD 380

SMITH & WESSON M&P BODYGUARD 380 ENGRAVED

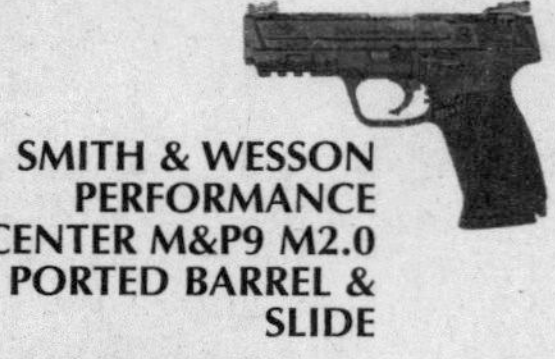
SMITH & WESSON PERFORMANCE CENTER M&P9 M2.0 PORTED BARREL & SLIDE

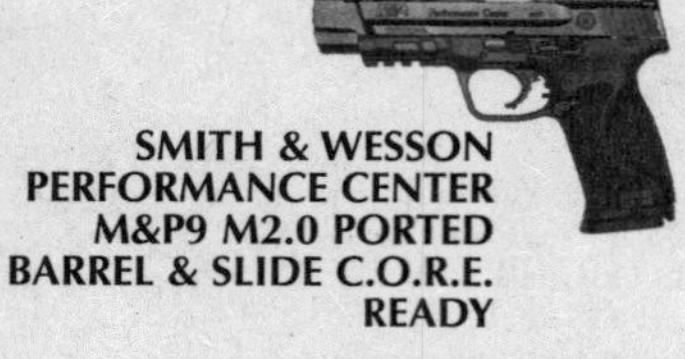
SMITH & WESSON PERFORMANCE CENTER M&P9 M2.0 PORTED BARREL & SLIDE C.O.R.E. READY

SMITH & WESSON PERFORMANCE CENTER M&P9 M2.0 PRO SERIES C.O.R.E. READY

SMITH & WESSON PERFORMANCE CENTER M&P40 M2.0 PORTED BARREL & SLIDE

SMITH & WESSON PERFORMANCE CENTER M&P40 M2.0 PORTED BARREL & SLIDE C.O.R.E. READY

M&P BODYGUARD 380

Action: DA semiautomatic
Grips: Synthetic
Barrel: 2.75 in.
Sights: Adjustable
Weight: 11.85 oz.
Caliber: .380 ACP
Capacity: 6+1 rounds
Features: Stainless steel drift adjustable sights; ergonomic grip; high-strength polymer frame; external takedown lever and slide stop; manual thumb safety; double action fire control (2nd strike compatibility); available with integral Crimson Trace; and with an engraved stainless slide
Standard:. $379.00
Red laser:. $449.00

M&P BODYGUARD 380 ENGRAVED

Action: Semiautomatic
Grips: Polymer
Barrel: 2.75 in.
Sights: Drift adjustable front and rear
Weight: 12 oz.
Caliber: .380 ACP
Capacity: 6 rounds
Features: Ultra-compact carry gun; DAO; custom machine-engraved matte silver slide
MSRP $405.00

PERFORMANCE CENTER M&P9 M2.0 PORTED BARREL & SLIDE

Action: Semiautomatic
Grips: Polymer
Barrel: 4.25 in., 5 in.
Sights: Green fiber optic front, adjustable red fiber optic rear
Weight: 27.7 oz., 29.8 oz.
Caliber: 9mm
Capacity: 10, 17 rounds
Features: Striker-fired pistol with a stainless steel barrel finished in Armonite; stainless slide finished in Armonite; four interchangeable palm swell size inserts; accessory rail; barrel and slide are ported; PC-tuned action; trigger stop
MSRP . . . . $720.00–$741.00

PERFORMANCE CENTER M&P9 M2.0 PORTED BARREL & SLIDE C.O.R.E. READY

Action: Semiautomatic
Grips: Polymer
Barrel: 4.25 in., 5 in.
Sights: White three-dot
Weight: 27.7 oz., 29.8 oz.
Caliber: 9mm
Capacity: 10, 17 rounds
Features: Striker-fired pistol with a stainless steel barrel finished in Armonite; four interchangeable palm swell size inserts; accessory rail; barrel and slide are ported; slide is C.O.R.E. and comes with optics mounting kit; larger slide stop; PC-tuned action; trigger stop
MSRP . . . . $720.00–$741.00

PERFORMANCE CENTER M&P9 M2.0 PRO SERIES C.O.R.E. READY

Action: Semiautomatic
Grips: Polymer
Barrel: 4.25 in., 5 in.
Sights: White three-dot
Weight: 29 oz.
Caliber: 9mm
Capacity: 10, 17 rounds
Features: Striker-fired pistol with a stainless steel barrel finished in Armonite; stainless slide finished in Armonite; four interchangeable palm swell size inserts; accessory rail; slide is C.O.R.E. and comes with optics mounting kit; larger slide stop; PC-tuned action; trigger stop
MSRP . . . . $720.00–$741.00

PERFORMANCE CENTER M&P40 M2.0 PORTED BARREL & SLIDE

Action: Semiautomatic
Grips: Polymer
Barrel: 4.25 in., 5 in.
Sights: Green fiber optic front, adjustable red fiber optic rear
Weight: 28.7 oz., 30.1 oz.
Caliber: .40 S&W
Capacity: 10, 15 rounds
Features: Striker-fired pistol with a stainless steel barrel finished in Armonite; stainless slide finished in Armonite; four interchangeable palm swell size inserts; accessory rail; barrel and slide are ported; slide is C.O.R.E. and includes mounting kit; enlarged slide stop
MSRP . . . . $720.00–$741.00

PERFORMANCE CENTER M&P40 M2.0 PORTED BARREL & SLIDE C.O.R.E. READY

Action: Semiautomatic
Grips: Polymer
Barrel: 4.25 in., 5 in.
Sights: White three-dot
Weight: 28.7 oz., 30.1 oz.
Caliber: .40 S&W
Capacity: 10, 15 rounds
Features: Striker-fired pistol with a stainless steel barrel finished in Armonite; stainless slide finished in Armonite; four interchangeable palm swell size inserts; accessory rail; slide is C.O.R.E. and comes with optics mounting kit; larger slide stop; PC-tuned action; trigger stop
MSRP . . . . $720.00–$741.00

Smith & Wesson

SMITH & WESSON PERFORMANCE CENTER M&P40 M2.0 PRO SERIES C.O.R.E. READY

SMITH & WESSON PERFORMANCE CENTER SW22 VICTORY TARGET MODEL 6-INCH CARBON FIBER BARREL

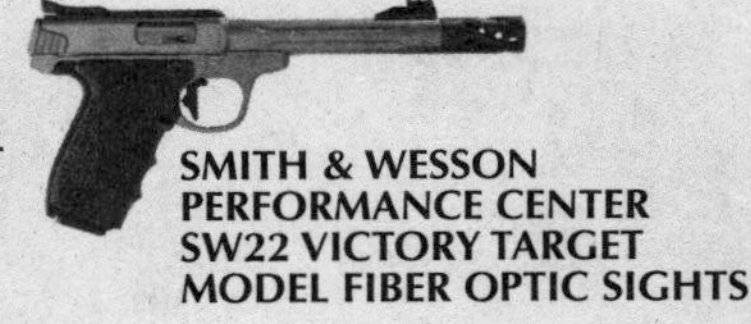

SMITH & WESSON PERFORMANCE CENTER SW22 VICTORY TARGET MODEL FIBER OPTIC SIGHTS

SMITH & WESSON SD9, SD40 FLAT DARK EARTH FRAME FINISH

SMITH & WESSON SD9, SD40 GRAY FRAME FINISH

SMITH & WESSON SD9 VE

SMITH & WESSON SW22 VICTORY

PERFORMANCE CENTER M&P40 M2.0 PRO SERIES C.O.R.E. READY

Action: Semiautomatic
Grips: Polymer
Barrel: 4.25 in., 5 in.
Sights: White three-dot
Weight: 29.4 oz.
Caliber: .40 S&W
Capacity: 10, 15 rounds
Features: Striker-fired pistol with a stainless steel barrel finished in Armonite; stainless slide finished in Armonite; four interchangeable palm swell size inserts; accessory rail; slide is C.O.R.E. and comes with optics mounting kit
MSRP . . . . $720.00–$741.00

PERFORMANCE CENTER SW22 VICTORY TARGET MODEL 6-INCH CARBON FIBER BARREL

Action: Semiautomatic
Grips: Tandemkross hiveGrip
Barrel: 6 in.
Sights: None
Weight: 33.1 oz.
Caliber: .22 LR
Capacity: 10 rounds
Features: An optics-ready target pistol with carbon fiber barrel; custom muzzle brake; Tandemkross hiveGrip with target thumb rest and texturing; top-side optics rail; flat face trigger; stainless steel frame; extended mag release; adjustable trigger stop
MSRP $706.00
With red-dot: $905.00

PERFORMANCE CENTER SW22 VICTORY TARGET MODEL FIBER OPTIC SIGHTS

Action: Semiautomatic
Grips: Tandemkross hiveGrip
Barrel: 6 in.
Sights: Adjustable fiber optic
Weight: 38.2 oz.
Caliber: .22 LR
Capacity: 10 rounds
Features: One for rimfire match competition, featuring a fluted target barrel; Tandemkross hiveGrip with thumb rest and texturing; flat face trigger; adjustable trigger stop; beveled magazine well; fiber optic sights with adjustable rear; custom muzzle break; Picatinny rail; stainless steel frame and barrel
MSRP $706.00

SD9, SD40 FLAT DARK EARTH FRAME FINISH

Action: Semiautomatic
Grips: Synthetic
Barrel: 4 in.
Sights: White three-dot
Weight: 22.3 oz.
Caliber: 9mm, .40 S&W
Capacity: 14, 16 rounds
Features: Self-Defense Trigger textured grip; accessory rail; slide serrations front; gray frame with matte black slide
MSRP $389.00

SD9, SD40 GRAY FRAME FINISH

Action: Semiautomatic
Grips: Synthetic
Barrel: 4 in.
Sights: White three-dot
Weight: 22.3 oz.
Caliber: 9mm, .40 S&W
Capacity: 14, 16 rounds
Features: Self-Defense Trigger textured grip; accessory rail; slide serrations front; frame is in Flat Dark Earth
MSRP $389.00

SD9 VE AND SD40 VE

Action: Striker Fired
Grips: Textured polymer

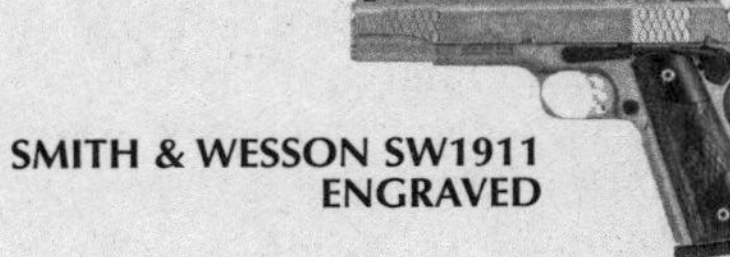

SMITH & WESSON SW1911 ENGRAVED

Barrel: 4 in.
Sights: White dot front, fixed 2-dot rear
Weight: 22.7 oz.
Caliber: 9mm, .40 S&W
Capacity: 10+1, 14+1, 16+1 rounds
Features: Lightweight polymer frame; front and rear slide serrations; Self Defense Trigger; ergonomic grip; Picatinny rail; two-tone finish Standard and low capacity
MSRP . . . . $389.00–$429.00

SW22 VICTORY

Action: SA
Grips: Polymer
Barrel: 5.5 in.
Sights: Green fiber optic front, adjustable fiber optic rear
Weight: 36 oz.
Caliber: .22 LR
Capacity: 10+1 rounds
Features: Removable interchangeable match-grade barrel; textured grip panels with finger cuts for easy magazine removal; Kryptek Highlander finish or stainless with threaded barrel
MSRP . . . . $428.00–$442.00

SW1911 ENGRAVED

Action: SA
Grips: Wood laminate E-Series
Barrel: 5 in.
Sights: White dot front, white 2-dot rear
Weight: 39.1 oz.
Caliber: .45 ACP
Capacity: 8+1 rounds
Features: Glass bead finish; machine scroll engraving; engraved, wooden presentation case
MSRP $1239.00

Springfield Armory

SPRINGFIELD ARMORY 911

SPRINGFIELD ARMORY 1911 EMP

SPRINGFIELD ARMORY 1911 EMP CHAMPION

SPRINGFIELD ARMORY 1911 EMP CHAMPION CONCEALED CARRY CONTOUR

SPRINGFIELD ARMORY 1911 LOADED

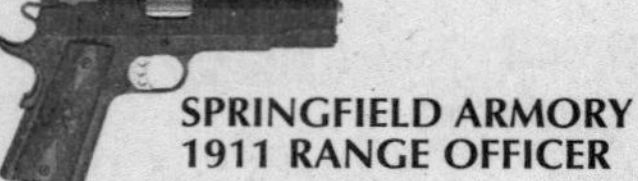

SPRINGFIELD ARMORY 1911 RANGE OFFICER

SPRINGFIELD ARMORY 1911 RANGE OFFICER CHAMPION

911

Action: Semiautomatic
Grips: G10, Hogue
Barrel: 2.7, 3 in.
Sights: ProGlo tritium front, white ***outline tritium rear***
Weight: 12.6–15.3 oz.
Caliber: .380 ACP, 9mm
Capacity: 6, 7 rounds
Features: Lightweight, aluminum-framed Carry gun with full-length guide rod, G10 grips, Octo-Grip texture on frontstrap and mainspring housing, night sights, ambidextrous extended thumb safety, trigger is set to five pounds. 9mm models available in Nitride with green G10 grips, Hogue rubber grips, Stainless with stainless slide, black frame and gray grips or grip laser. .380 models add all-over Desert FDE with Hogue grips; Cerakote Desert FDE frame with black nitride slide, black Sand Dune G10 grips; Platinum with clear hard-coat frame, Concrete Cerakote slide, engineered ivory grip panels; Titanium with all-over Cerakote Titanium finish, Blacked Out G10 grips; Cerakote Titanium frame with black nitride slide, black chevron G10 grips; Vintage Blue Cerakote frame with stainless slide, engineered ivory grips

9mm: . . . . $555.00–$580.00
.380: . . . . $429.00–$729.00

1911 EMP

Action: Semiautomatic
Grips: Thin line cocobolo wood
Barrel: 3 in.
Sights: Fixed low profile combat rear, dovetail
Weight: 26 oz.–33 oz.
Caliber: 9mm, .40 S&W
Capacity: 3–9 (9mm) or 3–8 (.40 S&W) rounds
Features: Forged stainless steel, satin finish; dual spring recoil system with full length guide rod

Black: $1104.00
Bi-Tone: $1249.00

1911 EMP 4-INCH CHAMPION

Action: SA semiautomatic
Grips: Cocobolo
Barrel: 4 in.
Sights: Three dot iron w/ fiber optic front and white dot rear
Weight: 31 oz. (9mm)
Caliber: 9mm, .40 S&W
Capacity: 9, 10 rounds
Features: Ambidextrous safety levers; match-grade barrel; Posi-Lock grip texture to the front strap; forged aluminum alloy frame with black hardcoat anodized finish

MSRP $1177.00

1911 EMP CHAMPION CONCEALED CARRY CONTOUR

Action: Semiautomatic
Grips: G10
Barrel: 4 in.
Sights: Fiber optic front, low-profile combat rear
Weight: 30.5 oz.
Caliber: 9mm
Capacity: 9 rounds
Features: Longer barrel; frame trimmed for concealment; bevel-cut mainspring housing; contouring to prevent snagging and printing; stainless steel match-grade bull barrel; fully supported feed ramp; satin slide; black hard coat anodized aluminum alloy frame; Posi-Lok texturing on rear and front straps; premium carry case; three magazines

MSRP $1220.00

1911 LOADED

Action: Semiautomatic
Grips: Synthetic
Barrel: 5 in.
Sights: Fixed combat, 3-dot tritium
Weight: 34–43 oz.
Caliber: .45 ACP
Features: Forged steel; integral accessory rail; GI-style recoil system. Six versions include Marine Corps Operator with gray G10 grips, Olive Drab Armory Kote frame and Black Armory Kote slide; Marine Corps Operator with Olive Drab Armory Kote frame, Black Armory Kote slide, and wraparound Pachmayr grips; Operator with all-over Black Armory Kote and black G10 grips; Loaded with Black-T slide, Parkerized frame, and cocobolo grips; Loaded Stainless with stainless frame and slide and cocobolo grips

Marine Corps Operator: . . $1308.00
Operator: $1409.00
Loaded: $950.00
Loaded Stainless: $1004.00

1911 RANGE OFFICER

Action: Semiautomatic
Grips: Cocobolo
Barrel: 5 in.
Sights: Adjustable
Weight: 41 oz.
Caliber: .45 ACP, 9mm
Capacity: 9 rounds
Features: Designed for competitive shooters, with GI-style recoil system, national match stainless barrel with fully supported ramp, Cross Cannon double diamond cocobolo grips, fiber optic front sight in shielded tube, flat mainspring housing, aluminum match trigger, skeletonized hammer

Parkerized: $942.00
Stainless: $1057.00
Parkerized with rail: $1042.00

1911 RANGE OFFICER CHAMPION

Action: Semiautomatic
Grips: Wood
Barrel: 4 in.
Sights: Fixed
Weight: 30 oz.
Caliber: .45 ACP
Capacity: 7 rounds
Features: Grips are Cross Cannon double diamond cocobolo; fiber optic front and low profile combat rear; dual spring recoil system with full length guide rod

MSRP $924.00

SPRINGFIELD ARMORY 1911 RANGE OFFICER ELITE OPERATOR

SPRINGFIELD ARMORY 1911 RONIN OPERATOR

SPRINGFIELD ARMORY 1911 TRP

SPRINGFIELD ARMORY DEFEND YOUR LEGACY 1911 MIL-SPEC

SPRINGFIELD ARMORY DEFEND YOUR LEGACY XD

SPRINGFIELD ARMORY HELLCAT MICRO-COMPACT OSP

SPRINGFIELD ARMORY SAINT PISTOL

1911 RANGE OFFICER ELITE OPERATOR

Action: Semiautomatic
Grips: G10
Barrel: 5 in.
Sights: Fiber optic front, Tactical Rack white dot rear
Weight: 41 oz.
Caliber: 10mm
Capacity: 9, 7 rounds
Features: Steel barrel; fully supported ramp; full-size frame of aluminum alloy; G-10 grips; Black-T surface treatment; Gen 2 trigger; GI recoil system; ambidextrous safety; forged steel slide; includes two magazines
MSRP $1145.00

1911 RONIN

Action: Semiautomatic
Grips: Laminate
Barrel: 4.25 in., 5 in.
Sights: Fiber optic front, tactical-rack white dot rear
Weight: 41 oz.
Caliber: 9mm, .45 ACP
Capacity: 8, 9 rounds
Features: A very nice full- or Commander-size pistol for competition or carry, with a duo-tone forged slide and frame; checkered "crossed cannon" laminate grips; hammer-forged barrel; magazines with basepad; grip safety with memory bump; Gen2 speed trigger;
MSRP $849.00

1911 TRP

Action: Semiautomatic
Grips: G10 composite
Barrel: 5 in.
Sights: Front tritium 3-dot, fixed low profile combat rear, dovetail
Weight: 42–45 oz.
Caliber: .45 ACP
Capacity: 2–7 rounds
Features: Forged National Match frames, National Match barrels, three-dot low-profile combat tritium sights, two-piece National Match guide rod, G10 grips. Five versions include: Black Armory Kote with gray/black grips; Stainless Steel with black grips; Operator with gray/black grips and rail; Operator Tactical Gray with gray/black grips and rail; Operator Black Armory Kote with black grips and full-length under-rail
Black Armory Kote: $1648.00
Stainless Steel:. $1648.00
Operator: $1730.00

DEFEND YOUR LEGACY 1911 MIL-SPEC

Action: Semiautomatic
Grips: Wood
Barrel: 5 in.
Sights: Three-dot combat
Weight: 39 oz.
Caliber: .45 ACP
Capacity: 7 rounds
Features: Faithful to GI originals with a fully forged frame and slide in Parkerized finish; checkered wood grips; match-grade barrel; GI-style recoil system
Black $640.00
Stainless. $849.00

DEFEND YOUR LEGACY XD

Action: Semiautomatic
Grips: Polymer
Barrel: 3 in.
Sights: Steel three-dot
Weight: 26 oz.
Caliber: 9mm
Capacity: 13 rounds
Features: A subcompact with great capacity; full-length guide rod with dual springs; forged steel slide with Melonite finish; steel barrel with Melonite finish;
MSRP $399.00

HELLCAT MICRO-COMPACT

Action: Semiautomatic
Grips: Polymer
Barrel: 3 in.
Sights: Tritium front, tactical-rack U-Dot rear
Weight: 17.9 oz.
Caliber: 9mm
Capacity: 11, 13 rounds
Features: A micro-compact with capacity and features that include a steel, hammer-forged barrel with Melonite finish; Adaptive Grip Texture; full-length guide rod; dual captive recoil springs; billet machined slide with Melonite finish; OSP is an optics-ready version
Standard . . . . $569.00–$610.00
OSP . . . . $599.00–$643.00
OSP with Shield SMSC red-dot $799.00

SAINT PISTOL

Action: Semiautomatic
Grips: Synthetic
Barrel: 7.5, 9 in.
Sights: None
Weight: 88–89 oz.
Caliber: 5.56 NATO
Capacity: 10, 30 rounds
Features: Forged 7075 T6 aluminum upper and lower; direct impingement pistol-length gas port; low-profile pinned gas block; SB Tactical stock; SBX-K forearm brace; GI-style charging handle; Bravo Company Mod 3 pistol grip; Springfield's own nickel-boron-coated G1 trigger; 1:7 twist Melonite-treated barrel; heavy Tungsten Carbine H buffer assembly; aluminum M-LOK free-floating handguard with locking tabs and a forward hand stop; rail space over the receiver and at the barrel end
MSRP $895.00

Springfield Armory

SPRINGFIELD ARMORY XD-E 3.3 SINGLE STACK

SPRINGFIELD ARMORY XD-E SINGLE-STACK

SPRINGFIELD ARMORY XD-M

SPRINGFIELD ARMORY XD-M ELITE

SPRINGFIELD ARMORY XD-M ELITE PRECISION

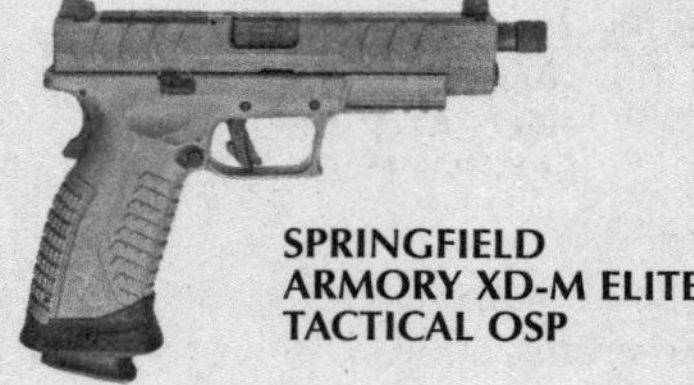
SPRINGFIELD ARMORY XD-M ELITE TACTICAL OSP

SPRINGFIELD ARMORY XD-S MOD.2

XD-E 3.3 SINGLE STACK

Action: Semiautomatic
Grips: Synthetic
Barrel: 3.3 in.
Sights: Fiber optic front, two-dot combat rear
Weight: 23–25 oz.
Caliber: 9mm, .45 ACP
Capacity: 6, 7, 8, 9 rounds
Features: Compact concealed carry pistol; hammer-forged steel barrel treated with Melonite; a true double/single-action with an exposed hammer; added grip texture
9mm: $542.00
.45 ACP: $580.00

XD-E 3.8-IN., 4.5-IN. SINGLE STACK

Action: Semiautomatic
Grips: Polymer
Barrel: 3.8 in., 4.5 in.
Sights: Fiber optic front, white dot rear
Weight: 24 oz., 25 oz.
Caliber: 9mm
Capacity: 8, 9 rounds
Features: Subcompact 9mm that comes with an eight-round flush and extended nine-round magazine; enhanced grip texture; DA/SA
MSRP $542.00

XD-M

Action: DA semiautomatic
Grips: Polymer
Barrel: 4.5 in., 5.25 in.
Sights: Three-dot
Weight: 27.5 oz.–32 oz.
Caliber: .45 ACP, 10mm
Features: "M" features include a full-length guide rod; backstraps and two magazines; "all-terrain" texture; deep slide serrations; match-grade barrel; standard and threaded models have 4.5-in. barrel; OSP threaded is in 10mm only; Competition variants have 5.25-in. barrel
Standard: $652.00
Threaded: $673.00
OSP Threaded: $695.00
Competition: $779.00

XD-M ELITE

Action: Semiautomatic
Grips: Polymer
Barrel: 3.8 in., 4.5 in.
Sights: Fiber optic front, tactical-rack U-Dot rear
Weight: 28 oz., 29 oz.
Caliber: 9mm
Capacity: 20 rounds
Features: Match Enhanced Trigger Assembly; removeable magwell; match-grade chamber; loaded chamber indicator; ambidextrous slide stop; forged steel slide with Melonite finish and front and rear slide serrations; hammer-forged steel barrel with Melonite finish
MSRP $590.00

XD-M ELITE PRECISION

Action: Semiautomatic
Grips: Polymer
Barrel: 5.25 in.
Sights: Fiber optic front, adjustable target rear
Weight: 30 oz.
Caliber: 9mm
Capacity: 22 rounds
Features: Match Enhanced Trigger Assembly; removeable magwell; match-grade chamber; loaded chamber indicator; ambidextrous slide stop; forged steel slide with Melonite finish and front and rear slide serrations
MSRP $653.00

XD-M ELITE TACTICAL OSP

Action: Semiautomatic
Grips: Polymer
Barrel: 5.28 in.
Sights: Suppressor-height co-witness
Weight: 30 oz.
Caliber: 9mm
Capacity: 22 rounds
Features: Match Enhanced Trigger Assembly; removeable magwell; match-grade chamber; loaded chamber indicator; ambidextrous slide stop; forged steel slide in Cerakote Desert flat dark earth, with front and rear slide serrations and optics ready
MSRP $709.00

XD-S MOD.2

Action: Semiautomatic
Grips: Polymer
Barrel: 3.3 in.
Sights: Fiber optic front; drift-adjustable steel rear
Weight: 21.5 oz.–23 oz.
Caliber: 9mm
Capacity: 7, 8 rounds
Features: A CCW gun featuring a dual-spring full-length guide rod; aggressive grip texturing; seven-round flush-fit mag; eight-round mag with Mid-Mag X-Tension
Standard: $425.00
With Crimson Trace red-dot: $549.00

Staccato 2011

STACCATO 2011
STACCATO XC

STACCATO 2011
STACCATO XL

STACCATO XC

Action: Semiautomatic
Grips: Synthetic
Barrel: 5 in.
Sights: Dawson fiber optic front, DUO rear
Weight: N/A
Caliber: 9mm
Capacity: 17, 20 rounds
Features: Gets the DUO (Dawson Universal Optic) Tactical Carry system which works with Leupold Delta Point Pro and Trijicon RMR red-dots with co-witness-height sights; competition bull barrel; Dawson 5.0 Adaptive Tool-less recoil system; 2011 G2 full-length grip with Tactical Advantage magwell
MSRP $4299.00

STACCATO XL

Action: Semiautomatic
Grips: Synthetic
Barrel: 5.4 in.
Sights: Dawson fiber optic front, adjustable STI rear
Weight: N/A
Caliber: 9mm, .40 S&W
Capacity: 15, 16, 18, 20 rounds
Features: The first of the Staccato line to be available in .40 S&W (as well as 9mm); bull barrel; ambidextrous safety; 2.5-lb. trigger; Dawson 5.4 Adaptive Tool-less recoil system; 2011 G2 grip with Tactical Advantage Magwell; billet steel frame; in Diamond Like all black or Tuxedo black frame/chrome slide
MSRP . . . . $3399.00–$3499.00

Standard Manufacturing Co.

STANDARD MANUFACTURING CO. SINGLE ACTION REVOLVER NICKEL PLATED

STANDARD MANUFACTURING CO. S333 THUNDERSTRUCK

STANDARD MANUFACTURING CO. SINGLE ACTION REVOLVER NICKEL PLATED C-COVERAGE ENGRAVING

S333 THUNDERSTRUCK

Action: Revolver
Grips: Polymer
Barrel: 1.25 in.
Sights: Ramp front, integral raised groove rear
Weight: N/A
Caliber: .22 Win. Mag.
Capacity: 8 rounds
Features: Interesting double-barrel revolver; each pull of the trigger fires two shots simultaneously; DAO
MSRP $429.00

SINGLE ACTION REVOLVER NICKEL PLATED

Action: Revolver
Grips: Walnut
Barrel: 4.75 in., 5.5 in., 7.5 in.
Sights: Blade front, groove rear
Weight: 40 oz.
Caliber: .45 LC
Capacity: 6 rounds
Features: A solid 4140 steel SA revolver with one- or two-piece figured walnut grips; full nickel-plating with fire-blued screws and pins
MSRP $1995.00

SINGLE ACTION REVOLVER NICKEL PLATED C-COVERAGE ENGRAVING

Action: Revolver
Grips: Walnut
Barrel: 4.75 in., 5.5 in., 7.5 in.
Sights: Blade front, groove rear
Weight: 40 oz.
Caliber: .45 LC
Capacity: 6 rounds
Features: Similar to Standard's full nickel-plated SA, but with 75% scroll engraving on frame, barrel, and cylinder; two-piece grip only
MSRP $3495.00

Steyr Arms

STEYR A2 MF

A2 MF

Action: Semiautomatic
Grips: Polymer
Barrel: 4.5 in.
Sights: Trapezoid
Weight: 27 oz.
Caliber: 9mm
Capacity: 10, 17 rounds
Features: MF stands for Modular Frame, which features interchangeable, textured backstraps and grips; trigger, drop, indirect firing pin safeties and manual lock; 5-pound trigger; under rail
MSRP $685.00

Stoeger Industries

STOEGER STR-9

STR-9

Action: Semiautomatic
Grips: Polymer
Barrel: 4.17 in.
Sights: Three-dot; tritium
Weight: 24 oz.
Caliber: 9mm
Capacity: 15 rounds
Features: Striker-fire pistol; double-stack magazine; aggressive slide serrations fore and aft; backstrap and grip texturing; fingergrooves; under rail. Three configurations: 1 magazine/1 backstrap; 3 magazines/3 backstraps; 3 magazines/3 backstraps with tritium sights
MSRP . . . . $329.00–$399.00

Taurus

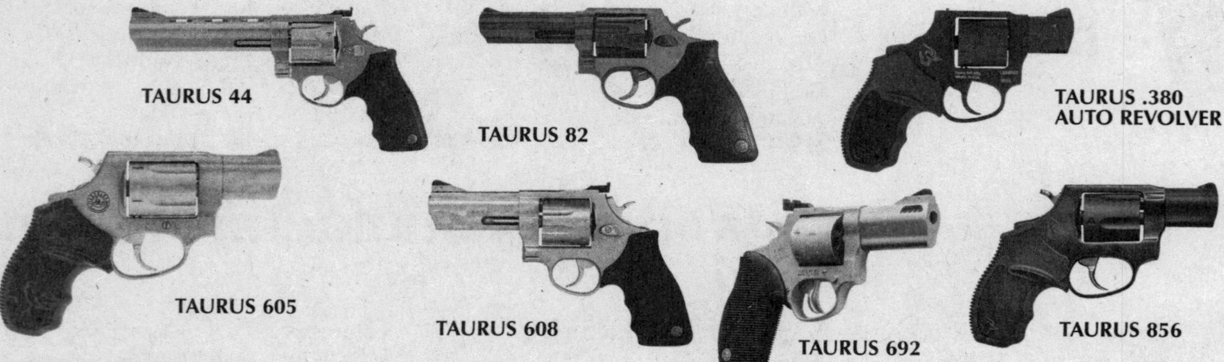

TAURUS 44 TAURUS 82 TAURUS .380 AUTO REVOLVER TAURUS 605 TAURUS 608 TAURUS 692 TAURUS 856

REVOLVERS

44

Action: Revolver
Grips: Soft rubber
Barrel: 4 in., 6.5 in., 8.4 in.
Sights: Fixed
Weight: 45–57 oz.
Caliber: .44 Mag.
Capacity: 6 rounds
Features: Transfer bar; ported barrel; matte stainless steel finish; double and single-action
4.5-, 6-in. barrel: $660.94
8.4-in barrel: $677.52

82

Action: Revolver
Grips: Rubber
Barrel: 4 in.
Sights: Fixed
Weight: 36.5 oz.
Caliber: .38 Spl. +P
Capacity: 6 rounds
Features: Transfer bar; steel construction with blued finish; single/double-action trigger
MSRP $431.35

.380 AUTO REVOLVER

Action: Revolver
Grips: Rubber
Barrel: 1.75 in.
Sights: Adjustable rear
Weight: 15.5 oz.
Caliber: .380 ACP
Capacity: 5 rounds
Features: Double-action trigger; fully enclosed hammer; blued or matte stainless finish; bobbed hammer
Blue: $488.15
Stainless: $524.27

605

Action: Revolver
Grips: Rubber
Barrel: 2 in.
Sights: Fixed
Weight: 24 oz.
Caliber: .357 Mag
Capacity: 5 rounds
Features: Transfer bar safety; steel construction with blued or stainless finish; single-double action trigger
MSRP . . . . $353.24–$376.59

608

Action: Revolver
Grips: Rubber
Barrel: 4 in., 6.5 in.
Sights: Fixed front, adjustable rear
Weight: 44 oz.–51 oz.
Caliber: .357 Mag
Capacity: 8 rounds
Features: Matte stainless steel finish; transfer bar; large frame; steel frame; Taurus security system; porting
MSRP $775.23

692

Action: Revolver
Grips: Rubber
Barrel: 3 in., 6.5 in.
Sights: Fixed front, adjustable rear
Weight: 35.27 oz., 45.85 oz.
Caliber: .357 Mag., 9mm
Capacity: 7 rounds
Features: User can swap out .38 Special/.357 Mag. cylinder for one in 9mm; unfluted cylinder and porting; 6.5-in. barrel has a vent rib; matte blue or matte stainless finish
Blue: . . . . $639.45–$652.50
Stainless: . . . . $691.95–$706.08

856

Action: Revolver
Grips: Rubber
Barrel: 2 in.
Sights: Serrated ramp front, notch rear
Weight: 16 oz., 22 oz.
Caliber: .38 Spec.
Capacity: 6 rounds
Features: Snub-nosed .38; ribbed rubber grips; matte blue, matte stainless, matte natural anodized and black oxide finishes; UL model is Ultralight 16 oz.; both versions +P rated
MSRP . . . . $341.86–$500.30

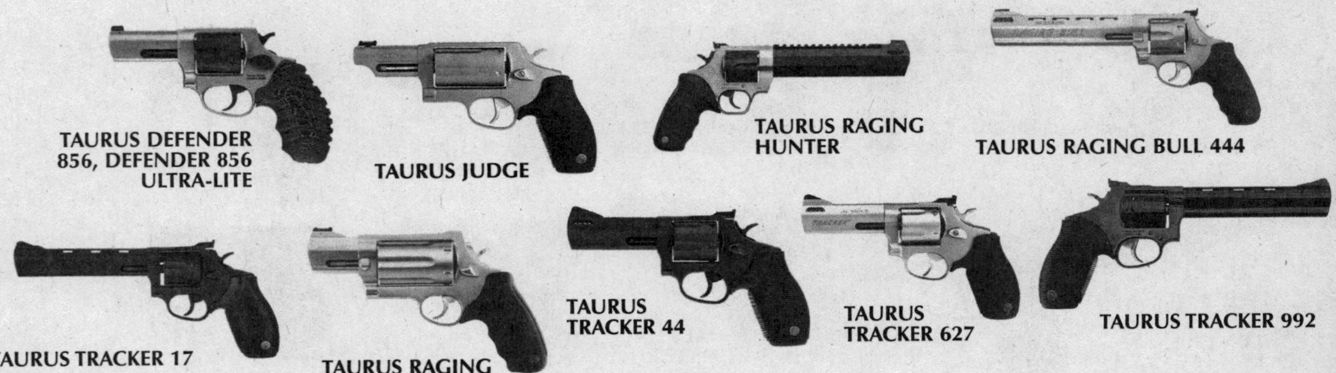

TAURUS DEFENDER 856, DEFENDER 856 ULTRA-LITE

TAURUS JUDGE

TAURUS RAGING HUNTER

TAURUS RAGING BULL 444

TAURUS TRACKER 17

TAURUS RAGING JUDGE 513

TAURUS TRACKER 44

TAURUS TRACKER 627

TAURUS TRACKER 992

DEFENDER 856, DEFENDER 856 ULTRA-LITE

Action: Revolver
Grips: Laminate, rubber
Barrel: 3 in.
Sights: Orange outline night sight front
Weight: 16 oz.–35 oz.
Caliber: .38 Spec.
Capacity: 6 rounds
Features: +P rated. Several configurations include: tungsten Cerakote finish with brown Altamont wood grips; matte stainless finish with Hogue rubber grips; matte stainless frame/barrel and matte black cylinder finishes with gray/black VZ laminate grips; hard-anodized black finish Hogue rubber grips; Ultra-Lite models in the matte stainless or hard anodized matte black
MSRP . . . . $389.88–$454.50

JUDGE

Action: DA/SA revolver
Grips: Taurus rubber grips
Barrel: 3 in.
Sights: Red fiber optic, fixed
Weight: 29–36.8 oz.
Caliber: .45 Colt/.410
Capacity: 5 rounds
Features: Firing pin block, transfer bar safety; compact frame; matte stainless steel finish; steel construction
MSRP . . . . $512.11–$560.02

RAGING BULL 444

Action: Revolver
Grips: Rubber w/cushioned insert
Barrel: 6.5 in., 8.38 in.
Sights: Partridge front, adjustable rear
Weight: 53 oz.–63 oz.
Caliber: .44 Mag.
Capacity: 6 rounds
Features: Steel construction with blued or stainless steel finish; transfer bar; dual lockup cylinder; porting; Taurus security system
MSRP $944.50

RAGING HUNTER

Action: Revolver
Grips: Rubber
Barrel: 5.12 in., 6.75 in., 8.375 in.
Sights: Fixed front, adjustable rear
Weight: 55 oz.
Caliber: .44 Mag.
Capacity: 6 rounds
Features: Optics rail; a steel sleeved barrel in an aluminum housing, porting, and cushioned grip inserts in all-over matte black or a two-tone with a stainless frame
Blue: . . . . $968.18–$928.25
Stainless/blue: . . . . $938.30–$983.33

RAGING JUDGE 513

Action: DA/SA revolver
Grips: Rubber with soft cushion insert
Barrel: 3 in., 6.5 in.
Sights: Fiber optic front, fixed rear
Weight: 60.6 oz.–73 oz.
Caliber: .410/.45 Colt, .454 Casull
Capacity: 6 rounds
Features: Stainless steel finish; "Raging Bull" backstrap for added cushioning
MSRP $1167.75

TRACKER 17

Action: Revolver
Grips: Rubber with ribs
Barrel: 6.5 in.
Sights: Fixed front, adjustable rear
Weight: 47 oz.
Caliber: .17 HMR
Capacity: 7 rounds
Features: Matte stainless steel or blued finish; transfer bar; steel frame; porting
Blue: $541.45
Stainless: $594.76

TRACKER 44

Action: Revolver
Grips: Rubber with ribs
Barrel: 4 in.
Sights: Fixed front, adjustable rear
Weight: 35 oz.
Caliber: .44 Mag.
Capacity: 5 rounds
Features: Matte stainless steel or blued finish; transfer bar; steel frame; barrel porting; vent rib
Blue: $578.12
Stainless: $594.70

TRACKER 627

Action: Revolver
Grips: Rubber with ribs
Barrel: 4, 6.5 in.
Sights: Fixed front, adjustable rear
Weight: 35–40 oz.
Caliber: .357 Mag.
Capacity: 6 rounds
Features: Matte stainless steel medium frame revolver; barrel porting; 6.5-inch barrel has topside vent rib
MSRP $534.82

TRACKER 992

Action: SA/DA revolver
Grips: Taurus Ribber
Barrel: 4 in., 6.5 in.
Sights: Adjustable
Weight: 55 oz.
Caliber: .22 LR
Capacity: 9 rounds
Features: The versatile Tracker 992 easily transforms from .22 LR to .22 Magnum in seconds with its breakthrough removable cylinder; perfect for plinking, target practice, or varmint hunting
Blue: $639.45
Stainless: $706.08

Taurus

SEMIAUTOMATICS

22 POLY

Action: DA semiautomatic
Grips: Polymer
Barrel: 2.3 in.
Sights: Fixed
Weight: 11.3 oz.
Caliber: .22 LR
Capacity: 8+1
Features: Polymer/blued steel construction; blued steel finish; tip-up barrel
MSRP . . . . $255.11–$299.30

92

Action: Semiautomatic
Grips: Checkered rubber
Barrel: 5 in.
Sights: Fixed-1 dot front, fixed-2 dots rear
Weight: 34 oz.
Caliber: 9mm
Capacity: 10+1 or 17+1 rounds
Features: Blued, stainless steel finish; steel/alloy construction; firing pin block, hammer decocker, manual safety
Blue: $544.27
Stainless: $555.67

1911 COMMANDER

Action: Semiautomatic
Grips: Synthetic
Barrel: 4.2 in.
Sights: Novak drift adjustable front and rear
Weight: 38 oz.
Caliber: .45 ACP
Capacity: 8 rounds
Features: Numerous finishes and grip combinations; Novak drift-adjustable sights; grip safety; manual safety
MSRP . . . . $626.27–$704.00

1911 OFFICER

Action: Semiautomatic
Grips: Synthetic
Barrel: 3.5 in.
Sights: Novak drift adjustable front and rear
Weight: 34.5 oz.
Caliber: .45 ACP
Capacity: 6 rounds
Features: Standard matte black finish or Cerakote finishes in tungsten, desert sand, and MS green; shortest model in the 1911 line
MSRP . . . . $639.45–$739.20

G2C

Action: Semiautomatic
Grips: Polymer
Barrel: 3.2 oz.
Sights: Blade front, adjustable rear
Weight: 22 oz.
Caliber: 9mm, .40 S&W
Capacity: 12, 10 rounds
Features: A double-stack striker-fire good for CCW, target practice, or competition
MSRP . . . . $272.20–$346.42

G2S

Action: Semiautomatic
Grips: Polymer
Barrel: 3.2 in.
Sights: Blade front, adjustable rear
Weight: 20 oz.
Caliber: 9mm, .40 S&W
Capacity: 7, 6 rounds
Features: A single-stack striker-fire for home-defense and target practice; various frame and slide color options available
MSRP . . . . $253.24–$346.42

G3

Action: Semiautomatic
Grips: Polymer
Barrel: 4 in.
Sights: White three-dot
Weight: 25 oz.
Caliber: 9mm
Capacity: 10, 15, 17 rounds
Features: A single-action striker-fire with a safety trigger; a carbons steel slide in matte black or a stainless steel slide in matte stainless; full-size frame
Standard $313.94
Tenifer . . . . $298.17–$345.23

SPECTRUM

Action: Semiautomatic
Grips: Soft-touch overmold
Barrel: 2.8 in.
Sights: Integral low-profile front and rear
Weight: 10 oz.
Caliber: .380 ACP
Capacity: 6 rounds
Features: Ultralight striker-fired micro-pistol; soft-touch overmold grip; slide serrations; soft-edged frame; reversible magazine release; customizable color options
MSRP $224.24

TH9

Action: Semiautomatic
Grips: Synthetic
Barrel: 3.54 in., 4.27 in.
Sights: Novak drift adjustable front and rear
Weight: 28.2 oz., 25 oz.
Caliber: 9mm
Capacity: 13, 19 rounds
Features: Lightweight polymer frame DA/SA; dual trigger safety system; ambidextrous controls; underbarrel Picatinny rail; interchangeable backstrap
MSRP . . . . $346.97–$376.95

TX22

Action: Semiautomatic
Grips: Polymer
Barrel: 4.1 in.
Sights: Blade front, notch rear
Weight: 17.3 oz.
Caliber: .22 LR
Capacity: 10 rounds
Features: A .22 pistol to fill the hands; striker-fire action; Taurus' Pittman Trigger System
MSRP $316.76

Taylor's & Co. Firearms

TAYLOR'S & CO. 1873 CATTLEMAN PHOTO ENGRAVED

TAYLOR'S & CO. 1873 GUNFIGHTER

TAYLOR'S & CO. 1873 TAYLOR GAMBLER

TAYLOR'S & CO. RUNNIN' IRON

TAYLOR'S & CO. SMOKE WAGON

1873 CATTLEMAN PHOTO ENGRAVED

Action: SA revolver
Grips: Walnut
Barrel: 4.75 in., 5.5 in., 7.5 in.
Sights: Fixed
Weight: 2 lb. 4 oz.–3 lb. 6 oz.
Caliber: .357 Mag., .45 LC
Capacity: 6 rounds
Features: Coin finish with charcoal blued screws; laser-engraved and hand chased; forged frame
MSRP $945.05

1873 GUNFIGHTER

Action: SA revolver
Grips: Walnut
Barrel: 5.5 in.
Sights: Fixed
Weight: 2 lb. 5 oz.
Caliber: .357 Mag., .45 Colt
Capacity: 6 rounds
Features: Special Army-sized grip; steel trigger guard and backstrap; blued finish with case-hardened frame; forged frame
Smooth grips: $654.62
Checkered grips: $623.08

1873 TAYLOR GAMBLER

Action: SA revolver
Grips: Walnut
Barrel: 4.75 in., 5.5 in.
Sights: Fixed
Weight: 2 lb. 5 oz.
Caliber: .357 Mag., .45 Colt
Capacity: 6 rounds
Features: Checkered walnut grip; blued color case-hardened frame
Standard: $618.24
Taylor tuned: $764.49

RUNNIN' IRON

Action: SA revolver
Grips: Checkered walnut
Barrel: 3.5 in., 4.75 in.
Sights: Wider fixed, open
Weight: 39 oz.
Caliber: .45 Colt, .357 Mag.
Capacity: 6 rounds
Features: Designed for the sport of mounted shooting; stainless or blued with low, wide hammer spur; checkered, one-piece gunfighter style grips in walnut or black polymer; wide trigger and extra clearance at front and rear of cylinder
Standard: . . . . $653.99–$679.23
Taylor tuned: . . . . . $800.24–$825.48

SMOKE WAGON

Action: SA revolver
Grips: Checkered wood
Barrel: 3.5 in., 4.75 in., 5.5 in.
Sights: Open rear sight groove, wide angle front sight blade
Weight: 40 oz.
Caliber: .357 Mag., .45 Colt, .44-40 Win.
Capacity: 6 rounds
Features: Low profile hammer; custom tuning, custom hammer and base pin springs; jig-cut positive angles on trigger and sears; wire bolt and trigger springs
Standard: . . . . $622.24–$630.65
Taylor tuned: . . . . . $768.49–$776.90

TNW Firearms

AERO SURVIVAL PISTOL

Action: Semiautomatic
Grips: Synthetic
Barrel: 8 in.
Sights: Flip-up front and rear
Weight: 88 oz.
Caliber: 9mm, 10mm, .40 S&W, .45 ACP, .460 Rowland, .357 SIG
Capacity: Varies with magazine
Features: Reduced SBR version of TNW's Aero Survival Rifle; compact, lightweight, and easily disassembled; takes Glock-style magazines; hard black anodized or variegated finishes in pink/black or green/black; some restricted state versions available
MSRP $899.00

TNW FIREARMS AERO SURVIVAL PISTOL

Traditions Firearms

TRADITIONS FIREARMS FRONTIER

TRADITIONS FIREARMS RAWHIDE

FRONTIER SERIES

Action: SA revolver
Grips: Simulated ivory or walnut
Barrel: 3.5 in., 4.75 in., 5.5 in., 7.5 in.
Sights: Front blade
Weight: N/A
Caliber: .357 Mag., .44 Mag., .45 Colt, .44-40 Win.
Capacity: 6 rounds
Features: 1873 single action revolvers; deep bluing and nickel frames and barrel or color case hardened frame; transfer bar safety system provides the highest lever of safety offered in an 1873 single action
MSRP . . . . $569.00–$689.00

RAWHIDE SERIES

Action: SA revolver
Grips: Walnut
Barrel: 4.75 in., 5.5 in., 7.5 in.
Sights: Front blade
Weight: N/A
Caliber: .45 Colt, .357 Mag., .22 LR, and .22 LR/.22 Mag.
Capacity: 6 rounds
Features: Quality single action shooter features at an affordable price; matte black finish that provides excellent corrosion resistance; transfer bar system provides the highest level of safety offered in an 1873 single action
MSRP . . . . $229.00–$474.00

Trailblazer Firearms

TRAILBLAZER FIREARMS LIFECARD .22LR

LIFECARD .22LR

Action: Single-shot
Grips: Aluminum
Barrel: 3 in.
Sights: None
Weight: 7 oz.
Caliber: .22LR
Capacity: 1 round
Features: Half-inch thick; barrel, bolt, and trigger are 4140 pre-hardened steel; handle is aluminum billet; folds to size of a stack of credit cards; full-size handle when unfolded; firearm will not fire when closed
MSRP $349.00

TriStar Sporting Arms

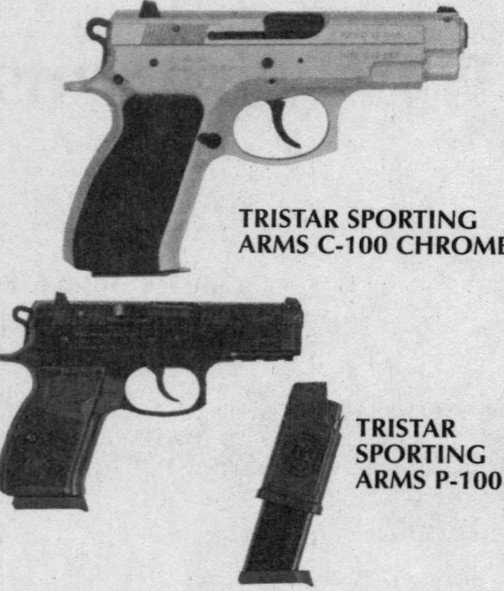

TRISTAR SPORTING ARMS C-100 CHROME

TRISTAR SPORTING ARMS P-100

C-100

Action: DA/SA semiautomatic
Grips: Polymer
Barrel: 3.9 in.
Sights: Rear dovetail, fixed front
Weight: 24.48 oz.–26.08 oz.
Caliber: 9mm
Capacity: 11, 15 rounds
Features: Produced to NATO specs; rear snag-free dovetail sights; fixed blade front sight; black polycoat finish; black polymer checkered grips; includes two magazines and a hard plastic case
Black Cerakote: $460.00
Tungsten Cerakote: $480.00

P-100

Action: Semiautomatic
Grips: Polymer
Barrel: 3.7 in.
Sights: Fixed front, rear dovetail
Weight: 2 lb. 5 oz.
Caliber: 9mm
Capacity: Detachable box, 11–15 rounds
Features: Steel frame and steel slide; double/single action; rear snag free dovetail sights and fixed blade front sight; Picatinny rail built into frame; Cerakote finish and black polymer checkered grips
MSRP $490.00

TriStar Sporting Arms

TRISTAR SPORTING ARMS T-100 BLUED

TRISTAR SPORTING ARMS P-120

P-120

Action: DA/SA semiautomatic
Grips: Polymer
Barrel: 4.7 in.
Sights: Rear dovetail, fixed front
Weight: 29.9 oz.
Caliber: 9mm
Capacity: 17 rounds
Features: Originally created for military use; constructed from steel alloy; blued or chrome finish; rear snag-free dovetail sights; fixed blade front sight; includes two magazines, cleaning kit, gun lock, and a black carrying case
Chrome: $510.00
Black Cerakote: $490.00

T-100

Action: DA/SA semiautomatic
Grips: Polymer
Barrel: 3.7 in.
Sights: Rear dovetail, fixed front
Weight: 26.24 oz.
Caliber: 9mm
Capacity: 15 rounds
Features: Compact pistol perfect for concealed carry; constructed from steel alloy; blued or chrome finish; rear snag-free dovetail sights; fixed blade front sight; includes two magazines, cleaning kit, gun lock, and a black carrying case
MSRP $460.00

Turnbull Restoration, Inc.

TURNBULL RESTORATION GOVERNMENT HERITAGE MODEL 1911

TURNBULL RESTORATION GOVERNMENT MODEL 1911

GOVERNMENT HERITAGE MODEL 1911

Action: Semiautomatic
Grips: Double-diamond walnut
Barrel: 5 in.
Sights: Titrium Kensights
Weight: 38 oz.
Caliber: .45 ACP
Capacity: 7 rounds
Features: Beavertail grip safety; steel parts, blue finished slide; color case hardened frame; checkered front strap
MSRP $3225.00

GOVERNMENT MODEL 1911

Action: Semiautomatic
Grips: Double-diamond walnut
Barrel: 5 in.
Sights: Titrium Kensights
Weight: 38 oz.
Caliber: .45 ACP
Capacity: 7 rounds
Features: Beavertail grip safety; steel parts, blue finished slide; blued frame; checkered front strap
MSRP $3025.00

Uberti

UBERTI 1851 NAVY CONVERSION

UBERTI 1851 NAVY CONVERSION WILD BILL

1851 NAVY CONVERSION

Action: SA revolver
Grips: Walnut
Barrel: 4.75 in., 5.5 in., 7.5 in.
Sights: Fixed, open
Weight: 42 oz.
Caliber: .38 Spl.
Capacity: 6 rounds
Features: Case-hardened frame octagonal barrel; brass backstrap and trigger guard; conversion revolver frames are retro-fitted with loading gates to accommodate metallic cartridges like the originals
MSRP $589.00

1851 NAVY CONVERSION WILD BILL

Action: Revolver
Grips: Simulated ivory
Barrel: 7.5 in.
Sights: Bead front, groove rear
Weight: 43 oz.
Caliber: .38 Special
Capacity: 6 rounds
Features: Based on the 1851 Navy with an unfluted barrel sporting light engraving; classic grip of simulated ivory; front bead; color case hardened frame; cylinder and barre in blue
MSRP $809.00

Uberti

UBERTI 1860 ARMY CONVERSION

UBERTI 1871–1872 OPEN-TOP CONVERSION

UBERTI 1873 SA CATTLEMAN

UBERTI 1873 .22 LR

UBERTI 1873 CATTLEMAN BONNEY

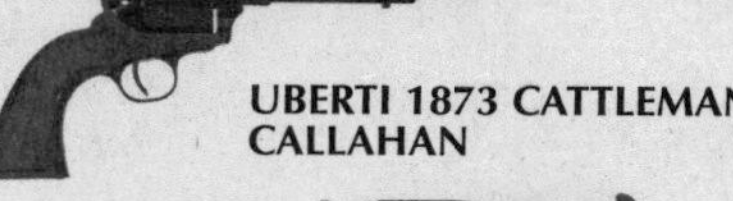
UBERTI 1873 CATTLEMAN CALLAHAN

UBERTI 1873 CATTLEMAN CODY MATCHING SET

UBERTI 1873 CATTLEMAN CHISHOLM

UBERTI 1873 CATTLEMAN DESPERADO

1860 ARMY CONVERSION

Action: SA revolver
Grips: Walnut
Barrel: 4.75 in., 5.5 in., 8 in.
Sights: Fixed, open
Weight: 42 oz.
Caliber: .38 Spl., .45 Colt
Capacity: 6 rounds
Features: Case-hardened frame; round barrel; steel backstrap and trigger guard; conversion revolver frames are retro-fitted with loading gates to accommodate metallic cartridges like the originals
MSRP. $619.00

1871–1872 OPEN-TOP CONVERSION

Action: SA revolver
Grips: Walnut
Barrel: 4.75 in., 5.5 in., 7.5 in.
Sights: Fixed, open
Weight: 42 oz.
Caliber: .38 Spl., .45 Colt
Capacity: 6 rounds
Features: 1872 model has steel backstrap and trigger guard; 1871 model has brass backstrap and trigger guard; case-hardened frame; round barrel; blued conversion revolver frames are retro-fitted with loading gates to accommodate metallic cartridges
1871 Navy: $549.00
1871 Army:. $579.00

1873 CATTLEMAN

Action: SA revolver
Grips: Walnut
Barrel: 4.75 in., 5.5 in., 7.5 in.
Sights: Fixed, open
Weight: 37 oz.
Caliber: .45 Colt
Capacity: 6 rounds
Features: Case-hardened frame; brass or steel backstrap and trigger guard; blued, nickel or stainless steel finish; fluted cylinder
Charcoal Blue: . . . . $669.00–$719.00
Nickel:. $689.00
Stainless: . . . .$679.00–$739.00

1873 CATTLEMAN .22 LR

Action: SA revolver
Grips: Walnut
Barrel: 4.75 in., 5.5 in., 7.5 in.
Sights: Fixed, open
Weight: 36.8 oz.
Caliber: .22 LR
Capacity: 6 and 12 round models
Features: Ideal for cowboy-action shooting practice; six-shot comes with brass or steel backstrap and trigger guard; case-hardened frame; blued finish
Six-shot:. $539.00
Twelve-shot: $589.00

1873 CATTLEMAN BONNEY

Action: Revolver
Grips: Simulated bison horn
Barrel: 5.5 in.
Sights: Blade front, groove rear
Weight: 37 oz.
Caliber: .45 LC
Capacity: 6 rounds
Features: Part of Uberti's 1873 Cattleman Series; SA; bird's head grip of simulated bison; color case hardened frame; blued barrel and cylinder
MSRP. $799.00

1873 CATTLEMAN CALLAHAN

Action: SA revolver
Grips: Walnut, black or mother-of-pearl synthetic
Barrel: 4.75 in., 6 in., 7.5 in.
Sights: Fixed
Weight: 42 oz.
Caliber: .44 Mag.
Capacity: 6 rounds
Features: Blued, stainless, case-hardened or Old West finish; target model has angled front target sight and adjustable notched rear blade
MSRP. $639.00

1873 CATTLEMAN CHISHOLM

Action: SA revolver
Grips: Checkered walnut
Barrel: 4.75 in., 5.5 in.
Sights: Fixed, open
Weight: 37 oz.
Caliber: .45 Colt
Capacity: 6 rounds
Features: Complete matte finished steel; fluted barrel
MSRP. $599.00

1873 CATTLEMAN CODY MATCHING SET

Action: SA revolver
Grips: Walnut
Barrel: 5.5 in.
Sights: Fixed, open
Weight: 37 oz.
Caliber: .45 Colt
Capacity: 6 rounds
Features: Fluted barrel; blued case-hardened frame; steel backstrap; trigger guard; the set shares matching serial numbers; available in nickel and ivory-style grip
MSRP. $1778.00

1873 CATTLEMAN DESPERADO

Action: SA revolver
Grips: Bison horn style
Barrel: 4.75 in., 5.5 in.
Sights: Fixed, open
Weight: 37 oz.
Caliber: .45 Colt
Capacity: 6 rounds
Features: Full nickel-plated steel; fluted barrel
MSRP. $889.00

UBERTI 1873 EL PATRÓN COWBOY MOUNTED SHOOTER (CMS)

UBERTI FIREARMS 1873 CATTLEMAN NEW MODEL DALTON

UBERTI FIREARMS 1873 SINGLE ACTION CATTLEMAN NEW MODEL DOC

UBERTI FIREARMS 1873 SINGLE ACTION CATTLEMAN NEW MODEL JESSE

UBERTI 1875 FRONTIER

UBERTI FIREARMS 1875 SINGLE ACTION ARMY OUTLAW FRANK

UBERTI 1890 SA POLICE REVOLVER

1873 CATTLEMAN EL PATRON COWBOY MOUNTED SHOOTER (CMS)

Action: SA revolver
Grips: Checkered walnut
Barrel: 3.5 in., 4 in.
Sights: EasyView
Weight: 37 oz.
Caliber: .45 Colt, .357 Mag.
Capacity: 6 rounds
Features: Blued or stainless steel finish; optional case-hardened frame; fluted barrel; fitted with U.S.-made Wolff springs; numbered cylinders
MSRP $669.00

1873 CATTLEMAN NEW MODEL DALTON

Action: Revolver
Grips: Pearl-style
Barrel: 5.5 in.
Sights: Blade front, notch rear
Weight: 36.8 oz.
Caliber: .357 Mag., .45 Colt
Capacity: 6 rounds
Features: Embellished with nearly full-coverage engraving; case-colored frame; polished blue barrel, hammer, trigger guard; based in the revolver owned by Bob Dalton of the famous Dalton gang
MSRP $1109.00

1873 SINGLE ACTION CATTLEMAN NEW MODEL DOC

Action: Revolver
Grips: Bison horn
Barrel: 5.5 in.
Sights: Metal blade front, receiver notch rear
Weight: 36.8 oz.
Caliber: .45 Colt
Capacity: 6 rounds
Features: Based on gambler and gunslinger Doc Holliday's revolver; short-barreled, nimble single-action 1873; all-over nickel-plating and pearl-style grips in a bird's-head design
MSRP $869.00

1873 SINGLE ACTION CATTLEMAN NEW MODEL JESSE

Action: Revolver
Grips: Pearl-style
Barrel: 4.75 in.
Sights: Metal blade front, receiver notch rear
Weight: 35.2 oz.
Caliber: .45 Colt
Capacity: 6 rounds
Features: Based on Jesse James' 1873 Colt; fluted cylinder; all-over polished blue finish; dark bison-horn grips
MSRP $759.00

1875 OUTLAW & FRONTIER

Action: SA revolver
Grips: Walnut
Barrel: 5.5 in. (Frontier), 7.5 in.
Sights: Fixed, open
Weight: 40–45 oz.
Caliber: .45 Colt
Capacity: 6 rounds
Features: Case-hardened or full nickel plated steel frame; steel backstrap and trigger guard; fluted cylinder
Outlaw case-hardened frame: $609.00
Outlaw full nickel-plating: . . $729.00
Frontier case-hardened frame: $609.00

1875 SINGLE ACTION ARMY OUTLAW FRANK

Action: Revolver
Grips: Ivory-style
Barrel: 7.5 in.
Sights: Metal blade front, receiver notch rear
Weight: 44.8 oz.
Caliber: .357 Mag., .45 Colt
Capacity: 6 rounds
Features: Replica of the 1875 Remington carried by outlaw Jesse James' brother Frank James; all-over nickel-plating; ivory-style grips; lanyard ring
MSRP $949.00

1890 SINGLE ACTION POLICE REVOLVER

Action: SA revolver
Grips: Walnut with lanyard ring
Barrel: 5.5 in.
Sights: Fixed, open
Weight: 42 oz.
Caliber: .45 Colt, .357 Mag.
Capacity: 6 rounds
Features: Blued steel frame, backstrap and trigger guard; fluted cylinder
MSRP $619.00

Uberti

UBERTI BIRD'S HEAD

UBERTI FIREARMS SHORT STROKE CMS PRO

UBERTI BISLEY

UBERTI STALLION

UBERTI FIREARMS EL PATRON GRIZZLY PAW

UBERTI TOP BREAK REVOLVER

BIRD'S HEAD

Action: SA revolver
Grips: Walnut
Barrel: 3.5 in., 4 in., 4.75 in., 5.5 in.
Sights: Fixed, open
Weight: 35 oz.
Caliber: .38 Spl., .45 Colt, .357 Mag.
Capacity: 6 rounds
Features: Case-hardened frame; steel backstrap and trigger guard; blued finish; bird head shape grip; Bird's Head Stallion Old West Defense is chambered in .38 Spl., has full matte finish, 3.5-in. barrel
Standard: . . . . $579.00–$589.00
Stallion Old West Defense: . . $589.00

BISLEY

Action: SA revolver
Grips: Bisley target style walnut
Barrel: 4.75 in., 5.5 in., 7.5 in.
Sights: Fixed, open
Weight: 40 oz.
Caliber: .45 Colt, .357 Mag.
Capacity: 6 rounds
Features: Case-hardened frame; steel backstrap and trigger guard; blued finish; fluted cylinder
MSRP $619.00

EL PATRON GRIZZLY PAW

Action: Revolver
Grips: Walnut
Barrel: 4.75 in., 5.5 in.
Sights: EasyView sights
Weight: 36.8 oz.
Caliber: .357 Mag., .45 Colt
Capacity: 6 rounds
Features: Made for those with larger hands ("grizzly paws"); checkered walnut 1860 Army grips; blued barrel and cylinder; blued, case-hardened frame; cylinder has numbered chambers
MSRP $659.00

SHORT STROKE CMS PRO

Action: Revolver
Grips: Walnut
Barrel: 3.5 in.
Sights: Blade front, notch rear
Weight: N/A
Caliber: .357 Mag., .45 Colt
Capacity: 6 rounds
Features: Designed specifically for cowboy action competition; short-stroke hammer that Uberti says has 20% less travel than other single-action revolvers; custom mainspring housing; checkered grip
MSRP . . . . $739.00–$909.00

STALLION

Action: SA revolver
Grips: Walnut
Barrel: 4.75 in., 5.5 in., 6.5 in.
Sights: Fixed, open
Weight: 32 oz.
Caliber: .22 LR, .22 LR/Mag.
Capacity: 6 or 10 round
Features: Case-hardened frame; brass or steel backstrap and trigger guard; blued finish; fluted cylinder
Stallion: . . . . $489.00–$559.00
Stallion 10-Shot: $529.00

TOP BREAK REVOLVERS

Action: SA revolver
Grips: Walnut or pearl-style
Barrel: 3.5 in., 5 in., 7 in.
Sights: Fixed, open
Weight: 40 oz.
Caliber: .45 Colt, .38 Spl., .44-40 Win.
Capacity: 6 rounds
Features: Full nickel plated steel or blued steel frame and blackstrap; case-hardened trigger guard
No. 3 Russian New Model blued frame: . . . . . . $1189.00–$1199.00
1875 No. 3 2nd Model blued frame: $1179.00
1875 No. 3 2nd Model full nickel-plating: $1589.00

Ultimate Arms, LLC

ULTIMATE ARMS MAGNA T5 COMMANDER TAC

ULTIMATE ARMS MAGNA T5 GOVERNMENT

MAGNA T5 COMMANDER MATCH, COMMANDER TAC

Action: Semiautomatic
Grips: Carbon fiber
Barrel: 4.25 in.
Sights: Blade front, drift-adjustable rear
Weight: 23 oz.
Caliber: .45 ACP
Capacity: 8 rounds
Features: Commander-length slide/barrel; full-size grip
MSRP $1999.00

MAGNA T5 GOVERNMENT MATCH, GOVERNMENT TAC

Action: Semiautomatic
Grips: Carbon fiber
Barrel: 5 in.
Sights: Fiber optic front, adjustable rear
Weight: 28 oz.
Caliber: .45 ACP
Capacity: 8 rounds
Features: A magnesium frame from forged billet makes this a strong and light full-size 1911 featuring a competition trigger; front and rear slide serrations; match-grade barrel
MSRP $1999.00

Volquartsen Firearms

VOLQUARTSEN FIREARMS BLACK MAMBA

VOLQUARTSEN FIREARMS SCORPION .22 LR

VOLQUARTSEN FIREARMS SCORPION .22 WMR

BLACK MAMBA

Action: Semiautomatic
Grips: Polymer
Barrel: 4.5 in., 6 in.
Sights: Front ramp blade, adjustable rear
Weight: N/A
Caliber: .22 LR
Capacity: 10 rounds
Features: A combination of Volquartsen's Scorpion target pistol and the takedown functionality of a Ruger 2245 frame; stainless steel threaded barrel with removeable compensator; Tandemkross hiveGrip; Volquartsen accurizing kit, DLC-coated competition bolt, magazine release, and magazine pads; choice of black, OD Green, or Flat Dark Earth upper; top and under rails; Hi-Viz fiber optic front sight available on some versions
MSRP . . . . $1342.00–$1714.00

SCORPION .22 LR

Action: Semiautomatic
Grips: Hogue
Barrel: 4.5 in., 6 in.
Sights: Front ramp fiber optic, adjustable target rear
Weight: 32 oz.
Caliber: .22 LR
Capacity: 10 rounds
Features: A 1911-angled frame with Hogue finger-groove grips; competition bolt; compensator; under and top rails; eye-catching finishes ranging from a full-coverage American flag to Battleworn grey and numerous grip options; some models available compensated; target or fiber optic sights
MSRP . . . . $1343.00–$1765.00

SCORPION .22 WMR

Action: Semiautomatic
Grips: G10
Barrel: 6 in.
Sights: Front ramp fiber optic, adjustable tritium rear
Weight: 67 oz.
Caliber: .22 WMR
Capacity: 9 rounds
Features: A dedicated small-game and varmint pistol with compensator; VZ Grips G10 panels in Predator Green; black nitride finish; under rail and topside rail; optional no sight version with black stainless finish; optional target sight version with black VZ Grip panels and black nitride finish
MSRP . . . . $1842.00–$2345.00

Walther Arms

WALTHER CCP (CONCEALED CARRY PISTOL)

WALTHER CREED

WALTHER P22

WALTHER CCP M2 .380

CCP (CONCEALED CARRY PISTOL)

Action: Semiautomatic
Grips: Synthetic
Barrel: 3.54 in.
Sights: Adjustable
Weight: 22.33 oz.
Caliber: 9mm
Capacity: 8+1 rounds
Features: Available in black or stainless steel; interchangeable front sight with white dot; adjustable rear sight; reversible magazine release
MSRP . . . . starting at $419.00

CCP M2 .380

Action: Semiautomatic
Grips: Polymer
Barrel: 3.54 in.
Sights: White three-dot
Weight: 19.4 oz.
Caliber: .380 ACP
Capacity: 8 rounds
Features: External safety; slide serrations front and rear; aggressive grip texture; reversible mag release; in a stainless slide, black slide, or a black slide with a built-in Viridian laser
MSRP . . . . $419.99–$479.99

CREED

Action: Semiautomatic
Grips: None
Barrel: 4 in.
Sights: Three-dot, low profile
Weight: 26.6 oz.
Caliber: 9mm
Capacity: 16, 10 rounds
Features: Economically priced, polymer frame; DAO pre-set trigger pistol; firing pin and drop safeties; ambidextrous magazine release button; 1913 Picatinny rail
MSRP $299.97

P22

Action: DA/SA semiautomatic
Grips: Polymer
Barrel: 3.42 in., 5 in.
Sights: 3-dot adjustable low-profile
Weight: 17 oz., 22 oz.
Caliber: .22 LR
Capacity: 10 rounds
Features: Threaded barrel, interchangeable with target barrel; loaded chamber indicator; external slide stop; 3 safeties; two magazine styles; available with integrated laser-set; available in black, nickel, and military finish; now available with laser, Target models with 5-in. barrels available in black, Flat Dark Earth, or nickel
MSRP . . . . starting at $299.99

Walther Arms

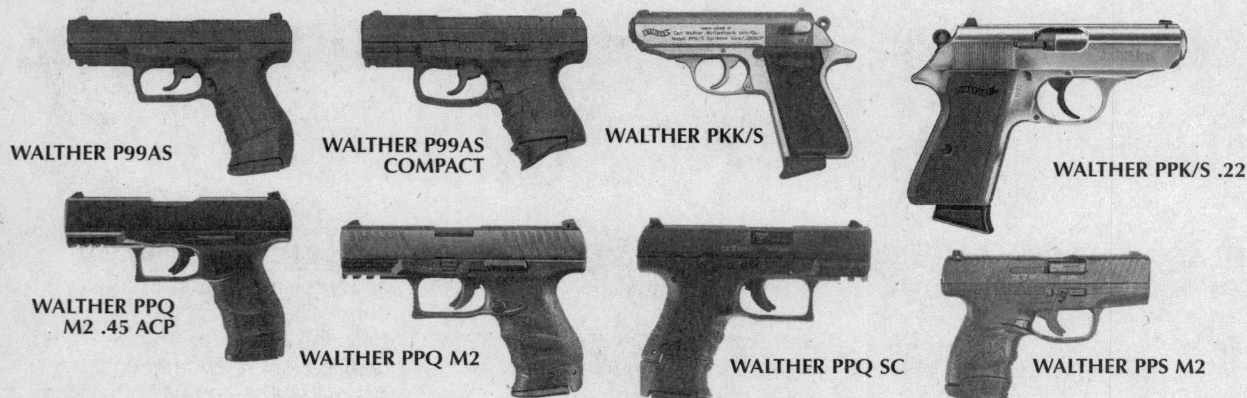

P99AS

Action: DA semiautomatic
Grips: Black polymer frame and grips
Barrel: 4 in. stainless steel with Tenifer finish
Sights: Front and rear tritium night
Weight: 24 oz.–25.6 oz.
Caliber: 9mm, .40 S&W
Capacity: 15 (9mm) or 12 (.40 S&W) rounds
Features: The first pistol with a firing pin block combines advantages of a traditional DA pull with SA trigger and a decocking button safety integrated into slide, allowing users the ability to decock the striker, preventing inadvertent firing in both DA and SA
MSRP . . . . starting at $604.99

P99AS COMPACT

Action: Striker-fired semiautomatic
Grips: Polymer
Barrel: 3.5 in.
Sights: 3-dot adjustable low-profile
Weight: 20.8 oz.–22.4 oz.
Caliber: 9mm, .40 S&W
Capacity: 10 (9mm) or 8 (.40 S&W) rounds
Features: Flat-bottom magazine buttplate, finger rest magazine buttplate; molded with a Weaver-style rail; interchangeable backstraps; hammerless striker system and integral safety devices come standard
MSRP . . . . starting at $604.99

PPK AND PPK/S

Action: DA/SA semiautomatic
Grips: Polymer
Barrel: 3.3 in.
Sights: Fixed, open
Weight: 22.4 oz. (PPK), 24 oz. (PPK/S)
Caliber: .380 ACP
Capacity: 6 (PPK) or 7 (PPK/S) rounds
Features: Firing pin safety; manual safety with decocking function; double- and single-action trigger; extended beaver tail; nickel plated or blued finish
MSRP . . . . $699.99–$829.99

PPK/S .22

Action: DA/SA semiautomatic
Grips: Polymer
Barrel: 3.3 in.
Sights: Fixed, open
Weight: 24 oz.
Caliber: .22 LR
Capacity: 10 rounds
Features: Manual safety; top strap waved to reduce glare; internal slide stop; iconic PPK/S frame; beaver tail extension; nickel plated or black finish
MSRP $329.99

PPQ M2 .45 ACP

Action: Striker-fired semiautomatic
Grips: Ergonomic polymer
Barrel: 4.25 in.
Sights: Three dot polymer
Weight: 28 oz.
Caliber: .45 ACP
Capacity: 12 rounds
Features: Custom Picatinny accessory rail; quick-defense trigger; ergonomic, non-slip, cross-directional grip surface; three safeties; Tenifer coating on slide and barrel; front and rear slide serrations; ambidextrous slide stop
MSRP $649.99

PPQ M2 9MM

Action: Striker-fired semiautomatic
Grips: Polymer
Barrel: 4 in., 4.1 in., 4.6 in., 5 in.
Sights: 3-dot adjustable low-profile
Weight: 24 oz. (9mm), 25.6 oz. (.40 S&W)
Caliber: 9mm
Capacity: 15 (9mm), 15/17 (9mm Navy SD) or 11 (.40 S&W) rounds
Features: Quick defense trigger; three safeties; Tenifer coated slide and barrel with matte finish
MSRP $519.99

PPQ SC

Action: Semiautomatic
Grips: Synthetic
Barrel: 3.5 in.
Sights: Three-dot, windage-adjustable rear
Weight: 21.2 oz.
Caliber: 9mm
Capacity: 10, 15 rounds
Features: Sub-Compact is easy to conceal; unique grip texturing; wide trigger guard with serrations on the front for extra purchase; accessory rail; low-profile snag-resistant sights; interchangeable backstraps; ambidextrous slide release; slide has a Tenifer coating
MSRP $499.99

PPS M2

Action: Striker-fired semiautomatic
Grips: Ergonomic polymer
Barrel: 3.18 in.
Sights: Three dot metal
Weight: 21.1 oz.
Caliber: 9mm
Capacity: 6, 7, 8 rounds
Features: Front and rear slide serrations; smooth, light trigger; ergonomic, non-slip, cross-directional grip surface; cocking indicator; chamber viewport; slide stop; magazine release conveniently placed for thumb operation; three magazine options; LE (Law Enforcement) variation comes equipped with phosphoric sights and three magazines
MSRP . . . . $399.99–$729.99

Walther Arms

WALTHER Q4 STEEL FRAME OR

WALTHER Q4 TAC

WALTHER Q5 MATCH

Q4 STEEL FRAME

Action: Semiautomatic
Grips: Polymer
Barrel: 4 in.
Sights: LPA with adjustable rear
Weight: 39.7 oz.
Caliber: 9mm
Capacity: 15 rounds
Features: Double-stack, steel-frame, striker-fire pistol that has an ergonomic wrap-around grip; extended beavertail; optics-ready slide; Picatinny accessory rail
MSRP . . . . $1449.99–$1549.99

Q4 TAC

Action: Semiautomatic
Grips: Synthetic
Barrel: 4.6 in.
Sights: Fiber optic front sight, adjustable target rear
Weight: 26 oz.
Caliber: 9mm
Capacity: 15, 17 rounds
Features: Ambidextrous slide stop and mag release; texturing on the grip; wide trigger guard with serrations for additional purchase; ergonomic and finger-grooved grip; magazine with finger rest; interchangeable backstraps for a custom fit; threaded barrel for suppressor add-ons; slide has been milled to be optics ready
MSRP $749.00

Q5 MATCH

Action: Semiautomatic
Grips: Synthetic
Barrel: 5 in.
Sights: Fiber optic front sight, adjustable target rear
Weight: 27.9 oz.
Caliber: 9mm
Capacity: 15 rounds
Features: Optics-ready slide; Picatinny rail; Walther ergonomic grip; ported slide; blue Quick Defense trigger; front and rear slide serrations; ambidextrous slide stop
MSRP . . . . $799.99–$829.99

Wilson Combat

WILSON COMBAT ACP, ACP COMMANDER, ACP COMPACT

WILSON COMBAT AR9 PISTOL

WILSON COMBAT ARP TACTICAL

WILSON COMBAT BILL WILSON CARRY PISTOL

ACP, ACP COMMANDER, ACP COMPACT

Action: Semiautomatic
Grips: G10
Barrel: 4 in., 4.25 in., 5 in.
Sights: Fiber optic front, battlesight rear
Weight: 36.9 oz.–41.6 oz.
Caliber: 9mm, .45 ACP
Capacity: 8, 10 rounds
Features: With a full-size carbon steel frame, this pistol gets a Bullet Proof tactical thumb safety and high-grip beavertail safety; G10 Eagle Claw grip panels ; carbon steel slide with Eagle Claw rear serrations
.45 ACP starting at: $2495.00
9mm starting at: $2595.00

AR9 PISTOL

Action: Semiautomatic
Grips: Synthetic
Barrel: 8 in., 11.3 in.
Sights: None
Weight: 86 oz.–96 oz.
Caliber: 9mm
Capacity: 10, 15, 17 rounds
Features: A pistol-caliber MSR pistol with billet aluminum lower and flat-top upper; Q-Comp flash hider on threaded muzzle; Bravo Company Mfg. pistol grip; Shockwave forearm support; Wilson's TTU M2 trigger; Armor-Tuff and hard-anodized finishes; M-LOK rail
MSRP . . . . .starting at $1995.00

ARP TACTICAL

Action: Semiautomatic
Grips: Synthetic
Barrel: 8 in., 11.3 in.
Sights: None
Weight: 99 oz.
Caliber: .223 Rem., .300 BLK, 6.8 SPC, 7.62x40 WT
Capacity: 20 rounds
Features: Billet flat-top upper and pistol-marked lower; carbine-length gas system; low-profile gas block; Wilson Combat ARP Tactical match-grade barrel, single-stage TTU trigger, and tactical trigger guard; Shockwave forearm support; Bravo Company Mfg. pistol grip; Accu-Tak flash hider on threaded muzzle; M-LOK rail
MSRP . . . . .starting at $2250.00

BILL WILSON CARRY PISTOL

Action: Semiautomatic
Grips: G10
Barrel: 4 in.
Sights: Gold bead front, battlesight rear
Weight: 29.63 oz.
Caliber: 9mm, .45 ACP
Capacity: 7, 8 rounds
Features: Very pretty CCW choice with ultrathin cherry G10 grips; match-grade fluted cone barrel with reverse flush-cut crown; fluted chamber; contoured magazine well; aluminum frame; light rail; X-TAC frontstrap and mainspring housing treatment; X-TAC rear slide cocking serrations; carry and ball endmill cuts
MSRP . . . . .starting at $3850.00

Wilson Combat

WILSON COMBAT CQB ELITE COMBAT

WILSON COMBAT CQB ELITE COMMANDER

WILSON COMBAT CQB ELITE PROFESSIONAL

WILSON COMBAT EDC X9

WILSON COMBAT EDC X9L

WILSON COMBAT EXPERIOR 5-IN. DOUBLE STACK

WILSON COMBAT EXPERIOR 6-IN. LONGSLIDE

CQB ELITE COMBAT

Action: Semiautomatic
Grips: G10
Barrel: 4 in.
Sights: Fiber optic front, battlesight rear
Weight: 36.8 oz.
Caliber: 9mm, .45 ACP, 10mm, .40 S&W, .38 Super
Capacity: 7, 8 rounds
Features: With a carbon steel compact frame and slide; tactical thumb safety, high-ride beavertail safety, round-butt magazine well, and magazine release; starburst G10 grips
MSRP . . . . starting at $3425.00

CQB ELITE COMMANDER

Action: Semiautomatic
Grips: G10
Barrel: 4.25 in.
Sights: Fiber optic front, battlesight rear
Weight: 38.3 oz.
Caliber: 9mm, .38 Super, .45 ACP
Capacity: 7, 8 rounds
Features: Similar to the CQB Compact, but with Wilson's Professional carbon steel frame and 4.25-in. match-grade barrel and bushing
.45 ACP: . . . . . . starting at $3425.00
9mm/.38 Super: . . . . . starting at $3535.00

CQB ELITE PROFESSIONAL

Action: Semiautomatic
Grips: G10
Barrel: 4 in.
Sights: Fiber optic front, battlesight rear
Weight: 44 oz.
Caliber: 9mm, .38 Super, .45 ACP
Capacity: 7, 8 rounds
Features: A combo of the Compact and the Commander, with Wilson's Professional-size frame and Compact 4-in. match-grade cone barrel
.45 ACP: . . . . . . starting at $3425.00
9mm/.38 Super: . . . starting at $3535.00

EDC X9

Action: Semiautomatic
Grips: G10
Barrel: 4 in.
Sights: Fiber optic front, battlesight rear
Weight: 29.9 oz.
Caliber: 9mm
Capacity: 15, 18 rounds
Features: Double-stack aluminum X frame; Bullet Proof concealment hammer, thumb safety, and magazine release; tri-top slide with external extractor; X-TAC treatment to front- and backstrap; reliability-enhanced cone barrel with a reverse flush-cut crown; fluted chamber and barrel
MSRP . . . . starting at $2895.00

EDC X9L

Action: Semiautomatic
Grips: G10
Barrel: 5 in.
Sights: Fiber optic front, battlesight rear
Weight: 32.4 oz.
Caliber: 9mm
Capacity: 15, 18 rounds
Features: Double-stack aluminum X frame; Bullet Proof concealment hammer, thumb safety, and magazine release; tri-top slide with external extractor; X-TAC treatment to front- and backstrap; reliability enhanced barrel and bushing with a reverse flush-cut crown; fluted chamber
MSRP . . . . starting at $2995.00

EXPERIOR 5-IN. DOUBLE STACK, COMMANDER DOUBLE-STACK, COMPACT DOUBLE-STACK

Action: Semiautomatic
Grips: G10
Barrel: 4 in., 4.25 in., 5 in.
Sights: Fiber optic front, battlesight rear
Weight: 30.5 oz.–41 oz.
Caliber: 9mm
Capacity: 15, 18 rounds
Features: A compact aluminum frame with a longer slide and features like frontstrap and mainspring housing with TRAK pattern texturing; aluminum mag well; Bullet Proof magazine release, concealment hammer safety, and tactical thumb safety; stainless steel slide
MSRP . . . . starting at $2995.00

EXPERIOR 6-IN. LONGSLIDE

Action: Semiautomatic
Grips: G10
Barrel: 6 in.
Sights: Fiber optic front, battlesight rear
Weight: 44.1 oz.
Caliber: 9mm, .45 ACP
Capacity: 8, 10 rounds
Features: Full-size carbon steel frame with WAVE rails; frontstrap, mainspring housing and G10 grips have TRAK pattern texturing; Bullet Proof round-butt mag well, magazine release; concealment beavertail grip safety, and tactical thumb safety
.45 ACP: . . . . . . starting at $3750.00
9mm: . . . . starting at $3850.00

Wilson Combat

WILSON COMBAT EXPERIOR FULL-SIZE

WILSON COMBAT EXPERIOR PROFESSIONAL

WILSON COMBAT PROTECTOR SERIES AR PISTOL

WILSON COMBAT TACTICAL CARRY COMMANDER

WILSON COMBAT VICKERS ELITE

WILSON COMBAT X-TAC ELITE COMMANDER

EXPERIOR FULL-SIZE, COMMANDER, COMMANDER COMPACT, COMPACT, SUB-COMPACT

Action: Semiautomatic
Grips: G10
Barrel: 4 in., 4.25 in., 5 in.
Sights: Fiber optic front, battlesight rear
Weight: 36.4 oz.–40.2 oz.
Caliber: 9mm, .45 ACP
Capacity: 8, 10 rounds
Features: Carbon steel frame with WAVE rails; frontstrap, mainspring housing and G10 grips have TRAK pattern texturing; Bullet Proof round-butt mag well, magazine release; concealment beavertail grip safety, and tactical thumb safety
.45 ACP: . . . . . . starting at $3750.00
9mm: . . . . starting at $3850.00

EXPERIOR PROFESSIONAL

Action: Semiautomatic
Grips: G10
Barrel: 4 in.
Sights: Fiber optic front, battlesight rear
Weight: 38.2 oz.
Caliber: 9mm, .45 ACP
Capacity: 8, 10 rounds
Features: Professional-size carbon steel frame with WAVE rails; frontstrap, mainspring housing and G10 grips have TRAK pattern texturing; Bullet Proof round-butt mag well, magazine release; concealment beavertail grip safety, and tactical thumb safety; carbon steel slide
.45 ACP: . . . . . . starting at $3750.00
9mm: . . . . starting at $3850.00

PROTECTOR SERIES AR PISTOL

Action: Semiautomatic
Grips: Synthetic
Barrel: 11.3 in.
Sights: None
Weight: 90 oz.
Caliber: .300 HAM'R, .223 Rem., .300 BLK
Capacity: 20 rounds
Features: A loaded MSR-platform pistol with most components by Wilson Combat, including forged upper/lower; match-grade stainless barrel; low-profile gas block; Q-Comp flash hider; M-LOK compatible handguard; two-stage TTU trigger group with tactical trigger guard
MSRP . . . . starting at $2099.95

TACTICAL CARRY COMMANDER

Action: Semiautomatic
Grips: G10
Barrel: 4.25 in.
Sights: Fiber optic front, battlesight rear
Weight: 37.8 oz.
Caliber: 9mm, .38 Super, .45 ACP
Capacity: 8, 10 rounds
Features: Wilson's Professional-size carbon steel frame with a match-grade barrel and bushing with a reverse flush-cut crown; fluted chamber; Bullet Proof concealment beavertail grip safety, tactical thumb safety, and magazine release; countersunk slide stop
.45 ACP: . . . . . . starting at $3750.00
9mm/.38 Super: starting at $3860.00

VICKERS ELITE

Action: Semiautomatic
Grips: G10
Barrel: 5 in.
Sights: Battlesight with gold bead front
Weight: 41.6 oz.
Caliber: 9mm, .45 ACP
Capacity: 8, 9 rounds
Features: A full-size competition gun designed with Larry Vickers, featuring a carbon steel frame; high-cut and checkered front strap; Bullet Proof mag well, mag release and thumb safety; carbon steel slide with heavy underside machine chamfering and serrations fore and aft; match-grade barrel with flush cut reverse crown; countersunk slide stop
9mm: $3960.00
.45 ACP: $3850.00

X-TAC ELITE COMMANDER

Action: Semiautomatic
Grips: G10
Barrel: 4.5 in.
Sights: Fiber optic front, battlesight rear
Weight: 44.3 oz.
Caliber: 9mm, .38 Super, .45 ACP
Capacity: 8, 10 rounds
Features: Wilson's Professional-size carbon steel frame with a slightly longer match-grade barrel with a reverse flush-cut crown; Bullet Proof high-ride beavertail grip safety, tactical thumb safety, and magazine release
.45 ACP: . . . . . . starting at $3650.00
9mm/.38 Super: starting at $3760.00

Wilson Combat

WILSON COMBAT X-TAC PROFESSIONAL

WILSON COMBAT X-TAC SUPERGRADE

WILSON COMBAT X-TAC SUPERGRADE COMMANDER

X-TAC PROFESSIONAL

Action: Semiautomatic
Grips: G10
Barrel: 4.25 in.
Sights: Fiber optic front, battlesight rear
Weight: 38 oz.
Caliber: 9mm, .38 Super, .45 ACP
Capacity: 8, 10 rounds
Features: Wilson's Professional-size carbon steel frame; Bullet Proof high-ride beavertail grip safety, tactical thumb safety, and magazine release
.45 ACP: . . . . . . starting at $2785.00
9mm/.38 Super: . . starting at $2895.00

X-TAC SUPERGRADE

Action: Semiautomatic
Grips: G10
Barrel: 5 in.
Sights: Fiber optic front, battlesight rear
Weight: 46 oz.
Caliber: 9mm, .38 Super, .45 ACP
Capacity: 8, 10 rounds
Features: The Supergrade has a full-size carbon steel frame with a round butt; Bullet Proof magazine release, tactical thumb safety, and high-ride beavertail grip safety; X-TAC frontstrap and mainspring housing treatment, rear slide cocking serrations
.45 ACP: . . . . . . starting at $4795.00
9mm/.38 Super: starting at $4905.00

X-TAC SUPERGRADE COMMANDER, COMPACT, PROFESSIONAL

Action: Semiautomatic
Grips: G10
Barrel: 4 in., 4.25 in.
Sights: Fiber optic front, battlesight rear
Weight: 38.4 oz.–43.3 oz.
Caliber: 9mm, .38 Super, .45 ACP
Capacity: 7, 8, 10 rounds
Features: Similar to the full-size Supergrade, but with a Professional-size frame in the Commander/ Professional; Compact has Officer's size frame
.45 ACP: . . . . . . starting at $4795.00
9mm/.38 Super: starting at $4905.00

Windham Weaponry

WINDHAM WEAPONRY 9MM GMC PISTOL

WINDHAM WEAPONRY 300 BLACKOUT PISTOL

WINDHAM WEAPONRY .450 THUMPER

9MM GMC PISTOL

Action: Semiautomatic
Grips: Synthetic
Barrel: 9 in.
Sights: None
Weight: 93 oz.
Caliber: 9mm
Capacity: 17 rounds
Features: GMC stands for "Glock Magazine Compatible"; semiauto blowback; five-position SB tactical arm brace; A2 grip; flat-top upper; Chromoly vanadium steel barrel with 1:10 right twist
MSRP $1592.00

300 BLACKOUT PISTOL

Action: Semiautomatic gas impingment system
Grips: Rubber
Barrel: 9 in.
Sights: None
Weight: 4 lb. 14 oz.
Caliber: .300 BLK
Capacity: Detachable box, 30+1 rounds
Features: Quick-detach swing swivel; 1:7 inch twist; Picatinny rail; hardcoat black anodize reciever finish with laser caliber identification; chrome-Lined barrel with A2-type flash suppressor
MSRP $1496.00

.450 THUMPER

Action: Semiautomatic
Grips: Synthetic
Barrel: 9 in.
Sights: Flip-up front and rear
Weight: 93 oz.
Caliber: .450 Bushmaster
Capacity: 5 rounds
Features: Designed specifically for the straight-wall .450 Bushmaster, with SB Tactical pistol arm brace; hardcoat black anodized receiver; mil-spec trigger; Magpul MBUS flip-up sights
MSRP $1640.00

BLACK POWDER

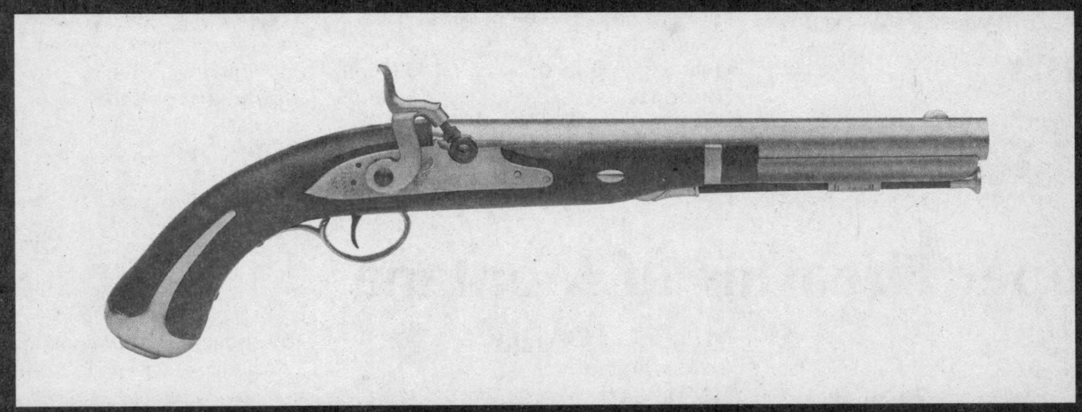

Cimarron Firearms

CIMARRON FIREARMS 1851 NAVY

CIMARRON FIREARMS CO. WALKER'S WALKER

1851 NAVY

Action: Revolver
Stock: Wood
Barrel: 7.5 in.
Sights: Front blade, groove
Weight: 2 lb. 11 oz.
Caliber: .36, .44
Features: Reproduction of the 1851 cap-and-ball revolver originally known as the Percussion Peacemaker; frame is engraved and finished in a case-hardened old silver finish; walnut grips are checkered; barrel is octagonal
Oval triggerguard: $364.88
London: $398.55

WALKER'S WALKER

Action: Revolver
Stock: Walnut
Barrel: 9 in.
Sights: Low blade front
Weight: 72 oz.
Caliber: .44
Features: A beefy revolver with a long barrel in limited edition and featuring a brass trigger guard; steel backstrap; one-piece grips; Cimarron's own original finish with military markings; ships in a glass and walnut presentation case
MSRP $778.80

BLACK POWDER

Cooper Firearms of Montana

COOPER FIREARMS OF MONTANA MUZZLELOADER

MUZZLELOADER

Action: Bolt/inline
Stock: Wood
Barrel: N/A
Sights: None
Weight: N/A
Caliber: .45, .50
Features: Synthetic and wood stock versions; left-hand available; fluted barrel; sealed and removeable plug; 209 shotgun primer ignition; adjustable single-stage trigger; synthetic stock available in Excalibur or Open Country Long-Range stocks; wood stock available in Classic, Custom Classic, Schnabel, and Jackson Game styles, and upgraded wood is available
Synthetic: $2275.00
Wood: $3395.00

CVA (Connecticut Valley Arms)

CONNECTICUT VALLEY ARMS (CVA) ACCURA MR CERAKOTE/NITRIDE

CVA ACCURA MR NITRIDE

CONNECTICUT VALLEY ARMS (CVA) ACCURA PR CERAKOTE/ NITRIDE

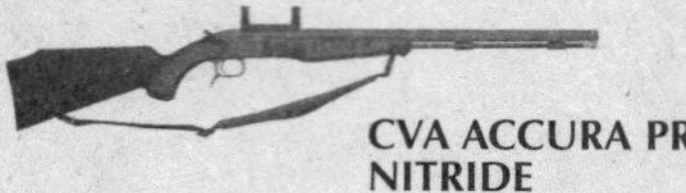
CVA ACCURA PR NITRIDE

ACCURA MR CERAKOTE/ NITRIDE

Action: Break-open
Stock: Synthetic
Barrel: 25 in.
Sights: None
Weight: 7 lb. 1 oz.
Caliber: .50
Features: Bergara barrel in bronze Cerakote/nitride finish; DuraSight DEAD-ON one-piece scope mount; Quake CLAW sling; reversible hammer spur
MSRP $589.00

ACCURA MR NITRIDE

Lock: Break-action in-line
Stock: Synthetic
Barrel: 25 in.
Sights: Scope mount
Weight: 6 lb. 6 oz.
Bore/Caliber: .50
Features: Aluminum frame; quick release breech plug; trigger guard actuated breeching action; Bergara barrel; neutral center of gravity trigger; premium SoftTouch stock with rubber grip panels; WeatherGuard barrel finish on the stainless steel barrel; Realtree Max-1 or black stock finishes; Quake Claw sling included; DuraSight Dead-On scope mount
MSRP . . . . $494.00–$684.00

ACCURA PR CERAKOTE/ NITRIDE

Action: Break-open
Stock: Synthetic
Barrel: 28 in.
Sights: None
Weight: 7 lb. 3 oz.
Caliber: .50
Features: The Accura PR (Plains Rifle) gets an upgrade with a 426 stainless Bergara barrel in Cerakote/nitride bronze finish; SoftTouch grip panels
MSRP $594.00

ACCURA PR NITRIDE

Action: Break-action
Stock: Synthetic
Barrel: 25 in.
Sights: None
Weight: 7 lb. 2 oz.
Caliber: .50
Features: 416 stainless steel, fluted, nitride-treated Bergara barrel; break-action is easy opening; disassembly can be performed by removing a single screw; Quick Release breech plug; reversible hammer spur; adjustable trigger; Palm Saver ramrod; Quake Claw sling; CrushZone recoil pad; ambidextrous stock; drilled and tapped for scope mounts; DuraSight DEAD-ON one-piece mount
MSRP . . . . $501.00–$701.00

CVA (Connecticut Valley Arms)

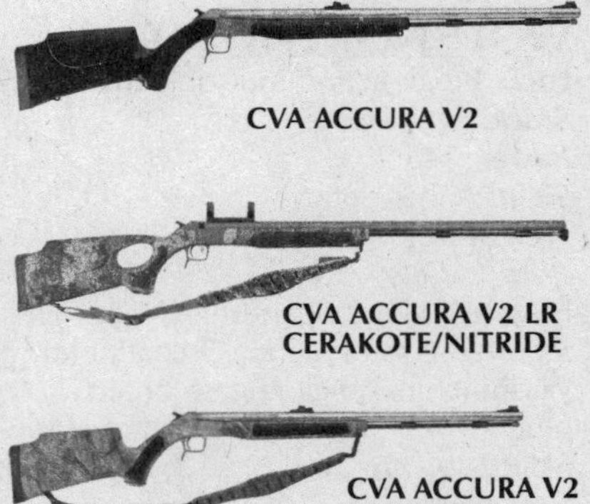

CVA ACCURA V2

CVA ACCURA V2 LR CERAKOTE/NITRIDE

CVA ACCURA V2 NORTHWEST

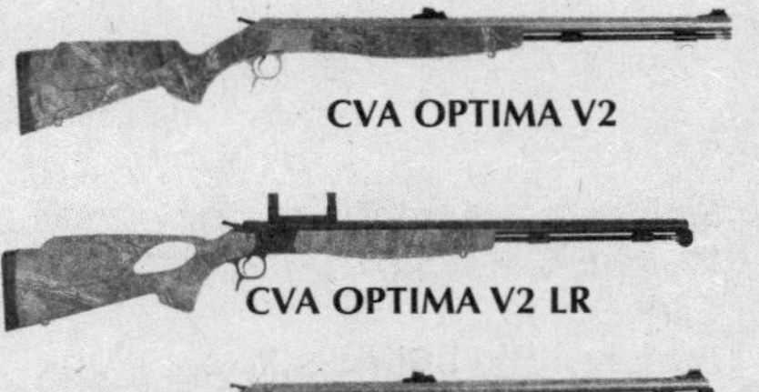

CVA OPTIMA V2

CVA OPTIMA V2 LR

CVA OPTIMA V2 NORTHWEST

CVA ARMS PARAMOUNT

CVA PARAMOUNT PRO

CVA PARAMOUNT PRO COLORADO

ACCURA V2

Lock: Break-action muzzleloading
Stock: Composite stock in standard or thumbhole
Barrel: 27 in.
Sights: DuraSight fiber optic
Weight: 7 lb. 5 oz.
Bore/Caliber: .50
Features: 416 stainless Bergara barrel; quick-release breech plug; CrushZone recoil pad; drilled and tapped for scope mount; SoftTouch coating and rubber grip panels; Quake Claw sling; with a variety of configuration choices, including standard or thumbhole stock, black or Realtree APG finishes, scope mount or fiber optic sights, black or stainless Nitride finished barrels
MSRP . . . . $482.00–$682.00

ACCURA V2 LR CERAKOTE/NITRIDE

Action: Break-open
Stock: Synthetic
Barrel: 30 in.
Sights: None
Weight: 7 lb. 10 oz.
Caliber: .45, .50
Features: Bergara barrel with bullet guiding muzzle that gets the Cerakote/nitride treatment in bronze; CVA Quick-Release breech plug; Quake CLAW sling; CrushZone recoil pad; reversible hammer spur; one-screw disassembly
MSRP $606.00

ACCURA V2 NORTHWEST

Lock: Break-action muzzleloading
Stock: Synthetic
Barrel: 27 in.
Sights: Fiber optics
Weight: 7 lb. 5 oz.
Bore/Caliber: .50
Features: Meets open-breech/ignition requirements of Idaho, Oregan, and Washington; quick release breech plug; in Realtree APG
MSRP $533.00

OPTIMA V2

Lock: Break-action muzzleloading
Stock: Realtree Xtra Green or black
Barrel: 26 in.
Sights: Fiber optic sights or mount
Weight: 6 lb. 10 oz.
Bore/Caliber: .50
Features: Modeled on Accura V2; stainless steel barrel; quick release breech plug; ambidextrous stock, thumbhole stock option; includes DuraSight Dead-On scope mount and ramrod
MSRP . . . . $304.00–$534.00

OPTIMA V2 LR

Action: Break-action
Stock: Synthetic
Barrel: 26 in.
Sights: None
Weight: 6 lb. 10 oz.
Caliber: .50
Features: Breech lever trigger-guard actuation; Optima's trigger and internal parts; finger-removable Quick-Release breech plug; PalmSaver ramrod; reversible hammer spur; DuraSight Dead-On scope mount; stainless steel barrel or Nitride treated; Realtree Xtra Green stock
MSRP . . . . $372.00–$534.00

OPTIMA V2 NORTHWEST

Lock: Break-action muzzleloading
Stock: Synthetic
Barrel: 26 in.
Sights: Fiber optics
Weight: 6 lb. 10 oz.
Bore/Caliber: .50
Features: Meets open-breech/ignition requirements of Idaho, Oregan, and Washington; quick release breech plug; stainless steel hardware and Realtree Xtra Green standard stock
MSRP $344.00

PARAMOUNT

Action: Bolt
Stock: Synthetic
Barrel: 26 in.
Sights: None
Weight: N/A
Caliber: .45
Features: Billed as the world's first long-range muzzleloader capable of killing shots 300 yards and beyond. Features include free-floating Bergara barrel; CVA VariFlame breech plus; aluminum chassis; takes new PowerBelt ELR bullets spedifically designed for this muzzleloader
MSRP $1094.00

PARAMOUNT PRO

Action: Bolt
Stock: Fiberglass
Barrel: 26 in.
Sights: None
Weight: 8 lb. 12 oz.
Caliber: .45
Features: Free-floating barrel of nitride-treated stainless steel; Grayboe stock; TriggerTech trigger; self-deploying ramrod; VariFlame breech plug; Quake CLAW flush cup sling; Cerakote finish in bronze
MSRP $1668.00

PARAMOUNT PRO COLORADO

Action: Bolt
Stock: Fiberglass
Barrel: 26 in.
Sights: Peep
Weight: 8 lb. 12 oz.
Caliber: .50
Features: Identical to the Paramount Pro, but with the addition of Williams peep sights
MSRP $1668.00

CVA (Connecticut Valley Arms)

CVA WOLF

CVA WOLF NORTHWEST

WOLF

Lock: Break-action in-line
Stock: Synthetic
Barrel: 24 in.
Sights: DuraSight fiber optic; includes 3–9x32mm KonusShot scope
Weight: 6 lb. 4 oz.
Bore/Caliber: .50
Features: Bullet-guiding muzzle; new tool-free QR breech plug system; ambidextrous compact or standard stock in black or camo; reversible hammer spur; blued or stainless barrel
MSRP . . . . $300.00–$372.00

WOLF NORTHWEST

Lock: Break-action muzzleloading
Stock: Synthetic
Barrel: 24 in.
Sights: Fiber optics
Weight: 6 lb. 4 oz.
Bore/Caliber: .50
Features: Meets open-breech/ignition requirements of Idaho, Oregan, and Washington; quick release breech plug
MSRP $237.00

Davide Pedersoli & C.

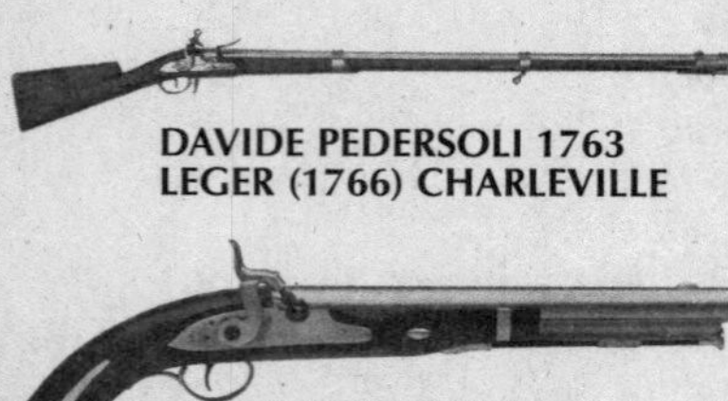

DAVIDE PEDERSOLI 1763 LEGER (1766) CHARLEVILLE

DAVIDE PEDERSOLI 1805 HARPER'S FERRY PERCUSSION PISTOL

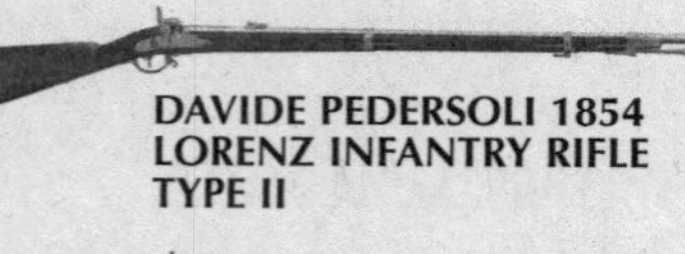

DAVIDE PEDERSOLI 1854 LORENZ INFANTRY RIFLE TYPE II

DAVIDE PEDERSOLI 1860 VOLUNTEER

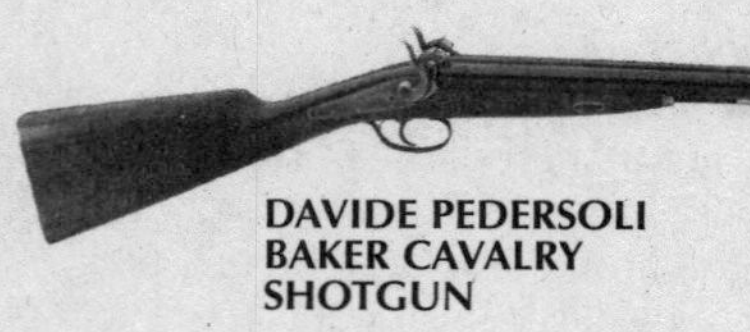

DAVIDE PEDERSOLI BAKER CAVALRY SHOTGUN

DAVIDE PEDERSOLI BOUTET 1ER EMPIRE

1763 LEGER (1766) CHARLEVILLE

Action: Dropping block
Stock: Walnut
Barrel: 44.7 in.
Sights: Open
Weight: 10 lb. 2 oz.
Caliber: .69
Magazine: None
Features: Creedmoor sight; tunnel front sight; replica of French infantry musket
MSRP $1625.00

1805 HARPER'S FERRY PERCUSSION PISTOL

Lock: Percussion cap
Stock: American walnut
Barrel: 10.06 in.
Sights: Bead front
Weight: 2 lb. 10.6 oz.
Bore/Caliber: .54
Features: Brass furniture; smooth bore; chromed and satin finished barrel; old silver case hardened lock
MSRP $685.00

1854 LORENZ INFANTRY RIFLE TYPE II

Action: Percussion
Stock: Walnut
Barrel: 37 in.
Sights: N/A
Weight: 9 lb.
Caliber: .54
Features: Conceived by the Austrian Lieutenant Joseph Lorenz; official production started in 1854, replacing the Augustin rifle among Austrian troops; used in Italy during the second Independence War, as well as in the Balkans; then largely exported to America, equipping both the Union and the Confederate armies, becoming one of the most used rifles during the American Civil War
MSRP $1735.00

1860 VOLUNTEER

Action: Percussion
Stock: Walnut
Barrel: 33 in.
Sights: Tunnel front, Creedmoor rear
Weight: 8 lb. 13 oz.
Caliber: .451
Features: The British N.R.A., for the first time, organized a national event held at Wimbledon in 1860, inspiring Pedersoli's Volunteer Rifle; broach rifled with an optimal twist for target shooting at 100-150 meters; oil-finished, hand-checkered stock
MSRP $1890.00

BAKER CAVALRY SHOTGUN

Lock: Percussion
Stock: Walnut
Barrel: 11.25 in.
Sights: None
Weight: 5 lb. 12 oz.
Bore/Caliber: 20 Ga.
Features: Single trigger back action, side-by-side shotgun; reproduces a gun made by London gunsmith Ezekiel Baker in 1850; case-hardened
MSRP $1280.00

BOUTET 1ER EMPIRE

Lock: Flintlock
Stock: Hardwood
Barrel: 10 in.
Sights: Fixed
Weight: 2 lb. 14 oz.
Bore/Caliber: .45
Features: Napoleon wrote with flattering appreciation about the style and prestige of the Boutet guns, which Pedersoli now proudly introduces with fine checkering on sides; metal buttplate; ramrod has horn tip; single set trigger; on lock two lines are engraved with MANUF RE/a Versailles.
MSRP $1415.00

Davide Pedersoli & C.

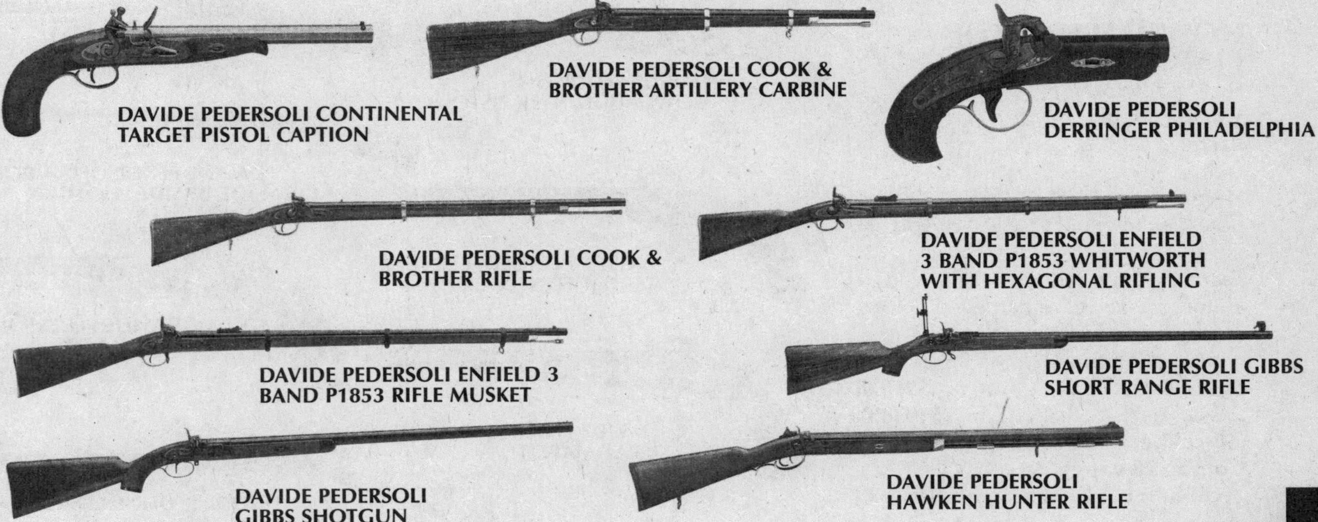

DAVIDE PEDERSOLI CONTINENTAL TARGET PISTOL CAPTION

DAVIDE PEDERSOLI COOK & BROTHER ARTILLERY CARBINE

DAVIDE PEDERSOLI DERRINGER PHILADELPHIA

DAVIDE PEDERSOLI COOK & BROTHER RIFLE

DAVIDE PEDERSOLI ENFIELD 3 BAND P1853 WHITWORTH WITH HEXAGONAL RIFLING

DAVIDE PEDERSOLI ENFIELD 3 BAND P1853 RIFLE MUSKET

DAVIDE PEDERSOLI GIBBS SHORT RANGE RIFLE

DAVIDE PEDERSOLI GIBBS SHOTGUN

DAVIDE PEDERSOLI HAWKEN HUNTER RIFLE

CONTINENTAL TARGET PISTOL

Action: Percussion, flintlock
Stock: Walnut
Barrel: 11 in.
Sights: Front, windage adjustable rear
Weight: 2 lb. 3 oz.
Caliber: .45, .44
Features: Reproduction of target pistol of Central European style; set trigger; octagonal barrel; chrome finished
Percussion: $585.00
Flintlock: $680.00

COOK & BROTHER ARTILLERY CARBINE

Lock: Caplock
Stock: Walnut
Barrel: 24 in.
Sights: None
Weight: 6 lb. 10 oz.
Bore/Caliber: .58
Features: Inspired by English model guns; brass garnitures; blued barrel; case-hardened lock
MSRP $1225.00

COOK & BROTHER RIFLE

Lock: Muzzleloading
Stock: Walnut
Barrel: 33 in.
Chokes: IC, M, F
Sights: Fixed
Weight: 8 lb. 10 oz.
Bore/Gauge: .58
Features: Brass garnitures; brown colour barrel
MSRP $1315.00

DERRINGER PHILADELPHIA

Lock: Percussion
Stock: Walnut
Barrel: 3.06 in.
Sights: None
Weight: 8.6 oz.
Bore/Caliber: .45
Features: Originally manufactured by John Henry Derringer; brass furniture; case-hardened lock; original markings on the lock: Derringer/Philadelphia
MSRP $550.00

ENFIELD 3 BAND P1853 RIFLE MUSKET

Lock: Percussion
Stock: Walnut
Barrel: 39 in.
Sights: Adjustable rear
Weight: 8 lb. 13 oz.
Bore/Caliber: .577
Features: Ladder rear sight with a slider assembled on a base with steps; steel barrel bands; brass furniture; ramrod tip is shaped with characteristic jag slot
MSRP $1315.00

ENFIELD 3 BAND P1853 WHITWORTH WITH HEXAGONAL RIFLING

Lock: Percussion cap
Stock: American walnut
Barrel: 36 in.
Sights: Creedmoor sight, tunnel front
Weight: 9 lb. 7.4 oz.
Bore/Caliber: .451
Features: Hammer-forged browned finish hexagonal barrel; lock parts with light colour case hardened finish
MSRP $2075.00

GIBBS SHORT RANGE RIFLE

Action: Percussion
Stock: Walnut
Barrel: 32 in.
Sights: Tunnel front, Creedmoor rear
Weight: 10 lb. 9.6 oz.
Caliber: .45
Features: Modeled on the original Gibbs; equipped with a barrel made for target shooting at 100-150 meters
MSRP $2125.00

GIBBS SHOTGUN

Lock: Percussion
Stock: Walnut
Barrel: 32.3 in.
Sights: None
Weight: 8 lb. 9 oz.
Bore/Caliber: 12 Ga.
Features: Octagonal to round barrel; case-hardened color-finished lock; grip and forend caps with ebony inserts; pistol grip stock
MSRP $1710.00

HAWKEN HUNTER RIFLE

Lock: Percussion, flintlock
Stock: Wood
Barrel: 28.4 in.
Chokes: IC, M, F
Sights: Adjustable rear, fixed front
Weight: 8 lb. 10 oz.
Bore/Gauge: .50, .54
Features: American walnut stock features a microcell thick butt plate; double set triggers
Percussion: $795.00
Percussion left-hand: $825.00
Flintlock: $855.00
Flintlock left-hand: $880.00

Davide Pedersoli & C.

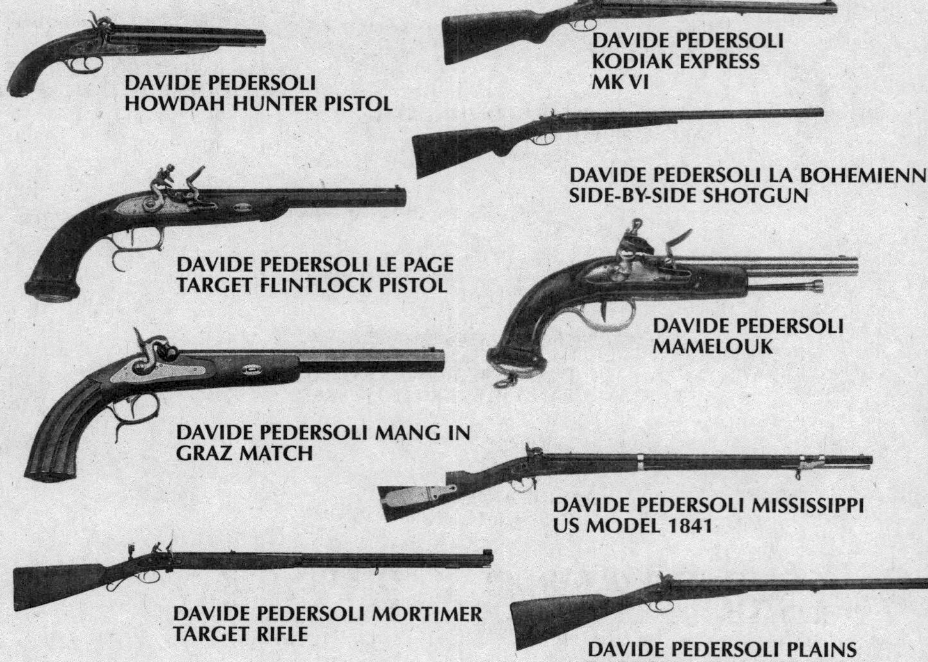
DAVIDE PEDERSOLI HOWDAH HUNTER PISTOL

DAVIDE PEDERSOLI KODIAK EXPRESS MK VI

DAVIDE PEDERSOLI LA BOHEMIENNE SIDE-BY-SIDE SHOTGUN

DAVIDE PEDERSOLI LE PAGE TARGET FLINTLOCK PISTOL

DAVIDE PEDERSOLI MAMELOUK

DAVIDE PEDERSOLI MANG IN GRAZ MATCH

DAVIDE PEDERSOLI MISSISSIPPI US MODEL 1841

DAVIDE PEDERSOLI MORTIMER TARGET RIFLE

DAVIDE PEDERSOLI PLAINS SHOTGUN "THE FAST BACK VACTION"

HOWDAH HUNTER PISTOL

Lock: Caplock
Stock: Walnut
Barrel: 11.25 in.
Sights: None
Weight: 5 lb. 1 oz.
Bore/Caliber: .45 LC, .45/.410, .50, .58
Features: Engraved locks with wild animal scenes; case-hardened color finish; checkered walnut pistol grip with steel butt cap
Shotgun: $910.00
.50-caliber: $1030.00
.58-caliber: $1045.00
Combo 20-gauge/.50-caliber: $1030.00

KODIAK EXPRESS MK VI

Lock: Percussion
Stock: Hardwood
Barrel: 24.25 in.
Sights: Creedmore
Weight: 10 lb. 2 oz.
Bore/Caliber: .50, .54, .58
Features: A very manageable gun, perfectly balanced; particularly suitable for wild boar hunting; practical rubber buttplate; half pistol grip stock; equipped with ghost sights
MSRP $1535.00

LA BOHEMIENNE SIDE-BY-SIDE SHOTGUN

Lock: Hinged breech muzzleloading
Stock: Checkered walnut
Barrel: 28 in.
Chokes: cyl/mod choke tubes
Weight: 7 lb.
Bore/Caliber: 12 Ga.
Features: Rust brown finish barrel; interchangeable chokes; color case-hardened frame; hand-engraved locks
MSRP $2200.00

LE PAGE TARGET PISTOL

Lock: Flintlock, percussion
Stock: Walnut
Barrel: 10.5 in.
Sights: Adjustable
Weight: 2 lb. 10 oz.
Bore/Caliber: .31, .36, .44 (percussion); .44, .45 (flintlock)
Features: Smoothbore .45 available; adjustable single-set trigger; brightly polished lock with a roller frizzen spring
Percussion: $1005.00
Flintlock: $1335.00

MAMELOUK

Lock: Flintlock
Stock: Hardwood
Barrel: 7.6 in.
Sights: Fixed
Weight: 1 lb. 10 oz.
Bore/Caliber: N/A
Features: Like all the firearms equipping Napoleon's Imperial Guards, the Mameluke pistols were made at the Manufacture of Versailles under the technical management of Nicolas-Noël Boutet; the trigger guard, buttcap, screw washers of the lock, and ramrod tip are brass
MSRP $735.00

MANG IN GRAZ MATCH

Lock: Percussion
Stock: Walnut
Barrel: 11.4 in.
Sights: Fixed
Weight: 2 lb. 10 oz.
Bore/Caliber: .38, .44
Features: Fluted grip; octagonal, rifled barrel in brown rust finish; adjustable single set trigger; breech plug shows a typical mask of the period; barrel and tang enriched with gold inlays
MSRP $1940.00

MISSISSIPPI US MODEL 1841

Lock: Percussion
Stock: Walnut
Barrel: 33 in.
Sights: Open rear
Weight: 9 lb. 8 oz.
Bore/Caliber: .54, .58
Features: Considered the best-looking ordnance rifle of its period; brass furniture; browned barrel; notched rear sight; case-hardened lock; ramrod with brass tip
MSRP $1345.00

MORTIMER TARGET RIFLE

Lock: Flintlock
Stock: English-style European walnut
Barrel: 36.4 in.
Sights: Target
Weight: 10 lb. 2 oz.
Bore/Caliber: .54
Features: Case-colored lock; stock has cheekpiece and hand checkering; 7-groove barrel
MSRP $2030.00

PLAINS SHOTGUN "THE FAST BACK ACTION"

Lock: Caplock
Stock: Walnut
Barrel: 27.5 in., 28.5 in.
Sights: None
Weight: 7 lb. 5 oz.–7 lb. 8 oz.
Bore/Caliber: 12, 20 Ga.
Features: Single trigger; side-by-side shotgun; fast second shot, thanks to back action lock reducing minor residues of black powder in lock parts
MSRP $1375.00

Davide Pedersoli & C.

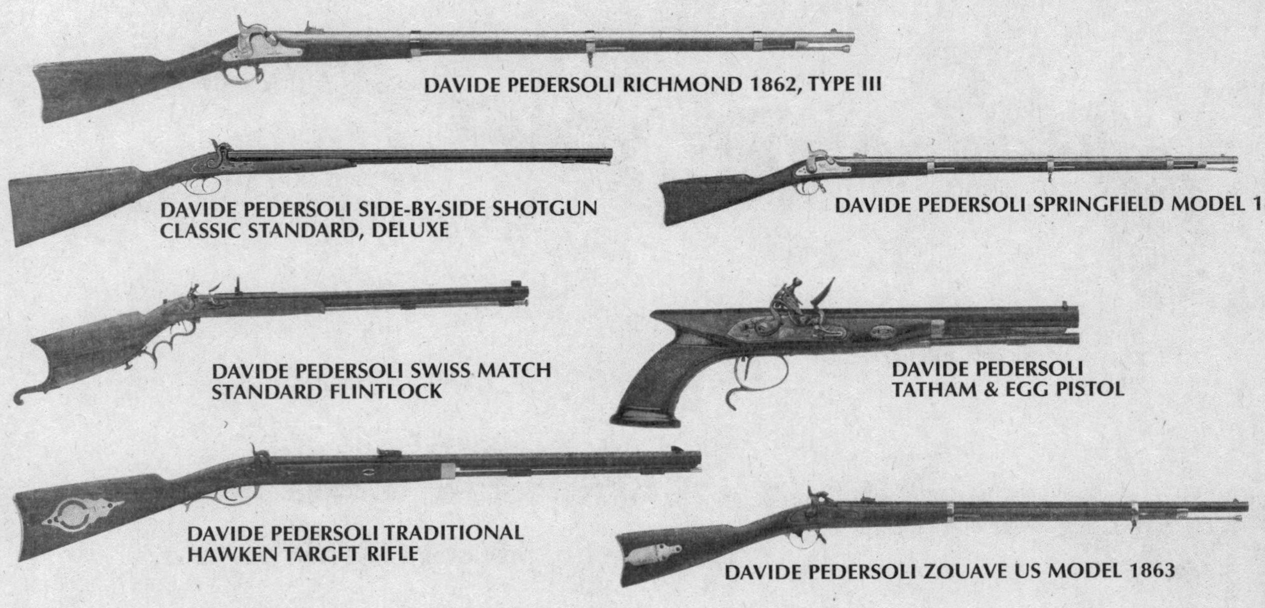

DAVIDE PEDERSOLI RICHMOND 1862, TYPE III

DAVIDE PEDERSOLI SIDE-BY-SIDE SHOTGUN CLASSIC STANDARD, DELUXE

DAVIDE PEDERSOLI SPRINGFIELD MODEL 1861 US

DAVIDE PEDERSOLI SWISS MATCH STANDARD FLINTLOCK

DAVIDE PEDERSOLI TATHAM & EGG PISTOL

DAVIDE PEDERSOLI TRADITIONAL HAWKEN TARGET RIFLE

DAVIDE PEDERSOLI ZOUAVE US MODEL 1863

RICHMOND 1862, TYPE III

Lock: Percussion
Stock: Walnut
Barrel: 39.75 in.
Sights: None
Weight: 9 lb. 14 oz.
Bore/Caliber: .58
Features: Manufactured based on the U.S. 1855 Model with the Maynard tape ignition system; except for the lock's profile, the brass buttplate, and the stock nose cap, the gun's appearance resembles the U.S. Model 1861
MSRP $1250.00

SIDE-BY-SIDE SHOTGUN CLASSIC, CLASSIC EXTRA DELUXE

Action: Percussion
Stock: Walnut
Barrel: 28.5 in.
Sights: Brass bead
Weight: 7 lb.
Caliber: 20 ga., 12 ga.
Features: Standard has a walnut stock, case-hardened receiver, and blued barrels; deluxe has wood, scroll-engraved receiver in a coin finish and rust-brown barrels
Classic: $1150.00
Extra Deluxe: $5105.00

SPRINGFIELD MODEL 1861 US

Lock: Caplock
Stock: Walnut
Barrel: 40 in.
Sights: None
Weight: 9 lb. 14 oz.
Bore/Caliber: .58
Features: More efficient than earlier smooth bored muskets used by both sides in the American Civil War; satin finish barrel; stock with three bands; coin-colored finish on the steel furniture
MSRP $1290.0

SWISS MATCH STANDARD FLINTLOCK

Lock: Flintlock
Stock: Walnut
Barrel: 30.8 in.
Sights: Adjustable
Weight: 16 lb. 5 oz.
Bore/Caliber: .40
Features: Octagonal conical profile barrel with rust brown finish; lock is case-hardened; steel ramrod; double-set trigger; steel hook buttplate
MSRP $3640.00

TATHAM & EGG PISTOL

Lock: Flintlock
Stock: Walnut
Barrel: 10.06 in.
Sights: Adjustable rear
Weight: 2 lb. 6.7 oz.
Bore/Caliber: .45 (smooth), .42
Features: Ergonomic grip; set trigger; PMG-quality trigger; case-hardened metal parts
MSRP $1425.00

TRADITIONAL HAWKEN TARGET RIFLE

Lock: Percussion, flintlock
Stock: Wood
Barrel: 28.4 in.
Chokes: IC, M, F
Sights: Adjustable rear, fixed front
Weight: 8 lb. 10 oz.
Bore/Gauge: .50, .54
Features: Double set trigger; adjustable buckhorn rear sight; American walnut stock is enriched with a brass patch box; left-handed version available
Percussion: $745.00
Percussion left-hand: $780.00
Flintlock: $805.00
Flintlock left-hand: $825.00

ZOUAVE US MODEL 1863

Lock: Percussion
Stock: Hardwood
Barrel: 33 in.
Sights: Front, rear
Weight: 9 lb. 4 oz.
Bore/Caliber: .58
Features: Intended for the U.S. Artillery Department and never distributed to any Civil War army division; features brass furnitures; ramrod with a tulip tip; three-leaf rear sight; two sling swivels; the lock shows the Eagle stamp and the U.S. letters in front of the hammer
MSRP $1315.00

Dixie Gun Works

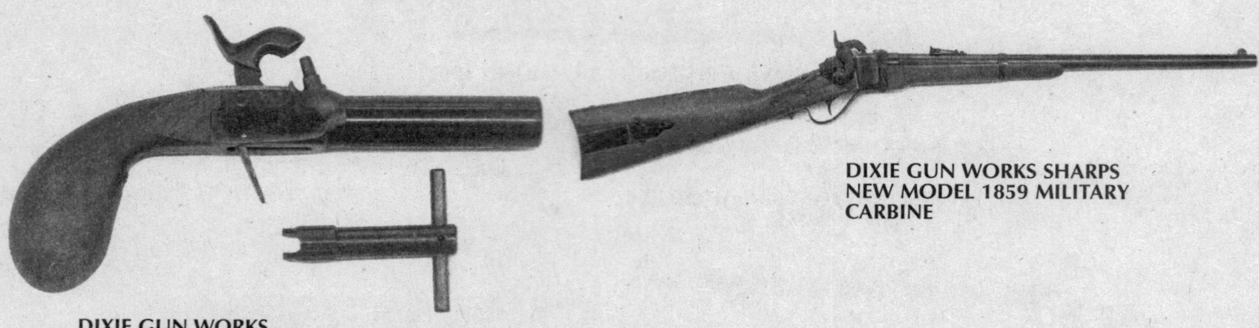

DIXIE GUN WORKS SHARPS NEW MODEL 1859 MILITARY CARBINE

DIXIE GUN WORKS PEDERSOLI SCREW BARREL PISTOL

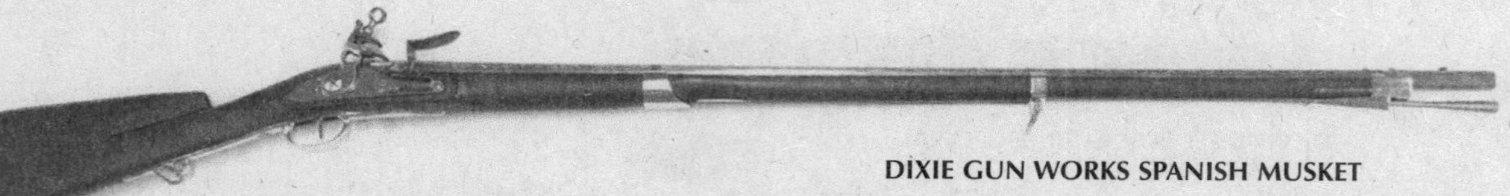

DIXIE GUN WORKS SPANISH MUSKET

BLACK POWDER

PEDERSOLI SCREW BARREL PISTOL

Lock: Traditional caplock
Stock: European walnut
Barrel: 3 in.
Sights: None
Weight: 12 oz.
Bore/Caliber: .44
Features: Color case-hardened lock; single folding trigger; combination nipple/barrel wrench included
MSRP $240.00

SHARPS NEW MODEL 1859 MILITARY CARBINE

Lock: Dropping block
Stock: Walnut
Barrel: 22 in.
Sights: Adjustable open
Weight: 8 lb.
Bore/Caliber: .54
Features: Steel furniture; color case-hardened; single trigger; single barrel band; saddle bar with ring
MSRP $1535.00

SPANISH MUSKET

Lock: Flintlock muzzleloading
Stock: Full, European walnut 56 in.
Barrel: 44.75 in.
Sights: Steel stud front
Weight: 10 lb.
Bore/Caliber: .68 round ball
Features: Brass buttplate, trigger guard, and barrel bands; bright steel sideplates; steel ramrod
MSRP $1450.00

EMF Company, Inc.

EMF 1860 ARMY REVOLVER

EMF 1863 REMINGTON POCKET STEEL

1860 ARMY REVOLVER

Lock: Caplock revolver
Stock: Walnut
Barrel: 8 in.
Sights: Fixed
Weight: 41.6 oz.
Bore/Caliber: .44
Features: Case-hardened frame; blued barrel
Brass: $265.00
Case-hardened: $285.00
Steel: $310.00
Old Silver: $335.00
Deluxe Engraved Old Silver: $605.00
London: $300.00
Old West frame $330.00
Snub-nosed casehardened: $335.00

1863 REMINGTON POCKET STEEL

Lock: Caplock revolver
Stock: Walnut
Barrel: 3.5 in.
Sights: Fixed
Weight: 21 oz.
Bore/Caliber: .36
Features: Steel frame, blued barrel
MSRP $405.00

Lyman

DEERSTALKER RIFLE

Lock: Traditional cap or flint
Stock: Walnut
Barrel: 24 in.
Sights: Fiber optic front and rear
Weight: 10 lb. 6 oz.
Bore/Caliber: .50, .54
Features: Quiet single trigger; metal blackened to avoid glare; black rubber recoil pad; left-hand available
MSRP . . . . $599.95–$708.95

GREAT PLAINS RIFLE

Lock: Traditional cap or flint
Stock: Walnut
Barrel: 32 in.
Sights: Adjustable open
Weight: 11 lb. 10 oz.
Bore/Caliber: .50, .54
Features: Double-set triggers; Hawken style percussion "snail" with clean-out screw; separate ramrod entry thimble and nose cap; left-hand available
Percussion: . . . . . $1164.95–$1240.95
Flintlock: . . . . $1138.00–$1240.95

PLAINS PISTOL

Lock: Percussion, flintlock
Stock: Walnut
Barrel: 6 in.
Sights: Fixed
Weight: 3 lb. 2 oz.
Bore/Caliber: .50, .54
Features: Blackened iron furniture; polished brass trigger guard and ramrod tips; hooked patent breech takes down quickly for easy cleaning
MSRP $445.95

TRADE RIFLE

Lock: Traditional cap or flint
Stock: Walnut
Barrel: 28 in.
Sights: Adjustable open
Weight: 10 lb. 13 oz.
Bore/Caliber: .50, .54
Features: Brass furniture; originally developed for the early Indian fur trade
Percussion: $607.50
Flintlock: $669.95

Shiloh Rifle

1874 CREEDMOOR TARGET RIFLE

Lock: Blackpowder cartridge
Stock: Walnut
Barrel: 32 in.
Sights: V aiming rear; blade front
Weight: 9 lb.
Bore/Caliber: All popular black powder cartridges from .38-55 to .50-90
Features: Pistol grip; single trigger; AA finish on American black walnut; polished barrel; octagon barrel; pewter tip
MSRP $3201.00

1874 QUIGLEY

Lock: Falling block
Stock: Walnut
Barrel: 34 in.
Sights: Semi buckhorn rear, midrange vernier tang, #111 globe aperture front
Weight: 12 lb. 8 oz.
Bore/Caliber: .45-70 Govt. or .45-110
Features: Military buttstock; patchbox; heavy octagonal barrel; pewter tip; Hartford collars; double set triggers; antique or standard color finish; gold inlay initials in gold oval
MSRP $3639.00

1877 #1 SHILOH ENGLISH RIFLE

Lock: Muzzleloading
Stock: Wood
Barrel: 26 in.–34 in.
Sights: Adjustable
Weight: N/A
Bore/Caliber: .38-55, .40-50BN, .40-50ST, .40-65, .40-70ST, .40-70BN, .40-90BN, .45-70, .45-90, .45-100
Features: Standard pistol grip; standard forearm; standard color cased; full or semi buckhorn rear sight; blade front sight; single trigger
MSRP $2250.00

Taylor's & Co. Firearms

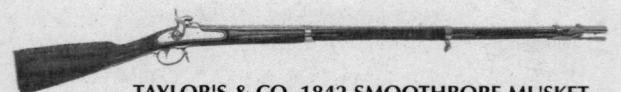

TAYLOR'S & CO. 1842 SMOOTHBORE MUSKET

TAYLOR'S & CO. 1847 WALKER

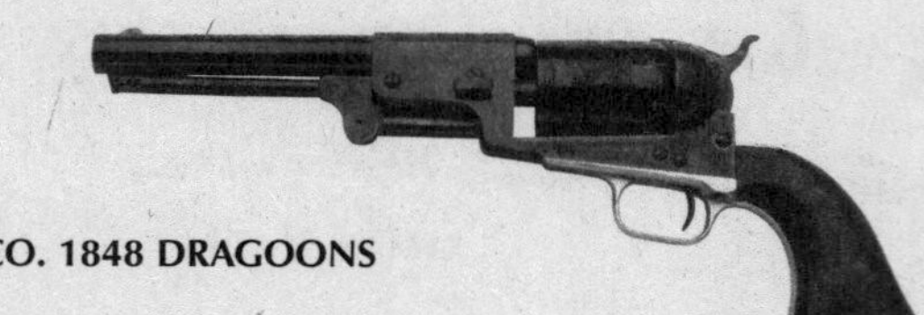

TAYLOR'S & CO. 1848 DRAGOONS

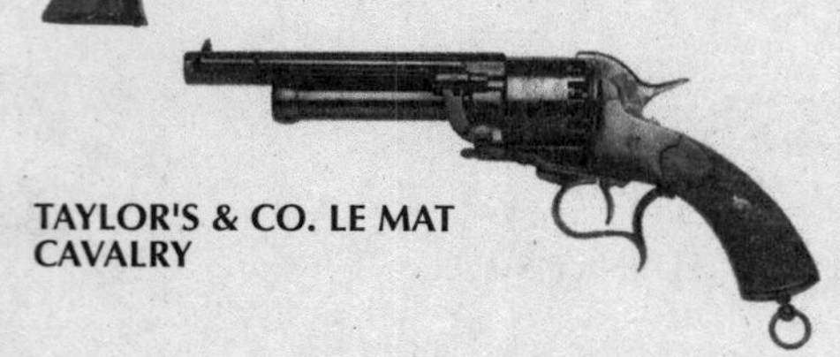

TAYLOR'S & CO. LE MAT CAVALRY

1842 SMOOTHBORE MUSKET

Lock: Percussion
Stock: Walnut
Barrel: 42 in.
Sights: Military style
Weight: 9 lb. 12 oz.
Bore/Caliber: .69
Features: The Springfield replica has all the features of the original, including a one-piece, oil-finished walnut stock; original-style barrel bands; and completely interchangeable parts; the percussion lock has a V-style mainspring; features the lock with stamping noting 1842 and Springfield; NSSA approved, with certificate of authenticity and a brass medallion featuring the model and serial number
MSRP $1219.83

1847 WALKER

Lock: Caplock revolver
Stock: Walnut
Barrel: 9 in.
Sights: Fixed
Weight: 4 lb. 12 oz.
Bore/Caliber: .44
Features: Blued finish; round barrel
Antique finish: $614.37
Case-hardened/blued: $483.52
Charcoal blue finish: $573.48

1848 DRAGOONS

Lock: Caplock revolver
Stock: Walnut
Barrel: 7.5 in.
Sights: Fixed
Weight: 4 lb.–4 lb. 14 oz.
Bore/Caliber: .44
Features: First used by the U.S. Army's Mounted Rifles 1st Cavalry in 1833 and they went on to see considerable use during the 1850 and during the Civil War; blued finish; six-round capacity; available in 1st, 2nd, and 3rd models, as well as the Whitney variation
1st, 2nd, 3rd: $475.33
Whitneyville: $483.52

LE MAT CAVALRY

Lock: Caplock revolver
Stock: Walnut
Barrel: 8 in.
Sights: Fixed
Weight: 5 lb.
Bore/Caliber: .44 or 20 Ga.
Features: Blued steel finish; nine-shot .44 caliber revolver with a 20 Ga. single-shot barrel was a favorite among Confederate cavalry troops; case-hardened hammer and trigger; lanyard ring; trigger guard with spur
MSRP $1242.80

Thompson/Center Arms

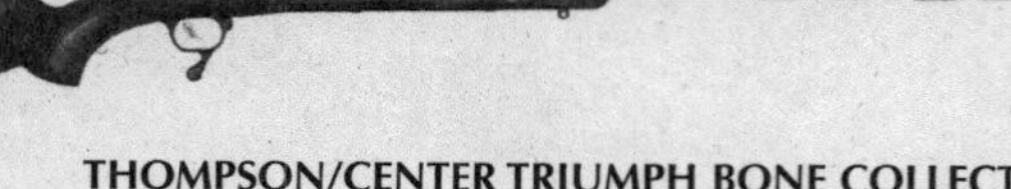

THOMPSON/CENTER ARMS IMPACT!SB

THOMPSON/CENTER TRIUMPH BONE COLLECTOR

IMPACT!SB

Action: Break-open
Stock: Synthetic
Barrel: 26 inv.
Sights: Fiber optic front, adjustable rear
Weight: 6 lb. 15 oz.
Caliber: .50
Features: Featuring a hand-removeable triple lead thread breech plug; Power Rod aluminum ramrod; single-0shot sliding hood design; adjustable stock with spacers. Five finish/stock options: blued/black; Silver Weather Shield/Realtree Edge; Silver Weather Shield/black; blued/Mossy Oak Bottomland; Silver Weather Shield/Mossy Oak Break-Up Country
MSRP . . . . $269.00–$332.00

TRIUMPH BONE COLLECTOR

Lock: In-line
Stock: Composite, black or Realtree AP HD camo
Barrel: 28 in.
Sights: Adjustable fiber optic
Weight: 6 lb. 8 oz.
Bore/Caliber: .50
Features: Blued, stainless, and weather shield finish; speed breech XT
MSRP . . . . $638.00–$720.00

Traditions Firearms

TRADITIONS FIREARMS 1851 NAVY REVOLVER

TRADITIONS FIREARMS 1858 ARMY REVOLVER

TRADITIONS FIREARMS 1860 ARMY REVOLVER

TRADITIONS FIREARMS BUCKSTALKER

TRADITIONS FIREARMS DEERHUNTER RIFLE

TRADITIONS FIREARMS HAWKEN WOODSMAN RIFLE

1851 NAVY REVOLVER

Lock: Caplock revolver
Stock: Walnut
Barrel: 7.5 in.
Sights: Fixed
Weight: 2 lb. 8 oz.
Bore/Caliber: .44, .36
Features: Octagonal barrel and lever-style loader; brass, antiqued, or old silver frame and guard
MSRP . . . . $267.00–$299.00

1858 ARMY REVOLVER

Lock: Caplock
Stock: Walnut
Barrel: 8 in.
Sights: Fixed
Weight: 2 lb. 12 oz.
Bore/Caliber: .44
Features: Octagonal barrel and lever style loader; brass frame and guard; top strap and post sights
MSRP $305.00

1860 ARMY REVOLVER

Lock: Caplock
Stock: Simulated ivory, walnut
Barrel: 8 in.
Sights: Fixed
Weight: 2 lb. 12 oz.
Bore/Caliber: .44
Features: Blued barrel and cylinder; choice of brass or case-hardened steel frames
Brass: $313.00
Steel: $344.00

BUCKSTALKER

Lock: Break-action muzzleloading
Stock: Synthetic
Barrel: 24 in.
Sights: Tru-Glo fiber optics
Weight: 7 lb. 8 oz.
Bore/Caliber: .50
Features: Dual safety system; nickel guard coating; synthetic black stock; blued or Cerakote brushed silver metalwork; Monte Carlo stock; drilled and tapped for a scope; sling swivel studs
Blued: $219.00
Cerakote silver: $254.00

DEERHUNTER RIFLE

Lock: Traditional cap or flint
Stock: Synthetic or hardwood
Barrel: 24 in.
Sights: Lite Optic adjustable
Weight: 6 lb.
Bore/Caliber: .50
Features: Octagonal performance barrels; blued or nickel barrel finish; percussion models are drilled and tapped to accept scope mounts; non-slip recoil pad; stock comes in black synthetic or hardwood
Hardwood: . . . . . . $323.00–$399.00
Synthetic: . . . . $269.00–$351.00

HAWKEN WOODSMAN RIFLE

Lock: Traditional cap or flint
Stock: Hardwood
Barrel: 28 in.
Sights: Adjustable rear hunting
Weight: 7 lb. 13 oz.
Bore/Caliber: .50
Features: Hooked breech for easy barrel removal; double-set triggers in an oversized glove-fitting trigger guard; inletted solid brass patch box; left-hand model available; octagonal blued barrel
Flintlock: $544.00
Percussion: $499.00

Traditions Firearms

TRADITIONS FIREARMS KENTUCKY PISTOL

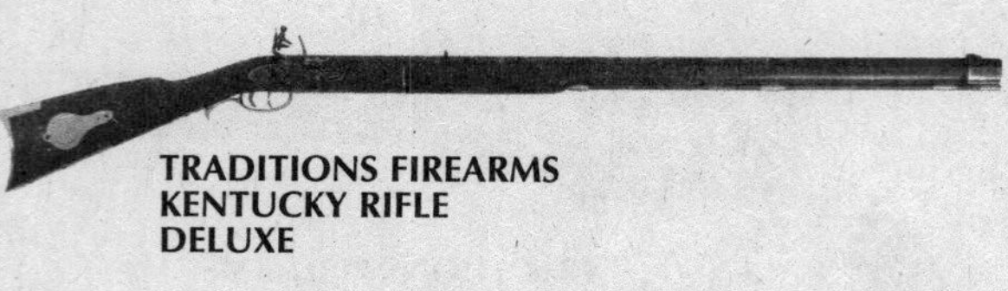

TRADITIONS FIREARMS KENTUCKY RIFLE DELUXE

TRADITIONS FIREARMS NITROFIRE

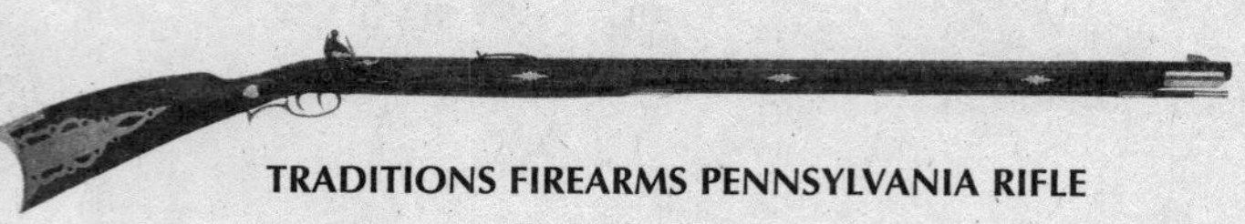

TRADITIONS FIREARMS PENNSYLVANIA RIFLE

TRADITIONS FIREARMS PURSUIT G4 ULTRALIGHT

TRADITIONS FIREARMS TRAPPER PISTOL

TRADITIONS FIREARMS VORTEK STRIKERFIRE

KENTUCKY PISTOL

Lock: Traditional caplock
Stock: Hardwood
Barrel: 10 in.
Sights: Fixed
Weight: 2 lb. 8 oz.
Bore/Caliber: .50
Features: Brass furniture; case-colored sidelock and brass ramrod thimble
MSRP $254.00

KENTUCKY RIFLE DELUXE

Action: Flintlock
Stock: Walnut
Barrel: 33.5 in.
Sights: Blade front, notch rear
Weight: N/A
Caliber: .50
Features: A handsome traditional flintlock with case-hardened flintlock; wooden ramrod; double-set triggers; 1:66 twist; brass furniture
MSRP $549.00

NITROFIRE

Action: Break-open
Stock: Synthetic
Barrel: 26 in.
Sights: None
Weight: N/A
Caliber: .50
Features: First muzzleloader to utilize Federal's Firestick propellant charge, which is breech loaded; projectiles load from muzzle; Elite XT trigger system with rebounding hammer, captive half-cock; Cerakote finish on metalwork; stocks in black and in camo by Mossy Oak, Realtree, and Go Wild
MSRP . . . . $549.00–$1220.00

PENNSYLVANIA RIFLE

Lock: Traditional cap or flint
Stock: Walnut
Barrel: 20 in.
Sights: Adjustable primitive style rear
Weight: 8 lb. 8 oz.
Bore/Caliber: .50
Features: Brass stock inlay ornamentation and toe plate; cheekpiece; solid brass patch box
Flintlock: $865.00
Percussion: $834.00

PURSUIT G4 ULTRALIGHT

Lock: Muzzleloading
Stock: Synthetic
Barrel: 26 in.
Chokes: IC, M, F
Sights: Fixed front, adjustable rear
Weight: 5 lb. 12 oz.
Bore/Gauge: .50
Features: Wider forend; Accelerator Breech Plug; Ultralight Chromoly Tapered, Fluted Barrel with Premium CeraKote Finish; LT-1 Alloy Frame; dual safety system - internal hammer block safety and trigger block safety; speed load system; soft touch camo stocks; Quick Relief Recoil Pad; Williams Fiber Optic Metal Sights; fast action release button; 1:28″ twist rifling; extended ambidextrous hammer extension; drilled and tapped for a scope; sling swivel studs; 209 shotgun primer ignition
MSRP . . . . $344.00–$539.00

TRAPPER PISTOL

Lock: Traditional cap or flint
Stock: Hardwood
Barrel: 9.75 in.
Sights: Primitive-style adjustable rear
Weight: 2 lb. 14 oz.
Bore/Caliber: .50
Features: Octagonal blued barrel; double set triggers
Flintlock: $385.00
Percussion: $344.00

VORTEK STRIKERFIRE

Lock: Strikerfire
Stock: Soft Touch synthetic
Barrel: 28 in.
Sights: Fiber optic
Weight: N/A
Bore/Caliber: .50
Features: This patent-pending rifle takes in-line muzzleloaders to the next level by taking away the external hammer and using an internal StrikerFire System; to cock the gun, simply slide the striker button forward until it locks and fire; the recessed de-cocking buttons allows for quick and quiet de-cocking of the firearm and the gun is also equipped with an automatic de-cocking mechanism—when the gun is opened, it is automatically de-cocked; also includes: two-stage trigger; CeraKote finish; Realtree Xtra, black, Mossy Oak Break-Up Country; most options available with 3-9x40mm Traditions Duplex scopes
MSRP . . . . $399.00–$654.00

UBERTI 1847 WALKER

UBERTI 1848 DRAGOON

UBERTI 1849 POCKET REVOLVER

UBERTI 1851 NAVY REVOLVER

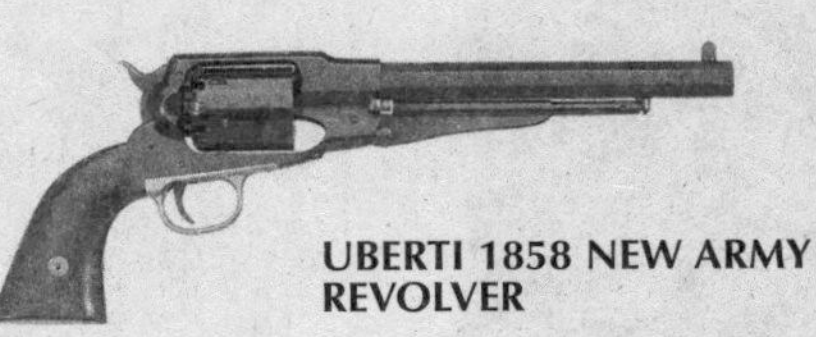
UBERTI 1858 NEW ARMY REVOLVER

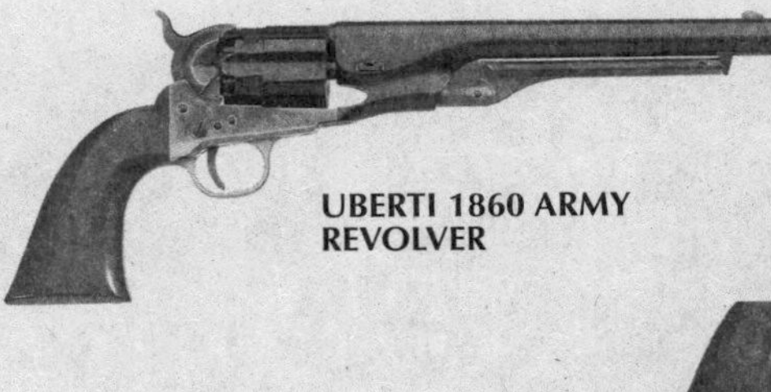
UBERTI 1860 ARMY REVOLVER

UBERTI 1861 NAVY REVOLVER

UBERTI 1862 POCKET NAVY REVOLVER

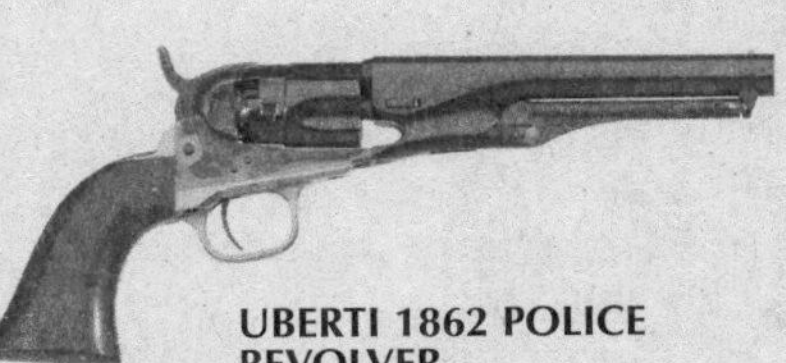
UBERTI 1862 POLICE REVOLVER

1847 WALKER

Lock: Caplock revolver
Stock: Walnut
Barrel: 9 in.
Sights: Fixed, open
Weight: 4 lb. 8 oz.
Bore/Caliber: .44
Features: Case-hardened frame, steel backstrap, brass trigger guard; blued finish
MSRP $489.00

1848 DRAGOON

Lock: Caplock revolver
Stock: Walnut
Barrel: 7.5 in.
Sights: Fixed, open
Weight: 4 lb. 2 oz.
Bore/Caliber: .44
Features: Case-hardened frame; steel or brass backstrap and trigger guard; engraved
2nd, 3rd Models: $479.00
Whitneyville: $489.00

1849 POCKET REVOLVER

Lock: Caplock revolver
Stock: Walnut
Barrel: 4 in.
Sights: Fixed, open
Weight: 1 lb. 8 oz.
Bore/Caliber: .31
Features: Case-hardened frame; brass backstrap and trigger guard; blued octagonal barrel; engraved
MSRP $389.00

1851 NAVY REVOLVER

Lock: Caplock revolver
Stock: Walnut
Barrel: 7.5 in.
Sights: Fixed, open
Weight: 2 lb. 10 oz.
Bore/Caliber: .36
Features: Color case-hardened frame; oval or squareback trigger guard; brass or steel backstrap and trigger guard; octagonal barrel (Leech-Rigdon model has round barrel)
MSRP . . . . $359.00–$389.00

1858 NEW ARMY REVOLVER

Lock: Caplock revolver
Stock: Walnut
Barrel: 8 in.
Sights: Fixed, open
Weight: 2 lb. 11 oz.
Bore/Caliber: .44
Features: Blued or stainless steel frame and backstrap; brass trigger guard; octagonal barrel
Blue: $409.00
Stainless: $509.00

1860 ARMY REVOLVER

Lock: Caplock revolver
Stock: Walnut
Barrel: 7.5 in.
Sights: Fixed, open
Weight: 2 lb. 10 oz.
Bore/Caliber: .44
Features: Case-hardened frame, steel backstrap, brass trigger guard; blued, round barrel
MSRP $389.00

1861 NAVY REVOLVER

Lock: Caplock revolver
Stock: Walnut
Barrel: 7.5 in.
Sights: Fixed, open
Weight: 2 lb. 10 oz.
Bore/Caliber: .36
Features: Case-hardened frame, steel or
brass backstrap and trigger guard
MSRP $389.00

1862 POCKET NAVY REVOLVER

Lock: Caplock revolver
Stock: Walnut
Barrel: 5.5 in., 6.5 in.
Sights: Fixed, open
Weight: 1 lb. 11 oz.
Bore/Caliber: .36
Features: Case-hardened frame; brass backstrap and trigger guard; octagonal, blued barrel
MSRP $409.00

1862 POLICE REVOLVER

Lock: Caplock revolver
Stock: Walnut
Barrel: 5.5 in., 6.5 in.
Sights: Fixed, open
Weight: 1 lb. 10 oz.
Bore/Caliber: .36
Features: Case-hardened frame; brass backstrap and trigger guard; fluted round barrel
MSRP $409.00

OPTICS

Accufire Technology

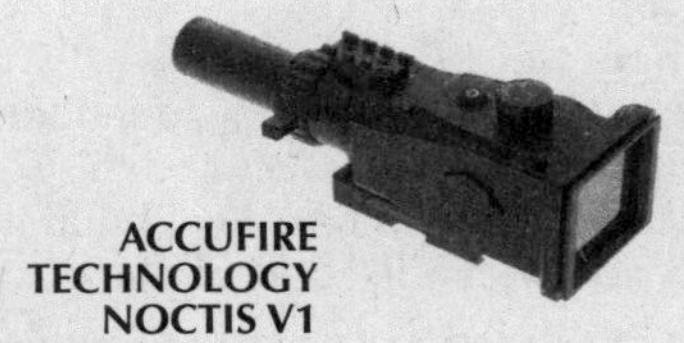
ACCUFIRE TECHNOLOGY NOCTIS V1

NOCTIS V1

Type: Nightvision
Power: 1–16X
Features: Compact day/night vision unit with loads of features, including HD-quality night vision; savable presets; ballistic calculations; fifty downloadable reticles; HD video recording in all light levels; built-in Wi-Fi
MSRP $699.00

ATN Corp.

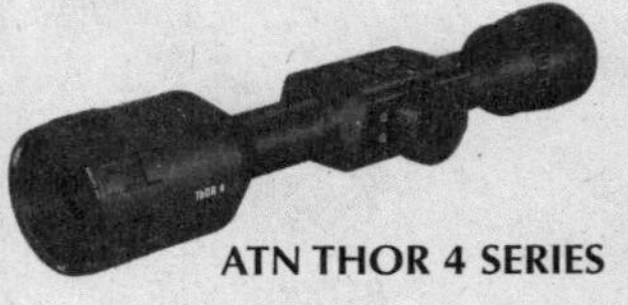
ATN THOR 4 SERIES

ATN X-SIGHT 4K BUCKHUNTER

ATN CORP. X-SIGHT 4K INT

ATN X-SIGHT 4K PRO

THOR 4 SERIES

Available in: 1.25–5x, 2–8x, 4.5–18x, 7–28x, 1-10x, 1.5–15x, 2.5–25x, 4–40x
Weight: 31 oz.–37 oz.
Length: 13.1–14.8 in.
Power: 1.25–5x, 2–8x, 4.5–18x, 7–28x, 1-10x, 1.5–15x, 2.5–25x, 4–40x
Main Dia.: 30mm
Eye Relief: 3.5 in.
Features: Thermal vision Smart HD scopes; Gen4 sensor that will display in black hot, white hot, or color modes; can record and stream video; Smart rangefinder; ballistic calculator that displays target profile and environmental conditions; 3D gyroscope; 3D accelerometer; recoil-activated video; e-barometer; microphone; SD card; HD display
MSRP . . . . $1999.00–$4799.00

X-SIGHT 4K BUCKHUNTER

Available in: 3–14x, 5–20x
Weight: 33.6 oz.
Length: 13.8 in.
Power: 3–14x, 5–20x
Main Dia.: 30mm
Eye Relief: 3.5 in.
Features: Smart scope; video records in 1080 Full HD; built-in rangefinder; ballistic calculator; recoil-activated and streaming video capabilities; a built-in compass; Smooth Zoom
3–14x: $599.00
5–20x: $699.00

X-SIGHT 4K INT

Available in: 3–14x, 5–20x
Weight: 33 oz.
Length: 13.8 in.
Power: 3–14X, 5–20X
Main Dia.: 30mm
Field of View: 460 ft.@1000 yd.
Eye Relief: 90mm
Features: A smart HD day/night riflescope with built-in SD card recording capabilities in 1080P full HD, streaming at 720p; spin to zoom wheel; one-shot zero capabilities; smart rangefinder; recoil-activated recording; 1280x720 HD micro display; 3D gyroscope and accelerometer
3–14X: $1199.00
5–20X: $1299.00

X-SIGHT 4K PRO

Available in: 3–14x, 5–20x
Weight: 33.6 oz.
Length: 13.8 in.
Power: 3–14x, 5–20x
Main Dia.: 30mm
Eye Relief: 3.5 in.
Features: Smart scope with day and night capabilities; video records in 1080 Full HD; built-in rangefinder that lets you zero in one shot; ballistic calculator; recoil-activated and streaming video capabilities; a built-in compass; Smooth Zoom
3–14x: $699.00
5–20x: $799.00

Barska

BARSKA AR6 1–6X24MM

BARSKA LEVEL HD, LEVEL HD FFP

AR6 1–6X24MM

Weight: 17.6 oz.
Length: 11 in.
Power: 1–6X
Obj. Dia.: 24mm
Main Dia.: 30mm
Exit Pupil: 4–11mm
Field of View: 75.78–12.79 ft @ 100 yds
Twilight Factor: 4.9–12
Eye Relief: 3.7 in.
Features: Water- and fogproof; red or green illuminated reticle; dual cantilever ring scope mount, flip-up scope caps
MSRP $282.99

LEVEL HD, LEVEL HD FFP

Available in: 1–4x24mm, 1–6x24mm
Weight: 16 oz.
Length: 10 in., 10.5 in.
Power: 1–4X, 1–6X
Obj. Dia.: 24mm
Main Dia.: 30mm
Exit Pupil: 5.88–2.29mm, 8–3.5mm
Field of View: 25–7.6 ft.@100 yd., 18.8 ft.–5.7 ft.@100 yd.
Eye Relief: 4.76–3.94 in., 3.9–3.5 in.
Features: Close and mid-range shooting applications will find favor with the scope featuring an illuminated HRS Quick Shot .223 BDC reticle; fully multi-coated optics; reticle can be red or green and adjusted for brightness; lockable turrets; 1–6X has first focal plane glass-etched reticle
MSRP . . . . $257.99–$447.99

Brownells

BROWNELLS RETRO CARRY HANDLE SCOPE

RETRO CARRY HANDLE SCOPE

Available in: 4x
Weight: 13.3 oz.
Length: 6.1 in.
Power: 4X
Obj. Dia.: 21mm
Main Dia.: 1 in.
Eye Relief: 3.11 in.
Features: Brownells says they found the original company that manufactured this sight during the 1970s and had them build this new version with a fixed focal plane
MSRP $299.99

Burris

BURRIS 2–7X SCOUT SCOPE

BURRIS DROPTINE RIFLESCOPE 4.5–14X42MM

BURRIS ELIMINATOR IV LASER

BURRIS FULLFIELD E1 3–9X40MM ILLUMINATED

BURRIS FULLFIELD IV

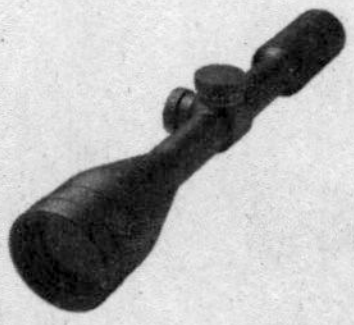

BURRIS MSR RIFLESCOPE 4.5–14X42MM

2–7X SCOUT SCOPE

Weight: 13 oz.
Length: 9.7 in.
Power: 2–7X
Obj. Dia.: 32mm
Main Dia.: 1 in.
Exit Pupil: 16–4.6mm
Field of View: 21–7 ft @ 100 yds
Twilight Factor: 8–15
Eye Relief: 11–21 in.
Features: Ballistic Plex reticle; fully multi-coated; variable power; low mounting capabilities; black matte finish; Scout also available in a fixed-power 2.75x20mm
X20: $299.00
X32: $479.00

DROPTINE RIFLESCOPE 4.5–14X42MM

Weight: 18 oz.
Length: 13 in.
Power: 4.5–14X
Obj. Dia.: 42mm
Main Dia.: 1 in.
Exit Pupil: 9–3mm
Field of View: 22–7.5 ft @ 100 yds
Twilight Factor: 13.75–24.25
Eye Relief: 3.1 in.–3.8 in.
Features: Nitrogen filled; multi-coated lenses; Ballistic Plex reticle or G2B Mil-Dot reticle; adjustable parallax; 3–9x50 also available
4.5–14X: $191.00
3–9X: . . . . $143.00–$155.00

ELIMINATOR IV LASERSCOPE

Available in: 4-16x50mm
Weight: 28.8 oz.
Length: 13.5 in.
Power: 4–16X
Obj. Dia.: 50mm
Exit Pupil: 16–4.2mm
Field of View: 33–9 ft.@100 yd.
Eye Relief: 3.5–4 in.
Features: Enhanced ballistic software with an onboard calculator and bluetooth laser activation; internal digital inclinometer; smart-dope card; built-in laser rangefinder; X96 rear focal plane reticle with five illumination settings; 50 MOA windage/elevation adjustment
MSRP $2039.00

FULLFIELD E1 3–9X40MM ILLUMINATED

Weight: 12 oz.
Length: 11.4 in.
Power: 3–9X
Obj. Dia.: 40mm
Main Dia.: 1 in.
Exit Pupil: 17–5mm
Field of View: 45–13 ft @ 100 yds
Twilight Factor: 10.95–18.97
Eye Relief: 3.1–4.1 in.
Features: A series of cascading dots to the left and right of the reticle help compensate for crosswinds. The dots represent a 10 mph crosswind (+/- 1.5-in. at 400 yds) for most hunting cartridges. For a 5 mph crosswind, halve the distance between dot and reticle. For 20 mph crosswind, simply double the distance. Also available in 4.5–14x42 and 6.5–20x50
3–9X: $227.00
4.5–14X: $263.00
6.5–20X: $347.00

FULLFIELD IV

Available in: 2.5–10x42mm, 3–12x42mm, 3–12x56mm, 4–16x50mm, 6–24x50mm
Weight: 16.8 oz.–18.4 oz.
Length: 11.6 in., 12 in.
Power: 2.5–10X, 3–12X, 4–16X, 6–24X
Obj. Dia.: 42mm, 50mm, 56mm
Main Dia.: 1 in., 30mm
Exit Pupil: 10.1–4.6mm, 11–4mm, 13.7–5.4mm, 1.8–3.4mm, 9.4–2.7mm
Field of View: 46–11 ft.@100 yd., 38–9 ft.@100 yd., 40–1 ft.@100 yd., 26–6.5 ft.@100 yd., 2–5.1 ft.@100 yd.
Eye Relief: 3.5–3.8 in., 3.5–3.9 in., 3.3–3.5 in.
Features: Fourth generation of economical rear focal plane Fullfields; nitrogen-field tubes, waterproof, shockproof, and fogproof; easy turn turret knobs, and multicoated lenses.
2.5–1X: . . . . $203.00–$239.00
3–12X42mm: . . . . . . $263.00–$335.00
3–12X56mm: $359.00
4–16X: . . . . $383.00–$455.00
6–24X: . . . . $479.00–$539.00

MSR RIFLESCOPE 4.5–14X42MM

Weight: 18 oz.
Length: 13 in.
Power: 4.5–14X
Obj. Dia.: 42mm
Main Dia.: 1 in.
Exit Pupil: 9–3mm
Field of View: 22–7.5 ft @ 100 yds
Twilight Factor: 13.75–24.25
Eye Relief: 3.1–3.8 in.
Features: Shock-, water-, and fog-proof; nitrogen filled; multi-coated lenses; Ballistic Plex reticle; adjustable parallax; 3–9x40 also available
4.5–14X: $335.00
3–9X: $239.00

Burris

BURRIS RT-6

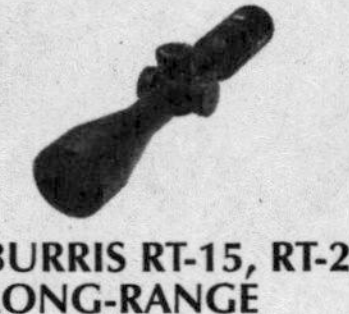
BURRIS RT-15, RT-25 LONG-RANGE

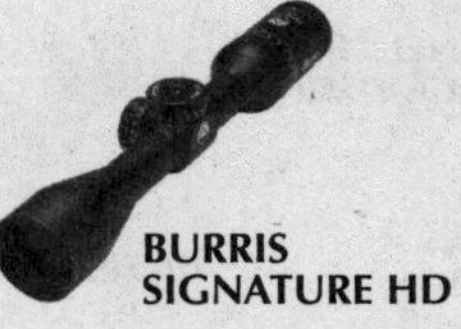
BURRIS SIGNATURE HD

BURRIS T.M.P.R. 3, T.M.P.R. 5

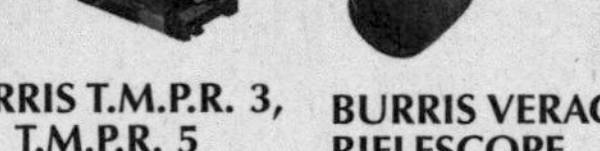

BURRIS VERACITY RIFLESCOPE 2–10X42MM

BURRIS XTR III TACTICAL

RT-6

Weight: 17.4 oz.
Length: 10.3 in.
Power: 1–6x24mm
Obj. Diameter: 24mm
Exit Pupil: 11.5 mm–5.2mm
Eye Relief: 3.3–4 in.
Field of View: 18.5–106 in.
Features: Intended for 3-gun competition; illuminated reticle; integrated adjustable throw lever; eleven brightness levels; tube is 30mm; ballistic AR mil reticle with trajectory compensation to 600 yards
MSRP $419.00

RT-15, RT-25 LONG-RANGE

Available in: 3–15x50mm
Weight: 23.2 oz., 24.8 oz.
Length: 13.2 in., 14.3 in.
Power: 3–15X, 5–25X
Obj. Dia.: 50mm, 56mm
Main Dia.: 30mm
Exit Pupil: 8–3.3mm, 8–2.2mm
Field of View: 37.5–7.5 ft.@100 yd., 22.5–4.5 ft.@100 yd.
Eye Relief: 3.5–3.8 in., 3.3–3.6 in.
Features: First focal plane scopes for distance shooting, adjustable throw lever, zero-stop click turrets, side parallax adjustment, SCR2 Mil reticle
3–15X: $719.00
5–25X: $839.00

SIGNATURE HD

Available in: 2–10x40mm, 3–15x44mm, 5–25x50mm
Weight: 17.6 oz.–24 oz.
Length: 11.7 in.–14.3 in.
Power: 2–10X, 3–15X, 5–25X
Obj. Dia.: 40mm, 44mm, 50mm
Main Dia.: 1 in., 30mm
Exit Pupil: 8–3.5mm, 8–3.3mm, 8–2.2mm
Field of View: 54–10.8 ft.@100 yd., 37.5–7.5 ft.@100 yd., 22.5–4.5 ft.@100 yd.
Eye Relief: 3.5–3.8 in., 3.3–3.6 in.
Features: Second focal plane scopes with multi-coated glass, push-pull locking turrets
2–10X: $431.00
3–15X: . . . . $575.00–$599.00
5–25X: . . . . $719.00–$875.00

T.M.P.R. 3, T.M.P.R. 5

Available in: 3x, 5x
Weight: 18.2 oz.
Length: 5.6 in.
Power: 3x, 5x
Obj. Dia.: 32mm
Field of View: 40 ft.
Eye Relief: 2.2 in.
Features: Modular combo optics package for law enforcement, self-defense, and action sports use; prism optic in 3x or 5x; Ballistic AR reticle; Burris' FastFire M3 red dot sight; Burris T.M.P.R. red laser; components may be purchased individually; ballistic reticle is illuminated digitally at seven levels with a choice of red, blue, or green viewing options; prism is night-vision compatible with three settings and three color choices; CR123 battery; quick-detach mounting base
3x: . . . . $839.00–$1259.00
5x: . . . . $899.00–$1319.00

VERACITY RIFLESCOPE 2–10X42MM

Weight: 22.7 oz.
Length: 13.5 in.
Power: 2–10X
Obj. Dia.: 42mm
Main Dia.: 30mm
Exit Pupil: 21–4.2mm
Field of View: 52–10.5 ft @ 100 yds
Twilight Factor: 9.17–20.49
Eye Relief: 3.5 in.–4.25 in.
Features: Ballistic E1 FFP MOA reticle with PTC technology; E1 Hunter knobs; parallax adjustment; 3–15x50, 4–20x50, and 5–25x50 also available
2–10X: $629.00
3–15X: $719.00
4–20X: $959.00
5–25X: $1079.00

XTR III TACTICAL

Available in: 3.3–18x50mm, 5.5–30x56mm
Weight: 29.8 oz., 32 oz.
Length: 13.3 in., 15.4 in.
Power: 3.3–18X, 5.5–30X
Obj. Dia.: 50mm, 56mm
Main Dia.: 34mm
Exit Pupil: 8.6–2.7mm, 8.6–1.8 in.
Field of View: 37.7–6.8 ft.@100 yd., 23–4.2 ft.@100 yd.
Eye Relief: 3.25–4 in.
Features: Premium first focal plane scopes with big fields of view, big adjustment range, "Dragon Scale" knurling at adjustment points, and optional Race dial with a writable surface
3.3–18X: . . . . $2039.00–$2099.00
5–30X: . . . . $2159.00–$2219.00

OPTICS

Bushnell Outdoor Products

BUSHNELL AR OPTICS 1–4X24MM

AR OPTICS 1–4X24MM

Weight: 17.3 oz.
Length: 3.6 in.
Power: 1–4X
Obj. Dia.: 24mm
Main Dia.: 30mm
Exit Pupil: 13–6mm
Field of View: 110–36 ft @ 100 yds
Twilight Factor: 4.9–9.8
Eye Relief: 3.6 in.
Features: Designed for tactical applications; first focal plane reticles in Drop-Zone 223, and illuminated BTR-1; fully multi-coated glass; anti-reflective coating on all air-to-glass surfaces; 120 MOA elevation, 140 MOA windage adjustment ranges
MSRP . . . . $149.99–$299.99

Bushnell Outdoor Products

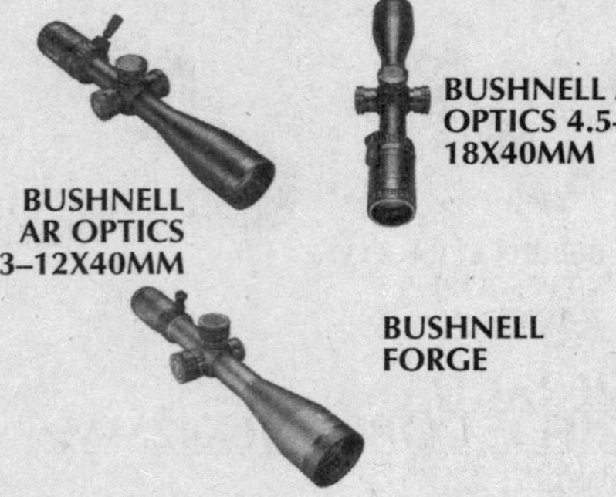

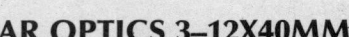

BUSHNELL ELITE TACTICAL XRS II

BUSHNELL ENGAGE

AR OPTICS 3–12X40MM

Weight: 21.3 oz.
Length: 12 in.
Power: 3–12X
Obj. Dia.: 40mm
Main Dia.: 1 in.
Exit Pupil: 13.7–3.7mm
Field of View: 33–11 ft @ 100 yds
Twilight Factor: 11–21.9
Eye Relief: 3.7 in.
Features: Target turrets; side parallax FOCUS; Drop Zone 223 reticle in the second focal plane; fully multicoated optics; 50 MOA elevation, 85 MOA windage adjustment range; Rainguard
MSRP $169.99

AR OPTICS 4.5–18X40MM

Weight: 21.5 oz.
Length: 12.4 in.
Power: 4.5–18X
Obj. Dia.: 40mm
Main Dia.: 1 in.
Exit Pupil: 8.6–2.3mm
Field of View: 22–7.3 ft @ 100 yds
Twilight Factor: 13.4–26.8
Eye Relief: 3.7 in.
Features: Target turrets; side parallax FOCUS; fully multi-coated optics; Drop-Zone second focal plane reticles available calibrated for 6.5 Creedmoor, .224 Valkyrie, .308 Win., and .223; 50 MOA elevation, 80 MOA windage adjustment range; Rainguard; multi-turret option also available with Windhold reticle and five different caliber turrets
MSRP . . . . $179.99–$269.99

ELITE TACTICAL DMR II, DMR II PRO

Weight: 34 oz.
Length: 13.2 in.
Power: 3.5–21x50mm
Obj. Diameter: 50mm
Exit Pupil: 10.4–2.4mm
Eye Relief: 3.74 in.
Field of View: 25.3–5.1 ft @ 100 yds
Features: Throwhammer lever allows instant magnification changes; EXO Barrier Protection repels water, dust, and other debris; IPX7 Waterproof construction; DMR II model offered with first focal plane G3, G3 illuminated or Horus H59 reticles; DMR II Pro gets upgraded ED Prime glass and first focal plane G3 reticle (no illumination); 100 MOA elevation, 60 MOA windage adjustment range
DMR II: . . . . $1199.99–$1299.99
DMR II Pro: $1599.99

ELITE TACTICAL XRS II

Available in: 4.5–30x50mm
Weight: 37.8 oz.
Length: 14.5 in.
Power: 4.5–30x
Obj. Dia.: 50mm
Main Dia.: 34mm
Exit Pupil: 9.3mm–1.6mm
Field of View: 24–3.6 ft.@100 yd.
Eye Relief: 3.74 in.
Features: Designed for long-range work; ED Prism Glass; Bushnell's EXO Barrier glass treatment that repels oil, water, dust and other contaminants; adjustments are 10 MILs per revolution; locking diopter feature ensures consistent focus; windage turret has a lock; elevation turret includes a RevLimiter Zero Stop that prevents the user from turning it past zero; first focal plane reticle/housing color combos in illuminated G3/gun metal gray, Horus H59/black, Horus Tremor3/matte black, or non-illuminated G3 in either black or Flat Dark Earth
MSRP: . . . . $1699.99–$1949.99

ENGAGE

Available in: 2–7x36mm, 3–9x40mm, 3–9x50mm, 4–12x40mm, 6–18x50mm, 2.5–10x44mm, 3–12x42mm, 4–16x44mm, 6–24x50mm
Weight: 11.4–23.7 oz.
Length: 12.8–14.3 in.
Power: 2–7x, 3–9x, 4–12x, 6–18x, 2.5–10x, 3–12x, 4–16x, 6–24x
Obj. Dia.: 36mm, 40mm, 50mm, 44mm, 42mm
Main Dia.: 1 in., 30mm
Exit Pupil: varies
Field of View: varies
Eye Relief: 3.5–4 in.
Features: New Deploy MOA reticle that is compatible with a range of calibers; locking turrets; toolless zero reset; EXO lens barrier; some models have side focus
MSRP . . . . $187.49–$467.99

FORGE

Available in: 4.5–27x50mm
Weight: 29.2 oz.
Length: 14.2 in.
Power: 4.5–27X
Obj. Dia.: 50mm
Main Dia.: 30mm
Field of View: 22.2–3.8 ft.@100 yd. (4.5–27X)
Eye Relief: 4 in. (4.5–27X)
Features: Exposed locking turrets; Ultra Wide Band coatings; RevLimiter zero stop; IPX7 waterproof construction; EXO Barrier Protection; second focal plane optics. Available in Black with Deploy MOA, Deploy MOA FFP, or Deploy MIL FFP reticles; Terrain finish available only with Deploy MOA or Deploy MOA FFP reticles; also available in a 1–8x30mm with an illuminated German No. 4 reticle
MSRP . . . . $779.95–$849.99

MATCH PRO

Available in: 6–24x50mm
Weight: 29.8 oz.
Length: 14.01 in.
Power: 6–24X
Obj. Dia.: 50mm
Main Dia.: 30mm
Field of View: 18–4 ft.@100 yd.
Eye Relief: 3.74 in.
Features: A heavyweight for today's distant target games, this first focal plane scope has choice of non-illuminated or illuminated Deploy Mil etched glass reticle; 65 MOA of elevation/windage adjustment
MSRP . . . . $449.99–$499.99

Bushnell Outdoor Products

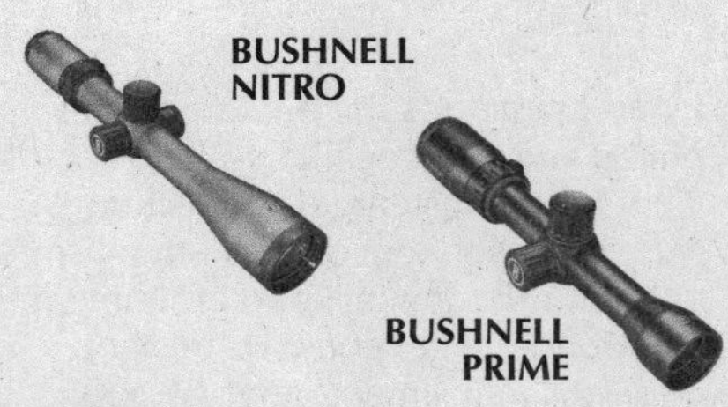
BUSHNELL NITRO

BUSHNELL PRIME

NITRO

Available in: 2.5–10x44mm, 3–12x44mm
Weight: 23.9 oz., 24.2 oz.
Length: 13.4 in.,13.7 in.
Power: 2.5–10X, 3–12X
Obj. Dia.: 44mm
Main Dia.: 30mm
Field of View: 37–9 ft.@100 yd. (2.5–10X), 34.8–8.6 ft.@100yd. (3–12X)
Eye Relief: 3.6 in.
Features: Designed for hunters working at close to middle ranges. Second focal plane copes have a matte gray or black finish; variety of Multi-Plex and Deploy reticles; capped target turrets; Ultra-Wide Band Coating; EXO Barrier Protection; IPX7 waterproofing
2.5–10X: $349.99
3–12X: $399.99

PRIME

Available in: 1–4x32mm, 3–9x40mm, 3–12x40mm, 4-12x40mm, 6–18x50mm
Weight: 13.4 oz., 16.6 oz., 17 oz., 18.6 oz., 19 oz.
Length: 10.4 in., 12.8 in., 12 in., 12.8 in., 15 in.
Power: 1–4X, 3–9X, 3–12X, 4–12X, 6–18X
Obj. Dia.: 32mm, 40mm, 50mm
Main Dia.: 1 in.
Field of View: 105–26 ft.@100 yd. (1–4X), 31–11 ft.@100 yd. (3–9X), 29–7.5 ft,@100 yd. (3–12X), 26–9 ft.@100 yd. (4–12X), 18–6 ft.@100 yd. (6–18X)
Eye Relief: 3.9 in. (1–4X), 3.3 in. (3–9X), 3.7 in. (3.5–10X), 3.5 in. (3–12X), 3.3 in. (4–12X), 3.5 n. (6–18X)
Features: Lightweight and compact second focal plane package in a power range for every target or hunting application. Features include multi-coated optics; EXO Barrier Protection; IPX7 waterproofing; Ultra Wide Band coatings; Multi-X reticle; 3–12X is a multi-turret design with six turrets calibrated for popular calibers, including two for muzzleloader loads
MSRP . . . . $129.99–$299.99

Cabela's

CABELA'S RIMFIRE RIFLESCOPE 3–9X40MM

CABELA'S LEVER ACTION 3–9X40MM

LEVER ACTION 3–9X40MM

Weight: 14.64 oz.
Length: 13 in.
Power: 3–9X
Obj.Dia.: 40mm
Main Dia.: 1 in.
Exit Pupil: 13.33–4.44mm
Field of View: 30.55–9.6 ft @ 100 yds
Twilight Factor: 10.95–18.97
Eye Relief: 5.5 in.
Features: Ballistic glass reticles specifically engineered for use with a particular Hornady LEVERevolution round; tube is machined aluminum and lenses are multi-coated; windage and elevation are adjustable in ¼ MOA clicks; in .45-70 Govt., .44 Mag., and .30-30 Win. reticles
MSRP $99.99

RIMFIRE RIFLESCOPE 3–9X40MM

Weight: 13.4 oz.
Length: 12 in.
Power: 3–9X
Obj.Dia.: 40mm
Main Dia.: 1 in.
Exit Pupil: 13.33–4.44mm
Field of View: 37.7–12.4 ft @ 100 yds
Twilight Factor: 10.95–18.97
Eye Relief: 4 in.
Features: For hunting, target shooting, or plinking with a rimfire rifle; parallax-free at 50 yards; multi-coated glass optics; extended eye relief and an expanded exit pupil; low-profile windage and elevation turrets; Duplex reticle; also available in 2-7x32, 4X
MSRP . . . . $49.99–$79.99

OPTICS

Carl Zeiss Sports Optics

CARL ZEISS SPORTS OPTICS CONQUEST V4

CONQUEST V4

Available in: 1–4x24mm, 3–12x56mm, 4–16x44mm, 6–24x50mm
Weight: 16.6 oz. (1–4x), 21.5 oz. (3–12x), 22.6 oz. (4–16x), 24.4 oz. (6-24x)
Length: 10.08 in. (1–4x), 14.5 in. (3–12x), 14 in. (4–16), 14.5 in. (6–24x)
Power: 1–4x, 3–12x, 4–16x, 6–24x
Obj. Dia.: 24mm, 56mm, 44mm, 50mm
Main Dia.: 30mm
Exit Pupil: 11.9–24mm (1–4x), 9.2–4.7mm (3–12x), 8.5–2.8mm (4–16x), 7.5–2.1mm (6–24x)
Field of View: 114–28.5 ft.@100 yd. (1–4x), 38–9.5 ft.@100 yd. (3–12x), 28.5–7.1 ft.@100 yd. (4–16x), 19–4.8 ft.@100 yd. (6–24x)
Twilight Factor: 3.5–9.8 (1–4x), 9.1–25.9 (3–12x), 11.5–26.5 (4–16x), 16.4–34.6 (6–24x)
Eye Relief: 3.5 in.
Features: Multiple reticles available, all second focal plane: 1–4x #60 illuminated center dot, ZQAR (on external turret option), 3–12x Z-Plex, Plex illuminated, 4–16x Z-Plex, ZMOA-2, 6–24x ZBR-1, ZMOA-1
MSRP . . . . $699.99–$1199.99

Carl Zeiss Sports Optics

CARL ZEISS SPORTS OPTICS VICTORY V8

VICTORY V8

Available in: 1–8x30mm, 1.8–14x50mm, 2.8–20x56mm, 4.8–35x60mm
Weight: 21 oz.–34 oz.
Length: 12 in.–15.75 in.
Power: 1–8X, 1.8–13.5X, 2.8–20X, 4.8–35X
Obj. Dia.: 30mm, 50mm, 56mm, 60mm
Main Dia.: 36mm
Exit Pupil: 9.9–3.9mm, 10.3–3.7mm, 9.8–2.8mm, 9.9–1.4mm
Field of View: 110–15 ft @ 100 yds, 63–8.5 ft @ 100 yds, 42–5.7 ft @ 100 yds, 24–3.3 ft @ 100 yds
Twilight Factor: 3.1–15.5; 5.1–26; 7.9–33; 13.6–45.8
Eye Relief: 3.75 in.
Features: Largest zoom range; interaction of 92 percent transmission; fluoride lens elements and SCHOTT HT glass ensures outstanding image quality and target resolution; large exit pupils and extremely large fields of view ensure fast target acquisition, an excellent overview of the hunting situation, no shadowing, and an immediate round image; compact design; generous adjustment range of 100 clicks enables you to stay on target at distances up to 600 yds; a fiber optic thinner than a human hair provides the finest illuminated dot in the world, resulting in 0.1188 in. subtension at 100 yds
MSRP . . . . $2749.99–$3999.99

C-More Systems

C-MORE SYSTEMS C3 1–6X24MM COMPETITION

C3 1–6X24MM COMPETITION

Available in: 1–6x24mm
Weight: 22 oz.
Length: 10.5 in.
Power: 1–6X
Obj. Dia.: 24mm
Main Dia.: 30mm
Exit Pupil: 12–4.1mm
Field of View: 108.3–19.8 ft @ 100 yds
Eye Relief: 4.25 in.
Features: Lockable windage and elevation turrets; TJ11 competition ballistic reticle with 1.5 in. illuminated red dot; 11 entensity settings; nitrogen filled; waterproof, fogproof, and shockproof; quick-zoom power adjustment ring; coated optics
MSRP $1999.99

EoTech

EOTECH VUDU SERIES

VUDU SERIES

Available in: 1–6x24mm, 1–8x24mm, 2.5–10x44mm, 3.5–18x50mm, 8–32x50mm, 5-25x50mm
Weight: 19.75 oz.–33.23 oz.
Length: 10.63 in.–14.84 in.
Power: 1–6X, 2.5–10X, 3.5–18X, 8–32X, 5-25X, 1–8X
Obj. Dia.: 24mm–50mm
Main Dia.: 30mm, 34mm
Exit Pupil: 11.4–4mm, 11.4–4.4mm, 10–2.4mm
Field of View: 105.8–17.7 ft @ 100 yds, 44–11 ft @100 yds, 30–6 ft @100 yds
Eye Relief: 3.15–4 in., 3.43–3.94 in., 3.39–3.94 in.
Features: Allows for fast target engagement at low power; at higher power provides the resolution and accuracy required to tackle longer shots; extremely clear XC High-Density glass; foversized and precision-machined turrets; EZ Chek zero stop feature; side-mounted parallax adjustment; 1–6X, 2.5-10X, 3.5–18X and 5–25X have first focal plane reticles, second focal plane reticles in the 8–32X and a second 3.5–18X model
FFP: . . . . $1249.99–$2099.99
SFP: . . . . $1399.99–$1799.99

GPO

GPO GPOTAC

GPOTAC

Length: 10.6 in.–15.5 in.
Power: 1–6x24mm, 1–8x24mm
Obj. Diameter: 24mm
Exit Pupil: Varies with model/magnification
Eye Relief: 3.54–4.33 in.
Field of View: Varies with model/magnification
Features: 1–8x model has a 34mm tube, 1–6x has a 30mm. Features of both include, iControl illumination with a custom Mil-Spec Horseshoe reticle, Double HD objective lenses, and oversized target turrets. These are first focal plane scopes; also now available in a 2.5–20x50 and a 4.5–27x50, both with illuminated reticles.
MSRP . . . . $1399.99–$1899.99

GPO

GPO PASSION 3X

GPO PASSION 4X

GPO PASSION 8X

PASSION 3X

Weight: 13.8 oz.–18.2 oz.
Length: 11.7 in.–13.2in.
Power: 3–9x40imm, 3–9x42mm, 4–12x42mm, 4–12x50i, 6–18X50mm
Obj. Diameter: 40mm, 42 mm
Exit Pupil: Varies with model/magnification
Eye Relief: 3.54–3.74 in.
Field of View: Varies with model/magnification
Features: Entry-level scopes; 1-in. tubes; generous eye relief; fast focus ocular lenses; proprietary lens coatings; metal turret caps; clicks are ¼-MOA; with or without illuminated reticles
MSRP . . . . $399.99–$699.99

PASSION 4X

Weight: 22.6 oz.–23.3 oz.
Length: 13.4 in. (3–12x56mm), 15.5 in. (6–24x50mm)
Power: 3–12x56mm, 6–24x50mm
Obj. Diameter: 50mm, 56mm
Exit Pupil: 19–4.7mm
Eye Relief: 3.54 in.
Field of View: 37–14 ft @ 100 yds
Features: Entry-level scopes; 30mm tubes; generous eye relief; fast focus ocular lenses; proprietary lens coatings; metal turret caps; clicks are .36-in. in the 3-12x model, ¼-MOA in the 6-24x model; 3-12x models come with standard or illuminated G4 reticle; 6-24X has Plex reticle; parallax free at 100m for 3-12x; 6-24mm has side-adjustment parallax correction
3–12X: $699.99
6–24X: $1149.99

PASSION 8X

Weight: 18 oz.
Length: 10.7 in.
Power: 1–8x24mm
Obj. Diameter: 24mm
Exit Pupil: 24–3mm
Eye Relief: 3.54 in.
Field of View: 108–14 ft @ 100 yds
Features: Premium optic; 30mm tube; generous eye relief; Super Zoom technology; proprietary lens coatings; PassionTrac quick-zero target turrets; G4 illuminated reticle; clicks are .36-in.; optic is parallax free at 100 meters
MSRP $1599.99

Hawke Sport Optics, LLC

HAWKE SPORT OPTICS .350 LEGEND

HAWKE SPORT OPTICS FRONTIER 30

HAWKE SPORT OPTICS FRONTIER 30 SF

HAWKE SPORT OPTICS FRONTIER 30 SF FFP

.350 LEGEND

Available in: 2.5–10x50mm, 3–12x56mm
Weight: 21.6 oz., 22.4 oz.
Length: 13.1 in., 13.7 in.
Power: 2.5–10X, 3–12X
Obj. Dia.: 50mm, 56mm
Main Dia.: 30mm
Exit Pupil: 20–5mm, 18–5mm
Field of View: 49.8–12.5 ft.@100 yd., 41.5–1.4 ft.@100 yd.
Eye Relief: 4 in.
Features: Designed specifically to partner with the .350 Legend straight-wall cartridge, with precise holdover points; illuminated 35 Legend reticle in the second focal plane
2.5–10X: $499.00
3–12X: $519.00

FRONTIER 30

Available in: 1–6x24mm
Weight: 19.7 oz.
Length: 10.4 in.
Power: 1–6X
Obj. Dia.: 24mm
Main Dia.: 30mm
Exit Pupil: 24–4mm
Field of View: 108–17.6 ft.@100 yd.
Eye Relief: 4 in.
Features: Designed for tactical applications with a wide field of view; generous eye relief; second focal plane; 21 layers fully multicoated; illuminated etched glass Tactical Dot (6X), L4A Dot or Circle Dot reticle with six brightness levels
MSRP . . . . $699.99–$729.99

FRONTIER 30 SF

Available in: 2.5–15x50mm, 4–24x50mm, 5–30x56mm
Weight: 23.4 oz., 24.5 oz.
Length: 13.7 in., 13.9 in.
Power: 2.5–15X, 4-24X, 5–30X
Obj. Dia.: 50mm, 56mm
Main Dia.: 30mm
Exit Pupil: 20–3mm (2.5–15X), ***10–2mm (5–30X), 12.5–2.1mm (4–24X)***
Field of View: 42–6.9 ft.@100 yd. (2.5–15X), 22.8–3.9 ft.@100 yd. (5–30X), 28.2–4.8 ft.@1000 yd. (4–24X)
Eye Relief: 4 in.
Features: Super tool for hunters especially those shooting magnum calibers, thanks to the 4-inch eye relief; big objective; side focus parallax adjustment; second focal plane; illuminated glass etched LR Dot or Mil Pro reticles
MSRP . . . . $849.99–$949.00

FRONTIER 30 SF FFP

Available in: 3–15x50mm, 5–25x56mm, 4–20X50mm
Weight: 26.3 oz., 28.8 oz., 22.2 oz.
Length: 13.2 in.
Power: 3–15X, 5–25X
Obj. Dia.: 50mm, 56mm
Main Dia.: 30mm
Exit Pupil: 16.7–3.3mm (3–15X), 11.2–2.3mm (5–25X), 12.5–2.5mm (4–20X)
Field of View: 36.7–7.3 ft.@100 yd. (3–15X), 21.7–4.3 ft.@100 yd. (5–25X), 28.5–5.7 ft.@100 yd. (4–20X)
Eye Relief: 4 in.
Features: A mid-size hunter's tool in the underutilized 5X category; 1/10 MRAD locking turrets; first focal Plane illuminated etched glass Mil Pro reticle with six brightness settings
MSRP . . . . $949.00–$1049.00

Hawke Sport Optics, LLC

HAWKE SPORT OPTICS VANTAGE

HAWKE SPORT OPTICS VANTAGE 30 WA FFP

HAWKE SPORT OPTICS VANTAGE 30 WA IR

HAWKE SPORT OPTICS VANTAGE SF

HAWKE SPORT OPTICS VANTAGE 30 WA SF IR

HAWKE SPORT OPTICS VANTAGE IR

VANTAGE

Available in: 4x32mm, 2–7x32mm, 3–9x4mm, 3–9x50, 4–12x40mm
Weight: 11.1 oz.–20.3 oz.
Length: 11.5 in.–13.8 in.
Power: 4X, 2–7X, 3–9X, 4–12X
Obj. Dia.: 32mm, 40mm, 50mm
Main Dia.: 1 in.
Exit Pupil: 8mm, 16–5mm, 13–4mm, 17–6mm, 10–3mm
Field of View: 28.5 ft.@100 yd., 46.6–14.1 ft.@100 yd., 39–12.7 ft.@100 yd., 33.6–11 ft.@100 yd., 26.2–8.7 ft.@100 yd.
Eye Relief: 3.5 in.
Features: A truly economical line of second focal plane all-purpose scopes that include adjustable objective options; glass-etched 30/30 Duplex or Mil-Dot reticles; ¼-MOA turrets
4X: . . . . $89.00–$99.00
2–7X: . . . . $109.00–$119.00
3–9x40: . . . . $119.00–$129.00
3–9x50: . . . . $129.0–$139.00
4–12X: $149.00

VANTAGE 30 WA FFP

Available in: 4–16x50mm, 6–24x50mm
Weight: 26.3 oz., 26.6 oz.
Length: 13.7 in., 14.9 in.
Power: 4–16X, 6–24mm
Obj. Dia.: 50mm
Main Dia.: 30mm
Exit Pupil: 12.5–3.1mm, 8.3–2.1mm
Field of View: 21–5.2 ft.@100 yd.
Eye Relief: 3.5 in.
Features: The only first focal plane models in the Vantage line, these two scopes have illuminated green/red reticles with five brightness settings; side-focus control; 1/10 MRAD locking turrets
4–16X: $469.00
6–24X: $489.00

VANTAGE 30 WA IR

Available in: 1–4x24mm, 1.5–6x44mm, 2.5–10x50mm, 3–9x42mm, 3–12x56mm
Weight: 14.9 oz.–23.6 oz.
Length: 11.1 in.–13.4 in.
Power: 1–4X, 1.5–6X, 2.5–10X, 3–9X, 3–12X
Obj. Dia.: 24mm, 42mm, 44mm, 50mm, 56mm
Main Dia.: 30mm
Exit Pupil: 24–6mm, 29.3–7.3mm, 20–5mm, 14–4.7mm, 18–5mm
Field of View: 126–31.5 ft.@100 yd., 80.4–19.8 ft.@100 yd., 50.4–12.6 ft.@100 yd., 42.2–13.1 ft.@100 yd., 42.8–1.7 ft.@100 yd.
Eye Relief: 3.5 in.
Features: Moving to a 30mm tube, this wide-angle series has illuminated glass-etched reticles with five brightness settings and in red and green; ½-MOA clicks
MSRP . . . . $259.00–$319.00

VANTAGE 30 WA SF IR

Available in: 4–16x50mm, 6–24x50mm
Weight: 26.1 oz., 26.3 oz.
Length: 13.7 in., 15.4 in.
Power: 4–16X, 6–24mm
Obj. Dia.: 50mm
Main Dia.: 30mm
Exit Pupil: 12.5–3.1mm, 8.3–2.1mm
Field of View: 28.8–7.8 ft.@100 yd., 20.7–5.4 ft.@100 yd.
Eye Relief: 3.5 in.
Features: All the features of the 30 WA IR, but with side-focus design; ¼-MOA clicks
4–16X: $399.00
6–24X: $419.00

VANTAGE IR

Available in: 2–7x32mm, 3–9x40mm, 3–9x50mm, 4–12x40mm, 4–12x50mm, 4–16x50mm, 6–24x50mm
Weight: 15.9 oz.–22 oz.
Length: 11.5 in.–15.6 in.
Power: 2–7X, 3–9X, 4–12X, 4–16X, 6–24X
Obj. Dia.: 32mm, 40mm, 50mm
Main Dia.: 1 in.
Exit Pupil: 16–5mm, 13–4mm, 17–6mm, 10–3.3mm, 13–4mm, 13–3mm, 8–2mm
Field of View: 46.6–14.1 ft.@100 yd., 39–12 ft.@100 yd., 33.6–11 ft.@100 yd., 26.2–8.7 ft.@100 yd., 26.2–8.7 ft.@100 yd.; 23.6–6.2 ft.@100 yd., 15.1–4.2 ft.@100 yd.
Eye Relief: 3.5 in.
Features: Illuminated reticles with five brightness settings; fast-focus eyeball; glass-etched reticle in green and red; some models have adjustable objective
MSRP . . . . $169.00–$259.00

VANTAGE SF

Available in: 3–12x44mm, 4–16x44mm, 6–24x44mm
Weight: 17.3 oz.–18.7 oz.
Length: 13.3 in.–14.7 in.
Power: 3–12X, 4–16X, 6–24X
Obj. Dia.: 44mm
Main Dia.: 1 in.
Exit Pupil: 15–4mm, 11–3mm, 7–2mm
Field of View: 30.6–77 ft.@100 yd., 22.9–5.8 ft.@100 yd., 15.3–3.8 ft.@100 yd.
Eye Relief: 3.5 in.
Features: Budget-friendly side-focus models; ¼-MOA clicks; fully multi-coated optics; 100 MOA elevation/windage; knurled posi-grip power selector; second focal plane ½ Mil Dot reticle
3–12X: $259.00
4–16X: $279.00
6–24X: $289.00

Hi-Lux Precision Optics

HI-LUX CMR4 1–4X24MM

HI-LUX M40 TACTICAL HUNTER 3-9X40MM

HI-LUX PRECISION OPTICS LEATHERWOOD ART M1000 PRO

HI-LUX LEATHERWOOD ART M1200

HI-LUX TOBY BRIDGES HIGH PERFORMANCE MUZZLELOADER

HI-LUX WM. MALCOLM 2.5X M73G4

HI-LUX WM. MALCOLM 6X LONG TELESCOPIC

HI-LUX WM. MALCOM 8X USMC SNIPER SCOPE

CLOSE TO MEDIUM RANGE (CMR4) 1–4X24MM

Weight: 16.5 oz.
Length: 10.2 in.
Power: 1–4X
Obj.Dia.: 24mm
Main Dia.: 30mm
Exit Pupil: 11.1–6mm
Field of View: 94.8–26.2 ft @ 100 yds
Twilight Factor: 4.89–9.79
Eye Relief: 3 in.
Features: Zero-locking turrets; large external target-style windage and elevation adjustment knobs; power-ring extended lever handle for power change; CMR ranging reticle for determining range and also BDC hold over value good for .223, .308, and other calibers; red illuminated reticle
MSRP $395.00

M40 TACTICAL HUNTER 3-9X40MM

Weight: 16.2 in.
Length: 12.5 in.
Power: 3–9X
Obj. Dia.: 40mm
Main Dia.: 1 in.
Exit Pupil: 13.3–4.4mm
Field of View: 37.7–12.6 ft @ 100 yds
Twilight Factor: 10.95–18.97
Eye Relief: 3.25 in.
Features: This is a dual focal plane reticle scope, with a glass-etched ranging reticle in the first focal plane and a .223/5.56 BDC reticle in the second
MSRP $249.00

LEATHERWOOD ART M1000 PRO

Available in: 2–10x42mm
Weight: 32 oz.
Length: 12 in.
Power: 2–10X
Obj. Dia.: 42mm
Main Dia.: 30mm
Eye Relief: 3.5 in.
Features: 50th anniversary of Jim Leatherwood's Automatic Ranging Trajectory (ART) scope; distance to target can be accomplished by framing targets of known size within the HR1 reticle or dialing the cam to a known distance, either way eliminating holdover guesswork
MSRP $515.00

LEATHERWOOD ART M1200

Weight: 29 oz.
Length: 15.5 in.
Power: 6–24X
Obj. Dia.: 50mm
Main Dia.: 30mm
Exit Pupil: 8.5–2mm
Field of View: 12–4 ft @ 100 yds
Twilight Factor: 17.32–34.64
Eye Relief: 3.25 in.
Features: Auto-ranging trajectory; multi-coated lenses; second focal plane; nitrogen gas filled; waterproof; ZRO-LOK system
MSRP $585.00

TOBY BRIDGES HIGH PERFORMANCE MUZZLELOADER 3–9X40MM

Weight: 15.8 oz.
Length: 12.5 in.
Power: 3–9X
Obj.Dia.: 40mm
Main Dia.: 1 in.
Exit Pupil: 13.3–4.4mm
Field of View: 39–13 ft @ 100 yds
Twilight Factor: 10.9–19
Eye Relief: 3.25 in.
Features: The TB/ML scope is designed for in-line ignition muzzleloaders and saboted bullets. It offers multiple reticles for shooting at ranges out to 250 yards.
MSRP $129.00

WM. MALCOLM 2.5X M73G4

Weight: 11.8 in.
Length: 8.3 oz.
Power: 2.5X
Obj. Dia.: 16mm
Main Dia.: ¾ in.
Exit Pupil: 4mm
Field of View: 24.9 ft @ 100 yds
Twilight Factor: 6.33
Eye Relief: 3.54 in.
Features: Built to bring the vintage sniper rifle competition shooter a top quality scope that surpasses the quality of the WWII originals used on the M1903A4 sniper rifles; modern erector tube and quality multi-coated lenses for superior light transmission; offers a minimum total of 60 MOA with either windage or elevation when those adjustments are at center
MSRP $385.00

WM. MALCOLM 6X LONG TELESCOPIC

Weight: 32.5 oz.
Length: 30.5 in.
Power: 6X
Obj.Dia.: 16mm
Main Dia.: .75 in.
Exit Pupil: 5.8mm
Field of View: 10 ft @ 100 yds
Twilight Factor: 9.79
Eye Relief: 4 in.
Features: A modern copy of the Model 1855 W. Malcolm riflescopes; early-style mounts for scoping original and replica 19th century breechloading rifles (Sharps, rolling block, high wall, etc.) or late period long-range percussion muzzleloading bullet rifles; ¾-in. (steel) scope tube; interchangeable front extension tubes to mount on rifles with barrels of 30 to 34 inches; also in 3x17-in. and 6x18-in. short Malcolms
MSRP $475.00

WM. MALCOLM 8X USMC SNIPER SCOPE

Weight: 25.4 oz.
Length: 22.1 in.
Power: 8X
Obj. Dia.: 31mm
Main Dia.: .75 in.
Exit Pupil: 4.2mm
Field of View: 11 ft @ 100 yds
Twilight Factor: 15.75
Eye Relief: 3.15 in.
Features: Fully multi-coated lens; fine cross reticle; elevation and wind adjustment ¼ MOA per click at the mounts
MSRP $575.00

Kahles

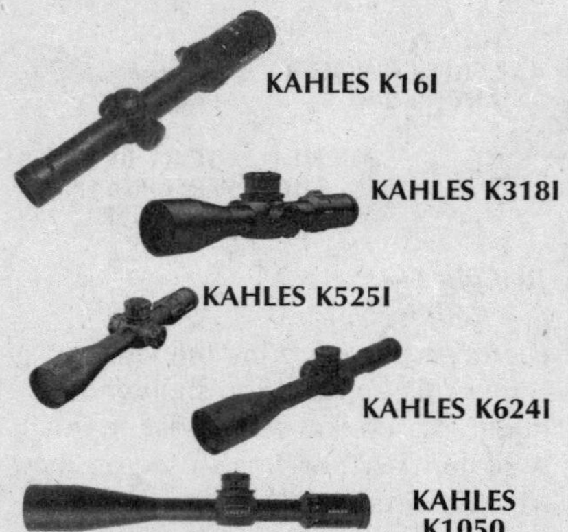

K16I
Weight: 16.9 oz.
Length: 10.9 in.
Power: 1–6X
Obj. Dia.: 24mm
Main Dia.: 30mm
Exit Pupil: 9.65–3.81mm
Field of View: 127–20.1 ft @ 100 yds
Twilight Factor: 4.9–12
Eye Relief: 3.74 in.
Features: Rear focal plane; illuminated; integrated magnification throw lever allows for instant magnification changes even in the most adverse environmental conditions
MSRP $1999.99

K318I
Available in: 3.5–18x50mm
Weight: 33.2 oz.
Length: 12.3 in.
Power: 3.5–18X
Obj. Dia.: 50mm
Main Dia.: 34mm
Field of View: 27.8–5.5 ft.@100 yd.
Eye Relief: 3.6 in.
Features: A solid scope for mid-range work with an illuminated reticle in the first focal plane; TWIST GUARD windage protection; reticle choices of MSR/Ki, SKMR3, and MOAK
MSRP $3299.00

K525I
Available in: 5–25x56mm
Weight: 34.2 oz.
Length: 14.8 in.
Power: 5–25X
Obj. Dia.: 56mm
Main Dia.: 34mm
Exit Pupil: 9.5–2.3mm
Field of View: 21.7–4.4 ft.@100 yd.
Eye Relief: 3.74 in.
Features: A big scope for big calibers going big distances featuring an elevation turret with integrated parallax wheel; illuminated first focal plane reticle in reticle choice of SKMR3, SKMR, MOAK, Mil4+, or MSR2/Ki; TWIST GUARD windage system prevents accidental dial movement
MSRP $3399.00

K624I
Weight: 33.5 oz.
Length: 15.9 in.
Power: 6–24X
Obj. Dia.: 56mm
Main Dia.: 34mm
Exit Pupil: 9.3–2.3mm
Field of View: 20–5.1 ft @ 100 yds
Twilight Factor: 18.33–36.66
Eye Relief: 3.54 in.
Features: Front focal plane; illuminated; adjustable parallax; specifically engineered for long range precision
MSRP $2999.00

K1050
Weight: 31.4 oz.
Length: 16.9 in.
Power: 10–50X
Obj. Dia.: 56mm
Main Dia.: 30mm
Exit Pupil: 15.1–5mm
Field of View: 9.5–2 ft @ 100 yds
Twilight Factor: 23.66–52.92
Eye Relief: 3.75 in.
Features: Rear focal plane; adjustable parallax; ultra-precise 1/8 MOA adjustments constructed of hardened steel
MSRP $3089.00

OPTICS

Konus

KONUS KONUSHOT 4X32MM

KONUS KONUSPRO EL-30

KONUS KONUSPRO M-30 4.5–16X40MM

KONUSHOT
Weight: 12.6 oz., 11.2 oz., 13.7 oz.
Length: 12.2 in., 12.2 in., 13.3 in.
Power: 3–9X, 3–12X
Obj. Dia.: 32mm, 40mm
Main Dia.: 1 in.
Exit Pupil: 8mm, 10.7–3.9mm, 13.3–3.3mm
Field of View: 25.5 ft @ 100 yds, 33.54–11.56 ft @ 100 yds, 27.4–6.9 ft @ 100 yds
Twilight Factor: 11.31, 9.8–16.97, 10.95–21.91
Eye Relief: 3.4 in., 3 in., 3 in.
Features: Shock-, water-, and fog-proof; nitrogen filled
3–9X: $109.99
3–12X: $84.99

KONUSPRO EL-30
Available in: 4–16x44mm
Weight: 23.39 oz.
Length: 13.1 in.
Power: 4–16X
Obj. Dia.: 44mm
Main Dia.: 30mm
Exit Pupil: 11–2.7mm
Field of View: 22.6–9.5 ft.@100 yd.
Eye Relief: 3.3–3 in.
Features: Utilizing LCD technology, the EL-30 features 10 interchangeable reticles; 1/10-Mil adjustments; locking tactical turrets
MSRP $489.99

KONUSPRO M-30
Weight: 17.6 oz., 21.1 oz., 28.9 oz., 31.7 oz., 30.6 oz., 32.3 oz.
Length: 11.6 in., 12.8 in., 16.4 in., 17.6 in., 18.4 in.
Power: 1–4X, 1.5–6X, 6.5–25X, 8.5–32X, 10–40X, 12.5–50X
Obj. Dia.: 24mm, 56mm, 44mm, 52mm, 52mm
Main Dia.: 30mm
Exit Pupil: 12–6mm, 18–7.3mm, 6.8–1.8mm, 6.1–1.6mm, 4.4–1.15mm, 5.2–1.4mm
Field of View: 100–25 ft @ 100 yds, 64–15.7 ft.@100 yds, 17–4.5 ft @100 yds, 13–3.3 ft @ 100 yds, 9.7–2.5 ft@100 yds, 11–2.8 ft @ 100 yds
Features: Engraved reticle in second focal plane; illuminated reticle; adjustable parallax
MSRP . . . . $369.99–$549.99

Konus

KONUS KONUSPRO PLUS 3–12X50MM

KONUSPRO PLUS

Weight: 25.7 oz.
Length: 16.4 in.
Power: 6–24X
Obj. Dia.: 50mm
Main Dia.: 1 in.
Exit Pupil: 8.3–2.1mm
Field of View: 16.2–4.45 ft @100 yds
Eye Relief: 3.4 in.
Features: engraved reticle in second focal plane; shock-, water-, and fog-proof; nitrogen filled; illuminated reticle
MSRP $229.99

Leapers, Inc.

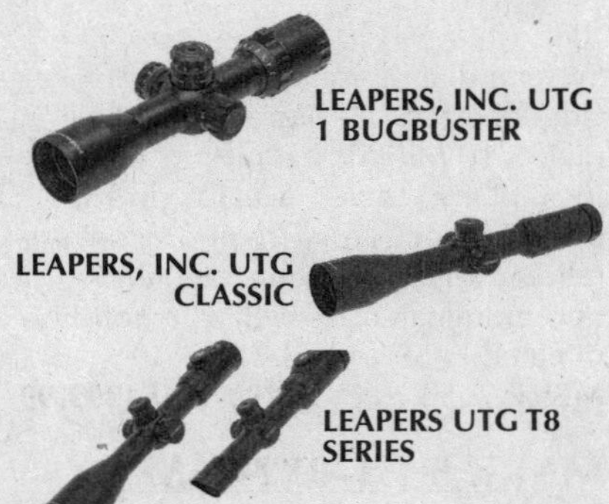

LEAPERS, INC. UTG 1 BUGBUSTER

LEAPERS, INC. UTG CLASSIC

LEAPERS UTG T8 SERIES

UTG 1 BUGBUSTER

Available in: 3–9x32mm, 3–12x32mm
Weight: 12 oz., 12.7 oz.
Length: 7.8, 8 in.
Power: 3–9X, 3–12X
Obj. Dia.: 32 mm
Main Dia.: 1 in.
Exit Pupil: 10.6–3.6 in., 10.6–2.7mm,
Field of View: 36.6–21.5 ft.@100 yd., 31–10 ft.@100 yd.
Eye Relief: 4.3–3.3 in.
Features: Compact scope with True Strength Platform; mil-dot range-estimating reticle; resettable target turrets; 2-inch sunshade; flip-up lens caps
MSRP . . . . $124.97–$149.97

UTG CLASSIC

Available in: 3–12x44mm
Weight: 19.2 oz.
Length: 12.8 in.
Power: 3–12X
Obj. Dia.: 44mm
Main Dia.: 30mm
Exit Pupil: 14.7–3.7mm
Field of View: 34–8.5 ft.@100 yd.
Eye Relief: 3.3–3 in.
Features: A utilitarian riflescope with the wire Mil-Dot reticle in the second focal plane; zero resetting target turrets; side parallax adjustment; ¼-MOA clicks
MSRP $114.97

UTG T8 SERIES

Available in: 1–8x28mm (Circle Dot & QD rings, Mil-dot, or Mil-dot & QD rings), 2–16x44mm
Weight: 18 oz.–22.6 oz.
Length: 10.2 in.–12.4 in.
Power: 1–8X, 2–16X
Obj. Dia.: 28mm, 44mm
Main Dia.: 30mm
Exit Pupil: 26.5–3.4mm, 22–2.7mm
Field of View: 99.5–13 ft @ 100 yds, 44.5–6.3 ft @ 100 yds
Eye Relief: 3.35–5 in., 3.5–4.1 in.
Features: Completely sealed and nitrogen filled; shockproof, fogproof, and rainproof; multi emerald–coated lenses for maximum light and edge-to-edge clarity; innovative EZ-TAP Illumination Enhancing (IE) System with red/green dual-color mode and 36 colors in multi-color mode to accommodate all weather/light conditions; one-click high-tech illumination memory feature
1–8X: $159.97
2–16X: $179.97

Leica Camera AG

LEICA MAGNUS I

LEICA PRS 5–30X56I

MAGNUS I

Weight: 19.2 oz.–27.7 oz.
Length: 10.7 in.–14.1 in.
Power: 1–6.3x24mm, 1.5–10x42mm, 1.8–12x50mm, 2.4–16x56mm,
Obj. Diameter: 24mm, 42mm, 50mm, 56 mm
Exit Pupil: Varies with model
Eye Relief: 3.5 in.
Field of View: Varies with model
Features: Zoom factor up to 6.7; bright day/night reticle illumination with brightness control; high contrast images and superior light transmission; new tooless scale zeroing; reduced dot subtensions; improved battery lifetime and exchange; slimmed eyepiece; redesigned illumination activation to prevent accidental on/off
MSRP . . . . $2299.00–$2899.00

PRS 5–30X56I

Available in: 5–30x56mm
Weight: 36.3 oz.
Length: 14.37 in.
Power: 5–30X
Obj. Dia.: 56mm
Main Dia.: 34mm
Exit Pupil: 9–2mm
Field of View: 8.2–1.3m@100m
Eye Relief: 3.5 in.
Features: Leica dives into the long-range game with a first focal plane 6X; huge elevation adjustment of 320/180 cm, 32/18 Mil (100m); illuminated dot/scale reticle; sunshade and throw lever included
MSRP $2699.00

Leupold & Stevens

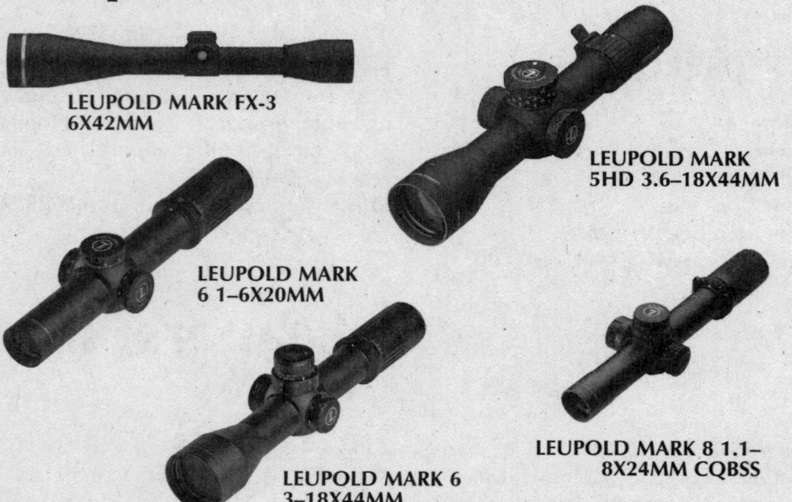

LEUPOLD MARK FX-3 6X42MM

LEUPOLD MARK 5HD 3.6–18X44MM

LEUPOLD MARK 6 1–6X20MM

LEUPOLD MARK 6 3–18X44MM

LEUPOLD MARK 8 1.1–8X24MM CQBSS

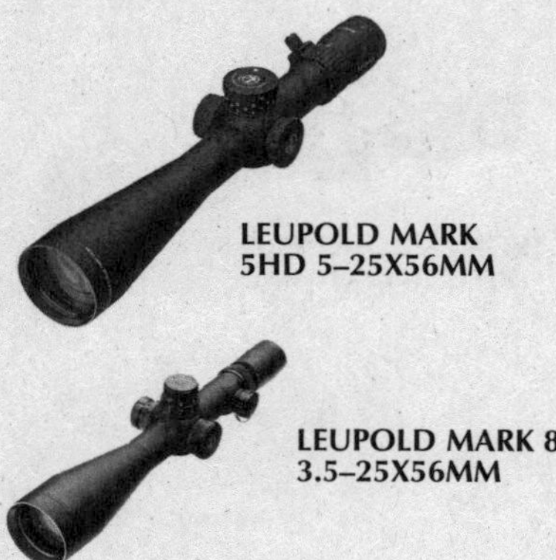

LEUPOLD MARK 5HD 5–25X56MM

LEUPOLD MARK 8 3.5–25X56MM

FX-3 6X42MM

Weight: 15 oz.
Length: 12.2 in.
Power: 6X
Obj.Dia.: 42mm
Main Dia.: 1 in.
Exit Pupil: 7mm
Field of View: 17.3 ft @ 100 yds
Twilight Factor: 15.87
Eye Relief: 4.4 in.
Features: Fixed-power riflescope; Twilight Light Management System; rear focal plane Wide Duplex reticle; ¼-MOA clicks
MSRP. $449.99

MARK 5HD 3.6–18X44MM

Available in: 3.6–18x44mm
Weight: 26 oz.
Length: 12.6 in.
Power: 3.6–18x
Obj. Dia.: 44mm
Main Dia.: 35mm
Exit Pupil: 2.4mm
Field of View: 28.4–5.8 ft.@100 yd.
Eye Relief: 3.54–3.82 in.
Features: Lighter than comparable scopes; 1/10-MIL click adjustments; side-focus parallax adjustment; choice of Horus H59, front focal Tremor 3, TMR illuminated, or TMR reticles; three full rotations of elevation adjustment; quick-throw lever
MSRP . . . . $1799.99–$2599.99

MARK 5HD 5–25X56MM

Available in: 5–25x56mm
Weight: 30 oz.
Length: 15.67 in.
Power: 5–25x
Obj. Dia.: 56mm
Main Dia.: 35mm
Exit Pupil: 2.2mm
Field of View: 20.5–4.2 ft.@100 yd.
Eye Relief: 3.58–3.82 in.
Features: Reticle choices include front focal TMR, first focal plane CCH, H-59, front focal Tremor 3, TMR illuminated, front focal Tremor 3 illuminated, and front focal TMR
MSRP . . . . $1999.99–$2799.99

MARK 6 1–6X20MM

Weight: 17 oz.
Length: 10.3 in.
Power: 1–6X
Obj. Dia.: 20mm
Main Dia.: 1.34 in.
Exit Pupil: 10.2–3.3mm
Field of View: 103.2–17.4 ft @ 100 yds
Twilight Factor: 4.5–11
Eye Relief: 3.7 in.
Features: Scratch-resistant lenses; Twilight Max HD Light Management System; dial illumination control; side-focus; M5C2 elevation control dial; 1/10 Mil click adjustments; first focal plane reticles available in CMR-W 7.62, CMR-W 5.56, or TMR-D reticles, all illuminated
MSRP. $2199.99

MARK 6 3–18X44MM

Weight: 23.6 oz.
Length: 11.9 in.
Power: 3–18X
Obj. Dia.: 44mm
Main Dia.: 1.34 in.
Exit Pupil: 10.3–2.4mm
Field of View: 36.8–6.3 ft @ 100 yds
Twilight Factor: 11.5–28.1
Eye Relief: 3.8–3.9 in.
Features: Scratch-resistant lenses; Twilight Max HD Light Management System; dial illumination control; side-focus; M5C2 elevation control dial; 1/10 Mil click adjustments; first focal plane reticles available in TMR (Mk), Tremor 2, and Tremor 3 configurations, all either illuminated and non-illuminated, as well as a non-illuminated H-59 reticle
MSRP . . . . $2199.99–$4399.99

MARK 8 1.1–8X24MM CQBSS

Weight: 23.2 oz.
Length: 11.75 in.
Power: 1.1–8x24mm
Obj. Diameter: 24mm
Eye Relief: 3.3–3.7 in.
Field of View: 14.7–92 ft @ 100 yds
Features: Scratch-resistant lenses; Twilight Max HD Light Management System; dial illumination control; easy grip power selector; M5B1 windage/elevation control; bullet drop compensation; 1/10 Mil click adjustments; first focal plane reticles available in H-27D, M-TMR, Mil-Dot, and CMR-W 7.62 designs, all illuminated
MSRP. . . . . $2999.99–$3799.99

MARK 8 3.5–25X56MM

Weight: 37 oz.
Length: 16 in.
Power: 3.5–25x56mm
Obj. Diameter: 56mm
Eye Relief: 3.3–3.7 in.
Field of View: 4.4–32.5 ft @ 100 yds
Features: Scratch-resistant lenses; Twilight Max HD Light Management System; dial illumination control; easy grip power selector; M5B2 windage/elevation control; bullet drop compensation; 1/10 Mil click adjustments; first focal plane reticles available in Tremor 2, Tremor 3, and TMR (Mk), all illuminated, plus the non-illuminated Horus H-59
MSRP. . . . . $2999.99–$4699.99

Leupold & Stevens

LEUPOLD & STEVENS VX-4.5HD SERVICE RIFLE 1–4.5X24MM

LEUPOLD VX-6HD

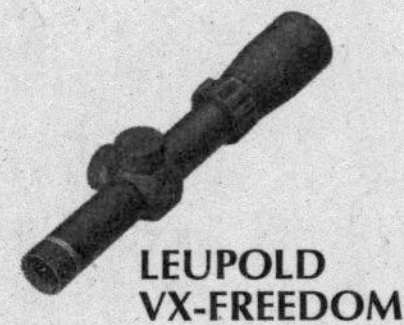

LEUPOLD VX-FREEDOM

LEUPOLD VX-FREEDOM MUZZLELOADER ULTIMATESLAM

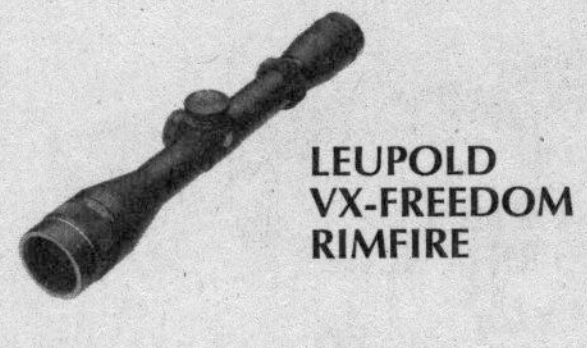

LEUPOLD VX-FREEDOM RIMFIRE

VX-4.5HD SERVICE RIFLE 1–4.5X24MM

Available in: 1–4.5x24mm
Weight: 13.4 oz.
Length: 10.76 in.
Power: 1–4.5X
Obj. Dia.: 24mm
Main Dia.: 30mm
Field of View: 123.2–26.2 ft.@100 yd.
Eye Relief: 3.82–3.7 in.
Features: As the name implies, this is one for Service Rifle matches and features true 1X magnification; Bull-Ring Post Reticle in the second focal plane and available with FireDot illumination; Guard-Ion lens coating
Standard reticle: $1399.99
Firedot reticle: $1499.99

VX-6HD

Weight: 13.4 oz.–23.4 oz.
Length: 11.2 in.–14.6 in.
Power: 1–6x24mm, 2–12x42mm, 3–18x44mm, 3–18x50mm, 4–24x52mm
Obj. Diameter: 24mm, 42mm, 44mm, 50mm, 52mm
Eye Relief: Varies with model
Field of View: Varies with model
Features: Twilight Max Light Management System; CDS-ZL2 dial locks; electronic level; fast-change magnification throw lever; flip-up lens covers; Zero Lock windage adjusment; reversible throw lever for quick-change magnification; Guard Ion lens coating; push-button illumination with power-off motion sensing technology; second generation argon/krypton waterproofing; 2–12X and 3–18X available in Sitka Subalpine camo
MSRP . . . . $1399.99–$2199.99

VX-FREEDOM

Available in: 3–9x40mm, 2–7x33mm,1.5–4x20mm, 1.5–4x28mm, 3-9x50mm, 4–12x40mm, 4–12x50mm, 3–9x40, 3–9x33mm, 6–18x40mm
Weight: 9.6 oz.–17 oz.
Length: 9.3 in.–14.61 in.
Power: 3–9x, 2–7x,1.5–4x, 1.5–4x, 3-9x, 4–12x, 4–12x, 3–9x, 3–9x, 6–18x
Obj. Dia.: 20mm, 28mm, 33mm, 40mm, 50mm
Main Dia.: 1 in.
Exit Pupil: Varies with model
Field of View: Varies with model
Eye Relief: Varies with model
Features: Twilight Light Management System; aluminum tubes; scratch-resistant lenses; ¼-MOA finger clicks; rear focal plane reticles. Multiple features and variations across the line, including Leupold's CDS (Custom Dial System), Fire Dot illumination technology, a wide range of reticle choices, a Scout model in 1.5–4x28mm, a 3–9x33mm with an EFR (Extended Focal Ring), a 3–9x40mm calibrated for the .450 Bushmaster and another for the .350 Legend
MSRP . . . . $349.99–$499.99

VX-FREEDOM MUZZLELOADER ULTIMATESLAM

Available in: 3–9x40mm
Weight: 12.2 oz.
Length: 12.39 in.
Power: 3–9x
Obj. Dia.: 40mm
Main Dia.: 1 in.
Field of View: 33.7–13.6 ft.@100 yd.
Eye Relief: 4.17
Features: Designed for muzzleloader pressures; houses an Ultimateslam reticle
MSRP $299.99

VX-FREEDOM RIMFIRE

Available in: 2–7x33mm, 3–9x40mm
Weight: 11.1 oz. (2–7x), 12.2 oz. (3–9x)
Length: 11.04 in. (2–7x), 12.39 in (3–9x)
Power: 2–7x, 3–9x
Obj. Dia.: 33mm, 40mm
Main Dia.: 1 in.
Exit Pupil: 5mm (2–7x), 4.7mm (3–9x)
Field of View: 43.8–17.8 ft.@100 yd. (2–7x), 33.7–13.6 ft.@100 yd. (3–9x)
Eye Relief: 4.17–3.7 in. (2–7x), 4.17–3.66 in. (3–9x)
Features: Rimfire MOA reticle; Twilight Light Management System; scratch-resistant lenses
MSRP $299.99

Lucid Optics, LLC

LUCID OPTICS L5 4-16X44MM RIFLE SCOPE

L5 4-16X44MM RIFLE SCOPE

Weight: 18 oz.
Length: 13.25 in.
Power: 4–16X
Obj. Dia.: 44mm
Main Dia.: 34mm
Exit Pupil: 11–3mm
Field of View: 25.5–8.5 ft @ 100 yds
Twilight Factor: 13.27–8
Eye Relief: 4.25 in.–3.25 in.
Features: Shock-, water-, and fog-proof; adjustable parallax; etched-glass reticle
MSRP $499.99

Lucid Optics, LLC

LUCID OPTICS L5 6-24X50 RIFLE SCOPE

LUCID OPTICS L7 1–6X24MM

LUCID OPTICS MLX RIFLE SCOPE

L5 6-24X50 RIFLE SCOPE

Weight: 24.5 oz.
Length: 15.5 in.
Power: 6–24X
Obj. Dia.: 50mm
Main Dia.: 30mm
Exit Pupil: 8.3–2mm
Field of View: 16.5–4.3 ft @ 100 yds
Twilight Factor: 17.32–34.64
Eye Relief: 4.25–3.25 in.
Features: Sniper-style rifle scope with the new L5 reticle; multi-coated lenses; 1/8 MOA turret click value; water-, fog-, and shockproof; matte black finish; available in STRELOK
MSRP $519.99

L7 1–6X24MM

Available in: 1–6x24mm
Weight: 20.40 oz.
Length: 10.75 in.
Power: 1–6X
Obj. Dia.: 34mm
Main Dia.: 30mm
Exit Pupil: 15–4mm
Field of View: 56–20 ft @ 100 yds
Eye Relief: 3.75–4 in.
Features: Edge-to-edge sharp, crisp image resolution through the entire magnification range; Lucid blue reticle illumination; windage and elevation turrets offer 60MOA either side of optical center; selectable magnification lever for fast changes to the zoom function
MSRP $499.99

MLX RIFLE SCOPE

Weight: 26 oz.
Length: 13.89 in.
Power: 4.5–18x44mm
Obj. Diameter: 44mm
Exit Pupil: 2.4–11mm
Eye Relief: 3.1–3.6 in.
Field of View: 8.5–25 ft @ 100 yds
Features: First focal plane scope; one-piece 6063 aluminum 30mm tube; Mil-based reticle; side parallax adjustment; 1/10 Mil tactile and audible click adjustments
MSRP $719.99

March Scopes/Deon Optical Design Corp.

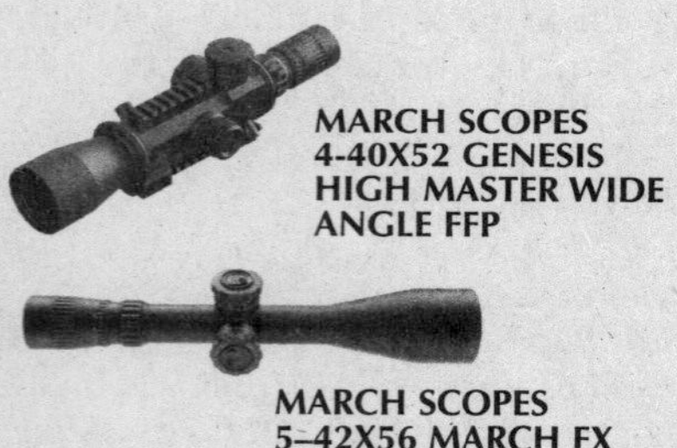
MARCH SCOPES 4-40X52 GENESIS HIGH MASTER WIDE ANGLE FFP

MARCH SCOPES 5–42X56 MARCH FX WIDE ANGLE

4-40X52 GENESIS HIGH MASTER WIDE ANGLE FFP

Available in: 4-40x52mm
Weight: 45.2 oz.
Length: 13 in.
Power: 4-40X
Obj. Dia.: 52mm
Main Dia.: 34mm
Features: Designed for ultra long-range applications (up to three miles); 10X zoom ratio; 86 MRAD elevation with .05-MRAD clicks; side focus 20m to infinity; tactical windage dial; Genesis body system tube adjusts on a horizontal/vertical pivot via a gimbled system with return springs keeping the guts tight against the turrets
MSRP $5500.00

5–42X56 MARCH FX WIDE ANGLE

Available in: 5–42x56mm
Weight: 33.5 oz.
Length: 14.1 in.
Power: 5-42X
Obj. Dia.: 56mm
Main Dia.: 34mm
Features: A premium competition model with a 26-degree wide-angle ocular lens with a fast-focus diopter; temperature tolerant anti-drift objective; turret-locking system with zero-set elevation; side focus; six illumination settings
MSRP $4200.00

Meopta USA

MEOPTA MEOSTAR R1 RD 1.5–6X42MM

MEOSTAR R1 SERIES

Weight: 18.87 oz., 20.6 oz., 15.87 oz., 21.87 oz., 18.27 oz., 24.16 oz.
Length: 12.09 in., 13.54 in., 13.03 in., 14.37 in., 12.91 in., 15.16 in..
Power: 1–4X, 1.5–6X, 3–10X, 3–12X, 4–12X, 4–16X
Power: 1–4X, 1.5–6X, 3–10X, 3–12X, 4–12X, 4–16X, 7X
Obj. Dia.: 22mm, 42mm, 50mm, 56mm, 40mm, 44mm
Main Dia.: 30mm, 25.4mm
Exit Pupil: 13.5–5.5mm, 14.8–7mm, 16.7–5mm, 14.8–4.6mm, 10–3.3mm, 11–2.8mm, 8mm
Field of View: 117.78–28.22 ft @ 100 yds, 73.49–22.31 ft @ 100 yds, 43.64–13.12 ft @ 100 yds, 36–11.15 ft @ 100 yds, 33.14–11.15 ft @ 100 yds, 16–4.46 ft @ 100 yds, 17.4 ft @ 100 yds
Twilight Factor: 4.69–9.38, 7.94–15.88, 12.25–22.36, 12.96–25.92, 12.65–21.91, 13.27–26.53, 19.8
Eye Relief: 3.31–3.47 in., 3.23–3.74 in., 3.15–3.23 in., 3.03–3.27 in., 3.58–3.15 in., 3.94–3.15 in., 3.3 in.
Features: Features MeoTrak IITM posi-click turret adjustments, nitrogen-purged tube, ion-assisted MeoBright and MeoShield lens coatings, MeoQuick fast focus; second focal plane models some with illuminated reticles
MSRP . . . . $1374.99–$1624.99

OPTICS

Meopta USA

MEOPTA MEOSTAR R2 1–6X24MM

MEOPTA USA OPTIKA6 FFP

MEOPTA USA OPTIKA6 SFP

MEOSTAR R2 SERIES

Weight: 17.64 oz., 20.32 oz., 21.02 oz., 22.93 oz.
Length: 11.69 in. 3.31–3.47 in., 3.23–3.74 in., 3.15–3.23 in., 3.03–3.27 in., 3.58–3.15 in., 3.94–3.15 in.
Power: 1–6X, 1.7–10X, 2–12X, 2.5–15X, 8X56
Obj. Dia.: 24mm, 42mm, 50mm, 56mm
Main Dia.: 30mm
Exit Pupil: varies with model
Field of View: varies with model
Twilight Factor: varies with model
Eye Relief: 3.54 in.
Features: Water- and fogproof; MeoLux ion-assisted multi-coatings for 99.8 percent light transmission; MeoQuick fast focus adsjutment; MeoClick tactile turret adjustments; MeoTrack windage and elevation controls; second focal plane illuminated reticles in 4C, 4K, BDC-2, and BDC-3 configurations
MSRP . . . . $1874.99–$2499.99

OPTIKA6 FFP

Available in: 1–6x24mm, 3–18x50mm, 3–18x56mm, 4.5–27x50mm, 5–30x56mm
Weight: 20.4 oz.–36.7 oz.
Length: 10.07 in.–15.44 in.
Power: 1–6X, 3–18X,4.5–27X, 5–30X
Obj. Dia.: 24mm, 50mm, 56mm
Main Dia.: 30mm, 34mm
Exit Pupil: 10–4mm, 9.5–2.8mm, 9.5–3.1mm, 9.5–1.9mm
Field of View: 109.5–18.9 ft.@100 yd., 33.6–5.7 ft.@100 yd., 33.3–5.7 ft.@100 yd., 21.9–3.6 ft.@100 yd., 24.6–3.6 ft.@100 yd.
Eye Relief: 3.94 in.
Features: First focal plane; parallax correction on all but 1–6X
MSRP . . . . $812.49–$1187.49

OPTIKA6 SFP

Available in: 1–6x24mm, 2.5–14x44mm, 3–18x50mm, 3–18x56mm, 4.5–27x50mm
Weight: 20.4 oz.–31.1 oz.
Length: 10.07 in.–14.21 in.
Power: 1–6X, 2.5–14X, 3–18X, 4.5–27X
Obj. Dia.: 24mm, 44mm, 50mm, 56mm
Main Dia.: 30mm
Exit Pupil: 10–4mm, 11–2.9mm, 9.5–2.8mm, 9.5–3.1mm, 9.5–1.9mm
Field of View: 109.5–19.9 ft.@100 yd., 39.9–6.9 ft.@100 yd., 33.6–5.7 ft.@100 yd., 33.3–5.7 ft.@100 yd., 21.9–3.6 ft.@100 yd.
Eye Relief: 3.94 in.
Features: Similar to the FFP line, but all with 30mm tubes and second focal plane design
MSRP . . . . $549.99–$749.99

Minox

MINOX ZE5.2 2–10X50MM

MINOX ZE5.2 3–15X56MM

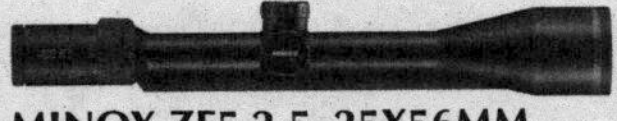

MINOX ZE5.2 5–25X56MM

MINOX ZP TAC SERIES 1–8X24MM

ZE5.2 2–10X50MM

Weight: 22.9 oz.
Length: 13.2 in.
Power: 2–10X
Obj. Dia.: 50mm
Main Dia.: 30mm
Exit Pupil: 11.4–5.1mm
Field of View: 55.2–11.5 ft @ 100 yds
Twilight Factor: 10–22.4
Eye Relief: 3.94 in.
Features: Illuminated central red-dot with eleven brightness settings; German A4, BDC, and Dot reticles available; finished with Minox's M* coating; Z-rail mount
MSRP $1799.00

ZE5.2 3–15X56MM

Weight: 26.1 oz.
Length: 14.6 in.
Power: 3–15X
Obj. Dia.: 56mm
Main Dia.: 30mm
Exit Pupil: 11.4–3.8mm
Field of View: 36.3–7.6 ft @ 100 yds
Twilight Factor: 13–29
Eye Relief: 3.94 in.
Features: Illuminated central red-dot with eleven brightness settings; automatic shut down to conserve battery; German A4, BDC, and Dot reticles available; finished with Minox's M* coating; Z-rail mount
MSRP $1899.00

ZE5.2 5–25X56MM

Weight: 27.9 oz.
Length: 16.9 in.
Power: 5–25X
Obj. Dia.: 56mm
Main Dia.: 30mm
Exit Pupil: 10.9–2.5mm
Field of View: 21.6–4.5 ft @ 100 yds
Twilight Factor: 16.7–37.4
Eye Relief: 3.94 in.
Features: Illuminated central red-dot with eleven brightness settings; automatic shut down to conserve battery; German A4, BDC, and Dot reticles available; finished with Minox's M* coating; Z-rail mount
MSRP $1902.00

ZP TAC SERIES 1–8X24MM

Weight: 24.5 oz.
Length: 11.6 in.
Power: 1–8X
Obj. Dia.: 24mm
Main Dia.: 34mm
Exit Pupil: 10.3–3mm
Field of View: 112.5–14.4 ft @ 100 yds
Twilight Factor: 4.9–13.86
Eye Relief: 3.5 in.
Features: Front focal plane; illuminated reticle; 3–15x50 and 5–25x56 also available
MSRP $3063.00

Nightforce Optics, Inc.

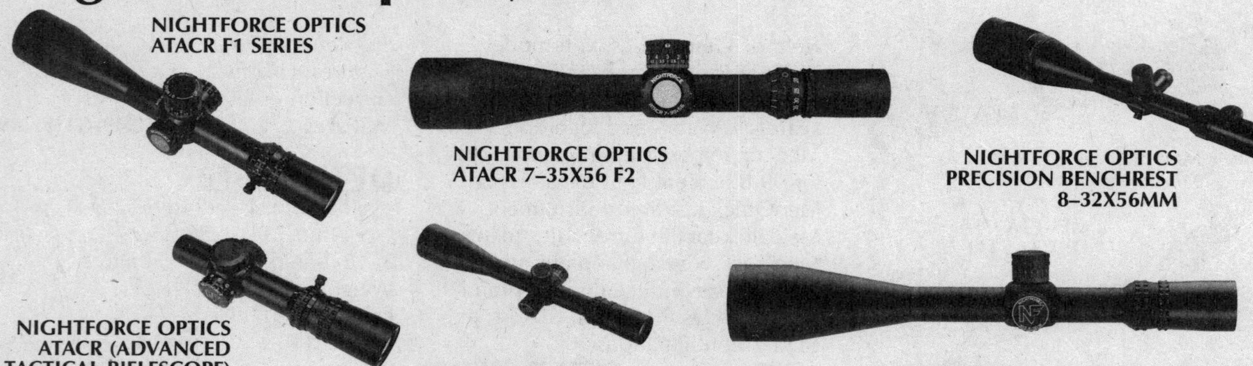

NIGHTFORCE OPTICS ATACR F1 SERIES

NIGHTFORCE OPTICS ATACR 7–35X56 F2

NIGHTFORCE OPTICS PRECISION BENCHREST 8–32X56MM

NIGHTFORCE OPTICS ATACR (ADVANCED TACTICAL RIFLESCOPE) 1-8X24 F1

NIGHTFORCE OPTICS NXS 5.5–22X50MM

NIGHTFORCE OPTICS NXS 8–32X56MM

ATACR F1 SERIES

Weight: 21, 30, 38 oz.
Length: 10.6, 12.6 in., 15.37 in.
Power: 1–8X, 4–16X, 5–25X, 7-35X
Obj. Dia.: 24mm, 42mm, 56mm
Main Dia.: 30, 34mm
Exit Pupil: 11.2–3.9mm, 10.3–2.7mm, 8.3–2.3mm,
6–1.6mm
Field of View: 96.1–13.1 ft.@100 yds, 26.9–6.9 ft @ 100 yds, 18.7–4.92 ft @ 100 yds, 14.97–3.44 ft
@ 100 yards
Eye Relief: 3.74 in., 3.35–3.54 in., 3.26–3.58 in.
Features: Front focal plane; multicoated lenses; eyepiece features enhanced engraving, an integrated Power Throw Lever (PTL) and an XtremeSpeed thread for making a fast diopter adjustment; adjustments are standard with the patented Nightforce Hi-Speed ZeroStop, and available in .1 Mrad (12 Mils per revolution) or .25 MOA (30 MOA per revolution) Increments. Available reticles as follows: 1–8X first focal plane FC-DM; 4-16X and 5-25X Horus H59 illuminated, Horus Tremor3 illuminated, Mil-C, Mil-R, Mil-XT, MOAR; 7–35X Horus Tremor3 illuminated, Mil-C, Mil-R, MOAR
1–8X: $2800.00
4-16X: . . . . $2400.00–$2750.00
5-25X: . . . . $2700.00–$3350.00
7-35X: . . . . $3600.00–$3850.00

ATACR 7–35X56 F2

Available in: 7–35x56mm
Weight: 39.3 oz.
Length: 16 in.
Power: 7–35X
Obj. Dia.: 56mm
Main Dia.: 34mm
Exit Pupil: 6mm (7X), 1.6mm (35X)
Field of View: 97–3.44 ft.@100 yd.
Eye Relief: 3.5 in.
Features: ED glass; 100 MOA total click travel; side parallax adjustment 11 yards to infinity; two-piece locking eyepiece adaptor; power-throw lever; Zero-Stop elevation adjustment; three 30 MOA or 12 MRAD rotation built-in quick-dial options; choice of MOAR-T or MIL-C reticles; second focal plane optics
MSRP $3100.00

NX8 1-8X24 F1

Available in: 1-8x24mm
Weight: 17 oz.
Length: 8.75 in.
Power: 1-8x
Obj. Dia.: 24mm
Main Dia.: 30mm
Exit Pupil: 7.9mm@1x–3.0mm@8x
Field of View: 106 ft.@100 yd.–13.2 ft. @100 yd.
Eye Relief: 3.75 in.
Features: Illuminated daytime reticle with multiple brightness levels; Power Throw Lever that permits fast magnification changes; first focal plane reticle
MSRP . . . . $1715.00–$1750.00

NXS 5.5–22X50MM

Weight: 31 oz.
Length: 15.1 in.
Power: 5.5–22X
Obj.Dia.: 50mm
Main Dia.: 30mm
Exit Pupil: 9.1–2.3mm
Field of View: 17.5–4.7 ft @ 100 yds
Twilight Factor: 16.58–33.16
Eye Relief: 3.8 in.
Features: Originally developed for the U.S. military's extreme long range shooting and hard target interdiction; 100 MOA of elevation travel make it ideal for use on the .50 BMG, allowing accurate shots to 2000 yards and beyond; slim profile, easily adaptable to a wide range of mounting systems
MSRP . . . . $1800.00–$2090.00

NXS 5.5–22X56MM

Weight: 32 oz.
Length: 15.2 in.
Power: 5.5–22X
Obj.Dia.: 56mm
Main Dia.: 30mm
Exit Pupil: 10.2–2.5mm
Field of View: 17.5–4.7 ft @ 100 yds
Twilight Factor: 17.54–35.09
Eye Relief: 3.9 in. ***F***eatures: Advanced field tactical riflescope for long-range applications; maximum clarity and resolution across the entire magnification range, exceptional low-light performance; available with ZeroStop technology and 1/8 and . MOA or .1 Mil-Radian adjustments; available with MOAR, MOAR-T, MIL-R, or MIL-DOT reticles
MSRP . . . . $1800.00–$2090.00

NXS 8–32X56MM

Weight: 34 oz.
Length: 15.9 in.
Power: 8–32X
Obj.Dia.: 56mm
Main Dia.: 30mm
Exit Pupil: 7–1.8mm
Field of View: 12.1–3.1 ft @ 100 yds
Twilight Factor: 21.16–42.33
Eye Relief: 3.8 in.
Features: For long-range hunting, competition, and target shooting; choice of five different reticles for the shooter's chosen application; offered with .125 MOA, .250 MOA or .1 Mil-Radian Hi-Speed adjustments; equipped with ZeroStop; second focal plane reticles available in MOAR, MOAR-T, NP-2DD, MIL-R, or MIL-DOT, all with analog illumination
MSRP . . . . $1900.00–$2190.00

Nightforce Optics, Inc.

NIGHTFORCE OPTICS NXS 5.5–22X56MM

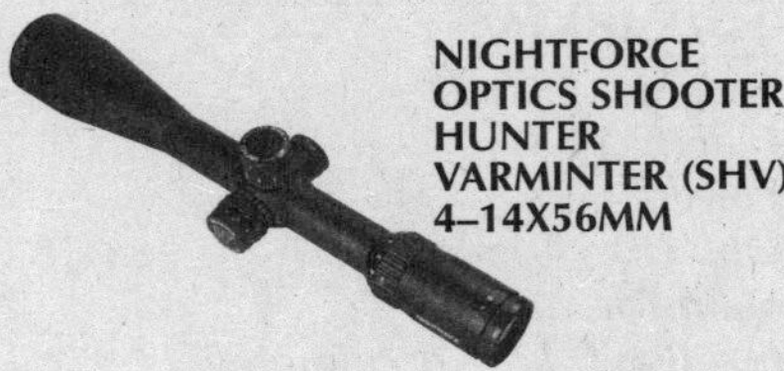

NIGHTFORCE OPTICS SHOOTER HUNTER VARMINTER (SHV) 4–14X56MM

PRECISION BENCHREST 8–32X56MM, 12-42X56MM

Weight: 36 oz.
Length: 16.6 in.
Power: 8–32X, 12-42X
Obj.Dia.: 56mm
Main Dia.: 30mm
Exit Pupil: 5.6–1.7mm, 4–1.4mm
Field of View: 9.4–3.1 ft @ 100 yds, 6.7–2.3 ft. @ 100 yds
Twilight Factor: 21.16–42.33
Eye Relief: 2.9 in.
Features: Superior resolution; adjustable objective; parallax adjustment from 25 yards to infinity; target adjustments calibrated in 1/8 click) MOA values, and can be re-indexed to zero after sighting in; eyepiece allows for fast reticle focusing; second plane reticles in a choice of NP-R2 or NP-2DD configurations with analog illumination
8-32X:. $1326.00
12-42X:. $1473.00

SHOOTER HUNTER VARMINTER (SHV) SERIES

Weight: 20.8 oz., 26.9 oz., 29.1 oz.
Length: 11.6 in., 14.8 in., 15.2 in.
Power: 3–10X, 4–14X, 5–20X
Obj. Dia.: 42mm, 56mm, 56mm
Main Dia.: 30mm
Exit Pupil: 10.7–4.4mm, 12–3.6mm, 8.7–2.5mm
Field of View: 34.9–11 ft @ 100 yds, 24.9–7.3 ft @ 100 yds, 17.9–5 ft @ 100 yds
Twilight Factor: 11.22–20.49, 14.97–28, 16.73–33.47
Eye Relief: 3.5 in., 3.15–3.54 in., 3.15–3.54 in.
Features: European-style fast-focus eyepiece, side parallax adjustment, capped .25-MOA adjustments, and multiple reticle choices, including illuminated options, at a consumer-friendly price point.
3–10X: $985.00
4–14x56mm:. . . . . $895.00–$1128.00
5–20X: . . . . $1195.00–$1345.00

Nikko Stirling

NIKKO STIRLING DIAMOND FFP

NIKKO STIRLING DIAMOND LONG RANGE

DIAMOND FFP

Weight: 24.2 oz.–24 oz.
Length: 13 in.–14.2 in.
Power: 4–16x44mm, 6–24x50mm
Obj. Diameter: 44mm, 50mm
Eye Relief: 3.9 in., 3.5 in.
Field of View: Varies with model
Features: First focal plane (FFP) optics allow for range-finding shot corrections via reticle; 30mm main body tube; glass-etched illuminated skeleton HMD or PRR reticles; fully multi-coated lenses; parallax turret houses illumination
MSRP. . . . . starting at $367.00

DIAMOND LONG RANGE

Available in: 4–16x50mm, 6–24x50mm, 10-40x56m
Weight: 16.5 oz.
Length: 14.2 in.
Power: 4–16X, 6–24X, 10-40X
Obj. Dia.: 50mm, 56mm
Main Dia.: 30mm
Field of View: 32.1–8 ft @ 100 yds, 21.4–5.4 ft @ 100 yds, 10.5–2.6 ft.@100 yds
Eye Relief: 4.5 in.
Features: Fully multi-coated lens; Zerostop turrets; dual-color red/green illumination settings; 4–16X features LR HMD reticle, 6–24X houses LR Hold Fast reticle
MSRP. . . . . starting at $283.00

Primary Arms

PRIMARY ARMS SLX 1–8X24MM FFP

PRIMARY ARMS SLX 2.5 COMPACT PRISM

SLX 1–8X24MM FFP

Available in: 1–8x24mm
Weight: 17.9 oz.
Power: 1–8X
Obj. Dia.: 24mm
Main Dia.: 30mm
Exit Pupil: 9–3mm
Field of View: 105–4.3 ft.@100 yd.
Eye Relief: 3.3–3.2 in.
Features: A first focal plane compact 8X with illuminated ACSS Raptor 5.56 reticle; capped, low-profile, finger-adjustable turrets; moveable and replaceable magnification ring fin; fully multi-coated lenses; ¼-MOA clicks
MSRP. $479.99

SLX 2.5 COMPACT PRISM

Available in: 2.5x32mm
Weight: 14.9 oz.
Power: 2.5X
Main Dia.: 30mm
Exit Pupil: 10.16mm
Field of View: 37.5 ft.@100 yd.
Eye Relief: 2.7 in.
Features: A workhorse CQB scope with an illuminated ACSS CQB-M1 reticle that has BDC ranging to 600 yards with .223/.308 applications; prism construction; Type II hardcoat anodized finish; ½-MOA clicks; optional Picatinny rail for red-dot piggybacking
MSRP. $199.00

Redfield

REDFIELD REVOLUTION 3–9X40MM

REDFIELD REVOLUTION/TAC 3–9X40MM

REVOLUTION SERIES

Weight: 11.1 oz., 12.6 oz., 14.5 oz., 13.1 oz.
Length: 11 in., 12.3 in., 12.4 in., 12.3 in.
Power: 2–7X, 3–9X, 4–12X
Obj. Dia.: 33mm, 40mm, 50mm
Main Dia.: 1 in.
Field of View: 43.2–17.3 ft @ 100 yds, 32.9–13.1 ft @ 100 yds, 33–13.1 ft @ 100 yds, 19.9–9.4 ft @ 100 yds
Twilight Factor: 8.12–15.2, 10.95–18.97, 12.25–21.21, 12.65–21.91
Eye Relief: 3.7–4.2 in., 3.7–4.2 in., 3.7–4.2 in., 3.7–4.9 in.
Features: 4-Plex or Accu-Range reticle; Illuminator Lens System with premium lenses and vapor-deposition multi-coatings; Accu-Trac windage and elevation adjustment system has resettable stainless steel ¼ MOA finger click adjustments
MSRP . . . . $160.99–$230.49

REVOLUTION/TAC 3–9X40MM

Weight: 12.6 oz.
Length: 12.3 in.
Power: 3–9X
Obj. Dia.: 40mm
Main Dia.: 1 in.
Exit Pupil: 12.1–4.7mm
Field of View: 32.9–13.1 ft @ 100 yds
Twilight Factor: 10.95–18.97
Eye Relief: 3.7 in.–4.2 in.
Features: Shock-, water-, and fogproof; nitrogen filled; vapor deposited, multi-coated illuminator lens system
MSRP $237.99

Riton Optics

RITON OPTICS CONQUER SERIES

RITON OPTICS TACTIX SERIES

RITON OPTICS PRIMAL SERIES

CONQUER SERIES

Available in: 3–15x44mm, 3–18x50mm, 3–24x50mm, 3–24x56mm, 4–32x56mm, 5–25x50mm, 6–24x50mm
Weight: 24 oz.–37 oz.
Length: 12.62 in.–15.37 in.
Power: 3–15X, 3–18X, 3–24X, 4–32X, 5–25X, 6–24X
Obj. Dia.: 44mm, 50mm, 56mm
Main Dia.: 30mm, 34mm
Exit Pupil: 14.7–2.9mm, 7.5–2.9mm, 6.6–2.2mm, 7–1.6mm, 10.2–2.2mm, 8.2–2.1mm
Field of View: 38.3–7.6 ft.@100 yd., 35–6.2 ft.@100 yd., 35–6.4 ft.@100 yd., 27–3.4 ft.@100 yd., 22.5–4.5 ft.@100 yd., 16.8–4.4 ft.@100 yd.
Eye Relief: 3.7 in., 3.4 in., 3.5 in., 3.5 in., 3.7 in., 3.9 in.
Features: This series of scopes vary in features, but all have removable throw levers, HD glass, fast focus eyepieces
MSRP . . . . $329.99–$1999.99

PRIMAL SERIES

Available in: 1–8x28mm, 3–9x40mm, 3–15x 44, 3–18x44, 4–16x44mm
Weight: 22 oz.–27 oz.
Length: 10.75 in.–13.37 in.
Power: 1–8X, 3–9X, 3–15X, 3–18X, 4–16X
Obj. Dia.: 28mm, 40mm, 44mm
Main Dia.: 1 in., 30mm, 34mm
Exit Pupil: 7.5–2.9mm, 10.6–3.5mm, 14.7–2.9mm, 8.2–2.8mm, 11–2.8mm
Field of View: 105.8–13.1 ft.@100 yd., 41–13 ft.@100 yd., 38.3–7.6 ft.@100 yd., 35–6.2 ft.@100 yd., 24.1–6.3 ft.@100 yd.
Eye Relief: 3.4 in., 3.9 in.
Features: The scopes in this series vary widely in features
MSRP . . . . $249.99–$1299.99

TACTIX SERIES

Available in: 1–6x24mm, 1–8x24mm, 1–8x28mm
Weight: 19.3 oz.–25 oz.
Length: 10.25 in.–10.9 in.
Power: 1–6X, 1–8X
Obj. Dia.: 24mm, 28mm
Main Dia.: 30mm
Exit Pupil: 8.5–4mm, 7.5–3mm, 7.5–2.9mm
Field of View: 111.2–18.33 ft.@100 yd., 105.8–13.1 ft.@100 yd.
Eye Relief: 3.5 in.
Features: Features in this series vary
MSRP . . . . $499.99–$1299.99

Schmidt & Bender

SCHMIDT & BENDER PM II HIGH POWER

SCHMIDT & BENDER POLAR T96

SCHMIDT & BENDER PM II ULTRA BRIGHT

EXOS

Available in: 3–21x50mm
Weight: 32.6 oz.
Length: 13.4 in.
Power: 3–21X
Obj. Dia.: 50mm
Main Dia.: 34mm
Exit Pupil: 11.4–2.5mm
Field of View: 13–1.9m@100m
Eye Relief: 3.5 in.
Features: Features an illuminated second focal plane D7 reticle with 11 settings and auto shutoff; locking elevation turret; Minimum Deviation System
MSRP . . . . $3299.99–$3999.99

PM II HIGH POWER

Available in: 5–45x56mm
Weight: 39.03 oz.
Length: 17 in.
Power: 5–45x
Obj. Dia.: 56mm
Main Dia.: 34mm
Exit Pupil: 8.8–1.2mm
Field of View: 7.8–.9m@100m
Twilight Factor: 16.7–50.2
Eye Relief: 3.54 in.
Features: Developed via a U.S. SOCOM request for a scope to cover extreme distances; reticles available include TReMoR2, H58, MSR, Police, P3L, H2CMR, H37, P4L, Klein, and P4LF
MSRP . . . . $5799.99–$6599.99

PM II ULTRA BRIGHT

Available in: 3–12x54mm, 4–16x56mm
Weight: 32.52 oz. (3–12x), 33.79 oz. (4–16x)
Length: 13.8 in. (3–12x), 15.2 in. (4–16x)
Power: 3-12x, 4–16x
Obj. Dia.: 54mm, 56mm
Main Dia.: 34mm
Exit Pupil: 12–4.5mm (3–12x), 12–3.5mm (4–16x)
Field of View: 12.5–3.1m@100m (3–12x), 9.4–2.3m@100m (4–16x)
Twilight Factor: 12.7–25.5 (3–12x), 15–29.9 (4–16x)
Eye Relief: 3.54 in.
Features: More than 96 percent light transmission; "reverse" design is rounder and sports flattened turrets; reticle choices include TReMoR3, P3L, and P4LF; other reticles can be installed at request
MSRP . . . . $3799.99–$4899.99

POLAR T96

Available in: 3–12x54mm, 4–16x56mm, 2.5–10x50mm
Weight: 23.92–28.57 oz.
Length: 13 in., 14 in.
Power: 3–12x, 4–16x, 2.5–10X
Obj. Dia.: 54mm, 56mm
Main Dia.: 34mm
Exit Pupil: 12–4.5mm (3-12x), 12–3.5mm (4–16x), 12–5mm (2.5–10x)
Field of View: 12.5–3.1m@100m, 9.4–3m@100m, 15–3.75m
Eye Relief: 3.54 in.
Features: Model is named based on its 96 percent light transmission; dusk-proof reticles; choice of reticle in the first or second focal plane; reticle choices include L7, L4, D7, and D4
MSRP . . . . $2299.99–$3699.99

OPTICS

Sightron

SIGHTRON USA S-TAC4-20X50FFPZSIRMH

S-TAC4-20X50FFPZSIRMH

Available in: 4–20x50mm
Weight: 25.6 oz.
Length: 15 in.
Power: 4–20X
Obj. Dia.: 50mm
Main Dia.: 30mm
Field of View: 22.2–4.36 ft.@100 yd.
Eye Relief: 3.9–3.7 in.
Features: A nice entry for long-range work, with ample eye relief and magnification; tactical resettable turret knobs; side focus; illuminated Mil-Hash 4 reticle in the first focal plane; fast-focus eyepiece; zoom ring lever
MSRP $999.00

SIG Sauer

SIG SAUER SIERRA3BDX

SIG SAUER SIERRA6 BDX

SIG SAUER TANGO4

SIG SAUER TANGO6

SIG SAUER WHISKEY3

SIERRA3BDX

Available in: 2.5x8x32mm, 3–18x44mm, 3.5–10x42mm, 4.5–14x44mm, 4.5–14x50mm, 6.5–20x52mm
Power: 2.5–8X, 3–18, X3.5–10X, 4.5–14X, 6.5–20X
Obj. Dia.: 32mm, 40mm, 42mm, 44mm, 50mm, 52mm
Main Dia.: 30mm
Exit Pupil: varies with model
Field of View: varies with model
Features: A rangefinder and scope all in one via SIG's BDX-R1 reticle--BDX stands for Ballistic Data Exchange--which includes an illuminated auto-holdover dot when the scope is paired with Sig's BDX-capable KILO rangefinders; SpectralCoat lenses; anti-cant digital LevelPlex technology; second focal plane
MSRP . . . . $519.99–$1039.99

SIERRA6BDX

Available in: 3–18x44mm, 2–12x40mm, 5–30x56mm
Weight: 23.8 oz., 30.04 oz.
Power: 3–18X, 2–12X, 5–30X
Obj. Dia.: 44mm, 40mm, 56mm
Main Dia.: 34mm, 30mm
Exit Pupil: 8.2–2.4mm, 8.4–3.3mm, 8.1–1.9mm
Field of View: 34.9–8 ft.@100 yd., 52.5–8.7 ft.@100 yd., 21–3.5 ft.@100 yd.
Eye Relief: 3.9 in., 3.7 in.
Features: A second focal plane riflescope with adjustments in ¼-MOA; eight daytime/two night vision settings; IPX7 waterproofing; Argon-gas purged; 60 MOA total windage/elevation adjustment
MSRP . . . . $1169.99–$1689.99

TANGO4

Available in: 1–4x24mm, 4–16x44mm, 6–24x50mm
Weight: 20.1 oz.–26.9 oz.
Length: 10 in.–15.6 in.
Power: 1–4X, 4–16X, 6–24X
Obj. Dia.: 24mm–50mm
Main Dia.: 30mm
Exit Pupil: 15.4–6.1mm, 22.9–5.1mm, 8–2.1mm
Field of View: 98–24 ft @ 100 yds, 24.3–6.1 ft @ 100 yds, 16.8–4.2 ft @ 100 yds
Eye Relief: 3.3 in.
Features: Low dispersion glass provides industry-leading optical clarity for any situation; offered in first focal plane with multiple, illuminated reticle options; MOTAC (Motion Activated Illumination) powers up when it senses motion and powers down when it does not; provides for optimum operational safety and enhanced battery life; dependable waterproof (IPX-7 rated for complete immersion up to 1 meter) and fogproof performance; LockDown Zero System features a resettable zero, zero-stop, and auto-locks down at zero
MSRP . . . . $649.99–$1039.99

TANGO6

Available in: 5–30x56mm
Weight: 39.5 oz.
Length: 15.3 in.
Power: 5–30X
Obj. Dia.: 24mm–56mm
Main Dia.: 30mm
Exit Pupil: 8.8–1.9mm
Field of View: 20.2–3.4 ft @ 100 yds
Eye Relief: 3.5–3.9 in.
Features: Offered in first focal plane; HDX optics extra-low dispersion glass combined with high transmittance glass provide industry-leading light transmission and optical clarity for any situation; LockDown Zero System features a resettable zero, zero-stop, and is lockable at any location
MSRP $2599.99

WHISKEY3

Available in: 2–7x32mm, 3–9x50mm, 4–12x40mm, 4–12x50mm
Weight: 14.8 oz.–18.8 oz.
Length: 11.2 in.–14 in.
Power: 2–7X, 3–9X, 4–12X
Obj. Dia.: 32mm–50mm
Main Dia.: 25.4mm
Exit Pupil: 15–4.5mm, 15–4.8mm, 15.1–5.6mm, 10–3.3mm
Field of View: 45.4–13.1 ft @ 100 yds, 33.9–11.3 ft @ 100 yds, 23.6–7.9 ft @ 100 yds
Eye Relief: 3.5 in.
Features: 3X optical zoom offered in second focal plane (SFP) with multiple reticle options; low dispersion glass provides industry-leading optical clarity for any situation; European-style eyepiece for a smooth, fast, and precise reticle adjustment; dependable waterproof (IPX-7 rated for complete immersion up to 1 meter) and fogproof performance
MSRP . . . . $169.99–$299.99

Simmons

SIMMONS .22 MAG 3–9X32MM

.22 MAG 3–9X32MM

Weight: 10 oz.
Length: 12 in.
Power: 3–9X
Obj. Dia.: 32mm
Main Dia.: 1 in.
Exit Pupil: 10.7–3.6mm
Field of View: 31.4–10.5 ft @ 100 yds
Twilight Factor: 9.8–17
Eye Relief: 3.75 in.
Features: One piece tube construction; fully coated optics; waterproof; fogproof; shockproof; Truplex reticle; RF Rings with available Adjustable Objective; matte or silver finish
MSRP . . . . $62.45–$73.99

Simmons

SIMMONS PROTARGET RIFLESCOPES

SIMMONS OPTICS PROTARGET RIMFIRE

SIMMONS WHITETAIL CLASSIC

PROTARGET RIFLESCOPES

Available in: 2.5–10x40mm, 4–16x40mm, 6–24x44
Weight: 20–20.4 oz.
Power: 2.5–10x, 4–16x, 6–24x
Obj. Dia.: 40mm
Main Dia.: 1 in.
Field of View: 31–10.5 ft.@100 yd. (2.5–10x), 33-8.6 ft.@100 yd. (4–16x), 17–4.5 ft.@100 yd. (6–24x)
Eye Relief: 3.9 in.
Features: Three dedicated rimfire scopes with TruPlex reticles and side parallax adjustment; 3–9x and 6–24x have turrets calibrated for .22 LR; 3–12x's turrets are calibrated for .17 HMR; 3–12x and 6–24x have side focus adjustment; multi-coated glass; matte finish; supplied with rings
MSRP . . . . $124.95–$171.45

PROTARGET RIMFIRE

Available in: 4x32, 2–7x32mm, 3–9x40mm
Weight: 8.8 oz.–11.2 oz.
Power: 4X, 2–7X, 3–9X
Obj. Dia.: 32mm, 40mm
Main Dia.: 1 in.
Exit Pupil: 8mm, 13.5–4.4mm, 13–4.2mm
Field of View: 26 ft.@100 yd., 49–15 ft.@100 yd., 32–11 ft.@100 yd.
Eye Relief: 3.5 in.
Features: Designed specifically for rimfire accuracy, this series of scopes feature a Truplex reticle; 35 MOA windage/elevation with ¼-MOA clicks; capped exposed turrets
MSRP . . . . $62.45–$77.95

WHITETAIL CLASSIC

Available in: 4x32mm, 1–4x20mm, 2–7x32mm, 3–9x40mm, 4–12x40mm, 6–24x50mm
Weight: 13.29–19.4 oz.
Length: 9.76–15.98 in.
Power: 4x, 1–4x, 2–7x, 3–9x, 4–12x, 6–24x
Obj. Dia.: 20, 32, 40, 50mm
Main Dia.: 1 in.
Exit Pupil: varies
Field of View: varies
Eye Relief: varies
Features: Five utilitarian zoom magnifications; second focal plane optics with 1-in. tubes; Black Granite finish and red highlights; waterproof, fog-proof, and shockproof
MSRP . . . . $64.95–$155.95

Steiner

STEINER GS3 SERIES 2–10X42MM

STEINER M7XI, M7XI IFS

STEINER T5XI SERIES

GS3 2–10X42MM

Weight: 18 oz.
Length: 13.5 in.
Power: 2–10X
Obj. Dia.: 42mm
Main Dia.: 30mm
Exit Pupil: 16.8–4.2mm
Field of View: 52–10.5 ft @ 100 yds
Twilight Factor: 9.17–20.49
Eye Relief: 3.5 in.–4.25 in.
Features: Rear focal plane; water- and fog-proof; nitrogen filled; 3–15x50, 3–15x56, and 4–20x50 also available
4–20X: $1379.99
3–15X: $1199.99
2–10X: $1059.99

M7XI, M7XI IFS

Available in: 4–28x56mm
Weight: 33.5 oz.
Length: 15.2 in.
Power: 4–28X
Obj. Dia.: 56mm
Main Dia.: 34mm
Field of View: 9–1.42m@100m
Eye Relief: 3.54 in.
Features: Designed for long-range applications but with a compact form; first focal plane optics; low-profile turrets; nitrogen-filled tube; water- and fog-proof; available reticles include MSR, MSR2, G2B, TReMor3; IFS version features Steiner's Intelligent Firing System
M7Xi: . . . . $3812.99–$4852.99
M7Xi IFS: . . . . . . $5750.99–$6784.99

T5XI SERIES

Weight: 19.4 oz., 29.8 oz., 33 oz.
Length: 11.3 in., 13.1 in., 16.6 in.
Power: 1–5X, 3–15X, 5–25X
Obj. Dia.: 24mm, 50mm, 56mm
Main Dia.: 30mm, 34mm, 34mm
Exit Pupil: 11–4.8mm, 12–3.4mm, 11.2–2.3mm
Field of View: 108–21m@ 100m, 36–7.3m@ 100m, 21.5–4.3m@100m
Twilight Factor: 4.9–10.95, 12.25–27.39, 16.73–37.42
Eye Relief: 3.5–4.3 in.
Features: The 1–5x24 is designed as a close-combat scope; medium-range 3–15x50 and long-range 5–25x56 scope come with illuminated etched glass featuring the new Special Competition Reticle (SCR) and Second Rotation Indicator that shows each mil of elevation through the indication window on the elevation turret; front focal plane; MOA SCR reticle added as an option in 2018
1–5X: $1804.99
3–15X: $2369.99
5–25X: $2610.99

Swarovski Optik

SWAROVSKI OPTIK X5(I) 3.5–18X50MM

SWAROVSKI OPTIK X5(I) 5–25X56 P 1/4 MOA

SWAROVSKI OPTIK Z3 3.3–10X42MM

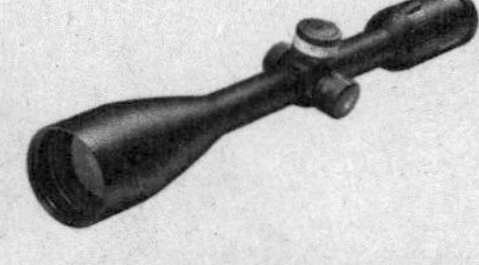

SWAROVSKI OPTIK Z5(I) 5–25X52MM

SWAROVSKI OPTIK Z6I 5–30X50MM P

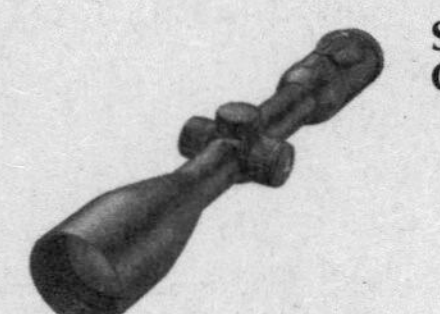
SWAROVSKI OPTIK Z8I

X5(I) 3.5–18X50MM

Weight: 28.6 oz.–32.1 oz.
Length: 14.4 in.–14.8 in.
Power: 3.5–18X
Obj. Dia.: 50mm
Main Dia.: 30mm
Exit Pupil: 9.5–2.8mm
Field of View: 30–6.3 ft @ 100 yds
Twilight Factor: 11–30
Eye Relief: 3.7 in.
Features: The X5(i) from SWAROVSKI OPTIK redefines accuracy; new spring retention system and turrets are part of the total package promoting accuracy and offering across the entire adjustment range an accurate impact point adjustment of ¼ MOA in terms of both elevation and windage even in the most extreme situations; use the SUBZERO function to go below the sight-in distance
MSRP $3110.00

X5(I) 5–25X56 P 1/4 MOA

Weight: 32.1 oz.
Length: 14.8 in.
Power: 5–25x56mm
Obj. Diameter: 56mm
Exit Pupil: 2.3–9.5mm
Field of View: 4.5–21 ft @ 100 yds
Features: High-luminosity rifle scope with 25x magnification; three reticle options; 30mm tube; 10 illumination brightness settings
MSRP $3332.00

Z3 3.3–10X42MM

Weight: 12.7 oz.
Length: 12.6 in.
Power: 3.3–10X
Obj.Dia.: 42mm
Main Dia.: 1 in.
Exit Pupil: 12.6–4.2mm
Field of View: 33–11.7 ft @ 100 yds
Twilight Factor: 11.22–20.49
Eye Relief: 3.5 in.
Features: Z3 riflescopes have a 3x zoom factor and are the lightest riflescopes in the Swarovski Optik line; perfect fit for many of today's lightweight rifles; reticles for the Z3 include the 4A, Plex, BRX, and BRX Heavy; also available in 3–10x40mm and 4–12x50mm
MSRP $832.00

Z5(I) 5–25X52MM

Weight: 17.5 oz.
Length: 14.6 in.
Power: 5–25X
Obj.Dia.: 52mm
Main Dia.: 1 in.
Exit Pupil: 9.6–2.1mm
Field of View: 21.9–4.5 ft @ 100 yds
Twilight Factor: 16.12–36.05
Eye Relief: 3.75 in.
Features: The Z5 Riflescope line features a 5x zoom factor; a third parallax-adjustment turret; and long eye relief; with reticles available in #4, Plex, Fine in the 5–25x, and BRX/BRH; also available with the ballistic turrets; also in 3.5–18x44mm, 2.4–12x50mm
5–25X: . . . . $1888.00–$1966.00
3.5–18X: . . . . $1399.00–$1854.00
2.4–12X: . . . . $1277.00–$1388.00

Z6I 5–30X50MM P

Weight: 22.6 oz.
Length: 15.67 in.
Power: 5–30X
Obj. Dia.: 48.2–50mm
Main Dia.: 30mm
Exit Pupil: 9.5–1.7mm
Field of View: 23.7–3.9 ft @ 100 yds
Twilight Factor: 14.1–38.7
Eye Relief: 3.74 in.
Features: New 2nd Generation scopes feature slimmer design that enables a clearer view of the controls and of the hunting situation; parallax turret also features a lock-in position at the 100 yds mark; more prominent ribbing on the magnification ring; 4A-I, 4W-I reticles available
MSRP $2433.00

Z8I

Weight: 18.2 oz.–25.6 oz.
Length: 14 in.–14.3 in.
Power: 1–8x24mm, 1.7–13.3x42mm, 2–16x50mm, 2.3–18x56mm
Obj. Diameter: 24, 42, 50, 56mm
Exit Pupil: Varies with model
Field of View: Varies with model
Features: Illuminated 8x zoom in a 30mm tube; Flexchange, a switchable reticle; multiple reticles to choose from
MSRP . . . . $2888.00–$3943.00

Tangent Theta

TANGENT THETA LONG-RANGE HUNTER

LONG-RANGE HUNTER

Available in: 3-15x50mm
Weight: 26.98 oz.
Length: 13.7 oz.
Power: 3–15X
Obj. Dia.: 50mm
Main Dia.: 30mm
Field of View: 7.3–1.6 degrees
Features: A premium riflescope for the hunter, with a first focal plane illuminated LRH MRAD reticle
MSRP $3729.00

OPTICS

Tangent Theta

TANGENT THETA PROFESSIONAL

PROFESSIONAL

Weight: 40.57 oz.
Length: 16.73 in.
Power: 5–25X
Obj. Dia.: 56mm
Main Dia.: 34mm
Exit Pupil: 11–2.3mm
Field of View: 7.6–1.6m @ 100m
Twilight Factor: 16.73–37.42
Eye Relief: 3.54 in.
Features: Water- and shockproof; adjustable parallax; illuminated reticle; 3–15x50 also available
5–25X: . . . . $4733.00–$5158.00
3–15X: $4113.00

Tasco

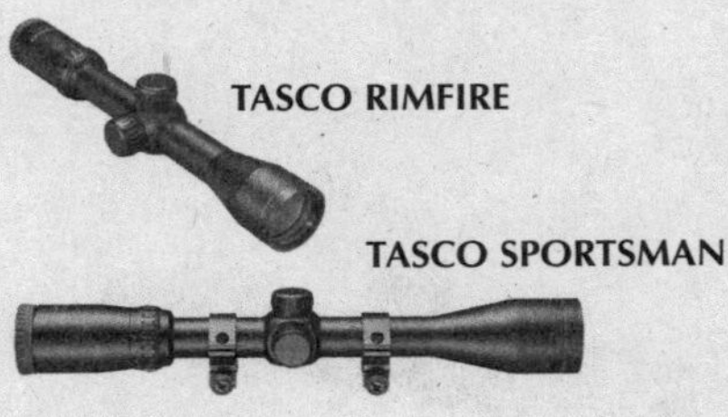
TASCO RIMFIRE

TASCO SPORTSMAN

RIMFIRE

Available in: 4x32mm, 2–7x32mm, 3–9x40mm
Weight: 4 oz.–11.6 oz.
Length: 11 in.–12.2 in.
Power: 4X, 2–7X, 3–9X
Obj. Dia.: 32mm, 40mm
Main Dia.: .75 in., 1 in.
Exit Pupil: 8mm, 14.3–4.6mm, 14–4.4mm
Field of View: 26 ft.@100 yd., 49–15 ft.@100 yd., 32–11 ft.@100 yd.
Eye Relief: 2.5–3.6 in.
Features: Very budget-friendly line of rimfire rifle scopes in a variety of fixed and variable powers to fit any job at hand
MSRP . . . . $31.19–$41.59

SPORTSMAN

Available in: 3–9x40mm, 3–9x50mm, 4-12x40mm, 6-24x44mm
Weight: 14.9 oz.–17.2 oz.
Length: 13 in.–13.5 in.
Power: 3–9X, 4-12X, 6–24X
Obj. Dia.: 40mm, 44mm, 50mm
Main Dia.: 1 in.
Exit Pupil: 100–4.6mm, 10.5–5.5mm, 10–3.5mm, 7.5–2.1mm
Field of View: 39–12.7 ft.@100 yd., 33-10 ft.@100 yd., 27–9 ft.@100 yd., 18.5–4.5 ft.@100 yd.
Eye Relief: 3.5 in.
Features: Economical line of scopes for centerfire rifles, with 1-in. main tubes; 30/30 reticle in the second focal plane
MSRP . . . . $57.19–$103.99

Tract Optics

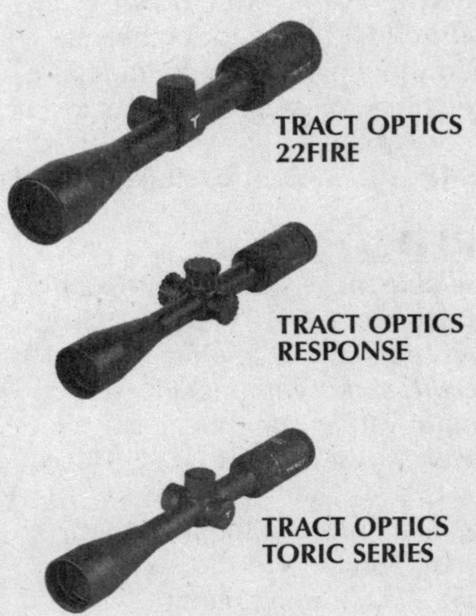
TRACT OPTICS 22FIRE

TRACT OPTICS RESPONSE

TRACT OPTICS TORIC SERIES

22FIRE

Weight: 15.2 oz. (3–9x40mm), 16 oz. (4–12x40mm)
Length: 12.2 in. (3–9x40mm), 13.9 in. (4–12x40mm)
Power: 3–9, 4–12
Obj. Diameter: 40mm
Exit Pupil: Varies with model
Eye Relief: 3.5 in.
Field of View: Varies with model
Features: 22Rifle line designed specifically to maximize accuracy with .22-caliber rifles; Impact BDC or T-Plex reticle; BDC designed for longer-distance work, while T-Plex is suitable for target practice and small-game hunting
3–9X: $194.00
4–12X: $224.00

RESPONSE

Weight: 19.6 oz.
Length: 13.1 in.
Power: 4–16X
Obj. Diameter: 42mm
Exit Pupil: 10.5–2.6mm
Eye Relief: 3.5 in.
Field of View: 22–2.5 ft @ 100 yds
Features: Response line consists of three scopes; intended for use with ARs/MSRs in the .223 reticles and the AR10 platform with the .308 reticle; exposed tactical type turrets; glassetched reticles with windage correction
MSRP $424.00

TORIC

Available in: 2–10x42mm, 3–15x42mm, 3–15x50mm
Weight: 18.6 oz.–22.3 oz.
Length: 13.2 in.–13.9 in.
Power: 2–10X, 3–15X, 3–15X
Obj. Dia.: 42mm–50mm
Main Dia.: 1 in.
Exit Pupil: 10.7–4.2mm, 10–2.8mm, 10–3.3mm
Field of View: 49–9.9 ft @ 100 yds, 34–6.9 ft @ 100 yds, 34.3–6.8 ft @ 100 yds
Eye Relief: 4 in.
Features: Schott HT glass; glass etched BDC and T-Plex reticle (w/ windage correction in the BDC)
2–10X: $694.00
3–15X: . . . . $754.00–$794.00

Tract Optics

TRACT OPTICS TORIC UHD 30MM

TORIC UHD 30MM

Available in: 4–20x59mm
Weight: 34 oz.
Length: 13.7 in.
Power: 4–20X
Obj. Dia.: 50mm
Main Dia.: 30mm
Exit Pupil: 12.5–2.5mm
Field of View: 24.5–4.9 ft.@100 yd.
Eye Relief: 3.9 in.
Features: One for the long-range game with first focal plane illuminated glass-etched reticle; quick-focus eyepiece; 11 brightness settings; magnification ring with rear-facing numbers; waterproof, fog-proof with Argon gas; locking turrets with zero stop; side focus parallax adjustment; choice of MRAD or MOA reticles
MSRP $1294.00

Trijicon

TRIJICON ACCUPOINT 4–16X50MM

TRIJICON ACOG WITH .300 BLK RETICLE 3X30MM

TRIJICON CREDO

TRIJICON CREDO HX

TRIJICON ASCENT

ACCUPOINT 4–16X50MM

Available in: 4–16x50mm
Weight: 24.2 oz.
Length: 13.9 in.
Power: 4–16x
Obj. Dia.: 50mm
Main Dia.: 30mm
Exit Pupil: 9.3–3.1mm
Field of View: 25.8–6.4 ft.@100 yd.
Eye Relief: 3.6–3.7 in.
Features: Fiber optic and tritium illuminated reticle; operates without a battery; illumination automatically adjusts to lighting conditions; aircraft-quality aluminum body; available with a standard Duplex crosshair in green, an MOA-Dot crosshair in green, a Mil-Dot crosshair in green, or a BAC triangle post in red, green, or yellow
MSRP . . . . $1399.00–$1499.00

ACOG WITH .300 BLK RETICLE 3X30MM

Weight: 11.64 oz.
Length: 6.1 in.
Power: 3X
Obj. Dia.: 30mm
Exit Pupil: 10mm
Field of View: 19.3 ft @ 100 yds
Twilight Factor: 9.5
Eye Relief: 1.9 in.
Features: TA60 Mount; designed for law enforcement and military applications; .300 BLK Ballistic Reticle for subsonic and supersonic rounds; bullet drop compensator; Bindon Aiming Concept (BAC), fiber optics & tritium illuminated; available with amber, green, or red crosshair reticle
MSRP $1407.00

ASCENT

Available in: 1–4x24mm, 3–12x40mm
Weight: 15.9 oz., 17.8 oz.
Length: varies with model
Power: 1–4X, 3–12X
Obj. Dia.: 24mm, 40mm
Main Dia.: 30mm
Exit Pupil: varies with model
Field of View: varies with model
Eye Relief: varies with model
Features: Tested to military standards, the two scopes in this line have anti-scratch glass, wide fields of view, knurled adjustment points, easy-focus eyepieces, and BDC Target Hold reticle in the second focal plane
1-4X: $650.00
3–12X: $699.00

CREDO

Available in: 1–4x24mm, 1–6x24mm, 1–8x28mm, 2–10x36mm, 2.5–10x56mm, 2.5–15x42mm, 2.5–15x56mm, 3–9x40mm, 4–16x50
Weight: varies with model
Length: varies with model
Power: 1–4X, 1–6X, 1-8X, 2–10X, 2.5–10X, 2.5–15X, 3–9X, 4–16X
Obj. Dia.: 24mm, 28mm, 36mm, 40mm, 42mm, 50mm, 56mm
Main Dia.: 1 in., 30mm, 34mm
Exit Pupil: varies with model
Field of View: varies with model
Eye Relief: varies with model
Features: Designed for both-eyes-open shooting, the Credo line has a wide range of variable powers to choose from
MSRP . . . . $799.00–$1799.00

CREDO HX

Available in: 1–4x24mm, 1–6x24mm, 1–8x28mm, 2.5–10x56mm, 2.5–15x42mm, 2.5–15x56mm, 4–16x50
Weight: varies with model
Length: varies with model
Power: 1–4X, 1–6X, 1-8X, 2.5–10X, 2.5–15X, 4–16X
Obj. Dia.: 24mm, 28mm, 42mm, 50mm, 56mm
Main Dia.: 30mm, 34mm
Exit Pupil: varies with model
Field of View: varies with model
Eye Relief: varies with model
Features: Similar to the Credo line, the HX designates reticles and power ranges for hunters
MSRP . . . . $999.00–$1799.00

Trijicon

TRIJICON HURON

TRIJICON TENMILE

TRIJICON TENMILE HX

TRIJICON VCOG 1–6X24MM RIFLESCOPE

HURON

Available in: 1–4x24mm, 2.5–10x40mm, 3–9x40mm, 3–12x40mm
Weight: varies with model
Length: varies with model
Power: 1–4X, 2.5–10X, 3-9X, 3-12X
Obj. Dia.: 24mm, 40mm
Main Dia.: 1 in., 30mm
Exit Pupil: varies with model
Field of View: varies with model
Eye Relief: varies with model
Features: Second focal plane reticle scopes designed for whitetail deer hunters, with aircraft-grade aluminum bodies, fast-focus eyepieces, BDC Hunter Holds reticle, ¼-MOA click adjustments, and wide fields of view
MSRP . . . . $650.00–$699.00

TENMILE

Available in: 3–18x44mm, 4–24x50mm, 4.5–30x56mm, 5–25x50mm, 5–50x56, 6–24x56mm
Weight: varies with model
Length: varies with model
Power: 3–18X, 4–24X, 4.5-30X, 5-25X, 5–50X, 6–24X
Obj. Dia.: 44mm, 50mm, 56mm
Main Dia.: 30mm, 34mm
Exit Pupil: varies with model
Field of View: varies with model
Eye Relief: varies with model
Features: Big tubes, big objectives, and big power ranges help those in the long-range game go the distance, and scopes include repositionable magnification knob, sunshade, battery, and Tenebraex flip lens caps
MSRP . . . . $1399.00–$2700.00

TENMILE HX

Available in: 3–18x44mm, 3–18x50mm, 5–25x50mm, 6-24x50mm
Weight: varies with model
Length: varies with model
Power: 3-18X, 5–25X, 6–24X
Obj. Dia.: 44mm, 50mm
Main Dia.: 30mm
Exit Pupil: varies with model
Field of View: varies with model
Eye Relief: varies with model
Features: Similar to the Tenmile series for target games, the HX here indicates powers and reticles suitable for hunting applications at distance
MSRP . . . . $1399.00–$2199.00

VCOG 1–6X24MM

Weight: 23.2 oz.
Length: 10.05 in.
Power: 1–6X
Obj. Dia.: 24mm
Exit Pupil: 10.4–3.8mm
Field of View: 95–15.9 ft @ 100 yds
Twilight Factor: 12
Eye Relief: 4 in.
Features: Designed and built in the U.S.; Mil Spec, hard-coat finish; 90 MOA of windage and elevation adjustment; fully multi-coated lenses; waterproof; seven different reticle choices, between centered crosshair and horseshoe/dot reticle; red illuminated reticle; six brightness settings; matte finish
MSRP . . . . $2800.00–$3050.00

Truglo

TRUGLO BUCKLINE

TRUGLO EMINUS

TRUGLO NEXUS

TRUGLO OMNIA

BUCKLINE

Available in: 3–9x32mm, 3–9x32mm, 3–9x40mm, 3–9x50mm, 4x32mm
Power: 3–9X, 4X
Obj. Dia.: 32mm, 40mm, 50mm
Main Dia.: .375 in., 1 in.
Features: Super economical scope series has a rubber-coated speed-focus eyepiece; BDC dot or Duplex reticles; fully coated lenses; water-resistant and fogproof; Weaver-style or 3/8-in. rings supplied
MSRP . . . .$29.99–$39.99

EMINUS

Available in: 3–9x42mm, 4–16x44mm, 6-24x50mm
Power: 3-9X, 4–16X, 6-24X
Obj. Dia.: 42mm, 44mm, 50mm
Main Dia.: 30mm
Features: A full-size scope for MSRs with side-focus wheel; illuminated TacPlex reticle; multi-coated lenses; hardcoat anodized matte black finish; leaf-spring turret control; ¼-MOA clicks; locking target turrets; supplied with APTUS-M1 mount
MSRP . . . . $248.99–$390.99

NEXUS

Available in: 3–9x42mm, 4–12x44mm
Power: 3–9X, 4–12X
Obj. Dia.: 42mm, 44mm
Features: Rubber-coated speed-focus eyepiece; non-illuminated BDC MOA-based or Duplex reticle
MSRP . . . . $131.99–$152.99

OMNIA

Available in: 1–4x24mm, 1–6x24mm, 1–8x24mm
Power: 1–4X, 1-6X, 1–8X
Obj. Dia.: 24mm
Main Dia.: 30mm
Features: A tactical sight with illuminated A.P.T.R. reticle; multi-coated lenses; hardcoat anodized matte black finish; leaf-spring turret control; ½-MOA clicks; locking target turrets
MSRP . . . . $248.99–$414.99

Truglo

TRUGLO TRU-BRITE 30

TRUGLO TRU-BRITE XTREME DUAL-COLOR TACTICAL COMPACT 4X32MM

TRU-BRITE 30

Available in: 1–4x24mm
Weight: 13.4 oz.–15.1 oz.
Length: 9.88 in.
Power: 1–4X
Obj. Dia.: 24mm
Main Dia.: 30mm
Field of View: 93.6–23.03 @ 100 yds
Eye Relief: 3.75 in.
Features: Includes two pre-calibrated BDC turrets in calibers .223 (55 grain) and .308 (168 grain) to engage targets up to 800 yards away; ½ MOA windage/elevation adjustments
MSRP $119.99

TRU-BRITE XTREME DUAL-COLOR TACTICAL COMPACT 4X32MM

Weight: 15.4 oz.
Length: 9.8 in.
Power: 4X
Obj. Dia.: 32mm
Main Dia.: 1 in.
Field of View: 20.79 ft @ 100 yds
Twilight Factor: 11.31
Eye Relief: 5.5 in.
Features: Illuminated reticle; fully coated lenses; durable, scratch-resistant, non-reflective matte finish
MSRP $103.99

U.S. Optics

U.S. OPTICS FOUNDATION SERIES

FOUNDATION SERIES

Available in: 1.8–10x42mm, 10x42mm, 3.2–17x50mm, 5–25x52mm
Weight: 25.7 oz.–33.4 oz.
Length: 12.98 in.–17.93 in.
Power: 1.8–10X, 10X, 3.2–17X, 5–25X
Obj. Dia.: 42mm, 50mm, 52mm
Main Dia.: 34mm
Exit Pupil: 3.2mm, 3mm
Field of View: 36–11 ft.@100 yd., 11.3 ft.@100 yd., 25.25–8 ft.@100 yd., 25.25–8 ft.@100 yd.
Eye Relief: 3.2 in.
Features: A U.S.-made line of premium optics that include aircraft-grade aluminum bodies, low-profile ER3K elevation knobs, capped US#1 windage knob, integrated and adjustable parallax, 180-degree magnification throw, choice of hard coat black anodized finish or a variety of Cerakote colors, reticles available in red, blue, or green illumination
MSRP . . . . starting at $1999.00

OPTICS

Vortex Optics

VORTEX CROSSFIRE II 3–12X56 AO

VORTEX CROSSFIRE II SCOUT

VORTEX DIAMONDBACK TACTICAL

CROSSFIRE II 3–12X56 AO

Weight: 21.1 oz.
Length: 14.3 in.
Power: 3–12X
Obj. Dia.: 56mm
Main Dia.: 30mm
Field of View: 36.7–9.2 ft @ 100 yds
Twilight Factor: 12.96–25.92
Eye Relief: 3.5 in.
Features: Second focal plane V-Brite illuminated reticle; capped reset turrets; adjustable objective; hard anodized finish
MSRP $369.99

CROSSFIRE II SCOUT

Available in: 2–7x32mm
Weight: 12 oz.
Length: 10.5 in.
Power: 2–7X
Obj. Dia.: 32mm
Main Dia.: 25.4mm
Field of View: 18.3–5.2 ft @ 100 yds
Eye Relief: 9.45 in.
Features: Fully multi-coated; second focal plane reticle; single-piece tube; capped reset turrets
MSRP $199.99

DIAMONDBACK TACTICAL

Weight: 16.2 oz., 23.1 oz., 24.6 oz.
Length: 12.5 in.
Power: 4–12x40mm, 4–16X44mm, 6–24X50mm
Obj. Diameter: 40mm, 44mm, 50mm
Eye Relief: 3.8 in., 3.9 in.
Field of View: 7.9–23.6 ft @ 100 yds (4–12x), 26.9–6.7 ft @ 100 yds, 18–4.5 ft @ 100 yds
Features: 3–9X and 4–12X have second focal plane reticle (VMR-1); 4–16X and 6–24X have first focal plane reticle (glass-etched EBR-2C MOA); XD lens elements; XR full multi-coatings; fast focus eyepiece; fiber optic turret rotation indicator
4–12X: $349.99
4–16X: $449.99
6–24X: $499.99

Vortex Optics

VORTEX GOLDEN EAGLE HD

VORTEX RAZOR HD AMG

VORTEX RAZOR HD GEN II SERIES 4.5–27X56MM

VORTEX RAZOR HD GEN II-E

VORTEX OPTICS RAZOR HD GEN III

VORTEX STRIKE EAGLE

VORTEX HS LR RFP SERIES 4–16X44MM

VORTEX VIPER HST SERIES 6–24X50MM

GOLDEN EAGLE HD

Available in: 15–60x52mm
Weight: 29.7 oz.
Length: 16.1 in.
Power: 15–60X
Obj. Dia.: 52mm
Main Dia.: 30mm
Field of View: 6.3–1.7 ft @ 100 yds
Eye Relief: 3.9 in.
Features: Apochromatic objective lens system uses index-matched lenses to correct color across the entire visual spectrum; extra-fine resolution turret
MSRP $1899.99

RAZOR HD AMG

Available in: 6–24x50mm
Weight: 28.8 oz.
Length: 15.2 in.
Power: 6–24X
Obj. Dia.: 50mm
Main Dia.: 30mm
Field of View: 20.4–5.1 ft @ 100 yds
Eye Relief: 3.6 in.
Features: ALO proprietary automated laser optical alignment process; apochromatic objective lens system uses index-matched lenses to correct color across the entire visual spectrum; optically indexed lenses; high-density, extra-low dispersion glass; first focal plane reticle; illuminated reticle; side focus adjustment
MSRP $3699.99

RAZOR HD GEN II 4.5–27X56MM

Weight: 48.5 oz.
Length: 14.4 in
Power: 4.5–27X
Obj. Dia.: 56mm
Main Dia.: 34mm
Field of View: 25.3–4.4 ft @ 100 yds
Twilight Factor: 15.87–38.88
Eye Relief: 3.7 in.
Features: Front focal plane; shock-, water-, and fogproof; adjustable parallax; illuminated reticle; glass-etched reticle; 3–18x50 also available
3–18X: $2499.99
4.5–27X: $2899.99

RAZOR HD GEN II-E

Available in: 1–6x24mm
Weight: 21.5 oz.
Length: 10.1 in.
Power: 1–6x
Obj. Dia.: 24mm
Main Dia.: 30mm
Field of View: 115.2–20.5 ft.@100 yd.
Eye Relief: 4 in.
Features: Optically indexed lens for clarity; XR Plus fully multi-coated lenses; HD lens elements; second focal plane reticle; illuminated center dot with intensity lock; Armor-Tek finish for reduced external wear; reticles include VRM-2 MOA, VRM-2 MRAD, and JM-1 BDC
MSRP $1999.99

RAZOR HD GEN III

Available in: 1-10x24mm
Weight: 21.5 oz.
Length: 10.1 in.
Power: 1-10X
Obj. Dia.: 24mm, 50mm
Main Dia.: 34mm
Field of View: 116–11.7 ft.@100 yd.
Eye Relief: 3.6 in.
Features: When everyone in the CQB scope game goes 8X, Vortex steps up the game with a first focal plane 10X
MSRP $2899.99

STRIKE EAGLE

Available in: 1–6x24mm, 1–8x24mm
Weight: 17.6 oz., 16.5 oz.
Length: 10.5 in., 10 in.
Power: 1–6X, 1–8X
Obj. Dia.: 24mm
Main Dia.: 30mm
Field of View: 116.5–19.2 ft @ 100 yds, 116,6–14.4 ft @ 100 yds
Eye Relief: 3.5 in., 4.1 in.
Features: Second focal plane; glass-etched, illuminated reticles in a lightweight package and with fast-focus eyepieces; reticle is the EBR-4
1–6X: $399.99
1–8X: $499.99

VIPER HUNTING SHOOTING LONG RANGE (HS LR) 4–16X50MM

Weight: 19.8 oz.
Length: 13.7 in.
Power: 4–16X
Obj. Dia.: 50mm
Main Dia.: 30mm
Field of View: 27.4–7.4 ft @ 100 yds
Twilight Factor: 13.27–26.53
Eye Relief: 4 in.
Features: Rear focal plane; shock-, water-, and fogproof; adjustable parallax; 4–16X features Dead-Hold BDC reticle; also available in a 6–24X50mm with a first focal plane XLR reticle
4–16X: $899.99
6–24X: $1249.99

VIPER HUNTING SHOOTING TACTICAL (HST) 6–24X50MM

Weight: 22.6 oz.
Length: 15.5 in.
Power: 6–24X
Obj. Dia.: 50mm
Main Dia.: 30mm
Field of View: 17.8–5.1 ft @ 100 yds
Twilight Factor: 17.32–34.64
Eye Relief: 4 in.
Features: Choice of VMR-1 MRAD or MOA reticles in the second focal plane; shock-, water-, and fogproof; adjustable parallax; 4–16x44 also available
4–16X: $849.99
6–24X: $949.99

Vortex Optics

VORTEX VIPER PST GEN II

VIPER PST GEN II

Weight: 22.7 oz.–31.2 oz.
Length: 10.9 in.–16 in.
Power: 1–6x24mm, 2–10x32mm, 3–15x44mm, 5–25x50mm
Obj. Diameter: 24mm, 32mm, 44mm, 50mm
Eye Relief: 3.4–3.8 in.
Field of View: Varies with model
Features: Extra-low dispersion (XD) glass; multiple anti-reflection coatings on all air-to-glass surfaces; glass-etched, illuminated reticles; Reticle and focal plane options available are: 1–6x VMR-2 MRAD or MOA second focal plane; 2–10x EBR-4 MRAD or MOA first focal plane; 3–15x EBR-4 MOA second focal plane or EBR-2C MRAD or MOA first focal plane; 5–25x EBR-4 MOA second focal plane or EBR-2C MRAD or MOA first focal plane.

1–6x: $899.99
2–10x: $1149.99
3–15x: . . . . $1099.99–$1199.99
5–25x: . . . . $1199.99–$1299.99

SIGHTS

Aimpoint

AIMPOINT 9000SC

AIMPOINT ACO

AIMPOINT MICRO H-2

AIMPOINT PRO

9000SC

Weight: 7.4 oz.
Length: 6.3 in.
Obj. Dia.: 38mm
Features: Ideal for short length action rifles, semi-automatic firearms, and magnum handguns; ACET technology for longer battery life; available in 2 or 4 MOA dot sizes; two-ring configuration for mounting; waterproof; matte finish
MSRP $462.00

ACO

Weight: 7.8 oz.
Length: 5.1 in.
Power: 1X
Features: Developed with the modern sporting rifle owner in mind, the ACO is ready to mount and shoot directly out of the box; 30mm aluminum alloy sight tube is paired with a rugged fixed height mount designed to provide absolute co-witness with AR-15 backup iron sights; 2 MOA red-dot to allow maximum target acquisition speed and accuracy at all distances; exclusive ACET technology allows for up to one year of constant-on use from a single DL1/3N battery; completely waterproof housing.
MSRP $399.00

MICRO H-2 AND T-2

Weight: 4.6 oz.–4.8 oz.
Length: 2.7 in.–3.16 in.
Power: 1X
Features: Advanced optical lenses for even better light transmission; can be used on shotguns, rifles, handguns or archery tackle; transparent front and rear flip-up lens covers are included; reinforced protection of the turrets for even greater ruggedness; 12 daylight settings; available in 2 MOA dot size; can be "piggybacked" on larger magnifying optics using an adapter.
H-2: . . . . $732.00–$1091.00
T-2:. . . . . $782.00–$910.00

PRO

Weight: 7.8 oz.
Length: 5.1 in.
Power: 1X
Features: Parallax free optic; 2 MOA dot for accurate target engagement at all distances; four night vision settings and six daylight settings; modular QRP2 mount includes removable spacer that indexes the sight at optimal height for co-witness, with the standard iron sights on AR15/M16/M4 carbine style weapons
MSRP $445.00

Armament Technology, Inc.

ARMAMENT TECHNOLOGY, INC. XOPTEK

XOPTEK

Type: Reflex sight
Weight: 1.3 oz.
Length: 1.8 in.
Power: 1X
Field of View: Infinite
Features: A tiny reflex red-dot available in either 4 MOA or 6 MOA dot size; average 34,000 hours battery life (CR2032); can be ordered to clamp on to a Picatinny rail or to fit Armament's ELCAN Spector products
MSRP $399.00

Barska

BARSKA 1X20 HQ RED DOT

BARSKA 1X30 HQ RED DOT

BARSKA 1X30 ION REFLEX SIGHT

BARSKA 1X40 ION REFLEX SIGHT

1X20 HQ RED DOT

Type: Red-dot
Weight: 7 oz.
Length: 2.95 in.
Power: 1X20mm
Obj. Dia.: 20mm
Exit Pupil: 18mm
Field of View: 36 ft.@100 yd.
Eye Relief: Unlimited
Features: Red-dot auto adjusts for external lighting conditions via a light sensor; integrated QD mount
MSRP $106.99

1X30 HQ RED DOT

Type: Red-dot
Weight: 10.8 oz.
Length: 4.13 in.
Power: 1X30mm
Obj. Dia.: 30mm
Exit Pupil: 26mm
Field of View: 57 ft.@100 yd.
Eye Relief: Unlimited
Features: Similar to the 1X20 version, including auto-adjusting brightness; 1 MOA adjustments
MSRP $117.99

1X30 ION REFLEX SIGHT

Type: Reflex sight
Weight: 3.9 oz.
Length: 2.37 in.
Power: 1X30mm
Obj. Dia.: 30mm
Exit Pupil: 26–20mm
Field of View: Unlimited
Eye Relief: Unlimited
Features: A compact, affordable reflex with choice of four reticle patterns; Picatinny rail mount
MSRP $94.99

1X40 ION REFLEX SIGHT

Type: Reflex sight
Weight: 6.2 oz.
Length: 3.6 in.
Power: 1X40mm
Obj. Dia.: 40mm
Exit Pupil: 28–44mm
Field of View: Unlimited
Eye Relief: Unlimited
Features: A slightly bigger reflex with choice of four reticles; quick release Picatinny/Weaver-type mount
MSRP $81.99

British Small Arms Co. (BSA)

BSA TACTICAL WEAPON ILLUMINATED SIGHT

TACTICAL WEAPON ILLUMINATED SIGHT

Weight: 22 oz.
Length: 8.75 in.
Power: 1X
Field of View: 3.7–19.3 ft @ 100 yds
Eye Relief: 2 in.
Features: Fully multicoated optics; easy one-piece mounting; 5/8-inch Weaver-style rail; illuminated red dot; rubber eye guard; output power: 5mW; wave length: 650 nm; attachable 140 lumen LED flashlight
With flashlight: $119.00

OPTICS

Browning

BROWNING BUCK MARK REFLEX SIGHT

BUCK MARK REFLEX SIGHT

Power: 1X
Field of View: 47 ft @ 100 yds
Eye Relief: Unlimited
Features: The Buck Mark has an aluminum housing, four red reticle patterns, a seven-position brightness rheostat powered by a lithium battery, and mounts on a standard Weaver-styled base
MSRP $69.99

Burris

BURRIS AR-536

AR-536

Weight: 18.75 oz.
Length: 5.75 in.
Power: 5X
Obj. Dia.: 36mm
Field of View: 20 ft @ 100 yds
Eye Relief: 2.5–3.5 in.
Features: Ballistic/CQTM lighted reticle; 600 yard range; multi-coated lenses; adjustable diopter; three Picatinny rail mounting points; black matte finish; max adj. 60 MOA; one-year warranty
MSRP $419.00

Burris

BURRIS FASTFIRE 3 BURRIS FASTFIRE 4 BURRIS FASTFIRE RD BURRIS RT-1 BURRIS RT-3

FASTFIRE 3

Weight: 0.9 oz.
Power: 1X
Features: 3 or 8 MOA dot; power button with three levels of brightness; low battery warning indicator and see-through protective cap; ideally suited for use on pistols and AR-15s where fast target acquisition is desired, the FastFire red-dot sight will also match up well with carbines, lever guns, and shotguns; available Picatinny mount
MSRP . . . . $287.00–$299.00

FASTFIRE 4

Type: Reflex sight
Weight: 1.6 oz.
Length: 1.9 in.
Field of View: Infinite
Features: Change between a 3 MOA red dot, 11 MOA red dot, or either in a red circle; removeable weather shield; impact-resistant housing
MSRP $455.00

FASTFIRE RD

Type: Red-dot
Weight: 6.4 oz.
Length: 2.8 in.
Obj. Dia.: 35.5mm
Field of View: Infinite
Features: Features a 2 MOA red dot; alloy housing; 90 MOA elevation/windage; 1 MOA click value; runs off a AAA battery
MSRP $299.00

RT-1

Type: Red-dot
Weight: 4.8 oz.
Length: 2.75 in.
Power: 1X
Obj. Dia.: 25mm
Field of View: Infinite
Features: True 1X magnification; 2 MOA red-dot; 45 MOA elevation/windage; ½-MOA clicks; CR2032 battery; comes with high and low base mounts
MSRP $359.00

RT-3

Type: Red-dot
Weight: 8.8 oz.
Length: 3.5 in.
Power: 3X
Obj. Dia.: 33.8mm
Field of View: Infinite
Features: True 3X magnification; 50 MOA elevation/windage; CR2032 battery; Ballistic 3X red dot reticle; integrated Picatinny rail mount
MSRP $455.00

Bushnell Outdoor Products

BUSHNELL AR OPTICS ADVANCE

BUSHNELL AR OPTICS FIRST STRIKE 2.0

BUSHNELL AR OPTICS TRS-26

AR OPTICS ADVANCE

Power: 1X
Features: 5-MOA dot; compact design compatible with a large selection of semiautomatic pistols
MSRP $159.99

AR OPTICS FIRST STRIKE 2.0

Type: Red dot
Weight: 2.1 oz.
Length: 2.4 in.
Power: 1X
Exit Pupil: 22 mm
Field of View: Unlimited
Eye Relief: Unlimited
Features: Five brightness settings; side battery compartment that requires no tools to access
MSRP $189.99

AR OPTICS TRS-26

Type: Red dot
Weight: 13.2 oz.
Power: 1x
Obj. Dia.: 26mm
Field of View: Unlimited
Eye Relief: Unlimited
Features: Compact red dot replacing an older version; brighter, five-setting dot; enhanced battery life; push-button controls
MSRP $149.99

C-More Systems

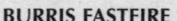

C-MORE SYSTEMS RTSB-V5

RTSB-V5

Type: Reflex sight
Field of View: Infinite
Features: V5-hardened electronics; motion-sensing system with auto-off; 1 MOA click adjustments; removeable battery tray eliminates need to rezero; choice of 3, 6, 8, or 10 MOA red dot
MSRP $389.00

Crimson Trace Corp.

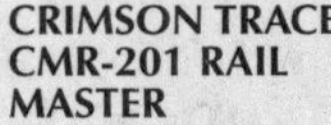
CRIMSON TRACE CMR-201 RAIL MASTER

CRIMSON TRACE CMR-204 RAIL MASTER PRO

CRIMSON TRACE CMR-205 RAIL MASTER PRO

CRIMSON TRACE CMR-206 RAIL MASTER PRO

CRIMSON TRACE CMR-207G RAIL MASTER PRO

CMR-201 RAIL MASTER

Type: Laser/light
Features: Made for Picatinny or Weaver rail-equipped pistol, rifles, and shotguns; ambidextrous "tap" on/off controls; 5mW red laser; five-minute auto shutoff
MSRP $164.99

CMR-204 RAIL MASTER PRO

Type: Laser/light
Features: Made for Picatinny or Weaver rail-equipped pistol, rifles, and shotguns; ambidextrous "tap" on/off controls; combination green laser with 100 Lumen white light; four modes include laser/light constant on, laser constant on, light constant on, and laser w/light dazzler
MSRP $389.99

CMR-205 RAIL MASTER PRO

Type: Laser/light
Features: Similar to the CMR-204, but with a red laser
MSRP $299.99

CMR-206 RAIL MASTER PRO

Type: Laser/light
Features: Made for Picatinny or Weaver rail-equipped pistol, rifles, and shotguns; ambidextrous "tap" on/off controls; 5mW green laser with momentary, strobe, and constant-on functionality; five-minute auto shutoff
MSRP $239.99

CMR-207G RAIL MASTER PRO

Type: Laser/light
Features: For any Picatinny/Weaver rail-equipped firearm, this is a combo laser and a 400 Lumen tactical light; choice of red or green laser
MSRP $249.99

Davide Pedersoli & C.

150 UNIVERSAL CREEDMOOR SIGHT, MIDDLE AND LONG RANGE, MODELS USA 465 AND 430

Features: Tang sight with elevation and windage adjustment in the eye piece; for long-distance target shooting both with muzzle-loading and breech-loading rifles; 2.1875–2.3125-in. between two mounting holes; 2- and 3-in. elevation adjustments
USA 430 Long Range: $395.00
USA 465 Middle Range: $395.00

ENGLISH REAR SIGHT, MODEL USA 428

Features: Rear sight with convex base, with two adjustable and folding leaves
Flat base: $80.00
Convex base: $135.00

FIBER OPTIC FRONT AND REAR SIGHT, MODEL USA 409

Features: Front sight and rear sight set for muzzleloading rifles (Model 410 for breechloaders); front sight with dovetail base; rear sight with base for octagonal barrel
From: $130.00

FOLDING FRONT SIGHT

Features: Globe sight for long-range when raised, or fold down for built-in blade for close range; ball/detent locking mechanism; 3/8-in. dovetail base; ½-in. high
From: $100.00

GHOST CREEDMOOR SIGHT-USA 422

Features: A tang sight inspired by some models in use in the 1800s, economic, functional, and useful for hunting; adjustable in elevation and windage; can fit several gun types; small eye piece ring enables a quick, instinctive aim at the target; when quickly shouldering the rifle, the open ring provides a clear sight picture with low light condition; distance between the two mounting holes is 1 ¾-in.
From: $80.00

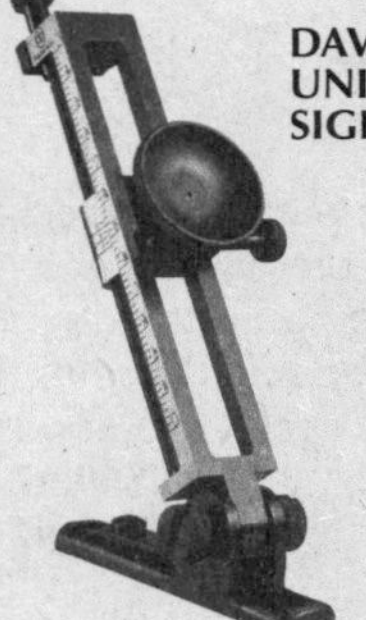
DAVIDE PEDERSOLI UNIVERSAL CREEDMOOR SIGHT–430

DAVIDE PEDERSOLI ENGLISH REAR SIGHT–428

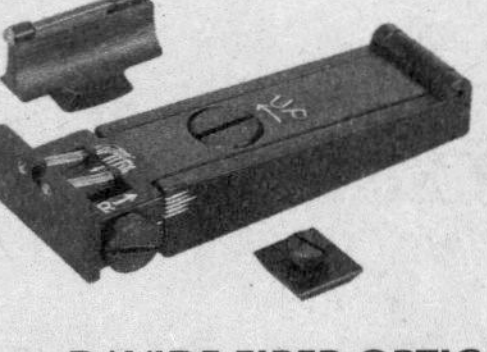
DAVIDE FIBER OPTIC FRONT AND REAR SIGHT–409

DAVIDE PEDERSOLI FOLDING FRONT SIGHT

DAVIDE PEDERSOLI GHOST CREEDMOOR SIGHT-USA 422

Davide Pedersoli & C.

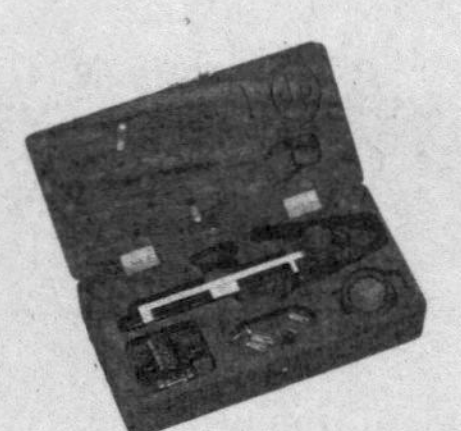

DAVIDE PEDERSOLI "SOULE TYPE" MIDDLE RANGE SET-170

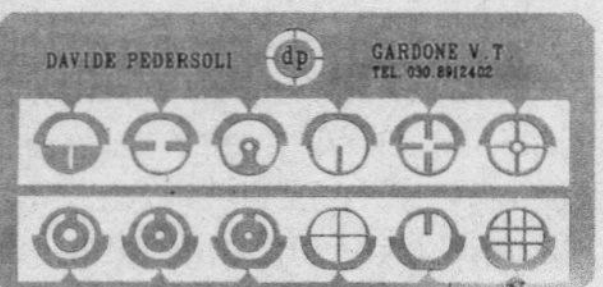

DAVIDE PEDERSOLI SPIRIT LEVEL TUNNEL SIGHT ADJUSTABLE–425

DAVIDE PEDERSOLI U.S. MODEL 1879 SPRINGFIELD TRAPDOOR REAR SIGHT–473

"SOULE TYPE" MIDDLE RANGE SET, MODEL USA 170

Features: Wooden-box set including Soule XL Middle Range Sight; tunnel front sight with a micrometric screw for windage adjustment, spirit level, and fifteen interchangeable inserts; professional "Hadley Style" eyepiece with eight varying diameter viewing holes, depending on available light, on a rotating disk which can be selected without disassembling or loosening the eyepiece, and a rubber ring on the eyepiece; six interchangeable glass bubbles (spirit level) with different colors for varying light conditions; 3-in. elevation adjustment

From: $755.00

SPIRIT LEVEL TUNNEL SIGHT ADJUSTABLE WITH 12 INSERTS SET, MODEL USA 425

Features: Spirit level tunnel sight with micrometer adjustment for windage, equipped with twelve interchangeable inserts; also available in 15 and 18 insert sets

From: $25.00

U.S. MODEL 1879 SPRINGFIELD TRAPDOOR REAR SIGHT, MODEL USA 473

Features: Sometimes referred to as "Buckhorn" style; used on Trapdoor rifles from 1874 until superseded by Buffington style in 1884; side ramps are graduated to 500 yds and the ladder to 1500 yds; slide has windage adjustment

From: $80.00

EOTech

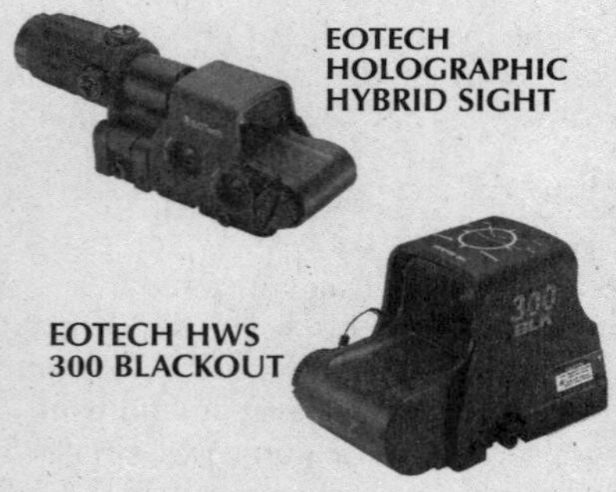

EOTECH HOLOGRAPHIC HYBRID SIGHT

EOTECH HWS 300 BLACKOUT

HOLOGRAPHIC HYBRID SIGHT (HHS)

Power: 3X
Eye Relief: 2.2 in.
Features: The HHS kits combine the speed of the EXPS holographic weapon sight and the extended range versatility of the G33 magnifier; available in three configurations: Sight I houses the EXPS3 red dot; Sight II houses the EXPS2 red dot; and the Sight III houses with the 518.2 red-dot that takes AA batteries

Sight I: $1239.00
Sight II: $1169.00
Sight III: $1089.00

HWS 300 BLACKOUT

Weight: 9 oz.
Length: 3.8 in.
Power: 1X
Field of View: 90 ft @ 100 yds
Eye Relief: Unlimited
Features: Designed with tactical shooters in mind, this optic offers a two-dot ballistic drop reticle that allows the shooter to zero either subsonic or supersonic rounds in the same reticle pattern; offered in the XPS2 platform, it is the shortest and lightest HWS sight available; its size and weight make it convenient for hunters, military and law enforcement officers to carry; the single compact lithium 123 battery configuration opens up more space on the rail for rear iron sights or magnifiers

MSRP $585.00

Firefield

FIREFIELD IMPACT XL, XLT

IMPACT XL, XLT

Type: Red dot
Weight: 5.6, 7.8 oz.
Length: 3.6 in.
Power: 1x
Eye Relief: Unlimited
Battery Life: 25–250 hours (XL); 40–250 hours (XLT)
Features: Multiple reticle options; AR-red coated lenses; parallax correction; ample windage; elevation adjustments; neoprene cover; adjustment tools; XLT has a quick-detach mount, digital controls, and a protective hood

XL: $59.97
XLT: $79.97

Firefield

FIREFIELD SPEEDSTRIKE

SPEEDSTRIKE

Type: Laser
Weight: 6.3 oz.
Length: 4.25 in.
Battery Life: 80 hours (red); 25 hours (green)
Laser Power Output: Less than 5 mw
Laser Wavelength: 632 nm
Features: Available in green; modular mount; windage and elevation adjustments can be made without tools; pressure-pad activated
MSRP . . . . $49.97–$79.97

Hi-Lux Precision Optics

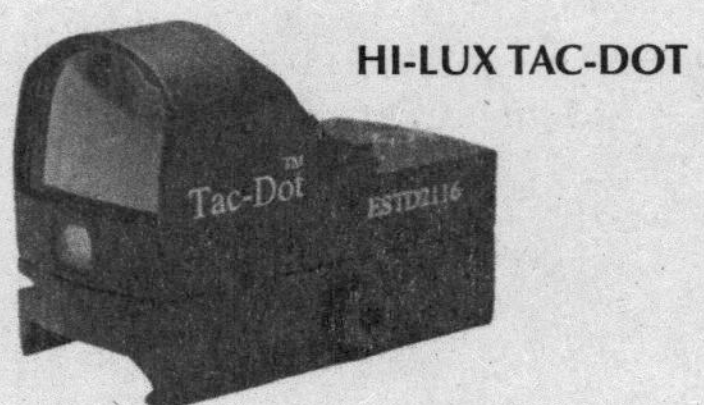

HI-LUX TAC-DOT

TAC-DOT

Weight: 2.1 oz.
Length: 2.5 in.
Power: 1X
Obj. Dia.: 21x16mm
Field of View: 30x22 ft @ 100 yds
Features: Elevation and windage adjustments are 50 MOA per revolution; special illumination circuit is designed to control the illuminated dot size in a consistent shape and size; dot size is 4 MOA; light sensor will control the brightness of the dot automatically based on the light situation
MSRP $99.00

HIVIZ

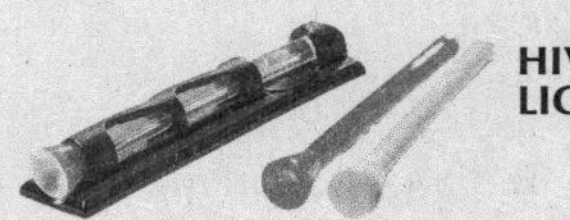

HIVIZ LIGHTWAVE

HIVIZ LIGHTWAVE H3

HIVIZ LIGHTWAVE H3 EXPRESS

LIGHTWAVE

Features: The wave design of the front sight housing produces a sharper, brighter sight; available in green, red, or white front with a two-dot adjustable green rear for a variety of rifles; as a single front for shotguns; and as a Lighwave front/rear pair for a variety of handguns
MSRP . . . . $86.99–$161.99

LIGHTWAVE H3

Features: Combines tritium with a fiber optic pipe for a brighter sight; all-steel construction; green front with choice of green or orange two-dot rear
MSRP $135.00

LIGHTWAVE H3 EXPRESS

Features: HiViz brings the competition to XS Sights, with a big front tritium/pip "dot" gathering light via the "wave" housing, sitting over a single fiber optic vertical line in the rear sight; green front with choice of orange or green rear
MSRP $135.00

OPTICS

Kahles

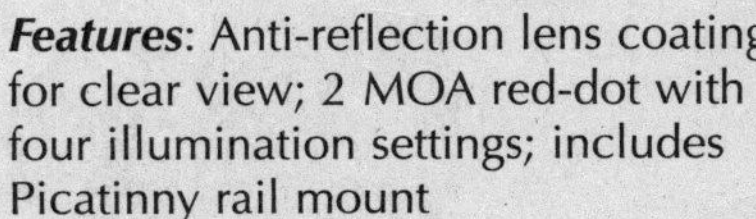

KAHLES HELIA RD

HELIA RD

Type: Reflex sight
Weight: 1.4 oz.
Length: 2.16 in.
Power: 1X
Obj. Dia.: 26X22mm
Features: Anti-reflection lens coating for clear view; 2 MOA red-dot with four illumination settings; includes Picatinny rail mount
MSRP $443.00

Konus

KONUS SIGHTPRO ATOMIC 2.0

SIGHTPRO ATOMIC 2.0

Weight: 3.8 oz.
Length: 2.4 in.
Power: 1X
Field of View: 76 ft @ 100 yds
Features: Illuminated reticle dots; fits both Picatinny and Weaver rails
MSRP $129.99

Konus

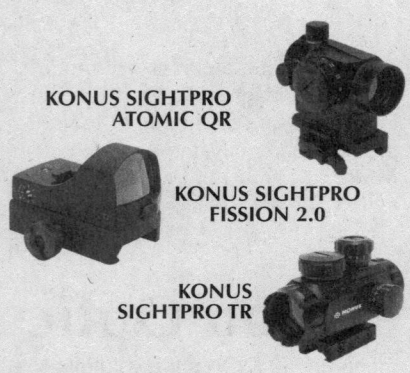

KONUS SIGHTPRO ATOMIC QR

KONUS SIGHTPRO FISSION 2.0

KONUS SIGHTPRO TR

SIGHTPRO ATOMIC QR

Weight: 6.5 oz.
Length: 2.5 in.
Power: 1X
Features: Illuminated reticle dots; fits both Picatinny and Weaver rails
MSRP $139.99

SIGHTPRO FISSION 2.0

Weight: 1.76 oz.
Length: 1.7 in.
Power: 1X
Field of View: 115 ft @ 100 yds
Features: Illuminated reticle dots; fits both Picatinny and Weaver rails
MSRP $179.99

SIGHTPRO PTS1

Weight: 14.1 oz.
Length: 12.2 in.
Power: 3X
Obj. Dia.: 32mm
Field of View: 36.6 ft @ 100 yds
Eye Relief: 4.5 in.
Features: Shock-, water-, and fog-proof; illuminated reticle dots; fits both Picatinny and Weaver rails
MSRP $399.99

SIGHTPRO TR

Weight: 13 oz.
Length: 4.75 in.
Power: 1X
Features: Illuminated reticle dots; four different reticle patterns
MSRP $139.99

Lasermax

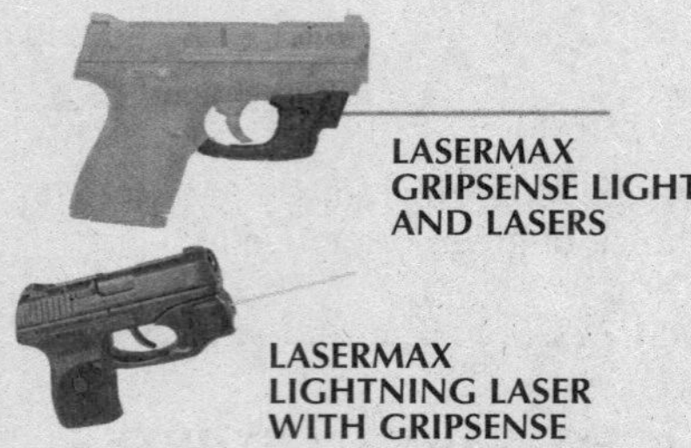

LASERMAX GRIPSENSE LIGHT AND LASERS

LASERMAX LIGHTNING LASER WITH GRIPSENSE

GRIPSENSE LIGHT AND LASERS

Type: Laser
Weight: 1.5 oz.
Battery Life: At least 4 hours
Laser Power Output: Less than 5 mw
Laser Wavelength: 510–535 nm
Red: $149.00
Green: $169.00

LIGHTNING LASER WITH GRIPSENSE

Type: Laser
Weight: .5 oz.
Features: Dual-activation via the GripSense technology that does not alter grip, or via push-button; steady or pulse beam; Rail Vise mounting technology; fits Picatinny or Weaver-type rails; red or green beam
MSRP . . . . $149.99–$199.99

Leapers, Inc.

LEAPERS UTG ITA RED/GREEN CLOSE QUARTERS BATTLE (CQB) T-DOT SIGHT

LEAPERS, INC. UTG REFLEX MICRO DOT

UTG ITA RED/GREEN CLOSE QUARTERS BATTLE (CQB) T-DOT SIGHT

Weight: 13.1 oz.
Length: 6.1 in.
Power: 1X
Field of View: 85 ft @ 100 yds
Eye Relief: Unlimited
Features: Completely sealed; shock-proof, fogproof; and rainproof; 4 MOA red/green single dot reticle or quick-to-acquire red/green T-dot reticle; premium zero lockable and zero resettable target turrets; TactEdge angled integral sunshade reduces glare off the lens while maintaining superb light transmission clarity
MSRP $67.97

UTG REFLEX MICRO DOT

Type: Reflex sight
Weight: 1.87 oz.
Length: 1.9 in.
Power: 1X
Exit Pupil: Unlimited
Eye Relief: Unlimited
Features: Anodized aluminum body; True Strength Platform; 4 MOA dot; 1 MOA click adjustment; red or green dot options
MSRP $89.97

Leica Camera AG

LEICA CAMERA AG TEMPUS ASPH

TEMPUS ASPH

Type: Reflex sight
Weight: 1.41 oz.
Power: 1X
Obj. Dia.: 21X25mm
Features: Utilizes an aspheric lens for a more exacting red-dot image; aluminum housing; choice of 2 or 3.5 MOA dot
MSRP $599.00

Leupold & Stevens

LEUPOLD DELTAPOINT PRO

DELTAPOINT PRO

Weight: 1.95 oz.
Length: 1.82 in.
Power: 1X
Eye Relief: Unlimited
Features: Water- and fogproof; DiamondCoat; removable, adjustable rear sight; tool-less, spring actuated battery compartment; illuminated reticle available
MSRP . . . . $399.99–$499.99

LEUPOLD & STEVENS VX-FREEDOM RDS

FREEDOM RDS

Type: Red-dot
Weight: 6.9 oz.
Length: 5.5 in.
Power: 1X
Features: 1MOA dot reticle; one version has ¼ MOA click adjustments, a second has exposed BDC elevation turrets designed for use with the .223 Rem. 55-grain load; built-in Motion Sensor Technology saves battery life
Optic only: $279.99
With mount: $299.99
With mount/BDC reticle: . . .$399.99

Lucid Optics, LLC

LUCID HD7 GEN III

LUCID OPTICS HDX

LUCID OPTICS LITL MO

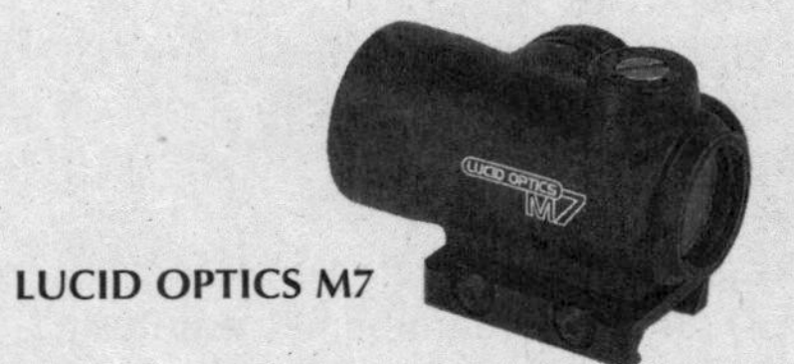

LUCID OPTICS M7

HD7 GEN III

Weight: 13 oz.
Length: 5.5 in.
Power: 1X
Obj.Dia.: 34mm
Field of View: 44 ft @ 100 yds
Eye Relief: Unlimited
Features: Third generation unit; integral Picatinny rail and reversible mounting pins for bullpup-style firearms; manual and a Auto-Brightness with twelve brightness settings; four operator-selectable reticles based on a 2 MOA dot with ½ MOA click adjustments; parallax free, it is powered by one AAA battery; the frame is cast aluminum armored in chemical rubber and is available with a 2x screw-in eyepiece; available in tan
Black:. $249.99
Tan: $259.99

HDX

Type: Red-dot
Weight: 11 oz.
Length: 4.35 in.
Field of View: Infinite
Features: Roughly have the weight of the original HD7, the HDx has a 3 MOA base; is shockproof up to .458 SOCOM; auto-brightness control
MSRP $299.99

LITL MO

Type: Reflex sight
Weight: 1 oz.
Obj. Dia.: 28X19mm
Field of View: Infinite
Features: Just one ounce! This micro reflex sight has a 3MOA red dot; ½-MOA adjustments; shockproof up to .458 SOCOM use
MSRP $349.99

M7

Type: Red-dot
Weight: 4.4 oz.
Length: 2.6 in.
Power: 1X
Obj. Dia.: 25mm
Field of View: Infinite
Features: A very small red dot optic with an M5 reticle that sports a 4 MOA red dot within a 32 MOA circle; Picatinny rail adaptor included; 11 brightness settings; modular mounting system
MSRP $309.99

Meopta USA

MEOPTA MEOMAG3 MAGNIFIER

MEOPTA MEORED 30

MEOMAG3 MAGNIFIER

Type: Magnifier
Weight: 7.48 oz.
Length: 4.65 in.
Power: 3x
Obj. Dia.: 20mm
Exit Pupil: 5.4 mm
Field of View: 7 degrees
Eye Relief: 60mm
Features: Works with both Meopta and other red dot sights on the market; works as a monocular; waterproof, shockproof, and fogproof; Meopta's Fast Opening Lens Covers; optional accessories include fixed, quick-release and hinge mounts, tactical carry pouch, and a hard case
MSRP **$1249.99**

MEORED 30

Weight: 1 oz.
Length: 1.85 in.
Power: 1X
Features: Ultra compact reflex red-dot sight; parallax free and designed for use on handguns with cut-out slides, AR platforms, or shotguns; dot size is 3 MOA; integrated MIL-STD 1913 mount; interface plate accepts a Docter mount; windage adjustment up to 180 MOA; elevation adjustment to 120 MOA; simple on/off button on left side of optic allows the user to adjust brightness level; one CR 2302 battery with a life of up to 300 hours; optic will auto-off after three hours of continuous operation if the on/off button hasn't been activated; MeoBright, MeoDrop, and MeoShield coatings are all featured
MSRP **$599.99**

Minox

MINOX RV1

RV1

Type: Red-dot
Weight: 3.38 oz.
Length: 2.51 in.
Power: 1X
Field of View: Infinite
Features: A very small and lightweight red-dot with a 2 MOA dot; 100 MOA elevation/windage in 1 MOA clicks; three night, six daylight, and extra-bright daylight settings; IPX7 waterproofing
MSRP **$460.00**

Riton Optics

RITON OPTICS X1 TACTIX ARD

RITON OPTICS X1 TACTIX RRD

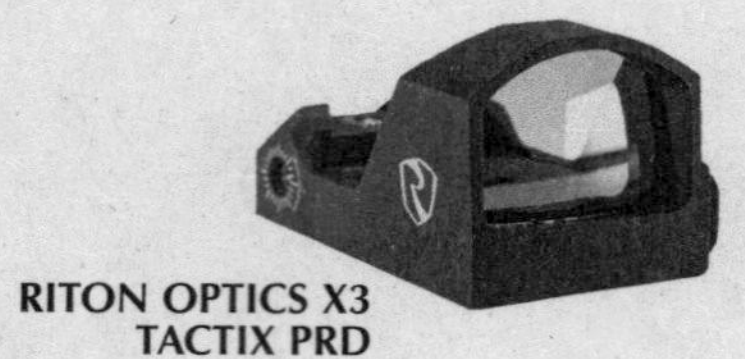

RITON OPTICS X3 TACTIX PRD

X1 TACTIX ARD

Type: Red-dot
Weight: 3.5 oz.
Length: 2.48 in.
Power: 1X
Obj. Dia.: 23mm
Field of View: Infinite
Features: In Riton's (X1) price level, this optic sports 120 MOA elevation/windage with 1-MOA clicks; parallax fixed at 50 yd., six brightness settings
MSRP **$199.99**

X1 TACTIX RRD

Type: Red-dot
Weight: 9.5 oz.
Length: 3.76 in.
Power: 1X
Obj. Dia.: 29mm
Main Dia.: 30mm
Field of View: Infinite
Features: A more substantial red-dot in Riton's budget-friendly (X1) family, this optic has a 30mm tube; 2 MOA dot with six brightness levels; 120 MOA elevation/windage with 1-MOA clicks; 40,000 hours battery life
MSRP **$199.99**

X3 TACTIX PRD

Type: Reflex red-dot
Weight: 1.12 oz.
Length: 1.8 in.
Power: 1X
Field of View: Infinite
Features: A micro reflex in Riton's (X3) price level family that features a 3 MOA red dot with six levels of illumination; 45 MOA total adjustment in 1 MOA increments
MSRP **$299.99**

Shield Sights

RMSC

Type: Reflex red dot
Weight: .57 oz.
Length: 17 in.
Power: 1x
Features: Reflex Mini Sight Compact; designed specifically for use on sub-compact pistols; with a 4 MOA or 8 MOA dot
MSRP . . . . $400.00–$470.00

RMSW

Type: Reflex sight
Power: 1X
Field of View: Unlimited
Eye Relief: Unlimited
Features: Model stands for Reflex Mini Sight Waterproof; gasket sealed and watertight to 20 meters for up to thirty minutes; hard-coated S1O2 polymer lens; 4 MOA or 8 MOA dot
MSRP . . . . $470.00–$570.00

SMS2

Type: Reflex sight
Power: 1X
Field of View: Unlimited
Eye Relief: Unlimited
Features: Updated "2.0" version of the original Shield Mini Sight (SMS); available with 1 MOA, 4 MOA, 8 MOA, or 65/1 MOA ring/dot
MSRP . . . . $310.00–$360.00

SHIELD SIGHTS RMSC

SHIELD SIGHTS RMSW

SHIELD SIGHTS SMS2

Sightmark

SIGHTMARK ULTRA SHOT A-SPEC

SIGHTMARK ULTRA SHOT M-SPEC FMS

SIGHTMARK ULTRA SHOT R-SPEC

ULTRA SHOT A-SPEC

Type: Reflex sight
Weight: 10.8 oz.
Length: 4.33 in.
Power: 1X
Obj. Dia.: 33X24mm
Field of View: Unlimited
Eye Relief: Unlimited
Features: The A stands for Advanced. Features include: scratch-resistant wide-angle lens; aluminum hood and shield; 120 MOA windage and elevation adjustments in 1 MOA clicks; recoil-rated up to .338-caliber; one-hour shutoff; battery life of 2000 hours
MSRP $179.99

ULTRA SHOT M-SPEC FMS, M-SPEC LQD

Type: Reflex sight
Weight: 9.6 oz.
Length: 4.01 in.
Power: 1X
Obj. Dia.: 33X24mm
Field of View: Unlimited
Eye Relief: Unlimited
Features: Useful across law enforcement, hunting, and target competition disciplines, this rugged reflex sight's feature includes: waterproof to 40 feet; ability to handle recoil up to .50 BMG; 12-hour auto off with five minute motion activation shutoff/on; 65 MOA dot; 120 MOA of windage and elevation adjustment in 1 MOA clicks; 2000 hours of battery life; integrated sunshade; quick-detach option with the LQD version
FMS: $239.99
LQD: $299.99

ULTRA SHOT R-SPEC

Type: Reflex sight
Weight: 10.7 oz.
Length: 4.33 in.
Power: 1X
Obj. Dia.: 33X24mm
Field of View: Unlimited
Eye Relief: Unlimited
Features: The R stands for Range. Features include: 10 brightness settings; 120 MOA of windage and elevation adjustment with 1 MOA clicks; choice of four each red or green reticles; one-hour auto shutoff
MSRP $155.99

SIG Sauer

SIG SAUER BRAVO3

BRAVO3

Type: Red-dot
Weight: 22 oz.
Length: 6.45 in.
Power: 3X
Obj. Dia.: 24mm
Exit Pupil: 8mm
Field of View: 10 degrees
Features: A 3X red dot in SIG's battlesight family with choice of .300 BLK or .223/5.56 NATO Horseshoe dot; 120 MOA windage/elevation with ½-MOA clicks; motion-activated illumination with eight daytime and three night vision settings
MSRP $459.99

SIG Sauer

SIG SAUER BRAVO5

SIG SAUER ECHO3

SIG SAUER JULIET4 MAGNIFIER

SIG SAUER LIMA365

SIG SAUER ROMEO-MSR

SIG SAUER ROMEO ZERO

SIG SAUER ROMEO1

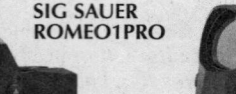

SIG SAUER ROMEO1PRO

SIG SAUER ROMEO3MAX

SIG SAUER ROMEO3XL

OPTICS

BRAVO5

Type: Red-dot
Weight: 23 oz.
Length: 6.45 in.
Power: 5X
Obj. Dia.: 30mm
Exit Pupil: 6.4mm
Field of View: 6 degrees
Features: Similar to the BRAVO3, including the same reticle choices, but in a 5X magnification
MSRP $519.99

ECHO3

Type: Reflex sight
Weight: 14.3 oz.
Length: 4.3 in.
Power: 1–6X, 2–12X
Obj. Dia.: 23mm
Features: A thermal imaging reflex sight with multiple reticles including active and custom fixed reticles; 11 color palettes; six brightness settings; 150 MOA elevation/windage travel
1–6X: $3899.99
2–12X: $5199.99

JULIET4 MAGNIFIER

Type: Magnifier
Weight: 12.5 oz.
Length: 4.2 in.
Power: 4X
Obj. Dia.: 24mm
Exit Pupil: 6mm
Field of View: 6.25 degrees
Eye Relief: 65mm
Features: Included spacers allow height adjustment; stand-alone or with red dot sight; aircraft grade CNC aluminum housing; quick release mount with recoil lugs; IPX-8 waterproofing of 20 meters per 1 hour; protectors for front thread-in lens and rear flip back lens
MSRP . . . . $519.99–$549.99

LIMA365

Type: Laser
Features: Designed specifically for SIG's P365 compact handgun, the rail-mounted laser is available in either red or green
MSRP . . . . $199.99–$259.99

ROMEO-MSR

Type: Reflex sight
Weight: 4.9 oz.
Length: 3.1 in.
Power: 1X
Obj. Dia.: 20mm
Features: Houses a green 2MOA dot; IPX7 waterproofing; ten day, two night vision illumination settings; 100 MOA total windage/elevation travel
Red dot:. $169.99
Green dot:. $189.99

ROMEO ZERO

Type: Reflex sight
Weight: 0.4 oz.
Length: 1.6 in.
Power: 1X
Obj. Dia.: 24mm
Features: Choice of 3 or 6 MOA dot in red; eight daytime illumination settings; 20,000-hour runtime
MSRP $259.99

ROMEO1

Weight: 0.8 oz.
Length: 1.8 in.
Power: 1X
Eye Relief: Unlimited
Features: Also available with a universal mount with rear sight dovetail adapters for the most popular handguns on the market; also available with either an M1913 Picatinny or KeyMod Rail interface for use with today's MSR platforms; molded glass aspheric lens with high performance coatings for superior light transmittance and zero distortion; manual illumination controls that remember your last used settings; MOTAC (Motion Activated Illumination) powers up when it senses motion and powers down when it does not; top-loading CR1632 battery, allowing for quick battery replacement without having to remove the sight from the firearm; extremely strong and lightweight aircraft grade CNC magnesium housing waterproof (IPX-7 rated for complete immersion up to 1 meter)
MSRP $389.99

ROMEO1PRO

Type: Reflex sight
Weight: 1 oz.
Length: 1.8 in.
Power: 1X
Obj. Dia.: 30mm
Features: Choice of 3 or 6 MOA dot; 10 daytime and two night vision illumination settings; 100 MOA total elevation/windage travel
Black:. $519.99
Flat dark earth: $549.99

ROMEO3MAX

Type: Reflex sight
Weight: 1.5 oz.
Length: 2.1 in.
Power: 1X
Obj. Dia.: 30mm
Features: Choice of 3 or 6 MOA dot; 10 daytime and two night vision illumination settings
MSRP $779.99

ROMEO3XL

Type: Reflex sight
Weight: 1.5 oz.
Length: 2.1 in.
Power: 1X
Obj. Dia.: 35mm
Features: Choice of 3 or 6 MOA dot; 10 daytime and two night vision illumination settings
MSRP $779.99

SIG Sauer

SIG SAUER ROMEO4H

SIG SAUER ROMEO4S

SIG SAUER ROMEO4T

SIG SAUER ROMEO5

SIG SAUER ROMEO7

SIG SAUER ROMEO8H

SIG SAUER ROMEO8T

ROMEO4H

Weight: 3.4 oz.
Power: 1X
Obj. Diameter: 20mm
Features: Designed for a AR-platform pistols, MSRs, and shotguns; four reticle options; side-loading battery has 50,000+ hours of life
MSRP . . . . $459.99–$519.99

ROMEO4S

Weight: 3.4 oz.
Power: 1X
Obj. Diameter: 20mm
Features: Solar powered red-dot runs in excess of 100,000+ with solar and battery usage; designed for AR-platform pistols, MSRs, and shotguns; lens caps and quick-release mount; four reticle choices
MSRP $589.99

ROMEO4T

Weight: 3.2 oz.
Power: 1X
Obj. Diameter: 20mm
Features: Solar powered red dot runs in excess of 100,000+ with solar and battery usage; designed for AR-platform pistols, MSRs, and shotguns; lens caps and quick-release mount; four reticle choices; tactical version designed for harsh environments
MSRP . . . . $719.99–$749.99

ROMEO5

Type: Red dot
Weight: 6 oz.
Length: 2.47 in.
Power: 1X
Obj. Dia.: 20mm
Eye Relief: Infinite
Features: Mounts on any platform; 2 MOA dot; motion-activated illumination; 10 brightness settings; front-mounting AAA battery or side-loading CR2032 battery; waterproof and fog-proof; Picatinny low mount and co-witness 1.41-inch riser mount included; torx tool; battery; lens cloth; lens covers; reticles include 2 MOA dot with 65 MOA circle, 2 MOA red dot, 2 MOA green dot with triangle holds
MSRP $199.99

ROMEO7

Weight: 12.5 oz.
Length: 4.75 in.
Power: 1X
Eye Relief: Unlimited
Features: Low dispersion glass lens design with high-performance coatings for excellent light transmittance and zero distortion; 2 MOA dot is optimal for close quarters battle to mid-range target engagement; MOTAC (Motion Activated Illumination) powers up when it senses motion and powers down when it does not; 62,500 hours of continuous battery life in medium illumination setting; ready to mount with a standard QD mount provided, but can be customized with vertical spacers to fit a variety of systems; dependable waterproof (IPX-7 rated for complete water immersion up to 1 meter)
MSRP $259.99

ROMEO8H

Type: Red-dot
Power: 1X
Obj. Dia.: 38mm
Eye Relief: Unlimited
Features: Similar to the 8T, but with a 2 MOA red ballistic circle dot
MSRP $649.99

ROMEO8T

Type: Red-dot
Power: 1X
Obj. Dia.: 38mm
Eye Relief: Unlimited
Features: Intended for use on MSR rifle platforms and on shotguns; 2 MOA/65 MOA circle reticle; MOTAC motion activated illumination power up/down; LED illumination for daytime use; four integrated user-selectable reticles; lens covers; ½ hex bolt mount; 100,000 hours battery life; waterproof and fog-proof
MSRP . . . .$779.99–$809.99

Steiner

STEINER DRS 1X

DRS 1X

Type: Reflex sight
Weight: 10.4 oz.
Length: 3.88 in.
Power: 1X
Features: Choice of three reticle options; seven illumination settings; 50 MOA windage and elevation adjustment
MSRP $749.99

Steiner

STEINER EOPTICS DBAL-RL

STEINER MICRO REFLEX SIGHT (MRS)

STEINER T536

STEINER TOR FUSION

STEINER TOR MINI

EOPTICS DBAL-RL

Type: Laser
Weight: 5.4 oz.
Length: 3.46 in.
Battery Life: 1.75 hours
Laser Power Output: Less than 5 mw
Laser Wavelength: 515–535 nm (green); 635–650 nm (red)
Features: Dual Beam Aiming Laser; includes both a light and a laser, fully programmable and capable of being dimmed in both infrared and visible modes; lasers are in green or red, visible or IR laser; the light is IR illuminator or white light; fully adjustable for windage and elevation; mounts on a standard Picatinny M1913 rail; remote switch operation
MSRP $1529.99

MICRO REFLEX SIGHT (MRS)

Weight: 2.5 oz.
Power: 1X
Eye Relief: Unlimited
Features: Picatinny mount; waterproof; holographic sight; adjustable for windage and elevation; illuminated
MSRP $562.99

T332, T432, T536

Type: Red-dot
Weight: 15.9 oz., 16.6 oz., 17.8 oz.
Length: 4.8 in., 5 in., 5.7 in.
Power: 3X, 4X, 5X
Obj. Dia.: 32mm
Field of View: 10.5m@100m
Eye Relief: 2.56 in.
Features: Intended mostly for AR-platform use, these T-dot red-dot sights are shockproof, fogproof, and waterproof and have 50 MOA elevation/windage travel
T332: $735.95
T432: $804.99
T536: $919.99

TOR FUSION

Type: Laser
Features: A rail-mounted combo white light and aiming laser; laser available in red or green; left and right activation buttons; mil-spec engineering; anodized aluminum housing; dustproof; splash-proof; windage and elevation adjustment screws; auto-mode that senses motion like draw from a holster and automatically turns on the laser; boost mode forces unit to maximum output
MSRP $401.99

TOR MINI

Type: Laser
Features: Similar to the Micro, but intended for rail mounting forward of the trigger guard. Red and green lasers available; low, medium, high, and high pulse modes plus setting memory; auto-on senses movement such as retrieval from a nightstand safe and automatically activates laser; ambidextrous use
MSRP $286.99

Trijicon

TRIJICON GLOCK SUPPRESSOR BRIGHT & TOUGH NIGHT SIGHTS

TRIJICON FIBER SIGHTS

TRIJICON HD XR NIGHT SIGHTS

TRIJICON MACHINE GUN REFLEX SIGHT (MGRS)

BRIGHT & TOUGH SUPPRESSOR NIGHT SIGHTS

Features: Three-dot iron sights; shock-resistant design; increase night-fire accuracy by as much as 5x; available for a wide variety of Glock, FNH, H&K, SIG Sauer, Smith & Wesson, and Springfield Armory handguns
MSRP $145.00

FIBER SIGHTS

Features: Front post is .110-inch wide with a .060-inch-diameter fiber; rear sight is blacked out with a .125-inch square notch, is steeply hooked for one-handed slide manipulation as needed, and has rounded edges to reduce snagging; red front installed, red and green replacements included
MSRP $105.00

HD XR NIGHT SIGHTS

Type: Night sights
Weight: 1.6 oz.
Length: 1.22 in.
Features: Thin front sight post provides a larger field of view; available for Beretta, FNH, GLOCK, H&K, Sig Sauer, Smith & Wesson, and Springfield Armory handguns; front sight choice of yellow or orange outline
Front sight only: $99.00
Front and rear: $175.00

MACHINE GUN REFLEX SIGHT (MGRS)

Weight: 66.9 oz.
Length: 8.78 in.
Power: 1x
Features: Created to withstand the constant, violent battering of machine guns; large objective lens with a 3-inch-by-2-inch viewing area; 35 MOA segmented circle reticle; centered 3 MOA dot for precise aiming at close combat to extended ranges; powered by a single CR123A battery that lasts 1000 hours of continuous operation
MSRP $4499.00

Trijicon

TRIJICON MINIATURE RIFLE OPTIC (MRO)

TRIJICON MINIATURE RIFLE OPTIC (MRO) PATROL

MINIATURE RIFLE OPTIC (MRO)

Weight: 4.1 oz.
Length: 2.6 in.
Power: 1X
Eye Relief: Unlimited
Features: Large viewing area; adjustable brightness settings; ambidextrous brightness control; easy-to-set adjusters; aircraft-grade aluminum housing; surface-flush adjusters; waterproof to 30 meters; single lithium battery
Green dot:. . . . . . . $613.00–$749.00
Red dot:. . . . . $579.00–$639.00

MINIATURE RIFLE OPTIC (MRO) PATROL

Type: Red dot
Weight: 5.1 oz.
Length: 4.1 in.
Power: 1X
Obj. Dia.: 25mm
Eye Relief: Infinite
Features: Lens covers; Kill Flash feature that eliminates glare; quick-release mount in full height or co-witness configurations; 70 MOAs of adjustment are in 0.5-MOA increments; runs for five years of continuous use on its 2032 battery; available without mount
MSRP . . . . $849.00–$919.00

Truglo

TRUGLO FIBER OPTIC PRO

TRUGLO SIGHT LINE HANDGUN LASER

TRUGLO TRITON 30MM TRI-COLOR TACTICAL TG8230GB

TRUGLO TRUTEC MICRO

TRUGLO TFX

FIBER OPTIC PRO

Features: Patented light reflector design; blacked-out rear with serrated anti-glare face
MSRP. $76.99

SIGHT LINE HANDGUN LASER

Type: Laser
Features: Red or green laser created for pistol Picatinny/Weaver, Glock and other rail mounts; pulse and constant beam modes; adjustable recoil lug
MSRP. . . . . $94.99–$174.99

TRITON 30MM TRI-COLOR TACTICAL RED DOT

Weight: 6.4 oz.
Length: 5.2 in.
Power: 1X
Obj. Dia.: 30mm
Features: Weaver style mount; multi-coated lenses; tri-color illuminated reticle; Model #TG8230B has 5 MOA single dot; Model #TG8230GB has 3 MOA center dot and surrounding aiming ring
Picatinny mount:. $98.99
Cantilever mount: $141.99

TRUTEC MICRO

Type: Reflex sight
Power: 1X
Obj. Dia.: 23X17mm
Eye Relief: Unlimited
Features: Ten brightness settings; compatible with most pistol optics mounting plates/platforms; shock-, water-, and fog-resistant; includes ABS hardshell cover; aluminum body
MSRP. $218.99

TFX

Features: Day/night sights with a combination of tritium and fiber optic pipe; white contrasting ring around front sight dot; for a wide range of handguns
MSRP. . . . . $76.99–$153.99

OPTICS

Vortex Optics

VORTEX CROSSFIRE

VORTEX SPARC AR

CROSSFIRE

Type: Red dot
Weight: 5.2 oz.
Length: 2.5 in.
Power: 1X
Eye Relief: Infinite
Features: Daylight-bright 2 MOA dot; 100 MOA of elevation and windage adjustment; parallax-free viewing
MSRP. $219.99

SPARC AR

Weight: 7.5 oz.
Length: 2.9 in.
Power: 1X
Eye Relief: Unlimited
Features: Fully multi-coated; bright red dot highly visible in daylight; ten variable illumination settings; waterproof, fogproof, and shockproof; hard anodized finish; twelve-hour auto-shutdown feature
MSRP. $274.99

Vortex Optics

VORTEX SPITFIRE AR PRISM

VORTEX STRIKEFIRE II

VORTEX VENOM

VORTEX VIPER

SPITFIRE AR PRISM
Weight: 11.2 oz.
Length: 4.3 in.
Power: 1X, 3X
Field of View: 29 ft @ 100 yds
Eye Relief: 3.8 in.
Features: Fully multi-coated; prism-based design; twelve variable illumination settings; waterpoof and shockproof; hard anodized finish; red or green reticle option
MSRP $349.99

STRIKEFIRE II
Weight: 7.2 oz.
Length: 5.6 in.
Power: 1X
Features: Shock-, water-, and fog-proof; illuminated red dot; red/green dot cantilever and low mount models available
MSRP $274.99

VENOM
Weight: 1.1 oz.
Length: 1.9 in.
Power: 1X
Eye Relief: Unlimited
Features: Bright red dot; Picatinny mount; choice of 3 or 6 MOA dots; machined aluminum housing
MSRP $349.99

VIPER
Weight: 1.37 oz.
Length: 1.8 in.
Power: 1X
Eye Relief: Unlimited
Features: Bright red dot; Picatinny mount; 6 MOA dot
MSRP $349.99

Williams Gun Sight Company

WILLIAMS GUN SIGHT COMPANY AR-15 FOLDING TACTICAL SIGHT

AR-15 FOLDING TACTICAL SIGHT
Features: CNC high-grade machined aluminum construction; upright lock; fit any Picatinny-style rail; windage and elevation adjustments
MSRP $139.95

XS Sights

XS SIGHTS DXT

XS SIGHTS DXT2 BIG DOT NIGHT SIGHTS

XS SIGHTS DXW

XS SIGHTS F8 NIGHT SIGHTS

DXT
Features: Defensive Express Tritium available in Big Dot or Standard Dot versions for the CZ P10C, Kimber Micro 9 and 380, and BerettaPico
MSRP . . . . $137.00–$212.00

DXT2 BIG DOT NIGHT SIGHTS
Features: Available in orange or yellow, the sight design naturally allows the shooter to focus on the front sight; dot absorbs light and glows when conditions aren't dark enough to sustain the visible glow of tritium; available for a wide variety of handgun models and with yellow or orange front sights
MSRP . . . . $69.99–$137.00

DXW
Features: Defensive Express White Rear available in Big Dot or Standard Dot versions for the CZ P10C, Kimber Micro 9 and 380, and Beretta Pico
MSRP . . . . $104.00–$175.99

F8 NIGHT SIGHTS
Type: Sights
Weight: 2.4 oz.
Features: Presents a figure 8 top-to-bottom alignment of front and rear sight; orange ring of the sight absorbs ambient light to glow in low light conditions; wide notch rear allows more light around the front sight for quicker acquisition and also reduces glare in daylight; available for a variety of GLOCK, Sig Sauer, Smith & Wesson, Springfield, and FNH pistols
MSRP $142.00

ATN Corp.

ATN LASERBALLISTICS 1000, 1500

LASERBALLISTICS 1000, 1500

Type: Rangefinder
Weight: 5.4 oz.
Length: 4.17 in.
Power: 6X
Features: Pairs with ATN's Smart HD Bluetooth scopes; gives the distance to your target in five seconds, then moves the reticle of those scopes accordingly via the mobile app for a shot in under 15 seconds; range is from 5–1000 yds (Model 1000) and 5–1500 yds (Model 1500); waterproof
1000: $279.00
1500: $349.00

Bushnell Outdoor Products

BUSHNELL NITRO 1800

BUSHNELL PRIME 1300/1700

NITRO 1800

Type: Rangefinder
Weight: 5.7 oz.
Length: 4.19 in.
Power: 6X
Obj. Dia.: 24mm
Features: With a stellar 2,000 yards reflective range (trees 1,200 yards, deer 800 yards), this is top choice for long-range target shooters more than hunters

MSRP $349.99

PRIME 1300, 1700

Type: Rangefinder
Weight: 5.9 oz.
Length: 4.27 in.
Power: 6X
Obj. Dia.: 24mm
Features: Running off a 3-volt CR2 battery; regular, bow, and rifle ARC modes; bull's-eye and brush scanning modes; IPX4 waterproofing; Rainguard glass coating; EXO Barrier
Prime 1300: $173.99
Prime 1700: $203.99

Hawk Sport Optics, LLC

HAWKE SPORT OPTICS VANTAGE

VANTAGE 400, 600, 900

Type: Rangefinder
Weight: 6 oz.
Length: 3.8 in.
Power: 6X
Obj. Dia.: 21mm
Field of View: 420 ft.@1000 yd.
Eye Relief: 0.7 in.
Features: BK7 prism; fully multi-coated lenses; standard, horizontal distance, angle, rain, and hunt modes; auto shut-off, water- and fog-proofed; ranging distances are 400, 600, and 900 meters relative to the same model numbers
400: $219.00
600: $239.00
900: $259.00

Kahles

KAHLES HELIA RF-M

HELIA RF-M

Type: Rangefinder
Weight: 7.5 oz.
Length: 4 in.
Power: 7X
Obj. Dia.: 25mm
Exit Pupil: 3.6mm
Field of View: 6.7 degrees
Eye Relief: 15mm
Features: A generous 7X rangefinder with an ergonomic housing; targeting to 2,000m; Enhanced Angle Compensation function; scan mode
MSRP $610.00

Leica Camera AG

LEICA CAMERA AG RANGEMASTER CRF 2400-R

RANGEMASTER CRF 2400-R

Type: Rangefinder
Weight: 6.5 oz.
Length: 4.5 in.
Power: 7X
Obj. Dia.: 24mm
Exit Pupil: 3.4mm
Field of View: 347 ft.@1,000 yd.
Eye Relief: 15mm
Features: Updated LED display adjusts to ambient light for better viewing; decimal results to 200 yards; equivalent horizontal range to 1200 yards
MSRP $550.00

Leica Camera AG

LEICA CAMERA AG RANGEMASTER CRF 2800 COM

LEICA RANGEMASTER CRF 3500.COM

RANGEMASTER CRF 2800 COM

Type: Rangefinder
Weight: 6.7 oz.
Power: 7X
Obj. Dia.: 24mm
Exit Pupil: 3.4mm
Field of View: 115m @1,000 yd.
Eye Relief: 15mm
Features: Leica's ABC ballistic system; measurements to 2800 yards; works in combination with Leica's hunting app to relay information via Bluetooth to calculate holdover and distance corrections for given environmental conditions
MSRP $749.00

RANGEMASTER CRF 3500. COM

Type: Rangefinder
Weight: 6.7 oz.
Power: 7X
Obj. Dia.: 24mm
Exit Pupil: 3.4mm
Field of View: 310 ft.@1000 yd.
Eye Relief: 15mm
Features: Ranging to 3,500 yards; user can create individual ballistic profiles to work with the Leica Hunting App, and information can be transferred to an Apple watch; meter/yard switchover
MSRP $1199.00

Leupold & Stevens

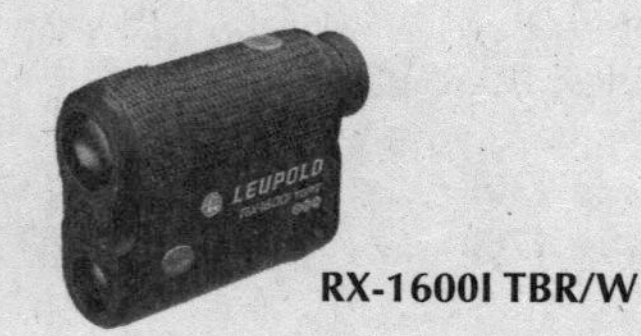

RX-1600I TBR/W

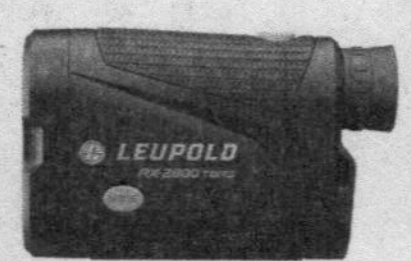

LEUPOLD RX-2800 TBR/W

RX-2800 TBR/W

Type: Rangefinder
Weight: 7.3 oz.
Length: 4.3 in.
Power: 7X
Field of View: 318 ft.@1000 yd.
Eye Relief: 16 mm
Features: Powered by Alpha IQ; OLED display; scan mode; trophy scale analysis; True Ballistic Range with Wind
MSRP $599.99

RX-1600I TBR/W

Type: Rangefinder
Weight: 7.8 oz.
Length: 3.8 in.
Power: 6X
Exit Pupil: 3.6mm
Field of View: 315 ft.@1000 yd.
Eye Relief: 17mm
Features: Fully multi-coated glass; Leupold's DNA technology; scan mode; choice of three reticles; line-of-sight distance; trophy scale technology; built-in inclinometer; True Ballistic Range with Wind; fold-down rubber eye cup; OLED display
MSRP $399.99

Newcon Optik

NEWCON OPTIK LRM 2K

NEWCON OPTIK LRM 1800S

LRM 2K

Type: Rangefinder
Weight: 5.8 oz.
Length: 4.17 in.
Power: 7X
Obj. Dia.: 24mm
Field of View: 7.5 degrees
Eye Relief: 16mm
Features: Very lightweight rangefinder capable of reading targets to 2,000 meters (about 1.24 miles); built-in inclinometer; bluetooth compatible and works with NC Cronus App; speed detection; yards/meters display; TOLED display; in green/black
MSRP $472.00

LRM 1800S

Type: Rangefinder
Weight: 15.69 oz.
Length: 5 in.
Power: 7X
Obj. Dia.: 25mm
Field of View: 8 degrees
Eye Relief: 15mm
Features: Built-in speed detector; last 10 reading recall; target quality indicator; reticle pattern selection; meters/yards readings; scan mode
MSRP $455.00

Newcon Optik

NEWCON OPTIK LRM 2200SI

NEWCON OPTIK LRM 3500M

LRM 2200SI

Type: Rangefinder
Weight: 15.69 oz.
Length: 5 in.
Power: 7X
Obj. Dia.: 25mm
Eye Relief: 15mm
Features: A compact monocular rangefinder capable of reading targets to 2,200 meters (about 1.36 miles); built-in inclinometer; bluetooth compatible and works with NC Cronus App; first/last target logic
MSRP $924.00

LRM 3500M

Type: Rangefinder
Weight: 16 oz.
Length: 4.6 in.
Power: 6.5X
Obj. Dia.: 30mm
Field of View: 7 degrees
Eye Relief: 20mm
Features: A full-featured rangefinder goes the distance to 5 km; etched reticle in mils; last ten readings recall; first/last target logic; declination correction; digital compass; user and target GPS coordinates; bluetooth capability/Android compatible; Kestrel ballistic calculator
MSRP $6235.00

Redfield

REDFIELD RAIDER 650 AND 650A

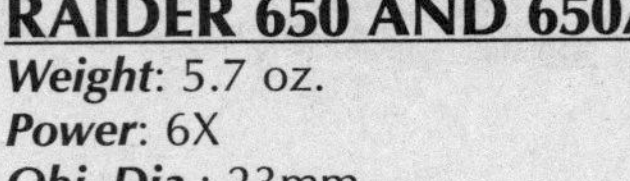

RAIDER 650 AND 650A

Weight: 5.7 oz.
Power: 6X
Obj. Dia.: 23mm
Range: up to 650 yd
Features: Fully multi-coated optics; high contrast LCD display; lightweight; compact; weatherproof; availabe in Mossy Oak in 650A model
MSRP $249.99

SIG Sauer

SIG SAUER KILO1800BDX 6X22MM

SIG SAUER KILO2200BDX 7X25MM

SIG SAUER KILO2400ABS

SIG SAUER KILO2400BDX 7X25MM

KILO1800BDX 6X22MM

Type: Rangefinder
Weight: 7.8 oz.
Length: 4.1in.
Power: 6X
Obj. Dia.: 22mm
Exit Pupil: 6 degrees
Eye Relief: 17mm
Features: Similar to the KILO1400BDX but with a slightly bigger aperture and eye relief; circle reticle; up to 2000 yards reflective ranging
MSRP . . . .
$519.99

KILO2200BDX 7X25MM

Type: Rangefinder
Weight: 7.5 oz.
Length: 4.4 in.
Power: 7X
Obj. Dia.: 25mm
Exit Pupil: 6.78 degrees
Eye Relief: 15mm
Features: Similar to the KILO1400BDX but at 7X and with a circle plus Milling grid reticle; ten illumination settings; gray body; up to 3400 yards reflective ranging
MSRP $649.99

KILO2400ABS

Weight: 7.5 oz.
Length: 4.2 in.
Power: 7X
Obj. Diameter: 25mm
Exit Pupil: 3.6mm
Eye Relief: 15mm
Field of View: 35.67 ft @ 100 yds
Features: LightWave DSP Technology ranges up to two miles; embedded applied ballistics calculator; integrated temperature, humidity, pressure, and compass; Milling reticle with 2.4 MRAD inner diameter and 3 MRAD outer diameter; user-selectable target modes feature last and best readings; Lumatic OLED display constantly monitors light conditions and adjusts display brightness accordingly; multi-position twist-up eyecup provides custom fit; tripod adaptor; smartphone jack WindMETER; stylus pen; lanyard; three spare batteries; ballistic nylon molle kit; nylon carry pouch; configurable reticle with three viewing options: center aiming circle only, center aiming circle and horizontal milling grid, or center aiming circle with horizontal and vertical milling grids; ranges up to two miles
MSRP $1689.99

KILO2400BDX 7X25MM

Type: Rangefinder
Weight: 7.5 oz.
Length: 4.4 in.
Power: 7X
Obj. Dia.: 25mm
Exit Pupil: 6.78 degrees
Eye Relief: 15mm
Features: Similar to the other rangefinders in the KILO BDX series but at 7X and with a circle plus Milling grid reticle; ten illumination settings; OD green body; up to 3400 yards reflective ranging
MSRP $1039.99

AMMUNITION

MUZZLELOADING BULLETS

BULLETS

Aguila Ammunition

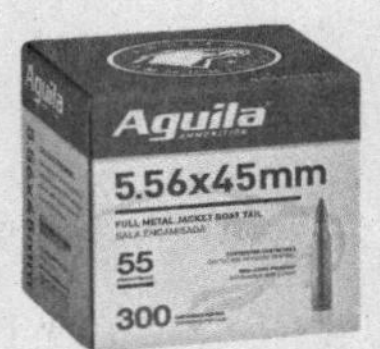

AGUILA 5.56X45MM

AGUILA MINISHELL

5MM REMINGTON SJHP

Features: The unusual 5mm necked rimfire round in a semi-jacketed hollowpoint; 2200 fps velocity
Available in: 5mm Remington (30 gr.)
Box 50: $37.99
Box 1000: $933.99

5.56X45MM

Features: Bulk packs of 300 rounds with full metal jacket boattails
Available in: 5.56x45mm (55 gr.)
Box 300: $254.99
Box 1200: $1122.99

MINISHELL

Description: SAAMI-approved in 2019, this 12 ga. 1.75-in. shotshell offers less recoil than traditional 2.75-in. shotshells
Available in: 12 ga. No. 7 ½ 5/8-oz. load, 12 ga. No. 4 Buck 5/8-oz. load, 12 ga. 7/8-oz. slug
Box of 20: . . . . $16.99–$24.99

Alexander Arms

ALEXANDER ARMS .50 BEOWULF

.50 BEOWULF

Features: Several configurations available, including 200-gr. frangible Inceptor ARX; 350-gr. Hornady XTP jacketed hollowpoint; 350-gr. plated round-shoulder; 400-gr. Hawk jacketed flat-point; 300-gr. Hornady FTX
Box 20: . . . . $44.99–$74.99

6.5 GRENDEL

Features: A long-range favorite available in 123-gr. Lapua Scenar hollowpoint; 120-gr. Nosler Ballistic Tip; 129-gr. Hornady SST
Box 20: $49.99

Allegiance Ammunition

ALLEGIANCE POWERSTRIKE

APEX TURKEY NINJA TSS

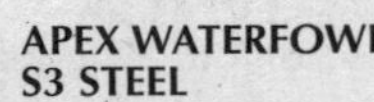
APEX WATERFOWL S3 STEEL

HOGSTRIKE

Features: A frangible round with a thick solid core that penetrates tough game hides and fragments into soft fluid tissue and creates devastating wound channels
Available in: .308 Win. (150 gr.), 5.56 NATO (80 gr., 100 gr.)
Box 20: . . . . $38.70–$49.02

ONESTRIKE

Features: A frangible offering intended for use where metal enclosures or crowds are a concern; HET High Energy Transfer frangible core; fragments on light barriers
Available in: 5.56 NATO (55 gr., 80 gr.), 9mm (90 gr.)
Box 20: . . . . $33.17–$38.70

POWERSTRIKE

Description: Jacketed frangible self-defense ammo
Available in: 9mm (95 gr., 115 gr.)
Box of 20: . . . . $32.42–$35.42

RANGESTRIKE

Features: A frangible round for target practice; USA made to NATO spec; same point of impact as the company's tactical line
Available in: 9mm (65 gr., 115 gr., 124 gr.)
Box 50: $31.00

SILENTSTRIKE

Features: A subsonic, frangible round made of compressed tungsten powder and with a high-density core that will penetrate even thick clothing; fragmentation of core occurs both horizontally and vertically upon hitting fluid-filled tissue
Available in: 5.56 NATO (80 gr., 95 gr. [non-frangible], 100 gr. [hybrid/subsonic], 110 gr.), .300 BLK (150 gr.), .308 Win. (150 gr.); 9mm (140 gr.)
Box 20: . . . . $32.06–$49.02

PREDATOR TSS

Description: A full lineup of 12-ga. shotshells loaded with Tungsten Super Shot for predator hunting
Available in: 12 ga. (3 in., 3 ½ in.)
Box of 5: . . . . $32.99–$58.49

TURKEY NINJA TSS

Description: You don't have to guess that this stuff is for serious turkey hunters with a unique No. 8.5 shot size
Available in: 12 ga. (3 in., 3 ½ in.), 20 ga. (3 in.), 28 ga. (2 ¾ in.), .410 (3 in.)
Box of 5: . . . . $35.49–$58.49

UPLAND BIRD TSS

Description: Utilizes Tungsten Super Shot
Available in: 12 ga. (2¾ in.), 20 ga. (2¾ in.); shot sizes #7.5, #8, #9 in both gauges
Box 10: . . . . $44.99–$59.99

WATERFOWL S3 STEEL

Description: A premium all-steel load for waterfowlers
Available in: 12 ga. (2¾ in.), 20 ga. (2¾ in.); #BB, #4, and #2 in 12-ga.; #4 and #2 in 20-ga.
Box 25: . . . . $20.99–$23.99

Apex Ammunition

WATERFOWL TSS

Description: Utilizes Apex's own Tungsten Super Shot
Available in: 12 ga. (2 ¾ in.), 20 ga. (2 ¾ in.); #7.5, #8, #9 in both gauges
Box 10: . . . . $44.99–$59.99

WATERFOWL TSS/S3 STEEL BLEND

Description: Shell holds a combination Tungsten Super Shot with S3 steel shot
Available in: 12 ga. (2¾ in., #BB, #4, or #2); 20 ga. (2¾ in., #4)
Box 25: . . . . $41.99–$43.99

Barnes Bullets

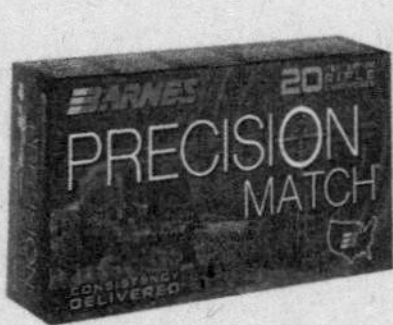

BARNES PRECISION MATCH

BARNES BULLETS VOR-TX EXPANDER SHOTSHELL

PRECISION MATCH

Features: Engineered for precision at extreme distances, with very low standard deviations; Loaded with Barnes match-grade OTM (Open Tip Match) boattail
Available in: 5.56 NATO, .308 Win., .300 Win. Mag., .338 Lapua Mag., 6.5 Creedmoor, 6mm Creedmoor, .260 Rem., .300 BLK, 6.5 Grendel
Box 20: . . . . $42.99–$168.99

RANGE AR

Features: Higher velocity, flatter trajectory, and ultimate accuracy; factory-fresh brass paired with a lead-free, copper-jacketed, zinc core OTFB (Open Tip Flat Base) provides excellent performance in ARs with quick twist barrels
Available in: 5.56x45mm, .300 BLK
Box of 20 5.56 NATO: $19.99
Box of 20 .300 BLK: $18.99

TAC-XPD

Features: Loaded with Barnes TAC-XP bullets, the all-copper construction and very large, deep hollow-point cavity expand, penetrate, and perform consistently and optimally for personal and home defense
Available in: .357 Mag., .380 ACP, 9mm Luger +P, .45 ACP +P, .40 S&W
Box 20: . . . . $28.49–$37.49

VOR-TX

Features: Provides maximum tissue and bone destruction, pass-through penetration, and devastating energy transfer; multiple grooves in the bullet's shank reduce pressure and improve accuracy; bullets open instantly on contact causing the nose to peel back into four sharp-edged copper petals
Available in: ***Rifle:*** .223 Rem., .22-250 Rem., 5.56 NATO, .243 Win., .25-06 Rem., 6.5 Grendel, 6.5 Creedmoor, .260 Rem., .270 Win., .270 WSM, 7mm-08 Rem., 7mm Rem. Mag., .30-30 Win., .308 Win., .30-06 Spfd., .300 BLK, .300 WSM, .300 Win. Mag., .300 RUM, .300 Wby. Mag., .338 Win. Mag., .338 Lapua Mag., .35 Whelen, .45-70 Gov't., 9.3X62mm, 7X64 Brenneke, .450 Bushmaster
Rifle LR: 6mm Creedmoor, 6.5 Creedmoor, .270 Win., 7mm Rem. Mag., 7mm RUM, .30-06 Spfd., .300 Win. Mag., .300 RUM, .338 RUM, .375 RUM
Hunting Handgun: .357 Mag., 10mm, .41 Rem. Mag., .44 Mag., .45 Colt, .454 Casull
Safari: .375 H&H Mag., .416 Rem. Mag., .416 Rigby, .458 Win. Mag., .458 Lott, .470 Nitro Express, .500 Nitro Express
Euro: 7x64 Brenneke, .308 Win., .30-06 Spfd., 8x57 JS, 9.3x62mm
Rifle: . . . . $41.99–$187.99
Rifle LR: . . . . $58.99–$109.99
Safari: . . . . $86.99–$232.99
Handgun: . . . . $37.99–$59.99

VOR-TX EXPANDER SHOTSHELL

Description: Rifle-like precision for slug shotguns; blue polymer-tipped all-copper body; flat trajectory
Available in: 12 ga. (3 in., 2 ¾ in.), 20 ga. (3 in., 2 ¾ in.)
Box of 5: . . . . $15.79–$17.49

Black Hills Ammunition

BLACK HILLS FACTORY NEW RIFLE

Rifle Ammunition

BLACK HILLS GOLD

Features: Bullets by Barnes; lead-free non-toxic rounds; high-performance hunting ammunition
Available in: .22–250 Rem., .243 Win., .25-06 Rem., .260 Rem., .270 Win., 7mm Rem. Mag., .300 Win. Mag., .308 Win., .30-06 Spfd., .338 Lapua; 6.5 Creedmoor
Box 20: . . . . $36.99–$135.99

FACTORY NEW RIFLE

Features: Bullets by manufacturers such as Hornady, Barnes, and Nosler; high-performance hunting ammunition; certain calibers available in Molycoat
Available in: .223 Rem., .308 Win. Match, .300 Win. Mag., .338 Lapua, .338 Norma Mag. , .300 Whisper, 5.56 NATO
Box 50: . . . . $83.99–$173.99

Black Hills Ammunition

Handgun Ammunition

COWBOY ACTION

Features: Designed to meet the needs of cowboy-action pistol shooters with its new virgin brass and premium-quality hard-cast bullets; velocities are moderate to provide low recoil and excellent accuracy
Available in: .32 H&R, .32-20 Win., .38 LC, .38 Spl., .38-40 Win., .44-40 Win., .44 Russian, .44 Spl., .44 Colt, .45 Schofield, .45 Colt, .38-55 Win., .357 Mag.
Box 50: . . . . $35.99–$59.99

FACTORY NEW HANDGUN

Features: Used by the U.S. Military in all four branches for its reliability
Available in: .32 H&R Mag., .380 ACP, 9mm Luger, .38 Spl., .357 Mag., .40 S&W, .44 Mag., .45 ACP
Box 20: . . . . $23.99–$71.99

HONEYBADGER

Features: A unique fluted projectile—not a hollowpoint—designed for self-defense purposes; a .45-70 load is likely suitable for ranch and varmint/predator work
Available in: .38 Spec. +P (100 gr.), .380 ACP (60 gr.), .44 Mag. (160 gr.), .44 Spec. (125 gr.), .45 ACP (235 gr.), .45-70 Gov't. (325 gr.), 9mm (100 gr.), .357 Mag. (127 gr.)
Box 20: . . . . $25.57–$69.31

Boss Shotshells

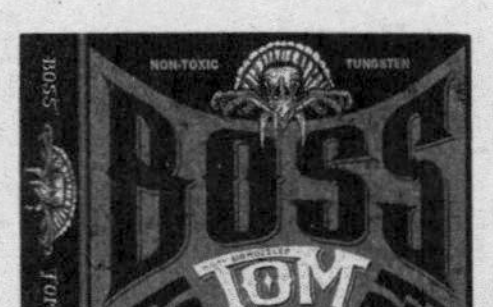

BOSS SHOTSHELLS TOM

TOM

Description: Dedicated copper-plated tungsten loads for a range of shotgun gauges/bores for the turkey hunter
Available in: 12 ga. (3 in., 2¾ in.), 20 ga. (3 in., 2¾ in.), 28-ga. (2¾ in), .410-bore (3-in.)
Box 5: . . . . $25.00–$60.00

UNMUZZLED

Features: A line of copper-plated Bismuth shells without the historically high cost; a variety of 3-inch and 2 ¾-inch 12 ga. and 20 ga. loads, 2 ¾-inch 16 and 28 ga., and 3-in. .410 bore loadings
Available in: 10 ga., 12 ga., 16 ga., 20 ga., 28 ga., .410 bore
Box 25: . . . . $27.00–$45.00

Brenneke USA

BRENNEKE CLOSE ENCOUNTER

BLACK MAGIC MAGNUM

Features: The Black Magic Magnum and Black Magic Short Magnum are two of the most powerful cartridges available on the market, offering tremendous knockdown power up to 100/60 yds; clean speed coating reduces lead fouling inside the barrel by almost 100 percent
Available in: 12 Ga. (3 in.)
Box 5: $17.99

BRENNEKE 28

Features: The moderate recoil makes the 28 Ga. a perfect slug for young hunters who will be introduced to slug shooting; 28 Ga. is a multi-talent: small game, home defense, and all around shooting
Available in: 28 Ga. (2¾ in.)
Box 5: $13.99

CLASSIC MAGNUM

Features: Invented by Wilhelm Brenneke in 1898, the classic is the ancestor of all modern shotgun slugs; this state-of-the-art slug provides long-range stopping power, consistently flat trajectories, and a patented B.E.T. wad column
Available in: 12 Ga. (2¾ in.), 16 Ga. (2¾ in.)
Box 5: $12.99

CLOSE ENCOUNTER

Features: The .410 Close Encounter is the perfect choice if you are a fan of 2½-in. .410/.45 revolvers. They are powerful without having bad recoil, and they have an incredible frontal area and the legendary Brenneke penetration
Available in: .410 (2½ in.)
Box 5: $10.15

HEAVY FIELD SHORT MAGNUM GREEN LIGHTNING

Features: The original "Emerald" slug with patented B.E.T wad and famous stopping power; for all barrel types; range up to 100 yds.
Available in: 12 Ga., 20 Ga. (2¾ in.)
MSRP $12.99

K.O. SLUG

Features: The KO is an improved Foster-type slug with excellent penetration; range up to 60 yds; for all barrel types
Available in: 12 Ga. (2¾ in.), 20 Ga. (2 ¾ in.)
MSRP $8.99

MAGNUM CRUSH

Features: Delivers a force of more than 3.800 ft/lbs, weighs a full 1 ½ oz. / 666 gr. and the flat trajectory is ideal for bigger game; special coating to reduce lead fouling and broad ribs for optimum groove engagement
Available in: 12 Ga. (3 in.)
Box 5: $12.34

Browning Ammunition

BROWNING BPT PERFORMANCE TARGET

BROWNING BXV PREDATOR & VARMINT

BPR PERFORMANCE RIMFIRE

Features: BPR provides reliability and performance in 22 long rifle ammunition that you can expect from The Best There Is in rimfire ammunition.
Available in: .22 LR
Box of 100:. $15.99

BPT PERFORMANCE TARGET

Features: BPT Performance Target is a premium training product that can be used to hone your handgun skills. It is a matched training counterpart to BXP Personal Defense.
Available in: .223 Rem., .38 Spec., .380 ACP, .40 S&W, .45 ACP, 9mm
Box of 50 handgun: . . $34.99–$59.99
Box of 20 .223 Rem.: $8.95

BPT TARGET LOAD

Features: BPT Performance Target utilizes premium, hard shot to help deliver tight patterns and maximum target breaking energy. The smooth hull allows for a sleek profile and smooth ejection.
Available in: 2¾-inch 12- (No. 7½, 8), 20- (No. 7½), 16- (No. 8) and 28-gauge (No. 7½); 2 ½-inch .410-boren (No. 7½)
Box of 25:. . . . . $11.99–$20.99

BXC BIG GAME

Features: BXC Controlled Expansion Terminal Tip is designed specifically for use on big game like elk, moose, mule deer, and bear. The Terminal Tip and bonded bullet design allow for deep penetration through thick, tough hide and bone. The brass tip, heavy bullet weight, and boat-tail are integral components to delivering precision accuracy, maximum downrange velocity, and long-range, on-target performance.
Available in: .270 Win., .30-06 Spfd., .300 Win. Mag., .300 WSM, .308 Win., 7mm Rem. Mag., 6.5 Creedmoor, .270 WSM, .28 Nosler
Box of 20:. . . . . $51.99–$81.99

BXD UPLAND

Features: BXD Upland Extra Distance launches premium-plated shot at high velocities to achieve premium in-the-field performance. Nickel-plated shot helps keep shot round resulting in high velocity retention and energy transfer as well as tighter downrange patterns.
Available in: 12 ga. (2¾ in.), 20 ga. (2¾ in.), 16 ga. (2¾ in.)
Box of 25: . . . . $18.99–$19.99

BXD WATERFOWL

Features: BXD Waterfowl Extra Distance is launched at high velocities utilizing an optimized long-range wad and plated round steel shot. Combining round steel with a cutting edge wad design results in a lethal combination of energy retention, penetration, and pattern density that is critical in achieving long-range performance. No. 2, 4, and BB shot sizes available in 12-gauge, No. 2 shot only for 20-gauge.
Available in: 12 (3 in., 3.5 in.), 20 (3 in.)
Box of 25:. . . . . $19.99–$21.99

BXR DEER

Features: BXR Rapid Expansion Matrix Tip is designed specifically for use on whitetail, blacktail, mule deer, and antelope. The proprietary matrix tip design allows for high downrange velocity and energy retention while also initiating rapid positive expansion. The jacket and tip combination yields precision accuracy and rapid energy transfer, and generates massive knockdown power.
Available in: .243 Win., .270 Win., .270 WSM, .30-06 Spfd., .30-30 Win., .300 Win. Mag., .300 WSM, .308 Win. 6.5 Creedmoor, 7mm Rem. Mag., 7mm-08, .350 Legend
Box of 20:. . . . . $38.99–$46.99

BXS DEER

Features: Solid copper expansion sabot slug designed to increase accuracy, penetration, and energy transfer
Available in: 12-ga. sabot slug, 00 Buckshot, or rifled slug, 20-ga. sabot slug, all in 5-count boxes; 20-count boxes of rifle cartridges in .270 Win., .30-06 Spfd., .300 Win. Mag., .300 WSM, .308 Win., 6.5 Creedmoor, 7mm Rem. Mag.
Sabot slugs:. $16.99
00 Buckshot: $7.99
Rifled slug: $4.99
Rifle cartridges:. . . . . $47.99–$75.99

BXV PREDATOR & VARMINT

Features: Polymer tip improves BC and results in flatter trajectory and higher downrange velocity
Available in: .223 Win., .243 Win., .22 Hornet, .22-250
Box of 20:. . . . . $28.99–$38.99

TSS TUNGSTEN TURKEY

Features: Super-dense loads for gobbler season; shot sizes BB, 6, 5, and 4 across magnum 12- and 20 ga. and .410-bore loads; duplex loads are also to be made available in smaller shot size combos
Available in: 12 ga. (3 ½ in., 3 in.), 20 ga. (3 in.), .410-bore (3 in.)
Box 10:. . . . . $28.99–$43.99

X-POINT DEFENSE

Features: BXP Personal Defense is designed for superior personal defense performance in reliability, expansion, and penetration. The X-Point is designed to shield the hollow point through intermediate barriers.
Available in: .380 ACP, 9mm. .40 S&W, 10mm Auto, .45 ACP
Box of 20:. . . . . $23.99–$24.99

CCI Ammunition

.22 WIN. MAG. MAXI MAG

Features: A favorite of varmint shooters; 40 gr. TMJ flat nose at 1875 fps, or 40 gr. jacketed HP at 1875 fps; both loads give over 1400 fps from a 6-in. revolver; clean-burning propellants keep actions cleaner; sure-fire CCI priming; reusable plastic box with dispenser lid
Available in: .22 Win. Mag.
Box of 50:. . . . . $16.49–$18.29

CCI Ammunition

CCI BLAZER 10MM

CCI MAXI-MAG POUR PACK

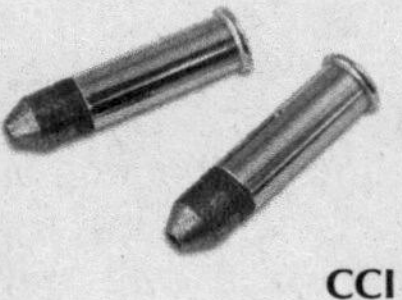

CCI GREEN TAG

CCI MAXI-MAG MEATEATER

A17 VARMINT TIP

Features: Optimized for feeding and function in the Savage Arms A17 semiautomatic rifle and can be fired through bolt-action .17 HMR firearms; 100 fps faster than other .17 HMR loads of the same weight; Varmint Tip bullet provides rapid expansion; CCI-made and primed case
Available in: .17 HMR
Box 50:..................$19.99
Box 2000:...............$802.99

A22 MAGNUM GAMEPOINT

Features: GamePoint bullet; designed around Savage's semiautomatic A22 Magnum rifle
Available in: .22 WMR (35 gr.)
Box 200:.................$87.99
Box 2000:...............$882.99

BIG 4

Features: Centerfire handgun shotshells with larger No. 4 pellets for extended range and penetration
Available in: .38 Spl., .44 Spl., .45 Colt, 9mm
Box 10:............$19.99–$38.49

BLAZER .22 LR BULK PACK

Features: A 525-count box of lead roundnose for hours of plinking fun
Available in: .22 LR (38 gr.)
Box of 425:...............$41.49
Box of 525:...............$48.49
Box of 1500:.............$145.99
Box of 3400:.............$329.99
Box of 5250:.............$493.99

BLAZER 9MM

Features: Designed for high-volume training; FMJ bullet in a reloadable brass case
Available in: 9mm (124 gr., 147 gr.)
Box 50:..................$46.99

BLAZER 10MM

Description: Full-power, full metal jacket 10mm loads in Blazer reloadable brass cases
Available in: 10mm (180 gr.)
Box of 50:...............$43.99

CLEAN-22

Features: A coated polymer bullet leaves no residue behind while reducing traditional copper and lead fouling, even in suppressors; sub-sonic and high-velocity loads; will cycle in semiautomatics
Available in: .22 LR (40 gr.)
Box 100:.................$13.79

CLEAN-22 PINK

Description: Bullets wear a pink polymer coating that reduces copper and lead fouling; a portion of the sales go to fight breast cancer; lead roundnose
Available in: .22 LR (40 gr.)
Box of 400:...............$40.99

CLEAN-22 SUPPRESSOR POUR PACK

Description: Uses polymer bullet coating to reduce barrel and suppressor fouling; reliable functioning in semiautomatic firearms; 1,000 fps
Available in: .22 LR (45 gr.)
Box of 200:...............$37.49

COPPER-22

Features: Non-lead, California-legal bullet; constructed from a unique mix of copper particles and polymer compressed into a potent, 21-grain hollow-point bullet
Available in: .22 LR
Box of 50:................$14.29

COPPER-22 MEATEATER

Description: One of three loads developed in partnership with hunting personality Steven Rinella; official rimfire ammunition of Rinella's MeatEater brand
Available in: .22 LR (21 gr.)
Box of 50:................$12.49

GREEN TAG

Features: Our first and still most-popular match rimfire product; tight manufacturing and accuracy specs mean you get the consistency and accuracy that the unforgiving field of competition demands; the rimfire match ammo leaves the muzzle sub-sonic which means no buffeting in the transonic zone; clean-burning propellants keep actions cleaner. Sure-fire CCI priming; reusable plastic box with dispenser lid
Available in: .22 LR (40 gr. lead round nose)
Box of 100:...............$28.99

HMR TNT

Features: A 17-gr. Speer TNT hollow point answers requests from varmint hunters and gives explosive performance over the .17's effective range; clean-burning propellants keep actions cleaner; sure-fire CCI priming; reusable plastic box with dispenser lid
Available in: .17 HMR 17-gr. TNT hollow point or 16-gr. lead-free green TNT solid hollow point
TNT, box 50:..............$19.99
TNT Green, box 50:........$19.49

LONG HV AND SHORT HV

Features: Designed for rimfire guns that require .22 Long and .22 Short ammunition; clean-burning propellants keep actions cleaner; sure-fire CCI priming; reusable plastic box with dispenser lid
Available in: .22 Short (29 gr. solid lead bullet), .22 Short (27 gr. hollow point bullet), .22 Long (29 gr. solid lead bullet)
Box of 100:...............$14.79

MAXI-MAG MEATEATER

Description: One of three loads developed in partnership with hunting personality Steven Rinella; official rimfire ammunition of Rinella's MeatEater brand
Available in: .22 WMR (40 gr.)
Box of 200:...............$69.99

MAXI-MAG POUR PACK

Description: "Milk"-carton bulk packs of 125
Available in: .22 WMR (40 gr.)
Box of 125:...............$52.99

MINI-MAG

Features: CCI's first rimfire product and still the most popular; Mini-Mag. hollow points are high-velocity products and offer excellent all-around performance for small game and varmints; clean-burning propellants keep actions cleaner; sure-fire CCI priming; reusable plastic box with dispenser lid
Available in: .22 LR (40 gr. gilded round nose or 36 gr. gilded lead hollow point)
Box 100:.................$12.79

CCI Ammunition

CCI VNT .17 MACH 2, .22 WMR

MINI-MAG MEATEATER

Description: One of three loads developed in partnership with hunting personality Steven Rinella; official rimfire ammunition of Rinella's MeatEater brand
Available in: .22 LR (36 gr.)
Box of 300: $37.49

MINI-MAG SEGMENTED HOLLOW POINT

Features: New bullet design splits into three equal parts upon impact
Available in: .22 LR (40 gr.)
Box 100: $15.99

PISTOL MATCH

Features: Designed expressly for high-end semiautomatic match pistols; singe-die tooling and great care in assembly lets you wring the last bit of accuracy from your precision pistol; clean-burning propellants keep actions cleaner; sure-fire CCI priming; reusable plastic box with dispenser lid
Available in: .22 LR (40 gr. lead round nose bullet)
Box 50: $15.29

QUIET-22

Features: Ideal for bolt-action and single shot .22 LR rifles (and perfectly safe in semiautomatics), this new reduced report cartridge generates ¼ the perceived noise level of standard velocity .22 LR
Available in: .22 LR
Box 50: . . . . $6.99–$9.49

QUIET-22 SEMI-AUTO

Features: Reduced report in a round that reliably cycles semiautomatics; noise reduced with or without suppressors; low velocity
Available in: .22 LR (45 gr., 735 fps)
Box of: 50
MSRP $6.49

SELECT .22 LR

Features: The .22 Long Rifle Select is built for semiautomatic competition; reliable operation, accuracy, and consistency make Select an ideal choice for competition shooters
Available in: .22 LR
Box of 100: $15.99

STANGERS .22 LR

Description: Named for the drawl of YouTube personality 22plinkster, this is CCI Stinger ammo in special edition packaging; varmint load at 1,640 fps
Available in: .22 LR (32 gr.)
Box of 100: $22.99

SUPPRESSOR 22 LONG RIFLE

Features: Subsonic velocity of 970 fps minimizes sound signature through suppressed firearms; HP bullet; consistent function in semiautomatic firearms; clean-burning powders
Available in: .22 LR
Box 50:. $9.39

VNT

Features: Special Speer VNT bullet design for varmint hunters favoring these speedy specialty rimfire rounds; polymer tip and thin jacket; nickel-plated cases
Available in: .17 Mach 2 (17 gr.), .22 WMR (30 gr.)
.17 Mach 2, box 50: $11.29
.17 HMR, box 100: $105.99
.22 WMR, box 50: $21.99

VNT POUR PACK

Description: Lots of varmint or plinking fun in "milk"-carton bulk packs of .22 WMR or .17 HMR
Available in: .17 HMR (17 gr.), .22 WMR (30 gr.)
Box 125: $52.99
Box 1250: $529.99

Cor-Bon

COR-BON MPR

CORBON HUNTER

Rifle

DPX, T-DPX RIFLE

Features: This is an optimum load for Law Enforcement; lead-free projectile; reduced recoil due to lighter weight projectile; deep penetration on soft tissue 12–17-in.
Available in: .223 Rem., .243 Win., .270 Win., .30-06 Spfd., .30-30 Win., .300 BLK, .300 Win. Mag., .308 Win., .338 Lapua, .338 RUM, .338 Win. Mag., .340 Wby. Mag., .444 Marlin, .458 SOCOM, 6.5-284 Norma, 7.62X39
Box 20: . . . . $39.99–$129.99

MULTI-PURPOSE RIFLE (MPR)

Features: Features a gilding metal jacket with a specially formulated lead core and a green acetal resin tip, which reduces drag, producing extremely high ballistic coefficient, and also creates more reliable feeding in magazine fed firearms; provides rapid, explosive expansion without excessive penetration; aerodynamic resin tip offers extreme accuracy at long-range precision competition and also improves feeding in magazine fed rifles; reliably expands for humane kills on varmints and deer-size game, giving just the right amount of penetration
Available in: .223 Rem., .22-250 Rem., 30-06 Spfd., .300 BLK, 300 Win. Mag., .308 Win.
Box 20: . . . . $39.99–$47.99

Handgun

DPX HANDGUN

Features: DPX is a solid copper hollowpoint bullet that combines the best of the lightweight high-speed JHPs and the heavyweight, deep-penetrating JHPs; the copper bullet construction allows it to conquer hard barriers like auto glass and steel
Available in: 10mm, .32 ACP, .357 Mag., .357 SIG, .375 JDJ, .38 Spec. +P, .38 Super +P, .380 ACP, .40 S&W, .400 CORBON, .44 Mag. .44 Spl., .45 ACP, .45 ACP +P, .45 Colt +P, .454 Casull, .460 S&W, .500 S&W, 9mm, 9mm +P
Box 20: . . . . $29.99–$84.99

Cor-Bon

GLASER SAFETY SLUG

Features: Originally designed for use by Sky Marshals on airplanes, today the slug is recommended for anyone concerned with over-penetration; copper jacket; filled with a compressed load of #12 or #6 lead shot, then capped with a round polymer ball that enhances feeding and reloading. Silver line is designed for more penetration than the blue line and is a preferred choice in colder climates where thick, heavy clothing would be prevalent
Available in:
Silver line: 10mm, .44 Mag.
Pow'RBall: 38 Spec. +P, .357 Mag., .38 Super +P, .380 ACP, 9mm +P, 9mm
Silver, box 20: . . . . . . $40.31–$44.99
Pow'RBall, box 20: . . . $31.99–$34.99

HUNTER

Features: Bone-breaking loads for the handgun hunter; expanding bullet varieties include Swift A-frame, Swift Scirocco II, Bonded Core Jacketed Soft Point, jacketed soft point, and jacketed hollowpoint; non-expanding bullets include Round Nose Penetrator, hard cast, and full metal jacket
Available in: .45 Colt +P, .454 Casull, .460 Rowland, .460 S&W Mag., .500 S&W Mag.
Box 20: . . . . $35.99–$84.99

D Dupleks USA

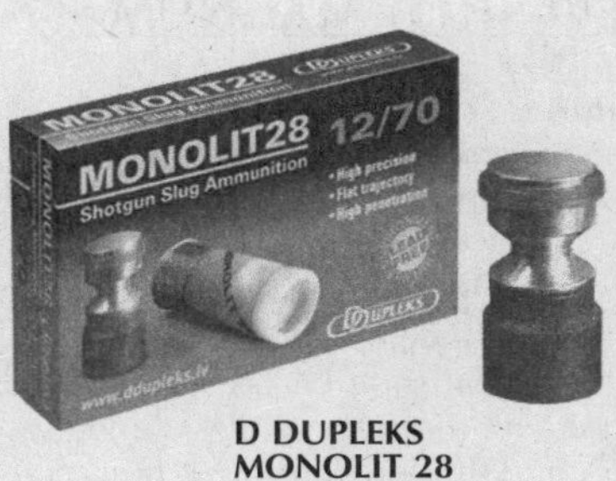

D DUPLEKS MONOLIT 28

DUPO 28

Description: An expanding slug of non-toxic steel and polyethylene construction; works in smoothbore and rifled barrels; 1,460 fps with 2,050 ft.-lb. of muzzle energy
Available in: 12 ga. (2 ¾ in.)
Box of 5: $11.99

HEXOLIT 32

Features: Expanding slug with polymer bearing bands that prevent slug contact with the barrel, so safe for use in both rifled and smoothbore barrels; one-piece wad column; six-piece fragmentation after hit; eco-friendly for use in areas that prohibit lead projectiles
Available in: 12 ga. (2 ¾ in.)
Box 5: $13.99

KAVIAR SLUG

Features: Home-defense frangible hollowpoint slug made of a combination of pellets and polyethylene; reduced recoil; also suitable for use on steel targets; designed for smoothbore, suitable for rifled bores
Available in: 12 ga. (2¾ in.)
Box 5: $14.99

MONOLIT 28

Description: A deep-penetrating slug of solid non-toxic steel/polyethylene construction; can be used in both smoothbores and rifled barrels; flat ogive; 1,460 fps/2,070 ft-lb. muzzle energy
Available in: 12 ga. (2 ¾ in.)
Box of 5: $8.99

MONOLIT 32

Features: A solid steel hunting slug suitable for both rifled and smooth bores; obstacle penetrating; one-piece wad; flat fore-front; self-stabilizing
Available in: 12 ga. (2 ¾ in.)
Box 5: $8.99

Eley

ELEY .38 SUPER COMP

.38 SUPER COMP

Description: A major power-factor round for IPSC/USPSA and 3-Gun competitors; rimless case; copper-jacketed bullet
Available in: .38 Super (124 gr.)
Box of 50: $25.99

Environ-Metal/Hevi-Shot

ENVIRON-METAL/ HEVI-SHOT HEVI-BISMUTH UPLAND

HEVI-BISMUTH UPLAND

Description: Bismuth loads in 12- and 20-ga., No. 5 only
Available in: 12 ga. (2 ¾ in.), 20 ga. (2 ¾ in.)
Box of 25: $52.99

HEVI-BISMUTH WATERFOWL

Description: Bismuth loads for the waterfowler
Available in: 10 ga. (3 ½ in.), 12 ga. (3 ½ in., 3 in., 2 ¾ in.), 16 ga. (2 ¾ in.), 20 ga. (3 in.), 28 ga. (2 ¾ in., 3 in.)
Box of 25: . . . . $50.99–$61.99

HEVI-DUTY CENTERFIRE

Features: Steel-safe frangible projectiles; non-toxic
Available in: 9mm
Box 50: $39.99

Environ-Metal/Hevi-Shot

ENVIRON-METAL/HEVI-SHOT HEVI-METAL LONGER RANGE

ENVIRON-METAL/ HEVI-SHOT HEVI-X STRUT

HEVI-HAMMER

Description: A unique duplex load of steel shot under Bismuth shot and with a layer of flax seed under the crimp
Available in: 12 ga. (3 in.), 20 ga. (3 in.)
Box of 25:. $32.99

HEVI-METAL LONGER RANGE

Description: Improved bismuth pellets are 16 percent denser than previous Hevi-Shot Heavier Than Steel shot
Available in: 10 ga. (3½ in.), 12 ga. (3½ in., 3 in., 2¾ in.), 20 ga. (3 in.)
Box of 25:. . . . . $27.99–$47.99

HEVI-METAL TURKEY

Features: A layered load that combines premium steel shot with HEVI-Shot pellets; timeless testing of various shot load methods found layering to provide the most pellets on target and the best knockdown performance
Available in: 12 Ga. (3 in., 3½ in.), 20 Ga. (3 in.)
Box 5:. . . . .$10.49–$13.99

HEVI-SHOT DEAD COYOTE!

Features: With these HEVI-Shot T-shot loads, you can be deadly at ranges you never thought possible with a 12 gauge; the 3-in. load pounds out 50 perfectly round pellets at 1,350 fps. 10 percent heavier than lead, 54 percent denser than steel; every 50 rounds includes a dry-storage box.
Available in: 12 Ga. (3 in., 3½ in.)
3-in., box 10: $83.99
3½-in., box 10:. $89.99

HEVI-SHOT HEVI-SNOW

Features: A high-speed, non-toxic load for skies full of snow geese
Available in: 12 ga. (3 in., 3 ½ in.); Shot sizes: 1, 2, BB, BBB
Box 25:. $18.99

HEVI-SHOT HEVI-X

Features: A tungsten-based load for waterfowl hunters in Hevi Metal's Deadlier at Distance line; allows hunters to shoot two shot sizes smaller than normal to put more pellets on target
Available in: 12 ga. (2 ¾ in., 3 in., 3 ½ in./ No. 2, 4, BB), 20 ga. (3 in./No. 2, 4), 28 ga. (2 ¾ in./No. 4, 6)
Box 25:. $41.99

HEVI-X STRUT

Description: A tungsten-based load for tom hunting; No. 6 Heavier Than Lead tungsten over No. 5 Heavier Than Steel Hevi-X
Available in: 12 ga. (3 in., 2 ¾ in.), 20 ga. (3 in.)
Box of 5: . . . .$23.99–$26.99

HEVI-SHOT MAGNUM BLEND

Features: Put more lethal pellets in your pattern with a combination of No. 5, 6, and 7 HEVI-13 shot, and boost your lethal range by 14 to 17 percent; buffered and moly-coated pellets produce a denser pattern than conventional shot; HEVI-13 delivers 40 percent more knockdown energy and up to 40 percent longer range than lead shells
Available in: 10 Ga. (3½-in.), 12 Ga. (3 in., 3½ in.) 20 Ga. (3 in.)
Box 5:. . . . . $32.99–$51.99

Federal Ammunition

FEDERAL AMERICAN EAGLE MSR AMMO CANS

FEDERAL BYOB

Rifle Ammunition

AMERICAN EAGLE BUCKETS

Description: Practice ammo in bulk and reasonably priced for hours of fun on the range
Available in: .223 Rem. (55 gr.)
Box 200:. $165.99
Box 300:. $248.99
Box 1000: . . . . $804.29–$829.99

AMERICAN EAGLE FULL METAL JACKET BOATTAIL

Features: Accurate, non-expanding bullets; flat shooting trajectory, leaves small exit holes in game, and put clean holes in paper; smooth, reliable feeding into semiautomatics
Available in: .223 Rem., 5.56 NATO, .224 Valkyrie, 6.5 Creedmoor, 6.5X55 Swedish Mauser, 6.8 Rem. SPC, .300 Blk. .308 Win., .30-06 Spfd., 7.62X39 Russian, .50 BMG
Box 20:. . . . .$22.49–$49.99
Box 10 .50 BMG: $66.99

AMERICAN EAGLE MSR AMMO CANS

Description: If .223/5.56 NATO is your game, this is how to stock up your ammo supply; all are full metal jacket boattails; comes in heavy-duty metal can
Available in: .223 Rem. (55 gr.), 5.56 NATO (55 gr.). 5.56 NATO (62 gr.)
Box 420:. . . . . $364.99–$366.99

BYOB

Features: Bulk rimfire in "Bring Your Own Bucket" packs
Available in: .17 HMR (17 gr. jacketed hollowpoint), .22 LR (36 gr. copper-plated hollowpoint), .22 WMR (50 gr. jacketed hollowpoint)
.22 LR: . . . . $45.99–$372.99
.17 HMR: . . . . $79.99–$639.99
.22 WMR:. . . . . $74.99–$591.99

EDGE TLR

Features: Uses the exclusive Slipstream polymer tip to initiate expansion at long range; at close the bullet's copper shank and bonded lead core retain weight for consistent, lethal penetration; long, sleek profile offers an extremely high BC; AccuChannel groove technology improves accuracy and reduces drag
Available in: .270 Win., .270 WSM, 7mm Rem. Mag., .308 Win., .30-06 Spfd., .300 Win. Mag., .300 WSM
Box 20:. . . . . $47.99–$59.99

FEDERAL HAMMERDOWN

FEDERAL PREMIUM CENTERFIRE SWIFT SCIROCCO II

FUSION RIFLE

Features: This specialized deer bullet electrochemically joins pure copper to an extreme pressure-formed core to ensure optimum performance. The result is high terminal energy on impact that radiates lethal shock throughout the target. This energy is optimized through mass weight retention, a top secretive tip-skiving process and superior bullet integrity.
Available in: .223 Rem., .22-250 Rem., .224 Valkyrie, .243 Win., .25-06 Rem., 6.5 Grendel, 6.5x55 Swedish Mauser, .260 Rem., 6.8 SPC, .270 Win., .270 WSM, 7mm-08, .280 Rem., 7mm Rem. Mag., 7mm WSM, 7.62x39 Soviet, .30-30 Win. 6.5 Creedmoor, .308 Win., .30-06 Spfd., .300 Win. Mag., .300 WSM, .338 Federal, .338 Win. Mag., .35 Whelen, .375 H&H Mag.,.45-70 Govt., .450 Bushmaster, .350 Legend
Box 20: . . . . $30.99–$74.99

GOLD MEDAL BERGER HYBRID

Features: Rounds feature a Berger bullet with a high BC to provide flat trajectories, less wind drift, and surgical long-range accuracy; Gold Medal match primers; Federal brass; specially formulated propellants
Available in: 6mm Creedmoor, 6.5 Creedmoor, .300 Win. Mag., .300 Norma Mag.
Box 20: . . . . $46.99–$133.99

GOLD MEDAL SIERRA MATCHKING BOATTAIL HOLLOWPOINT

Features: Long ranges are its specialty; excellent choice for everything from varmints to big game animals; tapered, boattail design provides extremely flat trajectories; higher downrange velocity for more energy at the point of impact; reduced wind drift
Available in: .223 Rem., .224 Valiyrie, 6mm Creedmoor, 6.5 Creedmoor, .260 Rem., .308 Win., 7.62x51 NATO, .30-06 Spfd., .300 Win. Mag., .338 Lapua Mag.
Box 20: . . . . $33.99–$139.99

HAMMERDOWN

Description: Designed for lever-action rifles; bullets optimized for terminal performance; nickel-plated cases
Available in: .357 Mag. (170 gr.), .327 Fed. (127 gr.), .44 Mag. (270 gr.), .45 Colt (250 gr.), .30-30 Win. (150 gr.), .45-70 Govt. (300 gr.)
Handgun, box 20: . . . $25.99–$36.99
Rifle, box 20: . . . . $34.99–$61.99

HUNTER MATCH .22 LONG RIFLE

Features: High-velocity long-range round; hollowpoint designed for optimum expansion at 100 yards; nickel-plated case
Available in: .22 LR
Box 50: $7.99

NON-TYPICAL

Features: New line designed for deer hunting; soft-point bullet with a concentric jacket
Available in: .243 Win., 6.5 Creedmoor, .270 Win., .30-30 Win., .308 Win., .30-06 Spfd., .300 Win. Mag., 7mm Rem. Mag. .450 Bushmaster, .350 Legend, 7mm-08 Rem.
Box 20: . . . . $28.99–$53.99

POWER-SHOK COPPER

Features: Copper-alloy construction; hollow-point design expands consistently; accurate, reliable performance; large wound channels and efficient energy transfer to the target; lead-free; California-legal; federal brass and primers
Available in: .243 Win, .270 Win., .308 Win., .30-06 Spfd., .300 Blackout, .300 Win. Mag., .300 WSM
Box 20: . . . . $33.99–$56.99

PREMIUM CENTERFIRE BARNES TSX

Features: One of Federal's most popular hunting designs resurrected. Deep hollowpoint, monolithic bullet design has more than 99% weight retention
Available in: .223 Rem., .224 Valkyrie, .243 Win., .25-06 Rem., 6.5 Creedmoor, .270 Win., .270 WSM, 7mm-08 Rem., .308 Win., .30-30 Win., .30-06 Spfd., 7mm Rem. Mag., .300 WSM, .300 Win. Mag.
Box 20: . . . . $37.99–$64.99

PREMIUM CENTERFIRE BERGER HYBRID HUNTER

Features: Features a low-drag bullet profile with a hybrid tangent/secant ogive design. Very high BC; Gold Medal primers; nickel-plated brass
Available in: 6.5 Creedmoor, .270 Win., .270 WSM, 7mm Rem. Mag., .280 Ackley Improved, .30-06 Spfd., .300 Win., .300 WSM
Box 20: . . . . $45.99–$64.99

PREMIUM CENTERFIRE NOSLER PARTITION

Features: Bullet features a partitioned lead core and shank that allows the front half to mushroom while the rear core remains intact for deep penetration and stopping power
Available in: .223 Rem., .22-250 Rem., 6mm Rem., .243 Win., .25-06 Rem., .270 Win., .270 WSM, .280 Rem., 7mm Rem. Mag., .30-30 Win., .308 Win. .30-06 Spfd., .300 Win. Mag., .300 WSM, .338 Win. Mag., .338 RUM, .375 H&H
Box 20: . . . . $36.99–$97.99

PREMIUM CENTERFIRE SIERRA GAMEKING BOATTAIL SOFTPOINT

Features: Proven performer on small game and thin-skinned medium game; aerodynamic tip for a flat trajectory; exposed soft point expands rapidly for hard hits, even as velocity slows at longer ranges
Available in: .243 Win., .25-06 Rem., .260 Rem., .270 Win., 7-30 Waters, 7mm Rem. Mag., .308 Win., .30-06 Spfd.
Box 20: . . . . $37.99–$51.99

PREMIUM CENTERFIRE SWIFT SCIROCCO II

Description: Advanced streamlined bullet design with a high B.C.; improved secant ogive; tapered copper jacket bonded to a lead core; polymer tip for low-velocity expansion
Available in: .243 Win. (90 gr.) 6.5 Creedmoor (130 gr.), .270 Win. (130 gr.), .270 WSM (130 gr.), 7mm Rem. Mag. (150 gr.), .308 Win. (165 gr.), .30-06 Spfd. (165 gr.), .300 Win. Mag. (180 gr.), .300 WSM (180 gr.)
Box of 20: . . . . $56.99–$71.99

Federal Ammunition

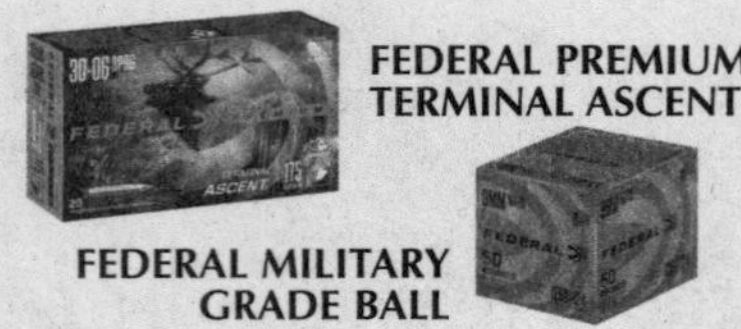
FEDERAL PREMIUM TERMINAL ASCENT

FEDERAL MILITARY GRADE BALL

PREMIUM CENTERFIRE TERMINAL ASCENT

Description: Long sleek bullets have high B.C. and Federal's AccuChannel groove technology that reduces drag and improves accuracy; Slipstream polymer tip; copper shank; bonded lead core
Available in: 6.5 Creedmoor (130 gr.), 6.5 PRC (130 gr.), .270 Win. (136 gr.), .270 WSM (136 gr.), .280 Ackley Improved (155 gr.), 7mm Rem. Mag. (155 gr.), .308 Win. (175 gr.), .30-06 Spfd. (175 gr.), .300 Win. Mag. (200 gr.), .300 WSM (200 gr.), .28 Nosler
Box of 20:. . . . . $53.99–$98.99

PREMIUM CENTERFIRE TROPHY BONDED TIP

Features: Built on the Trophy Bonded Bear Claw platform to provide deep penetration and high weight retention; sleek profile, with tapered heel and translucent polymer tip; nickel-plated; available as component
Available in: .223 Rem., .270 Win., .270 WSM, .270 Wby. Mag., 7mm-08 Rem., .280 Rem., 7mm Rem. Mag., 7mm WSM, 7mm Wby. Mag., 7mm STW, .308 Win., .30-06 Spfd., .300 H&H Mag., .300 Wby. Mag., .300 Win. Mag., .300 RUM, .300 WSM, .338 Federal, .338 Win. Mag.
Box 20:. . . . . $49.99–$107.99

PREMIUM SAFARI TROPHY BONDED BEAR CLAW

Features: Ideal for medium to large dangerous game; jacket and core are 100 percent fusion-bonded for reliable bullet expansion from 25 yds to extreme ranges; bullet retains 95 percent of its weight for deep penetration; hard solid copper base tapering to a soft, copper nose section for controlled expansion
Available in: .375 H&H, .416 Rigby, .416 Rem. Mag., .458 Win. Mag., .458 Lott, .470 NE
MSRP: . . . . $121.99–$327.99

PREMIUM SAFARI TROPHY BONDED SLEDGEHAMMER SOLID

Features: Use it on the largest, most dangerous game in the world; Jack Carter design maximizes stopping power; bonded bronze solid with a flat nose that minimizes deflection off bone and muscle for a deep straight wound channel
Available in: .375 H&H Mag., .416 Rigby, .416 Rem. Mag., .458 Win. Mag., .458 Lott, .470 NE
Box 20:. . . . . $137.99–$284.99

PREMIUM CENTERFIRE TROPHY COPPER MEATEATER

Description: The "official ammunition" of Steve Rinella's MeatEater brand; tipped bullet cavity; grooved bullet shank; boattail, polymer tip
Available in: .223 Rem., .243 Win., .25-06 Rem., 6.5 Creedmoor, .270 Win., .270 WSM, 7mm-08 Rem., .280 Rem., 7mm Rem. Mag., 7mm WSM, .30-30 Win., .308 Win., .30-06 Spfd., .300 Win. Mag., .300 WSM, .338 Federal, .338 Win. Mag., .338 Lapua Mag.
Box 20:. . . . . $35.99–$105.99

PREMIUM SAFARI WOODLEIGH HYDRO SOLID

Features: Provides safari hunters superb accuracy, consistent performance, and tremendous impact; special heavy jackets provide excellent weight retention, up to 100 percent for solids
Available in: 9.3x62 Mauser, 9.3x74 R, .370 Sako Mag., .375 H&H Mag., .416 Rigby, .416 Rem. Mag., .458 Win. Mag., 458 Lott, .470 NE, .500 NE
Box 20:. . . . . $141.99–$320.99

SYNTECH PCC

Description: Created specifically for better functionality in pistol-caliber carbine rifles, especially those used in competition; Total Synthetic Jacket reduces heat and fouling
Available in: 9mm (130 gr.)
Box of 50:. $26.99

VARMINT & PREDATOR

Features: A line of coyote and prairie dog ammo priced for high-volume shooters; V-Max bullets; Federal brass and primer
Available in: .204 Ruger, .22 Hornet, .222 Rem., .223 Rem., .224 Valkyrie, .22-250 Rem., .220 Swift, .243 Win., .25-06 Rem., 6.5 Creedmoor, .308 Win.
Box 20 or 50: . . . . . . $24.99–$135.99

V-SHOK SPEER TNT GREEN HOLLOWPOINT

Features: Brings non-tox technology to the Federal Premium V-Shok varmint hunting line; a totally lead-free bullet that couples explosive expansion with match-grade accuracy
Available in: .22 Hornet, .222 Rem., .223 Rem., .22-250 Rem.
Box 20:. . . . . $31.99–$34.99
Box 50 (.22 Hornet only):. . . .$86.99

Handgun Ammunition

AMERICAN EAGLE FULL METAL JACKET

Features: Good choice for range practice and reducing lead fouling in the barrel; jacket extends from the nose to the base, preventing bullet expansion and barrel leading; primarily as military ammunition for recreational shooting
Available in: 5.7X28, .25 ACP, .32 ACP, .327 Federal, .380 ACP, 9mm Luger, .357 SIG, .38 Spl., .40 S&W, 10mm, .45 ACP
Box 50:. . . . . $26.99–$66.99

AMERICAN EAGLE LEAD ROUND NOSE

Features: Great training round for practicing at the range; 100 percent lead with no jacket; excellent accuracy and very economical
Available in: .38 Spl.
Box 50:. $33.99

FUSION

Features: Bullet weights and velocities have been developed to be lethal on whitetails, without pounding the shooter
Available in: .357 Mag., 10mm Auto .44 Rem. Mag., .454 Casull, .460 S&W, .500 S&W, 50 Action Express
Box 20:. . . . . $27.99–$55.99

MILITARY GRADE BALL

Description: High-grade full-metal-jacket practice ammo that has a staked primer; mouth and primer sealed; NATO spec brass; assembled to NATO requirements
Available in: 9mm (124 gr.)
Box of 50:. $27.99

FEDERAL PRACTICE & DEFEND PACKS

FEDERAL PUNCH

FEDERAL SYNTECH BULK BUCKET

PERSONAL DEFENSE HST

Features: Provides near 100 percent weight retention through most barriers; consistent expansion, optimum penetration, and superior terminal performance, it's specially designed hollow point won't plug while passing through a variety of barriers
Available in: .380 ACP, 9mm, .40 S&W, 10mm Auto, .45 ACP
Box 20: . . . . $33.99–$44.99

PERSONAL DEFENSE HST MICRO

Features: Designed for subcompact and micro pistol platforms; available in .380 ACP, .38 Special +P, and 9mm with a deeply seated bullet that stabilizes powder burn rates and velocities
Available in: .380 ACP (99 gr.), 38 Special +P (130 gr.), 9mm (150-gr.)
Box 20: . . . . $33.99–$35.99

PERSONAL DEFENSE HYDRA-SHOK DEEP

Features: New version of Hydra-Shok, intended for better results when fired through barriers; 50-percent deeper penetration than original Hydra-Shok
Available in: .380 ACP, 9mm, .40 S&W, .45 ACP
Box 20: . . . . $32.99–$38.99

PERSONAL DEFENSE REVOLVER

Features: Economical personal defense round for revolvers; quick, positive expansion
Available in: .32 H&R Mag., .357 Mag.
.32 H&R, box 20: $28.99
.357 Mag, box 20: $32.99

PRACTICE & DEFEND PACKS

Description: Boxes of ballistically paired Syntech Training Match rounds (50 count) and HST self-defense loads (50 count)
Available in: 9mm (124 gr., 147 gr.), .40 S&W (180 gr.), .45 ACP (230 gr.)
Box of 100: . . . . $73.99–$88.99

PUNCH

Description: These personal defense loads get a Punch jacketed hollow-point bullet with a skived jacket and soft lead core; nickel-plated brass cases; sealed primer
Available in: .380 ACP (85 gr.), .38 Spec. +P (120 gr.), 9mm (124 gr.), .40 S&W (165 gr.), .45 ACP (230 gr.), 10mm Auto (200-gr.)
Box of 20: . . . . $20.99–$33.99

SOLID CORE

Description: Touted as hunting rounds, these are heavy-hitting bone-crushing rounds; Syntech jacket reduces fouling; super-hard lead core
Available in: 9mm +P (147 gr.), .357 Mag. (180 gr.), .40 S&W (200 gr.), 10mm Auto (200 gr.), .45 ACP +P (240 gr.), .44 Mag. (300 gr.)
Box of 20: . . . . $34.99–$39.99

SYNTECH ACTION PISTOL

Features: Designed for action shooting competitors; flat-nosed bullets help with steel target knockdown while reducing bullet fracturing and splash back; Federal's TSJ–Total Synthetic Jacket–reduces bore fouling; clean powders; Federal's lead-free Catalyst primer
Available in: 9mm (150 gr.), .40 S&W (205 gr.), .45 ACP (.220 gr.)
Box 50: . . . . $26.99–$34.99

SYNTECH BULK BUCKET

Description: Save money and practice more with these handgun rounds in bulk; lead-free Catalyst primer; Syntech projectiles with TSJ polymer jackets
Available in: 9mm (124 gr.), .40 S&W (165 gr.), .45 ACP (230 gr.)
9mm: . . . . $87.99–$240.99
.45 ACP: . . . . $210.99–$217.99

SYNTECH DEFENSE

Features: Hollowpoint design separates into three segments for additional trauma, while the core continues penetration; Catalyst lead-free primer; polymer jacket reduces fouling
Available in: 9mm (138 gr.), .40 S&W (175 gr.), .45 ACP (205 gr.)
Box 20: . . . . $22.99–$26.99

SYNTECH PCC

Features: A 9mmm load specifically developed for reliable functionality in pistol-caliber carbines; minimizes splashback so a great choice for competitors; synthetic jacket reduces fouling; lead-free Catalyst primer
Available in: 9mm (130 gr.)
Box 50: $26.99

SYNTECH RANGE

Features: Polymer-encapsulated bullet eliminates metal contact with the bore; Catalyst lead-free primer; no copper jacket means improved safety when used on steel targets; reduced recoil
Available in: 9mm, .40 S&W, .45 ACP
9mm: . . . . $26.99–$240.99
.40 S&W: . . . . $30.99–$217.99
.45 ACP: . . . . $34.99–$210.99

SYNTECH TRAINING MATCH

Features: Provides the same velocities, trajectories, and point of impact's as Federal's Personal Defense HST and Tactical HST loadings, but with a Catalyst lead-free primer and synthetic bullet jacket that reduces fouling; purple bullet color makes use as a training round easily identifiable
Available in: 9mm (124 gr., 147 gr.), .40 S&W (180 gr.), .45 ACP (230 gr.)
Box 50: . . . . $26.99–$34.99

Shotgun Ammunition

3RD DEGREE WITH HEAVYWEIGHT TSS MEATEATER

Description: The "official" turkey ammunition of Steve Rinella's MeatEater brand; three-stage payload of 20% No. 6 Flitestopper, 40% copper-plated No. 5, and 40% Heavyweight TSS shot; Flitecontrol Flex wad; portion of the proceeds go to benefit the National Wild Turkey Federation
Available in: 12 ga. (3½ in., 3 in.)
Box of 5: . . . . $28.99–$33.99

Federal Ammunition

FEDERAL BISMUTH MEATEATER

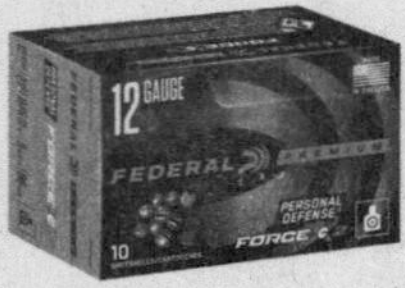

FEDERAL PERSONAL DEFENSE SHOTSHELLS FORCE X2

FEDERAL SPEED-SHOK SNOW GOOSE

BISMUTH MEATEATER

Description: A return to bismuth non-toxic shot makes this the "official" waterfowl/upland load for Steven Rinella's MeatEater brand; Flitecontrol Fex wad; lead-free Catalyst primer
Available in: 12 ga. (3 in., 2 ¾ in.), 20 ga. (3 in.)
Box of 25:. . . . . $62.99–$71.99

BLACK CLOUD FS STEEL

Available in: 10-gauge 3½-inch No. 2, BB; 12-gauge 3½-inch No. 3, 2, 1, BB, BBB; 12-gauge 3-inch No. 4, 3, 2, 1, BB, BBB; 12-gauge 2¾-inch No. 4, 3, 2, BB; 20-gauge 3-inch No. 4, 3, 2, 1
Box 25:. . . . . $24.99–$44.99

BLACK CLOUD TSS

Features: A new and improved duplex Black Cloud with Heavyweight Tungsten Super Shot pellets (60%) and Flitestopper Steel (40%) backed by Flitecontrol Flex wad; Catalyst lead-free primer
Available in: 12-gauge 3-in. 1¼-ounce load in No. 7 TSS/BB FS Steel or No. 9 TSS/No. 3 FS Steel; 20-gauge 2¾-inch 1 1/8-ounce load in No. 9 TSS/No. 3 FS Steel
Box 10:. . . . . $42.99–$47.99

GOLD MEDAL GRAND PAPER

Available in: 12 Ga. (2¾ in.) only, in 1 1/8-oz. loads of 7.5 or 8, or 1-oz. load of 8
Box of 25:. . . . . $15.99–$16.99

GOLD MEDAL GRAND PLASTIC

Available in: 12-gauge 2¾-inch No. 9, 8, 7½; general target shooting and dedicated competition loads available in a variety of velocities and payloads
Box of 25:. . . . . $12.99–$13.99

GRAND SLAM

Features: FLITECONTROL FLEX wad; load of copper-plated lead shot; 20 ga. is available in No. 5 only; 12 ga. is available in 4, 5, and 6; 10 ga. is available in 4 and 5
Available in: 10 ga. (3.5 in.), 12 ga. (2.75 in., 3 in., 3.5 in.), 20 ga. (3 in.)
Box 5:. . . . . $16.99–$27.99

HEAVYWEIGHT TSS

Features: Four duplex loads of HEAVYWEIGHT TSS (Tungsten Super Shot) and a single-size fine-shot TSS load provide superior pellet counts--more than double the pellet count of a No. 5 load in the same weight
Available in: 20-ga. 3-in., #7/#9, #8/#10, #9, or #7
Box 5:. . . . . $53.99–$63.99

HI-BIRD

Features: Two-piece wad features SoftCell technology to decrease perceived recoil and produce more consistent long-range patterns; dense long-range patterns and increased down-range energy
Available in: 12-gauge 2¾-inch No. 8, 7, 6, 5, 4
Box 25:. . . . . $13.99–$17.99

PERSONAL DEFENSE SHOTSHELLS

Features: Just as the name implies, buckshot loads for personal-/home-defense use; one of two 12-gauge loads keep shot column tight with Flitecontrol wad; .410 is suitable for revolver use
Available in: .410-bore (3-inch #4 Buck, #000 Buck; 2½-inch No. 4 shot, #000 Buck); 12-gauge (2¾-inch #00 Buck with Flitecontrol or #4 Buck without); 20-gauge (2¾-inch #4 Buck)
.410-bore, box 20: . . . $22.99–$26.99
12-ga., box 5:. $10.99

PERSONAL DEFENSE SHOTSHELLS FORCE X2

Description: Defensive loads of FX2 buckshot designed to split in two upon impact, doubling the number of wound channels; nine-pellet load
Available in: 12 ga. (2 ¾ in.)
Box of 10:. $22.99

PRAIRIE STORM FS STEEL

Available in: 12-gauge and 20-gauge 3-inch No. 4, 3
Box 25:. . . . . $25.99–$27.99

SHORTY

Features: Just 1¾-inches long, perfect for use in short-chambered older guns and offers performance similar to 2 ¾-inch shells
Available in: 12 ga.; Shot size: #4 Buck, rifled slug, 8
Box 10:. . . . . $7.99–$9.99

SPEED-SHOK SNOW GOOSE

Description: Just for snow goose hunters and their long, big limit seasons with two moderately priced steel loads
Available in: 12-ga. 3-in; No. 2 or BB
Box 25:. $18.99

SPEED-SHOK WATERFOWL

Available in: 10 ga. (3 ½ in., No. T, BBB, BB, 2); 12 ga. (3 ½ in., No. T, BBB, BB, 1, 2, 3, 4); 12 ga. (3 in., No. T, BBB, BB, 1, 2, 3, 4, 6); 12 ga. (2¾ in., No. BB, 2, 3, 4, 6); 16 ga. (2¾ in., No. BB, 2, 4); 20 ga. (3 in., No. 1, 2, 3, 4); 20 ga. (2¾ in., No. 4, 6, 7); 28 ga. (2¾ in., No. 6); .410-bore (3-in. No. 6)
Box 25:. . . . . $15.99–$39.99

TOP GUN, TOP GUN SUBSONIC

Available in: 12- or 20-gauge 2.75-inch in No. 7., 8, 9; multiple loadings available, including a subsonic load in 12-gauge in No. 7.
Box 5, 25, 100: . . . . . . $12.99–$41.99

TOP GUN SPORTING

Features: A dedicated sporting clays series of loads meant to speed velocities and minimize recoil; with an eight-segment crimp
Available in: 12 ga. (2 ¾ in. 1-ounce No. 7.5, 8); 20 ga. (2 ¾ in. 7/8-ounce 7.5, 8); 28 ga. (2 ¾ in. ¾-ounce No. 7.5, 8, 9); .410-bore (2 ½ in. ½-ounce No. 7.5, 8, 9)
Box 25:. . . . . $10.99–$17.99

Federal Ammunition

TOP GUN STEEL
Available in: 12 Ga., 20 Ga. (2¾ in.); Shot size: 7
Box 25:. $11.99

UPLAND STEEL
Features: Quail, woodcock, pheasant and other upland game on lands with traditional ammo restrictions are now easier to add to the dinner table with these high-velocity steel loads
Available in: 12 ga. (2¾ in. 11/8-ounce No. 6, 7.5); 20 ga. (2¾ in. ¾-ounce No. 5, 7.5)
Box 25:. . . . . $13.99–$26.99

Shotgun Slugs

TROPHY COPPER SABOT SLUG
Features: A copper slug that incorporates some of the most advanced technology in the industry; better accuracy, less drop, manageable recoil (similar to a .30-06 Spfd.) and consistent penetration and expansion; unique two-part sabot design achieves accuracy through a clean launch and improved projectile support
Available in: 12 Ga., 20 Ga. (2¾ in., 3 in.)
Box 5: . . . . $17.99–$19.99

TRUBALL RIFLED SLUG
Available in: 12, 20 Ga. (2¾ in., 3 in.)
Box 5:. . . . . $5.99–$7.99

Fiocchi USA

FIOCCHI RANGE DYNAMICS HANDGUN

Rifle Ammunition

EXTREMA RIFLE
Features: Combining the best bullets in the business with our precision-drawn brass cases gives you the best combination of value and performance; uses bullets like the Hornady SST, V Max, and Sierra Game King to provide a combination of accuracy, high ballistic coefficients, and reliable expansion
Available in: .204 Ruger, .222 Rem., .223 Rem., .22-50 Rem., .243 Win., 6.5 Creedmoor, .260 Rem., .270 Win., 6.5X55 Swedish Mauser, 7mm-08, .300 BLK, .308 Win., .30-06 Spfd., .300 Win. Mag., 7mm Rem. Mag.
Box 20:. . . . . $24.99–$88.99
Box 50 (.223 Rem., .204 Ruger): $59.99

EXTREMA SCIROCCO II RIFLE
Features: Big-game hunters get a dedicated cartridge modeled on the company's Extrema Rifle One loadings, but with polymer tipped Scirocco II boattail projectiles from Swift
Available in: .270 Win., 6.5 Creedmoor, .30-06 Spfd., 7mm Rem. Mag., .300 Win. Mag.
Box 20:. . . . . $54.99–$83.99

RANGE DYNAMICS RIFLE
Features: Training and target loads for rifle shooters, most calibers sold in bulk
Available in: .223 Rem., .300 BLK, .308 Win.
Box of: 100, 200
Box 100:. . . . . $114.99–$292.30

SHOOTING DYNAMICS RIFLE
Features: High-quality reloadable brass cases combined with quality full metal jacket, soft point, or flat soft point (for lever guns) make sure your shooting dollar goes further
Available in: 5.56 NATO, .223 Rem., .22-250 Rem., .243 Win., .25-06 Rem., 6.5 Creedmoor, .270 Win., 7mm-08 Rem., .300 BLK, .308 Win., .30-06 Spfd., 7.62x39 Russian, .45-70 Gov't.; .223 Rem., 5.56 NATO, .308, and 7.62x39 available in bulk quantities
Box 20:. . . . . $23.99–$63.99

Handgun Ammunition

COWBOY ACTION
Features: Loaded with brass reloadable cases, noncorrosive primers, smokeless powders, and lead bullets coated with lube to reduce leading in the barrel; velocity is on par with what you would expect from period-correct ammo while keeping the recoil to a minimum for timed Cowboy Action competition and to reduce wear and tear on older guns
Available in: .45 Colt, .44 Spec., .357 Mag., .38 Spec., .38 S&W Short, .32 S&W Long, .45-70 Gov't.
Box 50:. $59.99

RANGE DYNAMICS HANDGUN
Features: Training and target load sold in bulk; reloadable brass cases
Available in: .380 ACP, 9mm, .45 ACP
Box of:100, 200 rounds
9mm, box 100:. $64.99
.380, box 100:. $50.00
.45 ACP, box 200:. $120.00

XTP HANDGUN
Features: Combined with nickel-plated cases for positive feeding and extraction when you need it most, qualified primers and clean powders deliver the maximum performance for the ultimate hunting or self-defense application
Available in: .25 ACP, 7.65 Browning, .380 ACP, 9mm, .38 Spec., .38 Spec. +P, .357 Mag., .40 S&W, .45 ACP, .44 S&W Russian, .44 Mag.
MSRP . . . . $29.99–$41.99

Shotgun Ammunition

EXACTA TARGET LOADS
Features: Specifically for competitive shooters; the Target Load Line incldes Crusher, Paper Crusher, and Trap loads
Available in: 12 ga., 28 ga., .410-bore
Box 25:. $14.99

GOLDEN PHEASANT
Features: Golden Pheasant shot shells utilize a special hard, nickel-plated lead shot, based on Fiocchi's strict ballistic tolerances that ensure proven shot consistency and result in deeper penetration, longer ranges, and much tighter patterns
Available in: 12 Ga. (2¾ in., 3 in.), 16 Ga. (2¾ in.), 20, 28 Ga. (2¾ in., 3 in.); Shot sizes: 4, 5, 6, 7.5, 8, 9
Box of 25:. . . . . $19.99–$24.99

Fiocchi USA

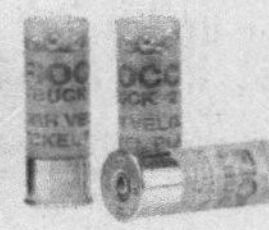

FIOCCHI NICKEL-PLATED BUCKSHOT

NICKEL-PLATED BUCKSHOT

Features: Harder pellets from the nickel plating mean better patterns, better penetration, and no buffer needed
Available in: 12 Ga. (2¾ in.); Shot sizes: 00, 4
Box of 10:................$13.99

WATERFOWL STEEL

HUNTING

Features: Treated steel pellets, the correct wad, and powders that perform in the cold conditions often encountered in waterfowl hunting deliver the kills a waterfowl hunter wants
Available in: 12 Ga. (2¾ in., 3 in.), 20 Ga. (3 in.); Shot sizes: T, BBB, BB, 1, 2, 3, 4, 5, 6
Box 25:.............$15.99–$22.99

GECO

RIFLE AMMUNITION

Features: A range of bullets for training and all types of hunting situations worldwide; GECO offers five different bullet types to cover every hunting situation; GECO PLUS for shooting big game, GECO EXPRESS for the long distance shot, GECO SOFTPOINT as the real all-rounder, GECO SWISS MATCH for .223 competitors, and GECO ZERO, a lead-free line for hunters; made in Germany, which means outstanding accuracy and reliable bullet performance
Available calibers: .223 Rem., .243 Win., .270 WSM, .270 Win., .280 Rem., .30-06 Spfd., .300 Win. Mag., .308 Win., 6.5x55 Swedish Mauser, 7mm Rem. Mag., 7x57, 7x57R, 7x64, 7x65R, 8x57 IRS, 8x57 IS, 9.3x62, 9.3x74R
MSRP..............$9.99–$29.99

RIMFIRE AMMUNITION

Features: Target shooters can always depend on the cartridges perfect functioning, consistent performance and good precision.; reliable rimfire ammunition to guarantee required standards of accuracy at a favorable price
Available in: .22 LR Rifle, .22 LR Semi-Auto
Box 500:...........$14.99–$39.99

PISTOL AMMUNITION

Features: GECO offers 18 loads with cartridges in nine different calibers;

GECO RIMFIRE AMMUNITION

these cover all relevant fields of application like precision shooting, dynamic sport disciplines, hunting, protection, and self-defense.
Available in: .38 Super, .40 S&W, .45ACP, 6.35 Browning, 7.65 Browning (.32 ACP), 9mm Browning Court (.380 ACP), 9mm, 9mm Makarov, 9x21., .357 Mag., .38 Spl. .357 SIG
Box 50:.............$8.49–$30.82

Grasso Holdings/GH Ammunition

GRASSO HOLDINGS/GH AMMUNITION TULAMMO

MAXXTECH

Features: Economical brass-cased ammunition for range practice; Boxer primed, full metal jacket except for the lead .22 LR rimfire
Available in: .380 ACP, 9mm, .40 S&W, .45 ACP, .22 LR, .223 Rem.
Box of: 50/100 (pistol), 20/50 (rifle), 250 (.22 LR)
MSRP.............$12.49–$19.29

TULAMMO

Features: Russian-made steel-cased ammo designed to be range-friendly by minimizing spark risks with a non-steel, brass-jacketed projectile; legal in all 50 states; Berdan primers
Available in: .223 Rem., .30 Carbine, .308 Win., 5.45x39mm, 7.62x39, 7.62x54R
Box 100:...........$34.99–$37.99
Box 50 (.45 ACP):..........$38.99

AMMUNITION

Honor Defense

HONOR DEFENSE FRANGIBLE HOLLOWPOINT

FRANGIBLE HOLLOWPOINT

Features: Previously available only to military and law enforcement, now available to the consumer market; handgun/pistol-caliber carbine rounds with a drilled hollowpoint that's frangible in soft tissue, is lead free, and housed in virgin brass; passes FBI light and heavy clothing, wallboard, plywood, and bare gel protocols
Available in: 9mm
Box 20:................. $19.99

Hornady Manufacturing

HORNADY SUPERFORMANCE MATCH

HORNADY OUTFITTER

Rifle Ammunition

AMERICAN GUNNER RIFLE

Features: The American Gunner line of ammunition is a collection of tried-and-true, versatile loads that are popular with shooters for their target shooting, hunting, or self-defense needs. Made in the USA with premium components, American Gunner ammunition combines generations of ballistics know-how with modern technology. Hornady introduces new rifle calibers to complement the handgun offerings currently available. These rifle options are loaded with match grade hollow point bullets for a broad range of use including self-defense, target shooting, and varmint/small game hunting.
Available in: .223 Rem., 6.5 Creedmoor, .300 BLK, .308 Win., 7.652x39
Box 50:. . . . . $54.99–$81.99

AMERICAN WHITETAIL

Features: Loaded with Hornady InterLock Bullets, optimized loads specifically for deer hunting, and select propellants for greater consistency
Available in: 6.5 Creedmoor, .243 Win., .25-06 Rem., .270 Win., 7mm-08 Rem., 7mm Rem. Mag, 30-30 Win., .308 Win., 30-06 Spfd., .300 Win. Mag, .300 WSM, .350 Legend, .450 Bushmaster
Box 20:. . . . . $30.99–$46.99

BLACK

Features: Designed to function across a wide variety of platforms including direct impingement, gas piston, suppressed, unsuppressed, inertia, bolt, pump, supersonic, subsonic, rifle, mid-length, carbine, or pistol; seven bullet types; 00 buckshot comes in a box of 10
Available in: 5.45x39, .223 Rem., 5.56 NATO, 6.5 Grendel, .224 Valkyrie, 6mm ARC, 6mm Creedmoor, 6.8mm SPC, .300 BLK, 7.62x39, .308 Win., .450 Bushmaster
Box 20:. . . . . $23.99–$45.99

CRITICAL DEFENSE RIFLE

Features: Corrosion-resistant nickel-plated cases; Critical Defense offers improved expansion with limited penetration in self-defense rifles
Available in: .223 Rem., .30 Carbine, .308 Win.
Box 20:. . . . . $32.99–$49.99

CUSTOM

Features: Depending on caliber, Custom ammo is loaded with Hornady SST, InterBond, InterLock, or V-MAX bullets
Available in: .22 Hornet, .218 Bee, .223 Rem., .243 Win., .250 Savage, 6.5 Grendel, .264 Win. Mag., 6.8 SPC, .275 Rigby, .308 Win., .300 BLK, .30-40 Krag, .300 H&H Mag., .303 British, .350 Legend, .358 Win., .405 Win., .450 Bushmaster
Box 20:. . . . . $33.99–$85.99

CUSTOM LITE

Features: CustomLite ammunition is recommended for children, women, and anyone new to the game; offer minimum recoil and a reduced muzzle blast; often paired with SST and RN bullets
Available in: .243 Win, 7mm-08 Rem., .308 Win., .30-06 Spfd.
From:. . . . . $42.99–$44.99

DANGEROUS GAME

Features: These bullets are among the largest offered by Hornady and feature the DGS (Dangerous Game Solid) and the DGX (Dangerous Game eXpanding); made with hard lead/antimony alloy cone and surrounded by a copper-clad steel jacket; straighter penetration comes from a flat meplat that creates more energy than traditional round bullets
Available in: 9.3x62 Mauser, 9.3x74R, .376 Steyr., .375 H&H, .375 H&H Superformance, .375 Ruger, .375 Ruger Superformance, .450/.400 Nitro Express, .416 Ruger, .416 Rem. Mag., .416 Rigby, .404 Jeffery, .450 Nitro Express 3.25-in., .450 Rigby, .458 Win. Mag. Superformance, .458 Win. Mag., .458 Lott, .470 Nitro Express 3.25-in., .500 Nitro Express
Box 20:. . . . . $65.99–$200.99

FRONTIER

Features: Frontier is American made; military grade; brass cases; wide variety of bullet weights and profiles
Available in: .223 Rem., 5.56 NATO, .300 BLK, 6.5 Grendel
Box 20:. . . . . $11.99–$19.99

LEVEREVOLUTION

Features: LEVERevolution bullets travel at a speed of 250 fps and have a faster muzzle velocity than most other conventional lever gun loads; are unbelievably accurate and offer incomparable terminal performance; available in FTX and MonoFlex
Available in: .25-35 Win., 7-30 Waters, .30-30 Win., .307 Win., .308 Marlin Express, .32 Win. Spec., .338 Marlin Express, .348 Win., .35 Rem., .444 Marlin, .45-70 Govt., .450 Marlin
Box 20:. . . . . $38.99–$76.99

MATCH

Features: Match bullets feature a boattail hollow point design that provides both accuracy and speed; these bullets' jackets feature near-zero wall thickness, which leads to uniformity throughout the jacket; case weight and internal capacity are also consistent throughout Match ammunition
Available in: .223 Rem., .224 Valkyrie, .260 Rem., 6mm ARC, 6mm Creedmoor, 6.5 Creedmoor, 6.5 PRC, .308 Win., .300 Win. Mag., .300 PRC, .338 Lapua Mag., .50 BMG (box 10)
Box 20:. . . . . $32.99–$154.99

OUTFITTER

Features: Dedicated hunting line of rifle cartridges featuring: corrosion-resistant, waterproof nickel-plated cases; monolithic copper alloy GMX bullets
Available in: .243 Win., .257 Wby. Mag., 6.5 Creedmoor, .270 Win., .270 WSM, 7mm WSM, 7mm Rem. Mag., .300 BLK, .308 Win., .30-06 Spfd., .300 WSM, .300 Win. Mag., .300 Wby. Mag., .300 RUM, .338 Win. Mag., .375 H&H Mag., .375 Ruger
Box 20:. . . . . $52.99–$111.99

Hornady Manufacturing

PRECISION HUNTER

Features: Best-in-class BCs, match-accurate hunting loads, topped with ELD-X Heat Shield Tip bullets
Available in: .243 Win., 6mm ARC, 6mm Creedmoor, .25-06 Rem., .257 Wby. Mag., 6.5 Creedmoor, 6.5 PRC, .270 Win., .270 WSM, 7mm-08 Rem., .280 Rem., .280 Ackley Improved, 7mm WSM, 7mm Rem. Mag., .28 Nosler, 7mm STW, .308 Win., .30-06 Spfd., .300 Rem. SAUM, .300 Ruger Compact Mag, .300 Win. Mag., .300 WSM, .300 Wby. Mag., .300 PRC, .300 RUM. .30-378 Wby. Mag., .338 Lapua Mag.
Box 20:. . . . . $42.99–$154.99

SUBSONIC .300 BLACKOUT

Features: Subsonic .300 Blackout wears a 190-gr. Sub-X (Subsonic eXpanding) bullet; lead core; gilded metal jacket; Flex Tip insert; muzzle velocity is 1,050 fps; muzzle energy is 465 ft-lbs.
Available in: .300 BLK, .30-30 Win., .450 Bushmaster, .45-70 Gov't. (1895 Marlin)
Box 20:. . . . . $36.99–$52.99

SUPERFORMANCE

Features: Superformance bullets are 100–200 fps faster than any other traditional type of bullet on the market today. In addition to their speed, they also offer minimal recoil, muzzle blast, temperature sensativity, and inaccuracies; these bullets are versatile and can be paired with all types of firearms, including semiautomatics, lever guns, and pump actions
Available in: .223 Rem., 5.56 NATO, .243 Win., 6mm Rem., 6mm Creedmoor, .25-06 Rem., .257 Roberts +P, .260 Rem., , 6.5 Creedmoor, 6.5x55 Swedish, .270 Win., 7mm-08 Rem., 7mm Rem. Mag., .300 Savage, .308 Win., .30 TC, .30-06 Spfd., .300 Ruger Compact Mag., .300 Win. Mag., .300 WSM, .338 Ruger Compact Mag., .338 Win. Mag., .35 Whelen, .444 Marlin
Box 20:. . . . . $31.99–$164.99

SUPERFORMANCE MATCH

Features: Achieves muzzle velocity 100 to 200 fps faster than conventional .308 Win. loads; AMAX or Hornady Boattail Hollowpoint Match bullets featuring AMP (Advanced Manufacturing Process) jackets
Available in: .223 Rem., 5.56 NATO, .308 Win.
Box 20:. . . . . $33.99–$52.99

Handgun Ammunition

AMERICAN GUNNER HANDGUN

Features: XTP (eXtreme Terminal Performance) bullets are exceptionally accurate and deliver excellent versatility and superior ballistic performance; propellants are matched to each load to ensure optimal pressure, velocity, volume and consistency from lot to lot; high quality primers and Hornady cases combine to deliver consistent shooting in the field
Available in: .380 ACP, .40 S&W, .45 ACP, 9mm, 9mm +P, .38 Spl., .357 Mag.
Box 25:. . . . . $24.99–$29.99

COWBOY

Features: These swaged bullets flatten instead of fragment when they reach their targets; diamond knurling ensures that the entire surface of the bullet is well-lubed
Available in: .44-40 Win., .45 Colt
Box 20:. . . . . $18.91–$20.32

CRITICAL DEFENSE HANDGUN

Features: Critical Defense bullets are custom-designed for individual loads, and their shiny silver nickel plating prevents bullet corrosion; Critical Defense ammunition is cannelured and crimped to avoid bullet setback, and clean burning and stable propellants reduce recoil
Available in: .25 ACP, .32 ACP, .32 NAA, 32 H&R Mag., .327 Fed. Mag., .380 ACP, 9mm, 9mm Lite, 9X18 Makarov, .38 Spec., .38 Spec. Lite, .38 Spec. +P, .357 Mag., .40 S&W, .44 Spec., .45 ACP, .45 Colt
Box 25:. . . . . $30.99–$36.99

HORNADY HANDGUN HUNTER

HORNADY AMERICAN GUNNER SHOTGUN

CRITICAL DUTY

Features: Features FlexLock Bullets, crimped and nickel-plated cases, interlocking bands, and a core made of high-antimony lead; these bullets are among the top choices of law enforcement and military professionals and highly reliable
Available in: .357 Mag., .40 S&W, .45 ACP +P, .357 SIG, 9mm, 9mm Luger +P, 10mm Auto
Box 25:. . . . . $33.99–$36.99

HANDGUN HUNTER

Description: A top-end choice for those pursing game with a handgun; MonoFlex projectiles contain a copper alloy; deep cavity has elastomer material that compresses upon impact before pushing out for rapid and wide expansion
Available in: 9mm +P (115 gr.), .357 Mag. (130 gr.), .40 S&W (135 gr.), 10mm Auto (135 gr.), .44 Mag. (200 gr.), .454 Casull (200 gr.), .460 S&W Mag. (200 gr.)
Box of 20, 25:. . . . . . . $39.99–$54.99

Shotgun Ammunition

AMERICAN GUNNER SHOTGUN

Features: Reduced recoil rifled slugs or 00 buckshot; rifled slug is 1 oz., 00 buck holds eight high-antimony swaged pellets
Available in: 12 ga.
Box 5:. . . . . $11.99–$15.99

AMERICAN WHITETAIL RIFLED SLUG

Features: Rifled slug for smooth-bore barrels; 12 gauge 1-ounce rifled, foster style slug or 325-grain InterLock slug; hollow point, tough lead-alloy core; 1,600 feet per second
Available in: 12 Ga.
Box 5:. . . . . $11.99–$15.99

CUSTOM LITE SHOTGUN SLUGS

Features: Delivers 25 percent less recoil than standard loads; for rifled barrels only; FTX bullet improves ballistic coefficient and aids in expansion; lower recoil and muzzle blast while maintaining accuracy and effectiveness out to 150 yds; innovative sabot design enhances accuracy
Available in: 12 Ga., 20 Ga. (2¾ in.)
Box 5:. $18.99

Hornady Manufacturing

HORNADY HEAVY MAGNUM COYOTE

HEAVY MAGNUM COYOTE

Features: Loaded with 1 ½ oz. of nickel plated lead shot in either a BB or 00 buckshot for close range predators; features Hornady Versatite wad for more impact on target; 1,300 fps
Available in: 12 Ga. (3 in., 00 buckshot or BB)
Box 10: $21.99

SST SLUGS

Features: Sharp points at the end of these slugs allow for faster and more accurate shooting; able to reach your target from an impressive 200 yards away; each shot delivers more than 1200 ft.-lbs. of energy
Available in: 12, 20 Ga. (2¾ in)
Box 5: . . . . $17.99–$18.99

Rimfire Ammunition

VARMINT EXPRESS RIMFIRE .17 HMR

Features: The 17 HMR is one of the most accurate rimfire bullets ever made; polymer tip fragments rapidly and dramatically on impact, and its flat trajectory adds to its accuracy and consistency
Available in: .17 HMR
Box 50: $20.99

VARMINT EXPRESS RIMFIRE .17 MACH 2

Features: These V-MAX bullets are known for their rapid fragmentation and consistent accuracy; these bullets are made in America and hand inspected; paired with Varmint Express products, ignition is fast and easy
Available in: .17 Mach2
Box 50: $12.99

VARMINT EXPRESS RIMFIRE .17 WSM

Features: 20 grain V-Max bullet that provides tack-driving accuracy; muzzle velocity of 3,000 feet per second; fills the gap between the rimfire 17 HMR and centerfire 17 Hornet
Available in: .17 WSM (20 gr.)
Box 50: $25.99

VARMINT EXPRESS RIMFIRE .22 WMR

Features: The .22 WMR guarantees accurate shooting from more than 125 feet; has a muzzle velocity of 2,200 fps and is one of the most requested products Hornady offers; available in 25, 30, and 45 gr.
Available in: .22 WMR
Box 50: $18.99

Inceptor Ammunition

INCEPTOR SPORT & CARRY COMBO

PREFERRED DEFENSE ARX

Features: Non-expanding projectile of a copper/polymer matrix for special critical defense use; 1780 fps, 633 ft.-lb.
Available in: 9mm, 9mm +P, .40 S&W, 10mm Auto, .45 ACP, .38 Spec., .357 Mag.
Box 20: $29.99

SPORT & CARRY COMBO

Description: They say to train with ammo ballistically equal to your carry ammo, and you can do that without breaking the bank with this combo pack that boasts 100 rounds of Inceptor's RNP roundnose practice ammo with 25 rounds of its hollow-point ARX Preferred Defense rounds
Available in: .380 ACP, 9mm +P, .40 S&W, .45 ACP, .38 Spec.
Box 120: $62.11

SPORT UTILITY-HANDGUN

Features: Lead-free injection-molded copper-polymer projectiles loaded to tight specifications in high-quality brass cases; RNP (Round Nose Precision) profile in handgun cartridges or with the SRR (Short-Range Rifle) in rifle cartridges
Available in: .380 ACP, 9mm, 9mm +P, .38 Spec., .40 S&W, .45 ACP
Box 50: . . . . $24.99–$32.34

Jarrett Rifles

TROPHY AMMUNITION

Features: Jarrett's high-performance cartridges are in ten round boxes; cases are from Norma with Jarrett's headstamp
Available in: .243 Win., .270 Win., 7mm Rem. Mag., .30-06 Spfd., .300 WM, .300 Jarrett, .375 H&H, .416 Rem. Mag.
MSRP . . . . $29.12–$82.81

JARRETT TROPHY AMMUNITION

Kent Cartridge

KENT CARTRIDGE BISMUTH UPLAND

BISMUTH UPLAND

Features: Bismuth-based shot is 24 percent denser than steel; safe to use in any choke; doesn't harm barrels; loaded to optimal velocities for max ballistic performance
Available in: 12- and 20-gauge 3- and 2 ¾-inch in No. 5 and 6; 16-gauge 2¾-inch in No. 5 only
Box of: 25
MSRP . . . . $31.99–$48.99

Kent Cartridge

KENT CARTRIDGE
TK7 PENETRATOR

BISMUTH WATERFOWL
Features: Bismuth-based shot is 24 percent denser than steel; safe to use in any choke; doesn't harm barrels; loaded to optimal velocities for max ballistic performance
Available in: 12-gauge 3½- and 3-inch in No. 3, 4; 12-gauge 2¾-inch in No. 4; 20-gauge 3-inch in No. 3, 4
Box 25:. . . . . $33.99–$37.99

ELITE LOW-RECOIL/ TRAINING
Features: The new Elite Low-Recoil/ Training load from Kent comes two ways: a 12-ga. 2.5-in. shell with a 0.75-oz. load, and a 12-ga. 2.75-in. shell with a 0.75-oz. load; loaded with No. 8 to muzzle velocity of 1,200 fps; Kent's Diamond Shot ensures solid break
Available in: 12 ga.
Case 250: $83.38

ELITE PRO TARGET
Features: Loaded with Diamond Shot; all 2.75 in. Shot sizes: 7.5, 8, 8.5
Available in: 12, 20 ga.
Case 250: $79.99

ELITE STEEL TARGET
Features: Two 12-ga. 2.75-in. loads: a 1-oz. load at 1,290 fps and a 0.75-oz. load at 1,215 fps, both in No. 7
Available in: 12 ga.
Box 25:. $8.49

ELITE TARGET
Features: Loaded with Diamond Shot; all 2.75 in. Shot sizes: 7.5, 8, 9
Available in: 12, 20 ga.
Case 250: $70.50

FASTEEL 2.0
Features: Zinc-plated shots; nickel-plated case heads; high-performance wad ensures consistent patterns in the coldest conditions; 12 ga. 3 ½-, 3-, 2¾-inch in a range of BB to No. 6; 20 ga. 3-inch in Nos. 2, 3, and 4
Available in: 12 ga., 20 ga.
Case 250: . . . . $174.98–$179.99

FIRST DOVE
Features: Consistent patterns; clean-burning powders; in 12-ga. 2.75-in. 1-oz. or 20-ga. 2.75-in. 0.75-oz., both in No. 7.5
Available in: 12, 20 ga.
Case 250: $69.99

STEEL DOVE
Features: Two 12-ga. 2.75-in. loads: a 1-oz. and a 1.125-oz.; One 20-ga. 2.75-in. 0.875-oz. load; Shot size: 6
Available in: 12, 20 ga.
Box 25:. $9.99

TK7 PENETRATOR
Features: A dedicated turkey load of No. 7 tungsten pellets offering high pellet count and manageable recoil. Available in a 3-inch 12 ga. load with a 1 5/8-ounce payload or a 3-inch 20 ga. load with a 1 3/8-ounce payload, both at 1100 fps.
Available in: 12 ga., 20 ga.
Box 5:. $34.99

Kynoch Ammunition

KYNOCH RIFLE AMMUNITION

Features: Kynoch hunting ammunition is now standardized on Woodleigh soft nosed and solid bullets, recognized world wide as the most reliable big game bullets currently manufactured; Kynamco offers virtually the whole range of classic British Nitro Express from its purpose-built factory
Available in: .300 Flanged, .303 British, .318 Westley Richards, 9.5X57 Mannlicher, .333 Jeffery Flanged. .350 Rigby, .400/.360 Westley Richards, .375 Flanged 2½-inch, .375 Flanged, .400 Purdey, .405 Winchester, .450/400 3- and 3½-inch, .416 Rigby, .404 Jeffery, .425 Westley Richards, .450 NE, .450 No. 2 NE, .450 Rigby, .577/.450 Martini Henry, .500/.450 NE, .500/.465 NE, .470 NE, .475 No. 2 Eley, .475 No. 2 Jeffery, .476 Westley Richards, .505 Gibbs, .500 Jeffery, .500 NE, .577 NE, .600 NE, .700 NE; currently available in the U.S. from M.W. Reynolds (mwreynolds.com) in Denver, Colorado.
MSRP . . . contact mwreynolds.com

Lapua

CENTERFIRE SPORT
Features: Lapua's extremely accurate target shooting cartridges are loaded with the best target bullets—Scenar, FMJBT, D46 and Lock Base; numerous world championships, Olympic championships, and other top competition gold medals, as well as many official world records in different disciplines, are shot with the Lapua cartridges
Available in: .222 Rem., .223 Rem., .243 Win., 6mm BR Norma, 6.5 Creedmoor, 6.5x47 Lapua, 6.5x55 Swedish, 7.62x39, .308 Win., .30-06 Spfd., 7.62x53R, .338 Lapua Mag.
Box 50:. . . . . $57.99–$214.99

Lapua

LAPUA NATURALIS (3RD GENERATION)

NATURALIS 3RD GENERATION

Features: Bullet mushrooming begins immediately on impact; bullet expands symmetrically and without shattering; gives a maximal shock effect to the hunted game; top premium copper bullet; 3rd Generation has updated bullet design with a monolithic pure copper body that can produce weight retention up to 100 percent; new boattail design eases reloading and improves ballistics; controlled expansion is procured via a polymer valve tip
Available in: .222 Rem., .243 Win., 6.5 Creedmoor, 6.5x47 Lapua, 6.5x55 Swedish Mauser, 7x64, 7x65R, ,308 Win., .30-06 Spfd., 8x57 JS, 8x57 JRS, 338 Lapua, 9.3X62
MSRP. . . . . starting at $69.99

Magnum Research

MAGNUM RESEARCH .429 DE MAGNUM

.429 DE MAGNUM

Features: Designed specifically for Magnum Research's 429 DE Mark XIX pistol; Starline brass; more energy and velocity than a .44 Mag.
Available in: .429 DE (240 gr.) soft-point, (210 gr.) hollowpoint
Box 20:. $42.00

Magtech Ammunition

SPORT SHOOTING HANDGUN

Features: The 100 percent solid copper hollow-point projectile features a six-petal hollow-point specifically designed to deliver tight groups, superior expansion, virtually 100 percent weight retention, and increased penetration over jacketed lead-core bullets
Available in: .25 ACP, .32 ACP, .32 S&W, .32 S&W Long, .380 ACP, 9mm, 9mm +P, 9X19 NATO, 9X21mm, .38 S&W, .38 Spec., .38 Spec. +P, .38 Super, .357 Mag., .40 S&W, 10mm Auto, .44040 Win., .44 Spec., .44 Mag., .45 G.A.P., .45 ACP, .454 Casull, .500 S&W
Box of 20, 50:. . . . . . .$34.99–$77.99

MAGTECH AMMUNITION

Nexus Ammunition

NEXUS AMMUNITION SUBSONIC

HUNTING GRADE

Features: Uses same proprietary loading methods as Nexus' Match line; lead projectiles
Available in: .223 Rem. (79-gr.), .300 BLK (125-gr.)
Box 20:. . . . .$35.99–$56.99

MATCH GRADE

Features: Proprietary loading process; competition-ready
Available in: .260 Rem., .223 Rem., .338 Lapua, .300 Win. Mag., .300 Norma, .308 Win., 6.5x47 Lapua, 6.5 Creedmoor
Box of 20:. . . . .$39.99–$75.99

POWDER CORE

Features: Heavy-metal powder core technology replaces solid lead in the projectile; improved spin stability; higher B.C.; improved shot-to-shot consistency
Available in: .223 Rem. (79-gr.)
Box of 20:. $35.99

SUBSONIC

Features: Subsonic ammo to pair with your favorite suppressor
Available in: .300 BLK (220-gr.), .308 Win. (175-, 220-gr.
Box 20:. . . . .$39.99–$59.99

Rifle Ammunition

AFRICAN PH

Features: Based on many generations of experience of reputable African Professional Hunters, this range of cartridges has been developed to optimize ballistic criteria such as bullet momentum, sectional density and deep, straight-line, bone-breaking penetration; loaded cartridges with Woodleigh softnose and solid bullets
Available in: .375 H&H, .375 Flanged Mag. NE, .505 Mag. Gibbs, .404 Jeffery, .458 Lott, .416 Rigby, .500 NE 3-in., .470 NE, 500/416 NE, .416 Rem., .500 NE, .450 Rigby, .500 Jeffery, .450 Rigby Rimless
Box 10:. . . . . $98.99–$209.99

BONDSTRIKE

Features: Long-range hunting application; polymer tip match-style boattail projectiles with proprietary bonding produce extreme wound channels; initial offerings all in 180 gr.
Available in: .308 Win., .30-06 Spfd., .300 Win. Mag., .300 WSM, .300 RUM
Box 20:. . . . . $69.99–$105.99

Norma Ammunition

NORMA RANGE & TRAINING FRANGIBLE

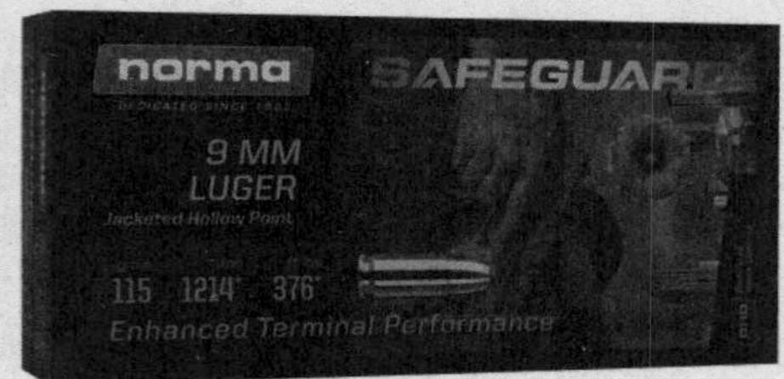

NORMA SAFEGUARD

HEXAGON

Description: Match-grade line of competition ammunition for handguns; consistent velocities; unique bullet has stabilizing grooves
Available in: .357 Mag. (180 gr.), 9mm (124 gr.), .45 ACP (200 gr.)
Box of 50:. $59.99

MHP

Features: High-expansion self-defense round with an all copper monolithic hollowpoint
Available in: 9mm (108 gr.)
Box of: 20
MSRP $35.49

RANGE & TRAINING

Description: Full metal jacket ball ammo for the practice range
Available in: .32 ACP (73 gr.), .380 ACP (95 gr.), 9mm (115 gr.), 9mm Makarov (95 gr.), .38 Spec. (158 gr.).357 Mag. (158 gr.), .40 S&W (180 gr.)
Box of 50:. . . . . $29.99–$41.79

RANGE & TRAINING FRANGIBLE

Description: An affordable line of frangible training ammunition; non-lead; great for use with steel targets
Available in: .40 S&W (122 gr.), .45 ACP (147 gr.)
Box of 50:. . . . . $37.99–$62.99

SAFEGUARD

Description: A jacketed hollowpoint designed for self-defense use
Available in: 9mm (115 gr., 124 gr.), .38 Spec. (158 gr.), .357 Mag. (158 gr.), .45 ACP (230 gr.)
Box of 50:. . . . . $32.49–$48.99

TACTICAL

Description: Reliable, consistent target-practice rounds with full metal jackets; 5.56 NATO also available with Penetrator bullets
Available in: .223 Rem. (55 gr.), 5.56 NATO (55 gr., 62 gr.), .308 Win. (150 gr.)
Box of 20:. . . . . $13.99–$28.99

Nosler

NOSLER SAFARI AMMUNITION

Rifle Ammunition

BALLISTIC TIP

Description: Dedicated whitetail round with a bullet that has a fully tapered jacket, lead alloy core, heavy jacketed base to improve mushrooming, and polymer tip
Available in: .243 Win. (90 gr.), 6mm Creedmoor (95 gr., 140 gr.), .25-06 (115 gr.) .260 Rem. (120 gr.), .270 Win. (130 gr., 140 gr.), 7mm Rem. (150 gr.), 7mm-08 Rem. (120 gr., 140 gr.), .280 Rem. (140 gr.), .280 Ackley Improved (140 gr.), 7.62x39 (123 gr.), .30-30 Win. (150 gr.), .308 Win. (125 gr.), .30-06 Spfd. (125 gr., 165 gr., 180 gr.), .300 Win. Mag. (180 gr.)
Box of 20:. . . . . $34.80–$49.15

MATCH GRADE

Features: Match Grade Ammunition consists of Nosler's precisely-designed Custom Competition bullet along with NoslerCustom Brass; each piece of brass is checked for correct length, neck-sized, chamfered, trued and flash holes are checked for proper alignment; powder charges are meticulously weighed and finished rounds are visually inspected and polished
Available in: .223 Rem., 5.56X45 .22 Nosler, 6mm Creedmoor, 6.5 Creedmoor, 6.5 Grendel, .260 Rem., 6.5-284 Norma, .26 Nosler, .28 Nosler, 6.8 SPC, .30 Nosler, .300 BLK, .308 Win., .300 Win. Mag., .33 Nosler, .338 Lapua Mag., .33 Nosler
Box 20: . . . . $30.80–$111.65

SAFARI

Features: Loaded with either the Partition or Nosler Solid and designed for the same point of impact with either bullet, Safari Ammunition provides the ultimate versatility for any dangerous game situation
Available in: .500 Jeffery, 505 Gibbs, 9.3x62 Mauser, .375 Flanged, .375 H&H, .404 Jeffery, .416 Rem. Mag., .416 Rigby, .450 Rigby, .458 Lott, .458 Win. Mag., .470 NE, .500 NE, .500/.416 NE
Box 20:. . . . . $99.90–$173.80

Nosler

NOSLER TROPHY GRADE LONG-RANGE

TROPHY GRADE

Features: Manufactured to Nosler's strictest quality standards, Trophy Grade Ammunition uses Nosler Custom Brass and Nosler Bullets to attain optimum performance, no matter where your hunting trip takes you. Whether you want your ammunition loaded with AccuBond, Partition Ballistic Tip or, E-Tip, NoslerCustom Trophy Grade Ammunition will have the right load for the right game.
Available in: .223 Rem., .22 Nosler, 6mm Creedmoor, .243 Win., .25-06 Rem., .257 Roberts, .257 Wby. Mag., 6.5 Creedmoor, 6.5x55 Swedish, .260 Rem., 6.5-284 Norma, .264 Win. Mag., .26 Nosler, .27 Nosler, .270 Win., .270 WSM, 7mm-08, 7x57 Mauser, .280 Rem., .28 Nosler, 7mm SAUM, .280 Ackley Improved, 7mm Rem. Mag., 7mm STW, 7mm RUM, .308 Win., .30–06 Spfd., .300 SAUM, .300 H&H, .300 WSM, .300 Win. Mag., .300 Wby. Mag., .30 Nosler, .30-378 Wby. Mag., .300 RUM, .325 WSM, .338 Win. Mag., .340 Wby. Mag., .338 RUM, .338 Lapua, .33 Nosler, .35 Whelen, 9.3X62, .375 H&H, .416 Rem. Mag.
Box 20: . . . . $51.60–$136.75

TROPHY GRADE LONG-RANGE

Description: More fuel for the fires stoking the long-range trend, these loaded with Nosler's Accubond Long-Range high B.C. bonded-core bullet; long ogive; boattail
Available in: 6.5–284 Norma (129 gr.), 6.5 Creedmoor (129 gr., 142 gr.), 6.5 Grendel (129 gr.), .26 Nosler (142 gr.), .260 Rem. (129 gr.), 6.5 PRC (142 gr.), .27 Nosler (165 gr.), .270 Wby. Mag. (150 gr.), .270 Win. (150 gr.), .270 WSM (150 gr.), .28 Nosler (175 gr.), .280 Ackley Improved (150 gr.), 7mm Rem. Mag. (168 gr.), 7mm RUM (175 gr.), 7mm STW (175 gr.), .308 Win. 1(68 gr.), .30-06 Spfd. (168 gr.), .30 Nosler (210 gr.), .300 RUM (210 gr.), .300 Win. Mag. (190 gr.), .300 WSM (190 gr.), .300 Wby. Mag. (210 gr.), .30-378 Wby. Mag. (210 gr.), .33 Nosler (265 gr.), 7mm-08 Rem. (150 gr.)
Box of 20: . . . . $46.30–$118.35

VARMAGEDDON

Features: Featuring a highly accurate polymer tip or hollow point combined with flat base design, Varmageddon products were created for the high-volume varmint shooter who requires the utmost precision; loaded with Nosler Custom Brass, Varmageddon ammunition provides the highest levels of performance for any varmint hunter
Available in: .17 Rem. Fireball, .17 Rem., .204 Ruger, .22 Hornet, .221 Rem. Fireball, .222 Rem., .223 Rem., .22 Nosler, .22-250 Rem., 6mm Creedmoor, .243 Win., 6.5 Grendel, .300 BLK, .308 Win.
Box 20: . . . . $29.25–$72.10

Handgun Ammunition

DEFENSE HANDGUN

Features: Bonded 'Performance' bullets for higher weight retention and maximum barrier penetration; either jacketed hollow point or polymer tipped configuration
Available in: 9mm +P, .40 S&W, .45 ACP +P
Box 20: . . . . $28.60–$32.85

NovX

NOVX RNP CROSSTRAINER, RNP +P CROSS TRAINER

ENGAGEMENT EXTREME, ENGAGMENT EXTREME +P

Features: Lead free; projectiles are a copper-polymer creation; cases are stainless steel; fluted bullet design; 65-gr. 9mm at 1,672 fps/358 ft-lbs standard pressure (1,710 fps/422 ft-lbs in the +P.)
Available in: 9mm, 9mm +P
Box 20: $31.99

CROSSTRAINER/ COMPETITION

Features: Roundnose design; 65-gr. at 1,600 fps, 347 ft-lbs standard pressure
Available in 9mm
Box 26: $26.99

PMC Ammunition

PMC BRONZE LINE - HANDGUN

Rifle Ammunition

BRONZE LINE - RIFLE

Features: For shooters and hunters who appreciate affordable quality ammunition, the PMC Bronze Line offers reliable performance for every shooting application; Full Metal Jacket (FMJ) bullet types
Available in: .223 Rem., .308 Win., 7.62x39, .50 BMG
Box 20: . . . . $10.99–$41.99

PMC Ammunition

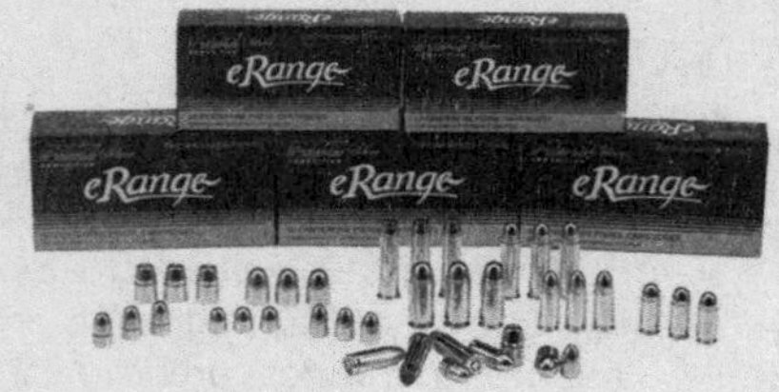

PMC ERANGE

X-TAC

Features: PMC's exacting adherence to precise specifications of military and law enforcement organizations assures that X-TAC ammunition will perform perfectly in that fraction of a second when a serious threat arises and your life is on the line
Available in: 5.56, 7.62x51
Box 20: . . . .$7.99–$15.99

X-TAC MATCH

Features: X-TAC ammo performance comined with Sierra Bullets' ballistics
Available in: .223 Rem., .308 Win., .50
.223, box 20: $23.49
.308, box 20: $25.79
.50 BMG, box 10: $82.99

Handgun Ammunition

BRONZE LINE - HANDGUN

Features: The same quality and dependability built into our Starfire ammunition is incorporated throughout our extensive line of PMC training ammunition and standard hollow point or soft point ammunition.
Available in: .25 ACP, .32 ACP, .380 ACP, .38 Spl., .38 Super +P, 9mm Luger, .357 Mag., 10mm ACP, .40 S&W, .44 S&W Spl., .44 Rem. Mag., .45 ACP
From: . . . .$16.99–$21.99

ERANGE

Features: PMC's eRange environmentally friendly ammunition utilizes a reduced hazard primer that is the first of this type in the industry, an encapsulated metal jacket (EMJ) bullet which completely encloses the surface of the bullet core with precision made copper alloy, and powder with clean-burning characteristics and smooth fire for increased barrel life
Available in: .380 ACP, .38 Spl., .38 Spl. +P, .357 Mag., 9mm Luger, .40 S&W, .44 Rem., .45 ACP
From: . . . . starting at $14.99

SFX

Features: A personal-defense load with "hyper-expanding" hollowpoint. Replaces the old Starfire line and meets current law enforcement ammo protocols
Available in: 9mm (124 gr.)
Box 20: $16.99

Polyfrang, LLC

POLYFRANG HANDGUN

Features: US-made lead-free and frangible cartridges for 9mm or .40 S&W; reduces splashback on steel targets; safe for use with suppressors
Available in: 9mm (90 gr.), .40 S&W (115 gr.)
Box 50: . . . . N/A

POLYFRANG RIFLE

Features: US-made lead-free and frangible cartridges; reduces splashback on steel targets; safe for use with suppressors; .223 comes 50 rounds to the box
Available in: .223 Rem/5.56 NATO. (45 gr.)
Box 20: . . . . N/A

POLYFRANG RIFLE

Remington Ammunition

REMINGTON HYPERSONIC BONDED

Rifle Ammunition

CORE-LOKT

Features: The bonded bullet retains up to 95 percent of its original weight with maximum penetration and energy transfer; features a progressively tapered jacket design, the Core-Lokt Ultra Bonded bullet initiates and controls expansion nearly 2x
Available in: .223 Rem., 6mm Rem., 6mm Creedmoor, .243 Win., .25-06 Rem., 6.5x55 Swedish Mauser, 6.5 Creedmoor, .260 Rem., .270 Win., .270 WSM. 7mm-08 Rem., .280 Rem., 7mm Rem. Mag., .30 Carbine, .30-30 Win., .300 Savage, .308 Win., .30-06 Spfd., .300 Win. Mag., .300 WSM, .300 Wby. Mag., .300 RUM, .303 British, .32 Win. Spec., .338 Win. Mag., .338 RUM, .35 Rem., .35 Whelen, .45-70 Gov't., .450 Bushmaster, .250 Savage, .25-20 Win., .257 Roberts, .264 Win. Mag., .300 RSAUM, .30-40 Krag, .308 Marlin Express, .30 Rem. AR, .444 Marlin, 7.62x39, 7mm RSAUM, 7mm RUM, 7x57 Mauser, 7x64 Brenneke
Box 20: . . . .$26.99–$116.99

HYPERSONIC BONDED

Features: Super-flat trajectories via a Core-Lokt Ultra Bonded projectile; souped up velocities; pointed soft point profile
Available in: .223 Rem., .243 Win., .270 Win., .30-06 Spfd., .300 Win. Mag., .308 Win.
Box 20: . . . .$35.99–$53.99

PREMIER MATCH

Features: Loaded with match-grade bullets, this ammunition employs special loading practices to ensure world-class performance and accuracy with every shot
Available in: .223 Rem., 6.8 SPC, .300 BLK, .308 Win.,. 6.5 Creedmoor, .260 Rem., 6mm Creedmoor
Box 20: . . . .$31.99–$48.99

Remington Ammunition

REMINGTON SUBSONIC RIFLE

PREMIER SCIROCCO BONDED

Features: A hunting round with a polymer-tipped boattail whose core is bonded to the jacket; deep penetration and high weight retention
Available in: .243 Win., .270 Win., 7mm Rem. Mag., 7mm RUM, .30-06 Spfd., .300 WSM, .300 Win. Mag., .300 RUM, 6.5 Creedmoor, .308 Win.
Box 20: . . . . $60.99–$93.99

SUBSONIC RIFLE

Features: A round resulting from the partnership of AAC and Remington; designed to work ideally with silencer-equipped firearms; special heel design reduces lead residue and fouling
Available in: .300 BLK
Box 20: $28.99

Handgun Ammunition

SUBSONIC HANDGUN

Features: A round resulting from the partnership of AAC and Remington; designed to work ideally with silencer-equipped firearms; special heel design reduces lead residue and fouling
Available in: 9mm, .45 ACP
Box 50: . . . . $22.99–$33.99

Rimfire Ammunition

PREMIER MAGNUM RIMFIRE

Features: Repackaged and repriced in 2019; .17 HMR in AccuTip; .22 Win. Mag. In Accutip, jacketed hollowpoint, or pointed softpoint
Available in: .17 HMR, .22 Win. Mag.
Box 50: . . . . $17.99–$19.99

Shotgun Ammunition

AMERICAN CLAY AND FIELD

Features: Nothing that flies stands a chance against these dual-purpose rounds. Expect the densest, most consistent patterns possible, no matter the day's pursuit. Featuring a premium STS primer, reloadable hull, our patented Power Piston wad, and high-hardness lead shot, they deliver flawless performance and consistent patterning, whether your target is winged or clay.
Available in: 12, 20, 28, .410
Box 25: . . . . $12.99–$15.99

GUN CLUB TARGET

Features: Loaded with Gun Club Grade Shot, Premier STS Primers, and Power Piston One-Piece Wads, these high-quality shells receive the same care in loading as top-of-the-line Premier STS and Nitro .27 shells
Available in: 12, 20 Ga. (2¾ in.); Shot sizes: 7.5, 8, 9
Box 25: $10.99

EXPRESS EXTRA LONG RANGE

Features: Suitable for everything from quail to farm predators
Available in: 12, 16, 20, 28 Ga. (2¾ in.), .410 (2½ in., 3 in.); Shot sizes: 2, 4, 5, 6, 7.5
From: . . . . $16.99–$28.99

HEAVY DOVE

Features: A sure bet for all kinds of upland game, ShurShot loads have earned the reputation as one of the best-balanced, best-pattering upland field loads available; shells combine an ideal balance of powder charge and shot payload to deliver effective velocities and near-perfect patterns with mild recoil for high-volume upland hunting situations
Available in: 12, 20 Ga. (2¾ in.); Shot sizes: 6, 7.5, 8
From: . . . . $11.99–$12.99

HYPERSONIC STEEL

Features: With unprecedented velocity and the highest downrange pattern energies ever achieved, Remington HyperSonic Steel takes lethality to new heights and lengths
Available in: 10 Ga. (3½ in.), 12 Ga. (3 in., 3½ in.), 20 Ga. (3 in.); Shot sizes: BB, BBB, 1, 2, 3, 4
From: . . . . $31.99–$42.99

NITRO PHEASANT

Features: Uses Remington's own Copper-Lokt copper-plated lead shot with high antimony content; hard shot stays rounder for truer flight, tighter patterns, and greater penetration; available in both high-velocity and magnum loadings
Available in: 12, 20 Ga. (2¾ in., 3 in.); Shot sizes: 4, 5, 6
From: . . . . $28.99–$31.99

NITRO-STEEL HIGH-VELOCITY

Features: Greater hull capacity means heavier charges and larger pellets, which makes these loads ideal for large waterfowl; delivers denser patterns for greater lethality and is zinc plated to prevent corrosion
Available in: 10 Ga. (3½ in.), 12 Ga. (2¾ in., 3 in., 3½ in.), 16 Ga. (2¾ in.), 20 Ga. (3 in.); Shot sizes: T, BBB, BB, 1, 2, 3, 4
From: . . . . $27.99–$28.99

NITRO TURKEY

Features: These loads contain Nitro Mag. extra-hard lead shot that is as hard and round as copper-plated shot; will pattern as well as other copper-plated, buffered loads without the higher cost
Available in: 12 Ga. (2¾ in., 3 in., 3½ in.), 20 Ga. (3 in.); Shot sizes: 4, 5, 6
Box 5, 10: . . . . $10.99–$16.99

PHEASANT

Features: For the broadest selection in game-specific Upland shotshells, Remington Upland Loads are the perfect choice with high-velocity and long-range performance for any pheasant hunting situation; standard high-base payloads feature Power Piston one-piece wads
Available in: 12, 16, 20 Ga. (2¾ in.); Shot sizes: 4, 5, 6, 7.5
From: . . . . $16.99–$26.99

PREMIER STS

Features: STS Target Loads have taken shot-to-shot consistency to a new performance level, setting the standard at all major skeet, trap, and sporting clays shooting across the country, while providing handloaders with unmatched reloading ease and hull longevity; available in most gauges, Premier STS shells are the most reliable, consistent, and reloadable shells you can shoot
Available in: 12, 20, 28 Ga. (2¾ in.), .410 (2½ in.); Shot sizes: 7.5, 8, 8.5, 9
From: . . . . $13.99–$18.99

Remington Ammunition

REMINGTON ULTIMATE DEFENSE SHOTSHELL .410-BORE

SPORTSMAN HI-SPEED STEEL

Features: Sportsman Hi-Speed Steel's sealed primer, high-quality steel shot, and consistent muzzle velocities combine to provide reliability in adverse weather, while delivering exceptional pattern density and retained energy; a high-speed steel load that is ideal for short-range high-volume shooting during early duck seasons or over decoys
Available in: 10 Ga. (3½ in.), 12 Ga. (2¾ in., 3 in., 3½ in.), 20 Ga. (2¾ in.); Shot sizes: BB, 1, 2, 3, 4, 6, 7
From:............. $15.99–$40.99

Shotgun Slugs & Buckshot

EXPRESS, EXPRESS MAGNUM BUCKSHOT

Features: A combination of heavy cushioning behind the shot column and a granulated polymer buffering helps maintain pellet roundness for tight, even patterns
Available in: 12 (2¾ in., 3 in., 3½ in.), 20 Ga. (2¾ in.); Shot sizes: 000, 00, 0, 1, 3, 4
Box 5:............. $7.99–$11.99

PREMIER ACCUTIP BONDED SABOT

Features: Guided by our new Power Port Tip, the AccuTip Bonded Sabot Slug delivers a degree of accuracy and terminal performance unmatched by any other we tested; yields over 95 percent weight retention thanks to its spiral nose cuts, bonded construction, and high-strength cartridge brass jacket; designed for fully-rifled barrels only
Available in: 12, 20 Ga. (2¾ in., 3 in.)
Box 5:............. $19.99–$22.99

SLUGGER HIGH VELOCITY

Features: This is the first high-velocity Foster-style lead slug which exits the barrel at 1800 fps, 13 percent faster than standard 1-oz. slugs; the 7/8 oz. Slugger High Velocity delivers 200 ft.-lbs. more energy at 50 yards with flatter trajectory on deer than standard 1-oz. slugs; designed for the avid deer hunter using smooth bore guns
Available in: 12 Ga. (2¾ in., 3 in.), 20 Ga. (2¾ in.)
Box 5:.............. $6.99–$8.99

SLUGGER RIFLED

Features: Remington redesigned their 12-gauge Slugger Rifled Slug for a 25 percent improvement in accuracy; at 1760 fps muzzle velocity, the 3-in. 12-gauge Magnum slug shoot 25 percent flatter than regular 12 gauge slugs
Available in: 12 Ga. (2¾ in., 3 in.), 16 Ga. (2¾ in.), 20 Ga. (2¾ in.), .410 (2½ in.)
Box 5:.............. $5.99–$9.99

ULTIMATE DEFENSE BUCKSHOT

Features: Dense patterns and big knock-down power; short-range patterns through smoothbores are tight; .410-bore loads house four lead 000 buckshot pellets
Available in: 12 ga 3 in., 2 ¾ in., 20 ga. 3 in., .410-bore 2 ½ in., 3 in. 12 ga. in 00 or No. 4 Buck; 20 ga. in No. 3 Buck; .410-bore in 000 Buck
12 ga., box 5.......... $7.99–$8.99
20 ga., box 5.............. $7.99
.410-bore, box 10 .... $22.99–$25.99

Rio Ammunition

RIO TARGET LOAD LOW RECOIL

ROYAL ECO BLUESTEEL

Description: Features an environmentally friendly water-soluble wad
Available in: 12 ga. (3 in.); No. BB, 2, 3, 4, 5, and 6
Case 250:............... $249.75

ROYAL PHEASANT

Features: A new line of copper-plated upland loads; designed for stopping power and patterns
Available in: 12, 20, 28 ga.
Case 250:............... $160.00

ROYAL TURKEY BUFFERED MAGNUM

Features: Offered in 12-ga. 3-in. with a Max Dram Equivalent and 1.75 oz. of shot, or a 3.5-in. Max Dram 2-oz. load in your choice of 4, 5, or 6 shot
Available in: 12 ga.
Box 10:................. $13.99

SPREADER

Features: Velocity of 1,350 fps; 25 percent higher dispersion than other spreader wads
Box 10:................. $4.19

TARGET LOAD LOW RECOIL

Features: A sound choice for new shooters; 12 ga. 2 ¾-inch 1-ounce, 2 ½ DE, 1,135 fps, Nos. 7, 7.5, 8, and 9
Available in: 28 ga., 12 ga.
Case 250:................ $69.99

VINTAGE 1896 PAPER

Features: Rio's line of five loads uses single-based powders for minimal fouling; unique dust-stopping membrane on primers; Kraft paper hulls; premium lead shot. Five 12 ga. 2¾-inch loadings: Paper Light 1 1/8 oz., 2¾ DE, No. 7.5, 8; Paper 1 1/8 oz., 3 DE, No. 7.5, 8, 9; Paper HC 1 1/8 oz., 3¼ DE, No. 7.5, 8; Paper Light 1 oz., 2 ¾ DE, No. 7.5, 8, 9; and Sporting 1-ounce, 3 DE, No. 7.5, 8
Box 25:................. $12.29

VINTAGE 1896 PAPER HELICE

Features: Designed specifically for the challenging game of Helice; three 12 ga. 1-ounce 2 ¾-inch loads, one at 3 DE and 1,250 fps, one at Max DE and 1,300 fps, and a third at Max DE in a high-velocity 1,350 fps, all in Nos. 7.5 and 8
Available in: 12 ga.
Box 10:................. N/A

Rio Ammunition

WING & TARGET LITE, HIGH VELOCITY

Features: A soft-shooting load offered in a Lite version with a 12 ga. 2¾-inch 1-ounce load at 1,150 fps and a High Velocity with the same payload at 1,350 fps; Nos. 7.5, 8
Available in: 12 ga.
Case 250: $79.99

Sierra Bullets

SIERRA PRAIRIE ENEMY

GAMECHANGER

Description: A line of centerfire rifle ammo for big-game hunters, these rounds sporting Sierra's Tipped GameKing projectile
Available in: .223 Rem., 6mm Creedmoor, .243 Win., 6.5 Creedmoor, .270 Win., 7mm Rem. Mag., .300 BLK., .308 Win., .30-06 Spfd., .300 Win. Mag.
Box of 20: . . . . $44.99–$79.99

PRAIRIE ENEMY

Description: A varmint getter loaded with Sierra's BlitzKing bullet
Available in: .22-250 Rem., .223 Rem., .204 Ruger, .243 Win., .224 Valkyrie, 6.5 Creedmoor
Box of 20: . . . . $39.99–$49.99

SIG Sauer

SIG SAUER 365 ELITE V-CROWN

Rifle Ammunition

ELITE BALL RIFLE

Features: Intended for training purposes with a full metal jacket projectile. Available in: 55-grain .223 Rem. with a muzzle velocity of 3,240 fps and 1,282 ft.-lb. of energy; 150-grain .308 Win. with a muzzle velocity of 2,900 fps and 2802 ft-lb. of energy
Available in: .300 BLK, .223 Rem.
Box 20: . . . . $15.95–$17.95

ELITE HUNTER TIPPED

Description: Long-range hunting application; deep penetration and impressive expansion thanks to concentric blackened jacket; improved B.C. with translucent yellow tip
Available in: .243 Win., .260 Rem., .270 Win., .30-06 Spfd., .308 Win., .300 Win. Mag., 6.5 Creedmoor, 6mm Creedmoor
Box of 20: . . . . $38.95–$53.95

ELITE MATCH GRADE OTM (OPEN TIP MATCH)

Features: Engineered to match the ballistics of SIG's V-Crown defensive ammo line as a more affordable match-grade loading
Available in: 6.5 Creedmoor, .30-06
Available in: 6mm Creedmoor, .30-06 Spfd., .300 Win. Mag., 6.5 Creedmoor, .223 Rem., .308 Win., .300 BLK
Box 20: . . . . $25.95–$57.95

VARMINT & PREDATOR

Features: Single-based extruded powders; smoke gray-tipped projectiles designed for expansion; match-grade accuracy; flat trajectories
Available in: .223 Rem. (40 gr.), .22-250 Rem. (40 gr.), .243 Win. (55 gr.)
MSRP . . . . $21.95–$31.95

Handgun Ammunition

365 ELITE FMJ

Features: Training ammo designed specifically for short-barreled handguns; offers reduced recoil; 1050 fps; 282 ft.-lb. energy
Available in: 9mm (115 gr.)
Box 50: $22.95

365 ELITE V-CROWN

Features: Carry ammo designed specifically for short-barreled handguns; offers reduced recoil; 1050 fps; 282 ft.-lb. energy
Available in: 9mm (115 gr.)
Box 20: $23.95

ELITE BALL M17

Features: Military-grade ammunition for 9mm handguns and carbine rifles capable of handling +P pressures. Muzzle velocity 1198 fps; muzzle energy 395 ft.-lb. Designed for training
Available in: 9mm +P
Box 50: $18.95

ELITE V-CROWN M17

Features: Military-grade ammunition for 9mm handguns and carbine rifles capable of handling +P pressures. Muzzle velocity 1198 fps; muzzle energy 395 ft.-lb. Designed with a stacked hollowpoint for maximum weight retention and expansion
Available in: 9mm +P
Box 20: $21.95

MATCH ELITE V-CROWN COMPETITION

Features: Designed for competitive handgun practitioners, specifically those shooting minor power factors; low recoil; coated nickel cases; velocities range from 860 to 900 fps
Available in: 9mm (115 gr., 147 gr.)
Box 50: $31.95

Speer

GOLD DOT 5.7X28MM

Description: The first time this round has been loaded for self-defense, featuring Speer's Gold Dot core/jacket bonding technology that all but eliminates jacket separation.
Available in: 5.7x28mm (40 gr.)
Box of 50:. $65.99

GOLD DOT G2

Description: Personal-defense rounds in standard bullet weights featuring an exclusive new shallow-dish nose design filled with an elastomer that, upon impact, is forced into several fissures internal to the bullet, forcing expansion
Available in: 9mm (147 gr.), .40 S&W (180 gr.), .45 ACP +P (230 gr.)
Box of 20:. . . . . $34.99–$39.99

GOLD DOT G2 CARRY GUN

Description: Personal-defense, compact pistol rounds featuring an exclusive new shallow-dish nose design filled with an elastomer that, upon impact, is forced into several fissures internal to the bullet, forcing expansion
Available in: 9mm (135 gr.)
Box of 20:. $34.95

GOLD DOT PERSONAL PROTECTION

Features: Well-respected expanding hollowpoint design used by law enforcement and consumers for defensive and personal protection; the .22 WMR round will feed reliably in sub-compact handguns and perform suitable through barrels as short as 2 inches

SPEER GOLD DOT G2

Available in: Handgun: .25 ACP, .32 ACP, .327 Fed. Mag., .380 ACP, 9mm, 9mm +P, .357 SIG, .357 Mag., .40 S&W, 10mm Auto, .44 Spec., .45 ACP Rifle: .223 Rem., .308 Win.
Handgun: . . . . $33.99–$39.99
Rifle: . . . . $29.99–$35.99

Steinel Ammunition

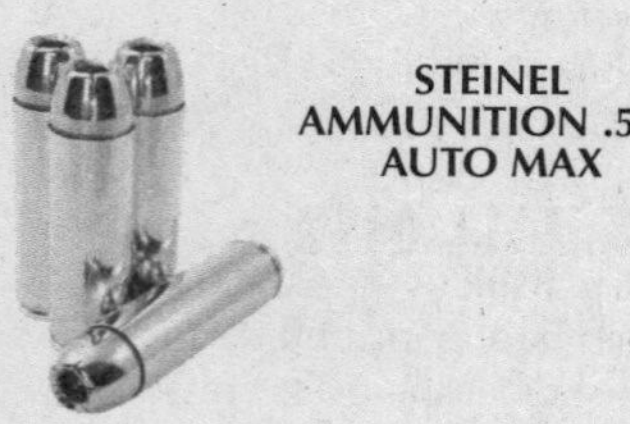

STEINEL AMMUNITION .500 AUTO MAX

RIFLE AMMUNITION

Features: A comprehensive line of custom premium rifle ammunition for some of the world's more unusual calibers; new Starline brass; Hodgdon powders
Available in: 12.7x42 (with a Hornady XTP or FP-XTP for use in Beowulf uppers); match-grade .223 Rem. softpoints; .30-30 with a Lehigh Defense Controlled Chaos hollowpoint); .308 Win. with a boattail hollowpoint; .357 Maximum with a Lehigh Defense Xtreme Penetrator bullet or a flat-nose soft-point for single-shot use; .44 Magnum ultimate solid copper hollowpoint Ultimate Deer or a hardcast, wide meplat WLNC Heavy Hitter bullet; .45 LC with a hardcast bullet and loaded only for modern lever rifles, T/C Contenders, and Ruger's Blackhawk, Super Blackhawk, Bisley, and Redhawk actions; .45-70 Gov't Goldilocks load intended for 100-yard shots on deer and loaded with a Hornady JHP; .45-70 Gov't High-Power load for other applications, a brass monolithic design for target work, and a light-recoil JHP for use in Trapdoor Springfields; .450 Bushmaster with an XTP Mag, FTX flex-tip or solid copper expanding hollowpoint Maker topping; .458 SOCOM in JHP, solid copper expanding hollowpoint Maker, FTX flex-tip, or brass monolithic bullets; .458 Win. in solid brass or dangerous game solids; .500 Auto Max for Big Horn Armory's AR500 in Lehigh Match Warhead brass, XTP Mag jacketed hollowpoint, or wide flatnose hardcast; 6.5X50 Arisaka in a softpoint; 6.5X52 Carcano in a roundnose or softpoint; 7.7X58 Japanese Arisaka in a softpoint or in an accurized full metal jacketed boattail; and just to throw in something normal, a full metal jacket .30-06 Spfd. for M1 Garand use
Box 20:. . . . . $17.49–$79.99

TB Ammunition, LLC

GPM QUADRA-SHOCK

Features: An economical lead-free alternative in a variety of rifle and pistol calibers; non-frangible bullets
Available in: .223 Rem., .243 Win., .270 Win., .30-06 Spfd., .30-30 Win., .300 AAC, .308 Win., .380 ACP, .40 S&W, .357 SIG, .45 ACP, 9mm
Box of: 20, 50
Rifle calibers:. . . . . . . $15.99–$39.99
Handgun calibers:. . . $26.99–$32.99

TB AMMUNITION, LLC GPM QUADRA-SHOCK

Weatherby

WEATHERBY MAGNUM

Features: Weatherby Magnum cartridges are loaded with a variety of popular bullet types for a wide range of shooting purposes

Available in: .224, .240, .257, 6.5-300, 6.5 RPM, .270, .30-378, .300, 7mm, .338-378, .340, .375, .378, .416, .460

MSRP . . . . $69.00–$179.00

WEATHERBY 6.5-300 WEATHERBY MAGNUM

Winchester Ammunition

WINCHESTER M-22 SUBSONIC

Rifle Ammunition

17 WINCHESTER SUPER MAGNUM

Features: A .27 caliber shellcase necked down to a .17 caliber bullet; surpasses the downrange velocity, energy, trajectory and wind bucking characteristics of both the .17 HMR and .22 WMR; available in Varmint HE, Varmint HV, and VarmintX lines.

Available in: .17 WSM

Box 50: . . . . $20.99–$24.99

BALLISTIC SILVERTIP

Features: Solid-based boattail design delivers excellent long-range accuracy; in .22 calibers, the ballistic plastic polycarbonate Silvertip bullet initiates rapid fragmentation; in medium to larger calibers, special jacket contours extend range and reduce cross-wind drift; harder lead core ensures proper bullet expansion

Available in: 6.5 Creedmoor, 6.8 Western,.22-250 Rem., .223 Rem., .223 WSSM, .243 Win., .243 WSSM, .25-06 Rem., .25 WSSM, .270 Win., .270 WSM, .280 Rem., .300 Win. Mag., .30–06 Spfd., .300 WSM, .30–30 Win., .308 Win., 7mm Rem. Mag., 7mm-08 Rem., 7mm WSM, .45-70 Gov't.

Box 20: . . . . $31.99–$59.99

DEER SEASON XP

Features: Large diameter polymer tip accelerates bullet expansion; built specifically for deer hunting and taking down big bucks; alloyed leather core; contoured jacket

Available in: .223 Rem., .243 Win., 25-06 Win., .270 Win., .270 WSM, .30-06 Spfd., .30-30 Win., .300 BLK, .300 Win. Mag., .350 Legend, 7.62X39, .450 Bushmaster, 6.5 Creedmoor, 7mm Rem. Mag., 7mm-08 Rem., 6.8 Spl.

Box 20: . . . . $24.99–$58.99

EXPEDITION BIG GAME

Features: Polymer tip; bonded alloyed lead core; jacket technology; Lubalox (black oxide) coating; controlled expansion

Available in: .270 Win., .270 WSM, .30-06 Spfd., .300 Win. Mag., .300 WSM, .325 WSM, .338 Win. Mag., .338 Lapua Mag., 7mm Rem. Mag.

Box 20: . . . . $49.99–$123.99

M-22 SUBSONIC

Features: Specifically designed to reliably function semiautomatic rifles and pistols at subsonic velocities. Subsonic velocities offer low noise in both suppressed and non-supressed firearms. Bullet is a black copper-plated roundnose.

Available in: .22 LR (45 gr.)

Box 100: $12.99
Box 2000: $274.99

MATCH

Features: Combining proven Winchester technology with proven bullets, the hollow point boat tail design provides the precision match shooters demand; sleek bullet profile, large boattail and small hollow point maximizes long-range accuracy

Available in: .223 Rem., 5.56 NATO, 6.5 Creedmoor, .308 Win., .338 Lapua, 6.5 PRC, 6.8 Western

Box 20: . . . . $37.99–$56.99

PDX1 DEFENDER

Features: Given the recent popularity of modern sporting rifles (MSR) among shooters and hunters, Winchester has designed a product using Split Core Technology (SCT) for personal defense; SCT technology, using a quick expansion front lead core and a deep driving bonded rear lead core, creates the ultimate .223 Rem. Home Defense load

Available in: .223 Rem., .308 Win., 7.62x39

Box 20: . . . . $41.99–$88.99

POWER MAX BONDED

Description: Featuring a contoured jacked bonded to a lead core; protected hollowpoint

Available in: .350 Legend (160 gr.), .223 Rem. (64 gr.), .243 Win. (100 gr.), .270 Win. (150 gr.), .270 WSM (130 gr.), .300 Win. Mag. (150 gr., 180 gr.), .300 WSM (150 gr.)

Box of 20: . . . . $28.99–$83.99

SUPER SUPPRESSED

Features: Optimized for suppressed rifles and specialty handguns with a fully encapsulated bullet backed by a brass disc that reduces fouling; reduced noise with subsonic speeds

Available in: .350 Legend (265 gr.), .300 BLK (200 gr.), .308 Win. (168 gr.)

Box 20: . . . . $19.99–$31.99

SUPER-X HOLLOW POINT

Available in: .204 Ruger, .218 Bee, .22 Hornet, .30-30 Win., .45-70 Gov't.

MSRP . . . . $32.99–$114.99

Winchester Ammunition

WINCHESTER AMMUNITION ACTIVE DUTY

SUPER-X HOLLOW SOFT POINT

Available in: .30 Carbine, .44 Rem. Mag.
Box 50:............$31.99–$57.99

SUPER-X JACKETED SOFT POINT

Available in: .22 Hornet, .22-250 Rem.
.22-250, box 20: $31.99
.22 Hornet, box 50: $55.99

SUPER-X LEAD

Available in: .32-20 Win.
Box of 50:................$64.99

SUPER-X POSITIVE EXPANDING POINT

Available in: .25-06 Rem., .25 WSSM
Box 20:............$48.99–$50.99

SUPER-X POWER CORE

Features: Start with a 95/5 copper alloy, integrate a highly engineered contoured cavity—and you have a new benchmark in lead-free big-game cartridges; features a devastating effective bullet with massive initial impact shock plus deep penetration and virtually 100 percent retained weight to assure maximum trauma to bone and vitals
Available in: .223 Rem., .243 Win., .270 Win., .270 WSM, .30-06 Spfd., .300 Win. Mag., .300 WSM, .30-30 Win., .308 Win., 7mm-08 Rem., 7mm Rem. Mag., 7mm WSM
Box 20:.................. N/A

SUPER-X POWER-POINT

Available in: .22-250 Rem., .223 Rem., .223 WSSM, .243 Win., .243 WSSM, .25-35 Win., .257 Roberts +P, .264 Win. Mag., .270 Win., .270 WSM, .284 Win., .300 Savage, .30-06 Spfd., .300 WSM, .30–30 Win., .303 British, .30-40 Krag, .307 Win., .308 Win., .300 Win. Mag., .325 WSM, .32 Win. Spl., .338 Win. Mag., .348 Win. Mag., .356 Win., 35 Rem., .375 Win., .38-40 Win., .38-55 Win., .44-40 Win., 6.5x55 Swede, 6mm Rem., 7.62x39mm, 7x57 Mauser, 7mm Rem. Mag., 7mm-08 Rem., 8x57 Mauser, .350 Legend, .450 Bushmaster
Box 20:...........$20.99–$105.99

USA READY

Features: Intended for competition and training; offered in a variety of common rifle and pistol cartridges; match grade primers; flat-nose or open-tip bullets depending on caliber
Available in: .223 Rem. (62 gr.), .300 BLK (125 gr.), .308 Win. (168 gr.), 6.5 Creedmoor (125 gr.), .45 ACP (230 gr.), .40 S&W (165 gr.), 9mm (115 gr.), 6.8 SPC (115 gr.)
Rifle, box 20: ....$19.99–$27.99
Handgun, box 50: ...$23.99–$38.99

VARMINT X

Features: Polymer tip, alloy jacket, lead core, and rapid fragmentation
Available in: .17 Hornet, .22 Hornet, .204 Ruger; .22-250 Rem.; .223 Rem.; .243 Win.
Box 20:............$26.99–$29.99

VARMINT X LEAD FREE

Features: Features zinc core technology used in Winchester's Super Clean pistol ammo
Available in: .22-250 Rem., .223 Rem., .243 Rem.
Box 20:............$22.95–$33.99

WWII VICTORY SERIES

Features: Intended to be a collector's item; standard FMJ ball; in special cartons and wood boxes
Available in: .30-06 Spfd., .30 Carbine
Box 20:................. $31.99

Handgun Ammunition

ACTIVE DUTY

Description: Winchester says this round was "selected to serve as the ammunition supplier for the U.S. Army Modular Handgun System;" loaded to M1152 military specifications; flat-nose full metal jacket; military-grade primer
Available in: 9mm (115 gr.)
Box of 100:...............$69.99

DEFENDER HANDGUN

Features: The Winchester Supreme Elite Bonded PDX1, which was chosen by the FBI as their primary service round, is engineered to maximize terminal ballistics, as defined by the demanding FBI test protocol, which simulates real-world threats
Available in: .357 Mag., .357 SIG, .380 ACP, .38 Spl., +P, .40 S&W, .45 Colt, .45 ACP, 9mm Luger +P, 9mm, 10mm Auto
Box of 20:..........$23.99–$39.99

DUAL BOND

Features: Dual Bond offers a large hollow point cavity, which provides consistent upsets at a variety of ranges and impact velocities; the heavy outer jacket is mechanically bonded to the inner bullet; inner bullet utilizes a proprietary bonding process for a combination of knockdown power, solid penetration, and significant tissue damage
Available in: .44 Rem. Mag., .454 Cassull, .460 S&W Mag., .500 S&W Mag.
Box 20:...........$46.99–$115.99

PLATINUM TIP HOLLOW POINT

Features: Patented notched reserve taper bullet jacket, plated heavy wall jacket, and two-part hollow point cavity for uniform bullet expansion, massive energy depot
Available in: .41 Rem. Mag., .44 Rem. Mag., .454 Casull, .500 S&W
Box 20:...........$34.99–$103.99

SUPER SUPPRESSED

Features: Optimized for suppressed handguns and PCCs with a fully encapsulated bullet backed by a brass disc that reduces fouling
Available in: 9mm (147 gr.), .45 ACP (230 gr.)
Box 50:............$34.99–$38.99

SUPER-X BLANK-BLACK POWDER

Available in: .32 S&W
Box 50:.................$43.99

SUPER-X BLANK-SMOKELESS

Available in: .38 Spl.
Box 50:.................$69.99

SUPER-X EXPANDING POINT

Available in: .25 ACP
Box 50:.................$40.99

AMMUNITION

Winchester Ammunition

SUPER-X JACKETED HOLLOW POINT
Available in: .357 Mag., .38 Spl. +P, .454 Casull, .45 Win. Mag., .460 S&W Mag., .500 S&W Mag.
Box 20: . . . . $28.99–$45.99
Box 50 (.357): $64.99

SUPER-X JACKETED SOFT POINT
Available in: .357 Mag.
Box 50: $84.99

SUPER-X LEAD ROUND NOSE
Available in: .32 Short Colt, .32 S&W Long, .32 S&W, .38 Spl., .38 S&W, .44 S&W Spl., .45 Colt
Box of 50: . . . . $35.09–$83.99

SUPER-X LEAD SEMI-WAD CUTTER
Available in: .38 Spl.
Box 50: $51.99

SUPER-X LEAD SEMI-WAD CUTTER HP
Available in: .38 Spl. +P
Box 50: $59.99

SUPER-X LEAD SEMI-WADCUTTER SUPER MATCH
Available in: .38 Spl.
Box 50: $43.99

SUPER-X SILVERTIP HOLLOW POINT
Available in: 10mm Auto, .32 ACP, .357 Mag., .380 ACP, .38 Super Auto +P, .38 Spl. +P, .38 Spl., .40 S&W, .41 Rem. Mag., .44 Rem. Mag., .44 S&W Spl., .45 ACP, .45 Colt, .45 GAP, 9x23 Win., 9mm Luger
Box 20, 50: . . . . $28.99–$64.99

USA FULL METAL JACKET (USA WHITE BOX)
Available in: .25 ACP, .32 ACP, .357 SIG, .38 Spec., .38 Super +P, .380 ACP, .40 S&W, .45 ACP, .45 G.A.P., 7.62X39 Tokarev, 9mm, 9mm Makarov, 9mm NATO, 10MM
From: . . . . $34.99–$69.99

W TRAIN & DEFEND
Features: A straightforward solution for new shooters interested in training to become more proficient with their personal defense ammunition; ballistically-matched ammunition pairs range-ready TRAIN (T) rounds with threat-stopping, technologically-driven DEFEND (D) rounds, each designed for less felt recoil
Available in: .38 Spl., .380 ACP, .40 S&W, 9mm, .45 ACP
Box of 50: . . . . $27.87–$32.75

WIN1911
Features: Provides a choice of personal defense or training ammunition that has been matched for ballistic performance and engineered for the same feel and function; high-accuracy, ballistically matched full metal jacket and jacketed hollow point offerings make this an ideal ammunition choice
Available in: .45 ACP
Box 50: . . . . $62.99–$69.39

WWII VICTORY SERIES
Features: Intended to be a collector's item;standard ball; period-correct loading for a muzzle velocity of 850 fps; special headstamp; packed in specialty carton and in wood boxes
Available in: .45 ACP (230 gr.)
Box 50: $21.99

Rimfire Ammunition

SUPER SUPPRESSED
Features: Designed for suppressed .22 LR rifles and handguns, featuring a black copperplated bullet with a roundnose profile; reduced muzzle flash; subsonic performance in both handguns and rifles
Available in: .22 LR (45 gr.)
Box 100: $12.99

SUPER-X #12 SHOT
Available in: .22 LR
Box 50: $19.99

SUPER-X FULL METAL JACKET
Available in: .22 Win. Mag.
Box 50: $15.99

SUPER-X JACKETED HOLLOW POINT
Available in: .17 HMR, .22 Win. Mag.
Box 50: . . . . $14.99–$15.99

SUPER-X LEAD ROUND NOSE
Available in: .22 LR, .22 Long, .22 Short
Box 100: $7.99

WINCHESTER WWII VICTORY SERIES (RIFLE)

WINCHESTER AMMUNITION AA SUPER SPORT SPORTING CLAYS

SUPER-X LEAD ROUND NOSE, STANDARD VELOCITY
Available in: .22 LR
Box of 50: $4.47

SUPER-X POWER-POINT PLATED LEAD HOLLOW POINT
Available in: .22 LR
Box 50: $10.99

VARMINT HIGH ENERGY
Available in: .22 LR, .22 Win. Mag., .17 WSM
Box of 50: $23.99

VARMINT HIGH VELOCITY
Available in: .22 Win. Mag., .17 HMR, .17 WSM
Box of 50: $20.99

Shotgun Ammunition

AA DIAMOND GRADE
Description: A top-end round for the competitive clay crowd; super-hard copper-plated shot
Available in: 12 ga. (2¾ in.)
Box of 25: $14.99

AA STEEL
Features: Steel shot; high-strength hull; AA wads
Available in: 12 (2¾ in.); Shot sizes: 7.5, 8
Box of 25: $12.99

AA SUPER SPORT SPORTING CLAYS
Description: Optimized for the wide variety of presentations sporting clays and FITASC shooters encounter; hard shot; recoil-reducing wad design
Available in: 12 ga. (2¾ in.), 28 ga. (2¾ in.)
Box of 25: . . . . $12.99–$14.99

Winchester Ammunition

WINCHESTER AMMUNITION ROOSTER XR

AA TARGET LOADS

Features: The hunter's choice for a wide variety of game bird applications, available in an exceptionally broad selection of loadings, from 12-gauge to .410 bore, with shot size options ranging from BBs all the way down to 9s—suitable for everything from quail to farm predators
Available in: 12, 20, 28 Ga. (2¾ in.), .410 (2½ in.); Shot sizes: 7.5, 8, 8.5, 9
Box 25:............$12.99–$14.99

AA TRAACKER

Features: Stay centered in the pattern all the way to the target; Shot-trap core design captures a portion of the shot to stabilize the wad; unique dove-tail petals allows the wad to spin-stabilize and track in the center of the pattern; available in bright orange for low light conditions and in black for bright light conditions
Available in: 12 Ga. (2 ¾ in.), 20 Ga. (2 ¾ in.)
Box 25:..................$10.99

BLIND SIDE MAGNUM PHEASANT

Features: High Packing density for increased powder charge with hinged wad results in 1675 fps; high velocity HEX Shot allows reduced leads and increased pellet energy; diamond cut wad design provides choke responsiveness for increased kill zone; Drylok Super Steel System keeps your powder dry
Available in: 12 (2¾ in., 3 in.)
Box: $28.99

BLIND SIDE WATERFOWL

Features: High Packing density for increased powder charge with hinged wad results in 1675 fps; high velocity HEX Shot allows reduced leads and increased pellet energy; diamond cut wad design provides choke responsiveness for increased kill zone; Drylok Super Steel System keeps your powder dry
Available in: 12 (2¾ in., 3 in., 3½ in.), 20 (3 in.)
Box: ....$20.99–$22.99

LONG BEARD XR

Features: Features Shot-Lok technology; offers the tightest patterns and longest shot capability of any traditional turkey load with twice the pellets in a 10-in. circle out to 60 yds
Available in: 12 Ga. (3 in., 3½ in.), 20 Ga. (3 in.)
Box 10:............$20.99–$22.99

ROOSTER LOK'D & LETHAL XR

Features: Protects shot during in-bore acceleration; shot launches from barrel near perfectly round for extremely tight long-range patterns; greater penetration over standard lead loads beyond 50 yards; devastating terminal on-target performances
Available in: 12 (2¾ in., 3 in.)
Box 15: ....$25.99–$30.99

SUPER PHEASANT

Available in: 12 Ga. (2¾ in., 3 in.), 20 Ga. (3 in.); Shot sizes: 4, 5, 6
Box 25:............$21.99–$26.99

SUPER TARGET

Available in: 12, 20 Ga. (2¾ in.); Shot sizes: 7, 7.5, 8, 9
Box 25:................. $9.99

SUPER-X TRIALS AND BLANKS

Available in: 10 Ga. (2⅞ in.), 12 Ga. (2¾ in.)
Box 25:............$27.99–$67.99

SUPER-X TURKEY LOADS

Available in: 12 Ga. (2¾ in., 3 in.); Shot sizes: 4, 5, 6
Box 10: .... $12.99–$13.99

SUPER-X XPERT HI-VELOCITY STEEL

Available in: 12 Ga. (2. in., 3 in., 3½ in.), 20 Ga. (3 in.); Shot sizes: BB, 1, 2, 3, 4
Box 25:............$12.99–$24.99

VARMINT-X

Features: Shot-Lok technology; 50 percent more pellets in a 10 in. circle at 40 yds; greater penetration over standard lead loads beyond 40 yds; devastating terminal on-target performance
Available in: 12 Ga. (3 in.); Shot size: BB
Box 10:.................$23.99

XPERT SNOW GOOSE

Features: Continuing the trend of ammo designed for specific species, XPERT Snow Goose uses features from Winchester's XPERT Steel and Blind Side lines, with XPERT Steel Shot and the Diamond Cut Wad; 12 ga. 3-inch BB, No. 1, No 2 1,475 fps; 12 ga. 3 ½-inch BB, No. 1. No. 2 1550 fps
Available in: 12 ga.
Box 25:................. $14.99

XTENDED RANGE BISMUTH

Features: A fresh non-lead alternative with the hard hits bismuth provides; patented Shot-Lok wad protects the shot from deformation during barrel travel; 12 ga. 3-inch 1 5/8-ounce No. 5 at 1200 fps is primarily a turkey load, but suitable for a variety of ducks as well
Available in: 12 ga.
Box 10:................. $38.99

Shotgun Ammunition–Slugs & Buckshot

DEER SEASON COPPER IMPACT XP

Features: Species-dedicated round for whitetail hunters featuring a wide polymer tip with a hollow nose; solid copper construction; streamlined, boattail profile
Available in: .243 Win. (85 gr.), .270 Win. (130 gr.), .300 Win. Mag. (150 gr.), .30-06 Spfd. (150 gr.), .308 Win. (150 gr.)
Box 20:................. $16.99

Winchester Ammunition

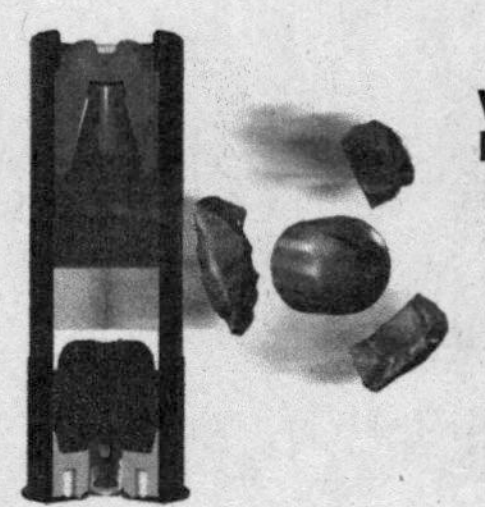

WINCHESTER AMMUNITION PDX1 DEFENDER SEGMENTING SLUG

DEER SEASON SHOTGUN SLUG

Features: A new species-dedicated shotgun slug for whitetail hunters; 1 1/8-ounce rifled slug; 1600 fps muzzle velocity; rear-stabilized wad
Available in: 12 ga.
Box 5:. $6.99

PDX1 12 SLUG AND BUCK

Features: The 12-gauge PDX1 Defender ammunition features a distinctive black hull, black oxide high-base head and three pellets of Grex buffered 00 plated buckshot nested on top of a 1 oz. rifled slug; an ideal, tight patterning personal defense load; slug/buckshot combination provides optimum performance at short and long ranges while compensating for aim error
Available in: 12 Ga. (2¾ in.)
Box 10:. . . . . $17.99–$33.99

PDX1 DEFENDER SEGMENTING SLUG

Features: The uniquely designed slug segments into three pieces when fired into FBI protocol barriers such as bare, light cloth, and heavy cloth covered ballistic gelatin; the round is designed to compensate for aim error over traditional slugs.
Available in: 12 Ga. (2¾ in.), 20 Ga. (2¾ in.)
Box 10: $22.99

SUPER-X BUCKSHOT

Available in: 12 Ga. (2¾ in., 3 in., 3½ in.), 20 Ga. (2¾ in.), .410 (2½ in., 3 in.); Shot sizes: 4, 3, 1, 00, 000
Box 5:. . . . . $6.99–$17.99

MUZZLELOADING BULLETS

Barnes Bullets

BARNES BULLETS SPIT-FIRE TMZ

EXPANDER MZ

Features: 100 percent copper with a large, hollow cavity; six copper petals with double-diameter expansion; full weight retention
Available in: .45 (195 gr.), .50 (250, 300 gr.), .54 (275, 325 gr.)
Box 15:. . . . . $19.99–$21.99

SPIT-FIRE MZ

Features: A streamlined semi-spitzer give, boattail base and tack-driving accuracy; six razor-sharp copper petals create massive shock, deep penetration, and double-diameter expansion; retains virtually 100 percent of its original weight; available in 15 and 24-bullet packs
Available in: .50 (245, 285 gr.)
Box 24:. $24.99

SPIT-FIRE TMZ

Features: 100 percent copper boattail design with streamlined polymer tip for faster expansion; expands at 1050 fps.; remains intact at extreme velocities; redesigned sabot loads faster while retaining tight gas seal
Available in: .50 (250, 290 gr.)
Box 15:. . . . . $19.99–$32.99
Box 24:. . . . . $29.99–$32.99

Harvester Muzzleloading (J-Ron, Inc.)

HARVESTER SCORPION PT GOLD

CRUSHED RIB SABOT

Features: 50 percent less loading friction; consistent ignition and superb accuracy
Available in: .45 (.400); .50 (.400, .429–.430, .451–.452)
Box 50:. . . . . $9.99–$10.99

SABER TOOTH BELTED

Features: Copper-clad belted bullets in Harvester Crush Rib Sabot
Available in: .50 (250, 270, 300, 350 gr.)
MSRP $15.99

SCORPION FUNNEL POINT MAG

Features: Electroplated copper plating does not separate from lead core; loaded in Harvester Crush Rib Sabots
Available in: .50 (240, 260, 300 gr.); .54 (240, 260, 300 gr.)
MSRP . . . . $9.99–$13.99

SCORPION PT GOLD

Features: Scorpion PT Gold Ballistic Tip Bullets are electroplated with copper plating that does not separate from lead core; offers greater accuracy at longer ranges than a hollow point; 3 percent antimony makes the bullet harder than pure lead
Available in: .45 (240, 260, 300 gr.); .50 ((240, 260, 300 gr.)
MSRP . . . . $15.99–$25.99

Hodgdon Powder Co.

TRIPLE SEVEN FIRESTAR PELLETS

Features: Star-shaped pellet designed for .50-caliber muzzleloaders utilizing 209 primers for ignition; long grooves provide more surface for ignition compared to traditional pellets
Available in: .50-caliber
Box 60:. . . . . $24.99–$31.99

HODGDON POWDER TRIPLE SEVEN FIRESTAR PELLETS

Hornady Manufacturing

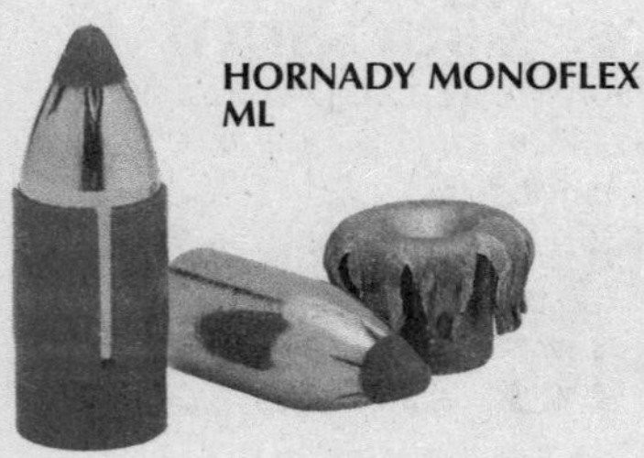

HORNADY MONOFLEX ML

GREAT PLAINS - PA CONICAL

Features: Delivers greater accuracy and more knock-down power; PA bullets are prelubed with special knurled grooves on the bearing surface to hold the lubricant on the bullet—no need for a patch or sabot
Available: in .50-caliber 240-grain
Box of 50: $13.99

MONOFLEX ML

Features: Constructed with the Hornady Flex Tip and retaining 95 percent of its original weight, it's available in both a High Speed/Low Drag sabot and Lock-N-Load Speed Sabot
Available in: .50 cal. sabot with .45 cal. (250 gr.) bullet
Box of 20:. $26.99

Knight Rifles

BLOODLINE BULLETS

Features: Individually machined, double knurled bullets for increased visual blood trails
Available in: .45 (185, 200 gr.); .50 (220, 250, 275, 300, 350 gr.); .52 (220, 275, 300, 350 gr.); .54 (325 gr.)
Box 20:. . . . . $25.49–$36.49

RED HOT BULLETS

Features: Saboted Barnes solid copper bullet with superior expansion
Available in: .45 (175, 195 gr.); .50 (250, 300, 350 gr.); .52 (275, 350, 375 gr.)
MSRP. . . . . $19.99–$33.13

KNIGHT RIFLES BLOODLINE BULLETS

PowerBelt Bullets

POWERBELT COPPER

AEROLITE

Features: Designed specifically for use with standard 100-grain loads; AeroLite's shape is noticeably longer and more aerodynamic than other PowerBelts of similar weight; longer length is made possible by the massive hollow point cavity that is filled by an oversized polycarbonate point
Available in: .45 (250 gr.), .50 (250, 300 gr.)
MSRP. $29.99

AEROTIP ELR

Features: Designed specifically for the CVA Paramount long-range bolt-action muzzleloader; 280-grain; .452 BC; best used in 1:22 twist
Type: ELR
Available in: .45
Box 15:. $29.99

COPPER

Features: Thin copper plating reduces bore friction while allowing for optimal bullet expansion; available in four tip designs: Hollow Point, AeroTip, Flat Point, and Steel Tip
Available in: .45 (195, 225, 275 gr.); .50 (223, 245, 295, 348, 405, 444 gr.); .54 (295, 348 gr.)
MSRP. . . . . $22.99–$56.99

PLATINUM

Features: Proprietary hard plating and aggressive bullet taper design for improved ballistic coefficient; large-size fluted gas check produces higher and more consistent pressures
Available in: .45 (223, 300 gr.); .50 (270, 300, 338 gr.)
MSRP. $24.99

PURE LEAD

Features: Pure lead, available in four different grain weights in Hollow Point and 444 in Flat Point
Available in: .50 (295, 348 gr.); .54 (345, 405 gr.)
Box 15:. $24.99

Swift Bullet Company

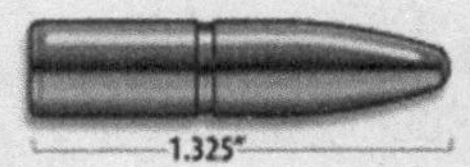

SWIFT A-FRAME MUZZLELOADING BULLETS

A-FRAME MUZZLELOADING BULLETS

Features: Muzzleloader and heavy revolver A-Frame bullets are one in the same; initiate expansion at 950 feet per second, expand to .65x their original caliber, and maintain 97% of their weight; virtually indestructible at velocities in excess of 3000 feet per second
Available in: .50 (240, 300 gr.); .54 (265, 325 gr.)
Box of 10:. $15.99

Thompson/Center Arms

MAXI-BALL

Features: An exceptionally accurate bullet and the preferred bullet for penetration needed for large game like elk; lubricating grooves (maxi wide grooves)
Available in: .50 (275, 350 gr.)
Box 20:. $22.99

SHOCK WAVE SABOTS

Features: Polymer tip spire point bullet with sabot; incorporates harder lead core with walls interlocked with the jacket for maximum weight retention and expansion; available with spire point or bonded bullets
Available in: Bonded Core in Super Glide Sabots .50 (250 gr.); Controlled Expansion in Super Glide Sabot .50 (250, 300 gr.); Bonded Core in Mag Express Sabots .50 (250, 300 gr.); Controlled Expansion in Mag Express Sabots .50 (200, 250, 300 gr.) and .45 (200 gr.)
MSRP. . . . . $18.99–$22.99

SUPER 45 XR SABOTS

Features: Centerfire weight performance without the recoil, Super 45 XR sabots have a flatter trajectory, provide deep penetration, and nearly 2 times the expansion of its original diameter.
Available in: .45 (155 gr.)
Box 30:. $19.99

THOMPSON/CENTER SHOCK WAVE SABOTS

Umarex

UUMAREX ARX

UMAREX/INCEPTOR ARX

Features: Designed in conjunction with PolyCase Ammunition Development Lab; SpeedBand sabot available calibers include .357, .40, and .45, while a .45-caliber option has Umarex's base-style SpeedBelt; acceptable for use in large-bore airguns, including Umarex's Hammer .50-caliber
Available in: .50
Box of 15:. $14.91

BULLETS

Due to extreme demand and limited supplies, pricing on components has varied too widely during 2021 to include MSRP here. Anticipating that prices will eventually settle down in 2022, we expect the 114th edition to include component MSRP. Purchasers of components should do their research across manufacturer, distributor, and retailer websites to assess availability and best pricing.

Barnes Bullets

Barnes continues to develop leading-edge products with a wide range of workability and functionality using an incredibly broad range of purpose-built components and ammunition. Barnes's most popular hunting bullets, the all-copper TSX line, also comes with a streamlined polymer tip. The Barnes Buster line can be used for both rifles and handguns.

Rifle Bullets

Banded Solids

Caliber & Description	9.3MM RN	9.3MM RN	416 RN	416 RN	404 JEFF RN	470 NITRO RN	505 GIBBS RN	500 NITRO FN	500 JEFF RN	50 BMG BORE RIDER	50 BMG BORE RIDER	577 NITRO FN	600 NITRO FN
Diameter, Inches	.366	.366	.416	.416	.422	.474	.504	.509	.510	.510	.510	.583	.618
Weight, Grains	250	286	350	400	400	500	525	570	535	750	800	750	900
Density	.267	.305	.289	.33	.321	.318	.295	.314	.294	.412	.439	.315	.337
Ballistic Coefficient	.214	.247	.217	.261	.261	.243	.267	.243	.238	1.070	1.095	.257	.380
Catalog Number	30466	30467	30520	30526	30536	30649	30685	30690	30694	30703	30707	30713	30714

From: N/A

LEGEND

Type of Bullet
- **BT** – Boattail
- **FB** – Flat Base
- **FN** – Flat Nose
- **RN** – Round Nose
- **S** – Spitzer
- **SP** – Soft Point
- **SS** – Semi-Spitzer

Barnes Buster

Caliber & Description	44 MAG. FN FB	454 CASULL FN FB	45/70 FN FB	500 S&W FN FB
Diameter, Inches	.429	.451	.458	.500
Weight, Grains	300	325	400	400
Density	.233	.228	.272	.229
Ballistic Coefficient	.241	.206	.242	.220
Catalog Number	30545	30572	30644	30672

Box 50: N/A

Barnes Bullets

Barnes Original

Caliber & Description	30-30 WIN FNSP	348 WIN FN SP	348 WIN FN SP	375 WIN FN SP	38/55 FN SP	38/55 FN SP	45/70 SSSP	45/70 FN SP	45/70 SSSP	45/70 FN SP	50/110 WIN FN SP	50/110 WIN FN SP
Diameter, Inches	.308	.348	.348	.375	.375	.377	.458	.458	.458	.458	.510	.510
Weight, Grains	190	220	250	255	255	255	300	300	400	400	300	450
Jckt.	-	.032	.032	.032	.032	.032	.032	.032	.032	.032	.032	.032
Density	.286	.260	.295	.259	.259	.256	.204	.204	.272	.272	.165	.247
Ballistic Coefficient	.296	.301	.327	.290	.290	.290	.291	.227	.389	.302	.183	.274
Catalog Number	30360	30437	30438	30496	30497	30498	30611	30612	30613	30614	30682	30683

From: N/A

LRX Bullets

Caliber & Description	22 BT	6MM BT	6.5MM BT	270 BT	7MM BT	7MM BT	7MM BT	30 BT	30 BT	30 BT	30 BT	338 BT	338 LAPUA BT	338 LAPUA BT	375 BT
Diameter, Inches	.224	.243	.264	.277	.284	.284	.284	.308	.308	.308	.308	.338	.338	.338	.375
Weight, Grains	77	95	127	129	139	145	168	175	190	200	212	250	265	280	270
Density	.216	230	.257	.240	.246	.257	.257	.264	.286	.301	.319	.313	.331	.350	.274
Ballistic Coefficient	.404	.436	.468	.463	.470	.486	.550	.508	.540	.546	.705	.602	.575	.667	.449
Catalog Number	30881	30862	30228	30262	30295	30282	30284	30318	30377	30374	30376	31150	30434	30432	30483

Box 50: N/A

Match Burner Bullets

Caliber & Description	22 FB	22 BT	22 BT	6MM FB	6MM BT	6MM BT	6.5MM BT	6.5MM BT	6.5MM BT	7MM BT	30 PALMA FB	30 BT
Diameter, Inches	.224	.224	.224	.243	.243	.243	.264	.264	.264	.284	.308	.308
Weight, Grains	52	69	85	68	105	112	120	140	145	171	155	175
Density	.148	.196	.242	.165	.254	.271	.246	.287	.297	.303	.233	.264
Ballistic Coefficient	.224	.339	.410	.267	.511	.624	.460	.586	.703	.645	.467	.521
Catalog Number	30160	30162	30164	30205	31120	31122	30234	31144	30102	30285	30381	30385

Box 100: N/A

LEGEND

Type of Bullet

BT – Boattail
FB – Flat Base
FN – Flat Nose
RN – Round Nose
S – Spitzer
SP – Soft Point
SS – Semi-Spitzer

Barnes Bullets

M/LE Reduced Ricochet, Limited Penetration (RRLP) Bullets

Caliber & Description	223/5.56 FB	6.8MM FB	30 FB	7.62X39 FB
Diameter, Inches	.224	.277	.308	.310
Weight, Grains	55	85	150	108
Density	.157	.158	.226	.161
Ballistic Coefficient	.225	.229	.357	.243
Catalog Number	30161	30252	30313	30390

From: N/A

M/LE TAC-TX Bullets

Caliber & Description	6.5mm BT	6.5mm BT	6.5mm BT	6.8mm BT	300 BLK	300 BLK	30 FB	30 BT	338 BT	338 BT	458 SOCOM BT
Diameter, Inches	.264	.264	.264	.277	.308	.308	.308	.308	.338	.338	.458
Weight, Grains	100	115	120	95	110	120	110	168	225	265	300
Density	.205	.236	.246	.177	.166	.181	.166	.253	.281	.331	.204
Ballistic Coefficient	.359	.387	.443	.292	.289	.358	.295	.470	.514	.575	.236
Catalog Number	30236	31142	30237	30253	30321	30320	30358	30359	30420	30419	30640

From: N/A

Multi-Purpose Green (MPG) Bullets

Caliber & Description	223 FB	6.8MM FB	30 FB	7.62X39 FB
Diameter, Inches	.224	.277	.308	.310
Weight, Grains	55	85	150	108
Density	.157	.158	.226	.161
Ballistic Coefficient	.225	.229	.357	.243
Catalog Number	30161	30249	30331	30388

From: N/A

LEGEND

Type of Bullet

- **BT** – Boattail
- **FB** – Flat Base
- **FN** – Flat Nose
- **RN** – Round Nose
- **S** – Spitzer
- **SP** – Soft Point
- **SS** – Semi-Spitzer

TSX Bullets

Caliber & Description	22 FB	22 FB	22 FB	22 FB	22 BT	22 BT	224 VALKYRIE BT	6MM BT	25 BT	25 FB	6.5MM BT	6.5MM FB	6.5MM BT	6.8MM FB	6.8MM BT	270 BT	270 BT
Diameter, Inches	.224	.224	.224	.224	.224	.224	.224	.243	.257	.257	.264	.264	.264	.277	.277	.277	.277
Weight, Grains	45	50	53	55	62	70	78	85	100	115	120	130	120	85	110	130	140
Density	.128	.142	.151	.157	.177	.199	.222	.206	.216	.249	.246	.266	.266	.158	.205	.242	.261
Ballistic Coefficient	.188	.197	.204	.209	.287	.314	.383	.333	.336	.335	.381	.365	.411	.246	.323	374	.404
Catalog Number	30176	30174	30180	30182	30190	30193	30204	30212	30222	30224	30244	30246	31140	30254	30260	30264	30266

Barnes Bullets

Caliber & Description	270 FB	7MM BT	7MM BT	7MM BT	7MM FB	7MM FB	30 FN FB	30 FB	30 BT	30 BT	30 BT	30 BT	30 BT	30 FB	7.62X39 BT
Diameter, Inches	.277	.284	.284	.284	.284	.284	.308	.308	.308	.308	.308	.308	.308	.308	.310
Weight, Grains	150	120	140	150	160	175	150	110	130	150	165	168	180	200	123
Density	.279	.213	.248	.266	.283	.310	.226	.166	.196	.226	.248	.253	.271	.301	.183
Ballistic Coefficient	.386	.349	.394	.408	.392	.417	.184	.264	.340	.369	.398	.404	.453	.423	.275
Catalog Number	30269	30287	30289	30293	30291	30294	30334	30341	30345	30347	30349	30351	30353	30356	30391

Caliber & Description	303/7.65MM FB	8MM BT	8MM BT	338 BT	338 BT	338 FB	338 FB	338 LAPUA BT	35 FB	35 FB	9.3MM FB	9.3MM FB	375 FB	375 FB	375 FB
Diameter, Inches	.311	.323	.323	.338	.338	.338	.338	.338	.358	.358	.366	.366	.375	.375	.375
Weight, Grains	150	180	200	185	210	225	250	285	200	225	250	286	235	270	300
Density	.222	.246	.274	.231	.263	.281	.313	.356	.223	.251	.267	.305	.239	.274	.305
Ballistic Coefficient	.322	.381	.421	.352	.404	.386	.425	.585	.284	.359	.361	.411	.270	.326	.357
Catalog Number	30393	30396	30398	30408	30410	30412	30415	30417	30455	30457	30469	30473	30486	30489	30491

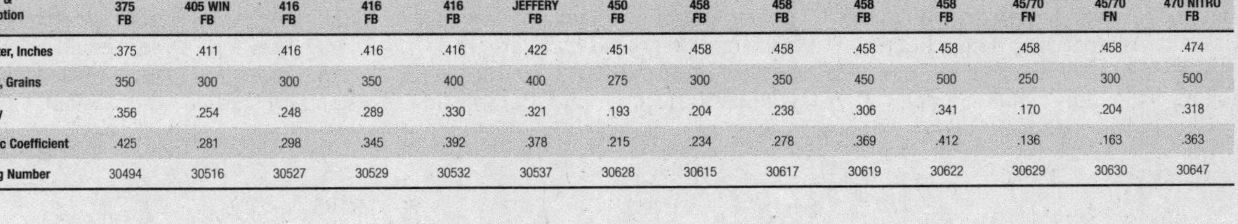

Caliber & Description	375 FB	405 WIN FB	416 FB	416 FB	416 FB	404 JEFFERY FB	450 FB	458 FB	458 FB	458 FB	458 FB	45/70 FN	45/70 FN	470 NITRO FB
Diameter, Inches	.375	.411	.416	.416	.416	.422	.451	.458	.458	.458	.458	.458	.458	.474
Weight, Grains	350	300	300	350	400	400	275	300	350	450	500	250	300	500
Density	.356	.254	.248	.289	.330	.321	.193	.204	.238	.306	.341	.170	.204	.318
Ballistic Coefficient	.425	.281	.298	.345	.392	.378	.215	.234	.278	.369	.412	.136	.163	.363
Catalog Number	30494	30516	30527	30529	30532	30537	30628	30615	30617	30619	30622	30629	30630	30647

Caliber & Description	505 GIBBS FB	500 NITRO FB	50 BMG BT	577 NITRO FB
Diameter, Inches	.505	.509	.510	.583
Weight, Grains	525	570	647	750
Density	.294	.314	.355	.315
Ballistic Coefficient	.320	.369	.572	.402
Catalog Number	30688	30692	30700	30712

From: N/A

VARMIN-A-TOR

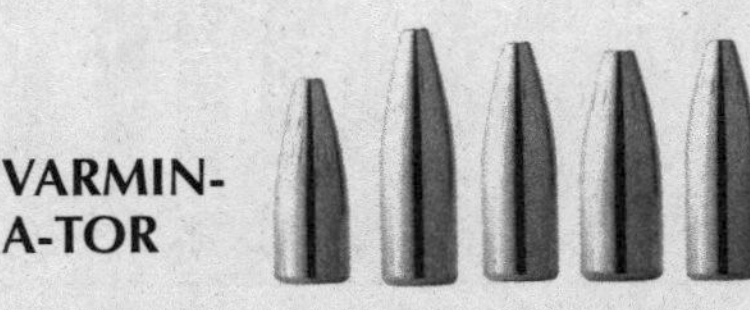

Caliber & Description	20 FB	22 FB	22 FB	6mm FB	6mm FB
Diameter, Inches	.204	.224	.224	.243	.243
Weight, Grains	32	40	50	58	72
Density	.110	.114	.142	.140	.174
Ballistic Coefficient	.159	.153	.192	.173	.208
Catalog Number	30092	30168	30178	30207	30210

From: N/A

VARMINT GRENADE

Caliber & Description	20 FB	22 HORNET FB	22 FB	223 FB	6MM FB
Diameter, Inches	.204	.224	.224	.224	.243
Weight, Grains	26	30	36	50	62
Density	.089	.085	.102	.142	.150
Ballistic Coefficient	.131	.101	.149	.183	.199
Catalog Number	30090	30170	30171	30198	30214

Box 100: N/A

Barnes Bullets

Handgun Bullets

M/LE TAC-XP Pistol Bullets

Caliber & Description	380 ACP	9MM	9MM	.357 SIG	38 SPL.	357 MAG.	10MM/40 S&W	10MM/40 S&W	10MM/40 S&W	44 SPL.	45 ACP/45 GAP	45 ACP
Diameter, Inches	.355	.355	.355	.355	.355	.357	.400	.400	.400	.429	.451	.451
Weight, Grains	80	95	115	125	110	125	125.	140	155	200	160	185
Density	.091	.108	.130	.142	.123	.140	.112	.125	.138	.155	.112	.130
Ballistic Coefficient	.107	.120	.167	.159	.156	.160	.113	.128	.189	.138	.133	.167
Catalog Number	30440	30444	30442	30446	30449	30451	30500	30502	30504	30539	30550	30552

Box 40: N/A

XPB Pistol Bullets

Caliber & Description	357 Mag.	41 Mag.	44 Mag.	44 Mag.	45 Colt	45 Colt	454 Casull	460 S&W	460 S&W	480 Ruger	500 S&W XPB	500 S&W XPB	500 S&W XPB
Diameter, Inches	.357	.410	.429	.429	.451	.451	.451	.451	.451	.475	.500	.500	.500
Weight, Grains	140	180	200	225	200	225	250	200	275	275	275	325	375
Density	.157	.153	.155	.175	.140	.158	.176	.140	.193	.174	.157	.186	.214
Ballistic Coefficient	.150	.126	.138	.166	-	.146	.141	.160	.215	.155	.141	.228	.261
Catalog Number	30453	30512	30541	30543	30556	30558	30562	30554	30548	30659	30663	30665	30667

Box 20: N/A

Berger Bullets

Famous for their superior performance in benchrest matches, Berger bullets also include hunting designs. From .17 to .30, all Bergers feature fourteen jackets with a wall concentricity tolerance of .0003. Lead cores are 99.9 percent pure and swaged in dies to within .0001 of a round. Berger's line includes several profiles: Match, Low Drag, Very Low Drag, Length Tolerant, and Maximum-Expansion, besides standard flat-base and boattail.

HUNTING

Caliber & Description	6mm VLD	6mm VLD	6mm	6mm VLD	6mm VLD	25 VLD"	6.5mm VLD	6.5mm VLD	270 VLD	270 Classic	270 VLD	270 VLD	7mm VLD	270 EOL	7mm VLD	7mm Classic	7mm VLD	7mm EOL	30 VLD	30 VLD	30 Classic	30 VLD	30 VLD	30 Classic	30 VLD	30 VLD	338 Elite	338 Elite
Diameter, Inches	.243	.243	.243	.243	.243	.257	.264	.264	.277	.277	.277	.277	.284	.277	.284	.284	.284	.284	.308	.308	.308	.308	.308	.308	.308	.308	.338	.338
Weight, Grains	87	95	95	105	115	115	130	140	130	130	140	150	140	170	168	168	180	195	155	168	168	175	185	185	190	210	250	300
Density	.210	.230	-	.254	.278	.249	.266	.287	.241	-	.260	.279	.248	-	.298	-	.319	.345	.233	.253	-	.264	.279	-	.286	.316	-	-
Ballistic Coefficient	.412	.480	.427	.532	.545	.466	.552	.612	.452	.497	.487	.531	.510	.662	.617	.604	.659	.754	.439	.473	.496	.498	.549	.547	.570	.631	.682	.818
Catalog Number	24524	24527	24570	24528	24530	25513	26503	26504	27501	27570	27502	27503	28503	27575	28501	28570	28502	28550	30508	30510	30570	30512	30513	30571	30514	30515	33554	33556

Box 100: N/A

AMMUNITION

Berger Bullets

TARGET

Caliber & Description	22 FBHP	22 FBHP	22 VLD	22 BTHP	22 VLD	22 VLD	22 VLD	22 LRBTHP	22 VLD	6mm FBHP	6mm BR	6mm BTHP	6mm FBHP	6mm FBHP	6mm BTHP	6mm VLD
Diameter, Inches	.224	.224	.224	.224	.224	.224	.224	.224	.224	.243	.243	.243	.243	.243	.243	.243
Weight, Grains	52	55	70	73	75	80	80.5	82	90	62	-	65	65	68	90	95
Density	.148	.157	.199	.208	.214	.228	.229	.233	.256	.150	-	.157	.157	.165	.218	.230
Ballistic Coefficient	.242	.262	.371	.343	.423	.445	.436	.444	.551	.253	.277	.270	.265	.280	.411	.480
Catalog Number	22408	22410	22418	22420	22421	22422	22427	22424	22423	24404	24407	24408	24409	24411	24425	24427

Caliber & Description	6mm BTHP	6mm VLD	6mm Hybrid	6mm BTHP	6mm VLD	6.5mm BTHP	6.5mm VLD	6.5mm VLD	6.5mm LRBTHP	6.5mm Hybrid	7mm VLD	7mm VLD	7mm Hybrid
Diameter, Inches	.243	.243	.243	.243	.243	.264	.264	.264	.264	.264	.284	.284	.284
Weight, Grains	105	105	105	108	115	120	130	140	140	140	168	180	180
Density	.254	.254	.254	.261	.278	.245	.266	.287	.287	.287	.298	.319	.319
Ballistic Coefficient	.493	.495	.547	.551	.545	.453	.552	.612	.592	.618	.617	.659	.674
Catalog Number	24428	24429	24433	24431	24430	26402	26403	26401	26409	26414	28401	28405	28407

Caliber & Description	30 FBHP	30 FBHP	30 VLD	30 Hybrid	30 LRBTHP	30 VLD	30 Hybrid	30 LRBTHP	30 VLD	30 Juggernaut	30 VLD	30 Hybrid
Diameter, Inches	.308	.308	.308	.308	.308	.308	.308	.308	.308	.308	.308	.308
Weight, Grains	115	150	155	155	155.5	168	168	175	175	185	185	185
Density	.183	.226	.233	.233	.234	.253	.253	.264	.264	.279	.279	.279
Ballistic Coefficient	.296	.398	.439	.483	.464	.473	.519	.515	.498	.560	.549	.569
Catalog Number	30421	30407	30408	30426	30416	30410	30425	30420	30412	30418	30413	30424

Caliber & Description	30 Hybrid	30 LRBTHP	30 VLD	30 Hybrid	30 Hybrid
Diameter, Inches	.308	.308	.308	.308	.308
Weight, Grains	200	210	210	215	230
Density	.301	.316	.316	-	-
Ballistic Coefficient	.624	.626	.631	.696	.743
Catalog Number	30427	30419	30415	30429	30430

Box 100: N/A

LEGEND

Type of Bullet

BT – Boattail
FB – Flat Base
HP – Hollow Point
LD – Low Drag
LR – Long Range
VLD – Very Low Drag

Berger Bullets

Varmint

Caliber & Description	17 FBHP	20 FBHP	20 BTHP	20 LRBTHP	22 FBHP	22 FBHP	22 FBHP	22 FBHP	22 FBHP	6mm LDHP	6mm FBHP	6mm LDHP
Diameter, Inches	.172	.204	.204	.204	.224	.224	.224	.224	.224	.243	.243	.243
Weight, Grains	25	35	40	55	40	52	55	60	64	69	80	88
Density	.121	.120	.137	.188	.114	.148	.157	.171	.182	.167	.194	.213
Ballistic Coefficient	.150	.176	.225	.381	.155	.197	.210	.278	.294	.291	.306	.391
Catalog Number	17308	20303	20304	20306	22303	22309	22311	22312	22316	24313	24321	24323

Box 100: N/A

LEGEND

Type of Bullet

- **BT** – Boat Tail
- **CT** – Combat Target
- **FMJ** – Full Metal Jacket
- **FP** – Flat Point
- **HB** – Hollow Base
- **L** – Lead
- **RN** – Round Nose
- **SP** – Spire Point
- **SX** – Super Explosive
- **SWC** – Semi-Wadcutter
- **WC** – Wadcutter

Hornady Bullets

Hornady's product line includes over 300 bullets, ranging from .17 caliber all the way up to the .50 caliber A-MAX bullet for the .50 BMG. Hornady is always working to originate the next technological innovation. From prairie dogs to dangerous game, they have the perfect bullet to meet every hunting and shooting need.

Rifle Bullets

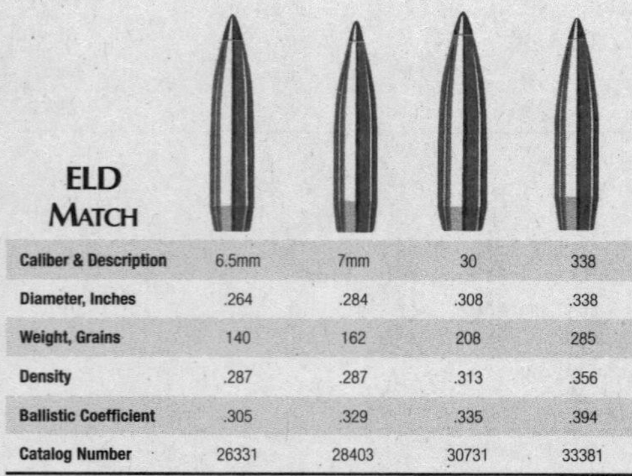

ELD Match

Caliber & Description	6.5mm	7mm	30	338
Diameter, Inches	.264	.284	.308	.338
Weight, Grains	140	162	208	285
Density	.287	.287	.313	.356
Ballistic Coefficient	.305	.329	.335	.394
Catalog Number	26331	28403	30731	33381

MSRP N/A

ELD-X

Caliber & Description	30	30	30	30	6.5mm	7mm	7mm
Diameter, Inches	.308	.308	.308	.308	.264	.284	.284
Weight, Grains	178	200	212	220	143	162	175
Density	.268	.301	.319	.331	.293	.287	.310
Ballistic Coefficient	.271	.315	.336	.325	.315	.315	.340
Catalog Number	3074	3076	3077	3078	2635	2840	2841

MSRP N/A

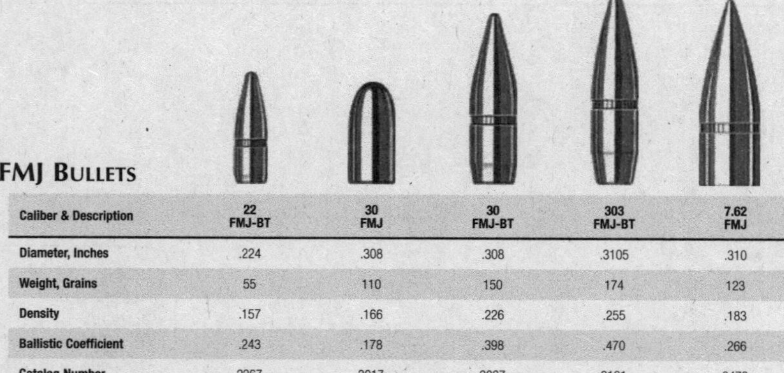

FMJ Bullets

Caliber & Description	22 FMJ-BT	30 FMJ	30 FMJ-BT	303 FMJ-BT	7.62 FMJ
Diameter, Inches	.224	.308	.308	.3105	.310
Weight, Grains	55	110	150	174	123
Density	.157	.166	.226	.255	.183
Ballistic Coefficient	.243	.178	.398	.470	.266
Catalog Number	2267	3017	3037	3131	3478

MSRP N/A

Hornady Bullets

INTERBOND

Caliber & Description	6mm BT	25 BT	6.5mm BT	270 BT	270 BT	7mm BT	7mm BT	30 BT	30 BT	30 BT	338 BT	416 RN
Diameter, Inches	.243	.257	.264	.277	.277	.284	.284	.308	.308	.308	.338	.416
Weight, Grains	85	110	129	130	150	139	154	150	165	180	225	400
Density	.206	.238	.264	.242	.279	.246	.525	.226	.248	.271	.281	.330
Ballistic Coefficient	.395	.390	.485	.460	.525	.486	.273	.415	.447	.480	.515	.311
Catalog Number	24539	25419	26209	27309	27409	28209	28309	30309	30459	30709	33209	41659

MSRP N/A

INTERLOCK

Caliber & Description	22 SP	6mm BT SP	25 SP	25 BTSP	25 RN	25 HP	6.5mm SP	6.5mm SP	6.5mm RN	6.5mm Carcano RN	270 SP	270 BTSP	270 SP	7mm BTSP	7mm SP	7mm SP	7mm BTSP	7mm RN	7mm SP
Diameter, Inches	.227	.243	.257	.257	.257	.257	.264	.264	.264	.268	.277	.277	.277	.284	.284	.284	.284	.284	.284
Weight, Grains	70	100	100	117	117	120	129	140	160	160	130	140	150	139	139	154	162	175	175
Density	.194	.242	.216	.253	.253	.260	.264	.287	.328	.321	.242	.261	.279	.246	.246	.273	.287	.310	.310
Ballistic Coefficient	.296	.405	.357	.391	.243	.394	.445	.465	.283	.275	.409	.486	.462	.453	.392	.433	.514	.285	.462
Catalog Number	2280	2453	2540	2552	2550	2560	2620	2630	2640	2645	2730	2735	2740	2825	2820	2830	2845	2855	2850

Caliber & Description	30 BTSP	30 RN	30 SP	30 BTSP	30 SP	30 FP	30 BTSP	30 RN	30 SP	30 BTSP	30 RN	7.62 SP	303 SP	303 RN	32 FP	8mm SP
Diameter, Inches	.308	.308	.308	.308	.308	.308	.308	.308	.308	.308	.308	.310	.312	.312	.321	.323
Weight, Grains	150	150	150	165	165	170	180	180	180	190	220	123	150	174	170	150
Density	.226	.226	.226	.248	.248	.256	.271	.271	.271	.286	.331	.183	.220	.255	.236	.205
Ballistic Coefficient	.349	.186	.338	.435	.387	.189	.452	.241	.425	.491	.300	.252	.361	.262	.249	.290
Catalog Number	3033	3035	3031	3045	3040	3060	3072	3075	3070	3085	3090	3140	3120	3130	3210	3232

Hornady Bullets

Caliber & Description	8mm RN	8mm SP	338 SP RP	338 SP RP	338 RN	338 SP RP	348 FP	35 RN	35 SP RP	35 SP RP	9.3 SP RP	375 FP	375 SP RP	375 SP RP
Diameter, Inches	.323	.323	.338	.338	.338	.338	.348	.358	.358	.358	.366	.375	.375	.375
Weight, Grains	170	195	200	225	250	250	200	200	200	250	286	220	225	270
Density	.233	.267	.250	.281	.313	.313	.236	.223	.223	.279	.305	.223	.229	.229
Ballistic Coefficient	.217	.410	.361	.397	.291	.431	.246	.195	.282	.375	.410	.217	.320	.380
Catalog Number	3235	3236	3310	3320	3330	3335	3410	3515	3510	3520	3560	3705	3706	3711

LEGEND

Type of Bullet

- **BT** – Boat Tail
- **CT** – Combat Target
- **FMJ** – Full Metal Jacket
- **FP** – Flat Point
- **HB** – Hollow Base
- **L** – Lead
- **RN** – Round Nose
- **SP** – Spire Point
- **SX** – Super Explosive
- **SWC** – Semi-Wadcutter
- **WC** – Wadcutter

Caliber & Description	405 FP	405 SP	416 RN	44 FP	45 HP	45 FP	45 RN	45 RN
Diameter, Inches	.411	.411	.416	.430	.458	.458	.458	.458
Weight, Grains	300	300	400	265	300	350	350	500
Density	.251	.251	.330	.205	.204	.238	.238	.341
Ballistic Coefficient	.215	.250	.311	.186	.197	.195	.189	.287
Catalog Number	41050	41051	4165	4300	4500	4503	4502	4504

LEGEND

Type of Bullet

- **BT** – Boat Tail
- **CT** – Combat Target
- **FMJ** – Full Metal Jacket
- **FP** – Flat Point
- **HB** – Hollow Base
- **L** – Lead
- **RN** – Round Nose
- **SP** – Spire Point
- **SX** – Super Explosive
- **SWC** – Semi-Wadcutter
- **WC** – Wadcutter

MSRP N/A

Match A-Max

Caliber & Description	6.5mm	22	22	22	6mm	6.5mm	6.5mm	6.5mm	7mm	30	30	30 MOLY	30	30	338 BT	50
Diameter, Inches	.264	.224	.224	.224	.243	.264	.264	.264	.284	.308	.308	.308	.308	.308	.338	.510
Weight, Grains	100	52	75	80	105	120	123	140	162	155	168	168	178	208	285	750
Density	.246	.148	.214	.228	.254	.246	.252	.287	.287	.233	.253	.253	.268	.313	.356	.412
Ballistic Coefficient	.390	.247	.435	.453	.500	.465	.510	.585	.625	.435	.475	.475	.495	.325	720	1.050
Catalog Number	26101	22492	22792	22832	24562	26172	26171	26332	28402	30312	30502	30504	30712	30732	3338	5165

MSRP N/A

SST

Caliber & Description	6mm	25	6.5mm	6.5mm	6.5mm	270	270	270	270	7mm SST	7mm SST	7mm SST	30	30	30	30
Diameter, Inches	.243	.257	.264	.264	.264	.277	.277	.277	.277	.284	.284	.284	.308	.308	.308	.308
Weight, Grains	95	117	123	129	140	120	130	140	150	139	154	162	125	150	150	165
Density	.230	.253	.252	.264	.287	.223	.242	.261	.279	.246	.273	.287	.185	.226	.226	.248
Ballistic Coefficient	.355	.390	.510	.485	.520	.400	.460	.495	.525	.486	.525	.550	.305	.415	.370	.447
Catalog Number	24532	25522	26173	26202	26302	2716	27302	27352	27402	28202	28302	28452	3019	30302	30303	30452

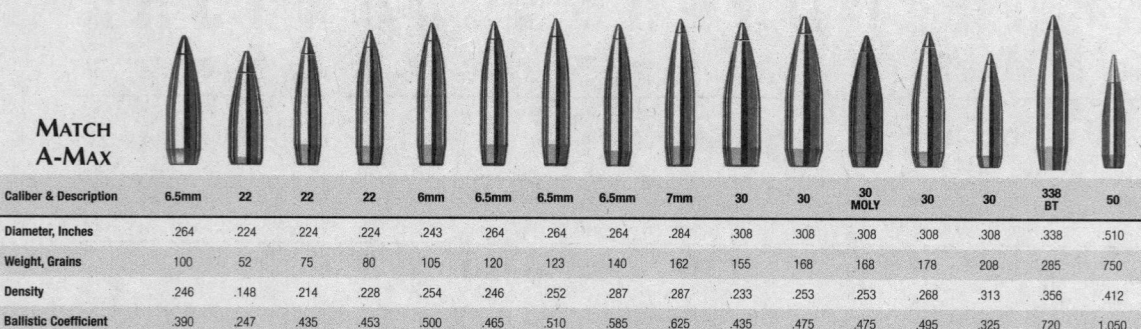

Hornady Bullets

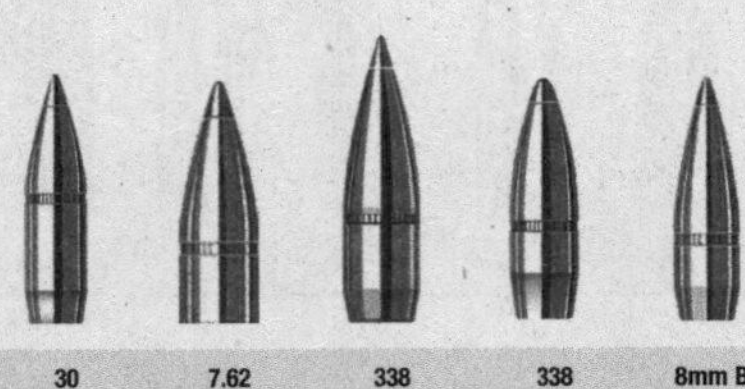

Caliber & Description	30	7.62	338	338	8mm BT
Diameter, Inches	.308	.310	.338	.338	
Weight, Grains	180	123	200	225	170
Density	.271	.183	.250	.281	.233
Ballistic Coefficient	.480	.260	.455	.515	.455
Catalog Number	30702	3142	33102	33202	3233

MSRP N/A

LEGEND

Type of Bullet

- **BT** – Boat Tail
- **CT** – Combat Target
- **FMJ** – Full Metal Jacket
- **FP** – Flat Point
- **HB** – Hollow Base
- **L** – Lead
- **RN** – Round Nose
- **SP** – Spire Point
- **SX** – Super Explosive
- **SWC** – Semi-Wadcutter
- **WC** – Wadcutter

Traditional Varmint

Caliber & Description	17 HP	20 SP	22 JET	22 Hornet	22 Hornet	22 HP BEE	22 SP
Diameter, Inches	.172	.204	.222	.223	.224	.224	.224
Weight, Grains	25	45	40	45	45	45	50
Density	.121	.155	.116	.129	.128	.128	.142
Ballistic Coefficient	.187	.245	.104	.202	.202	.108	.214
Catalog Number	1710	22008	2210	2220	2230	2229	2245

Caliber & Description	22 SP SX	22 SP	22 SP	22 SP SX	22 HP	22 SP	6mm HP
Diameter, Inches	.224	.224	.224	.224	.224	.224	.243
Weight, Grains	50	55	55	55	60	60	75
Density	.142	.157	.157	.157	.171	.171	.181
Ballistic Coefficient	.214	.235	.235	.235	.271	.264	.294
Catalog Number	2240	2265	2266	2260	2275	2270	2420

Caliber & Description	6mm BTHP	6mm SP	25 FP	25 HP	25 SP	270 SP	270 HP	270 BTHP	7mm HP	30 Short Jacket	30 SP	30 RN	30 SP
Diameter, Inches	.243	.243	.257	.257	.257	.277	.277	.277	.284	.308	.308	.308	.308
Weight, Grains	87	87	60	75	87	100	110	110	120	100	110	110	130
Density	.210	.210	.130	.162	.188	.186	.205	.205	.213	.151	.166	.166	.196
Ballistic Coefficient	.376	.327	.101	.257	.322	.307	.352	.360	.334	.152	.256	.150	.295
Catalog Number	2442	2440	2510	2520	2530	2710	2720	27200	2815	3005	3010	3015	3020

MSRP N/A

Hornady Bullets

V-Max

Caliber & Description	17	17	20	20	22	22	22	22 MOLY	22	22	22	22 MOLY	22	6mm
Diameter, Inches	.172	.172	.204	.204	.224	.224	.224	.224	.224	.224	.224	.224	.224	.243
Weight, Grains	20	25	32	40	35	40	50	50	53	55	55	55	60	58
Density	.097	.121	.110	.137	.100	.114	.142	.142	.151	.157	.157	.157	.171	.140
Ballistic Coefficient	.185	.230	.210	.275	.109	.200	.242	.242	.290	.255	.255	.255	.265	.250
Catalog Number	21710	17105	22004	22006	22252	22241	22261	22613	22265	22272	22271	22713	22281	22411

Caliber & Description	6mm	6mm	6mm	25	6.5mm	270	7mm	30
Diameter, Inches	.243	.243	.243	.257	.264	.277	.284	.308
Weight, Grains	65	75	87	75	95	110	120	110
Density	.157	.181	.210	.162	.195	.205	.213	.166
Ballistic Coefficient	.280	.330	.400	.290	.365	.370	.365	.290
Catalog Number	22415	22420	22440	22520	22601	22721	22810	23010

LEGEND

Type of Bullet

- **BT** – Boat Tail
- **CT** – Combat Target
- **FMJ** – Full Metal Jacket
- **FP** – Flat Point
- **HB** – Hollow Base
- **L** – Lead
- **RN** – Round Nose
- **SP** – Spire Point
- **SX** – Super Explosive
- **SWC** – Semi-Wadcutter
- **WC** – Wadcutter

MSRP N/A

Handgun Bullets

FMJ Bullets

Caliber & Description	9mm FMJ-RN	9mm FMJ-RN	10mm FMJ- FP	45 SWC	45 FMJ-RN	9mm FMJ	9mm FMJ-RN	10mm FMJ-FP	45 FMJ-CT
Diameter, Inches	.355	.355	.400	.451	.451	.355	.355	.400	.451
Weight, Grains	115	124	180	185	230	100	147	200	200
Density	.130	.141	N/A	.130	.162	.141	.167	.179	.140
Ballistic Coefficient	.140	.145	N/A	.068	.184	.158	.212	.182	.115
Catalog Number	35557	355771	400471	45137	45177	35527B	35597B	40077B	45157B

MSRP N/A

Frontier Lead Bullets

Caliber & Description	32 HBWC	32 SWC	38	38 HBWC	38 LRN	38 SWC	38 SWC HP	44 Cowboy	44 Cowboy
Diameter, Inches	.314	.314	.358	.358	.358	.358	.358	.427	.430
Weight, Grains	90	90	140	148	158	158	158	205	180
Density	.130	.130	.157	.165	.176	.176	.176	.161	.139
Ballistic Coefficient	.040	.096	.127	.047	.159	.135	.139	.123	.114
Catalog Number	10028	10008	10078	10208	10508	10408	10428	11208	11058

Hornady Bullets

Frontier/ Lead Bullets (cont.)

Caliber & Description	44 SWC	44 SWC HP	45 L-C/T	45 SWC	45 LRN	45 FP Cowboy
Diameter, Inches	.430	.430	.452	.452	.452	.454
Weight, Grains	240	240	200	200	230	255
Density	.185	.185	.140	.140	.162	.177
Ballistic Coefficient	.182	.204	.081	.070	.207	.117
Catalog Number	11108	11118	12208	12108	12308	12458

MSRP N/A

HAP Bullets

Caliber & Description	9mm	9mm	10mm	45	45	10mm	45
Diameter, Inches	.356	.356	.400	.451	.451	.400	.451
Weight, Grains	115	125	180	185	230	200	200
Density	.130	.141	.161	.130	.162	.179	.140
Ballistic Coefficient	.129	.158	.164	.139	.188	.199	151
Catalog Number	355281	355721	400421	451051	451611	40061B	45159B

MSRP N/A

LEGEND

Type of Bullet

BT – Boat Tail
CT – Combat Target
FMJ – Full Metal Jacket
FP – Flat Point
HB – Hollow Base
L – Lead
RN – Round Nose
SP – Spire Point
SX – Super Explosive
SWC – Semi-Wadcutter
WC – Wadcutter

XTP Bullets

Caliber & Description	30 RN	30 HP	32 HP	32 HP	32 HP	9mm HP	9mm HP	38 HP	9mm HP	38 FP
Diameter, Inches	.308	.309	.312	.312	.312	.355	.355	.357	.355	.357
Weight, Grains	86	90	60	85	100	90	115	110	124	125
Density	.130	.136	.088	.125	.147	.102	.130	.123	.141	.140
Ballistic Coefficient	.105	.115	.090	.145	.170	.099	.129	.131	.165	.148
Catalog Number	3100	31000	32010	32050	32070	35500	35540	35700	35571	35730

Caliber & Description	9mm HP	38 HP	38 HP	38 FP	38 HP	38 HP	9x18mm HP	10mm HP	10mm HP
Diameter, Inches	.355	.357	.357	.357	.357	.357	.365	.400	.400
Weight, Grains	147	125	140	158	158	180	95	155	180
Density	.167	.140	.157	.177	.177	.202	.102	.138	.161
Ballistic Coefficient	.212	.151	.169	.199	.206	.230	.127	.137	.164
Catalog Number	35580	35710	35740	35780	35750	35771	36500	40000	40040

Caliber & Description	10mm HP	41 HP	44 HP	44 HP	44 HP	44 HP	45 HP	45 HP	45 HP
Diameter, Inches	.400	.410	.430	.430	.430	.300	.451	.451	.451
Weight, Grains	200	210	180	200	240	300	185	200	230
Density	.179	.178	.139	.155	.185	.232	.130	.140	.162
Ballistic Coefficient	.199	.182	.138	.170	.205	.245	.139	.151	.188
Catalog Number	40060	41000	44050	44100	44200	44280	45100	45140	45160

Caliber & Description	45	45 HP	45 HP	45	475 MAG	50	500 MAG	500 FP
Diameter, Inches	.452	.452	.452	.452	.475	.500	.500	.500
Weight, Grains	240	250	300	300	325	300	350	500
Density	.168	.175	.210	.210	.206	.171	.192	.275
Ballistic Coefficient	.160	.146	.180	.200	.150	.120	.145	.185
Catalog Number	45220	45200	45230	45235	47500	50101	50100	50105

MSRP N/A

AMMUNITION

Lapua

Rifle Bullets

Lapua precision bullets are made from the best raw materials and meet the toughest precision specifications. Each bullet is subject to visual inspection and tested with advanced measurement devices.

D46
Manufactured to the strictest tolerances for concentricity, uniformity of shape, and weight; 7.62mm (.308) available
Box 100: . . . . N/A

D166
Superbly accurate FMJBT bullet for 7.62mm (.311) cartridges
Box 100: . . . . N/A

FMJ
Ten rounds loaded with Lapua's .30 S374 8.0/123gr FMJ bullet from 100m can easily achieve groupings less than; 30mm .224, 6.5mm, 7.62mm (.308, .311) available
Box 100: . . . . N/A

LOCK BASE
A distinctive Full Metal Jacket Boat Tail bullet that has many applications from sport shooting to battlefield; streamlined ballistic shape combined with patented base design; 7.62mm and .338 available
Box 100: . . . . N/A

MEGA
Soft point bullet with a protective copper jacket bullet at its best in the field and typically more than duplicates on impact; mechanical bonding locks the lead alloy in place; 6.5mm, 7.62mm, and 9.3mm available
Box 100: . . . . N/A

LAPUA NATURALIS THIRD GENERATION
Market leaders in terminal ballistic performance, and they can be used in hunting areas where lead-core bullets are prohibited. 5.69 (50 gr.), 6mm (90 gr.), 6.5mm (140 gr.), 7mm (155 gr.), 8mm (180 gr.), 9.3mm (250 gr.), .338 (231 gr.) available.
Box 50: . . . . N/A

SCENAR
Scenar Hollow Point Boat Tail bullets have the IBS World Record in 600 yard Heavy Gun 5-shot group (.404") and hold the official world ISSF record of 600 out of 600 possible; also available in Coated Silver Jacket version; .244, 6mm, 6.5mm, 7.62mm, and .338 available
Box 100: . . . . N/A

SCENAR-L
A refinement in all manufacturing steps that has resulted in closer weight tolerances, tighter jacket wall concentricity standards, and greater uniformity in every dimension, including the gilding metal cup, lead wire and jacket forming, ending up to core-jacket assembly, boat tail pressing, and tipping ; 6mm, 6.5mm, 7mm, and 7.62mm (.308) available
Box 100: . . . . N/A

LAPUA D46

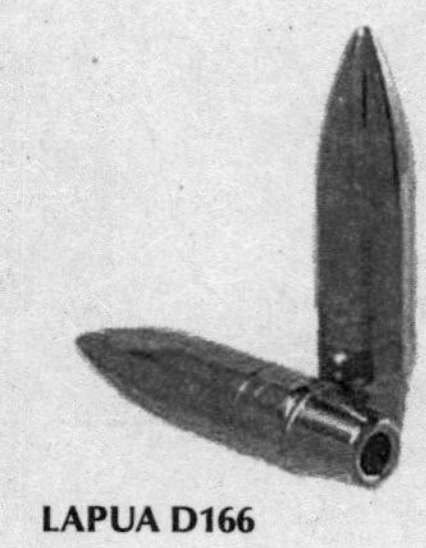
LAPUA D166

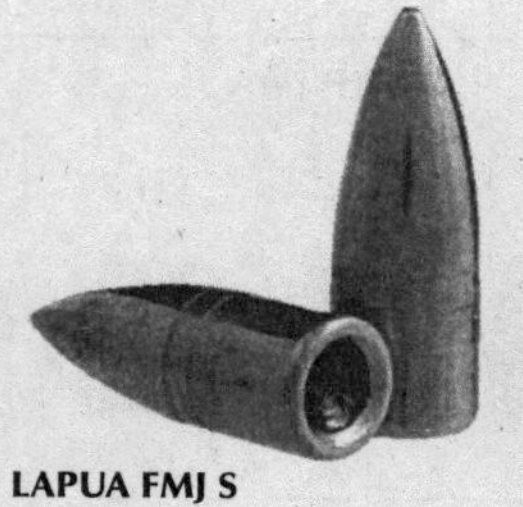
LAPUA FMJ S

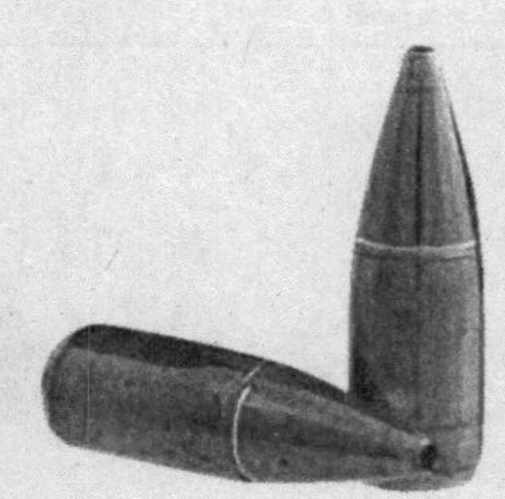
LAPUA HP

LAPUA LOCK BASE

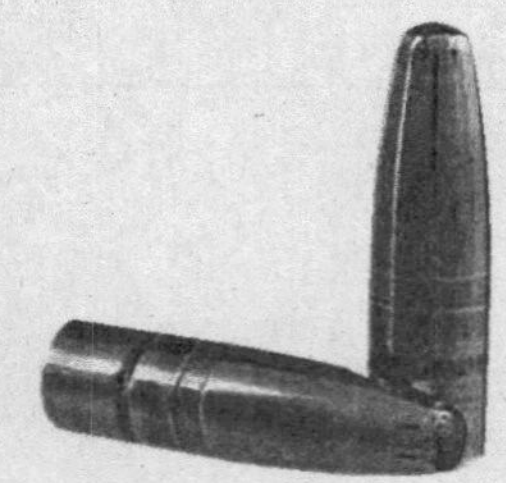
LAPUA MEGA

LAPUA NATURALIS THIRD GENERATION

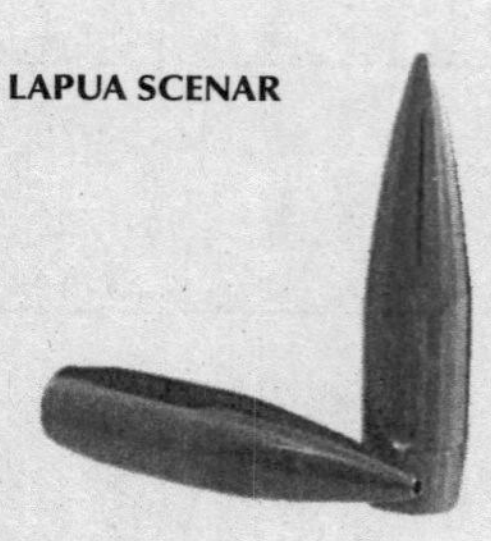
LAPUA SCENAR

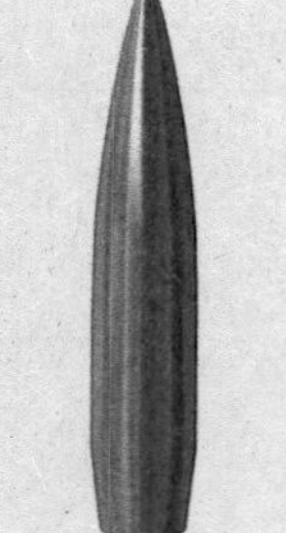
LAPUA SCENAR-L

AMMUNITION

Nosler Bullets

Rifle Bullets

Accubond

Caliber & Description	6mm S	25 SWT	6.5mm SWT	6.5mm	270 SWT	270 SWT	7mm SWT	7mm SWT	30 SWT	30 SWT	30 S	30 SWT	30 SWT
Diameter, inches	.243	.257	.264	.264	.277	.277	.277	.277	.284	.284	.308	.308	.308
Weight, Grains	90	110	130	140	100	110	130	140	140	160	125	150	165
Density	.218	.238	.266	.287	.186	.205	.242	.261	.248	.283	.188	.226	.248
Ballistic Coefficient	.376	.418	.488	.509	.323	.370	.435	.496	.485	.531	.366	.435	.475
Catalog Number	56357	53742	56902	57873	57845	54382	54987	54765	59992	54932	52165	56719	55602

Caliber & Description	30 S	30 S	8mm S	338 S	338 S	338 S	338 S	338 S	35 Whelen S	35 Whelen S	9.3mm S	375 S	375 S
Diameter, inches	.308	.308	.323	.338	.338	.338	.338	.338	.358	.358	.366	.375	.375
Weight, Grains	180	200	200	180	200	225	250	300	200	225	250	260	300
Density	.271	.301	.274	.225	.250	.281	.313	.375	.223	.251	.267	.264	.305
Ballistic Coefficient	.507	.588	.450	.372	.414	.550	.575	.720	.365	.421	.494	.473	.485
Catalog Number	54825	54618	54374	57625	56382	54357	57287	54851	54425	50712	59756	54413	53662

Box 50, 100: N/A

Ballistic Tip Hunting

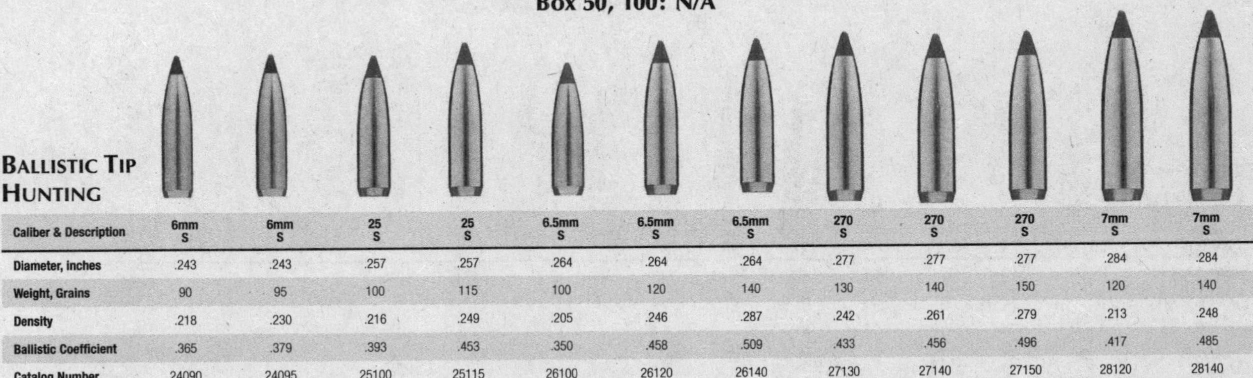

Caliber & Description	6mm S	6mm S	25 S	25 S	6.5mm S	6.5mm S	6.5mm S	270 S	270 S	270 S	7mm S	7mm S
Diameter, inches	.243	.243	.257	.257	.264	.264	.264	.277	.277	.277	.284	.284
Weight, Grains	90	95	100	115	100	120	140	130	140	150	120	140
Density	.218	.230	.216	.249	.205	.246	.287	.242	.261	.279	.213	.248
Ballistic Coefficient	.365	.379	.393	.453	.350	.458	.509	.433	.456	.496	.417	.485
Catalog Number	24090	24095	25100	25115	26100	26120	26140	27130	27140	27150	28120	28140

Caliber & Description	7mm S	30 S	30 S	30 S	30 S	30 S	8mm S
Diameter, inches	.284	.308	.308	.308	.308	.308	.323
Weight, Grains	150	125	150	165	168	180	180
Density	.266	.188	.226	.248	.253	.271	.247
Ballistic Coefficient	.493	.366	.435	.475	.490	.507	.394
Catalog Number	28150	30125	30150	30165	30168	30180	32180

Box 50: N/A

LEGEND

Type of Bullet		Type of Tip	
BT	Boat Tail	PT	Purple Tip
HP	Hollow Point	BT	Blue Tip
J	Jacketed	BrT	Brown Tip
PP	Protected Point	BuT	Buckskin Tip
RN	Round Nose	GT	Green Tip
S	Spitzer	GuT	Gunmetal Tip
SS	Semi Spitzer	MT	Maroon Tip
W	Whelen	OT	Olive Tip
		RT	Red Tip
		SLT	Soft Lead Tip
		YT	Yellow Tip

Nosler Bullets

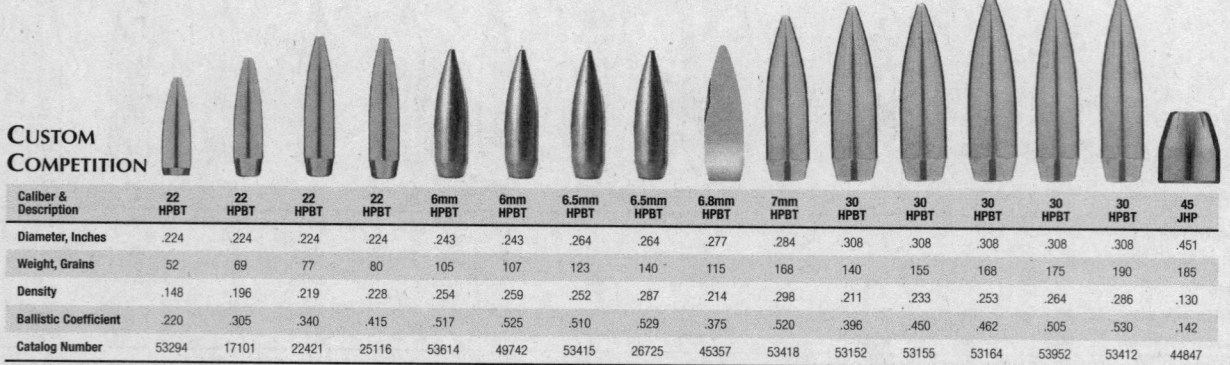

Ballistic Tip Varmint

Caliber & Description	204 S	204 S	22 S	22 S	22 S	22 S	6mm S	6mm S	6mm S	25 S
Diameter, inches	.204	.204	.224	.224	.224	.224	.243	.243	.243	.257
Weight, Grains	32	40	40	50	55	60	55	70	80	85
Density	.110	.137	.114	.142	.157	.171	.133	.169	.194	.184
Ballistic Coefficient	.206	.239	.221	.238	.27	.270	.276	.310	.329	.329
Catalog Number	35216	52111	39510	39522	39526	34992	24055	39532	24080	43004

Box 100: N/A

CT Ballistic Silvertip Hunting

Caliber & Description	6mm S	25 S	270 S	270 S	7mm S	7mm S	30 S	30 RN	30 S	30 S	8mm S	45-70 RN	338 S
Diameter, inches	.243	.257	.277	.277	.284	.284	.308	.308	.308	.308	.323	.458	.338
Weight, Grains	95	115	130	150	140	150	150	150	168	180	180	300	200
Density	.230	.249	.242	.279	.248	.266	.226	.226	.253	.271	.247	.204	.250
Ballistic Coefficient	.379	.453	.433	.496	.485	.493	.435	.232	.490	.507	.394	.191	.414
Catalog Number	51040	51050	51075	51100	51105	51110	51150	51165	51160	51170	51693	51834	51200

Box 50: N/A

Custom Competition

Caliber & Description	22 HPBT	22 HPBT	22 HPBT	22 HPBT	6mm HPBT	6mm HPBT	6.5mm HPBT	6.5mm HPBT	6.8mm HPBT	7mm HPBT	30 HPBT	30 HPBT	30 HPBT	30 HPBT	30 HPBT	45 JHP
Diameter, Inches	.224	.224	.224	.224	.243	.243	.264	.264	.277	.284	.308	.308	.308	.308	.308	.451
Weight, Grains	52	69	77	80	105	107	123	140	115	168	140	155	168	175	190	185
Density	.148	.196	.219	.228	.254	.259	.252	.287	.214	.298	.211	.233	.253	.264	.286	.130
Ballistic Coefficient	.220	.305	.340	.415	.517	.525	.510	.529	.375	.520	.396	.450	.462	.505	.530	.142
Catalog Number	53294	17101	22421	25116	53614	49742	53415	26725	45357	53418	53152	53155	53164	53952	53412	44847

Box 100, 250: N/A

E-TIP

Caliber& Description	6mm S	25 S	6.8mm S	270 S	7mm S	7mm S	30 S	30 S	30 S	8mm S	338 S	6.5MM S
Diameter, Inches	.243	.257	.277	.277	.284	.284	.308	.308	.308	.323	.338	264
Weight, Grains	90	100	85	130	140	150	150	168	180	180	200	120
Density	.218	.216	.158	.242	.248	.266	.226	.253	.271	.246	.250	.246
Ballistic Coefficient	.403	.409	.273	.459	.489	.498	.469	.503	.523	.427	.425	.497
Catalog Number	59165	59456	59543	59298	59955	59426	59378	59415	59180	59265	59186	59765

Box 50: N/A

Nosler Bullets

Partition

Caliber& Description	22 S	6mm S	6mm S	6mm S	25 S	25 S	25 S	6.5mm S	6.5mm S	6.5mm S	270 S	270 S	270 S	270 SS
Diameter, Inches	.224	.243	.243	.243	.257	.257	.257	.264	.264	.264	.277	.277	.277	.277
Weight, Grains	60	85	95	100	100	115	120	100	125	140	130	140	150	160
Density	.171	.206	.230	.242	.216	.249	.260	.205	.256	.287	.242	.261	.279	.298
Ballistic Coefficient	.228	.315	.365	.384	.377	.389	.391	.326	.4479	.490	.416	.432	.465	.434
Catalog Number	16316	16314	16315	35642	16317	16318	35643	16319	16320	16321	16322	35200	.16323	16324

Caliber & Description	7mm S	7mm S	7mm S	7mm S	30 S	30 S	30 RN	30 PP	30 S	30 S	30 SS	8mm S	338 S	338 S
Diameter, Inches	.284	.284	.284	.284	.308	.308	.308	.308	.308	.308	.308	.323	.338	.338
Weight, Grains	140	150	160	175	150	165	170	180	180	200	220	200	210	225
Density	.248	.266	.283	.310	.226	.248	.256	.271	.271	.301	.331	.274	.263	.281
Ballistic Coefficient	.434	.456	.475	.519	.387	.410	.252	.361	.474	.481	.351	.426	.400	.454
Catalog Number	16325	16326	16327	35645	16329	16330	16333	25396	16331	35626	16332	35277	16337	16336

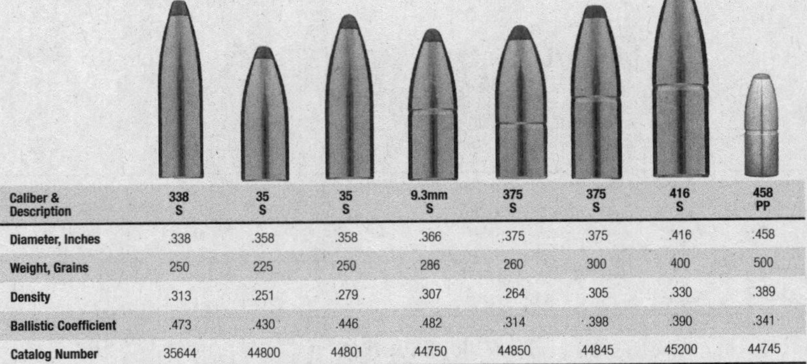

Caliber & Description	338 S	35 S	35 S	9.3mm S	375 S	375 S	416 S	458 PP
Diameter, Inches	.338	.358	.358	.366	.375	.375	.416	.458
Weight, Grains	250	225	250	286	260	300	400	500
Density	.313	.251	.279	.307	.264	.305	.330	.389
Ballistic Coefficient	.473	.430	.446	.482	.314	.398	.390	.341
Catalog Number	35644	44800	44801	44750	44850	44845	45200	44745

Box 25, 50: N/A

LEGEND

Type of Bullet
- **BT** – Boat Tail
- **HP** – Hollow Point
- **J** – Jacketed
- **PP** – Protected Point
- **RN** – Round Nose
- **S** – Spitzer
- **SS** – Semi Spitzer
- **W** – Whelen

Type of Tip
- **PT** – Purple Tip
- **BT** – Blue Tip
- **BrT** – Brown Tip
- **BuT** – Buckskin Tip
- **GT** – Green Tip
- **GuT** – Gunmetal Tip
- **MT** – Maroon Tip
- **OT** – Olive Tip
- **RT** – Red Tip
- **SLT** – Soft Lead Tip
- **YT** – Yellow Tip

Solid

Caliber & Description	9.3mm Solid	375 Solid	375 Solid	416 Solid	458 Solid	470 NE Solid
Diameter, Inches	.366	.375	.375	.416	.458	.474
Weight, Grains	286	260	300	400	500	500
Density	.305	.264	.305	.330	.341	.318
Ballistic Coefficient	.350	.254	.300	.289	.246	.237
Catalog Number	29825	29755	28451	23654	27452	28455

MSRP N/A

LEGEND

Type of Bullet
- **BT** – Boattail
- **FMJ** – Full Metal Jacket
- **J** – Jacketed
- **PP** – Protected Point
- **RN** – Round Nose
- **S** – Spitzer

Nosler Bullets

Varmageddon

Caliber& Description	17 FBHP	17 FB Tipped	20 FBHP	20 FB Tipped	22 FB Tipped	22 FBHP	22 FB Tipped	22 FBHP	22 FB Tipped	22 FBHP	6mm FBHP	6mm FB Tipped	6mm FB Tipped	30 FB Tipped
Diameter, Inches	.172	.172	.204	.204	.224	.224	.224	.224	.224	.224	.243	.243	.243	.308
Weight, Grains	20	20	32	32	35	40	40	55	55	62	55	55	70	110
Density	.097	.097	.110	.110	.100	.114	.114	.157	.157	.176	.133	.133	.169	.166
Ballistic Coefficient	.119	.183	.131	.204	.120	.158	.211	.210	.218	.251	.192	.252	.334	.293
Catalog Number	17205	17210	17215	17220	36763	17225	17230	17235	17240	35631	17245	17250	26123	34057

Box 100, 250: N/A

Handgun Bullets

Sporting Pistol

Caliber & Description	9mm JHP	9mm JHP	10mm JHP	10mm JHP	10mm JHP	10mm JHP	45 JHP	45 FMJ
Diameter, Inches	.355	.355	.400	.400	.400	.400	.451	.451
Weight, Grains	115	124	135	150	180	200	230	230
Density	.109	.141	.093	.106	.161	.179	.1625	.162
Ballistic Coefficient	.130	.118	.121	.134	.147	.163	.175	.183
Catalog Number	44848	43123	44852	44860	44885	44952	44922	44964

Box 250: N/A

LEGEND

Type of Bullet

BT – Boattail
FB – Flat Base
FN – Flat Nose
RN – Round Nose
S – Spitzer
SP – Soft Point
SS – Semi-Spitzer

Sporting Revolver

Caliber & Description	38 JHP	41 JHP	44 JHP	44 JHP	44 JHP	44 JHP	45 Colt JHP
Diameter, Inches	.357	.410	.429	.429	.429	.429	.451
Weight, Grains	158	210	200	240	240	300	250
Density	.182	.170	.151	.173	.177	.206	.177
Ballistic Coefficient	.177	.178	155	.186	.186	.233	.176
Catalog Number	44841	43012	44846	44842	44868	42069	43013

Box 100, 250: N/A

Sierra Bullets

Rifle Bullets

BlitzKing

Caliber & Description	20	20	224	224	224	6mm	6mm	257	257
Diameter, Inches	.204	.204	.224	.224	.224	.243	.243	.257	.257
Weight, Grains	32	39	40	50	55	55	70	70	90
Density	.110	.134	.114	.142	.157	.133	.169	.151	.195
Ballistic Coefficient	.221	.287	.196	.248	.185	.225	.299	.260	.388
Catalog Number	1032	1039	1440	1450	1455	1502	1507	1605	1616

From: N/A

Sierra Bullets

GameKing

Caliber & Description	22 FMJBT	22 SBT	22 HPBT	22 SBT	6mm HPBT	6mm FMJBT	6mm SBT	25 HPBT	25 SBT	25 SBT	25 HPBT	6.5mm HPBT
Diameter, Inches	.224	.224	.224	.224	.243	.243	.243	.257	.257	.257	.257	.264
Weight, Grains	55	55	55	65	85	90	100	90	100	117	120	130
Density	.157	.257	.157	.185	.206	.218	.242	.195	.216	.253	.260	.266
Ballistic Coefficient	.272	.250	.185	.303	.282	.387	.430	.250	.355	.410	.350	.355
Catalog Number	1355	1365	1390	1395	1530	1535	1560	1615	1625	1630	1650	1728

Caliber & Description	6.5mm SBT	270 SBT	270 HPBT	270 SBT	270 SBT	7mm HPBT	7mm SBT	7mm SBT	7mm SBT	7mm HPBT	7mm SBT	30 FMJBT
Diameter, Inches	.264	.277	.277	.277	.277	.284	.274	.284	.284	.284	.284	.308
Weight, Grains	140	130	140	140	150	140	140	150	160	160	175	150
Density	.287	.242	.261	.261	.279	.248	.248	.266	.283	.283	.310	.226
Ballistic Coefficient	.495	.436	.337	.457	.483	.375	.416	.436	.455	.384	.533	.408
Catalog Number	1730	1820	1835	1845	1840	1912	1905	1913	1920	1925	1940	2115

Caliber & Description	30 SBT	30 HPBT	30 SBT	30 SBT	30 SBT	8mm SBT	338 SBT	338 SBT	35 SBT	375 SBT	375 SBT
Diameter, Inches	.308	.308	.308	.308	.308	.323	.338	.338	.358	.375	.375
Weight, Grains	150	165	165	180	200	220	215	250	225	250	300
Density	.226	.248	.248	.271	.301	.301	.269	.313	.251	.254	.305
Ballistic Coefficient	.380	.363	.404	.501	.560	.521	.485	.565	.370	.353	.475
Catalog Number	2125	2140	2145	2160	2165	2420	2610	2600	2850	2950	3000

From: N/A

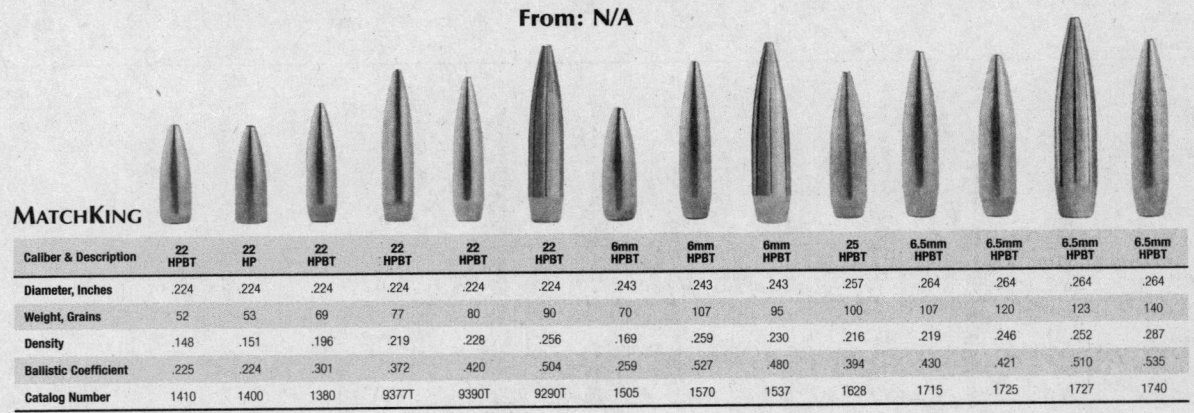

MatchKing

Caliber & Description	22 HPBT	22 HP	22 HPBT	22 HPBT	22 HPBT	22 HPBT	6mm HPBT	6mm HPBT	6mm HPBT	25 HPBT	6.5mm HPBT	6.5mm HPBT	6.5mm HPBT	6.5mm HPBT
Diameter, Inches	.224	.224	.224	.224	.224	.224	.243	.243	.243	.257	.264	.264	.264	.264
Weight, Grains	52	53	69	77	80	90	70	107	95	100	107	120	123	140
Density	.148	.151	.196	.219	.228	.256	.169	.259	.230	.216	.219	.246	.252	.287
Ballistic Coefficient	.225	.224	.301	.372	.420	.504	.259	.527	.480	.394	.430	.421	.510	.535
Catalog Number	1410	1400	1380	9377T	9390T	9290T	1505	1570	1537	1628	1715	1725	1727	1740

Sierra Bullets

MatchKing (cont.)

Caliber & Description	6.5mm HPBT	270 HPBT	270 HPBT	7mm HPBT	7mm HPBT	7mm HPBT	7mm HPBT	7mm HPBT	7mm HPBT	30 HP	30 HPBT	30 HPBT	30 HPBT	30 HPBT	30 HPBT	30 HPBT
Diameter, Inches	.264	.277	.277	.284	.284	.284	.284	.284	.284	.308	.308	.308	.308	.308	.308	.308
Weight, Grains	142	115	135	130	150	168	175	180	183	125	135	150	155	168	175	180
Density	.291	.214	.251	.230	.266	.298	.310	.319	.324	.188	.203	.226	.233	.253	.264	.271
Ballistic Coefficient	.595	.318	.488	.395	.429	.488	.608	.660	.707	.349	.390	.417	.450	.462	.505	.475
Catalog Number	1742	1815	1833	1903	1915	1930	1975	1980	1983	2121	2123	2190	2155	2200	2275	2220

Caliber & Description	30 HPBT	30 HPBT	30 HPBT	30 HPBT	30 HPBT	303 HPBT	8mm HPBT	338 HPBT	338 HPBT	375 HPBT
Diameter, Inches	.308	.308	.308	.308	.308	.311	.323	.338	.338	.375
Weight, Grains	190	200	210	220	240	174	200	250	300	350
Density	.286	.301	.316	.331	.361	.257	.274	.313	.375	.355
Ballistic Coefficient	.533	.565	.645	.629	.711	.499	.520	.587	.768	.805
Catalog Number	2210	2230	9240T	2240	9245T	2315	2415	2650	9300T	9350T

LEGEND
- **BT** – Boattail
- **FMJ** – Full Metal Jacket
- **FN** – Flat Nose
- **HC** – Hollow Cavity
- **HP** – Hollow Point
- **J** – Jacketed
- **RN** – Round Nose
- **S** – Spitzer
- **SMP** – Semi-Pointed
- **SP** – Soft Point

From: N/A

Pro-Hunter

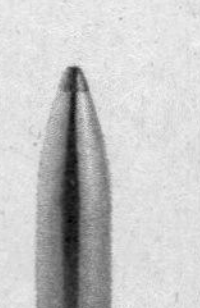
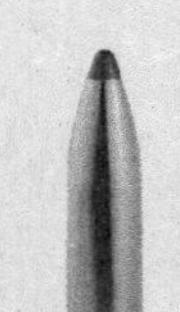
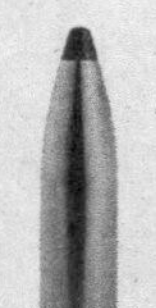

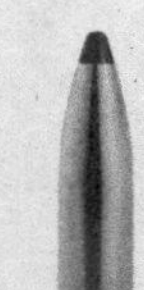
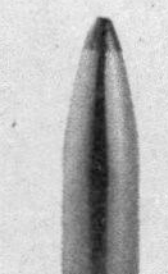

Caliber & Description	6mm S	25 S	25 S	6.5mm S	270 S	270 S	7mm S	7mm S	30 HP/FN	30 FN	30 FN
Diameter, Inches	.243	.257	.257	.264	.277	.277	.284	.284	.308	.308	.308
Weight, Grains	100	100	117	120	110	130	120	140	125	150	170
Density	.242	.216	.253	.246	.205	.242	.213	.248	.188	.226	.256
Ballistic Coefficient	.373	.330	.388	.356	.318	.370	.328	.377	.119	.185	.205
Catalog Number	1540	1620	1640	1720	1810	1830	1900	1910	2020	2000	2010

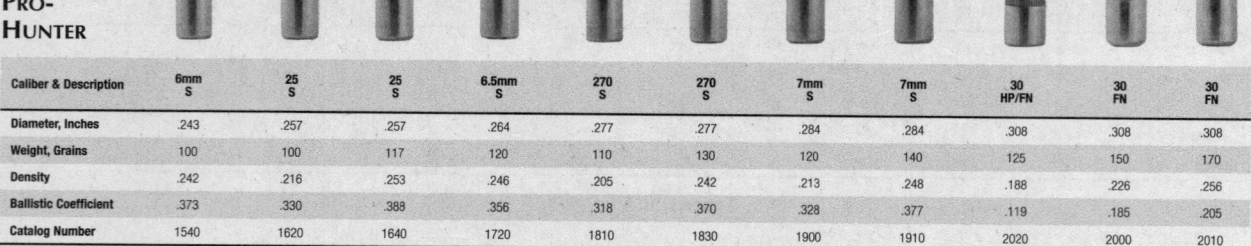

Caliber & Description	30 RN	30 FMJ	30 S	30 S	30 RN	30 S	30 RN	30 RN
Diameter, Inches	.308	.308	.308	.308	.308	.308	.308	.308
Weight, Grains	110	110	125	150	150	180	180	220
Density	.166	.166	.188	.226	.226	.271	.271	.331
Ballistic Coefficient	.144	.144	.279	.336	.200	.407	.240	.310
Catalog Number	2100	2105	2120	2130	2135	2150	2170	2180

Sierra Bullets

Pro-Hunter (cont.)

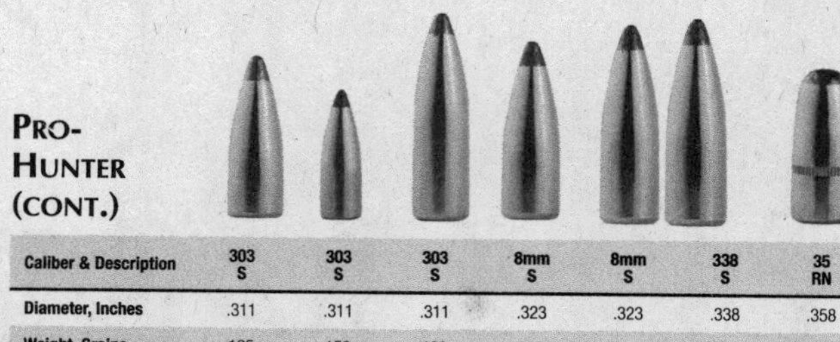

Caliber & Description	303 S	303 S	303 S	8mm S	8mm S	338 S	35 RN	375 FN	45-70 HP/FN
Diameter, Inches	.311	.311	.311	.323	.323	.338	.358	.375	.458
Weight, Grains	125	150	180	150	175	225	200	200	300
Density	.185	.222	.266	.205	.240	.281	.223	.203	.204
Ballistic Coefficient	.274	.344	.411	.336	.381	.462	.148	.195	.120
Catalog Number	2305	2300	2310	2400	2410	2620	2800	2900	8900

From: N/A

Varminter

Caliber & Description	22 Hornet	22 Hornet	22 Hornet	22 Hornet	22 HP
Diameter, Inches	.223	.223	.224	.224	.224
Weight, Grains	40	45	40	45	40
Density	.115	.129	.114	.128	.114
Ballistic Coefficient	.117	.132	.116	.131	.155
Catalog Number	1100	1110	1200	1210	1385

Caliber & Description	22 S	22 S	22 S	22 Blitz	22 Blitz	22 SMP	22 S	22 HP	22 SMP	6mm HP	6mm HP	6mm SBT Blitz	6mm S	25 HP	25 S	6.5mm HP	6.5mm HP	270 HP	7mm HP	30 HP
Diameter, Inches	.224	.224	.224	.224	.224	.224	.224	.224	.224	.243	.243	.243	.243	.257	.257	.264	.264	.277	.284	.308
Weight, Grains	45	50	50	50	55	55	55	60	63	60	75	80	85	75	87	85	100	90	100	110
Density	.128	.142	.142	.142	.157	.157	.157	.171	.179	.145	.181	.194	.206	.162	.188	.174	.205	.168	.177	.166
Ballistic Coefficient	.210	.192	.222	.222	.237	.204	.237	.246	.231	.182	.217	.319	.315	.189	.293	.225	.259	.195	.209	.177
Catalog Number	1310	1320	1330	1340	1345	1350	1360	1375	1370	1500	1510	1515	1520	1600	1610	1700	1710	1800	1895	2110

From: N/A

Tipped MatchKing

Caliber & Description	224	224	243	264	284	308	308	308	308
Diameter, Inches	.224	.224	.243	.264	.284	.308	.308	.308	.308
Weight, Grains	69	77	95	130	160	125	155	168	175
Density	.196	.219	.243	.264	.284	.188	.233	.253	.264
Ballistic Coefficient	.375	.420	.500	.518	.600	.343	.519	.535	.545
Catalog Number	7169	7177	7295	7430	7660	7725	7755	7768	7775

From: N/A

Handgun Bullets

Sports Master

Caliber & Description	30 RN	32 JHC	9mm JHP	9mm JHP	9mm JHP	38 JHP Blitz	38 JHP	38 JSP	38 JHP	38 JHC	38 JSP	10mm JHP	10mm JHP
Diameter, Inches	.308	.312	.355	.355	.355	.357	.357	.357	.357	.357	.357	.400	.400
Weight, Grains	85	90	90	115	125	110	125	125	140	158	158	135	150
Density	.128	.132	.102	.130	.142	.123	.140	.140	.157	.177	.177	.121	.134
Ballistic Coefficient	.102	.125	.095	.107	.124	.120	.133	.133	.0776	.100	.100	.105	.120
Catalog Number	8005	8030	8100	8110	8125	8300	8320	8310	8325	8360	8340	8425	8430

Sierra Bullets

Handgun Bullets

Caliber & Description	10mm JHP	10mm JHP	41 JHC	41 JHC	44 JHC	44 JHC	44 JHC	44 JSP	45 JHP	45 JHP	45 JHC	45 JSP	50 JHP	50 JSP
Diameter, Inches	.400	.400	.410	.410	.4295	.4295	.4295	.4295	.4515	.4515	.4515	.4515	.500	.500
Weight, Grains	165	180	170	210	180	210	240	300	185	230	240	300	350	400
Density	.147	.161	.144	.178	.139	.163	.186	.232	.130	.161	.168	.210	.200	.229
Ballistic Coefficient	.130	.140	.123	.165	.130	.160	.185	.230	.100	.145	.150	.192	.155	.185
Catalog Number	8445	8460	8500	8520	8600	8620	8610	8630	8800	8805	8820	8830	5350	5400

From: N/A

V-Crown

Caliber & Description	9mm JHP	9mm JHP	9mm JHP	10mm JHP	45 JHP
Diameter, Inches	.355	.355	.355	.400	.4515
Weight, Grains	90	124	125	165	200
Density	.109	.160	.168	.147	.143
Ballistic Coefficient	.094	.120	.122	.132	.118
Catalog Number	9990	9924	9925	9465	9820

Box 100: N/A

Speer Bullets

Rifle Bullets

Boat Tail Bullets

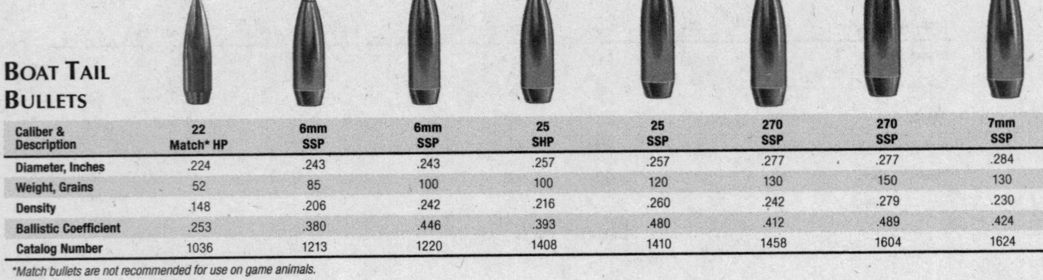

Caliber & Description	22 Match* HP	6mm SSP	6mm SSP	25 SHP	25 SSP	270 SSP	270 SSP	7mm SSP
Diameter, Inches	.224	.243	.243	.257	.257	.277	.277	.284
Weight, Grains	52	85	100	100	120	130	150	130
Density	.148	.206	.242	.216	.260	.242	.279	.230
Ballistic Coefficient	.253	.380	.446	.393	.480	.412	.489	.424
Catalog Number	1036	1213	1220	1408	1410	1458	1604	1624

Match bullets are not recommended for use on game animals.

Caliber & Description	7mm SSP	7mm Match* HP	7mm SSP	30 SSP	30 SSP	30 Match* HP	30 SSP	338 SSP	375 SSP
Diameter, Inches	.284	.284	.284	.308	.308	.308	.308	.338	.375
Weight, Grains	145	145	160	150	165	168	180	225	270
Density	.257	.257	.284	.226	.248	.253	.271	.281	.274
Ballistic Coefficient	.472	.468	.519	.417	.520	.534	.545	.497	.478
Catalog Number	1628	1631	1634	2022	2034	2040	2052	2406	2472

Match bullets are not recommended for use on game animals.

From: N/A

Speer Bullets

LEGEND

- **BT** – Boat Tail
- **FB** – Fusion Bonded
- **FMJ** – Full Metal Jacket
- **FN** – Flat Nose
- **GD** – Gold Dot
- **HC** – Hot-Cor
- **HP** – Hollow Point
- **L** – Lead
- **MHP** – Molybdenum Disulfide Impregnated
- **S** – Spitzer
- **SS** – Semi-Spitzer
- **SB** – For Short-Barrel Firearms
- **SP** – Soft Point
- **TMJ** – Encased-Core Full Jacket
- **RN** – Round Nose
- **SWC** – Semi-Wadcutter
- **UC** – Uni-Cor
- **WC** – Wadcutter

Grand Slam

Caliber & Description	6mm SP	25 HCSP	270 HCSP	270 HCSP	7mm HCSP	7mm HCSP	7mm HCSP	30 HCSP	30 HCSP	30 HCSP	338 HCSP	375 HCSP
Diameter, Inches	.243	.257	.277	.277	.284	.284	.284	.308	.308	.308	.338	.375
Weight, Grains	100	120	130	150	145	160	175	150	165	180	250	285
Density	.242	.260	.242	.279	.257	.283	.310	.226	.248	.271	.313	.290
Ballistic Coefficient	.327	.356	.332	.378	.353	.389	.436	.295	.354	.374	.436	.354
Catalog Number	1222	1415	1465	1608	1632	1638	1643	2026	2038	2063	2408	2473

From: N/A

Hot-Cor Bullets*

Caliber & Description	6mm SSP	25 SPFN	25 SSP	25 SSP	25 SSP	6.5mm SSP	6.5mm SSP	270 SSP	270 SSP	7mm SSP	7mm SPFN	7mm SSP
Diameter, Inches	.243	.257	.257	.257	.257	.264	.264	.277	.277	.284	.284	.284
Weight, Grains	90	75	87	100	120	120	140	130	150	130	130	145
Density	.218	.162	.188	.216	.260	.246	.287	.242	.279	.230	.230	.257
Ballistic Coefficient	.365	.135	.300	.334	.405	.392	.498	.383	.455	.394	.257	.416
Catalog Number	1217	1237	1241	1405	1411	1435	1441	1459	1605	1623	1625	1629

** Not recommended for lever-action rifles.*

Caliber & Description	7mm SSP	30 Spire SP	30 FNSP	30 SPFN	30 RNSP	30 SSP	30 Mag-Tip	30 SSP	30 SSP	30 SPRN	30 SSP	30 SSP	7.62x39 SSP
Diameter, Inches	.284	.308	.308	.308	.308	.308	.308	.308	.308	.308	.308	.308	.310
Weight, Grains	160	110	130	150	150	150	150	165	170	180	180	200	123
Density	.283	.166	.196	.226	.226	.226	.226	.248	.256	.271	.271	.301	.183
Ballistic Coefficient	.504	.245	.213	.255	.235	.377	.301	.444	.298	.304	.441	.478	.283
Catalog Number	1635	1855	2007	2011	2017	2023	2025	2035	2041	2047	2053	2211	2213

** Not recommended for lever-action rifles.*

Caliber & Description	303 SSP	303 RNSP	32 FNSP	8mm SSP	8mm SSSP	8mm SSP	338 SSP	35 FNSP	35 FNSP	35 SSP	9.3mm SSSP	375 SSSP	416 Mag-Tip	45 FNSP
Diameter, Inches	.311	.311	.321	.323	.323	.323	.338	.358	.358	.358	.366	.375	.416	.458
Weight, Grains	150	180	170	150	170	200	200	180	220	250	270	235	350	350
Density	.222	.266	.236	.205	.233	.274	.250	.201	.245	.279	.288	.239	.289	.238
Ballistic Coefficient	.351	.299	.283	.343	.311	.440	.426	.236	.286	.422	.361	.301	.332	.218
Catalog Number	2217	2223	2259	2277	2283	2285	2405	2435	2439	2453	2459	2471	2477	2478

From: N/A

Speer Bullets

Jacketed HP Bullets

Caliber & Description	22 Hornet	45
Diameter, Inches	.224	.458
Weight, Grains	33	300
Density	.094	.204
Ballistic Coefficient	.080	.206
Catalog Number	1014	2482

From: N/A

Special Purpose Bullets*

Caliber & Description	30 SPRN	30 HP	45 SPFN
Diameter, Inches	.308	.308	.458
Weight, Grains	100	110	400
Density	.151	.166	.272
Ballistic Coefficient	.144	.128	.259
Catalog Number	1805	1835	2479

From: N/A

TNT Bullets

Caliber & Description	204 HP	22 HP	22 HP	6mm HP	25 HP	6.5mm HP	270 HP	7mm HP	30 HP
Diameter, Inches	.204	.224	.224	.243	.247	.264	.277	.284	.308
Weight, Grains	39	50	55	70	87	90	90	110	125
Density	.134	.142	.157	.169	.188	.184	.168	.195	.188
Ballistic Coefficient	.202	.228	.233	.279	.337	.281	.303	.384	.341
Catalog Number	1015	1030	1032	1206	1246	1445	1446	1616	1986

From: N/A

Handgun Bullets

Gold Dot Bullets

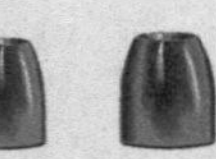

Caliber & Description	25 HP	32 Auto HP	327 Fed. Mag. HP	327 Fed. Mag. HP	380 Auto HP	9mm HP	9mm HP	9mm HP	357 SIG HP	38 Spl. HPSB	38 HPSB	357 Mag. HP	40/10mm HP
Diameter, Inches	.251	.312	.312	.312	.355	.355	.355	.355	.355	.357	.357	.357	.400
Weight, Grains	35	60	100	115	90	115	124	147	125	110	135	125	155
Density	.079	.088	.147	.168	.102	.130	.141	.167	.142	.123	.151	.177	.138
Ballistic Coefficient	.091	.118	.137	.180	.101	.125	.134	.164	.141	.117	.141	.140	.123
Catalog Number	3985	3986	3990	3988	3992	3994	3998	4002	4360	4009	4014	4012	4400

Caliber & Description	40/10mm HP	40/10mm HP	40/10mm HPSB	44 Spl. HP	44 Mag. HP	45 Auto HP	45 Auto HP	45 Auto HP	45 HPSB
Diameter, Inches	.400	.400	.400	.429	.429	.451	.451	.451	.451
Weight, Grains	165	180	180	200	210	185	200	230	230
Density	.147	.161	.161	.155	.163	.130	.140	.162	.162
Ballistic Coefficient	.138	.143	.148	.145	.154	.109	.138	.143	.148
Catalog Number	4397	4406	4401	4427	4428	4470	4478	4483	4482

LEGEND

- **BT** – Boat Tail
- **FB** – Fusion Bonded
- **FMJ** – Full Metal Jacket
- **FN** – Flat Nose
- **GD** – Gold Dot
- **HC** – Hot-Cor
- **HP** – Hollow Point
- **L** – Lead
- **MHP** – Molybdenum Disulfide Impregnated
- **S** – Spitzer
- **SS** – Semi-Spitzer
- **SB** – For Short-Barrel Firearms
- **SP** – Soft Point
- **TMJ** – Encased-Core Full Jacket
- **RN** – Round Nose
- **SWC** – Semi-Wadcutter
- **UC** – Uni-Cor
- **WC** – Wadcutter

From: N/A

Speer Bullets

Jacketed Bullets

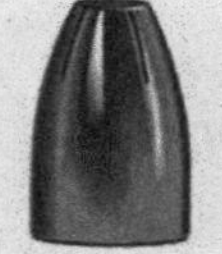      

Caliber & Description	9mm Luger FN JSP	38 Spl./357 Mag. JHP	38 Spl./357 Mag. JSP	38 Spl./357 Mag. JHP	38 Spl./357 Mag. JHP	38 Spl./357 Mag. JHP	38 Spl./357 Mag. JSP
Diameter, Inches	.355	.357	.357	.357	.357	.357	.357
Weight, Grains	124	110	125	125	140	158	158
Density	.141	.123	.140	.140	.157	.177	.177
Ballistic Coefficient	.115	.113	.129	.129	.145	.163	.164
Catalog Number	3997	4007	4011	4013	4203	4211	4217

Caliber & Description	44 Mag. JSP	44 Mag. JSP	45 Colt/460 S&W JHP	45 Colt/460 S&W JSP	50 Action Express JHP
Diameter, Inches	.429	.429	.451	.451	.186
Weight, Grains	240	300	260	300	325
Density	.186	.233	.183	.211	.186
Ballistic Coefficient	.169	.213	.183	.199	.169
Catalog Number	4454	4463	4481	4485	4495

LEGEND

FN	– Flat Nose	**S**	– Spitzer
HB	– Hollow Base	**SP**	– Soft Point
HC	– Hot-Cor	**SS**	– Semi-Spitzer
HP	– Hollow Point	**SWC**	– Semi-Wadcutter
J	– Jacketed	**WC**	– Wadcutter
RN	– Round Nose		

From: N/A

Lead Handgun Bullets

Caliber & Description	32 S&W HBWC	9mm Luger RN	38 HBWC	38 SWC	38 SWC HP	38 RN	44 SWC	45 Auto SWC	45 Auto RN	45 Colt SWC
Diameter, Inches	.314	.356	.358	.358	.358	.358	.430	.452	.452	.452
Weight, grains	98	125	148	158	158	158	240	200	230	250
Density	.142	.141	.165	.176	.176	.176	.185	.140	.161	.175
Ballistic Coefficient	.044	.155	.050	.123	.121	.170	.151	.078	.160	.117
Bulk Part No.	4600	4602	4618	4624	4628	4648	4661	4678	4691	4684
Bulk Count	1000	500	500	500	500	500	500	500	500	500

From: N/A

Swift Bullet Company

Rifle Bullets

The Scirocco II rifle bullet starts with a tough, pointed polymer tip that reduces air resistance, prevents tip deformation, and blends into the radius of its secant ogive nose section. The Scirocco II has a bonded core construction with a pure lead core encased in a tapered, progressively thickening jacket of pure copper. The Swift A-Frame bullet with its midsection wall of copper is less aerodynamic than the Scirocco, but it produces a broad mushroom while carrying almost all its weight through muscle and bone.

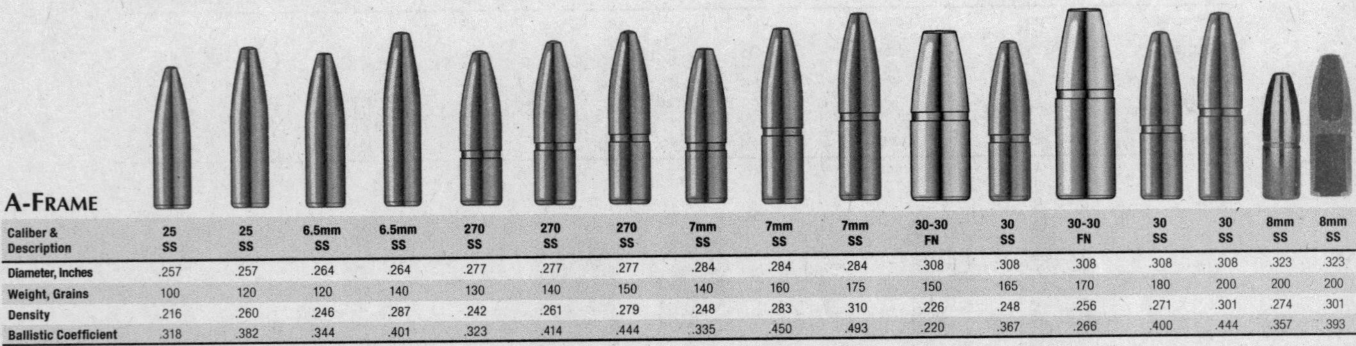

A-Frame

Caliber & Description	25 SS	25 SS	6.5mm SS	6.5mm SS	270 SS	270 SS	270 SS	7mm SS	7mm SS	7mm SS	30-30 FN	30 SS	30-30 FN	30 SS	30 SS	8mm SS	8mm SS
Diameter, Inches	.257	.257	.264	.264	.277	.277	.277	.284	.284	.284	.308	.308	.308	.308	.308	.323	.323
Weight, Grains	100	120	120	140	130	140	150	140	160	175	150	165	170	180	200	200	200
Density	.216	.260	.246	.287	.242	.261	.279	.248	.283	.310	.226	.248	.256	.271	.301	.274	.301
Ballistic Coefficient	.318	.382	.344	.401	.323	.414	.444	.335	.450	.493	.220	.367	.266	.400	.444	.357	.393

Caliber & Description	338 SS	338 SS	338 SS	348 FN	35 SS	35 SS	35 SS	9.3mm SS	9.3mm SS	9.3mm SS	375 SS	375 SS	375 SS	400 SS	400 SS
Diameter, Inches	.338	.338	.338	.348	.358	.358	.358	.366	.366	.366	.375	.375	.375	.410	.410
Weight, Grains	225	250	275	200	225	250	280	250	286	300	250	270	300	350	400
Density	.281	.313	.344	.236	.251	.279	.312	.267	.305	.320	.254	.274	.305	.297	.339
Ballistic Coefficient	.384	.427	.469	.245	.312	.347	.388	.285	.385	.342	.271	.349	.325	.321	.367

LEGEND

Type of Bullet

- **BT** – Boat Tail
- **CT** – Combat Target
- **FMJ** – Full Metal Jacket
- **FP** – Flat Point
- **HB** – Hollow Base
- **L** – Lead
- **RN** – Round Nose
- **SP** – Spire Point
- **SX** – Super Explosive
- **SWC** – Semi-Wadcutter
- **WC** – Wadcutter

Swift Bullet Company

Caliber & Description	416 SS	416 SS	404 SS	45-70 FN	458 FN	458 SS	458 SS	470 RN	505 RN	505 RN	50 FN	500 RN	500 RN
Diameter, Inches	.416	.416	.423	.457	.458	.458	.458	.475	.505	.505	.509	.509	.509
Weight, Grains	350	400	400	350	400	450	500	500	535	570	450	535	570
Density	.289	.330	.319	.238	.272	.307	.341	.329	.300	.319	.247	.294	.313
Ballistic Coefficient	.321	.367	.375	.172	.258	.325	.361	.364	.285	.306	.180	.285	.306

MSRP N/A

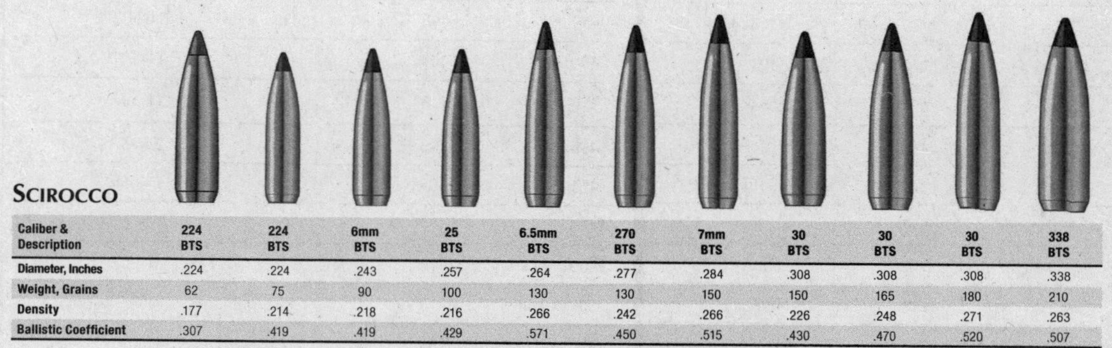

Scirocco

Caliber & Description	224 BTS	224 BTS	6mm BTS	25 BTS	6.5mm BTS	270 BTS	7mm BTS	30 BTS	30 BTS	30 BTS	338 BTS
Diameter, Inches	.224	.224	.243	.257	.264	.277	.284	.308	.308	.308	.338
Weight, Grains	62	75	90	100	130	130	150	150	165	180	210
Density	.177	.214	.218	.216	.266	.242	.266	.226	.248	.271	.263
Ballistic Coefficient	.307	.419	.419	.429	.571	.450	.515	.430	.470	.520	.507

MSRP N/A

LEGEND
BT – Boattail
FN – Flat Nose
HP – Hollow Point
RN – Round Nose
S – Spitzer
SS – Semi-Spitzer

Handgun Bullets

A-Frame Hunting Revolver Bullets

Caliber & Description	357 HP	357 HP	41 HP	44 HP	44 HP	44 HP	45 HP	45 HP	45 HP	50 HP
Diameter, Inches	.357	.357	.410	.430	.430	.430	.452	.452	.452	.499
Weight, Grains	158	180	210	240	280	300	265	300	325	325
Density	.177	.202	.178	.185	.216	.232	.185	.210	.227	.186
Ballistic Coefficient	.183	.189	.159	.119	.139	.147	.129	.153	.171	.135

MSRP N/A

LEGEND
BT – Boattail
FN – Flat Nose
HP – Hollow Point
RN – Round Nose
S – Spitzer
SS – Semi-Spitzer

Woodleigh Bullets

HYDROSTATICALLY STABILIZED

Hydrostatic stabilization is a method of producing pierced hollow bars to very precise concentricity to produce a bullet that resists deflection and achieves deep straight-line penetration. It's non-toxic and environmentally sensitive. It can be used in most nitro double and magazine rifles.

10–20 per box: N/A

Caliber	Diameter	"Weight, Grains"	Catalog Number
7mm	.284	140	H7mm
308	.308	150	H308A
308	.308	180	H308
303	.312	215	H303
8mm	.323	170	H8mm
338	.338	185	H338A
338	.338	225	H338
358	.358	225	H358
9.3	.366	232	H9.3A
9,3	.366	286	H9.3
375 Win.	.375	235	H375A
375	.375	300	H375
450/400 3"	.410	400	H450/400

Caliber	Diameter	"Weight, Grains"	Catalog Number
416	.416	400	H416
404 Jeffery	.422	400	H404
450	.458	325	H450BPE
45/70	.458	400	H45/70
458	.458	450	H458A
458	.458	480	H458
465	.468	480	H465
470	.474	500	H470
500	.510	570	H500
50 Alaskan	.510	400	H50 Alaskan
505	.505	525	H505
577	.585	750	H577

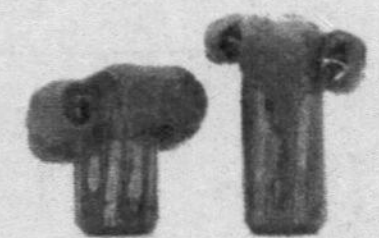

98% & 95% RETAINED WEIGHT 300 WIN MAG 180GR PP

458 X 500GN SN RECOVERED FROM BUFFALO

270 WIN 150GN PP 86% RETAINED WEIGHT

94% RETAINED WEIGHT 300 WIN MAG 180GR PP

500/465 RECOVERED FROM BUFFALO

Woodleigh Bullets

TRADITIONAL BULLETS

Fashioned from gilding-metal-clad steel 2mm thick, jackets on FMJ bullets are heavy at the nose for extra impact resistance. The jacket then tapers toward the base to assist rifling engraving. Woodleigh Weldcore Soft Nose bullets are made from 90/100 gilding metal (90 percent copper; 10 percent zinc) 1.6 mm thick.

50 per box: N/A

Caliber Diameter	Type	Weight, Grains	SD	BC	Catalog Number
6.5mm	PP SN	140	.287	.444	80
.264	PP SN	160	.328	.509	80A
	RN SN	160	.328	.285	80B
270 Win	PP SN	130	.242	.409	72
.277	PP SN	150	.279	.463	73
	PP SN	180	.334	.513	73A
7mm	PP SN	140	.248	.436	74
.284	PP SN	160	.283	.486	75
	PP SN	175	.310	.510	76
275 H&H	PP SN	160	.277	.474	77
.287	PP SN	175	.304	.509	78
308	PP SN	130	.189	.302	65I
.308	PP SN	150	.226	.310	65F
	PP SN	165	.248	.320	65A
	PP SN	180	.271	.376	65B
	RN SN	220	.331	.367	65C
	FMJ	220	.331	.359	65
30-30 .308	FN SN	150	.226	.246	65H
30-06 .308	PP SN	240	.361	.401	65G
300 Win. Mag.	PP SN	180	.271	.435	65D
.308	PP SN	200	.301	.450	65E
303 British	PP SN	174	.255	.362	68A
.312	RN SN	215	.316	.359	68
303/ 7.62x39mm .312	PP SN	130	.180	.295	68B
8mm	RN SN	196	.268	.315	64B
.323	RN SN	220	.301	.355	64C
	RN SN	250	.343	.403	64D
325 Win.	PP SN	200	.274	.406	64F
(8mm) .323	PP SN	220	.301	.448	64G
8x57 .318	RN SN	200	.283	.331	64E
318 WR	RN SN	250	.328	.420	63
.330	FMJ	250	.328	.364	64
333 Jeffery	RN SN	250	.322	.335	60
.333	RN SN	300	.386	.418	61
	FMJ	300	.386	.418	62
338 Fed	PP SN	180	.226	.361	56C
.338	PP SN	200	.251	.401	56D
33 Win. .338	FN SN	200	.246	.234	56E
338 Mag	PP SN	225	.281	.425	56A
.338	RN SN	250	.313	.332	56
	PP SN	250	.313	.431	56B
	FMJ	250	.313	.326	57
	RN SN	300	.375	.416	58
	FMJ	300	.375	.414	59
348 Win. .348	FN SN	250	.295	.281	348

Caliber Diameter	Type	Weight, Grains	SD	BC	Catalog Number
358	RN SN	225	.251	.263	51
.358	PP SN	225	.251	.372	51A
	FMJ	225	.251	.263	52
	RN SN	250	.279	.300	53
	PP SN	250	.279	.400	53A
	PP SN	275	.307	.450	53B
	RN SN	310	.346	.458	54
	FMJ	310	.346	.458	55
9.3	RN SN	250	.267	.281	47A
.366	PP SN	250	.267	.381	47C
	RN SN	286	.305	.321	47
	PP SN	286	.305	.396	47B
	FMJ	286	.305	.305	48
	RN SN	320	.341	.359	49
	PP SN	320	.341	.457	49A
	FMJ	320	.341	.341	50
375 Mag.	PP SN	235	.239	.310	42A
.375	RN SN	270	.274	.250	42
	PP SN	270	.274	.370	43A
	RN SN	300	.305	.277	44HD
	RN SN	300	.305	.277	44
	PP SN	300	.305	.380	45A
	FMJ	300	.305	.275	46
	RN SN	350	.356	.321	46B
	RN SN	350	.356	.323	46BHD
	PP SN	350	.356	.400	46C
	FMJ	350	.356	.307	46D
400 Purdey .405	RN SN	230	.200	.181	81
450/400 Nitro .408	RN SN	400	.344	.307	40A
450/400 Nitro .411	RN SN	400	.338	.307	40
450/400 Ruger .410	RN SN	400	.338	.307	40B
450/400 Ruger .408	FMJ	400	.344	.300	41A
.410 Ruger	FMJ	400	.338	.300	41
405 Win. .412	RN SN	300	.252	.194	71
416 Rigby	PP SN	340	.281	.330	39
.416	RN SN	410	.338	.307	37A
	FMJ	410	.338	.300	38
	RN SN	450	.371	.338	37B
	FMJ	450	.371	.330	38B"
416 Rem.	RN SN	400	.330	.305	37C
.416	FMJ	400	.330	.300	38C
	RN SN	450	.371	.338	37N
	FMJ	450	.371	.330	38N
404 Jeffery	RN SN	350	.281	.293	35
.422	RN SN	400	.321	.335	33A
	FMJ	400	.321	.330	34
	RN SN	450	.361	.360	33B
	FMJ	450	.361	.355	34B
10.75x68mm	RN SN	347	.277	.290	36
.423	FMJ	347	.277	.288	36A
444 Marlin .430	FN SN	280	.216	.186	444

Woodleigh Bullets

Caliber Diameter	Type	Weight, Grains	SD	BC	Catalog Number
425 WR .435	RN SN	410	.310	.222	31
	FMJ	410	.310	.221	32
11.2 Schuler .440	RN SN	401	.296	.325	67
458 Mag. .458	PP SN	400	.272	.340	30
	RN SN	480	.327	.328	24A
	FMJ	480	.327	.325	25A
	RN SN	500	.341	.310	26
	PP SN	500	.341	.378	26A
	FMJ	500	.341	.310	28
	RN SN	550	.375	.340	27
	FMJ	550	.375	.326	29
450 BPE .458	RN SN	350	.238	.250	30A
45/70 .458	FN SN	405	.276	.204	30B
	FN SN	300	.205	.196	30C
450 Nitro .458	RN SN	480	.327	.328	24
	FMJ	480	.327	.325	25
465 Nitro .468	RN SN	480	.313	.334	22
	FMJ	480	.313	.330	23
470 Nitro .474	RN SN	500	.318	.374	20
	FMJ	500	.318	.370	21
476 WR .476	RN SN	520	.328	.385	18
	FMJ	520	.328	.380	19
475 No. 2 .483	RN SN	480	.294	.309	15
	FMJ	480	.294	.300	16
475 No. 2 Jeffery .488	RN SN	500	.300	.315	13
	FMJ	500	.300	.300	14
500 S&W MAG .500	FN SN	400	.229	.182	83
505 Gibbs .505	RN SN	525	.294	.345	11
	FMJ	525	.294	.340	12
	PP SN	600	.336	.360	11A
	FMJ	600	.336	.360	12A
500 Jeffery .510	RN SN	535	.294	.350	9
	PP SN	535	.294	.310	9A
	FMJ	535	.294	.340	10
	PP SN	600	.330	.350	10B
	FMJ	600	.330	.355	10A
500 BP .510	RN SN	440	.242	.255	8
50 Alaskan & 50/110 Win. .510	FN SN	500	.275	.219	82
500 Nitro .510	RN SN	450	.247	.257	06A
	RN SN	570	.313	.368	6
	FMJ	570	.313	.350	7
577 BP Express .585	RN SN	650	.271	.292	5
577 Nitro .585	RN SN	650	.271	.292	3A
	RN SN	750	.313	.346	3
577 Nitro .584	FMJ	650	.272	.292	4A
	FMJ	750	.314	.351	4
600 Nitro .620	RN SN	900	.334	.371	1
	FMJ	900	.334	.334	2
700 Nitro .700	RN SN	1000	.292	.340	A
	FMJ	1000	.292	.340	B

AMMUNITION

BALLISTICS

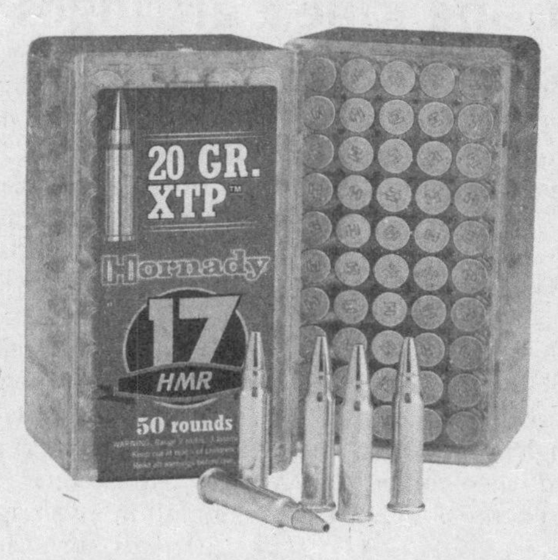

556 CENTERFIRE RIFLE BALLISTICS

590 LONG RANGE RIFLE

591 RIMFIRE BALLISTICS

593 CENTERFIRE HANDGUN BALLISTICS

Centerfire Rifle Ballistics

Comprehensive Ballistics Tables for Currently Manufactured Sporting Rifle Cartridges

No more collecting catalogs and peering at microscopic print to find out what ammunition is offered for a cartridge, and how it performs relative to other factory loads! *Shooter's Bible* has assembled the data for you, in easy-to-read tables, by cartridge.

Data is taken from manufacturers' charts; your chronograph readings may vary. Listings are not intended as recommendations. For example, the data for the .44 Magnum at 400 yards shows its effective range is much shorter. The lack of data for a 285-grain .375 H&H bullet beyond 300 yards does not mean the bullet has no authority farther out. Besides ammunition, the rifle, sights, conditions and shooter ability all must be considered when contemplating a long shot. Accuracy and bullet energy both matter when big game is in the offing.

Barrel length affects velocity, and at various rates depending on the load. As a rule, figure 50 fps per inch of barrel, plus or minus, if your barrel is longer or shorter than 22 inches.

Bullets are given by make, weight (in grains) and type. Most type abbreviations are self-explanatory: BT=Boat-Tail, FMJ=Full Metal Jacket, HP=Hollow Point, SP=Soft Point—except in Hornady listings, where SP is the firm's Spire Point. TNT and TXP are trademarked designations of Speer and Norma. XLC identifies a coated Barnes X bullet. HE indicates a Federal High Energy load, similar to the Hornady LM (Light Magnum) and HM (Heavy Magnum) cartridges.

Arc (trajectory) is based on a zero range published by the manufacturer, from 100 to 300 yards. If a zero does not fall in a yardage column, it lies halfway between—at 150 yards, for example, if the bullet's strike is "+" at 100 yards and "-" at 200.

.17 HORNET TO .222 REMINGTON

.17 Hornet

CARTRIDGE BULLET	RANGE, YARDS:	0	100	200	300	400
Hornady 15.5 NXT SPF		0	100	200	300	400
	velocity, fps:	3860	2924	2159	1531	1108
	energy, ft-lb:	513	294	160	81	42
	arc, inches:	-1.5	+1.4	0	-9.1	-33.7
Hornady 20 V-MAX		0	100	200	300	400
	velocity, fps:	3650	3077	2574	2122	1721
	energy, ft-lb:	592	420	294	200	132
	arc, inches:	-1.5	+1.1	0	-6.4	-20.7

.17 Remington

CARTRIDGE BULLET	RANGE, YARDS:	0	100	200	300	400
Rem. 20 AccuTip BT	velocity, fps:	4250	3594	3028	2529	2081
	energy, ft-lb:	802	574	407	284	192
	arc, inches:		+1.3	+1.3	-2.5	-11.8
Rem. 20 Fireball	velocity, fps	4000	3380	2840	2360	1930
	energy, ft-lb	710	507	358	247	165
	arc, inches		+1.6	+1.5	-2.8	-13.5
Rem. 25 HP Power-Lokt	velocity, fps:	4040	3284	2644	2086	1606
	energy, ft-lb:	906	599	388	242	143
	arc, inches:		+1.8	0	-3.3	-16.6

.204 Ruger

CARTRIDGE BULLET	RANGE, YARDS:	0	100	200	300	400
Federal 32 Nosler Ballistic Tip	velocity, fps	4030	3465	2968	2523	2119
	arc, inches		+0.7	0	-4.7	-14.9
Federal 40 Ballistic Tip	velocity, fps:	3650	3200	2790	2420	2080
	energy, ft-lb:	1185	910	695	520	385
	arc, inches:		+1.0	0	-5.4	-16.9
Hornady 32 V-Max	velocity, fps:	4225	3632	3114	2652	2234
	energy, ft-lb:	1268	937	689	500	355
	arc, inches:		+0.6	0	-4.2	-13.4
Hornady 40 V-Max	velocity, fps:	3900	3451	3046	2677	2335
	energy, ft-lb:	1351	1058	824	636	485
	arc, inches:		+0.7	0	-4.5	-13.9
Rem. 32 AccuTip	velocity, fps:	4225	3632	3114	2652	2234
	Energy, ft-lb:	1268	937	689	500	355
	Arc, inches:		+0.6	0	-4.1	-13.1
Rem. 40 AccuTip	velocity, fps:	3900	3451	3046	2677	2336
	energy, ft-lb:	1351	1058	824	636	485
	arc, inches:		+0.7	0	-4.3	-13.2
Win. 32 Ballistic Silver Tip	velocity, fps	4050	3482	2984	2537	2132
	energy, ft-lb	1165	862	632	457	323
	arc, inches		+0.7	0	-4.6	-14.7
Win. 34 HP	velocity, fps:	4025	3339	2751	2232	1775
	energy, ft-lb:	1223	842	571	376	238
	arc, inches:		+0.8	0	-5.5	-18.1

.218 Bee

CARTRIDGE BULLET	RANGE, YARDS:	0	100	200	300	400
Win. 46 Hollow Point	velocity, fps:	2760	2102	1550	1155	961
	energy, ft-lb:	778	451	245	136	94
	arc, inches:		0	-7.2	-29.4	

.22 Hornet

CARTRIDGE BULLET	RANGE, YARDS:	0	100	200	300	400
Federal 30 Speer TNT	velocity, fps:	3150	2150	1390	990	830
	energy, ft-lb:	660	310	130	65	45
	arc, inches:		+3.3	0	-22.8	-78.7
Federal 45 JSP	velocity, fps:	2690	2100	1590	1210	1000
	energy, ft-lb:	725	440	255	145	100
	arc, inches:		+3.3	0	-17.6	-59.5
Hornady 35 V-Max	velocity, fps:	3100	2278	1601	1135	929
	energy, ft-lb:	747	403	199	100	67
	arc, inches:		+2.8	0	-16.9	-60.4
Rem. 35 AccuTip	velocity, fps:	3100	2271	1591	1127	924
	energy, ft-lb:	747	401	197	99	66
	arc, inches:		+1.5	-3.5	-22.3	-68.4
Rem. 45 Pointed Soft Point	velocity, fps:	2690	2042	1502	1128	948
	energy, ft-lb:	723	417	225	127	90
	arc, inches:		0	-7.1	-30.0	
Rem. 45 Hollow Point	velocity, fps:	2690	2042	1502	1128	948
	energy, ft-lb:	723	417	225	127	90
	arc, inches:		0	-7.1	-30.0	
Win. 34 Jacketed HP	velocity, fps:	3050	2132	1415	1017	852
	energy, ft-lb:	700	343	151	78	55.
	arc, inches:		0	-6.6	-29.9	
Win. 45 Soft Point	velocity, fps:	2690	2042	1502	1128	948.
	energy, ft-lb:	723	417	225	127	90
	arc, inches:		0	-7.7	-31.3	
Win. 46 Hollow Point	velocity, fps:	2690	2042	1502	1128	948.
	energy, ft-lb:	739	426	230	130	92
	arc, inches:		0	-7.7	-31.3	

.221 Remington Fireball

CARTRIDGE BULLET	RANGE, YARDS:	0	100	200	300	400
Rem. 50 AccuTip BT	velocity, fps:	2995	2605	2247	1918	1622
	energy, ft-lb:	996	753	560	408	292
	arc, inches:		+1.8	0	-8.8	-27.1

.222 Remington

CARTRIDGE BULLET	RANGE, YARDS:	0	100	200	300	400
Federal 40 Ballistic Tip	velocity, fps:	3450	2990	2570	2190	1840
	energy, ft-lb:	1055	790	585	425	300
	arc, inches:		+1.2	0	-6.5	-20.4

Centerfire Rifle Ballistics

.222 REMINGTON TO .223 REMINGTON

CARTRIDGE BULLET	RANGE, YARDS:	0	100	200	300	400
Federal 43 Speer TNT	velocity, fps:	3400	2750	2180	1680	1290
	energy, ft-lb:	1105	720	450	270	160
	arc, inches:		+1.6	0	-9.2	-31.4
Federal 50 Hi-Shok	velocity, fps:	3140	2600	2120	1700	1350
	energy, ft-lb:	1095	750	500	320	200
	arc, inches:		+1.9	0	-9.7	-31.6
Federal 55 FMJ boat-tail	velocity, fps:	3020	2740	2480	2230	1990
	energy, ft-lb:	1115	915	750	610	484
	arc, inches:		+1.6	0	-7.3	-21.5
Hornady 40 V-Max	velocity, fps:	3600	3117	2673	2269	1911
	energy, ft-lb:	1151	863	634	457	324
	arc, inches:		+1.1	0	-6.1	-18.9
Hornady 50 V-Max	velocity, fps:	3140	2729	2352	2008	1710
	energy, ft-lb:	1094	827	614	448	325
	arc, inches:		+1.7	0	-7.9	-24.4
Norma 50 Soft Point	velocity, fps:	3199	2667	2193	1771	
	energy, ft-lb:	1136	790	534	348	
	arc, inches:		+1.7	0	-9.1	
Norma 50 FMJ	velocity, fps:	2789	2326	1910	1547	
	energy, ft-lb:	864	601	405	266	
	arc, inches:		+2.5	0	-12.2	
Norma 62 Soft Point	velocity, fps:	2887	2457	2067	1716	
	energy, ft-lb:	1148	831	588	405	
	arc, inches:		+2.1	0	-10.4	
PMC 50 Pointed Soft Point	velocity, fps:	3044	2727	2354	2012	1651
	energy, ft-lb:	1131	908	677	494	333
	arc, inches:		+1.6	0	-7.9	-24.5
PMC 55 Pointed Soft Point	velocity, fps:	2950	2594	2266	1966	1693
	energy, ft-lb:	1063	822	627	472	350
	arc, inches:		+1.9	0	-8.7	-26.3
Rem. 50 Pointed Soft Point	velocity, fps:	3140	2602	2123	1700	1350
	energy, ft-lb:	1094	752	500	321	202
	arc, inches:		+1.9	0	-9.7	-31.7
Rem. 50 HP Power-Lokt	velocity, fps:	3140	2635	2182	1777	1432
	energy, ft-lb:	1094	771	529	351	228
	arc, inches:		+1.8	0	-9.2	-29.6
Rem. 50 AccuTip BT	velocity, fps:	3140	2744	2380	2045	1740
	energy, ft-lb:	1094	836	629	464	336
	arc, inches:		+1.6	0	-7.8	-23.9
Win. 40 Ballistic Silvertip	velocity, fps:	3370	2915	2503	2127	1786
	energy, ft-lb:	1009	755	556	402	283
	arc, inches:		+1.3	0	-6.9	-21.5
Win. 50 Pointed Soft Point	velocity, fps:	3140	2602	2123	1700	1350
	energy, ft-lb:	1094	752	500	321	202
	arc, inches:		+2.2	0	-10.0	-32.3

.222 Remington Magnum

CARTRIDGE BULLET	RANGE, YARDS:	0	100	200	300	400
Nosler 40 BT	velocity, fps:	3600	3140	2726	2347	2000
	energy, ft-lb:	1150	876	660	489	355
	arc, inches:	-1.5	+1.0	0	-5.7	-17.8
Nosler 50 BT	velocity, fps:	3340	2917	2533	2179	1855
	energy, ft-lb:	1238	945	712	527	382
	arc, inches:	-1.5	+1.3	0	-6.8	-20.9

.223 Remington

CARTRIDGE BULLET	RANGE, YARDS:	0	100	200	300	400
Black Hills 36 Varmint Grenade	velocity, fps:	w3750				
	energy, ft-lb:	1124				
	arc, inches:					
Black Hills 40 Nosler B. Tip	velocity, fps:	3600				
	energy, ft-lb:	1150				
	arc, inches:					
Black Hills 50 V-Max	velocity, fps:	3300				
	energy, ft-lb:	1209				
	arc, inches:					
Black Hills 52 Match HP	velocity, fps:	3300				
	energy, ft-lb:	1237				
	arc, inches:					
Black Hills 55 Softpoint	velocity, fps:	3250				
	energy, ft-lb:	1270				
	arc, inches:					
Black Hills 55 TSX	velocity, fps:	3200				
	energy, ft-lb:	1250				
	arc, inches:					
Black Hills 60 SP or V-Max	velocity, fps:	3150				
	energy, ft-lb:	1322				
	arc, inches:					
Black Hills 60 Partition	velocity, fps:	3150				
	energy, ft-lb:	1322				
	arc, inches:					
Black Hills 62 TSX	velocity, fps:	3100				
	energy, ft-lb:	1323				
	arc, inches:					
Black Hills 68 Heavy Match	velocity, fps:	2850				
	energy, ft-lb:	1227				
	arc, inches:					
Black Hills 69 OTM	velocity, fps:	2875				
	energy, ft-lb:	1266				
	arc, inches:					
Black Hills 69 Sierra MK	velocity, fps:	2850				
	energy, ft-lb:	1245				
	arc, inches:					
Black Hills 73 Berger BTHP	velocity, fps:	2750				
	energy, ft-lb:	1226				
	arc, inches:					
Black Hills 75 Heavy Match	velocity, fps:	2750				
	energy, ft-lb:	1259				
	arc, inches:					
Black Hills 77 Sierra MKing	velocity, fps:	2750				
	energy, ft-lb:	1293				
	arc, inches:					
Black Hills 77 Tipped MatchKing	velocity, fps:	2750				
	energy, ft-lb:	1293				
	arc, inches:					
Federal 40 Ballistic Tip	velocity, fps:	3700	3210	2770	2370	2010
	energy, ft-lb:	1215	915	680	500	360
	arc, inches:		+0.9	0	-5.5	-17.3
Federal 43 Speer TNT	velocity, fps:	3600	2920	2330	1810	1390
	energy, ft-lb:	1235	810	515	315	185
	arc, inches:		+1.3	0	-7.9	-27.1
Federal 50 Jacketed HP	velocity, fps:	3400	2910	2460	2060	1700
	energy, ft-lb:	1285	940	675	470	320
	arc, inches:		+1.3	0	-7.1	-22.7
Federal 50 Speer TNT HP	velocity, fps:	3300	2860	2450	2080	1750
	energy, ft-lb:	1210	905	670	480	340
	arc, inches:		+1.4	0	-7.3	-22.6
Federal 52 Sierra MatchKing BTHP	velocity, fps:	3300	2860	2460	2090	1760
	energy, ft-lb:	1255	945	700	505	360
	arc, inches:		+1.4	0	-7.2	-22.4
Federal 55 Hi-Shok	velocity, fps:	3240	2750	2300	1910	1550
	energy, ft-lb:	1280	920	650	445	295
	arc, inches:		+1.6	0	-8.2	-26.1
Federal 55 FMJ boat-tail	velocity, fps:	3240	2950	2670	2410	2170
	energy, ft-lb:	1280	1060	875	710	575
	arc, inches:		+1.3	0	-6.1	-18.3
Federal 55 Sierra GameKing BTHP	velocity, fps:	3240	2770	2340	1950	1610
	energy, ft-lb:	1280	935	670	465	315
	arc, inches:		+1.5	0	-8.0	-25.3
Federal 55 Trophy Bonded	velocity, fps:	3100	2630	2210	1830	1500
	energy, ft-lb:	1175	845	595	410	275
	arc, inches:		+1.8	0	-8.9	-28.7
Federal 55 Nosler Bal. Tip	velocity, fps:	3240	2870	2530	2220	1920
	energy, ft-lb:	1280	1005	780	600	450
	arc, inches:		+1.4	0	-6.8	-20.8
Federal 55 Sierra BlitzKing	velocity, fps:	3240	2870	2520	2200	1910
	energy, ft-lb:	1280	1005	775	590	445
	arc, inches:		+-1.4	0	-6.9	-20.9

Centerfire Rifle Ballistics

.223 REMINGTON TO 5.6X52 R

CARTRIDGE BULLET	RANGE, YARDS:	0	100	200	300	400
Federal 60 Partition	velocity, fps:	3160	2740	2350	2000	1680
	energy, ft-lb:	1330	1000	735	530	375
	arc, inches:		+1.6	0	-7.9	-24.8
Federal 62 FMJ	velocity, fps:	3020	2650	2310	2000	1710
	energy, ft-lb:	1225	970	735	550	405
	arc, inches:		+1.7	0	-8.4	-25.5
Federal 64 Hi-Shok SP	velocity, fps:	3090	2690	2325	1990	1680
	energy, ft-lb:	1360	1030	770	560	400
	arc, inches:		+1.7	0	-8.2	-25.2
Federal 69 Sierra MatchKing BTHP	velocity, fps:	3000	2720	2460	2210	1980
	energy, ft-lb:	1380	1135	925	750	600
	arc, inches:		+1.6	0	-7.4	-21.9
Hornady 40 V-Max	velocity, fps:	3800	3305	2845	2424	2044
	energy, ft-lb:	1282	970	719	522	371
	arc, inches:		+0.8	0	-5.3	-16.6
Hornady 53 Hollow Point	velocity, fps:	3330	2882	2477	2106	1710
	energy, ft-lb:	1305	978	722	522	369
	arc, inches:		+1.7	0	-7.4	-22.7
Hornady 55 V-Max	velocity, fps:	3240	2859	2507	2181	1891
	energy, ft-lb:	1282	998	767	581	437
	arc, inches:		+1.4	0	-7.1	-21.4
Hornady 75 BTHP Superformance Match	velocity, fps:	2930	2695	2471	2259	2057
	energy, ft-lb:	1430	1209	1017	850	705
	arc, inches:		+1.7	0	-7.4	-21.6
Hornady 55 TAP-FPD	velocity, fps:	3240	2854	2500	2172	1871
	energy, ft-lb:	1282	995	763	576	427
	arc, inches:		+1.4	0	-7.0	-21.4
Hornady 55 Urban Tactical	velocity, fps:	2970	2626	2307	2011	1739
	energy, ft-lb:	1077	842	650	494	369
	arc, inches:		+1.5	0	-8.1	-24.9
Hornady 60 Soft Point	velocity, fps:	3150	2782	2442	2127	1837
	energy, ft-lb:	1322	1031	795	603	450
	arc, inches:		+1.6	0	-7.5	-22.5
Hornady 60 TAP-FPD	velocity, fps:	3115	2754	2420	2110	1824
	energy, ft-lb:	1293	1010	780	593	443
	arc, inches:		+1.6	0	-7.5	-22.9
Hornady 60 Urban Tactical	velocity, fps:	2950	2619	2312	2025	1762
	energy, ft-lb:	1160	914	712	546	413
	arc, inches:		+1.6	0	-8.1	-24.7
Hornady 75 BTHP Match	velocity, fps:	2790	2554	2330	2119	1926
	energy, ft-lb:	1296	1086	904	747	617
	arc, inches:		+2.4	0	-8.8	-25.1
Hornacy 75 TAP-FPD	velocity, fps:	2790	2582	2383	2193	2012
	energy, ft-lb:	1296	1110	946	801	674
	arc, inches:		+1.9	0	-8.0	-23.2
Hornady 75 BTHP Tactical	velocity, fps:	2630	2409	2199	2000	1814
	energy, ft-lb:	1152	966	805	666	548
	arc, inches:		+2.0	0	-9.2	-25.9
PMC 40 non-toxic	velocity, fps:	3500	2606	1871	1315	
	energy, ft-lb:	1088	603	311	154	
	arc, inches:		+2.6	0	-12.8	
PMC 50 Sierra BlitzKing	velocity, fps:	3300	2874	2484	2130	1809
	energy, ft-lb:	1209	917	685	504	363
	arc, inches:		+1.4	0	-7.1	-21.8
PMC 52 Sierra HPBT Match	velocity, fps:	3200	2808	2447	2117	1817
	energy, ft-lb:	1182	910	691	517	381
	arc, inches:		+1.5	0	-7.3	-22.5
PMC 53 Barnes XLC	velocity, fps:	3200	2815	2461	2136	1840
	energy, ft-lb:	1205	933	713	537	398
	arc, inches:		+1.5	0	-7.2	-22.2
PMC 55 HP boat-tail	velocity, fps:	3240	2717	2250	1832	1473
	energy, ft-lb:	1282	901	618	410	265
	arc, inches:		+1.6	0	-8.6	-27.7
PMC 55 FMJ boat-tail	velocity, fps:	3195	2882	2525	2169	1843
	energy, ft-lb:	1246	1014	779	574	415
	arc, inches:		+1.4	0	-6.8	-21.1
PMC 55 Pointed Soft Point	velocity, fps:	3112	2767	2421	2100	1806
	energy, ft-lb:	1182	935	715	539	398
	arc, inches:		+1.5	0	-7.5	-22.9

CARTRIDGE BULLET	RANGE, YARDS:	0	100	200	300	400
PMC 64 Pointed Soft Point	velocity, fps:	2775	2511	2261	2026	1806
	energy, ft-lb:	1094	896	726	583	464
	arc, inches:		+2.0	0	-8.8	-26.1
PMC 69 Sierra BTHP Match	velocity, fps:	2900	2591	2304	2038	1791
	energy, ft-lb:	1288	1029	813	636	492
	arc, inches:		+1.9	0	-8.4	-25.3
Rem. 50 AccuTip BT	velocity, fps:	3300	2889	2514	2168	1851
	energy, ft-lb:	1209	927	701	522	380
	arc, inches:		+1.4	0	-6.9	-21.2
Rem. 55 Pointed Soft Point	velocity, fps:	3240	2747	2304	1905	1554
	energy, ft-lb:	1282	921	648	443	295
	arc, inches:		+1.6	0	-8.2	-26.2
Rem. 55 HP Power-Lokt	velocity, fps:	3240	2773	2352	1969	1627
	energy, ft-lb:	1282	939	675	473	323
	arc, inches:		+1.5	0	-7.9	-24.8
Rem. 55 AccuTip BT	velocity, fps:	3240	2854	2500	2172	1871
	energy, ft-lb:	1282	995	763	576	427
	arc, inches:		+1.5	0	-7.1	-21.7
Rem. 55 Metal Case	velocity, fps:	3240	2759	2326	1933	1587
	energy, ft-lb:	1282	929	660	456	307
	arc, inches:		+1.6	0	-8.1	-25.5
Remington 62 Core-Lokt Ultra Bonded	velocity, fps:	3100	2695	2324	1983	1676
	energy, ft-lb:	1323	1000	743	541	386
	arc, inches:		+1.7			
Rem. 62 HP Match	velocity, fps:	3025	2572	2162	1792	1471
	energy, ft-lb:	1260	911	643	442	298
	arc, inches:		+1.9	0	-9.4	-29.9
Rem. 69 BTHP Match	velocity, fps:	3000	2720	2457	2209	1975
	energy, ft-lb:	1379	1133	925	747	598
	arc, inches:		+1.6	0	-7.4	-21.9
Win. 40 Ballistic Silvertip	velocity, fps:	3700	3166	2693	2265	1879.
	energy, ft-lb:	1216	891	644	456	314
	arc, inches:		+1.0	0	-5.8	-18.4
Win. 45 JHP	velocity, fps:	3600				
	energy, ft-lb:	1295				
	arc, inches:					
Win. 50 Ballistic Silvertip	velocity, fps:	3410	2982	2593	2235	1907.
	energy, ft-lb:	1291	987	746	555	404
	arc, inches:		+1.2	0	-6.4	-19.8
Win. 53 Hollow Point	velocity, fps:	3330	2882	2477	2106	1770
	energy, ft-lb:	1305	978	722	522	369
	arc, inches:		+1.7	0	-7.4	-22.7
Win. 55 Pointed Soft Point	velocity, fps:	3240	2747	2304	1905	1554.
	energy, ft-lb:	1282	921	648	443	295
	arc, inches:		+1.9	0	-8.5	-26.7
Win. 55 Super Clean NT	velocity, fps:	3150	2520	1970	1505	1165
	energy, ft-lb:	1212	776	474	277	166
	arc, inches:		+2.8	0	-11.9	-38.9
Win. 55 FMJ	velocity, fps:	3240	2854			
	energy, ft-lb:	1282	995			
	arc, inches:					
Win. 55 Ballistic Silvertip	velocity, fps:	3240	2871	2531	2215	1923
	energy, ft-lb:	1282	1006	782	599	451
	arc, inches:		+1.4	0	-6.8	-20.8
Win. 64 Power-Point	velocity, fps:	3020	2656	2320	2009	1724
	energy, ft-lb:	1296	1003	765	574	423
	arc, inches:		+1.7	0	-8.2	-25.1
Win. 64 Power-Point Plus	velocity, fps:	3090	2684	2312	1971	1664
	energy, ft-lb:	1357	1024	760	552	393
	arc, inches:		+1.7	0	-8.2	-25.4
Winchester 69 BTHP Match	velocity, fps:	3060	2740	2442	2163	1902
	energy, ft-lb:	1434	1150	913	716	554
	arc, inches:		+1.6	0	-7.4	-22.4

5.6x52 R

CARTRIDGE BULLET	RANGE, YARDS:	0	100	200	300	400
Norma 71 Soft Point	velocity, fps:	2789	2446	2128	1835	
	energy, ft-lb:	1227	944	714	531	
	arc, inches:		+2.1	0	-9.9	

Centerfire Rifle Ballistics

.22 PPC TO .220 SWIFT

.22 PPC

CARTRIDGE BULLET	RANGE, YARDS:	0	100	200	300	400
A-Square 52 Berger	velocity, fps:	3300	2952	2629	2329	2049
	energy, ft-lb:	1257	1006	798	626	485
	arc, inches:		+1.3	0	-6.3	-19.1

.225 Winchester

CARTRIDGE BULLET	RANGE, YARDS:	0	100	200	300	400
Win. 55 Pointed Soft Point	velocity, fps:	3570	3066	2616	2208	1838.
	energy, ft-lb:	1556	1148	836	595	412
	arc, inches:		+2.4	+2.0	-3.5	-16.3

.224 Weatherby Magnum

CARTRIDGE BULLET	RANGE, YARDS:	0	100	200	300	400
Wby. 55 Pointed Expanding	velocity, fps:	3650	3192	2780	2403	2056
	energy, ft-lb:	1627	1244	944	705	516
	arc, inches:		+2.8	+3.7	0	-9.8

.22-250 Remington

CARTRIDGE BULLET	RANGE, YARDS:	0	100	200	300	400
Black Hills 50 Nos. Bal. Tip	velocity, fps:	3700				
	energy, ft-lb:	1520				
	arc, inches:					
Black Hills 60 Nos. Partition	velocity, fps:	3550				
	energy, ft-lb:	1679				
	arc, inches:					
Federal 40 Nos. Bal. Tip	velocity, fps:	4150	3610	3130	2700	2300
	energy, ft-lb:	1530	1155	870	645	470
	arc, inches:		+0.6	0	-4.2	-13.2
Federal 40 Sierra Varminter	velocity, fps:	4000	3320	2720	2200	1740
	energy, ft-lb:	1420	980	660	430	265
	arc, inches:		+0.8	0	-5.6	-18.4
Federal 43 Speer TNT	velocity, fps:	4000	3250	2650	2070	1590
	energy, ft-lb:	1530	1010	655	405	240
	arc, inches:		+0.9	0	-6.1	-20.8
Federal 55 Hi-Shok	velocity, fps:	3680	3140	2660	2220	1830
	energy, ft-lb:	1655	1200	860	605	410
	arc, inches:		+1.0	0	-6.0	-19.1
Federal 55 Sierra BlitzKing	velocity, fps:	3680	3270	2890	2540	2220
	energy, ft-lb:	1655	1300	1020	790	605
	arc, inches:		+0.9	0	-5.1	-15.6
Federal 55 Sierra GameKing BTHP	velocity, fps:	3680	3280	2920	2590	2280
	energy, ft-lb:	1655	1315	1040	815	630
	arc, inches:		+0.9	0	-5.0	-15.1
Federal 55 Trophy Bonded	velocity, fps:	3600	3080	2610	2190	1810.
	energy, ft-lb:	1585	1155	835	590	400.
	arc, inches:		+1.1	0	-6.2	-19.8
Hornady 35 NTX Superformance Varmint	velocity, fps:	4450	3736	3128	2598	2125
	energy, ft-lb:	1539	1085	761	524	351
	arc, inches:		+0.5	0	-4.1	-13.4
Hornady 40 V-Max	velocity, fps:	4150	3631	3147	2699	2293
	energy, ft-lb:	1529	1171	879	647	467
	arc, inches:		+0.5	0	-4.2	-13.3
Hornady 50 V-Max	velocity, fps:	3800	3349	2925	2535	2178
	energy, ft-lb:	1603	1245	950	713	527
	arc, inches:		+0.8	0	-5.0	-15.6
Hornady 50 V-Max Superformance Varmint	velocity, fps:	4000	3517	3086	2696	2337
	energy, ft-lb:	1776	1373	1057	807	606
	arc, inches:		+0.7	0	-4.3	-13.5
Hornady 53 Hollow Point	velocity, fps:	3680	3185	2743	2341	1974.
	energy, ft-lb:	1594	1194	886	645	459
	arc, inches:		+1.0	0	-5.7	-17.8
Hornady 55 V-Max	velocity, fps:	3680	3265	2876	2517	2183
	energy, ft-lb:	1654	1302	1010	772	582
	arc, inches:		+0.9	0	-5.3	-16.1
Hornady 60 Soft Point	velocity, fps:	3600	3195	2826	2485	2169
	energy, ft-lb:	1727	1360	1064	823	627
	arc, inches:		+1.0	0	-5.4	-16.3
Norma 53 Soft Point	velocity, fps:	3707	3234	2809	1716	
	energy, ft-lb:	1618	1231	928	690	
	arc, inches:		+0.9	0	-5.3	
PMC 50 Sierra BlitzKing	velocity, fps:	3725	3264	2641	2455	2103
	energy, ft-lb:	1540	1183	896	669	491
	arc, inches:		+0.9	0	-5.2	-16.2
PMC 50 Barnes XLC	velocity, fps:	3725	3280	2871	2495	2152
	energy, ft-lb:	1540	1195	915	691	514.
	arc, inches:		+0.9	0	-5.1	-15.9.
PMC 55 HP boat-tail	velocity, fps:	3680	3104	2596	2141	1737
	energy, ft-lb:	1654	1176	823	560	368
	arc, inches:		+1.1	0	-6.3	-20.2
PMC 55 Pointed Soft Point	velocity, fps:	3586	3203	2852	2505	2178
	energy, ft-lb:	1570	1253	993	766	579
	arc, inches:		+1.0	0	-5.2	-16.0
Rem. 50 AccuTip BT (also in EtronX)	velocity, fps:	3725	3272	2864	2491	2147
	energy, ft-lb:	1540	1188	910	689	512
	arc, inches:		+1.7	+1.6	-2.8	-12.8
Rem. 55 Pointed Soft Point	velocity, fps:	3680	3137	2656	2222	1832
	energy, ft-lb:	1654	1201	861	603	410
	arc, inches:		+1.9	+1.8	-3.3	-15.5
Rem. 55 HP Power-Lokt	velocity, fps:	3680	3209	2785	2400	2046.
	energy, ft-lb:	1654	1257	947	703	511
	arc, inches:		+1.8	+1.7	-3.0	-13.7
Rem. 60 Nosler Partition (also in EtronX)	velocity, fps:	3500	3045	2634	2258	1914
	energy, ft-lb:	1632	1235	924	679	488
	arc, inches:		+2.1	+1.9	-3.4	-15.5
Win. 40 Ballistic Silvertip	velocity, fps:	4150	3591	3099	2658	2257
	energy, ft-lb:	1530	1146	853	628	453
	arc, inches:		+0.6	0	-4.2	-13.4
Win. 50 Ballistic Silvertip	velocity, fps:	3810	3341	2919	2536	2182
	energy, ft-lb:	1611	1239	946	714	529.
	arc, inches:		+0.8	0	-4.9	-15.2
Win. 55 Pointed Soft Point	velocity, fps:	3680	3137	2656	2222	1832
	energy, ft-lb:	1654	1201	861	603	410
	arc, inches:		+2.3	+1.9	-3.4	-15.9
Win. 55 Ballistic Silvertip	velocity, fps:	3680	3272	2900	2558	2240
	energy, ft-lb:	1654	1307	1027	799	613
	arc, inches:		+0.9	0	-5.0	-15.4
Win. 64 Power-Point	velocity, fps:	3500	3086	2708	2360	2038
	energy, ft-lb:	1741	1353	1042	791	590
	arc, inches:		+1.1	0	-5.9	-18.0

.220 Swift

CARTRIDGE BULLET	RANGE, YARDS:	0	100	200	300	400
Federal 52 Sierra MatchKing BTHP	velocity, fps:	3830	3370	2960	2600	2230
	energy, ft-lb:	1690	1310	1010	770	575
	arc, inches:		+0.8	0	-4.8	-14.9
Federal 55 Sierra BlitzKing	velocity, fps:	3800	3370	2990	2630	2310.
	energy, ft-lb:	1765	1390	1090	850	650
	arc, inches:		+0.8	0	-4.7	-14.4
Federal 55 Trophy Bonded	velocity, fps:	3700	3170	2690	2270	1880
	energy, ft-lb:	1670	1225	885	625	430
	arc, inches:		+1.0	0	-5.8	-18.5
Hornady 40 V-Max	velocity, fps:	4200	3678	3190	2739	2329
	energy, ft-lb:	1566	1201	904	666	482
	arc, inches:		+0.5	0	-4.0	-12.9
Hornady 50 V-Max	velocity, fps:	3850	3396	2970	2576	2215.
	energy, ft-lb:	1645	1280	979	736	545
	arc, inches:		+0.7	0	-4.8	-15.1
Hornady 50 SP	velocity, fps:	3850	3327	2862	2442	2060.
	energy, ft-lb:	1645	1228	909	662	471
	arc, inches:		+0.8	0	-5.1	-16.1
Hornady 55 V-Max	velocity, fps:	3680	3265	2876	2517	2183
	energy, ft-lb:	1654	1302	1010	772	582
	arc, inches:		+0.9	0	-5.3	-16.1
Hornady 60 Hollow Point	velocity, fps:	3600	3199	2824	2475	2156
	energy, ft-lb:	1727	1364	1063	816	619
	arc, inches:		+1.0	0	-5.4	-16.3
Norma 50 Soft Point	velocity, fps:	4019	3380	2826	2335	
	energy, ft-lb:	1794	1268	887	605	
	arc, inches:		+0.7	0	-5.1	

Centerfire Rifle Ballistics

.220 SWIFT TO .243 WINCHESTER

CARTRIDGE BULLET	RANGE, YARDS:	0	100	200	300	400
Rem. 50 Pointed Soft Point	velocity, fps:	3780	3158	2617	2135	1710
	energy, ft-lb:	1586	1107	760	506	325
	arc, inches:		+0.3	-1.4	-8.2	
Rem. 50 V-Max boat-tail (also in EtronX)	velocity, fps:	3780	3321	2908	2532	2185
	energy, ft-lb:	1586	1224	939	711	530
	arc, inches:		+0.8	0	-5.0	-15.4
Win. 40 Ballistic Silvertip	velocity, fps:	4050	3518	3048	2624	2238.
	energy, ft-lb:	1457	1099	825	611	445
	arc, inches:		+0.7	0	-4.4	-13.9
Win. 50 Pointed Soft Point	velocity, fps:	3870	3310	2816	2373	1972
	energy, ft-lb:	1663	1226	881	625	432
	arc, inches:		+0.8	0	-5.2	-16.7

.223 WSSM

CARTRIDGE BULLET	RANGE, YARDS:	0	100	200	300	400
Win. 55 Ballistic Silvertip	velocity, fps:	3850	3438	3064	2721	2402
	energy, ft-lb:	1810	1444	1147	904	704
	arc, inches:		+0.7	0	-4.4	-13.6
Win. 55 Pointed Softpoint	velocity, fps:	3850	3367	2934	2541	2181
	energy, ft-lb:	1810	1384	1051	789	581
	arc, inches:		+0.8	0	-4.9	-15.1
Win. 64 Power-Point	velocity, fps:	3600	3144	2732	2356	2011
	energy, ft-lb:	1841	1404	1061	789	574
	arc, inches:		+1.0	0	-5.7	-17.7

6mm PPC

CARTRIDGE BULLET	RANGE, YARDS:	0	100	200	300	400
A-Square 68 Berger	velocity, fps:	3100	2751	2428	2128	1850
	energy, ft-lb:	1451	1143	890	684	516
	arc, inches:		+1.5	0	-7.5	-22.6

6x70 R

CARTRIDGE BULLET	RANGE, YARDS:	0	100	200	300	400
Norma 95 Nosler Bal. Tip	velocity, fps:	2461	2231	2013	1809	
	energy, ft-lb:	1211	995	810	654	
	arc, inches:		+2.7	0	-11.3	

.243 Winchester

CARTRIDGE BULLET	RANGE, YARDS:	0	100	200	300	400
Black Hills 55 Nosler B. Tip	velocity, fps:	3800				
	energy, ft-lb:	1763				
	arc, inches:					
Black Hills 95 Nosler B. Tip	velocity, fps:	2950				
	energy, ft-lb:	1836				
	arc, inches:					
Federal 70 Nosler Bal. Tip	velocity, fps:	3400	3070	2760	2470	2200
	energy, ft-lb:	1795	1465	1185	950	755.
	arc, inches:		+1.1	0	-5.7	-17.1
Federal 70 Speer TNT HP	velocity, fps:	3400	3040	2700	2390	2100
	energy, ft-lb:	1795	1435	1135	890	685
	arc, inches:		+1.1	0	-5.9	-18.0
Federal 80 Sierra Pro-Hunter	velocity, fps:	3350	2960	2590	2260	1950
	energy, ft-lb:	1995	1550	1195	905	675
	arc, inches:		+1.3	0	-6.4	-19.7
Federal 85 Sierra GameKing BTHP	velocity, fps:	3320	3070	2830	2600	2380
	energy, ft-lb:	2080	1770	1510	1280	1070
	arc, inches:		+1.1	0	-5.5	-16.1
Federal 85 Trophy Copper	velocity, fps:	3200	2950	2710	2480	2270
	energy, ft-lb:	1935	1640	1385	1160	970
	arc, inches:		+1.3	0	-6.0	-17.6
Federal 90 Trophy Bonded	velocity, fps:	3100	2850	2610	2380	2160.
	energy, ft-lb:	1920	1620	1360	1130	935
	arc, inches:		+1.4	0	-6.1	-19.2
Federal 100 Hi-Shok	velocity, fps:	2960	2700	2450	2220	1990
	energy, ft-lb:	1945	1615	1330	1090	880
	arc, inches:		+1.6	0	-7.5	-22.0
Federal 100 Sierra GameKing BTSP	velocity, fps:	2960	2760	2570	2380	2210
	energy, ft-lb:	1950	1690	1460	1260	1080
	arc, inches:		+1.5	0	-6.8	-19.8
Federal 100 Nosler Partition	velocity, fps:	2960	2730	2510	2300	2100
	energy, ft-lb:	1945	1650	1395	1170	975.
	arc, inches:		+1.6	0	-7.1	-20.9
Hornady 58 V-Max Superformance Varmint	velocity, fps:	3925	3465	3052	2676	2330
	energy, ft-lb:	1984	1546	1200	922	699
	arc, inches:		+0.7	0	-4.4	-13.8
Hornady 75 Hollow Point	velocity, fps:	3400	2970	2578	2219	1890
	energy, ft-lb:	1926	1469	1107	820	595
	arc, inches:		+1.2	0	-6.5	-20.3
Hornady 80 GMX Superformance	velocity, fps:	3425	3081	2763	2468	2190
	energy, ft-lb:	2084	1686	1357	1082	852
	arc, inches:		+1.1	0	-5.7	-17.1
Hornady 87 SST Custom Lite	velocity, fps:	2800	2574	2359	2155	1961
	energy, ft-lb:	1514	1280	1075	897	743
	arc, inches:		+1.9	0	-8.1	-23.8
Hornady 95 SST Superformance	velocity, fps:	3185	2908	2649	2404	2172
	energy, ft-lb:	2140	1784	1480	1219	995
	arc, inches:		+1.3	0	-6.3	-18.6
Hornady 100 BTSP	velocity, fps:	2960	2728	2508	2299	2099
	energy, ft-lb:	1945	1653	1397	1174	979
	arc, inches:		+1.6	0	-7.2	-21.0
Hornady 100 BTSP LM	velocity, fps:	3100	2839	2592	2358	2138
	energy, ft-lb:	2133	1790	1491	1235	1014
	arc, inches:		+1.5	0	-6.8	-19.8
Norma 80 FMJ	velocity, fps:	3117	2750	2412	2098	
	energy, ft-lb:	1726	1344	1034	782	
	arc, inches:		+1.5	0	-7.5	
Norma 100 FMJ	velocity, fps:	3018	2747	2493	2252	
	energy, ft-lb:	2023	1677	1380	1126	
	arc, inches:		+1.5	0	-7.1	
Norma 100 Soft Point	velocity, fps:	3018	2748	2493	2252	
	energy, ft-lb:	2023	1677	1380	1126	
	arc, inches:		+1.5	0	-7.1	
Norma 100 Oryx	velocity, fps:	3018	2653	2316	2004	
	energy, ft-lb:	2023	1563	1191	892	
	arc, inches:		+1.7	0	-8.3	
PMC 80 Pointed Soft Point	velocity, fps:	2940	2684	2444	2215	1999
	energy, ft-lb:	1535	1280	1060	871	709
	arc, inches:		+1.7	0	-7.5	-22.1
PMC 85 Barnes XLC	velocity, fps:	3250	3022	2805	2598	2401
	energy, ft-lb:	1993	1724	1485	1274	1088
	arc, inches:		+1.6	0	-5.6	16.3
PMC 85 HP boat-tail	velocity, fps:	3275	2922	2596	2292	2009
	energy, ft-lb:	2024	1611	1272	991	761
	arc, inches:		+1.3	0	-6.5	-19.7
PMC 100 Pointed Soft Point	velocity, fps:	2743	2507	2283	2070	1869
	energy, ft-lb:	1670	1395	1157	951	776
	arc, inches:		+2.0	0	-8.7	-25.5
PMC 100 SP boat-tail	velocity, fps:	2960	2742	2534	2335	2144
	energy, ft-lb:	1945	1669	1425	1210	1021
	arc, inches:		+1.6	0	-7.0	-20.5
Rem. 75 AccuTip BT	velocity, fps:	3375	3065	2775	2504	2248
	energy, ft-lb:	1897	1564	1282	1044	842
	arc, inches:		+2.0	+1.8	-3.0	-13.3
Remington 80 Copper Solid Tipped	velocity, fps:	3350	3011	2696	2403	2128
	energy, ft-lb:	1993	1610	1291	1025	894
	arc, inches:		+1.2	0	-6.1	-18.1
Rem. 80 Pointed Soft Point	velocity, fps:	3350	2955	2593	2259	1951
	energy, ft-lb:	1993	1551	1194	906	676
	arc, inches:		+2.2	+2.0	-3.5	-15.8
Rem. 80 HP Power-Lokt	velocity, fps:	3350	2955	2593	2259	1951
	energy, ft-lb:	1993	1551	1194	906	676
	arc, inches:		+2.2	+2.0	-3.5	-15.8
Rem. 90 Nosler Bal. Tip (also in EtronX) or Scirocco	velocity, fps:	3120	2871	2635	2411	2199
	energy, ft-lb:	1946	1647	1388	1162	966
	arc, inches:		+1.4	0	-6.4	-18.8
Rem. 95 AccuTip	velocity, fps:	3120	2847	2590	2347	2118
	energy, ft-lb:	2053	1710	1415	1162	946
	arc, inches:		+1.5	0	-6.6	-19.5
Rem. 100 PSP Core-Lokt (also in EtronX)	velocity, fps:	2960	2697	2449	2215	1993
	energy, ft-lb:	1945	1615	1332	1089	882
	arc, inches:		+1.6	0	-7.5	-22.1
Rem. 100 PSP boat-tail	velocity, fps:	2960	2720	2492	2275	2069
	energy, ft-lb:	1945	1642	1378	1149	950
	arc, inches:		+2.8	+2.3	-3.8	-16.6
Speer 100 Grand Slam	velocity, fps:	2950	2684	2434	2197	
	energy, ft-lb:	1932	1600	1315	1072	
	arc, inches:		+1.7	0	-7.6	-22.4

Centerfire Rifle Ballistics

.243 WINCHESTER TO .25-06 REMINGTON

CARTRIDGE BULLET	RANGE, YARDS:	0	100	200	300	400
Win. 55 Ballistic Silvertip	velocity, fps:	4025	3597	3209	2853	2525
	energy, ft-lb:	1978	1579	1257	994	779
	arc, inches:		+0.6	0	-4.0	-12.2
Win. 80 Pointed Soft Point	velocity, fps:	3350	2955	2593	2259	1951.
	energy, ft-lb:	1993	1551	1194	906	676
	arc, inches:		+2.6	+2.1	-3.6	-16.2
Win. 95 Ballistic Silvertip	velocity, fps:	3100	2854	2626	2410	2203
	energy, ft-lb:	2021	1719	1455	1225	1024
	arc, inches:		+1.4	0	-6.4	-18.9
Win. 95 Supreme Elite XP3	velocity, fps	3100	2864	2641	2428	2225
	energy, ft-lb	2027	1730	1471	1243	1044
	a rc, inches		+1.4	0	-6.4	-18.7
Win. 100 Power-Point	velocity, fps:	2960	2697	2449	2215	1993
	energy, ft-lb:	1945	1615	1332	1089	882
	arc, inches:		+1.9	0	-7.8	-22.6.
Win. 100 Power-Point Plus	velocity, fps:	3090	2818	2562	2321	2092
	energy, ft-lb:	2121	1764	1458	1196	972
	arc, inches:		+1.4	0	-6.7	-20.0

6mm Remington

CARTRIDGE BULLET	RANGE, YARDS:	0	100	200	300	400
Federal 80 Sierra Pro-Hunter	velocity, fps:	3470	3060	2690	2350	2040
	energy, ft-lb:	2140	1665	1290	980	735
	arc, inches:		+1.1	0	-5.9	-18.2
Federal 100 Hi-Shok	velocity, fps:	3100	2830	2570	2330	2100
	energy, ft-lb:	2135	1775	1470	1205	985
	arc, inches:		+1.4	0	-6.7	-19.8
Federal 100 Nos. Partition	velocity, fps:	3100	2860	2640	2420	2220
	energy, ft-lb:	2135	1820	1545	1300	1090
	arc, inches:		+1.4	0	-6.3	-18.7
Hornady 95 SST Superformance	velocity, fps:	3235	2955	2693	2445	2211
	energy, ft-lb:	2207	1842	1530	1261	1031
	arc, inches:		+1.3	0	-6.1	-18.0
Hornady 100 SP boat-tail	velocity, fps:	3100	2861	2634	2419	2231
	energy, ft-lb:	2134	1818	1541	1300	1088
	arc, inches:		+1.3	0	-6.5	-18.9
Hornady 100 SPBT LM	velocity, fps:	3250	2997	2756	2528	2311
	energy, ft-lb:	2345	1995	1687	1418	1186
	arc, inches:		+1.6	0	-6.3	-18.2
Rem. 75 V-Max boat-tail	velocity, fps:	3400	3088	2797	2524	2267
	energy, ft-lb:	1925	1587	1303	1061	856
	arc, inches:		+1.9	+1.7	-3.0	-13.1
Rem. 100 PSP Core-Lokt	velocity, fps:	3100	2829	2573	2332	2104.
	energy, ft-lb:	2133	1777	1470	1207	983
	arc, inches:		+1.4	0	-6.7	-19.8
Rem. 100 PSP boat-tail	velocity, fps:	3100	2852	2617	2394	2183.
	energy, ft-lb:	2134	1806	1521	1273	1058
	arc, inches:		+1.4	0	-6.5	-19.1
Win. 100 Power-Point	velocity, fps:	3100	2829	2573	2332	2104
	energy, ft-lb:	2133	1777	1470	1207	983
	arc, inches:		+1.7	0	-7.0	-20.4

.243 WSSM

CARTRIDGE BULLET	RANGE, YARDS:	0	100	200	300	400
Win. 55 Ballistic Silvertip	velocity, fps:	4060	3628	3237	2880	2550
	energy, ft-lb:	2013	1607	1280	1013	794
	arc, inches:		+0.6	0	-3.9	-12.0
Win. 95 Ballistic Silvertip	velocity, fps:	3250	3000	2763	2538	2325
	energy, ft-lb:	2258	1898	1610	1359	1140
	arc, inches:		+1.2	0	5.7	16.9
Win. 95 Supreme Elite XP3	velocity, fps	3150	2912	2686	2471	2266
	energy, ft-lb	2093	1788	1521	1287	1083
	arc, inches		+1.3	0	-6.1	-18.0
Win. 100 Power Point	velocity, fps:	3110	2838	2583	2341	2112
	energy, ft-lb:	2147	1789	1481	1217	991
	arc, inches:		+1.4	0	-6.6	-19.7

.240 Weatherby Magnum

CARTRIDGE BULLET	RANGE, YARDS:	0	100	200	300	400
Wby. 87 Pointed Expanding	velocity, fps:	3523	3199	2898	2617	2352
	energy, ft-lb:	2397	1977	1622	1323	1069
	arc, inches:		+2.7	+3.4	0	-8.4
Wby. 90 Barnes-X	velocity, fps:	3500	3222	2962	2717	2484
	energy, ft-lb:	2448	2075	1753	1475	1233
	arc, inches:		+2.6	+3.3	0	-8.0
Wby. 95 Nosler Bal. Tip	velocity, fps:	3420	3146	2888	2645	2414
	energy, ft-lb:	2467	2087	1759	1475	1229
	arc, inches:		+2.7	+3.5	0	-8.4
Wby. 100 Pointed Expanding	velocity, fps:	3406	3134	2878	2637	2408
	energy, ft-lb:	2576	2180	1839	1544	1287
	arc, inches:		+2.8	+3.5	0	-8.4
Wby. 100 Partition	velocity, fps:	3406	3136	2882	2642	2415
	energy, ft-lb:	2576	2183	1844	1550	1294
	arc, inches:		+2.8	+3.5	0	-8.4

.25-20 Winchester

CARTRIDGE BULLET	RANGE, YARDS:	0	100	200	300	400
Rem. 86 Soft Point	velocity, fps:	1460	1194	1030	931	858
	energy, ft-lb:	407	272	203	165	141
	arc, inches:		0	-22.9	-78.9	-173.0
Win. 86 Soft Point	velocity, fps:	1460	1194	1030	931	858.
	energy, ft-lb:	407	272	203	165	141
	arc, inches:		0	-23.5	-79.6	-175.9

.25-35 Winchester

CARTRIDGE BULLET	RANGE, YARDS:	0	100	200	300	400
Win. 117 Soft Point	velocity, fps:	2230	1866	1545	1282	1097
	energy, ft-lb:	1292	904	620	427	313
	arc, inches:		+2.1	-5.1	-27.0	-70.1

.250 Savage

CARTRIDGE BULLET	RANGE, YARDS:	0	100	200	300	400
Rem. 100 Pointed SP	velocity, fps:	2820	2504	2210	1936	1684.
	energy, ft-lb:	1765	1392	1084	832	630
	arc, inches:		+2.0	0	-9.2	-27.7
Win. 100 Silvertip	velocity, fps:	2820	2467	2140	1839	1569
	energy, ft-lb:	1765	1351	1017	751	547
	arc, inches:		+2.4	0	-10.1	-30.5

.257 Roberts

CARTRIDGE BULLET	RANGE, YARDS:	0	100	200	300	400
Federal 120 Nosler Partition	velocity, fps:	2780	2560	2360	2160	1970
	energy, ft-lb:	2060	1750	1480	1240	1030
	arc, inches:		+1.9	0	-8.2	-24.0
Hornady 117 SP boat-tail	velocity, fps:	2780	2550	2331	2122	1925
	energy, ft-lb:	2007	1689	1411	1170	963
	arc, inches:		+1.9	0	-8.3	-24.4
Hornady 117 SP boat-tail LM	velocity, fps:	2940	2694	2460	2240	2031
	energy, ft-lb:	2245	1885	1572	1303	1071
	arc, inches:		+1.7	0	-7.6	-21.8
Hornady 117 SST Superformance	velocity, fps:	2946	2707	2480	2265	2060
	energy, ft-lb:	2255	1903	1598	1332	1102
	arc, inches:		+1.6	0	-7.3	-21.4
Rem. 117 SP Core-Lokt	velocity, fps:	2650	2291	1961	1663	1404
	energy, ft-lb:	1824	1363	999	718	512
	arc, inches:		+2.6	0	-11.7	-36.1
Win. 117 Power-Point	velocity, fps:	2780	2411	2071	1761	1488
	energy, ft-lb:	2009	1511	1115	806	576.
	arc, inches:		+2.6	0	-10.8	-33.0

.25-06 Remington

CARTRIDGE BULLET	RANGE, YARDS:	0	100	200	300	400
Black Hills 100 Nos. Bal. Tip	velocity, fps:	3200				
	energy, ft-lb:	2273				
	arc, inches:					
Black Hills 100 Barnes XLC	velocity, fps:	3200				
	energy, ft-lb:	2273				
	arc, inches:					
Black Hills 115 Barnes X	velocity, fps:	2975				
	energy, ft-lb:	2259				
	arc, inches:					

Centerfire Rifle Ballistics

.25-06 REMINGTON TO 6.5X55 SWEDISH

CARTRIDGE BULLET	RANGE, YARDS:	0	100	200	300	400
Federal 90 Sierra Varminter	velocity, fps:	3440	3040	2680	2340	2030
	energy, ft-lb:	2365	1850	1435	1100	825
	arc, inches:		+1.1	0	-6.0	-18.3
Federal 100 Barnes XLC	velocity, fps:	3210	2970	2750	2540	2330
	energy, ft-lb:	2290	1965	1680	1430	1205
	arc, inches:		+1.2	0	-5.8	-17.0
Federal 100 Nosler Bal. Tip	velocity, fps:	3210	2960	2720	2490	2280
	energy, ft-lb:	2290	1940	1640	1380	1150.
	arc, inches:		+1.2	0	-6.0	-17.5
Federal 100 Trophy Copper	velocity, fps:	3210	2970	2740	2520	2310
	energy, ft-lb:	2290	1955	1665	1410	1185
	arc, inches:		+1.2	0	-5.9	-17.2
Federal 115 Nosler Partition	velocity, fps:	2990	2750	2520	2300	2100
	energy, ft-lb:	2285	1930	1620	1350	1120
	arc, inches:		+1.6	0	-7.0	-20.8
Federal 115 Trophy Bonded	velocity, fps:	2990	2740	2500	2270	2050
	energy, ft-lb:	2285	1910	1590	1310	1075
	arc, inches:		+1.6	0	-7.2	-21.1
Federal 117 Sierra Pro Hunt.	velocity, fps:	2990	2730	2480	2250	2030
	energy, ft-lb:	2320	1985	1645	1350	1100
	arc, inches:		+1.6	0	-7.2	-21.4
Federal 117 Sierra GameKing	velocity, fps:	2990	2770	2570	2370	2190
BTSP	energy, ft-lb:	2320	2000	1715	1465	1240
	arc, inches:		+1.5	0	-6.8	-19.9
Hornady 90 GMX	velocity, fps:	3350	3001	2679	2378	2098
Superformance	energy, ft-lb:	2243	1799	1434	1130	879
	arc, inches:		+1.2	0	-6.0	-18.3
Hornady 117 SP boat-tail	velocity, fps:	2990	2749	2520	2302	2096
	energy, ft-lb:	2322	1962	1649	1377	1141
	arc, inches:		+1.6	0	-7.0	-20.7
Hornady 117 SP boat-tail LM	velocity, fps:	3110	2855	2613	2384	2168
	energy, ft-lb:	2512	2117	1774	1476	1220
	arc, inches:		+1.8	0	-7.1	-20.3
Hornady 117 SST	velocity, fps:	3110	2862	2627	2405	2193
Superformance	energy, ft-lb:	2513	2127	1793	1502	1249
	arc, inches:		+1.4	0	-6.4	-18.9
PMC 100 SPBT	velocity, fps:	3200	2925	2650	2395	2145
	energy, ft-lb:	2273	1895	1561	1268	1019
	arc, inches:		+1.3	0	-6.3	-18.6
PMC 117 PSP	velocity, fps:	2950	2706	2472	2253	2047
	energy, ft-lb:	2261	1900	1588	1319	1088
	arc, inches:		+1.6	0	-7.3	-21.5
Rem. 100 PSP Core-Lokt	velocity, fps:	3230	2893	2580	2287	2014
	energy, ft-lb:	2316	1858	1478	1161	901
	arc, inches:		+1.3	0	-6.6	-19.8
Rem. 115 Core-Lokt Ultra	velocity, fps:	3000	2751	2516	2293	2081
	energy, ft-lb:	2298	1933	1616	1342	1106
	arc, inches:		+1.6	0	-7.1	-20.7
Rem. 120 PSP Core-Lokt	velocity, fps:	2990	2730	2484	2252	2032
	energy, ft-lb:	2382	1985	1644	1351	1100
	arc, inches:		+1.6	0	-7.2	-21.4
Speer 120 Grand Slam	velocity, fps:	3130	2835	2558	2298	
	energy, ft-lb:	2610	2141	1743	1407	
	arc, inches:		+1.4	0	-6.8	-20.1
Win. 85 Ballistic Silvertip	velocity, fps	3470	3156	2863	2589	2331
	energy, ft-lb:	2273	1880	1548	1266	1026
	arc, inches:		+1.0	0	-5.2	-15.7
Win. 90 Pos. Exp. Point	velocity, fps:	3440	3043	2680	2344	2034
	energy, ft-lb:	2364	1850	1435	1098	827
	arc, inches:		+2.4	+2.0	-3.4	-15.0
Win. 110 AccuBond CT	velocity, fps:	3100	2870	2651	2442	2243
	energy, ft-lb:	2347	2011	1716	1456	1228
	arc, inches:		+1.4	0	-6.3	-18.5
Win. 115 Ballistic Silvertip	velocity, fps:	3060	2825	2603	2390	2188
	energy, ft-lb:	2391	2038	1729	1459	1223
	arc, inches:		+1.4	0	-6.6	-19.2
Win. 120 Pos. Pt. Exp.	velocity, fps:	2990	2717	2459	2216	1987
	energy, ft-lb:	2382	1967	1612	1309	1053
	arc, inches:		+1.6	0	-7.4	-21.8

.25 Winchester Super Short Magnum

CARTRIDGE BULLET	RANGE, YARDS:	0	100	200	300	400
Win. 85 Ballistic Silvertip	velocity, fps:	3470	3156	2863	2589	2331
	energy, ft-lb:	2273	1880	1548	1266	1026
	arc, inches:		+1.0	0	-5.2	-15.7
Win. 110 AccuBond CT	velocity, fps:	3100	2870	2651	2442	2243.
	energy, ft-lb:	2347	2011	1716	1456	1228
	arc, inches:		+1.4	0	-6.3	-18.5
Win. 115 Ballistic Silvertip	velocity, fps:	3060	2844	2639	2442	2254
	energy, ft-lb:	2392	2066	1778	1523	1298
	arc, inches:		+1.4	0	-6.4	-18.6
Win. 120 Pos. Pt. Exp.	velocity, fps:	2990	2717	2459	2216	1987
	energy, ft-lb:	2383	1967	1612	1309	1053
	arc, inches:		+1.6	0	-7.4	-21.8

.257 Weatherby Magnum

CARTRIDGE BULLET	RANGE, YARDS:	0	100	200	300	400
Federal 115 Nosler Partition	velocity, fps:	3150	2900	2660	2440	
2220						
	energy, ft-lb:	2535	2145	1810	1515	1260
	arc, inches:		+1.3	0	-6.2	-18.4
Federal 115 Trophy Bonded	velocity, fps:	3150	2890	2640	2400	2180
	energy, ft-lb:	2535	2125	1775	1470	1210
	arc, inches:		+1.4	0	-6.3	-18.8
Wby. 87 Pointed Expanding	velocity, fps:	3825	3472	3147	2845	2563
	energy, ft-lb:	2826	2328	1913	1563	1269
	arc, inches:		+2.1	+2.8	0	-7.1
Wby. 100 Pointed Expanding	velocity, fps:	3602	3298	3016	2750	2500
	energy, ft-lb:	2881	2416	2019	1680	1388
	arc, inches:		+2.4	+3.1	0	-7.7
Wby. 115 Nosler Bal. Tip	velocity, fps:	3400	3170	2952	2745	2547
	energy, ft-lb:	2952	2566	2226	1924	1656.
	arc, inches:		+3.0	+3.5	0	-7.9
Wby. 115 Barnes X	velocity, fps:	3400	3158	2929	2711	2504
	energy, ft-lb:	2952	2546	2190	1877	1601
	arc, inches:		+2.7	+3.4	0	-8.1
Wby. 117 RN Expanding	velocity, fps:	3402	2984	2595	2240	1921
	energy, ft-lb:	3007	2320	1742	1302	956
	arc, inches:		+3.4	+4.31	0	-11.1
Wby. 120 Nosler Partition	velocity, fps:	3305	3046	2801	2570	2350
	energy, ft-lb:	2910	2472	2091	1760	1471
	arc, inches:		+3.0	+3.7	0	-8.9

6.53 (.257) Scramjet

CARTRIDGE BULLET	RANGE, YARDS:	0	100	200	300	400
Lazzeroni 85 Nosler Bal. Tip	velocity, fps:	3960	3652	3365	3096	2844
	energy, ft-lb:	2961	2517	2137	1810	1526
	arc, inches:		+1.7	+2.4	0	-6.0
Lazzeroni 100 Nosler Part.	velocity, fps:	3740	3465	3208	2965	2735
	energy, ft-lb:	3106	2667	2285	1953	1661.
	arc, inches:		+2.1	+2.7	0	-6.7

6.5x50 Japanese

CARTRIDGE BULLET	RANGE, YARDS:	0	100	200	300	400
Norma 156 Alaska	velocity, fps:	2067	1832	1615	1423	
	energy, ft-lb:	1480	1162	904	701	
	arc, inches:		+4.4	0	-17.8	

6.5x52 Carcano

CARTRIDGE BULLET	RANGE, YARDS:	0	100	200	300	400
Norma 156 Alaska	velocity, fps:	2428	2169	1926	1702	
	energy, ft-lb:	2043	1630	1286	1004	
	arc, inches:		+2.9	0	-12.3	

6.5x55 Swedish

CARTRIDGE BULLET	RANGE, YARDS:	0	100	200	300	400
Federal 140 Hi-Shok	velocity, fps:	2600	2400	2220	2040	1860
	energy, ft-lb:	2100	1795	1525	1285	1080
	arc, inches:		+2.3	0	-9.4	-27.2

Centerfire Rifle Ballistics

6.5X55 SWEDISH TO 6.5 REMINGTON MAGNUM

CARTRIDGE BULLET	RANGE, YARDS:	0	100	200	300	400
Federal 140 Trophy Bonded	velocity, fps:	2550	2350	2160	1980	1810
	energy, ft-lb:	2020	1720	1450	1220	1015
	arc, inches:		+2.4	0	-9.8	-28.4
Federal 140 Sierra MatchKg.	velocity, fps:	2630	2460	2300	2140	2000
BTHP	energy, ft-lb:	2140	1880	1640	1430	1235
	arc, inches:		+16.4	+28.8	+33.9	+31.8
Hornady 129 SP LM	velocity, fps:	2770	2561	2361	2171	1994
	energy, ft-lb:	2197	1878	1597	1350	1138
	arc, inches:		+2.0	0	-8.2	-23.2
Hornady 140 SP Interlock	velocity, fps	2525	2341	2165	1996	1836
	energy, ft-lb:	1982	1704	1457	1239	1048
	arc, inches:		+2.4	0	-9.9	-28.5
Hornady140 SP LM	velocity, fps:	2740	2541	2351	2169	1999
	energy, ft-lb:	2333	2006	1717	1463	1242
	arc, inches:		+2.4	0	-8.7	-24.0
Norma 120 Nosler Bal. Tip	velocity, fps:	2822	2609	2407	2213	
	energy, ft-lb:	2123	1815	1544	1305	
	arc, inches:		+1.8	0	-7.8	
Norma 139 Vulkan	velocity, fps:	2854	2569	2302	2051	
	energy, ft-lb:	2515	2038	1636	1298	
	arc, inches:		+1.8	0	-8.4	
Norma 140 Nosler Partition	velocity, fps:	2789	2592	2403	2223	
	energy, ft-lb:	2419	2089	1796	1536	
	arc, inches:		+1.8	0	-7.8	
Norma 156 TXP Swift A-Fr.	velocity, fps:	2526	2276	2040	1818	
	energy, ft-lb:	2196	1782	1432	1138	
	arc, inches:		+2.6	0	-10.9	
Norma 156 Alaska	velocity, fps:	2559	2245	1953	1687	
	energy, ft-lb:	2269	1746	1322	986	
	arc, inches:		+2.7	0	-11.9	
Norma 156 Vulkan	velocity, fps:	2644	2395	2159	1937	
	energy, ft-lb:	2422	1987	1616	1301	
	arc, inches:		+2.2	0	-9.7	
Norma 156 Oryx	velocity, fps:	2559	2308	2070	1848	
	energy, ft-lb:	2269	1845	1485	1183	
	arc, inches:		+2.5	0	-10.6	
PMC 139 Pointed Soft Point	velocity, fps:	2850	2560	2290	2030	1790
	energy, ft-lb:	2515	2025	1615	1270	985
	arc, inches:		+2.2	0	-8.9	-26.3
PMC 140 HP boat-tail	velocity, fps:	2560	2398	2243	2093	1949
	energy, ft-lb:	2037	1788	1563	1361	1181
	arc, inches:		+2.3	0	-9.2	-26.4
PMC 140 SP boat-tail	velocity, fps:	2560	2386	2218	2057	1903
	energy, ft-lb:	2037	1769	1529	1315	1126
	arc, inches:		+2.3	0	-9.4	-27.1
PMC 144 FMJ	velocity, fps:	2650	2370	2110	1870	1650
	energy, ft-lb:	2425	1950	1550	1215	945
	arc, inches:		+2.7	0	-10.5	-30.9
Rem. 140 PSP Core-Lokt	velocity, fps:	2550	2353	2164	1984	1814
	energy, ft-lb:	2021	1720	1456	1224	1023
	arc, inches:		+2.4	0	-9.8	-27.0
Speer 140 Grand Slam	velocity, fps:	2550	2318	2099	1892	
	energy, ft-lb:	2021	1670	1369	1112	
	arc, inches:		+2.5	0	-10.4	-30.6
Win. 140 Soft Point	velocity, fps:	2550	2359	2176	2002	1836
	energy, ft-lb:	2022	1731	1473	1246	1048.
	arc, inches:		+2.4	0	-9.7	-28.1

6.5 Grendel

CARTRIDGE BULLET	RANGE, YARDS:	0	100	200	300	400
Hornady 123 A-MAX	velocity, fps:	2590	2420	2256	2099	1948
	energy, ft-lb:	1832	1599	1390	1203	1037
	arc, inches:	-2.4	+1.8	0	-8.6	-25.1
Hornady 123 SST	velocity, fps:	2620	2449	2284	2126	1974
	energy, ft-lb:	1875	1638	1425	1234	1064
	arc, inches:	-2.4	+1.7	0	-8.4	-24.5

6.5 Creedmoor

CARTRIDGE BULLET	RANGE, YARDS:	0	100	200	300	400
Hornady 120 GMX	velocity, fps:	3050	2850	2659	2476	2300
	energy, ft-lb:	2479	2164	1884	1634	1410
	arc, inches:	-1.5	+1.4	0	-6.3	-18.3
Hornady 129 SST	velocity, fps:	2950	2756	2571	2394	2223
	energy, ft-lb:	2493	2176	1894	1641	1415
	arc, inches:	-1.5	+1.5	0	-6.8	-19.7
Hornady 140 A-MAX	velocity, fps:	2710	2557	2410	2267	2129
	energy, ft-lb:	2283	2033	1805	1598	1410
	arc, inches:	-1.5	+1.9	0	-7.9	-22.6
Nosler 140 BT	velocity, fps:	2550	2380	2217	2060	1910
	energy, ft-lb:	2021	1761	1527	1319	1134
	arc, inches:	-1.5	+2.3	0	-9.4	-27.0

.260 Remington

CARTRIDGE BULLET	RANGE, YARDS:	0	100	200	300	400
Federal 140 Sierra GameKing	velocity, fps:	2750	2570	2390	2220	2060
BTSP	energy, ft-lb:	2350	2045	1775	1535	1315
	arc, inches:		+1.9	0	-8.0	-23.1
Federal 140 Trophy Bonded	velocity, fps:	2750	2540	2340	2150	1970
	energy, ft-lb:	2350	2010	1705	1440	1210
arc, inches:		+1.9	0	-8.4	-24.1	
Rem. 120 Nosler Bal. Tip	velocity, fps:	2890	2688	2494	2309	2131
	energy, ft-lb:	2226	1924	1657	1420	1210
	arc, inches:		+1.7	0	-7.3	-21.1
Rem. 120 AccuTip	velocity, fps:	2890	2697	2512	2334	2163
	energy, ft-lb:	2392	2083	1807	1560	1340
	arc, inches:		+1.6	0	-7.2	-20.7
Rem. 125 Nosler Partition	velocity, fps:	2875	2669	2473	2285	2105.
	energy, ft-lb:	2294	1977	1697	1449	1230
arc, inches:		+1.71	0	-7.4	-21.4	
Rem. 140 PSP Core-Lokt	velocity, fps:	2750	2544	2347	2158	1979
(and C-L Ultra)	energy, ft-lb:	2351	2011	1712	1448	1217
	arc, inches:		+1.9	0	-8.3	-24.0
Speer 140 Grand Slam	velocity, fps:	2750	2518	2297	2087	
	energy, ft-lb:	2351	1970	1640	1354	
	arc, inches:		+2.3	0	-8.9	-25.8

6.5-284

CARTRIDGE BULLET	RANGE, YARDS:	0	100	200	300	400
Norma 120 Nosler Bal. Tip	velocity, fps:	3117	2890	2674	2469	
	energy, ft-lb:	2589	2226	1906	1624	
	arc, inches:		+1.3	0	-6.2	
Norma 140 Nosler Part.	velocity, fps:	2953	2750	2557	2371	
	energy, ft-lb:	2712	2352	2032	1748	
	arc, inches:		+1.5	0	-6.8	

6.5-284 Norma

CARTRIDGE BULLET	RANGE, YARDS:	0	100	200	300	400
Nosler 120 Ballistic Tip	velocity, fps:	3000	2792	2594	2404	2223
	energy, ft-lb:	2398	2077	1793	1540	1316
	arc, inches:	-1.5	+1.4	0	-6.6	-17.1
Nosler 125 PT	velocity, fps:	3000	2788	2585	2392	2207
	energy, ft-lb:	2497	2157	1855	1588	1352
	arc, inches:	-1.5	+1.5	0	-6.7	-19.5
Nosler 130 AccuBond	velocity, fps:	2900	2709	2526	2351	2182
	energy, ft-lb:	2427	2118	1842	1595	1374
	arc, inches:	-1.5	+1.5	0	-6.9	-18.4

6.5 Remington Magnum

CARTRIDGE BULLET	RANGE, YARDS:	0	100	200	300	400
Nosler 125 PT	velocity, fps:	3025	2811	2608	2414	2228
	energy, ft-lb:	2539	2194	1888	1617	1377
	arc, inches:	-1.5	+1.5	0	-6.6	-19.1

Centerfire Rifle Ballistics

6.5 REMINGTON MAGNUM TO .270 WINCHESTER

CARTRIDGE BULLET	RANGE, YARDS:	0	100	200	300	400
Rem. 120 Core-Lokt PSP	velocity, fps:	3210	2905	2621	2353	2102
	energy, ft-lb:	2745	2248	1830	1475	1177
	arc, inches:		+2.7	+2.1	-3.5	-15.5

.264 WINCHESTER MAGNUM

CARTRIDGE BULLET	RANGE, YARDS:	0	100	200	300	400
Nosler 100 Ballistic Tip	velocity, fps:	3400	3105	2829	2569	2324
	energy, ft-lb:	2567	2141	1777	1465	1199
	arc, inches:	-1.5	+1.0	0	-5.5	-16.1
Nosler 130 AccuBond	velocity, fps:	3100	2900	2709	2527	2351
	energy, ft-lb:	2774	2428	2119	1843	1595
	arc, inches:	-1.5	+1.2	0	-6.0	-17.5
Rem. 140 PSP Core-Lokt	velocity, fps:	3030	2782	2548	2326	2114
	energy, ft-lb:	2854	2406	2018	1682	1389
	arc, inches:		+1.5	0	-6.9	-20.2
Win. 140 Power-Point	velocity, fps:	3030	2782	2548	2326	2114.
	energy, ft-lb:	2854	2406	2018	1682	1389
	arc, inches:		+1.8	0	-7.2	-20.8

6.8MM REMINGTON SPC

CARTRIDGE BULLET	RANGE, YARDS:	0	100	200	300	400
Hornady 110 BTHP (16-in. barrel)	velocity, fps:	2570	2332	2107	1895	1697
	energy, ft-lb:	1613	1328	1084	877	703
	arc, inches:	-2.4	+2.0	0	-9.9	-29.5
Hornady 120 SST (16-in. barrel)	velocity, fps:	2460	2250	2051	1863	1687
	energy, ft-lb:	1612	1349	1121	925	758
	arc, inches:	-2.4	+2.3	0	-10.5	-31.1
Rem. 115 Open Tip Match (and HPBT Match)	velocity, fps:	2800	2535	2285	2049	1828
	energy, ft-lb:	2002	1641	1333	1072	853
	arc, inches:		+2.0	0	-8.8	-26.2
Rem. 115 Metal Case	velocity, fps:	2800	2523	2262	2017	1789
	energy, ft-lb:	2002	1625	1307	1039	817
	arc, inches:		+2.0	0	-8.8	-26.2
Rem. 115 Sierra HPBT (2005; all vel. @ 2775)	velocity, fps:	2775	2511	2263	2028	1809
	energy, ft-lb:	1966	1610	1307	1050	835
	arc, inches:		+2.0	0	-8.8	-26.2.
Rem. 115 CL Ultra	velocity, fps:	2775	2472	2190	1926	1683
	energy, ft-lb:	1966	1561	1224	947	723
	arc, inches:		+2.1	0	-9.4	-28.2

.270 WINCHESTER

CARTRIDGE BULLET	RANGE, YARDS:	0	100	200	300	400
Black Hills 130 Nos. Bal. T.	velocity, fps:	2950				
	energy, ft-lb:	2512				
	arc, inches:					
Black Hills 130 Barnes XLC	velocity, ft-lb:	2950				
	energy, ft-lb:	2512				
	arc, inches:					
Federal 130 Barnes XLC And Triple Shock	velocity, fps:	3060	2840	2620	2420	2220
	energy, ft-lb:	2705	2320	1985	1690	1425
	arc, inches:		+1.4	0	-6.4	-18.9
Federal 130 Hi-Shok	velocity, fps:	3060	2800	2560	2330	2110
	energy, ft-lb:	2700	2265	1890	1565	1285
	arc, inches:		+1.5	0	-6.8	-20.0
Federal 130 Nosler Bal. Tip	velocity, fps:	3060	2840	2630	2430	2230
	energy, ft-lb:	2700	2325	1990	1700	1440
	arc, inches:		+1.4	0	-6.5	-18.8
Federal 130 Nos. Partition And Solid Base	velocity, fps:	3060	2830	2610	2400	2200
	energy, ft-lb:	2705	2310	19651665	1400	
	arc, inches:		+1.4	0	-6.5	-19.1
Federal 130 Sierra GameKing	velocity, fps:	3060	2830	2620	2410	2220
	energy, ft-lb:	2700	2320	1980	1680	1420
	arc, inches:		+1.4	0	-6.5	-19.0
Federal 130 Sierra Pro-Hunt.	velocity, fps:	3060	2830	2600	2390	2190
	energy, ft-lb:	2705	2305	1960	1655	1390
	arc, inches:	+1.4	0	-6.4	-19.0	
Federal 130 Trophy Bonded	velocity, fps:	3060	2810	2570	2340	2130
	energy, ft-lb:	2705	2275	1905	1585	1310
	arc, inches:		+1.5	0	-6.7	-19.8
Federal 130 Trophy Bonded Tip	velocity, fps:	3060	2840	2630	2430	2240
	energy, ft-lb:	2705	2330	2000	1710	1455
	arc, inches:		+1.4	0	-6.4	-18.7
Federal 140 Trophy Bonded	velocity, fps:	2940	2700	2480	2260	2060
	energy, ft-lb:	2685	2270	1905	1590	1315
	arc, inches:		+1.6	0	-7.3	-21.5
Federal 140 Trophy Bonded Tip	velocity, fps:	2950	2740	2550	2360	2180
	energy, ft-lb:	2705	2340	2015	1730	1475
	arc, inches:		+1.6	0	-6.9	-20.1
Federal 140 Tr. Bonded HE	velocity, fps:	3100	2860	2620	2400	2200.
	energy, ft-lb:	2990	2535	2140	1795	1500
	arc, inches:		+1.4	0	-6.4	-18.9
Federal 140 Nos. AccuBond	velocity, fps:	2950	2760	2580	2400	2230.
	energy, ft-lb:	2705	2365	2060	1790	1545
	arc, inches:		+1.5	0	-6.7	-19.6
Federal 150 Hi-Shok RN	velocity, fps:	2850	2500	2180	1890	1620
	energy, ft-lb:	2705	2085	1585	1185	870
	arc, inches:		+2.0	0	-9.4	-28.6
Federal 150 Sierra GameKing	velocity, fps:	2850	2660	2480	2300	2130
	energy, ft-lb:	2705	2355	2040	1760	1510
	arc, inches:		+1.7	0	-7.4	-21.4
Federal 150 Sierra GameKing HE	velocity, fps:	3000	2800	2620	2430	2260
	energy, ft-lb:	2995	2615	2275	1975	1700
	arc, inches:		+1.5	0	-6.5	-18.9
Federal 150 Nosler Partition	velocity, fps:	2850	2590	2340	2100	1880.
	energy, ft-lb:	2705	2225	1815	1470	1175
	arc, inches:		+1.9	0	-8.3	-24.4
Hornady 120 SST Custom Lite	velocity, fps:	2675	2288	1935	1619	1351
	energy, ft-lb:	1907	1395	998	699	486
	arc, inches:		+2.6	0	-12.0	-37.4
Hornady 130 GMX Superformance	velocity, fps:	3190	2975	2770	2575	2387
	energy, ft-lb:	2937	2554	2215	1913	1645
	arc, inches:		+1.2	0	-5.7	-16.8
Hornady 130 SST (or Interbond)	velocity, fps:	3060	2845	2639	2442	2254
	energy, ft-lb:	2700	2335	2009	1721	1467
	arc, inches:		+1.4	0	-6.6	-19.1
Hornady 130 SST LM (or Interbond)	velocity, fps:	3215	2998	2790	2590	2400
	energy, ft-lb:	2983	2594	2246	1936	1662
	arc, inches:		+1.2	0	-5.8	-17.0
Hornady 130 SST Superformance	velocity, fps:	3200	2984	2779	2583	2396
	energy, ft-lb:	2956	2570	2229	1926	1656
	arc, inches:		+1.2	0	-5.7	-16.7
Hornady 140 SP boat-tail	velocity, fps:	2940	2747	2562	2385	2214
	energy, ft-lb:	2688	2346	2041	1769	1524
	arc, inches:		+1.6	0	-7.0	-20.2
Hornady 140 SP boat-tail LM	velocity, fps:	3100	2894	2697	2508	2327.
	energy, ft-lb:	2987	2604	2261	1955	1684
	arc, inches:		+1.4	0	6.3	-18.3
Hornady 140 SST Superformance	velocity, fps:	3090	2894	2707	2568	2355
	energy, ft-lb:	2968	2604	2278	1986	1724
	arc, inches:		+1.3	0	-6.1	-17.6
Hornady 150 SP	velocity, fps:	2800	2684	2478	2284	2100
	energy, ft-lb:	2802	2400	2046	1737	1469
	arc, inches:		+1.7	0	-7.4	-21.6
Norma 130 SP	velocity, fps:	3140	2862	2601	2354	
	energy, ft-lb:	2847	2365	1953	1600	
	arc, inches:		+1.3	0	-6.5	
Norma 130 FMJ	velocity, fps:	2887	2634	2395	2169	
	energy, ft-lb:					
	arc, inches:		+1.8	0	-7.8	
Norma 150 SP	velocity, fps:	2799	2555	2323	2104	
	energy, ft-lb:	2610	2175	1798	1475	
	arc, inches:		+1.9	0	-8.3	
Norma 150 Oryx	velocity, fps:	2854	2608	2376	2155	
	energy, ft-lb:	2714	2267	1880	1547	
	arc, inches:		+1.8	0	-8.0	
PMC 130 Barnes X	velocity, fps:	2910	2717	2533	2356	2186
	energy, ft-lb:	2444	2131	1852	1602	1379
	arc, inches:		+1.6	0	-7.1	-20.4
PMC 130 SP boat-tail	velocity, fps:	3050	2830	2620	2421	2229
	energy, ft-lb:	2685	2312	1982	1691	1435
	arc, inches:		+1.5	0	-6.5	-19.0
PMC 130 Pointed Soft Point	velocity, fps:	2950	2691	2447	2217	2001
	energy, ft-lb:	2512	2090	1728	1419	1156
	arc, inches:		+1.6	0	-7.5	-22.1
PMC 150 Barnes X	velocity, fps:	2700	2541	2387	2238	2095
	energy, ft-lb:	2428	2150	1897	1668	1461
	arc, inches:		+2.0	0	-8.1	-23.1

Centerfire Rifle Ballistics

.270 WINCHESTER TO .270 WINCHESTER SHORT MAGNUM

CARTRIDGE BULLET	RANGE, YARDS:	0	100	200	300	400
PMC 150 SP boat-tail	velocity, fps:	2850	2660	2477	2302	2134
	energy, ft-lb:	2705	2355	2043	1765	1516.
	arc, inches:		+1.7	0	-7.4	-21.4
PMC 150 Pointed Soft Point	velocity, fps:	2750	2530	2321	2123	1936
	energy, ft-lb:	2519	2131	1794	1501	1248
	arc, inches:		+2.0	0	-8.4	-24.6
Rem. 100 Pointed Soft Point	velocity, fps:	3320	2924	2561	2225	1916
	energy, ft-lb:	2448	1898	1456	1099	815
	arc, inches:		+2.3	+2.0	-3.6	-16.2
Rem. 115 PSP Core-Lokt mr	velocity, fps:	2710	2412	2133	1873	1636
	energy, ft-lb:	1875	1485	1161	896	683
	arc, inches:		+1.0	-2.7	-14.2	-35.6
Rem. 130 PSP Core-Lokt	velocity, fps:	3060	2776	2510	2259	2022
	energy, ft-lb:	2702	2225	1818	1472	1180
	arc, inches:		+1.5	0	-7.0	-20.9
Rem. 130 Bronze Point	velocity, fps:	3060	2802	2559	2329	2110
	energy, ft-lb:	2702	2267	1890	1565	1285
	arc, inches:		+1.5	0	-6.8	-20.0
Rem. 130 Swift Scirocco	velocity, fps:	3060	2838	2677	2425	2232
	energy, ft-lb:	2702	2325	1991	1697	1438
	arc, inches:		+1.4	0	-6.5	-18.8
Rem. 130 AccuTip BT	velocity, fps:	3060	2845	2639	2442	2254
	energy, ft-lb:	2702	2336	2009	1721	1467
	arc, inches:		+1.4	0	-6.4	-18.6
Rem. 140 Swift A-Frame	velocity, fps:	2925	2652	2394	2152	1923
	energy, ft-lb:	2659	2186	1782	1439	1150
	arc, inches:		+1.7	0	-7.8	-23.2
Rem. 140 PSP boat-tail	velocity, fps:	2960	2749	2548	2355	2171
	energy, ft-lb:	2723	2349	2018	1724	1465
	arc, inches:		+1.6	0	-6.9	-20.1
Rem. 140 Nosler Bal. Tip	velocity, fps:	2960	2754	2557	2366	2187
	energy, ft-lb:	2724	2358	2032	1743	1487
	arc, inches:		+1.6	0	-6.9	-20.0
Rem. 140 PSP C-L Ultra	velocity, fps:	2925	2667	2424	2193	1975
	energy, ft-lb:	2659	2211	1826	1495	1212
	arc, inches:		+1.7	0	-7.6	-22.5
Rem. 150 SP Core-Lokt	velocity, fps:	2850	2504	2183	1886	1618
	energy, ft-lb:	2705	2087	1587	1185	872
	arc, inches:		+2.0	0	-9.4	-28.6
Rem. 150 Nosler Partition	velocity, fps:	2850	2652	2463	2282	2108
	energy, ft-lb:	2705	2343	2021	1734	1480
	arc, inches:		+1.7	0	-7.5	-21.6
Speer 130 Grand Slam	velocity, fps:	3050	2774	2514	2269	
	energy, ft-lb:	2685	2221	1824	1485	
	arc, inches:		+1.5	0	-7.0	-20.9
Speer 150 Grand Slam	velocity, fps:	2830	2594	2369	2156	
	energy, ft-lb:	2667	2240	1869	1548	
	arc, inches:		+1.8	0	-8.1	-23.6
Win. 130 Power-Point	velocity, fps:	3060	2802	2559	2329	2110
	energy, ft-lb:	2702	2267	1890	1565	1285.
	arc, inches:		+1.8	0	-7.1	-20.6
Win. 130 Power-Point Plus	velocity, fps:	3150	2881	2628	2388	2161
	energy, ft-lb:	2865	2396	1993	1646	1348
	arc, inches:		+1.3	0	-6.4	-18.9
Win. 130 Silvertip	velocity, fps:	3060	2776	2510	2259	2022.
	energy, ft-lb:	2702	2225	1818	1472	1180
	arc, inches:		+1.8	0	-7.4	-21.6
Win. 130 Ballistic Silvertip	velocity, fps:	3050	2828	2618	2416	2224
	energy, ft-lb:	2685	2309	1978	1685	1428
	arc, inches:		+1.4	0	-6.5	-18.9
Win. 140 AccuBond	velocity, fps:	2950	2751	2560	2378	2203
	energy, ft-lb:	2705	2352	2038	1757	1508
	arc, inches:		+1.6	0	-6.9	-19.9
Win. 140 Fail Safe	velocity, fps:	2920	2671	2435	2211	1999
	energy, ft-lb:	2651	2218	1843	1519	1242
	arc, inches:		+1.7	0	-7.6	-22.3
Win. 150 Power-Point	velocity, fps:	2850	2585	2336	2100	1879
	energy, ft-lb:	2705	2226	1817	1468	1175
	arc, inches:		+2.2	0	-8.6	-25.0
Win. 150 Power-Point Plus	velocity, fps:	2950	2679	2425	2184	1957
	energy, ft-lb:	2900	2391	1959	1589	1276
	arc, inches:		+1.7	0	-7.6	-22.6
Win. 150 Partition Gold	velocity, fps:	2930	2693	2468	2254	2051
	energy, ft-lb:	2860	2416	2030	1693	1402
	arc, inches:		+1.7	0	-7.4	-21.6
Win. 150 Supreme Elite XP3	velocity, fps:	2950	2763	2583	2411	2245
	energy, ft-lb:	2898	2542	2223	1936	1679
	arc, inches:		+1.5	0	-6.9	-15.5

.270 Winchester Short Magnum

CARTRIDGE BULLET	RANGE, YARDS:	0	100	200	300	400
Black Hills 140 AccuBond	velocity, fps:	3100				
	energy, ft-lb:	2987				
	arc, inches:					
Federal 130 Nos. Bal. Tip	velocity, fps:	3300	3070	2840	2630	2430
	energy, ft-lb:	3145	2710	2335	2000	1705
	arc, inches:		+1.1	0	-5.4	-15.8
Federal 130 Nos. Partition And Nos. Solid Base And Barnes TS	velocity, fps:	3280	3040	2810	2590	2380
	energy, ft-lb:	3105	2665	2275	1935	1635
	arc, inches:		+1.1	0	-5.6	-16.3
Federal 130 Trophy Copper	velocity, fps:	3280	3060	2850	2650	2460
	energy, ft-lb:	3105	2700	2345	2025	1745
	arc, inches:		+1.1	0	-5.4	-15.8
Federal 140 Nos. AccuBond	velocity, fps	3200	3000	2810	2630	2450
	energy, ft-lb:	3185	2795	2455	2145	1865
	arc, inches:		+1.2	0	-5.6	-16.2
Federal 140 Trophy Bonded	velocity, fps:	3130	2870	2640	2410	2200
	energy, ft-lb:	3035	2570	2160	1810	1500
	arc, inches:		+1.4	0	-6.3	18.7
Federal 140 Trophy Bonded Tip	velocity, fps:	3200	2980	2770	2580	2390
	energy, ft-lb:	3185	2765	2390	2060	1770
	arc, inches:		+1.2	0	-5.8	-16.7
Federal 150 Nos. Partition	velocity, fps:	3160	2950	2750	2550	2370
	energy, ft-lb:	3325	2895	2515	2175	1870
	arc, inches:		+1.3	0	-5.9	-17.0
Norma 130 FMJ	velocity, fps:	3150	2882	2630	2391	
	energy, ft-lb:					
	arc, inches:		+1.5	0	-6.4	
Norma 130 Ballistic ST	velocity, fps:	3281	3047	2825	2614	
	energy, ft-lb:	3108	2681	2305	1973	
	arc, inches:		+1.1	0	-5.5	
Norma 140 Barnes X TS	velocity, fps:	3150	2952	2762	2580	
	energy, ft-lb:	3085	2709	2372	2070	
	arc, inches:		+1.3	0	-5.8	
Norma 150 Nosler Bal. Tip	velocity, fps:	3280	3046	2824	2613	
	energy, ft-lb:	3106	2679	2303	1972	
	arc, inches:		+1.1	0	-5.4	
Norma 150 Oryx	velocity, fps:	3117	2856	2611	2378	
	energy, ft-lb:	3237	2718	2271	1884	
	arc, inches:		+1.4	0	-6.5	
Win. 130 Bal. Silvertip	velocity, fps:	3275	3041	2820	2609	2408
	energy, ft-lb:	3096	2669	2295	1964	1673
	arc, inches:		+1.1	0	-5.5	-16.1
Win. 140 AccuBond	velocity, fps:	3200	2989	2789	2597	2413
	energy, ft-lb:	3184	2779	2418	2097	1810
	arc, inches:		+1.2	0	-5.7	-16.5
Win. 140 Fail Safe	velocity, fps:	3125	2865	2619	2386	2165
	energy, ft-lb:	3035	2550	2132	1769	1457
	arc, inches:		+1.4	0	-6.5	-19.0
Win. 150 Ballistic Silvertip	velocity, fps:	3120	2923	2734	2554	2380.
	energy, ft-lb:	3242	2845	2490	2172	1886.
	arc, inches:		+1.3	0	-5.9	-17.2

Centerfire Rifle Ballistics

.270 WINCHESTER SHORT MAGNUM TO 7MM-08 REMINGTON

CARTRIDGE BULLET	RANGE, YARDS:	0	100	200	300	400
Win. 150 Power Point	velocity, fps:	3150	2867	2601	2350	2113
	energy, ft-lb:	3304	2737	2252	1839	1487
	arc, inches:		+1.4	0	-6.5	-19.4
Win. 150 Supreme Elite XP3	velocity, fps:	3120	2926	2740	2561	2389
	energy, ft-lb:	3242	2850	2499	2184	1901
	arc, inches:		+1.3	0	-5.9	-17.1

.270 Weatherby Magnum

CARTRIDGE BULLET	RANGE, YARDS:	0	100	200	300	400
Federal 130 Nosler Partition	velocity, fps:	3200	2960	2740	2520	2320
	energy, ft-lb:	2955	2530	2160	1835	1550
	arc, inches:		+1.2	0	-5.9	-17.3
Federal 130 Sierra GameKing BTSP	velocity, fps:	3200	2980	2780	2580	2400
	energy, ft-lb:	2955	2570	2230	1925	1655
	arc, inches:		+1.2	0	-5.7	-16.6
Federal 140 Trophy Bonded	velocity, fps:	3100	2840	2600	2370	2150.
	energy, ft-lb:	2990	2510	2100	1745	1440
	arc, inches:		+1.4	0	-6.6	-19.3
Federal 130 Trophy Bonded Tip	velocity, fps:	3200	2970	2760	2560	2360
	energy, ft-lb:	2955	2555	2200	1885	1610
	arc, inches:		+1.2	0	-5.9	-16.9
Wby. 100 Pointed Expanding	velocity, fps:	3760	3396	3061	2751	2462
	energy, ft-lb:	3139	2560	2081	1681	1346
	arc, inches:		+2.3	+3.0	0	-7.6
Wby. 130 Pointed Expanding	velocity, fps:	3375	3123	2885	2659	2444
	energy, ft-lb:	3288	2815	2402	2041	1724
	arc, inches:		+2.8	+3.5	0	-8.4
Wby. 130 Nosler Partition	velocity, fps:	3375	3127	2892	2670	2458.
	energy, ft-lb:	3288	2822	2415	2058	1744
	arc, inches:		+2.8	+3.5	0	-8.3
Wby. 140 Nosler Bal. Tip	velocity, fps:	3300	3077	2865	2663	2470.
	energy, ft-lb:	3385	2943	2551	2204	1896
	arc, inches:		+2.9	+3.6	0	-8.4
Wby. 140 Barnes X	velocity, fps:	3250	3032	2825	2628	2438
	energy, ft-lb:	3283	2858	2481	2146	1848
	arc, inches:		+3.0	+3.7	0	-8.7
Wby. 150 Pointed Expanding	velocity, fps:	3245	3028	2821	2623	2434
	energy, ft-lb:	3507	3053	2650	2292	1973
	arc, inches:		+3.0	+3.7	0	-8.7
Wby. 150 Nosler Partition	velocity, fps:	3245	3029	2823	2627	2439.
	energy, ft-lb:	3507	3055	2655	2298	1981
	arc, inches:		+3.0	+3.7	0	-8.

7-30 Waters

CARTRIDGE BULLET	RANGE, YARDS:	0	100	200	300	400
Federal 120 Sierra GameKing BTSP	velocity, fps:	2700	2300	1930	1600	1330.
	energy, ft-lb:	1940	1405	990	685	470
	arc, inches:		+2.6	0	-12.0	-37.6

7mm Mauser (7x57)

CARTRIDGE BULLET	RANGE, YARDS:	0	100	200	300	400
Federal 140 Sierra Pro-Hunt.	velocity, fps:	2660	2450	2260	2070	1890.
	energy, ft-lb:	2200	1865	1585	1330	1110
	arc, inches:		+2.1	0	-9.0	-26.1
Federal 140 Nosler Partition	velocity, fps:	2660	2450	2260	2070	1890.
	energy, ft-lb:	2200	1865	1585	1330	1110
	arc, inches:		+2.1	0	-9.0	-26.1
Federal 175 Hi-Shok RN	velocity, fps:	2440	2140	1860	1600	1380
	energy, ft-lb:	2315	1775	1340	1000	740
	arc, inches:		+3.1	0	-13.3	-40.1
Hornady 139 SP boat-tail	velocity, fps:	2700	2504	2316	2137	1965
	energy, ft-lb:	2251	1936	1656	1410	1192
	arc, inches:		+2.0	0	-8.5	-24.9
Hornady 139 SP Interlock	velocity, fps:	2680	2455	2241	2038	1846
	energy, ft-lb:	2216	1860	1550	1282	1052
	arc, inches:		+2.1	0	-9.1	-26.6
Hornady 139 SP boat-tail LM	velocity, fps:	2830	2620	2450	2250	2070
	energy, ft-lb:	2475	2135	1835	1565	1330
	arc, inches:		+1.8	0	-7.6	-22.1
Hornady 139 SP LM	velocity, fps:	2950	2736	2532	2337	2152.
	energy, ft-lb:	2686	2310	1978	1686	1429
	arc, inches:		+2.0	0	-7.6	-21.5
Hornady 139 SST Superformance	velocity, fps:	2760	2575	2397	2227	2063
	energy, ft-lb:	2351	2046	1774	1530	1314
	arc, inches:		+1.9	0	-7.9	-22.9
Norma 150 Soft Point	velocity, fps:	2690	2479	2278	2087	
	energy, ft-lb:	2411	2048	1729	1450	
	arc, inches:		+2.0	0	-8.8	
PMC 140 Pointed Soft Point	velocity, fps:	2660	2450	2260	2070	1890
	energy, ft-lb:	2200	1865	1585	1330	1110.
	arc, inches:		+2.4	0	-9.6	-27.3
PMC 175 Soft Point	velocity, fps:	2440	2140	1860	1600	1380
	energy, ft-lb:	2315	1775	1340	1000	740
	arc, inches:		+1.5	-3.6	-18.6	-46.8
Rem. 140 PSP Core-Lokt	velocity, fps:	2660	2435	2221	2018	1827
	energy, ft-lb:	2199	1843	1533	1266	1037
	arc, inches:		+2.2	0	-9.2	-27.4
Win. 145 Power-Point	velocity, fps:	2660	2413	2180	1959	1754
	energy, ft-lb:	2279	1875	1530	1236	990
	arc, inches:		+1.1	-2.8	-14.1	-34.4

7x57 R

CARTRIDGE BULLET	RANGE, YARDS:	0	100	200	300	400
Norma 150 FMJ	velocity, fps:	2690	2489	2296	2112	
	energy, ft-lb:	2411	2063	1756	1486	
	arc, inches:		+2.0	0	-8.6	
Norma 154 Soft Point	velocity, fps:	2625	2417	2219	2030	
	energy, ft-lb:	2357	1999	1684	1410	
	arc, inches:		+2.2	0	-9.3	
Norma 156 Oryx	velocity, fps:	2608	2346	2099	1867	
	energy, ft-lb:	2357	1906	1526	1208	
	arc, inches:		+2.4	0	-10.3	

7mm-08 Remington

CARTRIDGE BULLET	RANGE, YARDS:	0	100	200	300	400
Black Hills 140 AccuBond	velocity, fps:	2700				
	energy, ft-lb:					
	arc, inches:					
Federal 140 Nosler Partition	velocity, fps:	2800	2590	2390	2200	2020
	energy, ft-lb:	2435	2085	1775	1500	1265
	arc, inches:		+1.8	0	-8.0	-23.1
Federal 140 Nosler Bal. Tip And AccuBond	velocity, fps:	2800	2610	2430	2260	2100
	energy, ft-lb:	2440	2135	1840	1590	1360.
	arc, inches:		+1.8	0	-7.7	-22.3
Federal 140 Tr. Bonded HE	velocity, fps:	2950	2660	2390	2140	1900
	energy, ft-lb:	2705	2205	1780	1420	1120
	arc, inches:		+1.7	0	-7.9	-23.2
Federal 140 Trophy Copper	velocity, fps:	2800	2610	2440	2260	2100
	energy, ft-lb:	2435	2125	1845	1595	1370
	arc, inches:		+1.8	0	-7.7	-22.2
Federal 150 Sierra Pro-Hunt.	velocity, fps:	2650	2440	2230	2040	1860
	energy, ft-lb:	2340	1980	1660	1390	1150
	arc, inches:		+2.2	0	-9.2	-26.7
Hornady 120 SST Custom Lite	velocity, fps:	2675	2435	2207	1992	1790
	energy, ft-lb:	1907	1579	1298	1057	854
	arc, inches:		+2.2	0	-9.4	-27.5
Hornady 139 SP boat-tail LM	velocity, fps:	3000	2790	2590	2399	2216
	energy, ft-lb:	2777	2403	2071	1776	1515
	arc, inches:		+1.5	0	-6.7	-19.4
Norma 140 Ballistic ST	velocity, fps:	2822	2633	2452	2278	
	energy, ft-lb:	2476	2156	1870	1614	
	arc, inches:		+1.8	0	-7.6	
PMC 139 PSP	velocity, fps:	2850	2610	2384	2170	1969
	energy, ft-lb:	2507	2103	1754	1454	1197
	arc, inches:		+1.8	0	-7.9	-23.3
Rem. 120 Hollow Point	velocity, fps:	3000	2725	2467	2223	1992
	energy, ft-lb:	2398	1979	1621	1316	1058
	arc, inches:		+1.6	0	-7.3	-21.7
Rem. 140 PSP Core-Lokt	velocity, fps:	2860	2625	2402	2189	1988
	energy, ft-lb:	2542	2142	1793	1490	1228
	arc, inches:		+1.8	0	-7.8	-22.9
Rem. 140 PSP boat-tail	velocity, fps:	2860	2656	2460	2273	2094
	energy, ft-lb:	2542	2192	1881	1606	1363
	arc, inches:		+1.7	0	-7.5	-21.7

Centerfire Rifle Ballistics

7MM-08 REMINGTON TO .280 REMINGTON

CARTRIDGE BULLET	RANGE, YARDS:	0	100	200	300	400
Rem. 140 AccuTip BT	velocity, fps:	2860	2670	2488	2313	2145
	energy, ft-lb:	2543	2217	1925	1663	1431
	arc, inches:		+1.7	0	-7.3	-21.2
Rem. 140 Nosler Partition	velocity, fps:	2860	2648	2446	2253	2068
	energy, ft-lb:	2542	2180	1860	1577	1330
	arc, inches:		+1.7	0	-7.6	-22.0
Speer 145 Grand Slam	velocity, fps:	2845	2567	2305	2059	
	energy, ft-lb:	2606	2121	1711	1365	
	arc, inches:		+1.9	0	-8.4	-25.5
Win. 140 Power-Point	velocity, fps:	2800	2523	2268	2027	1802.
	energy, ft-lb:	2429	1980	1599	1277	1010
	arc, inches:		+2.0	0	-8.8	-26.0
Win. 140 Power-Point Plus	velocity, fps:	2875	2597	2336	2090	1859
	energy, ft-lb:	2570	1997	1697	1358	1075
	arc, inches:		+2.0	0	-8.8	26.0
Win. 140 Fail Safe	velocity, fps:	2760	2506	2271	2048	1839
	energy, ft-lb:	2360	1953	1603	1304	1051
	arc, inches:		+2.0	0	-8.8	-25.9
Win. 140 Ballistic Silvertip	velocity, fps:	2770	2572	2382	2200	2026
	energy, ft-lb:	2386	2056	1764	1504	1276
	arc, inches:		+1.9	0	-8.0	-23.8

7x64 Brenneke

CARTRIDGE BULLET	RANGE, YARDS:	0	100	200	300	400
Federal 160 Nosler Partition	velocity, fps:	2650	2480	2310	2150	2000
	energy, ft-lb:	2495	2180	1895	1640	1415
	arc, inches:		+2.1	0	-8.7	-24.9
Norma 140 AccuBond	velocity, fps:	2953	2759	2572	2394	
	energy, ft-lb:	2712	2366	2058	1782	
	arc, inches:		+1.5	0	-6.8	
Norma 154 Soft Point	velocity, fps:	2821	2605	2399	2203	
	energy, ft-lb:	2722	2321	1969	1660	
	arc, inches:		+1.8	0	-7.8	
Norma 156 Oryx	velocity, fps:	2789	2516	2259	2017	
	energy, ft-lb:	2695	2193	1768	1410	
	arc, inches:		+2.0	0	-8.8	
Norma 170 Vulkan	velocity, fps:	2756	2501	2259	2031	
	energy, ft-lb:	2868	2361	1927	1558	
	arc, inches:		+2.0	0	-8.8	
Norma 170 Oryx	velocity, fps:	2756	2481	2222	1979	
	energy, ft-lb:	2868	2324	1864	1478	
	arc, inches:		+2.1	0	-9.2	
Norma 170 Plastic Point	velocity, fps:	2756	2519	2294	2081	
	energy, ft-lb:	2868	2396	1987	1635	
	arc, inches:		+2.0	0	-8.6	
PMC 170 Pointed Soft Point	velocity, fps:	2625	2401	2189	1989	1801
	energy, ft lb:	2601	2175	1808	1493	1224
	arc, inches:		+2.3	0	-9.6	-27.9
Rem. 175 PSP Core-Lokt	velocity, fps:	2650	2445	2248	2061	1883
	energy, ft-lb:	2728	2322	1964	1650	1378
	arc, inches:		+2.2	0	-9.1	-26.4
Speer 160 Grand Slam	velocity, fps:	2600	2376	2164	1962	
	energy, ft-lb:	2401	2006	1663	1368	
	arc, inches:		+2.3	0	-9.8	-28.6
Speer 175 Grand Slam	velocity, fps:	2650	2461	2280	2106	
	energy, ft-lb:	2728	2353	2019	1723	
	arc, inches:		+2.4	0	-9.2	-26.2

7x65 R

CARTRIDGE BULLET	RANGE, YARDS:	0	100	200	300	400
Norma 150 FMJ	velocity, fps:	2756	2552	2357	2170	
	energy, ft-lb:	2530	2169	1850	1569	
	arc, inches:		+1.9	0	-8.2	
Norma 156 Oryx	velocity, fps:	2723	2454	2200	1962	
	energy, ft-lb:	2569	2086	1678	1334	
	arc, inches:		+2.1	0	-9.3	
Norma 170 Plastic Point	velocity, fps:	2625	2390	2167	1956	
	energy, ft-lb:	2602	2157	1773	1445	
	arc, inches:		+2.3	0	-9.7	
Norma 170 Vulkan	velocity, fps:	2657	2392	2143	1909	
	energy, ft-lb:	2666	2161	1734	1377	
	arc, inches:		+2.3	0	-9.9	
Norma 170 Oryx	velocity, fps:	2657	2378	2115	1871	
	energy, ft-lb:	2666	2135	1690	1321	
	arc, inches:		+2.3	0	-10.1	

.284 Winchester

CARTRIDGE BULLET	RANGE, YARDS:	0	100	200	300	400
Win. 150 Power-Point	velocity, fps:	2860	2595	2344	2108	1886
	energy, ft-lb:	2724	2243	1830	1480	1185
	arc, inches:		+2.1	0	-8.5	-24.8

.280 Remington

CARTRIDGE BULLET	RANGE, YARDS:	0	100	200	300	400
Federal 140 Sierra Pro-Hunt.	velocity, fps:	2990	2740	2500	2270	2060
	energy, ft-lb:	2770	2325	1940	1605	1320
	arc, inches:		+1.6	0	-7.0	-20.8
Federal 140 Trophy Bonded	velocity, fps:	2990	2630	2310	2040	1730
	energy, ft-lb:	2770	2155	1655	1250	925
	arc, inches:		+1.6	0	-8.4	-25.4
Federal 140 Trophy Bonded Tip	velocity, fps:	2950	2730	2520	2330	2140
	energy, ft-lb:	2705	2320	1980	1680	1420
	arc, inches:		+1.6	0	-7.0	-20.6
Federal 140 Tr. Bonded HE	velocity, fps:	3150	2850	2570	2300	2050
	energy, ft-lb:	3085	2520	2050	1650	1310
	arc, inches:		+1.4	0	-6.7	-20.0
Federal 140 Nos. AccuBond And Bal. Tip And Solid Base	velocity, fps:	3000	2800	2620	2440	2260
	energy, ft-lb:	2800	2445	2130	1845	1590
	arc, inches:		+1.5	0	-6.5	-18.9
Federal 150 Hi-Shok	velocity, fps:	2890	2670	2460	2260	2060
	energy, ft-lb:	2780	2370	2015	1695	1420
	arc, inches:		+1.7	0	-7.5	-21.8
Federal 150 Nosler Partition	velocity, fps:	2890	2690	2490	2310	2130
	energy, ft-lb:	2780	2405	2070	1770	1510.
	arc, inches:		+1.7	0	-7.2	-21.1
Federal 150 Nos. AccuBond	velocity, fps	2800	2630	2460	2300	2150
	energy, ft-lb:	2785	2455	2155	1885	1645
	arc, inches:		+1.8	0	-7.5	-21.5
Federal 160 Trophy Bonded	velocity, fps:	2800	2570	2350	2140	1940
	energy, ft-lb:	2785	2345	1960	1625	1340
	arc, inches:		+1.9	0	-8.3	-24.0
Hornady 139 SPBT LMmoly	velocity, fps:	3110	2888	2675	2473	2280.
	energy, ft-lb:	2985	2573	2209	1887	1604
	arc, inches:		+1.4	0	-6.5	-18.6
Hornady 139 SST Superformance	velocity, fps:	3090	2891	2700	2518	2343
	energy, ft-lb:	2947	2579	2250	1957	1694
	arc, inches:		+1.3	0	-6.1	-17.7
Norma 156 Oryx	velocity, fps:	2789	2516	2259	2017	
	energy, ft-lb:	2695	2193	1768	1410	
	arc, inches:		+2.0	0	-8.8	
Norma 170 Plastic Point	velocity, fps:	2707	2468	2241	2026	
	energy, ft-lb:	2767	2299	1896	1550	
	arc, inches:		+2.1	0	-9.1	
Norma 170 Vulkan	velocity, fps:	2592	2346	2113	1894	
	energy, ft-lb:	2537	2078	1686	1354	
	arc, inches:		+2.4	0	-10.2	
Norma 170 Oryx	velocity, fps:	2690	2416	2159	1918	
	energy, ft-lb:	2732	2204	1760	1389	
	arc, inches:		+2.2	0	-9.7	
Rem. 140 PSP Core-Lokt	velocity, fps:	3000	2758	2528	2309	2102
	energy, ft-lb:	2797	2363	1986	1657	1373
	arc, inches:		+1.5	0	-7.0	-20.5
Rem. 140 PSP boat-tail	velocity, fps:	2860	2656	2460	2273	2094
	energy, ft-lb:	2542	2192	1881	1606	1363
	arc, inches:		+1.7	0	-7.5	-21.7
Rem. 140 Nosler Bal. Tip	velocity, fps:	3000	2804	2616	2436	2263
	energy, ft-lb:	2799	2445	2128	1848	1593
	arc, inches:		+1.5	0	-6.8	-19.0

Centerfire Rifle Ballistics

.280 REMINGTON TO 7MM REMINGTON MAGNUM

CARTRIDGE BULLET	RANGE, YARDS:	0	100	200	300	400
Rem. 140 AccuTip	velocity, fps:	3000	2804	2617	2437	2265
	energy, ft-lb:	2797	2444	2129	1846	1594
	arc, inches:		+1.5	0	-6.8	-19.0
Rem. 150 PSP Core-Lokt	velocity, fps:	2890	2624	2373	2135	1912
	energy, ft-lb:	2781	2293	1875	1518	1217
	arc, inches:		+1.8	0	-8.0	-23.6
Rem. 165 SP Core-Lokt	velocity, fps:	2820	2510	2220	1950	1701
	energy, ft-lb:	2913	2308	1805	1393	1060.
	arc, inches:		+2.0	0	-9.1	-27.4
Speer 145 Grand Slam	velocity, fps:	2900	2619	2354	2105	
	energy, ft-lb:	2707	2207	1784	1426	
	arc, inches:		+2.1	0	-8.4	-24.7
Speer 160 Grand Slam	velocity, fps:	2890	2652	2425	2210	
	energy, ft-lb:	2967	2497	2089	1735	
	arc, inches:		+1.7	0	-7.7	-22.4
Win. 140 Fail Safe	velocity, fps:	3050	2756	2480	2221	1977
	energy, ft-lb:	2893	2362	1913	1533	1216
	arc, inches:		+1.5	0	-7.2	-21.5
Win. 140 Ballistic Silvertip	velocity, fps:	3040	2842	2653	2471	2297
	energy, ft-lb:	2872	2511	2187	1898	1640
	arc, inches:		+1.4	0	-6.3	-18.4

.280 Ackley Improved

CARTRIDGE BULLET	RANGE, YARDS:	0	100	200	300	400
Nosler 140 AccuBond	velocity, fps:	3150	2947	2753	2567	2389
	energy, ft-lb:	3084	2700	2355	2048	1774
	arc, inches:	-1.5	+1.1	0	-5.0	-16.8
Nosler 150 ABLR	velocity, fps:	2930	2775	2626	2482	2342
	energy, ft-lb:	2858	2565	2297	2052	1827
	arc, inches:	-1.5	+1.5	0	-6.6	-18.7
Nosler 160 Partition	velocity, fps:	2950	2752	2562	2380	2206
	energy, ft-lb:	3091	2690	2332	2013	1729
	arc, inches:	-1.5	+1.5	0	-6.7	-19.4

7mm Remington Magnum

CARTRIDGE BULLET	RANGE, YARDS:	0	100	200	300	400
A-Square 175 Monolithic Solid	velocity, fps:	2860	2557	2273	2008	1771
	energy, ft-lb:	3178	2540	2008	1567	1219
	arc, inches:		+1.92	0	-8.7	-25.9
Black Hills 140 Nos. Bal. Tip	velocity, fps:	3150				
	energy, ft-lb:	3084				
	arc, inches:					
Black Hills 140 Barnes XLC	velocity, fps:	3150				
	energy, ft-lb:	3084				
	arc, inches:					
Black Hills 140 Nos. Partition	velocity, fps:	3150				
	energy, ft-lb:	3084				
	arc, inches:					
Federal 140 Nosler Bal. Tip And AccuBond	velocity, fps:	3110	2910	2720	2530	2360.
	energy, ft-lb:	3005	2630	2295	1995	1725
	arc, inches:		+1.3	0	-6.0	-17.4
Federal 140 Nosler Partition	velocity, fps:	3150	2930	2710	2510	2320
	energy, ft-lb:	3085	2660	2290	1960	1670
	arc, inches:		+1.3	0	-6.0	-17.5
Federal 140 Trophy Bonded	velocity, fps:	3150	2910	2680	2460	2250.
	energy, ft-lb:	3085	2630	2230	1880	1575
	arc, inches:		+1.3	0	-6.1	-18.1
Federal 140 Trophy Copper	velocity, fps:	3150	2950	2760	2570	2400
	energy, ft-lb:	3085	2705	2360	2055	1785
	arc, inches:		+1.3	0	-5.9	-16.9
Federal 150 Hi-Shok	velocity, fps:	3110	2830	2570	2320	2090
	energy, ft-lb:	3220	2670	2200	1790	1450
	arc, inches:		+1.4	0	-6.7	-19.9
Federal 150 Nosler Bal. Tip	velocity, fps:	3110	2910	2720	2540	2370
	energy, ft-lb:	3220	2825	2470	2150	1865
	arc, inches:		+1.3	0	-6.0	-17.4
Federal 150 Nos. Solid Base	velocity, fps:	3100	2890	2690	2500	2310
	energy, ft-lb:	3200	2780	2405	2075	1775
	arc, inches:		+1.3	0	-6.2	-17.8
Federal 150 Sierra GameKing BTSP	velocity, fps:	3110	2920	2750	2580	2410
	energy, ft-lb:	3220	2850	2510	2210	1930
	arc, inches:		+1.3 0	-5.9	-17.0	
Federal 150 Trophy Copper	velocity, fps:	3025	2830	2650	2470	2300
	energy, ft-lb:	3045	2675	2335	2035	1765
	arc, inches:		+1.4	0	-6.4	-18.4
Federal 160 Barnes XLC	velocity, fps:	2940	2760	2580	2410	2240
	energy, ft-lb:	3070	2695	2360	2060	1785
	arc, inches:		+1.5	0	-6.8	-19.6
Federal 160 Sierra Pro-Hunt.	velocity, fps:	2940	2730	2520	2320	2140
	energy, ft-lb:	3070	2640	2260	1920	1620
	arc, inches:		+1.6	0	-7.1	-20.6
Federal 160 Nosler Partition	velocity, fps:	2950	2770	2590	2420	2250.
	energy, ft-lb:	3090	2715	2375	2075	1800
	arc, inches:		+1.5	0	-6.7	-19.4
Federal 160 Nos. AccuBond	velocity, fps:	2950	2770	2600	2440	2280.
	energy, ft-lb:	3090	2730	2405	2110	1845
	arc, inches:		+1.5	0	-6.6	-19.1
Federal 160 Trophy Bonded	velocity, fps:	2940	2660	2390	2140	1900
	energy, ft-lb:	3070	2505	2025	1620	1280.
	arc, inches:		+1.7	0	-7.9	-23.3
Federal 165 Sierra GameKing BTSP	velocity, fps:	2950	2800	2650	2510	2370.
	energy, ft-lb:	3190	2865	2570	2300	2050
	arc, inches:		+1.5	0	-6.4	-18.4
Federal 175 Hi-Shok	velocity, fps:	2860	2650	2440	2240	2060
	energy, ft-lb:	3180	2720	2310	1960	1640
	arc, inches:		+1.7	0	-7.6	-22.1
Federal 175 Trophy Bonded	velocity, fps:	2860	2600	2350	2120	1900
	energy, ft-lb:	3180	2625	2150	1745	1400
	arc, inches:		+1.8	0	-8.2	-24.0
Hornady 139 SPBT	velocity, fps:	3150	2933	2727	2530	2341
	energy, ft-lb:	3063	2656	2296	1976	1692
	arc, inches:		+1.2	0	-6.1	-17.7
Hornady 139 SPBT HMmoly	velocity, fps:	3250	3041	2822	2613	2413
	energy, ft-lb:	3300	2854	2458	2106	1797
	arc, inches:		+1.1 0	-5.7	-16.6	
Hornady 139 SST (or Interbond)	velocity, fps:	3150	2948	2754	2569	2391
	energy, ft-lb:	3062	2681	2341	2037	1764
	arc, inches:		+1.1	0	-5.7	-16.7
Hornady 139 SST Custom Lite	velocity, fps:	2800	2613	2434	2262	2097
	energy, ft-lb:	2420	2108	1829	1579	1357
	arc, inches:		+1.8	0	-7.7	-22.2
Hornady 139 SST LM (or Interbond)	velocity, fps:	3250	3044	2847	2657	2475
	energy, ft-lb:	3259	2860	2501	2178	1890
	arc, inches:		+1.1	0	-5.5	-16.2
Hornady 139 SPBT HMmoly	velocity, fps:	3250	3041	2822	2613	2413
	energy, ft-lb:	3300	2854	2458	2106	1797.
	arc, inches:		+1.1	0	-5.7	-16.6
Hornady 154 Soft Point	velocity, fps:	3035	2814	2604	2404	2212
	energy, ft-lb:	3151	2708	2319	1977	1674
	arc, inches:		+1.3	0	-6.7	-19.3
Hornady 154 SST (or Interbond)	velocity, fps:	3035	2850	2672	2501	2337
	energy, ft-lb:	3149	2777	2441	2139	1867
	arc, inches:		+1.4	0	-6.5	-18.7
Hornady 162 SP boat-tail	velocity, fps:	2940	2757	2582	2413	2251
	energy, ft-lb:	3110	2735	2399	2095	1823
	arc, inches:		+1.6	0	-6.7	-19.7
Hornady 162 SST Superformance	velocity, fps:	3030	2856	2689	2527	2372
	energy, ft-lb:	3302	2933	2600	2298	2023
	arc, inches:		+1.4	0	-6.2	-17.8
Hornady 175 SP	velocity, fps:	2860	2650	2440	2240	2060.
	energy, ft-lb:	3180	2720	2310	1960	1640
	arc, inches:		+2.0	0	-7.9	-22.7
Norma 140 Nosler Bal. Tip	velocity, fps:	3150	2936	2732	2537	
	energy, ft-lb:	3085	2680	2320	2001	
	arc, inches:		+1.2	0	-5.9	
Norma 140 Barnes X TS	velocity, fps:	3117	2912	2716	2529	
	energy, ft-lb:	3021	2637	2294	1988	
	arch, inches:		+1.3	0	-6.0	
Norma 150 Scirocco	velocity, fps:	3117	2934	2758	2589	
	energy, ft-lb:	3237	2869	2535	2234	
	arc, inches:		+1.2	0	-5.8	
Norma 156 Oryx	velocity, fps:	2953	2670	2404	2153	
	energy, ft-lb:	3021	2470	2002	1607	
	arc, inches:		+1.7	0	-7.7	

7MM REMINGTON MAGNUM TO 7MM WINCHESTER SHORT MAGNUM

CARTRIDGE BULLET	RANGE, YARDS:	0	100	200	300	400
Norma 170 Vulkan	velocity, fps:	3018	2747	2493	2252	
	energy, ft-lb:	3439	2850	2346	1914	
	arc, inches:		+1.5	0	-2.8	
Norma 170 Oryx	velocity, fps:	2887	2601	2333	2080	
	energy, ft-lb:	3147	2555	2055	1634	
	arc, inches:		+1.8	0	-8.2	
Norma 170 Plastic Point	velocity, fps:	3018	2762	2519	2290	
	energy, ft-lb:	3439	2880	2394	1980	
	arc, inches:		+1.5	0	-7.0	
PMC 140 Barnes X	velocity, fps:	3000	2808	2624	2448	2279
	energy, ft-lb:	2797	2451	2141	1863	1614
	arc, inches:		+1.5	0	-6.6	18.9
PMC 140 Pointed Soft Point	velocity, fps:	3099	2878	2668	2469	2279
	energy, ft-lb:	2984	2574	2212	1895	1614
	arc, inches:		+1.4	0	-6.2	-18.1
PMC 140 SP boat-tail	velocity, fps:	3125	2891	2669	2457	2255
	energy, ft-lb:	3035	2597	2213	1877	1580
	arc, inches:		+1.4	0	-6.3	-18.4
PMC 160 Barnes X	velocity, fps:	2800	2639	2484	2334	2189
	energy, ft-lb:	2785	2474	2192	1935	1703
	arc, inches:		+1.8	0	-7.4	-21.2
PMC 160 Pointed Soft Point	velocity, fps:	2914	2748	2586	2428	2276
	energy, ft-lb:	3016	2682	2375	2095	1840
	arc, inches:		+1.6	0	-6.7	-19.4
PMC 160 SP boat-tail	velocity, fps:	2900	2696	2501	2314	2135
	energy, ft-lb:	2987	2582	2222	1903	1620
	arc, inches:		+1.7	0	-7.2	-21.0
PMC 175 Pointed Soft Point	velocity, fps:	2860	2645	2442	2244	2957
	energy, ft-lb:	3178	2718	2313	1956	1644
	arc, inches:		+2.0	0	-7.9	-22.7
Remington 140 Copper Solid Tipped	velocity, fps:	3175	2964	2762	2570	2385
	energy, ft-lb:	3133	2730	2372	2053	1768
	arc, inches:		+1.4	0	-6.0	-17.6
Rem. 140 PSP Core-Lokt mr	velocity, fps:	2710	2482	2265	2059	1865
	energy, ft-lb:	2283	1915	1595	1318	1081
	arc, inches:		+1.0	-2.5	-12.8	-31.3
Rem. 140 PSP Core-Lokt	velocity, fps:	3175	2923	2684	2458	2243
	energy, ft-lb:	3133	2655	2240	1878	1564
	arc, inches:		+2.2	+1.9	-3.2	-14.2
Rem. 140 PSP boat-tail	velocity, fps:	3175	2956	2747	2547	2356
	energy, ft-lb:	3133	2715	2345	2017	1726
	arc, inches:		+2.2	+1.6	-3.1	-13.4
Rem. 150 AccuTip	velocity, fps:	3110	2926	2749	2579	2415
	energy, ft-lb:	3221	2850	2516	2215	1943
	arc, inches:		+1.3	0	-5.9	-17.0
Rem. 150 PSP Core-Lokt	velocity, fps:	3110	2830	2568	2320	2085
	energy, ft-lb:	3221	2667	2196	1792	1448
	arc, inches:		+1.3	0	-6.6	-20.2
Rem. 150 Nosler Bal. Tip	velocity, fps:	3110	2912	2723	2542	2367
	energy, ft-lb:	3222	2825	2470	2152	1867
	arc, inches:		+1.2	0	-5.9	-17.3
Rem. 150 Swift Scirocco	velocity, fps:	3110	2927	2751	2582	2419
	energy, ft-lb:	3221	2852	2520	2220	1948
	arc, inches:		+1.3	0	-5.9	-17.0
Rem. 160 Swift A-Frame	velocity, fps:	2900	2659	2430	2212	2006
	energy, ft-lb:	2987	2511	2097	1739	1430
	arc, inches:		+1.7	0	-7.6	-22.4
Rem. 160 Nosler Partition	velocity, fps:	2950	2752	2563	2381	2207
	energy, ft-lb:	3091	2690	2333	2014	1730
	arc, inches:		+0.6	-1.9	-9.6	-23.6
Rem. 175 PSP Core-Lokt	velocity, fps:	2860	2645	2440	2244	2057
	energy, ft-lb:	3178	2718	2313	1956	1644
	arc, inches:		+1.7	0	-7.6	-22.1
Speer 145 Grand Slam	velocity, fps:	3140	2843	2565	2304	
	energy, ft-lb:	3174	2602	2118	1708	
	arc, inches:		+1.4	0	-6.7	
Speer 175 Grand Slam	velocity, fps:	2850	2653	2463	2282	
	energy, ft-lb:	3156	2734	2358	2023	
	arc, inches:		+1.7	0	-7.5	-21.7
Win. 140 Fail Safe	velocity, fps:	3150	2861	2589	2333	2092
	energy, ft-lb:	3085	2544	2085	1693	1361
	arc, inches:		+1.4	0	-6.6	-19.5
Win. 140 Ballistic Silvertip	velocity, fps:	3100	2889	2687	2494	2310
	energy, ft-lb:	2988	2595	2245	1934	1659.
	arc, inches:		+1.3	0	-6.2	-17.9
Win. 140 AccuBond CT	velocity, fps:	3180	2965	2760	2565	2377
	energy, ft-lb:	3143	2733	2368	2044	1756
	arc, inches:		+1.2	0	-5.8	-16.9
Win. 150 Power-Point	velocity, fps:	3090	2812	2551	2304	2071
	energy, ft-lb:	3181	2634	2167	1768	1429
	arc, inches:		+1.5	0	-6.8	-20.2
Win. 150 Power-Point Plus	velocity, fps:	3130	2849	2586	2337	2102
	energy, ft-lb:	3264	2705	2227	1819	1472
	arc, inches:		+1.4	0	-6.6	-19.6
Win. 150 Ballistic Silvertip	velocity, fps:	3100	2903	2714	2533	2359
	energy, ft-lb:	3200	2806	2453	2136	1853
	arc, inches:		+1.3	0	-6.0	-17.5
Win. 160 AccuBond	velocity, fps:	2950	2766	2590	2420	2257
	energy, ft-lb:	3091	2718	2382	2080	1809
	arc, inches:		+1.5	0	-6.7	-19.4
Win. 160 Partition Gold	velocity, fps:	2950	2743	2546	2357	2176
	energy, ft-lb:	3093	2674	2303	1974	1682
	arc, inches:		+1.6	0	-6.9	-20.1
Win. 160 Fail Safe	velocity, fps:	2920	2678	2449	2331	2025
	energy, ft-lb:	3030	2549	2131	1769	1457
	arc, inches:		+1.7	0	-7.5	-22.0
Win. 175 Power-Point	velocity, fps:	2860	2645	2440	2244	2057
	energy, ft-lb:	3178	2718	2313	1956	1644
	arc, inches:		+2.0	0	-7.9	-22.7

7MM REMINGTON SHORT ULTRA MAGNUM

CARTRIDGE BULLET	RANGE, YARDS:	0	100	200	300	400
Rem. 140 PSP C-L Ultra	velocity, fps:	3175	2934	2707	2490	2283
	energy, ft-lb:	3133	2676	2277	1927	1620.
	arc, inches:		+1.3	0	-6.0	-17.7
Rem. 150 PSP Core-Lokt	velocity, fps:	3110	2828	2563	2313	2077
	energy, ft-lb:	3221	2663	2188	1782	1437
	arc, inches:		+2.5	+2.1	-3.6	-15.8
Rem. 160 Partition	velocity, fps:	2960	2762	2572	2390	2215
	energy, ft-lb:	3112	2709	2350	2029	1744
	arc, inches:		+2.6	+2.2	-3.6	-15.4
Rem. 160 PSP C-L Ultra	velocity, fps:	2960	2733	2518	2313	2117
	energy, ft-lb:	3112	2654	2252	1900	1592
	arc, inches:		+2.7	+2.2	-3.7	-16.2

7MM WINCHESTER SHORT MAGNUM

CARTRIDGE BULLET	RANGE, YARDS:	0	100	200	300	400
Federal 140 Nos. AccuBond	velocity, fps:	3250	3040	2840	2660	2470
	energy, ft-lb:	3285	2875	2515	2190	1900
	arc, inches:		+1.1	0	-5.5	-15.8
Federal 140 Nos. Bal. Tip	velocity, fps:	3310	3100	2900	2700	2520
	energy, ft-lb:	3405	2985	2610	2270	1975
	arc, inches:		+1.1	0	-5.2	15.2
Federal 150 Nos. Solid Base	velocity, fps:	3230	3010	2800	2600	2410
	energy, ft-lb:	3475	3015	2615	2255	1935
	arc, inches:		+1.3	0	-5.6	-16.3
Federal 150 Trophy Copper	velocity, fps:	3140	2940	2750	2570	2400
	energy, ft-lb:	3285	2885	2525	2205	1915
	arc, inches:		+1.3	0	-5.9	-16.9
Federal 160 Nos. AccuBond	velocity, fps:	3120	2940	2760	2590	2430
	energy, ft-lb:	3460	3065	2710	2390	2095
	arc, inches:		+1.3	0	-5.9	-16.8
Federal 160 Nos. Partition	velocity, fps:	3160	2950	2750	2560	2380.
	energy, ft-lb:	3545	3095	2690	2335	2015.
	arc, inches:		+1.2	0	-5.9	-16.9

Centerfire Rifle Ballistics

7MM WINCHESTER SHORT MAGNUM TO 7MM REMINGTON ULTRA MAGNUM

BALLISTICS

CARTRIDGE BULLET	RANGE, YARDS:	0	100	200	300	400
Federal 160 Barnes TS	velocity, fps:	2990	2780	2590	2400	2220
	energy, ft-lb:	3175	2755	2380	2045	1750
	arc, inches:		+1.5	0	-6.6	-19.4
Federal 160 Trophy Bonded	velocity, fps:	3120	2880	2650	2440	2230
	energy, ft-lb:	3460	2945	2500	2105	1765
	arc, inches:		+1.4	0	-6.3	-18.5
Federal 160 Trophy Bonded Tip	velocity, fps:	3000	2820	2640	2470	2310
	energy, ft-lb:	3195	2820	2480	2170	1895
	arc, inches:		+1.5	0	-6.4	-18.5
Win. 140 Bal. Silvertip	velocity, fps:	3225	3008	2801	2603	2414
	energy, ft-lb:	3233	2812	2438	2106	1812
	arc, inches:		+1.2	0	-5.6	-16.4
Win. 140 AccuBond CT	velocity, fps:	3225	3008	2801	2604	2415
	energy, ft-lb:	3233	2812	2439	2107	1812
	arc, inches:		+1.2	0	-5.6	-16.4
Win. 150 Power Point	velocity, fps:	3200	2915	2648	2396	2157
	energy, ft-lb:	3410	2830	23351911		1550
	arc, inches:		+1.3	0	-6.3	-18.6
Win. 160 AccuBond	velocity, fps:	3050	2862	2682	2509	2342
	energy, ft-lb:	3306	2911	2556	2237	1950
	arc, inches:		1.4	0	-6.2	-17.9
Win. 160 Fail Safe	velocity, fps:	2990	2744	2512	2291	2081
	energy, ft-lb:	3176	2675	2241	1864	1538
	arc, inches:		+1.6	0	-7.1	-20.8

7MM WEATHERBY MAGNUM

CARTRIDGE BULLET	RANGE, YARDS:	0	100	200	300	400
Federal 160 Nosler Partition	velocity, fps:	3050	2850	2650	2470	2290
	energy, ft-lb:	3305	2880	2505	2165	1865
	arc, inches:		+1.4	0	-6.3	-18.4
Federal 160 Sierra GameKing BTSP	velocity, fps:	3050	2880	2710	2560	2400
	energy, ft-lb:	3305	2945	2615	2320	2050
	arc, inches:		+1.4	0	-6.1	-17.4
Federal 160 Trophy Bonded	velocity, fps:	3050	2730	2420	2140	1880.
	energy, ft-lb:	3305	2640	2085	1630	1255
	arc, inches:		+1.6	0	-7.6	-22.7
Federal 160 Trophy Bonded Tip	velocity, fps:	3100	2910	2730	2560	2390
	energy, ft-lb:	3415	3015	2655	2330	2035
	arc, inches:		+1.3	0	-6.0	-17.2
Hornady 139 GMX Superformance	velocity, fps:	3300	3091	2891	2701	2519
	energy, ft-lb:	3361	2948	2580	2252	1958
	arc, inches:		+1.1	0	-5.2	-15.2
Hornady 154 Soft Point	velocity, fps:	3200	2971	2753	2546	2348.
	energy, ft-lb:	3501	3017	2592	2216	1885
	arc, inches:		+1.2	0	-5.8	-17.0
Hornady 154 SST (or Interbond)	velocity, fps:	3200	3009	2825	2648	2478
	energy, ft-lb:	3501	3096	2729	2398	2100
	arc, inches:		+1.2	0	-5.7	-16.5
Hornady 175 Soft Point	velocity, fps:	2910	2709	2516	2331	2154
	energy, ft-lb:	3290	2850	2459	2111	1803
	arc, inches:		+1.6	0	-7.1	-20.6
Wby. 139 Pointed Expanding	velocity, fps:	3340	3079	2834	2601	2380.
	energy, ft-lb:	3443	2926	2478	2088	1748
	arc, inches:		+2.9	+3.6	0	-8.7
Wby. 140 Nosler Partition	velocity, fps:	3303	3069	2847	2636	2434
	energy, ft-lb:	3391	2927	2519	2159	1841
	arc, inches:		+2.9	+3.6	0	-8.5
Wby. 150 Nosler Bal. Tip	velocity, fps:	3300	3093	2896	2708	2527
	energy, ft-lb:	3627	3187	2793	2442	2127
	arc, inches:		+2.8	+3.5	0	-8.2
Wby. 150 Barnes X	veloctiy, fps:	3100	2901	2710	2527	2352
	energy, ft-lb:	3200	2802	2446	2127	1842
	arc, inches:		+3.3	+4.0	0	-9.4
Wby. 154 Pointed Expanding	velocity, fps:	3260	3028	2807	2597	2397
	energy, ft-lb:	3634	3134	2694	2307	1964
	arc, inches:		+3.0	+3.7	0	-8.8
Wby. 160 Nosler Partition	velocity, fps:	3200	2991	2791	2600	2417
	energy, ft-lb:	3638	3177	2767	2401	2075.
	arc, inches:		+3.1	+3.8	0	-8.9
Wby. 175 Pointed Expanding	velocity, fps:	3070	2861	2662	2471	2288
	energy, ft-lb:	3662	3181	2753	2373	2034
	arc, inches:		+3.5	+4.2	0	-9.9

7MM DAKOTA

CARTRIDGE BULLET	RANGE, YARDS:	0	100	200	300	400
Dakota 140 Barnes X	velocity, fps:	3500	3253	3019	2798	2587
	energy, ft-lb:	3807	3288	2833	2433	2081
	arc, inches:		+2.0	+2.1	-1.5	-9.6
Dakota 160 Barnes X	velocity, fps:	3200	3001	2811	2630	2455
	energy, ft-lb:	3637	3200	2808	2456	2140
	arc, inches:		+2.1	+1.9	-2.8	-12.5

7MM STW

CARTRIDGE BULLET	RANGE, YARDS:	0	100	200	300	400
A-Square 140 Nos. Bal. Tip	velocity, fps:	3450	3254	3067	2888	2715
	energy, ft-lb:	3700	3291	2924	2592	2292
	arc, inches:		+2.2	+3.0	0	-7.3
A-Square 160 Nosler Part.	velocity, fps:	3250	3071	2900	2735	2576.
	energy, ft-lb:	3752	3351	2987	2657	2357
	arc, inches:		+2.8	+3.5	0	-8.2
A-Square 160 SP boat-tail	velocity, fps:	3250	3087	2930	2778	2631
	energy, ft-lb:	3752	3385	3049	2741	2460
	arc, inches:		+2.8	+3.4	0	-8.0
Federal 140 Trophy Bonded	velocity, fps:	3330	3080	2850	2630	2420
	energy, ft-lb:	3435	2950	2520	2145	1815
	arc, inches:		+1.1	0	-5.4	-15.8
Federal 150 Trophy Bonded	velocity, fps:	3250	3010	2770	2560	2350.
	energy, ft-lb:	3520	3010	2565	2175	1830
	arc, inches:		+1.2	0	-5.7	-16.7
Federal 160 Sierra GameKing BTSP	velocity, fps:	3200	3020	2850	2670	2530.
	energy, ft-lb:	3640	3245	2890	2570	2275
	arc, inches:		+1.1	0	-5.5	-15.7
Federal 160 Trophy Bonded Tip	velocity, fps:	3100	2910	2730	2560	2390
	energy, ft-lb:	3415	3015	2655	2330	2035
	arc, inches:		+1.3	0	-6.0	-17.2
Nosler 175 ABLR	velocity, fps:	2900	2760	2625	2493	2366
	energy, ft-lb:	3267	2960	2677	2416	2175
	arc, inches:	-1.5	+1.5	0	-6.6	-18.8
Rem. 140 PSP Core-Lokt	velocity, fps:	3325	3064	2818	2585	2364
	energy, ft-lb:	3436	2918	2468	2077	1737
	arc, inches:		+2.0	+1.7	-2.9	-12.8
Rem. 140 Swift A-Frame	velocity, fps:	3325	3020	2735	2467	2215
	energy, ft-lb:	3436	2834	2324	1892	1525
	arc, inches:		+2.1	+1.8	-3.1	-13.8
Speer 145 Grand Slam	velocity, fps:	3300	2992	2075	2435	
	energy, ft-lb:	3506	2882	2355	1909	
	arc, inches:		+1.2	0	-6.0	-17.8
Win. 140 Ballistic Silvertip	velocity, fps:	3320	3100	2890	2690	2499
	energy, ft-lb:	3427	2982	2597	2250	1941
	arc, inches:		+1.1	0	-5.2	-15.2
Win. 150 Power-Point	velocity, fps:	3250	2957	2683	2424	2181
	energy, ft-lb:	3519	2913	2398	1958	1584
	arc, inches:		+1.2	0	-6.1	-18.1
Win. 160 Fail Safe	velocity, fps:	3150	2894	2652	2422	2204
	energy, ft-lb:	3526	2976	2499	2085	1727
	arc, inches:		+1.3	0	-6.3	-18.5

7MM REMINGTON ULTRA MAGNUM

CARTRIDGE BULLET	RANGE, YARDS:	0	100	200	300	400
Nosler 175 ABLR	velocity, fps:	3040	2896	2756	2621	2490
	energy, ft-lb:	3590	3258	2952	2669	2409
	arc, inches:	-1.5	+1.3	0	-5.9	-16.9
Rem. 140 PSP Core-Lokt	velocity, fps:	3425	3158	2907	2669	2444
	energy, ft-lb:	3646	3099	2626	2214	1856
	arc, inches:		+1.8	+1.6	-2.7	-11.9
Rem. 140 Nosler Partition	velocity, fps:	3425	3184	2956	2740	2534
	energy, ft-lb:	3646	3151	2715	2333	1995
	arc, inches:		+1.7	+1.6	-2.6	-11.4
Rem. 160 Nosler Partition	velocity, fps:	3200	2991	2791	2600	2417
	energy, ft-lb:	3637	3177	2767	2401	2075
	arc, inches:		+2.1	+1.8	-3.0	-12.9

Centerfire Rifle Ballistics

7.21 (.284) FIREHAWK TO .30-30 WINCHESTER

7.21 (.284) Firehawk

CARTRIDGE BULLET	RANGE, YARDS:	0	100	200	300	400
Lazzeroni 140 Nosler Part.	velocity, fps:	3580	3349	3130	2923	2724
	energy, ft-lb:	3985	3488	3048	2656	2308
	arc, inches:		+2.2	+2.9	0	-7.0
Lazzeroni 160 Swift A-Fr.	velocity, fps:	3385	3167	2961	2763	2574
	energy, ft-lb:	4072	3565	3115	2713	2354
	arc, inches:		+2.6	+3.3	0	-7.8

7.5x55 Swiss

CARTRIDGE BULLET	RANGE, YARDS:	0	100	200	300	400
Norma 180 Soft Point	velocity, fps:	2651	2432	2223	2025	
	energy, ft-lb:	2810	2364	1976	1639	
	arc, inches:		+2.2	0	-9.3	
Norma 180 Oryx	velocity, fps:	2493	2222	1968	1734	
	energy, ft-lb:	2485	1974	1549	1201	
	arc, inches:		+2.7	0	-11.8	

7.62x39 Russian

CARTRIDGE BULLET	RANGE, YARDS:	0	100	200	300	400
Federal 123 Hi-Shok	velocity, fps:	2300	2030	1780	1550	1350
	energy, ft-lb:	1445	1125	860	655	500.
	arc, inches:		0	-7.0	-25.1	
Federal 124 FMJ	velocity, fps:	2300	2030	1780	1560	1360
	energy, ft-lb:	1455	1135	875	670	510
	arc, inches:		+3.5	0	-14.6	-43.5
PMC 123 FMJ	velocity, fps:	2350	2072	1817	1583	1368
	energy, ft-lb:	1495	1162	894	678	507
	arc, inches:		0	-5.0	-26.4	-67.8
PMC 125 Pointed Soft Point	velocity, fps:	2320	2046	1794	1563	1350
	energy, ft-lb:	1493	1161	893	678	505.
	arc, inches:		0	-5.2	-27.5	-70.6
Rem. 125 Pointed Soft Point	velocity, fps:	2365	2062	1783	1533	1320
	energy, ft-lb:	1552	1180	882	652	483
	arc, inches:		0	-6.7	-24.5	
Win. 123 Soft Point	velocity, fps:	2365	2033	1731	1465	1248
	energy, ft-lb:	1527	1129	818	586	425
	arc, inches:		+3.8	0	-15.4	-46.3

.30 Carbine

CARTRIDGE BULLET	RANGE, YARDS:	0	100	200	300	400
Federal 110 Hi-Shok RN	velocity, fps:	1990	1570	1240	1040	920
	energy, ft-lb:	965	600	375	260	210
	arc, inches:		0	-12.8	-46.9	
Federal 110 FMJ	velocity, fps:	1990	1570	1240	1040	920
	energy, ft-lb:	965	600	375	260	210
	arc, inches:		0	-12.8	-46.9	
Hornady 110 FTX (20-inch barrel)	velocity, fps:	2000	1601	1279	1067	
	energy, ft-lb:	977	626	399	278	
	arc, inches:		0	-12.9	-47.2	
Magtech 110 FMC	velocity, fps:	1990	1654			
	energy, ft-lb:	965	668			
	arc, inches:		0			
PMC 110 FMJ	(and RNSP)velocity, fps:	1927	1548	1248		
	energy, ft-lb:	906	585	380		
	arc, inches:		0	-14.2		
Rem. 110 Soft Point	velocity, fps:	1990	1567	1236	1035	923
	energy, ft-lb:	967	600	373	262	208
	arc, inches:		0	-12.9	-48.6	
Win. 110 Hollow Soft Point	velocity, fps:	1990	1567	1236	1035	923
	energy, ft-lb:	967	600	373	262	208
	arc, inches:		0	-13.5	-49.9	

.30 T/C Hornaday

CARTRIDGE BULLET	RANGE, YARDS:	0	100	200	300	400
Hornady 150	velocity, fps	3000	2772	2555	2348	
	energy, ft-lb	2997	2558	2176	1836	
	arc, inches	-1.5	+1.5	0	-6.9	
Hornady 165	velocity, fps	2850	2644	2447	2258	
	energy, ft-lb	2975	2560	2193	1868	
	arc, inches	-1.5	+1.7	0	-7.6	

.30-30 Winchester

CARTRIDGE BULLET	RANGE, YARDS:	0	100	200	300	400
Federal 125 Hi-Shok HP	velocity, fps:	2570	2090	1660	1320	1080
	energy, ft-lb:	1830	1210	770	480	320
	arc, inches:		+3.3	0	-16.0	-50.9
Federal 150 Hi-Shok FN	velocity, fps:	2390	2020	1680	1400	1180
	energy, ft-lb:	1900	1355	945	650	460
	arc, inches:		+3.6	0	-15.9	-49.1
Federal 170 Hi-Shok RN	velocity, fps:	2200	1900	1620	1380	1190
	energy, ft-lb:	1830	1355	990	720	535
	arc, inches:		+4.1	0	-17.4	-52.4
Federal 170 Sierra Pro-Hunt.	velocity, fps:	2200	1820	1500	1240	1060
	energy, ft-lb:	1830	1255	845	575	425
	arc, inches:		+4.5	0	-20.0	-63.5
Federal 170 Nosler Partition	velocity, fps:	2200	1900	1620	1380	1190
	energy, ft-lb:	1830	1355	990	720	535
	arc, inches:		+4.1	0	-17.4	-52.4
Hornady 150 Round Nose	velocity, fps:	2390	1973	1605	1303	1095
	energy, ft-lb:	1902	1296	858	565	399
	arc, inches:		0	-8.2	-30.0	
Hornady 160 Evolution	velocity, fps:	2400	2150	1916	1699	
	energy, ft-lb:	2046	1643	1304	1025	
	arc, inches:		+3.0	0.2	-12.1	
Hornady 170 Flat Point	velocity, fps:	2200	1895	1619	1381	1191
	energy, ft-lb:	1827	1355	989	720	535
	arc, inches:		0	-8.9	-31.1	
Norma 150 Soft Point	velocity, fps:	2329	2008	1716	1459	
	energy, ft-lb:	1807	1344	981	709	
	arc, inches:		+3.6	0	-15.5	
PMC 150 Starfire HP	velocity, fps:	2100	1769	1478		
	energy, ft-lb:	1469	1042	728		
	arc, inches:		0	-10.8		
PMC 150 Flat Nose	velocity, fps:	2300	1943	1627		
	energy, ft-lb:	1762	1257	881		
	arc, inches:		0	-7.8		
PMC 170 Flat Nose	velocity, fps:	2150	1840	1566		
	energy, ft-lb:	1745	1277	926		
	arc, inches:		0	-8.9		
Rem. 55 PSP (sabot) "Accelerator"	velocity, fps:	3400	2693	2085	1570	1187
	energy, ft-lb:	1412	886	521	301	172
	arc, inches:		+1.7	0	-9.9	-34.3
Rem. 150 SP Core-Lokt	velocity, fps:	2390	1973	1605	1303	1095
	energy, ft-lb:	1902	1296	858	565	399
	arc, inches:		0	-7.6	-28.8	
Rem. 170 SP Core-Lokt	velocity, fps:	2200	1895	1619	1381	1191
	energy, ft-lb:	1827	1355	989	720	535
	arc, inches:		0	-8.3	-29.9	
Rem. 170 HP Core-Lokt	velocity, fps:	2200	1895	1619	1381	1191.
	energy, ft-lb:	1827	1355	989	720	535
	arc, inches:		0	-8.3	-29.9	
Speer 150 Flat Nose	velocity, fps:	2370	2067	1788	1538	
	energy, ft-lb:	1870	1423	1065	788	
	arc, inches:		+3.3	0	-14.4	-43.7
Win. 150 Hollow Point	velocity, fps:	2390	2018	1684	1398	1177
	energy, ft-lb:	1902	1356	944	651	461
	arc, inches:		0	-7.7	-27.9	
Win. 150 Power-Point	velocity, fps:	2390	2018	1684	1398	1177
	energy, ft-lb:	1902	1356	944	651	461
	arc, inches:		0	-7.7	-27.9	
Win. 150 Silvertip	velocity,fps:	2390	2018	1684	1398	1177
	energy, ft-lb:	1902	1356	944	651	461
	arc, inches:		0	-7.7	-27.9	

Centerfire Rifle Ballistics

.30-30 Winchester to .308 Winchester

BALLISTICS

CARTRIDGE BULLET	RANGE, YARDS:	0	100	200	300	400
Win. 150 Power-Point Plus	velocity, fps:	2480	2095	1747	1446	1209
	energy, ft-lb:	2049	1462	1017	697	487
	arc, inches:		0	-6.5	-24.5	
Win. 170 Power-Point	velocity, fps:	2200	1895	1619	1381	1191
	energy, ft-lb:	1827	1355	989	720	535.
	arc, inches:		0	-8.9	-31.1	
Win. 170 Silvertip	velocity, fps:	2200	1895	1619	1381	1191
	energy, ft-lb:	1827	1355	989	720	535
	arc, inches:		0	-8.9	-31.1	

.300 Savage

CARTRIDGE BULLET	RANGE, YARDS:	0	100	200	300	400
Federal 150 Hi-Shok	velocity, fps:	2630	2350	2100	1850	1630
	energy, ft-lb:	2305	1845	1460	1145	885
	arc, inches:		+2.4	0	-10.4	-30.9
Federal 180 Hi-Shok	velocity, fps:	2350	2140	1940	1750	1570
	energy, ft-lb:	2205	1825	1495	1215	985
	arc, inches:		+3.1	0	-12.4	-36.1
Hornady 150 SST	velocity, fps:	2740	2499	2272	2056	1852
	energy, ft-lb:	2500	2081	1718	1407	1143
	arc, inches:		+2.1	0	-8.8	-25.8
Rem. 150 PSP Core-Lokt	velocity, fps:	2630	2354	2095	1853	1631
	energy, ft-lb:	2303	1845	1462	1143	806.
	arc, inches:		+2.4	0	-10.4	-30.9
Rem. 180 SP Core-Lokt	velocity, fps:	2350	2025	1728	1467	1252
	energy, ft-lb:	2207	1639	1193	860	626
	arc, inches:		0	-7.1	-25.9	
Win. 150 Power-Point	velocity, fps:	2630	2311	2015	1743	1500
	energy, ft-lb:	2303	1779	1352	1012	749
	arc, inches:		+2.8	0	-11.5	-34.4

.307 Winchester

CARTRIDGE BULLET	RANGE, YARDS:	0	100	200	300	400
Win. 180 Power-Point	velocity, fps:	2510	2179	1874	1599	1362
	energy, ft-lb:	2519	1898	1404	1022	742
	arc, inches:		+1.5	-3.6	-18.6	-47.1

.30-40 Krag

CARTRIDGE BULLET	RANGE, YARDS:	0	100	200	300	400
Rem. 180 PSP Core-Lokt	velocity, fps:	2430	2213	2007	1813	1632.
	energy, ft-lb:	2360	1957	1610	1314	1064
	arc, inches, s:		0	-5.6	-18.6	
Win. 180 Power-Point	velocity, fps:	2430	2099	1795	1525	1298
	energy, ft-lb:	2360	1761	1288	929	673
	arc, inches, s:		0	-7.1	-25.0	

7.62x54R Russian

CARTRIDGE BULLET	RANGE, YARDS:	0	100	200	300	400
Norma 150 Soft Point	velocity, fps:	2953	2622	2314	2028	
	energy, ft-lb:	2905	2291	1784	1370	
	arc, inches:		+1.8	0	-8.3	
Norma 180 Alaska	velocity, fps:	2575	2362	2159	1967	
	energy, ft-lb:	2651	2231	1864	1546	
	arc, inches:		+2.9	0	-12.9	
Winchester 180 FMJ	velocity, fps:	2580	2401	2230	2066	1909
	energy, ft-lb:	2658	2304	1987	1706	1457
	arc, inches:	-1.5	+2.6	0	-9.6	-27.3
Winchester 180 SP	velocity, fps:	2625	2302	2003	1729	1485
	energy, ft-lb:	2751	2117	1603	1195	882
	arc, inches:	-1.5	+2.9	0	-11.6	-34.9

.308 Marlin Express

CARTRIDGE BULLET	RANGE, YARDS:	0	100	200	300	400
Hornady 160	velocity, fps	2660	2438	2226	2026	1836
	energy, ft-lb	2513	2111	1761	1457	1197
	arc, inches	-1.5	+3.0	+1.7	-6.7	-23.5
Hornady 140 MonoFlex	velocity, fps:	2800	2532	2279	2040	1818
	energy, ft-lb:	2437	1992	1614	1294	1027
	arc, inches:	-1.5	+2.0	0	-8.7	-25.8

.308 Winchester

CARTRIDGE BULLET	RANGE, YARDS:	0	100	200	300	400
Black Hills 150 Nosler B. Tip	velocity, fps:	2800				
	energy, ft-lb:	2611				
	arc, inches:					
Black Hills 165 Nosler B. Tip (and SP)	velocity, fps:	2650				
	energy, ft-lb:	2573				
	arc, inches:					
Black Hills 168 Barnes X (and Match)	velocity, fps:	2650				
	energy, ft-lb:	2620				
	arc, inches:					
Black Hills 175 Match	velocity, fps:	2600				
	energy, ft-lb:	2657				
	arc, inches:					
Black Hills 180 AccuBond	velocity, fps:	2600				
	energy, ft-lb:	2701				
	arc, inches:					
Federal 150 Barnes XLC	velocity, fps:	2820	2610	2400	2210	2030
	energy, ft-lb:	2650	2265	1925	1630	1370
	arc, inches:		+1.8 0	-7.8	-22.9	
Federal 150 FMJ Boat-Tail	velocity, fps:	2820	2620	2430	2250	2070
	energy, ft-lb:	2650	2285	1965	1680	1430
	arc, inches:		+1.8 0	-7.7	-22.4	
Federal 150 Hi-Shok	velocity, fps:	2820	2530	2260	2010	1770
	energy, ft-lb:	2650	2140	1705	1345	1050
	arc, inches:		+2.0	0	-8.8	-26.3
Federal 150 Nosler Bal. Tip.	velocity, fps:	2820	2610	2410	2220	2040
	energy, ft-lb:	2650	2270	1935	1640	1380
	arc, inches:		+1.8	0	-7.8	-22.7
Federal 150 Trophy Copper	velocity, fps:	2820	2630	2440	2260	2090
	energy, ft-lb:	2650	2295	1980	1700	1455
	arc, inches:		+1.8	0	-7.6	-22.2
Federal 155 Sierra MatchKg. BTHP	velocity, fps:	2950	2740	2540	2350	2170
	energy, ft-lb:	2995	2585	2225	1905	1620
	arc, inches:		+1.9	0	-8.9	-22.6
Federal 165 Sierra GameKing BTSP	velocity, fps:	2700	2520	2330	2160	1990
	energy, ft-lb:	2670	2310	1990	1700	1450
	arc, inches:		+2.0	0	-8.4	-24.3
Federal 165 Trophy Bonded	velocity, fps:	2700	2440	2200	1970	1760
	energy, ft-lb:	2670	2185	1775	1425	1135
	arc, inches:		+2.2	0	-9.4	-27.7
Federal 165 Tr. Bonded HE	velocity, fps:	2870	2600	2350	2120	1890
	energy, ft-lb:	3020	2485	2030	1640	1310
	arc, inches:		+1.8	0	-8.2	-24.0
Federal 168 Sierra MatchKg. BTHP	velocity, fps:	2600	2410	2230	2060	1890
	energy, ft-lb:	2520	2170	1855	1580	1340.
	arc, inches:		+2.1	0	+8.9	+25.9
Federal 180 Hi-Shok	velocity, fps:	2620	2390	2180	1970	1780
	energy, ft-lb:	2745	2290	1895	1555	1270
	arc, inches:		+2.3	0	-9.7	-28.3
Federal 180 Nosler Partition	velocity, fps:	2620	2430	2240	2060	1890
	energy, ft-lb:	2745	2355	2005	1700	1430.
	arc, inches:		+2.2	0	-9.2	-26.5
Federal 180 Nosler Part. HE	velocity, fps:	2740	2550	2370	2200	2030
	energy, ft-lb:	3000	2600	2245	1925	1645
	arc, inches:		+1.9	0	-8.2	-23.5
Federal 180 Sierra Pro-Hunt.	velocity, fps:	2620	2410	2200	2010	1820
	energy, ft-lb:	2745	2315	1940	1610	1330
	arc, inches:		+2.3	0	-9.3	-27.1
Federal 180 Trophy Bonded Tip	velocity, fps:	2620	2450	2280	2120	1960
	energy, ft-lb:	2745	2390	2070	1790	1535
	arc, inches:		+2.2	0	-8.9	-25.5
Hornady 110 TAP-FPD	velocity, fps:	3165	2830	2519	2228	1957
	energy, ft-lb:	2446	1956	1649	1212	935
	arc, inches:		+1.4	0	-6.9	-20.9
Hornady 110 Urban Tactical	velocity, fps:	3170	2825	2504	2206	1937
	energy, ft-lb:	2454	1950	1532	1189	916
	arc, inches:		+1.5	0	-7.2	-21.2

CARTRIDGE BULLET	RANGE, YARDS:	0	100	200	300	400
Hornady 125 SST Custom Lite	velocity, fps:	2675	2389	2121	1871	1642
	energy, ft-lb:	1986	1584	1248	971	748
	arc, inches:		+2.3	0	-10.1	-30.1
Hornady 150 SP boat-tail	velocity, fps:	2820	2560	2315	2084	1866
	energy, ft-lb:	2648	2183	1785	1447	1160
	arc, inches:		+2.0	0	-8.5	-25.2
Hornady 150 SP LM	velocity, fps:	2980	2703	2442	2195	1964
	energy, ft-lb:	2959	2433	1986	1606	1285
	arc, inches:	+1.6 0	-7.5	-22.2		
Hornady 150 SST	velocity, fps:	2820	2593	2378	2174	1984
(or Interbond)	energy, ft-lb:	2648	2240	1884	1574	1311
	arc, inches:		+1.9	0	-8.1	-22.9
Hornady 150 SST LM	velocity, fps:	3000	2765	2541	2328	2127
(or Interbond)	energy, ft-lb:	2997	2545	2150	1805	1506
	arc, inches:		+1.5	0	-7.1	-20.6
Hornady 155 A-Max	velocity, fps:	2815	2610	2415	2229	2051
	energy, ft-lb:	2727	2345	2007	1709	1448
	arc, inches:		+1.9	0	-7.9	-22.6
Hornady 155 TAP-FPD	velocity, fps:	2785	2577	2379	2189	2008
	energy, ft-lb:	2669	2285	1947	1649	1387
	arc, inches:		+1.9	0	-8.0	-23.3
Hornady 165 GMX	velocity, fps:	2750	2550	2358	2174	1999
Superformance	energy, ft-lb:	2771	2381	2037	1732	1464
	arc, inches:		+1.9	0	-8.2	-23.8
Hornady 165 SP boat-tail	velocity, fps:	2700	2496	2301	2115	1937
	energy, ft-lb:	2670	2283	1940	1639	1375
	arc, inches:		+2.0	0	-8.7	-25.2
Hornady 165 SPBT LM	velocity, fps:	2870	2658	2456	2283	2078
	energy, ft-lb:	3019	2589	2211	1877	1583
	arc, inches:		+1.7	0	-7.5	-21.8
Hornady 165 SST LM	velocity, fps:	2880	2672	2474	2284	2103
(or Interbond)	energy, ft-lb:	3038	2616	2242	1911	1620
	arc, inches:		+1.6	0	-7.3	-21.2
Hornady 168 BTHP Match	velocity, fps:	2700	2524	2354	2191	2035.
	energy, ft-lb:	2720	2377	2068	1791	1545
	arc, inches:		+2.0	0	-8.4	-23.9
Hornady 168 BTHP Match	velocity, fps:	2640	2630	2429	2238	2056
LM	energy, ft-lb:	3008	2579	2201	1868	1577
	arc, inches:		+1.8	0	-7.8	-22.4
Hornady 168 A-Max Match	velocity fps:	2620	2446	2280	2120	1972
	energy, ft-lb:	2560	2232	1939	1677	1450
	arc, inches:		+2.6	0	-9.2	-25.6
Hornady 168 A-Max	velocity, fps:	2700	2491	2292	2102	1921
	energy, ft-lb:	2719	2315	1959	1648	1377
	arc, inches:		+2.4	0	-9.0	-25.9
Hornady 168 TAP-FPD	velocity, fps:	2700	2513	2333	2161	1996
	energy, ft-lb:	2719	2355	2030	1742	1486
	arc, inches:		+2.0	0	-8.4	-24.3
Hornady 178 BTHP Match	velocity, fps:	2600	2436	2278	2125	1979
	energy, ft-lb:	2672	2345	2050	1785	1548
	arc, inches:		+2.2	0	-8.9	-25.5
Hornady 180 A-Max Match	velocity, fps:	2550	2397	2249	2106	1974
	energy, ft-lb:	2598	2295	2021	1773	1557
	arc, inches:		+2.7	0	-9.5	-26.2
Norma 150 Nosler Bal. Tip	velocity, fps:	2822	2588	2365	2154	
	energy, ft-lb:	2653	2231	1864	1545	
	arc, inches:		+1.6	0	-7.1	
Norma 150 Soft Point	velocity, fps:	2861	2537	2235	1954	
	energy, ft-lb:	2727	2144	1664	1272	
	arc, inches:		+2.0	0	-9.0	
Norma 165 TXP Swift A-Fr.	velocity, fps:	2700	2459	2231	2015	
	energy, ft-lb:	2672	2216	1824	1488	
	arc, inches:		+2.1	0	-9.1	

CARTRIDGE BULLET	RANGE, YARDS:	0	100	200	300	400
Norma 180 Plastic Point	velocity, fps:	2612	2365	2131	1911	
	energy, ft-lb:	2728	2235	1815	1460	
	arc, inches:		+2.4	0	-10.1	
Norma 180 Nosler Partition	velocity, fps:	2612	2414	2225	2044	
	energy, ft-lb:	2728	2330	1979	1670	
	arc, inches:		+2.2	0	-9.3	
Norma 180 Alaska	velocity, fps:	2612	2269	1953	1667	
	energy, ft-lb:	2728	2059	1526	1111	
	arc, inches:		+2.7	0	-11.9	
Norma 180 Vulkan	velocity, fps:	2612	2325	2056	1806	
	energy, ft-lb:	2728	2161	1690	1304	
	arc, inches:		+2.5	0	-10.8	
Norma 180 Oryx	velocity, fps:	2612	2305	2019	1755	
	energy, ft-lb:	2728	2124	1629	1232	
	arc, inches:		+2.5	0	-11.1	
Norma 200 Vulkan	velocity, fps:	2461	2215	1983	1767	
	energy, ft-lb:	2690	2179	1747	1387	
	arc, inches:		+2.8	0	-11.7	
PMC 147 FMJ boat-tail	velocity, fps:	2751	2473	2257	2052	1859
	energy, ft-lb:	2428	2037	1697	1403	1150
	arc, inches:		+2.3	0	-9.3	-27.3
PMC 150 Barnes X	velocity, fps:	2700	2504	2316	2135.	1964
	energy, ft-lb:	2428	2087	1786	1518	1284
	arc, inches:		+2.0	0	-8.6	-24.7
PMC 150 Pointed Soft Point	velocity, fps:	2750	2478	2224	1987	1766
	energy, ft-lb:	2519	2045	1647	1315	1039
	arc, inches:		+2.1	0	-9.2	-27.1
PMC 150 SP boat-tail	velocity, fps:	2820	2581	2354	2139	1935
	energy, ft-lb:	2648	2218	1846	1523	1247.
	arc, inches:		+1.9	0	-8.2	-24.0
PMC 168 Barnes X	velocity, fps:	2600	2425	2256	2095	1940
	energy, ft-lb:	2476	2154	1865	1608	1379
	arc, inches:		+2.2	0	-9.0	-26.0
PMC 168 HP boat-tail	velocity, fps:	2650	2460	2278	2103	1936
	energy, ft-lb:	2619	2257	1935	1649	1399
	arc, inches:		+2.1	0	-8.8	-25.6
PMC 168 Pointed Soft Point	velocity, fps:	2559	2354	2160	1976	1803
	energy, ft-lb:	2443	2067	1740	1457	1212
	arc, inches:		+2.4	0	-9.9	-28.7
PMC 168 Pointed Soft Point	velocity, fps:	2600	2404	2216	2037	1866
	energy, ft-lb:	2476	2064	1709	1403	1142
	arc, inches:		+2.3	0	-9.8	-28.7
PMC 180 Pointed Soft Point	velocity, fps:	2550	2335	2132	1940	1760
	energy, ft-lb:	2599	2179	1816	1504	1238.
	arc, inches:		+2.5	0	-10.1	-29.5
PMC 180 SP boat-tail	velocity, fps:	2620	2446	2278	2117	1962
	energy, ft-lb:	2743	2391	2074	1790	1538
	arc, inches:		+2.2	0	-8.9	-25.4
Rem. 125 PSP C-L MR	velocity, fps:	2660	2348	2057	1788	1546
	energy, ft-lb:	1964	1529	1174	887	663
	arc, inches:		+1.1	-2.7	-14.3	-35.8
Rem. 150 PSP Core-Lokt	velocity, fps:	2820	2533	2263	2009	1774
	energy, ft-lb:	2648	2137	1705	1344	1048
	arc, inches:		+2.0	0	-8.8	-26.2
Rem. 150 PSP C-L Ultra	velocity, fps:	2620	2404	2198	2002	1818
	energy, ft-lb:	2743	2309	1930	1601	1320
	arc, inches:		+2.3	0	-9.5	-26.4
Rem. 150 Swift Scirocco	velocity, fps:	2820	2611	2410	2219	2037
	energy, ft-lb:	2648	2269	1935	1640	1381
	arc, inches:		+1.8	0	-7.8	-22.7
Rem. 165 AccuTip	velocity, fps:	2700	2501	2311	2129	1958.
	energy, ft-lb:	2670	2292	1957	1861	1401.
	arc, inches:		+2.0	0	-8.6	-24.8
Rem. 165 PSP boat-tail	velocity, fps:	2700	2497	2303	2117	1941.
	energy, ft-lb:	2670	2284	1942	1642	1379
	arc, inches:		+2.0	0	-8.6	-25.0
Rem. 165 Nosler Bal. Tip	velocity, fps:	2700	2613	2333	2161	1996
	energy, ft-lb:	2672	2314	1995	1711	1460
	arc, inches:		+2.0	0	-8.4	-24.3

Centerfire Rifle Ballistics

.308 WINCHESTER TO .30-06 SPRINGFIELD

CARTRIDGE BULLET	RANGE, YARDS:	0	100	200	300	400
Rem. 165 Swift Scirocco	velocity, fps:	2700	2513	2233	2161	1996
	energy, fps:	2670	2313	1994	1711	1459
	arc, inches:		+2.0	0	-8.4	-24.3
Rem. 168 HPBT Match	velocity, fps:	2680	2493	2314	2143	1979
	energy, ft-lb:	2678	2318	1998	1713	1460
	arc, inches:		+2.1	0	-8.6	-24.7
Rem. 180 SP Core-Lokt	velocity, fps:	2620	2274	1955	1666	1414
	energy, ft-lb:	2743	2066	1527	1109	799
	arc, inches:		+2.6	0	-11.8	-36.3
Rem. 180 PSP Core-Lokt	velocity, fps:	2620	2393	2178	1974	1782
	energy, ft-lb:	2743	2288	1896	1557	1269
	arc, inches:		+2.3	0	-9.7	-28.3
Rem. 180 Nosler Partition	velocity, fps:	2620	2436	2259	2089	1927.
	energy, ft-lb:	2743	2371	2039	1774	1485
	arc, inches:		+2.2	0	-9.0	-26.0
Speer 150 Grand Slam	velocity, fps:	2900	2599	2317	2053	
	energy, ft-lb:	2800	2249	1788	1404	
	arc, inches:		+2.1	0	-8.6	-24.8
Speer 165 Grand Slam	velocity, fps:	2700	2475	2261	2057	
	energy, ft-lb:	2670	2243	1872	1550	
	arc, inches:		+2.1	0	-8.9	-25.9
Speer 180 Grand Slam	velocity, fps:	2620	2420	2229	2046	
	energy, ft-lb:	2743	2340	1985	1674	
	arc, inches:		+2.2	0	-9.2	-26.6
Win. 150 Power-Point	velocity, fps:	2820	2488	2179	1893	1633
	energy, ft-lb:	2648	2061	1581	1193	888
	arc, inches:		+2.4	0	-9.8	-29.3
Win. 150 Power-Point Plus	velocity, fps:	2900	2558	2241	1946	1678
	energy, ft-lb:	2802	2180	1672	1262	938
	arc, inches:		+1.9	0	-8.9	-27.0
Win. 150 Partition Gold	velocity, fps:	2900	2645	2405	2177	1962
	energy, ft-lb:	2802	2332	1927	1579	1282.
	arc, inches:		+1.7	0	-7.8	-22.9
Win. 150 Ballistic Silvertip	velocity, fps:	2810	2601	2401	2211	2028
	energy, ft-lb:	2629	2253	1920	1627	1370.
	arc, inches:		+1.8	0	-7.8	-22.8
Win. 150 Fail Safe	velocity, fps:	2820	2533	2263	2010	1775
	energy, ft-lb:	2649	2137	1706	1346	1049
	arc, inches:		+2.0	0	-8.8	-26.2
Win. 150 Supreme Elite XP3	velocity, fps:	2825	2616	2417	2226	2044
	energy, ft-lb:	2658	2279	1945	1650	1392
	arc, inches:		+1.8	0	-7.8	-22.6
Win. 168 Ballistic Silvertip	velocity, fps:	2670	2484	2306	2134	1971
	energy, ft-lb:	2659	2301	1983	1699	1449
	arc, inches:		+2.1	0	-8.6	-24.8
Win. 168 HP boat-tail Match	velocity, fps:	2680	2485	2297	2118	1948
	energy, ft-lb:	2680	2303	1970	1674	1415
	arc, inches:		+2.1	0	-8.7	-25.1
Win. 180 Power-Point	velocity, fps:	2620	2274	1955	1666	1414
	energy, ft-lb:	2743	2066	1527	1109	799
	arc, inches:		+2.9	0	-12.1	-36.9
Win. 180 Silvertip	velocity, fps:	2620	2393	2178	1974	1782
	energy, ft-lb:	2743	2288	1896	1557	1269
	arc, inches:		+2.6	0	-9.9	-28.9

.30-06 Springfield

CARTRIDGE BULLET	RANGE, YARDS:	0	100	200	300	400
A-Square 180 M & D-T	velocity, fps:	2700	2365	2054	1769	1524
	energy, ft-lb:	2913	2235	1687	1251	928
	arc, inches:		+2.4	0	-10.6	-32.4
A-Square 220 Monolythic Solid	velocity, fps:	2380	2108	1854	1623	1424
	energy, ft-lb:	2767	2171	1679	1287	990
	arc, inches:		+3.1	0	-13.6	-39.9
Black Hills 150 Nosler B. Tip	velocity, fps:	2900				
	energy, ft-lb:	2770				
	arc, inches:					
Black Hills 165 Nosler B. Tip	velocity, fps:	2750				
	energy, ft-lb:	2770				
	arc, inches:					
Black Hills 168 Hor. Match	velocity, fps:	2700				
	energy, ft-lb:	2718				
	arc, inches:					
Black Hills 180 Barnes X	velocity, fps:	2650				
	energy, ft-lb:	2806				
	arc, inches:					
Black Hills 180 AccuBond	velocity, ft-lb:	2700				
	energy, ft-lb:					
	arc, inches:					
Federal 125 Sierra Pro-Hunt.	velocity, fps:	3140	2780	2450	2140	1850
	energy, ft-lb:	2735	2145	1660	1270	955
	arc, inches:		+1.5	0	-7.3	-22.3
Federal 150 Hi-Shok	velocity, fps:	2910	2620	2340	2080	1840
	energy, ft-lb:	2820	2280	1825	1445	1130
	arc, inches:		+1.8	0	-8.2	-24.4
Federal 150 Sierra Pro-Hunt.	velocity, fps:	2910	2640	2380	2130	1900
	energy, ft-lb:	2820	2315	1880	1515	1205
	arc, inches:		+1.7	0	-7.9	-23.3
Federal 150 Sierra GameKing BTSP	velocity, fps:	2910	2690	2480	2270	2070
	energy, ft-lb:	2820	2420	2040	1710	1430
	arc, inches:		+1.7	0	-7.4	-21.5
Federal 150 Nosler Bal. Tip	velocity, fps:	2910	2700	2490	2300	2110
	energy, ft-lb:	2820	2420	2070	1760	1485
	arc, inches:		+1.6	0	-7.3	-21.1
Federal 150 FMJ boat-tail	velocity, fps:	2910	2710	2510	2320	2150
	energy, ft-lb:	2820	2440	2100	1800	1535
	arc, inches:		+1.6	0	-7.1	-20.8
Federal 165 Sierra Pro-Hunt.	velocity, fps:	2800	2560	2340	2130	1920
	energy, ft-lb:	2875	2410	2005	1655	1360
	arc, inches:		+1.9	0	-8.3	-24.3
Federal 165 Sierra GameKing BTSP	velocity, fps:	2800	2610	2420	2240	2070.
	energy, ft-lb:	2870	2490	2150	1840	1580
	arc, inches:		+1.8	0	-7.8	-22.4
Federal 165 Sierra GameKing HE	velocity, fps:	3140	2900	2670	2450	2240.
	energy, ft-lb:	3610	3075	2610	2200	1845
	arc, inches:		+1.5	0	-6.9	-20.4
Federal 165 Nosler Bal. Tip	velocity, fps:	2800	2610	2430	2250	2080
	energy, ft-lb:	2870	2495	2155	1855	1585
	arc, inches:		+1.8	0	-7.7	-22.3
Federal 165 Trophy Bonded	velocity, fps:	2800	2540	2290	2050	1830.
	energy, ft-lb:	2870	2360	1915	1545	1230
	arc, inches:		+2.0	0	-8.7	-25.4
Federal 165 Tr. Bonded HE	velocity, fps:	3140	2860	2590	2340	2100
	energy, ft-lb:	3610	2990	2460	2010	1625.
	arc, inches:		+1.6	0	-7.4	-21.9
Federal 165 Trophy Copper	velocity, fps:	2800	2620	2450	2280	2120
	energy, ft-lb:	2870	2515	2190	1900	1645
	arc, inches:		+1.8	0	-7.6	-22.0
Federal 168 Sierra MatchKg. BTHP	velocity, fps:	2700	2510	2320	2150	1980
	energy, ft-lb:	2720	2350	2010	1720	1460
	arc, inches:		+16.2	+28.4	+34.1	+32.3
Federal 180 Barnes XLC	velocity, fps:	2700	2530	2360	2200	2040
	energy, ft-lb:	2915	2550	2220	1930	1670
	arc, inches:	+2.0	0	-8.3	-23.8	
Federal 180 Hi-Shok	velocity, fps:	2700	2470	2250	2040	1850
	energy, ft-lb:	2915	2435	2025	1665	1360
	arc, inches:		+2.1	0	-9.0	-26.4
Federal 180 Sierra Pro-Hunt. RN	velocity, fps:	2700	2350	2020	1730	1470
	energy, ft-lb:	2915	2200	1630	1190	860
	arc, inches:		+2.4	0	-11.0	-33.6
Federal 180 Nosler Partition	velocity, fps:	2700	2500	2320	2140	1970
	energy, ft-lb:	2915	2510	2150	1830	1550
	arc, inches:		+2.0	0	-8.6	-24.6

Centerfire Rifle Ballistics

.30-06 SPRINGFIELD TO .30-06 SPRINGFIELD

BALLISTICS

CARTRIDGE BULLET	RANGE, YARDS:	0	100	200	300	400
Federal 180 Nosler Part. HE	velocity, fps:	2880	2690	2500	2320	2150
	energy, ft-lb:	3315	2880	2495	2150	1845
	arc, inches:		+1.7	0	-7.2	-21.0
Federal 180 Sierra GameKing BTSP	velocity, fps:	2700	2540	2380	2220	2080
	energy, ft-lb:	2915	2570	2260	1975	1720
	arc, inches:		+1.9	0	-8.1	-23.1
Federal 180 Barnes XLC	velocity, fps:	2700	2530	2360	2200	2040.
	energy, ft-lb:	2915	2550	2220	1930	1670
	arc, inches:		+2.0	0	-8.3	-23.8
Federal 180 Sierra Pro-Hunt. RN	velocity, fps:	2700	2350	2020	1730	1470
	energy, ft-lb:	2915	2200	1630	1190	860
	arc, inches:		+2.4	0	-11.0	-33.6
Federal 180 Trophy Bonded	velocity, fps:	2700	2460	2220	2000	1800
	energy, ft-lb:	2915	2410	1975	1605	1290
	arc, inches:		+2.2	0	-9.2	-27.0
Federal 180 Tr. Bonded HE	velocity, fps:	2880	2630	2380	2160	1940
	energy, ft-lb:	3315	2755	2270	1855	1505
	arc, inches:		+1.8	0	-8.0	-23.3
Federal 180 Trophy Bonded Tip	velocity, fps:	2700	2520	2350	2190	2030
	energy, ft-lb:	2915	2540	2219	1910	1645
	arc, inches:		+2.0	0	-8.4	-23.9
Federal 200 Trophy Bonded	velocity, fps:	2540	2320	2120	1920	1740
	energy, ft-lb:	2865	2395	1990	1640	1345
	arc, inches:		+2.5	0	-10.1	-29.9
Federal 220 Sierra Pro-Hunt. RN	velocity, fps:	2410	2130	1870	1630	1420
	energy, ft-lb:	2835	2215	1705	1300	985
	arc, inches:		+3.1	0	-13.1	-39.3
Hornady 125 SST Custom Lite	velocity, fps:	2700	2412	2143	1891	1660
	energy, ft-lb:	2023	1615	1274	993	765
	arc, inches:		+2.3	0	-9.9	-29.5
Hornady 150 GMX Superformance	velocity, fps:	3080	2848	2628	2418	2218
	energy, ft-lb:	3159	2701	2300	1948	1639
	arc, inches:		+1.4	0	-6.4	-18.8
Hornady 150 SP	velocity, fps:	2910	2617	2342	2083	1843
	energy, ft-lb:	2820	2281	1827	1445	1131
	arc, inches:		+2.1	0	-8.5	-25.0
Hornady 150 SP LM	velocity, fps:	3100	2815	2548	2295	2058
	energy, ft-lb:	3200	2639	2161	1755	1410
	arc, inches:		+1.4	0	-6.8	-20.3
Hornady 150 SP boat-tail	velocity, fps:	2910	2683	2467	2262	2066.
	energy, ft-lb:	2820	2397	2027	1706	1421
	arc, inches:		+2.0	0	-7.7	-22.2
Hornady 150 SST (or Interbond)	velocity, fps:	2910	2802	2599	2405	2219
	energy, ft-lb:	3330	2876	2474	2118	1803
	arc, inches:		+1.5	0	-6.6	-19.3
Hornady 150 SST LM	velocity, fps:	3100	2860	2631	2414	2208
	energy, ft-lb:	3200	2724	2306	1941	1624
	arc, inches:		+1.4	0	-6.6	-19.2
Hornady 165 GMX Superformance	velocity, fps:	2940	2731	2532	2341	2158
	energy, ft-lb:	3167	2732	3248	2007	1706
	arc, inches:		+1.5	0	-7.0	-20.4
Hornady 165 SP boat-tail	velocity, fps:	2800	2591	2392	2202	2020
	energy, ft-lb:	2873	2460	2097	1777	1495
	arc, inches:		+1.8	0	-8.0	-23.3
Hornady 165 SPBT LM	velocity, fps:	3015	2790	2575	2370	2176
	energy, ft-lb:	3330	2850	2428	2058	1734
	arc, inches:		+1.6	0	-7.0	-20.1
Hornady 165 SST (or Interbond)	velocity, fps:	2800	2598	2405	2221	2046
	energy, ft-lb:	2872	2473	2119	1808	1534
	arc, inches:		+1.9	0	-8.0	-22.8
Hornady 165 SST LM	velocity, fps:	3015	2802	2599	2405	2219
	energy, ft-lb:	3330	2878	2474	2118	1803.
	arc, inches:		+1.5	0	-6.5	-19.3
Hornady 168 A-Max Garand Match	velocity, fps:	2710	2523	2343	2171	2006
	energy, ft-lb:	2739	2374	2048	1758	1501
	arc, inches:		+2.3	0	-8.6	-24.6
Hornady 168 HPBT Match	velocity, fps:	2790	2620	2447	2280	2120.
	energy, ft-lb:	2925	2561	2234	1940	1677.
	arc, inches:		+1.7	0	-7.7	-22.2
Hornady 180 SP	velocity, fps:	2700	2469	2258	2042	1846
	energy, ft-lb:	2913	2436	2023	1666	1362
	arc, inches:		+2.4	0	-9.3	-27.0
Hornady 180 SPBT LM	velocity, fps:	2880	2676	2480	2293	2114
	energy, ft-lb:	3316	2862	2459	2102	1786
	arc, inches:		+1.7	0	-7.3	-21.3
Norma 150 Nosler Bal. Tip	velocity, fps:	2936	2713	2502	2300	
	energy, ft-lb:	2872	2453	2085	1762	
	arc, inches:		+1.6	0	-7.1	
Norma 150 Soft Point	velocity, fps:	2972	2640	2331	2043	
	energy, ft-lb:	2943	2321	1810	1390	
	arc, inches:		+1.8	0	-8.2	
Norma 180 Alaska	velocity, fps:	2700	2351	2028	1734	
	energy, ft-lb:	2914	2209	1645	1202	
	arc, inches:		+2.4	0	-11.0	
Norma 180 Nosler Partition	velocity, fps:	2700	2494	2297	2108	
	energy, ft-lb:	2914	2486	2108	1777	
	arc, inches:		+2.1	0	-8.7	
Norma 180 Plastic Point	velocity, fps:	2700	2455	2222	2003	
	energy, ft-lb:	2914	2409	1974	1603	
	arc, inches:		+2.1	0	-9.2	
Norma 180 Vulkan	velocity, fps:	2700	2416	2150	1901	
	energy, ft-lb:	2914	2334	1848	1445	
	arc, inches:		+2.2	0	-9.8	
Norma 180 Oryx	velocity, fps:	2700	2387	2095	1825	
	energy, ft-lb:	2914	2278	1755	1332	
	arc, inches:		+2.3	0	-10.2	
Norma 180 TXP Swift A-Fr.	velocity, fps:	2700	2479	2268	2067	
	energy, ft-lb:	2914	2456	2056	1708	
	arc, inches:		+2.0	0	-8.8	
Norma 180 AccuBond	velocity, fps:	2674	2499	2331	2169	
	energy, ft-lb:	2859	2497	2172	1881	
	arc, inches:		+2.0	0	-8.5	
Norma 200 Vulkan	velocity, fps:	2641	2385	2143	1916	
	energy, ft-lb:	3098	2527	2040	1631	
	arc, inches:		+2.3	0	-9.9	
Norma 200 Oryx	velocity, fps:	2625	2362	2115	1883	
	energy, ft-lb:	3061	2479	1987	1575	
	arc, inches:		+2.3	0	-10.1	
PMC 150 X-Bullet	velocity, fps:	2750	2552	2361	2179	2005
	energy, ft-lb:	2518	2168	1857	1582	1339
	arc, inches:		+2.0	0	-8.2	-23.7
PMC 150 Pointed Soft Point	velocity, fps:	2773	2542	2322	2113	1916
	energy, ft-lb:	2560	2152	1796	1487	1222.
	arc, inches:		+1.9	0	-8.4	-24.6
PMC 150 SP boat-tail	velocity, fps:	2900	2657	2427	2208	2000
	energy, ft-lb:	2801	2351	1961	1623	1332
	arc, inches:		+1.7	0	-7.7	-22.5
PMC 150 FMJ	velocity, fps:	2773	2542	2322	2113	1916
	energy, ft-lb:	2560	2152	1796	1487	1222
	arc, inches:		+1.9	0	-8.4	-24.6
PMC 168 Barnes X	velocity, fps:	2750	2569	2395	2228	2067
	energy, ft-lb:	2770	2418	2101	1818	1565
	arc, inches:		+1.9	0	-8.0	-23.0
PMC 180 Barnes X	velocity, fps:	2650	2487	2331	2179	2034
	energy, ft-lb:	2806	2472	2171	1898	1652
	arc, inches:		+2.1	0	-8.5	-24.3
PMC 180 Pointed Soft Point	velocity, fps:	2650	2430	2221	2024	1839
	energy, ft-lb:	2807	2359	1972	1638	1351
	arc, inches:		+2.2	0	-9.3	-27.0
PMC 180 SP boat-tail	velocity, fps:	2700	2523	2352	2188	2030
	energy, ft-lb:	2913	2543	2210	1913	1646
	arc, inches:		+2.0	0	-8.3	-23.9
PMC 180 HPBT Match	velocity, fps:	2800	2622	2456	2302	2158
	energy, ft-lb:	3133	2747	2411	2118	1861
	arc, inches:		+1.8	0	-7.6	-21.7
Rem. 55 PSP (sabot) "Accelerator"	velocity, fps:	4080	3484	2964	2499	2080
	energy, ft-lb:	2033	1482	1073	763	528.
	arc, inches:		+1.4	+1.4	-2.6	-12.2
Rem. 125 PSP C-L MR	velocity, fps:	2660	2335	2034	1757	1509
	energy, ft-lb:	1964	1513	1148	856	632
	arc, inches:		+1.1	-3.0	-15.5	-37.4
Rem. 125 Pointed Soft Point	velocity, fps:	3140	2780	2447	2138	1853
	energy, ft-lb:	2736	2145	1662	1269	953.
	arc, inches:		+1.5	0	-7.4	-22.4
Rem. 150 AccuTip	velocity, fps:	2910	2686	2473	2270	2077
	energy, ft-lb:	2820	2403	2037	1716	1436
	arc, inches:		+1.8	0	-7.4	-21.5

Centerfire Rifle Ballistics

.30-06 SPRINGFIELD TO .300 BLACKOUT

BALLISTICS

CARTRIDGE BULLET	RANGE, YARDS:	0	100	200	300	400
Rem. 150 PSP Core-Lokt	velocity, fps:	2910	2617	2342	2083	1843
	energy, ft-lb:	2820	2281	1827	1445	1131
	arc, inches:		+1.8	0	-8.2	-24.4
Rem. 150 Bronze Point	velocity, fps:	2910	2656	2416	2189	1974
	energy, ft-lb:	2820	2349	1944	1596	1298
	arc, inches:		+1.7	0	-7.7	-22.7
Rem. 150 Nosler Bal. Tip	velocity, fps:	2910	2696	2492	2298	2112.
	energy, ft-lb:	2821	2422	2070	1769	1485
	arc, inches:		+1.6	0	-7.3	-21.1
Rem. 150 Swift Scirocco	velocity, fps:	2910	2696	2492	2298	2111
	energy, ft-lb:	2820	2421	2069	1758	1485
	arc, inches:		+1.6	0	-7.3	-21.1
Rem. 165 AccuTip	velocity, fps:	2800	2597	2403	2217	2039
	energy, ft-lb:	2872	2470	2115	1800	1523
	arc, inches:		+1.8	0	-7.9	-22.8
Rem. 165 PSP Core-Lokt	velocity, fps:	2800	2534	2283	2047	1825.
	energy, ft-lb:	2872	2352	1909	1534	1220
	arc, inches:		+2.0	0	-8.7	-25.9
Rem. 165 PSP boat-tail	velocity, fps:	2800	2592	2394	2204	2023
	energy, ft-lb:	2872	2462	2100	1780	1500
	arc, inches:		+1.8	0	-7.9	-23.0
Rem. 165 Nosler Bal. Tip	velocity, fps:	2800	2609	2426	2249	2080.
	energy, ft-lb:	2873	2494	2155	1854	1588
	arc, inches:		+1.8	0	-7.7	-22.3
Rem. 168 PSP C-L Ultra	velocity, fps:	2800	2546	2306	2079	1866
	energy, ft-lb:	2924	2418	1984	1613	1299
	arc, inches:		+1.9	0	-8.5	-25.1
Rem. 180 SP Core-Lokt	velocity, fps:	2700	2348	2023	1727	1466
	energy, ft-lb:	2913	2203	1635	1192	859
	arc, inches:		+2.4	0	-11.0	-33.8
Rem. 180 PSP Core-Lokt	velocity, fps:	2700	2469	2250	2042	1846
	energy, ft-lb:	2913	2436	2023	1666	1362
	arc, inches:		+2.1	0	-9.0	-26.3
Rem. 180 PSP C-L Ultra	velocity, fps:	2700	2480	2270	2070	1882
	energy, ft-lb:	2913	2457	2059	1713	1415
	arc, inches:		+2.1	0	-8.9	-25.8
Rem. 180 Bronze Point	velocity, fps:	2700	2485	2280	2084	1899.
	energy, ft-lb:	2913	2468	2077	1736	1441
	arc, inches:		+2.1	0	-8.8	-25.5
Rem. 180 Swift A-Frame	velocity, fps:	2700	2465	2243	2032	1833
	energy, ft-lb:	2913	2429	2010	1650	1343
	arc, inches:		+2.1	0	-9.1	-26.6
Rem. 180 Nosler Partition	velocity, fps:	2700	2512	2332	2160	1995
	energy, ft-lb:	2913	2522	2174	1864	1590
	arc, inches:		+2.0	0	-8.4	-24.3
Rem. 220 SP Core-Lokt	velocity, fps:	2410	2130	1870	1632	1422
	energy, ft-lb:	2837	2216	1708	1301	988
	arc, inches, s:		0	-6.2	-22.4	
Speer 150 Grand Slam	velocity, fps:	2975	2669	2383	2114	
	energy, ft-lb:	2947	2372	1891	1489	
	arc, inches:		+2.0	0	-8.1	-24.1
Speer 165 Grand Slam	velocity, fps:	2790	2560	2342	2134	
	energy, ft-lb:	2851	2401	2009	1669	
	arc, inches:		+1.9	0	-8.3	-24.1
Speer 180 Grand Slam	velocity, fps:	2690	2487	2293	2108	
	energy, ft-lb:	2892	2472	2101	1775	
	arc, inches:		+2.1	0	-8.8	-25.1
Win. 125 Pointed Soft Point	velocity, fps:	3140	2780	2447	2138	1853
	energy, ft-lb:	2736	2145	1662	1269	953
	arc, inches:		+1.8	0	-7.7	-23.0
Win. 150 Power-Point	velocity, fps:	2920	2580	2265	1972	1704
	energy, ft-lb:	2839	2217	1708	1295	967
	arc, inches:		+2.2	0	-9.0	-27.0
Win. 150 Power-Point Plus	velocity, fps:	3050	2685	2352	2043	1760
	energy, ft-lb:	3089	2402	1843	1391	1032
	arc, inches:		+1.7	0	-8.0	-24.3
Win. 150 Silvertip	velocity, fps:	2910	2617	2342	2083	1843
	energy, ft-lb:	2820	2281	1827	1445	1131
	arc, inches:		+2.1	0	-8.5	-25.0

CARTRIDGE BULLET	RANGE, YARDS:	0	100	200	300	400
Win. 150 Partition Gold	velocity, fps:	2960	2705	2464	2235	2019
	energy, ft-lb:	2919	2437	2022	1664	1358.
	arc, inches:		+1.6	0	-7.4	-21.7
Win. 150 Ballistic Silvertip	velocity, fps:	2900	2687	2483	2289	2103
	energy, ft-lb:	2801	2404	2054	1745	1473
	arc, inches:		+1.7	0	-7.3	-21.2
Win. 150 Fail Safe	velocity, fps:	2920	2625	2349	2089	1848
	energy, ft-lb:	2841	2296	1838	1455	1137
	arc, inches:		+1.8	0	-8.1	-24.3
Win. 165 Pointed Soft Point	velocity, fps:	2800	2573	2357	2151	1956
	energy, ft-lb:	2873	2426	2036	1696	1402
	arc, inches:		+2.2	0	-8.4	-24.4
Win. 165 Fail Safe	velocity, fps:	2800	2540	2295	2063	1846
	energy, ft-lb:	2873	2365	1930	1560	1249
	arc, inches:		+2.0	0	-8.6	-25.3
Win. 168 Ballistic Silvertip	velocity, fps:	2790	2599	2416	2240	2072
	energy, ft-lb:	2903	2520	2177	1872	1601
	arc, inches:		+1.8	0	-7.8	-22.5
Win. 180 Ballistic Silvertip	velocity, fps:	2750	2572	2402	2237	2080
	energy, ft-lb:	3022	2644	2305	2001	1728
	arc, inches:		+1.9	0	-7.9	-22.8
Win. 180 Power-Point	velocity, fps:	2700	2348	2023	1727	1466
	energy, ft-lb:	2913	2203	1635	1192	859
	arc, inches:		+2.7	0	-11.3	-34.4
Win. 180 Power-Point Plus	velocity, fps:	2770	2563	2366	2177	1997
	energy, ft-lb:	3068	2627	2237	1894	1594
	arc, inches:		+1.9	0	-8.1	-23.6
Win. 180 Silvertip	velocity, fps:	2700	2469	2250	2042	1846
	energy, ft-lb:	2913	2436	2023	1666	1362
	arc, inches:		+2.4	0	-9.3	-27.0
Win. 180 AccuBond	velocity, fps:	2750	2573	2403	2239	2082
	energy, ft-lb:	3022	2646	2308	2004	1732
	arc, inches:		+1.9	0	-7.9	-22.8
Win. 180 Partition Gold	velocity, fps:	2790	2581	2382	2192	2010
	energy, ft-lb:	3112	2664	2269	1920	1615
	arc, inches:		+1.9	0	-8.0	-23.2
Win. 180 Fail Safe	velocity, fps:	2700	2486	2283	2089	1904
	energy, ft-lb:	2914	2472	2083	1744	1450
	arc, inches:		+2.1	0	-8.7	-25.5
Win. 150 Supreme Elite XP3	velocity, fps:	2925	2712	2508	2313	2127
	energy, ft-lb:	2849	2448	2095	1782	1507
	arc, inches:		+1.6	0	-7.2	-20.8
Win. 180 Supreme Elite XP3	velocity, fps:	2750	2579	2414	2256	2103
	energy, ft-lb:	3022	2658	2330	2034	1768
	arc, inches:		+1.9	0	-7.8	-22.5

.300 BLK (.300 WHISPER)

CARTRIDGE BULLET	RANGE, YARDS:	0	100	200	300	400
Barnes 110 Tac/TX	velocity, fps:	2350	1810	1369		
	energy, ft-lb:	1349	800	458		
	arc, inches:	-1.5	-6.7	-55.5		
Black Hills 125 OTM	velocity, fps:	2200				
	energy, ft-lb:	1343				
	arc, inches					
Black Hills 220 OTM	velocity, fps:	1000				
	energy, ft-lb:	488				
	arc, inches					
Hornady 110 V-Max (16-inch barrel)	velocity, fps:	2375	2094	1834	1597	1389
	energy, ft-lb:	1378	1071	821	623	471
	arc, inches:		+3.20	0	-13.7	-41.0
Hornady 110 V-MAX	velocity, fps:	2375	2094	1834	1597	
	energy, ft-lb:	1378	1071	821	623	
	arc, inches:	-1.5	+3.2	0	-13.7	
Hornady 208 A-MAX	velocity, fps:	1020	987	959		
	energy, ft-lb:	480	450	424		
	arc, inches:	-1.5	0	-34.1		

Centerfire Rifle Ballistics

.300 H&H MAGNUM TO .300 WINCHESTER MAGNUM

.300 H&H Magnum

CARTRIDGE BULLET	RANGE, YARDS:	0	100	200	300	400
Federal 180 Barnes TSX	velocity, fps:	2880	2680	2480	2290	2120
	energy, ft-lb:	3315	2860	2460	2105	1790
	arc, inches:	-1.5	+1.7	0	-7.3	-21.3
Federal 180 Nosler Partition	velocity, fps:	2880	2620	2380	2150	1930
	energy, ft-lb:	3315	2750	2260	1840	1480
	arc, inches:		+1.8 0	-8.0	-23.4	
Federal 180 Trophy Bonded Tip	velocity, fps:	2880	2700	2520	2350	2180
	energy, ft-lb:	3315	2900	2530	2200	1900
	arc, inches:		+1.6	0	-7.1	-20.6
Handload, 165 Sierra HP	velocity, fps:	3000	2784	2579	2382	2195
	energy, ft-lb:	3297	2840	2436	2079	1764
	arc, inches:	-1.5	+1.5	0	-6.7	-19.5
Handload, 190 Hornady	velocity, fps:	2800	2615	2437	2266	2102
	energy, ft-lb:	3307	2884	2505	2166	1864
	arc, inches:	-1.5	+1.8	0	-7.7	-22.1
Hornady 180 InterBond	velocity, fps:	2870	2678	2493	2316	2146
	energy, ft-lb:	3292	2865	2484	2144	1841
	arc, inches:	-1.5	+1.	0	-7.3	-21.0
Win. 180 Fail Safe	velocity, fps:	2880	2628	2390	2165	1952
	energy, ft-lb:	3316	2762	2284	1873	1523
	arc, inches:		+1.8 0	-7.9	-23.2	

.308 Norma Magnum

CARTRIDGE BULLET	RANGE, YARDS:	0	100	200	300	400
Norma 180 TXP Swift A-Fr.	velocity, fps:	2953	2704	2469	2245	
	energy, ft-lb:	3486	2924	2437	2016	
	arc, inches:		+1.6	0	-7.3	
Norma 180 Oryx	velocity, fps:	2953	2630	2330	2049	
	energy, ft-lb:	3486	2766	2170	1679	
	arc, inches:		+1.8	0	-8.2	
Norma 200 Vulkan	velocity, fps:	2903	2624	2361	2114	
	energy, ft-lb:	3744	3058	2476	1985	
	arc, inches:	0	+1.8	0	-8.0	
Nosler 180 AB	velocity, fps:	2975	2787	2608	2435	2269
	energy, ft-lb:	3536	3105	2718	2371	2058
	arc, inches:	-1.5	+1.5	0	-6.6	-19.1

.300 Winchester Magnum

CARTRIDGE BULLET	RANGE, YARDS:	0	100	200	300	400
A-Square 180 Dead Tough	velocity, fps:	3120	2756	2420	2108	1820
	energy, ft-lb:	3890	3035	2340	1776	1324
	arc, inches:		+1.6	0	-7.6	-22.9
Black Hills 180 Nos. Bal. Tip	velocity, fps:	3100				
	energy, ft-lb:	3498				
	arc, inches:					
Black Hills 180 Barnes X	velocity, fps:	2950				
	energy, ft-lb:	3498				
	arc, inches:					
Black Hills 180 AccuBond	velocity, fps:	3000				
	energy, ft-lb:	3597				
	arc, inches:					
Black Hills 190 Match	velocity, fps:	2950				
	energy, ft-lb:	3672				
	arc, inches:					
Federal 150 Sierra Pro Hunt.	velocity, fps:	3280	3030	2800	2570	2360.
	energy, ft-lb:	3570	3055	2600	2205	1860
	arc, inches:		+1.1	0	-5.6	-16.4
Federal 150 Trophy Bonded	velocity, fps:	3280	2980	2700	2430	2190
	energy, ft-lb:	3570	2450	2420	1970	1590
	arc, inches:		+1.2	0	-6.0	-17.9
Federal 165 Trophy Copper	velocity, fps:	3050	2860	2680	2500	2330
	energy, ft-lb:	3410	2995	2620	2290	1990
	arc, inches:		+1.4	0	-6.3	-18.0
Federal 180 Sierra Pro Hunt.	velocity, fps:	2960	2750	2540	2340	2160
	energy, ft-lb:	3500	3010	2580	2195	1860
	arc, inches:		+1.6	0	-7.0	-20.3
Federal 180 Barnes XLC	velocity, fps:	2960	2780	2600	2430	2260
	energy, ft-lb:	3500	3080	2700	2355	2050
	arc, inches:		+1.5	0	-6.6	-19.2
Federal 180 Trophy Bonded	velocity, fps:	2960	2700	2460	2220	2000
	energy, ft-lb:	3500	2915	2410	1975	1605
	arc, inches:		+1.6	0	-7.4	-21.9
Federal 180 Tr. Bonded HE	velocity, fps:	3100	2830	2580	2340	2110
	energy, ft-lb:	3840	3205	2660	2190	1790
	arc, inches:		+1.4	0	-6.6	-19.7
Federal 180 Nosler Partition	velocity, fps:	2960	2700	2450	2210	1990
	energy, ft-lb:	3500	2905	2395	1955	1585
	arc, inches:		+1.6	0	-7.5	-22.1
Federal 190 Sierra MatchKg. BTHP	velocity, fps:	2900	2730	2560	2400	2240
	energy, ft-lb:	3550	3135	2760	2420	2115
	arc, inches:		+12.9	+22.5	+26.9	+25.1
Federal 200 Sierra GameKing BTSP	velocity, fps:	2830	2680	2530	2380	2240
	energy, ft-lb:	3560	3180	2830	2520	2230
	arc, inches:		+1.7	0	-7.1	-20.4
Federal 200 Nosler Part. HE	velocity, fps:	2930	2740	2550	2370	2200
	energy, ft-lb:	3810	3325	2885	2495	2145
	arc, inches:		+1.6	0	-6.9	-20.1
Federal 200 Trophy Bonded	velocity, fps:	2800	2570	2350	2150	1950
	energy, ft-lb:	3480	2935	2460	2050	1690
	arc, inches:		+1.9	0	-8.2	-23.9
Hornady 150 SP boat-tail	velocity, fps:	3275	2988	2718	2464	2224
	energy, ft-lb:	3573	2974	2461	2023	1648
	arc, inches:		+1.2	0	-6.0	-17.8
Hornady 150 SST (and Interbond)	velocity, fps:	3275	3027	2791	2565	2352
	energy, ft-lb:	3572	3052	2593	2192	1842
	arc, inches:		+1.2	0	-5.8	-17.0
Hornady 150 SST Custom Lite	velocity, fps:	2800	2582	2375	2177	1988
	energy, ft-lb:	2611	2220	1878	1578	1316
	arc, inches:		+1.9	0	-8.0	-23.5
Hornady 165 SP boat-tail	velocity, fps:	3100	2877	2665	2462	2269.
	energy, ft-lb:	3522	3033	2603	2221	1887
	arc, inches:		+1.3	0	-6.5	-18.5
Hornady 165 SST	velocity, fps:	3100	2885	2680	2483	2296
	energy, ft-lb:	3520	3049	2630	2259	1930
	arc, inches:		+1.4	0	-6.4	-18.6
Hornady 180 SP boat-tail	velocity, fps:	2960	2745	2540	2344	2157
	energy, ft-lb:	3501	3011	2578	2196	1859
	arc, inches:		+1.9	0	-7.3	-20.9
Hornady 180 SST	velocity, fps:	2960	2764	2575	2395	2222
	energy, ft-lb:	3501	3052	2650	2292	1974
	arc, inches:		+1.6	0	-7.0	-20.1.
Hornady 180 SPBT HM	velocity, fps:	3100	2879	2668	2467	2275
	energy, ft-lb:	3840	3313	2845	2431	2068
	arc, inches:		+1.4	0	-6.4	-18.7
Hornady 190 BTHP Match	velocity, fps:	2930	2760	2596	2438	2286
	energy, ft-lb:	3717	3297	2918	2574	2262
	arc, inches:		+1.5	0	-6.7	-19.3
Hornady 190 SP boat-tail	velocity, fps:	2900	2711	2529	2355	2187
	energy, ft-lb:	3549	3101	2699	2340	2018
	arc, inches:		+1.6	0	-7.1	-20.4
Norma 150 Nosler Bal. Tip	velocity, fps:	3250	3014	2791	2578	
	energy, ft-lb:	3519	3027	2595	2215	
	arc, inches:		+1.1	0	-5.6	
Norma 150 Barnes TS	velocity, fps:	3215	2982	2761	2550	
	energy, ft-lb:	3444	2962	2539	2167	
	arc, inches:		+1.2	0	-5.8	
Norma 165 Scirocco	velocity, fps:	3117	2921	2734	2554	
	energy, ft-lb:	3561	3127	2738	2390	
	arc, inches:		+1.2	0	-5.9	
Norma 180 Soft Point	velocity, fps:	3018	2780	2555	2341	
	energy, ft-lb:	3641	3091	2610	2190	
	arc, inches:		+1.5	0	-7.0	
Norma 180 Plastic Point	velocity, fps:	3018	2755	2506	2271	
	energy, ft-lb:	3641	3034	2512	2062	
	arc, inches:		+1.6	0	-7.1	
Norma 180 TXP Swift A-Fr.	velocity, fps:	2920	2688	2467	2256	
	energy, ft-lb:	3409	2888	2432	2035	
	arc, inches:		+1.7	0	-7.4	

Centerfire Rifle Ballistics

.300 WINCHESTER MAGNUM TO .300 REMINGTON SHORT ULTRA MAGNUM

CARTRIDGE BULLET	RANGE, YARDS:	0	100	200	300	400
Norma 180 AccuBond	velocity, fps:	2953	2767	2588	2417	
	energy, ft-lb:	3486	3061	2678	2335	
	arc, inches:		+1.5	0	-6.7	
Norma 180 Oryx	velocity, fps:	2920	2600	2301	2023	
	energy, ft-lb:	3409	2702	2117	1636	
	arc, inches:		+1.8	0	-8.4	
Norma 200 Vulkan	velocity, fps:	2887	2609	2347	2100	
	energy, ft-lb:	3702	3023	2447	1960	
	arc, inches:		+1.8	0	-8.2	
Norma 200 Oryx	velocity, fps:	2789	2510	2248	2002	
	energy, ft-lb:	3455	2799	2245	1780	
	arc, inches:		+2.0	0	-8.9	
PMC 150 Barnes X	velocity, fps:	3135	2918	2712	2515	2327
	energy, ft-lb:	3273	2836	2449	2107	1803
	arc, inches:		+1.3	0	-6.1	-17.7
PMC 150 Pointed Soft Point	velocity, fps:	3150	2902	2665	2438	2222
	energy, ft-lb:	3304	2804	2364	1979	1644.
	arc, inches:		+1.3	0	-6.2	-18.3
PMC 150 SP boat-tail	velocity, fps:	3250	2987	2739	2504	2281
	energy, ft-lb:	3517	2970	2498	2088	1733
	arc, inches:		+1.2	0	-6.0	-17.4
PMC 180 Barnes X	velocity, fps:	2910	2738	2572	2412	2258
	energy, ft-lb:	3384	2995	2644	2325	2037
	arc, inches:		+1.6	0	-6.9	-19.8
PMC 180 Pointed Soft Point	velocity, fps:	2853	2643	2446	2258	2077
	energy, ft-lb:	3252	2792	2391	2037	1724
	arc, inches:		+1.7	0	-7.5	-21.9
PMC 180 SP boat-tail	velocity, fps:	2900	2714	2536	2365	2200
	energy, ft-lb:	3361	2944	2571	2235	1935
	arc, inches:		+1.6	0	-7.1	-20.3
PMC 180 HPBT Match	velocity, fps:	2950	2755	2568	2390	2219
	energy, ft-lb:	3478	3033	2636	2283	1968
	arc, inches:		+1.5	0	-6.8	-19.7
Rem. 150 PSP Core-Lokt	velocity, fps:	3290	2951	2636	2342	2068
	energy, ft-lb:	3605	2900	2314	1827	1859
	arc, inches:		+1.6	0	-7.0	-20.2
Rem. 150 PSP C-L MR	velocity, fps:	2650	2373	2113	1870	1646
	energy, ft-lb:	2339	1875	1486	1164	902
	arc, inches:		+1.0	-2.7	-14.3	-35.8
Rem. 150 PSP C-L Ultra	velocity, fps:	3290	2967	2666	2384	2120
	energy, ft-lb:	3065	2931	2366	1893	1496
	arc, inches:		+1.2	0	-6.1	-18.4
Rem. 180 AccuTip	velocity, fps:	2960	2764	2577	2397	2224
	energy, ft-lb:	3501	3053	2653	2295	1976
	arc, inches:		+1.5	0	-6.8	-19.6
Rem. 180 PSP Core-Lokt	velocity, fps:	2960	2745	2540	2344	2157
	energy, ft-lb:	3501	3011	2578	2196	1424
	arc, inches:		+2.2	+1.9	-3.4	-15.0
Rem. 180 PSP C-L Ultra	velocity, fps:	2960	2727	2505	2294	2093
	energy, ft-lb:	3501	2971	2508	2103	1751
	arc, inches:		+2.7	+2.2	-3.8	-16.4
Rem. 180 Nosler Partition	velocity, fps:	2960	2725	2503	2291	2089
	energy, ft-lb:	3501	2968	2503	2087	1744
	arc, inches:		+1.6	0	-7.2	-20.9
Rem. 180 Nosler Bal. Tip	velocity, fps:	2960	2774	2595	2424	2259.
	energy, ft-lb:	3501	3075	2692	2348	2039
	arc, inches:		+1.5	0	-6.7	-19.3
Rem. 180 Swift Scirocco	velocity, fps:	2960	2774	2595	2424	2259
	energy, ft-lb:	3501	3075	2692	2348	2039
	arc, inches:		+1.5	0	-6.7	-19.3
Rem. 190 PSP boat-tail	velocity, fps:	2885	2691	2506	2327	2156
	energy, ft-lb:	3511	3055	2648	2285	1961
	arc, inches:		+1.6	0	-7.2	-20.8
Rem. 190 HPBT Match	velocity, fps:	2900	2725	2557	2395	2239
	energy, ft-lb:	3547	3133	2758	2420	2115
	arc, inches:		+1.6	0	-6.9	-19.9
Rem. 200 Swift A-Frame	velocity, fps:	2825	2595	2376	2167	1970
	energy, ft-lb:	3544	2989	2506	2086	1722
	arc, inches:		+1.8	0	-8.0	-23.5
Speer 180 Grand Slam	velocity, fps:	2950	2735	2530	2334	
	energy, ft-lb:	3478	2989	2558	2176	
	arc, inches:		+1.6	0	-7.0	-20.5
Speer 200 Grand Slam	velocity, fps:	2800	2597	2404	2218	
	energy, ft-lb:	3481	2996	2565	2185	
	arc, inches:		+1.8	0	-7.9	-22.9
Win. 150 Power-Point	velocity, fps:	3290	2951	2636	2342	2068.
	energy, ft-lb:	3605	2900	2314	1827	1424
	arc, inches:		+2.6	+2.1	-3.5	-15.4
Win. 150 Fail Safe	velocity, fps:	3260	2943	2647	2370	2110
	energy, ft-lb:	3539	2884	2334	1871	1483
	arc, inches:		+1.3	0	-6.2	-18.7
Win. 165 Fail Safe	velocity, fps:	3120	2807	2515	2242	1985
	energy, ft-lb:	3567	2888	2319	1842	1445
	arc, inches:		+1.5	0	-7.0	-20.0
Win. 180 Power-Point	velocity, fps:	2960	2745	2540	2344	2157
	energy, ft-lb:	3501	3011	2578	2196	1859
	arc, inches:		+1.9	0	-7.3	-20.9
Win. 180 Power-Point Plus	velocity, fps:	3070	2846	2633	2430	2236
	energy, ft-lb:	3768	3239	2772	2361	1999
	arc, inches:		+1.4	0	-6.4	-18.7
Win. 180 Ballistic Silvertip	velocity, fps:	2950	2764	2586	2415	2250
	energy, ft-lb:	3478	3054	2673	2331	2023
	arc, inches:		+1.5	0	-6.7	-19.4
Win. 180 AccuBond	velocity, fps:	2950	2765	2588	2417	2253
	energy, ft-lb:	3478	3055	2676	2334	2028
	arc, inches:		+1.5	0	-6.7	-19.4
Win. 180 Fail Safe	velocity, fps:	2960	2732	2514	2307	2110
	energy, ft-lb:	3503	2983	2528	2129	1780
	arc, inches:		+1.6	0	-7.1	-20.7
Win. 180 Partition Gold	velocity, fps:	3070	2859	2657	2464	2280
	energy, ft-lb:	3768	3267	2823	2428	2078
	arc, inches:		+1.4	0	-6.3	-18.3
Win. 150 Supreme Elite XP3	velocity, fps:	3260	3030	2811	2603	2404
	energy, ft-lb:	3539	3057	2632	2256	1925
	arc, inches:		+1.1	0	-5.6	-16.2
Win. 180 Supreme Elite XP3	velocity, fps:	3000	2819	2646	2479	2318
	energy, ft-lb:	3597	3176	2797	2455	2147
	arc, inches:		+1.4	0	-6.4	-18.5

.300 Remington Short Ultra Magnum

CARTRIDGE BULLET	RANGE, YARDS:	0	100	200	300	400
Rem. 150 PSP C-L Ultra	velocity, fps:	3200	2901	2672	2359	2112
	energy, ft-lb:	3410	2803	2290	1854	1485
	arc, inches:		+1.3	0	-6.4	-19.1
Rem. 165 PSP Core-Lokt	velocity, fps:	3075	2792	2527	2276	2040
	energy, ft-lb:	3464	2856	2339	1828	1525
	arc, inches:		+1.5	0	-7.0	-20.7
Rem. 180 Partition	velocity, fps:	2960	2761	2571	2389	2214
	energy, ft-lb:	3501	3047	2642	2280	1959
	arc, inches:		+1.5	0	-6.8	-19.7
Rem. 180 PSP C-L Ultra	velocity, fps:	2960	2727	2506	2295	2094
	energy, ft-lb:	3501	2972	2509	2105	1753
	arc, inches:		+1.6	0	-7.1	-20.9
Rem. 190 HPBT Match	velocity, fps:	2900	2725	2557	2395	2239
	energy, ft-lb:	3547	3133	2758	2420	2115
	arc, inches:		+1.6	0	-6.9	-19.9

Centerfire Rifle Ballistics

.300 WINCHESTER SHORT MAGNUM TO .300 WEATHERBY MAGNUM

.300 Winchester Short Magnum

CARTRIDGE BULLET	RANGE, YARDS:	0	100	200	300	400
Black Hills 175 Sierra MKing	velocity, fps:	2950				
	energy, ft-lb:	3381				
	arc, inches:					
Black Hills 180 AccuBond	velocity, fps:	2950				
	energy, ft-lb:	3478				
	arc, inches:					
Federal 150 Nosler Bal. Tip	velocity, fps:	3200	2970	2755	2545	2345
	energy, ft-lb:	3410	2940	2520	2155	1830.
	arc, inches:		+1.2	0	-5.8	-17.0
Federal 160 Trophy Bonded Tip	velocity, fps:	3130	2910	2710	2510	2320
	energy, ft-lb:	3590	3110	2680	2305	1970
	arc, inches:		+1.3	0	-6.0	-17.6
Federal 165 Nos. Partition	velocity, fps:	3130	2890	2670	2450	2250
	energy, ft-lb:	3590	3065	2605	2205	1855.
	arc, inches:		+1.3	0	-6.2	-18.2
Federal 165 Nos. Solid Base	velocity, fps:	3130	2900	2690	2490	2290
	energy, ft-lb:	3590	3090	2650	2265	1920
	arc, inches:		+1.3	0	-6.1	-17.8
Federal 180 Barnes TS And Nos. Solid Base	velocity, fps:	2980	2780	2580	2400	2220
	energy, ft-lbs:	3550	3085	2670	2300	1970
	arc, inches:		+1.5	0	-6.7	-19.5
Federal 180 Grand Slam	velocity, fps:	2970	2740	2530	2320	2130
	energy, ft-lb:	3525	3010	2555	2155	1810
	arc, inches:		+1.5	0	-7.0	-20.5
Federal 180 Trophy Bonded	velocity, fps:	2970	2730	2500	2280	2080
	energy, ft-lb:	3525	2975	2500	2085	1725
	arc, inches:		+1.5	0	-7.2	-21.0
Federal 180 Nosler Partition	velocity, fps:	2975	2750	2535	2290	2126
	energy, ft-lb:	3540	3025	2570	2175	1825
	arc, inches:		+1.5	0	-7.0	-20.3
Federal 180 Nos. AccuBond	velocity, fps:	2960	2780	2610	2440	2280
	energy, ft-lb:	3500	3090	2715	2380	2075
	arc, inches:		+1.5	0	-6.6	-19.0
Federal 180 Hi-Shok SP	velocity, fps:	2970	2520	2115	1750	1430
	energy, ft-lb:	3525	2540	1785	1220	820
	arc, inches:		+2.2	0	-9.9	-31.4
Norma 150 FMJ	velocity, fps:	2953	2731	2519	2318	
	energy, ft-lb:					
	arc, inches:		+1.6	0	-7.1	
Norma 150 Barnes X TS	velocity, fps:	3215	2982	2761	2550	
	energy, ft-lb:	3444	2962	2539	2167	
	arc, inches:		+1.2	0	-5.7	
Norma 180 Nosler Bal. Tip	velocity, fps:	3215	2985	2767	2560	
	energy, ft-lb:	3437	2963	2547	2179	
	arc, inches:		+1.2	0	-5.7	
Norma 180 Oryx	velocity, fps:	2936	2542	2180	1849	
	energy, ft-lb:	3446	2583	1900	1368	
	arc, inches:		+1.9	0	-8.9	
Win. 150 Power-Point	velocity, fps:	3270	2903	2565	2250	1958
	energy, ft-lb:	3561	2807	2190	1686	1277
	arc, inches:		+1.3	0	-6.6	-20.2
Win. 150 Ballistic Silvertip	velocity, fps:	3300	3061	2834	2619	2414
	energy, ft-lb:	3628	3121	2676	2285	1941
	arc, inches:		+1.1	0	-5.4	-15.9
Win. 165 Fail Safe	velocity, fps:	3125	2846	2584	2336	2102
	energy, ft-lb:	3577	2967	2446	1999	1619
	arc, inches:		+1.4	0	-6.6	-19.6
Win. 180 Ballistic Silvertip	velocity, fps:	3010	2822	2641	2468	2301.
	energy, ft-lb:	3621	3182	2788	2434	2116
	arc, inches:		+1.4	0	-6.4	-18.6
Win. 180 AccuBond	velocity, fps:	3010	2822	2643	2470	2304
	energy, ft-lb:	3622	3185	2792	2439	2121
	arc, inches:		+1.4	0	-6.4	-18.5
Win. 180 Fail Safe	velocity, fps:	2970	2741	2524	2317	2120
	energy, ft-lb:	3526	3005	2547	2147	1797
	arc, inches:		+1.6	0	-7.0	-20.5
Win. 180 Power Point	velocity, fps:	2970	2755	2549	2353	2166
	energy, ft-lb:	3526	3034	2598	2214	1875
	arc, inches:		+1.5	0	-6.9	-20.1
Win. 150 Supreme Elite XP3	velocity, fps:	3300	3068	2847	2637	2437
	energy, ft-lb:	3626	3134	2699	2316	1978
	arc, inches:		+1.1	0	-5.4	-15.8
Win. 180 Supreme Elite XP3	velocity, fps:	3010	2829	2655	2488	2326
	energy, ft-lb:	3621	3198	2817	2473	2162
	arc, inches:		+1.4	0	-6.4	-18.3

.300 Ruger Compact Magnum

CARTRIDGE BULLET	RANGE, YARDS:	0	100	200	300	400
Hornady 150 SST	velocity, fps:	3310	3065	2833	2613	2404
	energy, ft-lb:	3648	3128	2673	2274	1924
	arc, inches:	-1.5	+1.1	0	-5.4	-16.0
Hornady 165 GMX	velocity, fps:	3130	2911	2703	2504	2314
	energy, ft-lb:	3589	3105	2677	2297	1963
	arc, inches:	-1.5	+1.3	0	-6.1	-17.7
Hornady 180 SST	velocity, fps:	3040	2840	2649	2466	2290
	energy, ft-lb:	3693	3223	2804	2430	2096
	arc, inches:	-1.5	+1.4	0	-6.4	-18.5

.300 Weatherby Magnum

CARTRIDGE BULLET	RANGE, YARDS:	0	100	200	300	400
A-Square 180 Dead Tough	velocity, fps:	3180	2811	2471	2155	1863.
	energy, ft-lb:	4041	3158	2440	1856	1387
	arc, inches:		+1.5	0	-7.2	-21.8
A-Square 220 Monolythic Solid	velocity, fps:	2700	2407	2133	1877	1653
	energy, ft-lb:	3561	2830	2223	1721	1334
	arc, inches:		+2.3	0	-9.8	-29.7
Federal 180 Nosler Partition	velocity, fps:	3190	2980	2780	2590	2400
	energy, ft-lb:	4055	3540	3080	2670	2305
	arc, inches:		+1.2	0	-5.7	-16.7
Federal 180 Nosler Part. HE	velocity, fps:	3330	3110	2810	2710	2520
	energy, ft-lb:	4430	3875	3375	2935	2540
	arc, inches:		+1.0	0	-5.2	-15.1
Federal 180 Sierra GameKing BTSP	velocity, fps:	3190	3010	2830	2660	2490
	energy, ft-lb:	4065	3610	3195	2820	2480
	arc, inches:		+1.2	0	-5.6	-16.0
Federal 180 Trophy Bonded	velocity, fps:	3190	2950	2720	2500	2290
	energy, ft-lb:	4065	3475	2955	2500	2105
	arc, inches:		+1.3	0	-5.9	-17.5
Federal 180 Tr. Bonded HE	velocity, fps:	3330	3080	2850	2750	2410
	energy, ft-lb:	4430	3795	3235	2750	2320
	arc, inches:		+1.1	0	-5.4	-15.8
Federal 180 Trophy Copper	velocity, fps:	3100	2910	2740	2560	2400
	energy, ft-lb:	3840	3395	2990	2625	2300
	arc, inches:		+1.3	0	-6.0	-17.1
Federal 200 Trophy Bonded	velocity, fps:	2900	2670	2440	2230	2030
	energy, ft-lb:	3735	3150	2645	2200	1820
	arc, inches:		+1.7	0	-7.6	-22.2
Hornady 150 SST (or Interbond)	velocity, fps:	3375	3123	2882	2652	2434
	energy, ft-lb:	3793	3248	2766	2343	1973
	arc, inches:		+1.0	0	-5.4	-15.8
Hornady 165 GMX Superformance	velocity, fps:	3140	2921	2713	2515	2325
	energy, ft-lb:	3612	3126	2697	2317	1980
	arc, inches:		+1.3	0	-6.0	-17.5
Hornady 180 SP	velocity, fps:	3120	2891	2673	2466	2268.
	energy, ft-lb:	3890	3340	2856	2430	2055
	arc, inches:		+1.3	0	-6.2	-18.1
Hornady 180 SST	velocity, fps:	3120	2911	2711	2519	2335
	energy, ft-lb:	3890	3386	2936	2535	2180
	arc, inches:		+1.3	0	-6.2	-18.1
Rem. 180 PSP Core-Lokt	velocity, fps:	3120	2866	2627	2400	2184
	energy, ft-lb:	3890	3284	2758	2301	1905
	arc, inches:		+2.4	+2.0	-3.4	-14.9

Centerfire Rifle Ballistics

.300 WEATHERBY MAGNUM TO .303 BRITISH

BALLISTICS

CARTRIDGE BULLET	RANGE, YARDS:	0	100	200	300	400
Rem. 190 PSP boat-tail	velocity, fps:	3030	2830	2638	2455	2279
	energy, ft-lb:	3873	3378	2936	2542	2190.
	arc, inches:		+1.4	0	-6.4	-18.6
Rem. 200 Swift A-Frame	velocity, fps:	2925	2690	2467	2254	2052
	energy, ft-lb:	3799	3213	2701	2256	1870
	arc, inches:		+2.8	+2.3	-3.9	-17.0
Speer 180 Grand Slam	velocity, fps:	3185	2948	2722	2508	
	energy, ft-lb:	4054	3472	2962	2514	
	arc, inches:		+1.3	0	-5.9	-17.4
Wby. 150 Pointed Expanding	velocity, fps:	3540	3225	2932	2657	2399
	energy, ft-lb:	4173	3462	2862	2351	1916
	arc, inches:		+2.6	+3.3	0	-8.2
Wby. 150 Nosler Partition	velocity, fps:	3540	3263	3004	2759	2528
	energy, ft-lb:	4173	3547	3005	2536	2128
	arc, inches:		+2.5	+3.2	0	-7.7
Wby. 165 Pointed Expanding	velocity, fps:	3390	3123	2872	2634	2409
	energy, ft-lb:	4210	3573	3021	2542	2126
	arc, inches:		+2.8	+3.5	0	-8.5
Wby. 165 Nosler Bal. Tip	velocity, fps:	3350	3133	2927	2730	2542
	energy, ft-lb:	4111	3596	3138	2730	2367
	arc, inches:		+2.7	+3.4	0	-8.1
Wby. 180 Pointed Expanding	velocity, fps:	3240	3004	2781	2569	2366
	energy, ft-lb:	4195	3607	3091	2637	2237
	arc, inches:		+3.1	+3.8	0	-9.0
Wby. 180 Barnes X	velocity, fps:	3190	2995	2809	2631	2459
	energy, ft-lb:	4067	3586	3154	2766	2417
	arc, inches:		+3.1	+3.8	0	-8.7
Wby. 180 Bal. Tip	velocity, fps:	3250	3051	2806	2676	2503
	energy, ft-lb:	4223	3721	3271	2867	2504
	arc, inches:		+2.8	+3.6	0	-8.4
Wby. 180 Nosler Partition	velocity, fps:	3240	3028	2826	2634	2449
	energy, ft-lb:	4195	3665	3193	2772	2396
	arc, inches:		+3.0	+3.7	0	-8.6
Wby. 200 Nosler Partition	velocity, fps:	3060	2860	2668	2485	2308
	energy, ft-lb:	4158	3631	3161	2741	2366
	arc, inches:		+3.5	+4.2	0	-9.8
Wby. 220 RN Expanding	velocity, fps:	2845	2543	2260	1996	1751.
	energy, ft-lb:	3954	3158	2495	1946	1497
	arc, inches:		+4.9	+5.9	0	-14.6

.300 DAKOTA

CARTRIDGE BULLET	RANGE, YARDS:	0	100	200	300	400
Dakota 165 Barnes X	velocity, fps:	3200	2979	2769	2569	2377
	energy, ft-lb:	3751	3251	2809	2417	2070
	arc, inches:		+2.1	+1.8	-3.0	-13.2
Dakota 200 Barnes X	velocity, fps:	3000	2824	2656	2493	2336
	energy, ft-lb:	3996	3542	3131	2760	2423
	arc, inches:		+2.2	+1.5	-4.0	-15.2

.300 PEGASUS

CARTRIDGE BULLET	RANGE, YARDS:	0	100	200	300	400
A-Square 180 SP boat-tail	velocity, fps:	3500	3319	3145	2978	2817
	energy, ft-lb:	4896	4401	3953	3544	3172
	arc, inches:		+2.3	+2.9	0	-6.8
A-Square 180 Nosler Part.	velocity, fps:	3500	3295	3100	2913	2734
	energy, ft-lb:	4896	4339	3840	3392	2988
	arc, inches:		+2.3	+3.0	0	-7.1
A-Square 180 Dead Tough	velocity, fps:	3500	3103	2740	2405	2095
	energy, ft-lb:	4896	3848	3001	2312	1753
	arc, inches:		+1.1	0	-5.7	-17.5

.300 REMINGTON ULTRA MAGNUM

CARTRIDGE BULLET	RANGE, YARDS:	0	100	200	300	400
Federal 180 Trophy Bonded	velocity, fps:	3250	3000	2770	2550	2340
	energy, ft-lb:	4220	3605	3065	2590	2180
	arc, inches:		+1.2	0	-5.7	-16.8
Federal 180 Trophy Copper	velocity, fps:	3150	2960	2780	2610	2440
	energy, ft-lb:	3965	3505	3090	2715	2380
	arc, inches:		+1.2	0	-5.8	-16.6
Federal 200 Partition	velocity, fps:	3070	2870	2680	2490	2320
	energy, ft-lb:	4185	3655	3180	2760	2380
	arc, inches:		+1.4	0	-6.2	-18.0
Rem. 150 Swift Scirocco	velocity, fps:	3450	3208	2980	2762	2556
	energy, ft-lb:	3964	3427	2956	2541	2175
	arc, inches:		+1.7	+1.5	-2.6	-11.2
Remington 165 Copper Solid	velocity, fps:	3250	3035	2821	2617	2422
	energy, ft-lb:	3893	3373	2916	2602	2390
	arc, inches:		+1.4	0	-5.8	-16.7
Rem. 180 Nosler Partition	velocity, fps:	3250	3037	2834	2640	2454
	energy, ft-lb:	4221	3686	3201	2786	2407
	arc, inches:		+2.4	+1.8	-3.0	-12.7
Rem. 180 Swift Scirocco	velocity, fps:	3250	3048	2856	2672	2495
	energy, ft-lb:	4221	3714	3260	2853	2487
	arc, inches:		+2.0	+1.7	-2.8	-12.3
Rem. 180 PSP Core-Lokt	velocity, fps:	3250	2988	2742	2508	2287
	energy, ft-lb:	3517	2974	2503	2095	1741
	arc, inches:		+2.1	+1.8	-3.1	-13.6
Rem. 200 Nosler Partition	velocity, fps:	3025	2826	2636	2454	2279
	energy, ft-lb:	4063	3547	3086	2673	2308
	arc, inches:		+2.4	+2.0	-3.4	-14.6

.30-378 WEATHERBY MAGNUM

CARTRIDGE BULLET	RANGE, YARDS:	0	100	200	300	400
Nosler 210 ABLR	velocity, fps:	3040	2907	2778	2653	2531
	energy, ft-lb:	4308	3940	3599	3282	2987
	arc, inches:	-1.5	+1.3	0	-5.8	-16.6
Wby. 165 Nosler Bal. Tip	velocity, fps:	3500	3275	3062	2859	2665
	energy, ft-lb:	4488	3930	3435	2995	2603
	arc, inches:		+2.4	+3.0	0	-7.4
Wby. 180 Nosler Bal. Tip	velocity, fps:	3420	3213	3015	2826	2645
	energy, ft-lb:	4676	4126	3634	3193	2797
	arc, inches:		+2.5	+3.1	0	-7.5
Wby. 180 Barnes X	velocity, fps:	3450	3243	3046	2858	2678.
	energy, ft-lb:	4757	4204	3709	3264	2865
	arc, inches:		+2.4	+3.1	0	-7.4
Wby. 200 Nosler Partition	velocity, fps:	3160	2955	2759	2572	2392.
	energy, ft-lb:	4434	3877	3381	2938	2541
	arc, inches:		+3.2	+3.9	0	-9.1

7.82 (.308) WARBIRD

CARTRIDGE BULLET	RANGE, YARDS:	0	100	200	300	400
Lazzeroni 150 Nosler Part.	velocity, fps:	3680	3432	3197	2975	2764
	energy, ft-lb:	4512	3923	3406	2949	2546.
	arc, inches:		+2.1	+2.7	0	-6.6
Lazzeroni 180 Nosler Part.	velocity, fps:	3425	3220	3026	2839	2661
	energy, ft-lb:	4689	4147	3661	3224	2831
	arc, inches:		+2.5	+3.2	0	-7.5
Lazzeroni 200 Swift A-Fr.	velocity, fps:	3290	3105	2928	2758	2594.
	energy, ft-lb:	4808	4283	3808	3378	2988
	arc, inches:		+2.7	+3.4	0	-7.9

7.65X53 ARGENTINE

CARTRIDGE BULLET	RANGE, YARDS:	0	100	200	300	400
Norma 174 Soft Point	velocity, fps:	2493	2173	1878	1611	
	energy, ft-lb:	2402	1825	1363	1003	
	arc, inches:		+2.0	0	-9.5	
Norma 180 Soft Point	velocity, fps:	2592	2386	2189	2002	
	energy, ft-lb:	2686	2276	1916	1602	
	arc, inches:		+2.3	0	-9.6	

.303 BRITISH

CARTRIDGE BULLET	RANGE, YARDS:	0	100	200	300	400
Federal 150 Hi-Shok	velocity, fps:	2690	2440	2210	1980	1780
	energy, ft-lb:	2400	1980	1620	1310	1055
	arc, inches:		+2.2	0	-9.4	-27.6
Federal 180 Sierra Pro-Hunt.	velocity, fps:	2460	2230	2020	1820	1630
	energy, ft-lb:	2420	1995	1625	1315	1060
	arc, inches:		+2.8	0	-11.3	-33.2
Federal 180 Tr. Bonded HE	velocity, fps:	2590	2350	2120	1900	1700
	energy, ft-lb:	2680	2205	1795	1445	1160
	arc, inches:		+2.4	0	-10.0	-30.0
Hornady 150 Soft Point	velocity, fps:	2685	2441	2210	1992	1787
	energy, ft-lb:	2401	1984	1627	1321	1064
	arc, inches:		+2.2	0	-9.3	-27.4

Centerfire Rifle Ballistics

.303 British to .338 Federal

Cartridge Bullet	Range, yards:	0	100	200	300	400
Hornady 150 SP LM	velocity, fps:	2830	2570	2325	2094	1884.
	energy, ft-lb:	2667	2199	1800	1461	1185
	arc, inches:		+2.0	0	-8.4	-24.6
Hornady 174 BTHP	velocity, fps:	2430	2252	2082	1919	1765
	energy, ft-lb:	2281	1959	1674	1423	1204
	arc, inches:		+2.7	0	-10.7	-30.9
Norma 150 Soft Point	velocity, fps:	2723	2438	2170	1920	
	energy, ft-lb:	2470	1980	1569	1228	
	arc, inches:		+2.2	0	-9.6	
PMC 174 FMJ (and HPBT)	velocity, fps:	2400	2216	2042	1876	1720
	energy, ft-lb:	2225	1898	1611	1360	1143
	arc, inches:		+2.8	0	-11.2	-32.2
PMC 180 SP boat-tail	velocity, fps:	2450	2276	2110	1951	1799
	energy, ft-lb:	2399	2071	1779	1521	1294
	arc, inches:		+2.6	0	-10.4	-30.1
Rem. 180 SP Core-Lokt	velocity, fps:	2460	2124	1817	1542	1311
	energy, ft-lb:	2418	1803	1319	950	687
	arc, inches, s:		0	-5.8	-23.3	
Win. 180 Power-Point	velocity, fps:	2460	2233	2018	1816	1629
	energy, ft-lb:	2418	1993	1627	1318	1060
	arc, inches, s:		0	-6.1	-20.8	

7.7x58 Japanese Arisaka

Cartridge Bullet	Range, yards:	0	100	200	300	400
Norma 174 Soft Point	velocity, fps:	2493	2173	1878	1611	
	energy, ft-lb:	2402	1825	1363	1003	
	arc, inches:		+2.0	0	-9.5	
Norma 180 Soft Point	velocity, fps:	2493	2291	2099	1916	
	energy, ft-lb:	2485	2099	1761	1468	
	arc, inches:		+2.6	0	-10.5	

.32-20 Winchester

Cartridge Bullet	Range, yards:	0	100	200	300	400
Rem. 100 Lead	velocity, fps:	1210	1021	913	834	769
	energy, ft-lb:	325	231	185	154	131
	arc, inches:		0	-31.6	-104.7	
Win. 100 Lead	velocity, fps:	1210	1021	913	834	769
	energy, ft-lb:	325	231	185	154	131
	arc, inches:		0	-32.3	-106.3	

.32 Winchester Special

Cartridge Bullet	Range, yards:	0	100	200	300	400
Federal 170 Hi-Shok	velocity, fps:	2250	1920	1630	1370	1180
	energy, ft-lb:	1910	1395	1000	710	520
	arc, inches:		0	-8.0	-29.2	
Hornady 165 FTX	velocity, fps:	2410	2145	1897	1669	
	energy, ft-lb:	2128	1685	1318	1020	
	arc, inches:	-1.5	+3.0	0	-12.8	
Rem. 170 SP Core-Lokt	velocity, fps:	2250	1921	1626	1372	1175
	energy, ft-lb:	1911	1393	998	710	521
	arc, inches:		0	-8.0	-29.3	
Win. 170 Power-Point	velocity, fps:	2250	1870	1537	1267	1082
	energy, ft-lb:	1911	1320	892	606	442
	arc, inches:		0	-9.2	-33.2	

8mm Mauser (8x57)

Cartridge Bullet	Range, yards:	0	100	200	300	400
Federal 170 Hi-Shok	velocity, fps:	2360	1970	1620	1330	1120
	energy, ft-lb:	2100	1465	995	670	475
	arc, inches:		0	-7.6	-28.5	
Hornady 195 SP	velocity, fps:	2550	2343	2146	1959	1782
	energy, ft-lb:	2815	2377	1994	1861	1375
	arc, inches:		+2.3	0	-9.9	-28.8.
Hornady 195 SP (2005)	velocity, fps:	2475	2269	2074	1888	1714
	energy, ft-lb:	2652	2230	1861	1543	1271
	arc, inches:		+2.6	0	-10.7	-31.3
Norma 123 FMJ	velocity, fps:	2559	2121	1729	1398	
	energy, ft-lb:	1789	1228	817	534	
	arc, inches:		+3.2	0	-15.0	

Cartridge Bullet	Range, yards:	0	100	200	300	400
Norma 196 Oryx	velocity, fps:	2395	2146	1912	1695	
	energy, ft-lb:	2497	2004	1591	1251	
	arc, inches:		+3	0	-12.6	
Norma 196 Vulkan	velocity, fps:	2395	2156	1930	1720	
	energy, ft-lb:	2497	2023	1622	1289	
	arc, inches:		3.0	0	-12.3	
Norma 196 Alaska	velocity, fps:	2395	2112	1850	1611	
	energy, ft-lb:	2714	2190	1754	1399	
	arc, inches:		0	-6.3	-22.9	
Norma 196 Soft Point (JS)	velocity, fps:	2526	2244	1981	1737	
	energy, ft-lb:	2778	2192	1708	1314	
	arc, inches:		+2.7	0	-11.6	
Norma 196 Alaska (JS)	velocity, fps:	2526	2248	1988	1747	
	energy, ft-lb:	2778	2200	1720	1328	
	arc, inches:		+2.7	0	-11.5	
Norma 196 Vulkan (JS)	velocity, fps:	2526	2276	2041	1821	
	energy, ft-lb:	2778	2256	1813	1443	
	arc, inches:		+2.6	0	-11.0	
Norma 196 Oryx (JS)	velocity, fps:	2526	2269	2027	1802	
	energy, ft-lb:	2778	2241	1789	1413	
	arc, inches:		+2.6	0	-11.1	
PMC 170 Pointed Soft Point	velocity, fps:	2360	1969	1622	1333	1123
	energy, ft-lb:	2102	1463	993	671	476
	arc, inches:		+1.8	-4.5	-24.3	-63.8
Rem. 170 SP Core-Lokt	velocity, fps:	2360	1969	1622	1333	1123
	energy, ft-lb:	2102	1463	993	671	476
	arc, inches:		+1.8	-4.5	-24.3	-63.8.
Win. 170 Power-Point	velocity, fps:	2360	1969	1622	1333	1123
	energy, ft-lb:	2102	1463	993	671	476
	arc, inches:		+1.8	-4.5	-24.3	-63.8

.325 WSM

Cartridge Bullet	Range, yards:	0	100	200	300	400
Win. 180 Ballistic ST	velocity, fps:	3060	2841	2632	2432	2242
	energy, ft-lb:	3743	3226	2769	2365	2009
	arc, inches:		+1.4	0	-6.4	-18.7
Win. 200 AccuBond CT	velocity, fps:	2950	2753	2565	2384	2210
	energy, ft-lb:	3866	3367	2922	2524	2170
	arc, inches:		+1.5	0	-6.8	-19.8
Win. 220 Power-Point	velocity, fps:	2840	2605	2382	2169	1968
	energy, ft-lb:	3941	3316	2772	2300	1893
	arc, inches:		+1.8	0	-8.0	-23.3

8mm Remington Magnum

Cartridge Bullet	Range, yards:	0	100	200	300	400
A-Square 220 Monolythic Solid	velocity, fps:	2800	2501	2221	1959	1718
	energy, ft-lb:	3829	3055	2409	1875	1442
	arc, inches:		+2.1	0	-9.1	-27.6
Nosler 180 BT	velocity, fps:	3200	2923	2662	2416	2183
	energy, ft-lb:	4092	3414	2832	2333	1905
	arc, inches:	-1.5	+1.3	0	-6.2	-18.4
Rem. 200 Swift A-Frame	velocity, fps:	2900	2623	2361	2115	1885
	energy, ft-lb:	3734	3054	2476	1987	1577
	arc, inches:		+1.8	0	-8.0	-23.9

.338 Federal

Cartridge Bullet	Range, yards:	0	100	200	300	400
Federal 180 AccuBond	velocity, fps:	2830	2590	2350	2130	1930
	energy, ft-lb:	3200	2670	2215	1820	1480
	arc, inches:	-1.5	+1.8	0	-8.2	-23.9
Federal 185 Barnes TSX	velocity, fps:	2750	2500	2260	2030	1820
	energy, ft-lb:	3105	2560	2090	1695	1355
	arc, inches:	-1.5	+2.0	0	-8.9	-26.2
Federal 200 Tr. Bonded T	velocity, fps:	2630	2430	2240	2060	1890
	energy, ft-lb:	3070	2625	2230	1885	1580
	arc, inches:	-1.5	+2.2	0	-9.2	-26.3
Federal 210 Partition	velocity, fps:	2630	2410	2200	2010	1820
	energy, ft-lb:	3225	2710	2265	1880	1545
	arc, inches:	-1.5	+2.3	0	-9.4	-27.3

Centerfire Rifle Ballistics

.338 MARLIN EXPRESS TO .340 WEATHERBY MAGNUM

.338 Marlin Express

CARTRIDGE BULLET	RANGE, YARDS:	0	100	200	300	400
Hornady 200 FTX	velocity, fps:	2565	2365	2174	1992	`1820
	energy, ft-lb:	2922	2484	2099	1762	1471
	arc, inches:	-1.5	+3.0	+1.2	-7.9	-25.9

.338-06

CARTRIDGE BULLET	RANGE, YARDS:	0	100	200	300	400
A-Square 200 Nos. Bal. Tip	velocity, fps:	2750	2553	2364	2184	2011
	energy, ft-lb:	3358	2894	2482	2118	1796
	arc, inches:		+1.9	0	-8.2	-23.6
A-Square 250 SP boat-tail	velocity, fps:	2500	2374	2252	2134	2019
	energy, ft-lb:	3496	3129	2816	2528	2263
	arc, inches:		+2.4	0	-9.3	-26.0
A-Square 250 Dead Tough	velocity, fps:	2500	2222	1963	1724	1507
	energy, ft-lb:	3496	2742	2139	1649	1261
	arc, inches:		+2.8	0	-11.9	-35.5
Nosler 180 AB	velocity, fps:	2950	2698	2460	2234	2020
	energy, ft-lb:	3477	2909	2418	1994	1631
	arc, inches:	-1.5	+1.6	0	-7.4	-21.8
Nosler 225 AB	velocity, fps:	2600	2441	2287	2139	1997
	energy, ft-lb:	3376	2976	2614	2286	1992
	arc, inches:	-1.5	+2.2	0	-8.8	-25.3
Wby. 210 Nosler Part.	velocity, fps:	2750	2526	2312	2109	1916
	energy, ft-lb:	3527	2975	2403	2074	1712
	arc, inches:		+4.8	+5.7	0	-13.5

.338 Ruger Compact Magnum

CARTRIDGE BULLET	RANGE, YARDS:	0	100	200	300	400
Hornady 185 GMX	velocity, fps:	2980	2755	2542	2338	2143
	energy, ft-lb:	3647	3118	2653	2242	1887
	arc, inches:	-1.5	+1.5	0	-6.9	-20.3
Hornady 200 SST	velocity, fps:	2950	2744	2547	2358	2177
	energy, ft-lb:	3846	3342	2879	2468	2104
	arc, inches:	-1.5	+1.6	0	-6.9	-20.1
Hornady 225 SST	velocity, fps:	2750	2575	2407	2245	2089
	energy, ft-lb:	3778	3313	2894	2518	2180
	arc, inches:	-1.5	+1.9	0	-7.9	-22.7

.338 Winchester Magnum

CARTRIDGE BULLET	RANGE, YARDS:	0	100	200	300	400
A-Square 250 SP boat-tail	velocity, fps:	2700	2568	2439	2314	2193
	energy, ft-lb:	4046	3659	3302	2972	2669
	arc, inches:		+4.4	+5.2	0	-11.7
A-Square 250 Triad	velocity, fps:	2700	2407	2133	1877	1653
	energy, ft-lb:	4046	3216	2526	1956	1516
	arc, inches:		+2.3	0	-9.8	-29.8
Federal 200 Trophy Bonded Tip	velocity, fps:	2930	2720	2520	2320	2140
	energy, ft-lb:	3810	3280	2810	2395	2025
	arc, inches:		+1.6	0	-7.1	-20.7
Federal 210 Nosler Partition	velocity, fps:	2830	2600	2390	2180	1980
	energy, ft-lb:	3735	3160	2655	2215	1835
	arc, inches:		+1.8	0	-8.0	-23.3
Federal 225 Sierra Pro-Hunt.	velocity, fps:	2780	2570	2360	2170	1980
	energy, ft-lb:	3860	3290	2780	2340	1960
	arc, inches:		+1.9	0	-8.2	-23.7
Federal 225 Trophy Bonded	velocity, fps:	2800	2560	2330	2110	1900
	energy, ft-lb:	3915	3265	2700	2220	1800
	arc, inches:		+1.9	0	-8.4	-24.5
Federal 225 Tr. Bonded HE	velocity, fps:	2940	2690	2450	2230	2010
	energy, ft-lb:	4320	3610	3000	2475	2025
	arc, inches:		+1.7	0	-7.5	-22.0
Federal 225 Barnes XLC	velocity, fps:	2800	2610	2430	2260	2090
	energy, ft-lb:	3915	3405	2950	2545	2190
	arc, inches:		+1.8	0	-7.7	-22.2
Federal 250 Nosler Partition	velocity, fps:	2660	2470	2300	2120	1960
	energy, ft-lb:	3925	3395	2925	2505	2130.
	arc, inches:		+2.1	0	-8.8	-25.1
Federal 250 Nosler Part HE	velocity, fps:	2800	2610	2420	2250	2080
	energy, ft-lb:	4350	3775	3260	2805	2395
	arc, inches:		+1.8	0	-7.8	-22.5
Hornady 185 GMX Superformance	velocity, fps:	3080	2851	2633	2426	2228
	energy, ft-lb:	3897	3338	2848	2417	2038
	arc, inches:		+1.4	0	-6.4	-18.8
Hornady 200 SST Superformance	velocity, fps:	3030	2820	2620	2429	2246
	energy, ft-lb:	4077	3532	3049	2621	2240
	arc, inches:		+1.4	0	-6.5	-18.9
Hornady 225 Soft Point HM	velocity, fps:	2920	2678	2449	2232	2027
	energy, ft-lb:	4259	3583	2996	2489	2053
	arc, inches:		+1.8	0	-7.6	-22.0
Norma 225 TXP Swift A-Fr.	velocity, fps:	2740	2507	2286	2075	
	energy, ft-lb:	3752	3141	2611	2153	
	arc, inches:		+2.0	0	-8.7	
Norma 230 Oryx	velocity, fps:	2756	2514	2284	2066	
	energy, ft-lb:	3880	3228	2665	2181	
	arc, inches:		+2.0	0	-8.7	
Norma 250 Nosler Partition	velocity, fps:	2657	2470	2290	2118	
	energy, ft-lb:	3920	3387	2912	2490	
	arc, inches:		+2.1	0	-8.7	
PMC 225 Barnes X	velocity, fps:	2780	2619	2464	2313	2168
	energy, ft-lb:	3860	3426	3032	2673	2348.
	arc, inches:		+1.8	0	-7.6	-21.6
Rem. 200 Nosler Bal. Tip	velocity, fps:	2950	2724	2509	2303	2108
	energy, ft-lb:	3866	3295	2795	2357	1973
	arc, inches:		+1.6	0	-7.1	-20.8
Rem. 210 Nosler Partition	velocity, fps:	2830	2602	2385	2179	1983
	energy, ft-lb:	3734	3157	2653	2214	1834
	arc, inches:		+1.8	0	-7.9	-23.2
Rem. 225 PSP Core-Lokt	velocity, fps:	2780	2572	2374	2184	2003
	energy, ft-lb:	3860	3305	2815	2383	2004
	arc, inches:		+1.9	0	-8.1	-23.4
Rem. 225 PSP C-L Ultra	velocity, fps:	2780	2582	2392	2210	2036
	energy, ft-lb:	3860	3329	2858	2440	2071
	arc, inches:		+1.9	0	-7.9	-23.0
Rem. 225 Swift A-Frame	velocity, fps:	2785	2517	2266	2029	1808
	energy, ft-lb:	3871	3165	2565	2057	1633
	arc, inches:		+2.0	0	-8.8	-25.2
Rem. 250 PSP Core-Lokt	velocity, fps:	2660	2456	2261	2075	1898
	energy, ft-lb:	3927	3348	2837	2389	1999
	arc, inches:		+2.1	0	-8.9	-26.0
Speer 250 Grand Slam	velocity, fps:	2645	2442	2247	2062	
	energy, ft-lb:	3883	3309	2803	2360	
	arc, inches:		+2.2	0	-9.1	-26.2
Win. 200 Power-Point	velocity, fps:	2960	2658	2375	2110	1862
	energy, ft-lb:	3890	3137	2505	1977	1539
	arc, inches:		+2.0	0	-8.2	-24.3
Win. 200 Ballistic Silvertip	velocity, fps:	2950	2724	2509	2303	2108
	energy, ft-lb:	3864	3294	2794	2355	1972
	arc, inches:		+1.6	0	-7.1	-20.8
Win. 225 AccuBond	velocity, fps:	2800	2634	2474	2319	2170
	energy, ft-lb:	3918	3467	3058	2688	2353
	arc, inches:		+1.8	0	-7.4	-21.3
Win. 230 Fail Safe	velocity, fps:	2780	2573	2375	2186	2005
	energy, ft-lb:	3948	3382	2881	2441	2054
	arc, inches:		+1.9	0	-8.1	-23.4
Win. 250 Partition Gold	velocity, fps:	2650	2467	2291	2122	1960
	energy, ft-lb:	3899	3378	2914	2520	2134
	arc, inches:		+2.1	0	-8.7	-25.2

.340 Weatherby Magnum

CARTRIDGE BULLET	RANGE, YARDS:	0	100	200	300	400
A-Square 250 SP boat-tail	velocity, fps:	2820	2684	2552	2424	2299
	energy, ft-lb:	4414	3999	3615	3261	2935
	arc, inches:		+4.0	+4.6	0	-10.6
A-Square 250 Triad	velocity, fps:	2820	2520	2238	1976	1741
	energy, ft-lb:	4414	3524	2781	2166	1683
	arc, inches:		+2.0	0	-9.0	-26.8
Federal 225 Trophy Bonded	velocity, fps:	3100	2840	2600	2370	2150
	energy, ft-lb:	4800	4035	3375	2800	2310
	arc, inches:		+1.4	0	-6.5	-19.4

Centerfire Rifle Ballistics

.340 WEATHERBY MAGNUM TO .35 REMINGTON

CARTRIDGE BULLET	RANGE, YARDS:	0	100	200	300	400
Wby. 200 Pointed Expanding	velocity, fps:	3221	2946	2688	2444	2213
	energy, ft-lb:	4607	3854	3208	2652	2174
	arc, inches:		+3.3	+4.0	0	-9.9
Wby. 200 Nosler Bal. Tip	velocity, fps:	3221	2980	2753	2536	2329
	energy, ft-lb:	4607	3944	3364	2856	2409
	arc, inches:		+3.1	+3.9	0	-9.2
Wby. 210 Nosler Partition	velocity, fps:	3211	2963	2728	2505	2293
	energy, ft-lb:	4807	4093	3470	2927	2452
	arc, inches:		+3.2	+3.9	0	-9.5
Wby. 225 Pointed Expanding	velocity, fps:	3066	2824	2595	2377	2170
	energy, ft-lb:	4696	3984	3364	2822	2352
	arc, inches:		+3.6	+4.4	0	-10.7
Wby. 225 Barnes X	velocity, fps:	3001	2804	2615	2434	2260
	energy, ft-lb:	4499	3927	3416	2959	2551
	arc, inches:		+3.6	+4.3	0	-10.3
Wby. 250 Pointed Expanding	velocity, fps:	2963	2745	2537	2338	2149
	energy, ft-lb:	4873	4182	3572	3035	2563
	arc, inches:		+3.9	+4.6	0	-11.1
Wby. 250 Nosler Partition	velocity, fps:	2941	2743	2553	2371	2197
	energy, ft-lb:	4801	4176	3618	3120	2678
	arc, inches:		+3.9	+4.6	0	-10.9

.330 Dakota

CARTRIDGE BULLET	RANGE, YARDS:	0	100	200	300	400
Dakota 200 Barnes X	velocity, fps:	3200	2971	2754	2548	2350
	energy, ft-lb:	4547	3920	3369	2882	2452
	arc, inches:		+2.1	+1.8	-3.1	-13.4
Dakota 250 Barnes X	velocity, fps:	2900	2719	2545	2378	2217
	energy, ft-lb:	4668	4103	3595	3138	2727
	arc, inches:		+2.3	+1.3	-5.0	-17.5

.338 Remington Ultra Magnum

CARTRIDGE BULLET	RANGE, YARDS:	0	100	200	300	400
Federal 210 Nosler Partition	velocity, fps:	3025	2800	2585	2385	2190
	energy, ft-lb:	4270	3655	3120	2645	2230
	arc, inches:		+1.5	0	-6.7	-19.5
Federal 250 Trophy Bonded	velocity, fps:	2860	2630	2420	2210	2020
	energy, ft-lb:	4540	3850	3245	2715	2260.
	arc, inches:		+0.8	0	-7.7	-22.6
Rem. 250 Swift A-Frame	velocity, fps:	2860	2645	2440	2244	2057
	energy, ft-lb:	4540	3882	3303	2794	2347
	arc, inches:		+1.7	0	-7.6	-22.1
Rem. 250 PSP Core-Lokt	velocity, fps:	2860	2647	2443	2249	2064
	energy, ft-lb:	4540	3888	3314	2807	2363
	arc, inches:		+1.7	0	-7.6	-22.0

.338 Norma Magnum

CARTRIDGE BULLET	RANGE, YARDS:	0	100	200	300	400
Black Hills 300 MatchKing	velocity, fps:	2725				
	energy, ft-lb:	4946				
	arc, inches					

.338 Lapua

CARTRIDGE BULLET	RANGE, YARDS:	0	100	200	300	400
Black Hills 250 Sierra MKing	velocity, fps:	2950				
	energy, ft-lb:	4831				
	arc, inches:					
Black Hills 300 Sierra MKing	velocity, fps:	2800				
	energy, ft-lb:	5223				
	arc, inches:					
Hornady 250 BTHP Match	velocity, fps:	2900	2761	2626	2495	2368
	energy, ft-lb:	4668	4230	3827	3455	3112
	arc, inches:		+1.5	0	-6.6	-18.8
Hornady 285 BTHP	velocity, fps:	2745	2616	2491	2369	2251
	energy, ft-lb:	4768	4331	3926	3552	3206
	arc, inches:	-1.5	+1.8	0	-7.4	-21.0

CARTRIDGE BULLET	RANGE, YARDS:	0	100	200	300	600
Lapua 250 Scenar	velocity, fps:	2970	2823	2680	2539	2141
	energy, ft-lb:	4896	4424	3985	3579	2545
	arc, inches:	-1.5	+3.0	+4.0	0	-47.0
Lapua 300 Scenar	velocity, fps:	2723	2600	2482	2367	2042
	energy, ft-lb:	4938	4504	4102	3731	2778
	arc, inches:	-1.5	+4.0	+5.0	0	-54.0

CARTRIDGE BULLET	RANGE, YARDS:	0	100	200	300	400
Nosler 225 AB	velocity, fps:	3000	2826	2659	2498	2342
	energy, ft-lb:	4495	3990	3532	3117	2741
	arc, inches:	-1.5	+1.4	0	-6.3	-18.3

.338-378 Weatherby Magnum

CARTRIDGE BULLET	RANGE, YARDS:	0	100	200	300	400
Wby. 200 Nosler Bal. Tip	velocity, fps:	3350	3102	2868	2646	2434
	energy, ft-lb:	4983	4273	3652	3109	2631
	arc, inches:	0	+2.8	+3.5	0	-8.4
Wby. 225 Barnes X	velocity, fps:	3180	2974	2778	2591	2410.
	energy, ft-lb:	5052	4420	3856	3353	2902
	arc, inches:	0	+3.1	+3.8	0	-8.9
Wby. 250 Nosler Partition	velocity, fps:	3060	2856	2662	2475	2297
	energy, ft-lb:	5197	4528	3933	3401	2927
	arc, inches:	0	+3.5	+4.2	0	-9.8

8.59 (.338) Titan

CARTRIDGE BULLET	RANGE, YARDS:	0	100	200	300	400
Lazzeroni 200 Nos. Bal. Tip	velocity, fps:	3430	3211	3002	2803	2613
	energy, ft-lb:	5226	4579	4004	3491	3033
	arc, inches:		+2.5	+3.2	0	-7.6
Lazzeroni 225 Nos. Partition	velocity, fps:	3235	3031	2836	2650	2471
	energy, ft-lb:	5229	4591	4021	3510	3052
	arc, inches:		+3.0	+3.6	0	-8.6
Lazzeroni 250 Swift A-Fr.	velocity, fps:	3100	2908	2725	2549	2379
	energy, ft-lb:	5336	4697	4123	3607	3143
	arc, inches:		+3.3	+4.0	0	-9.3

.338 A-Square

CARTRIDGE BULLET	RANGE, YARDS:	0	100	200	300	400
A-Square 200 Nos. Bal. Tip	velocity, fps:	3500	3266	3045	2835	2634
	energy, ft-lb:	5440	4737	4117	3568	3081
	arc, inches:		+2.4	+3.1	0	-7.5
A-Square 250 SP boat-tail	velocity, fps:	3120	2974	2834	2697	2565.
	energy, ft-lb:	5403	4911	4457	4038	3652
	arc, inches:		+3.1	+3.7	0	-8.5
A-Square 250 Triad	velocity, fps:	3120	2799	2500	2220	1958
	energy, ft-lb:	5403	4348	3469	2736	2128
	arc, inches:		+1.5	0	-7.1	-20.4.

.338 Excaliber

CARTRIDGE BULLET	RANGE, YARDS:	0	100	200	300	400
A-Square 200 Nos. Bal. Tip	velocity, fps:	3600	3361	3134	2920	2715
	energy, ft-lb:	5755	5015	4363	3785	3274
	arc, inches:		+2.2	+2.9	0	-6.7
A-Square 250 SP boat-tail	velocity, fps:	3250	3101	2958	2684	2553
	energy, ft-lb:	5863	5339	4855	4410	3998
	arc, inches:		+2.7	+3.4	0	-7.8
A-Square 250 Triad	velocity, fps:	3250	2922	2618	2333	2066
	energy, ft-lb:	5863	4740	3804	3021	2370
	arc, inches:		+1.3	0	-6.4	-19.2

.348 Winchester

CARTRIDGE BULLET	RANGE, YARDS:	0	100	200	300	400
Win. 200 Silvertip	velocity, fps:	2520	2215	1931	1672	1443.
	energy, ft-lb:	2820	2178	1656	1241	925
	arc, inches:		0	-6.2	-21.9	

.357 Magnum

CARTRIDGE BULLET	RANGE, YARDS:	0	100	200	300	400
Federal 180 Hi-Shok HP Hollow Point	velocity, fps:	1550	1160	980	860	770
	energy, ft-lb:	960	535	385	295	235
	arc, inches:		0	-22.8	-77.9	-173.8
Win. 158 Jacketed SP	velocity, fps:	1830	1427	1138	980	883
	energy, ft-lb:	1175	715	454	337	274
	arc, inches:		0	-16.2	-57.0	-128.3

.35 Remington

CARTRIDGE BULLET	RANGE, YARDS:	0	100	200	300	400
Federal 200 Hi-Shok	velocity, fps:	2080	1700	1380	1140	1000
	energy, ft-lb:	1920	1280	840	575	445
	arc, inches:		0	-10.7	-39.3	

Centerfire Rifle Ballistics

.35 REMINGTON TO 9.3X74 R

CARTRIDGE BULLET	RANGE, YARDS:	0	100	200	300	400
Hornady 200 Evolution	velocity, fps:	2225	1963	1721	1503	
	energy, ft-lb:	2198	1711	1315	1003	
	arc, inches:		+3.0	-1.3	-17.5	
Rem. 150 PSP Core-Lokt	velocity, fps:	2300	1874	1506	1218	1039
	energy, ft-lb:	1762	1169	755	494	359
	arc, inches:		0	-8.6	-32.6	
Rem. 200 SP Core-Lokt	velocity, fps:	2080	1698	1376	1140	1001
	energy, ft-lb:	1921	1280	841	577	445
	arc, inches:		0	-10.7	-40.1	
Win. 200 Power-Point	velocity, fps:	2020	1646	1335	1114	985
	energy, ft-lb:	1812	1203	791	551	431
	arc, inches:		0	-12.1	-43.9	

.356 Winchester

CARTRIDGE BULLET	RANGE, YARDS:	0	100	200	300	400
Win. 200 Power-Point	velocity, fps:	2460	2114	1797	1517	1284
	energy, ft-lb:	2688	1985	1434	1022	732
	arc, inches:		+1.6	-3.8	-20.1	-51.2

.358 Winchester

CARTRIDGE BULLET	RANGE, YARDS:	0	100	200	300	400
Hornady 200 SP	velocity, fps:	2475	2180	1906	1655	1434
	energy, ft-lb:	2720	2110	1612	1217	913
	arc, inches:	-1.5	+2.9	0	-12.6	-37.9
Win. 200 Silvertip	velocity, fps:	2490	2171	1876	1610	1379
	energy, ft-lb:	2753	2093	1563	1151	844
	arc, inches:		+1.5	-3.6	-18.6	-47.2

.35 Whelen

CARTRIDGE BULLET	RANGE, YARDS:	0	100	200	300	400
Federal 225 Trophy Bonded	velocity, fps:	2600	2400	2200	2020	1840
	energy, ft-lb:	3375	2865	2520	2030	1690.
	arc, inches:		+2.3	0	-9.4	-27.3
Hornady 200 SP	velocity, fps:	2910	2585	2283	2001	1742
	energy, ft-lb:	3760	2968	2314	1778	1347
	arc, inches:	-1.5	+1.9	0	-8.6	-25.9
Rem. 200 Pointed Soft Point	velocity, fps:	2675	2378	2100	1842	1606
	energy, ft-lb:	3177	2510	1958	1506	1145
	arc, inches:		+2.3	0	-10.3	-30.8
Rem. 250 Pointed Soft Point	velocity, fps:	2400	2197	2005	1823	1652
	energy, ft-lb:	3197	2680	2230	1844	1515
	arc, inches:		+1.3	-3.2	-16.6	-40.0

.350 Remington Magnum

CARTRIDGE BULLET	RANGE, YARDS:	0	100	200	300	400
Nosler 225 PT	velocity, fps:	2550	2349	2158	1976	1804
	energy, ft-lb:	3248	2758	2327	1951	1626
	arc, inches:	-1.5	+2.4	0	-9.9	-28.7

.358 Norma Magnum

CARTRIDGE BULLET	RANGE, YARDS:	0	100	200	300	400
A-Square 275 Triad	velocity, fps:	2700	2394	2108	1842	1653
	energy, ft-lb:	4451	3498	2713	2072	1668
	arc, inches:		+2.3	0	-10.1	-29.8
Norma 250 TXP Swift A-Fr.	velocity, fps:	2723	2467	2225	1996	
	energy, ft-lb:	4117	3379	2748	2213	
	arc, inches:		+2.1	0	-9.1	
Norma 250 Woodleigh	velocity, fps:	2799	2442	2112	1810	
	energy, ft-lb:	4350	3312	2478	1819	
	arc, inches:		+2.2	0	-10.0	
Norma 250 Oryx	velocity, fps:	2756	2493	2245	2011	
	energy, ft-lb:	4217	3451	2798	2245	
	arc, inches:		+2.1	0	-9.0	

.358 STA

CARTRIDGE BULLET	RANGE, YARDS:	0	100	200	300	400
A-Square 275 Triad	velocity, fps:	2850	2562	2292	2039	1764
	energy, ft-lb:	4959	4009	3208	2539	1899.
	arc, inches:		+1.9	0	-8.6	-26.1

9.3x57

CARTRIDGE BULLET	RANGE, YARDS:	0	100	200	300	400
Norma 232 Vulkan	velocity, fps:	2329	2031	1757	1512	
	energy, ft-lb:	2795	2126	1591	1178	
	arc, inches:		+3.5	0	-14.9	
Norma 232 Oryx	velocity, fps:	2362	2058	1778	1528	
	energy, ft-lb:	2875	2182	1630	1203	
	arc, inches:		+3.4	0	-14.5	
Norma 285 Oryx	velocity, fps:	2067	1859	1666	1490	
	energy, ft-lb:	2704	2188	1756	1404	
	arc, inches:		+4.3	0	-16.8	
Norma 286 Alaska	velocity, fps:	2067	1857	1662	1484	
	energy, ft-lb:	2714	2190	1754	1399	
	arc, inches:		+4.3	0	-17.0	

9.3x62

CARTRIDGE BULLET	RANGE, YARDS:	0	100	200	300	400
Federal 286 Swift A-Frame	velocity, fps:	2360	2150	1950	1760	1580
	energy, ft-lb:	3535	2930	2405	1960	1590
	arc, inches:		+2.9	0	-11.6	-31.0
Federal 286 TSX	velocity, fps:	2360	2160	1970	1790	
	energy, ft-lb:	3535	2965	2465	2035	
	arc, inches:	-1.5	+3.0	0	-12.0	
Federal 286 Woodleigh Hydro	velocity, fps:	2360	2050	1760	1510	
	energy, ft-lb:	3535	2665	1975	1445	
	arc, inches::	-1.5	+3.4	0	-14.7	
Hornady 286 SP-HP	velocity, fps:	2350	2155	1961	1778	
	energy, ft-lb:	3537	2949	2442	2008	
	arc, inches:	-1.5	+3.0	0	-12.1	
Norma 232 Oryx	velocity, fps:	2625	2294	1988	1708	
	energy, ft-lb:	3535	2700	2028	1497	
	arc, inches:	-1.5	+2.5	0	-11.4	
Norma 250 A-Frame	velocity, fps:	2625	2322	2039	1778	
	energy, ft-lb:	3826	2993	2309	1755	
	arc, inches:	-1.5	+2.5	0	-10.9	
Norma 286 Plastic Point	velocity, fps:	2362	2141	1931	1736	
	energy, ft-lb:	3544	2911	2370	1914	
	arc, inches:	-1.5	+3.1	0	-12.4	
Nosler 250 AccuBond	velocity, fps:	2550	2376	2208	2048	1894
	energy, ft-lb:	3609	3133	2707	2328	1992
	arc, inches:	-1.5	+2.3	0	-9.5	-27.2
Nosler 286 Partition	velocity, fps:	2350	2179	2015	1859	1711
	energy, ft-lb:	3506	3014	2578	2194	1859
	arc, inches:	-1.5	+2.9	0	-11.5	-33.1

9.3x64

CARTRIDGE BULLET	RANGE, YARDS:	0	100	200	300	400
A-Square 286 Triad	velocity, fps:	2700	2391	2103	1835	1602
	energy, ft-lb:	4629	3630	2808	2139	1631
	arc, inches:		+2.3	0	-10.1	-30.8

.370 Sako

CARTRIDGE BULLET	RANGE, YARDS:	0	100	200	300	400
Federal 286 TSX	velocity, fps:	2550	2370	2190	2020	1860
	energy, ft-lb:	4130	3555	3045	2595	2195
	arc, inches:	-1.5	+2.4	0	-9.6	-27.5

370 Sako Magnum

CARTRIDGE BULLET	RANGE, YARDS:	0	100	200	300	400
Federal 286 Swift A-Frame	velocity, fps:	2550	2330	2120	1920	1730
	energy, ft-lb:	4130	3440	2845	2330	1900
	arc, inches:		+2.5	0	-10.1	-30.0
Federal 286 TSX	velocity, fps:	2550	2370	2190	2020	1860
	energy, ft-lb:	4130	3555	3045	2595	2195
	arc, inches:		+2.4	0	-9.5	-27.5
Federal 286 Woodleigh Hydro Solid	velocity, fps:	2550	2230	1920	1650	1410
	energy, ft-lb:	4130	3145	2350	1730	1265
	arc, inches:		+2.8	0	-12.4	-37.5

9.3x74 R

CARTRIDGE BULLET	RANGE, YARDS:	0	100	200	300	400
A-Square 286 Triad	velocity, fps:	2360	2089	1844	1623	
	energy, ft-lb:	3538	2771	2157	1670	
	arc, inches:		+3.6	0	-14.0	
Federal 286 Swift A-Frame	velocity, fps:	2360	2150	1950	1760	1580
	energy, ft-lb:	3535	2930	2405	1960	1590
	arc, inches:		+2.9	0	-11.6	-31.0
Federal 286 TSX	velocity, fps:	2360	2160	1970	1790	1630
	energy, ft-lb:	3535	2965	2465	2035	1675
	arc, inches:		+2.9	0	-11.1	-29.9
Federal 286 Woodleigh Hydro Solid	velocity, fps:	2360	2050	1760	1510	1300
	energy, ft-lb:	3535	2665	1975	1445	1065
	arc, inches:		+3.4	0	-14.7	-45.0
Hornady 286	velocity, fps	2360	2136	1924	1727	1545
	energy, ft-lb	3536	2896	2351	1893	1516
	arc, inches	-1.5	0	-6.1	-21.7	-49.0
Norma 232 Vulkan	velocity, fps:	2625	2327	2049	1792	
	energy, ft-lb:	3551	2791	2164	1655	
	arc, inches:		+2.5	0	-10.8	
Norma 232 Oryx	velocity, fps:	2526	2191	1883	1605	
	energy, ft-lb:	3274	2463	1819	1322	
	arc, inches:		+2.9	0	-12.8	

CARTRIDGE BULLET	RANGE, YARDS:	0	100	200	300	400
Norma 285 Oryx	velocity, fps:	2362	2114	1881	1667	
	energy, ft-lb:	3532	2829	2241	1758	
	arc, inches:		+3.1	0	-13.0	
Norma 286 Alaska	velocity, fps:	2362	2135	1920	1720	
	energy, ft-lb:	3544	2894	2342	1879	
	arc, inches:		+3.1	0	-12.5	
Norma 286 Plastic Point	velocity, fps:	2362	2135	1920	1720	
	energy, ft-lb:	3544	2894	2342	1879	
	arc, inches:		+3.1	0	-12.5	

.375 Winchester

CARTRIDGE BULLET	RANGE, YARDS:	0	100	200	300	400
Win. 200 Power-Point	velocity, fps:	2200	1841	1526	1268	1089
	energy, ft-lb:	2150	1506	1034	714	
	arc, inches:		0	-9.5	-33.8	

.375 Flanged

CARTRIDGE BULLET	RANGE, YARDS:	0	100	200	300	400
Nosler 300 PT	velocity, fps:	2400	2191	1993	1806	1632
	energy, ft-lb:	3836	3198	2646	2173	1775
	arc, inches:	-1.5	+2.9	0	-11.7	-34.0

.375 H&H Magnum

CARTRIDGE BULLET	RANGE, YARDS:	0	100	200	300	400
A-Square 300 SP boat-tail	velocity, fps:	2550	2415	2284	2157	2034
	energy, ft-lb:	4331	3884	3474	3098	2755
	arc, inches:		+5.2	+6.0	0	-13.3
A-Square 300 Triad	velocity, fps:	2550	2251	1973	1717	1496
	energy, ft-lb:	4331	3375	2592	1964	1491
	arc, inches:		+2.7	0	-11.7	-35.1
Federal 250 Trophy Bonded	velocity, fps:	2670	2360	2080	1820	1580
	energy, ft-lb:	3955	3100	2400	1830	1380
	arc, inches:		+2.4	0	-10.4	-31.7
Federal 270 Hi-Shok	velocity, fps:	2690	2420	2170	1920	1700
	energy, ft-lb:	4340	3510	2810	2220	1740
	arc, inches:		+2.4	0	-10.9	-33.3
Federal 300 Hi-Shok	velocity, fps:	2530	2270	2020	1790	1580
	energy, ft-lb:	4265	3425	2720	2135	1665
	arc, inches:		+2.6	0	-11.2	-33.3
Federal 300 Nosler Partition	velocity, fps:	2530	2320	2120	1930	1750
	energy, ft-lb:	4265	3585	2995	2475	2040
	arc, inches:		+2.5	0	-10.3	-29.9
Federal 300 Trophy Bonded	velocity, fps:	2530	2280	2040	1810	1610
	energy, ft-lb:	4265	3450	2765	2190	1725
	arc, inches:		+2.6	0	-10.9	-32.8
Federal 300 Tr. Bonded HE	velocity, fps:	2700	2440	2190	1960	1740
	energy, ft-lb:	4855	3960	3195	2550	2020
	arc, inches:		+2.2	0	-9.4	-28.0
Federal 300 Trophy Bonded Sledgehammer Solid	velocity, fps:	2530	2160	1820	1520	1280.
	energy, ft-lb:	4265	3105	2210	1550	1090
	arc, inches, s:		0	-6.0	-22.7	-54.6
Federal 300 TSX	velocity, fps:	2470	2240	2010	1800	1610
	energy, ft-lb:	4065	3325	2700	2170	1735
	arc, inches:		+2.7	0	-11.3	-33.6
Federal 300 Woodleigh Hydro Solid	velocity, fps:	2500	2180	1880	1610	1380
	energy, ft-lb:	4165	3160	2355	1735	1270
	arc, inches:		+2.9	0	-20.1	-46.3
Hornady 250 GMX Superformance	velocity, fps:	2890	2675	2471	2275	2088
	energy, ft-lb:	4636	3973	3388	2873	2421
	arc, inches:		+1.7	0	-7.4	-21.5
Hornady 270 SP HM	velocity, fps:	2870	2620	2385	2162	1957
	energy, ft-lb:	4937	4116	3408	2802	2296
	arc, inches:		+2.2	0	-8.4	-23.9
Hornady 300 FMJ RN HM	velocity, fps:	2705	2376	2072	1804	1560
	energy, ft-lb:	4873	3760	2861	2167	1621
	arc, inches:		+2.7	0	-10.8	-32.1
Norma 300 Soft Point	velocity, fps:	2549	2211	1900	1619	
	energy, ft-lb:	4329	3258	2406	1747	
	arc, inches:		+2.8	0	-12.6	
Norma 300 TXP Swift A-Fr.	velocity, fps:	2559	2296	2049	1818	
	energy, ft-lb:	4363	3513	2798	2203	
	arc, inches:		+2.6	0	-10.9	
Norma 300 Oryx	velocity, fps:	2559	2292	2041	1807	
	energy, ft-lb:	4363	3500	2775	2176	
	arc, inches:		+2.6	0	-11.0	
Norma 300 Barnes Solid	velocity, fps:	2493	2061	1677	1356	
	energy, ft-lb:	4141	2829	1873	1234	
	arc, inches:		+3.4	0	-16.0	
PMC 270 PSP	velocity, fps:					
	energy, ft-lb:					
	arc, inches:					
PMC 270 Barnes X	velocity, fps:	2690	2528	2372	2221	2076
	energy, ft-lb:	4337	3831	3371	2957	2582
	arc, inches:		+2.0	0	-8.2	-23.4
PMC 300 Barnes X	velocity, fps:	2530	2389	2252	2120	1993
	energy, ft-lb:	4263	3801	3378	2994	2644
	arc, inches:		+2.3	0	-9.2	-26.1
Rem. 270 Soft Point	velocity, fps:	2690	2420	2166	1928	1707
	energy, ft-lb:	4337	3510	2812	2228	1747
	arc, inches:		+2.2	0	-9.7	-28.7
Rem. 300 Swift A-Frame	velocity, fps:	2530	2245	1979	1733	1512
	energy, ft-lb:	4262	3357	2608	2001	1523
	arc, inches:		+2.7	0	-11.7	-35.0
Speer 285 Grand Slam	velocity, fps:	2610	2365	2134	1916	
	energy, ft-lb:	4310	3540	2883	2323	
	arc, inches:		+2.4	0	-9.9	
Speer 300 African GS Tungsten Solid	velocity, fps:	2609	2277	1970	1690	
	energy, ft-lb:	4534	3453	2585	1903	
	arc, inches:		+2.6	0	-11.7	-35.6
Win. 270 Fail Safe	velocity, fps:	2670	2447	2234	2033	1842
	energy, ft-lb:	4275	3590	2994	2478	2035
	arc, inches:		+2.2	0	-9.1	-28.7
Win. 300 Fail Safe	velocity, fps:	2530	2336	2151	1974	1806
	energy, ft-lb:	4265	3636	3082	2596	2173
	arc, inches:		+2.4	0	-10.0	-26.9

.375 Dakota

CARTRIDGE BULLET	RANGE, YARDS:	0	100	200	300	400
Dakota 270 Barnes X	velocity, fps:	2800	2617	2441	2272	2109
	energy, ft-lb:	4699	4104	3571	3093	2666
	arc, inches:		+2.3	+1.0	-6.1	-19.9
Dakota 300 Barnes X	velocity, fps:	2600	2316	2051	1804	1579
	energy, ft-lb:	4502	3573	2800	2167	1661
	arc, inches:		+2.4	-0.1	-11.0	-32.7

.375 Ruger

CARTRIDGE BULLET	RANGE, YARDS:	0	100	200	300	400
Hornady 250 GMX Superformance	velocity, fps:	2890	2675	2471	2275	2088
	energy, ft-lb:	4636	3973	3388	2873	2421
	arc, inches:		+1.7	0	-7.4	-21.5
Hornady 270 SP	velocity, fps:	2840	2600	2372	2156	1951
	energy, ft-lb:	4835	4052	3373	2786	2283
	arc, inches:	-1.5	+1.8	0	-8.0	-23.6
Hornady 300 Solid	velocity, fps	2660	2344	2050	1780	1536
	energy, ft-lb	4713	3660	2800	2110	1572
	arc, inches	-1.5	+2.4	0	-10.8	-32.6
Nosler 260 AB	velocity, fps:	2900	2703	2514	2333	2160
	energy, ft-lb:	4854	4217	3649	3143	2693
	arc, inches:	-1.5	+1.6	0	-7.1	-20.7

.375 Weatherby Magnum

CARTRIDGE BULLET	RANGE, YARDS:	0	100	200	300	400
A-Square 300 SP boat-tail	velocity, fps:	2700	2560	2425	2293	2166
	energy, ft-lb:	4856	4366	3916	3503	3125
	arc, inches:		+4.5	+5.2	0	-11.9
A-Square 300 Triad	velocity, fps:	2700	2391	2103	1835	1602
	energy, ft-lb:	4856	3808	2946	2243	1710
	arc, inches:		+2.3	0	-10.1	-30.8
Wby. 300 Nosler Part.	velocity, fps:	2800	2572	2366	2140	1963
	energy, ft-lb:	5224	4408	3696	3076	2541
	arc, inches:		+1.9	0	-8.2	-23.9

Centerfire Rifle Ballistics

.375 JRS TO .416 REMINGTON MAGNUM

.375 JRS

CARTRIDGE BULLET	RANGE, YARDS:	0	100	200	300	400
A-Square 300 SP boat-tail	velocity, fps:	2700	2560	2425	2293	2166.
	energy, ft-lb:	4856	4366	3916	3503	3125
	arc, inches:		+4.5	+5.2	0	-11.9
A-Square 300 Triad	velocity, fps:	2700	2391	2103	1835	1602
	energy, ft-lb:	4856	3808	2946	2243	1710
	arc, inches:		+2.3	0	-10.1	-30.8

.375 Remington Ultra Magnum

CARTRIDGE BULLET	RANGE, YARDS:	0	100	200	300	400
Nosler 260 AB	velocity, fps:	2950	2750	2560	2377	2202
	energy, ft-lb:	5023	4367	3783	3262	2799
	arc, inches:	-1.5	+1.6	0	-6.9	-19.9
Nosler 300 PT	velocity, fps:	2750	2524	2309	2105	1912
	energy, ft-lb:	5036	4244	3553	2953	2435
	arc, inches:	-1.5	+2.0	0	-8.5	-24.9
Rem. 270 Soft Point	velocity, fps:	2900	2558	2241	1947	1678
	energy, fps:	5041	3922	3010	2272	1689
	arc, inches:		+1.9	0	-9.2	-27.8
Rem. 300 Swift A-Frame	velocity, fps:	2760	2505	2263	2035	1822
	energy, fps:	5073	4178	3412	2759	2210
	arc, inches:		+2.0	0	-8.8	-26.1

.375 A-Square

CARTRIDGE BULLET	RANGE, YARDS:	0	100	200	300	400
A-Square 300 SP boat-tail	velocity, fps:	2920	2773	2631	2494	2360
	energy, ft-lb:	5679	5123	4611	4142	3710
	arc, inches:		+3.7	+4.4	0	-9.8
A-Square 300 Triad	velocity, fps:	2920	2596	2294	2012	1762
	energy, ft-lb:	5679	4488	3505	2698	2068
	arc, inches:		+1.8	0	-8.5	-25.5

.376 Steyr

CARTRIDGE BULLET	RANGE, YARDS:	0	100	200	300	400
Hornady 225 SP	velocity, fps:	2600	2331	2078	1842	1625
	energy, ft-lb:	3377	2714	2157	1694	1319
	arc, inches:		+2.5	0	-10.6	-31.4
Hornady 270 SP	velocity, fps:	2600	2372	2156	1951	1759
	energy, ft-lb:	4052	3373	2787	2283	1855
	arc, inches:		+2.3	0	-9.9	-28.9

.378 Weatherby Magnum

CARTRIDGE BULLET	RANGE, YARDS:	0	100	200	300	400
A-Square 300 SP boat-tail	velocity, fps:	2900	2754	2612	2475	2342
	energy, ft-lb:	5602	5051	4546	4081	3655
	arc, inches:		+3.8	+4.4	0	-10.0
A-Square 300 Triad	velocity, fps:	2900	2577	2276	1997	1747
	energy, ft-lb:	5602	4424	3452	2656	2034
	arc, inches:		+1.9	0	-8.7	-25.9
Wby. 270 Pointed Expanding	velocity, fps:	3180	2921	2677	2445	2225
	energy, ft-lb:	6062	5115	4295	3583	2968
	arc, inches:		+1.3	0	-6.1	-18.1
Wby. 270 Barnes X	velocity, fps:	3150	2954	2767	2587	2415
	energy, ft-lb:	5948	5232	4589	4013	3495
	arc, inches:		+1.2	0	-5.8	-16.7
Wby. 300 RN Expanding	velocity, fps:	2925	2558	2220	1908	1627.
	energy, ft-lb:	5699	4360	3283	2424	1764
	arc, inches:		+1.9	0	-9.0	-27.8
Wby. 300 FMJ	velocity, fps:	2925	2591	2280	1991	1725
	energy, ft-lb:	5699	4470	3461	2640	1983
	arc, inches:		+1.8	0	-8.6	-26.1

.38-40 Winchester

CARTRIDGE BULLET	RANGE, YARDS:	0	100	200	300	400
Win. 180 Soft Point	velocity, fps:	1160	999	901	827	
	energy, ft-lb:	538	399	324	273	
	arc, inches:		0	-23.4	-75.2	

.38-55 Winchester

CARTRIDGE BULLET	RANGE, YARDS:	0	100	200	300	400
Black Hills 255 FN Lead	velocity, fps:	1250				
	energy, ft-lb:	925				
	arc, inches:					
Win. 255 Soft Point	velocity, fps:	1320	1190	1091	1018	
	energy, ft-lb:	987	802	674	587	
	arc, inches:		0	-33.9	-110.6	

.41 Magnum

CARTRIDGE BULLET	RANGE, YARDS:	0	100	200	300	400
Win. 240 Platinum Tip	velocity, fps:	1830	1488	1220	1048	
	energy, ft-lb:	1784	1180	792	585	
	arc inches:		0	-15.0	-53.4	

.450/.400 Nitro Express

CARTRIDGE BULLET	RANGE, YARDS:	0	100	200	300	400
A-Square 400 Triad	velocity, fps:	2150	1910	1690	1490	
	energy, ft-lb:	4105	3241	2537	1972	
	arc, inches:		+4.4	0	-16.5	
Hornady 400 DGS, DGX	velocity, fps:	2050	1820	1609	1420	
	energy, ft-lb:	3732	2940	2298	1791	
	arc, inches:	-0.9	0	-9.7	-32.8	

.404 Jeffery

CARTRIDGE BULLET	RANGE, YARDS:	0	100	200	300	400
A-Square 400 Triad	velocity, fps:	2150	1901	1674	1468	1299
	energy, ft-lb:	4105	3211	2489	1915	1499
	arc, inches:		+4.1	0	-16.4	-49.1
Hornady 400 DGS, DGX	velocity, fps:	2300	2046	1809	1592	
	energy, ft-lb:	4698	3717	2906	2251	
	arc, inches:	-1.5	0	-6.9	-24.4	
Norma 450 Woodleigh SP	velocity, fps:	2150	2048	1949	1853	1760
	energy, ft-lb:	4620	4191	3795	3430	3096
	arc, inches:	-1.5	+.2	0	-2.5	-7.6

.405 Winchester

CARTRIDGE BULLET	RANGE, YARDS:	0	100	200	300	400
Hornady 300 Flatpoint	velocity, fps:	2200	1851	1545	1296	
	energy, ft-lb:	3224	2282	1589	1119	
	arc, inches:		0	-8.7	-31.9	
Hornady 300 SP Interlock	velocity, fps:	2200	1890	1610	1370	
	energy, ft-lb:	3224	2379	1727	1250	
	arc, inches:		0	-8.3	-30.2	

.416 Taylor

CARTRIDGE BULLET	RANGE, YARDS:	0	100	200	300	400
A-Square 400 Triad	velocity, fps:	2350	2093	1853	1634	1443
	energy, ft-lb:	4905	3892	3049	2371	1849
	arc, inches:		+3.2	0	-13.6	-39.8

.416 Hoffman

CARTRIDGE BULLET	RANGE, YARDS:	0	100	200	300	400
A-Square 400 Triad	velocity, fps:	2380	2122	1879	1658	1464
	energy, ft-lb:	5031	3998	3136	2440	1903
	arc, inches:		+3.1	0	-13.1	-38.7

.416 Remington Magnum

CARTRIDGE BULLET	RANGE, YARDS:	0	100	200	300	400
A-Square 400 Triad	velocity, fps:	2380	2122	1879	1658	1464
	energy, ft-lb:	5031	3998	3136	2440	1903
	arc, inches:		+3.1	0	-13.2	-38.7
Federal 400 Trophy Bonded	velocity, fps:	2400	2150	1920	1700	1500
Sledgehammer Solid	energy, ft-lb:	5115	4110	3260	2565	2005
	arc, inches:		0	-6.0	-21.6	-49.2
Federal 400 Trophy Bonded	velocity, fps:	2400	2180	1970	1770	1590
	energy, ft-lb:	5115	4215	3440	2785	2245
	arc, inches:		0	-5.8	-20.6	-46.9
Rem. 400 Swift A-Frame	velocity, fps:	2400	2175	1962	1763	1579
	energy, ft-lb:	5115	4201	3419	2760	2214
	arc, inches:		0	-5.9	-20.8	

Centerfire Rifle Ballistics

.416 RIGBY TO .45-70 GOVERNMENT

CARTRIDGE BULLET	RANGE, YARDS:	0	100	200	300	400
.416 RIGBY						
A-Square 400 Triad	velocity, fps:	2400	2140	1897	1673	1478
	energy, ft-lb:	5115	4069	3194	2487	1940
	arc, inches:		+3.0	0	-12.9	-38.0
Federal 400 Trophy Bonded	velocity, fps:	2370	2150	1940	1750	1570
	energy, ft-lb:	4990	4110	3350	2715	2190
	arc, inches:		0	-6.0	-21.3	-48.1
Federal 400 Trophy Bonded Sledgehammer Solid	velocity, fps:	2370	2120	1890	1660	1460
	energy, ft-lb:	4990	3975	3130	2440	1895
	arc, inches:		0	-6.3	-22.5	-51.5
Federal 410 Woodleigh Weldcore	velocity, fps:	2370	2110	1870	1640	1440
	energy, ft-lb:	5115	4050	3165	2455	1895
	arc, inches:		0	-7.4	-24.8	-55.0
Federal 410 Solid	velocity, fps:	2370	2110	2870	1640	1440
	energy, ft-lb:	5115	4050	3165	2455	1895
	arc, inches:		0	-7.4	-24.8	-55.0
Hornady 400 DGX, DGS	velocity, fps:	2415	2156	1915	1691	
	energy, ft-lb:	5180	4130	3256	2540	
	arc, inches:	-1.5	0	-6.0	-21.6	
Norma 400 TXP Swift A-Fr.	velocity, fps:	2350	2127	1917	1721	
	energy, ft-lb:	4906	4021	3266	2632	
	arc, inches:		+3.1	0	-12.5	
Norma 400 Barnes Solid	velocity, fps:	2297	1930	1604	1330	
	energy, ft-lb:	4687	3310	2284	1571	
	arc, inches:		+3.9	0	-17.7	
.416 RUGER						
Hornady 400 DGS, DGX	velocity, fps:	2400	2151	1917	1700	
	energy, ft-lb:	5116	4109	3264	2568	
	arc, inches:	-1.5	0	-6.0	-21.6	

.500/416 NITRO EXPRESS

CARTRIDGE BULLET	RANGE, YARDS:	0	50	100	150	200
Norma 450 Woodleigh SP	velocity, fps:	2100	1991	1886	1785	1688
	energy, ft-lb:	4408	3963	3556	3185	2849
	arc, inches:	-1.5	+.3	0	-2.7	-8.2

.416 DAKOTA

CARTRIDGE BULLET	RANGE, YARDS:	0	100	200	300	400
Dakota 400 Barnes X	velocity, fps:	2450	2294	2143	1998	1859
	energy, ft-lb:	5330	4671	4077	3544	3068
	arc, inches:		+2.5	-0.2	-10.5	-29.4
.416 WEATHERBY						
A-Square 400 Triad	velocity, fps:	2600	2328	2073	1834	1624
	energy, ft-lb:	6004	4813	3816	2986	2343
	arc, inches:		+2.5	0	-10.5	-31.6
Wby. 350 Barnes X	velocity, fps:	2850	2673	2503	2340	2182
	energy, ft-lb:	6312	5553	4870	4253	3700
	arc, inches:		+1.7	0	-7.2	-20.9
Wby. 400 Swift A-Fr.	velocity, fps:	2650	2426	2213	2011	1820
	energy, ft-lb:	6237	5227	4350	3592	2941
	arc, inches:		+2.2	0	-9.3	-27.1
Wby. 400 RN Expanding	velocity, fps:	2700	2417	2152	1903	1676
	energy, ft-lb:	6474	5189	4113	3216	2493
	arc, inches:		+2.3	0	-9.7	-29.3
Wby. 400 Monolithic Solid	velocity, fps:	2700	2411	2140	1887	1656
	energy, ft-lb:	6474	5162	4068	3161	2435
	arc, inches:		+2.3	0	-9.8	-29.7
10.57 (.416) METEOR						
Lazzeroni 400 Swift A-Fr.	velocity, fps:	2730	2532	2342	2161	1987
	energy, ft-lb:	6621	5695	4874	4147	3508
	arc, inches:		+1.9	0	-8.3	-24.0

CARTRIDGE BULLET	RANGE, YARDS:	0	100	200	300	400
.425 EXPRESS						
A-Square 400 Triad	velocity, fps:	2400	2136	1888	1662	1465
	energy, ft-lb:	5115	4052	3167	2454	1906
	arc, inches:		+3.0	0	-13.1	-38.3
.44-40 WINCHESTER						
Rem. 200 Soft Point	velocity, fps:	1190	1006	900	822	756
	energy, ft-lb:	629	449	360	300	254
	arc, inches:		0	-33.1	-108.7	-235.2
Win. 200 Soft Point	velocity, fps:	1190	1006	900	822	756
	energy, ft-lb:	629	449	360	300	254
	arc, inches:		0	-33.3	-109.5	-237.4
.44 REMINGTON MAGNUM						
Federal 240 Hi-Shok HP	velocity, fps:	1760	1380	1090	950	860
	energy, ft-lb:	1650	1015	640	485	395
	arc, inches:		0	-17.4	-60.7	-136.0
Rem. 210 Semi-Jacketed HP	velocity, fps:	1920	1477	1155	982	880
	energy, ft-lb:	1719	1017	622	450	361
	arc, inches:		0	-14.7	-55.5	-131.3
Rem. 240 Soft Point	velocity, fps:	1760	1380	1114	970	878
	energy, ft-lb:	1650	1015	661	501	411
	arc, inches:		0	-17.0	-61.4	-143.0
Rem. 240 Semi-Jacketed Hollow Point	velocity, fps:	1760	1380	1114	970	878
	energy, ft-lb:	1650	1015	661	501	411
	arc, inches:		0	-17.0	-61.4	-143.0
Rem. 275 JHP Core-Lokt	velocity, fps:	1580	1293	1093	976	896
	energy, ft-lb:	1524	1020	730	582	490
	arc, inches:		0	-19.4	-67.5	-210.8
Win. 210 Silvertip HP	velocity, fps:	1580	1198	993	879	795
	energy, ft-lb:	1164	670	460	361	295
	arc, inches:		0	-22.4	-76.1	-168.0
Win. 240 Hollow Soft Point	velocity, fps:	1760	1362	1094	953	861
	energy, ft-lb:	1650	988	638	484	395
	arc, inches:		0	-18.1	-65.1	-150.3
Win. 250 Platinum Tip	velocity, fps:	1830	1475	1201	1032	931
	energy, ft-lb:	1859	1208	801	591	481
	arc, inches:		0	-15.3	-54.7	-126.6.
.444 MARLIN						
Rem. 240 Soft Point	velocity, fps:	2350	1815	1377	1087	941
	energy, ft-lb:	2942	1755	1010	630	472
	arc, inches:		+2.2	-5.4	-31.4	-86.7
Hornady 265 Evolution	velocity, fps:	2325	1971	1652	1380	
	energy, ft-lb:	3180	2285	1606	1120	
	arc, inches:		+3.0	-1.4	-18.6	
Hornady 265 FP LM	velocity, fps:	2335	1913	1551	1266	
	energy, ft-lb:	3208	2153	1415	943	
	arc, inches:		+ 2.0	-4.9	-26.5	
Hornady 265 InterLock FP	velocity, fps:	2400	1974	1601	1295	
	energy, ft-lb:	3389	2294	1508	987	
	arc, inches:		+3.8	0	-17.5	
Rem. 240 Soft Point	velocity, fps:	2350	1815	1377	1087	941
	energy, ft-lb:	2942	1755	1010	630	472
	arc, inches:		+2.2	-5.4	-31.4	-86.7
.45-70 GOVERNMENT						
Black Hills 405 FPL	velocity, fps:	1250				
	energy, ft-lb:					
	arc, inches:					
Federal 300 Sierra Pro-Hunt. HP FN	velocity, fps:	1880	1650	1430	1240	1110
	energy, ft-lb:	2355	1815	1355	1015	810
	arc, inches:		0	-11.5	-39.7	-89.1
PMC 350 FNSP	velocity, fps:					
	energy, ft-lb:					
	arc, inches:					
Rem. 300 Jacketed HP	velocity, fps:	1810	1497	1244	1073	969
	energy, ft-lb:	2182	1492	1031	767	625
	arc, inches:		0	-13.8	-50.1	-115.7

Centerfire Rifle Ballistics

.45-70 GOVERNMENT TO .460 WEATHERBY MAGNUM

CARTRIDGE BULLET	RANGE, YARDS:	0	100	200	300	400
Rem. 405 Soft Point	velocity, fps:	1330	1168	1055	977	918
	energy, ft-lb:	1590	1227	1001	858	758
	arc, inches:		0	-24.0	-78.6	-169.4
Win. 300 Jacketed HP	velocity, fps:	1880	1650	1425	1235	1105
	energy, ft-lb:	2355	1815	1355	1015	810
	arc, inches:		0	-12.8	-44.3	-95.5
Win. 300 Partition Gold	velocity, fps:	1880	1558	1292	1103	988
	energy, ft-lb:	2355	1616	1112	811	651
	arc, inches:		0	-12.9	-46.0	-104.9.

.450 Bushmaster

CARTRIDGE BULLET	RANGE, YARDS:	0	100	200	300	400
Hornady 250 SST-ML	velocity, fps	2200	1840	1524	1268	
	energy, ft-lb	2686	1879	1289	893	
	arc, inches	-2.0	+2.5	-3.5	-24.5	

.450 Marlin

CARTRIDGE BULLET	RANGE, YARDS:	0	100	200	300	400
Hornady 325 FTX	velocity, fps:	2225	1887	1585	1331	
	energy, ft-lb:	3572	2569	1813	1278	
	arc, inches:	-1.5	+3.0	-2.2	-21.3	
Hornady 350 FP	velocity, fps:	2100	1720	1397	1156	
	energy, ft-lb:	3427	2298	1516	1039	
	arc, inches:		0	-10.4	-38.9	

.450 Nitro Express (3¼")

CARTRIDGE BULLET	RANGE, YARDS:	0	100	200	300	400
A-Square 465 Triad	velocity, fps:	2190	1970	1765	1577	
	energy, ft-lb:	4952	4009	3216	2567	
	arc, inches:		+4.3	0	-15.4	
Hornady 480 DGS, DGX	velocity, fps:	2150	1881	1635	1418	
	energy, ft-lb:	4927	3769	2850	2144	
	arc, inches:	-1.5	0	-8.4	-29.9	

.450 #2

CARTRIDGE BULLET	RANGE, YARDS:	0	100	200	300	400
A-Square 465 Triad	velocity, fps:	2190	1970	1765	1577	
	energy, ft-lb:	4952	4009	3216	2567	
	arc, inches:		+4.3	0	-15.4	

.458 Winchester Magnum

CARTRIDGE BULLET	RANGE, YARDS:	0	100	200	300	400
A-Square 465 Triad	velocity, fps:	2220	1999	1791	1601	1433
	energy, ft-lb:	5088	4127	3312	2646	2121
	arc, inches:		+3.6	0	-14.7	-42.5
Federal 350 Soft Point	velocity, fps:	2470	1990	1570	1250	1060
	energy, ft-lb:	4740	3065	1915	1205	870
	arc, inches:		0	-7.5	-29.1	-71.1
Federal 400 Trophy Bonded	velocity, fps:	2380	2170	1960	1770	1590
	energy, ft-lb:	5030	4165	3415	2785	2255
	arc, inches:		0	-5.9	-20.9	-47.1
Federal 500 Solid	velocity, fps:	2090	1870	1670	1480	1320
	energy, ft-lb:	4850	3880	3085	2440	1945
	arc, inches:		0	-8.5	-29.5	-66.2
Federal 500 Trophy Bonded	velocity, fps:	2090	1870	1660	1480	1310
	energy, ft-lb:	4850	3870	3065	2420	1915
	arc, inches:		0	-8.5	-29.7	-66.8
Federal 500 Trophy Bonded Sledgehammer Solid	velocity, fps:	2090	1860	1650	1460	1300
	energy, ft-lb:	4850	3845	3025	2365	1865
	arc, inches:		0	-8.6	-30.0	-67.8
Federal 510 Soft Point	velocity, fps:	2090	1820	1570	1360	1190
	energy, ft-lb:	4945	3730	2790	2080	1605
	arc, inches:		0	-9.1	-32.3	-73.9
Hornady 500 FMJ-RN HM	velocity, fps:	2260	1984	1735	1512	
	energy, ft-lb:	5670	4368	3341	2538	
	arc, inches:		0	-7.4	-26.4	
Norma 500 TXP Swift A-Fr.	velocity, fps:	2116	1903	1705	1524	
	energy, ft-lb:	4972	4023	3228	2578	
	arc, inches:		+4.1	0	-16.1	
Norma 500 Barnes Solid	velocity, fps:	2067	1750	1472	1245	
	energy, ft-lb:	4745	3401	2405	1721	
	arc, inches:		+4.9	0	-21.2	
Rem. 450 Swift A-Frame PSP	velocity, fps:	2150	1901	1671	1465	1289
	energy, ft-lb:	4618	3609	2789	2144	1659
	arc, inches:		0	-8.2	-28.9	
Speer 500 African GS Tungsten Solid	velocity, fps:	2120	1845	1596	1379	
	energy, ft-lb:	4989	3780	2828	2111	
	arc, inches:		0	-8.8	-31.3	
Speer African Grand Slam	velocity, fps:	2120	1853	1609	1396	
	energy, ft-lb:	4989	3810	2875	2163	
	arc, inches:		0	-8.7	-30.8	
Win. 510 Soft Point	velocity, fps:	2040	1770	1527	1319	1157
	energy, ft-lb:	4712	3547	2640	1970	1516
	arc, inches:		0	-10.3	-35.6	

.458 Lott

CARTRIDGE BULLET	RANGE, YARDS:	0	100	200	300	400
A-Square 465 Triad	velocity, fps:	2380	2150	1932	1730	1551
	energy, ft-lb:	5848	4773	3855	3091	2485
	arc, inches:		+3.0	0	-12.5	-36.4
Federal 500 TSX	velocity, fps:	2280	2090	1900	1730	1560
	energy, ft-lb:	5770	4825	4000	3305	2715
	arc, inches:	0	-6.4	-22.7	-50.7	
Hornady 500 RNSP or solid	velocity, fps:	2300	2022	1776	1551	
	energy, ft-lb:	5872	4537	3502	2671	
	arc, inches:		+3.4	0	-14.3	
Hornady 500 InterBond	velocity, fps:	2300	2028	1777	1549	
	energy, ft-lb:	5872	4535	3453	2604	
	arc, inches:		0	-7.0	-25.1	

CARTRIDGE BULLET	RANGE, YARDS:	0	50	100	150	200
Norma 500 Woodleigh SP	velocity, fps:	2100	1982	1868	1758	1654
	energy, ft-lb:	4897	4361	3874	3434	3039
	arc, inches:	-1.5	+.3	0	-2.8	-8.4

.450 Ackley

CARTRIDGE BULLET	RANGE, YARDS:	0	100	200	300	400
A-Square 465 Triad	velocity, fps:	2400	2169	1950	1747	1567
	energy, ft-lb:	5947	4857	3927	3150	2534
	arc, inches:		+2.9	0	-12.2	-35.8

.450 Rigby

CARTRIDGE BULLET	RANGE, YARDS:	0	50	100	150	200
Norma 550 Woodleigh SP	velocity, fps:	2100	1992	1887	1787	1690
	energy, ft-lb:	5387	4847	4352	3900	3491
	arc, inches:	-1.5	+.3	0	-2.7	-8.2

.460 Short A-Square

CARTRIDGE BULLET	RANGE, YARDS:	0	100	200	300	400
A-Square 500 Triad	velocity, fps:	2420	2198	1987	1789	1613
	energy, ft-lb:	6501	5362	4385	3553	2890
	arc, inches:		+2.9	0	-11.6	-34.2

.450 Dakota

CARTRIDGE BULLET	RANGE, YARDS:	0	100	200	300	400
Dakota 500 Barnes Solid	velocity, fps:	2450	2235	2030	1838	1658
	energy, ft-lb:	6663	5544	4576	3748	3051
	arc, inches:		+2.5	-0.6	-12.0	-33.8

.460 Weatherby Magnum

CARTRIDGE BULLET	RANGE, YARDS:	0	100	200	300	400
A-Square 500 Triad	velocity, fps:	2580	2349	2131	1923	1737
	energy, ft-lb:	7389	6126	5040	4107	3351
	arc, inches:		+2.4	0	-10.0	-29.4
Wby. 450 Barnes X	velocity, fps:	2700	2518	2343	2175	2013
	energy, ft-lb:	7284	6333	5482	4725	4050
	arc, inches:		+2.0	0	-8.4	-24.1

CARTRIDGE BULLET	RANGE, YARDS:	0	100	200	300	400
Wby. 500 RN Expanding	velocity, fps:	2600	2301	2022	1764	1533.
	energy, ft-lb:	7504	5877	4539	3456	2608
	arc, inches:		+2.6	0	-11.1	-33.5
Wby. 500 FMJ	velocity, fps:	2600	2309	2037	1784	1557
	energy, ft-lb:	7504	5917	4605	3534	2690
	arc, inches:	—	+2.5	0	-10.9	-33.0

.500/.465

CARTRIDGE BULLET	RANGE, YARDS:	0	100	200	300	400
A-Square 480 Triad	velocity, fps:	2150	1928	1722	1533	
	energy, ft-lb:	4926	3960	3160	2505	
	arc, inches:		+4.3	0	-16.0	

.470 Nitro Express

CARTRIDGE BULLET	RANGE, YARDS:	0	100	200	300	400
A-Square 500 Triad	velocity, fps:	2150	1912	1693	1494	
	energy, ft-lb:	5132	4058	3182	2478	
	arc, inches:		+4.4	0	-16.5	
Federal 500 Trophy Bond	velocity, fps:	2150	1890	1660	1450	
(and Sledgehammer solid)	energy, ft-lb:	5130	3975	3045	2320	
	arc, inches:	-1.5	0	-9.4	-29.3	
Hornady 500 DGX, DGS	velocity, fps:	2150	1885	1643	1429	
	energy, ft-lb:	5132	3946	2998	2267	
	arc, inches:	-1.5	0	-8.9	-30.9	

CARTRIDGE BULLET	RANGE, YARDS:	0	50	100	150	200
Norma 500 Woodleigh	velocity, fps:	2100	2002	1906	1814	1725
(soft and solid)	energy, ft-lb:	4897	4449	4035	3654	3304
	arc, inches:	-1.5	+.3	0	-2.7	-8.0

.470 Capstick

CARTRIDGE BULLET	RANGE, YARDS:	0	100	200	300	400
A-Square 500 Triad	velocity, fps:	2400	2172	1958	1761	1553
	energy, ft-lb:	6394	5236	4255	3445	2678
	arc, inches:		+2.9	0	-11.9	-36.1

.475 #2

CARTRIDGE BULLET	RANGE, YARDS:	0	100	200	300	400
A-Square 480 Triad	velocity, fps:	2200	1964	1744	1544	
	energy, ft-lb:	5158	4109	3240	2539	
	arc, inches:		+4.1	0	-15.6	

.475 #2 Jeffery

CARTRIDGE BULLET	RANGE, YARDS:	0	100	200	300	400
A-Square 500 Triad	velocity, fps:	2200	1966	1748	1550	
	energy, ft-lb:	5373	4291	3392	2666	
	arc, inches:		+4.1	0	-15.6	

.495 A-Square

CARTRIDGE BULLET	RANGE, YARDS:	0	100	200	300	400
A-Square 570 Triad	velocity, fps:	2350	2117	1896	1693	1513
	energy, ft-lb:	6989	5671	4552	3629	2899
	arc, inches:		+3.1	0	-13.0	-37.8

.50 BMG

CARTRIDGE BULLET	RANGE, YARDS:	0	100	200	300	400
Hornady 750 A-Max	velocity, fps:	2815	2727	2641	2557	2474
	energy, ft-lb:	13,196	12,386	11,619	10,889	10,196
	arc, inches:		+1.4	0	-6.4	-18.2

.500 Nitro Express (3")

CARTRIDGE BULLET	RANGE, YARDS:	0	100	200	300	400
A-Square 570 Triad	velocity, fps:	2150	1928	1722	1533	
	energy, ft-lb:	5850	4703	3752	2975	
	arc, inches:		+4.3	0	-16.1	

CARTRIDGE BULLET	RANGE, YARDS:	0	100	200	300	400
Federal 570 TSX	velocity, fps:	2100	1890	1700	1520	1370
	energy, ft-lb:	5580	4530	3655	2935	2355
	arc, inches:	0	-8.4	-28.7	-64.2	
Hornady 570 DGX, DGS	velocity, fps:	2150	1881	1635	1419	
	energy, ft-lb:	5850	4477	3384	2547	
	arc, inches:	-.9	0	-9.0	-31.1	

CARTRIDGE BULLET	RANGE, YARDS:	0	50	100	150	200
Norma 570 Woodleigh SP	velocity, fps:	2100	2000	1903	1809	1719
	energy, ft-lb:	5583	5064	4585	4145	3742
	arc, inches:	-1.5	+.3	0	-2.7	-8.0
50 BMG						
Hornady 750 A-MAX	velocity, fps:	2815	2727	2641	2557	2474
	energy, ft-lb:	13196	12386	11619	10889	10196
	arc, inches:	-1.8	+1.4	0	-6.4	-18.2

.500 Jeffery

CARTRIDGE BULLET	RANGE, YARDS:	0	50	100	150	200
Norma 570 Woodleigh SP	velocity, fps:	2200	2097	1997	1901	1807
	energy, ft-lb:	6127	5568	5050	4573	4134
	arc, inches:	-1.5	+.2	0	-2.4	-7.1

.500 A-Square

CARTRIDGE BULLET	RANGE, YARDS:	0	100	200	300	400
A-Square 600 Triad	velocity, fps:	2470	2235	2013	1804	1620
	energy, ft-lb:	8127	6654	5397	4336	3495
	arc, inches:		+2.7	0	-11.3	-33.5

.505 Gibbs

CARTRIDGE BULLET	RANGE, YARDS:	0	100	200	300	400
A-Square 525 Triad	velocity, fps:	2300	2063	1840	1637	
	energy, ft-lb:	6166	4962	3948	3122	
	arc, inches:		+3.6	0	-14.2	

CARTRIDGE BULLET	RANGE, YARDS:	0	50	100	150	200
Norma 600 Woodleigh SP	velocity, fps:	2100	1998	1899	1803	1711
	energy, ft-lb:	5877	5319	4805	4334	3904
	arc, inches:	-1.5	+.3	0	-2.7	-8.1

.577 Nitro Express

CARTRIDGE BULLET	RANGE, YARDS:	0	100	200	300	400
A-Square 750 Triad	velocity, fps:	2050	1811	1595	1401	
	energy, ft-lb:	6998	5463	4234	3267	
	arc, inches:		+4.9	0	-18.5	

.577 Tyrannosaur

CARTRIDGE BULLET	RANGE, YARDS:	0	100	200	300	400
A-Square 750 Triad	velocity, fps:	2460	2197	1950	1723	1516
	energy, ft-lb:	10077	8039	6335	4941	3825
	arc, inches:		+2.8	0	-12.1	-36.0

.600 Nitro Express

CARTRIDGE BULLET	RANGE, YARDS:	0	100	200	300	400
A-Square 900 Triad	velocity, fps:	1950	1680	1452	1336	
	energy, ft-lb:	7596	5634	4212	3564	
	arc, inches:		+5.6	0	-20.7	

.700 Nitro Express

CARTRIDGE BULLET	RANGE, YARDS:	0	100	200	300	400
A-Square 1000 Monolithic	velocity, fps:	1900	1669	1461	1288	
Solid	energy, ft-lb:	8015	6188	4740	3685	
	arc, inches:		+5.8	0	-22.2	

Long Range Rifle

6.6 CREEDMOOR TO .338 LAPUA

CARTRIDGE BULLET	RANGE, YARDS:	0	400	600	800	1000
6.6 Creedmoor						
Nosler 140 HPBT	velocity, fps:	2550	2229	1932	1662	1426
	energy, ft-lb:	2021	1544	1160	859	632
	arc, inches:	-1.5	0	-26.7	-90.9	-205.9
.264 Winchester Magnum						
Nosler 130 AccuBond	velocity, fps:	3100	2709	2350	2019	1718
	energy, ft-lb:	2773	2118	1594	1176	852
	arc, inches:	-1.5	0	-17.6	-60.6	-137.9
6.5-284 Norma						
Nosler 129 AccuBond	velocity, fps:	2965	2633	2324	2036	1771
Long Range	energy, ft-lb:	2517	1985	1547	1188	899
	arc, inches:	-1.5	0	-18.7	-63.2	-141.6
.270 WSM						
Nosler 150 AccuBond	velocity, fps:	2960	2661	2381	2118	1873
Long Range	energy, ft-lb:	2917	2358	1888	1495	1169
	arc, inches:	-1.5	0	-18.2	-61.1	-135.1
7mm Remington Magnum						
Nosler 168 AccuBond	velocity, fps:	2880	2598	2333	2084	1851
Long Range	energy, ft-lb:	3093	2518	2030	1620	1278
	arc, inches:	-1.5	0	-19.2	-64.0	-141.0
7mm STW						
Nosler 175 AccuBond	velocity, fps:	2900	2625	2366	2122	1893
Long Range	energy, ft-lb:	3267	2677	2175	1750	1393
	arc, inches:	-1.5	0	-18.8	-62.4	-137.1
7mm Remington Ultra Mag						
Nosler 175 AccuBond	velocity, fps:	3040	2756	2490	2239	2002
Long Range	energy, ft-lb:	3590	2952	2409	1948	1558
	arc, inches:	-1.5	0	-16.9	-56.2	-123.5
.308 Winchester						
Barnes 175 OTM						
velocity, fps:	2650	2318	2011	1730	1480	1272
energy, ft-lb:	2730	2089	1571	1163	852	629
arc, inches:	-1.5	0	-24.6	-83.8	-189. 9	-360.0
.300 WSM						
Nosler 190 AccuBond	velocity, fps:	2875	2588	2319	2066	1830
Long Range	energy, ft-lb:	3486	2826	2269	1801	1413
	arc, inches:	-1.5	0	-19.3	-64.7	-142.7

CARTRIDGE BULLET	RANGE, YARDS:	0	400	600	800	1000
.300 Winchester Magnum						
Barnes 220 OTM						
velocity, fps:	2700	2420	2158	1912	1685	1481
energy, ft-lb:	3562	2862	2275	1786	1387	1072
arc, inches:	-1.5	0	-22.4	-74.7	-165.4	-305.3
Nosler 190 AccuBond	velocity, fps:	2870	2583	2314	2062	1826
Long Range	energy, ft-lb:	3474	2816	2260	1794	1407
	arc, inches:	-1.5	0	-19.4	-64.9	-143.3
.300 Weatherby Magnum						
Nosler 210 AccuBond	velocity, fps:	2825	2575	2339	2115	1905
Long Range	energy, ft-lb:	3720	3092	2551	2087	1691
	arc, inches:	-1.5	0	-19.5	-64.6	-140.8
.300 Remington Ultra Mag						
Nosler 210 AccuBond	velocity, fps:	2920	2665	2424	2196	1980
Long Range	energy, ft-lb:	3975	3311	2740	2248	1828
	arc, inches:	-1.5	0	-18.1	-60.0	-130.8
.30-378 Weatherby Magnum						
Nosler 210 AccuBond	velocity, fps:	3040	2778	2531	2297	2076
Long Range	energy, ft-lb:	4308	3599	2987	2461	2009
	arc, inches:	-1.5	0	-16.6	-54.9	-119.7
.338 Remington Ultra Mag						
Nosler 300 AccuBond	velocity, fps:	2600	2359	2131	1916	1716
	energy, ft-lb:	4502	3707	3026	2447	1963
	arc, inches:	-1.5	0	-23.6	-77.9	-170.2
.338 Lapua						
Barnes 300 OTM						
velocity, fps:	2600	2375	2161	1958	1767	1591
energy, ft-lb:	4504	3757	3110	2554	2081	1687
arc, inches:	-1.5	0	-23.2	-76.4	-165.9	-300.1
Nosler 300 AccuBond	velocity, fps:	2650	2406	2176	1959	1755
	energy, ft-lb:	4677	3857	3154	2555	2053
	arc, inches:	-1.5	0	-22.6	-74.7	-163.1

Rimfire Ballistics

Rimfire cartridges have had a longer run than any centerfire you can name. Horace Smith and Daniel Wesson came up with the first successful .22 rimfires in the United States in 1857. Thirty years later the .22 Long Rifle arrived, courtesy of the J. Stevens Arms & Tool Company. It used 5 grains of black powder to drive a 40-grain bullet, shortly making the transition to smokeless in a case crimped on a heeled bullet. Remington produced the first modern high-speed load in 1930. Current .22 ammo includes myriad Long Rifle listings. The Long (essentially a Short bullet in a Long Rifle case), like the CB and WRF cartridges, is going the way of the dodo. The shot load of #12 "dust" has faded too, though it has dispatched many snakes, and was once hailed as just the ticket for barn mice and rats when you didn't want to perforate the boards. New rimfires have joined the versatile Long Rifle. The .22 WMR (Winchester Magnum Rimfire) came in 1959. More than four decades passed before Hornady necked down the WMR case to form the .17 HMR. A sibling on the CCI Stinger variation of the .22 LR appeared in 2004. Hornady dubbed it the .17 Mach 2. The newest .17, Winchester's Super Mag, arrived in 2013. The .17s and the .22 WMR feature jacketed hollowpoint and polymer-tipped bullets, just like centerfires.

This list is incomplete. For convenience (and given space constraints), it omits duplicate loads—those by the same manufacturer but under different labels). Units: velocity in feet per second, energy in foot-pounds, drop in inches.

.22 TO .17 HORNADY MAGNUM RIMFIRE

CARTRIDGE BULLET	LOAD	MUZZLE VEL./ENERGY	100-YD. VEL./ENERGY
.22			
CCI .22 CB Short	29-gr. RN	710/32	607/24
CCI .22 CB Long	29-gr. RN	710/32	607/24
CCI .22 Short	27-gr. HP	1105/73	868/45
CCI .22 Short	29-gr. RN	1080/75	857/47
CCI .22 Short	29-gr. Target RN	830/44	704/32
CCI .22 Long	29-gr. RN	1215/95	908/53
CCI .22 LR	21-gr. Short Range Green HP	1650/127	912/38
CCI .22 LR	31 gr. #12 birdshot	1000	
CCI .22 LR	32-gr. Stinger HP	1640/191	1066/81
CCI .22 LR	36-gr. HP	1260/127	1003/80
CCI .22 LR	40-gr. Tactical RN	1200/128	964/82
CCI .22 LR	40-gr. Mini-Mag RN	1235/135	998/88
CCI .22 LR	40-gr. Sub-sonic HP	1050/98	897/72
CCI .22 LR	40-gr. Velocitor HP	1435/183	1084/104
CCI .22 LR	40-gr. Small Game Bullet LFN	1235/135	992/87
CCI .22 LR	40-gr. Quiet-22 HP	710/45	640/36
CCI .22 LR	40-gr. Select RN	1200/128	964/82
CCI .22 LR	40-gr. Green Tag RN	1070/102	908/73
CCI .22 LR	45-gr. HP Suppressor	970/95	892/75
Federal .22 LR	25 gr. #12 birdshot		
Federal .22 LR	31-gr. Game-Shok HP	1430/140	1050/75
Federal .22 LR	36-gr. Champion HP	1260/125	1000/80
Federal .22 LR	38-gr. Game-Shok HP	1260/135	1010/85
Federal .22 LR	38-gr. Amer. Eagle HP	1260/135	1010/85
Federal .22 LR	40-gr. Prem. Gold Medal	1200/130	990/85
Federal .22 LR	40-gr. Game-Shok HP	1240/135	1010/90
Federal .22 LR	40-gr. Champion	1240/135	1010/90
Federal .22 LR	45-gr. Amer. Eagle Suppressed	1050/105	910/75
Lapua .22 LR	40-gr. Polar Biathlon	1106/109	914/74
Remington .22 Short	29-gr. RN	1095/77	903/52
Remington .22 LR	33-gr. CBee Low Noise HP	740/40	638/30
Remington .22 LR	33-gr. Yellow Jacket T. C.	1500/165	1075/85
Remington .22 LR	36-gr. Viper Truncated Cone	1410/159	1056/89
Remington .22 LR	36-gr. Cyclone HP	1280/131	1010/82
Remington .22 LR	38-gr. Sub-sonic HP	1050/93	901/69
Remington .22 LR	40-gr. Target	1150/117	976/85
Remington .22 LR	40-gr. Thunderbolt	1255/140	1017/92
Remington .22 LR	40-gr. Competition RN	1085/105	941/79
Winchester .22 Short	29-gr. RN	1095/77	903/52
Winchester .22 Long	29-gr. RN	770/38	681/30
Winchester .22 LR	31-gr. #12 birdshot	1000	
Winchester .22 LR	26-gr. Varmint LF HP	1650/157	1023/60
Winchester .22 LR	32-gr. Xpediter HP	1640/191	1078/83
Winchester .22 LR	29-gr. Super-X sub-sonic	770/38	681/30
Winchester .22 LR	36-gr. HP	1280/131	975/76
Winchester .22 LR	37-gr. Super-X HP	1280/135	1015/85
Winchester .22 LR	37-gr. Super Speed HP	1330/154	1038/88
Winchester .22 LR	37-gr. Varmint HE HP	1435/169	1080/96
Winchester .22 LR	40-gr. Super-X low-report	1065/101	922/76
Winchester .22 LR	40-gr. DynaPoint	1150/117	976/85
Winchester .22 LR	40-gr. M22 LRN Black	1255/140	1017/92
Winchester .22 LR	40-gr. Power-Point HP	1280/145	1001/89
Winchester .22 LR	40-gr. Super-X	1300/150	1038/96
Winchester .22 LR	40-gr. Hyper Speed HP	1435/183	1070/102
.17 Hornady Magnum Rimfire			
CCI .17 HMR	16-gr. TNT Green HP	2500/222	1642/96
CCI .17 HMR	17-gr. TNT JHP	2550/245	1757116
CCI .17 HMR	17-gr. Poly-Tip V-Max	2550/245	1915/138
CCI .17 HMR	20-gr. FMJ	2375/250	1776/140
CCI .17 HMR	20-gr. JSP	2375/250	1754/137
Federal .17 HMR	17-gr. Prem. V-Shok TNT JHP	2530/240	1800/125
Federal .17 HMR	17-gr. Prem. Hornady V-Max	2530/240	1880/135
Hornady .17 Mach 2	15.5-gr. NTX Lead-Free	2050/149	1450/75
Hornady .17 Mach 2	17-gr. V-Max	2100/166	1530/88

Rimfire Ballistics

.17 HORNADY MAGNUM RIMFIRE TO .22 WINCHESTER RIMFIRE

CARTRIDGE BULLET	LOAD	MUZZLE VEL./ENERGY	100-YD. VEL./ENERGY
Hornady .17 HMR	15.5-gr. NTX Lead-Free	2525/236	1829/119
Hornady .17 HMR	17-gr. V-Max	2550/245	1901/136
Hornady .17 HMR	20-gr. XTP	2375/250	1776/140
Remington.17 HMR	17-gr. AccuTip-V	2550/245	1901/136
Winchester .17 HMR	15.5-gr. Varmint LF NTX	2550/224	1901/124
Winchester .17 HMR	17-gr. Poly Tip V-Max	2550/245	1915/138
Winchester .17 HMR	20-gr. Super-X JHP	2375/250	1776/140

.22 Winchester Magnum Rimfire

CARTRIDGE BULLET	LOAD	MUZZLE VEL./ENERGY	100-YD. VEL./ENERGY
CCI .22 WMR	30 Maxi Mag HP + V	2200/322	1375/126
CCI .22 WMR	30 Poly-Tip V-Max	2200/322	1571/164
CCI .22 WMR	30 TNT JHP	2200/322	1405/131
CCI .22 WMR	30 TNT Green HP	2050/280	1317/116
CCI .22 WMR	40 Maxi Mag HP	1875/312	1319/155
CCI .22 WMR	40 Maxi Mag TMJ	1875/312	1366/166
CCI .22 WMR	40 GamePoint JSP	1875/312	1385/170
CCI .22 WMR	52 #12 birdshot	1000	
Federal .22 WMR	30-gr. Speer TNT HP	2200/320	1420/135
Federal .22 WMR	40-gr. FMJ	1880/315	1310/155
Hornady .22 WMR	30-gr. V-Max	2200/322	1421/134
Remington .22 WMR	33-gr. AccuTip-V	2000/293	1495/164
Remington .22 WMR	40-gr. JHP	1910/324	1350/162
Remington .22 WMR	40-gr. PSP	1910/324	1340/159
Winchester .22 WMR	28-gr. Varmint LF JHP	2200/301	1394/121
Winchester .22 WMR	30-gr. Varmint HV V-Max	2250/337	1490/148
Winchester .22 WMR	30-gr. Varmint HV JHP	2250/337	1450/140
Winchester .22 WMR	34-gr. Varmint HE JHP	2120/339	1437/156
Winchester .22 WMR	40-gr. Super-X JHP (and FMJ)	1910/324	1326/156
Winchester .22 WMR	45-gr. USA DynaPoint	1550/240	1147/131

.17 Winchester Super Mag.

CARTRIDGE BULLET	LOAD	MUZZLE VEL./ENERGY	100-YD. VEL./ENERGY
Winchester .17 Super Mag	20-gr. Varmint HV	3000/400	2504/278
Winchester .17 Super Mag	25-gr. Polymer Tip	2600/375	2230/276

.22 Winchester Rimfire

CARTRIDGE BULLET	LOAD	MUZZLE VEL./ENERGY	100-YD. VEL./ENERGY
CCI .22 WRF	45 JHP	1300/169	1013/103
Winchester .22 WRF	45 FN	1300/169	1023/105

Centerfire Handgun Ballistics

Data shown here is taken from manufacturers' charts; your chronograph readings may vary. Barrel lengths for pistol data vary, and depend in part on which pistols are typically chambered in a given cartridge. Velocity variations due to barrel length depend on the baseline bullet speed and the load. Velocity for the .30 Carbine, normally a rifle cartridge, was determined in a pistol barrel.

Listings are current as of February the year *Shooter's Bible* appears (not the cover year). Listings are not intended as recommendations. For example, the data for the .25 Auto gives velocity and energy readings to 100 yards. Few handgunners would call the little .25 a 100-yard cartridge.

Abbreviations: Bullets are designated by loading company, weight (in grains) and type, with these abbreviations for shape and construction: BJHP= brass-jacketed hollowpoint; FN=Flat Nose; FMC=Full Metal Case; FMJ=Full Metal Jacket; HP=Hollowpoint; L=Lead; LF=Lead-Free; +P=a more powerful load than traditionally manufactured for that round; RN=Round Nose; SFHP=Starfire (PMC) Hollowpoint; SP=Softpoint; SWC=Semi Wadcutter; TMJ=Total Metal Jacket; WC=Wadcutter; CEPP, SXT and XTP are trademarked designations of Lapua, Winchester and Hornady, respectively.

.25 AUTO TO .32 S&W LONG

.25 Auto

CARTRIDGE BULLET	RANGE, YARDS:	0	25	50	75	100
Federal 50 FMJ	velocity, fps:	760	750	730	720	700
	energy, ft-lb:	65	60	60	55	55
Hornady 35 JHP/XTP	velocity, fps:	900		813		742
	energy, ft-lb:	63		51		43
Magtech 50 FMC	velocity, fps:	760		707		659
	energy, ft-lb:	64		56		48
PMC 50 FMJ	velocity, fps:	754	730	707	685	663
	energy, ft-lb:	62				
Rem. 50 Metal Case	velocity, fps:	760		707		659
	energy, ft-lb:	64		56		48
Speer 35 Gold Dot	velocity, fps:	900		816		747
	energy, ft-lb:	63		52		43
Speer 50 TMJ (and Blazer)	velocity, fps:	760		717		677
	energy, ft-lb:	64		57		51
Win. 45 Expanding Point	velocity, fps:	815		729		655
	energy, ft-lb	66		53		42
Win. 50 FMJ	velocity, fps:	760		707		
	energy, ft-lb	64		56		

.30 Luger

CARTRIDGE BULLET	RANGE, YARDS:	0	25	50	75	100
Win. 93 FMJ	velocity, fps:	1220		1110		1040
	energy, ft-lb	305		255		225

7.62x25 Tokarev

CARTRIDGE BULLET	RANGE, YARDS:	0	25	50	75	100
PMC 93 FMJ	velocity and energy figures not available					

.30 Carbine

CARTRIDGE BULLET	RANGE, YARDS:	0	25	50	75	100
Win. 110 Hollow SP	velocity, fps:	1790		1601		1430
	energy, ft-lb	783		626		500

.32 Auto

CARTRIDGE BULLET	RANGE, YARDS:	0	25	50	75	100
Federal 65 Hydra-Shok JHP	velocity, fps:	950	920	890	860	830
	energy, ft-lb:	130	120	115	105	100
Federal 71 FMJ	velocity, fps:	910	880	860	830	810
	energy, ft-lb:	130	120	115	110	105
Hornady 60 JHP/XTP	velocity, fps:	1000		917		849
	energy, ft-lb:	133		112		96
Hornady 71 FMJ-RN	velocity, fps:	900		845		797
	energy, ft-lb:	128		112		100
Magtech 71 FMC	velocity, fps:	905		855		810
	energy, ft-lb:	129		115		103
Magtech 71 JHP	velocity, fps:	905		855		810
	energy, ft-lb:	129		115		103
PMC 60 JHP	velocity, fps:	980	849	820	791	763
	energy, ft-lb:	117				
PMC 70 SFHP	velocity, fps:	velocity and energy figures not available				
PMC 71 FMJ	velocity, fps:	870	841	814	791	763
	energy, ft-lb:	119				
Rem. 71 Metal Case	velocity, fps:	905		855		810
	energy, ft-lb:	129		115		97
Speer 60 Gold Dot	velocity, fps:	960		868		796
	energy, ft-lb:	123		100		84
Speer 71 TMJ (and Blazer)	velocity, fps:	900		855		810
	energy, ft-lb:	129		115		97
Win. 60 Silvertip HP	velocity, fps:	970		895		835
	energy, ft-lb	125		107		93
Win. 71 FMJ	velocity, fps:	905		855		
	energy, ft-lb	129		115		

.32 S&W

CARTRIDGE BULLET	RANGE, YARDS:	0	25	50	75	100
Rem. 88 LRN	velocity, fps:	680		645		610
	energy, ft-lb:	90		81		73
Win. 85 LRN	velocity, fps:	680		645		610
	energy, ft-lb	90		81		73

.32 S&W Long

CARTRIDGE BULLET	RANGE, YARDS:	0	25	50	75	100
Federal 98 LWC	velocity, fps:	780	700	630	560	500
	energy, ft-lb:	130	105	85	70	55
Federal 98 LRN	velocity, fps:	710	690	670	650	640
	energy, ft-lb:	115	105	100	95	90
Lapua 83 LWC	velocity, fps:	240		189*		149*
	energy, ft-lb:	154		95*		59*
Lapua 98 LWC	velocity, fps:	240		202*		171*
	energy, ft-lb:	183		130*		93*
Magtech 98 LRN	velocity, fps:	705		670		635
	energy, ft-lb:	108		98		88
Magtech 98 LWC	velocity, fps:	682		579		491
	energy, ft-lb:	102		73		52
Norma 98 LWC	velocity, fps:	787	759	732		683
	energy, ft-lb:	136	126	118		102
PMC 98 LRN	velocity, fps:	789	770	751	733	716
	energy, ft-lb:	135				
PMC 100 LWC	velocity, fps:	683	652	623	595	569
	energy, ft-lb:	102				
Rem. 98 LRN	velocity, fps:	705		670		635
	energy, ft-lb:	115		98		88

Centerfire Handgun Ballistics

.32 S&W Long to 9mm Luger

Cartridge Bullet	Range, yards:	0	25	50	75	100
Win. 98 LRN	velocity, fps:	705		670		635
	energy, ft-lb:	115		98		88

.32 Short Colt

Cartridge Bullet	Range, yards:	0	25	50	75	100
Win. 80 LRN	velocity, fps:	745		665		590
	energy, ft-lb	100		79		62

.32-20

Cartridge Bullet	Range, yards:	0	25	50	75	100
Black Hills 115 FPL	velocity, fps:	800				
	energy, ft-lb:					

.32 H&R Mag

Cartridge Bullet	Range, yards:	0	25	50	75	100
Black Hills 85 JHP	velocity, fps	1100				
	energy, ft-lb	228				
Black Hills 90 FPL	velocity, fps	750				
	energy, ft-lb					
Black Hills 115 FPL	velocity, fps	800				
	energy, ft-lb					
Federal 85 Hi-Shok JHP	velocity, fps:	1100	1050	1020	970	930
	energy, ft-lb:	230	210	195	175	165
Federal 95 LSWC	velocity, fps:	1030	1000	940	930	900
	energy, ft-lb:	225	210	195	185	170
Hornady 80 FTX		0		50 yds.		100.
	velocity, fps:	1150		1039		963
	energy, ft-lb:	235		192		165

.38 Special Lite, 4"bbl

Cartridge Bullet	Range, yards:	0	25	50	75	100
Hornady 90 FTX	velocity, fps:	1200		1037		938
	energy, ft-lb:	288		215		176

9mm Makarov

Cartridge Bullet	Range, yards:	0	25	50	75	100
Federal 90 Hi-Shok JHP	velocity, fps:	990	950	910	880	850
	energy, ft-lb:	195	180	165	155	145
Federal 90 FMJ	velocity, fps:	990	960	920	900	870
	energy, ft-lb:	205	190	180	170	160
Hornady 95 JHP/XTP	velocity, fps:	1000		930		874
	energy, ft-lb:	211		182		161
PMC 100 FMJ-TC	velocity, fps:	velocity and energy figures not available				
Speer 95 TMJ Blazer	velocity, fps:	1000		928		872
	energy, ft-lb:	211		182		161

9x21 IMI

Cartridge Bullet	Range, yards:	0	25	50	75	100
PMC 123 FMJ	velocity, fps:	1150	1093	1046	1007	973
	energy, ft-lb:	364				

9mm Luger

Cartridge Bullet	Range, yards:	0	25	50	75	100
Black Hills 115 JHP	velocity, fps:	1150				
	energy, ft-lb:	336				
Black Hills 115 FMJ	velocity, fps:	1150				
	energy, ft-lb:	336				
Black Hills 115 JHP +P	velocity, fps:	1300				
	energy, ft-lb:	431				
Black Hills 115 EXP JHP	velocity, fps:	1250				
	energy, ft-lb:	400				
Black Hills 124 JHP +P	velocity, fps:	1250				
	energy, ft-lb:	430				
Black Hills 124 JHP	velocity, fps:	1150				
	energy, ft-lb:	363				
Black Hills 124 FMJ	velocity, fps:	1150				
	energy, ft-lb:	363				
Black Hills 147 JHP subsonic	velocity, fps:	975				
	energy, ft-lb:	309				
Black Hills 147 FMJ subsonic	velocity, fps:	975				
	energy, ft-lb:	309				
Federal 105 EFMJ	velocity, fps:	1225	1160	1105	1060	1025
	energy, ft-lb:	350	315	285	265	245
Federal 115 Hi-Shok JHP	velocity, fps:	1160	1100	1060	1020	990
	energy, ft-lb:	345	310	285	270	250
Federal 115 FMJ	velocity, fps:	1160	1100	1060	1020	990
	energy, ft-lb:	345	310	285	270	250
Federal 124 FMJ	velocity, fps:	1120	1070	1030	990	960
	energy, ft-lb:	345	315	290	270	255
Federal 124 Hydra-Shok JHP	velocity, fps:	1120	1070	1030	990	960
	energy, ft-lb:	345	315	290	270	255
Federal 124 TMJ TMF Primer	velocity, fps:	1120	1070	1030	990	960
	energy, ft-lb:	345	315	290	270	255
Federal 124 Truncated FMJ	velocity, fps:	1120	1070	1030	990	960
Match	energy, ft-lb:	345	315	290	270	255
Federal 124 Nyclad HP	velocity, fps:	1120	1070	1030	990	960
	energy, ft-lb:	345	315	290	270	255
Federal 124 FMJ +P	velocity, fps:	1120	1070	1030	990	960
	energy, ft-lb:	345	315	290	270	255
Federal 135 Hydra-Shok JHP	velocity, fps:	1050	1030	1010	980	970
	energy, ft-lb:	330	315	300	290	280
Federal 147 Hydra-Shok JHP	velocity, fps:	1000	960	920	890	860
	energy, ft-lb:	325	300	275	260	240
Federal 147 Hi-Shok JHP	velocity, fps:	980	950	930	900	880
	energy, ft-lb:	310	295	285	265	255
Federal 147 FMJ FN	velocity, fps:	960	930	910	890	870
	energy, ft-lb:	295	280	270	260	250
Federal 147 TMJ TMF Primer	velocity, fps:	960	940	910	890	870
	energy, ft-lb:	300	285	270	260	245
Hornady 115 JHP/XTP	velocity, fps:	1155		1047		971
	energy, ft-lb:	341		280		241
Hornady 124 JHP/XTP	velocity, fps:	1110		1030		971
	energy, ft-lb:	339		292		259
Hornady 124 TAP-FPD	velocity, fps:	1100		1028		967
	energy, ft-lb:	339		291		257
Hornady 147 JHP/XTP	velocity, fps:	975		935		899
	energy, ft-lb:	310		285		264
Hornady 147 TAP-FPD	velocity, fps:	975		935		899
	energy, ft-lb:	310		285		264
Lapua 116 FMJ	velocity, fps:	365		319*		290*
	energy, ft-lb:	500		381*		315*
Lapua 120 FMJ CEPP Super	velocity, fps:	360		316*		288*
	energy, ft-lb:	505		390*		324*
Lapua 120 FMJ CEPP Extra	velocity, fps:	360		316*		288*
	energy, ft-lb:	505		390*		324*
Lapua 123 HP Megashock	velocity, fps:	355		311*		284*
	energy, ft-lb:	504		388*		322*
Lapua 123 FMJ	velocity, fps:	320		292*		272*
	energy, ft-lb:	410		342*		295*
Lapua 123 FMJ Combat	velocity, fps:	355		315*		289*
	energy, ft-lb:	504		397*		333*
Magtech 115 JHP +P	velocity, fps:	1246		1137		1056
	energy, ft-lb:	397		330		285
Magtech 115 FMC	velocity, fps:	1135		1027		961
	energy, ft-lb:	330		270		235
Magtech 115 JHP	velocity, fps:	1155		1047		971
	energy, ft-lb:	340		280		240
Magtech 124 FMC	velocity, fps:	1109		1030		971
	energy, ft-lb:	339		292		259
Norma 84 Lead Free Frangible	velocity, fps:	1411				
(Geco brand)	energy, ft-lb:	371				
Norma 124 FMJ	velocity, fps:	1120				
(Geco brand)	energy, fps:	341				
Norma 123 FMJ	velocity, fps:	1099	1032	980		899
	energy, ft-lb:	331	292	263		221
Norma 123 FMJ	velocity, fps:	1280	1170	1086		972
	energy, ft-lb:	449	375	323		259

Centerfire Handgun Ballistics

9MM LUGER TO .380 AUTO

CARTRIDGE BULLET	RANGE, YARDS:	0	25	50	75	100
PMC 75 Non-Toxic Frangible	velocity, fps:	1350	1240	1154	1088	1035
	energy, ft-lb:	303				
PMC 95 SFHP	velocity, fps:	1250	1239	1228	1217	1207
	energy, ft-lb:	330				
PMC 115 FMJ	velocity, fps:	1157	1100	1053	1013	979
	energy, ft-lb:	344				
PMC 115 JHP	velocity, fps:	1167	1098	1044	999	961
	energy, ft-lb:	350				
PMC 124 SFHP	velocity, fps:	1090	1043	1003	969	939
	energy, ft-lb:	327				
PMC 124 FMJ	velocity, fps:	1110	1059	1017	980	949
	energy, ft-lb:	339				
PMC 124 LRN	velocity, fps:	1050	1006	969	937	908
	energy, ft-lb:	304				
PMC 147 FMJ	velocity, fps:	980	965	941	919	900
	enerby, ft-lb:	310				
PMC 147 SFHP	velocity, fps:	velocity and energy figures not available				
Rem. 101 Lead Free Frangible	velocity, fps:	1220		1092		1004
	energy, ft-lb:	334		267		226
Rem. 115 FN Enclosed Base	velocity, fps:	1135		1041		973
	energy, ft-lb:	329		277		242
Rem. 115 Metal Case	velocity, fps:	1135		1041		973
	energy, ft-lb:	329		277		242
Rem. 115 JHP	velocity, fps:	1155		1047		971
	energy, ft-lb:	341		280		241
Rem. 115 JHP +P	velocity, fps:	1250		1113		1019
	energy, ft-lb:	399		316		265
Rem. 124 JHP	velocity, fps:	1120		1028		960
	energy, ft-lb:	346		291		254
Rem. 124 FNEB	velocity, fps:	1100		1030		971
	energy, ft-lb:	339		292		252
Rem. 124 BJHP	velocity, fps:	1125		1031		963
	energy, ft-lb:	349		293		255
Rem. 124 BJHP +P	velocity, fps:	1180		1089		1021
	energy, ft-lb:	384		327		287
Rem. 124 Metal Case	velocity, fps:	1110		1030		971
	energy, ft-lb:	339		292		259
Rem. 147 JHP subsonic	velocity, fps:	990		941		900
	energy, ft-lb:	320		289		264
Rem. 147 BJHP	velocity, fps:	990		941		900
	energy, ft-lb:	320		289		264
Speer 90 Frangible	velocity, fps:	1350		1132		1001
	energy, ft-lb:	364		256		200
Speer 115 JHP Blazer	velocity, fps:	1145		1024		943
	energy, ft-lb:	335		268		227
Speer 115 FMJ Blazer	velocity, fps:	1145		1047		971
	energy, ft-lb:	341		280		241
Speer 115 FMJ	velocity, fps:	1200		1060		970
	energy, ft-lb:	368		287		240
Speer 115 Gold Dot HP	velocity, fps:	1200		1047		971
	energy, ft-lb:	341		280		241
Speer 124 FMJ Blazer	velocity, fps:	1090		989		917
	energy, ft-lb:	327		269		231
Speer 124 FMJ	velocity, fps:	1090		987		913
	energy, ft-lb:	327		268		230
Speer 124 TMJ-CF (and Blazer)	velocity, fps:	1090		989		917
	energy, ft-lb:	327		269		231
Speer 124 Gold Dot HP	velocity, fps:	1150		1030		948
	energy, ft-lb:	367		292		247
Speer 124 Gold Dot HP+P	velocity, ft-lb:	1220		1085		996
	energy, ft-lb:	410		324		273
Speer 147 TMJ Blazer	velocity, fps:	950		912		879
	energy, ft-lb:	295		272		252
Speer 147 TMJ	velocity, fps:	985		943		906
	energy, ft-lb:	317		290		268
Speer 147 TMJ-CF (and Blazer)	velocity, fps:	985		960		924
	energy, ft-lb:	326		300		279
Speer 147 Gold Dot	velocity, fps:	985		960		924
	energy, ft-lb:	326		300		279
Win. 105 Jacketed FP	velocity, fps:	1200		1074		989
	energy, ft-lb:	336		269		228
Win. 115 Silvertip HP	velocity, fps:	1225		1095		1007
	energy, ft-lb:	383		306		259
Win. 115 Jacketed HP	velocity, fps:	1225		1095		
	energy, ft-lb:	383		306		
Win. 115 FMJ	velocity, fps:	1190		1071		
	energy, ft-lb:	362		293		
Win. 115 EB WinClean	velocity, fps:	1190		1088		
	energy, ft-lb:	362		302		
Win. 124 FMJ	velocity, fps:	1140		1050		
	energy, ft-lb:	358		303		
Win. 124 EB WinClean	velocity, fps:	1130		1049		
	energy, ft-lb:	352		303		
Win. 147 FMJ FN	velocity, fps:	990		945		
	energy, ft-lb:	320		292		
Win. 147 SXT	velocity, fps:	990		947		909
	energy, ft-lb:	320		293		270
Win. 147 Silvertip HP	velocity, fps:	1010		962		921
	energy, ft-lb:	333		302		277
Win. 147 JHP	velocity, fps:	990		945		
	energy, ft-lb:	320		291		
Win. 147 EB WinClean	velocity, fps:	990		945		
	energy, ft-lb:	320		291		

9 x 23 Winchester

CARTRIDGE BULLET	RANGE, YARDS:	0	25	50	75	100
Win. 124 Jacketed FP	velocity, fps:	1460		1308		
	energy, ft-lb:	587		471		
Win. 125 Silvertip HP	velocity, fps:	1450		1249		1103
	energy, ft-lb:	583		433		338

.38 S&W

CARTRIDGE BULLET	RANGE, YARDS:	0	25	50	75	100
Rem. 146 LRN	velocity, fps:	685		650		620
	energy, ft-lb:	150		135		125
Win. 145 LRN	velocity, fps:	685		650		620
	energy, ft-lb:	150		135		125

.38 Short Colt

CARTRIDGE BULLET	RANGE, YARDS:	0	25	50	75	100
Rem. 125 LRN	velocity, fps:	730		685		645
	energy, ft-lb:	150		130		115

.38 Long Colt

CARTRIDGE BULLET	RANGE, YARDS:	0	25	50	75	100
Black Hills 158 RNL	velocity, fps:	650				
	energy, ft-lb:					

.380 Auto

CARTRIDGE BULLET	RANGE, YARDS:	0	25	50	75	100
Black Hills 90 JHP	velocity, fps:	1000				
	energy, ft-lb:	200				
Black Hills 95 FMJ	velocity, fps:	950				
	energy, ft-lb:	190				
Federal 90 Hi-Shok JHP	velocity, fps:	1000	940	890	840	800
	energy, ft-lb:	200	175	160	140	130
Federal 90 Hydra-Shok JHP	velocity, fps:	1000	940	890	840	800
	energy, ft-lb:	200	175	160	140	130
Federal 95 FMJ	velocity, fps:	960	910	870	830	790
	energy, ft-lb:	190	175	160	145	130
Hornady 90 JHP/XTP	velocity, fps:	1000		902		823
	energy, ft-lb:	200		163		135

Centerfire Handgun Ballistics

.380 AUTO TO .38 SPECIAL

CARTRIDGE BULLET	RANGE, YARDS:	0	25	50	75	100
Magtech 85 JHP + P	velocity, fps:	1082		999		936
	energy, ft-lb:	221		188		166
Magtech 95 FMC	velocity, fps:	951		861		781
	energy, ft-lb:	190		156		128
Magtech 95 JHP	velocity, fps:	951		861		781
	energy, ft-lb:	190		156		128
PMC 77 NT/FR	velocity, fps:	1200	1095	1012	932	874
	energy, ft-lb:	223				
PMC 90 FMJ	velocity, fps:	910	872	838	807	778
	energy, ft-lb:	165				
PMC 90 JHP	velocity, fps:	917	878	844	812	782
	energy, ft-lb:	168				
PMC 95 SFHP	velocity, fps:	925	884	847	813	783
	energy, ft-lb:	180				
Rem. 88 JHP	velocity, fps:	990		920		868
	energy, ft-lb:	191		165		146
Rem. 95 FNEB	velocity, fps:	955		865		785
	energy, ft-lb:	190		160		130
Rem. 95 Metal Case	velocity, fps:	955		865		785
	energy, ft-lb:	190		160		130
Rem. 102 BJHP	velocity, fps:	940		901		866
	energy, ft-lb:	200		184		170
Speer 88 JHP Blazer	velocity, fps:	950		920		870
	energy, ft-lb:	195		164		148
Speer 90 Gold Dot	velocity, fps:	990		907		842
	energy, ft-lb:	196		164		142
Speer 95 TMJ Blazer	velocity, fps:	945		865		785
	energy, ft-lb:	190		160		130
Speer 95 TMJ	velocity, fps:	950		877		817
	energy, ft-lb:	180		154		133
Win. 85 Silvertip HP	velocity, fps:	1000		921		860
	energy, ft-lb:	189		160		140
Win. 95 SXT	velocity, fps:	955		889		835
	energy, ft-lb:	192		167		147
Win. 95 FMJ	velocity, fps:	955		865		
	energy, ft-lb:	190		160		
Win. 95 EB WinClean	velocity, fps:	955		881		
	energy, ft-lb:	192		164		

.38 Special

CARTRIDGE BULLET	RANGE, YARDS:	0	25	50	75	100
Black Hills 125 JHP +P	velocity, fps:	1050				
	energy, ft-lb:	306				
Black Hills 148 HBWC	velocity, fps:	700				
	energy, ft-lb:					
Black Hills 158 SWC	velocity, fps:	850				
	energy, ft-lb:					
Black Hills 158 CNL	velocity, fps:	800				
	energy, ft-lb:					
Federal 110 Hydra-Shok JHP	velocity, fps:	1000	970	930	910	880
	energy, ft-lb:	245	225	215	200	190
Federal 110 Hi-Shok JHP +P	velocity, fps:	1000	960	930	900	870
	energy, ft-lb:	240	225	210	195	185
Federal 125 Nyclad HP	velocity, fps:	830	780	730	690	650
	energy, ft-lb:	190	170	150	130	115
Federal 125 Hi-Shok JSP +P	velocity, fps:	950	920	900	880	860
	energy, ft-lb:	250	235	225	215	205
Federal 125 Hi-Shok JHP +P	velocity, fps:	950	920	900	880	860
	energy, ft-lb:	250	235	225	215	205
Federal 125 Nyclad HP +P	velocity, fps:	950	920	900	880	860
	energy, ft-lb:	250	235	225	215	205
Federal 129 Hydra-Shok JHP+P	velocity, fps:	950	930	910	890	870
	energy, ft-lb:	255	245	235	225	215
Federal 130 FMJ	velocity, fps:	950	920	890	870	840
	energy, ft-lb:	260	245	230	215	205
Federal 148 LWC Match	velocity, fps:	710	670	630	600	560
	energy, ft-lb:	165	150	130	115	105
Federal 158 LRN	velocity, fps:	760	740	720	710	690
	energy, ft-lb:	200	190	185	175	170
Federal 158 LSWC	velocity, fps:	760	740	720	710	690
	energy, ft-lb:	200	190	185	175	170
Federal 158 Nyclad RN	velocity, fps:	760	740	720	710	690
	energy, ft-lb:	200	190	185	175	170
Federal 158 SWC HP +P	velocity, fps:	890	870	860	840	820
	energy, ft-lb:	280	265	260	245	235
Federal 158 LSWC +P	velocity, fps:	890	870	860	840	820
	energy, ft-lb:	270	265	260	245	235
Federal 158 Nyclad SWC-HP+P	velocity, fps:	890	870	860	840	820
	energy, ft-lb:	270	265	260	245	235
Hornady 125 JHP/XTP	velocity, fps:	900		856		817
	energy, ft-lb:	225		203		185
Hornady 140 JHP/XTP	velocity, fps:	825		790		757
	energy, ft-lb:	212		194		178
Hornady 140 Cowboy	velocity, fps:	800		767		735
	energy, ft-lb:	199		183		168
Hornady 148 HBWC	velocity, fps:	800		697		610
	energy, ft-lb:	210		160		122
Hornady 158 JHP/XPT	velocity, fps:	800		765		731
	energy, ft-lb:	225		205		188
Lapua 123 HP Megashock	velocity, fps:	355		311*		284*
	energy, ft-lb:	504		388*		322*
Lapua 148 LWC	velocity, fps:	230		203*		181*
	energy, ft-lb:	254		199*		157*
Lapua 150 SJFN	velocity, fps:	325		301*		283*
	energy, ft-lb:	512		439*		388*
Lapua 158 FMJLF	velocity, fps:	255		243*		232*
	energy, ft-lb:	332		301*		275*
Lapua 158 LRN	velocity, fps:	255		243*		232*
	energy, ft-lb:	332		301*		275*
Magtech 125 JHP +P	velocity, fps:	1017		971		931
	energy, ft-lb:	287		262		241
Magtech 148 LWC	velocity, fps:	710		634		566
	energy, ft-lb:	166		132		105
Magtech 158 LRN	velocity, fps:	755		728		693
	energy, ft-lb:	200		183		168
Magtech 158 LFN	velocity, fps:	800		776		753
	energy, ft-lb:	225		211		199
Magtech 158 SJHP	velocity, fps:	807		779		753
	energy, ft-lb:	230		213		199
Magtech 158 LSWC	velocity, fps:	755		721		689
	energy, ft-lb:	200		182		167
Magtech 158 FMC-Flat	velocity, fps:	807		779		753
	energy, ft-lb:	230		213		199
PMC 85 Non-Toxic Frangible	velocity, fps:	1275	1181	1109	1052	1006
	energy, ft-lb:	307				
PMC 110 SFHP +P	velocity, fps:	velocity and energy figures not available				
PMC 125 SFHP +P	velocity, fps:	950	918	889	863	838
	energy, ft-lb:	251				
PMC 125 JHP +P	velocity, fps:	974	938	906	878	851
	energy, ft-lb:	266				
PMC 132 FMJ	velocity, fps:	841	820	799	780	761
	energy, ft-lb:	206				
PMC 148 LWC	velocity, fps:	728	694	662	631	602
	energy, ft-lb:	175				
PMC 158 LRN	velocity, fps:	820	801	783	765	749
	energy, ft-lb:	235				
PMC 158 JSP	velocity, fps:	835	816	797	779	762
	energy, ft-lb:	245				

Centerfire Handgun Ballistics

.38 SPECIAL TO .357 MAGNUM

CARTRIDGE BULLET	RANGE, YARDS:	0	25	50	75	100
PMC 158 LFP	velocity, fps:	800		761		725
	energy, ft-lb:	225		203		185
Rem. 101 Lead Free Frangible	velocity, fps:	950		896		850
	energy, ft-lb:	202		180		162
Rem. 110 SJHP	velocity, fps:	950		890		840
	energy, ft-lb:	220		194		172
Rem. 110 SJHP +P	velocity, fps:	995		926		871
	energy, ft-lb:	242		210		185
Rem. 125 SJHP +P	velocity, ft-lb:	945		898		858
	energy, ft-lb:	248		224		204
Rem. 125 BJHP	velocity, fps:	975		929		885
	energy, ft-lb:	264		238		218
Rem. 125 FNEB	velocity, fps:	850		822		796
	energy, ft-lb:	201		188		176
Rem. 125 FNEB +P	velocity, fps:	975		935		899
	energy, ft-lb:	264		242		224
Rem. 130 Metal Case	velocity, fps:	950		913		879
	energy, ft-lb:	261		240		223
Rem. 148 LWC Match	velocity, fps:	710		634		566
	energy, ft-lb:	166		132		105
Rem. 158 LRN	velocity, fps:	755		723		692
	energy, ft-lb:	200		183		168
Rem. 158 SWC +P	velocity, fps:	890		855		823
	energy, ft-lb:	278		257		238
Rem. 158 SWC	velocity, fps:	755		723		692
	energy, ft-lb:	200		183		168
Rem. 158 LHP +P	velocity, fps:	890		855		823
	energy, ft-lb:	278		257		238
Speer 125 JHP +P Blazer	velocity, fps:	945		898		858
	energy, ft-lb:	248		224		204
Speer 125 Gold Dot +P	velocity, fps:	945		898		858
	energy, ft-lb:	248		224		204
Speer 158 TMJ +P (and Blazer)	velocity, fps:	900		852		818
	energy, ft-lb:	278		255		235
Speer 158 LRN Blazer	velocity, fps:	755		723		692
	energy, ft-lb:	200		183		168
Speer 158 Trail Blazer LFN	velocity, fps:	800		761		725
	energy, ft-lb:	225		203		184
Speer 158 TMJ-CF +P	velocity, fps:	900		852		818
(and Blazer)	energy, ft-lb:	278		255		235
Win. 110 Silvertip HP	velocity, fps:	945		894		850
	energy, ft-lb:	218		195		176
Win. 110 Jacketed FP	velocity, fps:	975		906		849
	energy, ft-lb:	232		201		176
Win. 125 Jacketed HP	velocity, fps:	945		898		
	energy, ft-lb:	248		224		
Win. 125 Jacketed HP +P	velocity, fps:	945		898		858
	energy, ft-lb:	248		224		204
Win. 125 Jacketed FP	velocity, fps:	850		804		
	energy, ft-lb:	201		179		
Win. 125 Silvertip HP + P	velocity, fps:	945		898		858
	energy, ft-lb:	248		224		204
Win. 125 JFP WinClean	velocity, fps:	775		742		
	energy, ft-lb:	167		153		
Win. 130 FMJ	velocity, fps:	800		765		
	energy, ft-lb:	185		169		
Win. 130 SXT +P	velocity, fps:	925		887		852
	energy, ft-lb:	247		227		210
Win. 148 LWC Super Match	velocity, fps:	710		634		566
	energy, ft-lb:	166		132		105
Win. 150 Lead	velocity, fps:	845		812		
	energy, ft-lb:	238		219		
Win. 158 Lead	velocity, fps:	800		761		725
	energy, ft-lb:	225		203		185

CARTRIDGE BULLET	RANGE, YARDS:	0	25	50	75	100
Win. 158 LRN	velocity, fps:	755		723		693
	energy, ft-lb:	200		183		168
Win. 158 LSWC	velocity, fps:	755		721		689
	energy, ft-lb:	200		182		167
Win. 158 LSWC HP +P	velocity, fps:	890		855		823
	energy, ft-lb:	278		257		238

.38-40

CARTRIDGE BULLET	RANGE, YARDS:	0	25	50	75	100
Black Hills 180 FPL	velocity, fps:	800				
	energy, ft-lb:					

.38 Super

CARTRIDGE BULLET	RANGE, YARDS:	0	25	50	75	100
Federal 130 FMJ +P	velocity, fps:	1200	1140	1100	1050	1020
	energy, ft-lb:	415	380	350	320	300
PMC 115 JHP	velocity, fps:	1116	1052	1001	959	923
	energy, ft-lb:	318				
PMC 130 FMJ	velocity, fps:	1092	1038	994	957	924
	energy, ft-lb:	348				
Rem. 130 Metal Case	velocity, fps:	1215		1099		1017
	energy, ft-lb:	426		348		298
Win. 125 Silvertip HP +P	velocity, fps:	1240		1130		1050
	energy, ft-lb:	427		354		306
Win. 130 FMJ +P	velocity, fps:	1215		1099		
	energy, ft-lb:	426		348		

.357 Sig

CARTRIDGE BULLET	RANGE, YARDS:	0	25	50	75	100
Federal 125 FMJ	velocity, fps:	1350	1270	1190	1130	1080
	energy, ft-lb:	510	445	395	355	325
Federal 125 JHP	velocity, fps:	1350	1270	1190	1130	1080
	energy, ft-lb:	510	445	395	355	325
Federal 150 JHP	velocity, fps:	1130	1080	1030	1000	970
	energy, ft-lb:	420	385	355	330	310
Hornady 124 JHP/XTP	velocity, fps:	1350		1208		1108
	energy, ft-lb:	502		405		338
Hornady 147 JHP/XTP	velocity, fps:	1225		1138		1072
	energy, ft-lb:	490		422		375
PMC 85 Non-Toxic Frangible	velocity, fps:	1480	1356	1245	1158	1092
	energy, ft-lb:	413				
PMC 124 SFHP	velocity, fps:	1350	1263	1190	1132	1083
	energy, ft-lb:	502				
PMC 124 FMJ/FP	velocity, fps:	1350	1242	1158	1093	1040
	energy, ft-lb:	512				
Rem. 104 Lead Free Frangible	velocity, fps:	1400		1223		1094
	energy, ft-lb:	453		345		276
Rem. 125 Metal Case	velocity, fps:	1350		1146		1018
	energy, ft-lb:	506		422		359
Rem. 125 JHP	velocity, fps:	1350		1157		1032
	energy, ft-lb:	506		372		296
Speer 125 TMJ (and Blazer)	velocity, fps:	1350		1177		1057
	energy, ft-lb:	502		381		307
Speer 125 TMJ-CF	velocity, fps:	1350		1177		1057
	energy, ft-lb:	502		381		307
Speer 125 Gold Dot	velocity, fps:	1375		1203		1079
	energy, ft-lb:	525		402		323
Win. 105 JFP	velocity, fps:	1370		1179		1050
	energy, ft-lb	438		324		257
Win. 125 FMJ FN	velocity, fps:	1350		1185		
	energy, ft-lb	506		390		

.357 Magnum

CARTRIDGE BULLET	RANGE, YARDS:	0	25	50	75	100
Black Hills 125 JHP	velocity, fps:	1500				
	energy, ft-lb:	625				
Black Hills 158 CNL	velocity, fps:	800				
	energy, ft-lb:					
Black Hills 158 SWC	velocity, fps:	1050				
	energy, ft-lb:					

Centerfire Handgun Ballistics

.357 MAGNUM TO .40 S&W

CARTRIDGE BULLET	RANGE, YARDS:	0	25	50	75	100
Black Hills 158 JHP	velocity, fps:	1250				
	energy, ft-lb:					
Federal 110 Hi-Shok JHP	velocity, fps:	1300	1180	1090	1040	990
	energy, ft-lb:	410	340	290	260	235
Federal 125 Hi-Shok JHP	velocity, fps:	1450	1350	1240	1160	1100
	energy, ft-lb:	580	495	430	370	335
Federal 130 Hydra-Shok JHP	velocity, fps:	1300	1210	1130	1070	1020
	energy, ft-lb:	490	420	370	330	300
Federal 158 Hi-Shok JSP	velocity, fps:	1240	1160	1100	1060	1020
	energy, ft-lb:	535	475	430	395	365
Federal 158 JSP	velocity, fps:	1240	1160	1100	1060	1020
	energy, ft-lb:	535	475	430	395	365
Federal 158 LSWC	velocity, fps:	1240	1160	1100	1060	1020
	energy, ft-lb:	535	475	430	395	365
Federal 158 Hi-Shok JHP	velocity, fps:	1240	1160	1100	1060	1020
	energy, ft-lb:	535	475	430	395	365
Federal 158 Hydra-Shok JHP	velocity, fps:	1240	1160	1100	1060	1020
	energy, ft-lb:	535	475	430	395	365
Federal 180 Hi-Shok JHP	velocity, fps:	1090	1030	980	930	890
	energy, ft-lb:	475	425	385	350	320
Federal 180 Castcore	velocity, fps:	1250	1200	1160	1120	1080
	energy, ft-lb:	625	575	535	495	465
Hornady 125 JHP/XTP	velocity, fps:	1500		1314		1166
	energy, ft-lb:	624		479		377
Hornady 125 JFP/XTP	velocity, fps:	1500		1311		1161
	energy, ft-lb:	624		477		374
Hornady 140 Cowboy	velocity, fps:	800		767		735
	energy, ft-lb:	199		183		168
Hornady 140 JHP/XTP	velocity, fps:	1400		1249		1130
	energy, ft-lb:	609		485		397
Hornady 158 JHP/XTP	velocity, fps:	1250		1150		1073
	energy, ft-lb:	548		464		404
Hornady 158 JFP/XTP	velocity, fps:	1250		1147		1068
	energy, ft-lb:	548		461		400
Lapua 150 FMJ CEPP Super	velocity, fps:	370		527*		303*
	energy, ft-lb:	664		527*		445*
Lapua 150 SJFN	velocity, fps:	385		342*		313*
	energy, ft-lb:	719		569*		476*
Lapua 158 SJHP	velocity, fps:	470		408*		359*
	energy, ft-lb:	1127		850*		657*
Magtech 158 SJSP	velocity, fps:	1235		1104		1015
	energy, ft-lb:	535		428		361
Magtech 158 SJHP	velocity, fps:	1235		1104		1015
	energy, ft-lb:	535		428		361
PMC 85 Non-Toxic Frangible	velocity, fps:	1325	1219	1139	1076	1025
	energy, ft-lb:	331				
PMC 125 JHP	velocity, fps:	1194	1117	1057	1008	967
	energy, ft-lb:	399				
PMC 150 JHP	velocity, fps:	1234	1156	1093	1042	1000
	energy, ft-lb:	512				
PMC 150 SFHP	velocity, fps:	1205	1129	1069	1020	980
	energy, ft-lb:	484				
PMC 158 JSP	velocity, fps:	1194	1122	1063	1016	977
	energy, ft-lb:	504				
PMC 158 LFP	velocity, fps:	800		761		725
	energy, ft-lb:	225		203		185
Rem. 110 SJHP	velocity, fps:	1295		1094		975
	energy, ft-lb:	410		292		232
Rem. 125 SJHP	velocity, fps:	1450		1240		1090
	energy, ft-lb:	583		427		330
Rem. 125 BJHP	velocity, fps:	1220		1095		1009
	energy, ft-lb:	413		333		283
Rem. 125 FNEB	velocity, fps:	1450		1240		1090
	energy, ft-lb:	583		427		330

CARTRIDGE BULLET	RANGE, YARDS:	0	25	50	75	100
Rem. 158 SJHP	velocity, fps:	1235		1104		1015
	energy, ft-lb:	535		428		361
Rem. 158 SP	velocity, fps:	1235		1104		1015
	energy, ft-lb:	535		428		361
Rem. 158 SWC	velocity, fps:	1235		1104		1015
	energy, ft-lb:	535		428		361
Rem. 165 JHP Core-Lokt	velocity, fps:	1290		1189		1108
	energy, ft-lb:	610		518		450
Rem. 180 SJHP	velocity, fps:	1145		1053		985
	energy, ft-lb:	542		443		388
Speer 125 Gold Dot	velocity, fps:	1450		1240		1090
	energy, ft-lb:	583		427		330
Speer 158 JHP Blazer	velocity, fps:	1150		1104		1015
	energy, ft-lb:	535		428		361
Speer 158 Gold Dot	velocity, fps:	1235		1104		1015
	energy, ft-lb:	535		428		361
Speer 170 Gold Dot SP	velocity, fps:	1180		1089		1019
	energy, ft-lb:	525		447		392
Win. 110 JFP	velocity, fps:	1275		1105		998
	energy, ft-lb:	397		298		243
Win. 110 JHP	velocity, fps:	1295		1095		
	energy, ft-lb:	410		292		
Win. 125 JFP WinClean	velocity, fps:	1370		1183		
	energy, ft-lb:	521		389		
Win. 145 Silvertip HP	velocity, fps:	1290		1155		1060
	energy, ft-lb:	535		428		361
Win. 158 JHP	velocity, fps:	1235		1104		1015
	energy, ft-lb:	535		428		361
Win. 158 JSP	velocity, fps:	1235		1104		1015
	energy, ft-lb:	535		428		361
Win. 180 Partition Gold	velocity, fps:	1180		1088		1020
	energy, ft-lb:	557		473		416

.40 S&W

CARTRIDGE BULLET	RANGE, YARDS:	0	25	50	75	100
Black Hills 155 JHP	velocity, fps:	1150				
	energy, ft-lb:	450				
Black Hills 165 EXP JHP	velocity, fps:	1150 (2005: 1100)				
	energy, ft-lb:	483				
Black Hills 180 JHP	velocity, fps:	1000				
	energy, ft-lb:	400				
Black Hills 180 JHP	velocity, fps:	1000				
	energy, ft-lb:	400				
Federal 135 Hydra-Shok JHP	velocity, fps:	1190	1050	970	900	850
	energy, ft-lb:	420	330	280	245	215
Federal 155 FMJ Ball	velocity, fps:	1140	1080	1030	990	960
	energy, ft-lb:	445	400	365	335	315
Federal 155 Hi-Shok JHP	velocity, fps:	1140	1080	1030	990	950
	energy, ft-lb:	445	400	365	335	315
Federal 155 Hydra-Shok JHP	velocity, fps:	1140	1080	1030	990	950
	energy, ft-lb:	445	400	365	335	315
Federal 165 EFMJ	velocity, fps:	1190	1060	970	905	850
	energy, ft-lb:	520	410	345	300	265
Federal 165 FMJ	velocity, fps:	1050	1020	990	960	935
	energy, ft-lb:	405	380	355	335	320
Federal 165 FMJ Ball	velocity, fps:	980	950	920	900	880
	energy, ft-lb:	350	330	310	295	280
Federal 165 Hydra-Shok JHP	velocity, fps:	980	950	930	910	890
	energy, ft-lb:	350	330	315	300	290
Federal 180 High Antim. Lead	velocity, fps:	990	960	930	910	890
	energy, ft-lb:	390	365	345	330	315
Federal 180 TMJ TMF Primer	velocity, fps:	990	960	940	910	890
	energy, ft-lb:	390	370	350	330	315
Federal 180 FMJ Ball	velocity, fps:	990	960	940	910	890
	energy, ft-lb:	390	370	350	330	315

Centerfire Handgun Ballistics

.40 S&W TO .41 REMINGTON MAGNUM

CARTRIDGE BULLET	RANGE, YARDS:	0	25	50	75	100
Federal 180 Hi-Shok JHP	velocity, fps:	990	960	930	910	890
	energy, ft-lb:	390	365	345	330	315
Federal 180 Hydra-Shok JHP	velocity, fps:	990	960	930	910	890
	energy, ft-lb:	390	365	345	330	315
Hornady 155 JHP/XTP	velocity, fps:	1180		1061		980
	energy, ft-lb:	479		387		331
Hornady 155 TAP-FPD	velocity, fps:	1180		1061		980
	energy, ft-lb:	470		387		331
Hornady 180 JHP/XTP	velocity, fps:	950		903		862
	energy, ft-lb:	361		326		297
Hornady 180 TAP-FPD	velocity, fps:	950		903		862
	energy, ft-lb:	361		326		297
Magtech 155 JHP	velocity, fps:	1025		1118		1052
	energy, ft-lb:	500		430		381
Magtech 180 JHP	velocity, fps:	990		933		886
	energy, ft-lb:	390		348		314
Magtech 180 FMC	velocity, fps:	990		933		886
	energy, ft-lb:	390		348		314
PMC 115 Non-Toxic Frangible	velocity, fps:	1350	1240	1154	1088	1035
	energy, ft-lb:	465				
PMC 155 SFHP	velocity, fps:	1160	1092	1039	994	957
	energy, ft-lb:	463				
PMC 165 JHP	velocity, fps:	1040	1002	970	941	915
	energy, ft-lb:	396				
PMC 165 FMJ	velocity, fps:	1010	977	948	922	899
	energy, ft-lb:	374				
PMC 180 FMJ/FP	velocity, fps:	985	957	931	908	885
	energy, ft-lb:	388				
PMC 180 SFHP	velocity, fps:	985	958	933	910	889
	energy, ft-lb:	388				
Rem. 141 Lead Free Frangible	velocity, fps:	1135		1056		996
	energy, ft-lb:	403		349		311
Rem. 155 JHP	velocity, fps:	1205		1095		1017
	energy, ft-lb:	499		413		356
Rem. 165 BJHP	velocity, fps:	1150		1040		964
	energy, ft-lb:	485		396		340
Rem. 180 JHP	velocity, fps:	1015		960		914
	energy, ft-lb:	412		368		334
Rem. 180 FN Enclosed Base	velocity, fps:	985		936		893
	energy, ft-lb:	388		350		319
Rem. 180 Metal Case	velocity, fps:	985		936		893
	energy, ft-lb:	388		350		319
Rem. 180 BJHP	velocity, fps:	1015		960		914
	energy, ft-lb:	412		368		334
Speer 105 Frangible	velocity, fps:	1380		1128		985
	energy, ft-lb:	444		297		226
Speer 155 TMJ Blazer	velocity, fps:	1175		1047		963
	energy, ft-lb:	475		377		319
Speer 155 TMJ	velocity, fps:	1200		1065		976
	energy, ft-lb:	496		390		328
Speer 155 Gold Dot	velocity, fps:	1200		1063		974
	energy, ft-lb:	496		389		326
Speer 165 TMJ Blazer	velocity, fps:	1100		1006		938
	energy, ft-lb:	443		371		321
Speer 165 TMJ	velocity, fps:	1150		1040		964
	energy, ft-lb:	484		396		340
Speer 165 Gold Dot	velocity, fps:	1150		1043		966
	energy, ft-lb:	485		399		342
Speer 180 HP Blazer	velocity, fps:	985		951		909
	energy, ft-lb:	400		361		330
Speer 180 FMJ Blazer	velocity, fps:	1000		937		886
	energy, ft-lb:	400		351		313
Speer 180 FMJ	velocity, fps:	1000		951		909
	energy, ft-lb:	400		361		330
Speer 180 TMJ-CF (and Blazer)	velocity, fps:	1000		951		909
	energy, ft-lb:	400		361		330
Speer 180 Gold Dot	velocity, fps:	1025		957		902
	energy, ft-lb:	420		366		325
Win. 140 JFP	velocity, fps:	1155		1039		960
	energy, ft-lb:	415		336		286
Win. 155 Silvertip HP	velocity, fps:	1205		1096		1018
	energy, ft-lb	500		414		357
Win. 165 SXT	velocity, fps:	1130		1041		977
	energy, ft-lb:	468		397		349
Win. 165 FMJ FN	velocity, fps:	1060		1001		
	energy, ft-lb:	412		367		
Win. 165 EB WinClean	velocity, fps:	1130		1054		
	energy, ft-lb:	468		407		
Win. 180 JHP	velocity, fps:	1010		954		
	energy, ft-lb:	408		364		
Win. 180 FMJ	velocity, fps:	990		936		
	energy, ft-lb:	390		350		
Win. 180 SXT	velocity, fps:	1010		954		909
	energy, ft-lb:	408		364		330
Win. 180 EB WinClean	velocity, fps:	990		943		
	energy, ft-lb:	392		356		

10 MM AUTO

CARTRIDGE BULLET	RANGE, YARDS:	0	25	50	75	100
Federal 155 Hi-Shok JHP	velocity, fps:	1330	1230	1140	1080	1030
	energy, ft-lb:	605	515	450	400	360
Federal 180 Hi-Shok JHP	velocity, fps:	1030	1000	970	950	920
	energy, ft-lb:	425	400	375	355	340
Federal 180 Hydra-Shok JHP	velocity, fps:	1030	1000	970	950	920
	energy, ft-lb:	425	400	375	355	340
Federal 180 High Antim. Lead	velocity, fps:	1030	1000	970	950	920
	energy, ft-lb:	425	400	375	355	340
Federal 180 FMJ	velocity, fps:	1060	1025	990	965	940
	energy, ft-lb:	400	370	350	330	310
Hornady 155 JHP/XTP	velocity, fps:	1265		1119		1020
	energy, ft-lb:	551		431		358
Hornady 180 JHP/XTP	velocity, fps:	1180		1077		1004
	energy, ft-lb:	556		464		403
Hornady 200 JHP/XTP	velocity, fps:	1050		994		948
	energy, ft-lb:	490		439		399
PMC 115 Non-Toxic Frangible	velocity, fps:	1350	1240	1154	1088	1035
	energy, ft-lb:	465				
PMC 170 JHP	velocity, fps:	1200	1117	1052	1000	958
	energy, ft-lb:	543				
PMC 180 SFHP	velocity, fps:	950	926	903	882	862
	energy, ft-lb:	361				
PMC 200 TC-FMJ	velocity, fps:	1050	1008	972	941	912
	energy, ft-lb:	490				
Rem. 180 Metal Case	velocity, fps:	1150		1063		998
	energy, ft-lb:	529		452		398
Speer 200 TMJ Blazer	velocity, fps:	1050		966		952
	energy, ft-lb:	490		440		402
Win. 175 Silvertip HP	velocity, fps:	1290		1141		1037
	energy, ft-lb:	649		506		418

.41 REMINGTON MAGNUM

CARTRIDGE BULLET	RANGE, YARDS:	0	25	50	75	100
Federal 210 Hi-Shok JHP	velocity, fps:	1300	1210	1130	1070	1030
	energy, ft-lb:	790	680	595	540	495
PMC 210 TCSP	velocity, fps:	1290	1201	1128	1069	1021
	energy, ft-lb:	774				
PMC 210 JHP	velocity, fps:	1289	1200	1127	1068	1020
	energy, ft-lb:	774				
Rem. 210 SP	velocity, fps:	1300		1162		1062
	energy, ft-lb:	788		630		526

Centerfire Handgun Ballistics

.41 REMINGTON MAGNUM TO .45 AUTOMATIC (ACP)

CARTRIDGE BULLET	RANGE, YARDS:	0	25	50	75	100
Win. 175 Silvertip HP	velocity, fps:	1250		1120		1029
	energy, ft-lb:	607		488		412
Win. 240 Platinum Tip	velocity, ft-lb:	1250		1151		1075
	energy, ft-lb:	833		706		616

.44 Colt

CARTRIDGE BULLET	RANGE, YARDS:	0	25	50	75	100
Black Hills 230 FPL	velocity, fps:	730				
	energy, ft-lb:					

.44 Russian

CARTRIDGE BULLET	RANGE, YARDS:	0	25	50	75	100
Black Hills 210 FPL	velocity, fps:	650				
	energy, ft-lb:					

.44 Special

CARTRIDGE BULLET	RANGE, YARDS:	0	25	50	75	100
Black Hills 210 FPL	velocity, fps:	700				
	energy, ft-lb:					
Federal 200 SWC HP	velocity, fps:	900	860	830	800	770
	energy, ft-lb:	360	330	305	285	260
Federal 250 CastCore	velocity, fps:	1250	1200	1150	1110	1080
	energy, ft-lb:	865	795	735	685	645
Hornady 180 JHP/XTP	velocity, fps:	1000		935		882
	energy, ft-lb:	400		350		311
Magtech 240 LFN	velocity, fps:	750		722		696
	energy, ft-lb:	300		278		258
PMC 180 JHP	velocity, fps:	980	938	902	869	839
	energy, ft-lb:	383				
PMC 240 SWC-CP	velocity, fps:	764	744	724	706	687
	energy, ft-lb:	311				
PMC 240 LFP	velocity, fps:	750		719		690
	energy, ft-lb:	300		275		253
Rem. 246 LRN	velocity, fps:	755		725		695
	energy, ft-lb:	310		285		265
Speer 200 HP Blazer	velocity, fps:	875		825		780
	energy, ft-lb:	340		302		270
Speer 200 Trail Blazer LFN	velocity, fps:	750		714		680
	energy, ft-lb:	250		226		205
Speer 200 Gold Dot	velocity, fps:	875		825		780
	energy, ft-lb:	340		302		270
Win. 200 Silvertip HP	velocity, fps:	900		860		822
	energy, ft-lb:	360		328		300
Win. 240 Lead	velocity, fps:	750		719		690
	energy, ft-lb	300		275		253
Win. 246 LRN	velocity, fps:	755		725		695
	energy, ft-lb:	310		285		265

.44 Remington Magnum

CARTRIDGE BULLET	RANGE, YARDS:	0	25	50	75	100
Black Hills 240 JHP	velocity, fps:	1260				
	energy, ft-lb:	848				
Black Hills 300 JHP	velocity, fps:	1150				
	energy, ft-lb:	879				
Federal 180 Hi-Shok JHP	velocity, fps:	1610	1480	1370	1270	1180
	energy, ft-lb:	1035	875	750	640	555
Federal 240 Hi-Shok JHP	velocity, fps:	1180	1130	1080	1050	1010
	energy, ft-lb:	740	675	625	580	550
Federal 240 Hydra-Shok JHP	velocity, fps:	1180	1130	1080	1050	1010
	energy, ft-lb:	740	675	625	580	550
Federal 240 JHP	velocity, fps:	1180	1130	1080	1050	1010
	energy, ft-lb:	740	675	625	580	550
Federal 300 CastCore	velocity, fps:	1250	1200	1160	1120	1080
	energy, ft-lb:	1040	960	885	825	775
Hornady 180 JHP/XTP	velocity, fps:	1550		1340		1173
	energy, ft-lb:	960		717		550
Hornady 200 JHP/XTP	velocity, fps:	1500		1284		1128
	energy, ft-lb:	999		732		565
Hornady 240 JHP/XTP	velocity, fps:	1350		1188		1078
	energy, ft-lb:	971		753		619
Hornady 300 JHP/XTP	velocity, fps:	1150		1084		1031
	energy, ft-lb:	881		782		708
Magtech 240 SJSP	velocity, fps:	1180		1081		1010
	energy, ft-lb:	741		632		623
PMC 180 JHP	velocity, fps:	1392	1263	1157	1076	1015
	energy, ft-lb:	772				
PMC 240 JHP	velocity, fps:	1301	1218	1147	1088	1041
	energy, ft-lb:	900				
PMC 240 TC-SP	velocity, fps:	1300	1216	1144	1086	1038
	energy, ft-lb:	900				
PMC 240 SFHP	velocity, fps:	1300	1212	1138	1079	1030
	energy, ft-lb:	900				
PMC 240 LSWC-GCK	velocity, fps:	1225	1143	1077	1025	982
	energy, ft-lb:	806				
Rem. 180 JSP	velocity, fps:	1610		1365		1175
	energy, ft-lb:	1036		745		551
Rem. 210 Gold Dot HP	velocity, fps:	1450		1276		1140
	energy, ft-lb:	980		759		606
Rem. 240 SP	velocity, fps:	1180		1081		1010
	energy, ft-lb:	721		623		543
Rem. 240 SJHP	velocity, fps:	1180		1081		1010
	energy, ft-lb:	721		623		543
Rem. 275 JHP Core-Lokt	velocity, fps:	1235		1142		1070
	energy, ft-lb:	931		797		699
Speer 240 JHP Blazer	velocity, fps:	1200		1092		1015
	energy, ft-lb:	767		636		549
Speer 240 Gold Dot HP	velocity, fps:	1400		1255		1139
	energy, ft-lb:	1044		839		691
Speer 270 Gold Dot SP	velocity, fps:	1250		1142		1060
	energy, ft-lb:	937		781		674
Win. 210 Silvertip HP	velocity, fps:	1250		1106		1010
	energy, ft-lb:	729		570		475
Win. 240 Hollow SP	velocity, fps:	1180		1081		1010
	energy, ft-lb:	741		623		543
Win. 240 JSP	velocity, fps:	1180		1081		
	energy, ft-lb:	741		623		
Win. 250 Partition Gold	velocity, fps:	1230		1132		1057
	energy, ft-lb:	840		711		620
Win. 250 Platinum Tip	velocity, fps:	1250		1148		1070
	energy, ft-lb:	867		732		635

.44-40

CARTRIDGE BULLET	RANGE, YARDS:	0	25	50	75	100
Black Hills 200 RNFP	velocity, fps:	800				
	energy, ft-lb:					
Hornady 205 Cowboy	velocity, fps:	725		697		670
	energy, ft-lb:	239		221		204
Magtech 225 LFN	velocity, fps:	725		703		681
	energy, ft-lb:	281		247		232
PMC 225 LFP	velocity, fps:	725		723		695
	energy, ft-lb:	281		261		242
Win. 225 Lead	velocity, fps:	750		723		695
	energy, ft-lb:	281		261		242

.45 Automatic (ACP)

CARTRIDGE BULLET	RANGE, YARDS:	0	25	50	75	100
Black Hills 185 JHP	velocity, fps:	1000				
	energy, ft-lb:	411				
Black Hills 200 Match SWC	velocity, fps:	875				
	energy, ft-lb:	340				
Black Hills 230 FMJ	velocity, fps:	850				
	energy, ft-lb:	368				

Centerfire Handgun Ballistics

.45 AUTOMATIC (ACP) TO .45 GAP

CARTRIDGE BULLET	RANGE, YARDS:	0	25	50	75	100
Black Hills 230 JHP	velocity, fps:	850				
	energy, ft-lb:	368				
Black Hills 230 JHP +P	velocity, fps:	950				
	energy, ft-lb:	460				
Federal 165 Hydra-Shok JHP	velocity, fps:	1060	1020	980	950	920
	energy, ft-lb:	410	375	350	330	310
Federal 165 EFMJ	velocity, fps:	1090	1045	1005	975	942
	energy, ft-lb:	435	400	370	345	325
Federal 185 Hi-Shok JHP	velocity, fps:	950	920	900	880	860
	energy, ft-lb:	370	350	335	315	300
Federal 185 FMJ-SWC Match	velocity, fps:	780	730	700	660	620
	energy, ft-lb:	245	220	200	175	160
Federal 200 Exp. FMJ	velocity, fps:	1030	1000	970	940	920
	energy, ft-lb:	470	440	415	395	375
Federal 230 FMJ	velocity, fps:	850	830	810	790	770
	energy, ft-lb:	370	350	335	320	305
Federal 230 FMJ Match	velocity, fps:	855	835	815	795	775
	energy, ft-lb:	375	355	340	325	305
Federal 230 Hi-Shok JHP	velocity, fps:	850	830	810	790	770
	energy, ft-lb:	370	350	335	320	300
Federal 230 Hydra-Shok JHP	velocity, fps:	850	830	810	790	770
	energy, ft-lb:	370	350	335	320	305
Federal 230 FMJ	velocity, fps:	850	830	810	790	770
	energy, ft-lb:	370	350	335	320	305
Federal 230 TMJ TMF Primer	velocity, fps:	850	830	810	790	770
	energy, ft-lb:	370	350	335	315	305
Hornady 185 JHP/XTP	velocity, fps:	950		880		819
	energy, ft-lb:	371		318		276
Hornady 200 JHP/XTP	velocity, fps:	900		855		815
	energy, ft-lb:	358		325		295
Hornady 200 HP/XTP +P	velocity, fps:	1055		982		925
	energy, ft-lb:	494		428		380
Hornady 200 TAP-FPD	velocity, fps:	1055		982		926
	energy, ft-lbs:	494		428		380
Hornady 230 FMJ/RN	velocity, fps:	850		809		771
	energy, ft-lb:	369		334		304
Hornady 230 FMJ/FP	velocity, fps:	850		809		771
	energy, ft-lb:	369		334		304
Hornady 230 HP/XTP +P	velocity, fps:	950		904		865
	energy, ft-lb:	462		418		382
Hornady 230 TAP-FPD	velocity, fps:	950		908		872
	energy, ft-lb:	461		421		388
Magtech 185 JHP +P	velocity, fps:	1148		1066		1055
	energy, ft-lb:	540		467		415
Magtech 200 LSWC	velocity, fps:	950		910		874
	energy, ft-lb:	401		368		339
Magtech 230 FMC	veloctiy, fps:	837		800		767
	energy, ft-lb:	356		326		300
Magtech 230 FMC-SWC	velocity, fps:	780		720		660
	energy, ft-lb:	310		265		222
PMC 145 Non-Toxic Frangible	velocity, fps:	1100	1045	999	961	928
	energy, ft-lb:	390				
PMC 185 JHP	velocity, fps:	903	870	839	811	785
	energy, ft-lb:	339				
PMC 200 FMJ-SWC	velocity, fps:	850	818	788	761	734
	energy, ft-lb:	321				
PMC 230 SFHP	velocity, fps:	850	830	811	792	775
	energy, ft-lb:	369				
PMC 230 FMJ	velocity, fps:	830	809	789	769	749
	energy, ft-lb:	352				
Rem. 175 Lead Free Frangible	velocity, fps:	1020		923		851
	energy, ft-lb:	404		331		281

CARTRIDGE BULLET	RANGE, YARDS:	0	25	50	75	100
Rem. 185 JHP	velocity, fps:	1000		939		889
	energy, ft-lb:	411		362		324
Rem. 185 BJHP	velocity, fps:	1015		951		899
	energy, ft-lb:	423		372		332
Rem. 185 BJHP +P	velocity, fps:	1140		1042		971
	energy, ft-lb:	534		446		388
Rem. 185 MC	velocity, fps:	1015		955		907
	energy, ft-lb:	423		375		338
Rem. 230 FN Enclosed Base	velocity, fps:	835		800		767
	energy, ft-lb:	356		326		300
Rem. 230 Metal Case	velocity, fps:	835		800		767
	energy, ft-lb:	356		326		300
Rem. 230 JHP	velocity, fps:	835		800		767
	energy, ft-lb:	356		326		300
Rem. 230 BJHP	velocity, fps:	875		833		795
	energy, ft-lb:	391		355		323
Speer 140 Frangible	velocity, fps:	1200		1029		928
	energy, ft-lb:	448		329		268
Speer 185 Gold Dot	velocity, fps:	1050		956		886
	energy, ft-lb:	453		375		322
Speer 185 TMJ/FN	velocity, fps:	1000		909		839
	energy, ft-lb:	411		339		289
Speer 200 JHP Blazer	velocity, fps:	975		917		860
	energy, ft-lb:	421		372		328
Speer 200 Gold Dot +P	velocity, fps:	1080		994		930
	energy, ft-lb:	518		439		384
Speer 200 TMJ/FN	velocity, fps:	975		897		834
	energy, ft-lb:	422		357		309
Speer 230 FMJ (and Blazer)	velocity, fps:	845		804		775
	energy, ft-lb:	363		329		304
Speer 230 TMJ-CF (and Blazer)	velocity, fps:	845		804		775
	energy, ft-lb:	363		329		304
Speer 230 Gold Dot	velocity, fps:	890		845		805
	energy, ft-lb:	405		365		331
Win. 170 JFP	velocity, fps:	1050		982		928
	energy, ft-lb:	416		364		325
Win. 185 Silvertip HP	velocity, fps:	1000		938		888
	energy, ft-lb:	411		362		324
Win. 185 FMJ FN	velocity, fps:	910		861		
	energy, ft-lb:	340		304		
Win. 185 EB WinClean	velocity, fps:	910		835		
	energy, ft-lb:	340		286		
Win. 230 JHP	velocity, fps:	880		842		
	energy, ft-lb:	396		363		
Win. 230 FMJ	velocity, fps:	835		800		
	energy, ft-lb:	356		326		
Win. 230 SXT	velocity, fps:	880		846		816
	energy, ft-lb:	396		366		340
Win. 230 JHP subsonic	velocity, fps:	880		842		808
	energy, ft-lb:	396		363		334
Win. 230 EB WinClean	velocity, fps:	835		802		
	energy, ft-lb:	356		329		

.45 GAP

CARTRIDGE BULLET	RANGE, YARDS:	0	25	50	75	100
Federal 185 Hydra-Shok JHP	velocity, fps:	1090	1020	970	920	890
And Federal TMJ	energy, ft-lb:	490	430	385	350	320
Federal 230 Hydra-Shok	velocity, fps:	880	870	850	840	820
And Federal FMJ	energy, ft-lb:	395	380	3760	355	345
Win. 185 STHP	velocity, fps:	1000		938		887
	energy, ft-lb:	411		361		323
Win. 230 JHP	velocity, fps:	880		842		
	energy, ft-lb:	396		363		

Centerfire Handgun Ballistics

.45 GAP to .500 Smith & Wesson

Cartridge Bullet	Range, Yards:	0	25	50	75	100
Win. 230 EB WinClean	velocity, fps:	875		840		
	energy, ft-lb:	391		360		
Win. 230 FMJ	velocity, fps:	850		814		
	energy, ft-lb:	369		338		

.45 Winchester Magnum

Cartridge Bullet	Range, Yards:	0	25	50	75	100
Win. 260 Partition Gold	velocity, fps:	1200		1105		1033
	energy, ft-lb:	832		705		616
Win. 260 JHP	velocity, fps:	1200		1099		1026
	energy, ft-lb:	831		698		607

.45 Schofield

Cartridge Bullet	Range, Yards:	0	25	50	75	100
Black Hills 180 FNL	velocity, fps:	730				
	energy, ft-lb:					
Black Hills 230 RNFP	velocity, fps:	730				
	energy, ft-lb:					

.45 Colt

Cartridge Bullet	Range, Yards:	0	25	50	75	100
Black Hills 250 RNFP	velocity, fps:	725				
	energy, ft-lb:					
Federal 225 SWC HP	velocity, fps:	900	880	860	840	820
	energy, ft-lb:	405	385	370	355	340
Hornady 255 Cowboy	velocity, fps:	725		692		660
	energy, ft-lb:	298		271		247
Magtech 250 LFN	velocity, fps:	750		726		702
	energy, ft-lb:	312		293		274
PMC 250 LFP	velocity, fps:	800		767		736
	energy, ft-lb:	355		331		309
PMC 300 +P+	velocity, fps:	1250	1192	1144	1102	1066
	energy, ft-lb:	1041				
Rem. 225 SWC	velocity, fps:	960		890		832
	energy, ft-lb:	460		395		346
Rem. 250 RLN	velocity, fps:	860		820		780
	energy, ft-lb:	410		375		340
Speer 200 FMJ Blazer	velocity, fps:	1000		938		889
	energy, ft-lb:	444		391		351
Speer 230 Trail Blazer LFN	velocity, fps:	750		716		684
	energy, ft-lb:	287		262		239
Speer 250 Gold Dot	velocity, fps:	900		860		823
	energy, ft-lb:	450		410		376
Win. 225 Silvertip HP	velocity, fps:	920		877		839
	energy, ft-lb:	423		384		352
Win. 255 LRN	velocity, fps:	860		820		780
	energy, ft-lb:	420		380		345
Win. 250 Lead	velocity, fps:	750		720		692
	energy, ft-lb:	312		288		266

.454 Casull

Cartridge Bullet	Range, Yards:	0	25	50	75	100
Federal 300 Trophy Bonded	velocity, fps:	1630	1540	1450	1380	1300
	energy, ft-lb:	1760	1570	1405	1260	1130
Federal 360 CastCore	velocity, fps:	1500	1435	1370	1310	1255
	energy, ft-lb:	1800	1640	1500	1310	1260
Hornady 240 XTP-MAG	velocity, fps:	1900		1679		1483
	energy, ft-lb:	1923		1502		1172
Hornady 300 XTP-MAG	velocity, fps:	1650		1478		1328
	energy, ft-lb:	1813		1455		1175
Magtech 260 SJSP	velocity, fps:	1800		1577		1383
	energy, ft-lb:	1871		1437		1104
Rem. 300 Core-Lokt Ultra	velocity, fps:	1625		1472		1335
	energy, ft-lb:	1759		1442		1187
Speer 300 Gold Dot HP	velocity, fps:	1625		1477		1343
	energy, ft-lb:	1758		1452		1201
Win. 250 JHP	velocity, fps:	1300		1151		1047
	energy, ft-lb:	938		735		608
Win. 260 Partition Gold	velocity, fps:	1800		1605		1427
	energy, ft-lb:	1871		1485		1176
Win. 260 Platinum Tip	velocity, fps:	1800		1596		1414
	eneryg, ft-lb:	1870		1470		1154
Win. 300 JFP	velocity, fps:	1625		1451		1308
	energy, ft-lb:	1759		1413		1141

.460 Smith & Wesson

Cartridge Bullet	Range, Yards:	0	25	50	75	100
Federal 275 Expander	velocity, fps:	1800		1640		1500
	energy, ft-lb:	1980		1650		1370
Federal 300 A-Frame	velocity, fps:	1750		1510		1300
	energy, ft-lb:	2040		1510		1125
Hornady 200 SST	velocity, fps:	2250		2003		1772
	energy, ft-lb:	2248		1395		1081
Win. 260 Supreme Part. Gold	velocity, fps	2000		1788		1592
	energy, ft-lb	2309		1845		2012

.475 Linebaugh

Cartridge Bullet	Range, Yards:	0	25	50	75	100
Hornady 400 XTP-MAG	velocity, fps:	1300		1179		1093
	energy, ft-lb:	1501		1235		1060

.480 Ruger

Cartridge Bullet	Range, Yards:	0	25	50	75	100
Federal 275 Expander	velocity, fps:	1350		1190		1080
	energy, ft-lb:	1115		870		710
Hornady 325 XTP-MAG	velocity, fps:	1350		1191		1076
	energy, ft-lb:	1315		1023		835
Hornady 400 XTP-MAG	velocity, fps:	1100		1027		971
	energy, ft-lb:	1075		937		838
Speer 275 Gold Dot HP	velocity, fps:	1450		1284		1152
	energy, ft-lb:	1284		1007		810
Speer 325 SP	velocity, fps:	1350		1224		1124
	energy, ft-lb:	1315		1082		912

.50 Action Express

Cartridge Bullet	Range, Yards:	0	25	50	75	100
Hornady 300 XTP/HP	velocity, fps:	1475		1251		1092
	energy, ft-lb:	1449		1043		795
Speer 300 Gold Dot HP	velocity, fps:	1550		1361		1207
	energy, ft-lb:	1600		1234		970
Speer 325 UCHP	velocity, fps:	1400		1232		1106
	energy, ft-lb:	1414		1095		883

.500 Smith & Wesson

Cartridge Bullet	Range, Yards:	0	25	50	75	100
Federal 275 Expander	velocity, fps:	1660		1440		1250
	energy, ft-lb:	1680		1255		950
Federal 325 A-Frame	velocity, fps:	1800		1560		1350
	energy, ft-lb:	2340		1755		1315
Hornady 350 XTP Mag	velocity, fps:	1900		1656		1439
	energy, ft-lb:	2805		2131		1610
Hornady 500 FP-XTP	velocity, fps:	1425		1281		1164
	energy, ft-lb:	2254		1823		1505
Win. 350 Super-X	velocity, fps	1400		1231		1106
	energy, ft-lb	1523		1178		951
Win. 400 Platinum Tip	velocity, fps:	1800		1647		1505
	energy, ft-lb:	2877		2409		2012

Gunfinder Index

KBE>L

Gunfinder Index

Gunfinder Index

Gunfinder Index

GUNFINDER INDEX